Cloudy 222
236
Sanna bay

Cloudy 222
236
Sanna bay

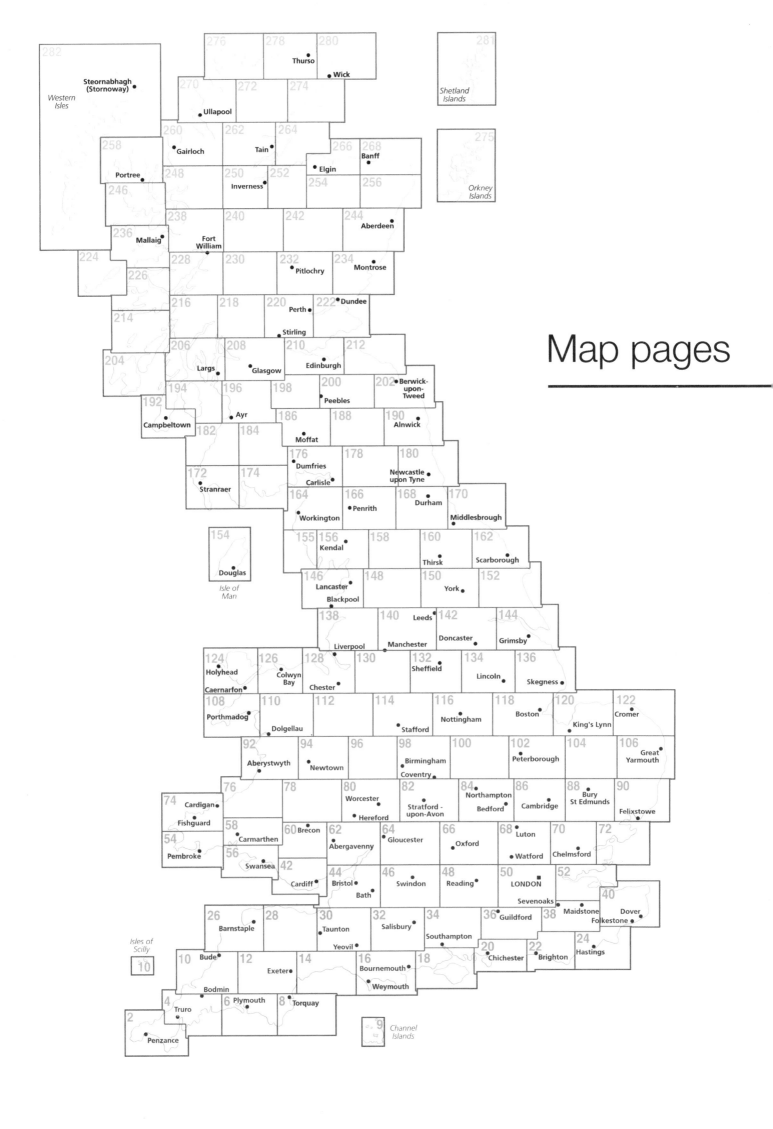

Map pages

5th edition August 2004

© Automobile Association Developments Limited 2004
Original edition printed 2000.

Ordnance Survey® This product includes mapping data licensed from Ordnance Survey® with the permission of the Controller of Her Majesty's Stationery Office.
© Crown copyright 2004. All rights reserved.
Licence number 399221.

Published by AA Publishing (a trading name of Automobile Association Developments Limited, whose registered office is Millstream, Maidenhead Road, Windsor, Berkshire SL4 5GD, UK. Registered number 1878835).

Mapping produced by the Cartography Department of The Automobile Association. This atlas has been compiled and produced from the Automaps database utilising electronic and computer technology (A02053).

ISBN 0 7495 4346 9 (flexibound)

A CIP catalogue record for this book is available from The British Library.

Printed in Italy by Spada Fratelli S.p.A., Roma.

The contents of this atlas are believed to be correct at the time of the latest revision. However, the publishers cannot be held responsible for loss occasioned to any person acting or refraining from action as a result of any material in this atlas, nor for any errors, omissions or changes in such material. This does not affect your statutory rights. The publishers would welcome information to correct any errors or omissions and to keep this atlas up to date. Please write to the Cartographic Editor, Publishing Division, The Automobile Association, Fanum House, Basing View, Basingstoke, Hampshire RG21 4EA, UK.

Information on National Parks in England provided by The Countryside Agency.

Information on National Nature Reserves in England provided by English Nature.

Information on National Parks, National Scenic Areas and National Nature Reserves in Scotland provided by Scottish Natural Heritage.

Information on National Parks and National Nature Reserves in Wales provided by The Countryside Council for Wales.

Information on Forest Parks provided by the Forestry Commission.

The RSPB sites shown are a selection chosen by the Royal Society for the Protection of Birds.

National Trust properties shown are a selection of those open to the public as indicated in the handbooks of the National Trust and the National Trust for Scotland.

AA 2005 SUPER SCALE BRITAIN

Scale 1:148,000 or 2.34 miles to 1 inch
(1.5 km to 1 cm)

Atlas contents

Map pages	inside front cover
Route planner	**II–VII**
Atlas symbols	**VIII–1**
Road maps 1:148,000 scale	**2–283**
Channel Islands 1:100,000 scale	9
Isle of Man 1:200,000 scale	154
Orkney Islands 1:450,000 scale	275
Shetland Islands 1:450,000 scale	281
Western Isles 1:480,000 scale	282–283
Index to place names	**284–369**
County, administrative area map	284–285

DUBLIN

Dún Laoghaire

To help you navigate safely
and easily, see the AA's
Ireland atlases...
www.theAA.com/bookshop

REPUBLIC
OF
IRELAND

Rosslare
Harbour

(Summer only)

St David's

Haverfordwest

Milford Haven
Pembroke Dock
Pembroke

Cork (Ringaskiddy)

Isles of
Scilly
inset

Newquay

Redruth
Camborne

Penzance

Land's End

Helston

Lizard

Holyhead
Anglesey
Bangor
Caernarfon
Bethesda
Betws-y-Coed
Llandudno
Conwy Abergele
Colwyn Bay
Rhyl
Holywell
Queensferry
Mold
Denbigh
Ruthin
Wrexham
Llangollen
Bala
Oswestry
Whitchurch
Pwllheli
Porthmadog
Abersoch
WALES
Barmouth
Dolgellau
Machynlleth
Welshpool
Newtown
Shrewsbury
Telford
Bridgnorth
WOLVERHAMPTON
Church Stretton
Cardigan Bay
Aberystwyth
Llangurig
Rhayader
Ludlow
Knighton
Leominster
Kidderminster
Bromsgro
Aberaeron
Tregaron
Lampeter
Llandrindod Wells
Kington
Worcester
Great Malvern
Ledbury
Tewkes
Cardigan
Newcastle Emlyn
Builth Wells
Hay-on-Wye
Hereford
Ross-on-Wye
Gloucester
Fishguard
Llandovery
Brecon
Abergavenny
Monmouth
Stroud
Carmarthen
Llandeilo
Merthyr Tydfil
Ebbw Vale
Cwmbran
Chepstow
St Clears
Tenby
Llanelli
Neath
Pontypridd
Newport
Avonmouth
BRISTOL
Swansea
Port Talbot
Bridgend
CARDIFF
Clevedon
Bath
Weston-super-Mare
Cheddar
Frome
Trow
Bristol Channel
Wells
Shepton Mallet
Ilfracombe
Lynton
Minehead
Lundy
Bridgwater
Glastonbury
Wincanton
Barnstaple
Bideford
Great Torrington
South Molton
Taunton
Yeovil
Shaftes
Ilminster
Sherborne
Blandford Forum
Bude
Hatherleigh
Tiverton
Chard
Crewkerne
Holsworthy
Crediton
Honiton
Axminster
Bridport
Okehampton
Exeter
Lyme Regis
Launceston
Dorchester
Wadebridge
Tavistock
Weymouth
Bodmin
Buckfastleigh
Newton Abbot
Fortuneswell
Liskeard
PLYMOUTH
Torquay
Lostwithiel
Saltash
Totnes
Paignton
Torpoint
Dartmouth
St Austell
Exmouth
Dawlish
Teignmouth
Truro
Kingsbridge
Falmouth

Guernsey
Jersey
St Malo

Santander
(Summer only)
Roscoff

ENGLISH

LIVERPOOL
Ormskirk
Skelmersdale
Bolton
Formby
Wigan
Crosby
St Helens
M
Birkenhead
Widnes
Altrinc
Runcorn
Warrington
Man
Knutsfor
Ellesmere Port
Northwich
Macc
Chester
Crewe
Kidgro
Nantwich
ST
Newcastle-under-Lyme
Market Drayton
Newport
Canno
Bromborough
Bromsgro
Dudle
Stourbridge
Halesow

Santa

Route Planner

Legend

- Motorway
- Toll motorway
- Primary route dual carriageway
- Primary route single carriageway
- Other A roads
- Vehicle ferry
- Vehicle ferry - fast catamaran
- Contact your local AA Service Centre on 0845 603 3111

To help you navigate safely and easily, see the AA's France and Europe atlases... www.theAA.com/bookshop

Scale: 0 10 20 30 miles / 0 10 20 30 40 kilometres

ENGLAND

FRANCE

CHANNEL

Strait of Dover

CHANNEL TUNNEL

Major roadworks Jct 12–15, due for completion early 2006

IV

To help you navigate safely
and easily, see the AA's
Ireland atlases...
www.theAA.com/bookshop

NORTHERN
IRELAND

REPUBLIC
OF
IRELAND

BELFAST
DUBLIN
Dún Laoghaire
Larne

IRISH
SEA

Isle of Man
Ramsey
Peel
Douglas
Castletown

WALES

Colonsay
Jura
Islay
Port Askaig
Port Ellen
Kennacraig
Tarbert
Lochgilphead
Inveraray
Arran
Campbeltown

Crianlarich
Crieff
Auchterarder
Callander
Dunblane
Kinross
Alloa
Stirling
Dunfermline
Rosyth
Edinburgh
EDINBURGH
Glenrothes
Kirkcaldy
St Andrews
Cupar
Dunbar
Dalkeith

Helensburgh
Dumbarton
Greenock
Dunoon
Clydebank
Largs
Paisley
GLASGOW
East Kilbride
Motherwell
Falkirk
Cumbernauld
Airdrie
Livingston
Peebles
Galashiels
Kelso
Selkirk
Jedburgh
Hawick
Coldstream

Ardrossan
Irvine
Kilwinning
Kilmarnock
Troon
Prestwick
Ayr
Maybole
Girvan
Cumnock
Strathaven
Lanark
Biggar
Moffat
Thornhill
Langholm
Otterburn

Stranraer
Cairnryan
Newton Stewart
New Galloway
Castle Douglas
Dumfries
Annan
Lockerbie
Longtown
Brampton
Hexham
Alston

Carlisle
Maryport
Cockermouth
Penrith
Brough
Workington
Keswick
Egremont
Ambleside
Windermere
Ravenglass
Kendal
Sedbergh
Millom
Kirkby Lonsdale

Barrow-in-Furness
Morecambe
Heysham
Lancaster
Settle
Fleetwood
Clitheroe
Blackpool
Preston
Blackburn
Southport
Bury
Formby
Ormskirk
Skelmersdale
Bolton
Rochdale
Crosby
Wigan
Aintree
St Helens
LIVERPOOL
Birkenhead
Widnes
Runcorn
Warrington
Altrincham
Manchester
Knutsford
Bromborough
Ellesmere Port
Northwich
Chester
Macclesfield
Crewe
Kidsgrove
Nantwich
Newcastle-under-Lyme
Stoke

Holyhead
Anglesey
Llandudno
Colwyn Bay
Rhyl
Bangor
Conwy
Abergele
Holywell
Queensferry
Mold
Denbigh
Ruthin
Caernarfon
Bethesda
Betws-y-Coed
Wrexham
Whitchurch
Pwllheli
Porthmadog
Bala
Llangollen
Oswestry
Market Drayton
Abersoch
Barmouth
Dolgellau
Welshpool
Newport
Shrewsbury
Telford
Cannock

NORTH
SEA

nouth

erwick-upon-Tweed

oler

Alnwick
A697
A1068 • Amble
A1

• Ashington
Morpeth ■
A1
A69

Tynemouth
North • South Shields
Shields 🅰🅰 🅰🅰
NEWCASTLE UPON TYNE
Gateshead ■ ■ **SUNDERLAND**
A692
nsett ■ A1
A691 Chester-le-Street
Durham 🅰🅰
A68 A689 **Hartlepool** 🅰🅰
Auckland A689
hard **Stockton-** **Middlesbrough** ■
stle A688 **on-Tees** ■
Guisborough
Darlington A66 Whitby ■
Richmond ■ A172 A171
Scotch A171
A684 Corner A19
A684 A169
Leyburn **Northallerton** A170 **Scarborough** 🅰🅰
Thirsk Helmsley Pickering A171
A170 • Filey
A64
Ripon ■ A165
A168 **Bridlington**
A61 Easingwold Malton
A1(M) A64
A59 A166 A614 • Driffield
A59 A59
Harrogate A1079 **York** 🅰🅰 A165
A65 Wetherby Market A1035 Beverley
Otley ■ Leeds A64 Weighton A164 • Beverley
A650 Bradford A19 A1079 A165
BRADFORD **LEEDS** A1(M) A63
alifax A58 Selby
M62 A645 A62 A63 M62 A63 🅰🅰 **KINGSTON UPON HULL**
Huddersfield **Wakefield** Pontefract Goole
A62 M1 A1 A19 M18 Thorne **Scunthorpe** Immingham
A61 A18 A180 **Grimsby**
am A628 **Barnsley** 🅰🅰 **Doncaster** M180 Cleethorpes
ESTER A616 A180
Glossop **Rotherham** Bawtry Brigg
ckport **SHEFFIELD** A631 Market A46 A18 A16
A57 Gainsborough Rasen Louth
M1 Retford A157 A16
Buxton A61 Worksop A1 A158 A52 Mablethorpe
A623 A57 A158
Bakewell Matlock Alfreton **Chesterfield** **Lincoln** Horncastle A158 • Skegness
A6 A617 A17 A52
N-TRENT **Mansfield** A52
Ashbourne Ilkeston Netherfield Newark- A17 Boston A52 The
DERBY Chilwell **NOTTINGHAM** on-Trent Sleaford A16 Wash
Nottingham Long A52 Grantham A17 King's
Uttoxeter East Eaton A52 Spalding Lynn
Midlands Loughborough A15 Bourne A151
ord **Burton upon** Melton Mowbray
Rugeley **Trent** A46 A1 A10
Lichfield Oakham Stamford Wisbech

🅰🅰 ══════ Motorway
══════ Toll motorway
══════ Primary route
dual carriageway
══════ Primary route
single carriageway
══════ Other A roads
Ⓥ Vehicle ferry
ⓒ Vehicle ferry -
fast catamaran
🅰🅰 Contact your local
AA Service Centre
on 0845 603 3111

Ⓥ Stavanger, Haugesund
Bergen, Kristiansand
Göteborg

Ⓥ IJmuiden

Ⓥ Rotterdam
(Europoort)
Zeebrugge

0 10 20 30 miles
0 10 20 30 40 kilometres

ENGLAND

Sheringham
Cromer
Hunstanton A149
A148 North Walsham
A149
Aylsham A140
Fakenham A1151 A149
A1065 Dereham A1067 **Norwich** A47 Caister-
Swaffham A47 on-Sea
Great

Western
Isles

Port Nis
(Port of Ness)

Scourie

O u t e r   H e b r i d e s

Steornabhagh
(Stornoway)

Isle of
Lewis

The Minch

Ullapool

Taransay

Tairbeart
(Tarbert)

Harris

Gairloch

Uibhist a Tuath
(North Uist)

Kinlochewe

Achnash

Loch nam Madadh
(Lochmaddy)

Uig

Beinn na Faoghla
(Benbecula)

Dunvegan

Portree

Uibhist a Deas
(South Uist)

Kyle of
Lochalsh

Isle
of
Skye

Loch Baghasdail
(Lochboisdale)

Barraigh
(Barra)

Sound of Barra

Armadale

Invergarry

Rùm

Mallaig

Inner Hebrides

Eigg

Fort Willia

Coll

Tobermory

Ballachulish

Lochaline

Tiree

Craignure
Isle of Mull

Oban

Tyndru

Fionnphort

A849

Inveraray

Colonsay

Lochgilphead

Helensbur

Dunoon

Port
Askaig

Jura

Tarbert

Greenock

Kennacraig

Largs

Islay

Ardrossan

Port Ellen

Arran

Irvine

Campbeltown

Troo
Prestwi
Ay

Maybole

Firth of
Clyde

Motorway

Toll motorway

Primary route
dual carriageway

Primary route
single carriageway

Other A roads

Vehicle ferry

Vehicle ferry -
fast catamaran

Contact your local
AA Service Centre
on 0845 603 3111

0   10   20   30 miles

0   10   20   30   40 kilometres

Atlas symbols

Motoring information

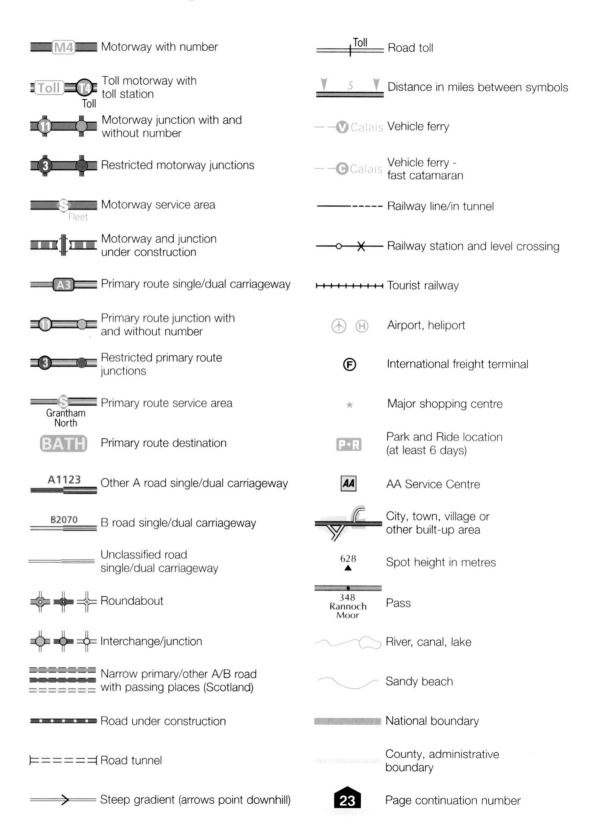

M4	Motorway with number
Toll / T4 Toll	Toll motorway with toll station
11	Motorway junction with and without number
3	Restricted motorway junctions
S Fleet	Motorway service area
	Motorway and junction under construction
A3	Primary route single/dual carriageway
	Primary route junction with and without number
3	Restricted primary route junctions
S Grantham North	Primary route service area
BATH	Primary route destination
A1123	Other A road single/dual carriageway
B2070	B road single/dual carriageway
	Unclassified road single/dual carriageway
	Roundabout
	Interchange/junction
	Narrow primary/other A/B road with passing places (Scotland)
	Road under construction
	Road tunnel
	Steep gradient (arrows point downhill)
Toll	Road toll
5	Distance in miles between symbols
V Calais	Vehicle ferry
C Calais	Vehicle ferry - fast catamaran
	Railway line/in tunnel
	Railway station and level crossing
	Tourist railway
✈ H	Airport, heliport
F	International freight terminal
★	Major shopping centre
P+R	Park and Ride location (at least 6 days)
AA	AA Service Centre
	City, town, village or other built-up area
628 ▲	Spot height in metres
348 Rannoch Moor	Pass
	River, canal, lake
	Sandy beach
	National boundary
	County, administrative boundary
23	Page continuation number

Touring information

Tourist Information Centre	RSPB site	Show jumping/equestrian circuit
Tourist Information Centre (seasonal)	National Nature Reserve (England, Scotland, Wales)	Motor-racing circuit
Visitor or heritage centre	Local nature reserve	Air show venue
Abbey, cathedral or priory	Forest drive	Ski slope – natural
Ruined abbey, cathedral or priory	National trail	Ski slope – artificial
Castle	Viewpoint	National Trust property
Historic house or building	Picnic site	National Trust for Scotland property
Museum or art gallery	Hill-fort	Other place of interest
Industrial interest	Roman antiquity	Boxed symbols indicate attractions within urban areas
Aqueduct or viaduct	Prehistoric monument	National Park
Garden	Battle site with year	National Scenic Area (Scotland)
Arboretum	Steam centre (railway)	Forest Park
Vineyard	Cave	Heritage coast
Country park	Windmill	Travelodge
Agricultural showground	Monument	Welcome Lodge
Theme park	Golf course	Days Inn Hotel
Farm or animal centre	County cricket ground	Welcome Break or Moto Burger King
Zoological or wildlife collection	Rugby Union national stadium	Kentucky Fried Chicken
Bird collection	International athletics stadium	
Aquarium	Horse racing	

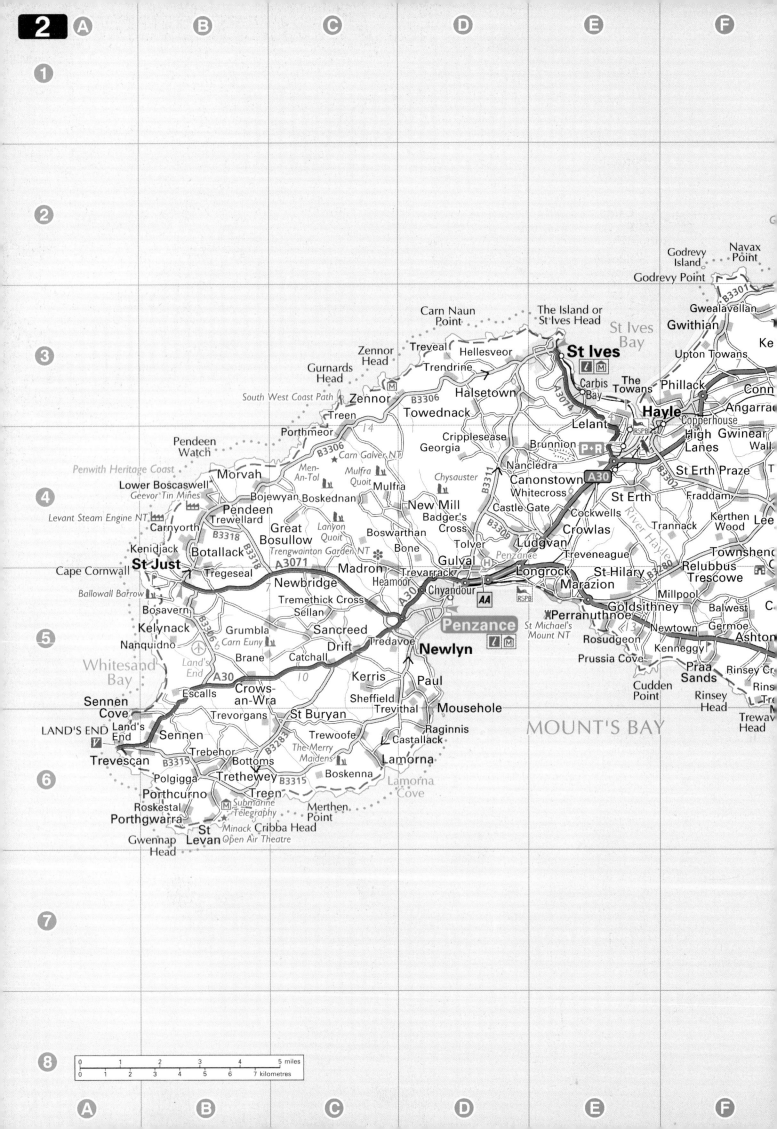

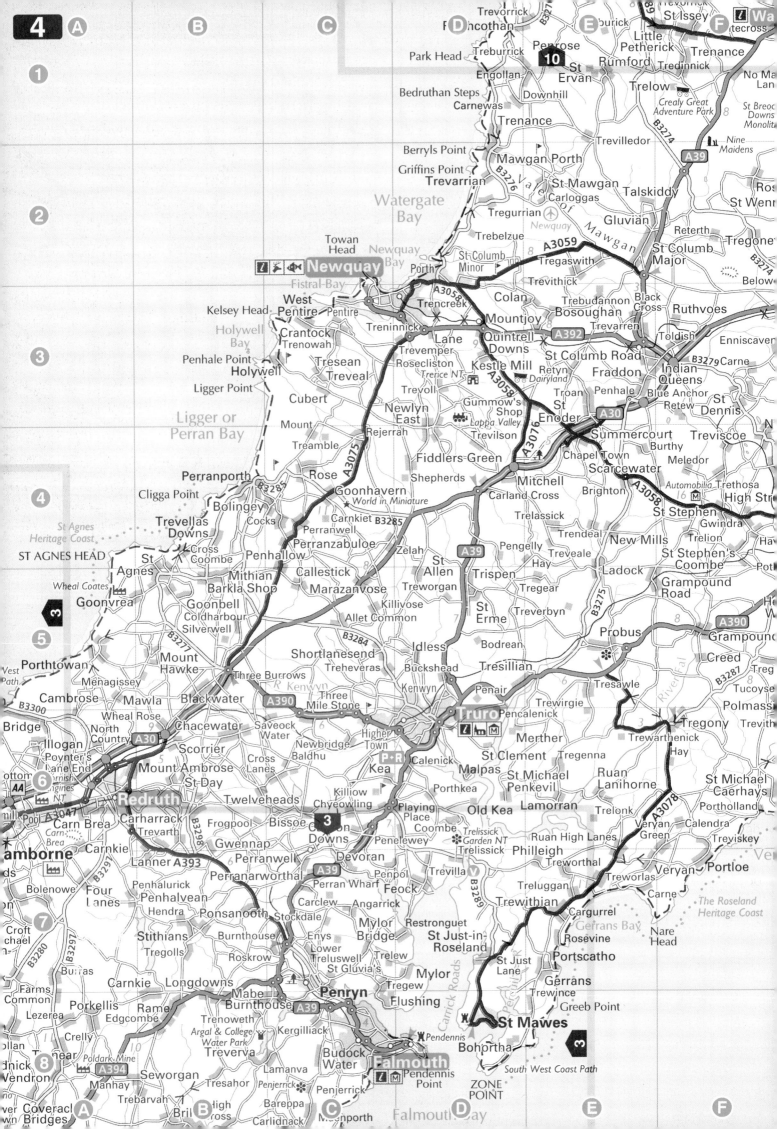

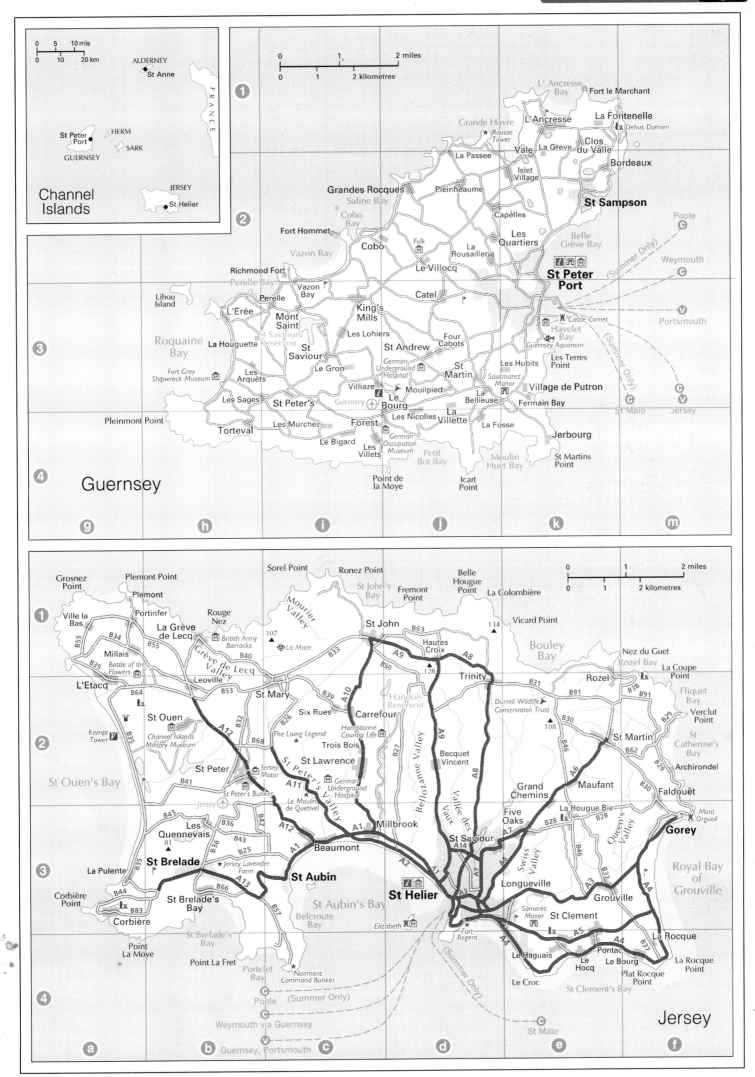

Channel Islands

FRANCE

ALDERNEY
• St Anne

St Peter
Port • HERM
GUERNSEY SARK

JERSEY
• St Helier

Guernsey

0 5 10 mls
0 10 20 km

L' Ancresse Bay
Fort le Marchant
L'Ancresse
La Fontenelle
Grande Havre
Dehus Dolmen
Rousse Tower
Vale
La Grève
Clos du Valle
La Passee
Islet Village
Bordeaux
Pleinheaume
Grandes Rocques
St Sampson
Saline Bay
Capelles
Cobo Bay
Les Quartiers
Belle Grève Bay
Fort Hommet
Folk
La Rousaillerie
Cobo
Le Villocq
St Peter Port
Vazon Bay
Catel
Richmond Fort
Castle Cornet
Perelle Bay
Vazon Bay
Havelet Bay
Lihou Island
Perelle
King's Mills
Four Cabots
Guernsey Aquarium
L'Erée
Mont Saint
Les Lohiers
St Andrew
Les Terres Point
Roquaine Bay
St Saviour Reservoir
German Underground Hospital
St Martin
Sausmarez Manor
La Houguette
St Saviour
Le Gron
Les Hubits
Fort Grey Shipwreck Museum
Villiaze
Mouilpied
La Bellieuse
Village de Putron
Les Arquets
Le Bourg
Fermain Bay
Les Sages
St Peter's
Guernsey
La Villette
Pleinmont Point
Les Murchez
Forest
Les Nicolles
La Fosse
Torteval
Le Bigard
Jerbourg
Le Villets
German Occupation Museum
St Martins Point
Point de la Moye
Petit Bot Bay
Moulin Huet Bay
Icart Point

0   1   2 miles
0   1   2 kilometres

Poole (Summer Only)
Weymouth
Portsmouth
St Malo (Summer Only)
Jersey

Jersey

Grosnez Point
Plemont Point
Sorel Point
Ronez Point
Belle Hougue Point
La Colombière
Plemont
St John's Bay
Fremont Point
Ville la Bas
Portinfer
Mourier Valley
St John
Vicard Point
Nez du Guet
Rozel Bay
La Grève de Lecq
Rouge Nez
British Army Barracks
La Mare
Hautes Croix
134
Bouley Bay
La Coupe Point
Millais
Grève de Lecq Valley
Trinity
Rozel
Battle of the Flowers
Leoville
128
Fliquet Bay
L'Etacq
St Mary
Six Rues
Handois Reservoir
Durrell Wildlife Conservation Trust
Verclut Point
St Ouen
Carrefour
108
St Martin
Channel Islands Military Museum
The Living Legend
Hamptonne Country Life
St Catherine's Bay
Kempt Tower
Trois Bois
Archirondel
St Ouen's Bay
St Lawrence
Bellozanne Valley
Becquet Vincent
Grand Chemins
Maufant
Faldouët
St Peter
Jersey Motor
German Underground Hospital
Vallée des Vaux
Five Oaks
La Hougue Bie
Mont Orgueil
St Peter's Bunker
Le Moulin de Quetivel
St Saviour
Queen's Valley
Gorey
Jersey
Les Quennevais
Millbrook
Longueville
Royal Bay of Grouville
81
Beaumont
Swiss Valley
Grouville
St Brelade
St Aubin
Samarès Manor
La Pulente
St Helier
St Clement
La Rocque
Corbière Point
St Aubin's Bay
Le Haguais
Pontac
Corbière
St Brelade's Bay
Belcroute Bay
Elizabeth
Le Bourg
La Rocque Point
Point La Moye
Fort Regent
Le Hocq
Plat Rocque Point
Point La Fret
Portelet Bay
Noirmont Command Bunker
Le Croc
St Clement's Bay
Poole (Summer Only)
Weymouth via Guernsey
Guernsey, Portsmouth
St Malo

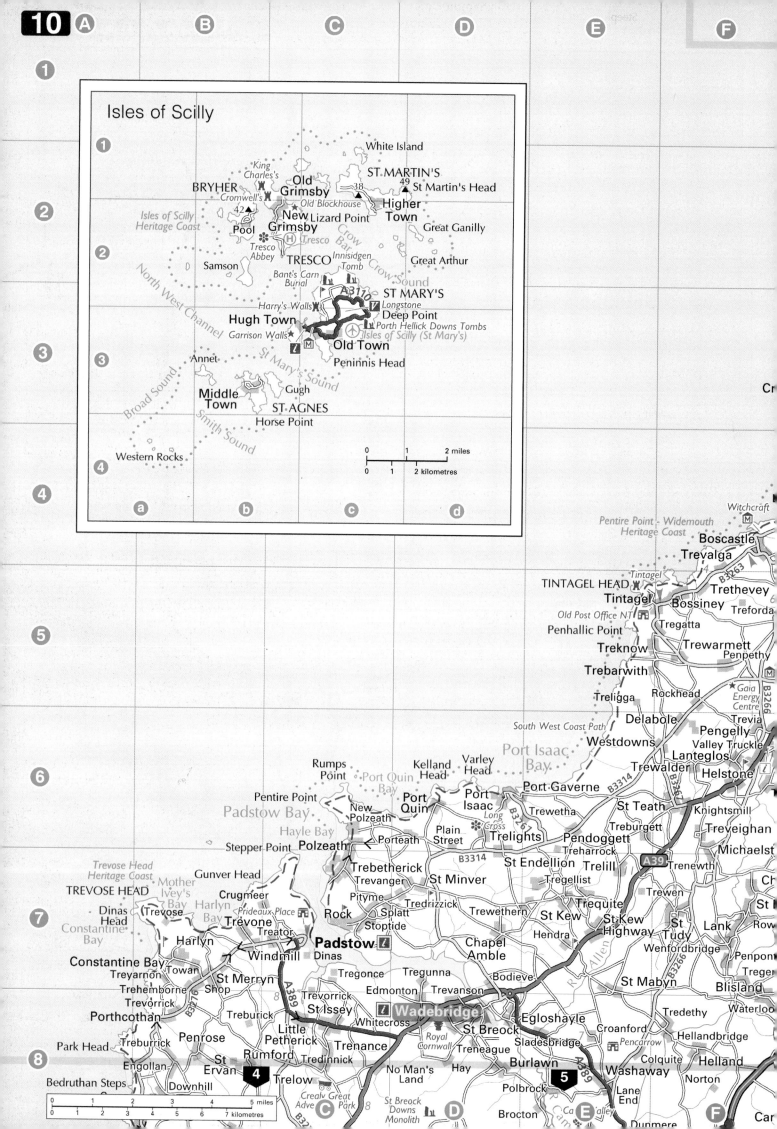

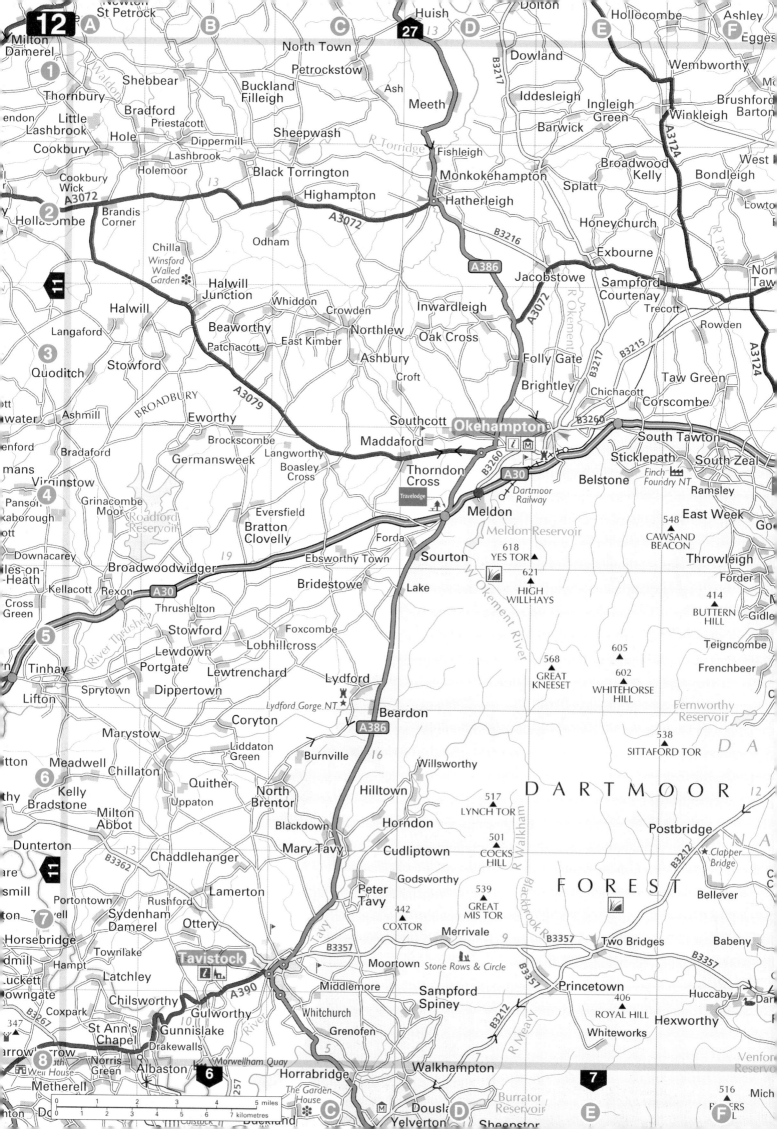

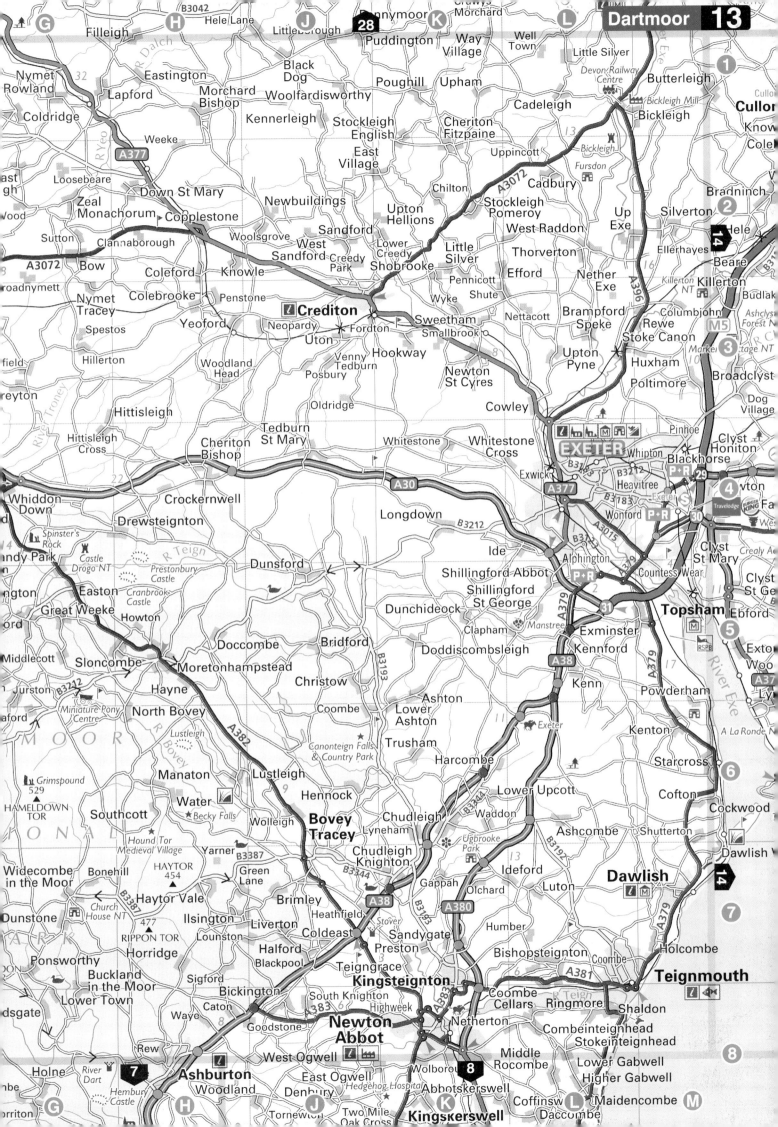

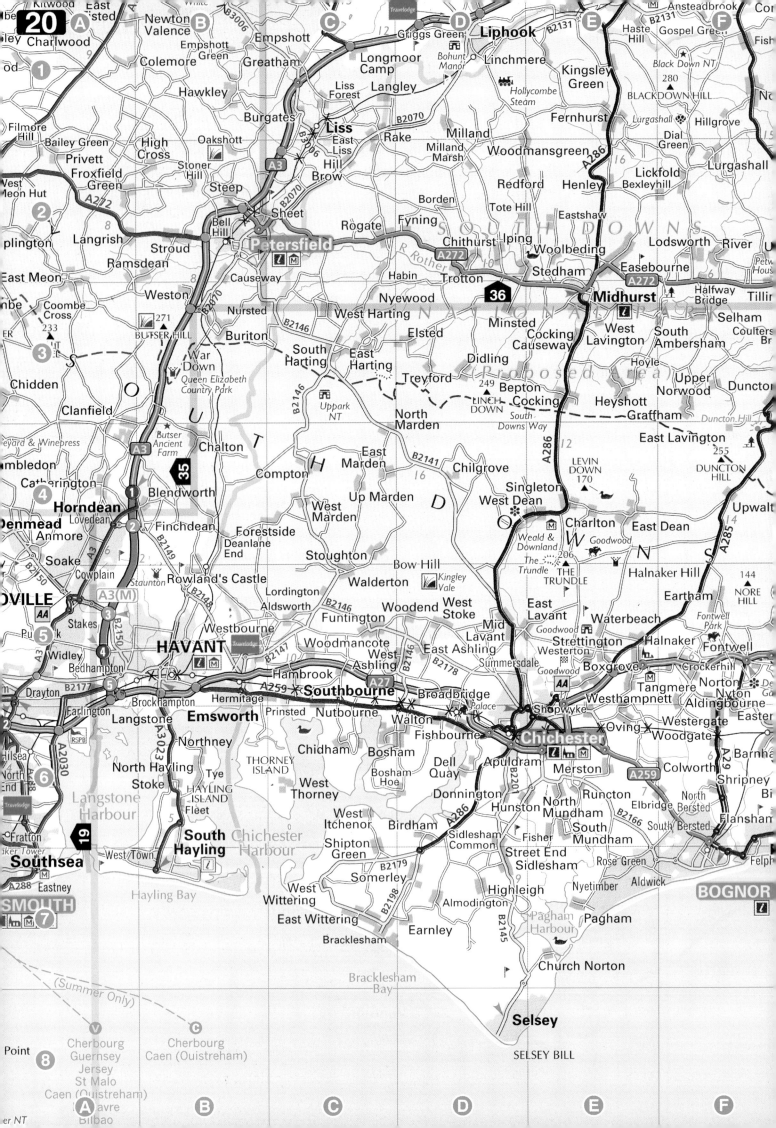

Horsham

St Leonards Forest

G **H** **J** **K**

Ifold
Plaistow
chapel
Bucks Gr
Slinfold
Broadbridge Heath
Court
Littlehaven
Doomsday Green
Ashfold Crossways
B2195
B2110
1
Hand
B211
Nyn
Sl
A23
2

Toyhorse Int Stud Farm
Park Street
Christ's Hospital
Denne Park
Manning's Heath
Lower Beeding
Slaugham
Ashfold Crossways
B2237
The Haven
Itchingfield
A264
AA
P+R
Warninglid
Leonardslee
B2115
Crabtree
Southwater Street
Monk's Gate
A281
Nuthurst
Maplehurst
Bookers
Bolney
2

Newpound Common
Five Oaks
Southwater Street
Southwater
Copsale
A23
3

obernoe
Common
Kirdford
Barns Green
A29
A272
Coneyhurst Common
Dragons Green
A24
West Grinstead
Cowfold
Crosspost
Twineham Green
Hickstead
3

Balls Cross
Wisborough Green
A272
Parbrook
Billingshurst
Brooks Green
Whitehall
Shipley
Littleworth
Wineham
Twineham
Hickstead
A2

Strood Green
Adversane
Broadford Bridge
Coolham
West Grinstead
B2135
Shermanbury
Sayers Common
Albourne Green

Petworth
Byworth
Bedham
North Heath
37
Gay Street
Broomer's Corner
Goose Green
Dial Post
Partridge Green
B2116
High Cross
Blackstone
Albourne
A272
A29
River Arun
Codmore Hill
Little Bognor
Broomershill
Holly Gate Cactus Garden
B2133
Henfield
West End
Nep Town
A281

Egdean
Fittleworth
Lower Fittleworth
Coates
Stopham
Nutbourne
West Chiltington
Thakeham
Spear Hill
Ashington
Ashurst
Woodmancote
A23
4

Barlavington
Roman Villa
A283
Pulborough
Marehill
Hardham
Greatham
Wiggonholt
Heath Common
Cootham
Hole Street
Wiston
Buncton
A2037
Small Dole
Woods Mill
Newtin
A283
B2138
Coldwaltham
Watersfield
RSPB
Parham
Storrington
Rock
B2135
Upper Beeding
Edburton
Poyning

BIGNOR HILL
225
West Burton
Bury
Amberley
B2139
212
Sullington
A283
Washington
Chanctonbury Ring
Bramber
Fulking
Devil's Dyke

Houghton
North Stoke
KITHURST HILL
South Downs Way
A24
Steyning
TRULEIGH HILL
213

HARROW HILL
167
North End
Findon
Botolphs
S
O

South Stoke
Burpham
Wepham
Wildfowl & Wetlands Trust
Cissbury Ring
Coombes
A283
5
Mile Oak
Hanglet
We
Blatch

Arundel
A27
Warningcamp
Poling Corner
Patching
Clapham
High Salvington
Lancing College Chapel
Old Shoreham
A27
Portslade

Binsted
Walberton
Crossbush
Hammerpot
HIGHDOWN HILL
Durrington
Salvington
Upper Cokeham
Sompting
A259
AA
Southwick
Portslade-by-Sea

North End
Tortington
Poling
Angmering
A2032
West Tarring
Broadwater
A2222
AA
Shoreham-by-Sea
A259

Lyminster
Wick
Hangleton
A259
Lancing
RSPB
H

Burndell
Ford
Rustington
Ferring
Kingston
Goring-by-Sea
West Worthing
A259
6

Climping
A259
Littlehampton
East Preston
Worthing
WORTHING

Ancton
Atherington
Elmer
dleton-on-Sea
22
7

GIS

| 0 | 1 | 2 | 3 | 4 | 5 miles |
| 0 | 1 | 2 | 3 | 4 | 5 | 6 | 7 kilometres |

8

G **H** **J** **K** **L** **M**

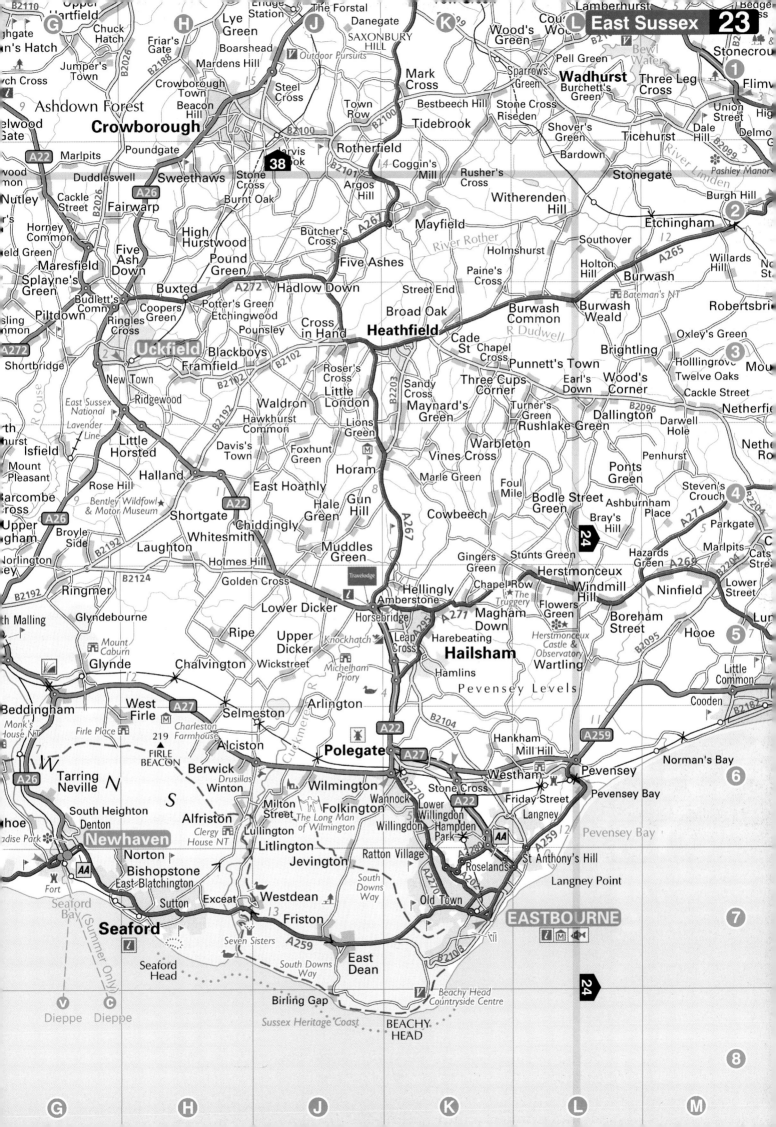

Michaels

Woodchurch

Brook Street

G

Leigh Green

B2082

The Leacon

H

South of England Rare Breeds Centre

Kenardington

Reading Street

B2080

Small Hythe

Smallhythe Place NT

Peening Quarter

ISLE OF OXNEY

Appledore

Appledore Heath

The Stocks

Stone

River Rother

Iden

Fairfield

Snargate

Brookland

A259

Rye Foreign

A259

Playden

Rye

Houghton Green

East Guldeford

WALLAND MARSH

7

B2089

Rye Harbour

Camber

Camber

Winchelsea Beach

Rye Bay

helsea

m

B12

og Hill

Cliff End

Bilsing

K

40

Hamstreet

Warehorne

A2070

Newchurch

R O M N E Y   M A R S H

Snave

Norwood

Brenzett Green

Brenzett

Ivychurch

Old Romney

A259

4

New Romney

B2075

Lydd

Lydd

RSPB

Pilot Inn

Power Station Visitor Centre

★ Old Lighthouse

DUNGENESS

Ruckinge

St Mary in the Marsh

Aeronautical Museum

Port Lymbne

Bridge

Donkey Street

Burmarsh

A259

Romney, Hythe & Dymchurch Railway

Hythe

9

Seabrook

Dymchurch

Martello Tower

St Mary's Bay

Littlestone-on-Sea

B2071

Greatstone-on-Sea

1

2

3

4

5

6

7

8

G **H** **J** **K** **L** **M**

J

Royal Military Canal

A   B   C   D   E   F

1

North West
Point

*Lundy
Heritage Coast*   LUNDY

2   ▲142

Marisco

Shutter Point   Surf Point

3

4   B A R N S T A P L E

O R

5   B I D E F O R D   B A

*Shipload
Bay*

HARTLAND POINT

Titchberry   Brownsham   *Hartland
Heritage C.*

Damehole
Point   *Hartland Abbey
& Garden*   Clovelly

Stoke   B3248   Velly   Buck's
Mills

Hartland Quay   Hartland   Higher   Hor
Clovelly   Cro

*Spekes Mill
Mouth*   Milford   Philham   6   Buck's
Cross   A39

Elmscott   *Milky Way*   Woolfardisworthy   Parkh

Hardisworthy   Cranford   Parkham
Ash

South
Hole

Welcombe   Ashmansworthy

Mead   Meddon   East
Putford

7   Darracott   East   Dinworthy   West
Woolley   Youlstone   Putfor

Gooseham   Eastcott   *16*   Colscott   Ha

Morwenstow   West Youlstone   Bradworthy

Higher Sharpnose Point   Shop   *Killarney
Springs*   Kimworthy   Bic

*South West
Coast Path*   Woodford   *Tamar
Lakes*   Darracott   Sutcombe

Lower Sharpnose Point   Kilkhampton   Alfardisworthy
Sutcombemill

8   Steeple Point   Stibb   Thurdon   Mi
Brocklands   Soldon   Dan

0 1 2 3 4 5 miles
0 1 2 3 4 5 6 7 kilometres   *Sandy
Mouth*   C   A39   D   **11**   E   Soldon   F
Cross

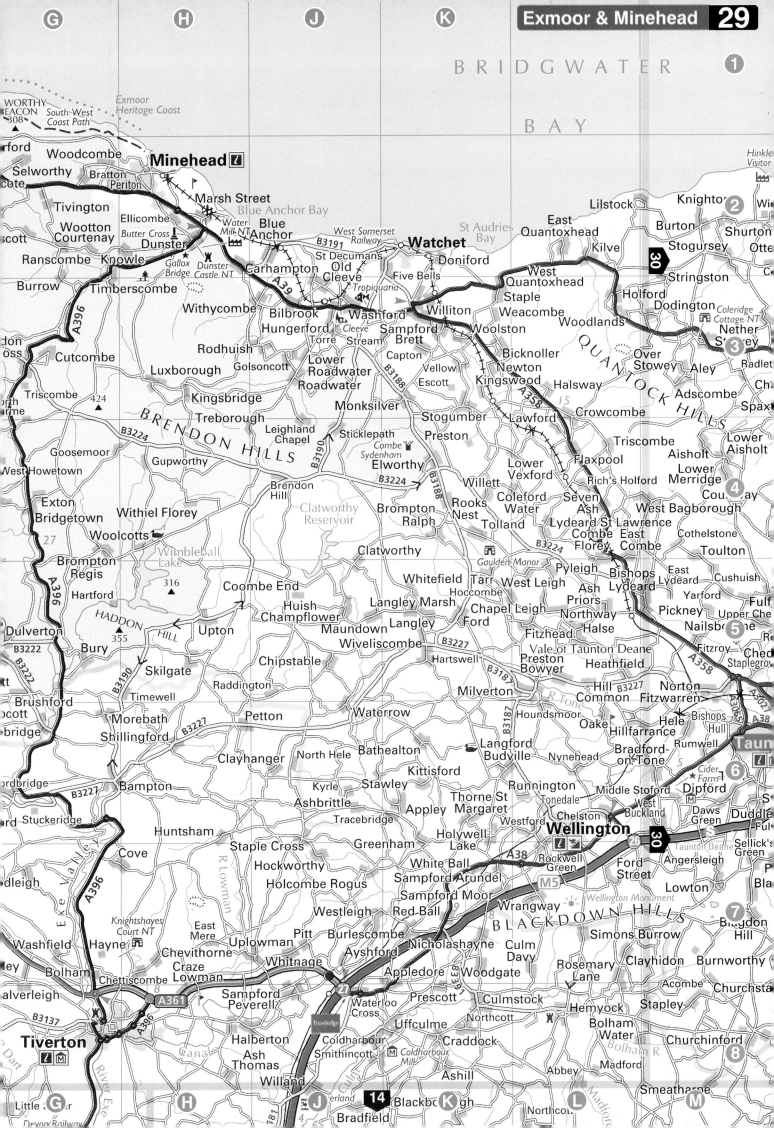

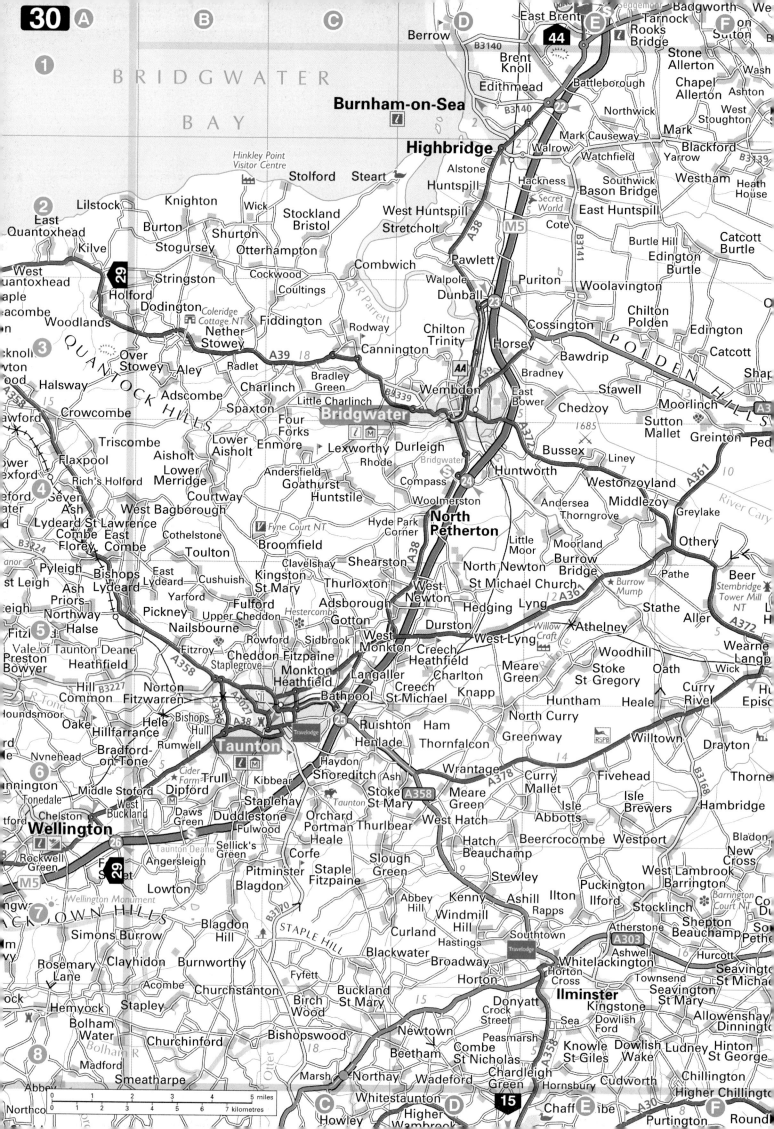

Cheddar

G H J 45 K Chewton Mendip Easton Bathway Clapton Chilcompton Stratton-on-the-Fosse Kilmersdon A362 Babington Buck Din

Draycott B3135 Emborough B3114 Downside Holcombe Newbury Upper Highbury Vobster Mells

Priddy East Water B3139 Gurney Slade Ham Vobster Little Green Whatley

Clewer Old Ditch Green Ore Binegar Nettlebridge Coleford

Cocklake Rodney Stoke A371 Ebbor Gorge Westbury-sub-Mendip A37 Ashwick Oakhill Stoke St Michael East End Leigh upon Mendip Chantry

Wedmore Latcham Easton Lower Milton Wookey Hole West Horrington Darshill Downside Dean Leighton A361 Cloford Trudoxh

Theale Henton Walcombe South Horrington East Horrington Shepton Mallet Doulting East Cranmore Wanstrow

Bagley Panborough Burcott Mill Wookey Dulcote Dinder Darshill Cranmore East Somerset Railway Chesterblade Higher Alham West Town

Bleadney Worth Coxley Wick Wells Croscombe West Compton Charlton Prestleigh Stoney Stratton Batcombe Upton Noble

Godney Southway North Town Pilton B3136 East Compton Westcombe Milton Clevedon SEAT HILL North Brewham

Meare Fish House Brindham North Wootton Westholme Royal Bath and West Showground Evercreech B3081 South Brewham King Alfred's Tower NT

Glastonbury A361 Street on the Fosse Pylle Lamyatt West End Bruton Hardwa

Glastonbury Tor NT Havyatt West Pennard Hambridge Wyke Champflower Dovecote

Northover Edgarley Woodland Street East Pennard Huxham Green Wraxall Ditcheat Ansford Cole Redlynch Stoney Stoke

Street Butleigh Wootton West Town Parbrook A37 Alhampton Clanville Pitcombe Shepton Montague Charlton Mus

Overleigh Coxbridge Tilham Street College Green Stone Hornblotton Green Alford Castle Cary Bratton Seymour Penselw

Baltonsborough Ham Street Four Foot Clanville Lovington Galhampton Hadspen Wincanton Bayford

Compton Dundon Butleigh Gosling Street Catsham Southwood West Lydford East Lydford North Barrow Yarlington A371

Dundon Silver Street Barton St David Kingweston Lydford on Fosse Wheathill Foddington South Barrow Brookhampton Woolston Lattiford Wi

Somerton Charlton Mackrell Babcary North Cadbury Blackford Holton Maperton

Pitney B3153 Charlton Adam Haynes Motor Museum Little Weston Compton Pauncefoot North Cheriton

Midney Kingsdon Downhead West Camel Sparkford South Cadbury South Cheriton Horsington

Upton South Hill Catsgore Podimore Queen Camel Sutton Montis Charlton Horethorne Abbas Comb

Long Sutton Travelodge Northover Bridgehampton Wales Marston Magna Corton Denham Stowell Templecombe

Knole Little Load Ilchester RNAS Yeovilton Fleet Air Arm Chilton Cantelo Rimpton Milborne Wick Yenston

Long Load Yeovilton Limington Ashington West Mudford Adber Sandford Orcas Milborne Port Henstridge Ash

Witcombe A37 Draycott A303 Yeovil Marsh Mudford Sock Mudford Poyntington Henstridge

Stapleton Coat Ash Tintinhull NT Chilthorne Domer Up Mudford Oborne Purse Caundle

Martock Treasurer's House NT Montacute Thorne Trent Nether Compton Stallen Goathill Stalbridge Weston

Norton sub Hamdon Stoke sub Hamdon AA Preston Plucknett Yeovil Over Compton Worldwide Butterflies Haydon North Wootton Allweston Stourton Caundle

Hurst NT Montacute House NT Odcombe A3088 Sherborne Folke Bishop's Caundle

Over Stratton Little Norton Brympton West Coker Barwick Bradford Abbas Thornford Lillington Longburton A3030 Caundle Marsh Holwell

West Chinnock East Chinnock Chiselborough Burton Stoford East Coker Leweston

Middle Chinnock Hardington Moor Hardington Mandeville Haselbury Plucknett Sutton Bingham Beer Hackett Knighton Boys Hill Crouch Hill Pleck King's

Crewkerne North Perrott G 15 H Hardington Marsh J Closwo K 16 Ryme Intrinseca Yetminster Hamlet Holnest L Sandhills East Pulham M

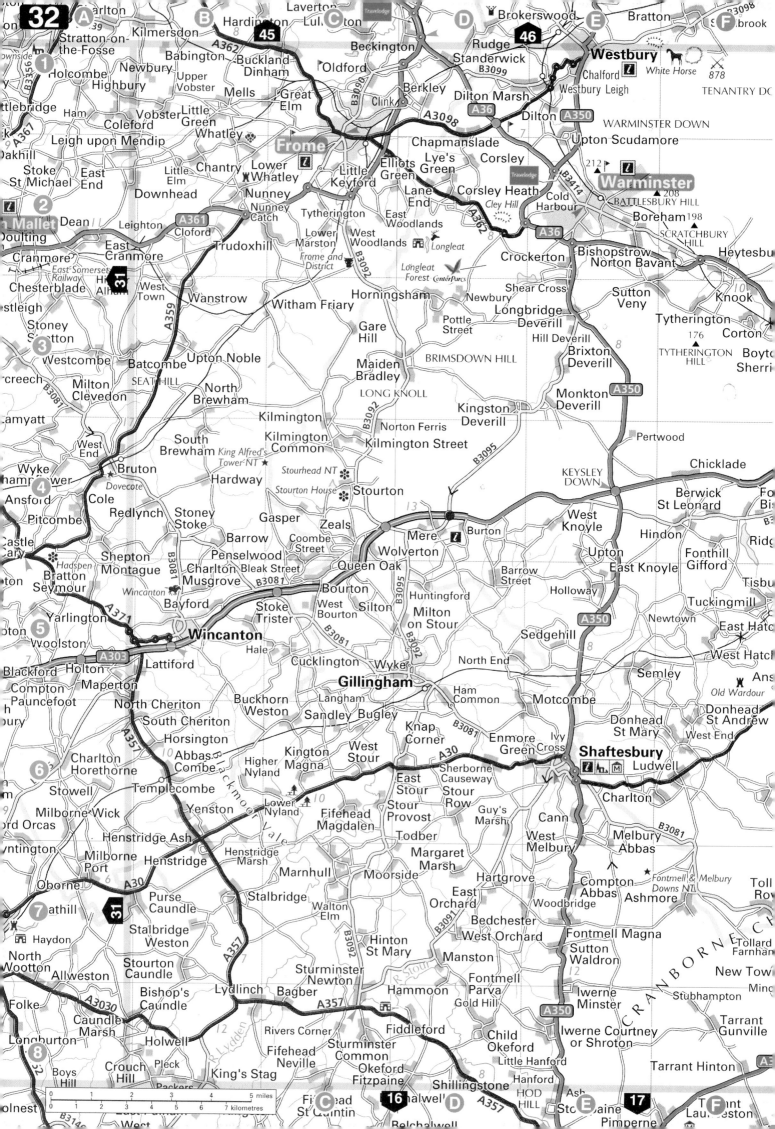

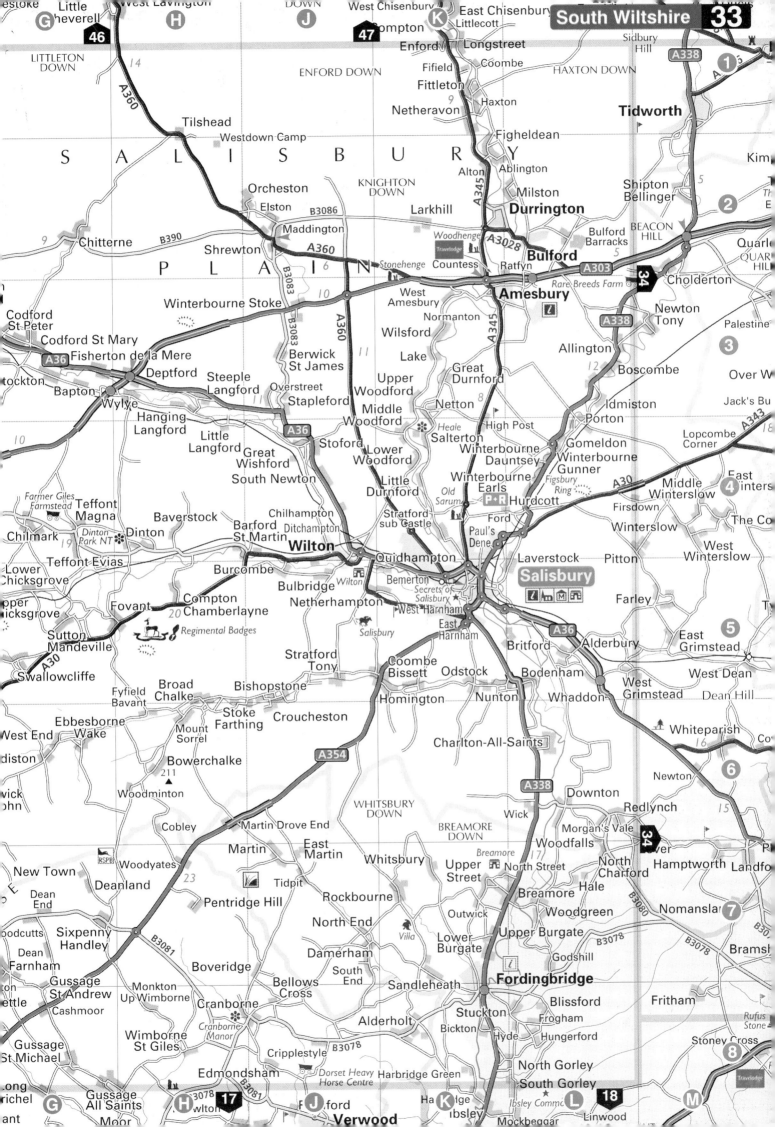

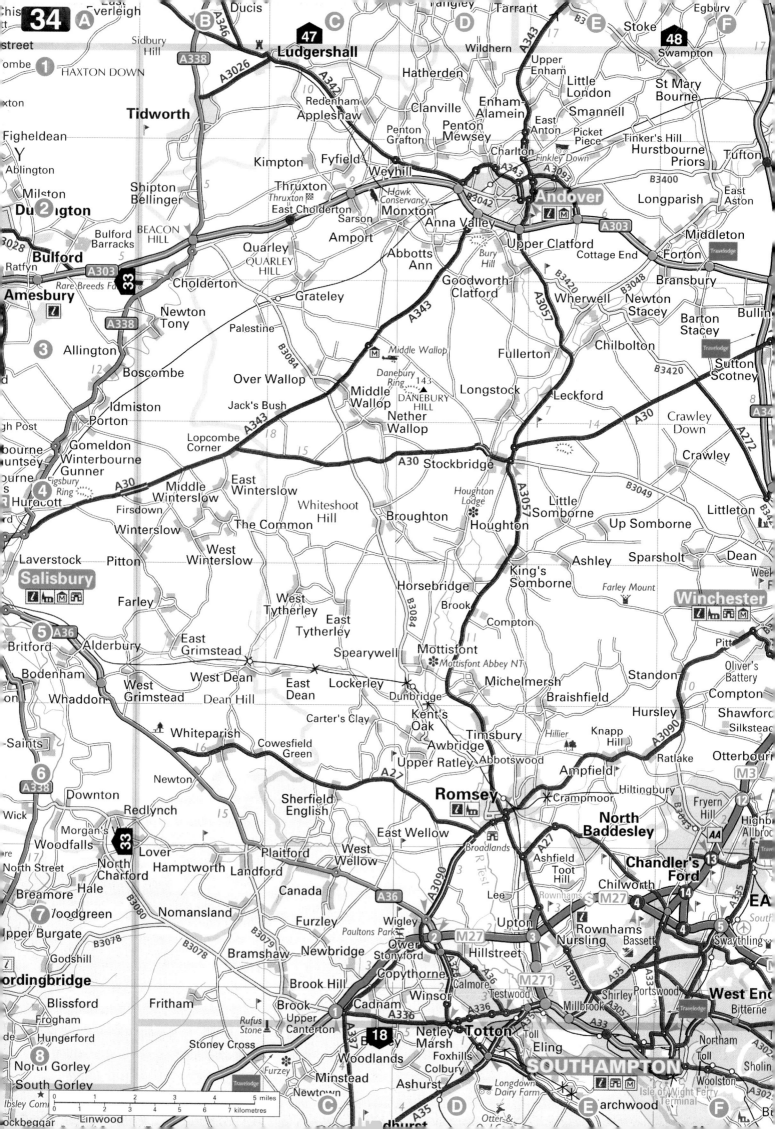

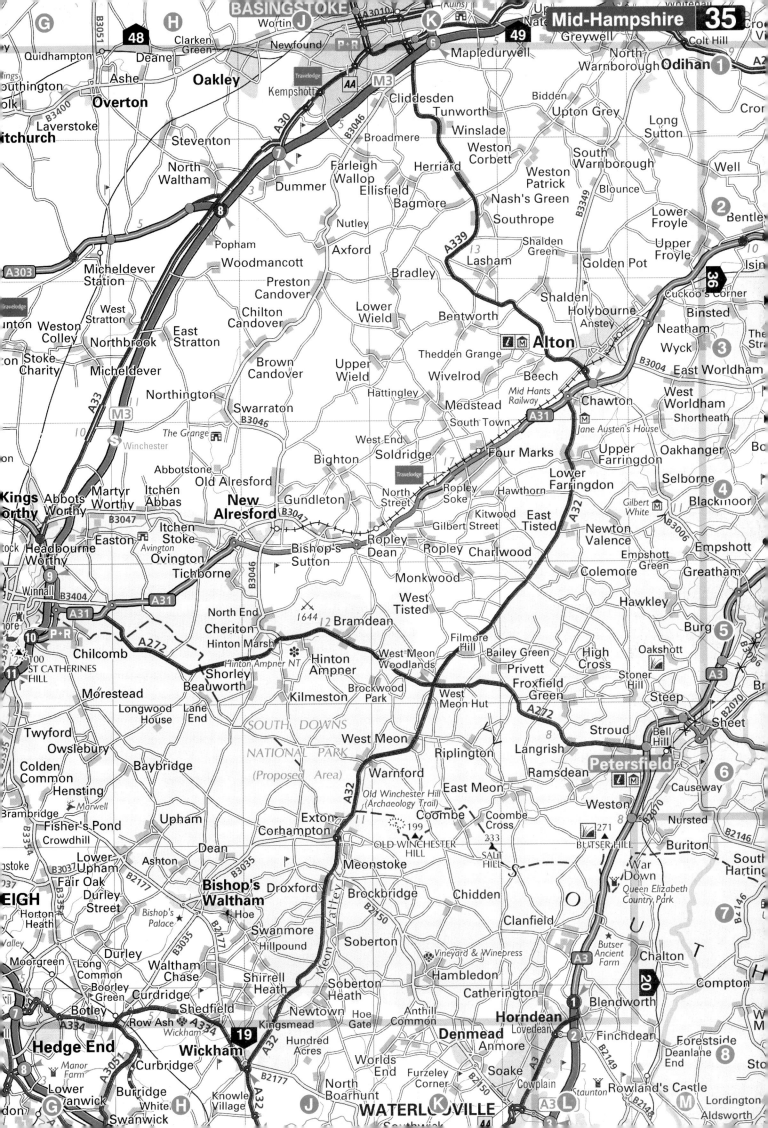

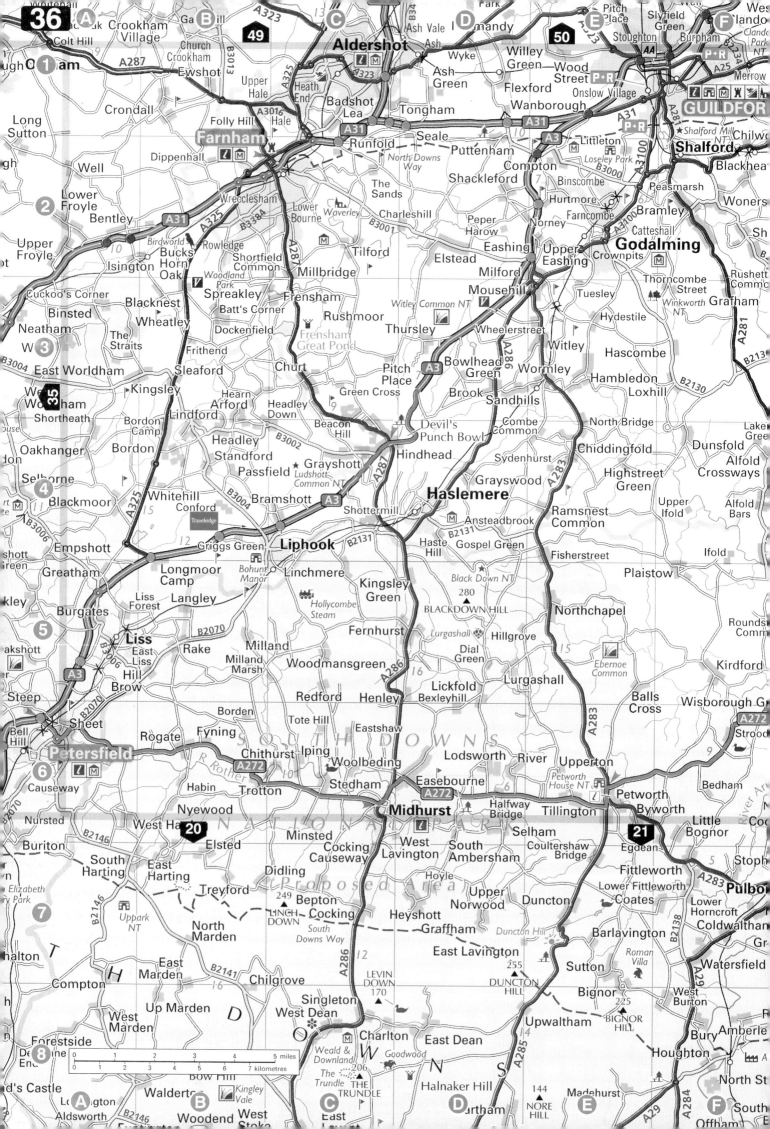

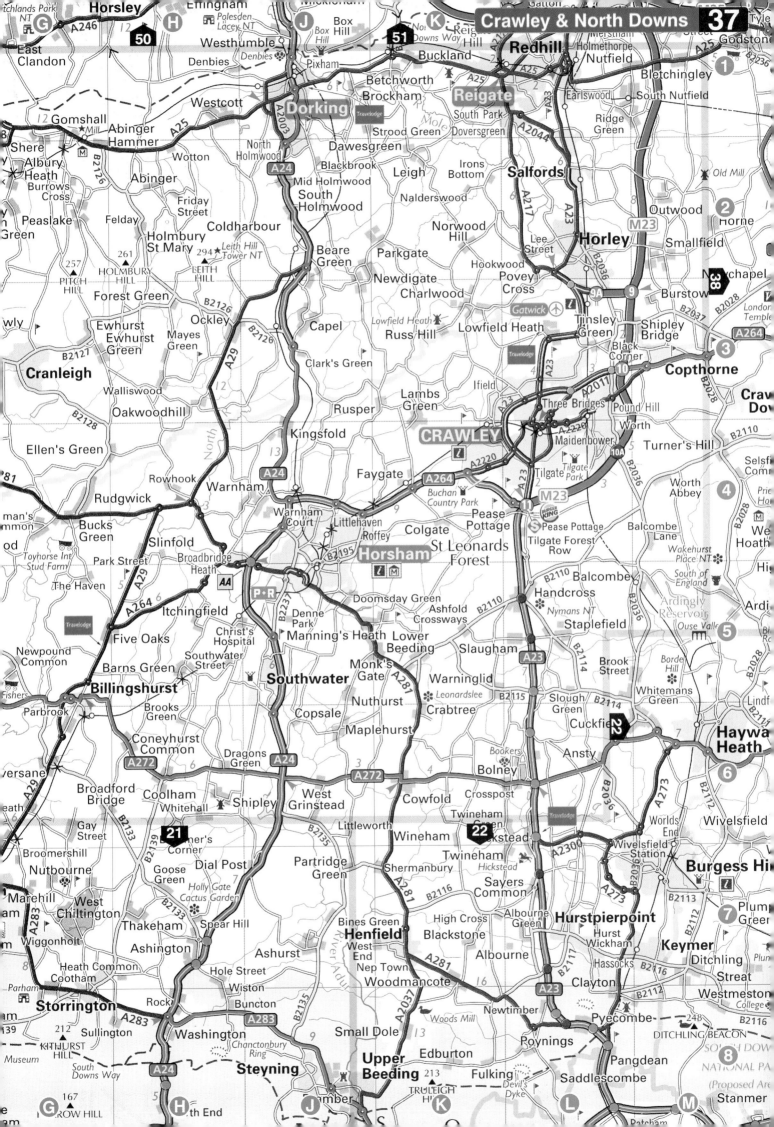

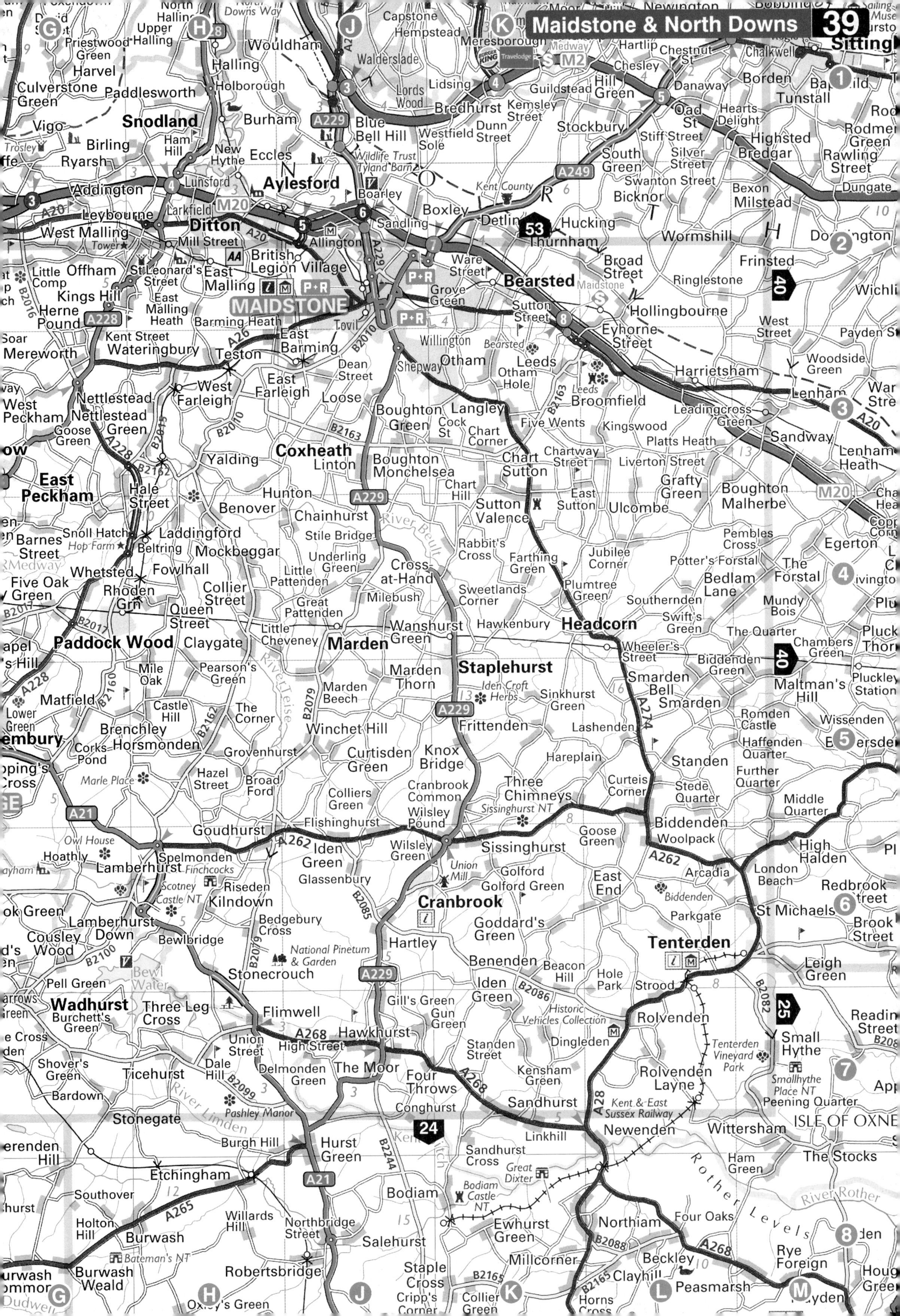
Sittingbourne
Wouldham
Halling
Snodland
Burham
Aylesford
Addington
Leybourne
Ditton
West Malling
East Malling
MAIDSTONE
Bearsted
Detling
Thurnham
Hollingbourne
Harrietsham
Lenham
Walderslade
Bredhurst
Boxley
Stockbury
Bicknor
Wormshill
Frinsted
Borden
Tunstall
Bredgar
Milstead
Teston
Wateringbury
Mereworth
East Farleigh
Loose
Coxheath
Linton
Boughton Monchelsea
Otham
Langley
Leeds
Broomfield
Kingswood
Chart Sutton
Sutton Valence
East Sutton
Ulcombe
Headcorn
Yalding
Nettlestead
East Peckham
Hunton
Benover
Laddingford
Collier Street
Paddock Wood
Claygate
Marden
Staplehurst
Frittenden
Smarden
Biddenden
Sissinghurst
Cranbrook
Goudhurst
Lamberhurst
Kilndown
Horsmonden
Brenchley
Matfield
Pembury
Benenden
Tenterden
Rolvenden
Hawkhurst
Flimwell
Wadhurst
Ticehurst
Stonegate
Etchingham
Hurst Green
Burwash
Robertsbridge
Salehurst
Bodiam
Sandhurst
Newenden
Northiam
Beckley
Peasmarsh
Wittersham
ISLE OF OXNEY
Rother Levels
River Rother
River Beult
River Teise
River Medway
Bewl Water
A20
A21
A26
A28
A229
A249
A262
A268
A274
A265
A228
M20
M2
40
53
24
25

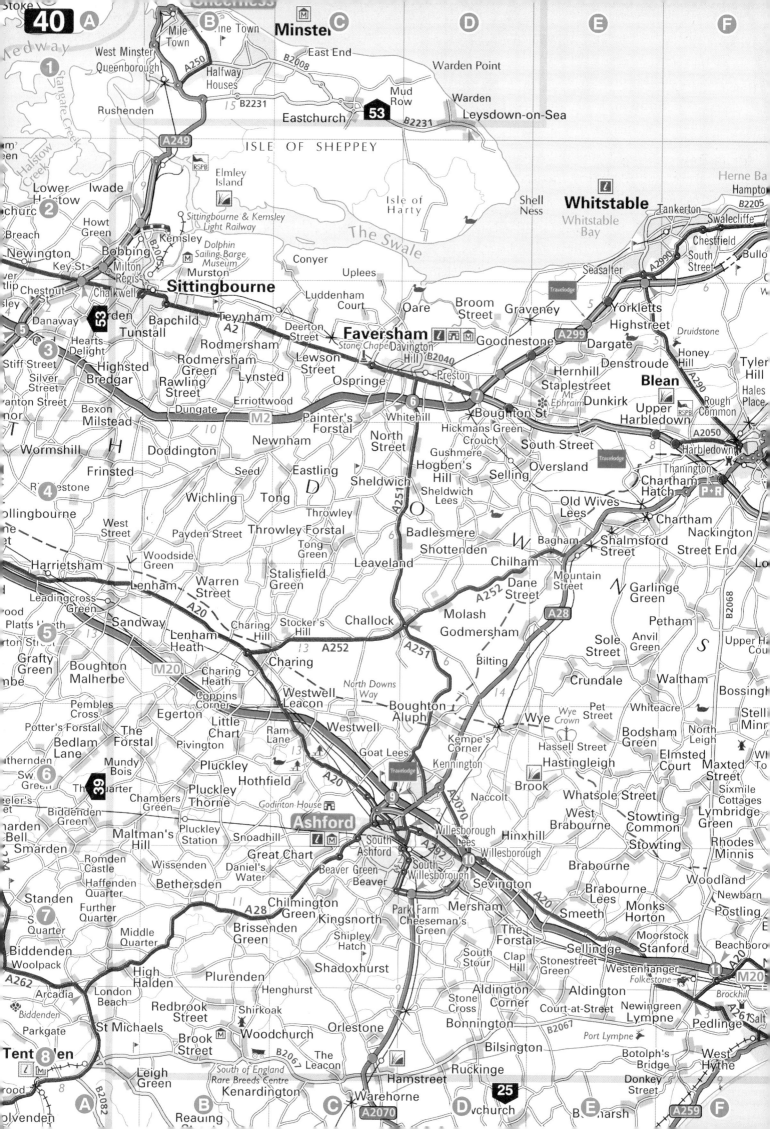

G H J K L

1

MARGATE
Foreness Point
Westgate on Sea
Westbrook
Cliftonville Kingsgate
Northdown
B2052
NORTH FORELAND
Minnis Bay
Birchington
Garlinge
Reading Street Lighthouse
B2052
Minnis Bay
Brooks End
Salmestone Grange
Lydden
Westwood
St Peter's
Broadstairs

2

Herne Bay
Bishopstone Reculver
Beltinge Hillborough
Eddington
Broomfield
Herne
Potten Street
St Nicholas at Wade
Boyden Gate
Sarre
Chislet
Acol
Manston
Haine
Manston
Travelodge
Dumpton
Hereson
St Lawrence
Ramsgate

Highstead
Maypole
Hoath
Hicks Forstal
Upstreet
West Stourmouth
Monkton Way
Cliffsend
Viking Ship 'Hugin'
Pegwell
Pegwell Bay

3

Hersden
Grove
East Stourmouth
R Stour
Minster
St Augustine's Cross
Westbere
Stodmarsh
Fordwich
Old Town Hall
Littlebourne
Preston Street
Elmstone
Cop Street
Hoaden
Weddington
Cooper Street
Richborough
Prince's
Sandwich Bay
Westmarsh
Paramour Street
Goldstone
Walmestone
Shatterling
Ash
Great Stonar
Sandwich
Royal St George's

4

terbury
Howletts
Bekesbourne Hill
Bramling
Ickham
Durlock
Guilton
Wingham Marshborough
Twitham
Staple
Barnsole
Stone Cross
Toll
Woodnesborough
Worth
Bekesbourne
Patrixbourne
Adisham
Ratling
Goodnestone
Eastry
Heronden
Statenborough
Ham
Hacklinge
Higham Park
Chillenden
Knowlton
West Street
Marley
Finglesham

5

ardres
hopsbourne
Kingston
Elmstead
Aylesham
Easole Street
Betteshanger
Great Mongeham
Sholden
Northbourne
The Downs
Deal
Marley
Derringstone
Womenswold
Holt St
Tilmanstone
Great Mongeham
Upper Deal
Barham
Woolage Village
Barfrestone
Elvington
Lower Eythorne
Sutton
East Studdal
Ripple
Walmer
Woolage Green
Eythorne
East Kent Railway
Mongeham
Ringwould
Breach
Shepherdswell
Ashley
Sutton Downs
Martin
Kingsdown
Bladbean
Denton
North Downs Way
West Langdon
A258

6

Wootton
Coldred
A2
Whitfield
East Langdon
St Margaret's at Cliffe
Geddinge
Temple Ewell
Guston
St Margaret's Bay
Selsted
Lydden
A256
West Cliffe
SOUTH FORELAND
North Elham
Ewell Minnis
Kearsney
River
Pines
Swingfield Minnis
Chilton
West Cliffe
Lighthouse NT
Swingfield Street
Wolverton
Buckland
Langdon Cliffs NT
South Foreland Heritage Coast

7

Ridge Row
Densole
Upper Standen
Alkham
St Radigund's
Maxton
Calais Dunkerque
Hawkinge
South Alkham
Drellingore
West Hougham
Farthingloe
DOVER
Boulogne
ttinge
minge
dlesworth
Lower Standen
Channel Tunnel Terminal
Battle of Britain
Capel le-Ferne
Satmar
A20
Peene
B2011
Samphire Hoe
Dover - Folkestone Heritage Coast
Channel Tunnel
gton
11A 12
Cheriton
Morehall
2
East Wear Bay
Calais

Horn Street
Sandgate
FOLKESTONE
Seabrook
A259

Hythe

5 miles / 7 kilometres

8

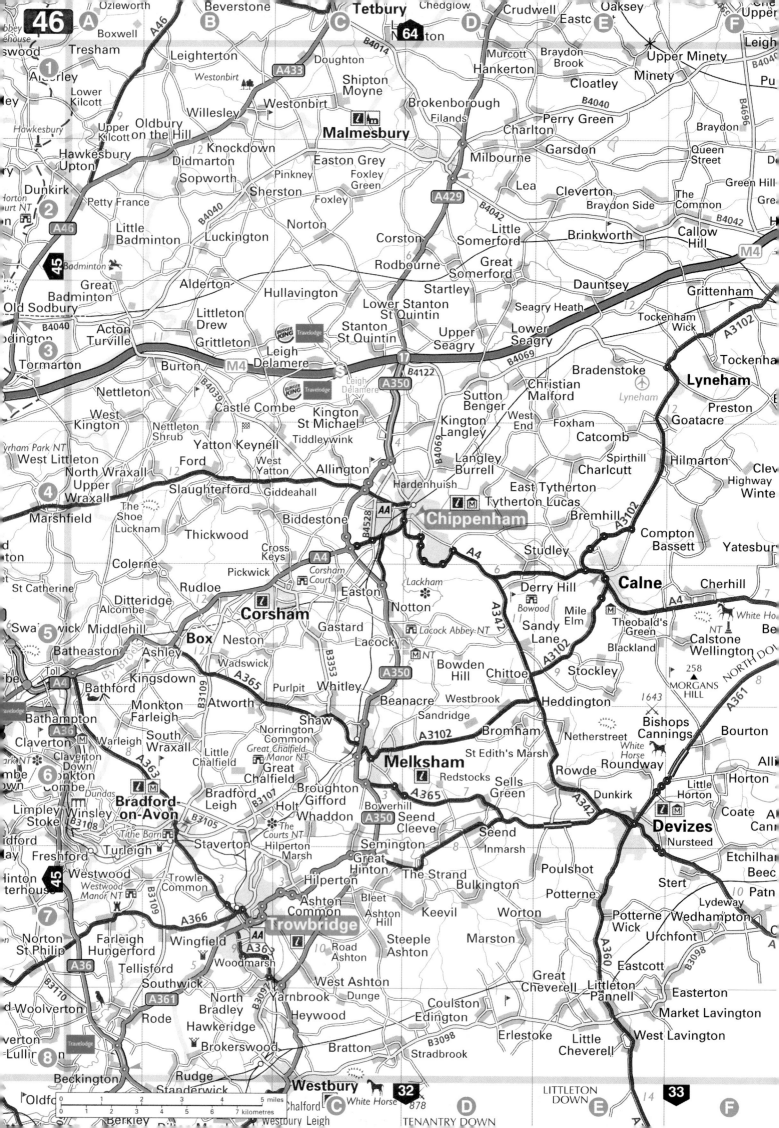

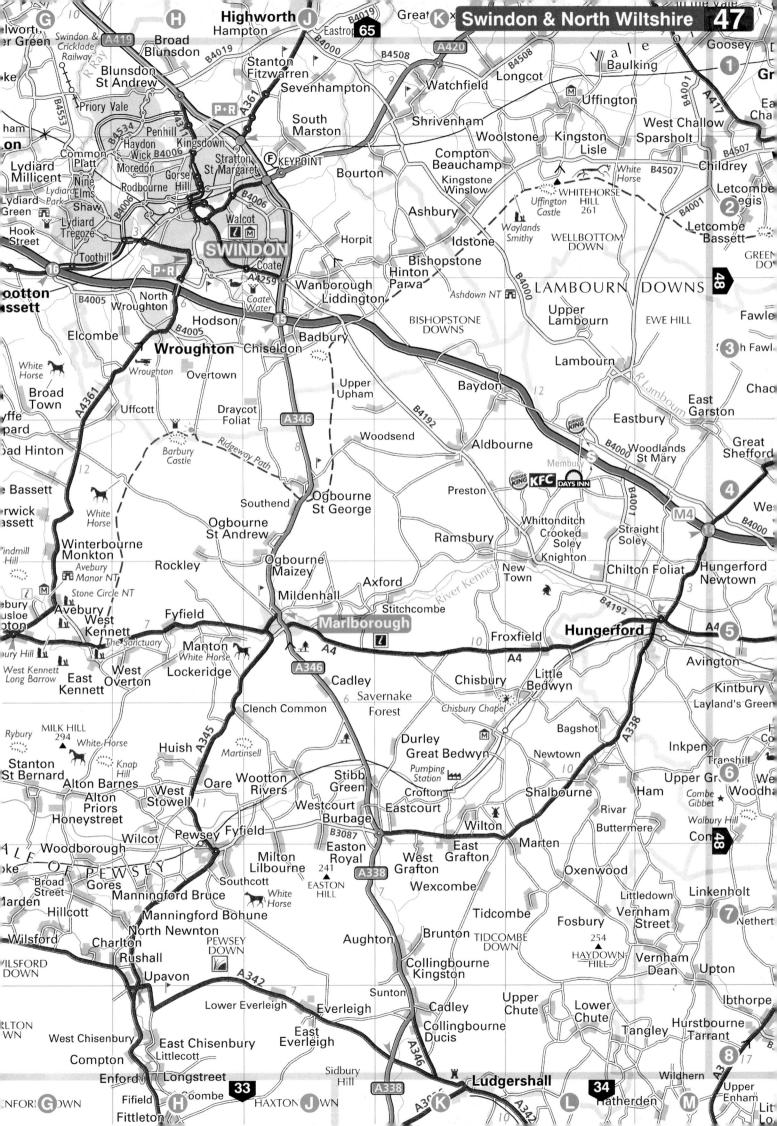

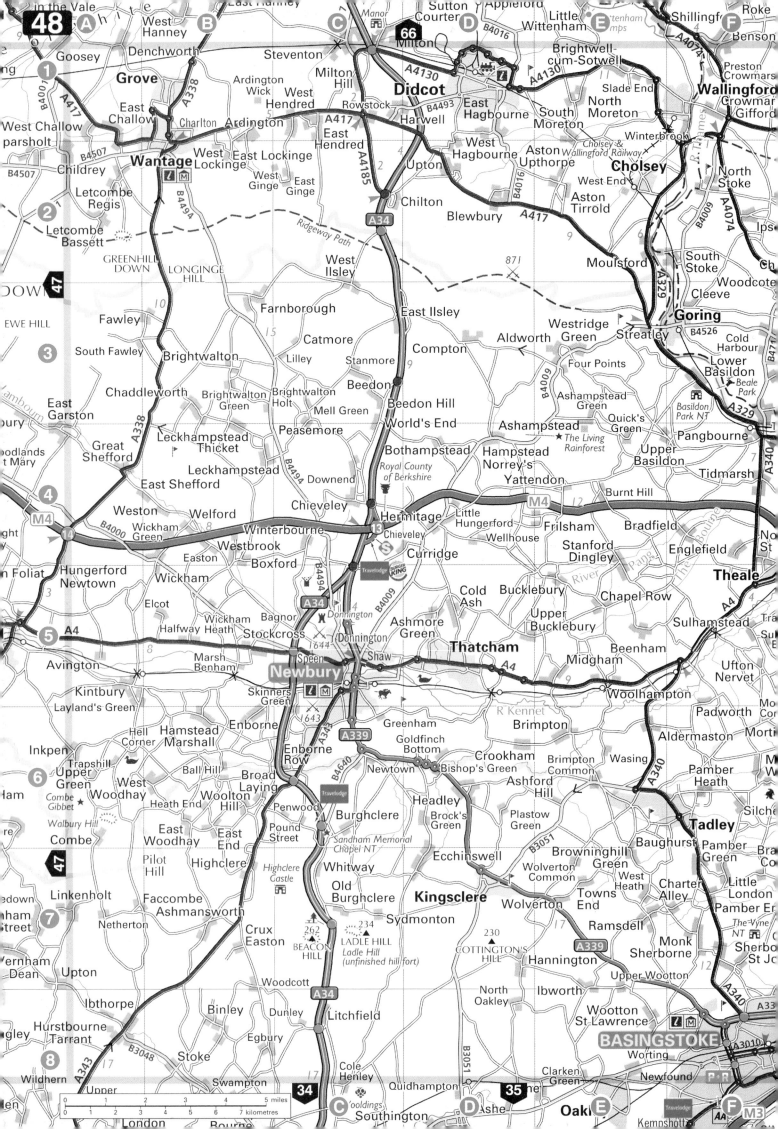

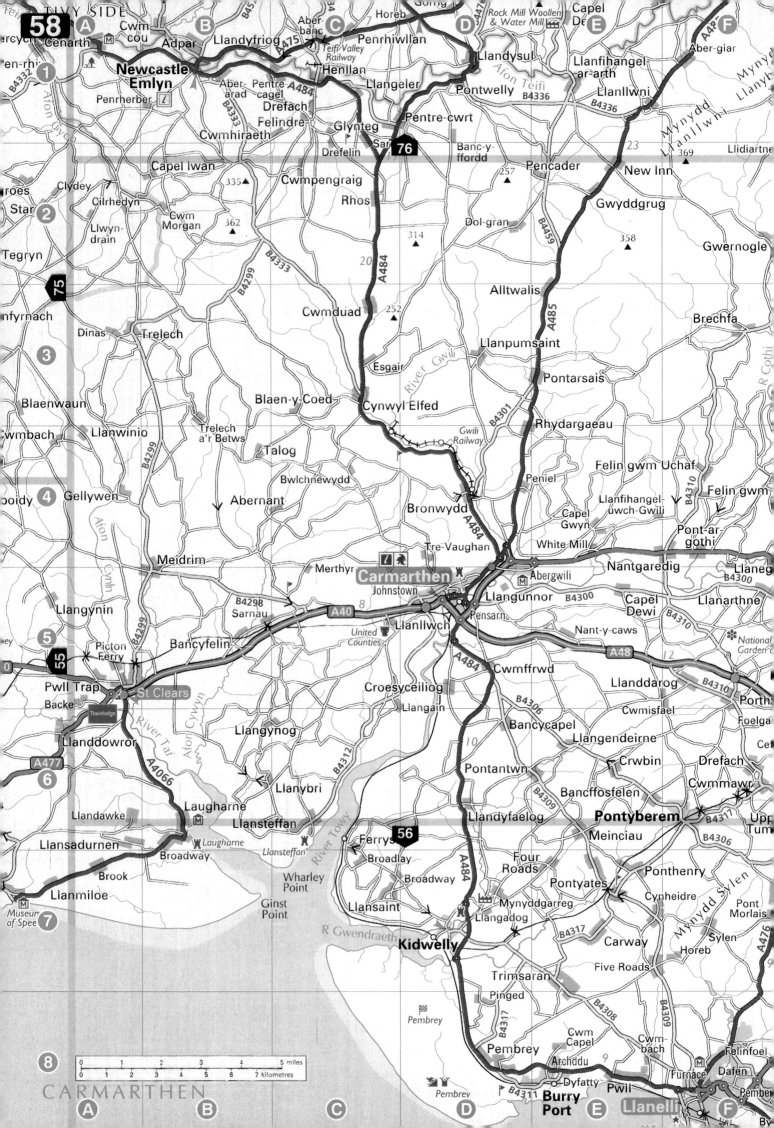

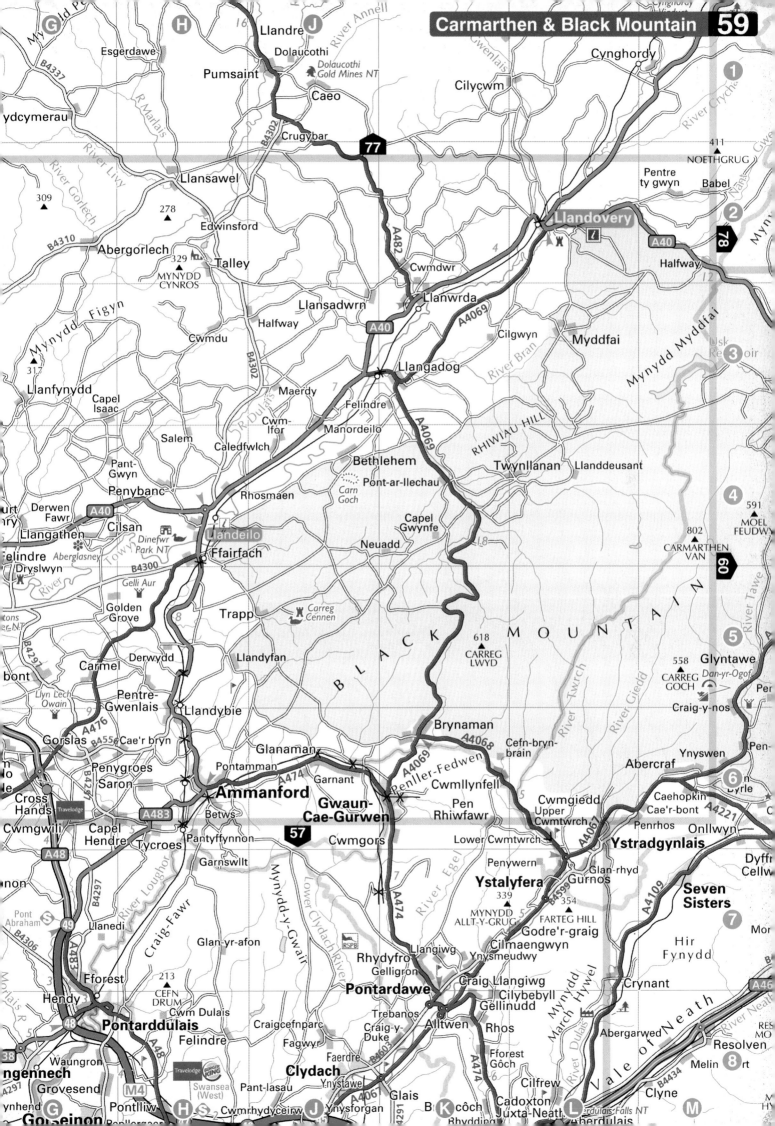

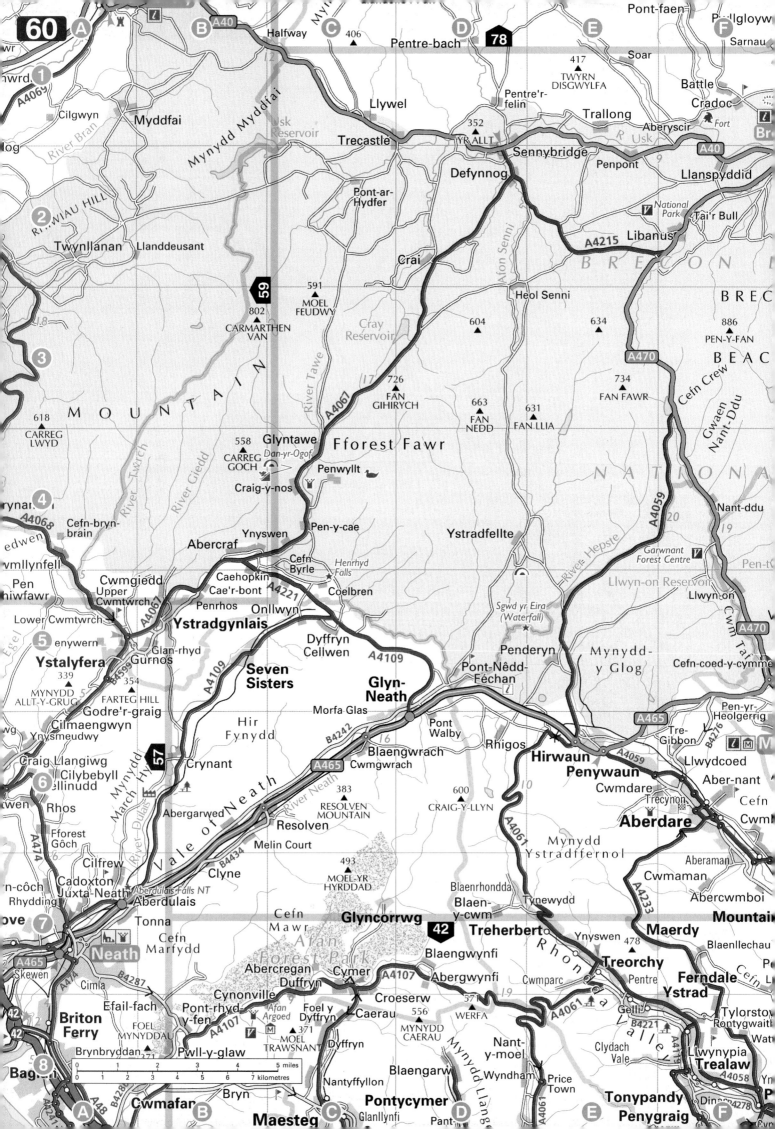

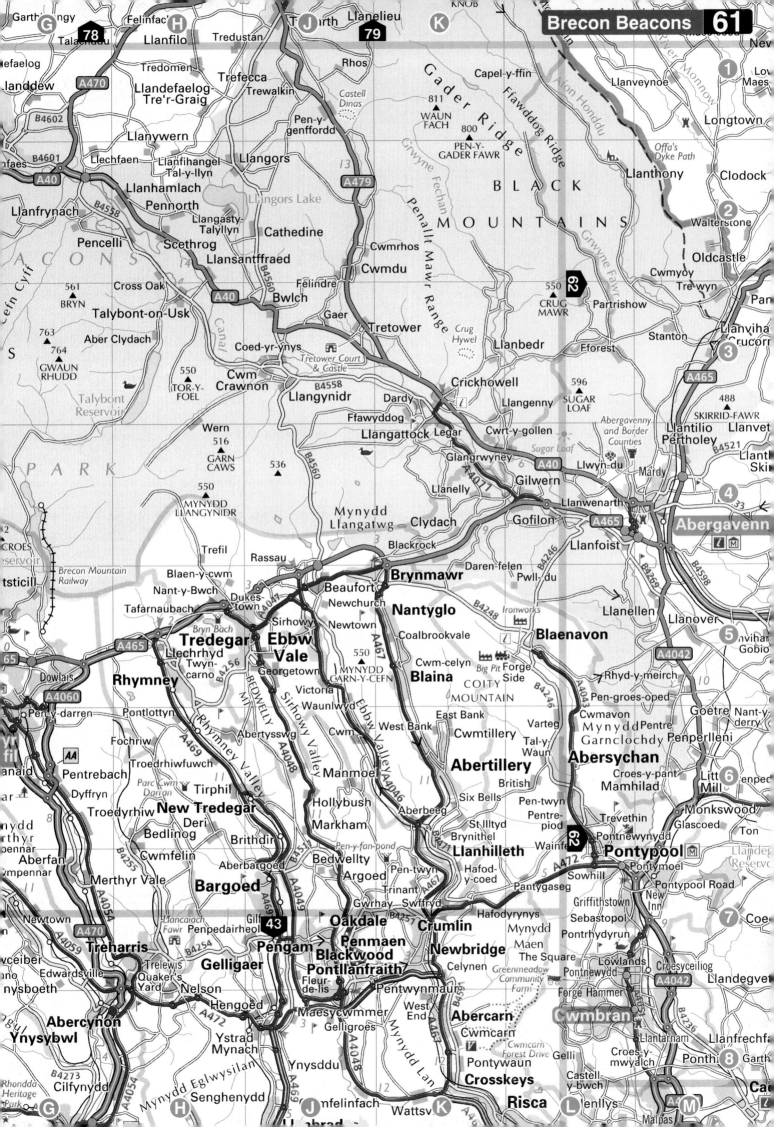

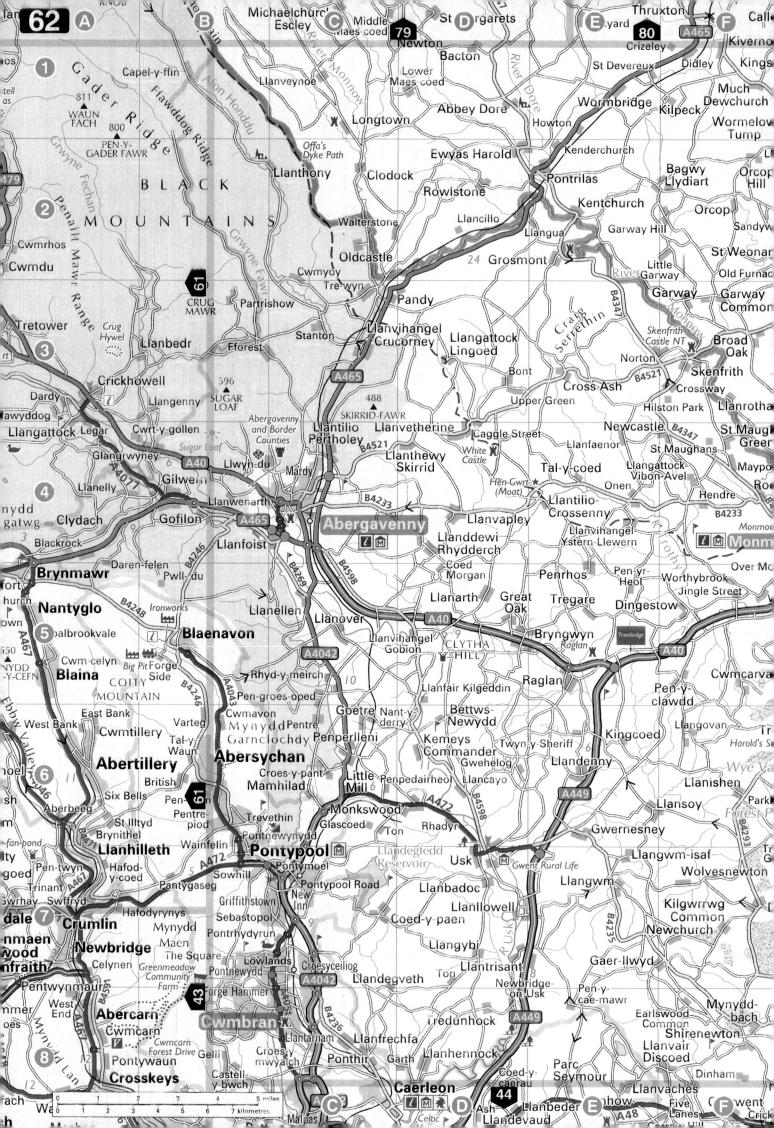

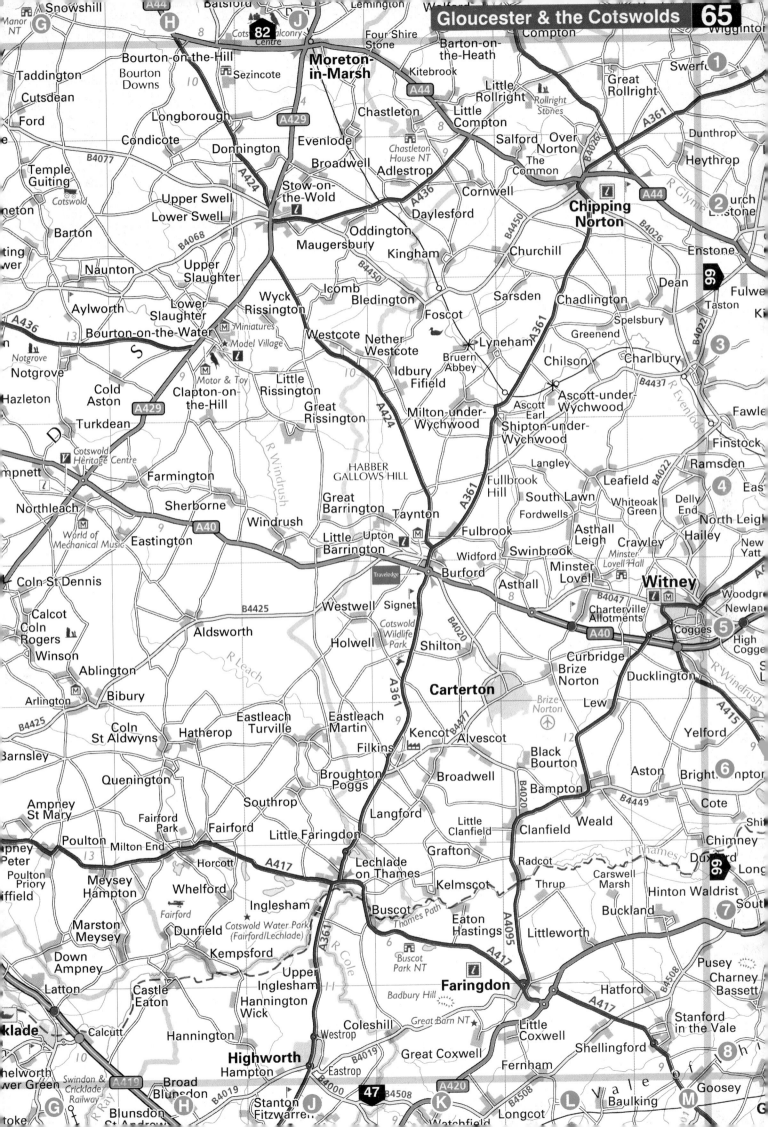

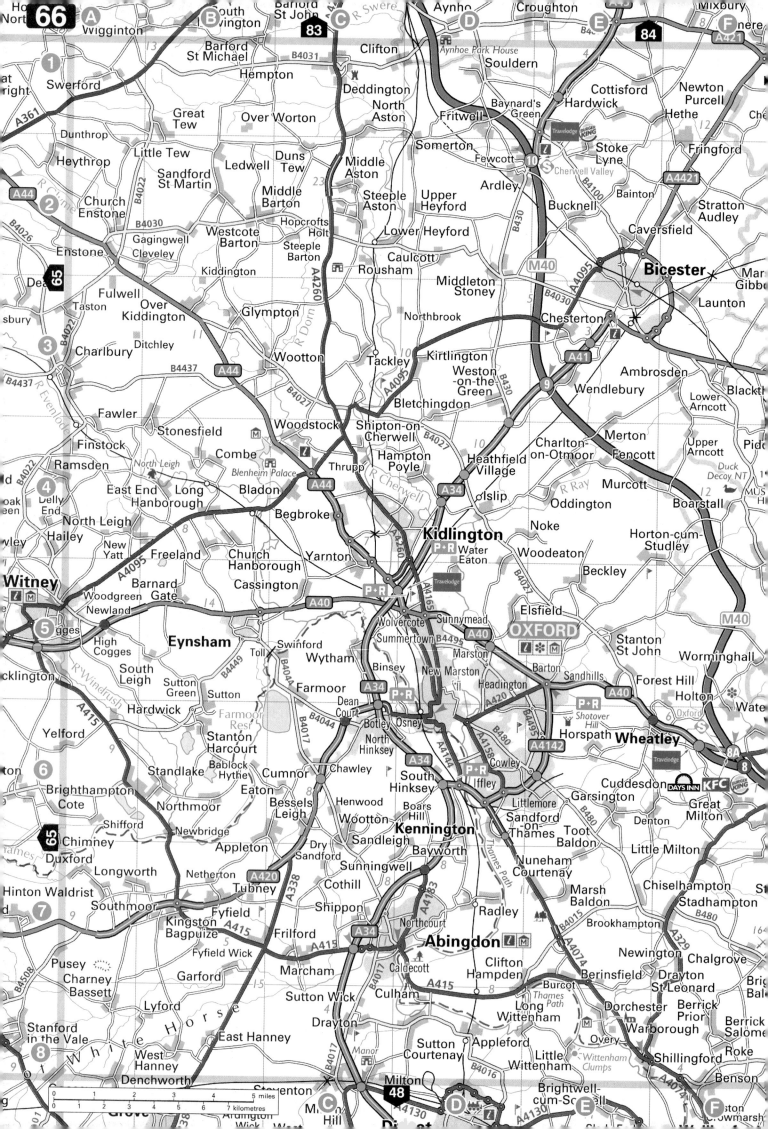

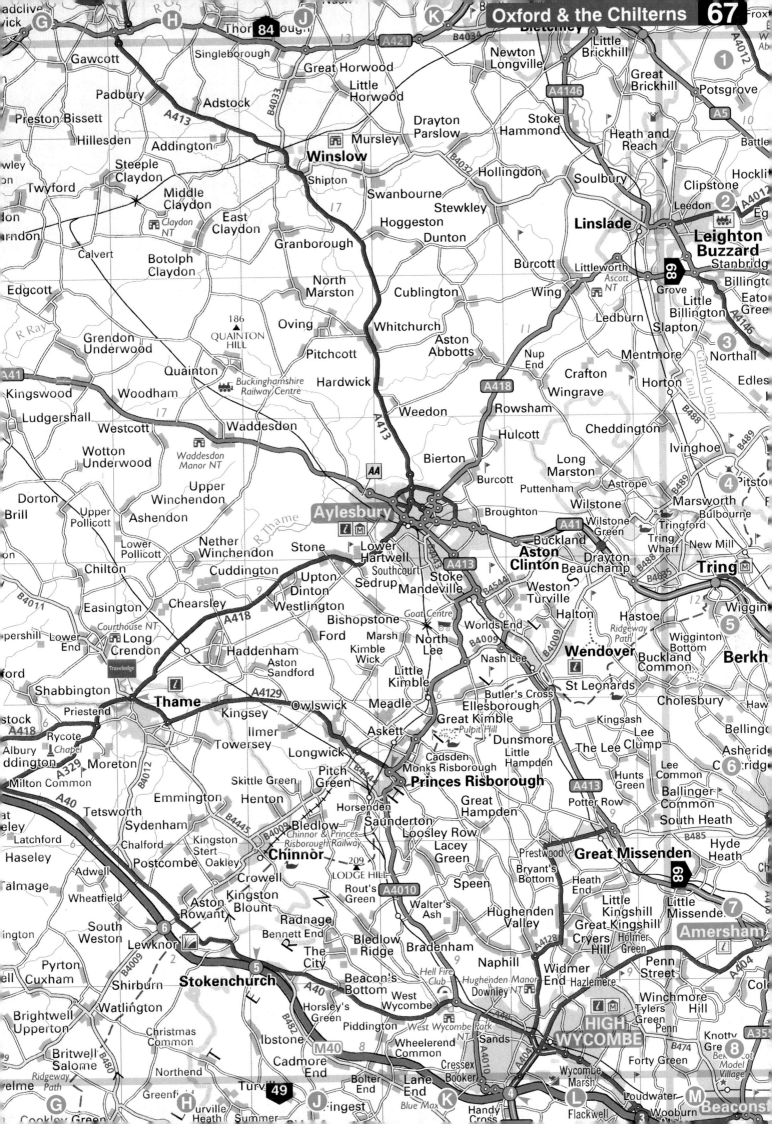

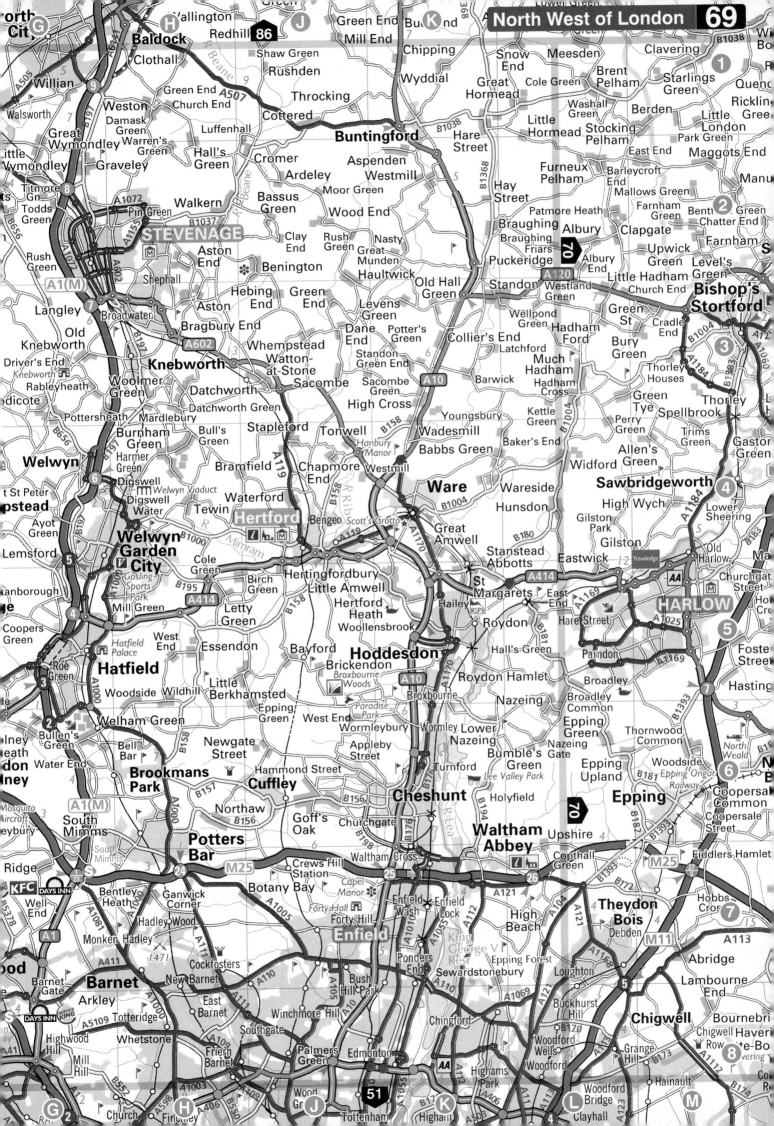

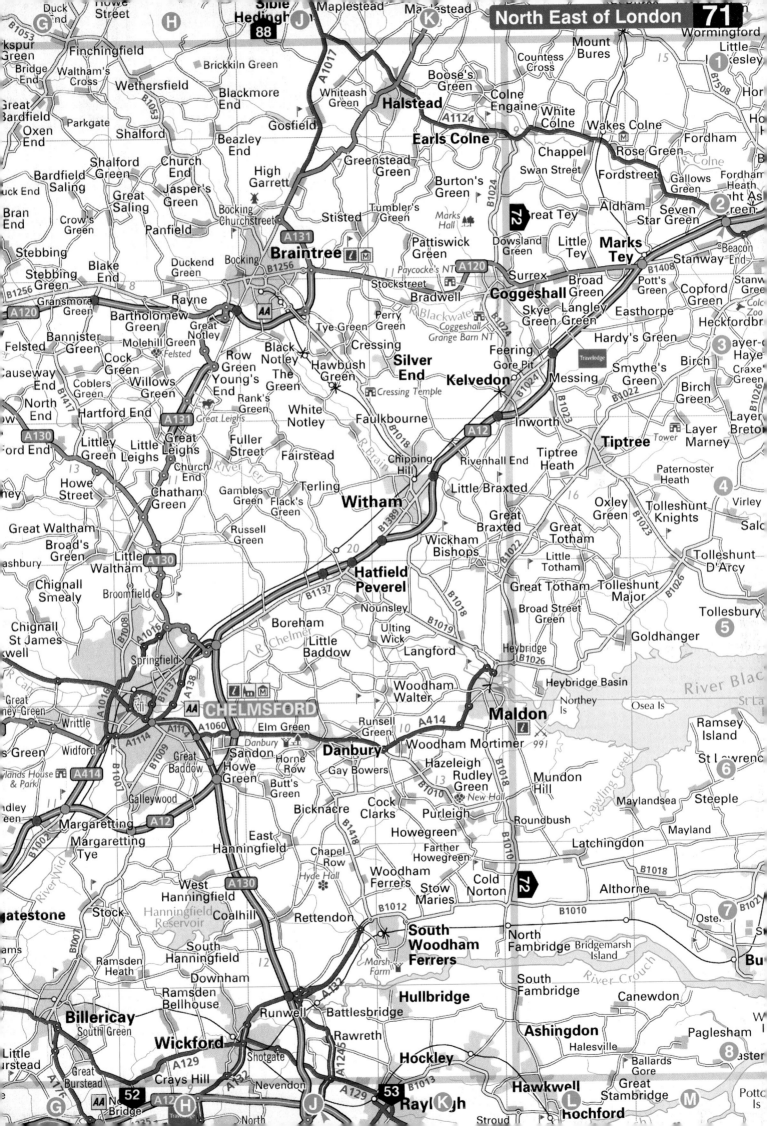

Brantham
Cattawade
atford /
Cottage N
Mistley Towers
Mistley
nningtree
New Mistley
ord
Mistley
Heath
Bradfield
Little
Bromley
Horsleycross
Street
Wix
ley
Great
Bromley
Little
Bentley
Tendring
Heath
Tendring Green
Goose
Green
Beaumont
ead
Hare Green
Tendring
Thorpe
Green
Thorpe-
le-Soken
Frating
Green
Frating
stead Row
Great
Bentley
Weeley
Aingers
Green
Thorrington
Weeley
Heath
ord
Cook's
Green
Little Clacton
Samson's
Corner
Hurst
Green
St Osyth
Rush
Green
ore
e
Point Clear
Jaywick
Colne Point
nt

Holbrook R
River Stour
Wrabness
RSPB
B1352
Bradfield Heath
A120
Wix
Green
Stones
Green
Goose
Green
B1414
B1035
B1033
B1441
B1414
A133
B1442
B1027
B1032

Street
Gate
International Fe
Terminal
Parkeston Quay
Parkeston
Upper
Dovercourt
Dovercourt
Harwich

Ramsey
Little
Oakley
Great
Oakley

Horsey
Island
Horsey Island

Kirby
le Soken
Kirby Cross
B1034
B1033

Great
Holland
Holland-
on-Sea
Great
Clacton
B1032

CLACTON-ON-SEA
ℹ

The Redoubt
Bath Side
Harwich
Harbour
M
Landguard Fort
Landguard
Point

Pennyhole
Bay

The Naze
**Walton on
the Naze**

Frinton-on-Sea

Hoek van Holland

Hoek van Holland
Cuxhaven
Esbjerg

90
19
A120
17
16
29

1
2
3
4
5
6
7
8

G
H
J
K
L
M

0   1   2   3   4   5 miles
0 1 2 3 4 5 6 7 kilometres

A   B   C   D   E   F

1

2

3

Rosslare Harbour   (Summer only)
Rosslare Harbour

STRUMBLE HEAD

4   Carregwast.

Pen Brush   Llanwnda

Pwllderi   Goodwick   Ocean L

Trefasser

Pembrokeshire   Manorowen   F
Coast Path   St Nicholas   Panteg

Ynys   Scledda
5   Daullyn   Granston
Carreg Sampson   Abercastle   A40
Llangloffan   Jordanston

Porthgain   Trefin   Mathry
Newbridge
Abereiddy   Llanrhian   16   A487   Castle   B4331   New
Berea   Square &   Morris
Croes-goch   Compass   Letterston
6   Tretio   Treglemais   Treffynnon   Welsh
ST DAVID'S HEAD   Treleddyd-fawr   Carnhedryn   Cerbyd   B4330   Hook   15
Whitesand   Rhodiad-   Caer   River Solva   Llandeloy
Bay   y-brenin   Farchell   Tancredston   Pont-yr-hafod   Wolf's
Bishops   Whitchurch   Middle Mill   Treffgarne   Castle
Palace   i   Owen   Hayscastle   Hayscastle
RAMSEY   St David's   Cross
ISLAND   Brawdy   Treffgarne
7   Nine   Solva   A487   Pen-y-cwn
RSPB   Wells   54   178
St David's Peninsula   Newgale   DUDWELL   Leweston
Heritage Coast   16   MT
Roch   Wolfsdale
PEMBROKESHIRE   Roch Gate
COAST   Simpson   Camrose
Rickets Head   NATIONAL PARK   Cross   Keeston   Pembrokeshire
Nolton Haven   Nolton   A487   County
Tangiers
8   Pelcomb Cross   Pelcomb
0 1 2 3 4 5 miles   Lambston   Glanafon
0 1 2 3 4 5 6 7 kilometres   Pelcomb
St Brides Bay   St Brides Bay   Druidston   Bridge
Heritage Coast   Sutton

A   B   C   D   E   F

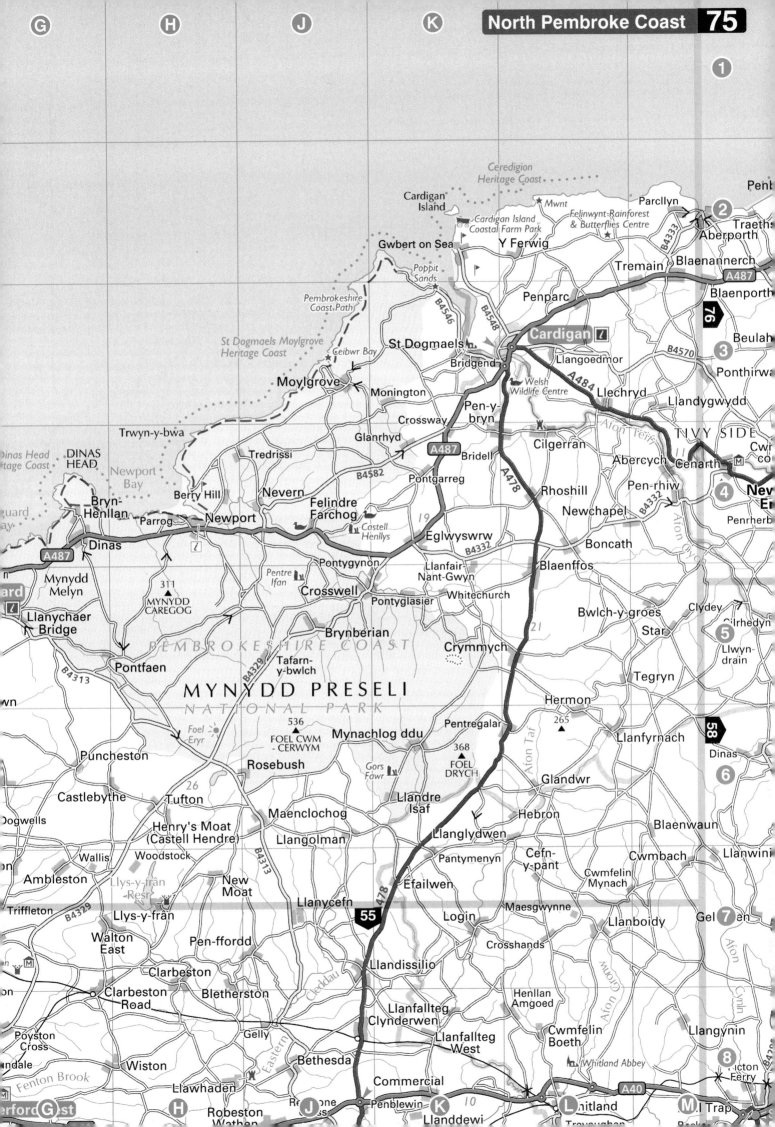

G H J K

1

Ceredigion
Heritage Coast

Cardigan
Island
★ Mwnt
Felinwynt-Rainforest
& Butterflies Centre
Parcllyn
2
Cardigan Island
Coastal Farm Park
Traeth
Aberporth
Gwbert on Sea
Y Ferwig
Tremain
Blaenannerch
Poppit
Sands
Penparc
A487
Blaenporth
Pembrokeshire
Coast Path
B4546
B4548
Cardigan i
76
Ceibwr Bay
St Dogmaels
Beulah
St Dogmaels Moylgrove
Heritage Coast
Bridgend
Llangoedmor
B4570
3
Moylgrove
Monington
Welsh
Wildlife Centre
Pen-y-
bryn
Ponthirwa
Crossway
A484
Llechryd
Llandygwydd
Trwyn-y-bwa
Glanrhyd
A487
Bridell
Cilgerran
TIVY SIDE
Cwi
Dinas Head
ritage Coast
DINAS
HEAD
Tredrissi
B4582
Pontgarreg
Abercych
Cenarth
co
Newport
Bay
Berry Hill
Nevern
Felindre
Farchog
19
A478
Rhoshill
Pen-rhiw
4
Nev
E
Bryn-
Henllan
Castell
Henllys
Eglwyswrw
Newchapel
B4332
Penrherb
Parrog
Newport
B4332
Boncath
Dinas
i
A487
Pontygynon
Llanfair
Nant-Gwyn
Blaenffos
Mynydd
Melyn
Pentre
Ifan
Crosswell
Whitechurch
Clydey
irhedyn
ard
i
311
MYNYDD
CAREGOG
Pontyglasier
Bwlch-y-groes
5
Llanychaer
Bridge
Brynberian
P E M B R O K E S H I R E   C O A S T
Crymmych
Star
Llwyn-
drain
Pontfaen
B4313
Tafarn-
y-bwlch
21
Tegryn
MYNYDD PRESELI
Hermon
58
N A T I O N A L   P A R K
Foel
Eryr
536
Pentregalar
265
Llanfyrnach
Dinas
Puncheston
FOEL CWM
- CERWYM
Mynachlog ddu
368
FOEL
DRYCH
Glandwr
6
Rosebush
Gors
Fawr
26
Castlebythe
Tufton
Llandre
Isaf
Hebron
Blaenwaun
Dogwells
Henry's Moat
(Castell Hendre)
Maenclochog
Llanglydwen
Cwmbach
Llanwini
Wallis
Llangolman
Pantymenyn
Cefn-
y-pant
Ambleston
Woodstock
Llys-y-frân
Resr
New
Moat
B4313
Efailwen
Cwmfelin
Mynach
Triffleton
B4329
Llanycefn
55
Maesgwynne
Gel 7 en
Walton
East
Llys-y-frân
Login
Llanboidy
Pen-ffordd
Crosshands
Clarbeston
Llandissilio
Henllan
Amgoed
Llangynin
Poyston
Cross
ndale
Clarbeston
Road
Bletherston
Llanfallteg
Clynderwen
Llanfallteg
West
Cwmfelin
Boeth
8
Wiston
Gelly
Bethesda
Whitland Abbey
icton
Ferry
Fenton Brook
Llawhaden
Commercial
A40
Trap
erford G est
H
J
Penblewin
K
10
hitland
M
Robeston
Wathen
Llanddewi
L
A40

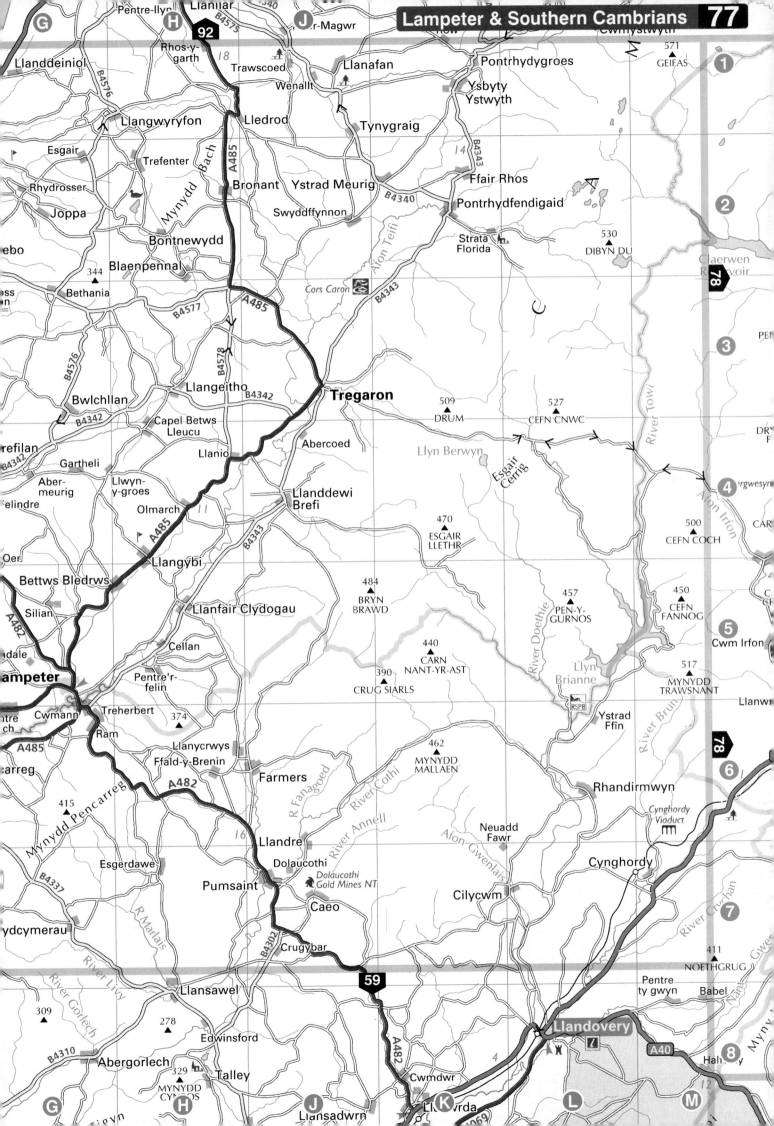

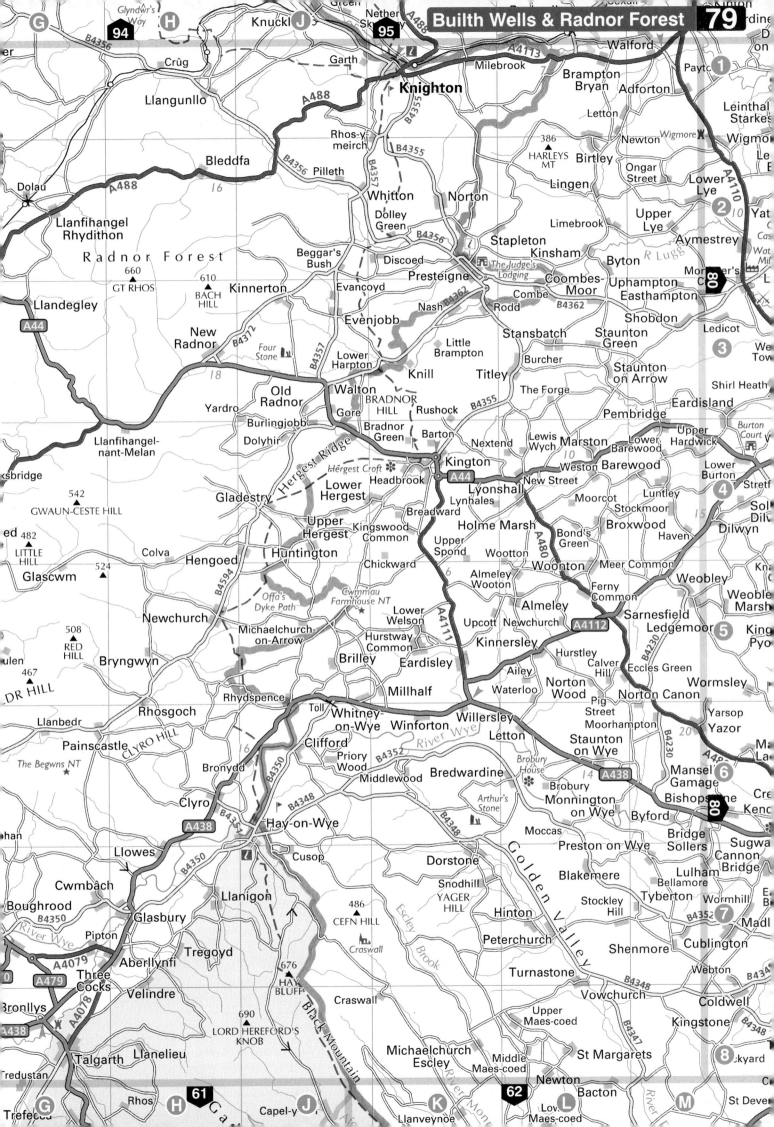

Kinton
avardine
Ludlow
Ludford
Knowbury
Hints
Dudnill
Bransley
uckto
owton on the Rock
ological Trail
Caynham
Hope
Knowl
Coreley
Bay

1
forton
Paytoe
Burrington
Overton
Ashford Carbonel
Bagot
Whitton
Greete
Nash
Bickley
Milson
Neen Sollars
Mamb

Elton
Aston
Ashford Bowdler
Bleathwood
Little Hereford
Boraston
Knighton on Teme
A456
Comr

ngar treet
Leinthall Starkes
Richards Castle
Middleton
Burford
Newnham
A

2
Upper Lye
Wigmore
Oreleton Common
Woofferton
Brimfield Cross
Berrington
Tenbury Wells
Rochford
Upper Rochford
Hanley William
Stoc
Or

Aymestrey
Yatton
Croft Ambrey
Ashley Moor
Comberton
Wyson
Brimfield
Berrington Green
Gallows Grave
Kyrewood
Hanley Child
St

R Lugg
Croft Castle NT
Orleton
Stony Cross
Middleton on the Hill
St Michaels
Miles Hope
Nineveh
Broadheath

79
ampton sthampton
Water Mill
Lucton
Bircher
Yarpole
Moreton Eye
Ashton
Berrington Hall NT
Leysters
Kyre Park
Bank Street
Upper Stoke Sapey
Sweet Green

hobdon
Ledicot
Lugg Green
Luston
The Hundred
Pateshall
Woonton
Grafton
Kyre Green
Wolferlow
Pie Corner

3
unton Arrow
Kingsland
Eyton
Kimbolton
Whyle
Bockleton
Collington

West Town
Cobnash
The Broad
Stockton
Grantsfield
Hatfield
Thornbury

Shirl Heath
Lawton
Cholstrey
Ebnall
Leominster
Pudleston
Old Church
Tedstone Wafer

Eardisland
B4529
Baron's Cross
Steen's Bridge
Docklow
Grendon Green
Edwyn Ralph
Edvin Loach

bridge
Monkland
A44
Newtown
Stretford
A44
Bredenbury
Sandy Cross
Low Brockham

4
Upper Hardwick
Ivington Green
Ivington
Stoke Prior
Humber
Marston Stannett
Bromyard Downs

Lower Burton
Stretford
Brierley
Wharton
Risbury
Bromyard

Luntle moor wood
Sollers Dilwyn
Aulden
Marlbrook
Risbury
Hegdon Hill
Birchyfield

Haven
Dilwyn
Birley
Upper Newton Hill
Bowley Town
Bowley
Pencombe
Stanford Bishop

5
common
Weobley
Knapton Green
Bush Bank
Hope under Dinmore
England's Gate
Little Cowarne
Munderfield Row
Munderfield Stocks

Ledgemoor
Weobley Marsh
Queenswood
Westhope
Bodenham
Maund Bryan
Stoke Cross
Be

cles Green
King's Pyon
Highway
Bodenham Moor
Pool Head
Ullingswick
Stoke Lacy
Bishop's Frome
Paunto

Wormsley
Canon Pyon
Wellington
Urdimarsh
The Vauld
Upper Town
Felton
Panks Bridge
Eves

ton Canon
Auberrow
Walker's Green
Preston Wynne
Moreton Jeffries
Much Cowarne
Five Bridges
Halmond Frome

6
Yarsop Yazor
Tillington Common
Marden
Wellington Marsh
Franklands Gate
Hillhampton
Burley Gate
Lower Egleton
Castle Frome
Fr

sell Gamage
Mansell Lacy
Tillington
Portway
Moreton on Lugg
Sutton St Nicholas
Ocle Pychard
Newtown
Upper Egleton
Stretton Grandison
Catle

Bishopstone
Brinsop
Credenhill
Burghill
Upper Lyde
Pipe and Lyde
Sutton Marsh Nunnington
Withington Marsh
Westhide
Monkhide
Canon Frome
Cold Green

yford
Kenchester
Stretton Sugwas
A49
Holmer
Shelwick
White Stone
Withington
A4103
Yarkhill
Lower Town

Bridge Sollers
The Weir NT
Sugwas Pool
Swainshill
Westfields
Lugwardine
Hagley
Shucknall
Weston Beggard
Ashperton
Swinmore Common

Lulham
ye
Cannon Bridge
Upper Breinton
King's Acre
AA
A465
A438
Bartestree
Perton
Stoke Edith
Tarrington
Munsley

7
Bellamore
Tyberton
Wormhill
Eaton Bishop
Breinton
Tupsley
Dormington
Hampton Bishop
Durlow Common
Putley Green
Trumpet
Plais

79
more
olington
Madley
Clehonger
Ruckhall
Warham
Hereford
Blackmarstone
Lower Bullingham
Rotherwas Chapel
Mordiford
Putley
Aylton
A438
Little Marcl

Webton
B4349
Grafton
Goose Pool
Bullinghope
Dinedor
Dinedor Hill
B4224
Woolhope
Kynaston
Rushall

Coldwell
Allensmore
Portway
Holme Lacy
Lower Buckenhill
Hellen's House
Preston

8
Kingstone
Hungerstone
Cobhall Common
Twyford Common
Aconbury
Newtown
Fownhope
Peartree Green
Much Marcle
Tillers Gre

ts
Thruxton
Cockyard
Crizeley
Kivernoll
A465
C
Little Dewchurch
Balling
D
Ladyridge
Brockhampton
E
63
F
Dym
St Mary

0 1 2 3 4 5 miles
0 1 2 3 4 5 6 7 kilometres

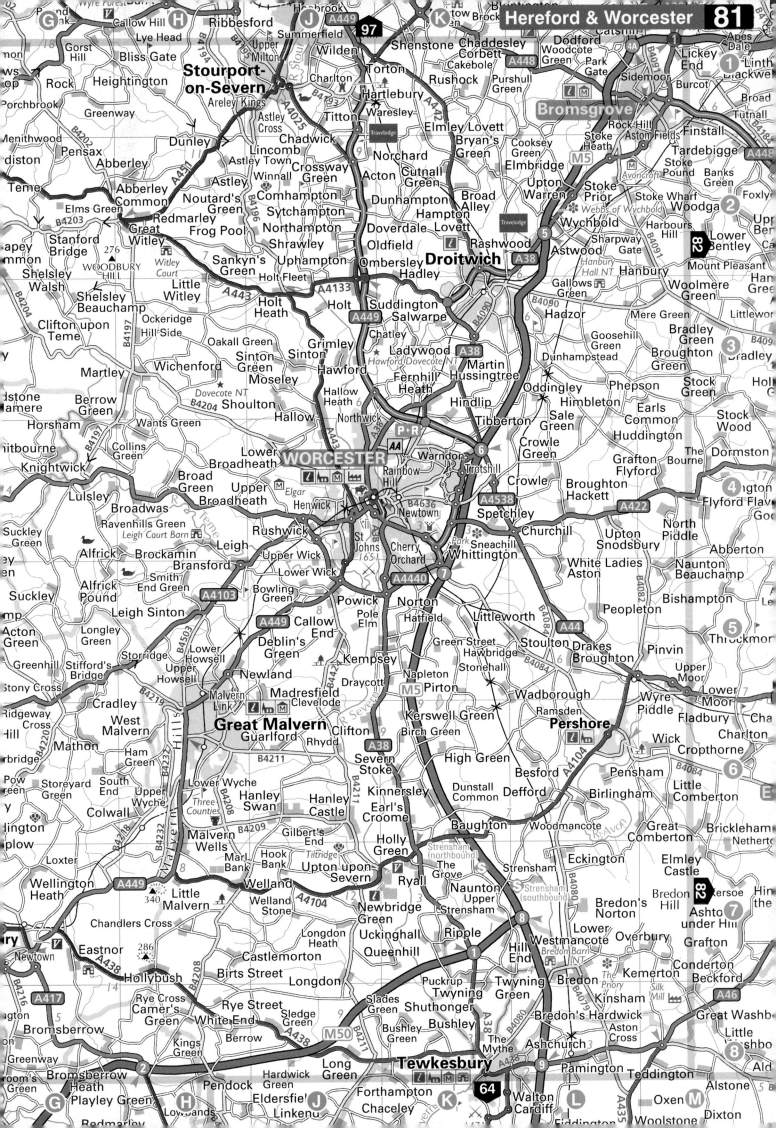

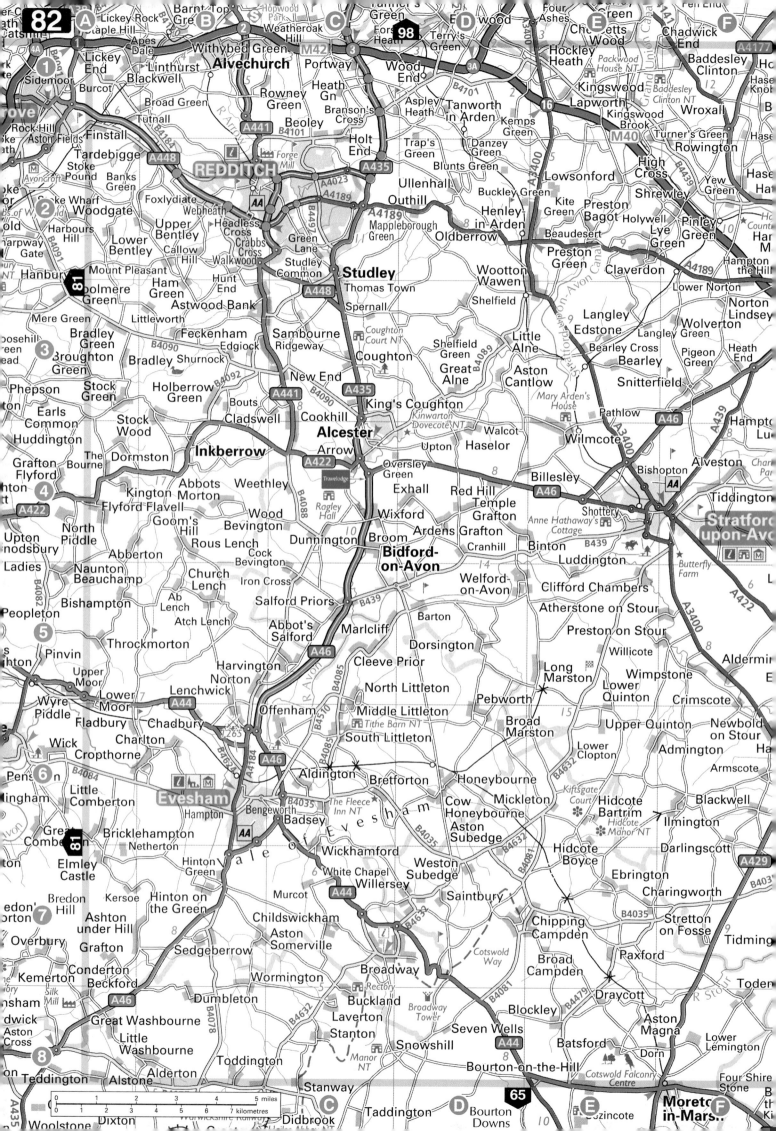

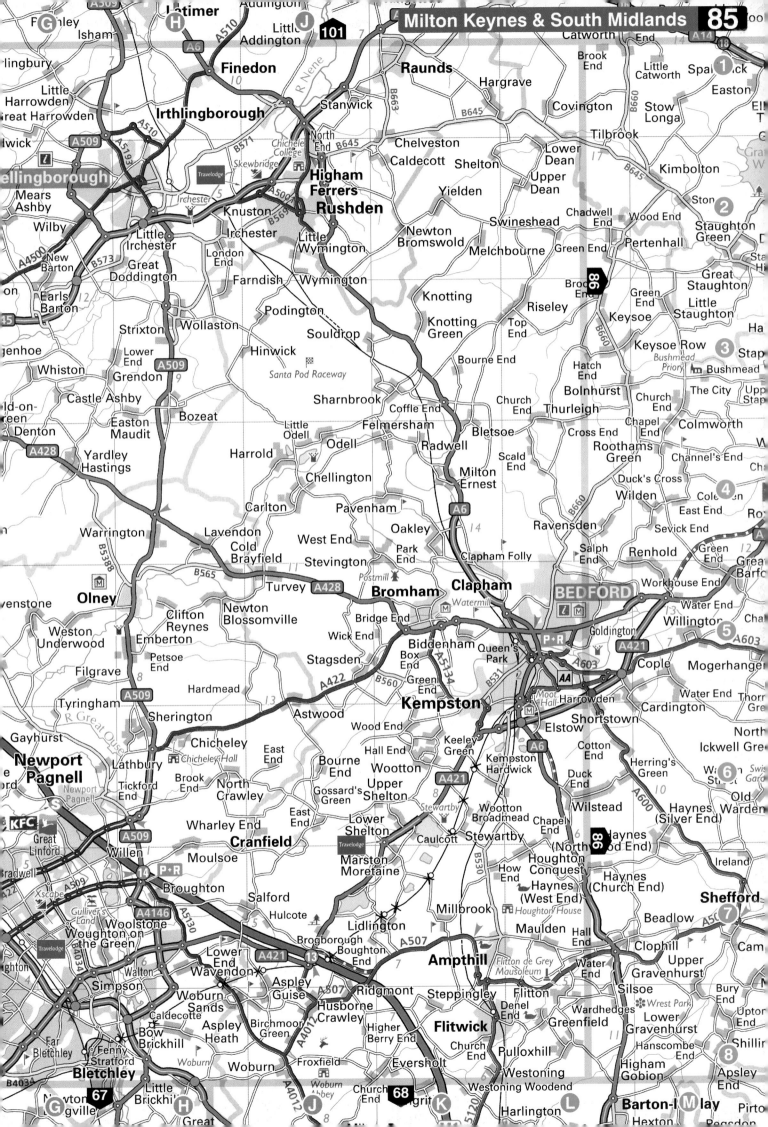

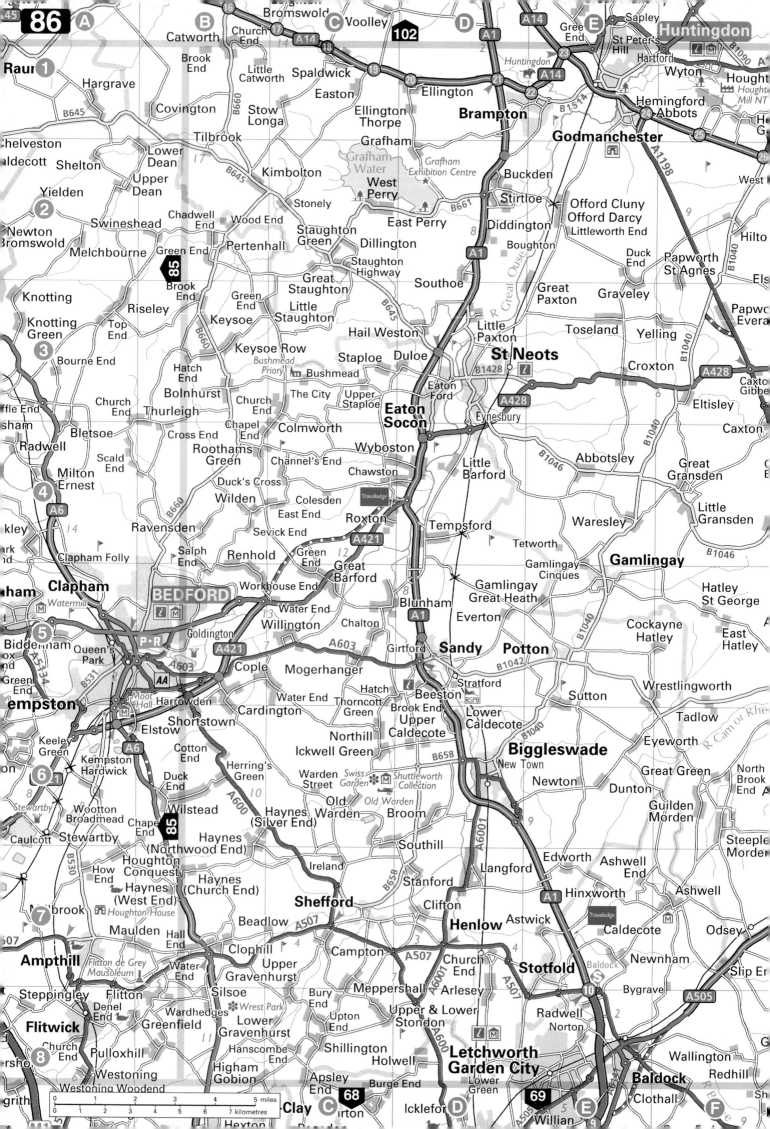

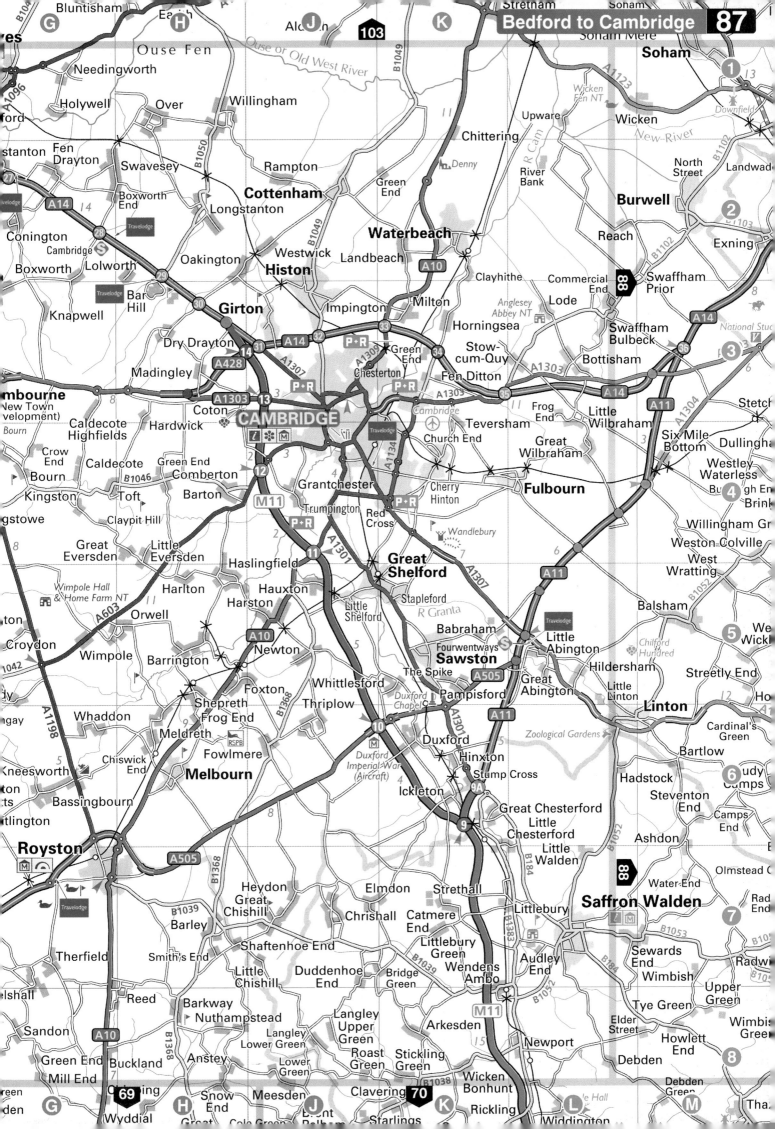

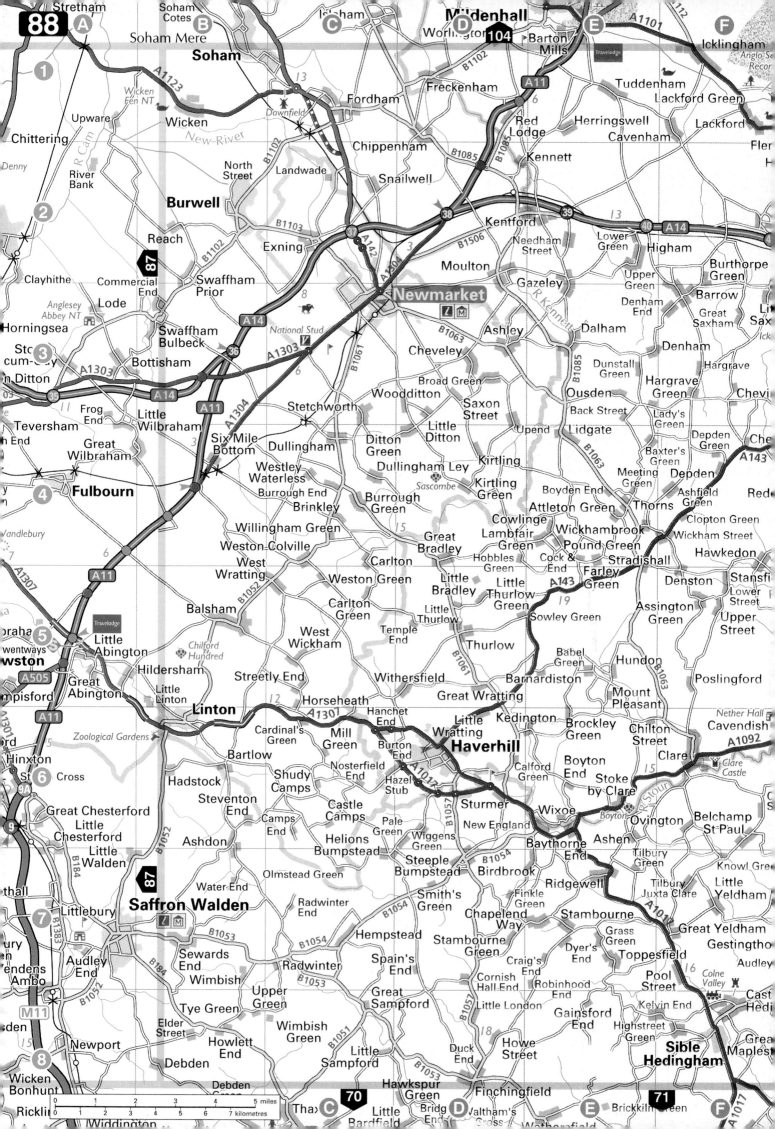

Bury St Edmunds · Stowmarket · Needham Market · Hadleigh · Long Melford · Sudbury

A143 · A1101 · A1088 · A14 · A134 · A1141 · A1071 · A131 · A12

105 · 72 · 90 · 06

Troston · Ampton · Ingham · Timworth · Brockley · Culford · Fornham St Martin · Timworth Green · Conyer's Green · Upper Town · Grimstone End · Ixworth · Ixworth Thorpe · Bardwell · Bangrove · Stanton · Upthorpe · Wattisfield · Walsham le Willows · West Street · Langham · Badwell Ash · Hunston · Stowlangtoft · Great Ashfield · Long Thurlow · Crowland · Allwood Green · Cranmer Green · Gislingham · Finningham · Westhorpe · Badwell Green · Wyverstone Street · Wyverstone · Wickham Street · Wickham Skeith · Cotton · Thornham Parva · Thornham Magna · Wickham Green · Brockford

Great Livermere · Great Barton · Pakenham · Thurston · Great Green · Norton · Norton Little Green · Elmswell · Tostock · Broadgrass Green · Base Green · Wetherden · Haughley Green · Haughley · Bacton · Bacton Green · Cow Green · Ford's Green · Canhams Green · Mendlesham · Gipping · Old Newton · Saxham Street · Stowupland · Middlewood Green · Mendlesham Green · Brown Street

Battlies Green · Thurston Planch · Beyton Gn · Kingshall Street · Beyton · Woolpit · Hessett · Drinkstone · Woolpit Green · Borley Green · Dagworth · Harleston · Onehouse · **Stowmarket** · Forward Green · Earl Stonham · Creeting St Mary · Combs Ford · Combs · **Needham Market** · Barking · Battisford · Battisford Tye · Ringshall · Lower Street · Baylham

Horringer · Rushbrooke · Rougham Green · Drinkstone Green · Clopton Green · Rattlesden · Buxhall Fen Street · Buxhall · Great Finborough · Mill Green · Hightown Green · Brettenham · Cross Green · Bird Street · Charles Tye · Ringshall Stocks · Barking Tye · Upper Street

High Green · Nowton · Sicklesmere · Bradfield St George · Maypole Green · Gedding · Poystreet Green · Felsham · Cockfield · Thorpe Green · Cooks Green · Hitcham Causeway · Wattisham · Nedging Tye · Great Bricett · Greenstreet Green · Offton · Naughton · Somersham · Little Blakenham · Flowton

Pinford End · Hawstead · Hawstead Green · Little Welnetham · Great Welnetham · Bradfield Combust · Bradfield St Clare · Bush Green · Hoggards Green · Oldhall Green · Cross Green · Great Green · Thorpe Morieux · Preston · Hitcham Street · Hitcham · Nedging · Ash Street · Whatfield · Elmsett · Aldham

Whepstead · Mickley Green · Stanningfield · Windsor Green · Lawshall · Lawshall Green · Shimpling Street · Alpheton · Kettlebaston · Bildeston · Monks Eleigh · Chelsworth · Semer · Stone Street · Sproughton · Burstall · Hintlesham · Washbrook · Chattisham · Copdock · Coles Green

Gulling Green · Melon Green · Harrow Green · Lawshall · Cross Green · Audley End · Shimpling · Bridge Street · Lavenham · Guildhall NT · Brent Eleigh · Swingleton Green · Milden · Lindsey Tye · Rose Green · Lindsey · St James Chapel · Kersey Tye · Kersey · Kersey Upland · Coram Street · **Hadleigh** · Duke Street · Whatfield

Hartest · Gifford's Hall · Boxted · Stanstead · Stanstead Street · Glemsford · Melford Hall NT · Kentwell Hall · **Long Melford** · Acton · Little Waldingfield · Great Waldingfield · Mill Green · Edwardstone · Groton · Horners Green · Calais Street · Hadleigh Heath · Bower House Tye · Polstead Heath · Layham · Raydon · Little Wenham

Pentlow · Liston · Newman's Green · Chilton · Cornard Tye · Newton · Boxford · Hagmore Green · Stone Street · Whitestreet Green · Shelley · Great Wenham · Capel St Mary · Bentley

Borley · **Sudbury** · Ballingdon · Great Cornard · Middleton · Little Cornard · Assington · Leavenheath · Stoke-by-Nayland · Polstead · Lower Raydon · Holton St Mary · Higham · Stratford St Mary · East Bergholt · East End

Belchamp Walter · Bulmer · Bulmer Tye · Great Henny · Henny Street · Twinstead · Rose Green · Dorking Tye · Honey Tye · Nayland · Thorington Street · Dedham

Wickham St Paul · Alphamstone · Lamarsh · Little Maplestead · Cross End · Pebmarsh · Mount Bures · Bures · Wissington · Wormingford · Horkesley Heath · Boxted · Boxted Cross · Langham · Stratford St Mary

R Lark · R Gipping · R Stour · R Box · R Brett · R Glem

Flatford Mill & Cottage NT · Carters · Mistley · Manningtree

G · H · J · K · 1 · 2 · 3 · 4 · 5 · 6 · 7 · 8

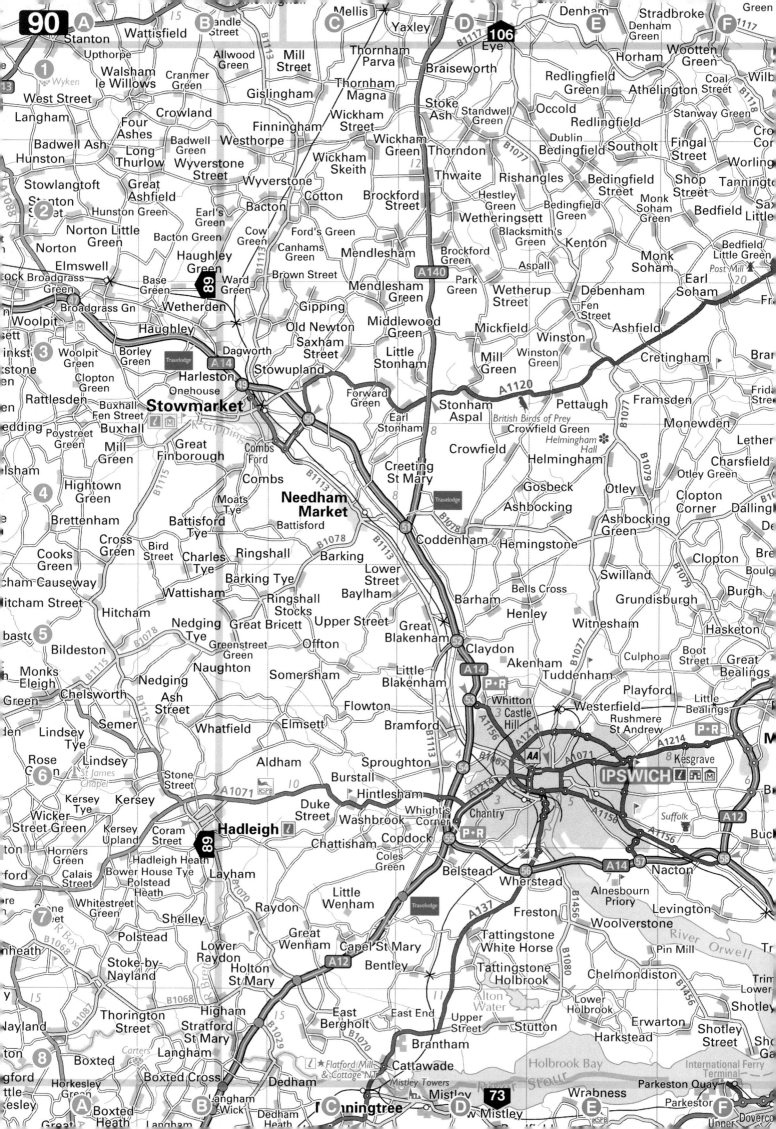

G   H   B1117   Walpol   J   107   T   ington   K   B1387

1

Huntingfield   Walpol   Bramfield

Laxfield   Heveningham
Ubbeston   Green   Pouy   Street   High Street   Darsham
rundish Street   Yoxford   Little   Street   Dunwich
ndish   Owl's   Green   Sibton   Grey Friars
Goddard's Corner   Peasenhall   A1120   Yoxford   B1125
Capon's   Green   Middleton Moor   Middleton   Westleton   Minsmere   RSPB
pole   Badingham   North Green   B1122   Eastbridge
Green   Bruisyard   A12   Theberton   Poplar Street
xtead   Dennington   Bruisyard   Street   7   East   Green   Leiston
Brabling   Green   B1120   Rendham   Kelsale   Sizewell Visitor Centre
ad   Cransford   Carlton   Saxmundham
79   Shawsgate   B1119   Knodishall   Sizewell
ham   Swefling   Great   Glemham   Benhall   Street   B1119   Sternfield   Leiston   M
North Green   Mill   Green   Benhall   Green   Coldfair   Green   Aldringham   Thorpe   Ness
Parham   B1116   Stratford   St Andrew   Friday   Street   Friston   B1353   Thorpeness
Kettleburgh   Silverlace   Green   Farnham   A1094   B1122   RSPB
Easton   Hacheston   Snape   A1094
n   Marlesford   Gromford   Snape Street
on   Little   Glemham   The Maltings   Aldeburgh
Wickham   Market   Lower   Hacheston   Blaxhall   B1069   Iken   River Alde   Aldeburgh   Bay
Pettistree   Campsea   Ash   Tunstall   High   Street
Upper   Ufford   10   Rendlesham   B1078
A12   Ufford   Lower Ufford   Chillesford   Sudbourne
Melton   Eyke   Friday   Street   B1084   Orford   Orford Ness
Woodbridge   Bromeswell   B1084   12   Butley   Butley High   Corner   Suffolk Heritage Coast
Sutton Hoo   NT   Capel   Green   Orfordness-   Havergate   RSPB
sham   B1083   Capel St Andrew   Boyton   River Ore
esham   Sutton   Shottisham   North Weir Point   Hollesley   Bay
ath   Waldringfield   Hollesley
well   Newbourne   Hemley   B1083   Ramsholt   Shingle   Street
am   River Deben   Alderton
Kirton   Bawdsey   Falkenham

Felixstowe Ferry

59   Old   Felixstowe
Walton   61
Felixstowe   i
doubt
Side   G   H   J   K   L   M
rwich   ndguard Fort
arbour   Landguard

1   2   3   4   5   6   7   8

0   1   2   3   4   5 miles
0   1   2   3   4   5   6   7 kilometres

A   B   C   D   E   F

1
Barmouth Bridge

Barmouth Bay

Fairbourne & Barmouth Steam Railway

Fairbourne

Arthog

Dyffry

110

CADER IDRIS
892

621

2
Friog

20

Llwyngwril

Afon Dysynni

Llanfihangel-y-pennant

Castell y Bere

Tal-y-llyn

B4405

Tal-y-llyn

Corri
Ucha

King Arthur's La
& Craft Ce

Llangelynin

Rhoslefain

A493

Peniarth

Abergynolwyn

667

3
Aber Dysynni

Llanegryn

Bryncrug

B4405

Dolgoch

Tal-y-Llyn Railway

Pantpe

Ynysymaengwyn

Pandy

Dolgoch Falls

633

TAREN HENDRE

Rhyd-yr-onnen

Pennal

Vall

Tywyn

5

Cwrt

4
Aberdyfi

A493

11

Dovey

Dery

Glaspwll

RSPB

Glandyfi

Eglwys Fach

Afon Dyfi (River Dovey)

Furnace

Ysgubor-y-Coed

447

PEN CARREG-GO

A487

Ynyslas

18

5
B4353

Llancynfelyn

Tre'r-ddol

Tre Taliesin

Borth

Staylittle

Tal-y-bont

Upper Borth

B4353

Dolybont

Ceredigion Heritage Coast

Llandre

Pen-y-garn

Rhyd-y pennau

6
Bow Street

Salem

Clarach Bay

Clarach

Penrhyncoch

Garth Penrhyncoch

Pen-bont Rhydybeddau

B45

A4159

Capel Dewi

Dollwen

Bwlch Nant Yr Arian

Aberystwyth

Waunfawr

Capel Bangor

Goginan

Ponter

P+R

Llanbadarn Fawr

Blaengeuffordd

Cwmbrwyno

Llywer
Silver L
Min

7
Penparcau

Rhydyfelin

Moriah

Rheidol Power Station

Aberffrwd

Ystumtuen

Aberystwyth and District

Capel Seion

12

A4120

Vale of Rheid

Llanfarian

Gors

New Cross

Pisgah

Mynydd
Buch

Blaenplwyf

A485

Afon Ystwyth

Llanfihangel-y-Creuddyn

Capel Trisant

Cnwch Coch

Pentre-llyn

Llanilar

B4340

B4575

Aber-Magwr

New Row

8
0   1   2   3   4   5 miles
0   1   2   3   4   5   6   7 kilometres

Ceredigion Heritage Coast

nddeiniol

16

Rhos-y-garth

18

Trawsco

77

Llanafan

A   B   C   D   E   F

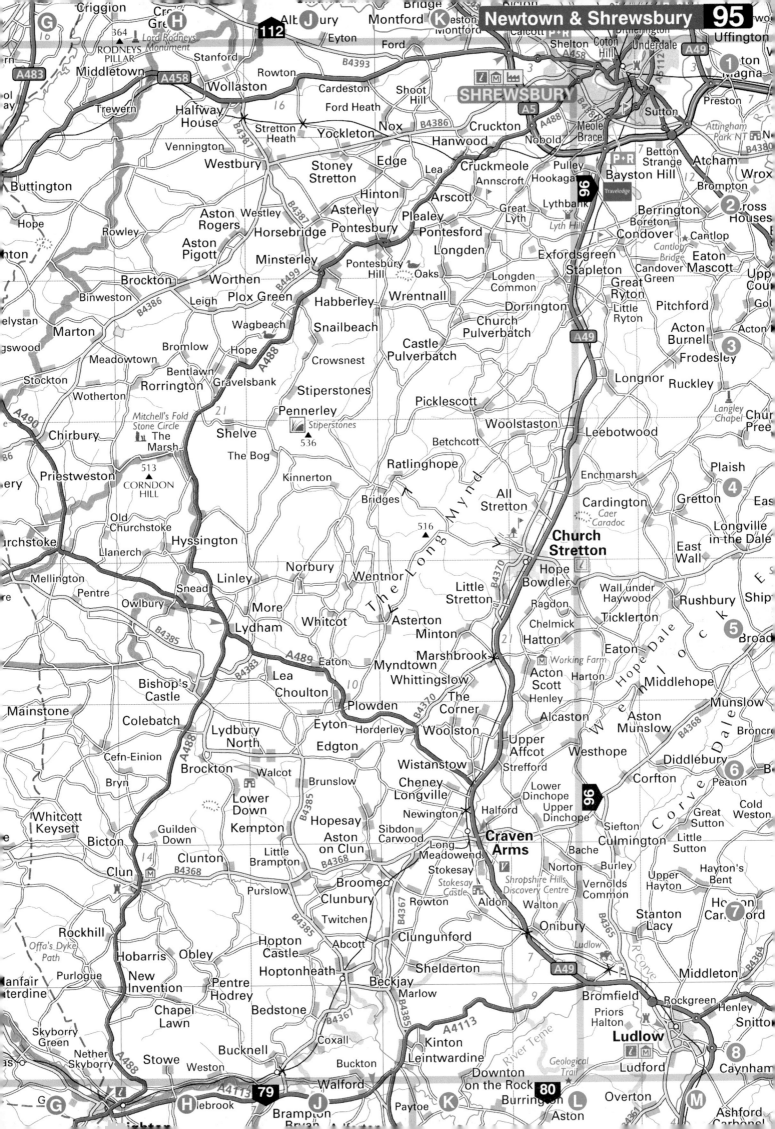

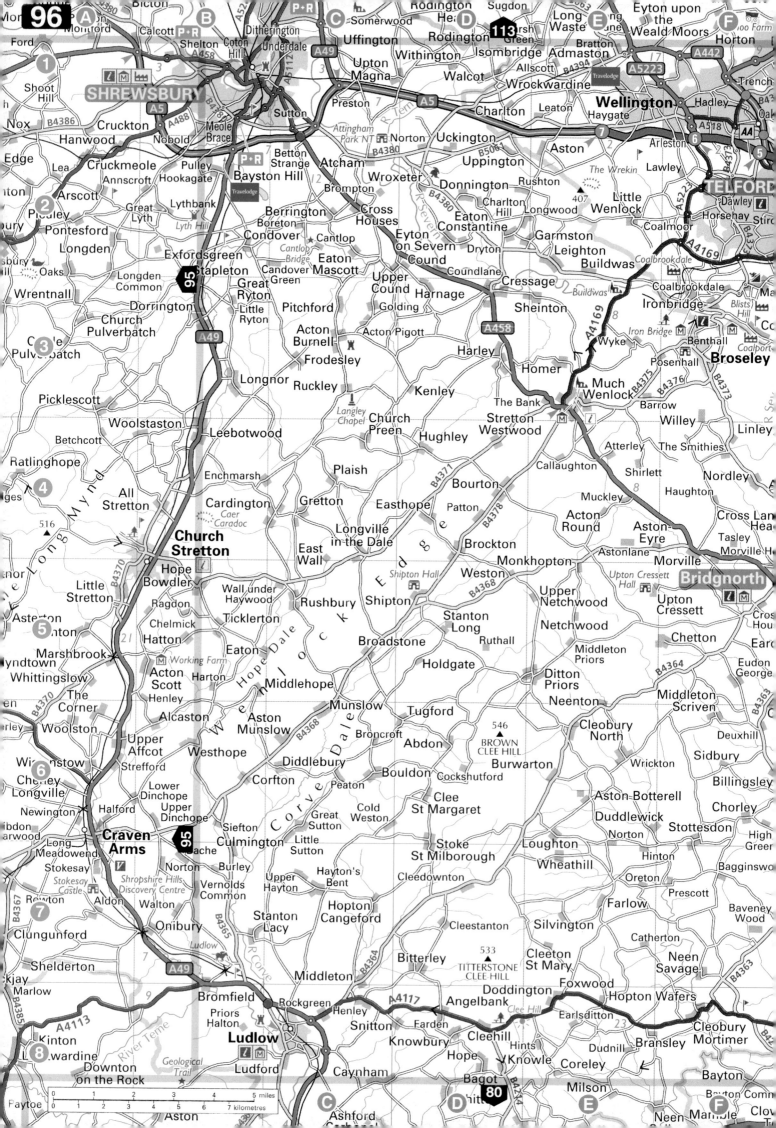

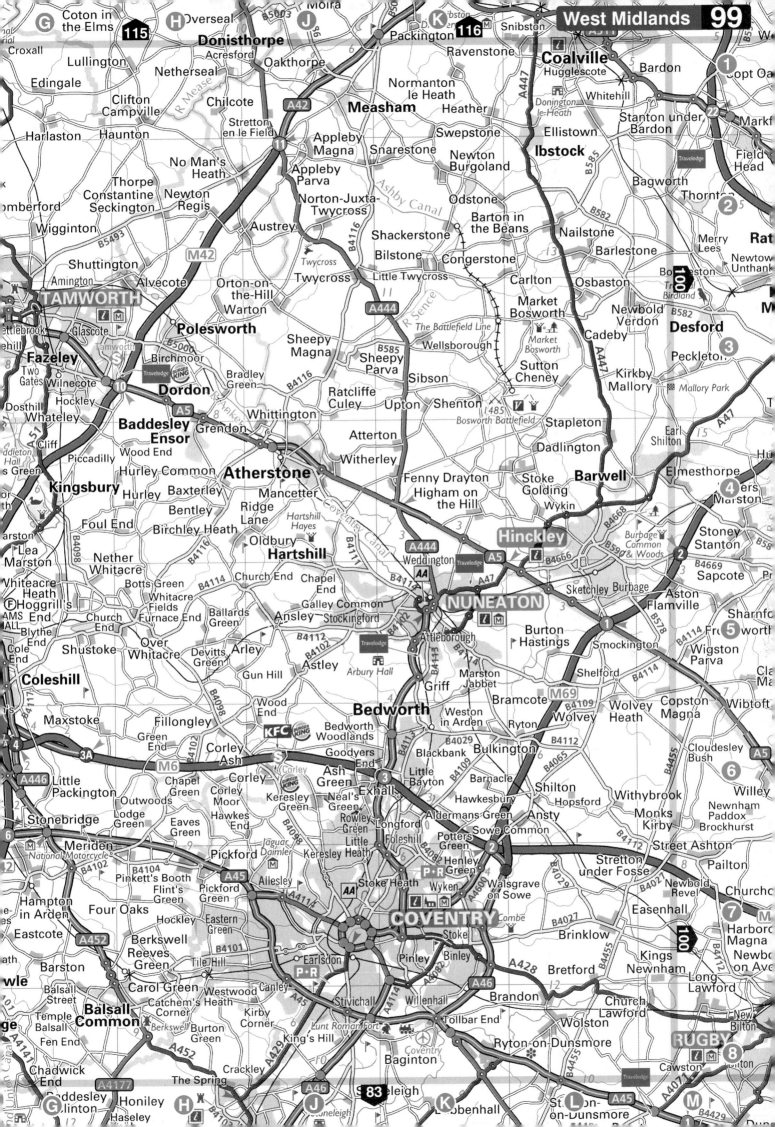

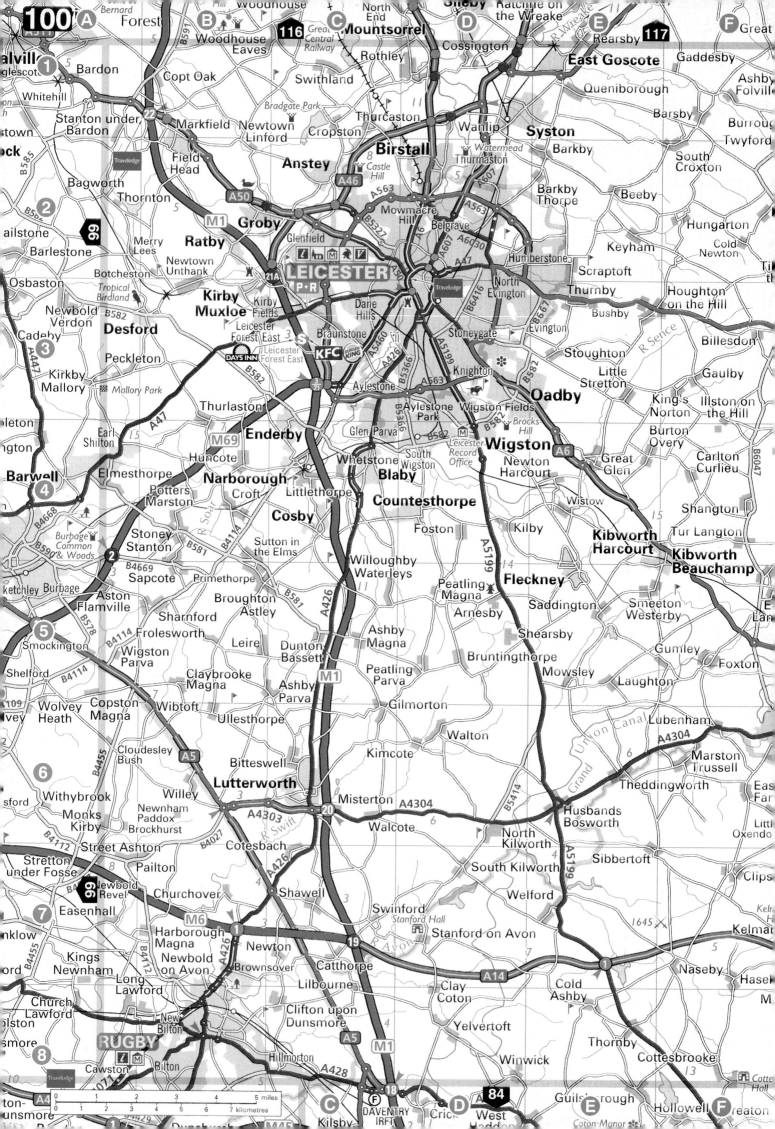

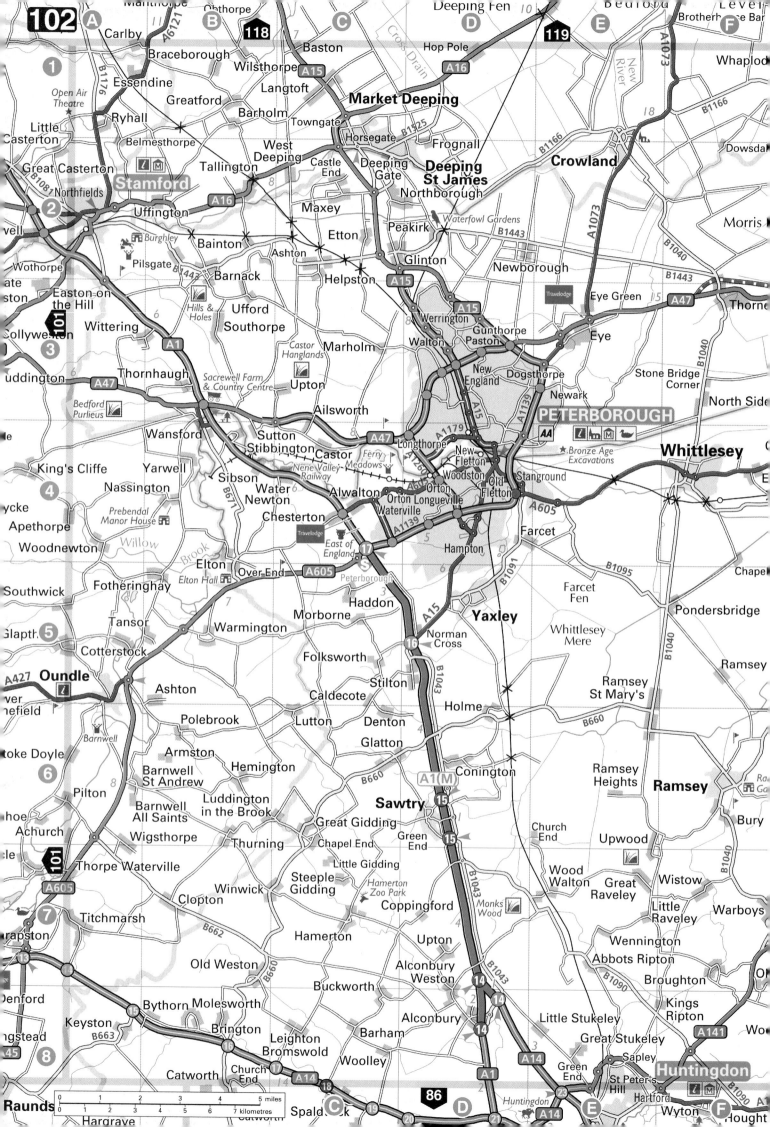

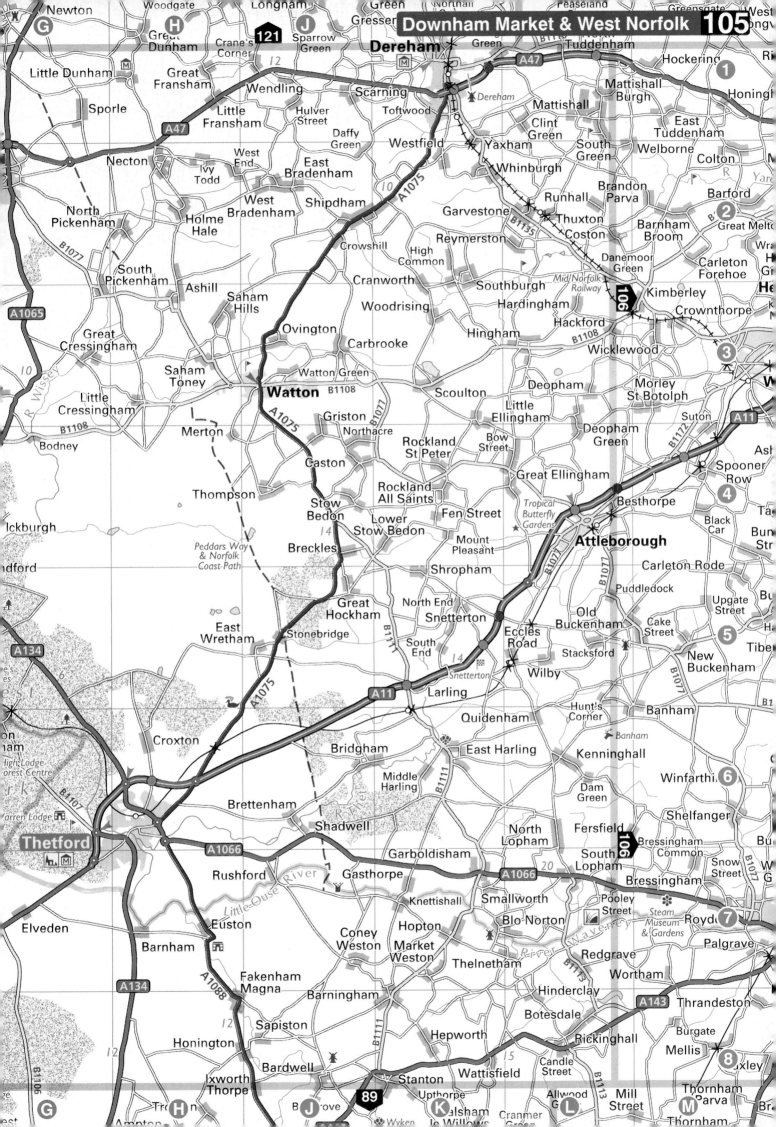

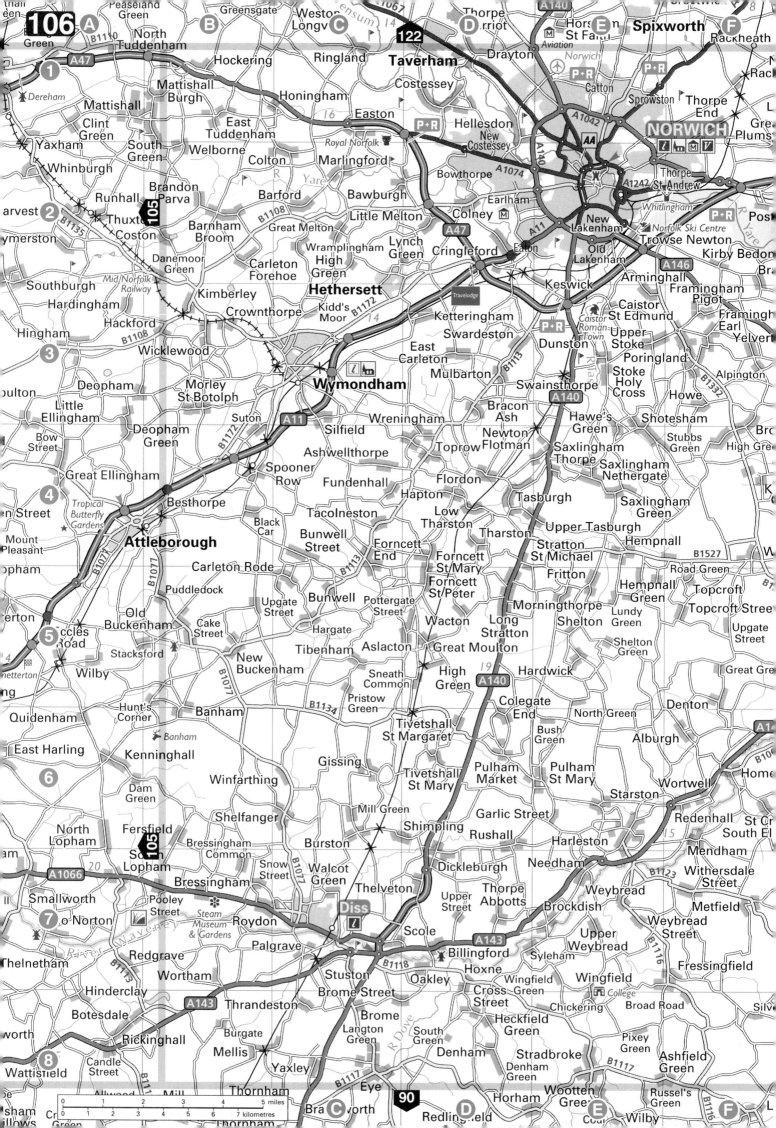

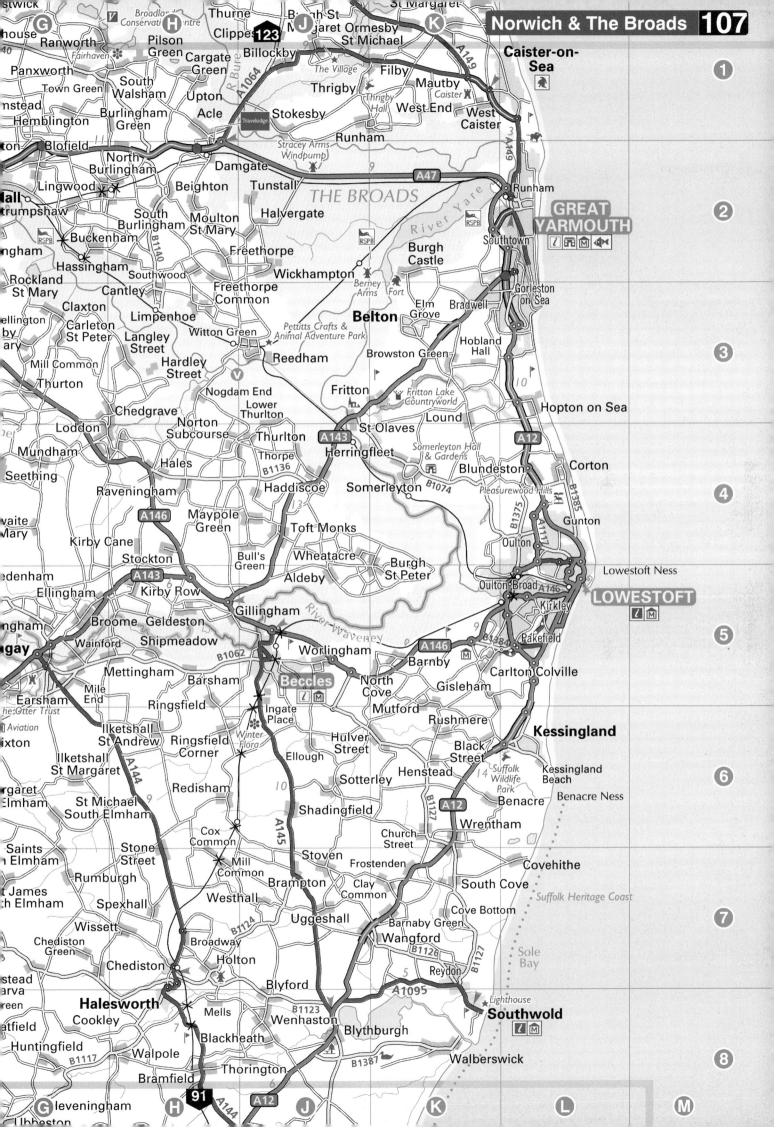

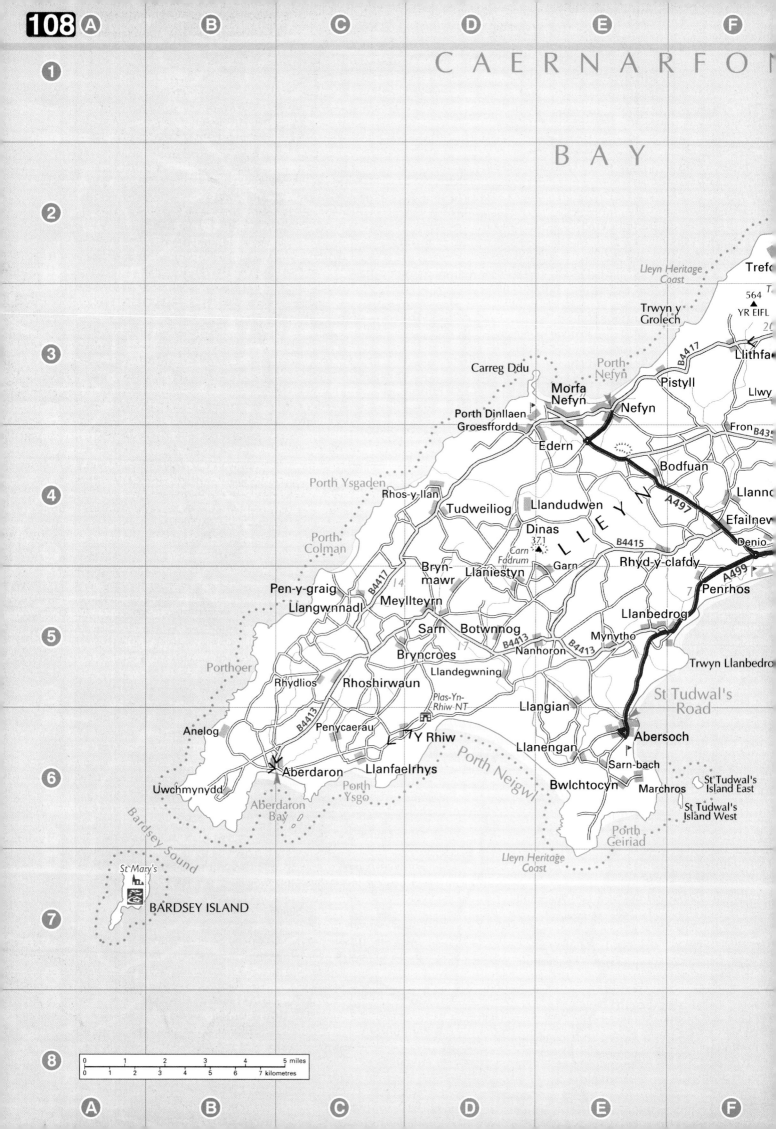

CAERNARFON
BAY

Lleyn Heritage Coast

Tref

564
YR EIFL

Trwyn y Grolech

Carreg Ddu

Porth Nefyn

B4417

Llithfa

Morfa Nefyn

Pistyll

Llwy

Porth Dinllaen
Groesffordd

Nefyn

Fron B43

Edern

Bodfuan

Porth Ysgaden

Llann

Rhos-y-llan

Llandudwen

LLEYN

A497

Tudweiliog

Efailnev

Dinas

371
Carn
Fadrum

B4415

Denio

Porth Colman

Bryn-mawr

Llaniestyn

Garn

Rhyd-y-clafdy

A499

Pen-y-graig

B4417
14

Penrhos

Meyllteyrn

7

Llangwnnadl

Llanbedrog

Sarn

Botwnnog

Mynytho

B4413

Porthoer

Bryncroes

1.7

Nanhoron

B4413

Trwyn Llanbedro

Llandegwning

St Tudwal's Road

Rhydlios

Rhoshirwaun

Plas-Yn-Rhiw NT

Llangian

Anelog

B4413

Penycaerau

Y Rhiw

Abersoch

Uwchmynydd

Aberdaron

Llanfaelrhys

Porth Neigwl

Llanengan

Sarn-bach

Porth Ysgo

Bwlchtocyn

Marchros

St Tudwal's Island East

Aberdaron Bay

Porth Geiriad

St Tudwal's Island West

Bardsey Sound

Lleyn Heritage Coast

St Mary's

BARDSEY ISLAND

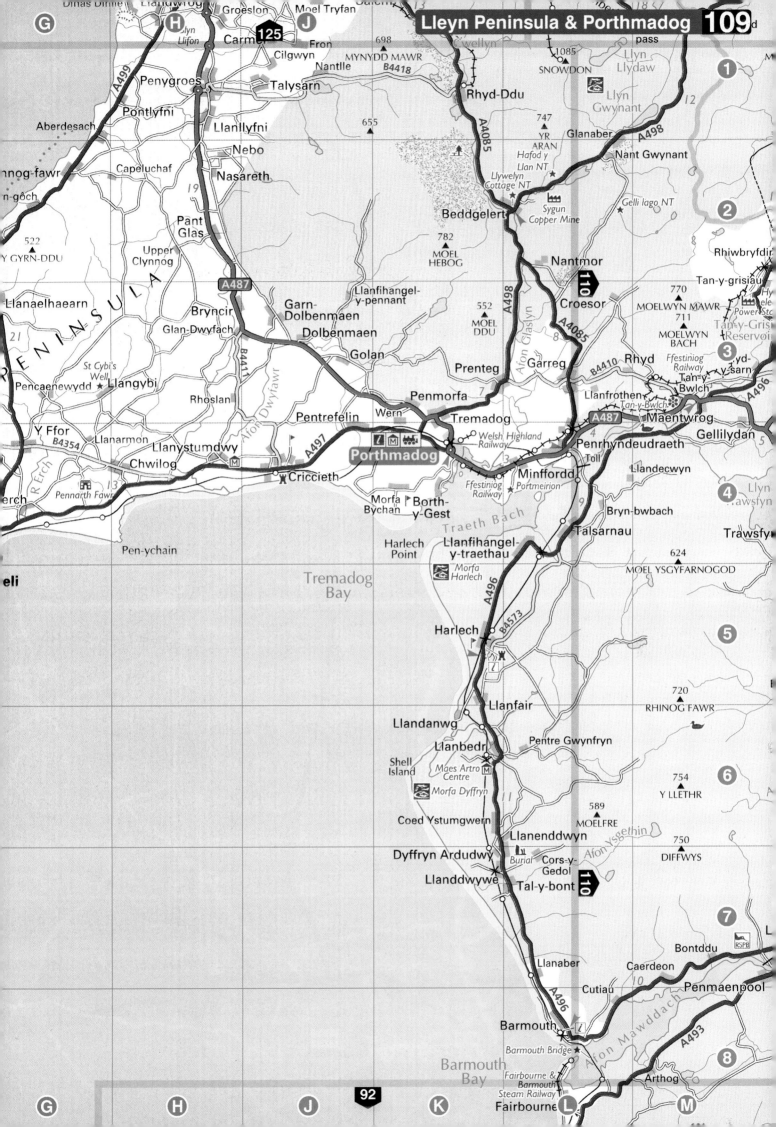

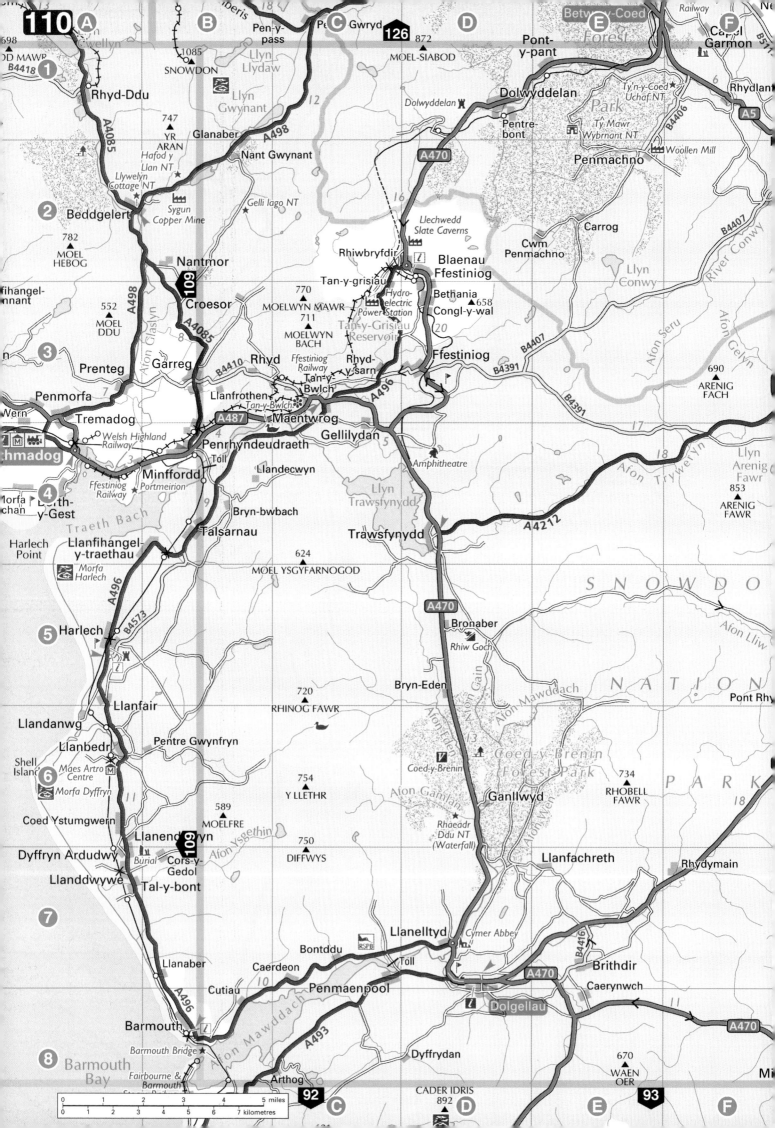

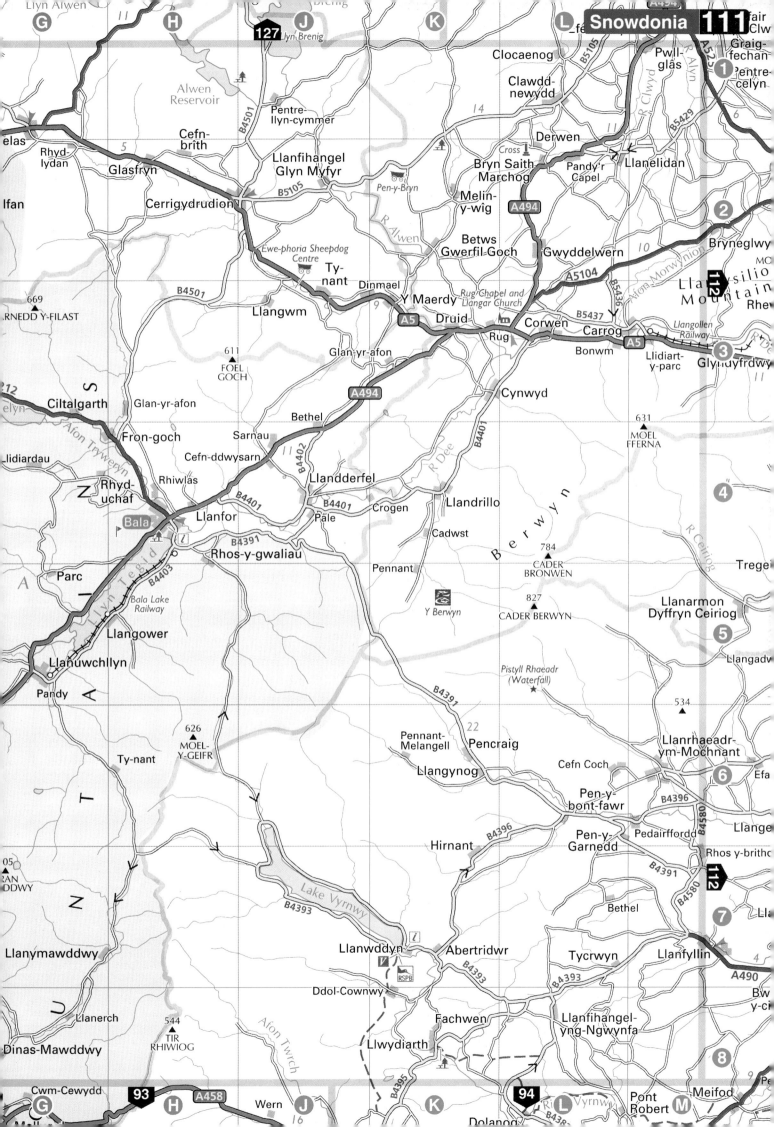

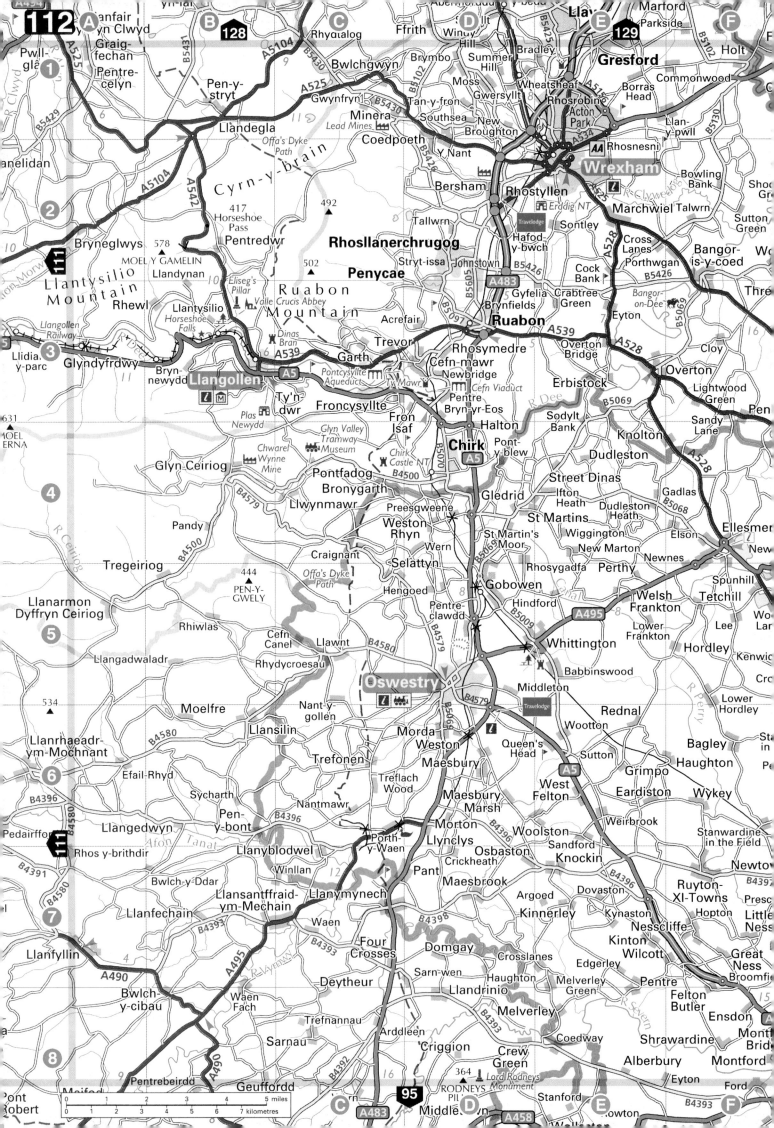

Chowley
Harthill
Higher Burwardsley
Bulkeley
Radmore Green
Clutton
Broxton
Barnhill
Barton
Fuller's Moor
Gallantry Bank
Ridley Green
Faddiley
Hollin Green
Burland
Rease Heath
Wistaston Green
Crewe Green
Wistaston
Willaston
Wells Green
Gresty Green
Shavington
Weston
Acton
Nantwich
Hough
Stretton
Bickerton
Cholmondeley Castle
Croxton Green
Gradeley Green
Stoneley Green
Ravensmoor
Butt Green
Haymoor Green
Chorlton
Stapeley Water
Stapeley
Wybunbury
Tilston
Duckington
Edge Green
Chorley
Horton Green
Hampton Green
Hetherson Green
Bickley Moss
Hack Green
Walgherton
Shocklach
Ebnal
Hampton Heath
Norbury Common
Secret Bunker
Chorlton Lane
Malpas
No Man's Heath
Bickley
Norbury
Wrenbury
Newtown
Hatherton
Hunsterson
Checkley
Gaunton's Bank
Pinsley Green
Aston
Broomhill Green
Bradley Green
Tushingham cum Grindley
Marbury
Marley Green
Newhall
Hankelow
Bridgemere
Check Green
Upper Threapwood
Oldcastle Heath
Bell o' th' Hill
Hollyhurst
Audlem
Tallarn Green
Higher Wych
Wirswall
Dodd's Green
Royal's Green
Buerton
Canal
Grindley Brook
Whitchurch
Burleydam
Lightwood Green
Kinsey Heath
Eglwys Cross
The Chequer
Coxbank
Woore
Redbrook
Broughall
Catteralslane
Wilkesley
Dorrington
Knighton
Bearstone
Bronington
Ash Magna
Adderley
Arowry
Alkington
Shropshire Union Canal
Ash Parva
Ightfield
Norton in Hales
Tilstock
Prees Heath
Calverhall
Muckleton
Betton
Steel Heath
Platt Lane
Hollinwood
Prees Higher Heath
Welsh End
Longslow
Sandylane
Bettisfield
Whixall
Moreton Say
Almington
Hookgate
Balmer Heath
Sandford
Longford
Blore
Coton
Prees
Bletchley
Market Drayton
Hales
Lyneal
Northwood
Quina Brook
Darliston
Prees Lower Heath
Fauls
Ternhill
Paddolgreen
Marchamley Wood
The Fouralls
Sutton
Chipnall
Newtown
Edstaston
Prees Green
Lostford
Woodseaves
Wolverley
Ryebank
Old Colhurst Manor
English Frankton
Lowe
Creamore Bank
Hawkstone
Wollerton
Cheswardine
Lipley
Hawkstone Park
Stoke Heath
Brownhead
Horton
Weston-under-Redcastle
Marchamley
Hodnet
Wistanswick
Loppington
Heathbrook
Heathcote
Lockleywood
Great Soudley
Wem
Wixhill
Hodnet Hall
Goldstone
Little Soudley
Noneley
Aston
Millgreen
Commonwood
Barkers Green
Bury Walls
Stoke upon Tern
Lee Brockhurst
Moston
Hungryhatton
Ashfields
Sleap
Burlton
Booley
Ollerton
Hinstock
Ellerton
Weston Lullingfields
Preston Brockhurst
Besford
High Hatton
Child's Ercall
Sambrook
Myddle
Alderton
Clive
Stanton upon Hine Heath
Peplow
Howle
Stanford Bridge
Grinshill
Eyton
Newton on the Hill
Yorton Heath
Moreton Corbet
Ellerdine Heath
Eaton upon Tern
Moretonmill
Harmer Hill
Shawbury
Edgebolton
Cold Hatton
Great Bolas
Chetwynd
Old Woods
Merrington
Preston Gubbals
Meeson
Cold Hatton Heath
Little Wytheford
Rowton
Tibberton
Hadnall
Cherrington
Great Wytheford
Waters Upton
Edgmond
Walford Heath
Bomere Heath
Astley
Bings
Moortown
Adeney
Leaton
Albrighton
Poynton Green
Walton
Longford
Fitz
High Ercall
Crudgington
Battlefield
Poynton
Cotwall
Tern
Kynnersley
Church Aston
Haughton
Cheswell
Rosehill
Harlescott
Haughmond Abbey
Roden
Longdon upon Tern
Sleapford
Preston upon the Weald Moors
Bicton
Rodington Heath
Sugdon
Long Waste
Long Lane
Eyton upon the Weald Moors
Muxton
Somerwood
Hoo Farm
Calcott
Ditherington
Marsh Green
Horton
Donnington
Shelton
Coton Hill
Underdale
Uffington
Rodington
Bratton
Admaston
Upton Magna
Withington
Isombridge
Allscott
Walcot
Wrockwardine
Trench
Lilyhill
Granville
Donnington Wood
Travelodge
A41
A49
A534
A530
A51
A500
A529
A525
A495
A53
A442
A528
A5124
A458
A5112
A518
A5223
B5069
B5395
B5476
B5063
B5065
B4397
B5067
B5062
B4380
B4394
B5060
B5071
B5415
B5026
1
2
3
4
5
6
7
8
G
H
J
K
L
M
129
130
96
114
P+R

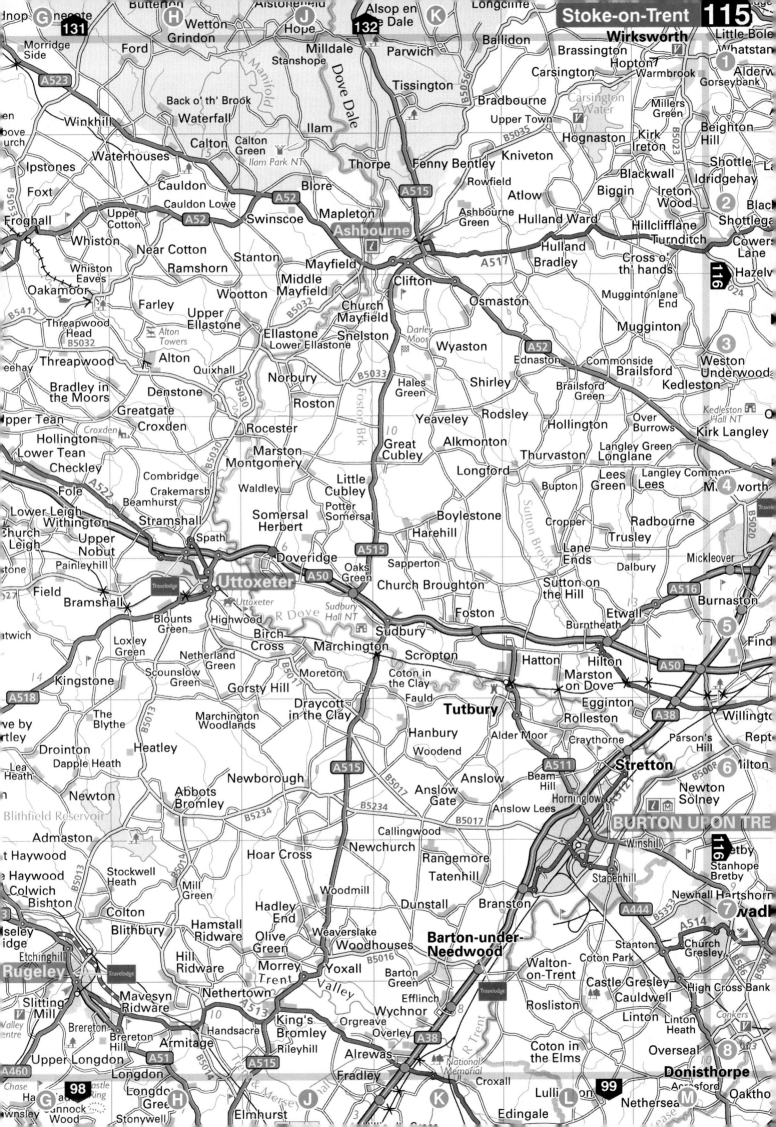

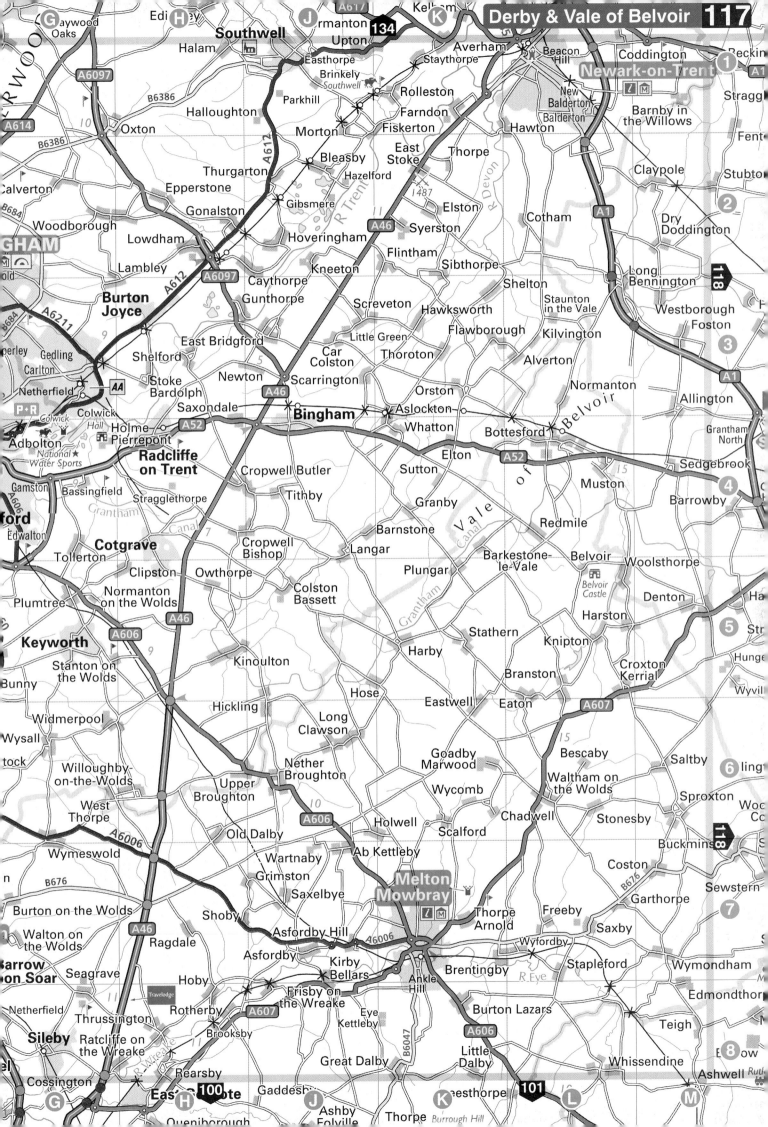

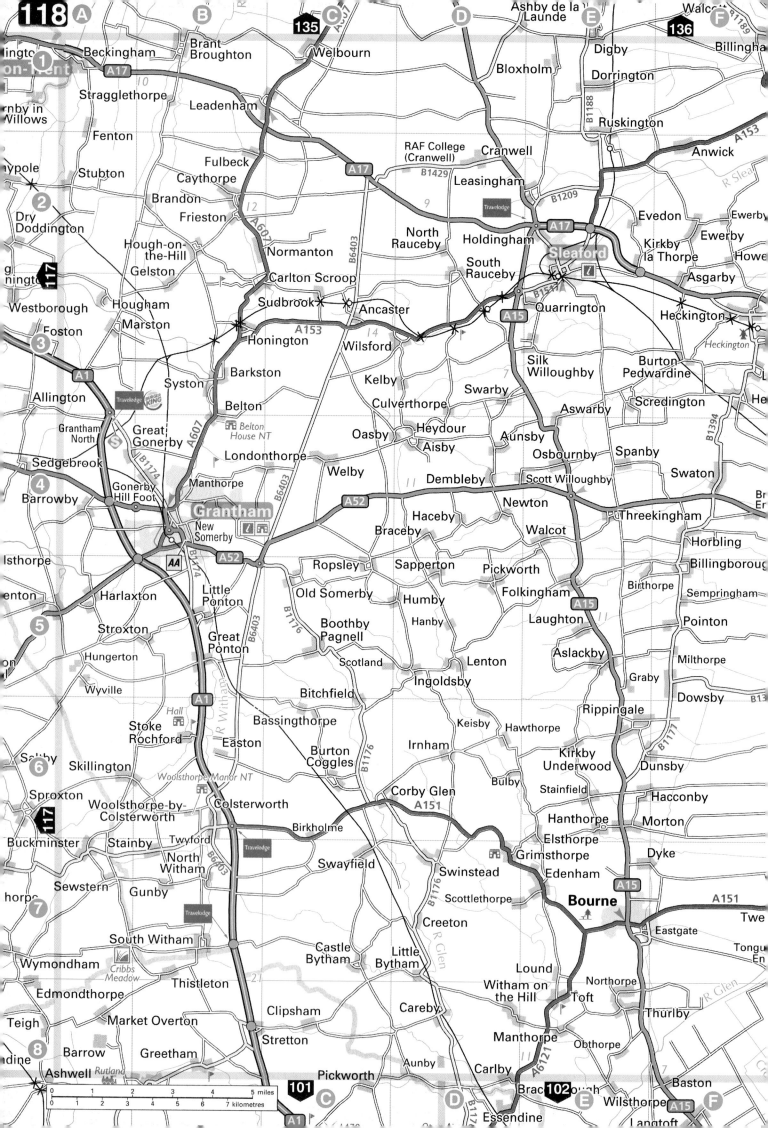

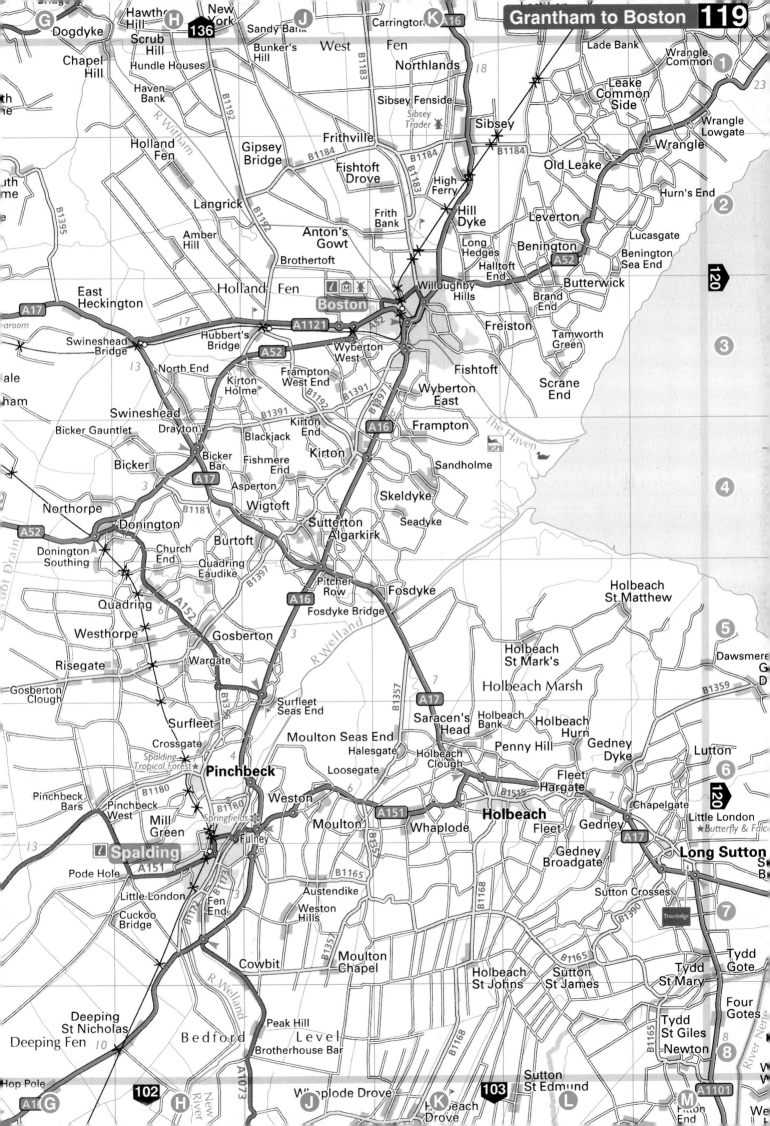

A   B   C   D   E   F

137

Friskney E dike

Wrangle
C on

1

Wrangle
Lowgate

Wrangle

Hurn's End

2

casgate

ington
End

119

3

THE WASH

4

ach
hew

Dawsmere

5

Gedney
Drove End

B1359

utton

6

119

apelgate

Little London
★ Butterfly & Falconry Park

Long Sutton

Sutton
Bridge

osses

Travelodge

7

Tydd
Gote

Tydd
St Mary

Walpole
Cross Keys

Walpole
St Andrew

Hay Green

**Terrington
St Clement**

Little
London

Clenchwarton
African Violet Centre

West
Lynn

A17

Tilney
All Saints

Four
Gotes

Walpole
St Peter

Tilney High End

A47

Tydd
St Giles

B1165

wton

Ingleborough

St John's
Highway

River Nene

8

West
Walton

Rattan Row

Tilney St
Lawrence

Saddle
Bow

Wiggenhall
St Germans

West
Winch

A10

Fitto

West Walton
Highway

103

Wiggenhall
St Mary t irgin

Holme ne
the Sea

Old
Hunstanton

Hunstanton

Ringstead

A149

Heacham

Norfolk
Lavender

Sedgeford

Snettisham

Park Farm
Southgate

Shernb

RSPB

Ingoldisthorpe

12

B1440

Dersingham

Doddshill

Wolferton

**Sandringha
West New**

Babingley River

A149

B1440

B1439

Castle Rising

Congham

North
Wootton

A148

Roydon

South Wootton

A148

A149

Pott
Row

Bawsey

Gaywood

B1145

Gayton

King's Lynn

Brow-of-
the-Hill

Ashwicke

A47

Middleton

East
Winch

North
Runcton

Blackborough
End

West
Bilney

Setchey

104

Pentney

Nar

0   1   2   3   4   5 miles

0   1   2   3   4   5   6   7 kilometres

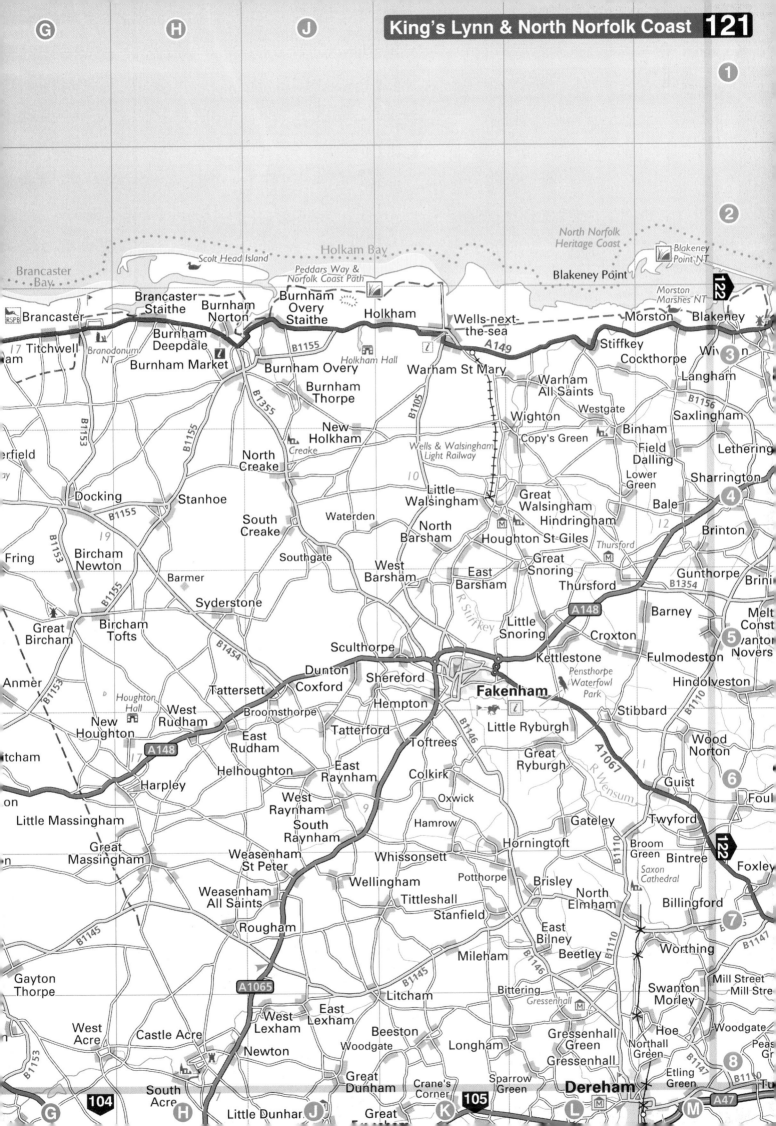

North Norfolk
Heritage Coast

Holkam Bay

Scolt Head Island

Peddars Way &
Norfolk Coast Path

Blakeney
Point NT

Brancaster
Bay

Blakeney Point

Morston
Marshes NT

RSPB Brancaster

Brancaster
Staithe

Burnham
Norton

Burnham
Overy
Staithe

Holkham

Wells-next-
the-sea

Morston

Blakeney

17 Titchwell
ham

Branodunum
NT

Burnham
Deepdale

Burnham Market

B1155

Holkham Hall

Warham St Mary

A149

Stiffkey
Cockthorpe

Wiv n

B1353

Burnham Overy

Burnham
Thorpe

B1105

Warham
All Saints

Westgate

Langham

B1156

Saxlingham

erfield

B1153

Docking

Stanhoe

B1155

Fring

B1153

Bircham
Newton

19

B1155

Great
Bircham

Bircham
Tofts

Barmer

Syderstone

New
Holkham

Creake

North
Creake

South
Creake

Southgate

Waterden

West
Barsham

Wighton

Copy's Green

Wells & Walsingham
Light Railway

10

Little
Walsingham

North
Barsham

East
Barsham

R Stiffkey

Great
Walsingham

Hindringham

Houghton St Giles

Great
Snoring

Thursford

Little
Snoring

Binham

Field
Dalling

Lower
Green

Thursford

Bale

12

A148

B1354

Barney

Lethering

Sharrington

Brinton

Gunthorpe

Brini

Melt
Const

anton
Novers

Croxton

Kettlestone

Hindolveston

Anmer

B1153

Houghton
Hall

New
Houghton

17

A148

Tattersett

West
Rudham

Broomsthorpe

Dunton
Coxford

Sculthorpe

Shereford

Hempton

B1146

Fakenham

Little Ryburgh

Pensthorpe
Waterfowl
Park

Stibbard

B1110

Wood
Norton

icham

Harpley

B1454

East
Rudham

Helhoughton

Tatterford

East
Raynham

Toftrees

Colkirk

Great
Ryburgh

A1067

R Wensum

Guist

Foul

on

Little Massingham

West
Raynham

South
Raynham

B1145

Oxwick

Hamrow

Gateley

Broom
Green

B1110

Twyford

Bintree

122

Foxley

n

Great
Massingham

Weasenham
St Peter

Weasenham
All Saints

Wellingham

Whissonsett

Potthorpe

Tittleshall

Stanfield

Horningtoft

Brisley

Saxon
Cathedral

North
Elmham

Billingford

B1147

Gayton
Thorpe

Rougham

Mileham

East
Bilney

Beetley

B1110

Worthing

B1146

Mill Street
Mill Stre

West
Acre

B1145

Castle Acre

West
Lexham

East
Lexham

A1065

Litcham

Beeston
Woodgate

Bittering

Gressenhall

Longham

Swanton
Morley

Hoe

Woodgate

Northall
Green

Peas
Gr

Newton

B1153

South
Acre

Great
Dunham

Crane's
Corner

Sparrow
Green

Gressenhall
Green

Gressenhall

Dereham

Etling
Green

B1147

B1110

A47

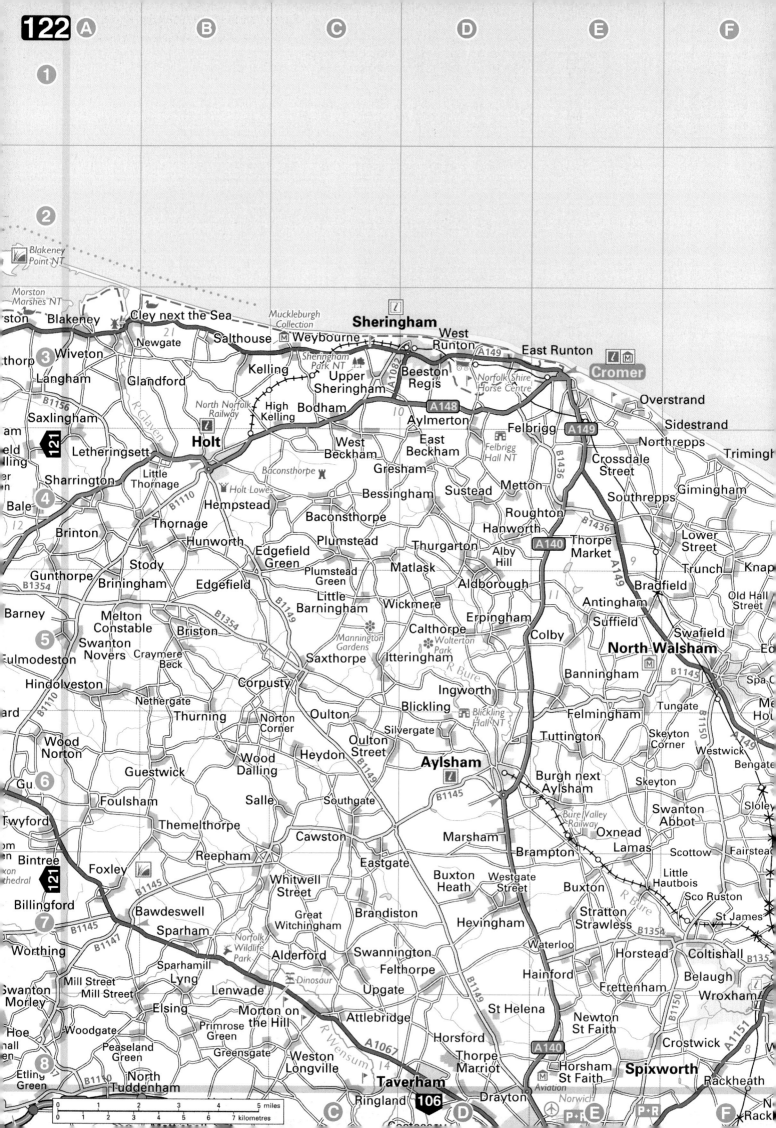

A B C D E F

1

2

Blakeney
Point NT

Morston
Marshes NT

ston Blakeney Cley next the Sea Muckleburgh Sheringham West
Newgate Salthouse Weybourne Collection Runton A149 East Runton Cromer

3 Wiveton Kelling Sheringham Beeston Norfolk Shire Overstrand
thorp Park NT Upper Regis Horse Centre
Langham Glandford North Norfolk Sheringham Aylmerton Sidestrand
Saxlingham Railway High Bodham Felbrigg Northrepps
121 Holt Kelling West East Felbrigg Crossdale Trimingh
Letheringsett Little Baconsthorpe Beckham Beckham Hall NT Metton Street Gimingham
Sharrington Thornage Holt Lowes Gresham Sustead Roughton Southrepps Lower
4 Hempstead Bessingham Hanworth Thorpe Street
Bale Brinton Thornage Baconsthorpe Thurgarton Alby A140 Market 9 Trunch Knap
Gunthorpe Hunworth Plumstead Hill Antingham Bradfield Old Hall
Stody Edgefield Matlask Aldborough Colby Suffield Swafield Street
Briningham Green Plumstead Little Wickmere Erpingham 11 North Walsham
Barney Edgefield Green Barningham Calthorpe Mannington Banningham Spa
5 Melton Briston Gardens Wolterton Ingworth B1145
Fulmodeston Constable Craymere Saxthorpe Itteringham Park Felmingham Tungate
Swanton Beck R Bure Blickling Skeyton Westwick
Hindolveston Novers Corpusty Blickling Tuttington Corner Bengate
Nethergate Oulton Hall NT Skeyton
6 Wood Thurning Norton Silvergate Aylsham Burgh next Swanton
Gu Norton Corner Heydon Oulton Aylsham Oxnead Abbot Sloley
Wood Street Bure Valley Lamas Scottow Fairstea
Twyford Guestwick Dalling Southgate B1145 Railway Brampton Little
7 Foulsham Salle Marsham Hautbois Sco Ruston St James
Bintree Foxley Cawston Buxton Westgate Buxton R Bure
121 Reepham Eastgate Heath Street Stratton Belaugh
Billingford Whitwell Brandiston Hevingham Strawless Horstead Coltishall
7 Bawdeswell Street Great Swannington Waterloo B1354
Worthing Sparham Witchingham Felthorpe Hainford Horstead Belaugh
Swanton Sparhamill Alderford Upgate Frettenham Wroxham
Morley Lyng Norfolk St Helena Newton
Mill Street Wildlife Dinosaur Horsford St Faith Crostwick
Hoe Elsing Park Morton on Thorpe Horsham Spixworth
8 Woodgate Primrose the Hill Attlebridge Marriot St Faith
Etling Peaseland Green Weston Aviation P+R Rackheath
Green Green Greensgate Longville Norwich P+R
B1110 North Ringland Taverham Drayton
Tuddenham 106

0 1 2 3 4 5 miles
0 1 2 3 4 5 6 7 kilometres

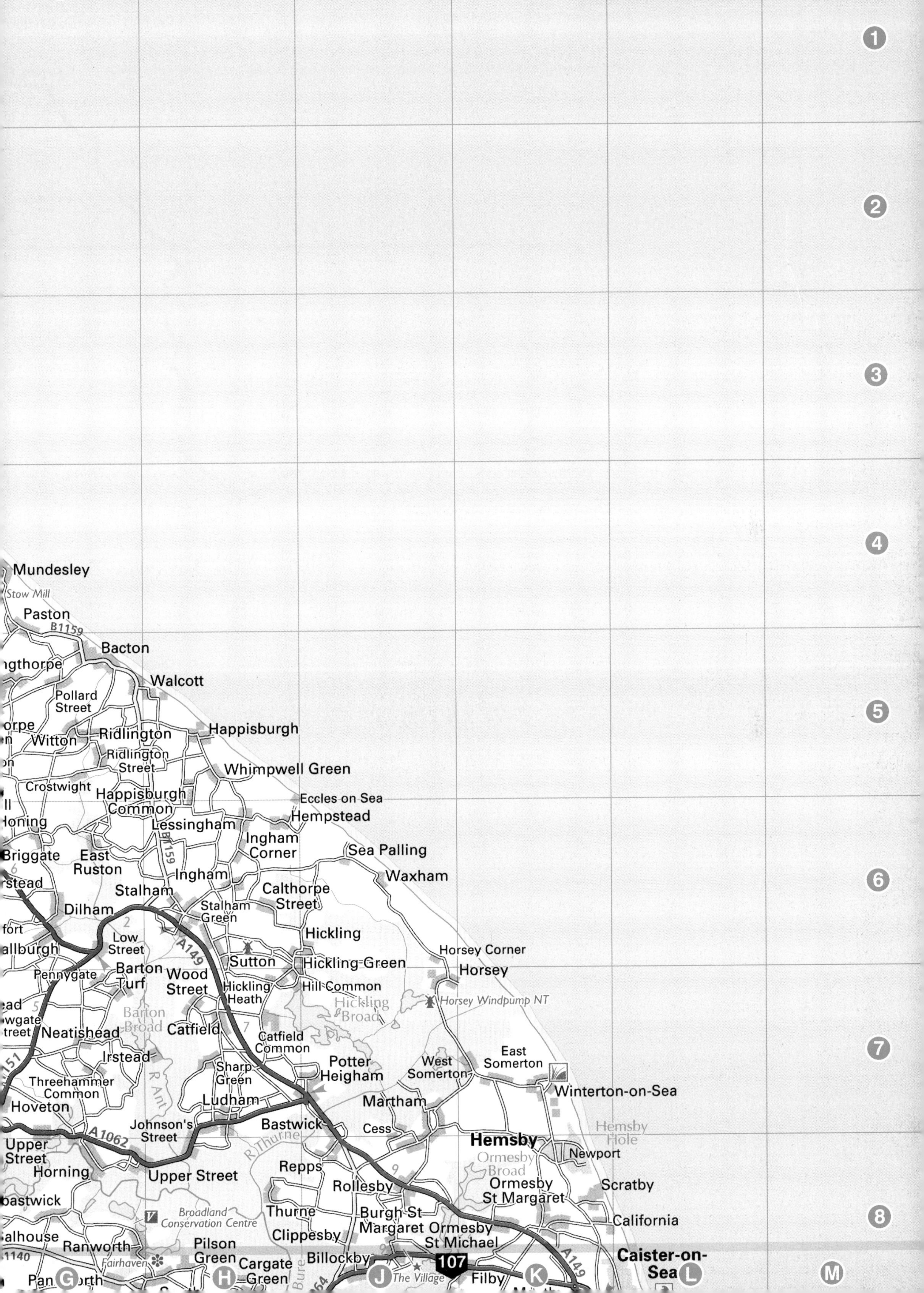

G H J K

1

2

3

4

Mundesley

Stow Mill

Paston

B1159

Bacton

ngthorpe

Walcott

Pollard
Street

orpe

Witton   Ridlington   Happisburgh

Ridlington
Street

Crostwight   Whimpwell Green

Happisburgh   Eccles on Sea

Honing   Common   Hempstead

Lessingham

Ingham   Ingham   Sea Palling
Corner

Briggate   East
Ruston   Ingham   Waxham

rstead   Stalham   Calthorpe
Street

Dilham   Stalham
Green

5

6

fort   Low
Street   Hickling   Horsey Corner

allburgh   Horsey

Pennygate   Barton   Wood   Sutton   Hickling Green
Turf   Street   Hickling   Hill Common

Hickling
Heath   *Hickling
Broad*   *Horsey Windpump NT*

*Barton
Broad*   Catfield   7

ead
wgate
treet   Neatishead   Catfield
Common

Irstead   Sharp   East
Green   West   Somerton

Threehammer   Ludham   Potter   Somerton
Common   Heigham   Winterton-on-Sea

Hoveton   Johnson's   Martham   *Hemsby
Street   Bastwick   Cess   Hole*

Upper   A1062   *R.Thurne*   Hemsby   Newport
Street
Horning   Upper Street   Repps   *Ormesby
Broad*   Scratby

bastwick   Rollesby   Ormesby
St Margaret   California

*Broadland
Conservation Centre*   Thurne   Burgh St
Margaret Ormesby

alhouse   Clippesby   St Michael

Ranworth   Pilson   Cargate   Billockby   **Caister-on-
1140   Green   Green   Sea**

Fairhaven

7

8

G   H   J   **107**   K   L   M

Pan   orth   *The Village*   Filby

A   B   C   D   E   F

1

The Skerries

North Anglesey Heritage Coast

Wylfa Head   Cemaes Bay

Cemlyn Bay

Hen Borth   NT

Cemaes

CARMEL HEAD

Tregele

A5

Llanfairynghornwy

Llanfechell

2

Dublin   V C

Holyhead Bay

Church Bay

Llanrhyddlad

Llanfflewyn

Llanbab

Dun Laoghaire   C

Llanfaethlu

3

North Stack

Breakwater Quarry

Gogarth Bay

Llandeusant

Llanfwrog

Stryd-y-Facsen

Elim

Llaingoch

Holyhead Mountain Hut Group

Holyhead

Llanfachraeth

Llanfigael

Llantrisant

Pen-llyn

South Stack

Penrhos-Feilw

Llanynghenedl

Penrhos

Llyn Llywenan

Holyhead Mountain Heritage Coast   RSPB

South Stack

Kingsland

3

A5

B5109

Penrhyn Mawr

Port Dafarch NT

Trefignath

A55

Valley   A5025

Bodedern

4

Treaddur Bay

B4545

Caergeiliog

Bryngwra

Four Mile Bridge

Llanfihangel yn Nhowyn

Llechylched

HOLY ISLAND

Llanfair-yn-Neubwll

Capel Gwyn

A44080

Rhoscolyn

Plas Cymyran

RSPB

Ty Newydd

5

Rhoscolyn Head

Cymyran Bay

Pencarni

Llanfaelog

Rhosneigr

A4080

Bryn Du

Barclodiad y Gawres

Porth Trecastell

6

Aberffraw

Llanga

Aberffraw Bay

Aberffraw Bay Heritage Coast

Malltraeth

7

Llanddwyn Isl

C A E R N A R F O N

B A Y

8

0   1   2   3   4   5 miles
0   1   2   3   4   5   6   7 kilometres

A   B   C   D   E   F

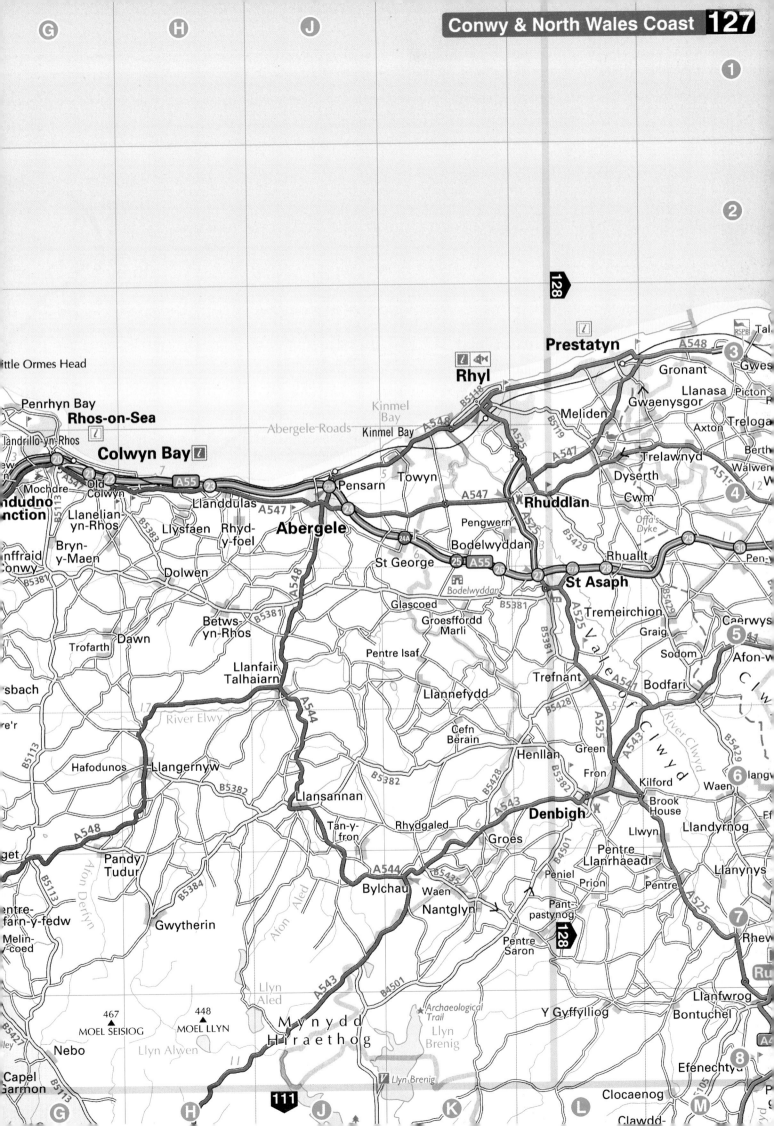

G H J

1

2

128

i

Prestatyn

RSPB Tal

A548

Gwes

ittle Ormes Head

Kinmel
Bay

Gronant

3

Llanasa Picton

Penrhyn Bay

Gwaenysgor

Treloga

Rhos-on-Sea

Abergele-Roads

i ◄►

Rhyl

Meliden

Axton

Berth

i

Kinmel Bay

A548

A525

Trelawnyd

Walwen

landrillo-yn-Rhos

B5118

B5119

A54?

Colwyn Bay *i*

A55

Towyn

Dyserth

12

4

ndudno

Mochdre

Old
Colwyn

7

23

Pensarn

A547

Cwm

nction

Llanddulas

A547

Rhuddlan

B5113

Llanelian-
yn-Rhos

B5383

A547

21

Pengwern

A525

Offa's
Dyke

29

30

Bryn-
y-Maen

Llysfaen

Rhyd-
y-foel

Abergele

20

Bodelwyddan

B5429

Rhuallt

Pen-

nffraid
Conwy

24A

St George

25 A55 26

27

28

St Asaph

B5381

Dolwen

A548

6

Bodelwyddan

A525 Vale

Tremeirchion

Caerwys

5

Glascoed

B5381

Graig

Dawn

Trofarth

Betws-
yn-Rhos

B5381

Groesffordd
Marli

Sodom

Afon-w

sbach

Pentre Isaf

A547

Trefnant

Bodfari

C

re'r

River Elwy

17

**Llanfair
Talhaiarn**

A544

Llannefydd

B5428

5

River Clwyd

C

l

w

y

d

Hafodunos

Llangernyw

B5382

Cefn
Berain

Henllan

B5382

B5429

6

langw

B5382

Green

Kilford

Waen

Llansannan

A543

Fron

Brook
House

Llandyrnog

Ef

Tan-y-
fron

Rhydgaled

6

Denbigh

Llwyn

A548

B5113

Pandy
Tudur

B5384

Groes

B4501

Pentre

Llandynog

get

A544

B5435

Peniel

Pentre
Llanrhaeadr

A525

Llanynys

ntre-
farn-y-fedw

Bylchau

Waen

Prion

Pentre

7

Rhew

Melin-
coed

Gwytherin

Nantglyn

Pant-
pastynog

Afon Aled

Pentre
Saron

128

Ru

Llanfwrog

Llyn
Aled

★ Archaeological
Trail

467
▲
MOEL SEISIOG

448
▲
MOEL LLYN

A543

Y Gyffylliog

Bontuchel

Nebo

Llyn Alwen

11

**Mynydd
Hiraethog**

Llyn
Brenig

8

Capel
Garmon

B5427

ley

V Llyn Brenig

111

Efenechty

Clocaenog

Clawdd-

G H J K L M

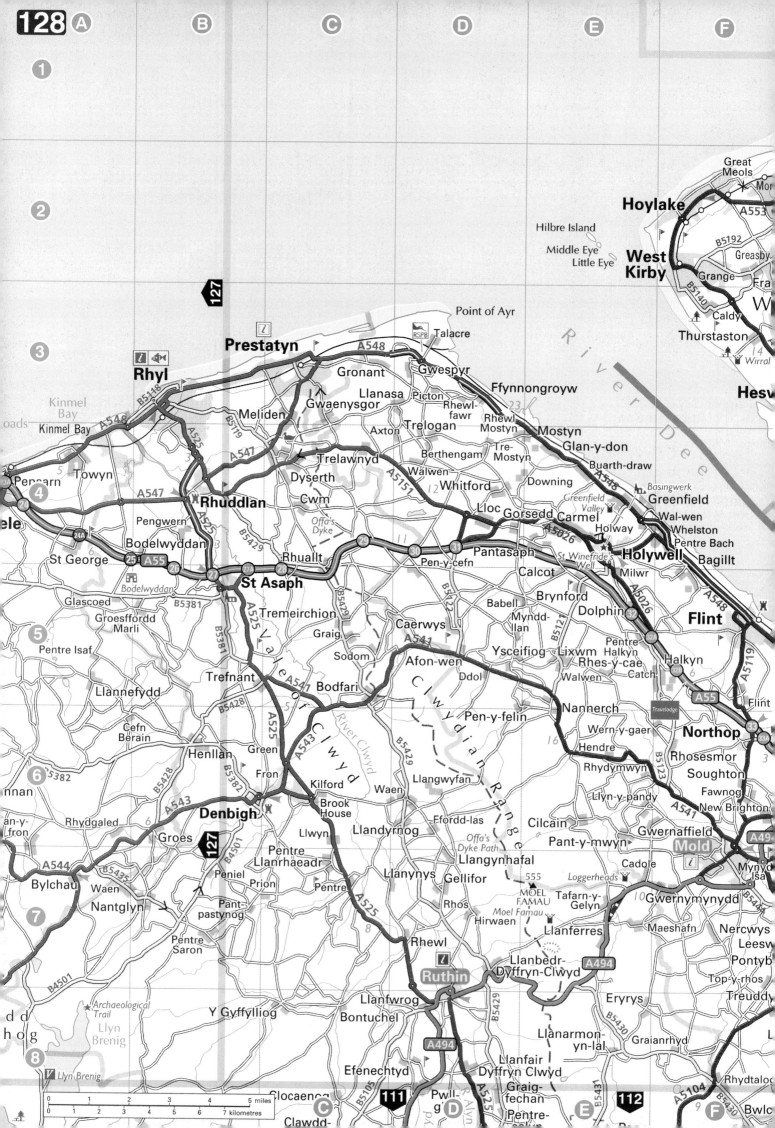

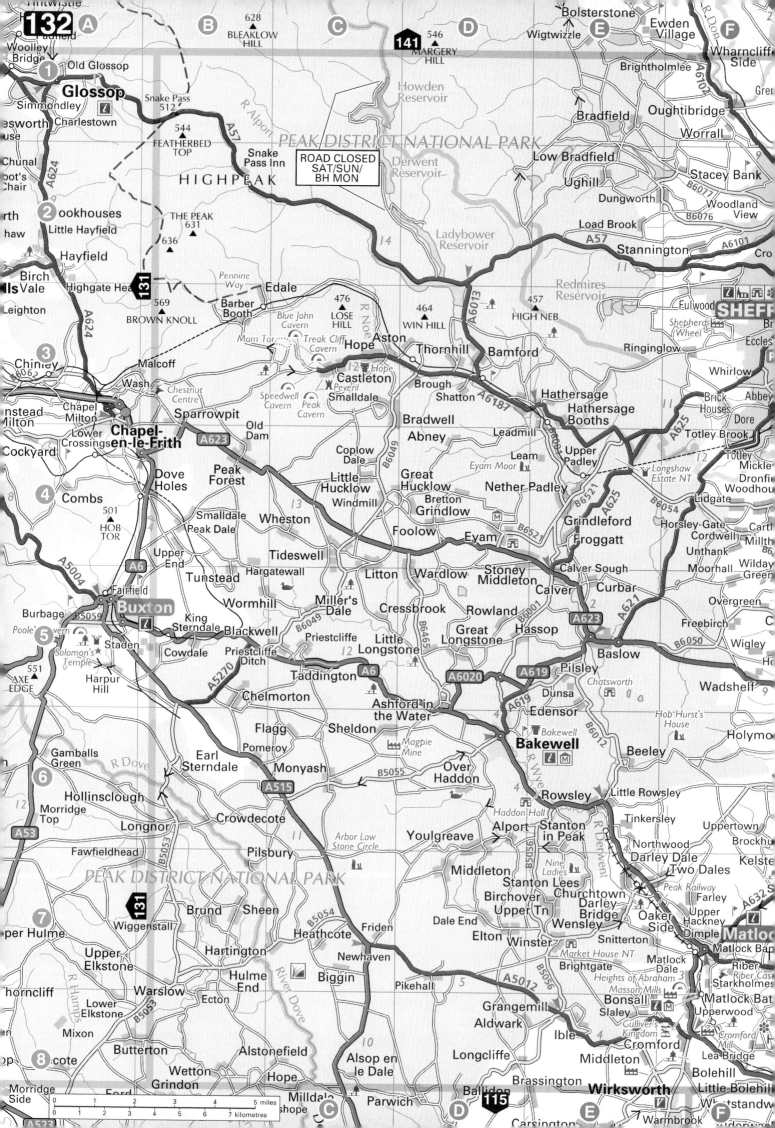

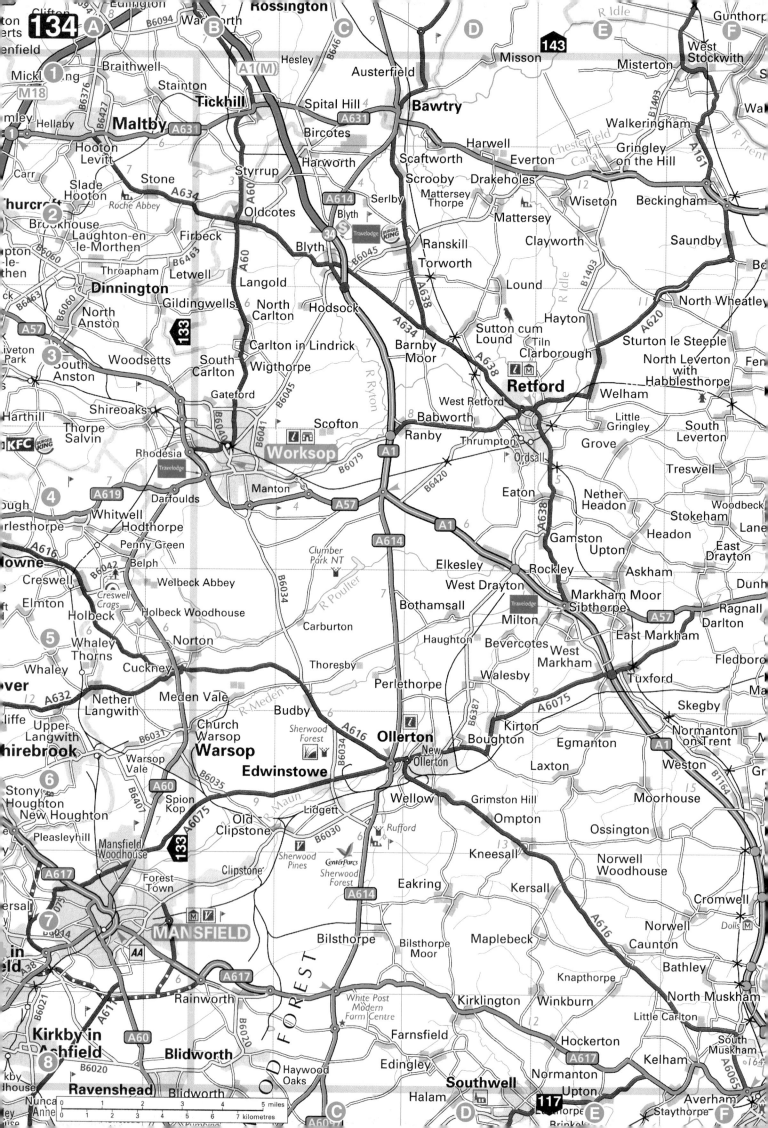

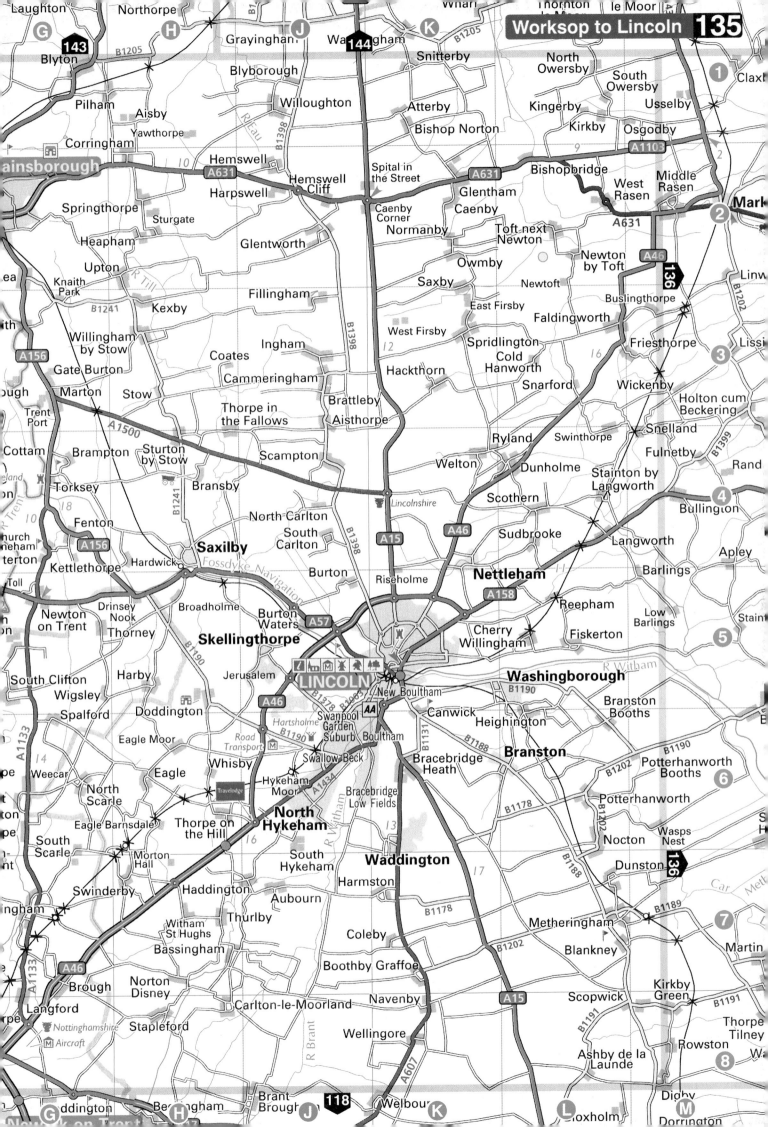

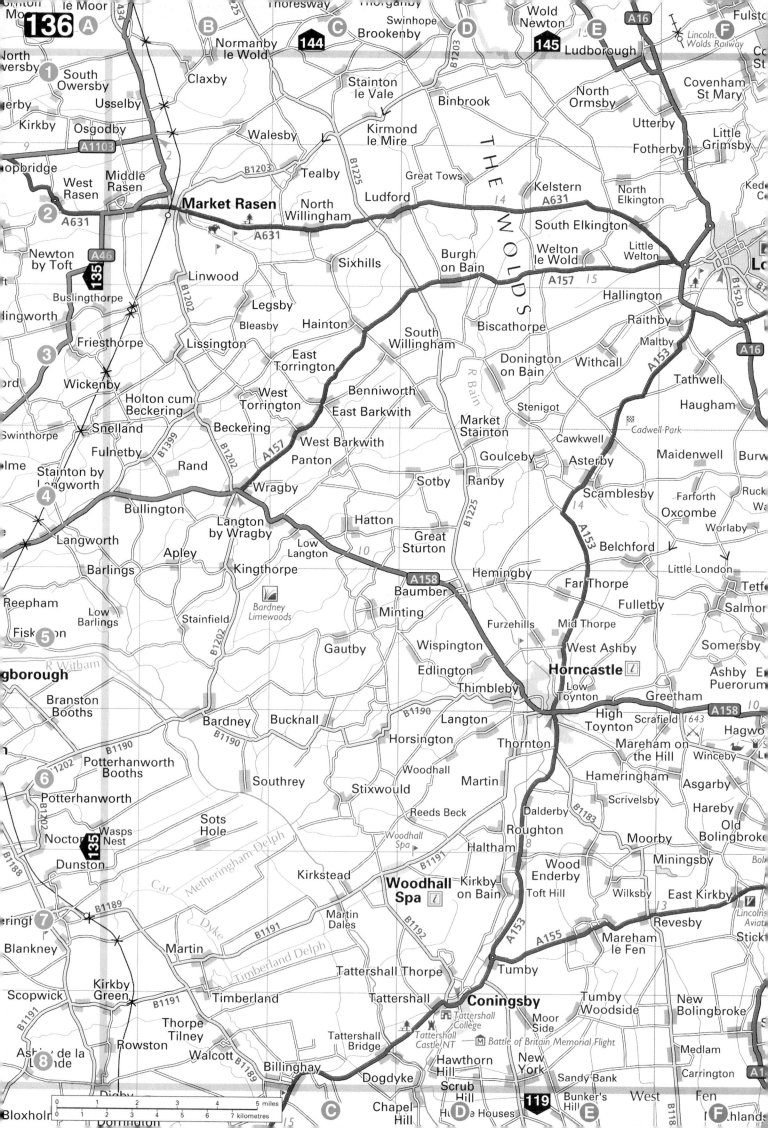

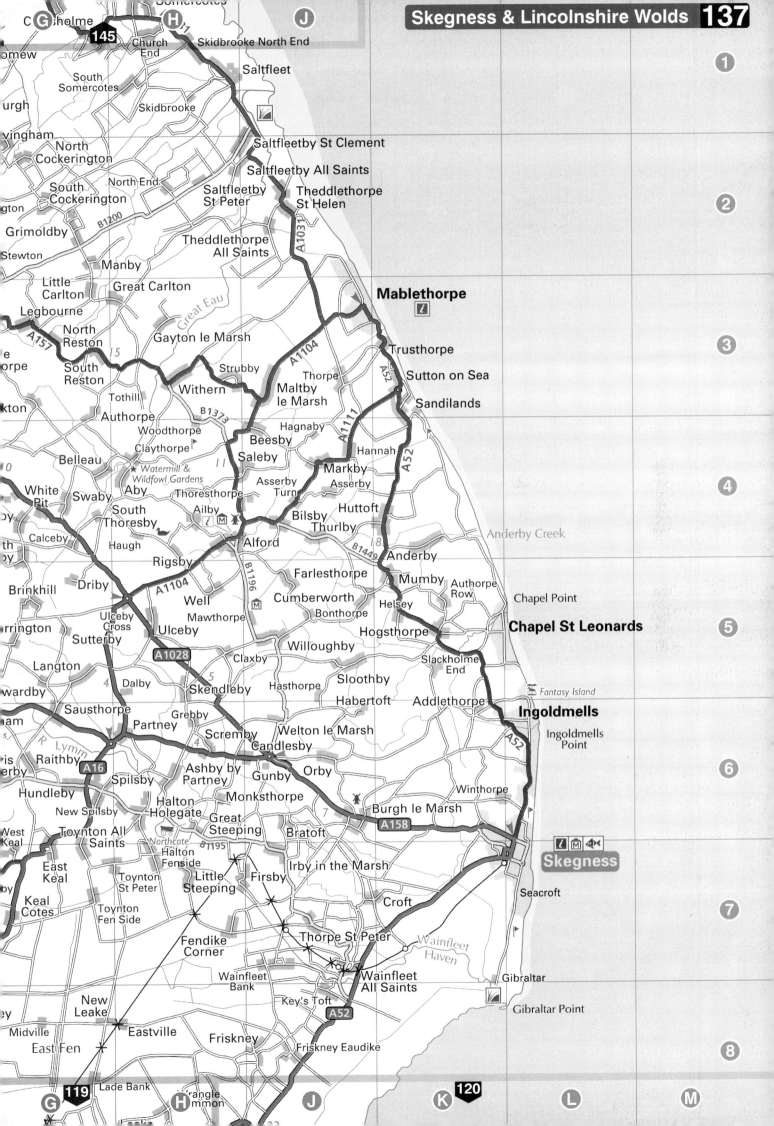

Skidbrooke North End
Saltfleet
Church End
Skidbrooke
South Somercotes
North Cockerington
North End
Saltfleetby St Clement
Saltfleetby All Saints
South Cockerington
Saltfleetby St Peter
Theddlethorpe St Helen
Grimoldby
Stewton
Theddlethorpe All Saints
Manby
Little Carlton
Great Carlton
Legbourne
Great Eau
Mablethorpe
North Reston
Gayton le Marsh
Trusthorpe
South Reston
Strubby
Thorpe
Sutton on Sea
Withern
Maltby le Marsh
Sandilands
Tothill
Authorpe
Hagnaby
Woodthorpe
Beesby
Hannah
Claythorpe
Saleby
Belleau
Markby
Watermill & Wildfowl Gardens
Asserby
Aby
Thoresthorpe
Asserby Turn
Huttoft
White Pit
Swaby
Ailby
Bilsby
South Thoresby
Thurlby
Calceby
Haugh
Alford
Anderby Creek
Rigsby
Anderby
Brinkhill
Driby
Farlesthorpe
Mumby
Authorpe Row
Well
Chapel Point
Ulceby Cross
Mawthorpe
Cumberworth
Helsey
Sutterby
Ulceby
Bonthorpe
Chapel St Leonards
Langton
Willoughby
Hogsthorpe
Dalby
Claxby
Slackholme End
Sausthorpe
Skendleby
Hasthorpe
Sloothby
Fantasy Island
Partney
Grebby
Habertoft
Addlethorpe
Ingoldmells
Raithby
Scremby
Welton le Marsh
Ingoldmells Point
Spilsby
Candlesby
Hundleby
Ashby by Partney
Gunby
Orby
New Spilsby
Halton Holegate
Monksthorpe
Winthorpe
Toynton All Saints
Great Steeping
Bratoft
Burgh le Marsh
Skegness
Northcote
Halton Fenside
Irby in the Marsh
East Keal
Toynton St Peter
Little Steeping
Firsby
Croft
Seacroft
Keal Cotes
Toynton Fen Side
Fendike Corner
Thorpe St Peter
Wainfleet Haven
New Leake
Wainfleet Bank
Wainfleet All Saints
Gibraltar
Eastville
Key's Toft
Gibraltar Point
East Fen
Friskney
Friskney Eaudike
Midville
Lade Bank

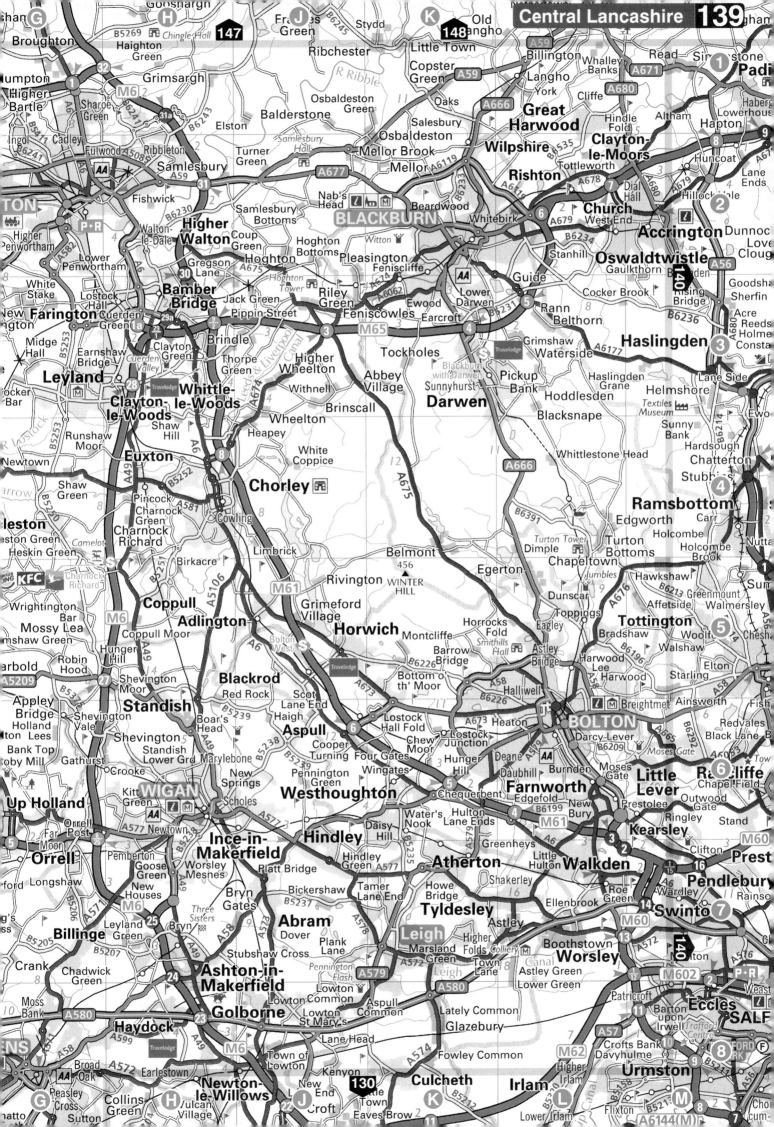

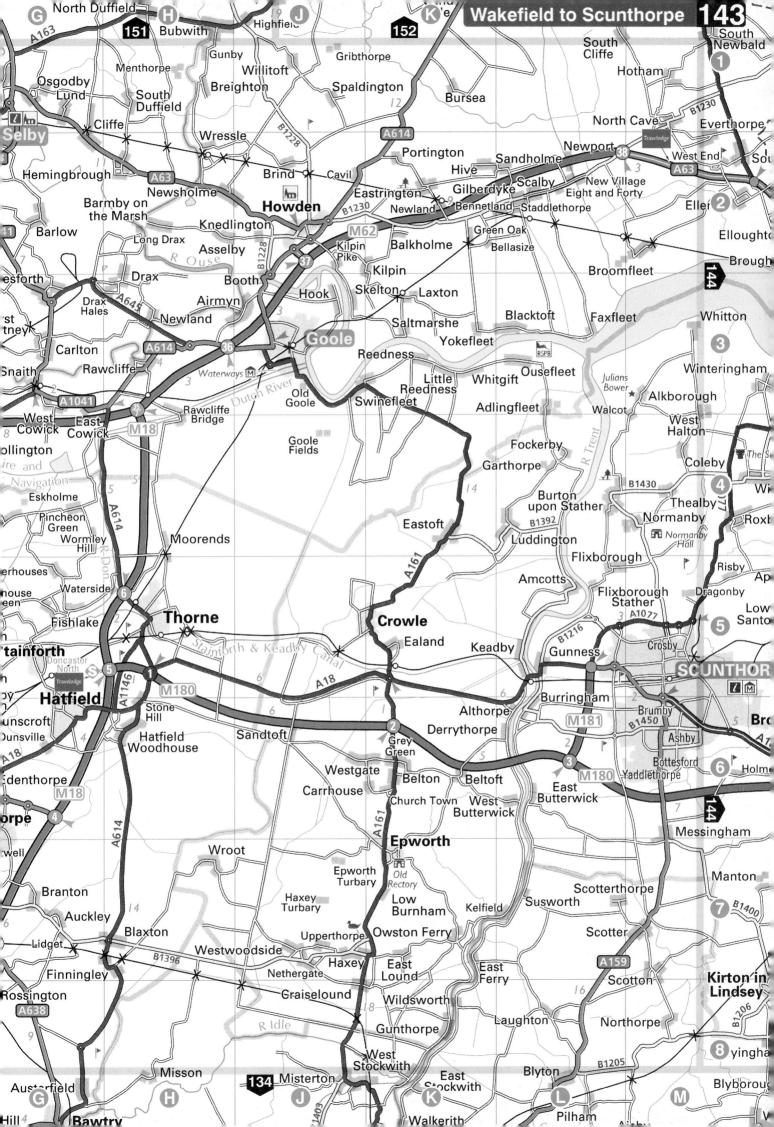

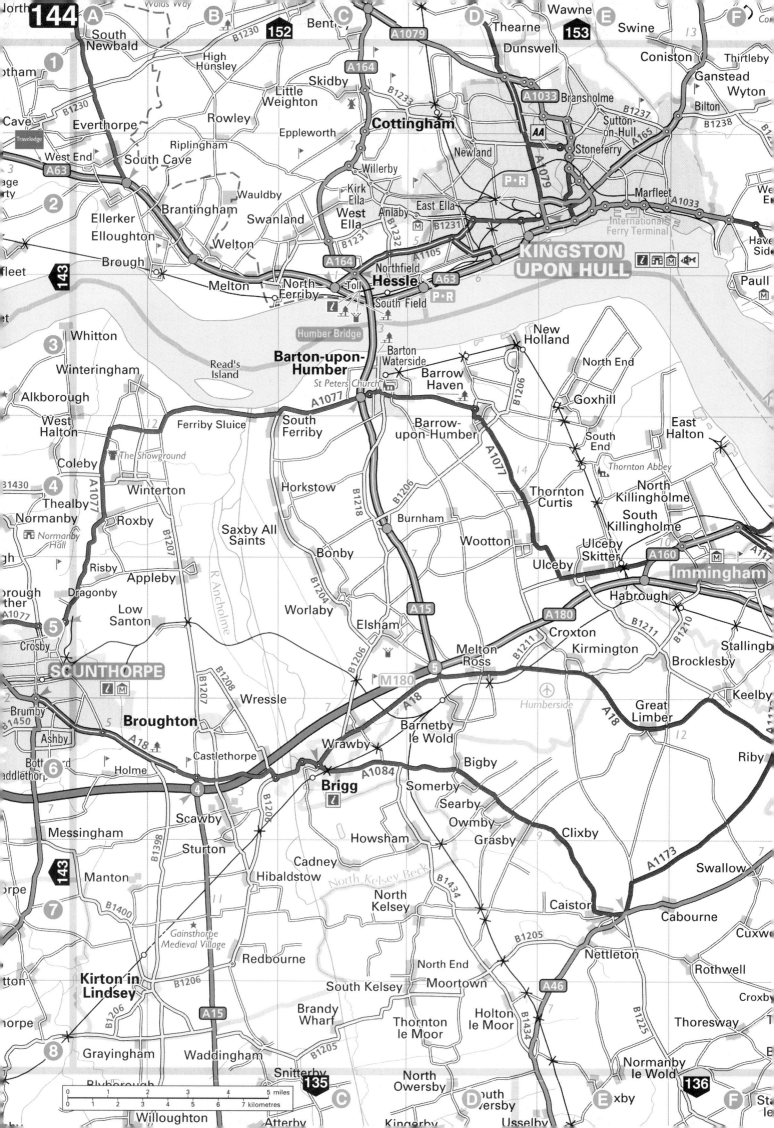

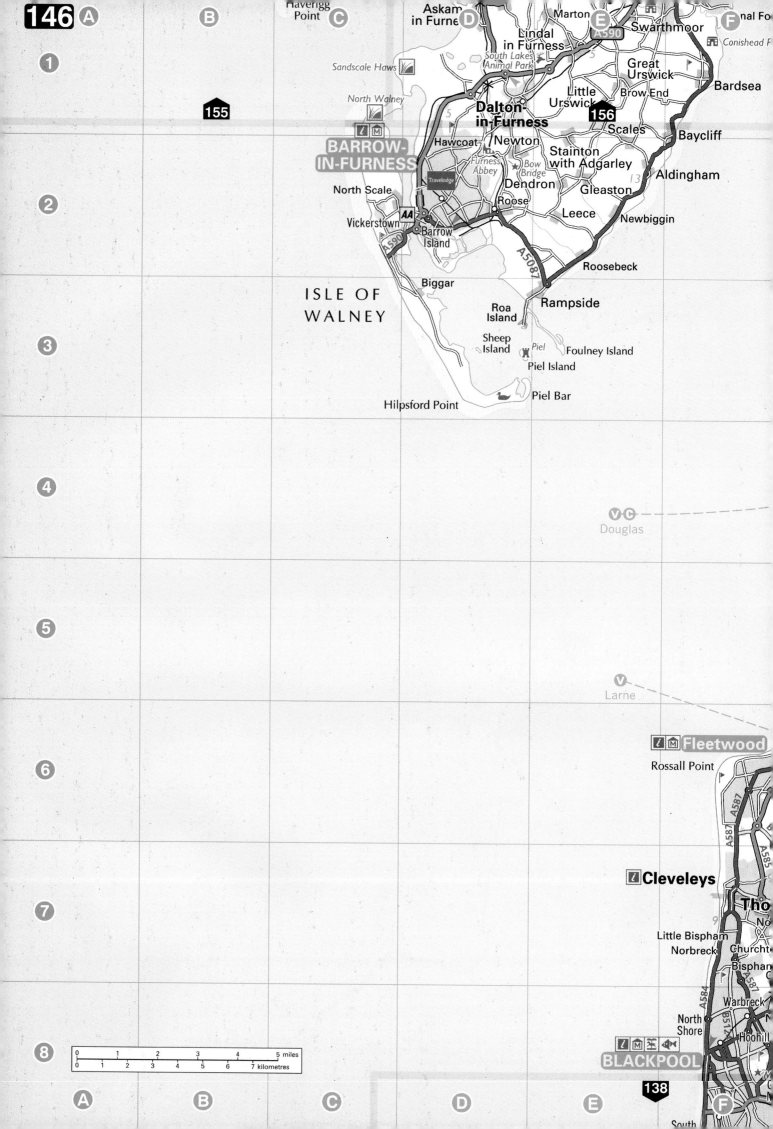

ISLE OF
WALNEY

Haverigg
Point

Askam
in Furne

Marton

Swarthmoor

nal Fo

Conishead

Lindal
in Furness

A590

Great
Urswick

Bardsea

South Lakes
Animal Park

Little
Urswick

Brow End

155

Sandscale Haws

156

Dalton-
in-Furness

North Walney

Scales

Baycliff

BARROW-
IN-FURNESS

Hawcoat

Newton

Stainton
with Adgarley

Aldingham

North Scale

Furness
Abbey

Bow
Bridge

Dendron

Gleaston

13

Travelodge

Roose

Newbiggin

Vickerstown

AA

Leece

A590

Barrow
Island

A5087

Roosebeck

Biggar

Roa
Island

Rampside

Sheep
Island

Piel

Foulney Island

Piel Island

Hilpsford Point

Piel Bar

V C
Douglas

V
Larne

Fleetwood

Rossall Point

A587

A587

A585

Cleveleys

Tho
No

9

Little Bispham

Norbreck

Churcht

Bisphan

A584

A581

Warbreck

B512

North
Shore

Hoohill

BLACKPOOL

138

South

0   1   2   3   4   5 miles
0 1 2 3 4 5 6 7 kilometres

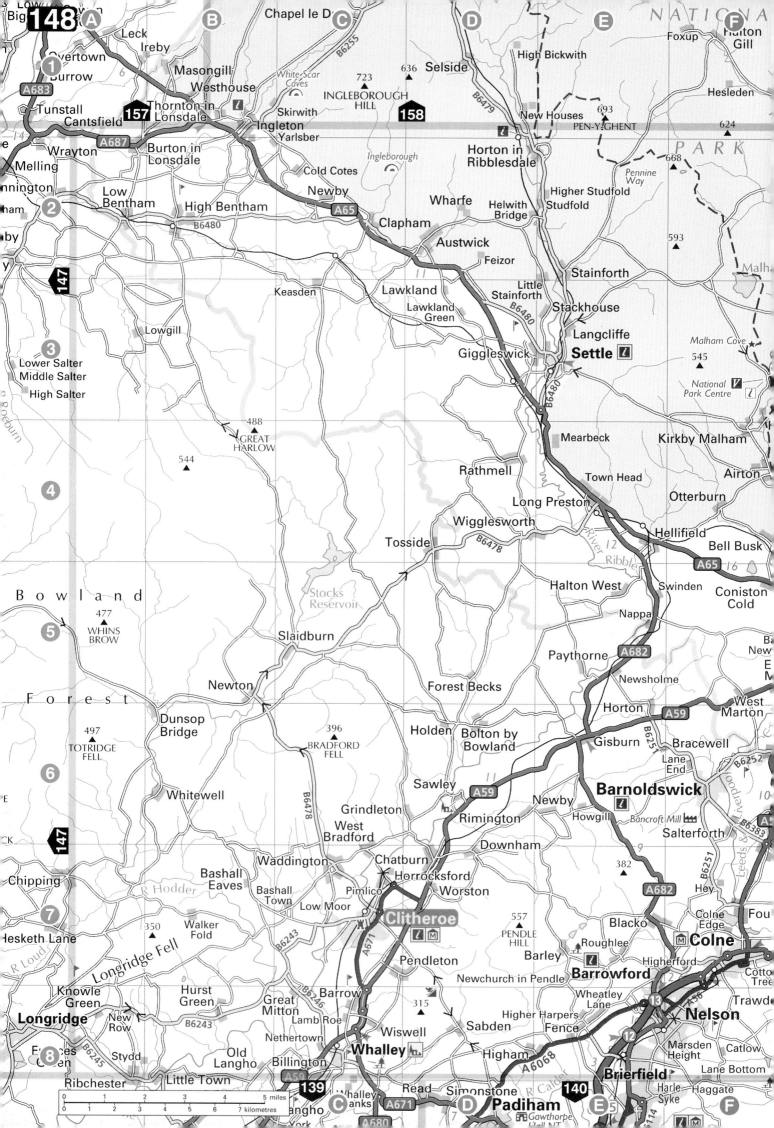

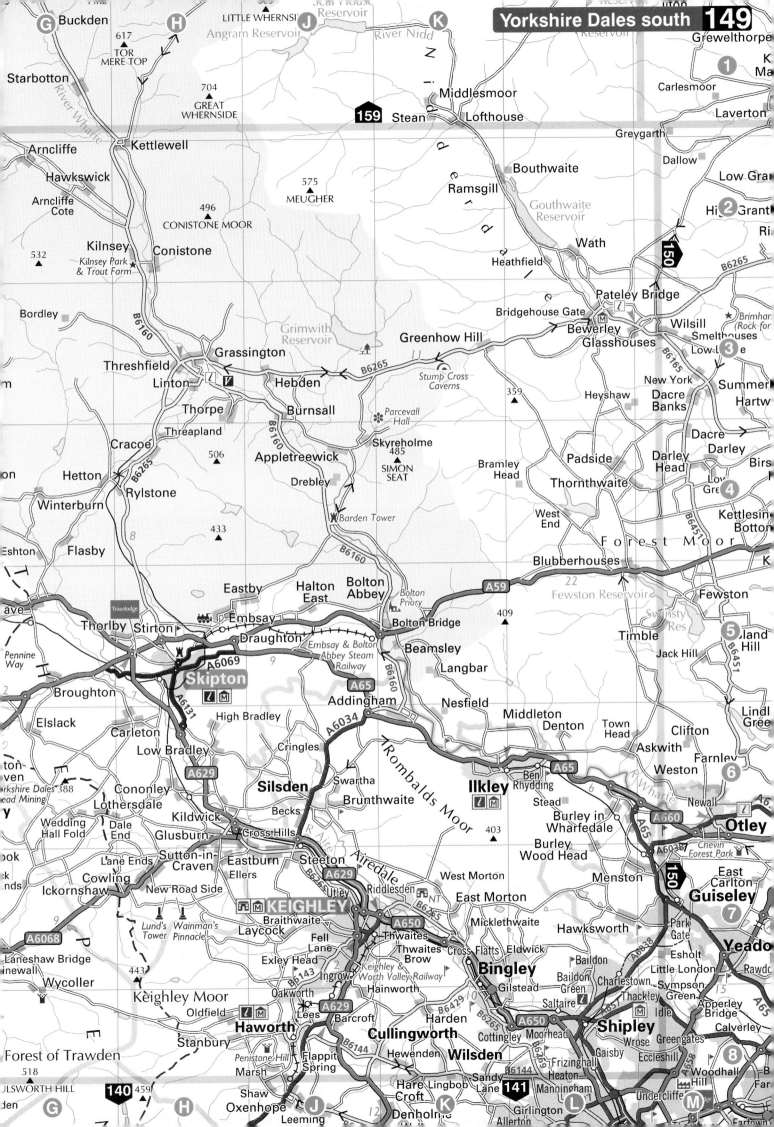

G Buckden
617
TOR MERE TOP
Starbotton
River Wharfe
Arncliffe
Hawkswick
Arncliffe Cote
532
Kilnsey
Kilnsey Park & Trout Farm
Conistone
Bordley
B6160
Threshfield
Grassington
Linton
Thorpe
Threapland
506
Cracoe
Hetton
B6265
Rylstone
Winterburn
Flasby
433
Eshton
Thorlby Stirton
Travelodge
Pennine Way
Broughton
Elslack
Carleton
Low Bradley
A629
Cononley
Lothersdale
Kildwick
Wedding Hall Fold
Dale End
Glusburn
Sutton-in-Craven
Cowling
Ickornshaw
A6068
Laneshaw Bridge
Wycoller
Forest of Trawden
518

LITTLE WHERNSIDE J
Angram Reservoir
704
GREAT WHERNSIDE
Kettlewell
575
MEUGHER
496
CONISTONE MOOR
Grimwith Reservoir
Hebden
Burnsall
Appletreewick
Drebley
Barden Tower
B6160
Eastby
Halton East
Bolton Abbey
Embsay
Draughton
Embsay & Bolton Abbey Steam Railway
Skipton
A6069
A6131
High Bradley
Cringles
Silsden
Becks
Brunthwaite
Swartha
Cross Hills
Eastburn
Ellers
Steeton
Utley
Riddlesden
KEIGHLEY
Braithwaite
Laycock
Fell Lane
Exley Head
Ingrow
Keighley & Worth Valley Railway
Hainworth
Lund's Tower
Wainman's Pinnacle
443
Keighley Moor
Oldfield
Lees
Barcroft
Haworth
Stanbury
Penistone Hill
Flappit Spring
Marsh
Shaw
Oxenhope
Leeming

River Nidd
Middlesmoor
159 Stean Lofthouse
Bouthwaite
Ramsgill
Gouthwaite Reservoir
Wath
Heathfield
Greenhow Hill
B6265
Stump Cross Caverns
Parcevall Hall
Skyreholme
485
SIMON SEAT
Bolton Priory
Bolton Bridge
A59
Beamsley
Langbar
409
A65
Addingham
A6034
Nesfield
Middleton
Denton
Ilkley
Ben Rhydding
Stead
Burley in Wharfedale
403
Burley Wood Head
West Morton
East Morton
Micklethwaite
Hawksworth
Thwaites
Thwaites Brow
Cross Flatts Eldwick
Bingley
Gilstead
Harden
Cullingworth
Wilsden
Hewenden
B6144
Hare Lingbob Croft
Denholme
140 459 G
H J K

Grewelthorpe
Carlesmoor
1
Laverton
Greygarth
Dallow
Low Gra
2 Hi Grant
Ri
B6265
Pateley Bridge
Bewerley
Glasshouses
Wilsill
Smelthouses
Low L e
3
New York
Dacre Banks
Heyshaw
Summer
Hartw
Dacre
Darley
Birs
359
Padside
Darley Head
Low
Gre 4
Thornthwaite
West End
Kettlesin
Botton
Forest Moor
Blubberhouses
22
Fewston Reservoir
Fewston
Timble
Swinsty Res
Jack Hill
5 land Hill
B6451
Town Head
Clifton
Askwith
Farnley
Weston
6
R Wharfe
Lindl Gree
A660
Newall
Otley
A6038
Chevin Forest Park
150
East Carlton
Menston
Guiseley
7
Park Gate
Yeado
Baildon
Little London
Esholt
Baildon Green
Charlestown
Sympson Green
Cottingley
Moorhead
Saltaire
Shipley
A650
Gaisby
Wrose
Greengates
Frizinghall
Heaton
Sandy Lane
141 Manningham
Girlington
Allerton
Idle
Calverley
Apperley Bridge
Thackley
Eccleshill
8
Woodhall
Hill
Undercliffe
L M

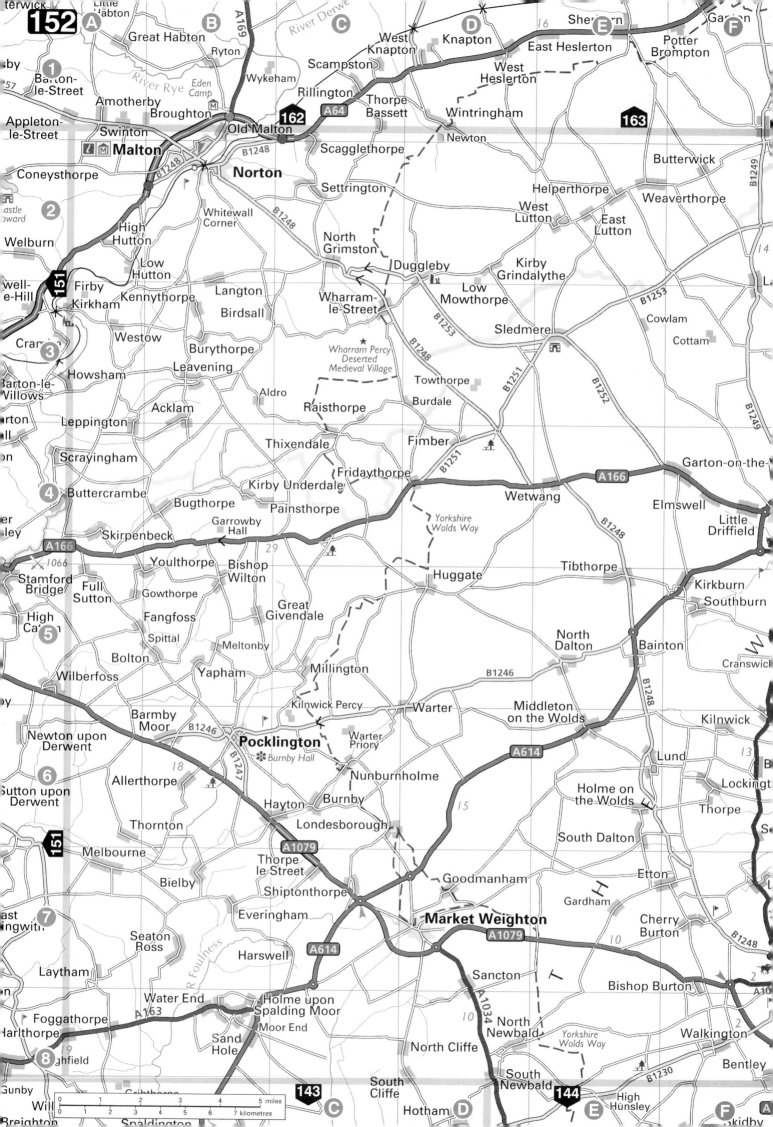

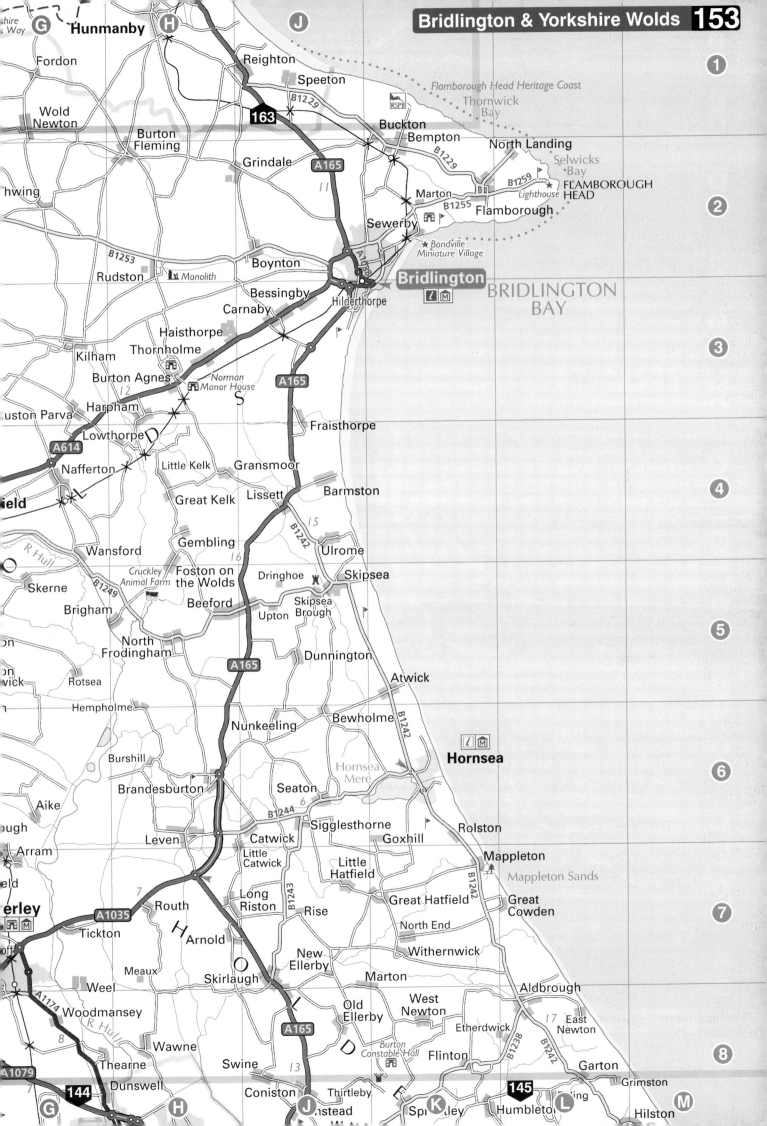

G H J 1

hire
Way
Hunmanby
Fordon
Reighton
Speeton
Flamborough Head Heritage Coast
Thornwick Bay
RSPB
Wold Newton
Burton Fleming
B1229
163
Buckton
Bempton
North Landing
Selwicks Bay
Grindale
A165
B1229
Lighthouse
FLAMBOROUGH HEAD
B1259
Marton
B1255
Flamborough
2
11
Sewerby
Boynton
Rudston
Monolith
Bondville Miniature Village
Bridlington
Bessingby
Hilderthorpe
BRIDLINGTON BAY
Carnaby
Haisthorpe
3
Thornholme
Kilham
Burton Agnes
S
Norman Manor House
A165
Harpham
uston Parva
Lowthorpe
D
Fraisthorpe
A614
Nafferton
Little Kelk
Gransmoor
4
L
 field
Great Kelk
Lissett
Barmston
Wansford
B1242
15
Gembling
Ulrome
R Hull
16
Foston on the Wolds
Dringhoe
Skipsea
Cruckley Animal Farm
Skerne
B1249
Beeford
Skipsea Brough
5
Brigham
Upton
North Frodingham
A165
Dunnington
Rotsea
Atwick
Hempholme
Bewholme
B1242
Nunkeeling
Burshill
i *M*
Hornsea
Hornsea Mere
6
Aike
Brandesburton
Seaton
ough
6
Leven
B1244
Sigglesthorne
Rolston
Arram
Catwick
Goxhill
Mappleton
7
Little Catwick
Little Hatfield
Mappleton Sands
erley
A1035
Routh
Long Riston
B1243
Rise
Great Hatfield
Great Cowden
7
Tickton
H
Arnold
North End
Meaux
O
Withernwick
Weel
Skirlaugh
New Ellerby
Marton
Aldbrough
A1174
Woodmansey
L
Old Ellerby
West Newton
Etherdwick
B1238
B1242
17
East Newton
R Hull
8
Wawne
D
A165
Burton Constable Hall
Flinton
Garton
A1079
Thearne
Swine
13
Grimston
Dunswell
Coniston
Thirtleby
145
Humbleto
Hilston
144
G H J nstead K Spiddley Humbleto L M

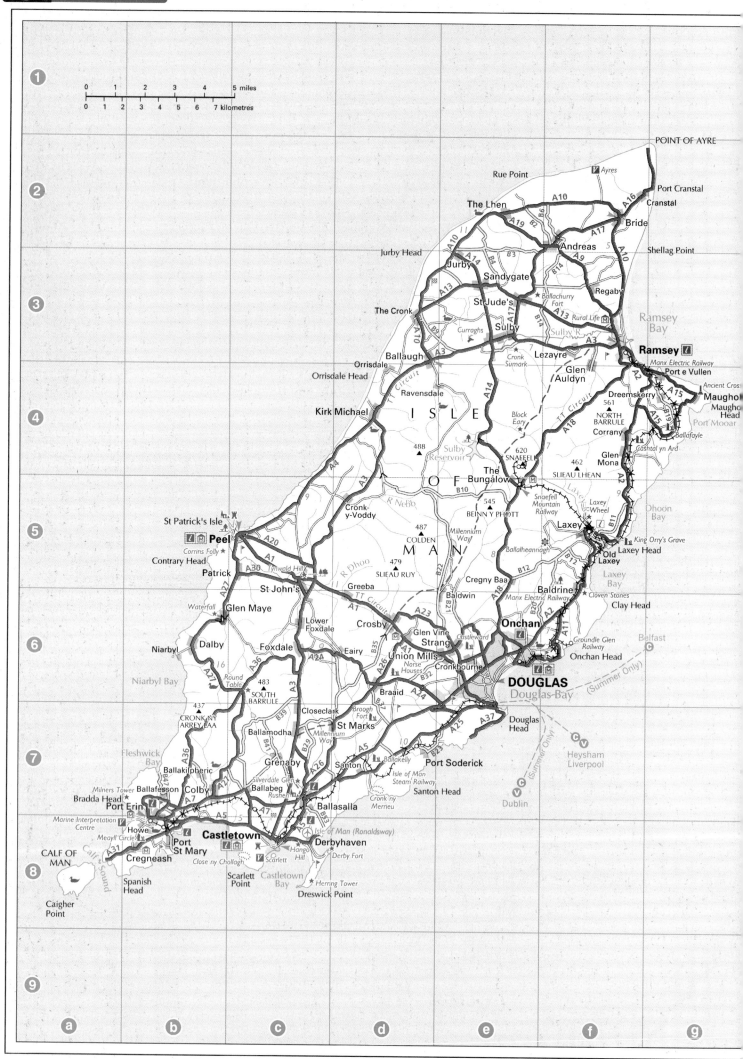

POINT OF AYRE

Rue Point

Ayres

Port Cranstal

The Lhen
A10
A16
Cranstal
A19
B6
A17
Bride
Andreas
5
A10
Shellag Point

Jurby Head
A10
A14
Jurby
A14
B4
B3
Sandygate
B14
A9
Regaby
A13
St Jude's
Ballachurry Fort
A13
Rural Life
Ramsey Bay

The Cronk
A17
Sulby
B14
Sulby R.
Ramsey

Currachs
Cronk Sumark
7
Lezayre
A3
Manx Electric Railway
Port e Vullen

Ballaugh
A3
Glen Auldyn
A2
Ancient Cross
Orrisdale
Dreemskerry
561
A15
Maughold
Orrisdale Head
Ravensdale
Block Eary
NORTH BARRULE
A18
Corrany
Maughold Head
Port Mooar

Kirk Michael
ISLE
Ballafayle
488
Sulby Reservoir
620
SNAEFELL
462
SLIEAU LHEAN
Glen Mona
A2
Cashtal yn Ard

OF
The Bungalow
A14
A3
A4
TT Circuit
B10
Snaefell Mountain Railway
Laxey Wheel
Dhoon Bay

St Patrick's Isle
R. Nebb
545
BEINN Y PHOTT
Laxey
B11

Peel
MAN
487
COLDEN
Millennium Way
9
Corrins Folly
A20
8
Ballalheannagh
King Orry's Grave
Contrary Head
A1
479
SLIEAU RUY
B22
B12
Laxey Head
Patrick
A30
Tynwald Hill
R. Dhoo
Old Laxey
A27
Cregny Baa
B12
Laxey Bay
Waterfall
St John's
TT Circuit
Baldwin
A18
Baldrine
Glen Maye
A1
Greeba
A23
B21
Manx Electric Railway
Lower Foxdale
Crosby
B20
A2
Clay Head
Dalby
Crosby
Glen Vine
Castleward
A11
Niarbyl
Foxdale
Eairy
B35
Strang
Onchan
A3
A26
Union Mills
Norse Houses
A18
Groundle Glen Railway
Niarbyl Bay
A27
Round Table
A36
A42A
B32
Cronkbourne
Onchan Head
483
SOUTH BARRULE
A3
Braaid
A24
DOUGLAS
Belfast
437
CRONK NY ARREY LAA
B39
Brough Fort
B37
Douglas Bay
Closeclark
Douglas Head
Ballamodha
Millennium Way
St Marks
A5
A25
A37
Fleshwick Bay
A36
B31
10
Ballakelly
Douglas Head
Heysham Liverpool
Grenaby
A26
Santon
Ballakilpheric
A27
Silverdale Glen
Port Soderick
Milners Tower
Ballafesson
Colby
Ballabeg
Rushen
Isle of Man Steam Railway
Santon Head
Dublin
Bradda Head
A7
A5
Cronk ny Merrieu
Port Erin
Ballabeg
Ballasalla
Marine Interpretation Centre
Howe
Meayll Circle
Port St Mary
A5
5
A7
Isle of Man (Ronaldsway)
A3
A5
Castletown
Derbyhaven
CALF OF MAN
A31
Cregneash
Hango Hill
Derby Fort
Spanish Head
Scarlett
Scarlett Point
Close ny Chollagh
Herring Tower
Caigher Point
Castletown Bay
Dreswick Point

1
2
3
4
5
6
7
8
9
a
b
c
d
e
f
g

G · · · · · St Bees H **Egremont** J K L
Wilton

G

River

LAKE

Worm Gill

164
Florence Mine
Carleton
Coulderton
Middletown
Haile
Nethertown
Blackbeck
Beckermet
Calder Bridge
Braystones
Ponsonby
Sellafield
Visitor
Centre
Gosforth
B5343
R Elten
Cross
Seascale
Hallsenna Moor
Drigg
Holmrook
Muncaster
Mill
13
Saltcoats
Ravenglass
Bath
House
Muncaster
Newbiggin
A595
Broad Oak
Lane End
Waberthwaite
Corney
Hycemoor
Selker Bay
Hyton
Bootle
Swinside Stone Circle
Annaside
600
BLACK
COMBE
Whitbeck
Gutterby Spa
Whicham
Silecroft
8
Kirksanton
Steel Green
Haverigg
Haverigg
Point
Sandscale Haws
146

HAYCOCK
KIRK
FELL
GREAT
ABLE
899
1
Wasdale
Head
NAT
691
SEATALLAN
978
SCAFELL
964
SCAFELL PIKE
Burnmoor
Tarn
P
Nether
Wasdale
Wellington
R Irt
2
Santon
Santon Bridge
Moorside
Eskdale
Green
Beckfoot
156
Boot
Hardknott
Fort
Hard
Pa
39
ESKDALE
652
HARTER
FELL
Ravenglass and Eskdale
Railway
River Esk
Devoke
Water
3
Hall
Dunnerdale
Rive
Loganbeck
Beckfoot
573
WHITFELL
Ulp a
4
Broughton
Mills
Lower
Hawthwaite
Duddon
Bridge
Br
5
Bro
Lady
Hall
Foxfie
A595
Hallthwaites
The Green
Arnaby
Bridge End
7
The Hill
Sand Side
156
6
Soutergate
Millom
Borwick
Rails
RSPB
Askam
in Furness
7
North Walney
Dal
in-F
BARROW-
IN-FURNESS
Hawcoat
Furness
Abbey
Travelodge
AA
North Scale
8
Vickerstown
row
Island
A590
M

0 1 2 3 4 5 miles
0 1 2 3 4 5 6 7 kilometres

G H J K L **M**

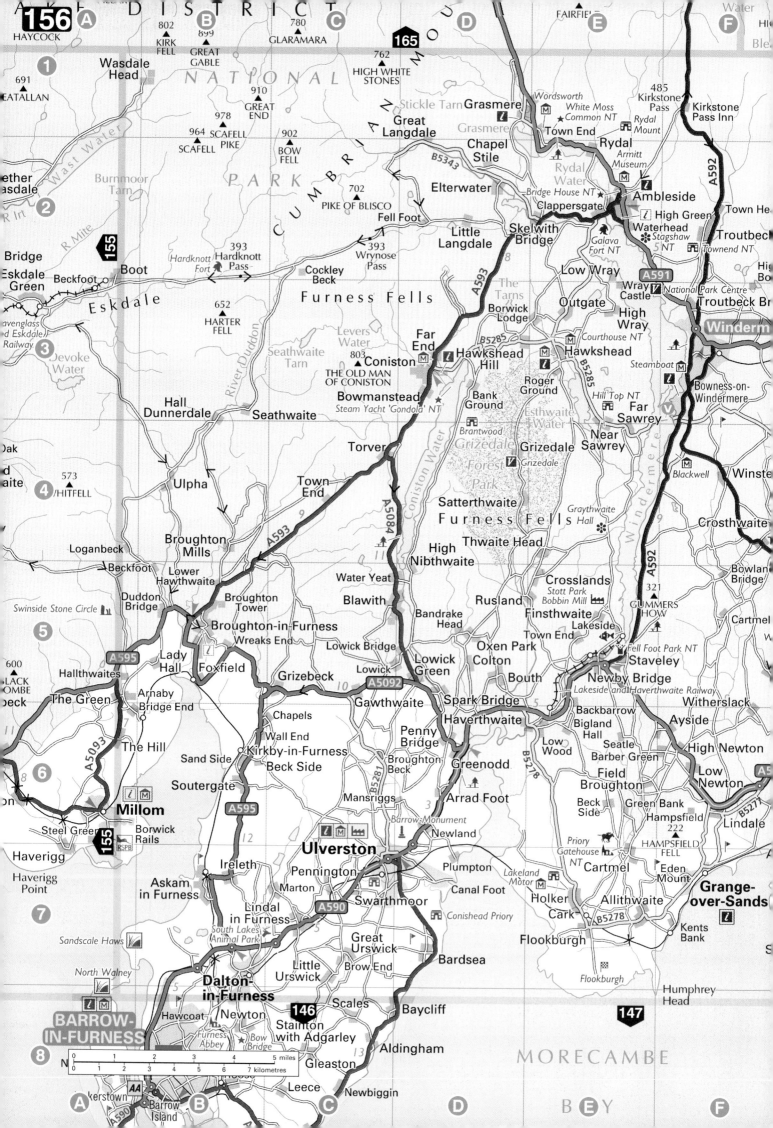

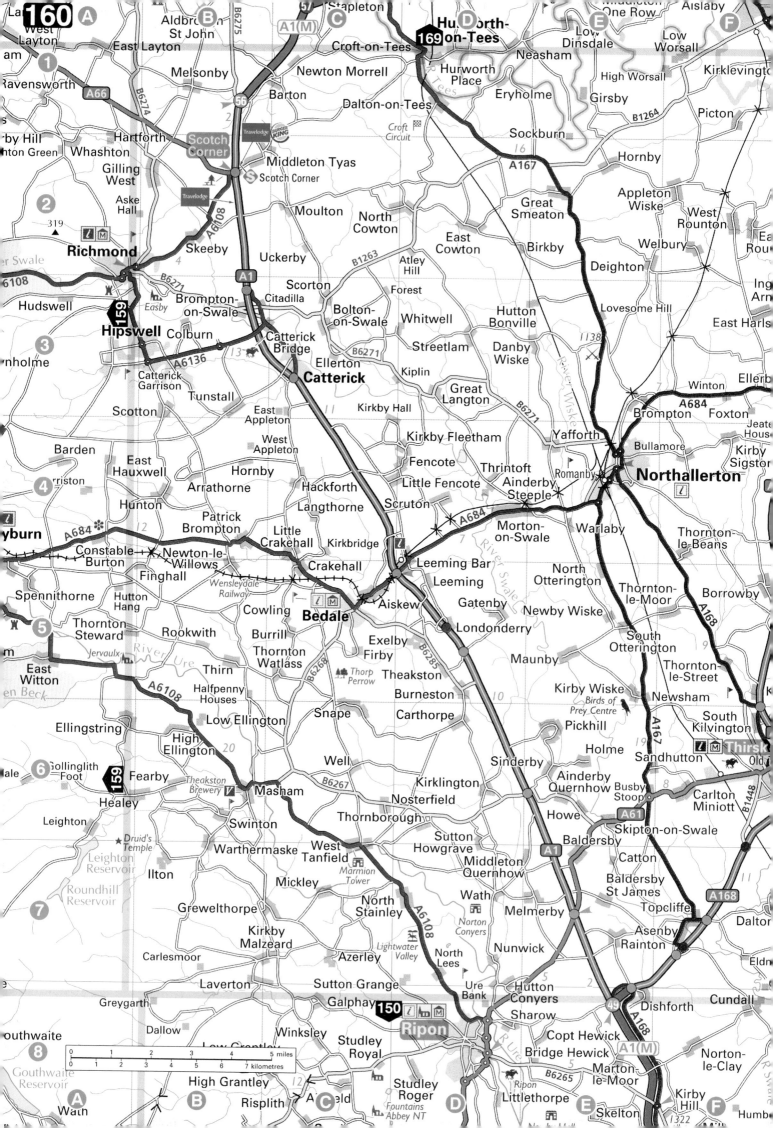

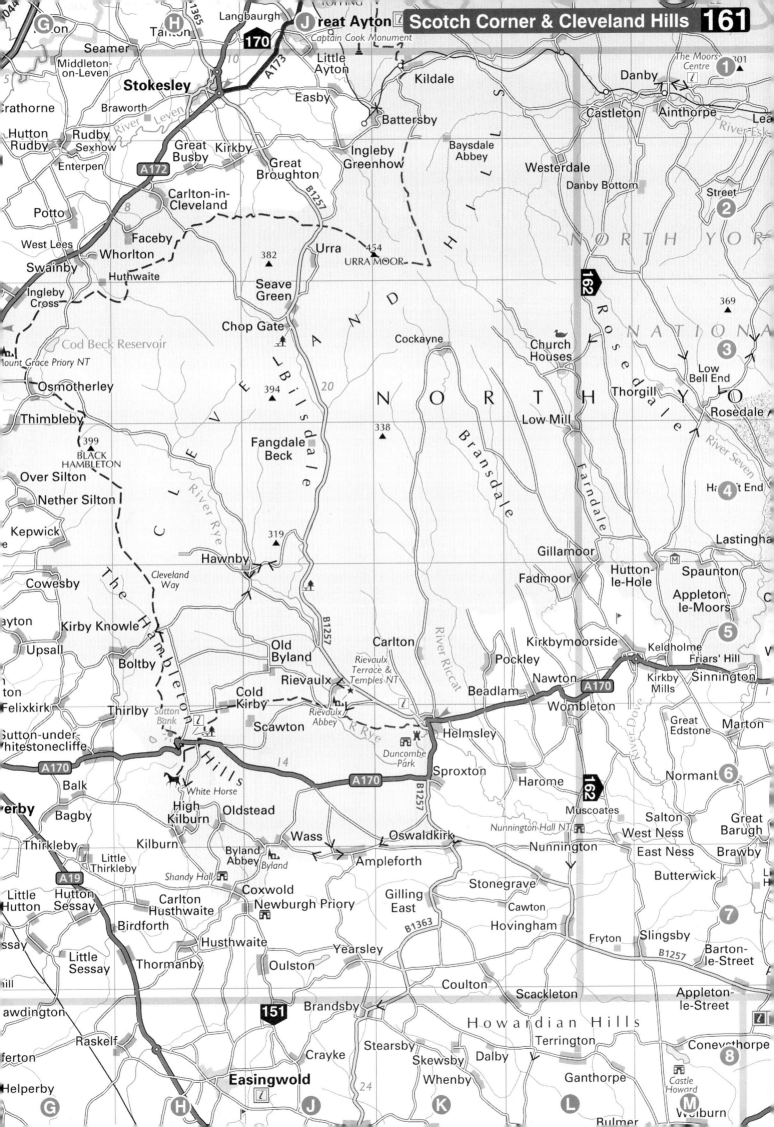

G · on
Seamer
Middleton-on-Leven
Stokesley
Crathorne
Braworth
Hutton Rudby
Rudby
Sexhow
Enterpen
Potto
West Lees
Swainby
Whorlton
Faceby
Huthwaite
Ingleby Cross
Mount Grace Priory NT
Osmotherley
Thimbleby
399 BLACK HAMBLETON
Over Silton
Nether Silton
Kepwick
ayton
Upsall
Cowesby
Kirby Knowle
Boltby
Thirlby
Felixkirk
ton
Sutton-under-Whitestonecliffe
erby
Balk
Bagby
Thirkleby
Little Thirkleby
Hutton Sessay
Little Hutton
ssay
Carlton Husthwaite
Birdforth
Thormanby
Little Sessay
awdington
Helperby
ferton
Raskelf

Langbaurgh
Tarlton
170
10
A173
A172
8
A172
20
The Hambleton Hills
Sutton Bank
14
White Horse
High Kilburn
Kilburn
Oldstead
Byland Abbey
Byland
Shandy Hall
Coxwold
Newburgh Priory
Husthwaite
Oulston
Wass
Ampleforth
Yearsley
Brandsby
151
Crayke
Easingwold
Stearsby
Skewsby
Whenby
24

reat Ayton
Captain Cook Monument
Little Ayton
Easby
Battersby
Ingleby Greenhow
Great Busby
Kirkby
Great Broughton
Carlton-in-Cleveland
Whorlton
382
Urra
454
URRA MOOR
Seave Green
Chop Gate
Cod Beck Reservoir
394
Fangdale Beck
River Rye
319
Hawnby
Cleveland Way
B1257
Old Byland
Rievaulx
Cold Kirby
Scawton
Rievaulx Abbey
Rievaulx Terrace & Temples NT
Carlton
River Riccal
Cockayne
338
Bransdale
NORTH
CLEVELAND Bilsdale

Kildale
Baysdale Abbey
Westerdale
Danby Bottom
H I L L S
Church Houses
Low Mill
Rosedale
Low Bell End
Thorgill
Farndale
Gillamoor
Fadmoor
Hutton-le-Hole
Appleton-le-Moors
Kirkbymoorside
Pockley
Nawton
A170
Beadlam
Wombleton
Helmsley
Sproxton
Duncombe Park
Harome
R Rye
Muscoates
Nunnington Hall NT
Nunnington
A170
B1257
Oswaldkirk
Gilling East
Gilling
B1363
Stonegrave
Cawton
Hovingham
Coulton
Scackleton
H o w a r d i a n   H i l l s
Terrington
Dalby
Ganthorpe
Castle Howard
Bulmer

The Moors Centre
Danby
Castleton
Ainthorpe
River Esk
Lea
Street
N O R T H   Y O R
369
N A T I O N A
Rosedale
Haut End
Lastingha
Spaunton
Keldholme
Friars' Hill
Kirkby Mills
Sinnington
Great Edstone
Marton
Normanl
Salton
West Ness
East Ness
Great Barugh
Brawby
Butterwick
Slingsby
Barton-le-Street
Fryton
Appleton-le-Street
Coneysthorpe
Welburn

A19
A170

1
2
3
4
5
6
7
8

G H J K L M

162
162
170
151

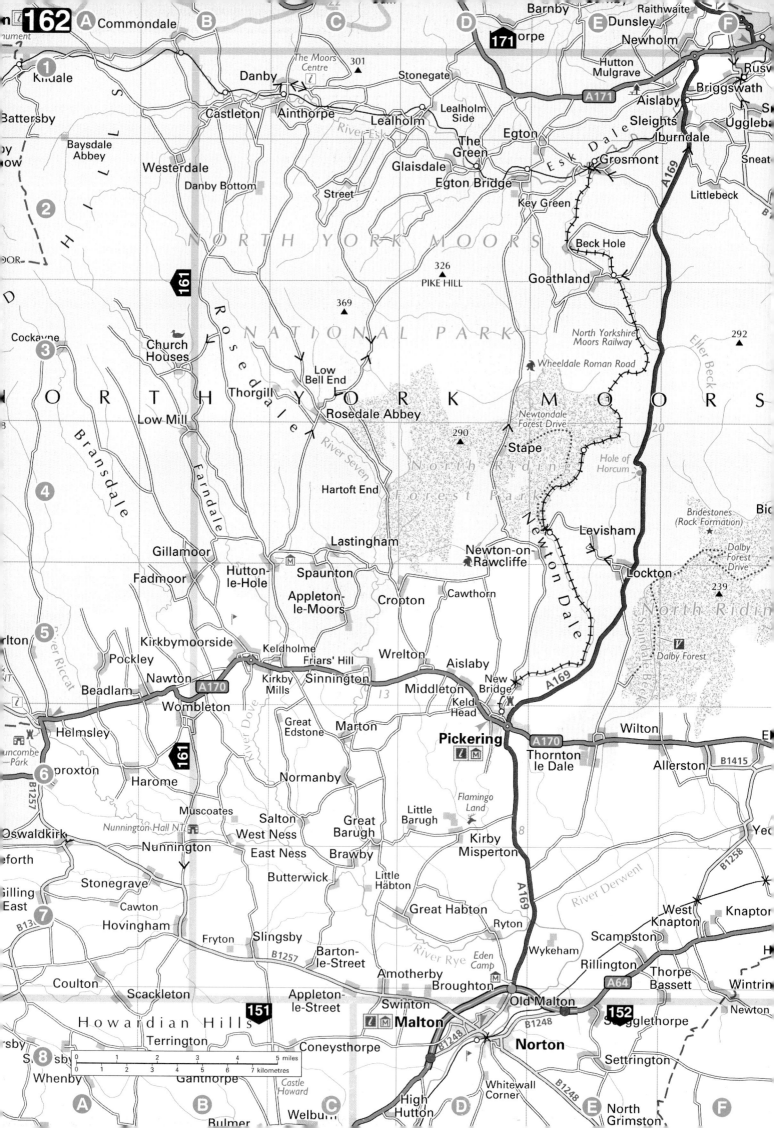

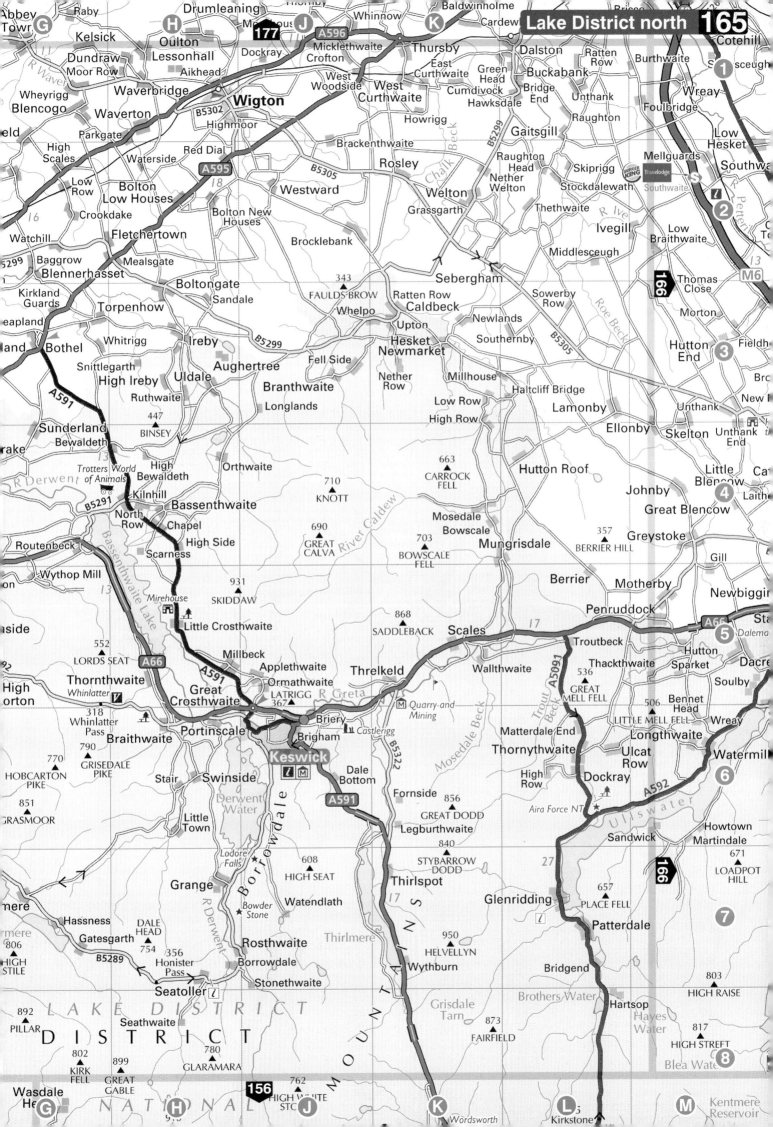

G H 179 J K Penrith & Weardale 167

Sinderho
Keirsley
Row
HANGMAN
HILL
River Derwent
Baybridge
Edmundb
khaugh
Ayle
B6295
Hunstanworth
1
South Tynedale
Railway
Limestone Brae
Spartylea
Blagill
572
HARTLEY
MOOR
478
NOOKTON
FELL
Ramshaw
B6294
Carr
Shield
Dirt Pot
Allenheads
Alston
540
BOLT'S LAW
Nenthall
Coalcleugh
2
Nenthead
627
Killhope
Summit
A689
20
Killhope Lead
Mining Centre
Lanehead
Cornriggs
Rookhope Burn
Rookhope
Garrigill
Cowshill
Wearhead
168
Crawleyside
Sta
B6277
Weardale
Eastgate
A689
3
Ireshopeburn
Westgate
R South Tyne
St John's
Chapel
Daddry
Shield
Brotherlee
Bri
22
747
BURNHOPE
SEAT
559
BLACK
HILL
653
OUTBERRY PLAIN
Bollihope Burn
4
Milburn
Forest
847
REAT DUN FELL
Harwood
Cow Green
Reservoir
Langdon Beck
Forest-in-
Teesdale
Ettersgill
601
CARRS HILL
River Tees
Cauldron Snout (Waterfall)
Moor House -
Upper Teesdale
B6277
High Force
(Waterfall)
Newbiggin
5
B6278
Dufton Fell
Pennine Way
Holwick
T
Middleton-
in-Teesdale
481
UFTON
PIKE
Maize Beck
672
MURTON FELL
e
e
B6282
Hill
fton
790
MICKLE
FELL
618
Bowbank
s
d
a
B6281
Keisley
Thringarth
Mickleton
Romaldk
746
HILTON FELL
10
6
Murton
Lune
Forest
Fish Loch
B6276
Grassholme
Reservoir
Hunderthwaite
Hilton
Selset
Reservoir
Hury
East
Briscoe
Coupland
562
IRON BAND
West
Briscoe
168
Larting
Great
Ormside
Balderhead
Reservoir
7
Eden Valley
Railway
Sandford
8
Hillbeck
North
Stainmore
Deepdale Beck
Warcop
A66
Great
Musgrave
Brough
Church
Brough
Brough
Sowerby
478
BELDOO HILL
A66
13
Bov
Bleatarn
Little
Musgrave
Kaber
Barras
The Otter Trust
Giln
Soulby
R Eden
B6259
A685
Stainmore Forest
Crosby
G et
Winton
158
Sleighthol
8
Waitby
Hartley
G H J K L M

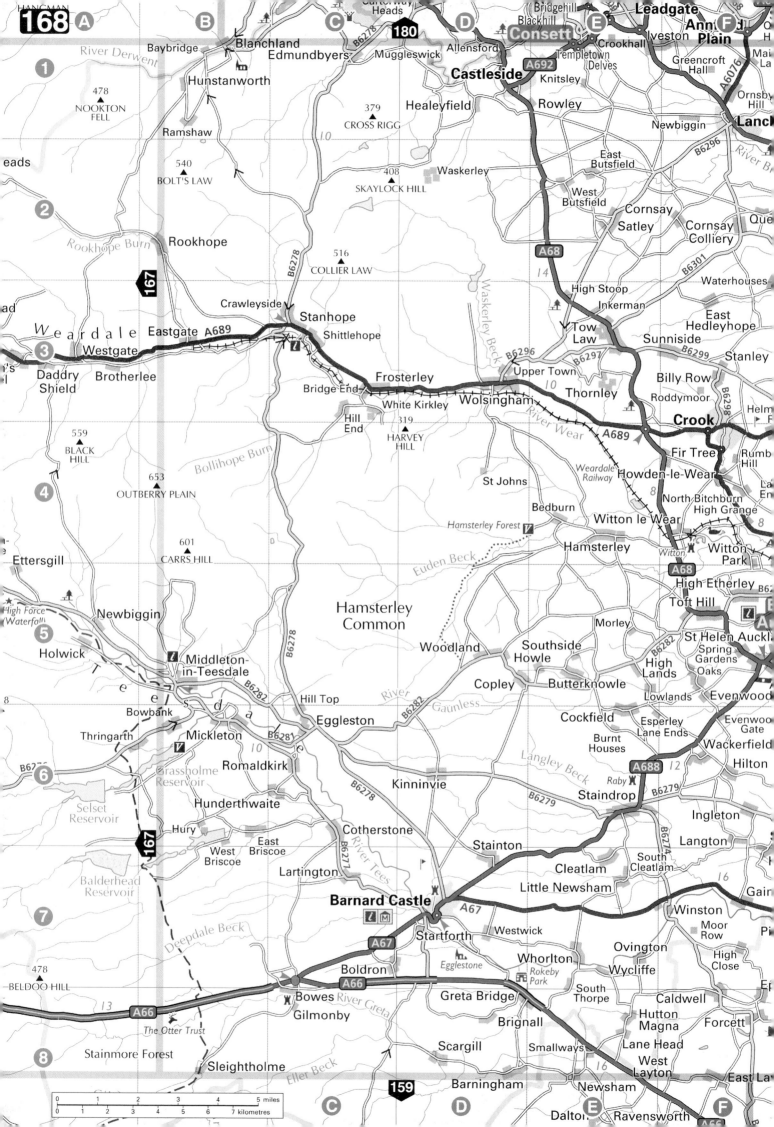

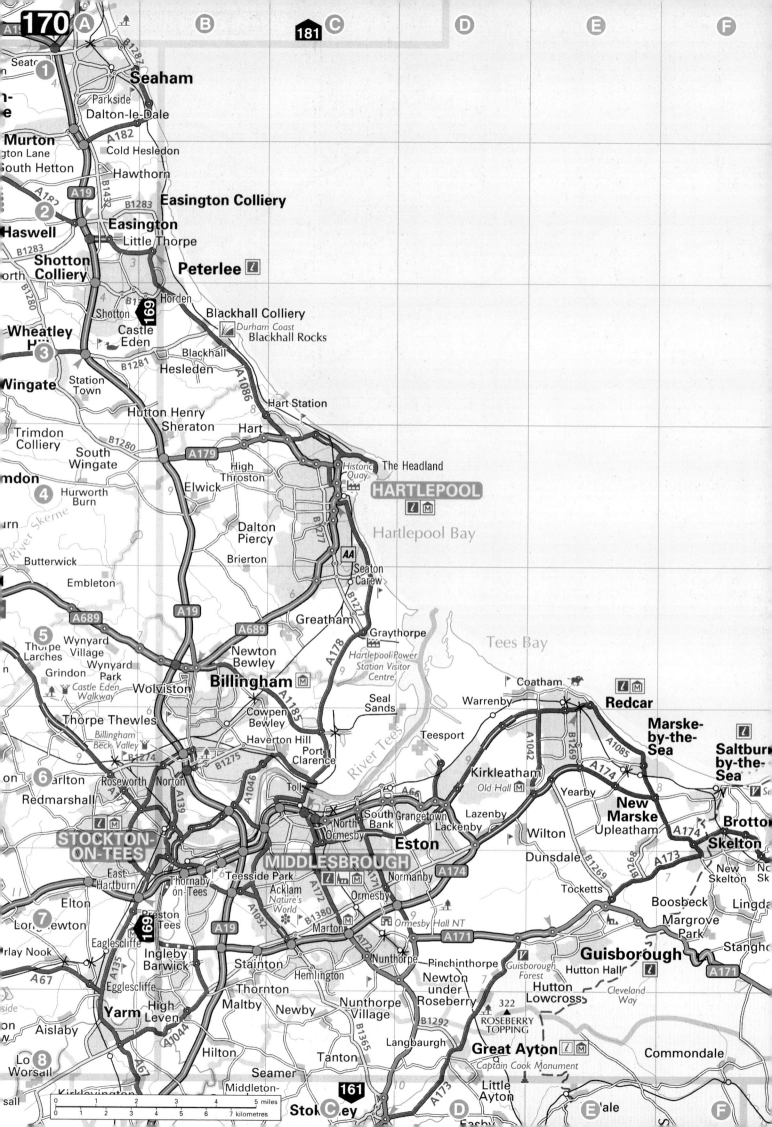

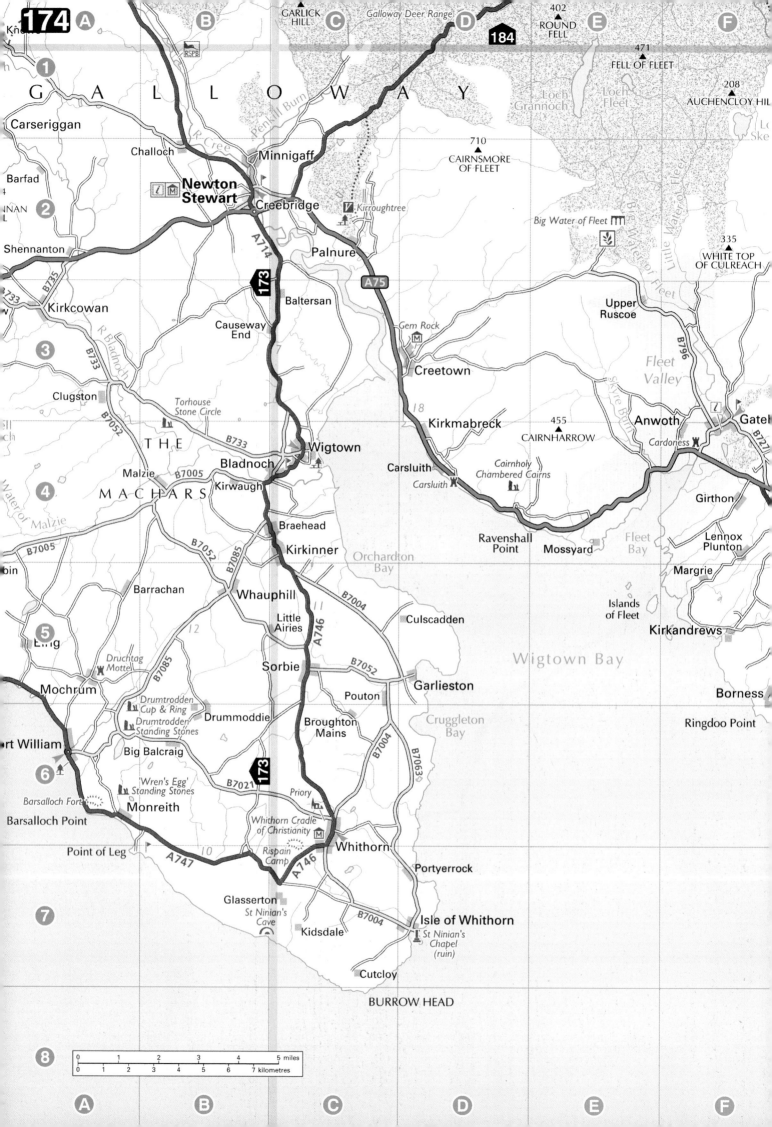

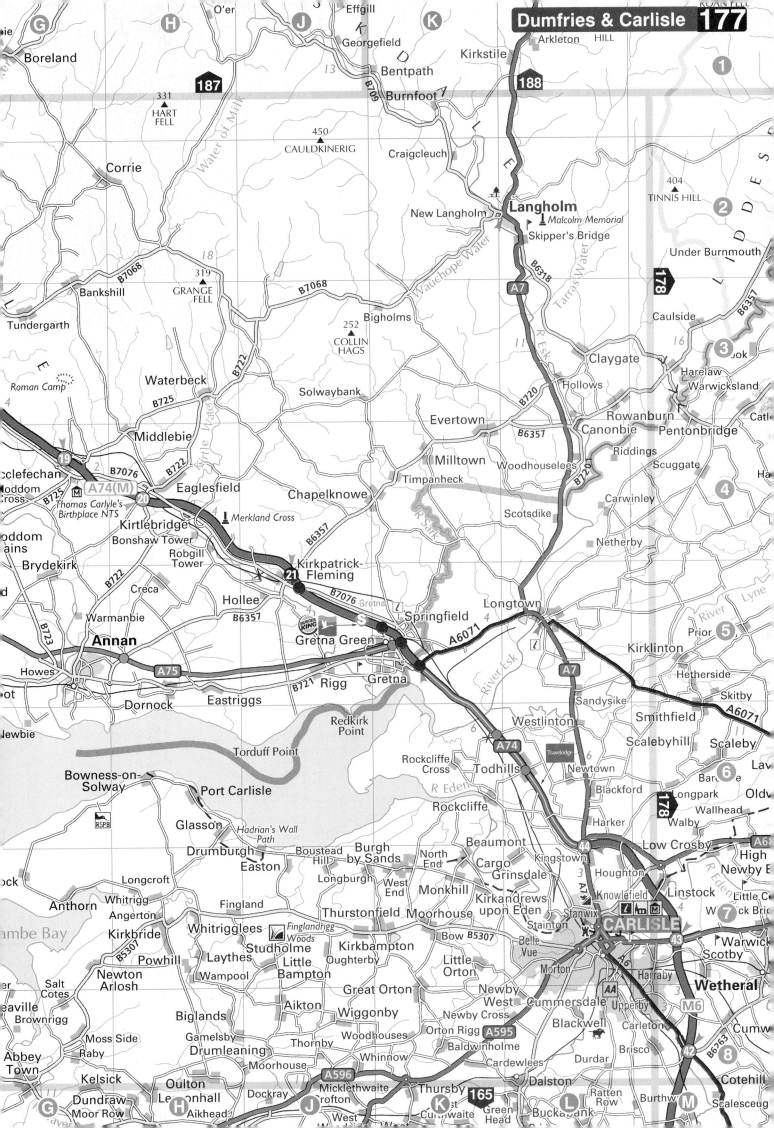

ROAN FELL
HILL

O'er
Effgill
Georgefield
Bentpath
Burnfoot
B709
Arkleton
Kirkstile
188

Boreland
331
HART FELL
187
Craigcleuch
New Langholm
Langholm
Malcolm Memorial
Skipper's Bridge

TINNIS HILL
404

Corrie
450
CAULDKINERIG

Under Burnmouth

178

Tundergarth
B7068
319
GRANGE FELL
B7068
Bigholms
252
COLLIN HAGS
Solwaybank
A7
B6318
R Esk
B6357

Bankshill

Caulside

Claygate
Harelaw
Warwicksland

Waterbeck
B725
Myrtle Water
B722
Hollows
B720

Roman Camp
4
Evertown
B6357
Rowanburn
Canonbie
Pentonbridge

Middlebie
19
B7076
B722
Milltown
Woodhouselees
Riddings
Scuggate

ecclefechan
Moddom Cross
A74(M)
20
Eaglesfield
Chapelknowe
Timpanheck
R Sark
Scotsdike
Carwinley

Thomas Carlyle's Birthplace NTS
Merkland Cross

oddom ains
Kirtlebridge
Bonshaw Tower
Robgill Tower
B6357
Netherby

Brydekirk
B722
Creca
Kirkpatrick-Fleming
21

Warmanbie
Hollee
B6357
B7076
Gretna
Springfield
Longtown
A7
Prior
5

Annan
B723
A75
BURGER KING
Gretna Green
S
Gretna
A6071
4
Kirklinton

Howes
B721
Rigg
Eastriggs
River Esk
Sandysike
Hetherside

ot
Dornock
Redkirk Point
6
Westlinton
A74
Smithfield
Skitby
A6071

ewbie
Torduff Point
Rockcliffe Cross
Todhills
Travelodge
Newtown
Scalebyhill
Scaleby

Bowness-on-Solway
Port Carlisle
R Eden
Rockcliffe
Blackford
6
178
Longpark
Oldw
Lav

Glasson
Hadrian's Wall Path
Burgh by Sands
North End
Beaumont
Kingstown
Harker
44
3
Low Crosby
Wallhead
Walby
A6

Drumburgh
Easton
Boustead Hill
Longburgh
West End
Cargo
Grinsdale
Houghton
Knowlefield
Linstock
High
Newby

Anthorn
Longcroft
Whitrigg
Angerton
Fingland
Thurstonfield
Moorhouse
Kirkandrews upon Eden
Monkhill
Stainton
Stanwix
4
7
Little C
Wick Bri

Kirkbride
Whitrigglees
Finglandrigg Woods
Bow B5307
CARLISLE
Belle Vue
43
Warwick
Scotby

Studholme
Kirkbampton
Oughterby
Little Orton
Morton
Harraby

B5307
Powhill
Laythes
Little Bampton
Great Orton
Newby
West
Cummersdale
Upperby
AA
3
M6
Wetheral

Newton Arlosh
Wampool
Aikton
Wiggonby
Newby Cross
Blackwell
Carleton
42
B6263
8

Salt Cotes
Biglands
Gamelsby
Thornby
Woodhouses
Orton Rigg
A595
Brisco
Cumw

eaville Brownrigg
Moss Side
Raby
Drumleaning
Moorhouse
Whinnow
Baldwinholme
Cardewlees
Durdar

Abbey Town
Kelsick
Oulton
Leconhall
Dockray
Crofton
Micklethwaite
Thursby
165
Dalston
Ratten Row
Burthw
Cotehill

Dundraw
Moor Row
Aikhead
West
A596
Buckabank
Green Head
Scalesceug

G
H
J
K
L
M

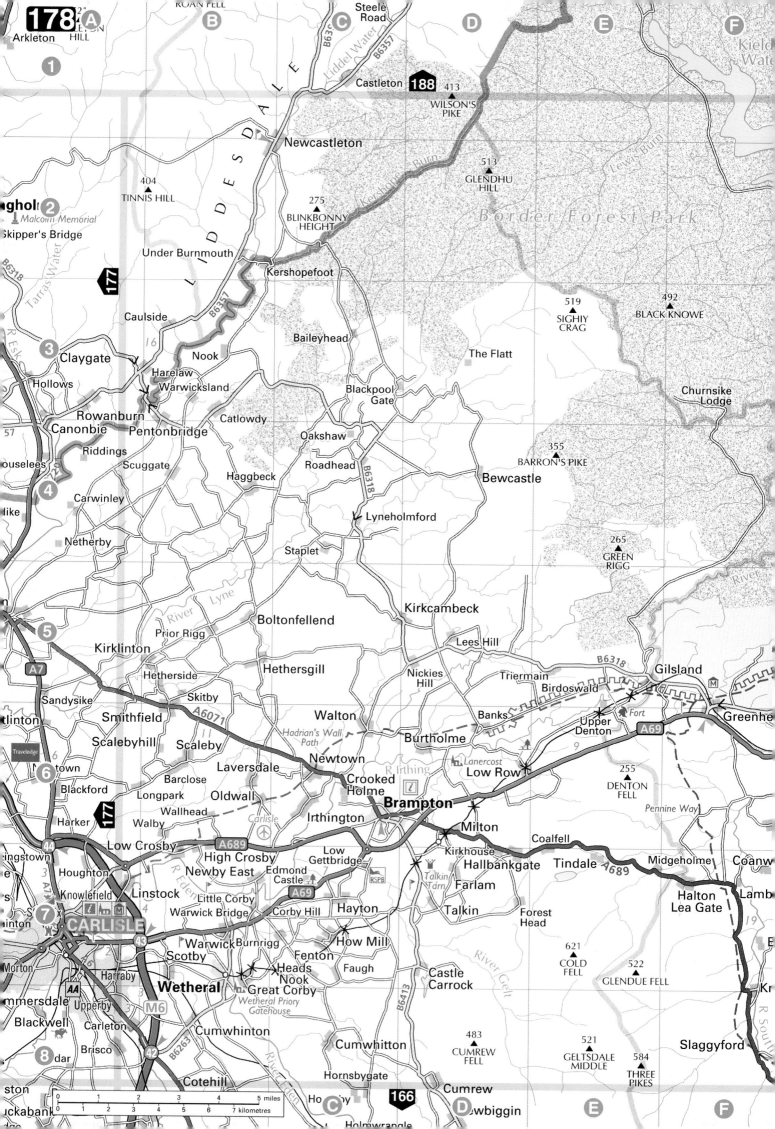

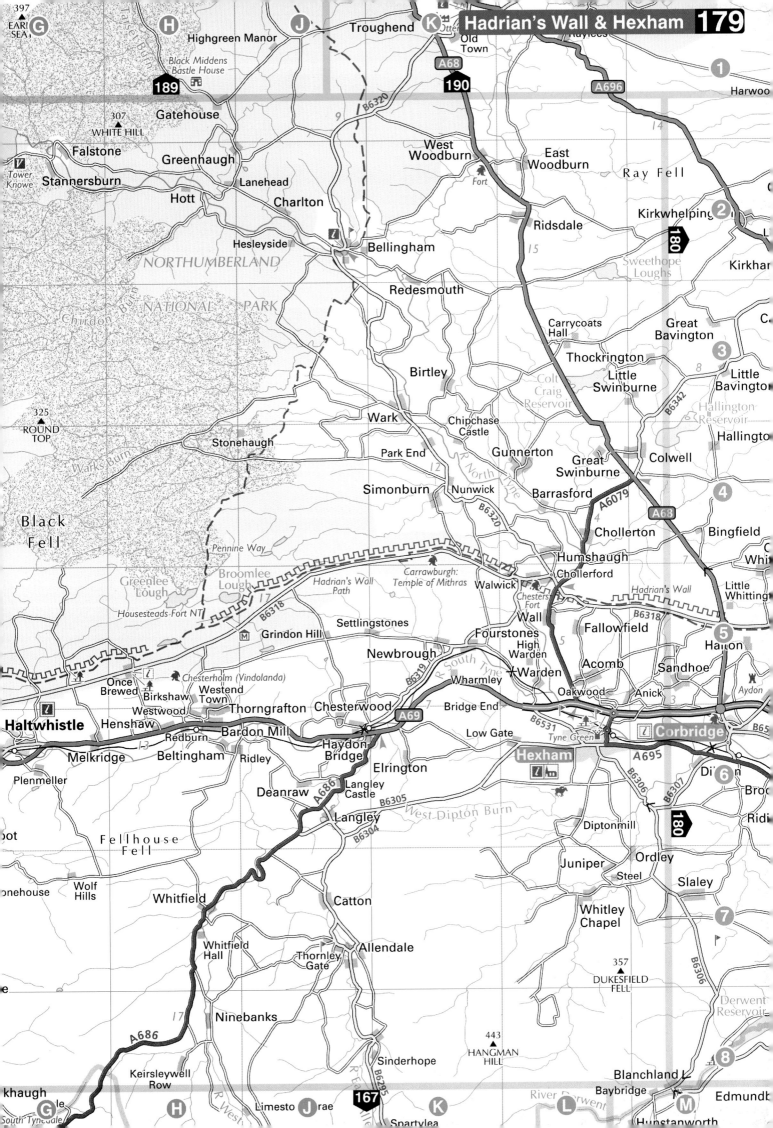

G H J Troughend K Old Town 1 Harwoo

189

EARL SEAT G

Highgreen Manor

Black Middens Bastle House

A68

190

A696

Gatehouse
307 ▲ WHITE HILL

West Woodburn
East Woodburn

Ray Fell

14

Falstone
Greenhaugh
Stannersburn
Tower Knowe V
Hott
Charlton
Lanehead

Fort

Ridsdale
Kirkwhelping n 2

A68 **180**

Kirkhar

Hesleyside
Bellingham
i

15

Sweethope Loughs

NORTHUMBERLAND

Redesmouth

Carrycoats Hall
Great Bavington

NATIONAL PARK

Chirdon Burn
Birtley

Thockrington
Little Swinburne
Little Bavington 3

8

B6342
Hallington Reservoir

Hallingto

325 ▲ ROUND TOP

Warks Burn

Wark
Stonehaugh

Chipchase Castle
Gunnerton
Great Swinburne
Barrasford
Colwell

Park End

12

R North Tyne

A6079

Simonburn
Nunwick
B6320
Chollerton
4
Bingfield

4

Whi

Black Fell

Pennine Way

Carrawburgh: Temple of Mithras
Walwick
Humshaugh
Chollerford
Little Whitting

Hadrian's Wall Path
Broomlee Lough

Hadrian's Wall
A68

Greenlee Lough

17

Chesters Fort

B6318

Wall
Fallowfield

Hadrian's Wall
B6318

5

Housesteads Fort NT

Settlingstones
Fourstones
Haltn

M Grindon Hill

Newbrough
High Warden
Acomb
Sandhoe

B6319

Aydon

Once Brewed
i
Chesterholm (Vindolanda)
Birkshaw
Westend Town
Thorngrafton
Chesterwood
A69
Bridge End
Low Gate
Warden
Wharmley
R South Tyne
Oakwood
Anick

3

Westwood
i
Haltwhistle
Henshaw
Bardon Mill
Haydon Bridge
Tyne Green
Corbridge

B6531

i

B65

Melkridge
Redburn
Beltingham
Ridley
Elrington
Hexham
i
A695
Di n
6

Plenmeller

13

Deanraw
Langley Castle
A686
B6306
180
B6307
Bro
Ridl

Fellhouse Fell

Langley
B6305
B6304
West Dipton Burn

Diptonmill

Juniper
Ordley
Steel
Slaley

Whitfield

Catton

Whitley Chapel

7

Wolf Hills

onehouse

Whitfield Hall
Thornley Gate
Allendale

357 ▲ DUKESFIELD FELL

B6306

Ninebanks

443 ▲ HANGMAN HILL

Derwent Reservoir

A686

17

Sinderhope

Blanchland

8

Keirsleywell Row

Baybridge

Edmundb

khaugh

G le
South Tynedale
H
rae J
Limesto
167
B6295
K
Spartylea
River Derwent
L
M
Hunstanworth

G **H** **J** **K**

A1068
Ellington
Linton
Lynemouth
A189
191 Beacon Point
Woodhorn
A197
Woodhorn Demesne
Hirst
North
Seaton
Newbiggin-by-the-Sea
Wansbeck
Riverside
eepwash
Stakeford
North Seaton Colliery
Guide Post
West Sleekburn
Scotland
Gate
Bomarsund
Cambois
North Blyth
dlington
East
Sleekburn
A193
Cowpen
Blyth
B1331
East
Hartford
Bebside
Newsham
A189
New
Delaval
A192
A1061
Shankhouse
New
Hartley
Seaton
Sluice
A193
ington
East
Cramlington
A192
Seaton
Hartley
19
B1326
Seaton Delaval
★ St Mary's Lighthouse
Seghill
Holywell
A190
ton
Annitsford
B1322
A192
A1148
Whitley Bay
rn
Dudley
Burradon
Earsdon
Backworth
Monkseaton
Cullercoats
Camperdown
Murton
A1056
Killingworth
Shiremoor
B1317
A191
Tynemouth
Forest Hall
New York
A19
A1058
Rising Sun
A193
★ v
south
A191
Jesmond
A1058
North Shields
sforth
A189
Longbenton
Willington Quay
A187
Bergen
Göteborg
Haugesund
IJmuiden
Kristiansand
Stavanger
Wallsend
Int. Ferry Terminal
Tolls
SOUTH SHIELDS
Heaton
A187
Tyne Tunnel
Westoe
A183
Walker
B1313
Jarrow
Harton
Marsden Bay
Byker
Hebburn
Monkton
Marsden
Souter Lighthouse NT
A185
A184
Felling
A19
A1300
Cleadon
Souter Point
Wardley
West Boldon
B1298
Whitburn
GATESHEAD
A194
Boldon Colliery
B1299
A1018
A183
Whitburn Bay
A167
Low Fell
B1288
East Boldon
A184
B129
Bowes Railway & Museum
A194(M)
Seaburn
Springwell
Usworth
A19
Hylton
Southwick
Roker
A1290
Castletown
Monkwearmouth
Wildfowl & Wetlands Trust
South Hylton
A183
Birtley
65
A1231
Grindon
SUNDERLAND
Portobello
WASHINGTON
Hendon
Ouston
64
Offerton
A183
A690
High Newport
B1405
Grangetown
Fatfield
Penshaw NT
Penshaw
Herrington
New Silksworth
Tunstall
63
A693
Shiney Row
New Herrington
Silksworth
B1286
Ryhope
Pelton Fell
A183
Philadelphia
Newbottle
A19
A1018
Chester-le-Street
Houghton Gate
Burnmoor
Houghton le Spring
169
High Dubmire
Seaham

G **H** **J** **K** **L** **M**

A B C D E F

1

2

Maide
B.

Maid

Turnberry

Turnberry

Turnberry
Bay

A77

3

340 Ailsa Craig

O

Girvan   Dounepark

Woodland

Pinmin

4

297
▲
GREY
HILL   Pinmore

A714

13

Lendalfoot

5

A77

B734

Bennane Head   **Colmonell**   9   *River Stinchar*   P

B734
B7044

6

Heronsford

Ballantrae   *Water of Tig*

C
Larne

V
Larne   *(Summer Only)*

Currarie
Port

437
▲
BENERAIRD

7

V C
Belfast

321
▲
CARLOCK HILL

387
▲
ALTIMEG HILL

Glen App

Milleur
Point

Corsewall Point

Lady
Bay

Lagganga
Standing St

8

Barnhills   **Portencalzie**   Glenwhilly

Cross

| 0 | 1 | 2 | 3 | 4 | 5 miles |
| 0 | 1 | 2 | 3 | 4 | 5 | 6 | 7 kilometres |

172

C D E F

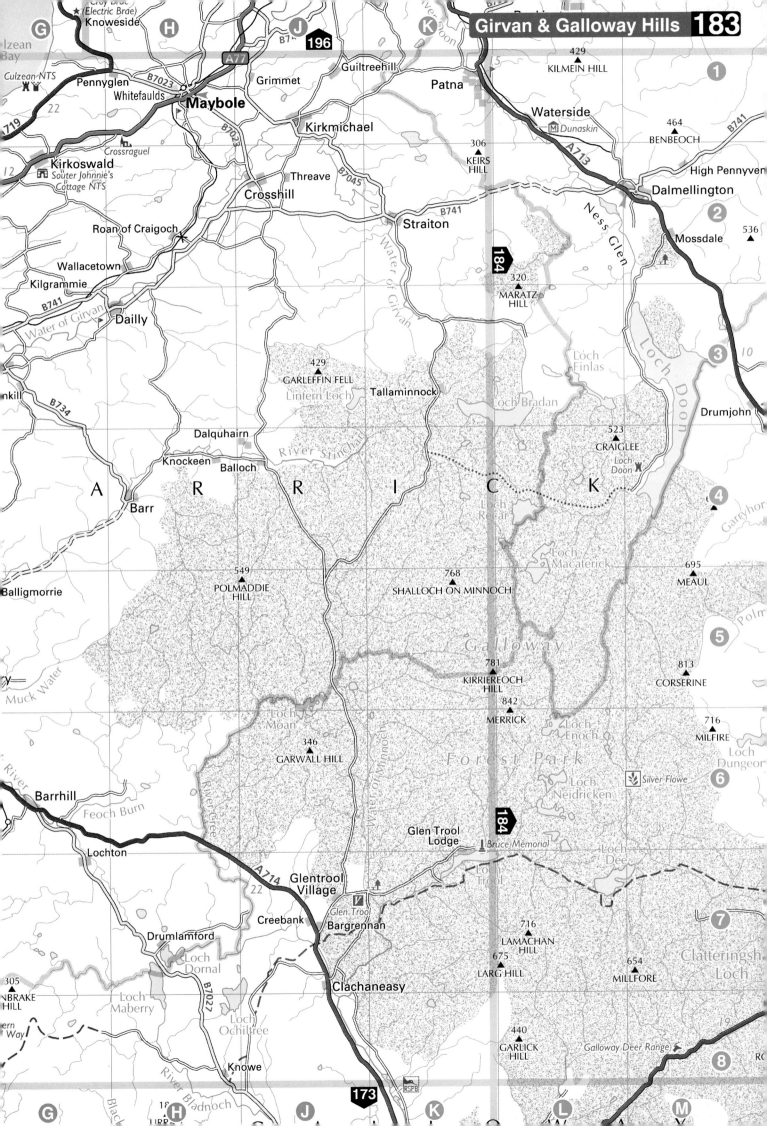

Croy Brae
(Electric Brae)
Knoweside

G H J **196** K

B7023

B71

Izean
Bay

Culzean NTS

Pennyglen Guiltreehill
Whitefaulds Grimmet Patna

Maybole

719

22 B7023 Kirkmichael

Waterside
Dunaskin KILMEIN HILL
429

12 Crossraguel

Kirkoswald Threave B7045 464
Souter Johnnie's Crosshill BENBEOCH B741
Cottage NTS 306 KEIRS High Pennyver
Straiton HILL Dalmellington

Roan of Craigoch **184** Mossdale 536

Wallacetown 320 2
Kilgrammie MARATZ Ness Glen
HILL

B741 Loch 3
Dailly Loch Finlas Doon
Water of Girvan Drumjohn

B734 429 Loch Bradan 523
GARLEFFIN FELL CRAIGLEE
Linfern Loch Tallaminnock Loch
Doon

Dalquhairn Loch
Recar 4
Knockeen Balloch Garryhor

A R R I C K

Barr Loch
Macaterick 695
Balligmorrie 549 768 MEAUL
POLMADDIE SHALLOCH ON MINNOCH
HILL 5
Galloway Polm

781 813
Muck Water KIRRIEREOCH CORSERINE
HILL
842 716
Loch MERRICK Loch MILFIRE
Moan Enoch Loch
346 Dungeon
GARWALL HILL Forest Park 6
Silver Flowe

Barrhill Loch
Feoch Burn Neidricken

River **184**
Lochton Glen Trool Loch
Lodge Bruce Memorial Dee
A714 Loch
Glentrool Trool 7
22 Village
Creebank Glen Trool
Bargrennan 716
Drumlamford LAMACHAN 654
HILL MILLFORE
Loch 675 Clatteringsh
Dornal Clachaneasy LARG HILL Loch
305
NBRAKE Loch
HILL Maberry 19
Loch
n Way Ochiltree 440
GARLICK
HILL Galloway Deer Range

Knowe 8

G H J **173** K L M
River Bladnoch RSPB

G H J

197 Kirkconnel
Kelloholm
A76
Crawick
GREEN LOWTHER
725 ▲ LOWTHER HILL
Nether Fiend
1

594 ▲ HARE HILL
Blackcraig
Newtown
Sanquhar
Dalveen

700 ▲ BLACKCRAIG
Kello Water
Mennock
Durisdeermill
BALLENCLI LAW
691 ▲
2

Euchan Water
23
Durisdeer
66 ▲

450 ▲ CLOUD HILL
478 ▲
Enterkinfoot
Gateslack

Polgown
River Nith
East Morton

475 ▲ COUNTAM
554 ▲ CAIRNKINNA HILL
186
A76
A702
Morton Loch
Morton
3

Cleuchhead
N
Drumlanrig

598 ▲ COLT HILL
I
Carronbridge
T
H
S
4

Big Carlae
Old Auchenbrack
Tibbers
Thornhill
Closeburnmill

Benbuie
Auchenhessnane
Burnhead
Penpont
D
Lo Ettr

Southern Upland Way
Shinnel Water
337 ▲ BENNAN
Scaur Water
Keir Mill
Cample

532 ▲ CORNHARROW HILL
Stenhouse
Tynron
9
Closeburn
4

Water of Ken
B729
Moniaive
Kirkland
A702
Keir Hills
Park
Kirkpatrick

15
Maxwelton
Breckonside
ligh dgirth
5

Glencrosh
385 ▲ WETHER HILL
Craigneston
Blackwood
Auldgirth
Dalsw

A702
13
431 ▲ BOGRIE HILL
Skelston
Snade
Lag
A76

Black Water
Sundaywell
Dunscore
Throughgate
17

quhairn
Loch Howie
Loch Urr
Upper Stepford
Holyw
6

Bogue
176
Twelve Apos
Newbri

B7075
392 ▲ SKEOCH HILL
Drumpark

A713
A712
Crochmore House
Te les
7

Balmaclellan
281 ▲ LARGLEAR HILL
Corsock
Shawhead
Cargen

Ironmacannie
25
Cargen

Knockvennie Smithy
B794
Eastlands
A75
Lochfoot
Lochrutton Loch
A711

A713
175
Kirkpatrick Durham
Crocketford
Auchenreoch Loch
Milton Loch
8

Mo le
Airds of Kells
16
Loch
Springholm
Milton
Beeswing
Lochobe Loch

G H J K L M

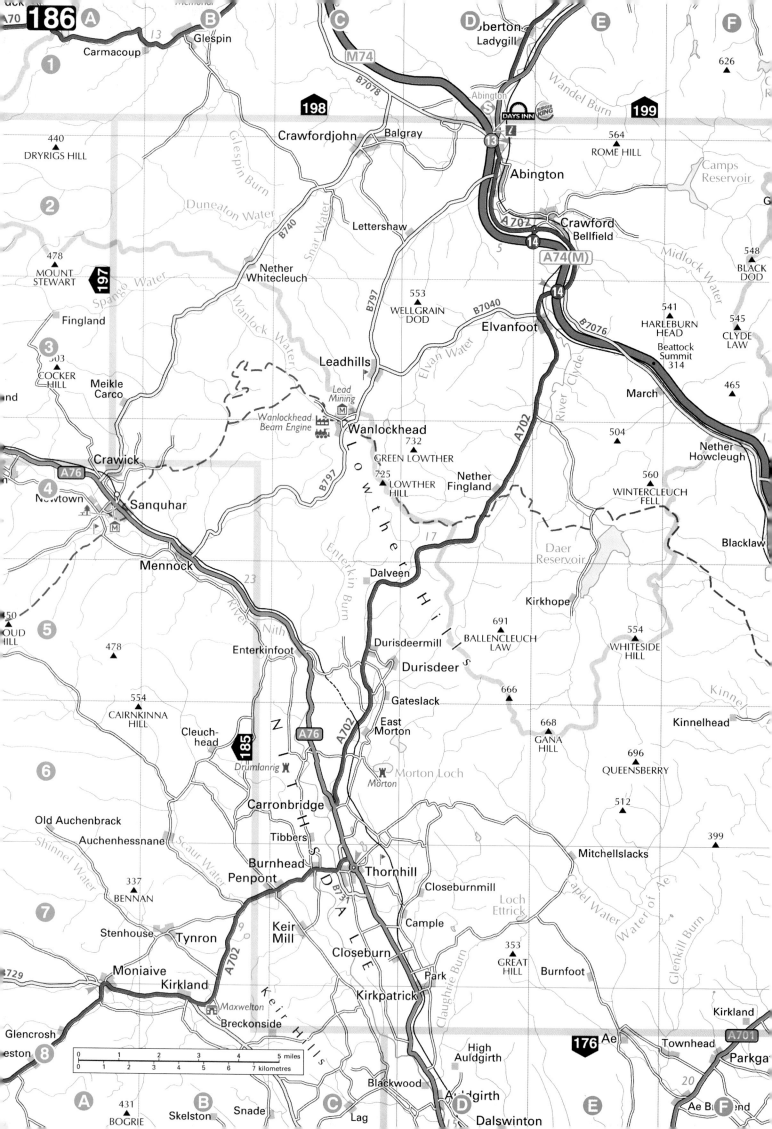

G H J K Yarrow

Stanhope

817
DOLLAR
LAW ▲

696
BLACK
LAW ▲

629 ▲

200

Gordon
Arms Hotel

Yarrow Feus

Sundhope

1

Crook
Inn

Oliver

199

Tweedsmuir

A701

River Tweed

Talla Reservoir

Talla Linnfoots

840
BROAD
LAW ▲

Megget
Reservoir

Cappercleuch

St Marys
Loch

E t t r i c

513 ▲

2

15

Gilmanscleuch

466
MOSSBRAE
HEIGHT ▲

188

dlieu

Fruid
Reservoir

Tibbie Shiels Inn

Chapelhope

Hopehouse

B709

6

weed's
Well

552
CRAIGINAID ▲

783 ▲

800
LOCHCRAIG
HEAD ▲

Loch
Skeen

822 ▲
WHITE COOMB ★
Grey Mare's Tail NTS
(Waterfall)

Birkhill

22

Ettrickhill

Ettrick

West Buccleuch
Hotel

B711

3

721 ▲

808
HART
FELL ▲

735 ▲
SADDLE
YOKE

624 ▲
BELL
CRAIG

Broadgairhill

498 ▲
LAW
KNEIS

De

728 ▲

A708

550 ▲
BLACK
KNOWE

B709

443 ▲
THE PIKE

16

423 ▲
CRIB
LAW

Borthwic

4

474 ▲
GREYGILL
FELL

Bridgend

Moffat Water

678 ▲
CAPEL FELL

692 ▲
ETTRICK
PEN

417 ▲

5

Moffat

A701

688 ▲
LOCH
FELL

Davington

White Esk

Rae Burn

476 ▲
STOCK HILL

Southern
Upland Way

Beattock

15

A701

R Annan

476 ▲
CRAIG
FELL

Johnstone

Samye Ling Monastery

Fort

6

B7076

Z

Eskdalemuir

Clerkhill

188

Lochwood

Newton Wamphray

Z

Z

A

B7020

Megget Water

492 ▲
BROAD

7

Ann's

Sandyford

B723

Castle
O'er

E
S

Effgill

Johnstonebridge

16

S

A

Annandale
Water

Gillesbie

Georgefield

B709

Kirksti

Dinwoodie

Dryfe Water

Boreland

13

Bentpath

Burnfoot

Courance

A74(M)

B7076

176

Z

331 ▲
HART
FELL

177

Water of Milk

450 ▲
CAULDKINERIG

8

Greyrigg

Jardine
Hall

Craigcleuch

Templand

ermill

Netnercleuch

umrue

G H D J Corrie K L M

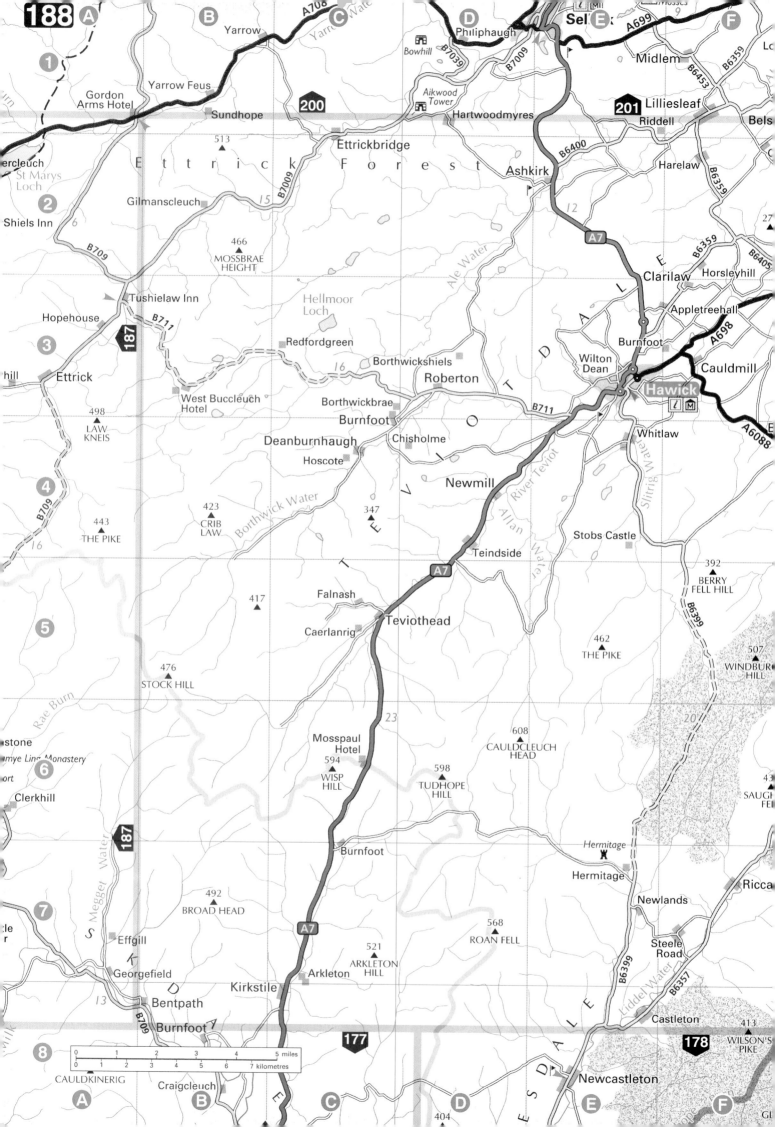

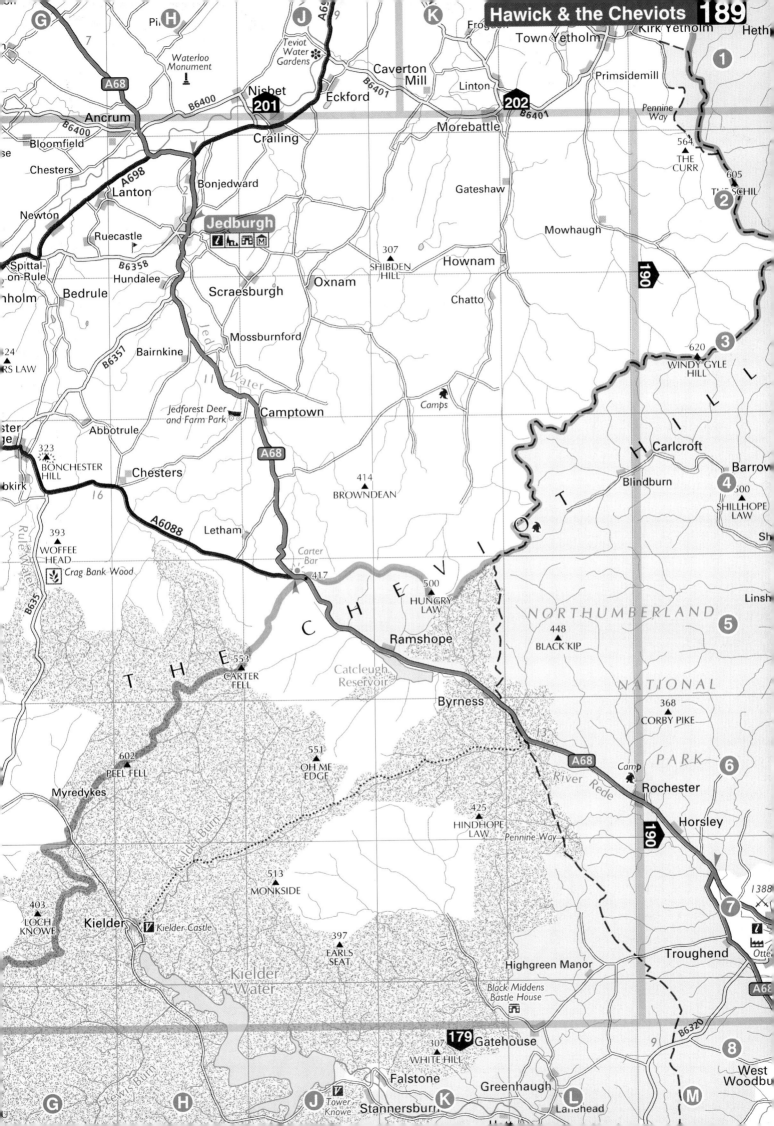

G
H
J
K
1

Town Yetholm
Kirk Yetholm
Heth

Pi
Waterloo
Monument
Teviot
Water
Gardens
Caverton
Mill
Frogdu
Primsidemill
Pennine
Way

A68
Nisbet
201
Eckford
B6401
Linton
202
564
THE
CURR

Ancrum
Crailing
B6400
Morebattle
B6401
605
THE SCHIL
2

Bloomfield
Bonjedward
Gateshaw
Mowhaugh

Chesters
Lanton
Newton
A698
Jedburgh
Hundalee
Ruecastle
B6358
Scraesburgh
Oxnam
307
SHIBDEN
HILL
Hownam
Gateshaw
190

Spittal-
on-Rule
Bedrule
Mossburnford
Chatto

holm
B6357
Bairnkine
Jed
Water
Camptown
Camps
620
WINDY GYLE
HILL
3

24
RS LAW
Jedforest Deer
and Farm Park
Abbotrule
Chesters
A68
414
BROWNDEAN
Carlcroft
Barrow

ster
ge
323
BONCHESTER
HILL
A6088
Letham
Blindburn
500
SHILLHOPE
LAW
4

bkirk
393
WOFFEE
HEAD
16
Crag Bank Wood
Carter
Bar
417
HUNGRY
500
LAW
NORTHUMBERLAND
448
BLACK KIP
5

Rule
Water
B635
Ramshope
THE
CHEVIOT
HILL
Linsh

553
CARTER
FELL
Catcleugh
Reservoir
NATIONAL

602
PEEL FELL
551
OH ME
EDGE
Byrness
368
CORBY PIKE

Myredykes
13
A68
Camp
River Rede
PARK
6

Kielder
Burn
425
HINDHOPE
LAW
Rochester
190
Horsley

403
LOCH
KNOWE
Kielder
Kielder Castle
513
MONKSIDE
Pennine Way
1388
7

397
EARLS
SEAT
Tarset Burn
Highgreen Manor
Troughend
Otte

Kielder
Water
Black Middens
Bastle House
A68

179
Gatehouse
B6320
9
8

Lewis Burn
307
WHITE HILL
Falstone
Greenhaugh
West
Woodbu

G
H
Tower
Knowe
J
Stannersburn
K
L
Lanehead
M

205

Muasdale

Glenacardoch
Point

Belloch

Glenbarr

MacAlister Clan

Cleongart

Bellochantuy Bay

Bellochantuy

454
BEINN AN TUIRC   Torr

319

408
BÒRD
MÒR

Sadde

194

396
SGREADAN
HILL

Ugadale

Tangy Loch

Glen Lussa

Kilkenzie

Peninver

Ardnacro
Bay

A83

Kilmichael

B842

Machrihanish
Bay

Campbeltown

Campbeltown

Machrihanish

B842

6

Island Dav

Drumlemble

B843

Kilkerran

Kildalloig

Campbeltown
Loch

Earadale Point

352
BEINN GHUILEAN

Achinhoan

385
THE
STATE

446
CNOC
MOY

10

Conie Glen

Glen Kerran

Dalsmeran

Ru S

Strone Glen

Glen Breakevie

Cattadale

B842

Polliwilline Bay

BEINN NA LICE

428

Carskey

Southend

Macharioch

Dunaverty

MULL OF KINTYRE

Carskey Bay

Sanda Sound

Sheep Island

Borgadalemore Point

Sanda Island

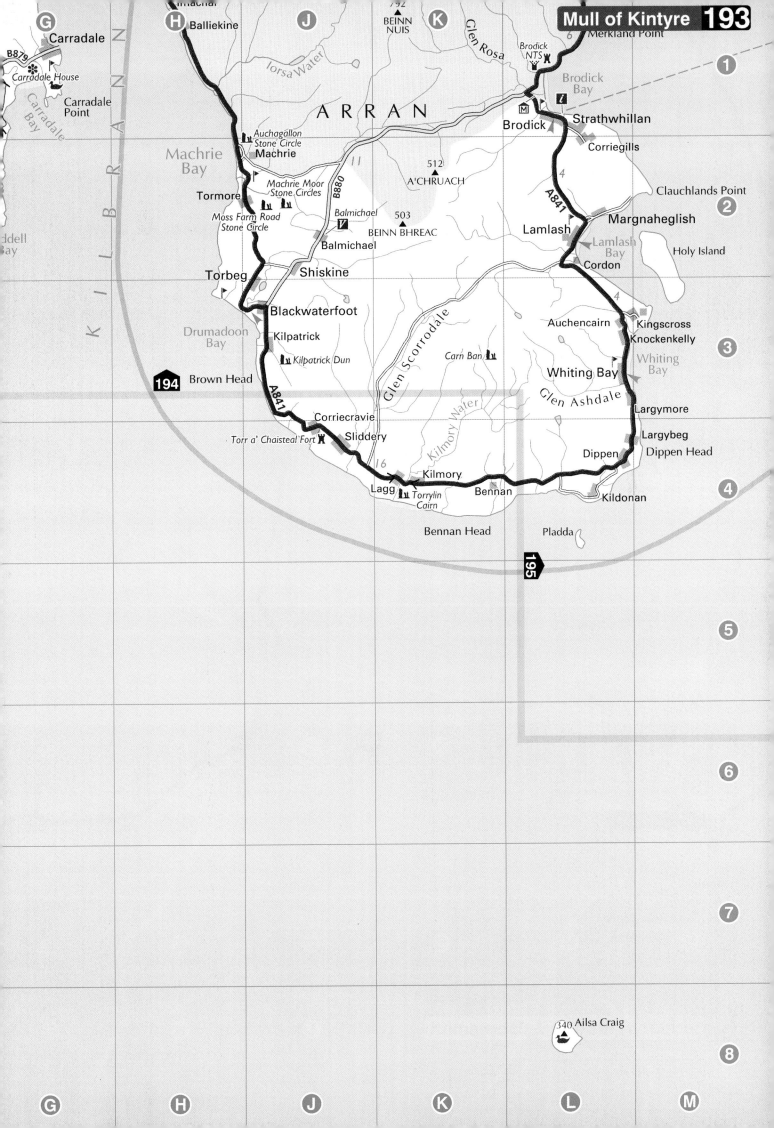

G Carradale
B879
Carradale House
Carradale Point
Carradale Bay

H Balliekine
J
BEINN NUIS 792
K
Glen Rosa
Merkland Point
Brodick NTS
6
Brodick Bay
1

Iorsa Water

A R R A N

Strathwhillan
Brodick
Corriegills

Machrie Bay
Auchagallon Stone Circle
Machrie
11
A841
Clauchlands Point
2

Tormore
Machrie Moor Stone Circles
B880
512
A'CHRUACH
Margnaheglish
Lamlash

Moss Farm Road Stone Circle
Balmichael
503
BEINN BHREAC
Holy Island
Lamlash Bay

Torbeg
Shiskine
Balmichael
Cordon

Blackwaterfoot
Auchencairn
Kingscross
Knockenkelly
3

Drumadoon Bay
Kilpatrick
Carn Ban
Whiting Bay
Whiting Bay

194 Brown Head
Kilpatrick Dun
Glen Scorrodale
Glen Ashdale

A841
Corriecravie
Largymore

Torr a' Chaisteal Fort
Sliddery
Kilmory Water
Largybeg
Dippen
Dippen Head

16
Kilmory
Bennan
Kildonan
4

Lagg
Torrylin Cairn

Bennan Head
Pladda
195

5

6

7

340 Ailsa Craig

8

G   H   J   K   L   M

G H J K

1

Ga H ty

Garroch Head

Little
Cumbrae
Island

207

Fairlie R

Hunsterston
Power Station

12

Drakemyre

Crosbie

Blackshaw

Munnoch

Dalry

A737

B780

B780

B780

B781

Dalgarven
Mill

Dalgarven

C U N

Portencross
Farland Head

B7048

**West
Kilbride**

B7047

Seamill

A78

B780

B778

Kilwinning

2

B785

annox

Corrie

A841

Ardrossan

Horse Isle

A78

A738

A738

Stevenston

Ardeer

Merkland Point

6

v

Saltcoats

196

3

Irvine

Maritime

Brodick
Bay

V

The Big Idea

Fullar

i

Strathwhillan

Corriegills

F I R T H

Irvine

Bay

Ga

Clauchlands Point

O F

4

841

Margnaheglish

ash

C L Y D E

Baras

Lamlash
Bay

Holy Island

Cordon

(Summer only)

C

Troon

4

Larne

Auchencairn

Kingscross

Knockenkelly

C

5

Belfast

0

Royal

Whiting

Bay

Pr

Whiting Bay

en Ashdale

Largymore

Ne

Largybeg

6

Ayr

Bay

Dippen

Dippen Head

i M A

Kildonan

196

adda

Doonfoo

Heads
of Ayr

Burns Cotta

Heads of Ayr

A719

Allo

7

Fisherton

Dunure

Culroy

Drumshang

Croy Brae
(Electric Brae)

Knoweside

8

Culzean
Bay

A7

Culzean

Pennyglen

Maybol

Whitefaulas

G H J K L M

182

Maidenhead

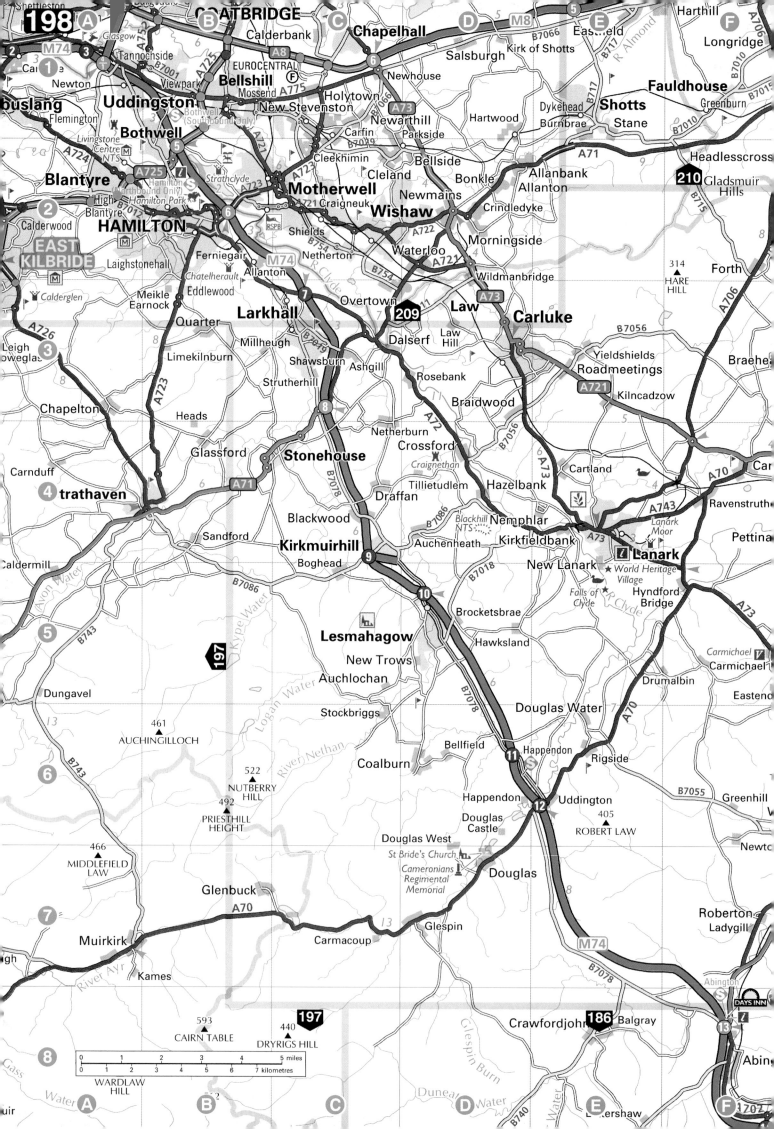

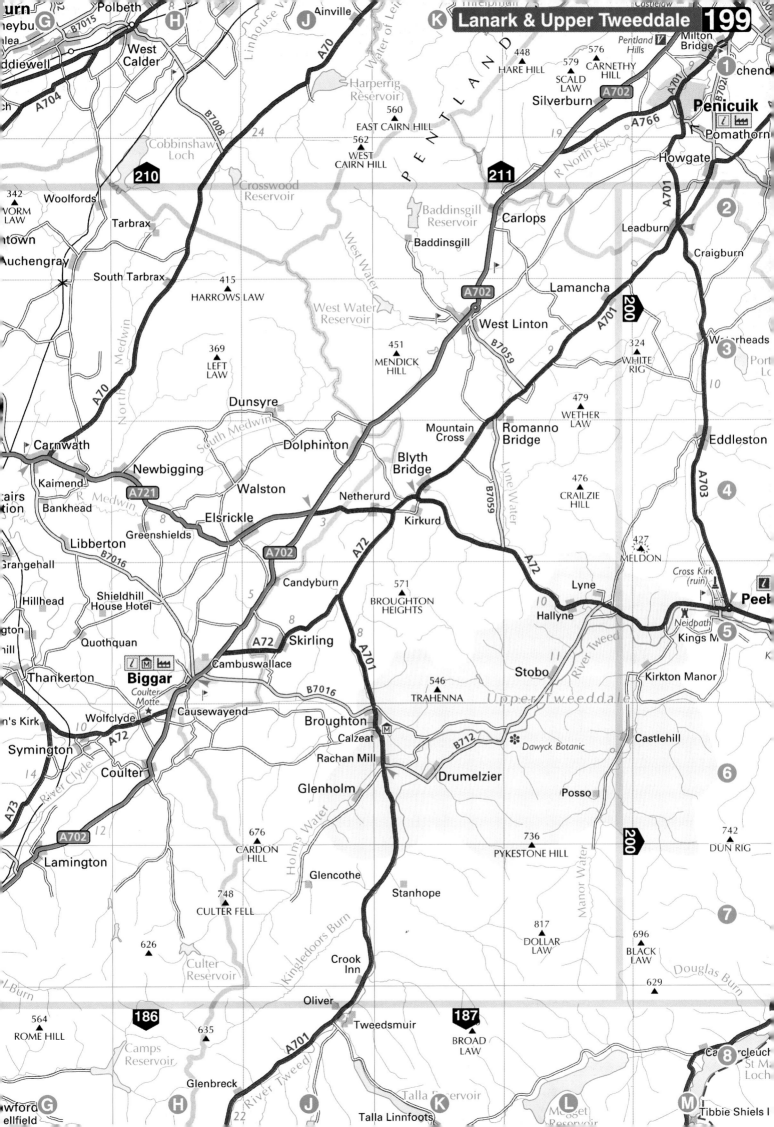

Polbeth

G B7015 ▢ **H** ▢ **J** Ainville ▢ **K** Water of Leith Castlelaw Pentland ▽ Milton Bridge

eybu
lea
West Calder
A70
448 HARE HILL
576
579 CARNETHY HILL
Pentland Hills
1 chend

ddiewell
A704
SCALD LAW
A702
560
EAST CAIRN HILL
Silverburn
A766
Penicuik
i ▦
Pomathorn

ch
West Calder
Harperrig Reservoir
24
562 WEST CAIRN HILL
A702
Carlops
R North Esk
Howgate
A701
2

Cobbinshaw Loch
210
Crosswood Reservoir
Baddinsgill Reservoir
211
Baddinsgill
Leadburn
Craigburn

342
WORM LAW
Woolfords
West Water
415 HARROWS LAW
A702
West Linton
Lamancha
A701
200
324 WHITE RIG
Waterheads
3

ntown
Tarbrax
West Water Reservoir
West Linton
B7059
479 WETHER LAW
Port Lo

Auchengray
South Tarbrax
369 LEFT LAW
451 MENDICK HILL
9
10

B7008
North Medwin
Dunsyre
South Medwin
Mountain Cross
Romanno Bridge
Lyne Water
476 CRAILZIE HILL
Eddleston
A703
4

Carnwath
Dolphinton
Blyth Bridge
B7059
427 MELDON
5 Kaimend
Newbigging
Walston
Netherurd
A72

cairs
tion
Bankhead
A721
R Medwin
Elsrickle
Kirkurd
Cross Kirk (ruin)
i
Peeb

Libberton
Greenshields
8
3
A702
A72
Lyne
Hallyne
5

Grangehall
B7016
Candyburn
5
571 BROUGHTON HEIGHTS
A72
10
Neidpath
5

Hillhead
Shieldhill House Hotel
8
Stobo
River Tweed
Kings M

gton
Quothquan
Skirling
8
A701
Kirkton Manor

Thankerton
A72
Cambuswallace
546 TRAHENNA
Upper Tweeddale
11

Biggar
Coulter Motte ★
Causewayend
Broughton
M
Castlehill
6

n's Kirk
10
Wolfclyde
A72
Calzeat
B712
Dawyck Botanic

Symington
14
Coulter
Rachan Mill
Drumelzier
Posso

River Clyde
A73
A702
12
Glenholm
Holms Water
736 PYKESTONE HILL
Manor Water
200
742 DUN RIG

Lamington
676 CARDON HILL
Glencothe
817 DOLLAR LAW
696 BLACK LAW
7

748 CULTER FELL
Stanhope
629

564
ROME HILL
626
Culter Reservoir
Kingledoors Burn
Crook Inn
Douglas Burn

l-Burn

186
635
Oliver
187
BROAD LAW
8
Ca rcleuch
St Ma
Loch

Camps Reservoir
A701
R iver Tweed
Tweedsmuir
817
DOLLAR LAW

wford
ellfield
G Glenbreck **H** 22 **J** Talla Reservoir **K** Talla Linnfoots **L** Megget Reservoir **M** Tibbie Shiels I

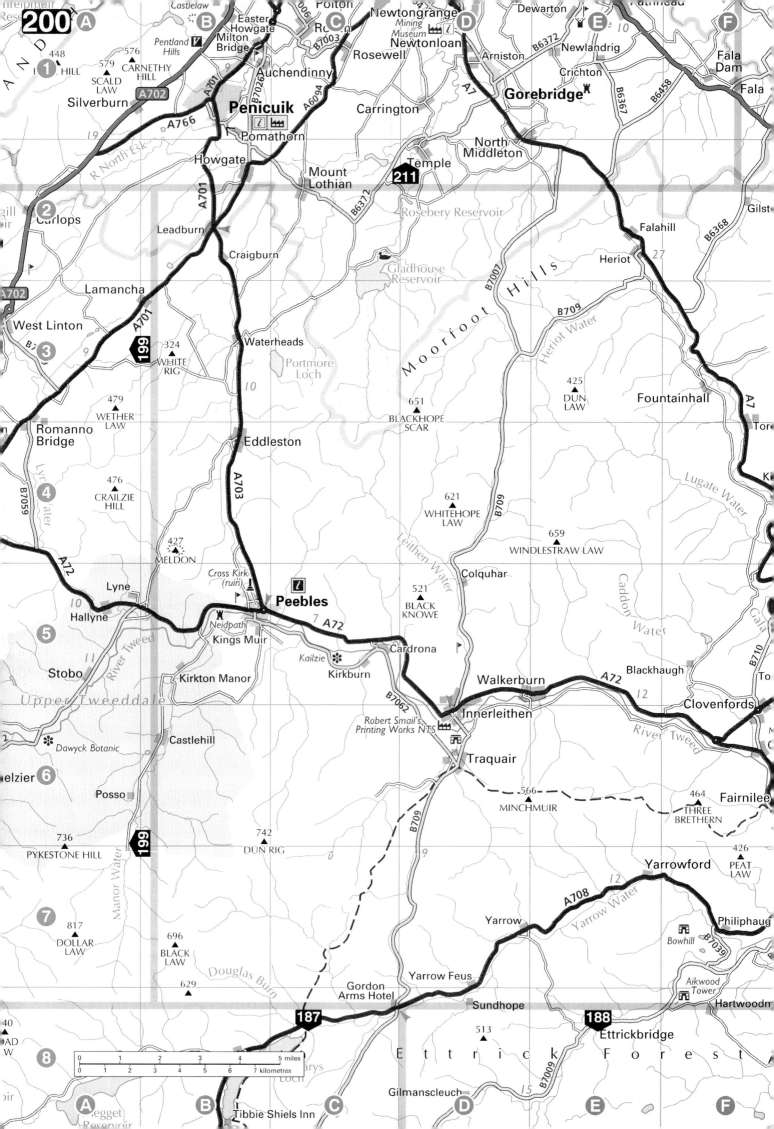

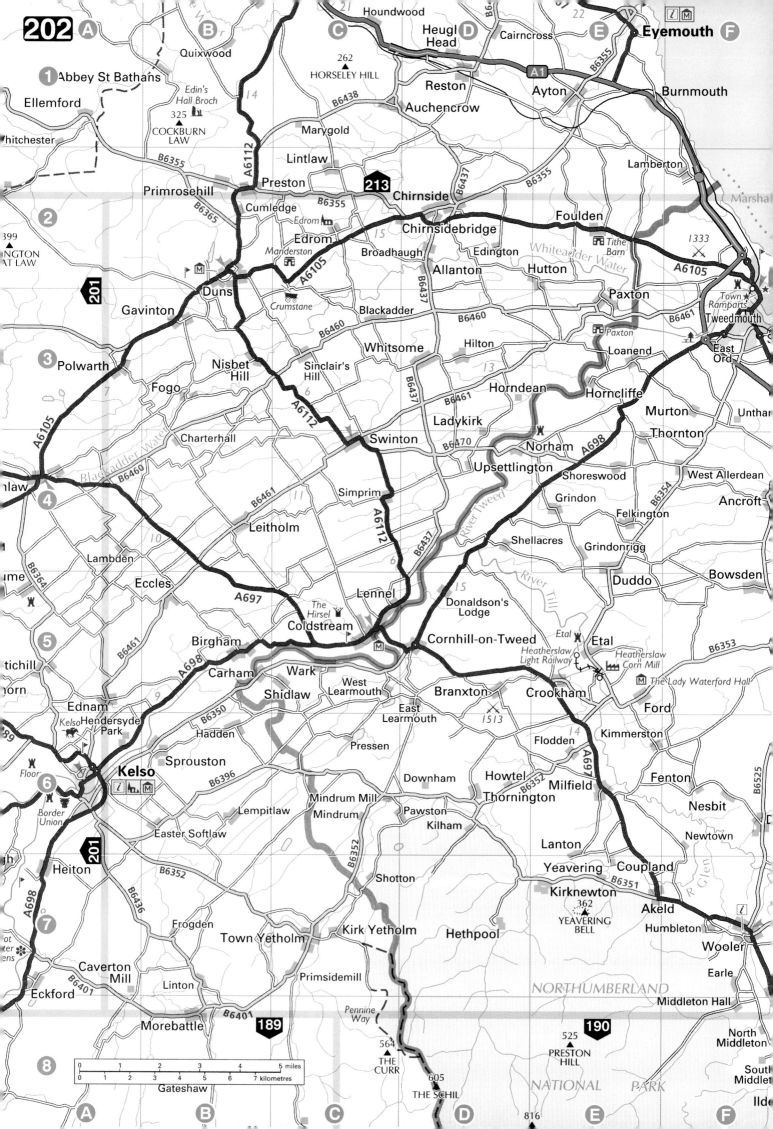

G H J

1

2

ws Bay

Northumberland Heritage Coast

ck-upon-Tweed

3

Huds
Head

erston

Cheswick

Goswick

CAUSEWAY
FLOODED
AT HIGH TIDE

4

Haggerston

Beal

Fenham

HOLY ISLAND

Holy
Island

Lindisfarne NT

*Lindisfarne
Priory*

Castle Point

Guile Point

6353

Kyloe

East
Kyloe

Fenwick

Buckton

Smeafield

Elwick

Ross

*Longstone
Lighthouse*

NT

FARNE
ISLANDS

5

owick

Detchant

Holburn

St Cuthbert's
Cave NT

Middleton

Low
Middleton

Easington

Budle
Bay

Bamburgh

Staple
Sound

Inner
Sound

*North Northumberland
Heritage Coast*

Hetton
Steads

North
Hazelrigg

Belford

Outchester

Waren
Mill

Budle

B1342

Bamburgh

B1340

Glororum

New
Shoreston

6

ton

South
Hazelrigg

B6349

Spindlestone

Burton

Bradford

B1341

Seahouses

East
Horton

on

Warenton

Bellshill

Lucker

Elford

North Sunderland

B6348

Adderstone

Newham

Beadnell

Chatton

Warenford

Swinhoe

B1340

*Beadnell
Bay*

7

A1

River Till

Ros
Castle NT

Newstead

Chathill

Tughall

Newton-by-the-Sea

ewtown

Chillingham

Ellingham

Preston

14

rn

190

Wild Cattle
Park

Hepburn

267
CATERAN
HILL

Brownieside

Preston
Pele Tower

Doxford

191

Brunton

Christon
Bank

Embleton

*Embleton
Bay*

8

Old Bewick

A69

B6

North
Charlton

347

Falloden

B1339

Dunstan
Steads

*Dunstanburgh
NT*

Ditchbur

South
Charlton

G H J K L M

ISLAY

214

G H J K

214 215

G'a' **G** il
H
J
K

lbric

1

Loch na
Danna
Island

St Cormacs
Chapel

Ellary

506
▲
SCRINADLE

398
▲
BEINN
TARSUINN

Kilmory Knap
Chapel

Kilmory

Loch Caolispo

2

Jura Forest

784
▲
BEINN
AN OIR

Paps of Jura

Kilmory Bay

Point of Knap

Loch a'
Chnuic Bhric

734
▲

24

206

Dru

Jura

560
▲
GLASS BHEINN

Dr

3
C hengan

Coulaghailt

Feolin Ferry

529
▲
DUBHA
BHEINN

Keils

Craighouse

Small
Isles

A846

Kilberry Sculptured Stones ★

Kilberry

342
▲
BRAT
BHEINN

Rudha na Gaillich

Kilberry Head

Keppoch Point

213
▲
CRUACH AIR

Cabrach

Tiretigan

Am Fraoch
Eilean

Rudha na Tràille

4

Loch Stornoway

Brosdale
Island

McArthur's
Head

NAM
EANN

EIGEIR

Port Askaig - Kennacraig

V

W

Rona n Point **5**

Ardp

Rudha Liath

Ardtalla

Kinerarach

Claggain
Bay

Tarbert

Sound of Gigha

Kintour

Ardmore
Point

GIGHA

Rhunahaorine
Point

6

Kildalton
Cross

V

Ardminish

Rhunahaorine

194

Eilean
a' Chuirn

Port Ellen - Kennacraig

Achamore

V

Tayinloan

Rudha na
Gainmhich

Cara

7

A83

Muasdale

8

Glenacardoch
Point

Belloch

Barr Water

G
H
192
J
K
L
Gl barr
M

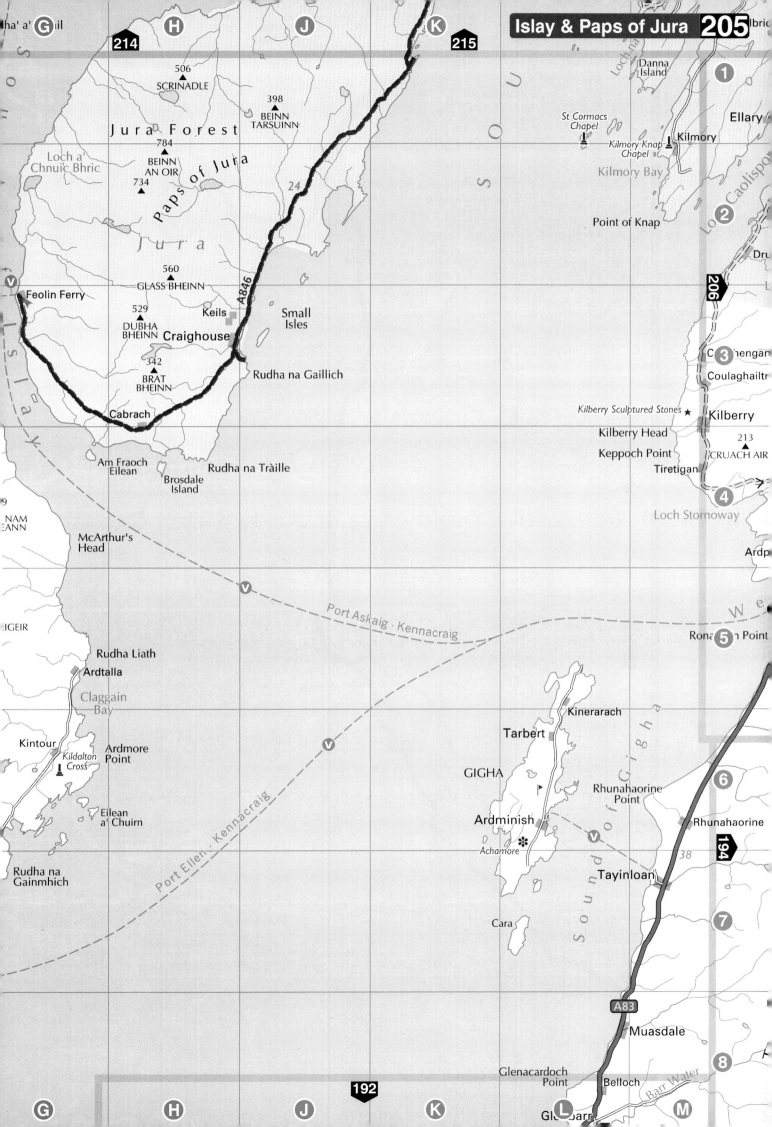

A · B · C · D · 216 · E · F

A83
B8002
A816

1

Kilmahumaig
Bellanoch
Dunadd Fort
Kilmichael Gla y
Loch
shan
Asknish
B8000
Lochgair
Crinan Canal
Barnluasgan
Cairnbaan
Middle Kames

Carsaig Bay
Lochgilphead
i
Càm Loch
Kilmory Woodland Park
Carrick
Largiemore
435
CRUACH CHUILCEACH

2
Tayvallich
215
Achnamara
Kilmichael of Inverlussa
Ardrishaig
Shirvan
Otter Ferry
Kilmodan Sculptured Stones
Ballimore

Knapdale
Taynish
331
BEINN BHEAG
A83

466
CRUACH LUSACH
Brenfield
Fearnoch

3
Is Chapel
B8024
Kilfinan Bay
Kilfinan
454
BEINN BHREAC

Kilbride
Sween
Lochead
Drum
B8000

Danna Island
Achahoish

Ellary
Erines

4
Knap el
Kilmory
Bay
561
SLIABH GAOIL
Auchenlochan
Tighr

Ormsary
Stonefield Castle Hotel
Kames

Knap
Druimdrishaig
480
DUBH CHREAG
Glenan Bay
Millhouse

5
Loch nan Torran
An Tairbeart
Glenralloch
Blair's Ferry
Portavadie
207
CNOC NA CARRAIGE

Cretshengan
Tarbert
i
West Tarbert

Coulaghailtro
343
CRUACH AN T SORCHAIN
Kilbride Bay
Ardlamont

ured Stones ★
Kilberry
Torinturk
A83
Ardlamont Bay

6
Head
h Point
213
CRUACH AIRDE
B8024
422
CNOC A' BHAILE-SHOIS
Ardlamo Point

Tiretigan
Kennacraig
(Winter Only)

205
Whitehouse
V

Loch noway
Kilchamaig
B8001

7
Ardpatrick
Skipness
Skipness
Chapel
Skipness Point

Portachoillan
Clachan
West Loch Tarbert
Claonaig
B8001

Ronachan Point
B842
V (Summer Only)

Ronachan
Loch Ciaran
R
Soune

8
Loch Garasdale
Cock Of Arran

Crossaig
194
Lochra
E
F

G H J 217 K

CRUACH AN LOCHAIN

Dunans Castle

618 BE BHE
Bernice
Whistlefield Inn
643
742 BEINN MHOR
Argyll Forest Park
Sligrachan
657 CREACHAN MOR

BEINN CHAORACH
Garelochhead
655 BEI THARSUINN 1
A814

Rockville
Greenfield
B872
Coulport
Glen Fruin
Shandon
Ballymenoch 2

643 CLACH BHEINN
Glenmassen
664 BEINN RUADH
Ardentinny
548 STRONCHULLIN HILL

B833
Clynder
Rhu
Rosneath
208 He

601 SGORACH MÒR
Benmore Younger
Benmore
Glen Massen

Cove
Kilcreggan
3

432 CRUACH NAN CUILEAN
Loch Tarsan
606
Rashfield
Ardbeg
Kilmun
A880
Strone

Firth of

Stronafian
B836
Glen Lean
Clachaig
Kilmun
Holy Loch

Ardmore

daruel
611 CRUACH NAN CAPULL
Glenkin
Sandbank
Ardnadam
A815
Hunter's Quay
Kirn

Gourock

Ardgowan
Cloch Point
Larkfield
Braeside
A78
GREENOCK

7
A886
Glenstriven
503 BISHOP'S SEAT
Dunoon

Ashton
Lyle Hill

Stronafian
Loch Striven
Ardhallow

A770
Chrisswell
8
8

Bute
505 BEINN BHREAC
Ardentraive

391 KILMARNOCK HILL
Dunan

Lunderston Bay
Ardgowan
Loch Thom
Gryfe Reservoir

Colintraive
Altgaltraig

322 BEINN RUADH
Innellan

Inverkip
Shielhill
Garvock
Cairncurran

ubodach
Kyles of Bute
A886

A815
Wemyss Bay

441 CREUCH HILL
5

B U T E
267 KAMES HILL
Ardmaleish

Toward
Toward Quay

Skelmorlie
Upper Skelmorlie
6

Kilbride
Ardyre Point
Port Bannatyne

Bogany Point

A78

Knock Castle
522 HILL OF STAKE
6

ildavanan
B875
St Colmac
Ardbeg

Quarter
Routenburn

Ettrick Bay

Rothesay
A844
St Mary's Chapel (ruin)
Ardencraig
Ascog
Loch Ascog

Skelmorlie Aisle
Vikingar!
Largs

483 IRISH LAW

B878
Ballanlay
A844
Loch Fada
Kerrycroy

GREAT CUMBRAE ISLAND

Kelburn
Kelburn Country Centre

A760
14

Midpark
Meikle Kilmory
B881
Mount Stuart
Bruchag

Fairlie

371 COCK LAW

Camphill Reservoir
Kilbirnie

Ardscalpsie Bay
Kingarth
B881
B896
B899

Millport
B899
B896

Stravanan Bay
Kilchattan Bay
Kilchattan

St Blane's Church

Fairlie Roads

f B u t e
Garrochty

Garroch Head

Little Cu Isla
195
Hunterston Power Station
Crosbie
ngarnoch
B784 B780

G H J K L Drake yre M

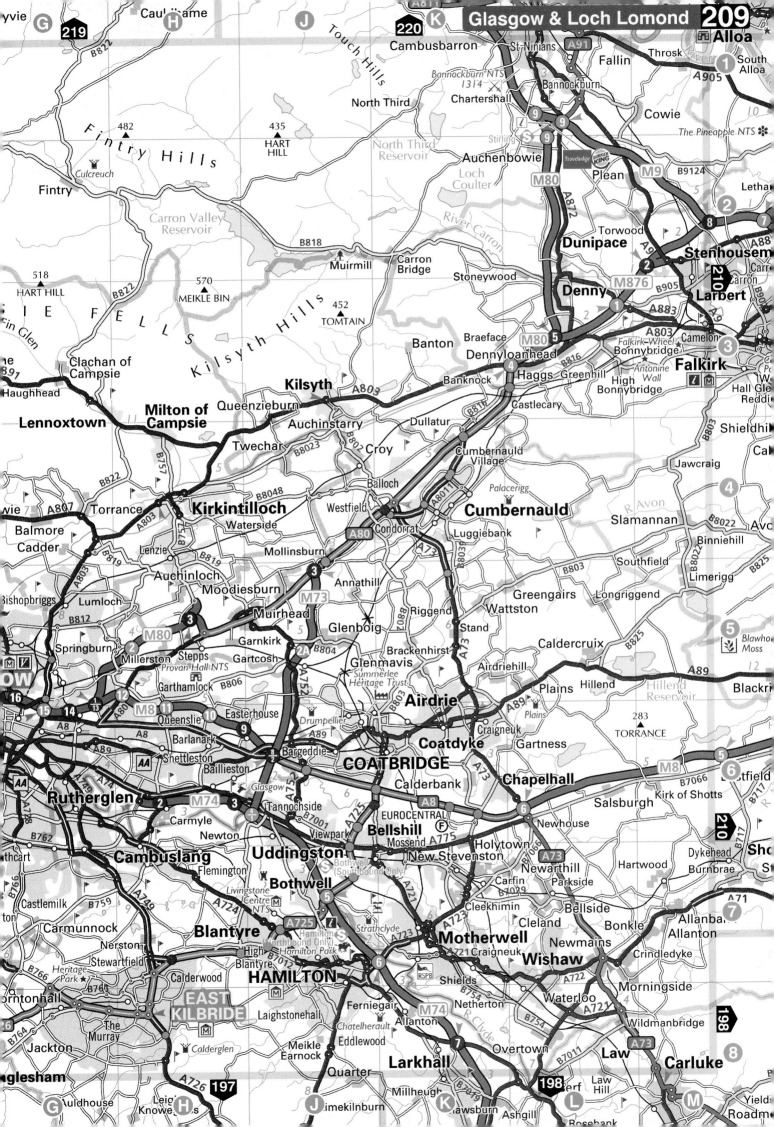

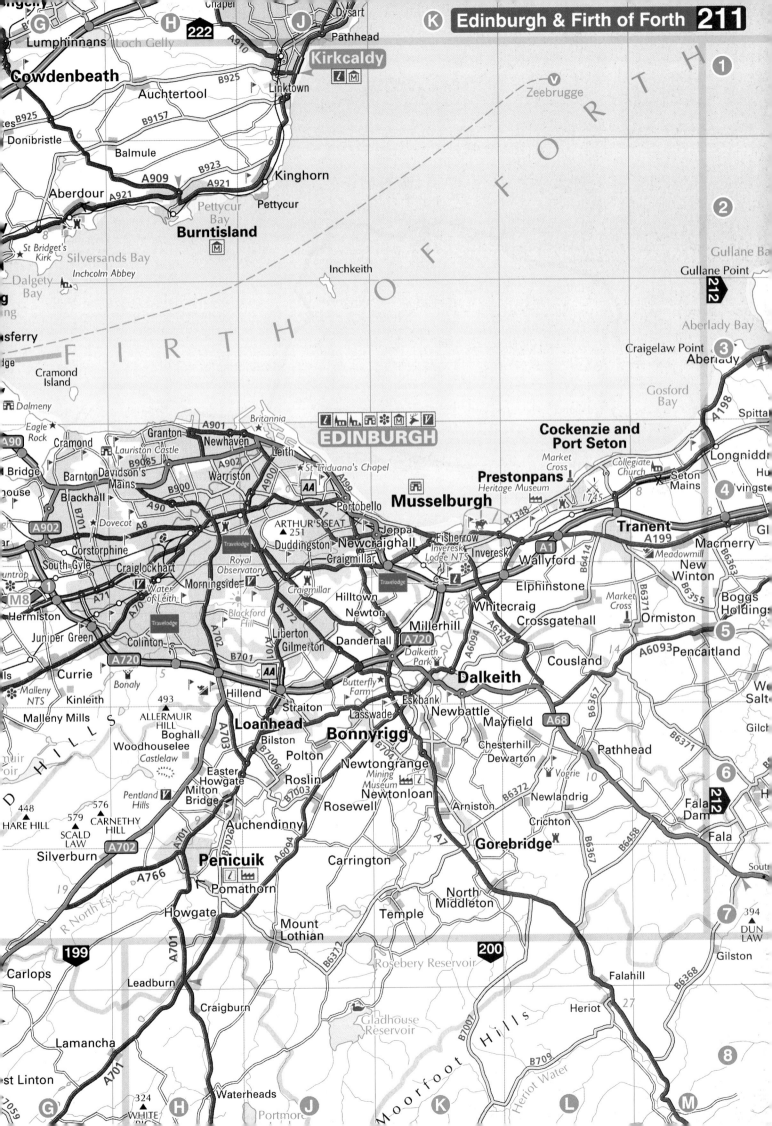

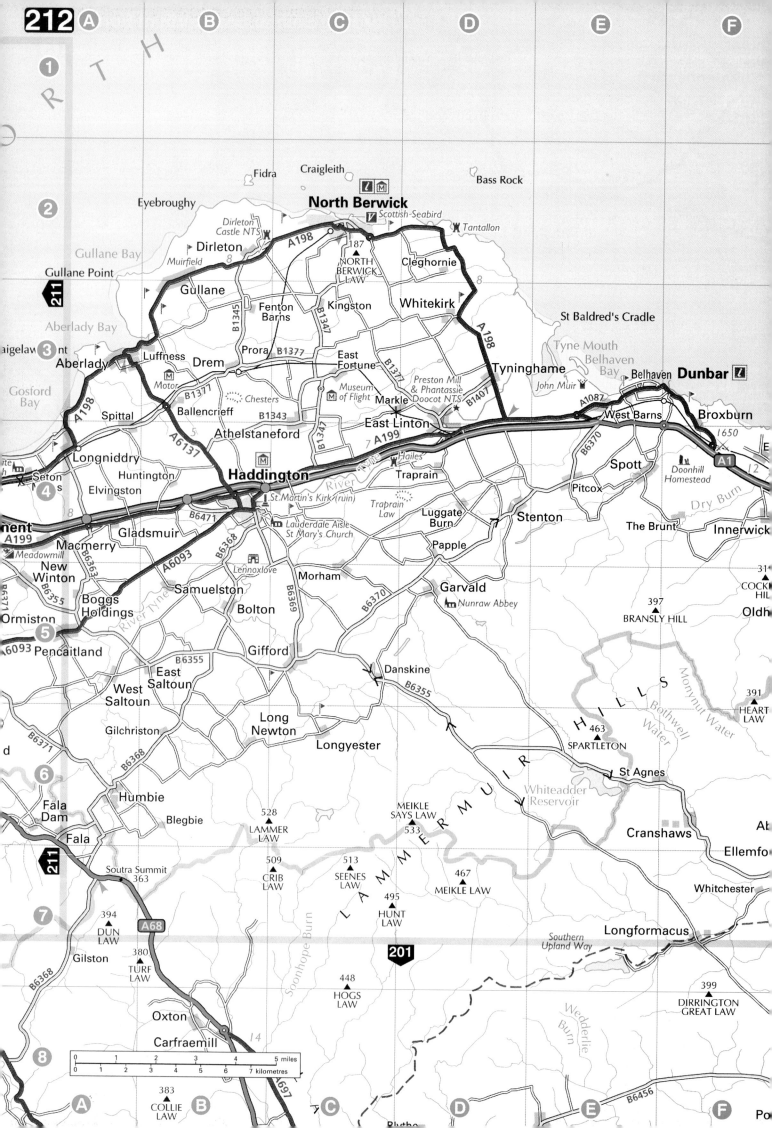

G H J

1
2
3
4
5
6
7
8

Ness

Chapel Point

Torness Power Station
Thorntonloch

rowhill

Reed Point
Cove Pease Bay
Collegiate Church
Cockburnspath Siccar Point
Fast Castle Head

A1107 **ST ABB'S HEAD**

196 ▲ BROWN RIG Coldingham Loch

cks

Ecclaw

St Abbs

Grantshouse **Coldingham** Coldingham Bay

Southern Upland Way **Butterdean** A1107 22

Eye Water 21 Houndwood B6438 Eyemouth

Quixwood Heugh Head Cairncross

t Bathans 262 ▲ HORSELEY HILL Reston A1 Ayton Burnmouth

Edin's Hall Broch B6438 Auchencrow

325 ▲ COCKBURN LAW Marygold B6355

B6355 Lintlaw A6112 Lamberton Marshall Meadows Bay

Primrosehill **Preston** B6437 B6355

Cumledge Chirnside North Northumber

B6365 Edrom **202** Foulden

Edrom Chirnsidebridge Tithe Barn 1333

Manderston Broadhaugh Edington Whiteadder Water A6105 **Berwick-upo**

Duns A6105 Allanton Hutton Town Ramparts Barracks

Crumstane Paxton

Gavinton Blackadder B6461 **Tweedmouth** Spittal

B6460 Paxton East Ord Huds Head

h Nisbet Hill Sinclair's Hill Whitsome Hilton 13 Loanend **Scremerston**

G H J K L M

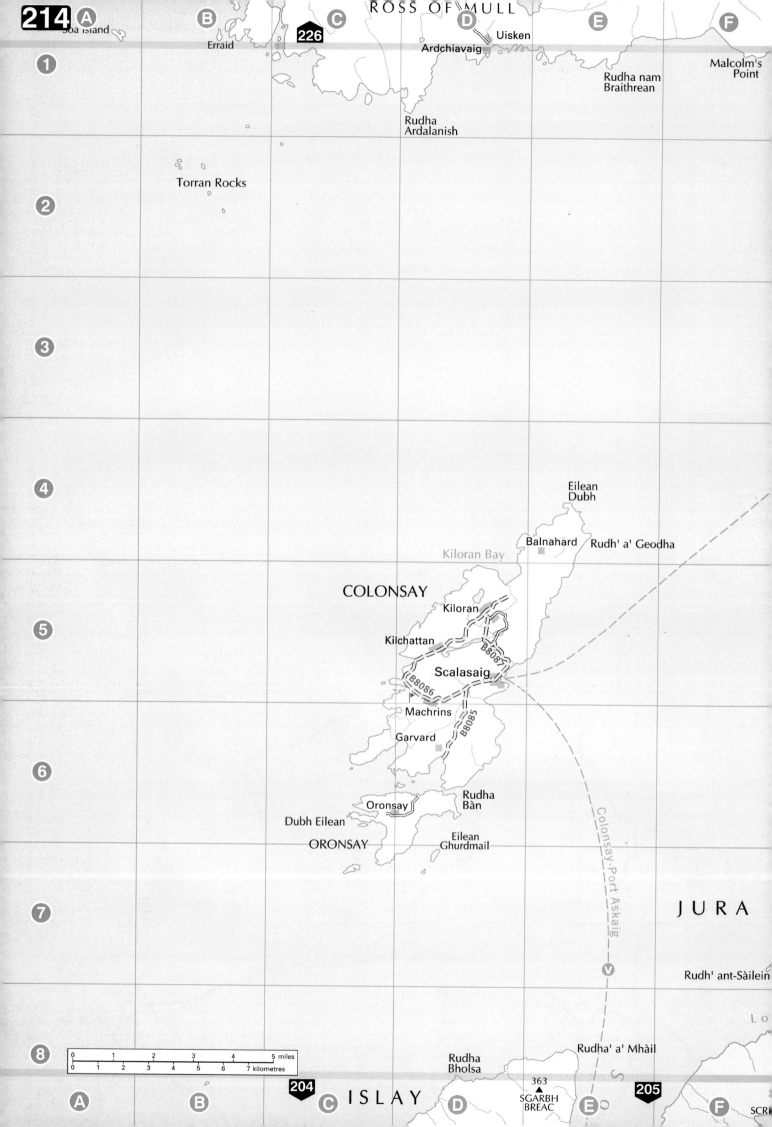

ROSS OF MULL

Soa Island

A

Erraid

B

226

C

Uisken

Ardchiavaig

D

E

Malcolm's Point

F

1

Rudha nam Braithrean

Rudha Ardalanish

Torran Rocks

2

3

4

Eilean Dubh

Balnahard

Rudh' a' Geodha

Kiloran Bay

COLONSAY

Kiloran

B8087

5

Kilchattan

Scalasaig

B8086

Machrins

B8085

Garvard

6

Oronsay

Rudha Bàn

Dubh Eilean

ORONSAY

Eilean Ghurdmail

Colonsay-Port Askaig

7

JURA

Rudh' ant-Sàilein

V

8

Rudha' a' Mhàil

Rudha Bholsa

204

C   ISLAY

D

363
SGARBH BREAC

205

E

F

SCR

Lo

0   1   2   3   4   5 miles
0   1   2   3   4   5   6   7 kilometres

A   B   C   D   E   F

Dubh

G   H   J   K

227

1

FIRTH

Colonsay : Oban

Garbh Eileach

Eilean
Dubh Mòr

GARVELLACHS
★ Monastery & Beehive Cells

Eileach
an Naoimh

LUNGA

Scarba, Lunga

and the

Garvellachs

SCARBA

448
▲
CRUACH SCARBA

Gulf of Corryvreckan

Glengarrisdale
Bay

295
▲
CRUACH NA
SEILCHEIG

Glendebadel Bay

364
▲
BEN
GARRISDALE

Corpach Bay

466
▲
BEINN
BHREAC

Glen Grundale

Lussa River

Lealt Burn

453
▲
RAINBERG MÒR

an-Bay

A846

Ardlussa

Lussa
Point

Loch
Righ Mòr

T a r b e r t

205

G   H   J   K

Insh
Island

Clachan-Seil

SEIL

Ellanbeich   Easdale   Balvicar

B844

Easdale   B8003

V

Cuan Ferry Village

Cullipool
House   Torsay
Island   LUING

Degnish

Loch Melfort

Arduaine
Garden NTS   Arduaine

216

SHUNA

Toberonochy

Shuna
Point

Cra
Hav

Craigdhu

Ardfern   Kintr

En Mhic

En Righ

Craignish Point

Aird   Loch Craignish

Island
Macaskin   Slockavulli
Temple Wood
Stone Circle

Ri Cruin C
Poltalloc

Loch Crinan

Crinan

Kilmahumaig

Bellanoch

Crinan River
B8025   B841

Carsaig Bay

Tayvallich

Achnamara

Kilmichael of Inverlus

Knapdale   **206**

Taynish

331
▲
BEINN
BHEA

466
▲
CRUACH
LUSACH

Loch Sween

B8025

Keills Chapel

Loch na Cille

Kilbride
Sween

Danna
Island

Lochead

hahoish

L   M

1
2
3
4
5
6
7
8

G H 229 J K 1

River Noe

River Orchy B8074

771
▲
BEINN UDLAIDH

Glen St

988
▲
BEINN EUNAICH

648
▲
BEINN
DONACHAN

River Lochy

Tyndrum

we Ironworks
Inverawe

1124
▲
BEN
CRUACHAN

Pass of Brander

B8077

Kilchurn ⚓

Stronmilchan

Inverlochy

Glen Lochy

A85

Glen Lochy

2

1130
▲
BEN LUI

River Awe

Cruachan
Reservoir

Lochawe

Cruachan
Power Station

Upper
Kinchrackine

Dalmally

1028
▲
BEN OSS

977
▲
BEINN
DUBHCHRA

Nant B845

A819

636
▲

218

739
▲

LOCH-LOMOND-AND-T

NATIONAL P

Ardanaiseig ❋
Ardanaiseig Hotel

Hayfield

hrenan

Taychreggan
Hotel

Cladich

Portsonachan
Hotel

B840

we

Lochan
Shira

3

947
▲
BEINN
BHUIDHE

Glen Fyne

A82

arghour

589
▲
CRUACH
MHOR

Glen Aray

A819

Glen Shira

Glenfyne
Lodge

645
▲
MAOL BREAC

uil

4

658
▲
CLACHAN
HILL

942
▲
BEN
VORLICH

Bell Tower

Ardkinglas
Woodland
Garden ❋

Cairndow

Loch
Sloy

Inverglas

5

Inveraray Castle 🏰
Inveraray
Inveraray Jail ★

Loch Shira

Loch Fyne

Ardno

Glen Kinglas

1011
▲
BEN IME

912
▲
BEINN AN
LOCHAIN

Rest and be thankful

925
▲
BEINN NARNAIN

416
▲
CRUACH
TAIRBEIRT

Argyll Wildlife Park

A83

St Catherines

565
▲
CRUACH
NAN CAPULL

B839

B828

Glen
Croe

881
▲
THE
COBBLER

Succoth

Arrochar

6

Douglas Water

Auchindrain 🏛
Township

A815

845
▲
BEN
DONICH

A83

Ardgartan ℹ

Strachur

Argyll Forest Park

Lochgoilhead

661
▲
BEN
REACH

Furnace

A886

Balliemore

River Cur

Corrow

Douglas Pier

218

Glen Doug

7

Newton

Glenbranter

L

779
▲
BEINN
BHEULA

Loch Goil

A814

734
▲
DOUNE
HILL

stle
hlan

480
▲
CRUACH
NAN CAPULL

Invernoaden

A

Arddarroch

702
▲
BEINN EICH
Edentaggart

8

505
▲
CRUACH AN
LOCHAIN

arry

A886

Loch
Eck

W

A815

Carrick Castle

Portincaple

Whistlefield

713
▲
BEINN
CHAORACH

55

15

618
▲
BEINN
BHEAG

207

Whistlefield
Inn

657
▲
CREA
MC

A814

arelochhead

G

Dunans Castle

742
▲

H

J

rest Park

Sligrachan

K

L

arochhead

M

THARSUINN

Newton

A | **B** | **C** 229 | **D** | **E** 230 | **F**

1
988
BEINN EUNAICH
648
BEINN DONACHAN
771
BEINN UDLAIDH
818
BEINN CHAORACH

2
Ichurn
Stronmilchan
Upper Kinchrackine
Inverlochy
Dalmally
A85
Glen Lochy
River Orchy
River Lochy
12
B8074
B8077
A819
Tyndrum
A82
Ben Lui
Strath Fillan
Loch Lubhair
5
1130
BEN LUI
Inverherive Hotel

3
636
217
739
1028
BEN OSS
977
BEINN DUBHCHRAIG
LOCH LOMOND AND THE TROSSACHS NATIONAL PARK
Crianlarich
Glen Falloch
West Highland Way
Falls of Falloch

4
Lochan Shira
947
BEINN BHUIDHE
Glenfyne Lodge
658
CLACHAN HILL
Glen Fyne
645
MAOL BREAC
Ardlui
A82
17
946
BEINN A' CHROIN
LOCH LOMOND AN
865
STOB A' CH
747
MEALL MÒR

5
Glen Shira
Cairndow
Ardkinglas Woodland Garden
Ardno
ch Fyne
11
10
942
BEN VORLICH
Loch Sloy
Inveruglas
Loch
Inversnaid Hotel
RSPB
Stronachlachar
Loch Arklet
B829

6
St Catherines
565
CRUACH NAN CAPULL
B839
Glen Kinglas
912
BEINN AN LOCHAIN
B828
Rest and be thankful
Glen Croe
1011
BEN IME
925
BEINN NARNAIN
881
THE COBBLER
Succoth
416
CRUACH TAIRBEIRT
Arrochar
A83
Ardgartan
Argyll Forest Park
845
BEN DONICH
217
Tarbet
2
633
CRUINN A' BHEINN
Queen Elizabeth Forest Park
973
BEN LOMOND
Loch Chon

7
nvernoaden
779
BEINN BHEULA
Corrow
Douglas Pier
Lochgoilhead
River Gail
Loch Goil
661
BEN REACH
Glen Douglas
Inverbeg
Rowardennan Lodge
Rowardennan Hotel
596
BEINN UIRD

8
618
BEINN BHEAG
Loch Eck
A815
Whistlefield Inn
Bernice
rgyll Fo
657
Sligrachan
Carrick Castle
Portincaple
Arddarroch
A814
Whistlefield
A814
207
lochhead
734
DOUNE HILL
702
BEINN EICH
Edentaggart
713
BEINN CHAORACH
655
BEINN THARSUINN
Glen Luss
A82
Inchlonaig
Luss
Aldoch
208
586
BEN VRACKIE
Qu
Loch Lomond

0 1 2 3 4 5 miles
0 1 2 3 4 5 6 7 kilometres

A | **B** | **C** | **D** | **E** | **F**

G 230 H J Finlarig 231

Killin
Falls of Dochart ★
Breadalbane Folklore Centre
CREAG UCHDAG ▲ 879
RUADH MHEALL ▲ 682

HEATHAICH
Bovain E
Auchlyne
River Dochart
A85 Dochart
A85ll

B R A
Glen Beich
Loch Lednock
Inve
Glen L

MEALL AN FHIODHAIN ▲ 778
SRÒN MHOR ▲ 671
Dalveich
Lochearnhead
St Fillans 220 A85

Loch Earn
River Earn
Glen Le

A84
Balquhidder Auchtubh
Craigruie Tulloch
Kingshouse Hotel
Ardvorlich
Glen Vorlich

Loch Voil
Loch Doine
TROSSACHS NATIONAL PARK
Ballimore Strathyre
BEN VORLICH ▲ 985
STUC A' CHROIN ▲ 975
Dalchruin

5
14
Ardchullarie More
MEALL ODHAR ▲ 630

BENVANE ▲ 818
MEALL CALA ▲ 671
Queen Elizabeth Forest Park
Loch Lubnaig

6
BEN LEDI ▲ 876
Kilmahog Woollen Mill

Katrine
Falls of Leny ★
Kilmahog
Callander
Upper Drumbane

The Trossachs
Loch Katrine Pier
Brig o'Turk
10 A821 Coilantogle
Rob Roy and Trossachs
A84 8

BEINN BHREAC ▲ 700
BEN VENUE ▲ 729
Loch Achray
Queen Elizabeth Forest Park
Lendrick
Loch Venachar
A81
6
Drumvaich
ndie
Burn of Cambus
Buchany

Altskeith Hotel
A821 7
Loch Drunkie
Menteith Hills
BEINN DEARG ▲ 427
B822
220
Deanston
Doun

ochard
Loch Ard
Milton
Queen Elizabeth Forest Park
4 A81
Aberfoyle
Port of Menteith
Farmlife Centre
Ruskie
Goodie Water
Thornhill
B8032
B826
Doune
Meldrum

izabeth Park
Duchray Water
Inchmahome
Lake of Menteith
A873 13
air Dr
7

ELRIG ▲ 208
Cunninghame Graham Memorial NTS
Gartmore
Dykehead
Flanders Moss
River Forth
B8034
B822
19
B8031
B8075

Dalmary
A81
B835
Arnprior
B8037
Kippen
Gargunnock

Auchentroig
A811
Buchlyvie
209
B822
Cauldhame
8

PARK
West Highland Way
G H J K L M
Touch Hills
Milto Buchanan

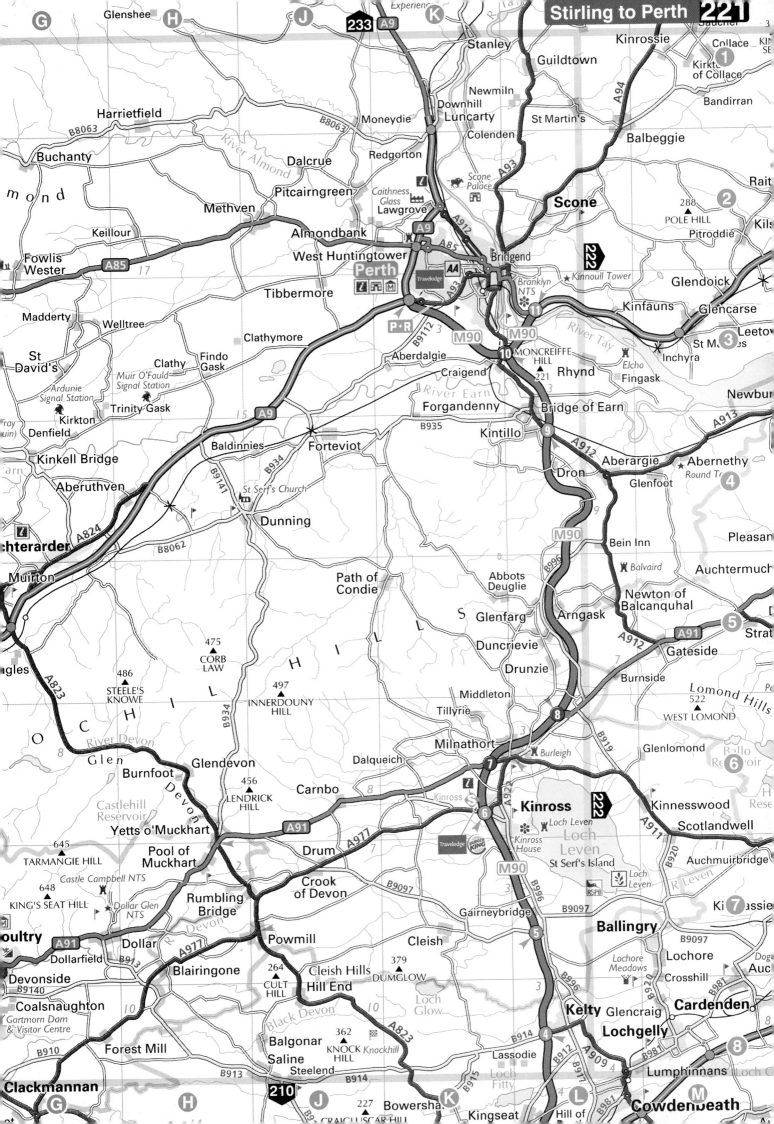

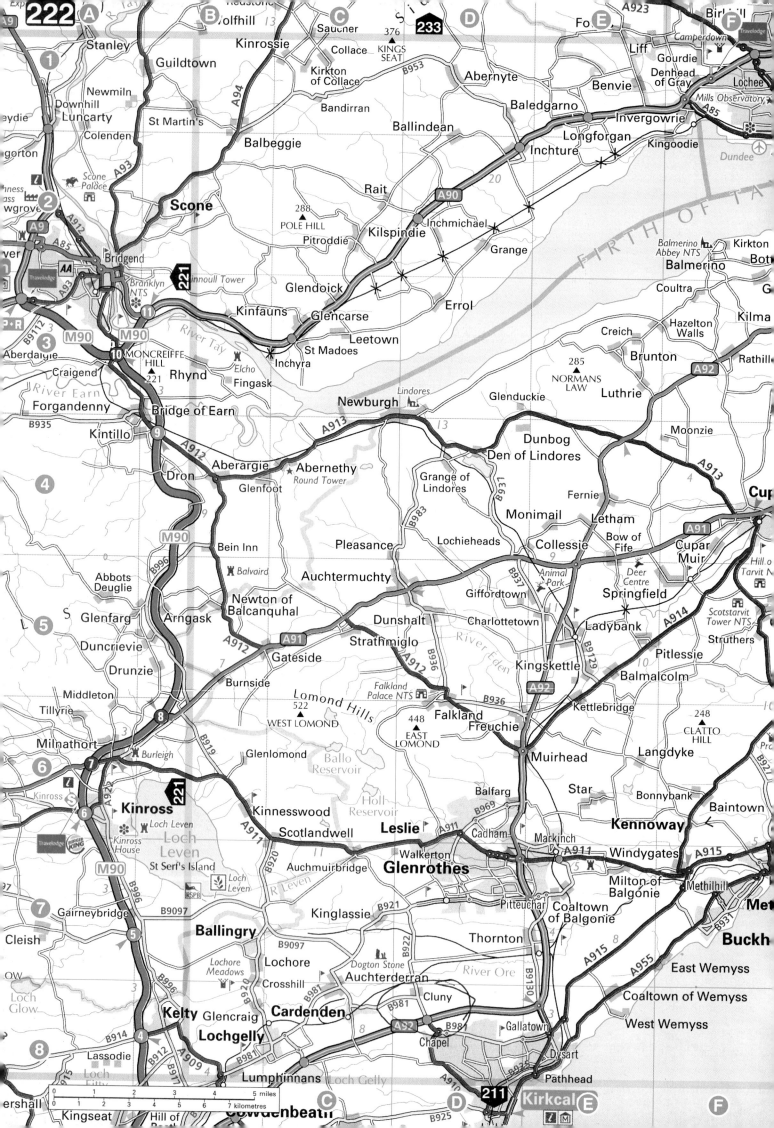

1

2

3

4

5

6

7

8

G H J K

Burnside of
Fintry
Mains of
Fintry
Douglas
and Angus
Baldovie
234
B961
B962
A92
A930
noustie
Carnoustie
Buddon

A90
B960
B959
Monifieth
Barnhill
Broughty
Ferry
Broughty
BUDDON
NESS

North Carr
Lightship
DUNDEE
Toll
A92 Tay Bridge
Tayport
Newport-
on-Tay
Wormit
B946
A914
B945
Scottish National Golf Centre
Tentsmuir Point
Tentsmuir Point

oint
HM
Frigate
'Unicorn'

ST ANDREWS
BAY

A919
13
Leuchars
RAF Leuchars
ie
Balmullo
13
A914
Guardbridge
River Eden
Kincaple
A91
St Andrews
St Andrews
brae
airsie
10
Strathkinness
Kemback
Botanic
Gardens
Brownhills
B939
Craigtoun
A917
10
Boarhills
Blebocraigs
Denhead
Stravithie
B9131
Kingsbarns
gend
B939
Pitscottie
A915
Cameron
Reservoir
Dunino
Balcomie
Links
FIFE NESS
Ceres
Baldinnie
B940
12
Radernie
Kingsmuir
10
othie
Peat
Inn
B941
New
Gilston
Lathones
Lochty
B940
Scotland's
Secret Bunker
B9171
Crail
Woodside
Largoward
Carnbee
Kellie
Castle NTS
Easter Pitkierie
4
A917
Upper
Largo
A915
Arncroach
B9171
Wester
Pitkierie
B9131
Kilrenny
Cellardyke
Lundin
Mill
Colinsburgh
B942
Newton of
Balcormo
Fisheries
Museum
Anstruther
Drumeldrie
A917
B941
B942
6
Pittenweem
Lundin
Links
Lower
Largo
Kilconquhar
6
St Monans
ven
Largo Bay
Earlsferry
Elie
Isle of May

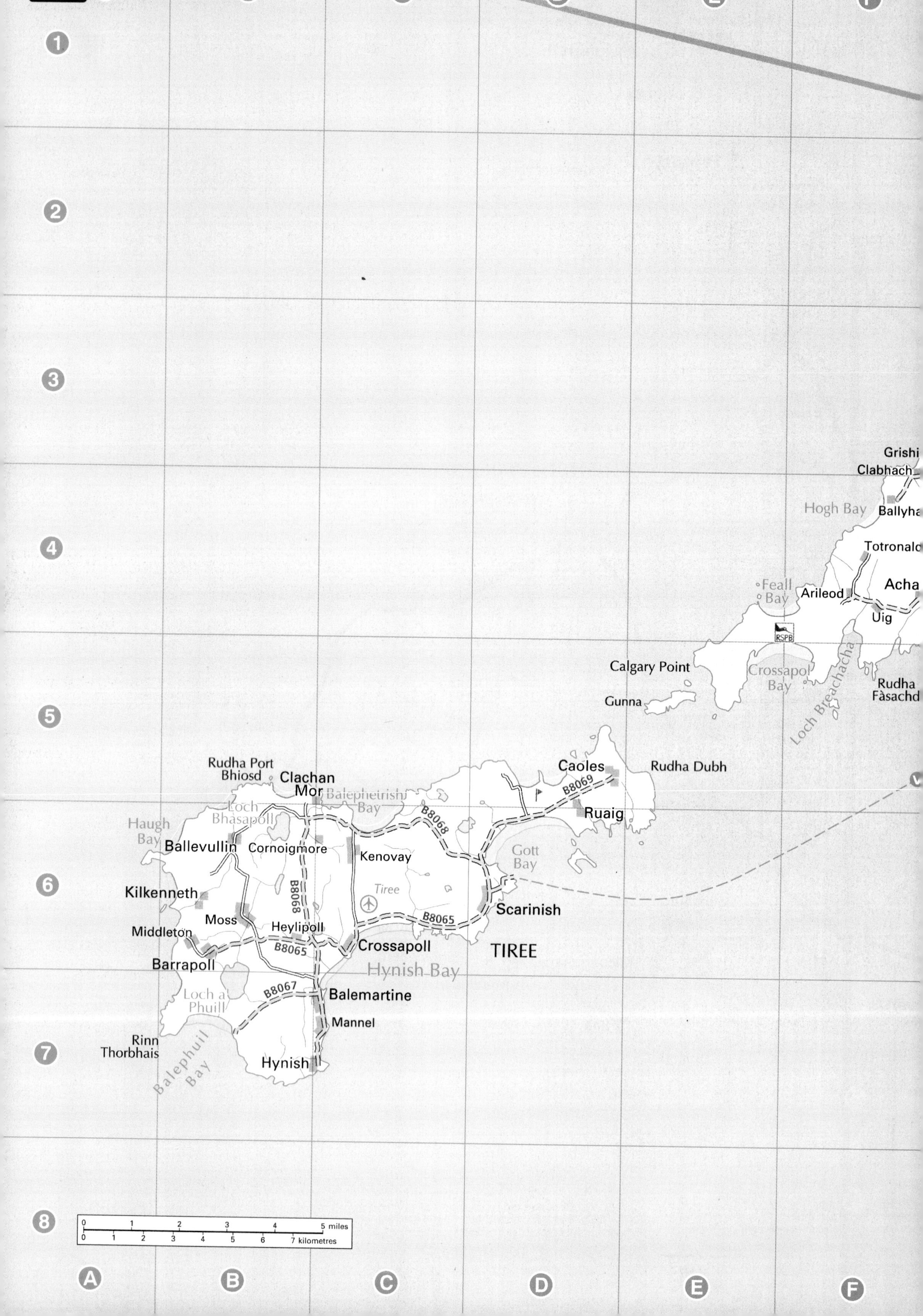

A B C D E F

1

2

3

Grishi
Clabhach

Hogh Bay   Ballyha

4

Totronald

Feall   Arileod   Acha
Bay

Uig

RSPB

Calgary Point   Crossapol   Rudha
Bay   Fàsachd

Gunna   Loch Breachacha

5

Rudha Port   Clachan   Caoles   Rudha Dubh
Bhiosd   Mor   Balepheirish   B8069
Loch   Bay   B8068   Ruaig
Bhasapoll
Haugh   Kenovay   Gott
Bay   Ballevullin   Cornoigmore   Bay

6

Kilkenneth   Tiree   Scarinish
B8068
Moss   Heylipoll   B8065
Middleton   B8065   Crossapoll   TIREE
Barrapoll   Hynish Bay
Loch a   B8067   Balemartine
Phuill
Mannel

7

Rinn   Balephuil   Hynish
Thorbhais   Bay

8

A B C D E F

G H J K L

1

Sanna Point

Sanna Bay

Sanna Bay

Portuairk   Achnaha

4

MEALL I

Ardnamurchan
Point

Achosnich

B8007

2

236
Bagh a Chaisteil
(Castlebay)
Loch Baghasdail
(Lochboisdale)

236

Eilean Mòr

Rudha
Mòr

Rudha
Sgor-innis

342
BEINN
NA SEILG

Kilch

i

Bousd   Sorisdale

Ormsaigmore

3

*Cliad
Bay*

B8072

Ardmore Point

ch
iad

B8071

ost

Sorne
Point

Glengorm Castle

Quinish Point

Arinagour

COLL

Coll - Oban

To

mory

i

4

292
'S AIRDE
BEINN

Eilean
Ornsay

nd

Caliach Point

Dervaig

Achnadrish Lodge

B8073

444
SPEINNE

5

Calgary

5

Loch Frisa

Calgary Bay

Ensay

342
CÀRN MÒR

Treshnish Point

Rudh' a' Chaoil

Burg

390
CNOC AN DÀ CHINN

Fanmore

6

Ballygown

Fladda

Loch

Eas Fors (Waterfall)

3

Lunga

**TRESHNISH
ISLES**

Gometra

226

Tuath

19

BE
NAN

Oskamull

7

ULVA

Bac Mòr or Dutchmans Cap

Eorsa

Bac Beag

Little Colonsay

Inch Kenneth
*Inchkenneth Chapel
(ruin)*

B8035 17

Staffa

*Loch na Keal,
Isle of Mull*

Balnahard

8

Fingal's Cave

226

G H J K L M

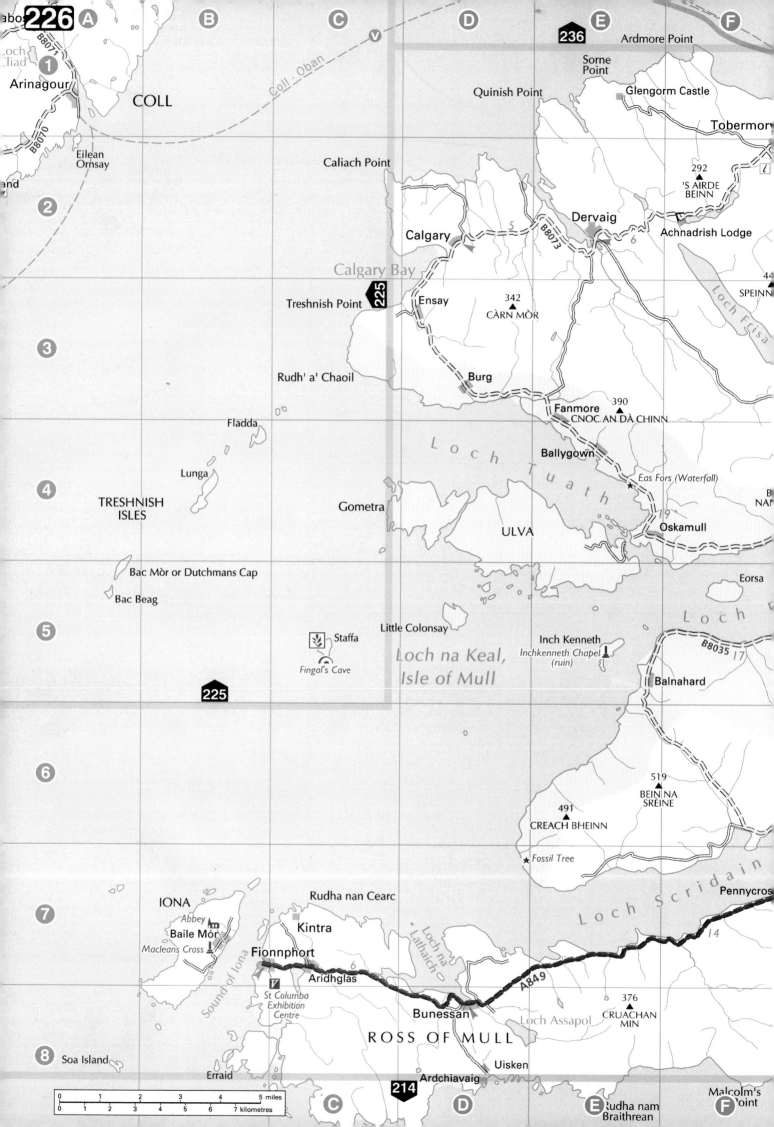

A B C D E F

1

COLL

Arinagour

Eilean
Ornsay

and

2

Caliach Point

236 Ardmore Point

Sorne
Point

Quinish Point

Glengorm Castle

Tobermor

292
'S AIRDE
BEINN

i

Dervaig

Calgary

B8073

Achnadrish Lodge

Calgary Bay

Treshnish Point 225 Ensay

44
SPEINN

Loch Frisa

342
CÀRN MÒR

3

Rudh' a' Chaoil

Burg

Fanmore

390
CNOC AN DÀ CHINN

Fladda

Ballygown

Eas Fors (Waterfall)

B
NAI

Loch Tuath

Lunga

4

TRESHNISH
ISLES

Gometra

ULVA

Oskamull

19

Bac Mòr or Dutchmans Cap

Eorsa

Bac Beag

Loch

5

Little Colonsay

Staffa

Inch Kenneth

Inchkenneth Chapel
(ruin)

B8035 17

Fingal's Cave

Loch na Keal,
Isle of Mull

Balnahard

225

6

519
BEIN NA
SRÈINE

491
CREACH BHEINN

Fossil Tree

Loch Scridain

Pennycros

7

IONA

Rudha nan Cearc

Abbey

Baile Mòr

Kintra

Macleans Cross

Fionnphort

Loch na Lathaich

A849

14

Aridhglas

St Columba
Exhibition
Centre

Bunessan

376
CRUACHAN
MIN

Loch Assapol

ROSS OF MULL

8

Soa Island

Erraid

Uisken

Ardchiavaig

214

Malcolm's
Point

Rudha nam
Braithrean

0 1 2 3 4 5 miles
0 1 2 3 4 5 6 7 kilometres

C D E F

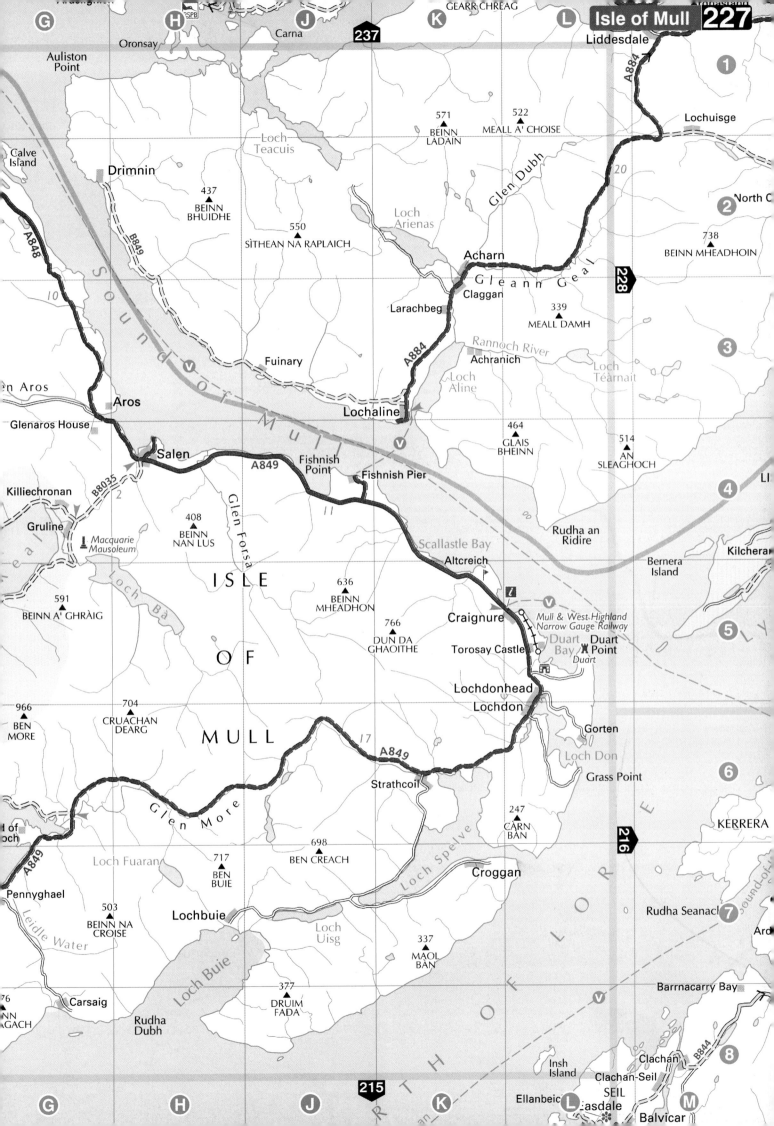

G · H · J · 237 · K · L · 1

GEARR CHREAG

Liddesdale

Oronsay

Carna

Auliston
Point

Lochuisge

A884

1

571 ▲
BEINN
LADAIN

522 ▲
MEALL A' CHOISE

2 North C

Calve
Island

Loch
Teacuis

Glen Dubh

20

Drimnin

437 ▲
BEINN
BHUIDHE

738 ▲
BEINN MHEADHOIN

B849

Loch
Arienas

A848

550 ▲
SÌTHEAN NA RAPLAICH

Acharn

Gleann Geal

228

2

n Aros

10

Fuinary

Larachbeg

Claggan

Rannoch River

339 ▲
MEALL DAMH

3

Aros

Sound of Mull

Achranich

Loch
Téarnait

Glenaros House

Loch
Aline

Salen

A849

Fishnish
Point

Lochaline

464 ▲
GLAIS
BHEINN

514 ▲
AN
SLEAGHOCH

4

Killiechronan

B8035

2

Fishnish Pier

Gruline

Macquarie
Mausoleum

408 ▲
BEINN
NAN LUS

Glen Forsa

11

Scallastle Bay

Rudha an
Ridire

Bernera
Island

Kilchera

5

Loch Bà

ISLE

Altcreich

i

Craignure

Mull & West Highland
Narrow Gauge Railway

V

591 ▲
BEINN A' GHRÀIG

636 ▲
BEINN
MHEADHON

766 ▲
DUN DA
GHAOITHE

Torosay Castle

Duart
Bay

Duart
Point

Duart

OF

Lochdonhead

966 ▲
BEN
MORE

704 ▲
CRUACHAN
DEARG

Lochdon

Gorten

MULL

247 ▲
CÀRN
BÀN

Strathcoil

A849

17

Loch Don

Grass Point

6

Glen More

Loch Fuaran

717 ▲
BEN
BUIE

698 ▲
BEN CREACH

Loch Spelve

216

KERRERA

d of
och

A849

Croggan

Rudha Seanacl

7

Pennyghael

503 ▲
BEINN NA
CROISE

Lochbuie

Loch
Uisg

337 ▲
MAOL
BÀN

Ard

Leidle Water

Carsaig

Rudha
Dubh

Loch
Buie

377 ▲
DRUIM
FADA

Barrnacarry Bay

V

76
NN
GACH

Insh
Island

Clachan

B844

8

Clachan-Seil

SEIL

G · H · J · 215 · K · L · Easdale · M · Balvicar

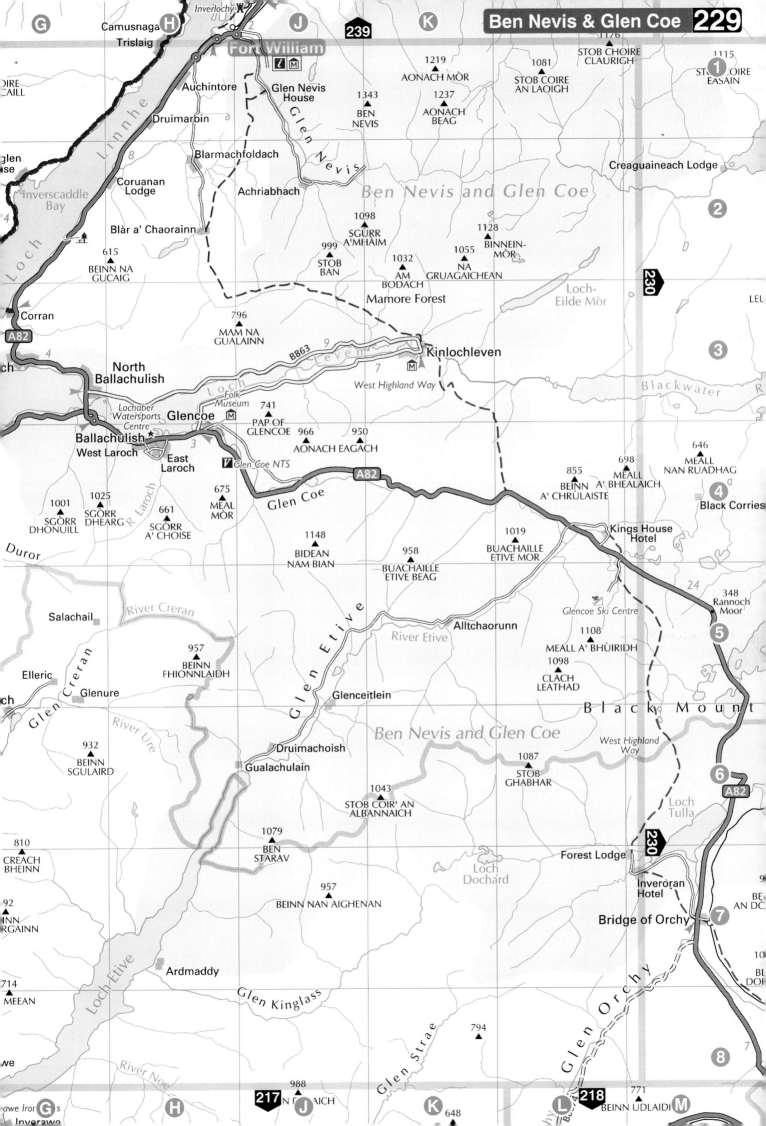

G H J 239 K

Camusnaga
Trislaig

Inverlochy

Fort William

Auchintore

Glen Nevis House

Druimarbin

Glen Nevis

Blarmachfoldach

Achriabhach

Ben Nevis and Glen Coe

1219
AONACH MÒR

1176
STOB CHOIRE
CLAURIGH

1115
STOB COIRE
EASÀIN

1
1081
STOB COIRE
AN LAOIGH

1343
BEN
NEVIS

1237
AONACH
BEAG

Creaguaineach Lodge

DOIRE
CAILL

Linnhe

2

glen
se

Inverscaddle
Bay

Loch

Coruanan
Lodge

Blàr a' Chaorainn

615
BEINN NA
GUCAIG

4

Corran

A82

4

1098
SGURR
A'MHAIM

999
STOB
BAN

1032
AM
BODACH

1055
NA
GRUAGAICHEAN

1128
BINNEIN-
MÒR

Mamore Forest

Loch-
Eilde Mòr

230

LEU

3

796
MAM NA
GUALAINN

B863

9

Leven

Kinlochleven

7

West Highland Way

Blackwater

North
Ballachulish

Loch

Folk
Museum

Lochaber
Watersports
Centre

Glencoe

Ballachulish

West Laroch

East
Laroch

741
PAP OF
GLENCOE

Glen Coe NTS

966
AONACH EAGACH

950

855
BEINN
A' CHRULAISTE

698
MEALL
A' BHEALAICH

646
MEALL
NAN RUADHAG

4

Black Corries

R Laroch

1001
SGÒRR
DHONUILL

1025
SGÒRR
DHEARG

661
SGÒRR
A' CHOISE

675
MEALL
MÒR

Glen Coe

A82

1019
BUACHAILLE
ETIVE MÒR

Kings House
Hotel

Duror

1148
BIDEAN
NAM BIAN

958
BUACHAILLE
ETIVE BEAG

24

348
Rannoch
Moor

5

River Creran

Salachail

Glen Etive

Glencoe Ski Centre

1108
MEALL A' BHÙIRIDH

Elleric

957
BEINN
FHIONNLAIDH

Alltchaorunn

River Etive

1098
CLACH
LEATHAD

Glen Creran

Glenure

Glenceitlein

Black Mount

ch

River Ure

Ben Nevis and Glen Coe

West Highland Way

932
BEINN
SGULAIRD

Druimachoish

Gualachulain

1087
STOB
GHABHAR

Loch
Etive

Glen

810
CREACH
BHEINN

1043
STOB COIR' AN
ALBANNAICH

Forest Lodge

230

Loch
Tulla

92
NN
RGAINN

1079
BEN
STARAV

Loch
Dochard

Inveroran
Hotel

BE
AN DO

Ardmaddy

957
BEINN NAN AIGHENAN

Bridge of Orchy

7

714
MEEAN

Glen Kinglass

Glen Strae

794

Glen Orchy

8

River Noe

988

awe Iron s
Inverawe

G H 217 J AICH K 648 L 218 218 M
771
BEINN UDLAIDH

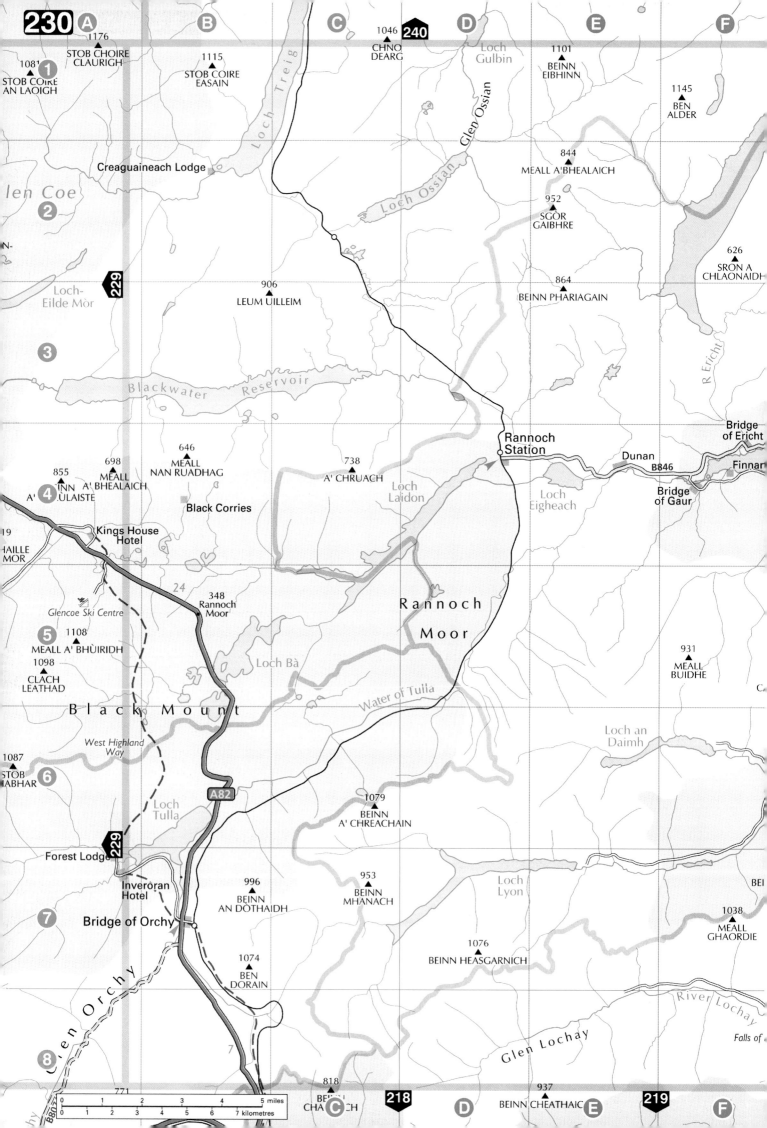

A | B | C | D | E | F

1176 ▲
STOB CHOIRE
CLAURIGH

1115 ▲
STOB COIRE
EASAIN

1046 ▲
CHNO
DEARG

Loch
Gulbin

1101 ▲
BEINN
EIBHINN

1081 ▲
STOB COIRE
AN LAOIGH

1

1145 ▲
BEN
ALDER

Creaguaineach Lodge

Glen Ossian

844 ▲
MEALL A'BHEALAICH

len Coe

2

Loch Ossian

952 ▲
SGOR
GAIBHRE

626 ▲
SRON A
CHLAONAIDH

Loch-
Eilde Mòr

229

906 ▲
LEUM UILLEIM

864 ▲
BEINN PHARIAGAIN

3

Blackwater   Reservoir

Bridge
of Ericht

646 ▲
MEALL
NAN RUADHAG

738 ▲
A' CHRUACH

Rannoch
Station

Dunan

B846

Finnar

698 ▲
MEALL
A' BHEALAICH

855 ▲

Loch
Laidon

Loch
Eigheach

Bridge
of Gaur

R Ericht

INN
ULAISTE

4

A'

Black Corries

19

Kings House
Hotel

Ra n n o c h

931 ▲
MEALL
BUIDHE

HAILLE
MOR

Mo o r

24

348
Rannoch
Moor

Glencoe Ski Centre

1108 ▲
MEALL A' BHÙIRIDH

5

Loch Bà

1098 ▲
CLACH
LEATHAD

B l a c k   M o u n t

Water of Tulla

Loch an
Daimh

*West Highland
Way*

1087 ▲
STOB
ABHAR

6

A82

1079 ▲
BEINN
A' CHREACHAIN

Loch
Tulla

229

Forest Lodge

Inveroran
Hotel

996 ▲
BEINN
AN DÒTHAIDH

953 ▲
BEINN
MHANACH

Loch
Lyon

BEI

1038 ▲
MEALL
GHAORDIE

7

Bridge of Orchy

1076 ▲
BEINN HEASGARNICH

1074 ▲
BEN
DORAIN

Gle n   Lochay

G le n   O r c h y

8

771

818 ▲
BEIN
CHA

River Lochy

Falls of

937 ▲
BEINN CHEATHAIC

B80

0   1   2   3   4   5 miles
0 1 2 3 4 5 6 7 kilometres

C

D

E

F

G **H** **J** **241** **K**

A' MHARCONAICH

Loch Fri

1008
▲
BEINN UDLAMAIN

991
▲
SGAIRNEACH
MHOR

Dalnaspidal

Loch Garry

Glen Garry

20

Dalnacardoch

A9

1

Bruar Water

491
▲
CRAIG
BHAGAILTEACH

Glen

2

Cla Donnachaidh

Loch Con

Loch Errochty

841
▲
BEINN
MHOLACH

G

Trinafour

Glen

Calvine

Bruar

Pitagowan

232 Struan

Blair

B847

Errochty

892
▲
BEINN
A' CHUALLAICH

511
▲
TORR
DUBH

Tay Forest Park

TU

3

Tressait

B8019

Queen's View

Tay Forest Park

7 B846

Loch Tummel

Loch Tumm

ichonan

16

Loch Rannoch

Kinloch
Rannoch

Drumchastle

R Tummel

Dunalastair

Dunalastair
Water

Tummel
Bridge

Foss

Frenich

13

Tay Forest Park

Inverhadden

Tempar

Daloist

Carie

Camghouran

780
▲
FARRAGON
HILL

4

Tay Forest Park

780
▲
MEALL
TAIRNEACHAN

De

Loch
Glassie

Tay Forest Park

1081
▲
SCHIEHALLION

Glengoulandie
Deer Park

B846

Loch Rannoch and Glen Lyon

745
▲
MEALL A' MHUIC

824
▲
BEINN
DEARG

1027
▲
CÀRN
GORM

1042
▲
CÀRN
MAIRG

14

Menzies

5

Camserney

We

Coshieville

Dull

G

Keltneyburn

Dewars

en Lyon

Bridge of Balgie

River Lyon

Fortingall

Tay
Forest
Park

River Tay

Croftmoraig
Stone Circle

6

Fearnan

Kenmore

A827

232

E

780
▲
MEALL
LUAIDHE

924
▲
MEALL A' CHOIRE
LEITH

1116
▲
MEALL
GARBH

1000
▲
MEALL
GREIGH

Acharn

The Crannog
Centre

N

DIGHREAG

1214
▲
BEN LAWERS

Loch Tay

Leckbuie

713
▲
BEINN
BHREAC

Glen Quaic

MEAL

7

Lochan na
Làirige

Lawers

25

A

River Quaich

B

864
▲
SRÒN A' CHAOINEIDH

802
▲
MEALL NAM
FUARAN

Ben Lawers

Ben Lawers
Mountain NTS

A827

Milton
Morenish

Morenish

Ardeonaig
Hotel

L

8

River Almond

Killin

Finlarig

Dochart

Breadalbane
Folklore Centre

G **H** **219** **J** **K** **220** **L** **M**

682

879
▲
CREAG
UCHDAG

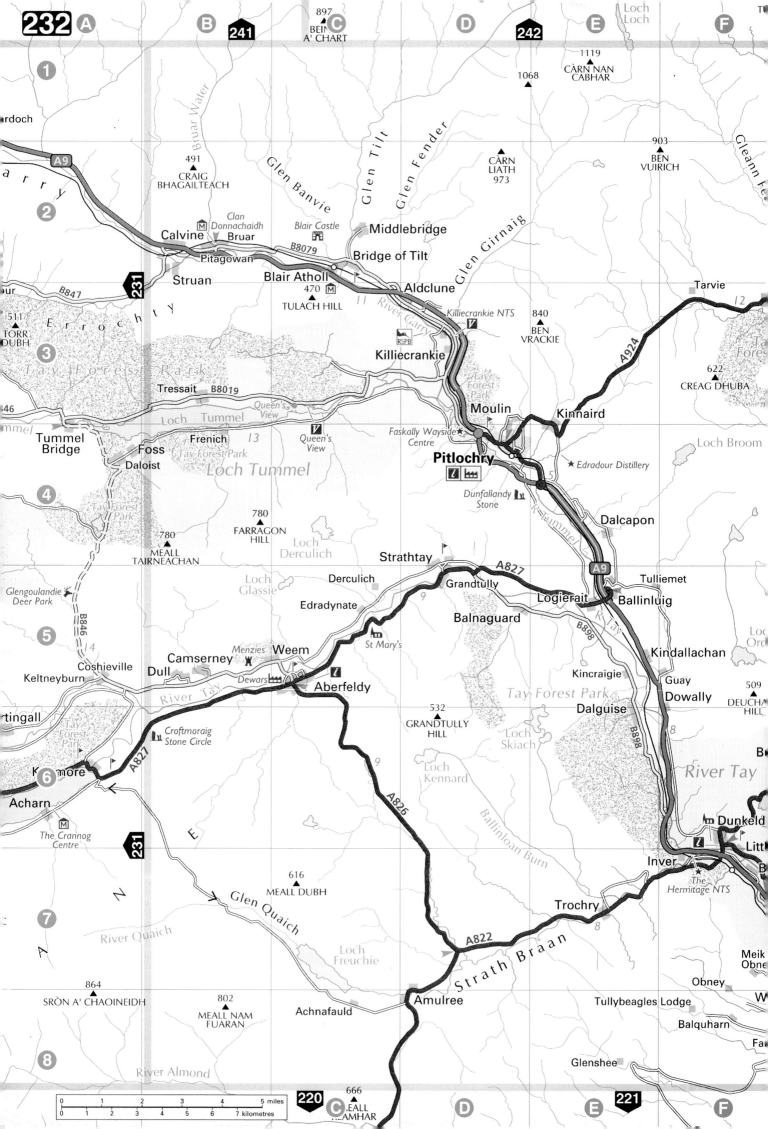

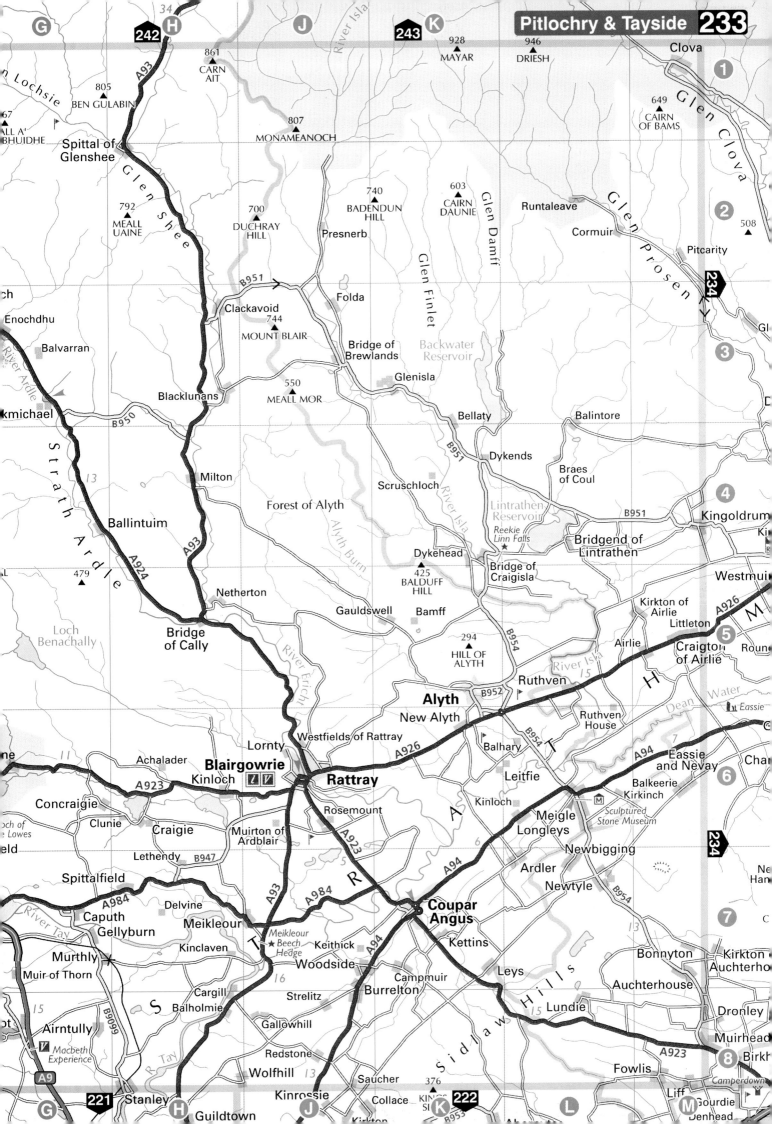

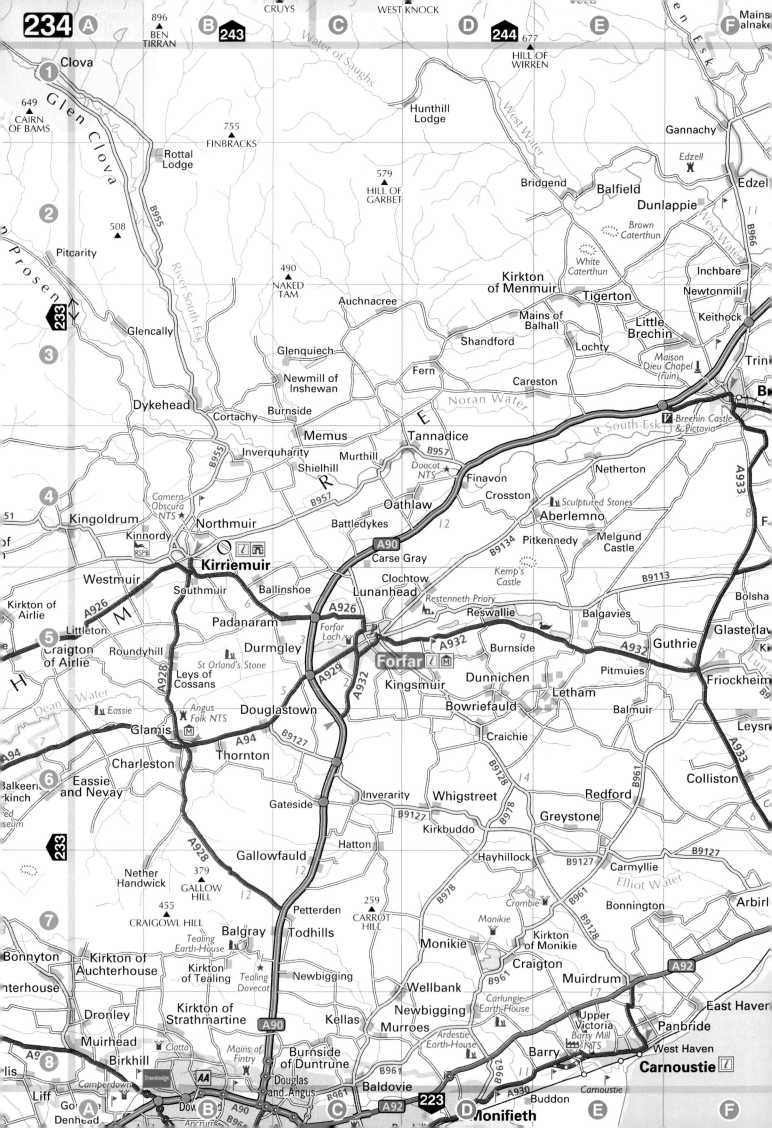

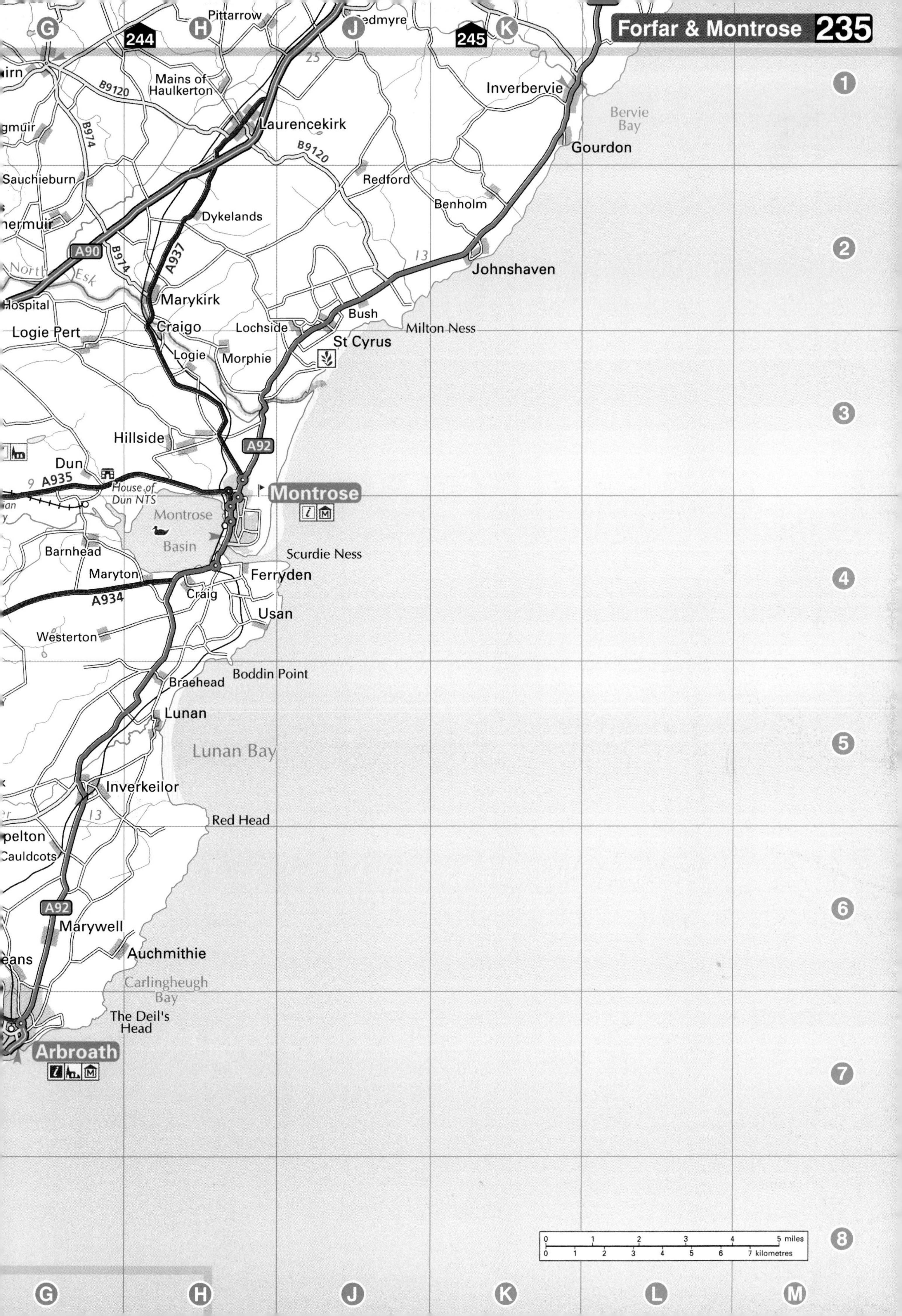

G H J K

Pittarrow

edmyre

Inverbervie

1

Mains of
Haulkerton

Bervie
Bay

B9120

Gourdon

Laurencekirk

B9120

Redford

2

Dykelands

Benholm

A90

Johnshaven

B974

North Esk

Marykirk

Bush

Milton Ness

Hospital

Craigo

Lochside

St Cyrus

Logie Pert

Logie

Morphie

3

Hillside

A92

Dun

A935

House of
Dun NTS

Montrose

9

Montrose
Basin

Scurdie Ness

4

Barnhead

Maryton

Ferryden

Craig

A934

Usan

Westerton

Boddin Point

Braehead

Lunan

5

Lunan Bay

Inverkeilor

13

Red Head

pelton

Cauldcots

6

A92

Marywell

Auchmithie

eans

Carlingheugh
Bay

The Deil's
Head

Arbroath

7

| 0 | 1 | 2 | 3 | 4 | 5 miles |
| 0 | 1 | 2 | 3 | 4 | 5 | 6 | 7 kilometres |

8

A   B   C   D   E   F

MULLACH MÒR

Rudha na Roinne

A Bhrideanach

246

Kinloch

Loch Scresort

570
ORVAL

RÙM

810
ASKIVAL

763
SGÙRR NAN GILLEAN

The Small Isles

Rudha nam Meirleach

Sound of Rum

Bay of Laig

Cleadale

299
AN CRUACHAN

Rudha an Fhasaidh

Laig

EIGG

Kildo

393
AN SGÙRR

Sandavor

Eilean nan Each

MUCK

Sound of Eigg

Eilean Chathastail

Port Mor

Sanna Point

Sanna Bay

Sanna Bay

Portuairk

Achnaha

Ardnamurchan Point

Achosnich

MEALL

B8007

342
BEINN NA SEILG

Kilc

Ormsaigmore

Eilean Mòr

Bagh a Chaisteil (Castlebay)
Loch Baghasdail (Lochboisdale)

Rudha Mòr

Rudha Sgor-innis

225

Bousd

Sorisdale

Cliad Bay

B8072

abost

B8071

Loch Cliad

0   1   2   3   4   5 miles
0   1   2   3   4   5   6   7 kilometres

Coll – Oban

Arinagour

Ardmore Point

Sorne P

226

Glasgow Castle

A   B   C   D   E   F

KNOYD

G **H** **J** **v** **K**

247

1

Sleat

Ard Thurinish

Point of Sleat

Inverie Bay

Dub

Rudha Raonuill

Courteachan

Mallaig

Mallaigvaig

Marine World

547

CÀRN A'GHOBHAIR

Loch Nevis

854

BEINN BH

Glasnacardoch Bay

Loch an Nostaire

437

SGÙRR BHUIDHE

Stoul

2

lesmor

Beoraidbeg

Morar

Bracora

Bracorina

Tarbet

238 Swordland

Glenancross

B8008

A830

Loch Morar

Lettermorar

Meoble

3

710

MEITH BH

Eilean Ighe

Bunacaimb

503

CÀRN A' MHÀDAIDH-RUAIDH

River Meoble

Back of Keppoch

Luinga Mhòr

Arisaig

Loch nan Ceall

600

SIDHEAN MÒR

10

Prince Charlie's Cairn

Kinlochnanuagh

Loch

Rudh' Arisaig

103

CRUACH DOIRE

Druimindarroch

Arisaig House

Loch nan Uamh

Polnish

Lochailort

4

Loch Eilt

Sound of Arisaig

Rudha Choalais

Ardnish

Peanmeanach

Loch Ailort

Inverailort

A861

877

ROIS-BHEINN

5

Smearisary

Glenuig

21

712

664

BEINN GAIRE

Eilean Shona

Rudha Aird Druimnich

Loch Moidart

Tioram

Kinlochmoidart

Glen Forsian

Loch

Ockle Point

Morar, Moidart and Ardnamurchan

239

Ardmolich

BEINN BHREAC

Glen Moidart

MOIDART

6

Loch S

Imory

Ockle

Ardtoe

B8044

Shielfoot

Dalnabreck

Glen Hurich

Glen Hurich

Branault

356

BEINN BHREAC

Kentra

Blain

Mingarrypark

228

Polloch

Loch Doilet

Arevegaig

ARDNAMURCHAN

437

Acharacle

Claish Moss

SUNAR

Loch Mudle

A861

846

BEINN RESIPOL

7

527

BEN HIANT

19

Glenbeg

Salen

Resipole

12

Loch Sunart

Glenborrodale

Laga

512

BEN LAGA

B8007

Loch

Glencripesdale

339

GEÀRR CHREAG

Camasine

Woodend

An

St

Ardslignish

RSPB

Carna

Camasachoire

Ardnastang

8

Oronsay

Auliston Point

Liddesdale

A884

G **H** 227 **J** **K** **L** **M**

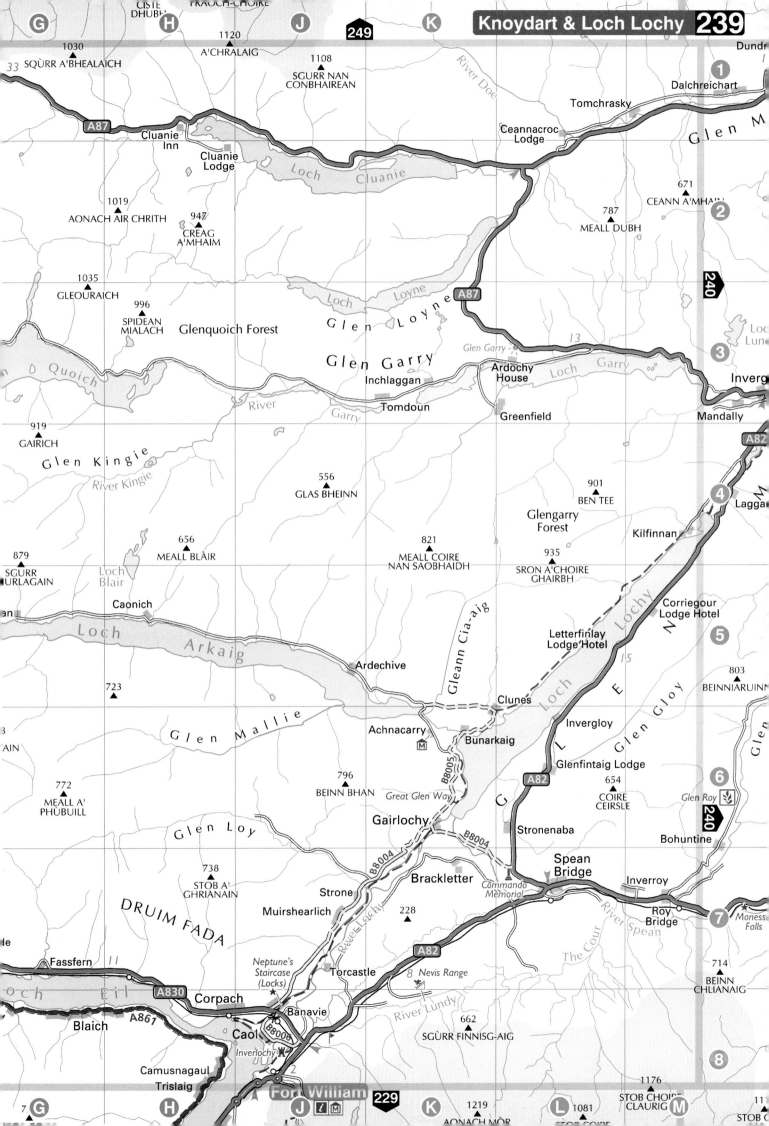

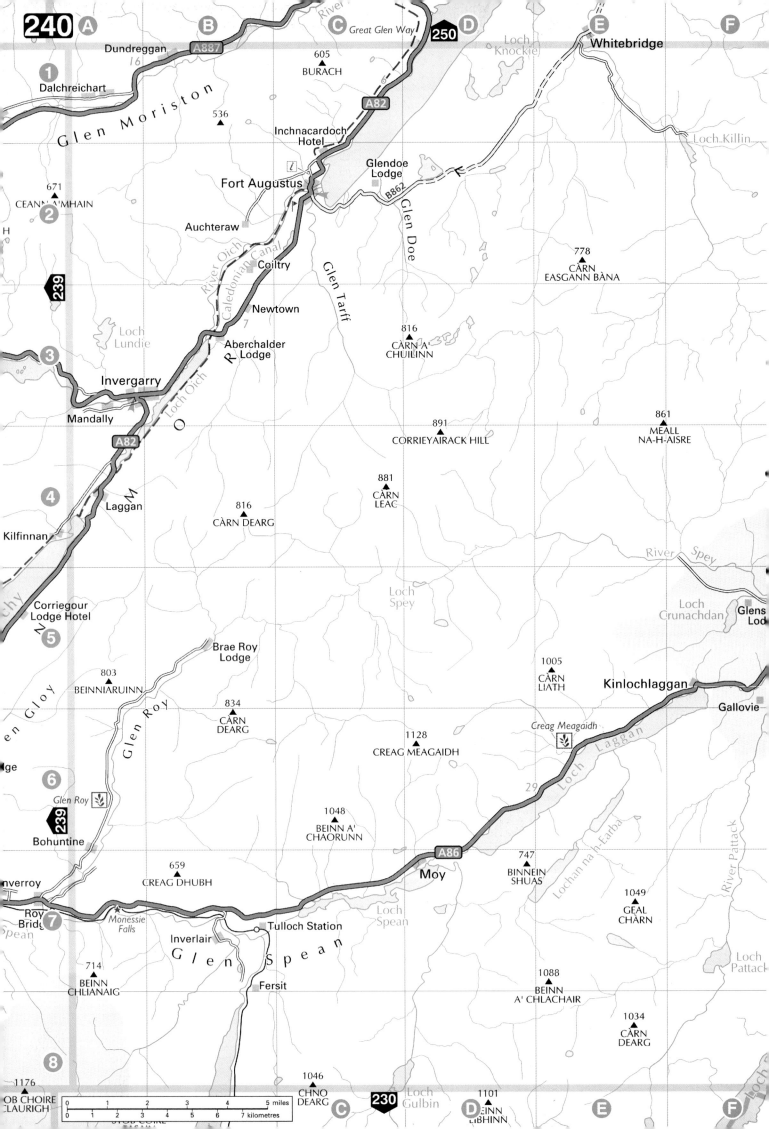

G   251 H   J   252

810
CÀRN NA SAOBHAIDHE

745
CNOC
FRAING

1

Avien

790
CÀRN COIRE
NA H-EASGAINN

824
GEAL-CHÀRN MÒR

Craigellachie

810
ÀRN NA
CHE MAOILE

River Eskin

729
CAIRN
DULNAN

Inve

Loch
Alvie

2

A9

813
CALPA
MÒR

B9152

M o n a d h l i a t h   M o u n t a i n s

Raitts Burn

B970

10

Kincraig

855
SGARAMAN
NAM FIADH

878
CÀRN AN
FHREICEADAIN

Highland
Wildlife Park

Loch
Insh

242

Feshiebridge

3

928
A CHAILLEACH

Highland
Folk

Farr

Insh

941
CÀRN
BÀN

M

Kingussie
Pitmain

Lynchat

Inveruglass

842
CÀRN AN
LETH-CHOIN

Turus Tim

M

RSPB

Insh
Marshes

Drumguish

Glen Feshie

River Feshie

Newtonmore

A9

Ruthven

Ruthven
Barracks

4

12

Ralia

Glentromie
Lodge

River Tromie

Glen Markie

A86

Glentruim
House

627
MEALL
BUIDHE

Glenfeshie
Lodge

Blargie Laggan   Balgowan

Phoines

5

MULLAC
A BH

A86

Catlodge

Etteridge

593
GARBH-
MHEALL MÒR

857
CÀRN
DEARG MÒR

Glenfes

CK
IG

Strathmashie
House

Crubenmore

768
MEALLACH
MHÒR

15

Loch
Coaldair

A9

Loch na
Cuaich

6

9

A889

898
BAGHA-
CLOICHE

Loch an
t-Seilich

910
LEATHAD AN
TOABHAIN

Distillery

Glen Truim

242   R

Dalwhinnie

Gaick Forest

G

7

896
IEALL
UAIDH

941
CÀRN NA CAIM

Loch an Dùin

1007
BEINN
DEARG

1008
UDLAMAIN

769
CREAGAN
MÒR

926
GLAS
MHEALL MÒR

814
SRON A'
CHLEIRICH

8

975
A' MHARCONAICH

459
Drumochter
Summit

BEINN
A' CHART

G   Dalnaspida H   231 J   K   L   232 M

SGAIRNEACH

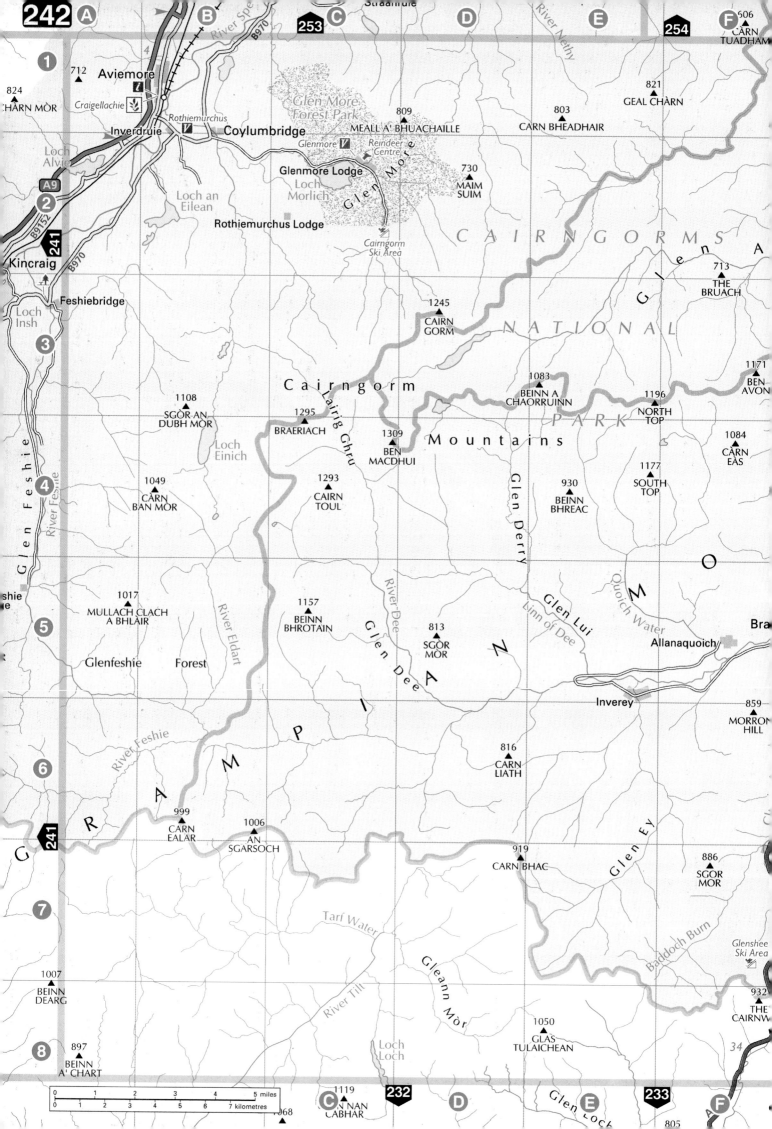

A **B** **253** **C** **D** **E** **254** **F**

1

▲ 712 Aviemore

824
▲ CHÀRN MÒR

i

Craigellachie

Rothiemurchus
Inverdruie

Coylumbridge

Glen More
Forest Park

809
▲ MEALL A' BHUACHAILLE

803
▲ CARN BHEADHAIR

821
▲ GEAL CHÀRN

606
▲ CÀRN
TUADHAM

Loch
Alvie

A9

2

B9152

Glenmore *i*

Reindeer
Centre

Glenmore Lodge

Loch
Morlich

730
▲ MAIM
SUIM

Loch an
Eilean

Rothiemurchus Lodge

C A I R N G O R M S

713
▲ THE
BRUACH

G l e n   A

241

Kincraig

B9170

Cairngorm
Ski Area

N A T I O N A L

3

Feshiebridge

Loch
Insh

1245
▲ CAIRN
GORM

1171
▲ BEN
AVON

Cairngorm

1083
▲ BEINN A
CHAORRUINN

1196
▲ NORTH
TOP

P A R K

1108
▲ SGÒR AN
DUBH MÒR

1295
▲ BRAERIACH

Lairig Ghru

M o u n t a i n s

1084
▲ CARN
EÀS

Loch
Einich

1309
▲ BEN
MACDHUI

1177
▲ SOUTH
TOP

4

1049
▲ CÀRN
BAN MÒR

1293
▲ CAIRN
TOUL

930
▲ BEINN
BHREAC

Glen Feshie

River Feshie

Glen Derry

M
O

5

1017
▲ MULLACH CLACH
A BHLÀIR

1157
▲ BEINN
BHROTAIN

River Dee

Glen Lui

Quoich Water

Linn of Dee

Bra

813
▲ SGÒR
MÒR

Allanaquoich

Glenfeshie   Forest

River Eldart

Glen Dee

A

N

P

I

Inverey

859
▲ MORRON
HILL

6

River Feshie

816
▲ CARN
LIATH

Glen Ey

A

M

241

999
▲ CARN
EALAR

1006
▲ AN
SGARSOCH

919
▲ CARN BHAC

886
▲ SGOR
MOR

R

G

7

Tarf Water

Glenshee
Ski Area

Baddoch Burn

1007
▲ BEINN
DEARG

River Tilt

Gleann Mòr

1050
▲ GLAS
TULAICHEAN

932
▲ THE
CAIRNW

8

897
▲ BEINN
A' CHART

Loch
Loch

0   1   2   3   4   5 miles
0 1 2 3 4 5 6   7 kilometres

1119
▲ N NAN
CABHAR

C **232** **D** Glen Loch **E** **233** **F**

068
▲

805

G Blairnamarrow
H
254
J
718
▲ THE SOCACH
Kirkton of Glenbuchat
Bellabeg
Strathdon
Forbestown
Glenkindie
Towie
1

637 Lecht Summit
Lecht Ski Area
Roughpark
A944
8
Heughhead
Boltenstone

792 ▲ CARN EALASAID
Garchory
A97
9
2

710 ▲ CRAIG VEANN
Milltown
Migvie
244
Corrachre

River Avon
Cock Bridge
Corgarff ✕
Corgarff
749 ▲ MONA GOWAN
Logie Coldstone
3

829 ▲ BROWN COW HILL
744 ▲ CARN A' BHACAIN
A939
872 ▲ MORVEN

Loch Builg
N
S
12
Candacraig
Cambus o' May
B9119
8
Loch

900 ▲ CULARDOCH
743 ▲ GEALLAIG HILL
Coilacriech
Bridge of Gairn
B972
Milton of Tullich
4 Tillyca

A
B976
Dee
River
Ballater
Pannanich Wells Hotel
B976

N T
Balmoral Castle
Crathie
Littlemill
i
531 ▲ BLACK CRAIG

618 ▲ MEALL GORM
Easter Balmoral
Balnacroft
B976
Birkhall

Inver
600 ▲ CREAG NAN GALL
596 ▲ THE COYLES OF MUICK
699 ▲ CAIRN LEUCHAN
5 7 ▲ CLACHAN YELL

Keiloch
A93
Glen Gelder
Glen Muick
River Muick
938 ▲ MOUNT KEEN

Balmoral Forest
1154 ▲ LOCHNAGAR
720 ▲ FASHEILACH
6
244

1045 ▲ CAIRN TAGGART
Loch Callater
Loch Muick
Spittal of Glenmuick
Glen Mark

996 ▲ BROAD CAIRN
832 ▲ EASTERBALLOCH
Inverm
7

1018 ▲ CÀRN AN TUIRC
831 ▲ LAIR OF ALDARARIE
Glen Lee
Loch Lee

1067 ▲ GLAS MAOL
Glen Doll
River Isla
739 ▲ CRUYS

928 ▲ MAYAR
946 DRI
896 ▲ BEN TIRRAN
8

G
H
233
J
K Clova
234
L
M
Water of Saug

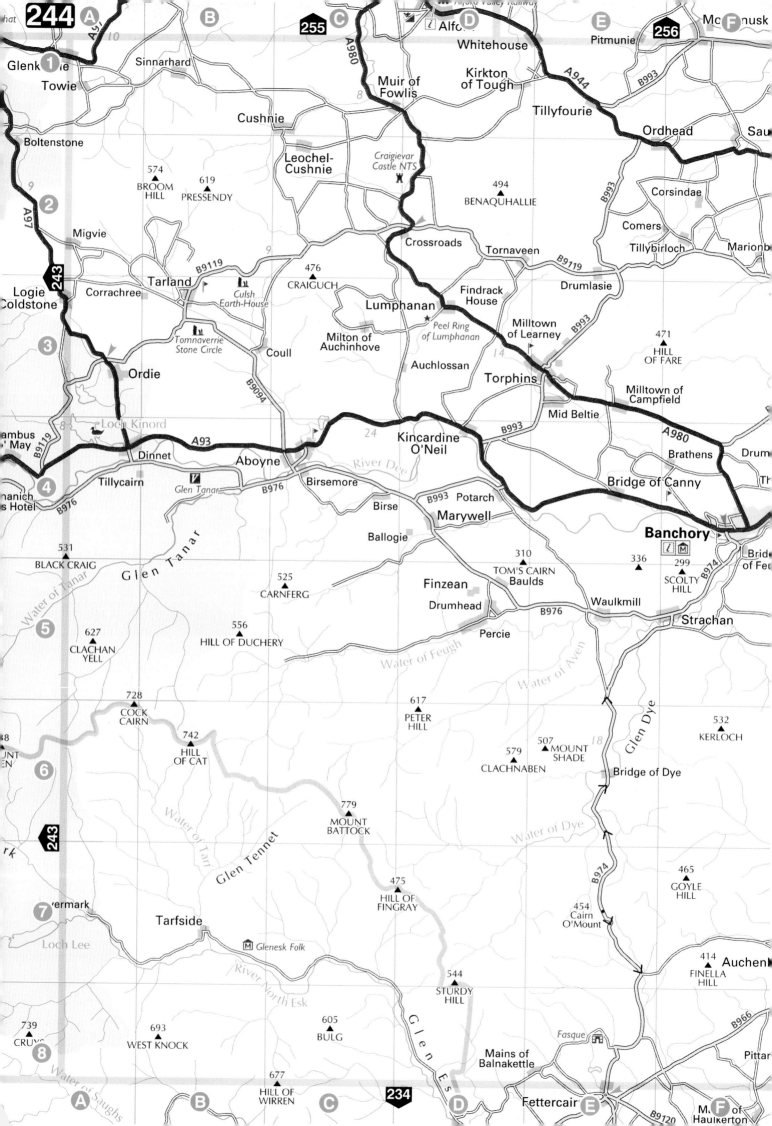

G H J K 256 257 K B9...

Kergy
Kintore
Cottown
Leylodge
Blackburn
Clinterty
Overton
Parkhill House
Blackdog
Dyce
Aberdeen
Stoneywood
Denmore
P+R
Bridge of Don
Kirkwall Lerwick
Lyne of Skene
Skene House
Millbuie
Buscksburn
Bankhead
Castle er NTS
Brimmond Hill
Northfield
Old Aberdeen
AA
unecht
Westhill
Kingswells
Kittybrewster
Kirkton of Skene
Kingsford
B9119
ABERDEEN
Travelodge
Garlogie
Carnie
Elrick
Ruthrieston
Torry
Nigg Bay
Echt
Redhill
Cullerlie Stone Circle
Easter Ord
Blacktop
Mannofield
Cults
Kincorth
AA
nderberry
Cullerlie
Benthoul
Bieldside
Banchory-Devenick
Nigg
Altens Haven
Hirn
Drum NTS
Craigton
Milltimber
Kingcausie
Charlestown
Cove Bay
Myrebird
Park
Peterculter
B9077
Marywell
Crathes NTS
A93
Maryculter
Hillside
Crathes
Durris
Denside
Auchlee
Findon
Portlethen
Cammachmore Bay
yal Deeside Railway
Woodlands
Cairngrassie
Downies
Crossroads
Elsick House
Cammachmore
Cookney
Newtonhill
A957
Netherley
Skateraw
MONGOUR
Muchalls
Doonie Point
A90
HILL OF TRUSTA
Mowtie
Garron Point
Stonehaven Bay
EACHIE HILL
Elfhill
Kirktown of Fetteresso
Stonehaven
Tannachie
Dunnottar
Goosecruives
New Mill
Crawton
Drumlithie
Temple of Fiddes
Trelong Bay
Glenbervie
Mondynes
Catterline
Kinneff
Todhead Point
Fordoun
B967
Arbuthnott
A92
Redmyre

G H 235 J K L M
Inverbervie

A B C 258 D E F

1

BHEAG

368
▲
BEINN NA
BOINEID

Harlosh
Island
Colbost
Point

Tarner
Island

Os

Bracadale

Coillore

Struan

Loch Bracadale

Ullinish
Lodge Hotel

Wiay

23

Loch Duagrich

Mug

O
F

2

Idrigill
Point

Oronsay

Portnalong

Fiskavaig

Rudha nan Clach

Loch Harport

B8009

Fernilea

Drynoch

A863

S

439
▲
ROINEVAL

369
▲
ARNAVAL

Carbost

Merkadale

Glen Drynoc

3

Talisker
Bay

Talisker

447
▲
BEINN
BHREAC

Glen Eynort

Grula

369
▲
BEINN BHREA

4

Loch Eynort

434
▲
AN CRUACHIN

Glenbrittle House

Bualintur

974
▲
SGÙR
A' GHEAD

C u i

10

SGÙ
ALASD

5

Loch Brittle

Rudh' an Dùnain

225
▲
CEANN NA BEINNE

Soay Sound

6

Rudh
Aongha

7

CANNA

210
▲
CÀRN A' GHAILL

A'Chill

Garrisdale Point

Canna
Harbour

Rudha
Shamhnan Insir

Sanday

C
U
I
L
L
I
N

8

Sound of Canna

302
▲
MULLACH
MÒR

Rudha na Roi

0 1 2 3 4 5 miles
0 1 2 3 4 5 6 7 kilometres

A Bhrideanach

236

570
▲
ORVAL

Kinloch

Loch
Scresort

A B C D E F

G   H   J   259

412
BEN
TIANAVAIG

444
DÙN CAAN

1

A87
agill

9
Camastianavaig
Tianavaig
Bay
Ollach
Clachan
Oskaig

Rudha na' Leac

Toscaig

River Toscaig

B883
Inverarish

310
BEINN NA LEAC

Caolas Mòr

2

The Braes
444
BEN LEE
Peinchorran
V
Suisnish
Point
Eyre
Point

Eilean
Meadhonach
Eilean
Mòr

CROWLIN ISLANDS

Port-an-Eor

Drumbu

Sconser

SCALPAY

248

3

gachan

773
GLAMAIG

67
Longay

Badicaul

A87
Loch Ainort
17
Dunan
Luib

Caolas Scalpay

396
MULLACH
NA CARN

27
Pabay

Kyle of Lochalsh
Skye Bridge
Toll

965
AN GILLEAN

564
GLAS BHEIN
MHÒRN
Luib Folk
M

Corry
Broadford
Bay
Waterloo

Lower
Breakish

A87
Kyleakin

The Cuillin Hills

732
BEINN NA
CAILLICH
708
BEINN
DEORG MHÒR
Broadford
Harrapool

Skulamus

Upper
Breakish

9

732
SGURR NA
COINNICH

4

Hills

927
BLAVEN

B8083
Torrin
14

B8083

Loch
Coruisk

Loch na
Crèitheach

A851

605
BEN ASLÀK

894
GARS
HEINN

Kirkibost

300
BEINN
NAN CARN
Heast

561
BEINN NA
SEAMRAIG

5

Loch
Slapin

9

Loch
Scavaig

344
BEN
MEABOST

Suisnish

Drumfearn

Sandaig
Island

NN
EAC

Rudha
Suisnish

Loch Eishort

Duisdalemore

Loch na Dal

6

-chlach

Elgol

Glasnakille

298
SGORACH
BREAC

Isleornsay

Ornsay

Rudh' Ard
Slisneach

OAY

Strathaird
Point

Tokavaig

Ord River

17

238

Tarskavaig

Achnacloich

Loch nam
Uamph

Teangue

Knock

Inverguser

Tarskavaig Bay

Ferrindonald

Knock
Bay

7

Kilmore

Kilbeg

Airor

S

Clan Donald
Ardvasar
Calligarry

A851
Armadale

O
U
N
D

O
F

S
L
E
A
T

Sandaig

518
DRUIM NA
CLUAIN-AIRIDHE

Aird of
Sleat

Sandaig Bay

8

Ard
Thurinish
237

Point
of Sleat

V

Rudha
Raonuill

Inverie
Bay

G   H   J   K   L   M

Courteachan

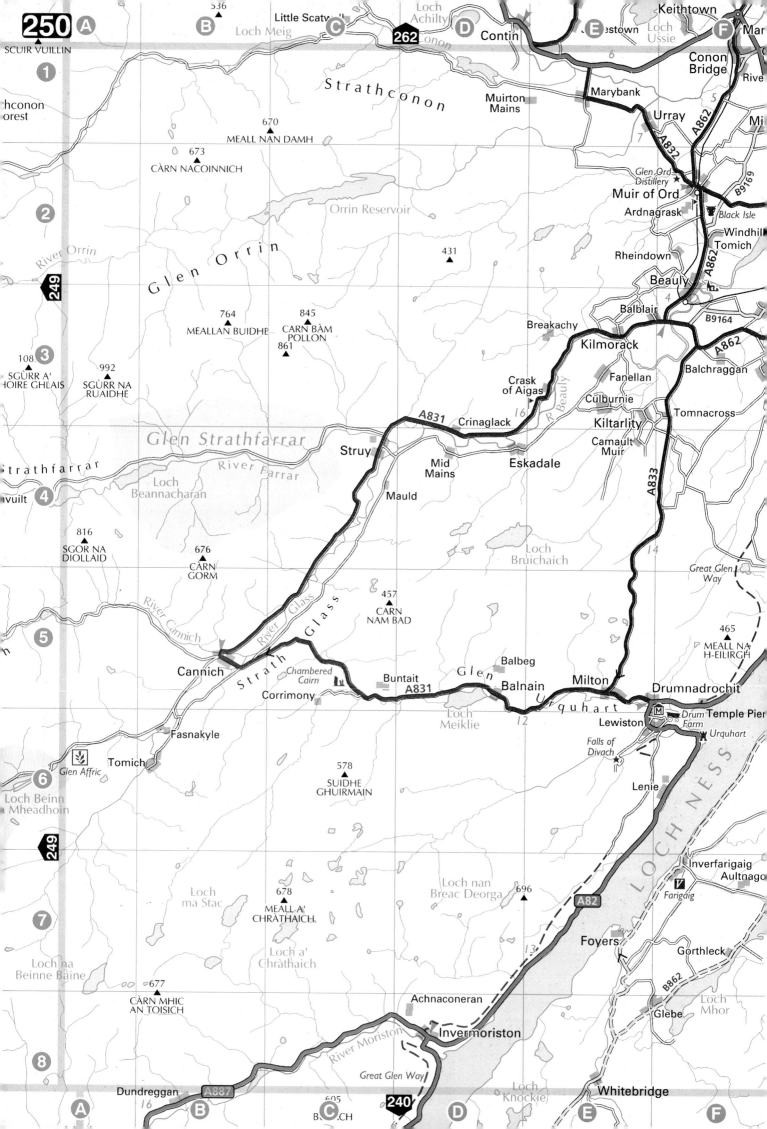

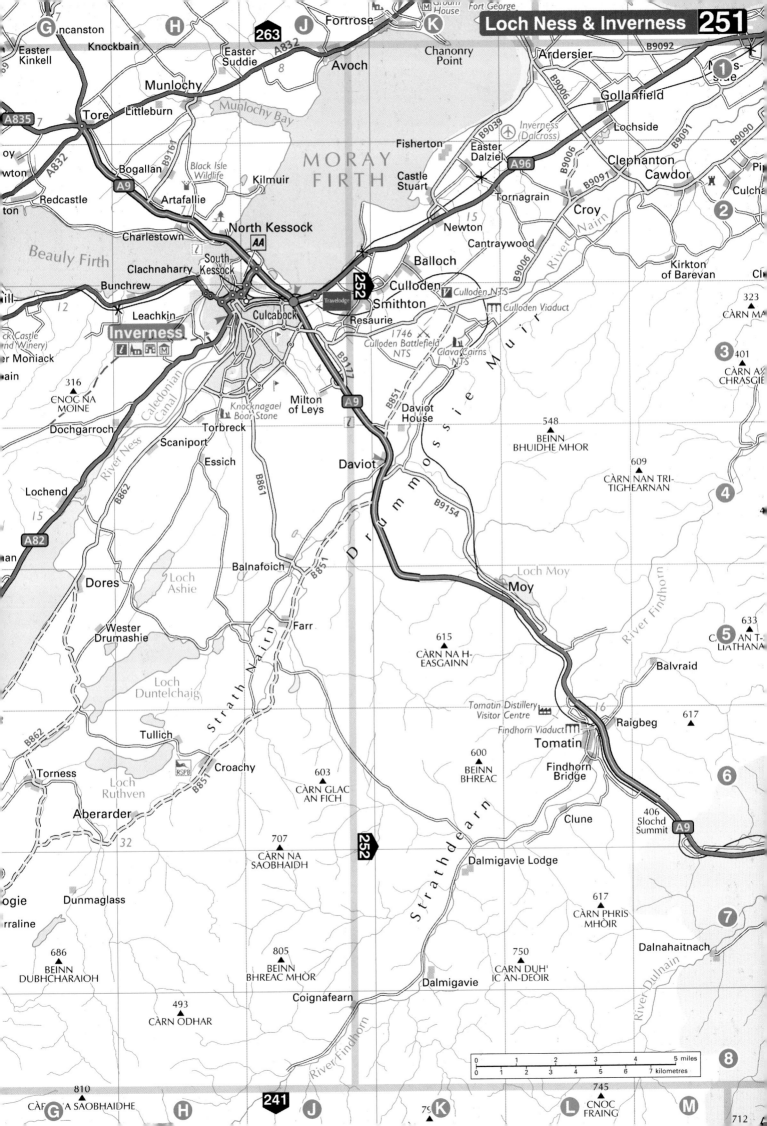

G **H** **J** **K**

Fort George
Fortrose
Groam House

Easter Kinkell
Knockbain
Easter Suddie
A832
263
Avoch
Chanonry Point
Ardersier
B9092
B9006
Gollanfield
Lochside
B9091
B9090
Clephanton
Cawdor
Culcha
Pi

Munlochy
Littleburn
Munlochy Bay
MORAY FIRTH
Fisherton
Inverness (Dalcross)
Easter Dalziel
A96
Tornagrain
Croy
River Nairn
Kirkton of Barevan

Tore
Bogallan
A9
Black Isle Wildlife
Kilmuir
Castle Stuart
Newton
Cantraywood
B9006
2

A835
Redcastle
Artafallie
Charlestown
North Kessock
AA
Balloch
Culloden
Culloden NTS
Culloden Viaduct
Clava Cairns NTS
BEINN BHUIDHE MHOR 548
3 401
CÀRN A' CHRASGIE
323
CÀRN MA

Beauly Firth
Clachnaharry
South Kessock
Bunchrew
Leachkin
252
Smithton
Resaurie
Travelodge
1746 Culloden Battlefield NTS

Inverness
Culcabock
Drummossie Muir
B9177
B851
Daviot House
609 CÀRN NAN TRI-TIGHEARNAN
4

CNOC NA MOINE 316
Dochgarroch
Torbreck
Scaniport
Essich
Knocknagael Boar Stone
Milton of Leys
A9
Daviot
B9154

Caledonian Canal
River Ness
B862
B861
Lochend
A82
Loch Ashie
Balnafoich
Loch Moy
Moy
River Findhorn

Dores
Wester Drumashie
B851
Farr
CÀRN NA H-EASGAINN 615
633
CA AN T-LIATHANA
5

Loch Duntelchaig
Strath Nairn
Balvraid
Tomatin Distillery Visitor Centre
Findhorn Viaduct
Raigbeg
617

Tullich
RSPB
Croachy
CÀRN GLAC AN FICH 603
BEINN BHREAC 600
Tomatin
Findhorn Bridge

Torness
Loch Ruthven
Aberarder
32
CÀRN NA SAOBHAIDH 707
252
Clune
Slochd Summit 406
A9
6

Dunmaglass
Dalmigavie Lodge
CÀRN PHRÌS MHÒIR 617
7

ogie
rraline
Strathdearn
Dalnahaitnach
River Dulnain

810
CÀF A SAOBHAIDHE
BEINN DUBHCHARAIOH 686
BEINN BHREAC MHÒR 805
CÀRN DUH' IC AN-DEOIR 750
Dalmigavie
Coignafearn

493 CÀRN ODHAR

0 — 5 miles
0 — 7 kilometres

8

G **H** **J** **K** **L** **M**
241
79
CNOC FRAING 745
712

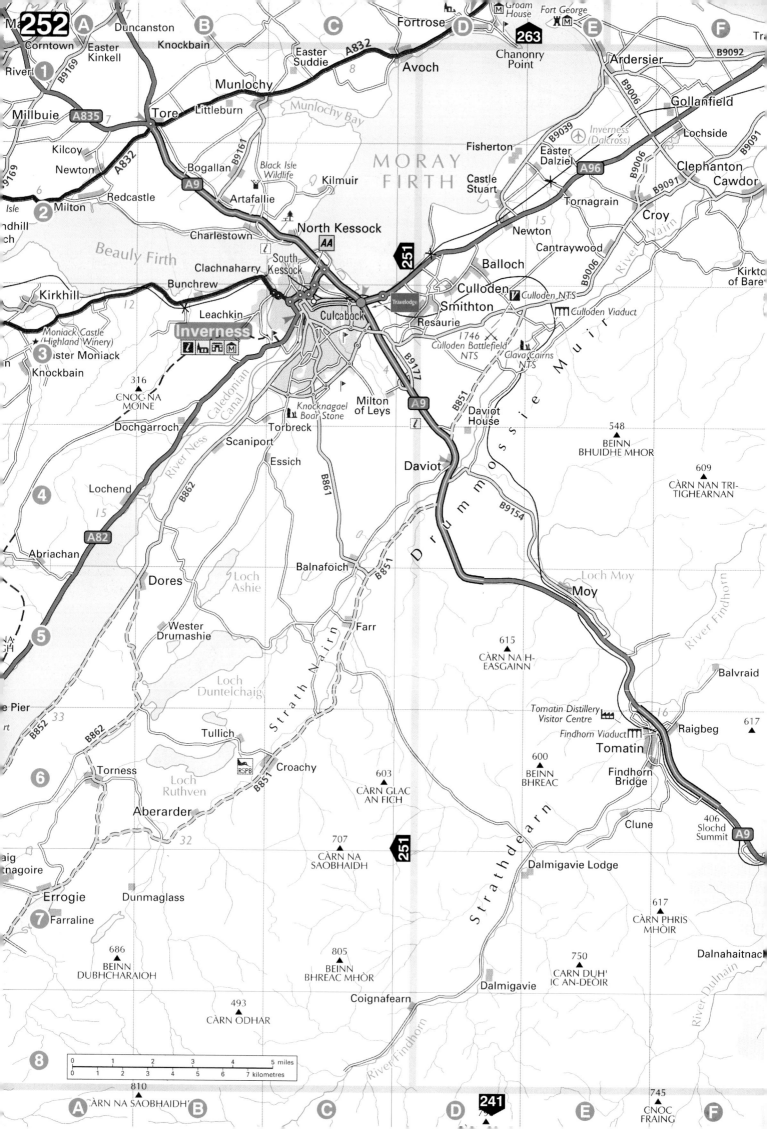

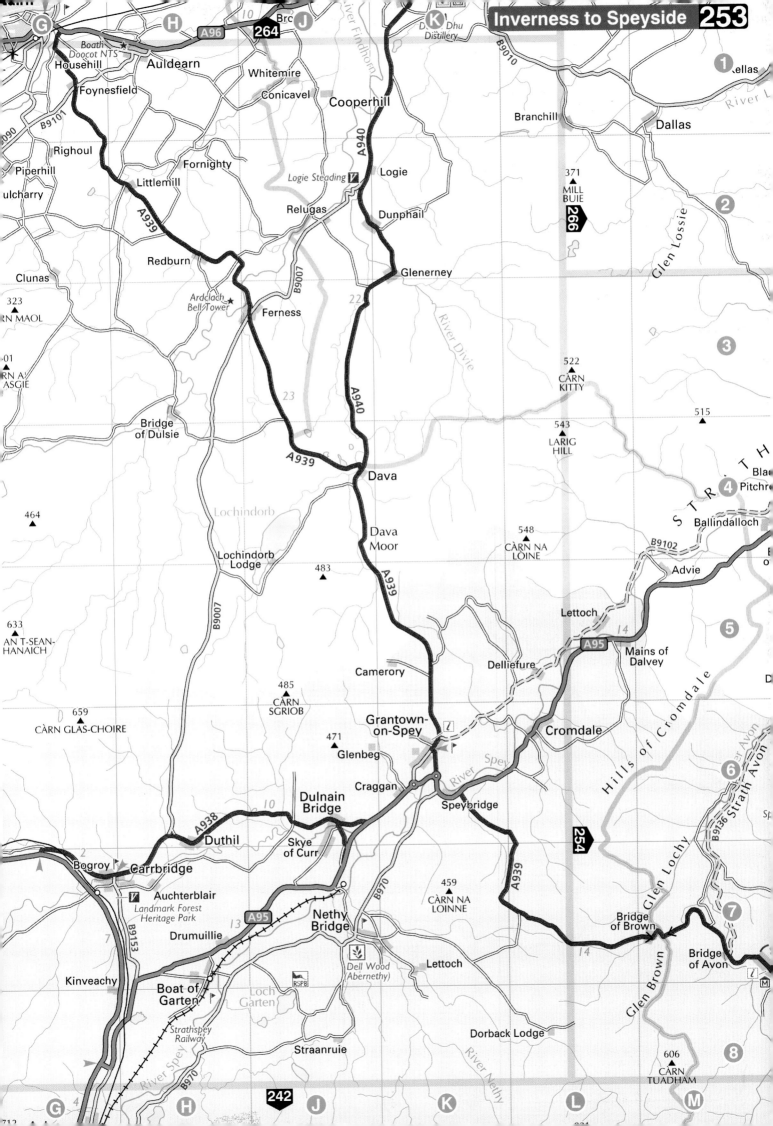

G
H
A96
10
Brc J
River Findhorn
K
Dhu
Distillery
B9010
Inverness to Speyside 253
1
ellas
River L

Boath
Doocot NTS
Househill
Auldearn
Whitemire
Conicavel
Cooperhill
Branchill
Dallas
Foynesfield
B9101
B9090
Righoul
Fornighty
A940
Logie
Logie Steading V
371
MILL
BUIE
266
2
Glen Lossie
Piperhill
Littlemill
A939
Relugas
Dunphail
lcharry
Redburn
B9007
Glenerney
22
522
CÀRN
KITTY
3
Clunas
Ardclach
Bell Tower ★
Ferness
River Divie
543
LARIG
HILL
515
323
RN MAOL ▲
23
A940
01
RN A'
ASGIE ▲
Bridge
of Dulsie
A939
Dava
S T R A T H
Black
548
CÀRN NA
LOINE
4
Pitchro
464 ▲
Lochindorb
Dava
Moor
Ballindalloch
B9102
Advie
Lochindorb
Lodge
A939
483 ▲
Lettoch
14
5
633
AN T-SEAN-
HANAICH ▲
B9007
Camerory
Delliefure
A95
Mains of
Dalvey
485 ▲
CÀRN
SGRIOB
Grantown-
on-Spey i
Cromdale
Hills of Cromdale
659
CÀRN GLAS-CHOIRE ▲
471 ▲
Glenbeg
River Spey
Speybridge
254
Avon
6
B9136 Strath Avon
Dulnain
Bridge
10
Craggan
A938
A938
Duthil
Skye
of Curr
B970
459
CÀRN NA
LOINNE ▲
A939
Glen Lochy
Bridge
of Brown
7
Begroy
Carrbridge
Auchterblair
V
Landmark Forest
Heritage Park
13 A95
Nethy
Bridge
Lettoch
Bridge
of Avon
i
M
B9153
Drumuillie
Dell Wood
(Abernethy)
Glen Brown
Kinveachy
RSPB
Boat of
Garten
Loch
Garten
Dorback Lodge
River Nethy
8
Strathspey
Railway
River Spey
B970
Straanruie
606
CÀRN
TUADHAM ▲

G
H
242
J
K
L
M

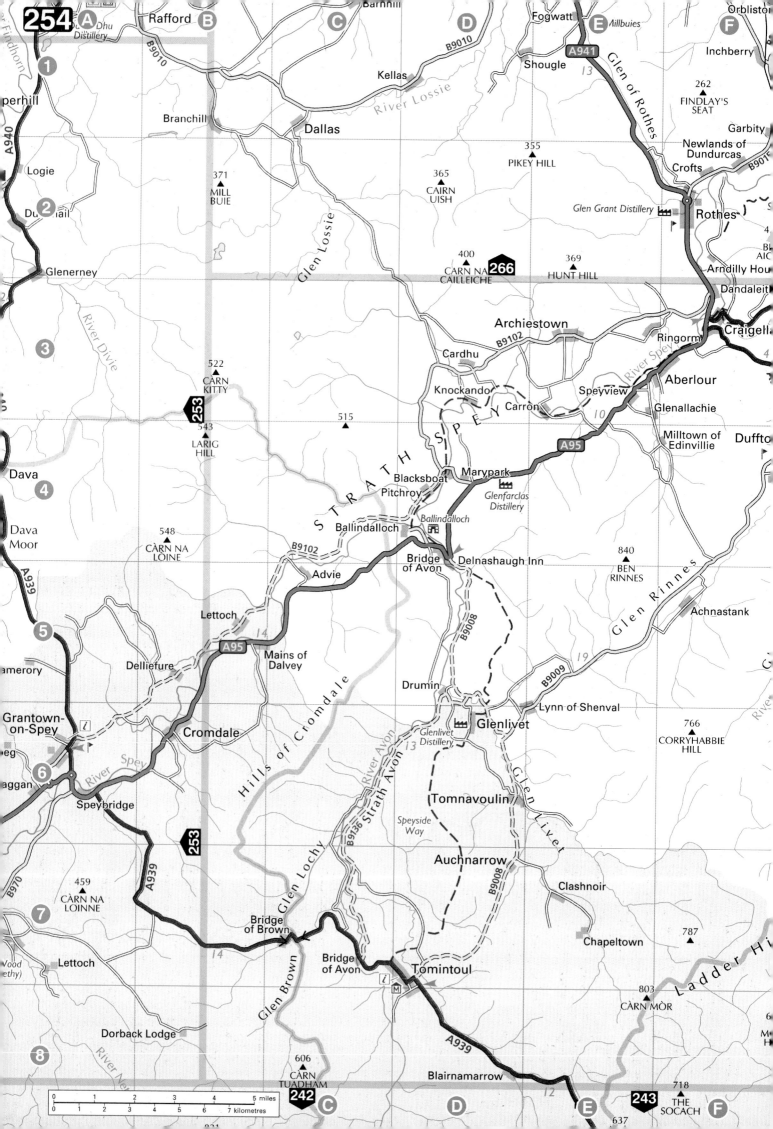

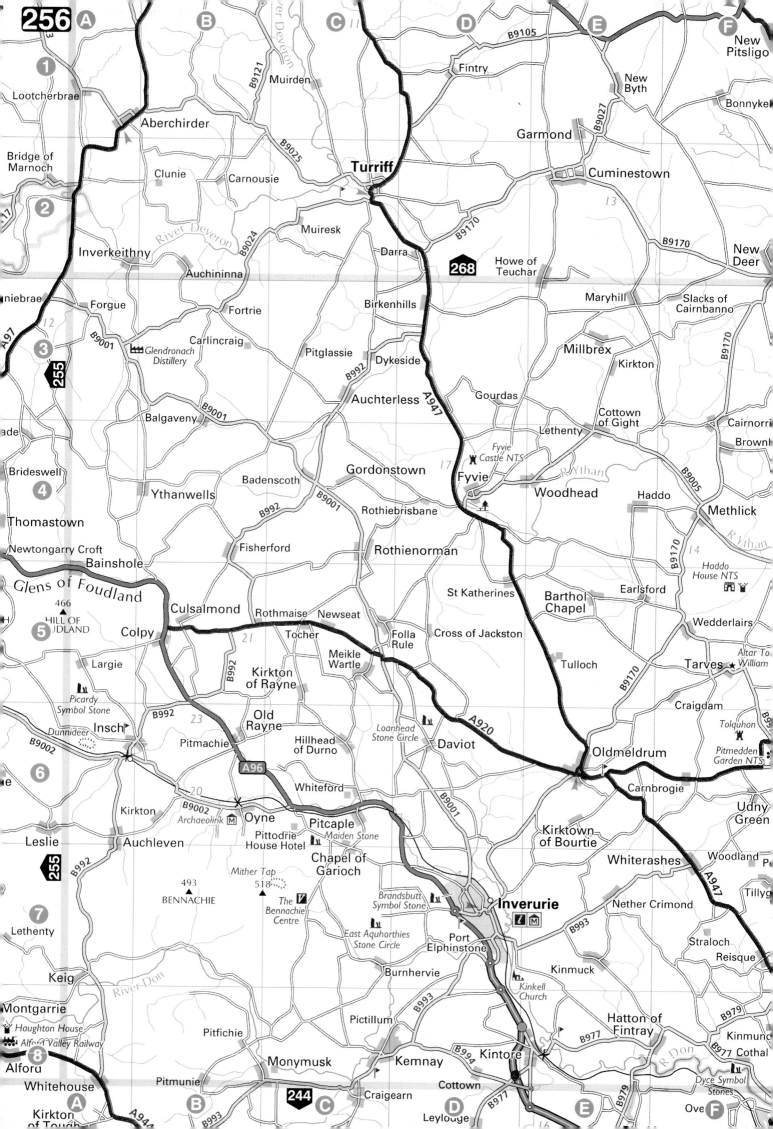

G H J K

1

B9093
Strichen
WAUGHTON HILL H
Crimond
K Blackhill
18
A952

New
Leeds
B9093
Leys
Denhead
Backfolds
Kirktown
St Fergus

Fetterangus
Rora
A981
A950
6
Deer
Abbey
Dunshillock
Inverugie
Buchanhaven
A90
River Ugie
Peterhead
M

2

Maud
B9106
Aden
Mintlaw
Longside
Inverugie
Buchanhaven
B9029
B9029
Old
Deer
269
A950
9
Peterhead
Bay
B9028
Blackhill of
Clackriach
Stuartfield
Inverquhomery
Burnhaven

3

Drymuir
Bulwark
Millbreck
Nether
Kinmundy
Hillhead
of Cocklaw
Buchan
Ness
Nethermuir
Clola
Little
Dens
Stirling
Boddam
B9030
Kinnadie
Blackhill
Lendrum
Terrace
Auchnagatt
12
Kinknockie
Longhaven

4

Inkhorn
Coldwells
Blackhill
A952
Hatton
Auchiries
A90
Bullers
of Buchan
Arthrath
Muirtack
14
17
Slains
North Haven
A948
Bogbrae
Chapel
Hill
Cruden Bay

5

Ythanbank
Birness
A975
Whinnyfold
Bay of
Cruden
Auchedly
Artrochie
The Skares
Kinharrachie
Ellon
P+R
B9005
Kirkton of
Logie Buchan
Kirktown of Slains

6

Esslemont
A920
10
Collieston
Itmedden
Logierieve
32
Forvie
Housieside
B9000
B9000
A90
B9000
Newburgh
Udny Station
Foveran
A975

7

Culterucullen
Delfrigs
17
Causeyend
B979
Balmedie
wmachar
B999
Belhelvie
Balmedie
Whitecairns
B977
B977
B999

8

0 1 2 3 4 5 miles
0 1 2 3 4 5 6 7 kilometres

Potterton
245
B999
rkhill
use
Black Dog

G H J K L M

A   B   C   D   E   F

1

2

3

4

5

6

7

8

Fladda-chùain

Rudha Hun

Lùb Score

Tairbeart
(Tarbert)

Borneskitaig

Kilmuir

Kilva

Balgown

Lini

Totscore

Idrigill

Uig Bay

Loch Snizort

283
BEN
GEARY

Geary

Gillen

Hallin

A87

16

Waternish Point

Ascrib
Islands

Trumpan

Ardmore
Point

DUNVEGAN
HEAD

Isay

Mingay

Stein

Lusta

Loch
Bay

214
BEN
DIUBAIG

Greshornish
House
Hotel

Loch Greshornish

Loch Snizort B

Kir

Claigan

Bay

B886

Loch Dunvegan

327
BEINN
BHREAC

22

Treaslane

Flashader

A850

Borreraig

Uig

Upperglen

Edinbane

Bernisdale

Loch
Pooltiel

Feriniquarrie

Totaig

Oisgill Bay

Glendale

B884

Colbost

Dunvegan

A850

Sk

Milovaig

Lephin

Colbost Croft

Giant Angus MacAskill

Kilmuir

Waterstein

Toy

Skinidin

Lonmore

265
BEN
AKETIL

271
CRUACHAN BEINN
A' CHEARCAILL

Neist
Point

Roskhill

Moonen Bay

Caroy River

Roag

Ramasaig

469
HEALAVAL
MORE

Orbost

Vatten

I
S
L
E

Hoe Rape

488
HEALAVAL
BHEAG

Harlosh

Glen Ose

A863

Hoe Point

368
BEINN NA
COINEID

246

Harlosh
Island

Tarner
Island

Colbost
Point

Ose

Loch Caroy

Bracadale

Du

0   1   2   3   4   5 miles

0   1   2   3   4   5   6   7 kilometres

A   B   C   D   E   F

Loch nam Madadh
(Lochmaddy)

G H J K L

1
2
3
4
5
6
7
8

G H J K L M

an Trodday

North Duntulm
Kilmaluag

Museum
and Life

Flodigarry
Eilean Flodigarry

Poldorais

542
MEAL NA SUIREAMACH
Digg

Staffin Bay
Staffin Island

Brogaig

Stenscholl
Staffin

464
BIODA BUIDHE

Kilt Rock Waterfall
Ellishader

Trotternish

Marishader
Valtos

611
BEINN EDRA
Garros
Rudha nam Brathairean

Culnaknock

River Conon

Peinlich
Lealt
Tote

A855

608
CREAG A' LAIN

nnisdal

451
BEINN A' SGÀ

Old Man of Storr
719
THE STORR

Loch a' Bhràige

RONA

South

260

Red Point

Rudha na Fearn

Ob Chuaig

Callakille

Kensaleyre

River Romesdal

River Haulton

16

Loch Leathan

Loch Fada

Lonbain

B8036

Carbost
Borve

Drumuie

Glengrasco

A855

312

Torvaig

Portree
Seafield

417
BEINN NA GRÈINE
Penifiler
412
BEN TIANAVAIG

Glenmore

Glenvarragill

Mugeary

A87

Camastianav
Tianavaig
Oskaig

247 DÙN CAAN
444

Rudha na' Leac

Eilean Tigh

Eilean Fladday

SOUND OF RAASAY

Manish Point
Loch Arnish
Torran
Umachan

Arnish

Brochel

RAASAY

INNER SO

248

Applecross Bay

Milton

Aird Dhu'

Toscaig

G

H 270

J Ardmair

K 271

Scoraig

Annat Bay

Rhireavach

635 BEINN GHOBHLACH

Morefield

Ullapool

Glen Achall

Loch an Daimh

Loch Achall

558 BEINN EILIDEACH

A835

Badrallach

Leckmelm

677 MEALL NAM BRADHAN

Badcaul

Ardessie

Camusnagaul

32

Ardcharnich

642 MEALL DUBH

Loch a' Choire Mhòir

262

764 SÀIL MHOR

Dundonnell

Ardindrean

Letters

Inverlael

647 CÀRN MÒR

Lochan Gaineamhaich

Loch na Sealga

1062 AN TEALLACH

Strathnasheallag Forest

507 CÀRN BHIORAIN

Inverbroom

R Broom

12

R Broom

1081 BEINN DEARG

906 BEINN DEARG MHOR

Auchindrean

387 CARN BREAC BEAG

Braemore

Corrieshalloch Gorge

4

Loch Coire Làir

Falls of Measach

618 MEALL LEACACHAIN

601 MEALL AN T-SITHE

A832

974 SGÙRRBÀN

1019 MULLACH COIRE MHIC FHEARCHAIR

Loch a' Bhraoin

Loch Droma

662 BEINN LIATH BHEAG

5

Lochan Fada

999 A' CHAILLEACH

1109 SGÙRR MÒR

981 SLIOCH

680 BEINN DEARG

6

Cabvie Lodge

680 BEINN A' MHÙINIDH

711 BEINN NAN RAMH

Fannich Lodge

Loch Fannich

Kinlochewe Forest

262

558 AN CABAR

Beinn Eighe

Incheril

933 FIONN BHEINN

Achanalt

7 A832

Kinlochewe

Glen Docherty

Strath Bran

Loch Achanalt

A832

10

Achnasheen

Loch a' Chroisg

Loch Fhiarlaid

Loch Gowan

249

847

867 SCUIR VUILLIN

550

538 CARN

G

H

J

K

L

M 8

A B C D E F

271

272

261

1

1

Loch an
Daimh

2

677
▲
ME_LL _AM
BRA_HAN

Loch a'
Choire Mhòir

261

_MÒR

3

Strath Mulzie

Gleann Beag

Giasha Burn

412
▲
CREAG
LOISGTE

701
▲
CARN A'
CHOIN DEIRG

Croik

BEINN
ULBHAIDH

506
▲
MEALL
DHEIRGIDH

463
▲
BREAC BHEINN

Brealangwell
Lodge

Strathcarron

River Carron

Glencalvie Forest

634
▲
CÀRN BHREN

842
▲
CARN
BAN

628
▲

Crom Loch

710
▲
BEINN
THARSUINN

838
▲
CÀRN
CHUINNEAG

4

1081
▲
BEINN
DEARG

Loch
Còire Làir

_HAIN

771
▲
MEALL A'
GHRIANAIN

Strathvaich Forest

Loch
Vaich

602
▲
CÀRN CAS NAN GABHAR

E A

Loch a'
Chaorunn

742
▲
BEINN
NAN EUN

Loch
Morie

5

Loch
Droma

N
HEAG

742
▲
TOM
BÀN MÒR

Loch
Glascarnoch

Aultguish
Inn

20

A835

737
▲
MEALL
MOR

Loch Glass

6

680
▲
BEINN
DEARG

600
▲

Corriemoille Forest

Inchbae
Lodge Hotel

479
▲

Strath Garve

🌱 Ben Wyvis

1045
▲
BEN WYVIS

Glen Glass

261

558
▲
AN CABAR

439
▲
CÀRN NA
DUBH CHOILLE

Lochluichart

Corriemoille

761
▲
LITTLE
WYVIS

484
▲
CLOCH MHÒR

7

Ach__lt

A832

16

Loch Luichart

Gorstan

Garve

Loch
Garve

Auchterneed

A834

Dingwall

Mou_
H

8

867
▲
SCUIR VUILLIN

579
▲
SGÙRR MARCASAIDH

536
▲

Little Scatwell

Loch Meig

R Conon

Loch
Achilty

A835

6

Rogie
Falls
★

Strathpeffer

Ⓜ Highland Museum
of Childhood

Gower

Jamestown

Loch
Ussie

Keithtown

Conon
Brid_

River

Mar_

250

C D E F

0	1	2	3	4	5 miles
0 1 2 3 4 5 6					7 kilometres

G | 272 | **H** | **J** | 273 | **K**

Sleasdairidh

349
BEINN
DONUILL

Cambusavie
Platform

Loch Fleet

1

River Evelix

Badninish

Skelbo

Skelbo Street

Fourpenny

Embo

A836

Achvaich

Rearquhar

Birichin

7

Embo Street

Pitgrudy

Kyle of
Sutherland

Lower
Gledfield

Bonar
Bridge

Loch
Migdale

Astle

Evelix

B9168

A949

Camore

Dornoch

Ardgay

A949

Spinningdale

10

Clashmore

A9

3

Kincardine

Upper Ardchronie

A836

Whiteface

Cuthill

264

Innis Mhor

2

Dornoch Firth

Ferrytown

15

Ardmore

Cambuscurrie
Bay

Ferry Point

Dornoch Firth

3

Struie Hill

Edderton

A836

Ferry Point

Glenmorangie
Distillery

Morangie

Inver

477
BEINN CLACH
AN FHEADAIN

19

Aultnamain Inn

284

Tain

M

Toulva

R O S S

692
BEINN
THARSUINN

379
CNOC AN
T-SABHAIL

B9165

Loch
Eye

Rhi ie

Fearn

4

B9176

6

Newfield

Hill of
Fearn

B9166

Tullich

Baln

Rusdale

Ardross

Ballchraggan

Arabella

Shandwick

Bali

Shand

Kildary

B9175

Ankerville

5

River Alness

Achandunie

Milton

Pitcalnie

Rhicullen

A9

Delny

Kilmuir

Nigg

523
CNOC
CEISLEIN

Millcraig

Tomich

8

Barbaraville

Moultavie

Achnagarron

Balintraid

Nigg Bay

Alness

B817

Saltburn

Balnapaling

Dalmore

Invergordon

Cromarty

6

2

Evanton

Cromarty Firth

Balblair

Resolis

Udale
Bay

Cromarty
Bay

B9163

Hugh Miller's Cottage NTS

Newton

Teanord

5

B9163

Allerton

Navity

ullie

Clanland
& Seapoint

Cullicudden

Brae

RSPB

Jemimaville

264

Upper Eathie

M R

7

Findon
Mains

B9169

B L A C K   I S L E

A832

10

Whiteness Head

62

A9

Culbokie

255
MOUNT
EAGLE

Killen

Raddery

RSPB

Nair

B9163

7

Duncanston

Easter
Kinkell

Knockbain

251

Easter
Suddie

A832

8

Avoch

Fortrose

Rosemarkie

Groam
House

Fort George

252

Chanonry
oint

Ard ier

L

M

Moss
side

8

Tradespark

B9092

G | **H** | **J** | **K**

A   B   C   **273**   D   E   F

1

Cambusavie Platform
Loch Fleet
Badninish
Skelbo
Skelbo Street
Fourpenny
Achvaich
velix
Rearquhar
Birichin
Embo
Astle
B9168
Embo Street
Evelix
A949
Pitgrudy
2 *ingda*
Clashmore
A9
Camore
Dornoch
10
Whiteface
3
Camore
Dornoch
i
Cuthill
263
Tarbat Ness
rnoch Firth
Ferrytown
Innis Mhor
Brucefield
Wilkhaven
Dornoch Firth
Ardmore
Cambuscurrie Bay
Ferry Point
Portmahomack
3 *erton*
A836
Inver
Rockfield
Glenmorangie Distillery
B9165
Morangie
Arboll
Toulvaddie
284
Tain
Loch Eye
Rhynie
4
379
Fearn
Balmuchy
OC AN
ABHAIL
Newfield
B9165
Hill of Fearn
Hilton of Cadboll Chapel (ruin)
rn
B9166
Tullich
Hilton
Ballchraggan
Arabella
Shandwick
Balintore
Kildary
Shandwick Bay
Milton
Ankerville
5
Delny
Kilmuir
B9175
Pitcalnie
Barbaraville
Nigg
A9
ich
Nigg Bay
Balintraid
nagarron
B817
Saltburn
Balnapaling
Invergordon
6
Mair
Cromarty
Cromarty Bay
Udale Bay
B9163
Hugh Miller's Cottage NTS
RSPB
Newton
Allerton
263
Navity
Jemimaville
Upper Eathie
7
A832
B9160
E
Culbin Forest
Kintessack
Raddery
MORAY FIRTH
RSPB
Rosemarkie
Groam House
Brodie Castle NTS
Dyk
8 *Fo* *se*
Fort George
Nairn
Brodie
Chanonry
Tradespark
Booth Doocot NTS
A96
Avo
B9092
252
253
Moss-side
Household
learn
Whitem

| 0 | 1 | 2 | 3 | 4 | 5 miles |
| 0 | 1 | 2 | 3 | 4 | 5 | 6 | 7 kilometres |

A   B   C   D   E   F

G   H   J   K   L

1

2

3

4

5

266

Branderburgh

Stotfield

B9040

Lossiemouth

Burghead
Well

Hopeman   Burnside

Burghead   Duffus   Kinneddar

6

Cummingston   St Peter's Kirk
& Parish Cross

B9012   B9013   B9012

Roseisle   Duffus   Loch
Spynie

B9135

College of
Roseisle   Spynie
Palace   B9103

Stonewells
Lochill   Kings
on S

Burghead Bay

B9089   Quarrywood   A941

Findhorn   Hempriggs   Bishopmill   Calcots   Viewfield   Binns
Farm

B9011   Newton   Innesmill

Kinloss   Coltfield   A96   **Elgin**   Urquhart

Findhorn
Bay   Alves   Glen Moray
Distillery   Lhanbryde   The
Lochs

7

Kincorth
House   **266**   Kilbuiack   New Elgin

Sueno's Stone   Grange Hall   Linkwood   Mosstodloc

Muir of
Miltonduff   Crofts
of Dipple

Forres   Pluscarden   Clackmarras   B9103

Longmorn   Orbl...on

Califer   Barnhill

Rafford   Fogwatt   Millbuies   Inchberry   8

Dallas Dhu
Distillery   B9010   B9015

G   **253**   H   J   K   Shougle   L   Glen   M

B9010   Kellas   262

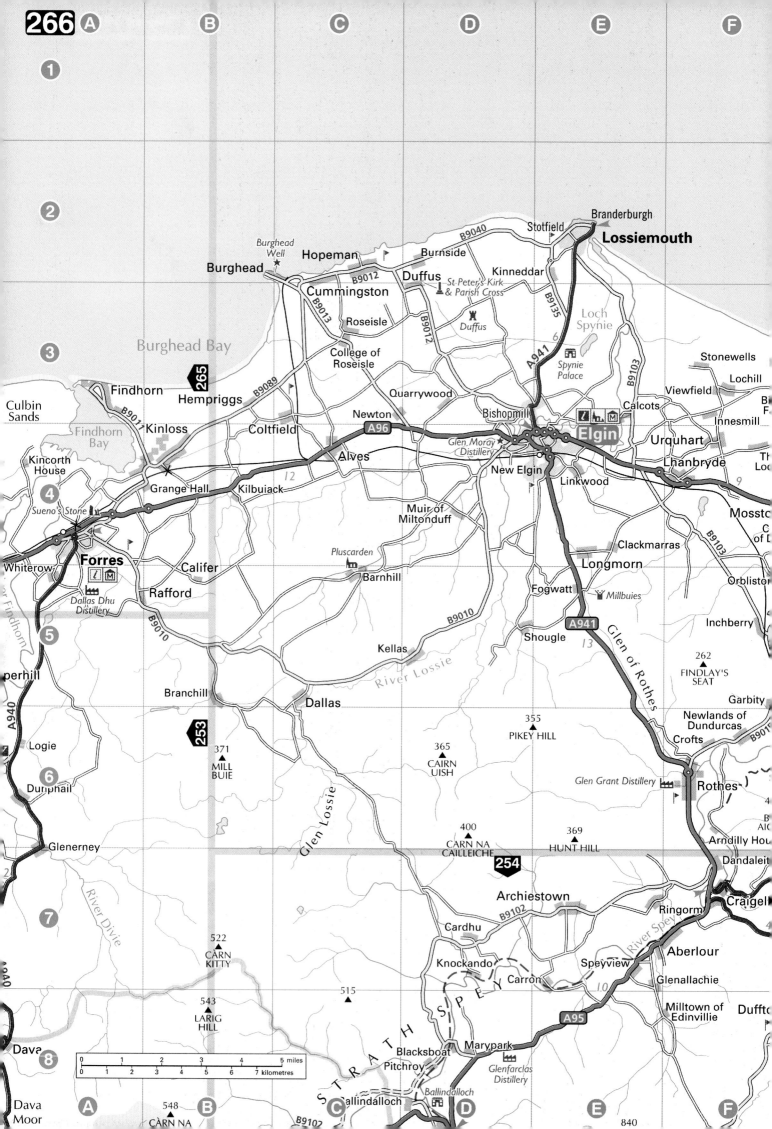

A B C D E F

1

2

B9040

Stotfield
Lossiemouth
Branderburgh

Burnside

Burghead
Well
Hopeman
Burghead

Kinneddar

Duffus
B9012

St Peter's Kirk
& Parish Cross

Cummingston
B9013

Roseisle
B9012
Duffus

Loch
Spynie

B9135

3

Burghead Bay

College of
Roseisle

A941

Spynie
Palace

Stonewells

Lochill

Findhorn
265
Hempriggs

B9089

Quarrywood

Viewfield

Calcots

Innesmill

Culbin
Sands
B9011
Kinloss

Newton

Bishopmill

Elgin

Urquhart

Findhorn Bay

Coltfield

A96

Glen Moray
Distillery

Lhanbryde

Kincorth
House

Alves

New Elgin

Mosstc

4

Sueno's Stone

Grange Hall
Kilbuiack

12

Muir of
Miltonduff

Linkwood

Clackmarras

Forres

Pluscarden

Longmorn

Orblistor

Whiterow

Califer

Barnhill

Fogwatt

Millbuies

Inchberry

Rafford

Dallas Dhu
Distillery

B9010

B9010

Kellas

River Lossie

Shougle

A941

13

262
FINDLAY'S
SEAT

Garbity

5

perhill

A940

Branchill

Dallas

Glen of Rothes

Newlands of
Dundurcas
Crofts

B901

253

371
MILL
BUIE

355
PIKEY HILL

Glen Grant Distillery

Rothes

6

Logie

365
CAIRN
UISH

B
AIC
of L

Dunphail

400
CARN NA
CAILLEICHE

369
HUNT HILL

Arndilly Hou

Glenerney

Glen Lossie

254

Dandaleit

7

River Divie

Archiestown

B9102

Ringorm

Craigel

522
CÀRN
KITTY

Cardhu

River Spey

Aberlour

Knockando

Speyview

Glenallachie

543
LARIG
HILL

515

Carron

10

Milltown of
Edinvillie

Duffto

A95

8

Dava

0 1 2 3 4 5 miles
0 1 2 3 4 5 6 7 kilometres

Blacksboat
Pitchroy

Marypark

S T R A T H S P E Y

Dava
Moor

548
CÀRN NA

Glenfarclas
Distillery

Ballindalloch
Ballindalloch

840

B9102

A B C D E F

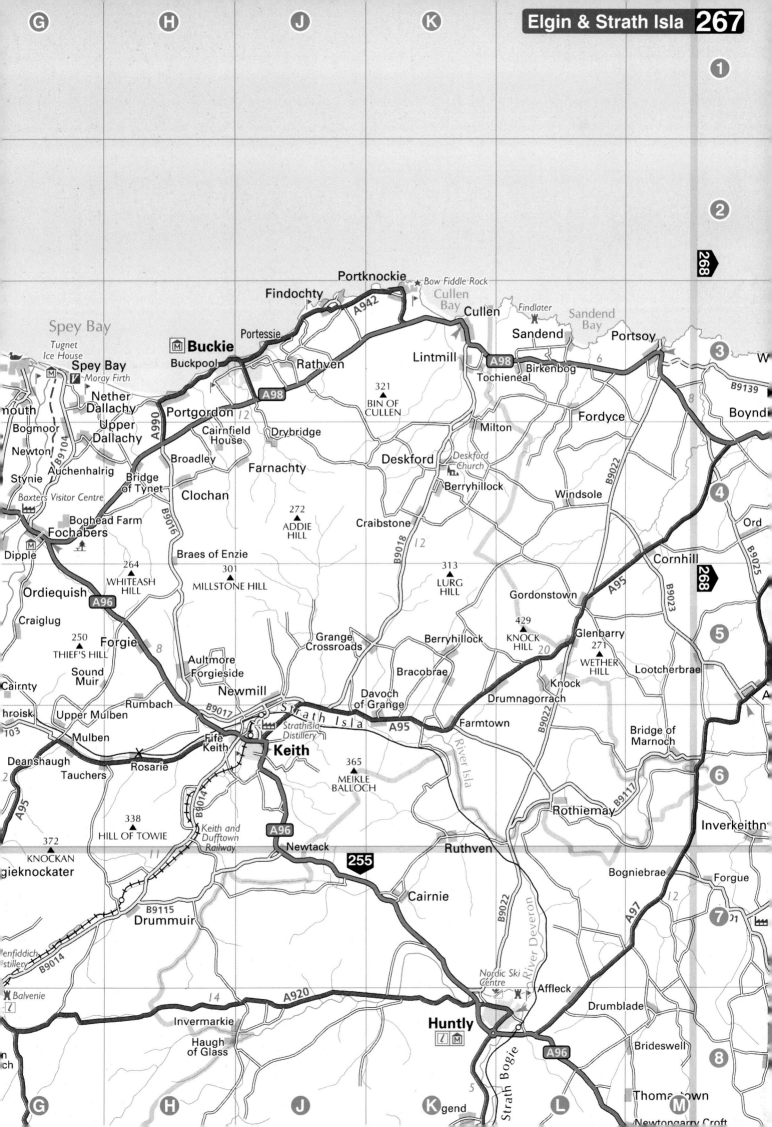

G   H   J   K

1

2

268

Spey Bay

Portknockie
Findochty   ★ Bow Fiddle Rock
                             Cullen Bay
Portessie   Cullen
Tugnet
Ice House   A942   Findlater   Sandend
Spey Bay   Sandend   Bay
Moray Firth   **Buckie**   Portsoy
              Buckpool   Rathven   Lintmill   3
Nether   Tochieneal A98 Birkenbog
Dallachy   A98   B9139
nouth   Portgordon 12   321   Fordyce   Boyndi
Bogmoor   Upper   BIN OF   Milton
Newton   Dallachy   Cairnfield Drybridge CULLEN
Stynie   House   4
Auchenhalrig Bridge Broadley   Farnachty   Deskford
           of Tynet   Deskford   Windsole
Baxters Visitor Centre   Clochan   Church
                                             Berryhillock   B9022
Fochabers   Boghead Farm   Craibstone
Dipple   272   B9018 12   Cornhill
Ordiequish   264 WHITEASH ADDIE   268
           WHITEASH HILL   HILL   301   313   B9023 B9025
Craiglug   HILL   MILLSTONE HILL LURG   Ord
       A96   HILL   Gordonstown   5
Forgie 250   Braes of Enzie   429 Glenbarry 271
       THIEF'S HILL   KNOCK   WETHER
Sound   Aultmore   Grange   HILL   20   HILL Lootcherbrae
Cairnty Muir   Forgieside Crossroads Berryhillock
       Rumbach   Newmill   Bracobrae   Knock
hroisk Upper Mulben   B9017   Strath Isla Davoch   Drumnagorrach Bridge of
103   Strathisla of Grange A95 Farmtown   Marnoch
Mulben   Fife   Distillery   B9117   6
Deanshaugh   Keith   **Keith**   River Isla   Inverkeithn
Tauchers Rosarie   365   Rothiemay
A95   MEIKLE
                             BALLOCH   Bogniebrae Forgue
338   Keith and   Ruthven   A97 12   7
HILL OF TOWIE   Dufftown   01
372   Railway   Newtack 255   Cairnie   B9022
KNOCKAN   River Deveron
gieknockater B9115   Brideswell
       Drummuir   Nordic Ski
enfiddich   Centre Affleck Drumblade
stilley B9014   A920   **Huntly**
Balvenie   14   Invermarkie
              Haugh   A96   Strath Bogie Brideswell
              of Glass   8
G   H   J   K gend   L   Strath Bogie M
                                        Thoma own
                                        Newtongarry Croft

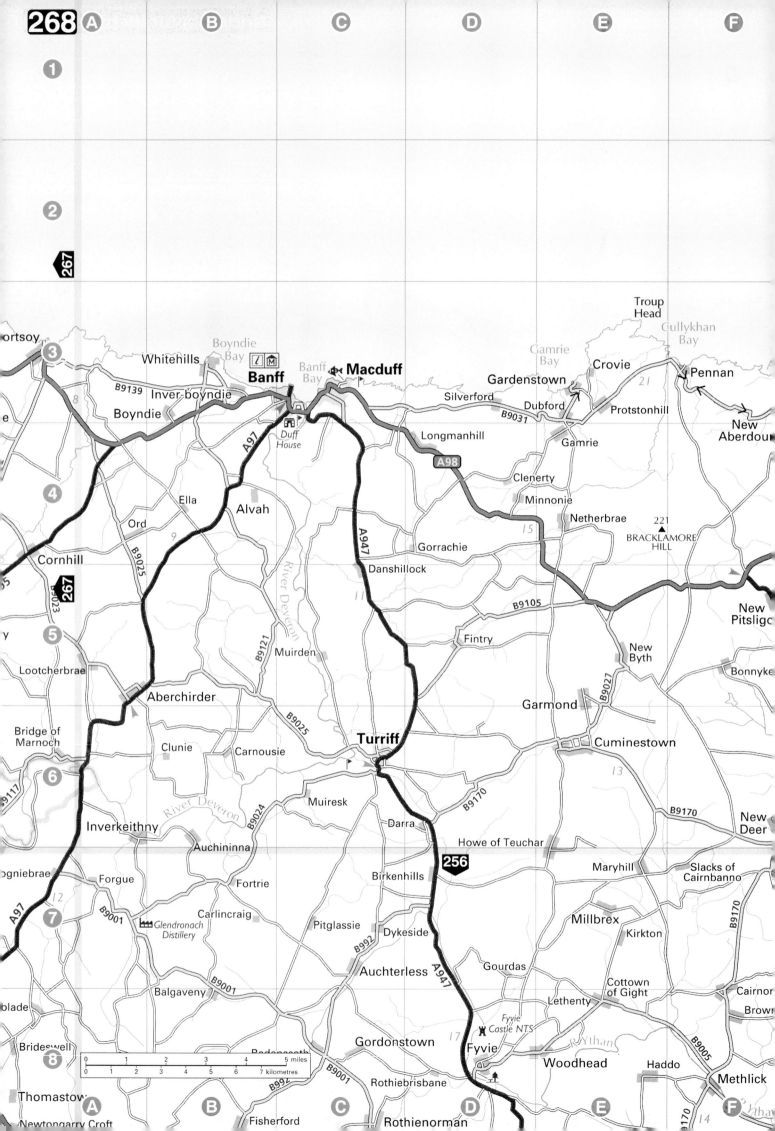

G H J K

1

2

Rosehearty
Pittulie
Lighthouse M Kinnaird Head
Sandhaven
Peathill
aigiefold
Fraserburgh ℹ
Percyhorner
Kirktown
Fraserburgh Bay
Maggie's Hoosie
Cairnbulg
Inverallochy
B9031
Coburby
Pitblae
Whitelinks Bay
ndlie
Mid Ardlaw
B9032
A90
St Combs
A98
Memsie
B9033
Rathen
Crofts of Savoch
Memsie Cairn
Newburgh
Lonmay
Rattray Head
234
WAUGHTON HILL
A981
RSPB
Loch of Strathbeg
B9093
A952
Crimond
Blackhill
Strichen
18
New Leeds
B9093
Leys
Denhead
Backfolds
Kirktown
St Fergus
Fetterangus
Rora
A981 A950
6
Deer Abbey
Dunshillock
River Ugie
A90
Maud
B9106
Aden
Mintlaw
Longside
Inverugie
Buchanhaven
Peterhead M
B9029
B9029
Old Deer
257
Inverquhomery
A950
A982
Peterhead Bay
Blackhill of Clackriach
Stuartfield
9
Hillhead of Cocklaw
Burnhaven
B9028
Drymuir
Bulwark
Millbreck
Nether Kinmundy
Buchan Ness
Nethermuir
Clola
Little Dens
Stirling
Boddam
B9030
Kinnadie
Blackhill
Lendrum Terrace
uchnagatt
12
Kinknockie
Blackhill
Longhaven
Inkhorn
A948
Coldwells
A952
A90
Auchiries
Bullers of Buchan
North Haven
Arthra
Muirtack
14
Hatton
17
☓ *Slains*
Cruden Bay

G H J K L M

3

4

5

6

7

8

A   B   C   D   E   F

1

2

Point of Stoer

OLDANY
ISLAND

Eddrach
Bay

**Culkein
Drumbeg**

Old Man
of Stoer

Culkein

Clashnessie
Bay

Oldany

Drumbeg

Achnacarnin

Clashmore

Nedd

Clashnessie

Loch
Poll

Stoer

3

Clachtoll

B869

Bay of Clachtoll

Rhicarn

Loch
Beannac

Achmelvich
Bay

A837

Achmelvich

Baddidarrach

Lochinver

Soyea Island

Loch Inver

Assyr

Strathan

4

Inverkirkaig

River Kirkaig

Fionn
Loch

Rhu
Coigach

Eilean Mòr

Enard Bay

Rubha Mòr

5

Reiff

Achnahaird

Loch
Sionasc

Altandhu

Eilean Mullagrach

Loch
Osgaig

Isle Ristol

612
STAC POLLAIDH

Polbain

Glas-leac Mòr

769
CUL BEA

6

SUMMER ISLES

Achiltibuie

Loch
Lurgainn

Tanera
Beg

Badentarbat
Bay

Polglass

Steornabhagh
(Stornoway)

Tanera
Mòr

C O I G A C H

Glas-leac Beag

Horse
Island

Horse
Sound

652
BEN MORE
COIGACH

7

Eilean Dubh

Achduart

Culnacraig

Priest
Island

Strathcanair

Leac Dhonn

Isle
Martin

Strath

Greenstone
Point

Cailleach Head

A835

8

Rudha Beag

Ardmair

0   1   2   3   4   5 miles
0 1 2 3 4 5 6 7 kilometres

tic Point

C

261

Scoraig

D

Rhireavach

Annat
Bay

E

Mo F ld

635

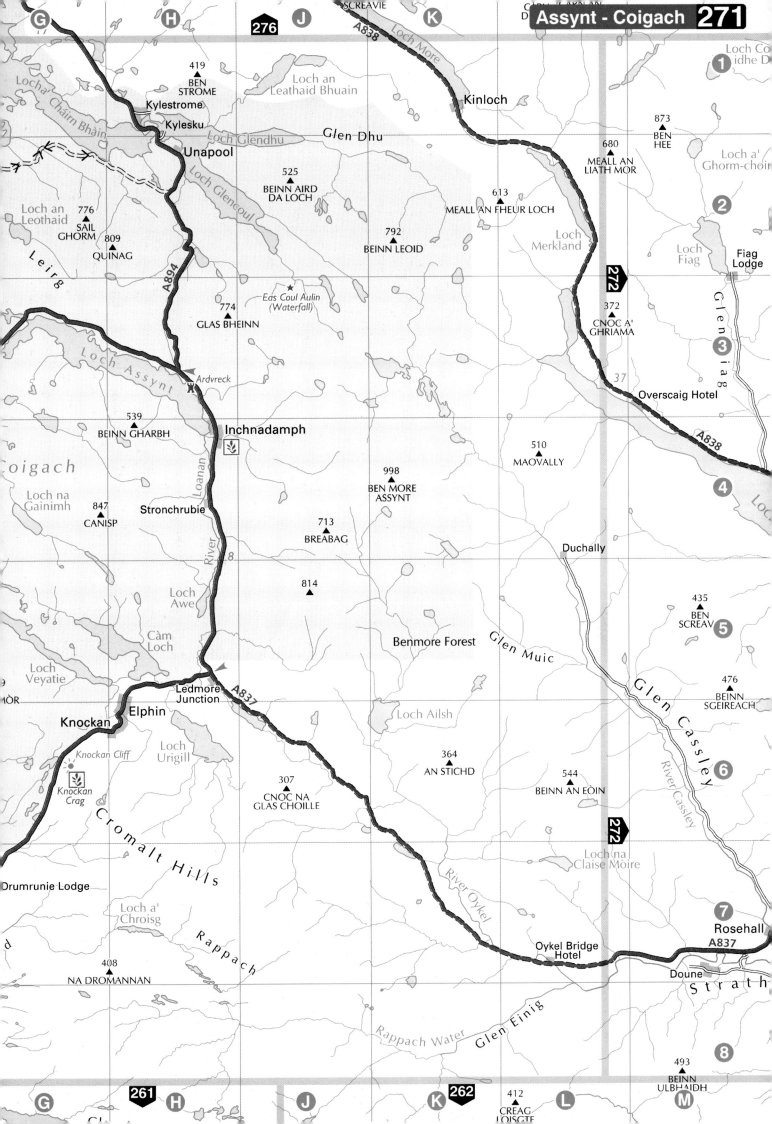

G H 276 J A838 Loch More K

Loch Co idhe D 1

Locha Chàirn Bhàin

419 ▲
BEN
STROME

Loch an
Leathaid Bhuain

Kinloch

873 ▲
BEN
HEE

Loch a'
Ghorm-choir

Kylestrome

Kylesku

Loch Glendhu

Glen Dhu

680 ▲
MEALL AN
LIATH MOR

Unapool

Loch Glencoul

525 ▲
BEINN AIRD
DA LOCH

613 ▲
MEALL AN FHEUR LOCH

Loch
Merkland

2

Loch
Fiag

Fiag
Lodge

Loch an
Leothaid

776 ▲
SAIL
GHORM

Leirg

809 ▲
QUINAG

792 ▲
BEINN LEOID

272

3

Glen Fiag

774 ▲
GLAS BHEINN

Eas Coul Aulin
(Waterfall) ★

372 ▲
CNOC A'
GHRIAMA

A894

Loch Assynt

Ardvreck

37

Overscaig Hotel

Loch

Coigach

539 ▲
BEINN GHARBH

Inchnadamph

A838

4

847 ▲
CANISP

Loch na
Gainimh

Stronchrubie

Loanan

River

510 ▲
MAOVALLY

998 ▲
BEN MORE
ASSYNT

713 ▲
BREABAG

Duchally

435 ▲
BEN
SCREAV

5

Loch Awe

814 ▲

Càm
Loch

Loch
Veyatie

MOR

476 ▲
BEINN
SGEIREACH

Glen Muic

Benmore Forest

Glen Cassley

Ledmore
Junction

A837

Loch Ailsh

River Cassley

6

Knockan

Elphin

Loch
Urigill

364 ▲
AN STICHD

544 ▲
BEINN AN EÒIN

Knockan Cliff ☼

Knockan
Crag

307 ▲
CNOC NA
GLAS CHOILLE

272

Loch na
Claise Mòire

Cromalt Hills

Rappach

River Oykel

7

Drumrunie Lodge

Loch a'
Chroisg

408 ▲
NA DROMANNAN

Rosehall

A837

Oykel Bridge
Hotel

Doune

Strath

d

Rappach Water

Glen Einig

493 ▲
BEINN
ULBHAIDH

8

G 261 H J K 262 L M

412 ▲
CREAG
LOISGTE

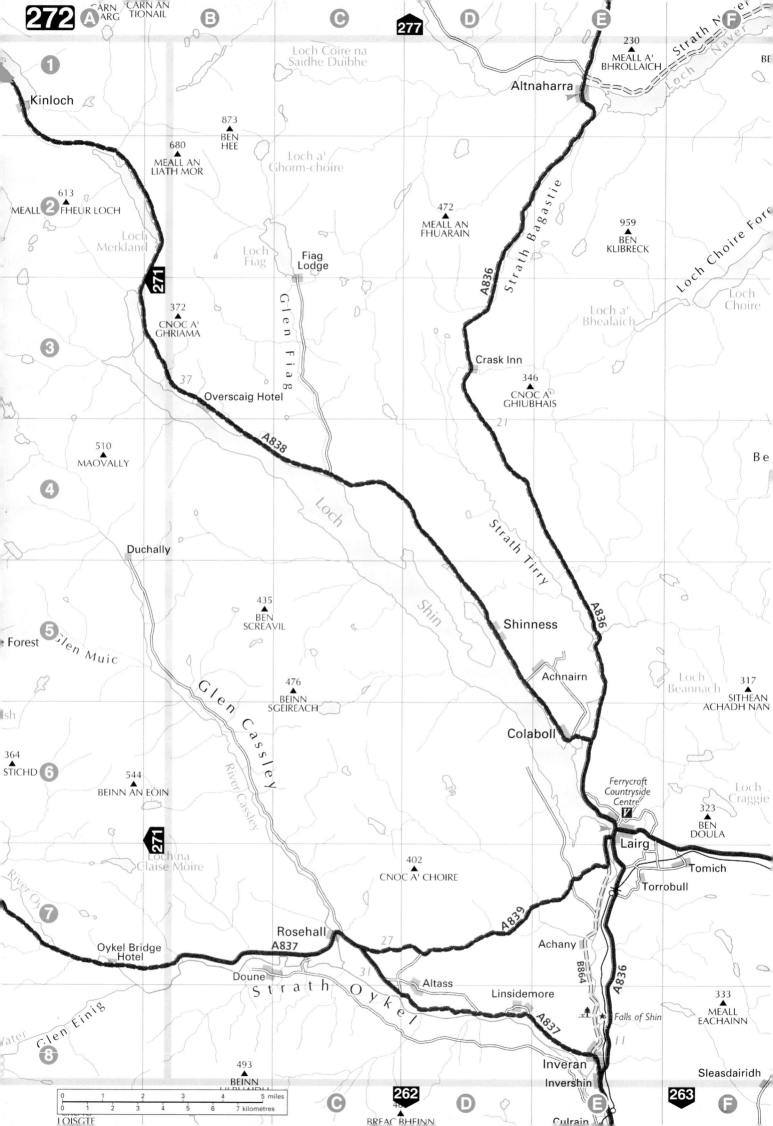

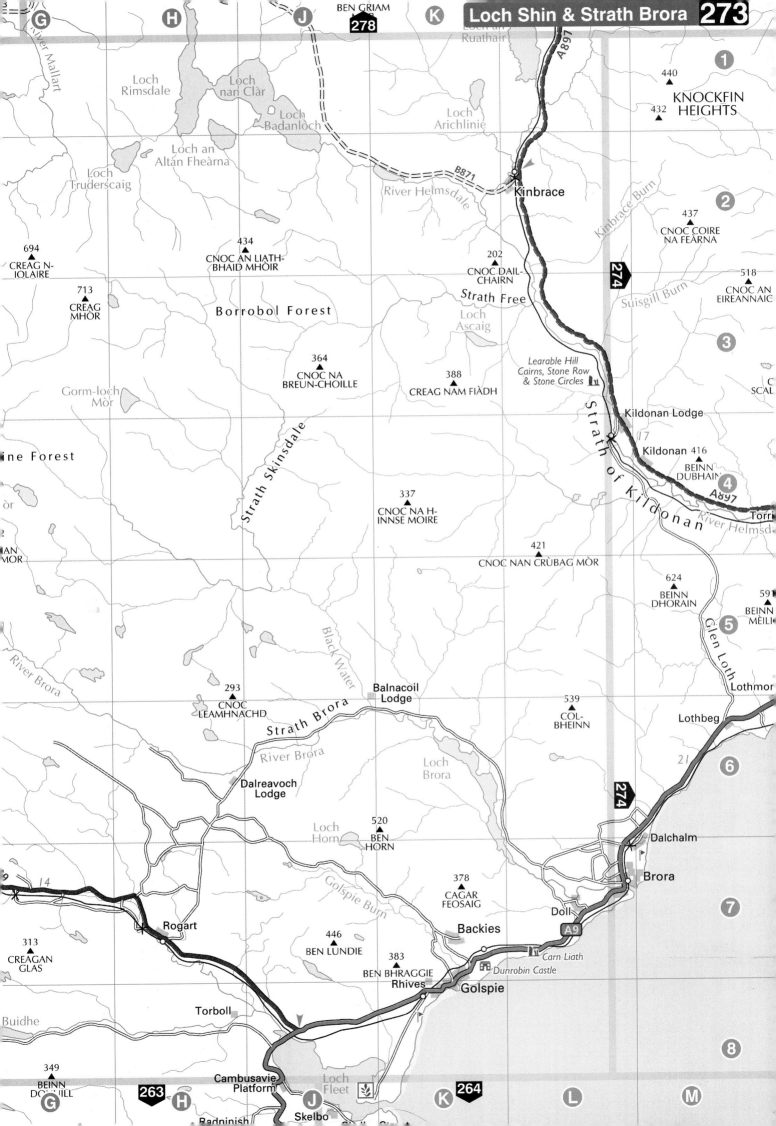

G H J K
BEN GRIAM **278**
Loch an Ruathair
A897

1
440
KNOCKFIN
HEIGHTS
432

River Mallart
Loch Rimsdale
Loch nan Clàr
Loch Badanloch

Loch Arichlinie
Loch an Altán Fheàrna
B871
River Helmsdale
Kinbrace
274
437 **2**
CNOC COIRE
NA FEÀRNA
Loch Truderscaig

694
CREAG N-IOLAIRE
434
CNOC AN LIATH-BHAID MHÒIR
202
CNOC DAIL-CHAIRN
Strath Free
Kinbrace Burn

518
CNOC AN EIREANNAIC

713
CREAG MHÒR
Borrobol Forest
Loch Ascaig
Suisgill Burn
3

Gorm-loch Mòr
364
CNOC NA BREUN-CHOILLE
388
CREAG NAM FIÀDH
Learable Hill
Cairns, Stone Row
& Stone Circles
Kildonan Lodge
C
SCAL

ne Forest
Strath Skinsdale
Kildonan 416
BEINN DUBHAIN
A897
Strath of Kildonan

òr
IAN
MÒR
337
CNOC NA H-INNSE MOIRE
Torri
River Helmsd

421
CNOC NAN CRÙBAG MÒR
624
BEINN DHORAIN
59
BEINN MÈILI
5

River Brora
Black Water
293
CNOC LEAMHNACHD
Balnacoil Lodge
Glen Loth
Lothmor

Strath Brora
River Brora
539
COL-BHEINN
Lothbeg

Dalreavoch Lodge
Loch Brora
21
6

Loch Horn
520
BEN HORN
274
Dalchalm

9 14
Loch Horn
378
CAGAR FEOSAIG
Brora
Doll
7

Rogart
Backies
A9
Carn Liath

313
CREAGAN GLAS
446
BEN LUNDIE
383
BEN BHRAGGIE
Rhives
Golspie
Dunrobin Castle

Torboll

Buidhe
349
BEINN DO HILL
263
Cambusavie Platform
Loch Fleet
264

G H J K L M **8**

Badninish
Skelbo

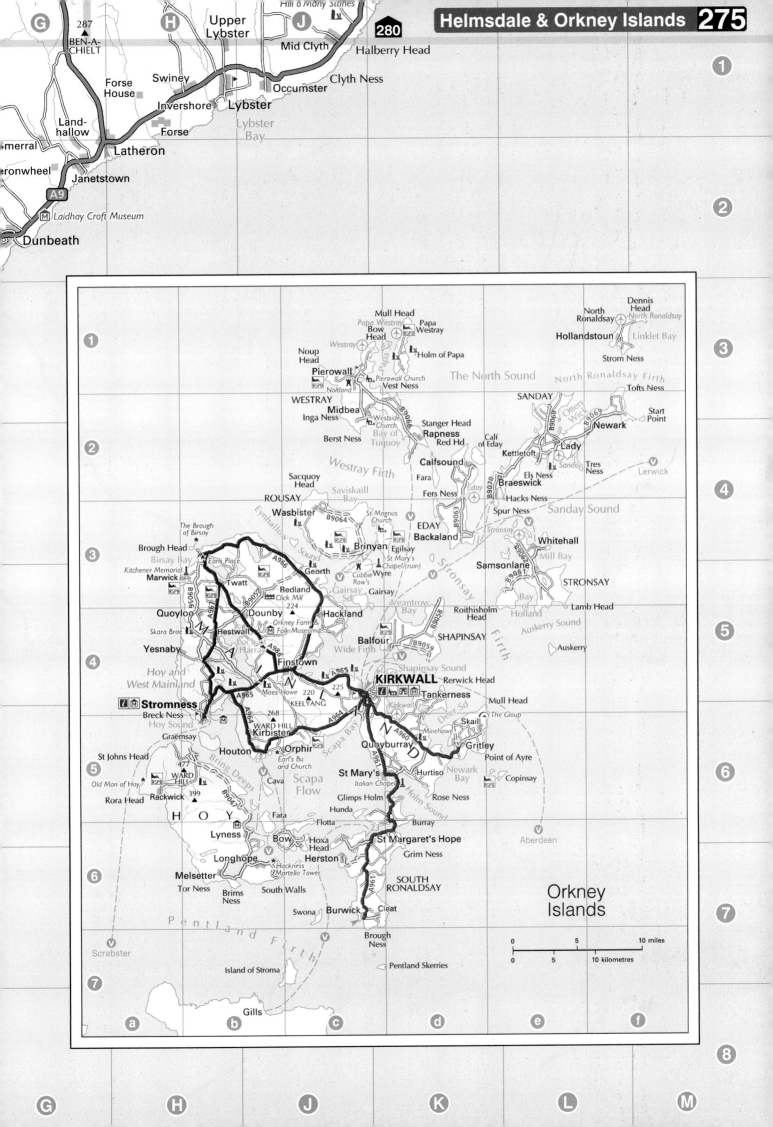

Orkney
Islands

CAPE WRATH

Cléit
Dhubh

Faraid
Head

371
SGRIBHIS-
BHEINN

297
CNOC A
GHIUBHAIS

300
MAOVALLY

Balnakeil
Bay

THE PARPH

Balnakeil   *i*

457
FASHVEN

Durness
Sangomor

Sandwood
Bay

Loch Airigh
na Beinne

Keolda

Sandwood
Loch

Rudh' an Fhir Leithe

485
CREAG
RIABACH

468
BEINN
DEARG MHÒR

464
MEALL
NA MÒINE

331
GHLAS-
BHEINN

489
MEALL
NA CRÀ

Sheigra

Strath Shinary

521
FARVEALL

19

773
BEINN
SPIONNAIDH

Balchreick
Blairmore

355
AN
SOCACH

801
CRANSTACKIE

Oldshoremore

Loch Clash

Kinlochbervie
Badcall

B801

Achriesgill

Strath Dionard

River Dionard

Strath Beag

Loch Inchard

Rhiconich

Loch na
Claise Càrnaich

Rudha Ruadh

Skerricha

A838

908
FOINAVEN

Fanagmore

Loch Laxford

North-west Sutherland

Loch na Tuadh

Tarbet

Foindle

**HANDA
ISLAND**

River Laxford

786
ARKLE

Scourie
Bay

7

Laxford
Bridge

A894

Scourie

729
SÀBHAL BEAG

Scourie More

Loch
Stack

Badcall

721
BEN STACK

Loch a'
Mhuilinn

Badcall
Bay

386
BEN
AUSKAIRD

Strath Stack

Achfary

333
BEN
SCREAVIE

800

796
CÀRN
DEARG

757
CARN A'
TIONAIL

**Rudh' a'
Mhucard**

17

A838

Loch M.

419
BEN

Eddrachillis

ANY
ND

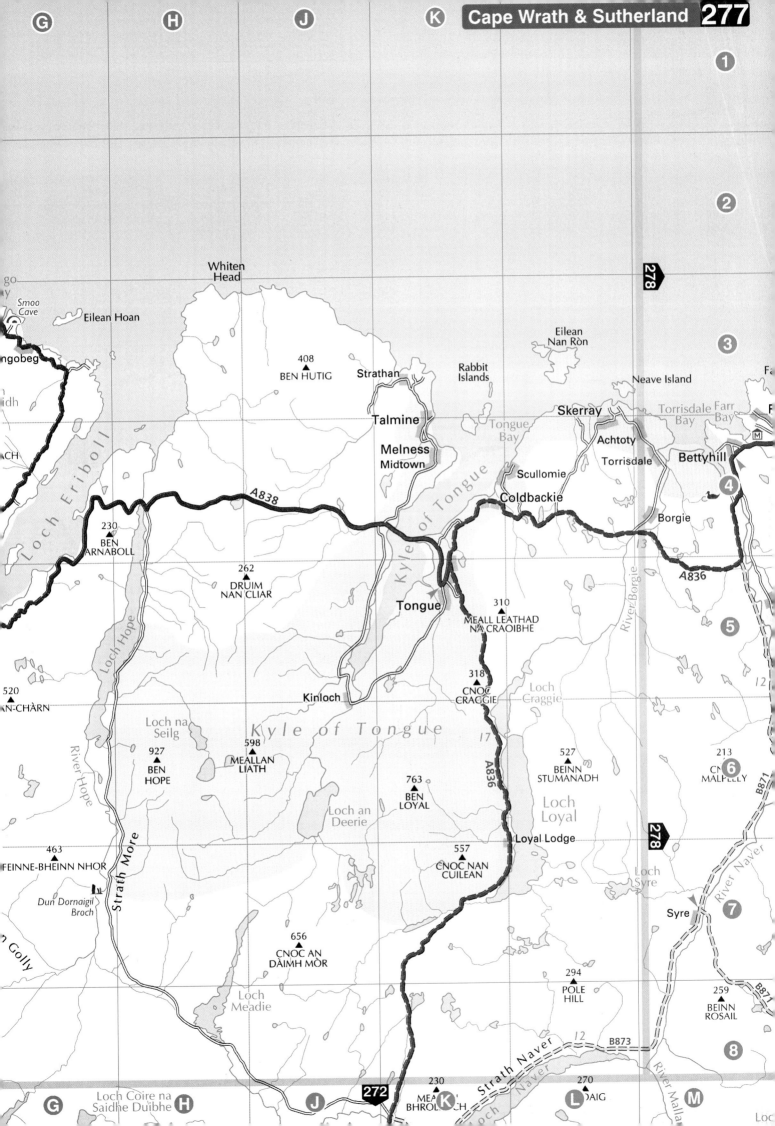

① ② ③ ④ ⑤ ⑥ ⑦ ⑧

278

Smoo
Cave

Eilean Hoan

ngobeg

idh

CH

Loch Eriboll

Whiten
Head

408
▲
BEN HUTIG

Strathan

Talmine

Melness
Midtown

230
▲
BEN
ARNABOLL

A838

262
▲
DRUIM
NAN CLIAR

Kyle of Tongue

Tongue

310
▲
MEALL LEATHAD
NA CRAOIBHE

Rabbit
Islands

Eilean
Nan Ròn

Neave Island

Skerray

Achtoty

Torrisdale

Scullomie

Coldbackie

Tongue
Bay

Torrisdale Farr
Bay Bay

Bettyhill

M

Borgie

13

A836

River Borgie

520
▲
AN-CHÀRN

Loch Hope

Loch na
Seilg

927
▲
BEN
HOPE

598
▲
MEALLAN
LIATH

Kinloch

318
▲
CNOC
CRAGGIE

Loch
Craggie

Loch Craggie

17

Kyle of Tongue

763
▲
BEN
LOYAL

Loch an
Deerie

527
▲
BEINN
STUMANADH

213
▲
CN
MALPELLY

6

A836

Loch
Loyal

278

463
▲
FEINNE-BHEINN NHOR

Strath More

River Hope

Dun Dornaigil
Broch

Loyal Lodge

557
▲
CNOC NAN
CUILEAN

Loch
Syre

Syre

River Naver

7

B871

259
▲
BEINN
ROSAIL

n Golly

656
▲
CNOC AN
DÀIMH MÒR

Loch
Meadie

294
▲
POLE
HILL

B871

272

230
▲
MEA
BHROL CH

270
▲
DAIG

12

B873

Strath Naver

Loch Naver

River Mallai

8

Loch Coire na
Saidhe Duibhe

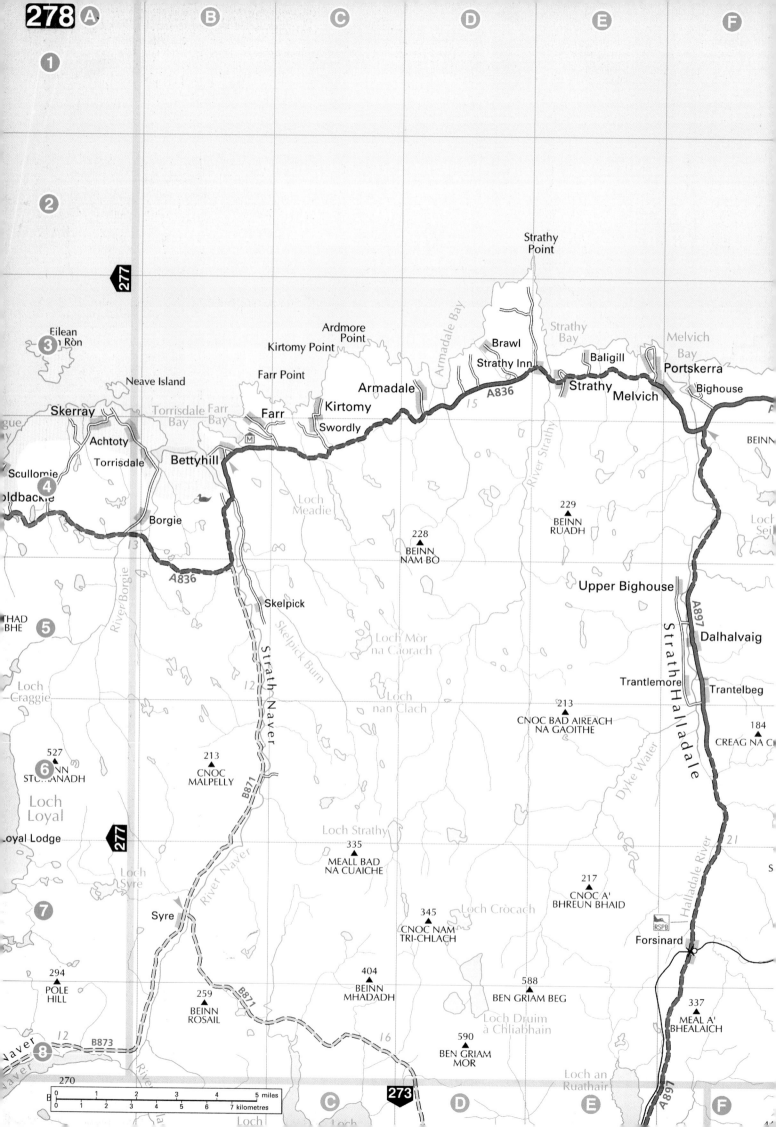

A   B   C   D   E   F

1

2

◀ 277

3   Eilean
    Ròn

Skerray

Neave Island

Achtoty

Torrisdale

Scullomie

oldbackie   4

Borgie

THAD
BHE   5

Loch
Craggie

527
NN
STORMANADH   6

Loch
Loyal

277

oyal Lodge

Loch
Syre

7

Syre

294
POLE
HILL

8   270

B873

Naver
Naver

River

Torrisdale Farr
Bay   Bay

Bettyhill

Loch
Meadie

A836

Skelpick

Strath Naver

13

12

Skelpick Burn

CNOC
MALPELLY
213

B871

River Naver

B871

259
BEINN
ROSAIL

Ardmore
Point

Kirtomy Point

Farr Point

Farr

Kirtomy

Swordly

228
BEINN
NAM BÒ

Loch Mòr
na Caorach

Loch
nan Clach

Loch Strathy

335
MEALL BAD
NA CUAICHE

345
CNOC NAM
TRI-CHLACH

404
BEINN
MHADADH

590
BEN GRIAM
MOR

Armadale

Armadale Bay

Strathy
Bay

Brawl

Strathy Inn

A836

15

River Strathy

Strathy
Point

Baligill

Strathy

229
BEINN
RUADH

213
CNOC BAD AIREACH
NA GAOITHE

Dyke Water

Loch Cròcach

588
BEN GRIAM BEG

Loch Druim
à Chliabhain

16

Melvich
Bay

Portskerra

Melvich

Bighouse

BEINN

Upper Bighouse

Loch
Sei

Strath Halladale

A897

Dalhalvaig

Trantlemore

Trantelbeg

184
CREAG NA C

217
CNOC A'
BHREUN BHAID

21

Halladale River

RSPB

Forsinard

337
MEAL A'
BHEALAICH

Loch an
Ruathair

A897

12

273

0   1   2   3   4   5 miles
0   1   2   3   4   5   6   7 kilometres

A   B   C   D   E   F

1

DUNNET HEAD
▲ 127
Briga Head

121
▲
DUNNET
HILL
Brough

St John's
Loch
B855

2
West Dunnet
Dunnet
Dunnet
Bay

Stromness
V

Holborn
Head

Castlehill
280
Murkle
Castletown
Gre

Scrabster
A836
A836
5

A9
Thurso Bay
Thurso
i M

Olrig
House
Tai
3
B876

St Mary's
Chapel (ruin)
Crosskirk
A836

Bridge of Forss
B874

Weydale

16
Buldoo
Skiall
Lythmore
Glengolly

Hilliclay
Bower

Dounreay
Visitor Centre
Achreamie
Sandside
Bay
Isauld
Upper
Dounreay
Cnoc Freiceadain
Long Cairns
Shebster
Westfield

Sordale
B874

Reay
Forss Water

Knockdee
A9
Roadside
B874

242
▲
BEINN
RATHA

Loch
Calder

Clayock
Gillock
4 Halcro

Broubster
B870

Loch
Scarmclate
B874

Shurrery
Halkirk

Loch Watten

290
▲
BEIN NAM
BAD MHÒR
Loch
Scye
Shurrery
Lodge

Harpsdale
176
▲
SPITTAL
HILL
21

243
▲
CNOC AN
OARAIN BHÀIN
Loch
Shurrery
Dorrery
Scotscalder
Station
Spittal
Watten
5
B870
Backlass

160
▲
BRAIGH FÉITH HEMIGAL
132
DRUIM A'
CHRACAIRNIE
River Thurso
Mybster
Loch of
Toftingall

Loch Tuim
Ghlais
203
▲
CNOC PREAS
A'MHADAIDH
200
▲
CNOC BEUL
NA FAIRE
Loch
Caluim

Westerdale
23
6

Strath Beg

275
CNOC
N GALL
Altnabreac Station

136
▲
BEINN CHÀITEAG
280
A9
7 BALLH
HIL

Rumsdale Water
Strathmore Water
Loch
More
Loch
Ruard
Achavanich
Loch
Stemster
14

Dalnawillan Lodge
Loch an
Thulachan
Loch
Sand
Loch
Rangag
248
▲
STEMSTER HILL

348
▲
BEN
ALISKY
226
▲
COIRE
NA BEINN
287
▲
BEN-A-
CHIELT
8 U
L

Glut Water
G Lodge
H
274
J
K
CNOCAN
L
M
Forse
Swiney

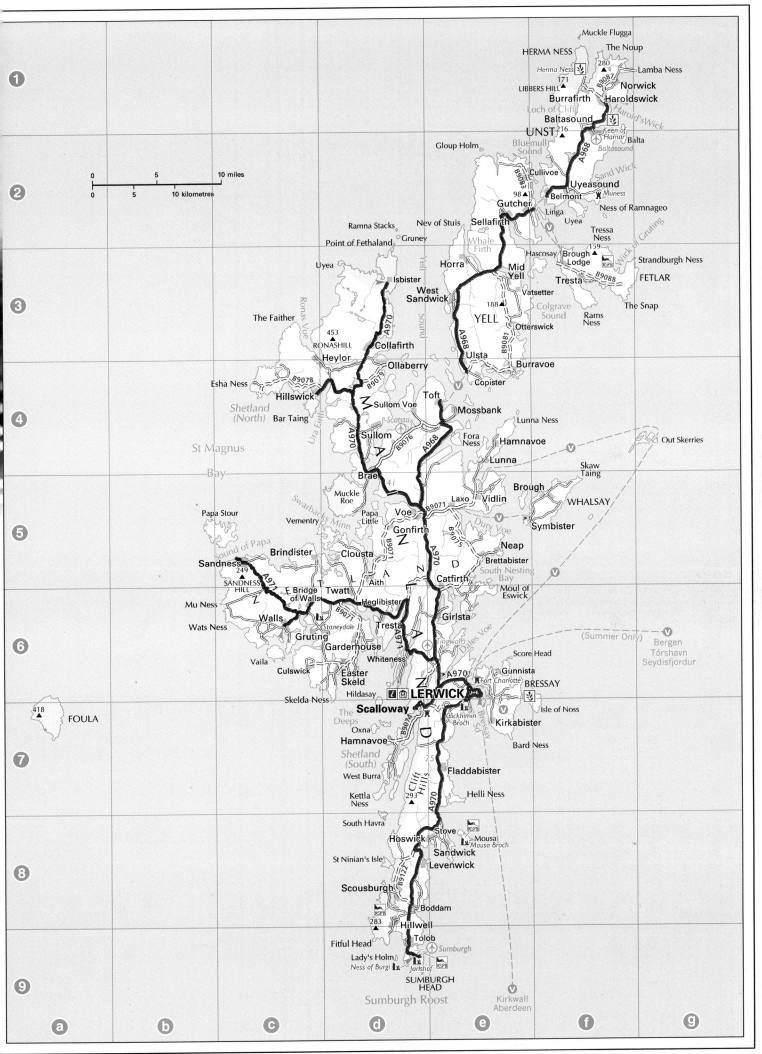

Muckle Flugga
The Noup
HERMA NESS
Herma Ness
280
LIBBERS HILL
171
Lamba Ness
Norwick
Burrafirth
Haroldswick
Baltasound
Loch of Cliff
UNST
216
Balta
Keen of Hamar
Baltasound
Gloup Holm
Bluemull
Sound
A968
Sand Wick
Cullivoe
Uyeasound
98
Belmont
Gutcher
Linga
Ness of Ramnageo
Ramna Stacks
Nev of Stuis
Muness
Gruney
Sellafirth
Uyea
Point of Fethaland
Whale
Firth
Hascosay
Tressa
Ness
Uyea
Horra
Brough
Lodge
159
Strandburgh Ness
Isbister
Mid
Yell
Tresta
RSPB
B9088
FETLAR
West
Sandwick
The Snap
The Faither
Vatsetter
A970
YELL
188
The Faither
Ronas Voe
RONASHILL
453
Collafirth
Otterswick
Rams
Ness
A968
Heylor
Ollaberry
Ulsta
Copister
Burravoe
Esha Ness
B9078
B9079
Hillswick
Lunna Ness
Shetland
(North)
Sullom Voe
Toft
Mossbank
Bar Taing
Scatsta
Fora
Ness
Hamnavoe
Out Skerries
St Magnus
B9076
Sullom
A970
Lunna
Skaw
Taing
Bay
Brae
41
Brough
WHALSAY
Muckle
Roe
Laxo
Vidlin
Papa Stour
Swarbacks Minn
Papa
Little
B9071
Symbister
Papa Stour
Vementry
Voe
Neap
Gonfirth
Brettabister
Sound of Papa
Brindister
Clousta
B9071
Moul of
Eswick
Sandness
Aith
Catfirth
South Nesting
Bay
SANDNESS
HILL
249
A971
Twatt
Heglibister
Girlsta
Mu Ness
E Bridge
of Walls
Score Head
Wats Ness
Walls
B9071
Tresta
Girlsta
Gunnista
Staneydale
A971
Bergen
Tórshavn
Seydisfjordur
Gruting
Garderhouse
Tingwall
BRESSAY
Vaila
Whiteness
A970
Fort Charlotte
Isle of Noss
Culswick
Easter
Skeld
LERWICK
Kirkabister
FOULA
418
Hildasay
Scalloway
Clickhimin
Broch
Skelda Ness
Bard Ness
The
Deeps
B9074
Oxna
Fladdabister
Helli Ness
Hamnavoe
Shetland
(South)
Clift Hills
West Burra
293
A970
Kettla
Ness
South Havra
Stove
RSPB
St Ninian's Isle
Hoswick
Mousa
Mousa Broch
Sandwick
Levenwick
Scousburgh
Boddam
RSPB
283
Hillwell
Fitful Head
Tolob
Lady's Holm
Sumburgh
Ness of Burgi
Jarlshof
RSPB
SUMBURGH
HEAD
Kirkwall
Aberdeen
Sumburgh Roost

Scale

0 — 5 — 10 miles
0 — 5 — 10 kilometres

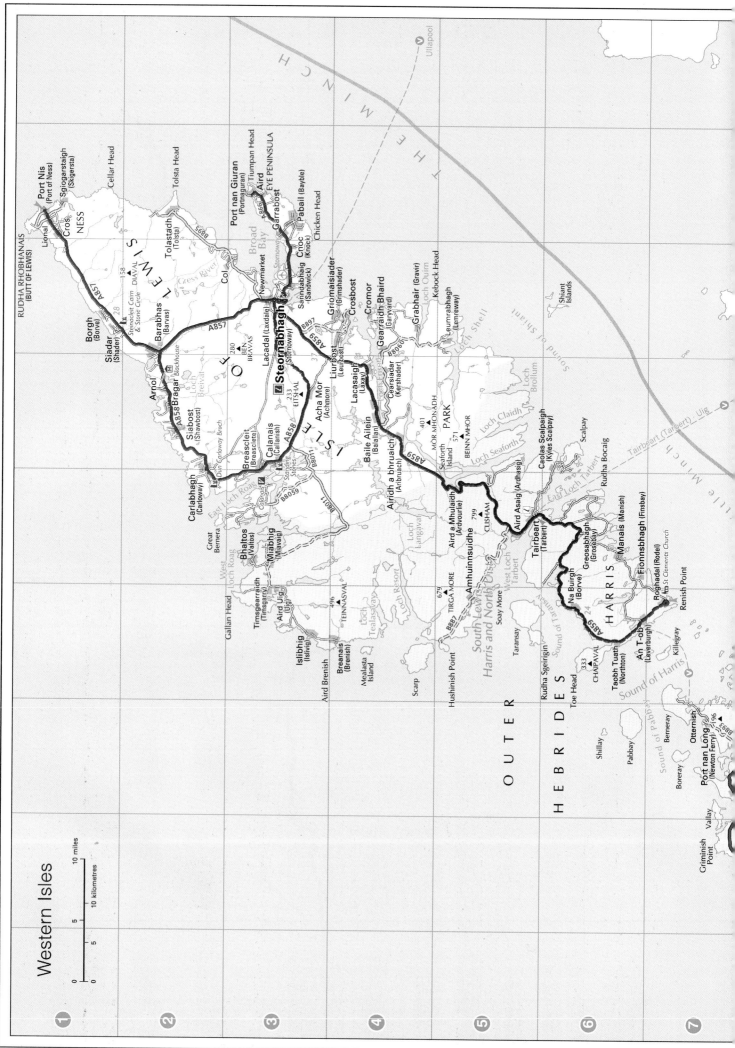

Western Isles

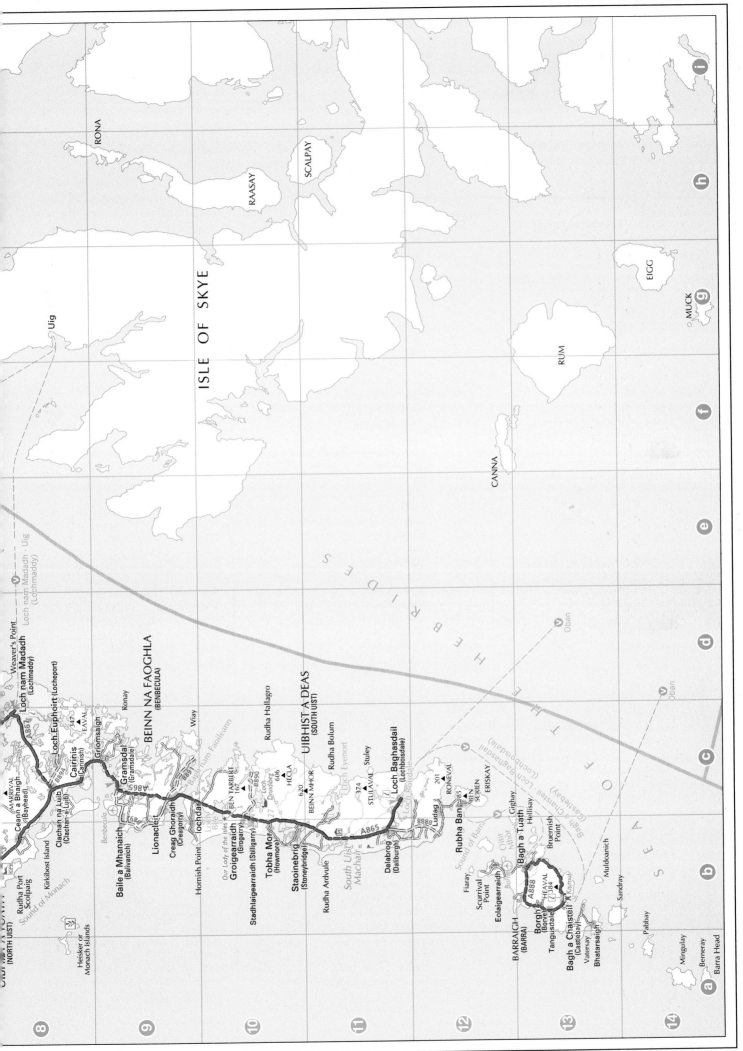

ISLE OF SKYE

RONA

SCALPAY

RAASAY

EIGG

MUCK

RUM

CANNA

OBAN

Uig

Loch nam Madadh · Uig
(Lochmaddy)

THE HEBRIDES

THE SEA OF

Oban

Oban

Weaver's Point

Loch nam Madadh
(Lochmaddy)

Loch Euphoirt (Lochport)

MARRIVAL

Ceann a Bhaigh
(Bayhead)

A867

Cairinis
(Carinish)

B894

B893

Clachan na Luib
(Clachan-a-Luib)

Griomsaigh

EAVAL
347

Gramsdal
(Gramsdale)

A865

B891

Ronay

Wiay

BEINN NA FAOGHLA
(BENBECULA)

Baile a Mhanaich
(Balivanich)

B895

Benbecula

Lionacleit

Creag Ghoraidh
(Creagorry)

Iochdar

Hornish Point

Stadhlaigearraidh (Stilligarry)

Groigearraidh
(Grogarry)

Loch Bì

Our Lady of the Isles

BEN TARBERT
167

B890

Baghasdail Faoileann

Druidibeg
Loch

HECLA
606

620
BEINN MHOR

Rudha Hallagro

UIBHIST A DEAS
(SOUTH UIST)

Rudha Bolum

Loch Eynort

Stuley

Tobha Mor
(Howmore)

Staoinebrig
(Stoneybridge)

Rudha Ardvule

South Uist
Machair

STULAVAL
374

A865

Dalabrog
(Daliburgh)

Loch Baghasdail
(Lochboisdale)

Loch

201
RONEVAL

Ludag

B888

Bagh a' Chaisteil · Lochbaisdale
(Castlebay · Lochboisdale)

Rubha Ban

Eoligearraidh

Fiaray

Scurrival
Point

BEN
SCRIEN
285

ERISKAY

Sound of Barra

Oitir
Mhor

Gighay

Hellisay

Bagh a Tuath

Bruernish
Point

BARRAIGH
(BARRA)

Borgh
(Borve)

Tangusdale

A888

HEAVAL
384
Kisimul

Bagh a Chaisteil
(Castlebay)

Vatersay

Bhatarsaigh

Muldoanich

Sandray

Pabbay

Mingulay

Bernaray

Barra Head

Rudha Port
Scolpaig

Kirkibost Island

Heisker or
Monach Islands

Sound of Monach

(NORTH UIST)

Index to place names

This index lists places appearing in the main-map section of the atlas in alphabetical order. The reference before each name gives the atlas page number and grid reference of the square in which the place appears. The map shows counties, unitary authorities and administrative areas, together with a list of the abbreviated name forms used in the index.

England

BaNES	**Bath & N E Somerset (18)**
Barns	**Barnsley (19)**
Beds	**Bedfordshire**
Birm	**Birmingham**
Bl w D	**Blackburn with Darwen (20)**
Bmouth	**Bournemouth**
Bolton	**Bolton (21)**
Bpool	**Blackpool**
Brad	**Bradford (22)**
Br & H	**Brighton and Hove (23)**
Br For	**Bracknell Forest (24)**
Bristl	**City of Bristol**
Bucks	**Buckinghamshire**
Bury	**Bury (25)**
C Derb	**City of Derby**
C KuH	**City of Kingston upon Hull**
C Leic	**City of Leicester**
C Nott	**City of Nottingham**
C Pete	**City of Peterborough**
C Plym	**City of Plymouth**
C Port	**City of Portsmouth**
C Sotn	**City of Southampton**
C Stke	**City of Stoke**
Calder	**Calderdale (26)**
Cambs	**Cambridgeshire**
Ches	**Cheshire**
Cnwll	**Cornwall**
Covtry	**Coventry**
Cumb	**Cumbria**
Darltn	**Darlington (27)**
Derbys	**Derbyshire**
Devon	**Devon**
Donc	**Doncaster (28)**
Dorset	**Dorset**
Dudley	**Dudley (29)**
Dur	**Durham**
E R Yk	**East Riding of Yorkshire**
E Susx	**East Sussex**
Essex	**Essex**
Gatesd	**Gateshead (30)**
Gloucs	**Gloucestershire**
Gt Lon	**Greater London**
Halton	**Halton (31)**
Hants	**Hampshire**
Hartpl	**Hartlepool (32)**
Herefs	**Herefordshire**
Herts	**Hertfordshire**
IoS	**Isles of Scilly**
IoW	**Isle of Wight**
Kent	**Kent**
Kirk	**Kirklees (33)**
Knows	**Knowsley (34)**
Lancs	**Lancashire**
Leeds	**Leeds**
Leics	**Leicestershire**
Lincs	**Lincolnshire**
Lpool	**Liverpool**
Luton	**Luton**
M Keyn	**Milton Keynes**

Manch	**Manchester**
Medway	**Medway**
Middsb	**Middlesbrough**
NE Lin	**North East Lincolnshire**
N Linc	**North Lincolnshire**
N Som	**North Somerset (35)**
N Tyne	**North Tyneside (36)**
N u Ty	**Newcastle upon Tyne**
N York	**North Yorkshire**
Nhants	**Northamptonshire**
Norfk	**Norfolk**
Notts	**Nottinghamshire**
Nthumb	**Northumberland**
Oldham	**Oldham (37)**
Oxon	**Oxfordshire**
Poole	**Poole**
R & Cl	**Redcar and Cleveland**
Readg	**Reading**
Rochdl	**Rochdale (38)**
Rothm	**Rotherham (39)**
Rutlnd	**Rutland**
S Glos	**South Gloucestershire (40)**
S on T	**Stockton-on-Tees (41)**
S Tyne	**South Tyneside (42)**
Salfd	**Salford (43)**
Sandw	**Sandwell (44)**
Sefton	**Sefton (45)**
Sheff	**Sheffield**
Shrops	**Shropshire**
Slough	**Slough (46)**
Solhll	**Solihull (47)**
Somset	**Somerset**
St Hel	**St Helens (48)**
Staffs	**Staffordshire**
Sthend	**Southend-on-Sea**
Stockp	**Stockport (49)**
Suffk	**Suffolk**
Sundld	**Sunderland**
Surrey	**Surrey**
Swindn	**Swindon**
Tamesd	**Tameside (50)**
Thurr	**Thurrock (51)**
Torbay	**Torbay**
Traffd	**Trafford (52)**
W & M	**Windsor & Maidenhead (53)**
W Berk	**West Berkshire**
W Susx	**West Sussex**
Wakefd	**Wakefield (54)**
Warrtn	**Warrington (55)**
Warwks	**Warwickshire**
Wigan	**Wigan (56)**
Wilts	**Wiltshire**
Wirral	**Wirral (57)**
Wokham	**Wokingham (58)**
Wolves	**Wolverhampton (59)**
Worcs	**Worcestershire**
Wrekin	**Telford and Wrekin (60)**
Wsall	**Walsall (61)**
York	**York**

Scotland

Abers	**Aberdeenshire**
Ag & B	**Argyll & Bute**
Angus	**Angus**
Border	**Borders**
C Aber	**City of Aberdeen**
C Dund	**City of Dundee**
C Edin	**City of Edinburgh**
C Glas	**City of Glasgow**
Clacks	**Clackmannanshire (1)**
D & G	**Dumfries & Galloway**
E Ayrs	**East Ayrshire**
E Duns	**East Dunbartonshire (2)**
E Loth	**East Lothian**
E Rens	**East Renfrewshire (3)**
Falk	**Falkirk**
Fife	**Fife**
Highld	**Highland**
Inver	**Inverclyde (4)**
Mdloth	**Midlothian (5)**
Moray	**Moray**
N Ayrs	**North Ayrshire**
N Lans	**North Lanarkshire (6)**
Ork	**Orkney Islands**
P & K	**Perth & Kinross**
Rens	**Renfrewshire (7)**
S Ayrs	**South Ayrshire**
Shet	**Shetland Islands**
S Lans	**South Lanarkshire**
Stirlg	**Stirling**
W Duns	**West Dunbartonshire (8)**
W Isls	**Western Isles**
W Loth	**West Lothian**

Wales

Blae G	**Blaenau Gwent (9)**
Brdgnd	**Bridgend (10)**
Caerph	**Caerphilly (11)**
Cardif	**Cardiff**
Carmth	**Carmarthenshire**
Cerdgn	**Ceredigion**
Conwy	**Conwy**
Denbgs	**Denbighshire**
Flints	**Flintshire**
Gwynd	**Gwynedd**
IoA	**Isle of Anglesey**
Mons	**Monmouthshire**
Myr Td	**Merthyr Tydfil (12)**
Neath	**Neath Port Talbot (13)**
Newpt	**Newport (14)**
Pembks	**Pembrokeshire**
Powys	**Powys**
Rhondd	**Rhondda Cynon Taff (15)**
Swans	**Swansea**
Torfn	**Torfaen (16)**
V Glam	**Vale of Glamorgan (17)**
Wrexhm	**Wrexham**

Channel Islands & Isle of Man

Guern	**Guernsey**
Jersey	**Jersey**
IoM	**Isle of Man**

ORKNEY ISLANDS

SHETLAND ISLANDS

WESTERN

ISLES

HIGHLAND

MORAY

S C O T L A N D

ABERDEENSHIRE

Aberdeen

ANGUS

PERTH & KINROSS

Dundee

ARGYLL & BUTE

STIRLING

FIFE

1

FALK

Edinburgh

E LOTH

8   2

W

4   LOTH

Glasgow   6

7   5

3

BORDERS

NORTH AYRSHIRE

S LANS

E AYRS

S AYRS

DUMFRIES & GALLOWAY

NORTHUMBERLAND

Newcastle upon Tyne   36

30   42

Sunderland

CUMBRIA

DURHAM   32

27 41 R & CL

Middlesbrough

IoM

NORTH YORKSHIRE

York   EAST RIDING OF YORKSHIRE

Blackpool   LANCASTER   22   Leeds   Kingston upon Hull

26

20   33   54   N LINCS   N E LINCS

21 25 38

IoA   56 37   19   28

45   34 43 50

48   52   39

Liverpool   55 49   Manchester

57   31   Sheffield

CONWY

FLINTS   CHESHIRE   DERBYS   NOTTS   LINCOLNSHIRE

DENBGS

WREXHAM   Stoke-on-Trent   Nottingham

GWYNEDD   Derby

STAFFS   LEICS   RUTLAND   NORFOLK

60   Peterborough

POWYS   SHROPSHIRE   59 61   Leicester   CAMBS

29 44 Birmingham

47   Coventry   NHANTS   SUFFOLK

CERDGN   WORCS   WARWKS   Milton Keynes   BEDS

HEREFS   Luton   ESSEX

PEMBKS   CARMTH   W A L E S   E N G L A N D   HERTS

GLOUCS   OXON   Southend-on-Sea

12   MONS   BUCKS   GREATER   51

13   9   16   Swindon   Reading   53 46   LONDON   MEDWAY

15 11   14   40   W BERKS   58 24

10   Cardiff   Bristol   Swindon   SURREY   KENT

17   35   18   WILTSHIRE   HAMPSHIRE   W SUSX   E SUSX   23

SOMERSET   Southampton

DEVON   DORSET   Portsmouth

Bournemouth   IoW

CORNWALL   Poole

Torbay   CHANNEL ISLANDS   Guernsey

Plymouth   Jersey

IoS

A

246 C7 **A'Chill** Highld
117 J7 **Ab Kettleby** Leics
82 B5 **Ab Lench** Worcs
32 B6 **Abbas Combe** Somset
81 H2 **Abberley** Worcs
81 G2 **Abberley Common** Worcs
72 E3 **Abberton** Essex
82 A4 **Abberton** Worcs
191 G3 **Abberwick** Nthumb
70 E5 **Abbess Roding** Essex
29 L8 **Abbey** Devon
62 D1 **Abbey Dore** Herefs
131 J8 **Abbey Green** Staffs
30 D7 **Abbey Hill** Somset
213 G6 **Abbey St Bathans** Border
177 G8 **Abbey Town** Cumb
139 J3 **Abbey Village** Lancs
52 A3 **Abbey Wood** Gt Lon
78 E1 **Abbeycwmhir** Powys
132 F3 **Abbeydale** Sheff
147 L5 **Abbeystead** Lancs
131 K2 **Abbot's Chair** Derbys
82 C5 **Abbot's Salford** Warwks
189 G4 **Abbotrule** Border
27 G8 **Abbots Bickington** Devon
115 H6 **Abbots Bromley** Staffs
221 K5 **Abbots Deuglie** P & K
68 E6 **Abbots Langley** Herts
45 G4 **Abbots Leigh** N Som
82 B4 **Abbots Morton** Worcs
102 E7 **Abbots Ripton** Cambs
35 G4 **Abbots Worthy** Hants
16 A5 **Abbotsbury** Dorset
27 G5 **Abbotsham** Devon
8 C1 **Abbotskerswell** Devon
8 B5 **Abbotsleigh** Devon
86 E4 **Abbotsley** Cambs
35 H4 **Abbotstone** Hants
34 D6 **Abbotswood** Hants
17 J2 **Abbott Street** Dorset
34 D2 **Abbotts Ann** Hants
95 J7 **Abcott** Shrops
96 D6 **Abdon** Shrops
63 K4 **Abenhall** Gloucs
61 H3 **Aber Clydach** Powys
76 B7 **Aber-arad** Carmth
76 C7 **Aber-banc** Cerdgn
76 F7 **Aber-giar** Carmth
92 E8 **Aber-Magwr** Cerdgn
77 G4 **Aber-meurig** Cerdgn
60 F6 **Aber-nant** Rhondd
76 E3 **Aberaeron** Cerdgn
60 F7 **Aberaman** Rhondd
93 J2 **Aberangell** Gwynd
251 H6 **Aberarder** Highld
222 B4 **Aberargie** P & K
76 E3 **Aberarth** Cerdgn
57 K7 **Aberavon** Neath
61 J7 **Aberbargoed** Caerph
61 K6 **Aberbeeg** Blae G
221 G3 **Abercairny** P & K
61 G6 **Abercanaid** Myr Td
43 K3 **Abercarn** Caerph
74 D5 **Abercastle** Pembks
93 H3 **Abercegir** Powys
240 B3 **Aberchalder Lodge** Highld
268 A5 **Aberchirder** Abers
77 J4 **Abercoed** Cerdgn
59 M6 **Abercraf** Powys
42 C2 **Abercregan** Neath
60 F7 **Abercwmboi** Rhondd
75 M4 **Abercych** Pembks
43 G3 **Abercynon** Rhondd
221 K3 **Aberdalgie** P & K
60 F6 **Aberdare** Rhondd
108 C6 **Aberdaron** Gwynd
245 L2 **Aberdeen** C Aber
109 G1 **Aberdesach** Gwynd
211 G2 **Aberdour** Fife
57 L5 **Aberdulais** Neath
92 D4 **Aberdyfi** Gwynd
78 F6 **Aberedw** Powys
74 C6 **Abereiddy** Pembks
109 G4 **Abererch** Gwynd
61 G7 **Aberfan** Myr Td
232 C5 **Aberfeldy** P & K
124 F6 **Aberffraw** IOA
92 E7 **Aberffrwd** Cerdgn
150 F8 **Aberford** Leeds
219 H7 **Aberfoyle** Stirlg
42 D5 **Abergarw** Brdgnd
60 B6 **Abergarwed** Neath

62 C4 **Abergavenny** Mons
127 J4 **Abergele** Conwy
59 G2 **Abergorlech** Carmth
78 A4 **Abergwesyn** Powys
58 D5 **Abergwili** Carmth
93 G3 **Abergwydol** Powys
126 C5 **Abergwyngregyn** Gwynd
92 E2 **Abergynolwyn** Gwynd
94 C5 **Aberhafesp** Powys
93 H4 **Aberhosan** Powys
42 D5 **Aberkenfig** Brdgnd
212 A3 **Aberlady** E Loth
234 E4 **Aberlemno** Angus
93 G2 **Aberllefenni** Powys
79 H7 **Aberllynfi** Powys
254 E3 **Aberlour** Moray
129 G8 **Abermorddu** Flints
94 E4 **Abermule** Powys
58 C4 **Abernant** Carmth
222 C4 **Abernethy** P & K
222 D1 **Abernyte** P & K
76 A5 **Aberporth** Cerdgn
108 E6 **Abersoch** Gwynd
62 B6 **Abersychan** Torfn
42 F6 **Aberthin** V Glam
61 K6 **Abertillery** Blae G
43 H4 **Abertridwr** Caerph
111 K7 **Abertridwr** Powys
61 H6 **Abertysswg** Caerph
221 H4 **Aberuthven** P & K
60 F1 **Aberyscir** Powys
92 C7 **Aberystwyth** Cerdgn
66 C7 **Abingdon** Oxon
37 H2 **Abinger** Surrey
37 G2 **Abinger Hammer** Surrey
84 F3 **Abington** Nhants
186 D2 **Abington** S Lans
86 F6 **Abington Pigotts** Cambs
65 G5 **Ablington** Gloucs
33 K2 **Ablington** Wilts
132 D4 **Abney** Derbys
115 G2 **Above Church** Staffs
244 C4 **Aboyne** Abers
139 J7 **Abram** Wigan
250 F4 **Abriachan** Highld
70 C7 **Abridge** Essex
45 L4 **Abson** S Glos
84 C6 **Abthorpe** Nhants
137 H4 **Aby** Lincs
151 J6 **Acaster Malbis** York
151 J7 **Acaster Selby** N York
27 M4 **Accott** Devon
139 M2 **Accrington** Lancs
224 F4 **Acha** Ag & B
282 f3 **Acha Mor** W Isls
206 B3 **Achahoish** Ag & B
233 H6 **Achalader** P & K
228 E8 **Achaleven** Ag & B
261 M7 **Achanalt** Highld
263 H5 **Achandunie** Highld
272 E7 **Achany** Highld
237 K3 **Acharacle** Highld
227 K2 **Acharn** Highld
231 L6 **Acharn** P & K
279 L7 **Achavanich** Highld
270 D7 **Achduart** Highld
276 D8 **Achfary** Highld
270 D6 **Achiltibuie** Highld
192 F5 **Achinhoan** Ag & B
248 F3 **Achintee** Highld
248 D4 **Achintraid** Highld
270 E3 **Achmelvich** Highld
248 D5 **Achmore** Highld
282 f3 **Achmore** W Isls
270 D2 **Achnacarnin** Highld
239 K6 **Achnacarry** Highld
247 J6 **Achnacloich** Highld
250 D8 **Achnaconeran** Highld
228 C7 **Achnacroish** Ag & B
226 F2 **Achnadrish Lodge** Ag & B
232 C8 **Achnafauld** P & K
263 J6 **Achnagarron** Highld
236 F6 **Achnaha** Highld
270 D5 **Achnahaird** Highld
272 E5 **Achnairn** Highld
228 C3 **Achnalea** Highld
206 B2 **Achnamara** Ag & B
261 K8 **Achnasheen** Highld
249 G2 **Achnashellach Lodge** Highld
254 F5 **Achnastank** Moray
236 E7 **Achosnich** Highld
227 K3 **Achranich** Highld
279 H3 **Achreamie** Highld
229 J2 **Achriabhach** Highld

276 D5 **Achriesgill** Highld
277 M4 **Achtoty** Highld
102 A6 **Achurch** Nhants
263 J1 **Achvaich** Highld
280 E5 **Ackergill** Highld
170 C7 **Acklam** Middsb
152 B3 **Acklam** N York
97 H4 **Ackleton** Shrops
191 J6 **Acklington** Nthumb
142 C3 **Ackton** Wakefd
142 C4 **Ackworth Moor Top** Wakefd
107 H1 **Acle** Norfk
98 E6 **Acock's Green** Birm
41 J2 **Acol** Kent
179 L5 **Acomb** Nthumb
151 J5 **Acomb** York
30 B8 **Acombe** Somset
80 C8 **Aconbury** Herefs
140 B3 **Acre** Lancs
112 D3 **Acrefair** Wrexhm
99 J1 **Acresford** Derbys
113 K1 **Acton** Ches
17 J6 **Acton** Dorset
51 G3 **Acton** Gt Lon
114 C3 **Acton** Staffs
89 H6 **Acton** Suffk
81 J2 **Acton** Worcs
80 F5 **Acton Beauchamp** Herefs
130 B4 **Acton Bridge** Ches
96 C3 **Acton Burnell** Shrops
81 G5 **Acton Green** Herefs
112 E1 **Acton Park** Wrexhm
96 C3 **Acton Pigott** Shrops
96 E4 **Acton Round** Shrops
95 L5 **Acton Scott** Shrops
114 E7 **Acton Trussell** Staffs
46 A3 **Acton Turville** S Glos
114 B6 **Adbaston** Staffs
31 K6 **Adber** Dorset
117 G4 **Adbolton** Notts
113 L3 **Adderley** Shrops
203 J7 **Adderstone** Nthumb
210 C6 **Addiewell** W Loth
149 K6 **Addingham** Brad
67 H2 **Addington** Bucks
51 K6 **Addington** Gt Lon
52 E7 **Addington** Kent
51 J5 **Addiscombe** Gt Lon
50 D6 **Addlestone** Surrey
50 D6 **Addlestonemoor** Surrey
137 K6 **Addlethorpe** Lincs
113 M7 **Adeney** Wrekin
68 D5 **Adeyfield** Herts
94 C3 **Adfa** Powys
79 M1 **Adforton** Herefs
41 H4 **Adisham** Kent
65 K2 **Adlestrop** Gloucs
143 L3 **Adlingfleet** E R Yk
131 H4 **Adlington** Ches
139 J5 **Adlington** Lancs
115 G7 **Admaston** Staffs
96 E1 **Admaston** Wrekin
82 E6 **Admington** Warwks
76 B7 **Adpar** Cerdgn
30 D5 **Adsborough** Somset
30 B3 **Adscombe** Somset
67 H1 **Adstock** Bucks
84 B5 **Adstone** Nhants
131 H2 **Adswood** Stockp
37 G6 **Adversane** W Susx
254 C5 **Advie** Highld
141 K2 **Adwalton** Leeds
67 G7 **Adwell** Oxon
142 E6 **Adwick Le Street** Donc
142 D7 **Adwick upon Dearne** Donc
176 C1 **Ae** D & G
176 D2 **Ae Bridgend** D & G
139 M5 **Affetside** Bury
255 L4 **Affleck** Abers
16 F4 **Affpuddle** Dorset
249 K7 **Affric Lodge** Highld
128 D5 **Afon-wen** Flints
8 C2 **Afton** Devon
18 E6 **Afton** IOW
159 K5 **Agglethorpe** N York
129 J2 **Aigburth** Lpool
153 G6 **Aike** E R Yk
166 B1 **Aiketgate** Cumb
165 H1 **Aikhead** Cumb
177 J8 **Aikton** Cumb
137 H4 **Ailby** Lincs
79 L5 **Ailey** Herefs
102 C4 **Ailsworth** C Pete
160 E6 **Ainderby Quernhow** N York

160 E4 **Ainderby Steeple** N York
73 G3 **Aingers Green** Essex
138 C5 **Ainsdale** Sefton
138 C5 **Ainsdale-on-Sea** Sefton
166 C2 **Ainstable** Cumb
139 M3 **Ainsworth** Bury
162 C1 **Ainthorpe** N York
138 D8 **Aintree** Sefton
210 F6 **Ainville** W Loth
216 B7 **Aird** Ag & B
172 D3 **Aird** D & G
282 h3 **Aird** W Isls
282 e5 **Aird a Mhulaidh** W Isls
282 e5 **Aird Asaig** W Isls
248 A4 **Aird Dhubh** Highld
227 G6 **Aird of Kinloch** Ag & B
247 J8 **Aird of Sleat** Highld
282 d3 **Aird Uig** W Isls
216 F1 **Airdeny** Ag & B
209 K6 **Airdrie** N Lans
209 K5 **Airdriehill** N Lans
216 F1 **Airds Bay** Ag & B
175 G1 **Airds of Kells** D & G
282 f4 **Airidh a bhruaich** W Isls
175 J3 **Airieland** D & G
233 M5 **Airlie** Angus
143 J3 **Airmyn** E R Yk
233 G8 **Airntully** P & K
247 M7 **Airor** Highld
210 B2 **Airth** Falk
148 F4 **Airton** N York
135 H1 **Aisby** Lincs
118 D4 **Aisby** Lincs
158 D3 **Aisgill** Cumb
7 K3 **Aish** Devon
8 C3 **Aish** Devon
30 B4 **Aisholt** Somset
160 C5 **Aiskew** N York
162 F1 **Aislaby** N York
162 D5 **Aislaby** N York
169 L8 **Aislaby** S on T
135 J3 **Aisthorpe** Lincs
281 d5 **Aith** Shet
202 E7 **Akeld** Nthumb
84 D7 **Akeley** Bucks
90 D5 **Akenham** Suffk
6 E1 **Albaston** Cnwll
112 E8 **Alberbury** Shrops
22 C4 **Albourne** W Susx
22 C4 **Albourne Green** W Susx
113 H7 **Albrighton** Shrops
97 H3 **Albrighton** Shrops
106 F6 **Alburgh** Norfk
70 B2 **Albury** Herts
67 G6 **Albury** Oxon
37 G2 **Albury** Surrey
70 B2 **Albury End** Herts
37 G2 **Albury Heath** Surrey
122 D5 **Alby Hill** Norfk
263 G8 **Alcaig** Highld
95 L6 **Alcaston** Shrops
82 C4 **Alcester** Warwks
98 D7 **Alcester Lane End** Birm
23 H6 **Alciston** E Susx
46 A5 **Alcombe** Wilts
102 D8 **Alconbury** Cambs
102 D7 **Alconbury Weston** Cambs
150 F3 **Aldborough** N York
122 D5 **Aldborough** Norfk
47 K4 **Aldbourne** Wilts
153 L8 **Aldbrough** E R Yk
169 G8 **Aldbrough St John** N York
68 B4 **Aldbury** Herts
147 J4 **Aldcliffe** Lancs
232 D3 **Aldclune** P & K
91 K4 **Aldeburgh** Suffk
107 J5 **Aldeby** Norfk
68 F7 **Aldenham** Herts
115 L6 **Alder Moor** Staffs
33 L5 **Alderbury** Wilts
116 D2 **Aldercar** Derbys
122 C7 **Alderford** Norfk
33 K8 **Alderholt** Dorset
45 M1 **Alderley** Gloucs
131 G4 **Alderley Edge** Ches
99 K6 **Aldermans Green** Covtry
48 E6 **Aldermaston** W Berk
82 F5 **Alderminster** Warwks
129 K8 **Aldersey Green** Ches
36 C1 **Aldershot** Hants
82 B8 **Alderton** Gloucs
84 E6 **Alderton** Nhants
113 H6 **Alderton** Shrops
91 H7 **Alderton** Suffk
46 B2 **Alderton** Wilts

Alderwasley - Ardeonaig Hotel 287

116 A1 **Alderwasley** Derbys
150 C2 **Aldfield** N York
129 K7 **Aldford** Ches
101 L3 **Aldgate** Rutlnd
72 D2 **Aldham** Essex
90 B6 **Aldham** Suffk
20 F5 **Aldingbourne** W Susx
146 E2 **Aldingham** Cumb
40 E8 **Aldington** Kent
82 C6 **Aldington** Worcs
40 E7 **Aldington Corner** Kent
255 G6 **Aldivalloch** Moray
208 B1 **Aldochlay** Ag & B
95 K7 **Aldon** Shrops
164 F1 **Aldoth** Cumb
103 J8 **Aldreth** Cambs
98 D3 **Aldridge** Wsall
91 K3 **Aldringham** Suffk
152 B3 **Aldro** N York
65 H5 **Aldsworth** Gloucs
20 C5 **Aldsworth** W Susx
255 G6 **Aldunie** Moray
132 E8 **Aldwark** Derbys
151 G3 **Aldwark** N York
20 E7 **Aldwick** W Susx
101 M7 **Aldwincle** Nhants
48 E3 **Aldworth** W Berk
208 C3 **Alexandria** W Duns
30 B3 **Aley** Somset
26 E8 **Alfardisworthy** Devon
14 D3 **Alfington** Devon
36 F4 **Alfold** Surrey
36 F4 **Alfold Bars** W Susx
36 F4 **Alfold Crossways** Surrey
255 M8 **Alford** Abers
137 H4 **Alford** Lincs
31 K4 **Alford** Somset
133 H8 **Alfreton** Derbys
81 H4 **Alfrick** Worcs
81 G5 **Alfrick Pound** Worcs
23 H6 **Alfriston** E Susx
119 J4 **Algarkirk** Lincs
31 K4 **Alhampton** Somset
143 M3 **Alkborough** N Linc
63 M6 **Alkerton** Gloucs
83 J6 **Alkerton** Oxon
41 H6 **Alkham** Kent
113 H4 **Alkington** Shrops
115 K4 **Alkmonton** Derbys
46 F6 **All Cannings** Wilts
107 G7 **All Saints South Elmham** Suffk
95 L4 **All Stretton** Shrops
8 B4 **Allaleigh** Devon
242 F5 **Allanaquoich** Abers
209 M7 **Allanbank** N Lans
202 D2 **Allanton** Border
209 M7 **Allanton** N Lans
209 K8 **Allanton** S Lans
63 J6 **Allaston** Gloucs
34 F6 **Allbrook** Hants
98 F4 **Allen End** Warwks
70 C4 **Allen's Green** Herts
179 J7 **Allendale** Nthumb
167 K2 **Allenheads** Nthumb
168 D1 **Allensford** Dur
80 B8 **Allensmore** Herefs
116 B5 **Allenton** C Derb
28 D5 **Aller** Devon
30 F5 **Aller** Somset
164 E3 **Allerby** Cumb
14 B4 **Allercombe** Devon
28 F2 **Allerford** Somset
162 F6 **Allerston** N York
152 B6 **Allerthorpe** E R Yk
141 H1 **Allerton** Brad
263 K6 **Allerton** Highld
129 J2 **Allerton** Lpool
142 C2 **Allerton Bywater** Leeds
150 F4 **Allerton Mauleverer** N York
99 J7 **Allesley** Covtry
116 B4 **Allestree** C Derb
4 C5 **Allet Common** Cnwll
101 H3 **Allexton** Leics
131 J6 **Allgreave** Ches
53 H3 **Allhallows** Medway
53 H3 **Allhallows-on-Sea** Medway
260 D8 **Alligin Shuas** Highld
114 D7 **Allimore Green** Staffs
15 K4 **Allington** Dorset
53 G7 **Allington** Kent
117 M3 **Allington** Lincs
46 C4 **Allington** Wilts
46 F6 **Allington** Wilts
33 L3 **Allington** Wilts
156 E7 **Allithwaite** Cumb
220 F8 **Alloa** Clacks
164 E2 **Allonby** Cumb
130 E5 **Allostock** Ches
196 C7 **Alloway** S Ayrs
30 F8 **Allowenshay** Somset
97 G4 **Allscott** Shrops
96 E1 **Allscott** Wrekin
129 G6 **Alltami** Flints
229 K5 **Alltchaorunn** Highld
78 F6 **Alltmawr** Powys
58 E3 **Alltwalis** Carmth
57 K4 **Alltwen** Neath
76 F6 **Alltyblaca** Cerdgn
31 L8 **Allweston** Dorset
90 B1 **Allwood Green** Suffk
79 L5 **Almeley** Herefs
79 L5 **Almeley Wooton** Herefs
17 H3 **Almer** Dorset
142 F6 **Almholme** Donc
113 M4 **Almington** Staffs
20 D7 **Almodington** W Susx
221 J2 **Almondbank** P & K
141 J5 **Almondbury** Kirk
45 J2 **Almondsbury** S Glos
151 G3 **Alne** N York
90 E7 **Alnesbourn Priory** Suffk
263 H6 **Alness** Highld
190 E4 **Alnham** Nthumb
191 J4 **Alnmouth** Nthumb
191 H3 **Alnwick** Nthumb
50 F2 **Alperton** Gt Lon
89 H8 **Alphamstone** Essex
89 H5 **Alpheton** Suffk
13 L4 **Alphington** Devon
106 F3 **Alpington** Norfk
132 D6 **Alport** Derbys
130 B7 **Alpraham** Ches
72 F3 **Alresford** Essex
115 K8 **Alrewas** Staffs
130 F8 **Alsager** Ches
114 C2 **Alsagers Bank** Staffs
132 C8 **Alsop en le Dale** Derbys
167 G2 **Alston** Cumb
15 G2 **Alston** Devon
44 E8 **Alston Sutton** Somset
82 A8 **Alstone** Gloucs
30 D2 **Alstone** Somset
114 D7 **Alstone Green** Staffs
132 C8 **Alstonefield** Staffs
28 C6 **Alswear** Devon
140 E7 **Alt** Oldham
270 C5 **Altandhu** Highld
11 J6 **Altarnun** Cnwll
272 D8 **Altass** Highld
227 K5 **Altcreich** Ag & B
207 G4 **Altgaltraig** Ag & B
140 A1 **Altham** Lancs
72 D7 **Althorne** Essex
143 L6 **Althorpe** N Linc
279 H7 **Altnabreac Station** Highld
216 C2 **Altnacraig** Ag & B
272 E1 **Altnaharra** Highld
142 B3 **Altofts** Wakefd
133 G6 **Alton** Derbys
35 L3 **Alton** Hants
115 H3 **Alton** Staffs
33 K2 **Alton** Wilts
47 G6 **Alton Barnes** Wilts
16 D2 **Alton Pancras** Dorset
47 G6 **Alton Priors** Wilts
130 E2 **Altrincham** Traffd
219 G6 **Altskeith Hotel** Stirlg
220 F7 **Alva** Clacks
268 B4 **Alvah** Abers
129 L5 **Alvanley** Ches
116 C5 **Alvaston** C Derb
82 B1 **Alvechurch** Worcs
99 H3 **Alvecote** Warwks
33 G6 **Alvediston** Wilts
97 G6 **Alveley** Shrops
27 J6 **Alverdiscott** Devon
19 K4 **Alverstoke** Hants
19 K6 **Alverstone** IOW
141 M3 **Alverthorpe** Wakefd
117 L3 **Alverton** Notts
266 C4 **Alves** Moray
65 K6 **Alvescot** Oxon
45 J1 **Alveston** Gloucs
82 F4 **Alveston** Warwks
137 G2 **Alvingham** Lincs
63 J7 **Alvington** Gloucs
102 C4 **Alwalton** Cambs
190 C5 **Alwinton** Nthumb
150 C7 **Alwoodley** Leeds
150 D7 **Alwoodley Gates** Leeds
233 K5 **Alyth** P & K
119 H2 **Amber Hill** Lincs
133 G8 **Amber Row** Derbys
116 B1 **Ambergate** Derbys
64 B6 **Amberley** Gloucs
21 H4 **Amberley** W Susx
23 K5 **Amberstone** E Susx
191 K5 **Amble** Nthumb
97 K6 **Amblecote** Dudley
141 H2 **Ambler Thorn** Brad
156 E2 **Ambleside** Cumb
75 G7 **Ambleston** Pembks
66 F3 **Ambrosden** Oxon
143 L5 **Amcotts** N Linc
103 J7 **America** Cambs
68 B7 **Amersham** Bucks
68 B7 **Amersham on the Hill** Bucks
114 F6 **Amerton** Staffs
33 K3 **Amesbury** Wilts
282 d5 **Amhuinnsuidhe** W Isls
99 G3 **Amington** Staffs
176 D2 **Amisfield Town** D & G
125 H1 **Amlwch** IOA
59 H6 **Ammanford** Carmth
162 C7 **Amotherby** N York
34 E6 **Ampfield** Hants
161 J7 **Ampleforth** N York
64 F6 **Ampney Crucis** Gloucs
65 G6 **Ampney St Mary** Gloucs
65 G6 **Ampney St Peter** Gloucs
34 C2 **Amport** Hants
85 K7 **Ampthill** Beds
89 H1 **Ampton** Suffk
55 K5 **Amroth** Pembks
232 D8 **Amulree** P & K
68 F4 **Amwell** Herts
282 d6 **An t-Ob** W Isls
228 C3 **Anaheilt** Highld
118 C3 **Ancaster** Lincs
94 E6 **Anchor** Shrops
202 F4 **Ancroft** Nthumb
189 H1 **Ancrum** Border
21 G6 **Ancton** W Susx
137 K4 **Anderby** Lincs
30 E4 **Andersea** Somset
30 C4 **Andersfield** Somset
17 G3 **Anderson** Dorset
130 C4 **Anderton** Ches
6 E4 **Anderton** Cnwll
34 D2 **Andover** Hants
64 F3 **Andoversford** Gloucs
154 f2 **Andreas** IOM
108 B6 **Anelog** Gwynd
51 J5 **Anerley** Gt Lon
129 J1 **Anfield** Lpool
2 F3 **Angarrack** Cnwll
3 K4 **Angarrick** Cnwll
96 D8 **Angelbank** Shrops
30 B7 **Angersleigh** Somset
177 H7 **Angerton** Cumb
54 D6 **Angle** Pembks
21 H6 **Angmering** W Susx
158 F3 **Angram** N York
151 H6 **Angram** N York
3 H7 **Angrouse** Cnwll
179 L5 **Anick** Nthumb
264 C5 **Ankerville** Highld
117 K7 **Ankle Hill** Leics
144 C2 **Anlaby** E R Yk
121 G5 **Anmer** Norfk
19 L1 **Anmore** Hants
34 D2 **Anna Valley** Hants
177 G5 **Annan** D & G
155 K5 **Annaside** Cumb
248 E1 **Annat** Highld
209 J5 **Annathill** N Lans
196 E6 **Annbank** S Ayrs
116 E1 **Annesley** Notts
116 E1 **Annesley Woodhouse** Notts
180 E8 **Annfield Plain** Dur
208 F5 **Anniesland** C Glas
181 G4 **Annitsford** N Tyne
95 L2 **Annscroft** Shrops
138 D2 **Ansdell** Lancs
31 L4 **Ansford** Somset
99 J5 **Ansley** Warwks
115 L6 **Anslow** Staffs
115 K6 **Anslow Gate** Staffs
115 K6 **Anslow Lees** Staffs
36 D4 **Ansteadbrook** Surrey
35 L3 **Anstey** Hants
87 H8 **Anstey** Herts
100 C2 **Anstey** Leics
223 K6 **Anstruther** Fife
37 L6 **Ansty** W Susx
99 L6 **Ansty** Warwks
33 G5 **Ansty** Wilts
16 E2 **Ansty Cross** Dorset
19 L1 **Anthill Common** Hants
50 C6 **Anthonys** Surrey
177 G7 **Anthorn** Cumb
122 E5 **Antingham** Norfk
119 J2 **Anton's Gowt** Lincs
6 D4 **Antony** Cnwll
130 C3 **Antrobus** Ches
3 G5 **Antron** Cnwll
11 M2 **Anvil Corner** Devon
40 E5 **Anvil Green** Kent
118 F2 **Anwick** Lincs
174 F4 **Anwoth** D & G
51 L7 **Aperfield** Gt Lon
82 A1 **Apes Dale** Worcs
102 A4 **Apethorpe** Nhants
114 D7 **Apeton** Staffs
136 B5 **Apley** Lincs
133 H4 **Apperknowle** Derbys
64 B2 **Apperley** Gloucs
150 B8 **Apperley Bridge** Brad
180 C7 **Apperley Dene** Nthumb
158 E4 **Appersett** N York
228 E6 **Appin** Ag & B
144 B5 **Appleby** N Linc
99 J2 **Appleby Magna** Leics
99 J2 **Appleby Parva** Leics
69 J6 **Appleby Street** Herts
166 F6 **Appleby-in-Westmorland** Cumb
248 A3 **Applecross** Highld
27 H5 **Appledore** Devon
29 K7 **Appledore** Devon
25 H2 **Appledore** Kent
25 H1 **Appledore Heath** Kent
66 D8 **Appleford** Oxon
176 F2 **Applegarth Town** D & G
142 A5 **Applehaigh** Wakefd
34 C1 **Appleshaw** Hants
165 J5 **Applethwaite** Cumb
129 M2 **Appleton** Halton
66 C6 **Appleton** Oxon
130 B3 **Appleton** Warrtn
151 J7 **Appleton Roebuck** N York
130 C3 **Appleton Thorn** Warrtn
160 F2 **Appleton Wiske** N York
162 C5 **Appleton-le-Moors** N York
162 C7 **Appleton-le-Street** N York
188 F3 **Appletreehall** Border
149 J4 **Appletreewick** N York
29 K6 **Appley** Somset
139 G6 **Appley Bridge** Lancs
19 J7 **Apse Heath** IOW
86 C8 **Apsley End** Beds
20 D6 **Apuldram** W Susx
264 C5 **Arabella** Highld
234 F7 **Arbirlot** Angus
264 D3 **Arboll** Highld
49 H5 **Arborfield** Wokham
49 J5 **Arborfield Cross** Wokham
133 G3 **Arbourthorne** Sheff
235 G7 **Arbroath** Angus
245 H8 **Arbuthnott** Abers
39 L6 **Arcadia** Kent
56 E4 **Archddu** Carmth
169 H7 **Archdeacon Newton** Darltn
208 C3 **Archencarroch** W Duns
254 E3 **Archiestown** Moray
9 f2 **Archirondel** Jersey
130 F7 **Arclid Green** Ches
217 H2 **Ardanaiseig Hotel** Ag & B
248 D4 **Ardaneaskan** Highld
248 D4 **Ardarroch** Highld
204 F7 **Ardbeg** Ag & B
207 H5 **Ardbeg** Ag & B
207 K2 **Ardbeg** Ag & B
261 K2 **Ardcharnich** Highld
214 D1 **Ardchiavaig** Ag & B
216 F5 **Ardchonnel** Ag & B
219 K4 **Ardchullarie More** Stirlg
218 C8 **Arddarroch** Ag & B
112 C8 **Arddleen** Powys
239 J5 **Ardechive** Highld
196 B3 **Ardeer** N Ayrs
69 J2 **Ardeley** Herts
248 D6 **Ardelve** Highld
208 B2 **Arden** Ag & B
82 D4 **Ardens Grafton** Warwks
216 C2 **Ardentallen** Ag & B
207 K2 **Ardentinny** Ag & B
207 G4 **Ardentraive** Ag & B
231 J8 **Ardeonaig Hotel** Stirlg

252 E1 **Ardersier** Highld
261 H2 **Ardessie** Highld
216 C6 **Ardfern** Ag & B
263 G2 **Ardgay** Highld
229 G3 **Ardgour** Highld
207 L4 **Ardgowan** Inver
207 K4 **Ardhallow** Ag & B
282 e5 **Ardhasig** W Isls
260 C8 **Ardheslaig** Highld
261 K2 **Ardindrean** Highld
38 A7 **Ardingly** W Susx
48 B1 **Ardington** Oxon
48 B1 **Ardington Wick** Oxon
206 F6 **Ardlamont** Ag & B
72 F1 **Ardleigh** Essex
72 F1 **Ardleigh Heath** Essex
233 L7 **Ardler** P & K
66 D2 **Ardley** Oxon
70 D4 **Ardley End** Essex
218 D4 **Ardlui** Ag & B
215 J6 **Ardlussa** Ag & B
229 H7 **Ardmaddy** Ag & B
270 F8 **Ardmair** Highld
207 H5 **Ardmaleish** Ag & B
205 L6 **Ardminish** Ag & B
237 K6 **Ardmolich** Highld
208 A3 **Ardmore** Ag & B
263 J3 **Ardmore** Highld
207 K3 **Ardnadam** Ag & B
250 F2 **Ardnagrask** Highld
248 E4 **Ardnarff** Highld
228 B3 **Ardnastang** Highld
217 J5 **Ardno** Ag & B
239 L3 **Ardochy House** Highld
206 B7 **Ardpatrick** Ag & B
206 D2 **Ardrishaig** Ag & B
263 H5 **Ardross** Highld
195 L3 **Ardrossan** N Ayrs
142 B6 **Ardsley** Barns
141 M3 **Ardsley East** Leeds
237 H8 **Ardslignish** Highld
205 G5 **Ardtalla** Ag & B
237 J6 **Ardtoe** Highld
216 B5 **Arduaine** Ag & B
263 G7 **Ardullie** Highld
247 K7 **Ardvasar** Highld
219 K3 **Ardvorlich** P & K
282 e5 **Ardvourlie** W Isls
172 D5 **Ardwell** D & G
140 C8 **Ardwick** Manch
81 H1 **Areley Kings** Worcs
237 J7 **Arevegaig** Highld
36 B3 **Arford** Hants
61 J7 **Argoed** Caerph
112 E7 **Argoed** Shrops
78 D3 **Argoed Mill** Powys
23 J2 **Argos Hill** E Susx
282 f4 **Aribruach** W Isls
226 C7 **Aridhglas** Ag & B
224 F4 **Arileod** Ag & B
225 G4 **Arinagour** Ag & B
216 D2 **Ariogan** Ag & B
237 J3 **Arisaig** Highld
237 K4 **Arisaig House** Highld
150 E4 **Arkendale** N York
87 K8 **Arkesden** Essex
147 L2 **Arkholme** Lancs
159 H2 **Arkle Town** N York
164 F3 **Arkleby** Cumb
188 C7 **Arkleton** D & G
69 G7 **Arkley** Gt Lon
142 F6 **Arksey** Donc
133 H5 **Arkwright Town** Derbys
64 D2 **Arle** Gloucs
164 D7 **Arlecdon** Cumb
83 J5 **Arlescote** Warwks
86 D7 **Arlesey** Beds
96 F1 **Arleston** Wrekin
130 C3 **Arley** Ches
99 H5 **Arley** Warwks
63 L5 **Arlingham** Gloucs
27 L3 **Arlington** Devon
23 J5 **Arlington** E Susx
65 G5 **Arlington** Gloucs
27 L3 **Arlington Beccott** Devon
278 D3 **Armadale** Highld
247 K7 **Armadale** Highld
210 B5 **Armadale** W Loth
164 F5 **Armaside** Cumb
166 C2 **Armathwaite** Cumb
106 E3 **Arminghall** Norfk
115 H8 **Armitage** Staffs
141 H5 **Armitage Bridge** Kirk
141 L1 **Armley** Leeds
82 F6 **Armscote** Warwks

114 E2 **Armshead** Staffs
102 B6 **Armston** Nhants
143 G6 **Armthorpe** Donc
225 G3 **Arnabost** Ag & B
156 A5 **Arnaby** Cumb
149 G2 **Arncliffe** N York
149 G2 **Arncliffe Cote** N York
223 J6 **Arncroach** Fife
266 F6 **Arndilly House** Moray
17 J5 **Arne** Dorset
100 D5 **Arnesby** Leics
140 F8 **Arnfield** Derbys
221 L5 **Arngask** P & K
238 D2 **Arnisdale** Highld
259 K7 **Arnish** Highld
211 K6 **Arniston** Mdloth
282 f2 **Arnol** W Isls
153 H7 **Arnold** E R Yk
117 G2 **Arnold** Notts
219 K8 **Arnprior** Stirlg
157 G7 **Arnside** Cumb
227 G3 **Aros** Ag & B
113 G4 **Arowry** Wrexhm
156 D6 **Arrad Foot** Cumb
153 G7 **Arram** E R Yk
160 B4 **Arrathorne** N York
19 J6 **Arreton** IOW
260 B8 **Arrina** Highld
87 G5 **Arrington** Cambs
218 D6 **Arrochar** Ag & B
82 C4 **Arrow** Warwks
98 C8 **Arrowfield Top** Worcs
95 K2 **Arscott** Shrops
251 H2 **Artafallie** Highld
150 C6 **Arthington** Leeds
101 G7 **Arthingworth** Nhants
110 C8 **Arthog** Gwynd
257 H4 **Arthrath** Abers
150 E8 **Arthursdale** Leeds
257 J5 **Artrochie** Abers
21 G5 **Arundel** W Susx
164 E6 **Asby** Cumb
207 J6 **Ascog** Ag & B
50 A5 **Ascot** W & M
83 H8 **Ascott** Warwks
65 L3 **Ascott Earl** Oxon
65 L3 **Ascott-under-Wychwood** Oxon
160 F7 **Asenby** N York
117 J7 **Asfordby** Leics
117 J7 **Asfordby Hill** Leics
118 F3 **Asgarby** Lincs
136 F6 **Asgarby** Lincs
12 C1 **Ash** Devon
8 C5 **Ash** Devon
32 E8 **Ash** Dorset
52 D6 **Ash** Kent
41 J4 **Ash** Kent
30 D6 **Ash** Somset
31 G6 **Ash** Somset
36 D1 **Ash** Surrey
36 D1 **Ash Green** Surrey
99 J6 **Ash Green** Warwks
113 J4 **Ash Magna** Shrops
28 D6 **Ash Mill** Devon
113 J4 **Ash Parva** Shrops
29 L5 **Ash Priors** Somset
89 K6 **Ash Street** Suffk
29 H8 **Ash Thomas** Devon
49 L8 **Ash Vale** Surrey
48 E4 **Ashampstead** W Berk
48 E4 **Ashampstead Green** W Berk
90 E4 **Ashbocking** Suffk
90 E4 **Ashbocking Green** Suffk
115 K2 **Ashbourne** Derbys
115 K2 **Ashbourne Green** Derbys
29 J6 **Ashbrittle** Somset
24 C4 **Ashburnham Place** E Susx
7 L1 **Ashburton** Devon
12 C3 **Ashbury** Devon
47 K2 **Ashbury** Oxon
143 M6 **Ashby** N Linc
137 H6 **Ashby by Partney** Lincs
145 H7 **Ashby cum Fenby** NE Lin
135 L8 **Ashby de la Launde** Lincs
100 F1 **Ashby Folville** Leics
100 C5 **Ashby Magna** Leics
100 C5 **Ashby Parva** Leics
136 F5 **Ashby Puerorum** Lincs
84 B2 **Ashby St Ledgers** Nhants
107 G3 **Ashby St Mary** Norfk
116 B3 **Ashby-de-la-Zouch** Leics
81 L8 **Ashchurch** Gloucs
13 L6 **Ashcombe** Devon
44 C6 **Ashcombe** N Som

31 G3 **Ashcott** Somset
88 B6 **Ashdon** Essex
35 H1 **Ashe** Hants
72 E6 **Asheldham** Essex
88 B6 **Ashen** Essex
67 H4 **Ashendon** Bucks
68 B6 **Asheridge** Bucks
34 E7 **Ashfield** Hants
63 H2 **Ashfield** Herefs
220 D6 **Ashfield** Stirlg
90 F3 **Ashfield** Suffk
88 F4 **Ashfield Green** Suffk
106 F8 **Ashfield Green** Suffk
113 M6 **Ashfields** Shrops
37 K5 **Ashfold Crossways** W Susx
27 J4 **Ashford** Devon
7 K5 **Ashford** Devon
40 D6 **Ashford** Kent
50 D4 **Ashford** Surrey
80 C1 **Ashford Bowdler** Shrops
80 C1 **Ashford Carbonel** Shrops
48 E6 **Ashford Hill** Hants
132 D5 **Ashford in the Water** Derbys
198 C3 **Ashgill** S Lans
29 K8 **Ashill** Devon
105 H3 **Ashill** Norfk
30 D7 **Ashill** Somset
72 C8 **Ashingdon** Essex
181 G1 **Ashington** Nthumb
17 K3 **Ashington** Poole
31 J6 **Ashington** Somset
21 K4 **Ashington** W Susx
188 E2 **Ashkirk** Border
19 G3 **Ashlett** Hants
64 A2 **Ashleworth** Gloucs
64 B2 **Ashleworth Quay** Gloucs
88 D3 **Ashley** Cambs
130 F3 **Ashley** Ches
28 B8 **Ashley** Devon
18 A3 **Ashley** Dorset
64 D8 **Ashley** Gloucs
34 E4 **Ashley** Hants
18 C4 **Ashley** Hants
41 J5 **Ashley** Kent
101 H5 **Ashley** Nhants
114 B4 **Ashley** Staffs
46 B5 **Ashley** Wilts
68 B6 **Ashley Green** Bucks
17 M2 **Ashley Heath** Dorset
80 B2 **Ashley Moor** Herefs
48 B7 **Ashmansworth** Hants
26 F7 **Ashmansworthy** Devon
63 M7 **Ashmead Green** Gloucs
11 M3 **Ashmill** Devon
32 F7 **Ashmore** Dorset
48 D5 **Ashmore Green** W Berk
83 G4 **Ashorne** Warwks
133 G7 **Ashover** Derbys
133 G7 **Ashover Hay** Derbys
83 H1 **Ashow** Warwks
80 E7 **Ashperton** Herefs
8 B3 **Ashprington** Devon
27 L8 **Ashreigney** Devon
68 C4 **Ashridge Park** Herts
50 F7 **Ashtead** Surrey
102 B2 **Ashton** C Pete
129 L6 **Ashton** Ches
2 F5 **Ashton** Cnwll
6 D1 **Ashton** Cnwll
13 K5 **Ashton** Devon
35 H7 **Ashton** Hants
80 C2 **Ashton** Herefs
207 L4 **Ashton** Inver
84 E5 **Ashton** Nhants
102 B5 **Ashton** Nhants
30 F1 **Ashton** Somset
46 C7 **Ashton Common** Wilts
46 C7 **Ashton Hill** Wilts
64 F8 **Ashton Keynes** Wilts
82 A7 **Ashton under Hill** Worcs
130 F1 **Ashton upon Mersey** Traffd
45 G5 **Ashton Watering** N Som
139 H7 **Ashton-in-Makerfield** Wigan
140 E7 **Ashton-under-Lyne** Tamesd
18 E2 **Ashurst** Hants
38 D5 **Ashurst** Kent
21 L4 **Ashurst** W Susx
38 B6 **Ashurstwood** W Susx
11 M3 **Ashwater** Devon
86 F7 **Ashwell** Herts
101 J1 **Ashwell** Rutlnd
30 E7 **Ashwell** Somset
86 E7 **Ashwell End** Herts
106 C4 **Ashwellthorpe** Norfk
31 K1 **Ashwick** Somset

120 F7 **Ashwicken** Norfk
97 K5 **Ashwood** Staffs
156 B7 **Askam in Furness** Cumb
160 B2 **Aske Hall** N York
142 F5 **Askern** Donc
15 M4 **Askerswell** Dorset
67 K6 **Askett** Bucks
166 C6 **Askham** Cumb
134 E5 **Askham** Notts
151 H6 **Askham Bryan** York
151 H6 **Askham Richard** York
206 E1 **Asknish** Ag & B
159 G4 **Askrigg** N York
149 L6 **Askwith** N York
118 E5 **Aslackby** Lincs
106 D5 **Aslacton** Norfk
117 K3 **Aslockton** Notts
31 G3 **Asney** Somset
90 E2 **Aspall** Suffk
164 F2 **Aspatria** Cumb
69 K2 **Aspenden** Herts
131 K2 **Aspenshaw** Derbys
119 J4 **Asperton** Lincs
114 C5 **Aspley** Staffs
85 J8 **Aspley Guise** Beds
85 H8 **Aspley Heath** Beds
82 C1 **Aspley Heath** Warwks
139 J6 **Aspull** Wigan
139 J8 **Aspull Common** Wigan
143 H2 **Asselby** E R Yk
137 J4 **Asserby** Lincs
137 J4 **Asserby Turn** Lincs
89 J7 **Assington** Suffk
88 F5 **Assington Green** Suffk
131 G5 **Astbury** Ches
84 D4 **Astcote** Nhants
136 E4 **Asterby** Lincs
95 J2 **Asterley** Shrops
95 K5 **Asterton** Shrops
65 L5 **Asthall** Oxon
65 L4 **Asthall Leigh** Oxon
263 K2 **Astle** Highld
142 B2 **Astley** Leeds
113 H7 **Astley** Shrops
99 J5 **Astley** Warwks
139 L7 **Astley** Wigan
81 H2 **Astley** Worcs
96 F4 **Astley Abbots** Shrops
139 L5 **Astley Bridge** Bolton
81 J1 **Astley Cross** Worcs
139 L7 **Astley Green** Wigan
81 H2 **Astley Town** Worcs
98 D5 **Aston** Birm
130 A4 **Aston** Ches
113 K2 **Aston** Ches
132 D3 **Aston** Derbys
129 G6 **Aston** Flints
80 B3 **Aston** Herefs
80 B1 **Aston** Herefs
69 H3 **Aston** Herts
65 M6 **Aston** Oxon
133 J3 **Aston** Rothm
113 H6 **Aston** Shrops
97 H5 **Aston** Shrops
114 B3 **Aston** Staffs
114 D6 **Aston** Staffs
114 E5 **Aston** Staffs
49 J2 **Aston** Wokham
96 E2 **Aston** Wrekin
67 K3 **Aston Abbotts** Bucks
96 E6 **Aston Botterell** Shrops
82 D3 **Aston Cantlow** Warwks
67 L4 **Aston Clinton** Bucks
63 K3 **Aston Crews** Herefs
81 L8 **Aston Cross** Gloucs
69 H2 **Aston End** Herts
81 M2 **Aston Fields** Worcs
100 A5 **Aston Flamville** Leics
130 A4 **Aston Heath** Ches
63 K3 **Aston Ingham** Herefs
130 C8 **Aston juxta Mondrum** Ches
83 L5 **Aston le Walls** Nhants
82 E8 **Aston Magna** Gloucs
96 C6 **Aston Munslow** Shrops
95 J7 **Aston on Clun** Shrops
95 H2 **Aston Pigott** Shrops
95 H2 **Aston Rogers** Shrops
67 H7 **Aston Rowant** Oxon
67 J5 **Aston Sandford** Bucks
82 B7 **Aston Somerville** Worcs
82 D7 **Aston Subedge** Gloucs
48 E2 **Aston Tirrold** Oxon
48 E2 **Aston Upthorpe** Oxon
96 E4 **Aston-Eyre** Shrops
116 C5 **Aston-upon-Trent** Derbys

96 E4 **Astonlane** Shrops
83 L7 **Astrop** Nhants
67 L4 **Astrope** Herts
86 E7 **Astwick** Beds
133 J6 **Astwith** Derbys
85 J5 **Astwood** M Keyn
81 L2 **Astwood** Worcs
82 B3 **Astwood Bank** Worcs
118 E4 **Aswarby** Lincs
137 G5 **Aswardby** Lincs
82 B5 **Atch Lench** Worcs
96 C2 **Atcham** Shrops
16 E4 **Athelhampton** Dorset
90 F1 **Athelington** Suffk
30 E5 **Athelney** Somset
212 C4 **Athelstaneford** E Loth
19 G7 **Atherfield Green** IOW
27 L6 **Atherington** Devon
21 G6 **Atherington** W Susx
30 F7 **Atherstone** Somset
99 J4 **Atherstone** Warwks
82 F5 **Atherstone on Stour** Warwks
139 K7 **Atherton** Wigan
160 D2 **Atley Hill** N York
115 L2 **Atlow** Derbys
248 E4 **Attadale** Highld
116 E5 **Attenborough** Notts
135 K1 **Atterby** Lincs
133 G2 **Attercliffe** Sheff
96 E4 **Atterley** Shrops
99 K4 **Atterton** Leics
105 L4 **Attleborough** Norfk
99 K5 **Attleborough** Warwks
122 C8 **Attlebridge** Norfk
88 E4 **Attleton Green** Suffk
153 K5 **Atwick** E R Yk
46 B6 **Atworth** Wilts
80 C6 **Auberrow** Herefs
135 J7 **Aubourn** Lincs
257 G5 **Auchedly** Abers
244 F7 **Auchenblae** Abers
209 L2 **Auchenbowie** Stirlg
175 K4 **Auchencairn** D & G
176 C2 **Auchencairn** D & G
195 G5 **Auchencairn** N Ayrs
213 J7 **Auchencrow** Border
211 H6 **Auchendinny** Mdloth
199 G2 **Auchengray** S Lans
267 H4 **Auchenhalrig** Moray
198 D4 **Auchenheath** S Lans
185 K4 **Auchenhessnane** D & G
206 F4 **Auchenlochan** Ag & B
196 C2 **Auchenmade** N Ayrs
173 G4 **Auchenmalg** D & G
196 D2 **Auchentiber** N Ayrs
219 J8 **Auchentroig** Stirlg
261 K4 **Auchindrean** Highld
268 B6 **Auchininna** Abers
197 G6 **Auchinleck** E Ayrs
209 H5 **Auchinloch** N Lans
209 J4 **Auchinstarry** N Lans
229 H1 **Auchintore** Highld
257 K4 **Auchiries** Abers
245 K4 **Auchlee** Abers
256 A6 **Auchleven** Abers
198 C5 **Auchlochan** S Lans
244 D3 **Auchlossan** Abers
219 H1 **Auchlyne** Stirlg
197 G5 **Auchmillan** E Ayrs
235 G6 **Auchmithie** Angus
222 C7 **Auchmuirbridge** Fife
234 C3 **Auchnacree** Angus
257 G3 **Auchnagatt** Abers
254 D7 **Auchnarrow** Moray
172 B3 **Auchnotteroch** D & G
267 G6 **Auchroisk** Moray
221 G4 **Auchterarder** P & K
240 B2 **Auchteraw** Highld
253 H7 **Auchterblair** Highld
260 C4 **Auchtercairn** Highld
222 C8 **Auchterderran** Fife
233 M7 **Auchterhouse** Angus
256 C3 **Auchterless** Abers
222 D5 **Auchtermuchty** Fife
262 E7 **Auchterneed** Highld
211 H1 **Auchtertool** Fife
248 D6 **Auchtertyre** Highld
219 J3 **Auchtubh** Stirlg
280 E3 **Auckengill** Highld
143 G2 **Auckley** Donc
140 D8 **Audenshaw** Tamesd
113 L3 **Audlem** Ches
114 C2 **Audley** Staffs
87 L7 **Audley End** Essex
89 G7 **Audley End** Essex

89 G4 **Audley End** Suffk
114 C7 **Audmore** Staffs
97 K6 **Audnam** Dudley
165 H3 **Aughertree** Cumb
151 L8 **Aughton** E R Yk
138 E6 **Aughton** Lancs
147 L2 **Aughton** Lancs
133 J2 **Aughton** Rothm
47 K7 **Aughton** Wilts
138 E6 **Aughton Park** Lancs
253 H1 **Auldearn** Highld
80 B4 **Aulden** Herefs
176 B2 **Auldgirth** D & G
197 J1 **Auldhouse** S Lans
248 F7 **Ault a' chruinn** Highld
133 J6 **Ault Hucknall** Derbys
260 D2 **Aultbea** Highld
260 B3 **Aultgrishin** Highld
262 B6 **Aultguish Inn** Highld
267 H5 **Aultmore** Moray
250 F7 **Aultnagoire** Highld
263 J4 **Aultnamain Inn** Highld
118 D8 **Aunby** Lincs
14 B3 **Aunk** Devon
118 D4 **Aunsby** Lincs
45 H1 **Aust** S Glos
119 J7 **Austendike** Lincs
134 D1 **Austerfield** Donc
140 E6 **Austerlands** Oldham
142 B1 **Austhorpe** Leeds
141 H6 **Austonley** Kirk
99 J2 **Austrey** Warwks
148 D2 **Austwick** N York
137 G3 **Authorpe** Lincs
137 K5 **Authorpe Row** Lincs
47 G5 **Avebury** Wilts
47 G5 **Avebury Trusloe** Wilts
52 C3 **Aveley** Thurr
64 C7 **Avening** Gloucs
117 K1 **Averham** Notts
7 K5 **Aveton Gifford** Devon
242 B1 **Aviemore** Highld
48 A5 **Avington** W Berk
251 J1 **Avoch** Highld
18 A4 **Avon** Dorset
83 K5 **Avon Dassett** Warwks
210 B4 **Avonbridge** Falk
45 G3 **Avonmouth** Bristl
7 K3 **Avonwick** Devon
34 D6 **Awbridge** Hants
45 H2 **Awkley** S Glos
14 D2 **Awliscombe** Devon
63 L5 **Awre** Gloucs
116 E3 **Awsworth** Notts
97 J7 **Axborough** Worcs
44 E8 **Axbridge** Somset
35 J2 **Axford** Hants
47 K5 **Axford** Wilts
15 G3 **Axminster** Devon
14 F4 **Axmouth** Devon
128 D4 **Axton** Flints
169 H6 **Aycliffe** Dur
180 B5 **Aydon** Nthumb
63 J6 **Aylburton** Gloucs
167 G1 **Ayle** Cumb
14 B4 **Aylesbeare** Devon
67 K4 **Aylesbury** Bucks
145 G6 **Aylesby** NE Lin
52 F7 **Aylesford** Kent
41 H5 **Aylesham** Kent
100 C3 **Aylestone** C Leic
100 D3 **Aylestone Park** C Leic
122 D4 **Aylmerton** Norfk
122 D6 **Aylsham** Norfk
80 F7 **Aylton** Gloucs
65 G3 **Aylworth** Gloucs
80 A2 **Aymestrey** Herefs
83 L8 **Aynho** Nhants
69 G4 **Ayot Green** Herts
69 G4 **Ayot St Lawrence** Herts
69 G4 **Ayot St Peter** Herts
196 C6 **Ayr** S Ayrs
159 H5 **Aysgarth** N York
29 J7 **Ayshford** Devon
156 F6 **Ayside** Cumb
101 J3 **Ayston** Rutlnd
70 E4 **Aythorpe Roding** Essex
213 K6 **Ayton** Border
160 C7 **Azerley** N York

B

8 D2 **Babbacombe** Torbay
116 E3 **Babbington** Notts

112 E5 **Babbinswood** Shrops
69 K4 **Babbs Green** Herts
31 J5 **Babcary** Somset
59 M2 **Babel** Carmth
88 E5 **Babel Green** Suffk
128 E5 **Babell** Flints
12 F7 **Babeny** Devon
32 B1 **Babington** Somset
66 B6 **Bablock Hythe** Oxon
87 K5 **Babraham** Cambs
134 D3 **Babworth** Notts
125 H3 **Bachau** IOA
95 L7 **Bache** Shrops
94 F5 **Bacheldre** Powys
24 F5 **Bachelor's Bump** E Susx
115 H1 **Back o' th' Brook** Staffs
237 J3 **Back of Keppoch** Highld
88 E3 **Back Street** Suffk
275 d3 **Backaland** Ork
156 E5 **Backbarrow** Cumb
58 A5 **Backe** Carmth
269 J5 **Backfolds** Abers
129 J5 **Backford** Ches
129 J5 **Backford Cross** Ches
273 K7 **Backies** Highld
280 B5 **Backlass** Highld
44 F5 **Backwell** N Som
181 H4 **Backworth** N Tyne
98 F6 **Bacon's End** Solhll
122 C4 **Baconsthorpe** Norfk
62 D1 **Bacton** Herefs
123 G5 **Bacton** Norfk
90 C2 **Bacton** Suffk
90 B2 **Bacton Green** Suffk
140 C3 **Bacup** Lancs
260 C5 **Badachro** Highld
47 J3 **Badbury** Swindn
84 A3 **Badby** Nhants
276 B7 **Badcall** Highld
276 C5 **Badcall** Highld
261 G2 **Badcaul** Highld
114 E1 **Baddeley Edge** C Stke
114 E1 **Baddeley Green** C Stke
82 F1 **Baddesley Clinton** Warwks
99 H4 **Baddesley Ensor** Warwks
270 E3 **Baddidarrach** Highld
199 K2 **Baddinsgill** Border
256 C4 **Badenscoth** Abers
255 G7 **Badenyon** Abers
11 J5 **Badgall** Cnwll
103 J4 **Badgeney** Cambs
97 H3 **Badger** Shrops
2 D4 **Badger's Cross** Cnwll
52 B6 **Badgers Mount** Kent
64 C3 **Badgeworth** Gloucs
44 E8 **Badgworth** Somset
11 J5 **Badharlick** Cnwll
248 B6 **Badicaul** Highld
91 G2 **Badingham** Suffk
40 D4 **Badlesmere** Kent
187 G2 **Badlieu** Border
280 B6 **Badlipster** Highld
261 G1 **Badluachrach** Highld
263 K1 **Badninish** Highld
261 H2 **Badrallach** Highld
82 C6 **Badsey** Worcs
36 C1 **Badshot Lea** Surrey
142 D5 **Badsworth** Wakefd
89 K2 **Badwell Ash** Suffk
89 K2 **Badwell Green** Suffk
136 F5 **Bag Enderby** Lincs
32 C8 **Bagber** Dorset
161 G6 **Bagby** N York
64 E5 **Bagendon** Gloucs
96 F7 **Bagginswood** Shrops
165 G2 **Baggrow** Cumb
283 b13 **Bagh a Chaisteil** W Isls
283 b13 **Bagh a Tuath** W Isls
40 E4 **Bagham** Kent
128 F4 **Bagillt** Flints
99 K8 **Baginton** Warwks
57 K6 **Baglan** Neath
141 K1 **Bagley** Leeds
112 F6 **Bagley** Shrops
31 G2 **Bagley** Somset
35 K2 **Bagmore** Hants
114 E1 **Bagnall** Staffs
48 C5 **Bagnor** W Berk
96 D8 **Bagot** Shrops
49 M6 **Bagshot** Surrey
47 L6 **Bagshot** Wilts
45 K2 **Bagstone** S Glos
116 D1 **Bagthorpe** Notts
99 M2 **Bagworth** Leics
62 F2 **Bagwy Llydiart** Herefs

149 L7 **Baildon** Brad
149 L7 **Baildon Green** Brad
283 c9 **Baile a Mhanaich** W Isls
282 f4 **Baile Ailein** W Isls
226 B7 **Baile Mor** Ag & B
35 K5 **Bailey Green** Hants
178 C3 **Baileyhead** Cumb
141 J3 **Bailiff Bridge** Calder
209 H6 **Baillieston** C Glas
147 J4 **Bailrigg** Lancs
159 G4 **Bainbridge** N York
256 A5 **Bainshole** Abers
102 B2 **Bainton** C Pete
152 E5 **Bainton** E R Yk
66 E2 **Bainton** Oxon
222 F6 **Baintown** Fife
189 H3 **Bairnkine** Border
52 B3 **Baker Street** Thurr
69 L4 **Baker's End** Herts
132 D6 **Bakewell** Derbys
111 H4 **Bala** Gwynd
282 f4 **Balallan** W Isls
250 D5 **Balbeg** Highld
222 B1 **Balbeggie** P & K
250 E3 **Balblair** Highld
263 J6 **Balblair** Highld
142 E7 **Balby** Donc
175 K5 **Balcary** D & G
250 F3 **Balchraggan** Highld
276 B4 **Balchreick** Highld
37 M5 **Balcombe** W Susx
37 M4 **Balcombe Lane** W Susx
223 L5 **Balcomie Links** Fife
160 E7 **Baldersby** N York
160 E7 **Baldersby St James** N York
139 J1 **Balderstone** Lancs
140 D5 **Balderstone** Rochdl
117 L1 **Balderton** Notts
4 C6 **Baldhu** Cnwll
223 G5 **Baldinnie** Fife
221 J4 **Baldinnies** P & K
86 E8 **Baldock** Herts
234 C8 **Baldovie** C Dund
154 f5 **Baldrine** IOM
24 E4 **Baldslow** E Susx
154 e6 **Baldwin** IOM
114 B3 **Baldwin's Gate** Staffs
38 B5 **Baldwin's Hill** Surrey
177 K8 **Baldwinholme** Cumb
121 M4 **Bale** Norfk
222 D1 **Baledgarno** P & K
224 C7 **Balemartine** Ag & B
211 G5 **Balerno** C Edin
222 D6 **Balfarg** Fife
234 E2 **Balfield** Angus
275 d4 **Balfour** Ork
208 F1 **Balfron** Stirlg
256 B4 **Balgaveny** Abers
234 E5 **Balgavies** Angus
221 J8 **Balgonar** Fife
172 E6 **Balgowan** D & G
241 H4 **Balgowan** Highld
258 F3 **Balgown** Highld
172 B3 **Balgracie** D & G
234 B7 **Balgray** Angus
186 C2 **Balgray** S Lans
51 H4 **Balham** Gt Lon
233 L6 **Balhary** P & K
233 H8 **Balholmie** P & K
278 E3 **Baligill** Highld
233 L4 **Balintore** Angus
264 D5 **Balintore** Highld
263 K5 **Balintraid** Highld
283 c9 **Balivanich** W Isls
161 G6 **Balk** N York
233 M6 **Balkeerie** Angus
143 K2 **Balkholme** E R Yk
114 D1 **Ball Green** C Stke
131 K8 **Ball Haye Green** Staffs
48 B6 **Ball Hill** Hants
64 B7 **Ball's Green** Gloucs
154 c7 **Ballabeg** IOM
229 H4 **Ballachulish** Highld
154 b7 **Ballafesson** IOM
154 b7 **Ballakilpheric** IOM
154 c7 **Ballamodha** IOM
207 G6 **Ballanlay** Ag & B
182 D6 **Ballantrae** S Ayrs
72 C8 **Ballards Gore** Essex
99 H5 **Ballards Green** Warwks
154 c7 **Ballasalla** IOM
243 L4 **Ballater** Abers
154 d3 **Ballaugh** IOM
263 K5 **Ballchraggan** Highld
212 B3 **Ballencrieff** E Loth

224 B6 **Ballevullin** Ag & B
115 K1 **Ballidon** Derbys
194 D3 **Balliekine** N Ayrs
217 H7 **Balliemore** Ag & B
183 G5 **Balligmorrie** S Ayrs
206 E2 **Ballimore** Ag & B
219 H4 **Ballimore** Stirlg
254 D4 **Ballindalloch** Moray
222 D2 **Ballindean** P & K
89 H7 **Ballinger Common** Bucks
67 M6 **Ballingham** Herefs
63 H1 **Ballingry** Fife
222 B7 **Ballinluig** P & K
232 E5 **Ballinshoe** Angus
234 B5 **Ballintuim** P & K
233 G4 **Balloch** Highld
252 D2 **Balloch** N Lans
209 K4 **Balloch** P & K
220 E3 **Balloch** S Ayrs
183 J4 **Balloch** W Duns
208 C3 **Ballogie** Abers
244 D4 **Balls Cross** W Susx
36 E5 **Balls Green** E Susx
38 D6 **Ballygown** Ag & B
226 E4 **Ballygrant** Ag & B
204 F3 **Ballyhaugh** Ag & B
224 F4 **Ballymenoch** Ag & B
208 A2 **Balmacara** Highld
248 C6 **Balmaclellan** D & G
185 G7 **Balmae** D & G
175 H6 **Balmaha** Stirlg
208 C1 **Balmalcolm** Fife
222 E5 **Balmangan** D & G
175 G5 **Balmedie** Abers
257 H8 **Balmer Heath** Shrops
113 G4 **Balmerino** Fife
222 F2 **Balmerlawn** Hants
18 D3 **Balmichael** N Ayrs
194 E5 **Balmore** E Duns
209 G4 **Balmuchy** Highld
264 D4 **Balmuir** Angus
234 E5 **Balmule** Fife
211 H2 **Balmullo** Fife
223 G3 **Balnacoil Lodge** Highld
273 J5 **Balnacra** Highld
248 F3 **Balnacroft** Abers
243 J5 **Balnafoich** Highld
251 J4 **Balnaguard** P & K
232 D5 **Balnahard** Ag & B
226 E5 **Balnahard** Ag & B
214 E4 **Balnain** Highld
250 D5 **Balnakeil** Highld
276 F3 **Balnapaling** Highld
264 B6 **Balne** N York
142 F4 **Balquharn** P & K
232 F8 **Balquhidder** Stirlg
219 H3 **Balsall Common** Solhll
99 G8 **Balsall Heath** Birm
98 D6 **Balsall Street** Solhll
99 G8 **Balscote** Oxon
83 J6 **Balsham** Cambs
88 B5 **Baltasound** Shet
281 f1 **Balterley** Staffs
114 B2 **Balterley Green** Staffs
114 B2 **Balterley Heath** Staffs
114 A2 **Baltersan** D & G
174 C3 **Baltonsborough** Somset
31 J4 **Balvarran** P & K
233 G3 **Balvicar** Ag & B
216 B4 **Balvraid** Highld
248 D8 **Balvraid** Highld
252 F5 **Balwest** Cnwll
2 F5 **Bamber Bridge** Lancs
139 H3 **Bamber's Green** Essex
70 E3 **Bamburgh** Nthumb
203 K6 **Bamff** P & K
233 K5 **Bamford** Derbys
132 D3 **Bamford** Rochdl
140 C5 **Bampton** Cumb
166 C7 **Bampton** Devon
29 G6 **Bampton** Oxon
65 L6 **Bampton Grange** Cumb
166 C7 **Banavie** Highld
239 J8 **Banbury** Oxon
83 K7 **Banc-y-ffordd** Carmth
76 D7 **Bancffosfelen** Carmth
58 E6 **Banchory** Abers
244 F4 **Banchory-Devenick** Abers
245 K3 **Bancycapel** Carmth
58 D6 **Bancyfelin** Carmth
58 B5 **Bandirran** P & K
222 C1 **Bandrake Head** Cumb
156 D5 **Banff** Abers
268 C3 **Bangor** Gwynd
125 K5

138 D6 **Bangor's Green** Lancs
112 F2 **Bangor-is-y-coed** Wrexhm
11 H3 **Bangors** Cnwll
89 J1 **Bangrove** Suffk
106 B6 **Banham** Norfk
18 D2 **Bank** Hants
156 D3 **Bank Ground** Cumb
148 F5 **Bank Newton** N York
80 E3 **Bank Street** Worcs
141 H3 **Bank Top** Calder
139 G6 **Bank Top** Lancs
176 D5 **Bankend** D & G
233 G8 **Bankfoot** P & K
197 H8 **Bankglen** E Ayrs
245 K2 **Bankhead** C Aber
199 G4 **Bankhead** S Lans
209 K3 **Banknock** Falk
178 D6 **Banks** Cumb
138 E4 **Banks** Lancs
82 A2 **Banks Green** Worcs
177 G3 **Bankshill** D & G
122 E5 **Banningham** Norfk
71 G3 **Bannister Green** Essex
209 L1 **Bannockburn** Stirlg
51 H7 **Banstead** Surrey
7 K6 **Bantham** Devon
209 K3 **Banton** N Lans
44 E7 **Banwell** N Som
40 B3 **Bapchild** Kent
33 G3 **Bapton** Wilts
87 H3 **Bar Hill** Cambs
282 g2 **Barabhas** W Isls
196 C4 **Barassie** S Ayrs
263 K5 **Barbaraville** Highld
132 B3 **Barber Booth** Derbys
156 F6 **Barber Green** Cumb
196 E7 **Barbieston** S Ayrs
157 K6 **Barbon** Cumb
130 B8 **Barbridge** Ches
28 C2 **Barbrook** Devon
84 A1 **Barby** Nhants
228 F7 **Barcaldine** Ag & B
83 G7 **Barcheston** Warwks
178 B6 **Barclose** Cumb
22 F4 **Barcombe** E Susx
23 G4 **Barcombe Cross** E Susx
149 J8 **Barcroft** Brad
159 L4 **Barden** N York
38 F4 **Barden Park** Kent
70 F1 **Bardfield End Green** Essex
71 G2 **Bardfield Saling** Essex
136 B6 **Bardney** Lincs
99 M1 **Bardon** Leics
179 H6 **Bardon Mill** Nthumb
209 G4 **Bardowie** E Duns
39 G7 **Bardown** E Susx
208 B4 **Bardrainney** Inver
156 D7 **Bardsea** Cumb
150 E7 **Bardsey** Leeds
140 D7 **Bardsley** Oldham
105 J8 **Bardwell** Suffk
147 J3 **Bare** Lancs
3 K5 **Bareppa** Cnwll
79 M4 **Barewood** Herefs
173 J2 **Barfad** D & G
106 C2 **Barford** Norfk
83 G3 **Barford** Warwks
83 K8 **Barford St John** Oxon
33 J4 **Barford St Martin** Wilts
83 K8 **Barford St Michael** Oxon
41 H5 **Barfrestone** Kent
116 B2 **Bargate** Derbys
209 J6 **Bargeddie** N Lans
61 J7 **Bargoed** Caerph
183 J7 **Bargrennan** D & G
102 C8 **Barham** Cambs
41 G5 **Barham** Kent
90 D5 **Barham** Suffk
102 B1 **Barholm** Lincs
100 E2 **Barkby** Leics
100 E2 **Barkby Thorpe** Leics
113 H6 **Barkers Green** Shrops
117 K4 **Barkestone-le-Vale** Leics
49 J5 **Barkham** Wokham
51 L2 **Barking** Gt Lon
90 C4 **Barking** Suffk
90 C5 **Barking Tye** Suffk
51 L1 **Barkingside** Gt Lon
141 G4 **Barkisland** Calder
4 B5 **Barkla Shop** Cnwll
118 B3 **Barkston** Lincs
151 G8 **Barkston Ash** N York
87 H8 **Barkway** Herts
209 H6 **Barlanark** C Glas
114 D4 **Barlaston** Staffs

21 G4 **Barlavington** W Susx
133 J4 **Barlborough** Derbys
143 G1 **Barlby** N York
99 L2 **Barlestone** Leics
87 H7 **Barley** Herts
148 E7 **Barley** Lancs
142 B8 **Barley Hole** Rothm
70 B2 **Barleycroft End** Herts
101 J2 **Barleythorpe** Rutlnd
53 K1 **Barling** Essex
135 M5 **Barlings** Lincs
175 K3 **Barlochan** D & G
133 G5 **Barlow** Derbys
180 E6 **Barlow** Gatesd
143 G2 **Barlow** N York
152 B6 **Barmby Moor** E R Yk
143 H2 **Barmby on the Marsh** E R Yk
121 H5 **Barmer** Norfk
39 J2 **Barming Heath** Kent
194 C2 **Barmollack** Ag & B
109 L8 **Barmouth** Gwynd
169 J7 **Barmpton** Darltn
153 J4 **Barmston** E R Yk
107 K7 **Barnaby Green** Suffk
216 F8 **Barnacarry** Ag & B
102 B2 **Barnack** C Pete
99 K6 **Barnacle** Warwks
168 D7 **Barnard Castle** Dur
66 B5 **Barnard Gate** Oxon
88 E5 **Barnardiston** Suffk
175 L3 **Barnbarroch** D & G
142 D7 **Barnburgh** Donc
107 K5 **Barnby** Suffk
142 F6 **Barnby Dun** Donc
117 M1 **Barnby in the Willows** Notts
134 D3 **Barnby Moor** Notts
172 D7 **Barncorkrie** D & G
52 B4 **Barnehurst** Gt Lon
51 G4 **Barnes** Gt Lon
39 G4 **Barnes Street** Kent
69 H7 **Barnet** Gt Lon
69 G8 **Barnet Gate** Gt Lon
144 D6 **Barnetby le Wold** N Linc
121 M5 **Barney** Norfk
105 H7 **Barnham** Suffk
20 F6 **Barnham** W Susx
106 B2 **Barnham Broom** Norfk
235 G4 **Barnhead** Angus
223 H1 **Barnhill** C Dund
113 H1 **Barnhill** Ches
266 C5 **Barnhill** Moray
182 B8 **Barnhills** D & G
168 D8 **Barningham** Dur
105 K8 **Barningham** Suffk
145 G7 **Barnoldby le Beck** NE Lin
148 F6 **Barnoldswick** Lancs
37 H5 **Barns Green** W Susx
142 D5 **Barnsdale Bar** Donc
142 A6 **Barnsley** Barns
65 G6 **Barnsley** Gloucs
97 G5 **Barnsley** Shrops
41 J4 **Barnsole** Kent
27 K4 **Barnstaple** Devon
70 F3 **Barnston** Essex
129 G3 **Barnston** Wirral
117 J4 **Barnstone** Notts
98 C8 **Barnt Green** Worcs
211 G4 **Barnton** C Edin
130 C5 **Barnton** Ches
102 A6 **Barnwell All Saints** Nhants
102 A6 **Barnwell St Andrew** Nhants
64 B3 **Barnwood** Gloucs
80 B4 **Baron's Cross** Herefs
13 G2 **Barons Wood** Devon
166 C2 **Baronwood** Cumb
183 H4 **Barr** S Ayrs
173 J5 **Barrachan** D & G
224 B6 **Barrapoll** Ag & B
167 J8 **Barras** Cumb
179 L4 **Barrasford** Nthumb
130 B7 **Barrets Green** Ches
208 E7 **Barrhead** E Rens
183 G6 **Barrhill** S Ayrs
87 H5 **Barrington** Cambs
30 F7 **Barrington** Somset
3 G3 **Barripper** Cnwll
196 D1 **Barrmill** N Ayrs
216 C3 **Barrnacarry Bay** Ag & B
280 C2 **Barrock** Highld
64 C2 **Barrow** Gloucs
148 C8 **Barrow** Lancs
118 A8 **Barrow** Rutlnd
96 E3 **Barrow** Shrops
32 B4 **Barrow** Somset
88 F3 **Barrow** Suffk

139 K5 **Barrow Bridge** Bolton
190 B4 **Barrow Burn** Nthumb
45 G5 **Barrow Gurney** N Som
144 D3 **Barrow Haven** N Linc
133 H4 **Barrow Hill** Derbys
146 D2 **Barrow Island** Cumb
138 F7 **Barrow Nook** Lancs
32 D5 **Barrow Street** Wilts
116 F8 **Barrow upon Soar** Leics
116 B6 **Barrow upon Trent** Derbys
45 J7 **Barrow Vale** BaNES
130 D8 **Barrow's Green** Ches
129 M2 **Barrow's Green** Halton
146 D2 **Barrow-in-Furness** Cumb
144 D4 **Barrow-upon-Humber** N Linc
104 B3 **Barroway Drove** Norfk
118 A4 **Barrowby** Lincs
101 L3 **Barrowden** Rutlnd
148 E7 **Barrowford** Lancs
234 E8 **Barry** Angus
43 H7 **Barry** V Glam
43 H8 **Barry Island** V Glam
100 F1 **Barsby** Leics
107 H5 **Barsham** Suffk
99 G7 **Barston** Solhll
80 D7 **Bartestree** Herefs
256 E5 **Barthol Chapel** Abers
71 H3 **Bartholomew Green** Essex
114 B1 **Barthomley** Ches
18 D1 **Bartley** Hants
98 C7 **Bartley Green** Birm
88 B6 **Bartlow** Cambs
87 H4 **Barton** Cambs
113 G1 **Barton** Ches
166 C5 **Barton** Cumb
65 G2 **Barton** Gloucs
79 K4 **Barton** Herefs
138 D6 **Barton** Lancs
147 K8 **Barton** Lancs
160 C1 **Barton** N York
66 E5 **Barton** Oxon
8 D2 **Barton** Torbay
82 D5 **Barton** Warwks
104 E2 **Barton Bendish** Norfk
64 B7 **Barton End** Gloucs
115 K7 **Barton Green** Staffs
66 F1 **Barton Hartshorn** Bucks
151 L3 **Barton Hill** N York
116 E5 **Barton in Fabis** Notts
99 L2 **Barton in the Beans** Leics
104 E8 **Barton Mills** Suffk
101 J7 **Barton Seagrave** Nhants
31 J4 **Barton St David** Somset
34 F3 **Barton Stacey** Hants
28 B3 **Barton Town** Devon
123 G7 **Barton Turf** Norfk
140 A8 **Barton upon Irwell** Salfd
144 C3 **Barton Waterside** N Linc
68 D1 **Barton-le-Clay** Beds
162 C7 **Barton-le-Street** N York
151 M3 **Barton-le-Willows** N York
18 C5 **Barton-on-Sea** Hants
83 G8 **Barton-on-the-Heath** Warwks
115 K7 **Barton-under-Needwood** Staffs
144 C3 **Barton-upon-Humber** N Linc
141 M6 **Barugh** Barns
141 M6 **Barugh Green** Barns
282 g2 **Barvas** W Isls
103 L8 **Barway** Cambs
99 L4 **Barwell** Leics
12 E1 **Barwick** Devon
69 K3 **Barwick** Herts
31 J8 **Barwick** Somset
150 F8 **Barwick in Elmet** Leeds
112 F7 **Baschurch** Shrops
83 J3 **Bascote** Warwks
83 J3 **Bascote Heath** Warwks
89 L3 **Base Green** Suffk
114 F1 **Basford Green** Staffs
148 B7 **Bashall Eaves** Lancs
148 C7 **Bashall Town** Lancs
18 C4 **Bashley** Hants
52 F1 **Basildon** Essex
48 F8 **Basingstoke** Hants
132 E5 **Baslow** Derbys
30 E2 **Bason Bridge** Somset
44 B2 **Bassaleg** Newpt
201 K4 **Bassendean** Border
165 H4 **Bassenthwaite** Cumb
34 F7 **Bassett** C Sotn
87 G6 **Bassingbourn** Cambs
117 G4 **Bassingfield** Notts
135 H7 **Bassingham** Lincs
118 C6 **Bassingthorpe** Lincs

69 J2 **Bassus Green** Herts
38 F2 **Basted** Kent
102 C1 **Baston** Lincs
123 J8 **Bastwick** Norfk
44 C7 **Batch** Somset
68 D8 **Batchworth** Herts
68 D8 **Batchworth Heath** Herts
16 B2 **Batcombe** Dorset
31 M3 **Batcombe** Somset
130 D4 **Bate Heath** Ches
68 F4 **Batford** Herts
45 L6 **Bath** BaNES
73 K1 **Bath Side** Essex
45 M5 **Bathampton** BaNES
29 K6 **Bathealton** Somset
45 M5 **Batheaston** BaNES
46 A5 **Bathford** BaNES
210 C5 **Bathgate** W Loth
134 F7 **Bathley** Notts
11 K7 **Bathpool** Cnwll
30 C5 **Bathpool** Somset
210 B5 **Bathville** W Loth
45 H8 **Bathway** Somset
141 K3 **Batley** Kirk
82 E8 **Batsford** Gloucs
7 L7 **Batson** Devon
36 B3 **Batt's Corner** Surrey
161 K1 **Battersby** N York
51 H4 **Battersea** Gt Lon
7 H5 **Battisborough Cross** Devon
90 C4 **Battisford** Suffk
89 L4 **Battisford Tye** Suffk
24 D4 **Battle** E Susx
60 F1 **Battle** Powys
30 E1 **Battleborough** Somset
64 D3 **Battledown** Gloucs
234 C4 **Battledykes** Angus
113 H8 **Battlefield** Shrops
71 J8 **Battlesbridge** Essex
68 B2 **Battlesden** Beds
29 G5 **Battleton** Somset
89 H2 **Battlies Green** Suffk
18 E4 **Battramsley Cross** Hants
141 J4 **Battyeford** Kirk
81 K6 **Baughton** Worcs
48 E7 **Baughurst** Hants
244 D5 **Baulds** Abers
47 L1 **Baulking** Oxon
136 D5 **Baumber** Lincs
64 E6 **Baunton** Gloucs
96 F7 **Baveney Wood** Shrops
33 H4 **Baverstock** Wilts
106 D2 **Bawburgh** Norfk
122 A7 **Bawdeswell** Norfk
30 E3 **Bawdrip** Somset
91 H7 **Bawdsey** Suffk
120 E7 **Bawsey** Norfk
134 C1 **Bawtry** Donc
140 A2 **Baxenden** Lancs
88 E4 **Baxter's Green** Suffk
99 H4 **Baxterley** Warwks
258 D6 **Bay** Highld
147 K5 **Bay Horse** Lancs
282 h3 **Bayble** W Isls
35 H6 **Baybridge** Hants
168 B1 **Baybridge** Nthumb
146 F2 **Baycliff** Cumb
47 L3 **Baydon** Wilts
69 J5 **Bayford** Herts
32 B5 **Bayford** Somset
283 b8 **Bayhead** W Isls
38 D3 **Bayley's Hill** Kent
90 C5 **Baylham** Suffk
66 E1 **Baynard's Green** Oxon
161 K1 **Baysdale Abbey** N York
63 H2 **Baysham** Herefs
96 B2 **Bayston Hill** Shrops
88 E6 **Baythorne End** Essex
96 F8 **Bayton** Worcs
81 G1 **Bayton Common** Worcs
66 D6 **Bayworth** Oxon
45 L5 **Beach** BaNES
84 E7 **Beachampton** Bucks
104 E2 **Beachamwell** Norfk
41 G7 **Beachborough** Kent
45 H1 **Beachley** Gloucs
14 E2 **Beacon** Devon
72 D2 **Beacon End** Essex
38 D7 **Beacon Hill** E Susx
39 K6 **Beacon Hill** Kent
117 L1 **Beacon Hill** Notts
36 C3 **Beacon Hill** Surrey
67 J8 **Beacon's Bottom** Bucks
50 B1 **Beaconsfield** Bucks
161 L5 **Beadlam** N York

86 C7 **Beadlow** Beds
203 L7 **Beadnell** Nthumb
27 K7 **Beaford** Devon
142 E3 **Beal** N York
203 H4 **Beal** Nthumb
6 D2 **Bealbury** Cnwll
11 L7 **Bealsmill** Cnwll
115 L6 **Beam Hill** Staffs
115 H4 **Beamhurst** Staffs
15 L2 **Beaminster** Dorset
180 F8 **Beamish** Dur
149 K5 **Beamsley** N York
52 C4 **Bean** Kent
46 C5 **Beanacre** Wilts
190 F3 **Beanley** Nthumb
12 C5 **Beardon** Devon
139 K2 **Beardwood** Bl w D
14 A2 **Beare** Devon
37 J2 **Beare Green** Surrey
82 E3 **Bearley** Warwks
82 E3 **Bearley Cross** Warwks
169 G2 **Bearpark** Dur
208 F4 **Bearsden** E Duns
39 K2 **Bearsted** Kent
114 A4 **Bearstone** Shrops
98 C6 **Bearwood** Birm
17 L3 **Bearwood** Poole
187 G6 **Beattock** D & G
70 E5 **Beauchamp Roding** Essex
132 F3 **Beauchief** Sheff
82 E2 **Beaudesert** Warwks
61 J5 **Beaufort** Blae G
18 F3 **Beaulieu** Hants
18 E2 **Beaulieu Road Station** Hants
250 F2 **Beauly** Highld
126 B4 **Beaumaris** IOA
177 K7 **Beaumont** Cumb
73 H2 **Beaumont** Essex
9 c3 **Beaumont** Jersey
169 J7 **Beaumont Hill** Darltn
82 F1 **Beausale** Warwks
35 J5 **Beauworth** Hants
40 C7 **Beaver** Kent
40 C7 **Beaver Green** Kent
12 B3 **Beaworthy** Devon
71 H1 **Beazley End** Essex
129 H3 **Bebington** Wirral
181 G3 **Bebside** Nthumb
107 J5 **Beccles** Suffk
138 F3 **Becconsall** Lancs
157 K3 **Beck Foot** Cumb
162 E2 **Beck Hole** N York
104 D7 **Beck Row** Suffk
156 B6 **Beck Side** Cumb
156 E6 **Beck Side** Cumb
97 H3 **Beckbury** Shrops
51 K5 **Beckenham** Gt Lon
136 B3 **Beckering** Lincs
155 J1 **Beckermet** Cumb
104 F4 **Beckett End** Norfk
164 E1 **Beckfoot** Cumb
155 L3 **Beckfoot** Cumb
156 B5 **Beckfoot** Cumb
82 A8 **Beckford** Worcs
47 G5 **Beckhampton** Wilts
118 A1 **Beckingham** Lincs
134 F2 **Beckingham** Notts
46 A8 **Beckington** Somset
95 J7 **Beckjay** Shrops
24 F3 **Beckley** E Susx
18 C4 **Beckley** Hants
66 E5 **Beckley** Oxon
149 J6 **Becks** Brad
157 K5 **Beckside** Cumb
51 L3 **Beckton** Gt Lon
150 C5 **Beckwithshaw** N York
52 A2 **Becontree** Gt Lon
9 d2 **Becquet Vincent** Jersey
160 C5 **Bedale** N York
168 E4 **Bedburn** Dur
32 E7 **Bedchester** Dorset
43 G4 **Beddau** Rhondd
109 L2 **Beddgelert** Gwynd
23 G5 **Beddingham** E Susx
51 J6 **Beddington** Gt Lon
51 H5 **Beddington Corner** Gt Lon
90 F2 **Bedfield** Suffk
90 F2 **Bedfield Little Green** Suffk
85 L5 **Bedford** Beds
39 H6 **Bedgebury Cross** Kent
36 F6 **Bedham** W Susx
20 A5 **Bedhampton** Hants
90 E2 **Bedingfield** Suffk
90 E2 **Bedingfield Green** Suffk
90 E2 **Bedingfield Street** Suffk

150 C3 **Bedlam** N York
39 M4 **Bedlam Lane** Kent
181 G3 **Bedlington** Nthumb
61 H6 **Bedlinog** Myr Td
45 H5 **Bedminster** Bristl
45 H5 **Bedminster Down** Bristl
68 E6 **Bedmond** Herts
114 F7 **Bednall** Staffs
189 G3 **Bedrule** Border
95 J8 **Bedstone** Shrops
43 J4 **Bedwas** Caerph
61 J7 **Bedwellty** Caerph
99 K6 **Bedworth** Warwks
99 K6 **Bedworth Woodlands** Warwks
100 E2 **Beeby** Leics
35 L3 **Beech** Hants
114 D4 **Beech** Staffs
49 G6 **Beech Hill** W Berk
47 G7 **Beechingstoke** Wilts
48 C3 **Beedon** W Berk
48 C3 **Beedon Hill** W Berk
153 H5 **Beeford** E R Yk
132 E6 **Beeley** Derbys
145 G7 **Beelsby** NE Lin
48 E5 **Beenham** W Berk
49 K4 **Beenham's Heath** W & M
11 G4 **Beeny** Cnwll
14 F5 **Beer** Devon
30 F4 **Beer** Somset
31 K8 **Beer Hackett** Dorset
30 D6 **Beercrocombe** Somset
8 B6 **Beesands** Devon
137 J4 **Beesby** Lincs
8 B6 **Beeson** Devon
86 D5 **Beeston** Beds
129 M7 **Beeston** Ches
141 L2 **Beeston** Leeds
121 K8 **Beeston** Norfk
116 E4 **Beeston** Notts
122 D3 **Beeston Regis** Norfk
176 A5 **Beeswing** D & G
157 H6 **Beetham** Cumb
30 D8 **Beetham** Somset
121 L7 **Beetley** Norfk
43 K5 **Began** Cardif
66 C4 **Begbroke** Oxon
103 J2 **Begdale** Cambs
55 J5 **Begelly** Pembks
79 J2 **Beggar's Bush** Powys
141 L3 **Beggarington Hill** Leeds
94 F7 **Beguildy** Powys
107 H2 **Beighton** Norfk
133 J3 **Beighton** Sheff
115 M1 **Beighton Hill** Derbys
222 B4 **Bein Inn** P & K
208 B8 **Beith** N Ayrs
41 G4 **Bekesbourne** Kent
41 G4 **Bekesbourne Hill** Kent
122 F7 **Belaugh** Norfk
97 L7 **Belbroughton** Worcs
16 F1 **Belchalwell** Dorset
16 F1 **Belchalwell Street** Dorset
88 F6 **Belchamp Otten** Essex
88 F6 **Belchamp St Paul** Essex
89 G7 **Belchamp Walter** Essex
136 E4 **Belchford** Lincs
203 H6 **Belford** Nthumb
100 D2 **Belgrave** C Leic
212 E3 **Belhaven** E Loth
257 H8 **Belhelvie** Abers
255 J6 **Belhinnie** Abers
69 H6 **Bell Bar** Herts
148 F4 **Bell Busk** N York
97 L7 **Bell End** Worcs
97 L7 **Bell Heath** Worcs
35 M6 **Bell Hill** Hants
113 H2 **Bell o' th' Hill** Ches
243 K1 **Bellabeg** Abers
79 M7 **Bellamore** Herefs
216 B8 **Bellanoch** Ag & B
143 K2 **Bellasize** E R Yk
233 K3 **Bellaty** Angus
177 L7 **Belle Vue** Cumb
142 A4 **Belle Vue** Wakefd
137 G4 **Belleau** Lincs
159 K4 **Bellerby** N York
12 F7 **Bellever** Devon
198 D6 **Bellfield** S Lans
186 E2 **Bellfield** S Lans
68 B6 **Bellingdon** Bucks
179 J2 **Bellingham** Nthumb
192 D1 **Belloch** Ag & B
192 D2 **Bellochantuy** Ag & B
33 J8 **Bellows Cross** Dorset

90 D5 **Bells Cross** Suffk
38 F6 **Bells Yew Green** E Susx
209 J7 **Bellshill** N Lans
203 J7 **Bellshill** Nthumb
209 L7 **Bellside** N Lans
210 D6 **Bellsquarry** W Loth
45 J6 **Belluton** BaNES
102 A2 **Belmesthorpe** Rutlnd
139 K4 **Belmont** Bl w D
51 H6 **Belmont** Gt Lon
196 C7 **Belmont** S Ayrs
281 f2 **Belmont** Shet
255 H8 **Belnacraig** Abers
4 F3 **Belowda** Cnwll
116 B2 **Belper** Derbys
116 B2 **Belper Lane End** Derbys
133 L4 **Belph** Derbys
180 D3 **Belsay** Nthumb
201 J8 **Belses** Border
7 L3 **Belsford** Devon
68 D7 **Belsize** Herts
90 D7 **Belstead** Suffk
12 E4 **Belstone** Devon
139 L3 **Belthorn** Lancs
41 G2 **Beltinge** Kent
179 H6 **Beltingham** Nthumb
143 K6 **Beltoft** N Linc
116 D7 **Belton** Leics
118 B3 **Belton** Lincs
143 K6 **Belton** N Linc
107 K3 **Belton** Norfk
101 H3 **Belton** Rutlnd
39 H4 **Beltring** Kent
52 B3 **Belvedere** Gt Lon
117 L5 **Belvoir** Leics
19 L6 **Bembridge** IOW
114 D1 **Bemersley Green** C Stke
33 K5 **Bemerton** Wilts
153 K2 **Bempton** E R Yk
149 L6 **Ben Rhydding** Brad
107 K6 **Benacre** Suffk
185 H4 **Benbuie** D & G
228 D7 **Benderloch** Ag & B
39 K6 **Benenden** Kent
180 D8 **Benfieldside** Dur
122 F6 **Bengates** Norfk
69 J4 **Bengeo** Herts
82 B6 **Bengeworth** Worcs
91 J3 **Benhall Green** Suffk
91 H3 **Benhall Street** Suffk
235 K2 **Benholm** Abers
151 H4 **Beningbrough** N York
69 J2 **Benington** Herts
119 L2 **Benington** Lincs
119 L2 **Benington Sea End** Lincs
125 J3 **Benllech** IOA
207 J2 **Benmore** Ag & B
11 K4 **Bennacott** Cnwll
193 K4 **Bennan** N Ayrs
166 B6 **Bennet Head** Cumb
143 L2 **Bennetland** E R Yk
67 J7 **Bennett End** Bucks
136 D3 **Benniworth** Lincs
39 H4 **Benover** Kent
66 F8 **Benson** Oxon
70 D2 **Bentfield Green** Essex
96 F3 **Benthall** Shrops
64 C4 **Bentham** Gloucs
245 H3 **Benthoul** C Aber
95 H3 **Bentlawnt** Shrops
142 E6 **Bentley** Donc
152 F8 **Bentley** E R Yk
36 A2 **Bentley** Hants
90 D7 **Bentley** Suffk
99 H4 **Bentley** Warwks
69 H7 **Bentley Heath** Herts
98 F8 **Bentley Heath** Solhll
28 B4 **Benton** Devon
188 B8 **Bentpath** D & G
28 C4 **Bentwichen** Devon
35 K3 **Bentworth** Hants
222 E1 **Benvie** Angus
15 M2 **Benville** Dorset
103 G5 **Benwick** Cambs
82 C1 **Beoley** Worcs
237 K2 **Beoraidbeg** Highld
20 D3 **Bepton** W Susx
70 C1 **Berden** Essex
6 E2 **Bere Alston** Devon
6 E2 **Bere Ferrers** Devon
17 G3 **Bere Regis** Dorset
74 C6 **Berea** Pembks
3 G6 **Berepper** Cnwll
106 F3 **Bergh Apton** Norfk
31 G4 **Berhill** Somset

66 E7 **Berinsfield** Oxon
63 K7 **Berkeley** Gloucs
63 K7 **Berkeley Heath** Gloucs
63 L7 **Berkeley Road** Gloucs
68 C5 **Berkhamsted** Herts
32 D1 **Berkley** Somset
99 H7 **Berkswell** Solhll
51 J3 **Bermondsey** Gt Lon
248 C7 **Bernera** Highld
207 J1 **Bernice** Ag & B
258 F6 **Bernisdale** Highld
66 F8 **Berrick Prior** Oxon
66 F8 **Berrick Salome** Oxon
274 F3 **Berriedale** Highld
165 L5 **Berrier** Cumb
94 E3 **Berriew** Powys
202 F4 **Berrington** Nthumb
96 C2 **Berrington** Shrops
80 D2 **Berrington** Worcs
80 D2 **Berrington Green** Worcs
44 C8 **Berrow** Somset
81 H8 **Berrow** Worcs
81 H3 **Berrow Green** Worcs
141 H5 **Berry Brow** Kirk
27 H7 **Berry Cross** Devon
27 K2 **Berry Down Cross** Devon
63 H4 **Berry Hill** Gloucs
75 H4 **Berry Hill** Pembks
8 B3 **Berry Pomeroy** Devon
51 L7 **Berry's Green** Gt Lon
267 K5 **Berryhillock** Moray
267 K4 **Berryhillock** Moray
27 K2 **Berrynarbor** Devon
112 D2 **Bersham** Wrexhm
128 D4 **Berthengam** Flints
23 H6 **Berwick** E Susx
47 G4 **Berwick Bassett** Wilts
180 E4 **Berwick Hill** Nthumb
33 J3 **Berwick St James** Wilts
32 F6 **Berwick St John** Wilts
32 F4 **Berwick St Leonard** Wilts
202 F3 **Berwick-upon-Tweed** Nthumb
117 L6 **Bescaby** Leics
138 E5 **Bescar** Lancs
113 J6 **Besford** Shrops
81 L6 **Besford** Worcs
140 E6 **Besom Hill** Oldham
142 F7 **Bessacarr** Donc
66 C6 **Bessels Leigh** Oxon
140 B6 **Besses o' th' Barn** Bury
153 J3 **Bessingby** E R Yk
122 D4 **Bessingham** Norfk
38 F7 **Bestbeech Hill** E Susx
106 B4 **Besthorpe** Norfk
135 G6 **Besthorpe** Notts
116 F2 **Bestwood Village** Notts
152 F6 **Beswick** E R Yk
95 K4 **Betchcott** Shrops
37 K1 **Betchworth** Surrey
77 G3 **Bethania** Cerdgn
110 D3 **Bethania** Gwynd
125 J6 **Bethel** Gwynd
111 J4 **Bethel** Gwynd
125 G5 **Bethel** IOA
111 L7 **Bethel** Powys
40 B7 **Bethersden** Kent
126 C6 **Bethesda** Gwynd
55 J3 **Bethesda** Pembks
59 J4 **Bethlehem** Carmth
51 K2 **Bethnal Green** Gt Lon
114 B2 **Betley** Staffs
52 D4 **Betsham** Kent
41 J5 **Betteshanger** Kent
15 J3 **Bettiscombe** Dorset
113 G4 **Bettisfield** Wrexhm
113 M4 **Betton** Shrops
96 C2 **Betton Strange** Shrops
44 C1 **Bettws** Newpt
77 H5 **Bettws Bledrws** Cerdgn
94 D4 **Bettws Cedewain** Powys
76 B5 **Bettws Evan** Cerdgn
62 D6 **Bettws-Newydd** Mons
278 B4 **Bettyhill** Highld
42 D4 **Betws** Brdgnd
59 H6 **Betws** Carmth
125 K8 **Betws Garmon** Gwynd
111 K2 **Betws Gwerfil Goch** Denbgs
126 F8 **Betws-y-Coed** Conwy
127 H5 **Betws-yn-Rhos** Conwy
76 B6 **Beulah** Cerdgn
78 C5 **Beulah** Powys
22 E6 **Bevendean** Br & H
134 D5 **Bevercotes** Notts
153 G7 **Beverley** E R Yk

64 B8 **Beverstone** Gloucs
63 K7 **Bevington** Gloucs
165 H4 **Bewaldeth** Cumb
178 D4 **Bewcastle** Cumb
97 H8 **Bewdley** Worcs
149 L3 **Bewerley** N York
153 J6 **Bewholme** E R Yk
39 H6 **Bewlbridge** Kent
24 D5 **Bexhill** E Susx
52 B4 **Bexley** Gt Lon
52 A4 **Bexleyheath** Gt Lon
36 D6 **Bexleyhill** W Susx
53 J7 **Bexon** Kent
104 C3 **Bexwell** Norfk
89 J3 **Beyton** Suffk
89 J3 **Beyton Green** Suffk
282 e3 **Bhaltos** W Isls
283 b13 **Bhatarsaigh** W Isls
45 K1 **Bibstone** S Glos
65 G5 **Bibury** Gloucs
66 E3 **Bicester** Oxon
99 G7 **Bickenhill** Solhll
119 H4 **Bicker** Lincs
119 H4 **Bicker Bar** Lincs
119 H4 **Bicker Gauntlet** Lincs
139 J7 **Bickershaw** Wigan
138 F7 **Bickerstaffe** Lancs
113 H1 **Bickerton** Ches
8 B7 **Bickerton** Devon
151 G5 **Bickerton** N York
190 E6 **Bickerton** Nthumb
114 D8 **Bickford** Staffs
27 J4 **Bickington** Devon
13 J8 **Bickington** Devon
13 M1 **Bickleigh** Devon
7 G2 **Bickleigh** Devon
27 J5 **Bickleton** Devon
113 J2 **Bickley** Ches
51 L5 **Bickley** Gt Lon
163 G4 **Bickley** N York
80 E1 **Bickley** Worcs
113 J2 **Bickley Moss** Ches
71 J6 **Bicknacre** Essex
29 K3 **Bicknoller** Somset
53 J7 **Bicknor** Kent
33 K8 **Bickton** Hants
80 B2 **Bicton** Herefs
113 G8 **Bicton** Shrops
95 G6 **Bicton** Shrops
38 E5 **Bidborough** Kent
35 L1 **Bidden** Hants
39 L5 **Biddenden** Kent
39 M5 **Biddenden Green** Kent
85 K5 **Biddenham** Beds
46 B4 **Biddestone** Wilts
44 D8 **Biddisham** Somset
84 C7 **Biddlesden** Bucks
190 D4 **Biddlestone** Nthumb
131 H7 **Biddulph** Staffs
131 H8 **Biddulph Moor** Staffs
27 H5 **Bideford** Devon
82 D5 **Bidford-on-Avon** Warwks
129 G2 **Bidston** Wirral
152 B7 **Bielby** E R Yk
245 K3 **Bieldside** C Aber
19 H8 **Bierley** IOW
67 K4 **Bierton** Bucks
173 K6 **Big Balcraig** D & G
185 G3 **Big Carlae** D & G
260 B4 **Big Sand** Highld
7 K5 **Bigbury** Devon
7 J6 **Bigbury-on-Sea** Devon
144 D6 **Bigby** Lincs
146 D3 **Biggar** Cumb
199 H5 **Biggar** S Lans
115 L2 **Biggin** Derbys
132 C7 **Biggin** Derbys
142 E1 **Biggin** N York
51 L7 **Biggin Hill** Gt Lon
86 D6 **Biggleswade** Beds
177 K3 **Bigholms** D & G
278 F3 **Bighouse** Highld
35 J4 **Bighton** Hants
156 E6 **Bigland Hall** Cumb
177 H8 **Biglands** Cumb
21 G4 **Bignor** W Susx
164 D8 **Bigrigg** Cumb
116 E3 **Bilborough** C Nott
29 J3 **Bilbrook** Somset
97 K3 **Bilbrook** Staffs
151 H6 **Bilbrough** N York
280 C5 **Bilbster** Highld
169 G6 **Bildershaw** Dur
89 K5 **Bildeston** Suffk
11 J4 **Billacott** Cnwll

71 G8 **Billericay** Essex
100 F3 **Billesdon** Leics
82 D4 **Billesley** Warwks
118 F5 **Billingborough** Lincs
139 G7 **Billinge** St Hel
121 M7 **Billingford** Norfk
106 D7 **Billingford** Norfk
170 B6 **Billingham** S on T
136 C8 **Billinghay** Lincs
142 C6 **Billingley** Barns
37 G5 **Billingshurst** W Susx
96 F6 **Billingsley** Shrops
68 B3 **Billington** Beds
148 C8 **Billington** Lancs
114 D7 **Billington** Staffs
107 J1 **Billockby** Norfk
168 F3 **Billy Row** Dur
147 K7 **Bilsborrow** Lancs
137 J4 **Bilsby** Lincs
21 G6 **Bilsham** W Susx
40 D8 **Bilsington** Kent
134 C7 **Bilsthorpe** Notts
134 C7 **Bilsthorpe Moor** Notts
211 J6 **Bilston** Mdloth
98 B4 **Bilston** Wolves
99 K2 **Bilstone** Leics
40 D5 **Bilting** Kent
144 F1 **Bilton** E R Yk
151 G6 **Bilton** N York
150 D4 **Bilton** N York
191 J4 **Bilton** Nthumb
100 B8 **Bilton** Warwks
191 J4 **Bilton Banks** Nthumb
136 D1 **Binbrook** Lincs
169 G4 **Binchester Blocks** Dur
16 D5 **Bincombe** Dorset
31 K1 **Binegar** Somset
21 L3 **Bines Green** W Susx
49 K4 **Binfield** Br For
49 H3 **Binfield Heath** Oxon
180 A4 **Bingfield** Nthumb
117 J3 **Bingham** Notts
16 E2 **Bingham's Melcombe** Dorset
149 K7 **Bingley** Brad
113 J7 **Bings** Shrops
121 L4 **Binham** Norfk
99 K7 **Binley** Covtry
48 B8 **Binley** Hants
17 G5 **Binnegar** Dorset
209 M4 **Binniehill** Falk
266 F3 **Binns Farm** Moray
36 E2 **Binscombe** Surrey
66 C5 **Binsey** Oxon
19 K5 **Binstead** IOW
36 A3 **Binsted** Hants
21 G5 **Binsted** W Susx
82 D4 **Binton** Warwks
121 M7 **Bintree** Norfk
95 H3 **Binweston** Shrops
72 D3 **Birch** Essex
140 C6 **Birch** Rochdl
17 G2 **Birch Close** Dorset
115 J5 **Birch Cross** Staffs
72 D3 **Birch Green** Essex
69 J5 **Birch Green** Herts
81 K6 **Birch Green** Worcs
130 A7 **Birch Heath** Ches
129 M5 **Birch Hill** Ches
131 K2 **Birch Vale** Derbys
30 C8 **Birch Wood** Somset
121 G5 **Bircham Newton** Norfk
121 G5 **Bircham Tofts** Norfk
70 D3 **Birchanger** Essex
141 H4 **Birchencliffe** Kirk
80 B2 **Bircher** Herefs
98 D5 **Birchfield** Birm
43 J5 **Birchgrove** Cardif
38 B7 **Birchgrove** E Susx
57 K5 **Birchgrove** Swans
41 J2 **Birchington** Kent
99 H4 **Birchley Heath** Warwks
99 H3 **Birchmoor** Warwks
85 J8 **Birchmoor Green** Beds
132 E7 **Birchover** Derbys
130 C2 **Birchwood** Warrtn
80 E4 **Birchyfield** Herefs
134 C2 **Bircotes** Notts
89 K5 **Bird Street** Suffk
88 E7 **Birdbrook** Essex
161 G7 **Birdforth** N York
20 D6 **Birdham** W Susx
83 K2 **Birdingbury** Warwks
64 D4 **Birdlip** Gloucs
178 E5 **Birdoswald** Cumb
141 K6 **Birds Edge** Kirk

70 E5 **Birds Green** Essex
152 B3 **Birdsall** N York
97 H6 **Birdsgreen** Shrops
15 J2 **Birdsmoorgate** Dorset
142 A7 **Birdwell** Barns
63 L3 **Birdwood** Gloucs
202 B5 **Birgham** Border
263 K2 **Birichin** Highld
139 H5 **Birkacre** Lancs
160 D2 **Birkby** N York
138 C5 **Birkdale** Sefton
267 L3 **Birkenbog** Abers
129 H2 **Birkenhead** Wirral
256 D3 **Birkenhills** Abers
141 K2 **Birkenshaw** Kirk
243 K5 **Birkhall** Abers
234 A8 **Birkhill** Angus
187 J3 **Birkhill** D & G
118 C6 **Birkholme** Lincs
142 E2 **Birkin** N York
141 L2 **Birks** Leeds
179 H5 **Birkshaw** Nthumb
80 B4 **Birley** Herefs
133 G1 **Birley Carr** Sheff
52 E6 **Birling** Kent
191 K5 **Birling** Nthumb
23 J8 **Birling Gap** E Susx
81 L6 **Birlingham** Worcs
98 D6 **Birmingham** Birm
232 F7 **Birnam** P & K
257 H5 **Birness** Abers
244 C4 **Birse** Abers
244 C4 **Birsemore** Abers
141 K3 **Birstall** Kirk
100 D2 **Birstall** Leics
150 B4 **Birstwith** N York
118 E5 **Birthorpe** Lincs
181 G7 **Birtley** Gatesd
79 L2 **Birtley** Herefs
179 K3 **Birtley** Nthumb
81 H7 **Birts Street** Worcs
101 J3 **Bisbrooke** Rutlnd
136 D3 **Biscathorpe** Lincs
5 H4 **Biscovey** Cnwll
28 C6 **Bish Mill** Devon
49 K2 **Bisham** W & M
82 A5 **Bishampton** Worcs
169 G5 **Bishop Auckland** Dur
152 F7 **Bishop Burton** E R Yk
169 J4 **Bishop Middleham** Dur
150 D3 **Bishop Monkton** N York
135 K1 **Bishop Norton** Lincs
45 H7 **Bishop Sutton** BaNES
150 C3 **Bishop Thornton** N York
152 B5 **Bishop Wilton** E R Yk
95 H5 **Bishop's Castle** Shrops
32 B8 **Bishop's Caundle** Dorset
64 D2 **Bishop's Cleeve** Gloucs
80 F5 **Bishop's Frome** Herefs
70 F3 **Bishop's Green** Essex
48 D6 **Bishop's Green** W Berk
83 J4 **Bishop's Itchington** Warwks
64 B2 **Bishop's Norton** Gloucs
28 D6 **Bishop's Nympton** Devon
114 B5 **Bishop's Offley** Staffs
70 C3 **Bishop's Stortford** Herts
35 J4 **Bishop's Sutton** Hants
83 H3 **Bishop's Tachbrook** Warwks
27 K5 **Bishop's Tawton** Devon
35 H7 **Bishop's Waltham** Hants
97 J2 **Bishop's Wood** Staffs
135 L2 **Bishopbridge** Lincs
209 G5 **Bishopbriggs** E Duns
266 E3 **Bishopmill** Moray
46 F6 **Bishops Cannings** Wilts
50 B5 **Bishops Gate** Surrey
30 B6 **Bishops Hull** Somset
29 M5 **Bishops Lydeard** Somset
41 G5 **Bishopsbourne** Kent
13 L7 **Bishopsteignton** Devon
34 F7 **Bishopstoke** Hants
57 G7 **Bishopston** Swans
67 J5 **Bishopstone** Bucks
23 G7 **Bishopstone** E Susx
80 A6 **Bishopstone** Herefs
41 G2 **Bishopstone** Kent
47 K2 **Bishopstone** Swindn
33 J5 **Bishopstone** Wilts
32 E2 **Bishopstrow** Wilts
30 C8 **Bishopswood** Somset
45 H5 **Bishopsworth** Bristl
151 J6 **Bishopthorpe** York
169 K6 **Bishopton** Darltn
208 D5 **Bishopton** Rens
82 E4 **Bishopton** Warwks

44 D2 **Bishton** Newpt
115 G7 **Bishton** Staffs
64 C6 **Bisley** Gloucs
50 B7 **Bisley** Surrey
50 B7 **Bisley Camp** Surrey
146 F7 **Bispham** Bpool
138 F5 **Bispham Green** Lancs
3 K3 **Bissoe** Cnwll
18 A3 **Bisterne** Hants
38 E3 **Bitchet Green** Kent
118 C6 **Bitchfield** Lincs
27 K3 **Bittadon** Devon
7 K3 **Bittaford** Devon
121 K8 **Bittering** Norfk
96 D7 **Bitterley** Shrops
34 F8 **Bitterne** C Sotn
100 C6 **Bitteswell** Leics
45 K5 **Bitton** S Glos
49 H2 **Bix** Oxon
100 C4 **Blaby** Leics
65 L6 **Black Bourton** Oxon
180 E5 **Black Callerton** N u Ty
106 B4 **Black Car** Norfk
37 L3 **Black Corner** W Susx
230 B4 **Black Corries** Highld
228 E8 **Black Crofts** Ag & B
4 E3 **Black Cross** Cnwll
13 J1 **Black Dog** Devon
180 C4 **Black Heddon** Nthumb
140 A6 **Black Lane** Bury
149 G7 **Black Lane Ends** Lancs
150 D7 **Black Moor** Leeds
71 J3 **Black Notley** Essex
57 H6 **Black Pill** Swans
107 K6 **Black Street** Suffk
55 G5 **Black Tar** Pembks
12 B2 **Black Torrington** Devon
202 C3 **Blackadder** Border
8 B4 **Blackawton** Devon
99 K6 **Blackbank** Warwks
155 J1 **Blackbeck** Cumb
14 C1 **Blackborough** Devon
120 E8 **Blackborough End** Norfk
23 J3 **Blackboys** E Susx
116 B2 **Blackbrook** Derbys
114 B4 **Blackbrook** Staffs
37 J2 **Blackbrook** Surrey
245 J1 **Blackburn** Abers
139 K2 **Blackburn** Bl w D
133 H1 **Blackburn** Rothm
210 C6 **Blackburn** W Loth
185 G1 **Blackcraig** E Ayrs
130 F5 **Blackden Heath** Ches
245 L1 **Blackdog** Abers
12 C6 **Blackdown** Devon
15 J2 **Blackdown** Dorset
176 F8 **Blackdyke** Cumb
142 A5 **Blacker** Barns
142 B7 **Blacker Hill** Barns
51 M4 **Blackfen** Gt Lon
19 G3 **Blackfield** Hants
177 L6 **Blackford** Cumb
220 F5 **Blackford** P & K
30 F2 **Blackford** Somset
31 L5 **Blackford** Somset
140 B6 **Blackford Bridge** Bury
116 B7 **Blackfordby** Leics
19 H8 **Blackgang** IOW
211 G4 **Blackhall** C Edin
170 B3 **Blackhall** Dur
170 B3 **Blackhall Colliery** Dur
200 F5 **Blackhaugh** Border
72 E3 **Blackheath** Essex
51 K4 **Blackheath** Gt Lon
98 B6 **Blackheath** Sandw
107 J8 **Blackheath** Suffk
36 F2 **Blackheath** Surrey
257 J4 **Blackhill** Abers
269 K5 **Blackhill** Abers
257 K3 **Blackhill** Abers
180 D8 **Blackhill** Dur
269 G7 **Blackhill of Clackriach** Abers
14 A4 **Blackhorse** Devon
24 D4 **Blackhorse Hill** E Susx
119 H4 **Blackjack** Lincs
28 E3 **Blackland** Somset
46 E5 **Blackland** Wilts
186 F4 **Blacklaw** D & G
140 C7 **Blackley** Manch
233 H3 **Blacklunans** P & K
80 C7 **Blackmarstone** Herefs
42 E4 **Blackmill** Brdgnd
36 A4 **Blackmoor** Hants
44 F6 **Blackmoor** N Som
141 H5 **Blackmoorfoot** Kirk

70 F6 **Blackmore** Essex
71 H1 **Blackmore End** Essex
68 F4 **Blackmore End** Herts
210 E3 **Blackness** Falk
36 B3 **Blacknest** Hants
50 B5 **Blacknest** W & M
148 E7 **Blacko** Lancs
146 F8 **Blackpool** Bpool
8 C5 **Blackpool** Devon
13 J7 **Blackpool** Devon
178 C3 **Blackpool Gate** Cumb
210 A5 **Blackridge** W Loth
3 G4 **Blackrock** Cnwll
61 K4 **Blackrock** Mons
45 G1 **Blackrock** Mons
139 J5 **Blackrod** Bolton
254 D4 **Blacksboat** Moray
176 D5 **Blackshaw** D & G
140 E2 **Blackshaw Head** Calder
90 D2 **Blacksmith's Green** Suffk
139 L3 **Blacksnape** Bl w D
22 C4 **Blackstone** W Susx
66 F3 **Blackthorn** Oxon
89 H3 **Blackthorpe** Suffk
143 L3 **Blacktoft** E R Yk
245 J3 **Blacktop** C Aber
115 L2 **Blackwall** Derbys
4 B5 **Blackwater** Cnwll
49 K7 **Blackwater** Hants
19 H6 **Blackwater** IOW
30 C7 **Blackwater** Somset
194 D5 **Blackwaterfoot** N Ayrs
177 L8 **Blackwell** Cumb
169 H8 **Blackwell** Darltn
132 C5 **Blackwell** Derbys
133 J7 **Blackwell** Derbys
82 F6 **Blackwell** Warwks
82 A1 **Blackwell** Worcs
63 M2 **Blackwellsend Green** Gloucs
43 J2 **Blackwood** Caerph
176 B2 **Blackwood** D & G
198 C4 **Blackwood** S Lans
131 H8 **Blackwood Hill** Staffs
129 J6 **Blacon** Ches
41 G6 **Bladbean** Kent
174 C4 **Bladnoch** D & G
66 C4 **Bladon** Oxon
30 F6 **Bladon** Somset
78 C7 **Blaen Dyryn** Powys
58 C3 **Blaen-y-Coed** Carmth
61 H5 **Blaen-y-cwm** Blae G
60 D7 **Blaen-y-cwm** Rhondd
75 M2 **Blaenannerch** Cerdgn
110 D2 **Blaenau Ffestiniog** Gwynd
61 L5 **Blaenavon** Torfn
75 L5 **Blaenffos** Pembks
42 D3 **Blaengarw** Brdgnd
92 E7 **Blaengeuffordd** Cerdgn
60 C6 **Blaengwrach** Neath
42 D2 **Blaengwynfi** Neath
42 F7 **Blaenllechau** Rhondd
77 H2 **Blaenpennal** Cerdgn
92 C8 **Blaenplwyf** Cerdgn
76 A5 **Blaenporth** Cerdgn
60 D7 **Blaenrhondda** Rhondd
75 M6 **Blaenwaun** Carmth
93 H8 **Blaenycwm** Cerdgn
45 G7 **Blagdon** N Som
30 B7 **Blagdon** Somset
8 C3 **Blagdon** Torbay
30 B7 **Blagdon Hill** Somset
167 G1 **Blagill** Cumb
138 F6 **Blaguegate** Lancs
239 G8 **Blaich** Highld
237 K6 **Blain** Highld
61 K5 **Blaina** Blae G
232 C2 **Blair Atholl** P & K
220 C7 **Blair Drummond** Stirlg
206 F5 **Blair's Ferry** Ag & B
233 J6 **Blairgowrie** P & K
221 H7 **Blairingone** P & K
220 E7 **Blairlogie** Stirlg
207 K2 **Blairmore** Ag & B
276 B4 **Blairmore** Highld
254 D8 **Blairnamarrow** Moray
63 K4 **Blaisdon** Gloucs
71 H3 **Blake End** Essex
97 J8 **Blakebrook** Worcs
97 K7 **Blakedown** Worcs
114 F2 **Blakeley Lane** Staffs
130 A5 **Blakemere** Ches
79 L7 **Blakemere** Herefs
7 M3 **Blakemore** Devon
98 C3 **Blakenall Heath** Wsall
63 K5 **Blakeney** Gloucs

122 A3 **Blakeney** Norfk
114 A2 **Blakenhall** Ches
97 K4 **Blakenhall** Wolves
97 J7 **Blakeshall** Worcs
84 C5 **Blakesley** Nhants
168 B1 **Blanchland** Nthumb
150 B5 **Bland Hill** N York
17 H1 **Blandford Camp** Dorset
17 G1 **Blandford Forum** Dorset
17 G2 **Blandford St Mary** Dorset
208 F3 **Blanefield** Stirlg
135 L7 **Blankney** Lincs
209 J7 **Blantyre** S Lans
229 H2 **Blar a' Chaorainn** Highld
241 G4 **Blargie** Highld
229 H2 **Blarmachfoldach** Highld
18 A2 **Blashford** Hants
101 H4 **Blaston** Leics
101 L4 **Blatherwycke** Nhants
156 C5 **Blawith** Cumb
184 F6 **Blawquhairn** D & G
91 J4 **Blaxhall** Suffk
143 H7 **Blaxton** Donc
180 F6 **Blaydon** Gatesd
31 H2 **Bleadney** Somset
44 C7 **Bleadon** N Som
32 C4 **Bleak Street** Somset
40 F3 **Blean** Kent
136 B3 **Bleasby** Lincs
117 J2 **Bleasby** Notts
147 L6 **Bleasdale** Lancs
167 G7 **Bleatarn** Cumb
80 D1 **Bleathwood** Herefs
223 G4 **Blebocraigs** Fife
79 H2 **Bleddfa** Powys
65 K3 **Bledington** Gloucs
67 J6 **Bledlow** Bucks
67 J7 **Bledlow Ridge** Bucks
46 C7 **Bleet** Wilts
212 B6 **Blegbie** E Loth
166 E4 **Blencarn** Cumb
165 G1 **Blencogo** Cumb
35 L8 **Blendworth** Hants
165 G2 **Blennerhasset** Cumb
66 D3 **Bletchingdon** Oxon
37 M1 **Bletchingley** Surrey
85 G8 **Bletchley** M Keyn
113 K5 **Bletchley** Shrops
55 H3 **Bletherston** Pembks
85 K4 **Bletsoe** Beds
48 D2 **Blewbury** Oxon
122 D6 **Blickling** Norfk
134 B8 **Blidworth** Notts
117 G1 **Blidworth Bottoms** Notts
189 L4 **Blindburn** Nthumb
164 F4 **Blindcrake** Cumb
38 A4 **Blindley Heath** Surrey
10 F7 **Blisland** Cnwll
81 G1 **Bliss Gate** Worcs
33 L8 **Blissford** Hants
84 D4 **Blisworth** Nhants
115 H7 **Blithbury** Staffs
176 F8 **Blitterlees** Cumb
105 H4 **Blo Norton** Norfk
82 E8 **Blockley** Gloucs
107 G2 **Blofield** Norfk
189 G2 **Bloomfield** Border
114 A4 **Blore** Staffs
115 J2 **Blore** Staffs
35 L2 **Blounce** Hants
115 H5 **Blounts Green** Staffs
138 D4 **Blowick** Sefton
83 K8 **Bloxham** Oxon
118 E1 **Bloxholm** Lincs
98 E3 **Bloxwich** Wsall
17 G4 **Bloxworth** Dorset
149 L6 **Blubberhouses** N York
4 E3 **Blue Anchor** Cnwll
29 J2 **Blue Anchor** Somset
52 F6 **Blue Bell Hill** Kent
138 C7 **Blundellsands** Sefton
107 L4 **Blundeston** Suffk
86 C5 **Blunham** Beds
47 H1 **Blunsdon St Andrew** Swindn
97 K8 **Bluntington** Worcs
103 H8 **Bluntisham** Cambs
6 C2 **Blunts** Cnwll
82 D2 **Blunts Green** Warwks
114 D2 **Blurton** C Stke
135 J1 **Blyborough** Lincs
107 J8 **Blyford** Suffk
97 H1 **Blymhill** Staffs
97 J1 **Blymhill Lawn** Staffs
134 C2 **Blyth** Notts
181 H3 **Blyth** Nthumb

199 K4 **Blyth Bridge** Border
107 J8 **Blythburgh** Suffk
201 J3 **Blythe** Border
114 F3 **Blythe Bridge** Staffs
99 G5 **Blythe End** Warwks
114 F3 **Blythe Marsh** Staffs
135 G1 **Blyton** Lincs
210 D3 **Bo'ness** Falk
139 H6 **Boar's Head** Wigan
223 K4 **Boarhills** Fife
19 K2 **Boarhunt** Hants
53 G7 **Boarley** Kent
66 D6 **Boars Hill** Oxon
140 C4 **Boarsgreave** Lancs
38 E6 **Boarshead** E Susx
66 F4 **Boarstall** Bucks
12 C4 **Boasley Cross** Devon
253 H7 **Boat of Garten** Highld
263 G5 **Boath** Highld
53 J6 **Bobbing** Kent
97 H5 **Bobbington** Staffs
70 D6 **Bobbingworth** Essex
5 L3 **Bocaddon** Cnwll
3 H7 **Bochym** Cnwll
71 J2 **Bocking** Essex
71 J2 **Bocking Churchstreet** Essex
80 D3 **Bockleton** Worcs
5 K3 **Boconnoc** Cnwll
257 L3 **Boddam** Abers
281 d8 **Boddam** Shet
64 C2 **Boddington** Gloucs
124 F4 **Bodedern** IOA
127 K4 **Bodelwyddan** Denbgs
80 C5 **Bodenham** Herefs
33 L5 **Bodenham** Wilts
80 D5 **Bodenham Moor** Herefs
125 G2 **Bodewryd** IOA
128 C5 **Bodfari** Denbgs
125 G4 **Bodffordd** IOA
108 E4 **Bodfuan** Gwynd
122 C3 **Bodham** Norfk
24 E2 **Bodiam** E Susx
83 K7 **Bodicote** Oxon
10 D7 **Bodieve** Cnwll
5 K4 **Bodinnick** Cnwll
23 L4 **Bodle Street Green** E Susx
5 H2 **Bodmin** Cnwll
105 G4 **Bodney** Norfk
125 G6 **Bodorgan** IOA
4 D5 **Bodrean** Cnwll
40 E6 **Bodsham Green** Kent
5 H3 **Bodwen** Cnwll
99 G4 **Bodymoor Heath** Warwks
251 H2 **Bogallan** Highld
257 J4 **Bogbrae** Abers
212 A5 **Boggs Holdings** E Loth
211 H6 **Boghall** Mdloth
210 C5 **Boghall** W Loth
198 C5 **Boghead** S Lans
267 G4 **Boghead Farm** Moray
267 G4 **Bogmoor** Moray
235 G1 **Bogmuir** Abers
255 M3 **Bogniebrae** Abers
20 F7 **Bognor Regis** W Susx
253 G7 **Bogroy** Highld
185 G6 **Bogue** D & G
6 E1 **Bohetherick** Devon
3 L4 **Bohortha** Cnwll
240 A6 **Bohuntine** Highld
2 B4 **Bojewyan** Cnwll
5 H2 **Bokiddick** Cnwll
169 G6 **Bolam** Dur
180 D2 **Bolam** Nthumb
7 K7 **Bolberry** Devon
129 M2 **Bold Heath** St Hel
98 E4 **Boldmere** Birm
181 J6 **Boldon Colliery** S Tyne
18 E4 **Boldre** Hants
168 C7 **Boldron** Dur
134 F2 **Bole** Notts
133 G5 **Bole Hill** Derbys
132 F8 **Bolehill** Derbys
3 H3 **Bolenowe** Cnwll
29 G7 **Bolham** Devon
29 L8 **Bolham Water** Devon
4 C4 **Bolingey** Cnwll
131 J4 **Bollington** Ches
131 H4 **Bollington Cross** Ches
63 L4 **Bollow** Gloucs
37 L6 **Bolney** W Susx
86 B3 **Bolnhurst** Beds
234 F5 **Bolshan** Angus
133 J5 **Bolsover** Derbys
141 G5 **Bolster Moor** Kirk
141 L8 **Bolsterstone** Sheff

161 H5 **Boltby** N York
243 M2 **Boltenstone** Abers
67 J8 **Bolter End** Bucks
139 L6 **Bolton** Bolton
166 E6 **Bolton** Cumb
212 B5 **Bolton** E Loth
152 B5 **Bolton** E R Yk
191 G3 **Bolton** Nthumb
149 K5 **Bolton Abbey** N York
149 K5 **Bolton Bridge** N York
148 D6 **Bolton by Bowland** Lancs
159 K5 **Bolton Hall** N York
147 J2 **Bolton le Sands** Lancs
165 H2 **Bolton Low Houses** Cumb
165 H2 **Bolton New Houses** Cumb
151 H7 **Bolton Percy** N York
147 J2 **Bolton Town End** Lancs
142 C7 **Bolton Upon Dearne** Barns
160 C3 **Bolton-on-Swale** N York
178 B5 **Boltonfellend** Cumb
165 H3 **Boltongate** Cumb
11 H7 **Bolventor** Cnwll
181 G2 **Bomarsund** Nthumb
113 G7 **Bomere Heath** Shrops
263 G2 **Bonar Bridge** Highld
228 F8 **Bonawe** Ag & B
144 C5 **Bonby** N Linc
75 L4 **Boncath** Pembks
189 G4 **Bonchester Bridge** Border
19 K8 **Bonchurch** IOW
79 L4 **Bond's Green** Herefs
12 F2 **Bondleigh** Devon
147 J6 **Bonds** Lancs
2 D4 **Bone** Cnwll
13 G7 **Bonehill** Devon
99 G3 **Bonehill** Staffs
98 D2 **Boney Hay** Staffs
208 C3 **Bonhill** W Duns
97 J3 **Boningale** Shrops
189 H2 **Bonjedward** Border
209 M7 **Bonkle** N Lans
234 F7 **Bonnington** Angus
40 D8 **Bonnington** Kent
222 F6 **Bonnybank** Fife
209 L3 **Bonnybridge** Falk
268 F5 **Bonnykelly** Abers
211 J6 **Bonnyrigg** Mdloth
233 M7 **Bonnyton** Angus
132 E8 **Bonsall** Derbys
177 H4 **Bonshaw Tower** D & G
62 D3 **Bont** Mons
93 J3 **Bont-Dolgadfan** Powys
110 C7 **Bontddu** Gwynd
137 J5 **Bonthorpe** Lincs
77 H2 **Bontnewydd** Cerdgn
125 J7 **Bontnewydd** Gwynd
128 C8 **Bontuchel** Denbgs
43 G7 **Bonvilston** V Glam
111 L3 **Bonwm** Denbgs
57 J6 **Bonymaen** Swans
27 J3 **Boode** Devon
8 D4 **Boohay** Devon
49 K1 **Booker** Bucks
113 J6 **Booley** Shrops
201 J4 **Boon** Border
114 C2 **Boon Hill** Staffs
35 G8 **Boorley Green** Hants
170 F7 **Boosbeck** R & Cl
71 K1 **Boose's Green** Essex
11 K3 **Boot** Cnwll
155 M3 **Boot** Cumb
90 F5 **Boot Street** Suffk
141 G2 **Booth** Calder
143 J3 **Booth** E R Yk
131 H3 **Booth Green** Ches
141 G2 **Booth Town** Calder
135 K7 **Boothby Graffoe** Lincs
118 C5 **Boothby Pagnell** Lincs
139 L7 **Boothstown** Salfd
84 F2 **Boothville** Nhants
155 K5 **Bootle** Cumb
138 D8 **Bootle** Sefton
130 E5 **Boots Green** Ches
159 H2 **Booze** N York
80 E1 **Boraston** Shrops
9 k2 **Bordeaux** Guern
53 J6 **Borden** Kent
36 B6 **Borden** W Susx
177 G8 **Border** Cumb
149 G3 **Bordley** N York
36 B4 **Bordon** Hants
36 B4 **Bordon Camp** Hants
71 J5 **Boreham** Essex
32 E2 **Boreham** Wilts
24 B5 **Boreham Street** E Susx

69 G7 **Borehamwood** Herts
187 J8 **Boreland** D & G
258 B6 **Boreraig** Highld
7 M4 **Boreston** Devon
96 C2 **Boreton** Ches
282 g1 **Borgh** W Isls
283 b13 **Borgh** W Isls
278 B4 **Borgie** Highld
175 G5 **Borgue** D & G
274 F3 **Borgue** Highld
89 G6 **Borley** Essex
89 G6 **Borley Green** Essex
89 K3 **Borley Green** Suffk
258 F2 **Borneskitaig** Highld
174 F5 **Borness** D & G
38 F2 **Borough Green** Kent
150 E3 **Boroughbridge** N York
112 E1 **Borras Head** Wrexhm
116 C4 **Borrowash** Derbys
171 H7 **Borrowby** N York
160 F5 **Borrowby** N York
165 H7 **Borrowdale** Cumb
210 D3 **Borrowstoun** Falk
52 F5 **Borstal** Medway
92 D5 **Borth** Cerdgn
109 K4 **Borth-y-Gest** Gwynd
188 C3 **Borthwickbrae** Border
188 D3 **Borthwickshiels** Border
259 G7 **Borve** Highld
282 g1 **Borve** W Isls
283 b13 **Borve** W Isls
282 d6 **Borve** W Isls
147 K1 **Borwick** Lancs
156 E3 **Borwick Lodge** Cumb
156 A6 **Borwick Rails** Cumb
2 B5 **Bosavern** Cnwll
80 F6 **Bosbury** Herefs
5 H1 **Boscarne** Cnwll
10 F4 **Boscastle** Cnwll
17 M4 **Boscombe** Bmouth
33 L3 **Boscombe** Wilts
5 H4 **Boscoppa** Cnwll
20 C6 **Bosham** W Susx
20 D6 **Bosham Hoe** W Susx
54 F7 **Bosherston** Pembks
2 C4 **Boskednan** Cnwll
2 C6 **Boskenna** Cnwll
131 H6 **Bosley** Ches
4 E3 **Bosoughan** Cnwll
151 M4 **Bossall** N York
10 F5 **Bossiney** Cnwll
40 F5 **Bossingham** Kent
28 F1 **Bossington** Somset
130 C6 **Bostock Green** Ches
119 K3 **Boston** Lincs
150 F6 **Boston Spa** Leeds
2 C4 **Boswarthan** Cnwll
5 G6 **Boswinger** Cnwll
2 B4 **Botallack** Cnwll
69 J7 **Botany Bay** Gt Lon
100 B2 **Botcheston** Leics
105 L8 **Botesdale** Suffk
180 F2 **Bothal** Nthumb
48 D4 **Bothampstead** W Berk
134 D5 **Bothamsall** Notts
165 G3 **Bothel** Cumb
15 L4 **Bothenhampton** Dorset
209 J7 **Bothwell** S Lans
68 B6 **Botley** Bucks
35 G8 **Botley** Hants
66 C6 **Botley** Oxon
67 H2 **Botolph Claydon** Bucks
40 F8 **Botolph's Bridge** Kent
21 L5 **Botolphs** W Susx
117 L4 **Bottesford** Leics
143 M6 **Bottesford** N Linc
87 L3 **Bottisham** Cambs
139 K5 **Bottom o' th' Moor** Bolton
138 F2 **Bottom of Hutton** Lancs
222 F2 **Bottomcraig** Fife
140 D3 **Bottoms** Calder
2 B6 **Bottoms** Cnwll
99 H5 **Botts Green** Warwks
6 E3 **Botusfleming** Cnwll
108 D5 **Botwnnog** Gwynd
38 D4 **Bough Beech** Kent
79 G7 **Boughrood** Powys
86 D2 **Boughton** Cambs
84 E2 **Boughton** Nhants
104 D3 **Boughton** Norfk
134 D6 **Boughton** Notts
40 D6 **Boughton Aluph** Kent
85 J7 **Boughton End** Beds
39 J3 **Boughton Green** Kent

39 M3 **Boughton Malherbe** Kent
39 J3 **Boughton Monchelsea** Kent
40 D3 **Boughton Street** Kent
171 H7 **Boulby** R & Cl
140 F3 **Boulder Clough** Calder
18 F5 **Bouldnor** IOW
96 C6 **Bouldon** Shrops
90 F5 **Boulge** Suffk
55 G4 **Boulston** Pembks
135 J6 **Boultham** Lincs
87 G4 **Bourn** Cambs
118 E7 **Bourne** Lincs
85 J6 **Bourne End** Beds
85 K3 **Bourne End** Beds
49 L2 **Bourne End** Bucks
68 C6 **Bourne End** Herts
70 D8 **Bournebridge** Essex
98 D6 **Bournebrook** Birm
17 L4 **Bournemouth** Bmouth
64 C6 **Bournes Green** Gloucs
53 K2 **Bournes Green** Sthend
98 B8 **Bournheath** Worcs
63 L8 **Bournstream** Gloucs
98 D7 **Bournville** Birm
32 C5 **Bourton** Dorset
44 D6 **Bourton** N Som
47 K2 **Bourton** Oxon
96 D4 **Bourton** Shrops
46 F6 **Bourton** Wilts
83 K1 **Bourton on Dunsmore** Warwks
65 J1 **Bourton-on-the-Hill** Gloucs
65 H3 **Bourton-on-the-Water** Gloucs
225 H3 **Bousd** Ag & B
177 J7 **Boustead Hill** Cumb
156 D5 **Bouth** Cumb
149 L2 **Bouthwaite** N York
82 B3 **Bouts** Worcs
219 J1 **Bovain** Stirlg
50 B3 **Boveney** Bucks
33 J7 **Boveridge** Dorset
13 J6 **Bovey Tracey** Devon
68 C6 **Bovingdon** Herts
49 K2 **Bovingdon Green** Bucks
70 D6 **Bovinger** Essex
16 F5 **Bovington** Dorset
16 F5 **Bovington Camp** Dorset
177 K7 **Bow** Cumb
13 G2 **Bow** Devon
8 B3 **Bow** Devon
51 K2 **Bow** Gt Lon
275 C6 **Bow** Ork
85 H8 **Bow Brickhill** M Keyn
222 E4 **Bow of Fife** Fife
92 D6 **Bow Street** Cerdgn
105 L4 **Bow Street** Norfk
168 B6 **Bowbank** Dur
64 B6 **Bowbridge** Gloucs
169 J3 **Bowburn** Dur
19 H6 **Bowcombe** IOW
14 D4 **Bowd** Devon
201 H7 **Bowden** Border
8 C5 **Bowden** Devon
46 D5 **Bowden Hill** Wilts
130 E2 **Bowdon** Traffd
280 B4 **Bower** Highld
45 H4 **Bower Ashton** Bristl
31 G7 **Bower Hinton** Somset
89 K7 **Bower House Tye** Suffk
142 B2 **Bower's Row** Leeds
33 H6 **Bowerchalke** Wilts
46 C6 **Bowerhill** Wilts
280 B3 **Bowermadden** Highld
114 C4 **Bowers** Staffs
53 G1 **Bowers Gifford** Essex
210 E1 **Bowershall** Fife
168 C7 **Bowes** Dur
147 K7 **Bowgreave** Lancs
176 D5 **Bowhouse** D & G
11 H6 **Bowithick** Cnwll
138 E6 **Bowker's Green** Lancs
200 F5 **Bowland** Border
156 F5 **Bowland Bridge** Cumb
140 C6 **Bowley** Rochdl
80 C5 **Bowley** Herefs
80 C5 **Bowley Town** Herefs
36 D3 **Bowlhead Green** Surrey
141 J2 **Bowling** Brad
208 D4 **Bowling** W Duns
112 F2 **Bowling Bank** Wrexhm
81 J5 **Bowling Green** Worcs
156 D3 **Bowmanstead** Cumb
204 D4 **Bowmore** Ag & B

177 H6 **Bowness-on-Solway** Cumb
156 F3 **Bowness-on-Windermere** Cumb
234 D5 **Bowriefauld** Angus
165 K4 **Bowscale** Cumb
202 F5 **Bowsden** Nthumb
157 H3 **Bowston** Cumb
106 D2 **Bowthorpe** Norfk
64 B7 **Box** Gloucs
46 B5 **Box** Wilts
85 K5 **Box End** Beds
51 G8 **Box Hill** Surrey
11 H2 **Box's Shop** Cnwll
63 K3 **Boxbush** Gloucs
63 L4 **Boxbush** Gloucs
89 K7 **Boxford** Suffk
48 B4 **Boxford** W Berk
20 E5 **Boxgrove** W Susx
53 G7 **Boxley** Kent
68 D6 **Boxmoor** Herts
89 K8 **Boxted** Essex
89 G5 **Boxted** Suffk
72 E1 **Boxted Cross** Essex
72 E1 **Boxted Heath** Essex
64 A8 **Boxwell** Gloucs
87 G2 **Boxworth** Cambs
87 G2 **Boxworth End** Cambs
88 E4 **Boyden End** Suffk
41 H2 **Boyden Gate** Kent
115 K4 **Boylestone** Derbys
268 B3 **Boyndie** Abers
269 G4 **Boyndlie** Abers
153 J2 **Boynton** E R Yk
16 C1 **Boys Hill** Dorset
234 F5 **Boysack** Angus
133 G5 **Boythorpe** Derbys
11 L4 **Boyton** Cnwll
91 J6 **Boyton** Suffk
32 F3 **Boyton** Wilts
70 F5 **Boyton Cross** Essex
88 E6 **Boyton End** Suffk
85 H3 **Bozeat** Nhants
154 d6 **Braaid** IOM
91 G2 **Brabling Green** Suffk
40 E7 **Brabourne** Kent
40 E7 **Brabourne Lees** Kent
280 D2 **Brabstermire** Highld
246 E1 **Bracadale** Highld
102 B1 **Braceborough** Lincs
135 K6 **Bracebridge Heath** Lincs
135 J6 **Bracebridge Low Fields** Lincs
118 D4 **Braceby** Lincs
148 F6 **Bracewell** Lancs
133 G7 **Brackenfield** Derbys
209 K5 **Brackenhirst** N Lans
165 J1 **Brackenthwaite** Cumb
150 C5 **Brackenthwaite** N York
20 C7 **Bracklesham** W Susx
239 K7 **Brackletter** Highld
84 B7 **Brackley** Nhants
84 C7 **Brackley Hatch** Nhants
49 L5 **Bracknell** Br For
220 E5 **Braco** P & K
267 K5 **Bracobrae** Moray
106 D3 **Bracon Ash** Norfk
237 L2 **Bracora** Highld
237 L2 **Bracorina** Highld
11 M4 **Bradaford** Devon
115 K1 **Bradbourne** Derbys
169 J5 **Bradbury** Dur
84 C5 **Bradden** Nhants
5 K2 **Braddock** Cnwll
114 D1 **Bradeley** C Stke
67 K7 **Bradenham** Bucks
46 E3 **Bradenstoke** Wilts
14 B1 **Bradfield** Devon
73 H1 **Bradfield** Essex
122 F5 **Bradfield** Norfk
132 E1 **Bradfield** Sheff
48 F4 **Bradfield** W Berk
89 H4 **Bradfield Combust** Suffk
130 D7 **Bradfield Green** Ches
73 H1 **Bradfield Heath** Essex
89 H4 **Bradfield St Clare** Suffk
89 H3 **Bradfield St George** Suffk
141 J1 **Bradford** Brad
11 G7 **Bradford** Cnwll
12 A1 **Bradford** Devon
203 J6 **Bradford** Nthumb
180 C3 **Bradford** Nthumb
31 K8 **Bradford Abbas** Dorset
46 B6 **Bradford Leigh** Wilts
16 C4 **Bradford Peverell** Dorset
46 B6 **Bradford-on-Avon** Wilts
30 B6 **Bradford-on-Tone** Somset

Bradiford - Brightlingsea 295

27 K4 **Bradiford** Devon
19 K6 **Brading** IOW
129 M4 **Bradley** Ches
115 L2 **Bradley** Derbys
35 K3 **Bradley** Hants
141 J4 **Bradley** Kirk
159 J6 **Bradley** N York
145 G6 **Bradley** NE Lin
114 D7 **Bradley** Staffs
98 B4 **Bradley** Wolves
82 A3 **Bradley** Worcs
112 E1 **Bradley** Wrexhm
113 H2 **Bradley Green** Ches
30 C3 **Bradley Green** Somset
99 H3 **Bradley Green** Warwks
82 A3 **Bradley Green** Worcs
115 H3 **Bradley in the Moors** Staffs
45 J3 **Bradley Stoke** S Glos
117 G5 **Bradmore** Notts
30 E3 **Bradney** Somset
27 L4 **Bradninch** Devon
14 A2 **Bradninch** Devon
131 K8 **Bradnop** Staffs
79 K4 **Bradnor Green** Herefs
15 L4 **Bradpole** Dorset
139 L5 **Bradshaw** Bolton
141 G2 **Bradshaw** Calder
141 G5 **Bradshaw** Kirk
11 M6 **Bradstone** Devon
130 E7 **Bradwall Green** Ches
132 C3 **Bradwell** Derbys
27 J2 **Bradwell** Devon
71 K3 **Bradwell** Essex
85 G7 **Bradwell** M Keyn
107 K3 **Bradwell** Norfk
72 E5 **Bradwell Waterside** Essex
72 E5 **Bradwell-on-Sea** Essex
26 E8 **Bradworthy** Devon
263 H7 **Brae** Highld
281 d4 **Brae** Shet
240 B5 **Brae Roy Lodge** Highld
209 K3 **Braeface** Falk
235 H5 **Braehead** Angus
173 K4 **Braehead** D & G
198 F3 **Braehead** S Lans
243 G5 **Braemar** Abers
274 E2 **Braemore** Highld
261 L4 **Braemore** Highld
233 L4 **Braes of Coul** Angus
267 H4 **Braes of Enzie** Moray
207 L4 **Braeside** Inver
275 e2 **Braeswick** Ork
216 E5 **Braevallich** Ag & B
169 H6 **Brafferton** Darltn
150 F2 **Brafferton** N York
84 F3 **Brafield-on-the-Green** Nhants
282 f2 **Bragar** W Isls
69 H3 **Bragbury End** Herts
198 D3 **Braidwood** S Lans
115 L3 **Brailsford** Derbys
115 L3 **Brailsford Green** Derbys
63 K5 **Brain's Green** Gloucs
71 J2 **Braintree** Essex
90 D1 **Braiseworth** Suffk
34 E6 **Braishfield** Hants
149 J7 **Braithwaite** Brad
165 H6 **Braithwaite** Cumb
133 K1 **Braithwell** Donc
142 C4 **Braken Hill** Wakefd
21 L5 **Bramber** W Susx
35 G6 **Brambridge** Hants
116 E4 **Bramcote** Notts
99 L5 **Bramcote** Warwks
35 J5 **Bramdean** Hants
106 F2 **Bramerton** Norfk
69 H4 **Bramfield** Herts
107 H8 **Bramfield** Suffk
90 D6 **Bramford** Suffk
131 H3 **Bramhall** Stockp
150 F7 **Bramham** Leeds
150 C7 **Bramhope** Leeds
133 H4 **Bramley** Derbys
49 G7 **Bramley** Hants
141 K1 **Bramley** Leeds
133 K1 **Bramley** Rothm
36 F2 **Bramley** Surrey
48 F7 **Bramley Corner** Hants
49 G7 **Bramley Green** Hants
149 L4 **Bramley Head** N York
41 H4 **Bramling** Kent
13 L3 **Brampford Speke** Devon
86 E1 **Brampton** Cambs
178 C6 **Brampton** Cumb
166 F6 **Brampton** Cumb
135 G4 **Brampton** Lincs
122 E6 **Brampton** Norfk
142 C7 **Brampton** Rothm
107 J7 **Brampton** Suffk
63 J2 **Brampton Abbotts** Herefs
101 H6 **Brampton Ash** Nhants
79 L1 **Brampton Bryan** Herefs
133 J2 **Brampton-en-le-Morthen** Rothm
115 H5 **Bramshall** Staffs
34 C7 **Bramshaw** Hants
49 H6 **Bramshill** Hants
36 C4 **Bramshott** Hants
31 G5 **Bramwell** Somset
71 G2 **Bran End** Essex
237 G6 **Branault** Highld
121 G3 **Brancaster** Norfk
121 H3 **Brancaster Staithe** Norfk
169 G3 **Brancepeth** Dur
266 B5 **Branchill** Moray
119 L3 **Brand End** Lincs
63 L2 **Brand Green** Gloucs
266 E2 **Branderburgh** Moray
153 H6 **Brandesburton** E R Yk
90 F3 **Brandeston** Suffk
12 A2 **Brandis Corner** Devon
122 C7 **Brandiston** Norfk
169 G3 **Brandon** Dur
118 B2 **Brandon** Lincs
190 F3 **Brandon** Nthumb
104 F6 **Brandon** Suffk
99 L8 **Brandon** Warwks
104 C5 **Brandon Bank** Norfk
104 C5 **Brandon Creek** Norfk
106 B2 **Brandon Parva** Norfk
151 J1 **Brandsby** N York
144 C8 **Brandy Wharf** Lincs
2 B5 **Brane** Cnwll
17 L4 **Branksome** Poole
17 L4 **Branksome Park** Poole
34 F2 **Bransbury** Hants
135 H4 **Bransby** Lincs
14 E5 **Branscombe** Devon
81 H5 **Bransford** Worcs
18 B4 **Bransgore** Hants
144 E1 **Bransholme** C KuH
96 E8 **Bransley** Shrops
82 C1 **Branson's Cross** Worcs
117 L5 **Branston** Leics
135 K6 **Branston** Lincs
115 L7 **Branston** Staffs
135 L6 **Branston Booths** Lincs
19 J7 **Branstone** IOW
118 B1 **Brant Broughton** Lincs
90 D8 **Brantham** Suffk
164 E5 **Branthwaite** Cumb
165 J3 **Branthwaite** Cumb
144 B2 **Brantingham** E R Yk
143 G7 **Branton** Donc
190 F3 **Branton** Nthumb
150 F3 **Branton Green** N York
202 D5 **Branxton** Nthumb
129 M7 **Brassey Green** Ches
115 L1 **Brassington** Derbys
38 D2 **Brasted** Kent
51 M8 **Brasted Chart** Kent
244 F4 **Brathens** Abers
137 J6 **Bratoft** Lincs
135 J3 **Brattleby** Lincs
29 G2 **Bratton** Somset
46 C8 **Bratton** Wilts
96 E1 **Bratton** Wrekin
12 B4 **Bratton Clovelly** Devon
27 M3 **Bratton Fleming** Devon
31 L5 **Bratton Seymour** Somset
69 K2 **Braughing** Herts
70 B2 **Braughing Friars** Herts
83 M2 **Braunston** Nhants
101 H2 **Braunston** Rutlnd
100 C3 **Braunstone** Leics
27 J4 **Braunton** Devon
162 C7 **Brawby** N York
54 D2 **Brawdy** Pembks
278 D3 **Brawl** Highld
161 H1 **Braworth** N York
49 L3 **Bray** W & M
11 L7 **Bray Shop** Cnwll
24 B4 **Bray's Hill** E Susx
101 G6 **Braybrooke** Nhants
46 F1 **Braydon** Wilts
64 E8 **Braydon Brook** Wilts
46 E2 **Braydon Side** Wilts
28 B4 **Brayford** Devon
155 H2 **Braystones** Cumb
150 C6 **Braythorn** N York
142 F2 **Brayton** N York
49 L3 **Braywick** W & M
49 L4 **Braywoodside** W & M
11 K4 **Brazacott** Cnwll
53 H6 **Breach** Kent
41 G6 **Breach** Kent
68 F3 **Breachwood Green** Herts
113 G4 **Breaden Heath** Shrops
116 B4 **Breadsall** Derbys
63 L7 **Breadstone** Gloucs
79 K4 **Breadward** Herefs
3 G5 **Breage** Cnwll
250 E3 **Breakachy** Highld
262 F1 **Brealangwell Lodge** Highld
63 J6 **Bream** Gloucs
33 L7 **Breamore** Hants
44 C7 **Brean** Somset
282 d4 **Breanais** W Isls
140 F3 **Brearley** Calder
150 D4 **Brearton** N York
282 f3 **Breascleit** W Isls
282 f3 **Breasclete** W Isls
116 D5 **Breaston** Derbys
58 F3 **Brechfa** Carmth
234 F3 **Brechin** Angus
105 J4 **Breckles** Norfk
185 L5 **Breckonside** D & G
61 G2 **Brecon** Powys
131 H2 **Bredbury** Stockp
24 E4 **Brede** E Susx
80 E4 **Bredenbury** Herefs
91 G4 **Bredfield** Suffk
53 J7 **Bredgar** Kent
53 G6 **Bredhurst** Kent
81 L7 **Bredon** Worcs
81 L8 **Bredon's Hardwick** Worcs
81 L7 **Bredon's Norton** Worcs
79 L6 **Bredwardine** Herefs
116 C7 **Breedon on the Hill** Leics
210 C7 **Breich** W Loth
139 L6 **Breightmet** Bolton
143 H1 **Breighton** E R Yk
80 B7 **Breinton** Herefs
46 E4 **Bremhill** Wilts
28 B5 **Bremridge** Devon
39 H5 **Brenchley** Kent
11 L1 **Brendon** Devon
28 D1 **Brendon** Devon
29 J4 **Brendon Hill** Somset
206 D3 **Brenfield** Ag & B
282 d4 **Brenish** W Isls
180 F4 **Brenkley** N u Ty
89 J5 **Brent Eleigh** Suffk
30 E1 **Brent Knoll** Somset
7 K3 **Brent Mill** Devon
70 B1 **Brent Pelham** Herts
50 F3 **Brentford** Gt Lon
117 K7 **Brentingby** Leics
70 E8 **Brentwood** Essex
25 J2 **Brenzett** Kent
25 J2 **Brenzett Green** Kent
115 G8 **Brereton** Staffs
130 F6 **Brereton Green** Ches
130 F6 **Brereton Heath** Ches
115 G8 **Brereton Hill** Staffs
106 B7 **Bressingham** Norfk
106 B7 **Bressingham Common** Norfk
116 A7 **Bretby** Derbys
99 L7 **Bretford** Warwks
82 C6 **Bretforton** Worcs
157 J2 **Bretherdale Head** Cumb
138 F4 **Bretherton** Lancs
281 e5 **Brettabister** Shet
105 J6 **Brettenham** Norfk
89 K4 **Brettenham** Suffk
132 D4 **Bretton** Derbys
129 H7 **Bretton** Flints
51 J8 **Brewer Street** Surrey
70 E3 **Brewers End** Essex
97 K2 **Brewood** Staffs
16 F4 **Briantspuddle** Dorset
70 E2 **Brick End** Essex
132 F3 **Brick Houses** Sheff
69 J5 **Brickendon** Herts
68 E6 **Bricket Wood** Herts
71 H1 **Brickkiln Green** Essex
82 A6 **Bricklehampton** Worcs
154 f2 **Bride** IOM
164 F4 **Bridekirk** Cumb
75 L4 **Bridell** Pembks
12 C4 **Bridestowe** Devon
255 M4 **Brideswell** Abers
13 J5 **Bridford** Devon
3 H2 **Bridge** Cnwll
41 G4 **Bridge** Kent
85 K5 **Bridge End** Beds
165 L1 **Bridge End** Cumb
156 A6 **Bridge End** Cumb
7 K5 **Bridge End** Devon
168 C3 **Bridge End** Dur
71 G1 **Bridge End** Essex
118 F4 **Bridge End** Lincs
179 L5 **Bridge End** Nthumb
50 D7 **Bridge End** Surrey
87 K7 **Bridge Green** Essex
150 D2 **Bridge Hewick** N York
255 L8 **Bridge of Alford** Abers
220 D7 **Bridge of Allan** Stirlg
254 D4 **Bridge of Avon** Moray
254 C7 **Bridge of Avon** Moray
231 G6 **Bridge of Balgie** P & K
233 J3 **Bridge of Brewlands** Angus
254 C7 **Bridge of Brown** Highld
233 H5 **Bridge of Cally** P & K
244 E4 **Bridge of Canny** Abers
233 K4 **Bridge of Craigisla** Angus
175 J3 **Bridge of Dee** D & G
245 L2 **Bridge of Don** C Aber
253 H3 **Bridge of Dulsie** Highld
244 E6 **Bridge of Dye** Abers
221 L3 **Bridge of Earn** P & K
230 F4 **Bridge of Ericht** P & K
244 F4 **Bridge of Feugh** Abers
279 J3 **Bridge of Forss** Highld
243 K4 **Bridge of Gairn** Abers
230 F4 **Bridge of Gaur** P & K
267 M6 **Bridge of Marnoch** Abers
230 B7 **Bridge of Orchy** Ag & B
232 C2 **Bridge of Tilt** P & K
267 H4 **Bridge of Tynet** Moray
281 c6 **Bridge of Walls** Shet
208 C6 **Bridge of Weir** Rens
28 B8 **Bridge Reeve** Devon
80 A6 **Bridge Sollers** Herefs
89 H5 **Bridge Street** Suffk
129 K5 **Bridge Trafford** Ches
45 K4 **Bridge Yate** S Glos
164 E5 **Bridgefoot** Cumb
31 J6 **Bridgehampton** Somset
180 D8 **Bridgehill** Dur
149 L3 **Bridgehouse Gate** N York
19 K3 **Bridgemary** Hants
113 M2 **Bridgemere** Ches
255 K4 **Bridgend** Abers
204 E4 **Bridgend** Ag & B
234 E2 **Bridgend** Angus
42 D5 **Bridgend** Brdgnd
75 L3 **Bridgend** Cerdgn
165 L7 **Bridgend** Cumb
187 G4 **Bridgend** D & G
7 G5 **Bridgend** Devon
223 G5 **Bridgend** Fife
255 H5 **Bridgend** Moray
221 L2 **Bridgend** P & K
210 D4 **Bridgend** W Loth
233 L4 **Bridgend of Lintrathen** Angus
11 K2 **Bridgerule** Devon
95 J4 **Bridges** Shrops
11 L4 **Bridgetown** Devon
29 G4 **Bridgetown** Somset
105 J6 **Bridgham** Norfk
97 G5 **Bridgnorth** Shrops
98 B2 **Bridgtown** Staffs
30 D3 **Bridgwater** Somset
153 K3 **Bridlington** E R Yk
15 K4 **Bridport** Dorset
63 H2 **Bridstow** Herefs
148 E8 **Brierfield** Lancs
142 B5 **Brierley** Barns
63 J4 **Brierley** Gloucs
80 C4 **Brierley** Herefs
97 L6 **Brierley Hill** Dudley
170 B5 **Brierton** Hartpl
165 J6 **Briery** Cumb
219 J6 **Brig o'Turk** Stirlg
144 C6 **Brigg** N Linc
123 G6 **Briggate** Norfk
162 F1 **Briggswath** N York
164 E4 **Brigham** Cumb
165 J6 **Brigham** Cumb
153 H5 **Brigham** E R Yk
141 J3 **Brighouse** Calder
19 G7 **Brighstone** IOW
132 E7 **Brightgate** Derbys
66 A6 **Brighthampton** Oxon
132 F1 **Brightholmlee** Sheff
12 E3 **Brightley** Devon
24 C3 **Brightling** E Susx
73 G4 **Brightlingsea** Essex

22 D6 **Brighton** Br & H
4 E4 **Brighton** Cnwll
138 C7 **Brighton le Sands** Sefton
210 B3 **Brightons** Falk
6 D3 **Brightor** Cnwll
48 B3 **Brightwalton** W Berk
48 B3 **Brightwalton Green** W Berk
48 B3 **Brightwalton Holt** W Berk
90 F6 **Brightwell** Suffk
67 G8 **Brightwell Baldwin** Oxon
67 G8 **Brightwell Upperton** Oxon
48 E1 **Brightwell-cum-Sotwell** Oxon
168 D8 **Brignall** Dur
145 H7 **Brigsley** NE Lin
157 G5 **Brigsteer** Cumb
101 L6 **Brigstock** Nhants
67 G4 **Brill** Bucks
3 J5 **Brill** Cnwll
79 J5 **Brilley** Herefs
80 C2 **Brimfield** Herefs
80 C2 **Brimfield Cross** Herefs
133 H5 **Brimington** Derbys
13 J7 **Brimley** Devon
64 D4 **Brimpsfield** Gloucs
48 E6 **Brimpton** W Berk
48 E6 **Brimpton Common** W Berk
64 C6 **Brimscombe** Gloucs
129 G3 **Brimstage** Wirral
132 F3 **Brincliffe** Sheff
143 J2 **Brind** E R Yk
31 H3 **Brindham** Somset
281 c5 **Brindister** Shet
139 J3 **Brindle** Lancs
97 H1 **Brineton** Staffs
101 J5 **Bringhurst** Leics
102 B8 **Brington** Cambs
122 A5 **Briningham** Norfk
117 J1 **Brinkely** Notts
137 G5 **Brinkhill** Lincs
88 C4 **Brinkley** Cambs
99 L7 **Brinklow** Warwks
46 E2 **Brinkworth** Wilts
139 J3 **Brinscall** Lancs
44 E8 **Brinscombe** Somset
44 F6 **Brinsea** N Som
116 D2 **Brinsley** Notts
80 B6 **Brinsop** Herefs
133 H2 **Brinsworth** Rothm
122 A4 **Brinton** Norfk
275 c3 **Brinyan** Ork
178 A8 **Brisco** Cumb
121 L7 **Brisley** Norfk
45 J5 **Brislington** Bristl
40 B7 **Brissenden Green** Kent
45 H4 **Bristol** Bristl
122 B5 **Briston** Norfk
7 G2 **Brisworthy** Devon
140 C3 **Britannia** Lancs
33 L5 **Britford** Wilts
61 J6 **Brithdir** Caerph
110 E7 **Brithdir** Gwynd
61 L6 **British** Torfn
52 F7 **British Legion Village** Kent
57 K6 **Briton Ferry** Neath
67 G8 **Britwell Salome** Oxon
8 D4 **Brixham** Torbay
7 G4 **Brixton** Devon
51 J4 **Brixton** Gt Lon
32 E3 **Brixton Deverill** Wilts
84 E1 **Brixworth** Nhants
65 L5 **Brize Norton** Oxon
81 K2 **Broad Alley** Worcs
47 H1 **Broad Blunsdon** Swindn
82 E7 **Broad Campden** Gloucs
141 H4 **Broad Carr** Calder
33 H5 **Broad Chalke** Wilts
140 C3 **Broad Clough** Lancs
39 H5 **Broad Ford** Kent
72 C2 **Broad Green** Essex
81 H4 **Broad Green** Worcs
82 A1 **Broad Green** Worcs
54 D4 **Broad Haven** Pembks
104 B8 **Broad Hill** Cambs
47 G4 **Broad Hinton** Wilts
48 B6 **Broad Laying** Hants
82 D6 **Broad Marston** Worcs
114 C2 **Broad Meadow** Staffs
155 K4 **Broad Oak** Cumb
24 E3 **Broad Oak** E Susx
23 K3 **Broad Oak** E Susx
49 H8 **Broad Oak** Hants
62 F3 **Broad Oak** Herefs
41 G3 **Broad Oak** Kent
139 G8 **Broad Oak** St Hel

106 F8 **Broad Road** Suffk
24 F4 **Broad Street** E Susx
70 E4 **Broad Street** Essex
39 L2 **Broad Street** Kent
53 G4 **Broad Street** Medway
47 G7 **Broad Street** Wilts
72 B5 **Broad Street Green** Essex
47 G3 **Broad Town** Wilts
71 G4 **Broad's Green** Essex
131 K1 **Broadbottom** Tamesd
20 D6 **Broadbridge** W Susx
37 H4 **Broadbridge Heath** W Susx
14 A3 **Broadclyst** Devon
208 B4 **Broadfield** Inver
55 K6 **Broadfield** Pembks
247 K4 **Broadford** Highld
37 G6 **Broadford Bridge** W Susx
187 K4 **Broadgairhill** Border
103 H2 **Broadgate** Lincs
89 K3 **Broadgrass Green** Suffk
202 D2 **Broadhaugh** Border
130 E2 **Broadheath** Traffd
80 F2 **Broadheath** Worcs
14 C2 **Broadhembury** Devon
8 B2 **Broadhempston** Devon
135 H5 **Broadholme** Notts
24 F3 **Broadland Row** E Susx
56 C3 **Broadlay** Carmth
70 B5 **Broadley** Essex
140 C4 **Broadley** Lancs
267 H4 **Broadley** Moray
70 B5 **Broadley Common** Essex
16 D5 **Broadmayne** Dorset
35 J2 **Broadmere** Hants
63 J4 **Broadmoor** Gloucs
55 J5 **Broadmoor** Pembks
13 G2 **Broadnymett** Devon
15 K3 **Broadoak** Dorset
63 K4 **Broadoak** Gloucs
129 J7 **Broadoak** Wrexhm
41 L2 **Broadstairs** Kent
63 G6 **Broadstone** Mons
17 K3 **Broadstone** Poole
96 C5 **Broadstone** Shrops
81 H4 **Broadwas** Worcs
69 H3 **Broadwater** Herts
21 K6 **Broadwater** W Susx
97 J7 **Broadwaters** Worcs
56 B3 **Broadway** Carmth
56 C3 **Broadway** Carmth
54 E4 **Broadway** Pembks
30 D7 **Broadway** Somset
107 H7 **Broadway** Suffk
82 C7 **Broadway** Worcs
63 H5 **Broadwell** Gloucs
65 J2 **Broadwell** Gloucs
65 K6 **Broadwell** Oxon
83 K2 **Broadwell** Warwks
16 C6 **Broadwey** Dorset
15 K2 **Broadwindsor** Dorset
12 E1 **Broadwood Kelly** Devon
12 A5 **Broadwoodwidger** Devon
79 L6 **Brobury** Herefs
259 K7 **Brochel** Highld
147 K7 **Brock** Lancs
48 D6 **Brock's Green** Hants
81 H4 **Brockamin** Worcs
35 J7 **Brockbridge** Hants
106 E7 **Brockdish** Norfk
97 K8 **Brockencote** Worcs
18 D3 **Brockenhurst** Hants
198 D5 **Brocketsbrae** S Lans
90 D2 **Brockford Green** Suffk
90 D2 **Brockford Street** Suffk
84 C3 **Brockhall** Nhants
37 J1 **Brockham** Surrey
64 D2 **Brockhampton** Gloucs
64 F3 **Brockhampton** Gloucs
20 B5 **Brockhampton** Hants
63 H1 **Brockhampton** Herefs
16 D1 **Brockhampton Green** Dorset
141 J5 **Brockholes** Kirk
133 G6 **Brockhurst** Derbys
100 A6 **Brockhurst** Warwks
165 J2 **Brocklebank** Cumb
144 E5 **Brocklesby** Lincs
44 F5 **Brockley** N Som
89 G1 **Brockley** Suffk
88 E6 **Brockley Green** Suffk
89 G4 **Brockley Green** Suffk
166 C3 **Brockleymoor** Cumb
97 K5 **Brockmoor** Dudley
12 B3 **Brockscombe** Devon
95 H3 **Brockton** Shrops
97 G3 **Brockton** Shrops

95 H6 **Brockton** Shrops
96 D4 **Brockton** Shrops
114 C5 **Brockton** Staffs
63 G6 **Brockweir** Gloucs
35 K5 **Brockwood Park** Hants
64 C4 **Brockworth** Gloucs
5 G1 **Brocton** Cnwll
114 F7 **Brocton** Staffs
195 G4 **Brodick** N Ayrs
264 F8 **Brodie** Moray
142 D6 **Brodsworth** Donc
259 H3 **Brogaig** Highld
85 J7 **Brogborough** Beds
130 D5 **Broken Cross** Ches
131 H5 **Broken Cross** Ches
46 D1 **Brokenborough** Wilts
46 B8 **Brokerswood** Wilts
129 H3 **Bromborough** Wirral
106 C8 **Brome** Suffk
106 C8 **Brome Street** Suffk
91 G5 **Bromeswell** Suffk
165 G1 **Bromfield** Cumb
96 B8 **Bromfield** Shrops
85 K5 **Bromham** Beds
46 D6 **Bromham** Wilts
141 M7 **Bromley** Barns
97 K5 **Bromley** Dudley
51 L5 **Bromley** Gt Lon
97 G4 **Bromley** Shrops
51 L5 **Bromley Common** Gt Lon
72 F2 **Bromley Cross** Essex
95 H3 **Bromlow** Shrops
53 G5 **Brompton** Medway
160 E3 **Brompton** N York
163 G6 **Brompton** N York
96 C2 **Brompton** Shrops
29 K4 **Brompton Ralph** Somset
29 G4 **Brompton Regis** Somset
160 B3 **Brompton-on-Swale** N York
63 J2 **Bromsash** Herefs
81 G8 **Bromsberrow** Gloucs
81 G8 **Bromsberrow Heath** Gloucs
81 M1 **Bromsgrove** Worcs
114 B8 **Bromstead Heath** Staffs
80 F4 **Bromyard** Herefs
80 F4 **Bromyard Downs** Herefs
110 D5 **Bronaber** Gwynd
77 H2 **Bronant** Cerdgn
96 C6 **Broncroft** Shrops
76 B6 **Brongest** Cerdgn
113 H3 **Bronington** Wrexhm
79 G8 **Bronllys** Powys
58 D4 **Bronwydd** Carmth
79 J6 **Bronydd** Powys
112 C4 **Brongarth** Shrops
56 A3 **Brook** Carmth
34 C8 **Brook** Hants
34 D5 **Brook** Hants
18 F6 **Brook** IOW
40 E6 **Brook** Kent
36 D3 **Brook** Surrey
37 G2 **Brook** Surrey
86 B3 **Brook End** Beds
86 D5 **Brook End** Beds
86 B1 **Brook End** Cambs
85 H6 **Brook End** M Keyn
34 C7 **Brook Hill** Hants
128 C6 **Brook House** Denbgs
70 E8 **Brook Street** Essex
40 B8 **Brook Street** Kent
89 G5 **Brook Street** Suffk
22 D2 **Brook Street** W Susx
106 F3 **Brooke** Norfk
101 J2 **Brooke** Rutlnd
145 G8 **Brookenby** Lincs
208 C6 **Brookfield** Rens
66 F7 **Brookhampton** Oxon
31 K5 **Brookhampton** Somset
147 K3 **Brookhouse** Lancs
133 K2 **Brookhouse** Rothm
130 F7 **Brookhouse Green** Ches
131 K2 **Brookhouses** Derbys
25 J2 **Brookland** Kent
130 F2 **Brooklands** Traffd
69 H6 **Brookmans Park** Herts
94 E3 **Brooks** Powys
41 J2 **Brooks End** Kent
37 H6 **Brooks Green** W Susx
117 H8 **Brooksby** Leics
64 B4 **Brookthorpe** Gloucs
104 E4 **Brookville** Norfk
50 B7 **Brookwood** Surrey
86 D6 **Broom** Beds
169 H2 **Broom** Dur
133 J1 **Broom** Rothm

82 C4 **Broom** Warwks
121 L6 **Broom Green** Norfk
142 C7 **Broom Hill** Barns
17 K2 **Broom Hill** Dorset
116 F2 **Broom Hill** Notts
97 L8 **Broom Hill** Worcs
40 D3 **Broom Street** Kent
81 G8 **Broom's Green** Gloucs
107 G5 **Broome** Norfk
95 K7 **Broome** Shrops
97 K7 **Broome** Worcs
191 G4 **Broome Park** Nthumb
130 D3 **Broomedge** Warrtn
21 K3 **Broomer's Corner** W Susx
21 H3 **Broomershill** W Susx
71 H5 **Broomfield** Essex
39 L3 **Broomfield** Kent
41 G2 **Broomfield** Kent
30 B4 **Broomfield** Somset
112 F7 **Broomfields** Shrops
143 M2 **Broomfleet** E R Yk
50 B5 **Broomhall** W & M
180 B6 **Broomhaugh** Nthumb
191 J6 **Broomhill** Nthumb
113 K2 **Broomhill Green** Ches
180 C6 **Broomley** Nthumb
121 J6 **Broomsthorpe** Norfk
274 B7 **Brora** Highld
96 F3 **Broseley** Shrops
119 J8 **Brotherhouse Bar** Lincs
167 L3 **Brotherlee** Dur
119 J2 **Brothertoft** Lincs
142 D3 **Brotherton** N York
170 F6 **Brotton** R & Cl
279 J4 **Broubster** Highld
167 J7 **Brough** Cumb
132 D3 **Brough** Derbys
144 B2 **Brough** E R Yk
280 B2 **Brough** Highld
135 G7 **Brough** Notts
281 f5 **Brough** Shet
281 f3 **Brough Lodge** Shet
167 J8 **Brough Sowerby** Cumb
113 J3 **Broughall** Shrops
199 K6 **Broughton** Border
67 K4 **Broughton** Bucks
102 F7 **Broughton** Cambs
129 H7 **Broughton** Flints
34 C4 **Broughton** Hants
139 G1 **Broughton** Lancs
85 H7 **Broughton** M Keyn
144 B6 **Broughton** N Linc
149 G5 **Broughton** N York
162 D8 **Broughton** N York
101 H8 **Broughton** Nhants
83 K7 **Broughton** Oxon
140 B7 **Broughton** Salfd
114 B5 **Broughton** Staffs
42 D7 **Broughton** V Glam
100 C5 **Broughton Astley** Leics
156 C6 **Broughton Beck** Cumb
46 C6 **Broughton Gifford** Wilts
81 M3 **Broughton Green** Worcs
81 L4 **Broughton Hackett** Worcs
174 C6 **Broughton Mains** D & G
156 B4 **Broughton Mills** Cumb
164 E4 **Broughton Moor** Cumb
65 K6 **Broughton Poggs** Oxon
156 B5 **Broughton Tower** Cumb
156 B5 **Broughton-in-Furness** Cumb
223 H1 **Broughty Ferry** C Dund
156 C7 **Brow End** Cumb
120 E7 **Brow-of-the-Hill** Norfk
35 J3 **Brown Candover** Hants
138 D5 **Brown Edge** Lancs
114 E1 **Brown Edge** Staffs
129 K6 **Brown Heath** Ches
131 G8 **Brown Lees** Staffs
90 C3 **Brown Street** Suffk
98 D5 **Brown's Green** Birm
158 B2 **Brownber** Cumb
113 G5 **Brownheath** Shrops
256 F4 **Brownhill** Abers
223 J4 **Brownhills** Fife
98 D2 **Brownhills** Wsall
191 H2 **Brownieside** Nthumb
48 E7 **Browninghill Green** Hants
131 G7 **Brownlow Heath** Ches
164 D6 **Brownrigg** Cumb
177 G8 **Brownrigg** Cumb
64 C6 **Browns Hill** Gloucs
26 E5 **Brownsham** Devon
100 B7 **Brownsover** Warwks
7 K4 **Brownston** Devon
107 K3 **Browston Green** Norfk

163 G4 **Broxa** N York
69 K5 **Broxbourne** Herts
212 F3 **Broxburn** E Loth
210 E4 **Broxburn** W Loth
191 J3 **Broxfield** Nthumb
70 E2 **Broxted** Essex
113 H1 **Broxton** Ches
79 L4 **Broxwood** Herefs
23 G4 **Broyle Side** E Susx
280 D8 **Bruan** Highld
232 B2 **Bruar** P & K
264 E3 **Brucefield** Highld
207 J7 **Bruchag** Ag & B
129 K7 **Bruera** Ches
65 K3 **Bruern Abbey** Oxon
204 C4 **Bruichladdich** Ag & B
91 H2 **Bruisyard** Suffk
91 H2 **Bruisyard Street** Suffk
143 M6 **Brumby** N Linc
132 B7 **Brund** Staffs
107 G2 **Brundall** Norfk
91 G1 **Brundish** Suffk
91 G1 **Brundish Street** Suffk
2 D4 **Brunnion** Cnwll
95 J6 **Brunslow** Shrops
180 F4 **Brunswick Village** N u Ty
141 L2 **Bruntcliffe** Leeds
149 J6 **Brunthwaite** Brad
100 D5 **Bruntingthorpe** Leics
222 E3 **Brunton** Fife
191 J1 **Brunton** Nthumb
47 K7 **Brunton** Wilts
29 G5 **Brushford** Somset
12 F1 **Brushford Barton** Devon
31 L4 **Bruton** Somset
81 K2 **Bryan's Green** Worcs
17 G1 **Bryanston** Dorset
67 L7 **Bryant's Bottom** Bucks
177 G5 **Brydekirk** D & G
112 H1 **Brymbo** Wrexhm
31 H7 **Brympton** Somset
130 B5 **Bryn** Ches
42 B3 **Bryn** Neath
95 H6 **Bryn** Shrops
139 H7 **Bryn** Wigan
124 F5 **Bryn Du** IOA
139 J7 **Bryn Gates** Wigan
42 F4 **Bryn Golau** Rhondd
111 L2 **Bryn Saith Marchog** Denbgs
110 B4 **Bryn-bwbach** Gwynd
57 K5 **Bryn-coch** Neath
110 D5 **Bryn-Eden** Gwynd
75 G4 **Bryn-Henllan** Pembks
108 D5 **Bryn-mawr** Gwynd
112 B3 **Bryn-newydd** Denbgs
94 D3 **Bryn-penarth** Powys
128 F6 **Bryn-y-bal** Flints
127 G4 **Bryn-y-Maen** Conwy
112 D3 **Bryn-yr-Eos** Wrexhm
59 K6 **Brynaman** Carmth
75 J5 **Brynberian** Pembks
57 L6 **Brynbryddan** Neath
42 F5 **Bryncae** Rhondd
42 D5 **Bryncethin** Brdgnd
109 H3 **Bryncir** Gwynd
108 C5 **Bryncroes** Gwynd
92 D3 **Bryncrug** Gwynd
112 A2 **Bryneglwys** Denbgs
112 D3 **Brynfields** Wrexhm
128 E5 **Brynford** Flints
124 F4 **Bryngwran** IOA
62 D5 **Bryngwyn** Mons
79 H5 **Bryngwyn** Powys
76 B5 **Brynhoffnant** Cerdgn
138 E2 **Bryning** Lancs
61 K6 **Brynithel** Blae G
61 J5 **Brynmawr** Blae G
42 D5 **Brynmenyn** Brdgnd
57 H6 **Brynmill** Swans
42 F5 **Brynna** Rhondd
125 K7 **Brynrefail** Gwynd
125 H2 **Brynrefail** IOA
42 F5 **Brynsadler** Rhondd
125 H6 **Brynsiencyn** IOA
125 J3 **Brynteg** IOA
246 F4 **Bualintur** Highld
128 E4 **Buarth-draw** Flints
83 J1 **Bubbenhall** Warwks
151 M8 **Bubwith** E R Yk
208 D1 **Buchanan Smithy** Stirlg
269 L6 **Buchanhaven** Abers
221 G2 **Buchanty** P & K
220 C6 **Buchany** Stirlg
219 J8 **Buchlyvie** Stirlg
26 F6 **Buck's Cross** Devon

26 F6 **Buck's Mills** Devon
165 L1 **Buckabank** Cumb
86 D2 **Buckden** Cambs
159 G7 **Buckden** N York
107 G2 **Buckenham** Norfk
14 D2 **Buckerell** Devon
7 L2 **Buckfast** Devon
7 L2 **Buckfastleigh** Devon
222 F7 **Buckhaven** Fife
63 G4 **Buckholt** Mons
32 C6 **Buckhorn Weston** Dorset
69 L8 **Buckhurst Hill** Essex
267 J3 **Buckie** Moray
84 D8 **Buckingham** Bucks
67 L4 **Buckland** Bucks
7 K6 **Buckland** Devon
82 C8 **Buckland** Gloucs
18 E4 **Buckland** Hants
87 G8 **Buckland** Herts
41 J6 **Buckland** Kent
65 M7 **Buckland** Oxon
37 K1 **Buckland** Surrey
27 G6 **Buckland Brewer** Devon
68 A5 **Buckland Common** Bucks
32 C1 **Buckland Dinham** Somset
12 B1 **Buckland Filleigh** Devon
13 G7 **Buckland in the Moor** Devon
6 F1 **Buckland Monachorum** Devon
16 D2 **Buckland Newton** Dorset
16 C6 **Buckland Ripers** Dorset
30 C8 **Buckland St Mary** Somset
7 L5 **Buckland-Tout-Saints** Devon
48 E5 **Bucklebury** W Berk
18 F4 **Bucklers Hard** Hants
90 F6 **Bucklesham** Suffk
129 G7 **Buckley** Flints
82 E2 **Buckley Green** Warwks
129 G6 **Buckley Mountain** Flints
130 E3 **Bucklow Hill** Ches
118 A7 **Buckminster** Leics
114 E2 **Bucknall** C Stke
136 C6 **Bucknall** Lincs
66 E2 **Bucknell** Oxon
95 J8 **Bucknell** Shrops
267 H3 **Buckpool** Moray
37 G4 **Bucks Green** W Susx
68 D7 **Bucks Hill** Herts
36 B3 **Bucks Horn Oak** Hants
245 K2 **Bucksburn** C Aber
4 D5 **Buckshead** Cnwll
153 K1 **Buckton** E R Yk
95 J8 **Buckton** Herefs
203 H5 **Buckton** Nthumb
102 C8 **Buckworth** Cambs
134 C5 **Budby** Notts
11 J2 **Budd's Titson** Cnwll
114 B2 **Buddileigh** Staffs
223 J1 **Buddon** Angus
11 H2 **Bude** Cnwll
6 C3 **Budge's Shop** Cnwll
14 A3 **Budlake** Devon
203 J6 **Budle** Nthumb
14 C6 **Budleigh Salterton** Devon
23 H3 **Budlett's Common** E Susx
3 K5 **Budock Water** Cnwll
113 L3 **Buerton** Ches
84 D4 **Bugbrooke** Nhants
8 B5 **Bugford** Devon
131 G7 **Buglawton** Ches
5 G3 **Bugle** Cnwll
32 C6 **Bugley** Dorset
152 B4 **Bugthorpe** E R Yk
96 E2 **Buildwas** Shrops
78 E4 **Builth Road** Powys
78 E5 **Builth Wells** Powys
68 B4 **Bulbourne** Herts
33 J5 **Bulbridge** Wilts
118 D6 **Bulby** Lincs
279 H3 **Buldoo** Highld
33 L2 **Bulford** Wilts
33 L2 **Bulford Barracks** Wilts
113 J1 **Bulkeley** Ches
99 K6 **Bulkington** Warwks
46 D7 **Bulkington** Wilts
27 G8 **Bulkworthy** Devon
125 G1 **Bull Bay** IOA
69 H4 **Bull's Green** Herts
107 J4 **Bull's Green** Norfk
160 F4 **Bullamore** N York
116 B1 **Bullbridge** Derbys
49 L5 **Bullbrook** Br For
69 G6 **Bullen's Green** Herts
63 M3 **Bulley** Gloucs
164 E3 **Bullgill** Cumb

80 C7 **Bullinghope** Herefs
34 F3 **Bullington** Hants
136 A4 **Bullington** Lincs
84 F6 **Bullington End** M Keyn
41 G2 **Bullockstone** Kent
89 G7 **Bulmer** Essex
151 L2 **Bulmer** N York
89 G7 **Bulmer Tye** Essex
52 D2 **Bulphan** Thurr
14 E4 **Bulstone** Devon
68 C6 **Bulstrode** Herts
50 C1 **Bulstrode Park** Bucks
24 D5 **Bulverhythe** E Susx
257 G3 **Bulwark** Abers
116 F3 **Bulwell** C Nott
101 L4 **Bulwick** Nhants
69 L6 **Bumble's Green** Essex
237 J3 **Bunacaimb** Highld
239 K6 **Bunarkaig** Highld
130 A8 **Bunbury** Ches
130 A8 **Bunbury Heath** Ches
251 H3 **Bunchrew** Highld
21 K4 **Buncton** W Susx
248 E6 **Bundalloch** Highld
226 D8 **Bunessan** Ag & B
107 G5 **Bungay** Suffk
119 J1 **Bunker's Hill** Lincs
204 F2 **Bunnahabhain** Ag & B
117 G5 **Bunny** Notts
250 C5 **Buntait** Highld
69 K1 **Buntingford** Herts
106 C5 **Bunwell** Norfk
106 C4 **Bunwell Street** Norfk
115 L4 **Bupton** Derbys
131 L5 **Burbage** Derbys
99 L5 **Burbage** Leics
47 K6 **Burbage** Wilts
79 L3 **Burcher** Herefs
39 G7 **Burchett's Green** E Susx
49 K3 **Burchett's Green** W & M
33 J5 **Burcombe** Wilts
66 E7 **Burcot** Oxon
82 A1 **Burcot** Worcs
97 G4 **Burcote** Shrops
67 K4 **Burcott** Bucks
67 L2 **Burcott** Bucks
152 D3 **Burdale** N York
89 H8 **Bures** Essex
65 K5 **Burford** Oxon
80 D2 **Burford** Shrops
226 D3 **Burg** Ag & B
106 B8 **Burgate** Suffk
36 A5 **Burgates** Hants
68 F1 **Burge End** Herts
22 E3 **Burgess Hill** W Susx
90 F5 **Burgh** Suffk
177 K7 **Burgh by Sands** Cumb
107 K2 **Burgh Castle** Norfk
51 H7 **Burgh Heath** Surrey
24 C2 **Burgh Hill** E Susx
137 J6 **Burgh le Marsh** Lincs
122 E6 **Burgh next Aylsham** Norfk
136 D2 **Burgh on Bain** Lincs
123 J8 **Burgh St Margaret** Norfk
107 K5 **Burgh St Peter** Norfk
48 C6 **Burghclere** Hants
266 C2 **Burghead** Moray
49 G5 **Burghfield** W Berk
49 G5 **Burghfield Common** W Berk
80 B6 **Burghill** Herefs
142 E5 **Burghwallis** Donc
52 F6 **Burham** Kent
20 B3 **Buriton** Hants
113 K1 **Burland** Ches
5 G1 **Burlawn** Cnwll
64 C6 **Burleigh** Gloucs
29 K7 **Burlescombe** Devon
16 E4 **Burleston** Dorset
8 B5 **Burlestone** Devon
18 C3 **Burley** Hants
101 J1 **Burley** Rutlnd
96 B7 **Burley** Shrops
80 E6 **Burley Gate** Herefs
149 L6 **Burley in Wharfedale** Brad
18 C3 **Burley Lawn** Hants
18 B3 **Burley Street** Hants
149 L7 **Burley Wood Head** Brad
113 K3 **Burleydam** Ches
107 H1 **Burlingham Green** Norfk
79 J3 **Burlingjobb** Powys
97 H1 **Burlington** Shrops
113 G6 **Burlton** Shrops
25 L1 **Burmarsh** Kent
83 G7 **Burmington** Warwks
142 F2 **Burn** N York

142 A8 **Burn Cross** Sheff
147 G7 **Burn Naze** Lancs
220 C6 **Burn of Cambus** Stirlg
131 G1 **Burnage** Manch
115 M5 **Burnaston** Derbys
166 C7 **Burnbanks** Cumb
210 A7 **Burnbrae** N Lans
152 C6 **Burnby** E R Yk
21 G6 **Burndell** W Susx
139 L6 **Burnden** Bolton
140 D5 **Burnedge** Rochdl
157 H3 **Burneside** Cumb
160 D5 **Burneston** N York
45 K6 **Burnett** BaNES
188 C4 **Burnfoot** Border
188 F3 **Burnfoot** Border
186 E7 **Burnfoot** D & G
177 K1 **Burnfoot** D & G
188 C6 **Burnfoot** D & G
221 H6 **Burnfoot** P & K
50 A3 **Burnham** Bucks
144 D4 **Burnham** N Linc
121 H3 **Burnham Deepdale** Norfk
69 H4 **Burnham Green** Herts
121 H3 **Burnham Market** Norfk
121 H3 **Burnham Norton** Norfk
121 J3 **Burnham Overy** Norfk
121 J3 **Burnham Overy Staithe** Norfk
121 J3 **Burnham Thorpe** Norfk
72 D7 **Burnham-on-Crouch** Essex
30 D1 **Burnham-on-Sea** Somset
257 L3 **Burnhaven** Abers
186 C7 **Burnhead** D & G
256 C7 **Burnhervie** Abers
97 H3 **Burnhill Green** Staffs
169 G1 **Burnhope** Dur
196 D1 **Burnhouse** N Ayrs
163 H4 **Burniston** N York
140 C1 **Burnley** Lancs
181 H8 **Burnmoor** Dur
213 L6 **Burnmouth** Border
180 E7 **Burnopfield** Dur
178 C7 **Burnrigg** Cumb
149 J3 **Burnsall** N York
234 D5 **Burnside** Angus
234 C3 **Burnside** Angus
222 B5 **Burnside** Fife
266 D2 **Burnside** Moray
210 E4 **Burnside** W Loth
234 C8 **Burnside of Duntrune** Angus
72 F2 **Burnt Heath** Essex
48 E4 **Burnt Hill** W Berk
168 E6 **Burnt Houses** Dur
23 H2 **Burnt Oak** E Susx
150 C4 **Burnt Yates** N York
50 D8 **Burntcommon** Surrey
115 L5 **Burntheath** Derbys
3 K4 **Burnthouse** Cnwll
211 H2 **Burntisland** Fife
98 D2 **Burntwood** Staffs
98 D2 **Burntwood Green** Staffs
12 C6 **Burnville** Devon
30 B7 **Burnworthy** Somset
50 C8 **Burpham** Surrey
21 H5 **Burpham** W Susx
181 G4 **Burradon** N Tyne
190 D5 **Burradon** Nthumb
281 f1 **Burrafirth** Shet
3 H4 **Burras** Cnwll
6 E2 **Burraton** Cnwll
7 H4 **Burraton** Devon
281 e4 **Burravoe** Shet
166 F7 **Burrells** Cumb
233 J7 **Burrelton** P & K
27 K4 **Burridge** Devon
15 H1 **Burridge** Devon
19 J2 **Burridge** Hants
160 C5 **Burrill** N York
143 L6 **Burringham** N Linc
27 L7 **Burrington** Devon
80 B1 **Burrington** Herefs
44 F7 **Burrington** N Som
88 C4 **Burrough End** Cambs
88 C4 **Burrough Green** Cambs
101 G1 **Burrough on the Hill** Leics
157 K7 **Burrow** Lancs
29 G2 **Burrow** Somset
30 E5 **Burrow Bridge** Somset
50 B6 **Burrowhill** Surrey
37 G2 **Burrows Cross** Surrey
56 E6 **Burry** Swans
56 E6 **Burry Green** Swans
56 E5 **Burry Port** Carmth
138 E5 **Burscough** Lancs

138 F5 **Burscough Bridge** Lancs
143 K1 **Bursea** E R Yk
153 H6 **Burshill** E R Yk
19 H2 **Bursledon** Hants
114 D2 **Burslem** C Stke
90 C6 **Burstall** Suffk
15 K2 **Burstock** Dorset
106 C6 **Burston** Norfk
114 E5 **Burston** Staffs
37 M3 **Burstow** Surrey
145 G2 **Burstwick** E R Yk
158 F5 **Burtersett** N York
178 D6 **Burtholme** Cumb
88 F2 **Burthorpe Green** Suffk
165 M1 **Burthwaite** Cumb
4 E4 **Burthy** Cnwll
30 F2 **Burtle Hill** Somset
119 J4 **Burtoft** Lincs
129 H5 **Burton** Ches
129 L7 **Burton** Ches
16 D4 **Burton** Dorset
18 B5 **Burton** Dorset
135 J5 **Burton** Lincs
203 K6 **Burton** Nthumb
55 G5 **Burton** Pembks
30 B2 **Burton** Somset
31 H8 **Burton** Somset
46 B3 **Burton** Wilts
32 D4 **Burton** Wilts
153 H3 **Burton Agnes** E R Yk
15 L4 **Burton Bradstock** Dorset
118 C6 **Burton Coggles** Lincs
83 J5 **Burton Dassett** Warwks
70 D2 **Burton End** Essex
88 D6 **Burton End** Suffk
153 H2 **Burton Fleming** E R Yk
99 H8 **Burton Green** Warwks
129 H7 **Burton Green** Wrexhm
99 L5 **Burton Hastings** Warwks
148 A2 **Burton in Lonsdale** N York
117 H3 **Burton Joyce** Notts
101 K8 **Burton Latimer** Nhants
117 K8 **Burton Lazars** Leics
150 D3 **Burton Leonard** N York
117 G7 **Burton on the Wolds** Leics
100 E4 **Burton Overy** Leics
118 F3 **Burton Pedwardine** Lincs
145 H2 **Burton Pidsea** E R Yk
142 D2 **Burton Salmon** N York
143 L4 **Burton upon Stather** N Linc
115 L6 **Burton upon Trent** Staffs
135 J5 **Burton Waters** Lincs
71 K2 **Burton's Green** Essex
157 H7 **Burton-in-Kendal** Cumb
130 A1 **Burtonwood** Warrtn
129 L8 **Burwardsley** Ches
96 E6 **Burwarton** Shrops
24 B2 **Burwash** E Susx
23 L3 **Burwash Common** E Susx
23 L3 **Burwash Weald** E Susx
88 B2 **Burwell** Cambs
137 G4 **Burwell** Lincs
125 G1 **Burwen** IOA
275 c6 **Burwick** Ork
140 B5 **Bury** Bury
102 F6 **Bury** Cambs
29 G5 **Bury** Somset
21 G4 **Bury** W Susx
86 C8 **Bury End** Beds
68 B7 **Bury End** Bucks
70 C3 **Bury Green** Herts
89 G2 **Bury St Edmunds** Suffk
152 B3 **Burythorpe** N York
208 F7 **Busby** E Rens
160 E6 **Busby Stoop** N York
65 J7 **Buscot** Wilts
235 J2 **Bush** Abers
11 J1 **Bush** Cnwll
80 B5 **Bush Bank** Herefs
106 E6 **Bush Green** Norfk
89 H4 **Bush Green** Suffk
69 J7 **Bush Hill Park** Gt Lon
97 L3 **Bushbury** Wolves
100 E3 **Bushby** Leics
68 E8 **Bushey** Herts
68 F8 **Bushey Heath** Herts
81 K8 **Bushley** Worcs
81 K8 **Bushley Green** Worcs
86 C3 **Bushmead** Beds
46 F3 **Bushton** Wilts
166 E2 **Busk** Cumb
135 M3 **Buslingthorpe** Lincs
64 C6 **Bussage** Gloucs
30 E4 **Bussex** Somset
140 D3 **Butcher Hill** Calder

23 J2 **Butcher's Cross** E Susx
45 G6 **Butcombe** N Som
31 H4 **Butleigh** Somset
31 H4 **Butleigh Wootton** Somset
67 K5 **Butler's Cross** Bucks
116 F2 **Butler's Hill** Notts
83 H5 **Butlers Marston** Warwks
91 J5 **Butley** Suffk
91 J5 **Butley High Corner** Suffk
113 L1 **Butt Green** Ches
114 C1 **Butt Lane** Staffs
71 J6 **Butt's Green** Essex
151 M4 **Buttercrambe** N York
213 H6 **Butterdean** Border
168 E5 **Butterknowle** Dur
14 A1 **Butterleigh** Devon
116 C1 **Butterley** Derbys
165 G7 **Buttermere** Cumb
47 M6 **Buttermere** Wilts
114 C2 **Butters Green** Staffs
141 H2 **Buttershaw** Brad
233 G6 **Butterstone** P & K
114 C3 **Butterton** Staffs
131 L8 **Butterton** Staffs
169 K5 **Butterwick** Dur
119 L3 **Butterwick** Lincs
162 C7 **Butterwick** N York
152 F7 **Butterwick** N York
95 G2 **Buttington** Powys
97 G7 **Buttonbridge** Shrops
97 G7 **Buttonoak** Shrops
19 G2 **Butts Ash** Hants
11 K2 **Buttsbear Cross** Cnwll
89 K4 **Buxhall** Suffk
89 K3 **Buxhall Fen Street** Suffk
23 H3 **Buxted** E Susx
131 L5 **Buxton** Derbys
122 E7 **Buxton** Norfk
122 D7 **Buxton Heath** Norfk
61 J3 **Bwlch** Powys
112 B8 **Bwlch-y-cibau** Powys
112 B7 **Bwlch-y-Ddar** Powys
94 C4 **Bwlch-y-ffridd** Powys
75 M5 **Bwlch-y-groes** Pembks
94 B8 **Bwlch-y-sarnau** Powys
112 C1 **Bwlchgwyn** Wrexhm
77 G3 **Bwlchllan** Cerdgn
58 C4 **Bwlchnewydd** Carmth
108 E6 **Bwlchtocyn** Gwynd
76 D5 **Bwlchyfadfa** Cerdgn
57 G5 **Bwlchymyrdd** Swans
180 F7 **Byermoor** Gatesd
169 J3 **Byers Green** Dur
169 G4 **Byers Green** Dur
83 M4 **Byfield** Nhants
50 D6 **Byfleet** Surrey
79 M6 **Byford** Herefs
86 F7 **Bygrave** Herts
181 G6 **Byker** N u Ty
161 J6 **Byland Abbey** N York
127 K7 **Bylchau** Conwy
130 E6 **Byley** Ches
57 G5 **Bynea** Carmth
201 K4 **Byrewalls** Border
189 K5 **Byrness** Nthumb
14 B6 **Bystock** Devon
102 B8 **Bythorn** Cambs
79 L2 **Byton** Herefs
180 C6 **Bywell** Nthumb
36 E6 **Byworth** W Susx

C

27 G6 **Cabbacott** Devon
144 F7 **Cabourne** Lincs
205 H3 **Cabrach** Ag & B
255 H6 **Cabrach** Moray
147 J6 **Cabus** Lancs
261 K6 **Cabvie Lodge** Highld
23 G2 **Cackle Street** E Susx
24 C3 **Cackle Street** E Susx
24 E3 **Cackle Street** E Susx
13 L2 **Cadbury** Devon
28 B7 **Cadbury Barton** Devon
209 G4 **Cadder** E Duns
68 D3 **Caddington** Beds
200 F6 **Caddonfoot** Border
23 K3 **Cade Street** E Susx
142 E7 **Cadeby** Donc
99 L3 **Cadeby** Leics
13 L1 **Cadeleigh** Devon
3 J8 **Cadgwith** Cnwll
222 D6 **Cadham** Fife
130 D1 **Cadishead** Salfd

57 H5 **Cadle** Swans
139 G2 **Cadley** Lancs
47 J5 **Cadley** Wilts
47 K8 **Cadley** Wilts
67 J8 **Cadmore End** Bucks
34 C8 **Cadnam** Hants
144 C7 **Cadney** N Linc
128 E7 **Cadole** Flints
43 H7 **Cadoxton** V Glam
57 L5 **Cadoxton Juxta-Neath** Neath
67 K6 **Cadsden** Bucks
111 K4 **Cadwst** Denbgs
59 H6 **Cae'r bryn** Carmth
59 M6 **Cae'r-bont** Powys
125 J7 **Caeathro** Gwynd
59 M6 **Caehopkin** Powys
135 K2 **Caenby** Lincs
135 K2 **Caenby Corner** Lincs
77 J7 **Caeo** Carmth
74 C6 **Caer Farchell** Pembks
42 C3 **Caerau** Brdgnd
43 H6 **Caerau** Cardif
110 C7 **Caerdeon** Gwynd
124 E4 **Caergeiliog** IOA
129 G8 **Caergwrle** Flints
126 F5 **Caerhun** Conwy
188 C5 **Caerlanrig** Border
44 D1 **Caerleon** Newpt
125 H7 **Caernarfon** Gwynd
43 J4 **Caerphilly** Caerph
94 B5 **Caersws** Powys
76 C4 **Caerwedros** Cerdgn
44 F1 **Caerwent** Mons
128 D5 **Caerwys** Flints
110 E8 **Caerynwch** Gwynd
62 D4 **Caggle Street** Mons
126 C3 **Caim** IOA
283 C8 **Cairinis** W Isls
206 C1 **Cairnbaan** Ag & B
269 J3 **Cairnbulg** Abers
213 K6 **Cairncross** Border
208 A5 **Cairncurran** Inver
217 K5 **Cairndow** Ag & B
210 D2 **Cairneyhill** Fife
267 H4 **Cairnfield House** Moray
172 C5 **Cairngarroch** D & G
245 K4 **Cairngrassie** Abers
255 K3 **Cairnie** Abers
256 F3 **Cairnorrie** Abers
172 D1 **Cairnryan** D & G
267 G5 **Cairnty** Moray
107 L1 **Caister-on-Sea** Norfk
144 E7 **Caistor** Lincs
106 E3 **Caistor St Edmund** Norfk
106 B5 **Cake Street** Norfk
81 K1 **Cakebole** Worcs
89 K7 **Calais Street** Suffk
282 f3 **Calanais** W Isls
19 G6 **Calbourne** IOW
137 G4 **Calceby** Lincs
128 E5 **Calcot** Flints
65 G5 **Calcot** Gloucs
49 G4 **Calcot** W Berk
49 G4 **Calcot Row** W Berk
266 E3 **Calcots** Moray
41 G3 **Calcott** Kent
95 K1 **Calcott** Shrops
150 E4 **Calcutt** N York
65 G8 **Calcutt** Wilts
165 K3 **Caldbeck** Cumb
159 K5 **Caldbergh** N York
102 C5 **Caldecote** Cambs
87 G4 **Caldecote** Cambs
86 E7 **Caldecote** Herts
84 D5 **Caldecote** Nhants
87 G3 **Caldecote Highfields** Cambs
85 K2 **Caldecott** Nhants
66 D7 **Caldecott** Oxon
101 J4 **Caldecott** Rutlnd
85 H8 **Caldecotte** M Keyn
155 J2 **Calder Bridge** Cumb
141 M4 **Calder Grove** Wakefd
147 K6 **Calder Vale** Lancs
209 K6 **Calderbank** N Lans
140 E4 **Calderbrook** Rochdl
209 L5 **Caldercruix** N Lans
197 J3 **Caldermill** S Lans
140 D4 **Caldermore** Rochdl
209 H7 **Calderwood** S Lans
44 F1 **Caldicot** Mons
98 C4 **Caldmore** W Mids
168 F8 **Caldwell** N York
128 F3 **Caldy** Wirral
59 J4 **Caledfwlch** Carmth
4 F6 **Calendra** Cnwll

4 D6 **Calenick** Cnwll
88 D6 **Calford Green** Suffk
275 d2 **Calfsound** Ork
226 D2 **Calgary** Ag & B
265 H8 **Califer** Moray
210 B4 **California** Falk
123 K8 **California** Norfk
7 K4 **California Cross** Devon
116 B7 **Calke** Derbys
259 M5 **Callakille** Highld
219 K5 **Callander** Stirlg
282 f3 **Callanish** W Isls
96 E4 **Callaughton** Shrops
4 C5 **Callestick** Cnwll
247 K7 **Calligarry** Highld
6 D1 **Callington** Cnwll
115 K6 **Callingwood** Staffs
80 C8 **Callow** Herefs
81 J5 **Callow End** Worcs
46 F2 **Callow Hill** Wilts
97 G8 **Callow Hill** Worcs
82 B2 **Callow Hill** Worcs
80 D2 **Callows Grave** Worcs
34 D7 **Calmore** Hants
64 F5 **Calmsden** Gloucs
46 E5 **Calne** Wilts
133 H5 **Calow** Derbys
19 H3 **Calshot** Hants
6 E1 **Calstock** Cnwll
46 F5 **Calstone Wellington** Wilts
122 D5 **Calthorpe** Norfk
123 H7 **Calthorpe Street** Norfk
166 B3 **Calthwaite** Cumb
148 F4 **Calton** N York
115 H2 **Calton** Staffs
115 H2 **Calton Green** Staffs
130 B7 **Calveley** Ches
132 E5 **Calver** Derbys
79 L5 **Calver Hill** Herefs
132 E5 **Calver Sough** Derbys
113 K4 **Calverhall** Shrops
29 G8 **Calverleigh** Devon
150 B8 **Calverley** Leeds
67 G2 **Calvert** Bucks
84 F7 **Calverton** M Keyn
117 G2 **Calverton** Notts
232 B2 **Calvine** P & K
176 F8 **Calvo** Cumb
199 K6 **Calzeat** Border
63 M7 **Cam** Gloucs
248 F6 **Camas Luinie** Highld
228 B3 **Camasachoirce** Highld
237 L8 **Camasine** Highld
247 G1 **Camastianavaig** Highld
250 E4 **Camault Muir** Highld
25 H3 **Camber** E Susx
49 L6 **Camberley** Surrey
51 J4 **Camberwell** Gt Lon
143 G3 **Camblesforth** N York
180 B2 **Cambo** Nthumb
181 H2 **Cambois** Nthumb
3 G3 **Camborne** Cnwll
87 G3 **Cambourne** Cambs
87 J3 **Cambridge** Cambs
63 L6 **Cambridge** Gloucs
4 A5 **Cambrose** Cnwll
220 E8 **Cambus** Clacks
243 M4 **Cambus o' May** Abers
263 L1 **Cambusavie Platform** Highld
220 D8 **Cambusbarron** Stirlg
220 D8 **Cambuskenneth** Stirlg
209 H7 **Cambuslang** S Lans
199 H5 **Cambuswallace** S Lans
51 H2 **Camden Town** Gt Lon
45 J7 **Cameley** BaNES
10 F6 **Camelford** Cnwll
209 M3 **Camelon** Falk
81 H8 **Camer's Green** Worcs
253 K5 **Camerory** Highld
45 K7 **Camerton** BaNES
164 D4 **Camerton** Cumb
231 G4 **Camghouran** P & K
201 J7 **Camieston** Border
245 K4 **Cammachmore** Abers
135 J3 **Cammeringham** Lincs
263 L2 **Camore** Highld
192 E4 **Campbeltown** Ag & B
181 G4 **Camperdown** N Tyne
186 D7 **Cample** D & G
233 K7 **Campmuir** Angus
210 E5 **Camps** W Loth
88 C6 **Camps End** Cambs
142 E5 **Campsall** Donc
91 H4 **Campsea Ash** Suffk
86 C7 **Campton** Beds

189 J4 **Camptown** Border
54 F3 **Camrose** Pembks
232 B5 **Camserney** P & K
261 H2 **Camusnagaul** Highld
239 H8 **Camusnagaul** Highld
248 A3 **Camusteel** Highld
248 A3 **Camusterrach** Highld
34 C7 **Canada** Hants
156 D7 **Canal Foot** Cumb
55 H4 **Canaston Bridge** Pembks
243 K4 **Candacraig** Abers
105 L8 **Candle Street** Suffk
137 H6 **Candlesby** Lincs
96 C2 **Candover Green** Shrops
199 J5 **Candyburn** Border
49 G3 **Cane End** Oxon
72 C8 **Canewdon** Essex
17 K2 **Canford Bottom** Dorset
17 L5 **Canford Cliffs** Poole
17 K4 **Canford Heath** Poole
17 K3 **Canford Magna** Poole
90 C2 **Canhams Green** Suffk
280 D2 **Canisbay** Highld
133 H2 **Canklow** Rothm
99 J7 **Canley** Covtry
32 E6 **Cann** Dorset
250 B5 **Cannich** Highld
51 L3 **Canning Town** Gt Lon
30 C3 **Cannington** Somset
98 B2 **Cannock** Staffs
98 D1 **Cannock Wood** Staffs
80 A7 **Cannon Bridge** Herefs
80 F6 **Canon Frome** Herefs
80 B5 **Canon Pyon** Herefs
177 L4 **Canonbie** D & G
84 B5 **Canons Ashby** Nhants
2 E4 **Canonstown** Cnwll
40 F4 **Canterbury** Kent
107 H3 **Cantley** Norfk
96 C2 **Cantlop** Shrops
43 J6 **Canton** Cardif
252 E2 **Cantraywood** Highld
147 M1 **Cantsfield** Lancs
53 G2 **Canvey Island** Essex
135 K6 **Canwick** Lincs
11 J4 **Canworthy Water** Cnwll
239 J8 **Caol** Highld
282 f6 **Caolas Scalpaigh** W Isls
224 D5 **Caoles** Ag & B
239 H5 **Caonich** Highld
39 G4 **Capel** Kent
37 J3 **Capel** Surrey
92 E7 **Capel Bangor** Cerdgn
77 H4 **Capel Betws Lleucu** Cerdgn
125 H3 **Capel Coch** IOA
126 E8 **Capel Curig** Conwy
76 C5 **Capel Cynon** Cerdgn
58 E5 **Capel Dewi** Carmth
76 E6 **Capel Dewi** Cerdgn
127 G8 **Capel Garmon** Conwy
91 J5 **Capel Green** Suffk
58 E4 **Capel Gwyn** Carmth
124 F4 **Capel Gwyn** IOA
59 K4 **Capel Gwynfe** Carmth
59 G6 **Capel Hendre** Carmth
59 G3 **Capel Isaac** Carmth
58 B2 **Capel Iwan** Carmth
41 H7 **Capel le Ferne** Kent
43 H5 **Capel Llanilltern** Cardif
125 G5 **Capel Mawr** IOA
92 D7 **Capel Seion** Cerdgn
91 J5 **Capel St Andrew** Suffk
90 C7 **Capel St Mary** Suffk
92 F8 **Capel Trisant** Cerdgn
92 D7 **Capel-Dewi** Cerdgn
61 L1 **Capel-y-ffin** Powys
125 K6 **Capel-y-graig** Gwynd
9 j2 **Capelles** Guern
109 H2 **Capeluchaf** Gwynd
126 E4 **Capelulo** Conwy
129 J5 **Capenhurst** Ches
147 K2 **Capernwray** Lancs
180 C3 **Capheaton** Nthumb
208 D7 **Caplaw** E Rens
91 G2 **Capon's Green** Suffk
187 K2 **Cappercleuch** Border
53 G6 **Capstone** Medway
8 C4 **Capton** Devon
29 K3 **Capton** Somset
233 G7 **Caputh** P & K
117 J3 **Car Colston** Notts
11 K8 **Caradon Town** Cnwll
208 E3 **Carbeth Inn** Stirlg
5 G3 **Carbis** Cnwll
2 E3 **Carbis Bay** Cnwll

246 E2 **Carbost** Highld
259 G7 **Carbost** Highld
133 G2 **Carbrook** Sheff
105 J3 **Carbrooke** Norfk
134 C5 **Carburton** Notts
5 H4 **Carclaze** Cnwll
3 K3 **Carclew** Cnwll
142 E6 **Carcroft** Donc
222 C8 **Cardenden** Fife
95 J1 **Cardeston** Shrops
177 K8 **Cardewlees** Cumb
254 D3 **Cardhu** Moray
43 J6 **Cardiff** Cardif
75 L3 **Cardigan** Cerdgn
88 C6 **Cardinal's Green** Cambs
86 B5 **Cardington** Beds
96 C4 **Cardington** Shrops
5 J1 **Cardinham** Cnwll
172 E8 **Cardrain** D & G
200 C5 **Cardrona** Border
208 B3 **Cardross** Ag & B
172 E8 **Cardryne** D & G
177 G7 **Cardurnock** Cumb
118 D8 **Careby** Lincs
234 E3 **Careston** Angus
55 H6 **Carew** Pembks
55 H6 **Carew Cheriton** Pembks
55 H6 **Carew Newton** Pembks
63 H1 **Carey** Herefs
209 K7 **Carfin** N Lans
201 G2 **Carfraemill** Border
107 H1 **Cargate Green** Norfk
176 C4 **Cargen** D & G
176 C4 **Cargenbridge** D & G
233 H8 **Cargill** P & K
177 L7 **Cargo** Cumb
6 E2 **Cargreen** Cnwll
3 M4 **Cargurrel** Cnwll
202 B5 **Carham** Nthumb
29 H2 **Carhampton** Somset
3 J3 **Carharrack** Cnwll
231 H4 **Carie** P & K
283 c8 **Carinish** W Isls
19 H6 **Carisbrooke** IOW
156 E7 **Cark** Cumb
6 E3 **Carkeel** Cnwll
282 e2 **Carlabhagh** W Isls
4 D4 **Carland Cross** Cnwll
169 G7 **Carlbury** Darltn
102 A1 **Carlby** Lincs
190 B4 **Carlcroft** Nthumb
141 J7 **Carlecotes** Barns
3 G5 **Carleen** Cnwll
160 B7 **Carlesmoor** N York
178 A8 **Carleton** Cumb
166 C5 **Carleton** Cumb
155 J1 **Carleton** Cumb
146 F7 **Carleton** Lancs
149 H6 **Carleton** N York
142 D4 **Carleton** Wakefd
106 B2 **Carleton Forehoe** Norfk
106 C5 **Carleton Rode** Norfk
107 G3 **Carleton St Peter** Norfk
3 K5 **Carlidnack** Cnwll
171 G6 **Carlin How** R & Cl
256 E2 **Carlincraig** Abers
45 K7 **Carlingcott** BaNES
177 L7 **Carlisle** Cumb
4 E2 **Carloggas** Cnwll
199 K2 **Carlops** Border
282 e2 **Carloway** W Isls
142 B5 **Carlton** Barns
85 J4 **Carlton** Beds
88 C4 **Carlton** Cambs
142 A2 **Carlton** Leeds
99 L2 **Carlton** Leics
159 J5 **Carlton** N York
161 K5 **Carlton** N York
143 G3 **Carlton** N York
117 G3 **Carlton** Notts
169 K6 **Carlton** S on T
91 J2 **Carlton** Suffk
107 K5 **Carlton Colville** Suffk
100 F4 **Carlton Curlieu** Leics
88 C5 **Carlton Green** Cambs
161 H7 **Carlton Husthwaite** N York
134 B3 **Carlton in Lindrick** Notts
160 F6 **Carlton Miniott** N York
118 B3 **Carlton Scroop** Lincs
161 H2 **Carlton-in-Cleveland** N York
135 H8 **Carlton-le-Moorland** Lincs
134 F7 **Carlton-on-Trent** Notts
5 H4 **Carluddon** Cnwll
198 D3 **Carluke** S Lans
5 H4 **Carlyon Bay** Cnwll

198 C7 **Carmacoup** S Lans
58 D5 **Carmarthen** Carmth
59 G5 **Carmel** Carmth
128 E4 **Carmel** Flints
125 J8 **Carmel** Gwynd
198 F5 **Carmichael** S Lans
3 H6 **Carminowe** Cnwll
209 G7 **Carmunnock** C Glas
209 H6 **Carmyle** C Glas
234 E6 **Carmyllie** Angus
3 H3 **Carn Brea** Cnwll
248 F7 **Carn-gorm** Highld
153 J3 **Carnaby** E R Yk
223 J6 **Carnbee** Fife
221 J6 **Carnbo** P & K
256 F6 **Carnbrogie** Abers
248 E6 **Carndu** Highld
197 J2 **Carnduff** S Lans
3 K6 **Carne** Cnwll
4 E7 **Carne** Cnwll
4 F3 **Carne** Cnwll
196 F4 **Carnell** E Ayrs
4 D1 **Carnewas** Cnwll
147 K2 **Carnforth** Lancs
74 C6 **Carnhedryn** Pembks
3 G4 **Carnhell Green** Cnwll
245 H2 **Carnie** Abers
3 H4 **Carnkie** Cnwll
3 H3 **Carnkie** Cnwll
4 C4 **Carnkiet** Cnwll
93 L4 **Carno** Powys
238 D4 **Carnoch** Highld
210 D1 **Carnock** Fife
3 K3 **Carnon Downs** Cnwll
268 B6 **Carnousie** Abers
234 E8 **Carnoustie** Angus
199 G4 **Carnwath** S Lans
2 B4 **Carnyorth** Cnwll
99 H7 **Carol Green** Solhll
4 F4 **Carpalla** Cnwll
159 H5 **Carperby** N York
140 B4 **Carr** Bury
133 K2 **Carr** Rothm
141 M3 **Carr Gate** Wakefd
167 J1 **Carr Shield** Nthumb
133 J5 **Carr Vale** Derbys
194 C3 **Carradale** Ag & B
253 G7 **Carrbridge** Highld
140 E7 **Carrbrook** Tamesd
9 c2 **Carrefour** Jersey
125 G2 **Carreglefn** IOA
143 K6 **Carrhouse** N Linc
206 E2 **Carrick** Ag & B
217 K8 **Carrick Castle** Ag & B
210 D3 **Carriden** Falk
136 F8 **Carrington** Lincs
211 K7 **Carrington** Mdloth
130 E1 **Carrington** Traffd
5 G3 **Carrismerry** Cnwll
110 E2 **Carrog** Conwy
111 L3 **Carrog** Denbgs
210 A3 **Carron** Falk
254 E3 **Carron** Moray
209 K2 **Carron Bridge** Stirlg
186 C6 **Carronbridge** D & G
210 A2 **Carronshore** Falk
44 E1 **Carrow Hill** Mons
208 B6 **Carruth House** Inver
176 E4 **Carrutherstown** D & G
169 J2 **Carrville** Dur
179 L3 **Carrycoats Hall** Nthumb
227 G8 **Carsaig** Ag & B
234 C4 **Carse Gray** Angus
173 H1 **Carseriggan** D & G
176 C7 **Carsethorn** D & G
51 H6 **Carshalton** Gt Lon
115 L1 **Carsington** Derbys
192 D6 **Carskey** Ag & B
174 D4 **Carsluith** D & G
184 E4 **Carsphairn** D & G
198 F4 **Carstairs** S Lans
198 F4 **Carstairs Junction** S Lans
65 L7 **Carswell Marsh** Oxon
34 C6 **Carter's Clay** Hants
70 D5 **Carters Green** Essex
65 L5 **Carterton** Oxon
180 C8 **Carterway Heads** Dur
5 G4 **Carthew** Cnwll
160 D6 **Carthorpe** N York
190 E5 **Cartington** Nthumb
198 E4 **Cartland** S Lans
132 F4 **Cartledge** Derbys
156 E7 **Cartmel** Cumb
156 F5 **Cartmel Fell** Cumb
56 E3 **Carway** Carmth

177 L4 **Carwinley** Cumb
64 B6 **Cashe's Green** Gloucs
33 G8 **Cashmoor** Dorset
66 C5 **Cassington** Oxon
169 K3 **Cassop Colliery** Dur
2 C6 **Castallack** Cnwll
126 F6 **Castell** Conwy
62 B8 **Castell-y-bwch** Torfn
157 K6 **Casterton** Lancs
5 J3 **Castle** Cnwll
121 H8 **Castle Acre** Norfk
85 G3 **Castle Ashby** Nhants
159 J4 **Castle Bolton** N York
98 F5 **Castle Bromwich** Solhll
118 C7 **Castle Bytham** Lincs
94 E2 **Castle Caereinion** Powys
88 C6 **Castle Camps** Cambs
178 D7 **Castle Carrock** Cumb
31 L4 **Castle Cary** Somset
46 B3 **Castle Combe** Wilts
116 D6 **Castle Donington** Leics
175 J2 **Castle Douglas** D & G
65 H7 **Castle Eaton** Swindn
169 L3 **Castle Eden** Dur
102 C2 **Castle End** C Pete
80 F6 **Castle Frome** Herefs
2 D4 **Castle Gate** Cnwll
157 H4 **Castle Green** Cumb
50 B6 **Castle Green** Surrey
115 M7 **Castle Gresley** Derbys
88 F8 **Castle Hedingham** Essex
39 H5 **Castle Hill** Kent
90 D6 **Castle Hill** Suffk
172 D3 **Castle Kennedy** D & G
217 G8 **Castle Lachlan** Ag & B
74 E6 **Castle Morris** Pembks
187 K7 **Castle O'er** D & G
95 K3 **Castle Pulverbatch** Shrops
120 E6 **Castle Rising** Norfk
140 E3 **Castle Street** Calder
252 D2 **Castle Stuart** Highld
283 b13 **Castlebay** W Isls
75 H6 **Castlebythe** Pembks
209 L3 **Castlecary** Falk
142 C3 **Castleford** Wakefd
200 B6 **Castlehill** Border
280 B3 **Castlehill** Highld
208 C4 **Castlehill** W Duns
54 E7 **Castlemartin** Pembks
209 G7 **Castlemilk** C Glas
81 H7 **Castlemorton** Worcs
168 D1 **Castleside** Dur
84 F6 **Castlethorpe** M Keyn
144 B6 **Castlethorpe** N Linc
188 E8 **Castleton** Border
132 C3 **Castleton** Derbys
162 B1 **Castleton** N York
43 L5 **Castleton** Newpt
140 C5 **Castleton** Rochdl
16 D7 **Castletown** Dorset
280 A3 **Castletown** Highld
154 C8 **Castletown** IOM
181 J7 **Castletown** Sundld
150 C6 **Castley** N York
105 J4 **Caston** Norfk
102 C4 **Castor** C Pete
57 G7 **Caswell Bay** Swans
131 K5 **Cat and Fiddle** Ches
44 D1 **Cat's Ash** Newpt
194 E1 **Catacol** N Ayrs
63 G6 **Catbrook** Mons
128 F5 **Catch** Flints
2 C5 **Catchall** Cnwll
99 H8 **Catchem's Corner** Solhll
180 E8 **Catchgate** Dur
133 H2 **Catcliffe** Rothm
46 E4 **Catcomb** Wilts
30 F3 **Catcott** Somset
30 F2 **Catcott Burtle** Somset
9 j3 **Catel** Guern
51 J7 **Caterham** Surrey
123 H7 **Catfield** Norfk
123 H7 **Catfield Common** Norfk
281 e6 **Catfirth** Shet
51 K4 **Catford** Gt Lon
138 F1 **Catforth** Lancs
209 G7 **Cathcart** C Glas
61 J2 **Cathedine** Powys
141 G2 **Catherine Slack** Brad
98 F7 **Catherine-de-Barnes** Solhll
35 L8 **Catherington** Hants
15 J4 **Catherston Leweston** Dorset
96 E7 **Catherton** Shrops
19 J2 **Catisfield** Hants
80 F6 **Catley** Herefs

140 C4 **Catley Lane Head** Rochdl
241 H5 **Catlodge** Highld
148 F8 **Catlow** Lancs
178 B3 **Catlowdy** Cumb
87 K7 **Catmere End** Essex
48 C3 **Catmore** W Berk
13 H8 **Caton** Devon
147 K3 **Caton** Lancs
147 L3 **Caton Green** Lancs
13 G7 **Cator Court** Devon
197 G6 **Catrine** E Ayrs
24 C4 **Catsfield** E Susx
24 C4 **Catsfield Stream** E Susx
31 H5 **Catsgore** Somset
31 J4 **Catsham** Somset
98 B8 **Catshill** Worcs
97 G4 **Catstree** Shrops
192 D6 **Cattadale** Ag & B
150 F5 **Cattal** N York
90 C8 **Cattawade** Suffk
147 K7 **Catterall** Lancs
113 J3 **Catteralslane** Shrops
160 C3 **Catterick** N York
160 B3 **Catterick Bridge** N York
160 B3 **Catterick Garrison** N York
166 B4 **Catterlen** Cumb
245 J7 **Catterline** Abers
151 H6 **Catterton** N York
36 E2 **Catteshall** Surrey
100 C7 **Catthorpe** Leics
89 H2 **Cattishall** Suffk
16 B3 **Cattistock** Dorset
179 J7 **Catton** Cumb
160 E7 **Catton** N York
106 E1 **Catton** Norfk
153 J6 **Catwick** E R Yk
86 B1 **Catworth** Cambs
64 D5 **Caudle Green** Gloucs
85 K6 **Caulcott** Beds
66 D2 **Caulcott** Oxon
235 G6 **Cauldcots** Angus
219 L8 **Cauldhame** Stirlg
188 F3 **Cauldmill** Border
115 H2 **Cauldon** Staffs
115 H2 **Cauldon Lowe** Staffs
115 L8 **Cauldwell** Derbys
176 B7 **Caulkerbush** D & G
178 B3 **Caulside** D & G
31 L8 **Caundle Marsh** Dorset
97 J7 **Caunsall** Worcs
134 E7 **Caunton** Notts
35 M6 **Causeway** Hants
157 G5 **Causeway End** Cumb
173 K3 **Causeway End** D & G
71 G3 **Causeway End** Essex
199 H6 **Causewayend** S Lans
176 F8 **Causewayhead** Cumb
220 D8 **Causewayhead** Stirlg
191 H7 **Causey Park** Nthumb
191 H7 **Causey Park Bridge** Nthumb
257 H7 **Causeyend** Abers
88 F6 **Cavendish** Suffk
88 F1 **Cavenham** Suffk
66 E2 **Caversfield** Oxon
49 H4 **Caversham** Readg
114 F3 **Caverswall** Staffs
202 A7 **Caverton Mill** Border
143 J2 **Cavil** E R Yk
252 F2 **Cawdor** Highld
136 E4 **Cawkwell** Lincs
151 J8 **Cawood** N York
6 E5 **Cawsand** Cnwll
122 C6 **Cawston** Norfk
100 A8 **Cawston** Warwks
162 D5 **Cawthorn** N York
141 L6 **Cawthorne** Barns
161 K7 **Cawton** N York
86 F3 **Caxton** Cambs
87 G4 **Caxton End** Cambs
86 F3 **Caxton Gibbet** Cambs
80 D1 **Caynham** Shrops
118 B2 **Caythorpe** Lincs
117 J2 **Caythorpe** Notts
163 J6 **Cayton** N York
283 b8 **Ceann a Bhaigh** W Isls
239 L1 **Ceannacroc Lodge** Highld
282 f4 **Cearsiadar** W Isls
63 G6 **Ceciliford** Mons
44 B1 **Cefn** Newpt
127 K6 **Cefn Berain** Conwy
60 C5 **Cefn Byrle** Powys
112 C5 **Cefn Canel** Powys
111 L6 **Cefn Coch** Powys
42 C5 **Cefn Cribwr** Brdgnd
42 C5 **Cefn Cross** Brdgnd

43 K5 **Cefn Mably** Caerph
111 H2 **Cefn-brith** Conwy
59 K6 **Cefn-bryn-brain** Carmth
60 F5 **Cefn-coed-y-cymmer** Myr Td
111 J4 **Cefn-ddwysarn** Gwynd
95 G6 **Cefn-Einion** Shrops
112 D3 **Cefn-mawr** Wrexhm
129 H8 **Cefn-y-bedd** Wrexhm
75 L7 **Cefn-y-pant** Carmth
59 G6 **Cefneithin** Carmth
78 B6 **Cefngorwydd** Powys
61 G7 **Cefnpennar** Rhondd
125 J4 **Ceint** IOA
77 H5 **Cellan** Cerdgn
223 K6 **Cellardyke** Fife
114 F2 **Cellarhead** Staffs
166 C5 **Celleron** Cumb
43 K3 **Celynen** Caerph
124 F1 **Cemaes** IOA
93 H2 **Cemmaes** Powys
93 H3 **Cemmaes Road** Powys
76 A7 **Cenarth** Cerdgn
74 D6 **Cerbyd** Pembks
223 G5 **Ceres** Fife
16 C2 **Cerne Abbas** Dorset
65 G7 **Cerney Wick** Gloucs
125 G5 **Cerrigceinwen** IOA
111 J2 **Cerrigydrudion** Conwy
123 J7 **Cess** Norfk
125 J7 **Ceunant** Gwynd
64 B1 **Chaceley** Gloucs
4 B6 **Chacewater** Cnwll
84 D8 **Chackmore** Bucks
83 L6 **Chacombe** Nhants
82 B6 **Chadbury** Worcs
140 D6 **Chadderton** Oldham
140 D6 **Chadderton Fold** Oldham
116 C4 **Chaddesden** C Derb
97 K8 **Chaddesley Corbett** Worcs
12 B7 **Chaddlehanger** Devon
48 B3 **Chaddleworth** W Berk
65 M3 **Chadlington** Oxon
83 H4 **Chadshunt** Warwks
117 K6 **Chadwell** Leics
114 B8 **Chadwell** Shrops
86 B2 **Chadwell End** Beds
52 A1 **Chadwell Heath** Gt Lon
52 E3 **Chadwell St Mary** Thurr
81 J2 **Chadwick** Worcs
82 F1 **Chadwick End** Solhll
139 G7 **Chadwick Green** St Hel
15 H1 **Chaffcombe** Somset
52 D3 **Chafford Hundred** Thurr
13 G5 **Chagford** Devon
22 F3 **Chailey** E Susx
103 J3 **Chainbridge** Cambs
39 J4 **Chainhurst** Kent
17 K1 **Chalbury** Dorset
17 K1 **Chalbury Common** Dorset
51 J7 **Chaldon** Surrey
19 H8 **Chale** IOW
19 H7 **Chale Green** IOW
68 C8 **Chalfont Common** Bucks
68 C8 **Chalfont St Giles** Bucks
50 C1 **Chalfont St Peter** Bucks
64 C6 **Chalford** Gloucs
67 H7 **Chalford** Oxon
32 E1 **Chalford** Wilts
68 C2 **Chalgrave** Beds
66 F7 **Chalgrove** Oxon
52 E4 **Chalk** Kent
70 F5 **Chalk End** Essex
49 H3 **Chalkhouse Green** Oxon
15 J1 **Chalkway** Somset
53 J6 **Chalkwell** Kent
7 J6 **Challaborough** Devon
28 B3 **Challacombe** Devon
173 K2 **Challoch** D & G
40 C5 **Challock** Kent
16 B2 **Chalmington** Dorset
68 C2 **Chalton** Beds
86 C5 **Chalton** Beds
20 B4 **Chalton** Hants
50 B3 **Chalvey** Slough
23 H5 **Chalvington** E Susx
40 B6 **Chambers Green** Kent
68 D7 **Chandler's Cross** Herts
34 F7 **Chandler's Ford** Hants
81 H7 **Chandlers Cross** Worcs
86 C4 **Channel's End** Beds
32 B2 **Chantry** Somset
90 D6 **Chantry** Suffk
165 H4 **Chapel** Cumb
222 D8 **Chapel** Fife
150 D8 **Chapel Allerton** Leeds

30 F1 **Chapel Allerton** Somset
10 D7 **Chapel Amble** Cnwll
84 E2 **Chapel Brampton** Nhants
114 C4 **Chapel Chorlton** Staffs
23 K3 **Chapel Cross** E Susx
85 L6 **Chapel End** Beds
86 B4 **Chapel End** Beds
102 C6 **Chapel End** Cambs
99 J5 **Chapel End** Warwks
140 B6 **Chapel Field** Bury
99 H6 **Chapel Green** Warwks
83 L3 **Chapel Green** Warwks
142 F3 **Chapel Haddlesey** N York
257 K4 **Chapel Hill** Abers
119 G1 **Chapel Hill** Lincs
63 G7 **Chapel Hill** Mons
150 D6 **Chapel Hill** N York
95 H8 **Chapel Lawn** Shrops
158 C7 **Chapel le Dale** N York
29 L5 **Chapel Leigh** Somset
131 L3 **Chapel Milton** Derbys
256 C7 **Chapel of Garioch** Abers
172 D6 **Chapel Rossan** D & G
23 L5 **Chapel Row** E Susx
71 J7 **Chapel Row** Essex
48 E5 **Chapel Row** W Berk
137 K5 **Chapel St Leonards** Lincs
156 D2 **Chapel Stile** Cumb
4 E4 **Chapel Town** Cnwll
131 L3 **Chapel-en-le-Frith** Derbys
102 F4 **Chapelbridge** Cambs
88 E7 **Chapelend Way** Essex
119 L6 **Chapelgate** Lincs
209 K6 **Chapelhall** N Lans
187 K2 **Chapelhope** Border
177 K4 **Chapelknowe** D & G
156 B6 **Chapels** Cumb
234 F6 **Chapelton** Angus
27 K5 **Chapelton** Devon
197 K1 **Chapelton** S Lans
139 L4 **Chapeltown** Bl w D
254 E7 **Chapeltown** Moray
142 A8 **Chapeltown** Sheff
11 L4 **Chapmans Well** Devon
32 D1 **Chapmanslade** Wilts
69 J4 **Chapmore End** Herts
72 C2 **Chappel** Essex
6 B1 **Charaton** Cnwll
15 H1 **Chard** Somset
15 H2 **Chard Junction** Somset
30 D8 **Chardleigh Green** Somset
15 G2 **Chardstock** Devon
63 L8 **Charfield** S Glos
64 D3 **Chargrove** Gloucs
40 B5 **Charing** Kent
40 B5 **Charing Heath** Kent
40 B5 **Charing Hill** Kent
82 E7 **Charingworth** Gloucs
65 M3 **Charlbury** Oxon
45 L5 **Charlcombe** BaNES
46 E4 **Charlcutt** Wilts
83 G4 **Charlecote** Warwks
98 C4 **Charlemont** W Mids
28 B4 **Charles** Devon
89 L5 **Charles Tye** Suffk
36 D2 **Charleshill** Surrey
234 B6 **Charleston** Angus
149 L8 **Charlestown** Brad
245 L3 **Charlestown** C Aber
140 E2 **Charlestown** Calder
5 H4 **Charlestown** Cnwll
131 L1 **Charlestown** Derbys
16 C6 **Charlestown** Dorset
210 E2 **Charlestown** Fife
260 C5 **Charlestown** Highld
251 H2 **Charlestown** Highld
140 B7 **Charlestown** Salfd
131 K1 **Charlesworth** Derbys
30 C3 **Charlinch** Somset
222 E5 **Charlottetown** Fife
51 L3 **Charlton** Gt Lon
34 D2 **Charlton** Hants
68 F2 **Charlton** Herts
83 M8 **Charlton** Nhants
179 J2 **Charlton** Nthumb
48 B1 **Charlton** Oxon
30 D5 **Charlton** Somset
31 K2 **Charlton** Somset
45 K8 **Charlton** Somset
50 D5 **Charlton** Surrey
20 E4 **Charlton** W Susx
32 F6 **Charlton** Wilts
46 D1 **Charlton** Wilts
47 G7 **Charlton** Wilts
81 J1 **Charlton** Worcs

82 B6 **Charlton** Worcs
96 D1 **Charlton** Wrekin
64 F2 **Charlton Abbots** Gloucs
31 J5 **Charlton Adam** Somset
96 D2 **Charlton Hill** Shrops
31 L6 **Charlton Horethorne** Somset
64 D3 **Charlton Kings** Gloucs
31 H5 **Charlton Mackrell** Somset
17 H2 **Charlton Marshall** Dorset
32 B5 **Charlton Musgrove** Somset
17 H2 **Charlton on the Hill** Dorset
33 L6 **Charlton-all-Saints** Wilts
66 E4 **Charlton-on-Otmoor** Oxon
35 K4 **Charlwood** Hants
37 K3 **Charlwood** Surrey
16 C4 **Charminster** Dorset
15 H4 **Charmouth** Dorset
67 G2 **Charndon** Bucks
66 A8 **Charney Bassett** Oxon
139 H4 **Charnock Green** Lancs
139 H4 **Charnock Richard** Lancs
90 F4 **Charsfield** Suffk
39 K3 **Chart Corner** Kent
39 K3 **Chart Hill** Kent
39 K3 **Chart Sutton** Kent
48 E7 **Charter Alley** Hants
202 B4 **Charterhall** Border
45 G7 **Charterhouse** Somset
209 L1 **Chartershall** Stirlg
65 L5 **Charterville Allotments** Oxon
40 E4 **Chartham** Kent
40 E4 **Chartham Hatch** Kent
68 B6 **Chartridge** Bucks
39 L3 **Chartway Street** Kent
49 J4 **Charvil** Wokham
83 M4 **Charwelton** Nhants
98 D2 **Chase Terrace** Staffs
98 D2 **Chasetown** Staffs
65 K1 **Chastleton** Oxon
11 L2 **Chasty** Devon
148 D7 **Chatburn** Lancs
114 B4 **Chatcull** Staffs
43 K4 **Chatham** Caerph
53 G5 **Chatham** Medway
71 H4 **Chatham Green** Essex
203 K7 **Chathill** Nthumb
81 J3 **Chatley** Worcs
53 G4 **Chattenden** Medway
70 C2 **Chatter End** Essex
103 H6 **Chatteris** Cambs
140 B4 **Chatterton** Lancs
90 C6 **Chattisham** Suffk
189 K3 **Chatto** Border
203 G7 **Chatton** Nthumb
68 D3 **Chaul End** Beds
28 C6 **Chawleigh** Devon
66 C6 **Chawley** Oxon
86 C4 **Chawston** Beds
35 L3 **Chawton** Hants
63 L4 **Chaxhill** Gloucs
49 G3 **Chazey Heath** Oxon
115 G3 **Cheadle** Staffs
131 G2 **Cheadle** Stockp
131 G2 **Cheadle Heath** Stockp
131 G2 **Cheadle Hulme** Stockp
51 H6 **Cheam** Gt Lon
50 B5 **Cheapside** W & M
67 H5 **Chearsley** Bucks
114 D6 **Chebsey** Staffs
49 G2 **Checkendon** Oxon
114 A2 **Checkley** Ches
115 G4 **Checkley** Staffs
114 A2 **Checkley Green** Ches
88 F4 **Chedburgh** Suffk
44 F8 **Cheddar** Somset
68 A4 **Cheddington** Bucks
114 F1 **Cheddleton** Staffs
114 F1 **Cheddleton Heath** Staffs
30 C5 **Cheddon Fitzpaine** Somset
64 D8 **Chedglow** Wilts
107 H3 **Chedgrave** Norfk
15 L2 **Chedington** Dorset
107 G7 **Chediston** Suffk
107 G7 **Chediston Green** Suffk
64 F5 **Chedworth** Gloucs
30 E3 **Chedzoy** Somset
140 B4 **Cheesden** Rochdl
40 D7 **Cheeseman's Green** Kent
140 C7 **Cheetham Hill** Manch
28 C8 **Cheldon** Devon
130 F5 **Chelford** Ches
116 C5 **Chellaston** C Derb
85 J4 **Chellington** Beds
97 G5 **Chelmarsh** Shrops
95 L5 **Chelmick** Shrops

90 E7 Chelmondiston Suffk
132 B5 Chelmorton Derbys
71 H5 Chelmsford Essex
98 F6 Chelmsley Wood Solhll
51 H3 Chelsea Gt Lon
52 A6 Chelsfield Gt Lon
51 K7 Chelsham Surrey
29 L6 Chelston Somset
89 K5 Chelsworth Suffk
64 D3 Cheltenham Gloucs
85 K1 Chelveston Nhants
44 F5 Chelvey N Som
45 J6 Chelwood BaNES
38 B7 Chelwood Common E Susx
38 B7 Chelwood Gate E Susx
64 E8 Chelworth Wilts
65 G8 Chelworth Lower Green Wilts
65 G8 Chelworth Upper Green Wilts
95 K6 Cheney Longville Shrops
68 C7 Chenies Bucks
63 G8 Chepstow Mons
139 K6 Chequerbent Bolton
103 K2 Chequers Corner Norfk
46 F5 Cherhill Wilts
64 C7 Cherington Gloucs
83 G7 Cherington Warwks
28 C2 Cheriton Devon
35 J5 Cheriton Hants
41 G7 Cheriton Kent
56 E6 Cheriton Swans
13 H4 Cheriton Bishop Devon
13 K1 Cheriton Fitzpaine Devon
55 G7 Cheriton or Stackpole Elidor Pembks
113 L7 Cherrington Wrekin
152 F7 Cherry Burton E R Yk
87 K4 Cherry Hinton Cambs
81 K4 Cherry Orchard Worcs
135 L5 Cherry Willingham Lincs
50 D5 Chertsey Surrey
16 E3 Cheselbourne Dorset
68 B6 Chesham Bucks
140 B5 Chesham Bury
68 B7 Chesham Bois Bucks
69 K6 Cheshunt Herts
53 J6 Chesley Kent
98 B2 Cheslyn Hay Staffs
99 G8 Chessetts Wood Warwks
50 F6 Chessington Surrey
129 J6 Chester Ches
169 H1 Chester Moor Dur
181 G8 Chester-le-Street Dur
31 L3 Chesterblade Somset
133 G5 Chesterfield Derbys
98 E2 Chesterfield Staffs
211 L6 Chesterhill Mdloth
189 G2 Chesters Border
189 H4 Chesters Border
102 C4 Chesterton Cambs
87 K3 Chesterton Cambs
64 E7 Chesterton Gloucs
66 E3 Chesterton Oxon
97 H4 Chesterton Shrops
114 C2 Chesterton Staffs
83 H4 Chesterton Green Warwks
179 J6 Chesterwood Nthumb
40 F2 Chestfield Kent
53 J6 Chestnut Street Kent
7 K3 Cheston Devon
114 A5 Cheswardine Shrops
113 M8 Cheswell Wrekin
203 G4 Cheswick Nthumb
98 E8 Cheswick Green Solhll
16 B1 Chetnole Dorset
29 H7 Chettiscombe Devon
103 L6 Chettisham Cambs
32 F8 Chettle Dorset
96 F5 Chetton Shrops
66 F1 Chetwode Bucks
114 A7 Chetwynd Wrekin
114 B8 Chetwynd Aston Wrekin
88 D3 Cheveley Cambs
52 A7 Chevening Kent
19 G6 Cheverton IOW
88 F3 Chevington Suffk
191 K6 Chevington Drift Nthumb
29 H7 Chevithorne Devon
45 H6 Chew Magna BaNES
139 K6 Chew Moor Bolton
45 H6 Chew Stoke BaNES
45 K5 Chewton Keynsham BaNES
45 H8 Chewton Mendip Somset
12 E3 Chichacott Devon
85 H6 Chicheley M Keyn
20 E6 Chichester W Susx

16 C6 Chickerell Dorset
106 E8 Chickering Suffk
32 F4 Chicklade Wilts
79 K4 Chickward Herefs
35 K7 Chidden Hants
36 E4 Chiddingfold Surrey
23 J4 Chiddingly E Susx
38 D4 Chiddingstone Kent
38 E4 Chiddingstone Causeway Kent
15 K4 Chideock Dorset
20 C6 Chidham W Susx
141 L3 Chidswell Kirk
48 C4 Chieveley W Berk
71 G5 Chignall Smealy Essex
71 G5 Chignall St James Essex
70 B8 Chigwell Essex
70 C8 Chigwell Row Essex
34 E3 Chilbolton Hants
35 G5 Chilcomb Hants
15 M4 Chilcombe Dorset
45 J8 Chilcompton Somset
99 H1 Chilcote Leics
32 D8 Child Okeford Dorset
113 L6 Child's Ercall Shrops
129 J4 Childer Thornton Ches
48 A2 Childrey Oxon
82 C7 Childswickham Worcs
129 K2 Childwall Lpool
68 F5 Childwick Bury Herts
68 F5 Childwick Green Herts
16 B3 Chilfrome Dorset
20 D4 Chilgrove W Susx
40 E4 Chilham Kent
33 J4 Chilhampton Wilts
12 B2 Chilla Devon
12 B6 Chillaton Devon
41 J4 Chillenden Kent
19 H6 Chillerton IOW
91 J5 Chillesford Suffk
203 G8 Chillingham Nthumb
8 B6 Chillington Devon
30 F8 Chillington Somset
33 G4 Chilmark Wilts
40 C7 Chilmington Green Kent
65 L3 Chilson Oxon
12 A8 Chilsworthy Cnwll
11 L1 Chilsworthy Devon
68 E3 Chiltern Green Beds
31 H7 Chilthorne Domer Somset
67 G5 Chilton Bucks
13 K2 Chilton Devon
169 H5 Chilton Dur
41 J6 Chilton Kent
48 C2 Chilton Oxon
89 H6 Chilton Suffk
35 J3 Chilton Candover Hants
31 J6 Chilton Cantelo Somset
47 L5 Chilton Foliat Wilts
30 E3 Chilton Polden Somset
88 E6 Chilton Street Suffk
30 D3 Chilton Trinity Somset
116 E4 Chilwell Notts
34 E7 Chilworth Hants
36 F2 Chilworth Surrey
65 M7 Chimney Oxon
49 G7 Chineham Hants
69 K8 Chingford Gt Lon
131 L3 Chinley Derbys
67 J6 Chinnor Oxon
179 K4 Chipchase Castle Nthumb
114 A5 Chipnall Shrops
88 D1 Chippenham Cambs
46 D4 Chippenham Wilts
68 D6 Chipperfield Herts
69 K1 Chipping Herts
147 M7 Chipping Lancs
82 E7 Chipping Campden Gloucs
71 K4 Chipping Hill Essex
65 L2 Chipping Norton Oxon
70 E6 Chipping Ongar Essex
45 L3 Chipping Sodbury S Glos
83 L5 Chipping Warden Nhants
29 J5 Chipstable Somset
38 D2 Chipstead Kent
51 H7 Chipstead Surrey
95 G4 Chirbury Shrops
112 D4 Chirk Wrexhm
202 D2 Chirnside Border
202 C2 Chirnsidebridge Border
47 G7 Chirton Wilts
47 K5 Chisbury Wilts
31 G7 Chiselborough Somset
47 J3 Chiseldon Swindn
66 E7 Chiselhampton Oxon

188 D4 Chisholme Border
51 L5 Chislehurst Gt Lon
41 H2 Chislet Kent
140 F2 Chisley Calder
68 E6 Chiswell Green Herts
51 G3 Chiswick Gt Lon
87 H6 Chiswick End Cambs
131 K2 Chisworth Derbys
24 E3 Chitcombe E Susx
36 C6 Chithurst W Susx
87 K1 Chittering Cambs
33 G2 Chitterne Wilts
28 B6 Chittlehamholt Devon
27 L5 Chittlehampton Devon
28 B8 Chittlehampton Devon
46 D5 Chittoe Wilts
8 A7 Chivelstone Devon
27 J4 Chivenor Devon
172 E3 Chlenry D & G
50 B6 Chobham Surrey
34 B2 Cholderton Wilts
68 B5 Cholesbury Bucks
179 L5 Chollerford Nthumb
179 L4 Chollerton Nthumb
130 C7 Cholmondeston Ches
48 E2 Cholsey Oxon
80 B3 Cholstrey Herefs
161 J3 Chop Gate N York
181 G2 Choppington Nthumb
180 D7 Chopwell Gatesd
113 J1 Chorley Ches
139 H4 Chorley Lancs
96 F6 Chorley Shrops
98 D1 Chorley Staffs
68 D7 Chorleywood Herts
68 C7 Chorleywood West Herts
114 A2 Chorlton Ches
113 G2 Chorlton Lane Ches
130 F1 Chorlton-cum-Hardy Manch
95 J5 Choulton Shrops
129 L8 Chowley Ches
87 J7 Chrishall Essex
207 L4 Chrisswell Inver
37 H5 Christ's Hospital W Susx
103 K4 Christchurch Cambs
18 B5 Christchurch Dorset
63 H4 Christchurch Gloucs
44 D1 Christchurch Mons
46 D3 Christian Malford Wilts
129 K6 Christleton Ches
67 H8 Christmas Common Oxon
44 D7 Christon N Som
191 J2 Christon Bank Nthumb
13 J5 Christow Devon
38 D6 Chuck Hatch E Susx
13 K6 Chudleigh Devon
13 K7 Chudleigh Knighton Devon
28 B8 Chulmleigh Devon
131 L2 Chunal Derbys
139 L2 Church Lancs
114 A8 Church Aston Wrekin
84 D2 Church Brampton Nhants
167 J7 Church Brough Cumb
115 K5 Church Broughton Derbys
3 H8 Church Cove Cnwll
49 K8 Church Crookham Hants
114 C8 Church Eaton Staffs
85 J8 Church End Beds
68 C3 Church End Beds
85 K8 Church End Beds
85 L3 Church End Beds
86 C3 Church End Beds
86 D7 Church End Beds
102 B8 Church End Cambs
102 E6 Church End Cambs
103 G7 Church End Cambs
87 K4 Church End Cambs
70 F3 Church End Essex
71 H2 Church End Essex
71 H2 Church End Essex
51 H1 Church End Gt Lon
49 G7 Church End Hants
68 E5 Church End Herts
69 H1 Church End Herts
70 C3 Church End Herts
119 H5 Church End Lincs
145 L8 Church End Lincs
99 H5 Church End Warwks
99 H5 Church End Warwks
66 A2 Church Enstone Oxon
151 H8 Church Fenton N York
14 E3 Church Green Devon
115 M7 Church Gresley Derbys
66 B4 Church Hanborough Oxon
130 C6 Church Hill Ches

98 C1 Church Hill Staffs
161 L3 Church Houses N York
17 H6 Church Knowle Dorset
135 G4 Church Laneham Notts
100 F5 Church Langton Leics
99 M8 Church Lawford Warwks
130 F8 Church Lawton Ches
115 G4 Church Leigh Staffs
82 B5 Church Lench Worcs
115 J3 Church Mayfield Staffs
130 C7 Church Minshull Ches
20 E7 Church Norton W Susx
96 C4 Church Preen Shrops
95 K3 Church Pulverbatch Shrops
84 C4 Church Stowe Nhants
88 F6 Church Street Essex
52 F4 Church Street Kent
107 K6 Church Street Suffk
95 L4 Church Stretton Shrops
143 K6 Church Town N Linc
43 G4 Church Village Rhondd
133 L6 Church Warsop Notts
116 D5 Church Wilne Derbys
63 M3 Churcham Gloucs
98 C2 Churchbridge Staffs
64 C3 Churchdown Gloucs
72 E8 Churchend Essex
98 C5 Churchfield Birm
69 K6 Churchgate Herts
70 C5 Churchgate Street Essex
27 L3 Churchill Devon
15 G2 Churchill Devon
44 E7 Churchill N Som
65 L2 Churchill Oxon
97 K7 Churchill Worcs
81 L4 Churchill Worcs
30 B8 Churchinford Somset
100 B7 Churchover Warwks
30 B7 Churchstanton Somset
95 G4 Churchstoke Powys
7 K5 Churchstow Devon
145 J8 Churchthorpe Lincs
146 F7 Churchtown Bpool
10 F7 Churchtown Cnwll
132 E7 Churchtown Derbys
28 B2 Churchtown Devon
147 J7 Churchtown Lancs
138 D4 Churchtown Sefton
178 F3 Churnsike Lodge Nthumb
8 D4 Churston Ferrers Torbay
36 C3 Churt Surrey
129 K8 Churton Ches
141 L2 Churwell Leeds
109 H4 Chwilog Gwynd
2 D5 Chyandour Cnwll
3 G6 Chyanvounder Cnwll
3 K3 Chyeowling Cnwll
3 G6 Chyvarloe Cnwll
94 E3 Cil Powys
128 E6 Cilcain Flints
76 F3 Cilcennin Cerdgn
94 F3 Cilcewydd Powys
57 L5 Cilfrew Neath
43 H3 Cilfynydd Rhondd
75 L4 Cilgerran Pembks
59 K3 Cilgwyn Carmth
109 J1 Cilgwyn Gwynd
76 F4 Ciliau-Aeron Cerdgn
57 K4 Cilmaengwyn Neath
78 D5 Cilmery Powys
58 A2 Cilrhedyn Pembks
59 H4 Cilsan Carmth
111 G3 Ciltalgarth Gwynd
57 K4 Cilybebyll Neath
77 L7 Cilycwm Carmth
57 L5 Cimla Neath
97 L4 Cinder Hill Wolves
63 K4 Cinderford Gloucs
50 B3 Cippenham Slough
64 F6 Cirencester Gloucs
160 B3 Citadilla N York
51 J3 City Gt Lon
42 F6 City V Glam
125 H2 City Dulas IOA
224 F3 Clabhach Ag & B
207 J3 Clachaig Ag & B
216 B3 Clachan Ag & B
228 D6 Clachan Ag & B
206 B7 Clachan Ag & B
247 H1 Clachan Highld
224 C5 Clachan Mor Ag & B
283 C8 Clachan na Luib W Isls
209 G3 Clachan of Campsie E Duns
283 C8 Clachan-a-Luib W Isls
216 B3 Clachan-Seil Ag & B

302 Clachaneasy - Coed-y-caerau

183 J7 Clachaneasy D & G
251 H2 Clachnaharry Highld
270 D3 Clachtoll Highld
233 H3 Clackavoid P & K
210 B1 Clackmannan Clacks
266 E4 Clackmarras Moray
73 J4 Clacton-on-Sea Essex
217 H3 Cladich Ag & B
82 C3 Cladswell Worcs
227 K3 Claggan Highld
258 C6 Claigan Highld
45 K7 Clandown BaNES
35 L7 Clanfield Hants
65 L6 Clanfield Oxon
13 H2 Clannaborough Devon
34 D1 Clanville Hants
31 K4 Clanville Somset
206 D7 Claonaig Ag & B
40 D7 Clap Hill Kent
17 K2 Clapgate Dorset
70 C2 Clapgate Herts
85 K5 Clapham Beds
13 L5 Clapham Devon
51 H4 Clapham Gt Lon
148 C2 Clapham N York
21 J5 Clapham W Susx
85 K5 Clapham Folly Beds
156 E2 Clappersgate Cumb
15 J1 Clapton Somset
45 J8 Clapton Somset
44 F4 Clapton-in-Gordano N Som
65 H3 Clapton-on-the-Hill Gloucs
28 B6 Clapworthy Devon
92 D6 Clarach Cerdgn
180 E6 Claravale Gatesd
55 H3 Clarbeston Pembks
55 G3 Clarbeston Road Pembks
134 E3 Clarborough Notts
88 F6 Clare Suffk
175 J2 Clarebrand D & G
176 E5 Clarencefield D & G
150 E4 Clareton N York
180 B5 Clarewood Nthumb
188 F3 Clarilaw Border
37 J3 Clark's Green Surrey
35 H1 Clarken Green Hants
208 F7 Clarkston E Rens
270 D2 Clashmore Highld
263 K2 Clashmore Highld
270 E2 Clashnessie Highld
254 E7 Clashnoir Moray
221 H3 Clathy P & K
221 H3 Clathymore P & K
255 L6 Clatt Abers
94 B4 Clatter Powys
70 F4 Clatterford End Essex
29 J4 Clatworthy Somset
147 K7 Claughton Lancs
147 L3 Claughton Lancs
129 G2 Claughton Wirral
30 C4 Clavelshay Somset
82 E2 Claverdon Warwks
44 F5 Claverham N Som
70 C1 Clavering Essex
97 H5 Claverley Shrops
46 A6 Claverton BaNES
45 M6 Claverton Down BaNES
43 G6 Clawdd-coch V Glam
111 L1 Clawdd-newydd Denbgs
157 H7 Clawthorpe Cumb
11 L3 Clawton Devon
136 B1 Claxby Lincs
137 H5 Claxby Lincs
151 L4 Claxton N York
107 G3 Claxton Norfk
107 K7 Clay Common Suffk
100 D8 Clay Coton Nhants
133 H7 Clay Cross Derbys
69 J2 Clay End Herts
100 B5 Claybrooke Magna Leics
83 K5 Claydon Oxon
90 D5 Claydon Suffk
177 L3 Claygate D & G
39 H4 Claygate Kent
50 F6 Claygate Surrey
38 F2 Claygate Cross Kent
51 L1 Clayhall Gt Lon
29 J6 Clayhanger Devon
98 D3 Clayhanger Wsall
29 L7 Clayhidon Devon
24 F3 Clayhill E Susx
18 D2 Clayhill Hants
87 K2 Clayhithe Cambs
279 L4 Clayock Highld
87 G4 Claypit Hill Cambs
63 M6 Claypits Gloucs
117 M2 Claypole Lincs
137 H4 Claythorpe Lincs
141 H2 Clayton Brad
142 C6 Clayton Donc
22 D4 Clayton W Susx
139 H3 Clayton Green Lancs
141 L5 Clayton West Kirk
139 M2 Clayton-le-Moors Lancs
139 H3 Clayton-le-Woods Lancs
134 E2 Clayworth Notts
236 F3 Cleadale Highld
181 J6 Cleadon S Tyne
7 G2 Clearbrook Devon
63 H5 Clearwell Gloucs
63 H5 Clearwell Meend Gloucs
169 H8 Cleasby N York
275 c6 Cleat Ork
168 E7 Cleatlam Dur
164 D7 Cleator Cumb
164 D7 Cleator Moor Cumb
141 J3 Cleckheaton Kirk
96 D6 Clee St Margaret Shrops
96 D7 Cleedownton Shrops
96 D8 Cleehill Shrops
209 K7 Cleekhimin N Lans
96 D7 Cleestanton Shrops
145 J6 Cleethorpes NE Lin
96 E7 Cleeton St Mary Shrops
44 F5 Cleeve N Som
48 F3 Cleeve Oxon
64 E2 Cleeve Hill Gloucs
82 C5 Cleeve Prior Worcs
212 D2 Cleghornie E Loth
80 B7 Clehonger Herefs
221 K7 Cleish P & K
209 L7 Cleland N Lans
52 B5 Clement Street Kent
68 C4 Clement's End Beds
216 E2 Clenamacrie Ag & B
47 H6 Clench Common Wilts
120 D7 Clenchwarton Norfk
268 D4 Clenerty Abers
97 L7 Clent Worcs
96 F8 Cleobury Mortimer Shrops
96 E6 Cleobury North Shrops
192 D2 Cleongart Ag & B
252 F2 Clephanton Highld
187 L6 Clerkhill D & G
185 K3 Cleuch-head D & G
46 F4 Clevancy Wilts
44 E5 Clevedon N Som
66 B2 Cleveley Oxon
146 F7 Cleveleys Lancs
81 J6 Clevelode Worcs
46 E2 Cleverton Wilts
31 G1 Clewer Somset
122 A3 Cley next the Sea Norfk
166 E5 Cliburn Cumb
35 K1 Cliddesden Hants
99 G4 Cliff Warwks
25 G4 Cliff End E Susx
139 L1 Cliffe Lancs
52 F4 Cliffe Medway
169 G7 Cliffe N York
143 G2 Cliffe N York
52 F4 Cliffe Woods Medway
79 J6 Clifford Herefs
150 F7 Clifford Leeds
82 E5 Clifford Chambers Warwks
63 K2 Clifford's Mesne Gloucs
41 K2 Cliffsend Kent
86 D7 Clifton Beds
45 H4 Clifton Bristl
116 F4 Clifton C Nott
141 J3 Clifton Calder
166 C5 Clifton Cumb
115 K3 Clifton Derbys
142 E8 Clifton Donc
138 F2 Clifton Lancs
150 B6 Clifton N York
180 F2 Clifton Nthumb
66 C1 Clifton Oxon
140 A7 Clifton Salfd
81 J6 Clifton Worcs
151 J5 Clifton York
99 H1 Clifton Campville Staffs
166 D5 Clifton Dykes Cumb
66 D7 Clifton Hampden Oxon
85 H5 Clifton Reynes M Keyn
100 C8 Clifton upon Dunsmore Warwks
81 G3 Clifton upon Teme Worcs
41 L1 Cliftonville Kent
21 G6 Climping W Susx
32 C1 Clink Somset
150 C4 Clint N York
105 L1 Clint Green Norfk
245 J1 Clinterty C Aber
201 J6 Clintmains Border
93 H1 Clipiau Gwynd
123 J8 Clippesby Norfk
118 C8 Clipsham Rutlnd
100 F7 Clipston Nhants
117 H5 Clipston Notts
68 B2 Clipstone Beds
134 B7 Clipstone Notts
148 C7 Clitheroe Lancs
113 H6 Clive Shrops
144 E7 Clixby Lincs
46 E1 Cloatley Wilts
111 L1 Clocaenog Denbgs
267 H4 Clochan Moray
234 D5 Clochtow Angus
129 M2 Clock Face St Hel
94 F2 Cloddiau Powys
62 C2 Clodock Herefs
32 B2 Cloford Somset
257 J3 Clola Abers
86 B7 Clophill Beds
102 B7 Clopton Nhants
90 F4 Clopton Suffk
90 F4 Clopton Corner Suffk
88 F4 Clopton Green Suffk
89 K3 Clopton Green Suffk
9 k1 Clos du Valle Guern
186 D7 Closeburn D & G
186 D7 Closeburnmill D & G
154 c7 Closeclark IOM
16 A1 Closworth Somset
69 H1 Clothall Herts
129 M6 Clotton Ches
100 A6 Cloudesley Bush Warwks
140 E6 Clough Oldham
140 D3 Clough Foot Calder
141 H4 Clough Head Calder
163 H4 Cloughton N York
163 H3 Cloughton Newlands N York
281 d5 Clousta Shet
233 M1 Clova Angus
26 E6 Clovelly Devon
200 F6 Clovenfords Border
228 F3 Clovulin Highld
140 B2 Clow Bridge Lancs
133 K4 Clowne Derbys
81 G1 Clows Top Worcs
112 F3 Cloy Wrexhm
239 H1 Cluanie Inn Highld
239 H2 Cluanie Lodge Highld
11 K4 Clubworthy Cnwll
173 J3 Clugston D & G
95 H7 Clun Shrops
253 G2 Clunas Highld
95 J7 Clunbury Shrops
252 E6 Clune Highld
239 K6 Clunes Highld
95 K7 Clungunford Shrops
268 B6 Clunie Abers
233 H6 Clunie P & K
95 H7 Clunton Shrops
222 D8 Cluny Fife
45 J7 Clutton BaNES
113 G1 Clutton Ches
45 J7 Clutton Hill BaNES
125 K7 Clwt-y-bont Gwynd
61 K4 Clydach Mons
57 J4 Clydach Swans
42 E3 Clydach Vale Rhondd
208 E5 Clydebank W Duns
75 M5 Clydey Pembks
47 G3 Clyffe Pypard Wilts
207 L2 Clynder Ag & B
55 J3 Clynderwen Carmth
60 B7 Clyne Neath
109 G2 Clynnog-fawr Gwynd
79 H6 Clyro Powys
14 A4 Clyst Honiton Devon
14 B2 Clyst Hydon Devon
14 A5 Clyst St George Devon
14 B3 Clyst St Lawrence Devon
14 A4 Clyst St Mary Devon
282 g3 Cnoc W Isls
92 E8 Cnwch Coch Cerdgn
11 K7 Coad's Green Cnwll
133 G4 Coal Aston Derbys
98 C3 Coal Pool Wsall
90 F1 Coal Street Suffk
96 F3 Coalbrookdale Wrekin
61 K5 Coalbrookvale Blae G
198 D6 Coalburn S Lans
180 D6 Coalburns Gatesd
167 J2 Coalcleugh Nthumb
63 M6 Coaley Gloucs
178 E7 Coalfell Cumb
71 J7 Coalhill Essex
96 F2 Coalmoor Wrekin
45 K3 Coalpit Heath S Glos
114 C1 Coalpit Hill Staffs
96 F3 Coalport Wrekin
221 G8 Coalsnaughton Clacks
222 E7 Coaltown of Balgonie Fife
222 E8 Coaltown of Wemyss Fife
116 D8 Coalville Leics
178 F7 Coanwood Nthumb
31 G6 Coat Somset
209 J6 Coatbridge N Lans
209 K6 Coatdyke N Lans
47 J2 Coate Swindn
46 F6 Coate Wilts
102 F4 Coates Cambs
64 E7 Coates Gloucs
135 G3 Coates Lincs
135 H3 Coates Lincs
21 G3 Coates W Susx
170 E5 Coatham R & Cl
169 H6 Coatham Mundeville Darltn
27 L5 Cobbaton Devon
64 D4 Coberley Gloucs
80 B8 Cobhall Common Herefs
52 E5 Cobham Kent
50 E7 Cobham Surrey
71 G3 Coblers Green Essex
33 H6 Cobley Dorset
80 B3 Cobnash Herefs
9 j2 Cobo Guern
114 D2 Cobridge C Stke
269 G3 Coburby Abers
88 E4 Cock & End Suffk
133 H5 Cock Alley Derbys
112 E2 Cock Bank Wrexhm
82 C5 Cock Bevington Warwks
243 J2 Cock Bridge Abers
71 K6 Cock Clarks Essex
71 G3 Cock Green Essex
24 F3 Cock Marling E Susx
39 K3 Cock Street Kent
161 K3 Cockayne N York
86 F5 Cockayne Hatley Beds
213 G5 Cockburnspath Border
211 L4 Cockenzie and Port Seton E Loth
139 G3 Cocker Bar Lancs
139 L3 Cocker Brook Lancs
147 J5 Cockerham Lancs
164 F4 Cockermouth Cumb
68 E2 Cockernhoe Green Herts
141 K2 Cockersdale Leeds
57 H6 Cockett Swans
168 E6 Cockfield Dur
89 H4 Cockfield Suffk
69 H7 Cockfosters Gt Lon
20 E3 Cocking W Susx
20 E3 Cocking Causeway W Susx
8 D2 Cockington Torbay
31 G1 Cocklake Somset
191 J7 Cockle Park Nthumb
156 C2 Cockley Beck Cumb
104 F3 Cockley Cley Norfk
49 J3 Cockpole Green Wokham
4 C4 Cocks Cnwll
96 D6 Cockshutford Shrops
113 G5 Cockshutt Shrops
121 L3 Cockthorpe Norfk
2 E4 Cockwells Cnwll
14 A6 Cockwood Devon
30 B2 Cockwood Somset
131 L4 Cockyard Derbys
80 A8 Cockyard Herefs
90 D4 Coddenham Suffk
129 K8 Coddington Ches
81 G6 Coddington Herefs
117 L1 Coddington Notts
33 G3 Codford St Mary Wilts
33 G3 Codford St Peter Wilts
69 G3 Codicote Herts
21 H3 Codmore Hill W Susx
116 C2 Codnor Derbys
45 L3 Codrington S Glos
97 K3 Codsall Staffs
97 J2 Codsall Wood Staffs
62 D5 Coed Morgan Mons
129 G7 Coed Talon Flints
109 K6 Coed Ystumgwern Gwynd
76 C6 Coed-y-Bryn Cerdgn
44 D1 Coed-y-caerau Newpt

62 C7 **Coed-y-paen** Mons
61 J3 **Coed-yr-ynys** Powys
125 H3 **Coedana** IOA
42 F4 **Coedely** Rhondd
44 B2 **Coedkernew** Newpt
112 D1 **Coedpoeth** Wrexhm
112 E8 **Coedway** Powys
60 C5 **Coelbren** Powys
8 D1 **Coffinswell** Devon
85 K3 **Coffle End** Beds
13 M6 **Cofton** Devon
98 C8 **Cofton Hackett** Worcs
43 J7 **Cogan** V Glam
84 F3 **Cogenhoe** Nhants
65 M5 **Cogges** Oxon
71 K3 **Coggeshall** Essex
23 K2 **Coggin's Mill** E Susx
251 J8 **Coignafearn** Highld
243 K4 **Coilacriech** Abers
219 K5 **Coilantogle** Stirlg
246 E1 **Coillore** Highld
240 B2 **Coiltry** Highld
42 D5 **Coity** Brdgnd
282 g3 **Col** W Isls
272 E6 **Colaboll** Highld
4 E3 **Colan** Cnwll
14 C5 **Colaton Raleigh** Devon
258 C7 **Colbost** Highld
160 B3 **Colburn** N York
18 E2 **Colbury** Hants
166 F6 **Colby** Cumb
154 b7 **Colby** IOM
122 E5 **Colby** Norfk
72 E2 **Colchester** Essex
48 D5 **Cold Ash** W Berk
100 E8 **Cold Ashby** Nhants
45 L4 **Cold Ashton** S Glos
65 H3 **Cold Aston** Gloucs
55 J4 **Cold Blow** Pembks
85 H5 **Cold Brayfield** M Keyn
148 C2 **Cold Cotes** N York
80 F6 **Cold Green** Herefs
135 L3 **Cold Hanworth** Lincs
68 F4 **Cold Harbour** Herts
48 F3 **Cold Harbour** Oxon
32 E2 **Cold Harbour** Wilts
113 K7 **Cold Hatton** Wrekin
113 K7 **Cold Hatton Heath** Wrekin
169 L2 **Cold Hesledon** Dur
142 B5 **Cold Hiendley** Wakefd
84 C4 **Cold Higham** Nhants
161 H6 **Cold Kirby** N York
100 F2 **Cold Newton** Leics
11 H5 **Cold Northcott** Cnwll
71 K7 **Cold Norton** Essex
101 H2 **Cold Overton** Leics
96 C6 **Cold Weston** Shrops
277 K4 **Coldbackie** Highld
158 C2 **Coldbeck** Cumb
22 E5 **Coldean** Br & H
13 J7 **Coldeast** Devon
140 E2 **Colden** Calder
35 G6 **Colden Common** Hants
91 K3 **Coldfair Green** Suffk
103 J3 **Coldham** Cambs
4 B5 **Coldharbour** Cnwll
29 J8 **Coldharbour** Devon
63 H6 **Coldharbour** Gloucs
37 H2 **Coldharbour** Surrey
213 K6 **Coldingham** Border
114 D5 **Coldmeece** Staffs
41 J6 **Coldred** Kent
13 G1 **Coldridge** Devon
202 C5 **Coldstream** Border
21 H3 **Coldwaltham** W Susx
80 A8 **Coldwell** Herefs
257 H4 **Coldwells** Abers
31 L4 **Cole** Somset
99 G5 **Cole End** Warwks
69 H5 **Cole Green** Herts
70 B1 **Cole Green** Herts
34 F1 **Cole Henley** Hants
8 A5 **Cole's Cross** Devon
95 H6 **Colebatch** Shrops
7 G3 **Colebrook** C Plym
14 B1 **Colebrook** Devon
13 H3 **Colebrooke** Devon
135 K7 **Coleby** Lincs
143 M4 **Coleby** N Linc
13 H2 **Coleford** Devon
63 H5 **Coleford** Gloucs
31 L1 **Coleford** Somset
29 L4 **Coleford Water** Somset
106 D6 **Colegate End** Norfk
17 K2 **Colehill** Dorset

69 G4 **Coleman Green** Herts
38 C6 **Coleman's Hatch** E Susx
113 G5 **Colemere** Shrops
35 L5 **Colemore** Hants
97 G4 **Colemore Green** Shrops
221 K1 **Colenden** P & K
116 C8 **Coleorton** Leics
46 B5 **Colerne** Wilts
15 J2 **Coles Cross** Dorset
90 C7 **Coles Green** Suffk
64 E4 **Colesbourne** Gloucs
86 C4 **Colesden** Beds
68 B8 **Coleshill** Bucks
65 K8 **Coleshill** Oxon
99 G5 **Coleshill** Warwks
14 C2 **Colestocks** Devon
45 H7 **Coley** BaNES
37 K4 **Colgate** W Susx
223 H6 **Colinsburgh** Fife
211 H5 **Colinton** C Edin
207 G4 **Colintraive** Ag & B
121 K6 **Colkirk** Norfk
222 C1 **Collace** P & K
281 d3 **Collafirth** Shet
7 L7 **Collaton** Devon
8 B4 **Collaton** Devon
8 C3 **Collaton St Mary** Torbay
31 J4 **College Green** Somset
266 C3 **College of Roseisle** Moray
49 K6 **College Town** Br For
222 D4 **Collessie** Fife
28 B7 **Colleton Mills** Devon
52 B1 **Collier Row** Gt Lon
39 H4 **Collier Street** Kent
69 K3 **Collier's End** Herts
24 E3 **Collier's Green** Kent
39 J5 **Colliers Green** Kent
169 J1 **Colliery Row** Sundld
257 J6 **Colliston** Abers
176 D4 **Collin** D & G
47 K8 **Collingbourne Ducis** Wilts
47 K7 **Collingbourne Kingston** Wilts
150 E6 **Collingham** Leeds
135 G7 **Collingham** Notts
80 F3 **Collington** Herefs
84 E4 **Collingtree** Nhants
130 A1 **Collins Green** Warrtn
81 G4 **Collins Green** Worcs
234 F6 **Colliston** Angus
14 C2 **Colliton** Devon
101 M3 **Collyweston** Nhants
182 E5 **Colmonell** S Ayrs
86 C4 **Colmworth** Beds
65 G5 **Coln Rogers** Gloucs
65 H6 **Coln St Aldwyns** Gloucs
65 G5 **Coln St Dennis** Gloucs
50 C3 **Colnbrook** Slough
103 H8 **Colne** Cambs
148 F7 **Colne** Lancs
141 J4 **Colne Bridge** Kirk
148 F7 **Colne Edge** Lancs
71 K1 **Colne Engaine** Essex
106 D2 **Colney** Norfk
69 G6 **Colney Heath** Herts
68 F6 **Colney Street** Herts
256 B5 **Colpy** Abers
200 D5 **Colquhar** Border
10 E8 **Colquite** Cnwll
26 F7 **Colscott** Devon
159 L6 **Colsterdale** N York
118 B6 **Colsterworth** Lincs
117 J5 **Colston Bassett** Notts
49 H8 **Colt Hill** Hants
39 G4 **Colt's Hill** Kent
266 C3 **Coltfield** Moray
122 F7 **Coltishall** Norfk
156 D5 **Colton** Cumb
142 B1 **Colton** Leeds
151 H6 **Colton** N York
106 C2 **Colton** Norfk
115 G7 **Colton** Staffs
13 M3 **Columbjohn** Devon
79 H4 **Colva** Powys
175 L4 **Colvend** D & G
81 H6 **Colwall** Herefs
179 M4 **Colwell** Nthumb
115 G7 **Colwich** Staffs
117 G3 **Colwick** Notts
42 E6 **Colwinston** V Glam
20 F6 **Colworth** W Susx
127 G4 **Colwyn Bay** Conwy
14 F4 **Colyford** Devon
14 F4 **Colyton** Devon
7 L7 **Combe** Devon
8 C5 **Combe** Devon

79 L3 **Combe** Herefs
66 B4 **Combe** Oxon
48 A6 **Combe** W Berk
17 J3 **Combe Almer** Dorset
36 E4 **Combe Common** Surrey
45 M6 **Combe Down** BaNES
8 C2 **Combe Fishacre** Devon
29 L4 **Combe Florey** Somset
45 L7 **Combe Hay** BaNES
27 K2 **Combe Martin** Devon
14 E2 **Combe Raleigh** Devon
30 D8 **Combe St Nicholas** Somset
13 L8 **Combeinteignhead** Devon
130 C4 **Comberbach** Ches
99 G2 **Comberford** Staffs
87 H4 **Comberton** Cambs
80 C2 **Comberton** Herefs
15 G4 **Combpyne** Devon
115 H4 **Combridge** Staffs
83 H5 **Combrook** Warwks
131 L4 **Combs** Derbys
90 B4 **Combs** Suffk
90 B4 **Combs Ford** Suffk
30 C2 **Combwich** Somset
244 F2 **Comers** Abers
81 J2 **Comhampton** Worcs
55 K3 **Commercial** Pembks
87 L3 **Commercial End** Cambs
93 H3 **Commins Coch** Powys
138 C1 **Common Edge** Bpool
164 D6 **Common End** Cumb
6 A1 **Common Moor** Cnwll
47 G2 **Common Platt** Wilts
133 G4 **Common Side** Derbys
170 F8 **Commondale** N York
130 A5 **Commonside** Ches
115 L3 **Commonside** Derbys
113 H6 **Commonwood** Shrops
112 F1 **Commonwood** Wrexhm
30 D4 **Compass** Somset
131 J2 **Compstall** Stockp
175 G4 **Compstonend** D & G
8 C2 **Compton** Devon
34 D5 **Compton** Hants
34 F5 **Compton** Hants
97 J6 **Compton** Staffs
36 E2 **Compton** Surrey
48 D3 **Compton** W Berk
20 C4 **Compton** W Susx
47 H8 **Compton** Wilts
32 E7 **Compton Abbas** Dorset
64 F4 **Compton Abdale** Gloucs
46 F4 **Compton Bassett** Wilts
47 K2 **Compton Beauchamp** Oxon
44 E7 **Compton Bishop** Somset
33 H5 **Compton Chamberlayne** Wilts
45 J6 **Compton Dando** BaNES
31 H4 **Compton Dundon** Somset
30 F7 **Compton Durville** Somset
45 H3 **Compton Greenfield** S Glos
45 G7 **Compton Martin** BaNES
31 L5 **Compton Pauncefoot** Somset
16 B4 **Compton Valence** Dorset
83 H5 **Compton Verney** Warwks
210 D1 **Comrie** Fife
220 D3 **Comrie** P & K
229 G2 **Conaglen House** Highld
248 E6 **Conchra** Highld
233 G6 **Concraigie** P & K
147 J4 **Conder Green** Lancs
81 M7 **Conderton** Worcs
65 H2 **Condicote** Gloucs
209 K4 **Condorrat** N Lans
96 B2 **Condover** Shrops
64 B3 **Coney Hill** Gloucs
105 J7 **Coney Weston** Suffk
37 H6 **Coneyhurst Common** W Susx
151 M2 **Coneysthorpe** N York
150 E4 **Coneythorpe** N York
36 B4 **Conford** Hants
11 K6 **Congdon's Shop** Cnwll
99 K2 **Congerstone** Leics
120 F6 **Congham** Norfk
24 D2 **Conghurst** Kent
110 D3 **Congl-y-wal** Gwynd
131 G2 **Congleton** Ches
44 E6 **Congresbury** N Som
97 K1 **Congreve** Staffs
176 C5 **Conheath** D & G
253 J1 **Conicavel** Moray
136 D8 **Coningsby** Lincs
102 D6 **Conington** Cambs
87 G2 **Conington** Cambs

142 D8 **Conisbrough** Donc
145 L8 **Conisholme** Lincs
156 D3 **Coniston** Cumb
144 F1 **Coniston** E R Yk
148 F5 **Coniston Cold** N York
149 H2 **Conistone** N York
129 G6 **Connah's Quay** Flints
228 E8 **Connel** Ag & B
197 H8 **Connel Park** E Ayrs
2 F3 **Connor Downs** Cnwll
250 F1 **Conon Bridge** Highld
149 H6 **Cononley** N York
114 F2 **Consall** Staffs
180 D8 **Consett** Dur
159 L4 **Constable Burton** N York
140 B3 **Constable Lee** Lancs
3 J5 **Constantine** Cnwll
10 B7 **Constantine Bay** Cnwll
262 D8 **Contin** Highld
126 F4 **Conwy** Conwy
40 C2 **Conyer** Kent
89 H2 **Conyer's Green** Suffk
24 C6 **Cooden** E Susx
73 J3 **Cook's Green** Essex
12 A1 **Cookbury** Devon
11 M2 **Cookbury Wick** Devon
49 L2 **Cookham** W & M
49 L2 **Cookham Dean** W & M
49 L2 **Cookham Rise** W & M
82 C3 **Cookhill** Warwks
107 G8 **Cookley** Suffk
97 J7 **Cookley** Worcs
49 G1 **Cookley Green** Oxon
245 J5 **Cookney** Abers
89 K4 **Cooks Green** Suffk
22 F4 **Cooksbridge** E Susx
81 L1 **Cooksey Green** Worcs
114 E3 **Cookshill** Staffs
5 J1 **Cooksland** Cnwll
70 F6 **Cooksmill Green** Essex
130 B5 **Cookson Green** Ches
169 H4 **Cookson's Green** Dur
37 H6 **Coolham** W Susx
53 G4 **Cooling** Medway
52 F4 **Cooling Street** Medway
3 G3 **Coombe** Cnwll
3 L3 **Coombe** Cnwll
13 J5 **Coombe** Devon
13 L7 **Coombe** Devon
14 C4 **Coombe** Devon
63 M8 **Coombe** Gloucs
35 K6 **Coombe** Hants
33 K1 **Coombe** Wilts
33 K5 **Coombe Bissett** Wilts
13 L8 **Coombe Cellars** Devon
35 K6 **Coombe Cross** Hants
29 J5 **Coombe End** Somset
64 C2 **Coombe Hill** Gloucs
17 G5 **Coombe Keynes** Dorset
8 D2 **Coombe Pafford** Torbay
32 C4 **Coombe Street** Somset
21 L5 **Coombes** W Susx
79 L3 **Coombes-Moor** Herefs
98 B6 **Coombeswood** Dudley
41 J3 **Cooper Street** Kent
139 J6 **Cooper Turning** Bolton
38 D3 **Cooper's Corner** Kent
253 J1 **Cooperhill** Moray
23 H3 **Coopers Green** E Susx
69 G5 **Coopers Green** Herts
70 C6 **Coopersale Common** Essex
70 C6 **Coopersale Street** Essex
21 J4 **Cootham** W Susx
41 J3 **Cop Street** Kent
90 D6 **Copdock** Suffk
72 D3 **Copford Green** Essex
150 D3 **Copgrove** N York
281 e4 **Copister** Shet
86 C5 **Cople** Beds
141 G3 **Copley** Calder
168 D5 **Copley** Dur
140 E8 **Copley** Tamesd
132 C4 **Coplow Dale** Derbys
151 J6 **Copmanthorpe** York
114 C5 **Copmere End** Staffs
147 H7 **Copp** Lancs
11 H2 **Coppathorne** Cnwll
114 E7 **Coppenhall** Staffs
130 D8 **Coppenhall Moss** Ches
2 F3 **Copperhouse** Cnwll
97 G7 **Coppicegate** Shrops
102 D7 **Coppingford** Cambs
40 B5 **Coppins Corner** Kent
13 H2 **Copplestone** Devon
139 H5 **Coppull** Lancs

139 H5 **Coppull Moor** Lancs
37 J6 **Copsale** W Susx
139 K1 **Copster Green** Lancs
99 M5 **Copston Magna** Warwks
98 F7 **Copt Heath** Solhll
150 D2 **Copt Hewick** N York
100 B1 **Copt Oak** Leics
70 B7 **Copthall Green** Essex
11 K4 **Copthorne** Cnwll
37 M3 **Copthorne** W Susx
121 L4 **Copy's Green** Norfk
34 C8 **Copythorne** Hants
89 K6 **Coram Street** Suffk
52 C2 **Corbets Tey** Gt Lon
9 a3 **Corbiere** Jersey
180 B6 **Corbridge** Nthumb
101 K5 **Corby** Nhants
118 C6 **Corby Glen** Lincs
178 B7 **Corby Hill** Cumb
195 G5 **Cordon** N Ayrs
132 F4 **Cordwell** Derbys
96 E8 **Coreley** Shrops
49 L2 **Cores End** Bucks
30 C7 **Corfe** Somset
17 J6 **Corfe Castle** Dorset
17 J3 **Corfe Mullen** Dorset
96 B6 **Corfton** Shrops
243 J2 **Corgarff** Abers
35 J6 **Corhampton** Hants
39 G5 **Corks Pond** Kent
99 J6 **Corley** Warwks
99 J6 **Corley Ash** Warwks
99 H6 **Corley Moor** Warwks
233 L2 **Cormuir** Angus
89 H7 **Cornard Tye** Suffk
13 G5 **Corndon** Devon
138 E1 **Corner Row** Lancs
155 K4 **Corney** Cumb
169 J4 **Cornforth** Dur
267 M4 **Cornhill** Abers
202 D5 **Cornhill-on-Tweed** Nthumb
140 D3 **Cornholme** Calder
88 D7 **Cornish Hall End** Essex
224 C6 **Cornoigmore** Ag & B
167 K2 **Cornriggs** Dur
168 F2 **Cornsay** Dur
168 F2 **Cornsay Colliery** Dur
262 F8 **Corntown** Highld
42 D6 **Corntown** V Glam
65 K2 **Cornwell** Oxon
7 H3 **Cornwood** Devon
8 B4 **Cornworthy** Devon
239 H8 **Corpach** Highld
122 C5 **Corpusty** Norfk
244 B3 **Corrachree** Abers
5 G5 **Corran** Cnwll
238 D2 **Corran** Highld
229 G3 **Corran** Highld
154 f4 **Corrany** IOM
177 G2 **Corrie** D & G
195 G2 **Corrie** N Ayrs
193 J4 **Corriecravie** N Ayrs
195 G4 **Corriegills** N Ayrs
239 M5 **Corriegour Lodge Hotel** Highld
262 C7 **Corriemoille** Highld
250 C5 **Corrimony** Highld
135 H2 **Corringham** Lincs
52 F2 **Corringham** Thurr
93 G2 **Corris** Gwynd
92 F2 **Corris Uchaf** Gwynd
217 K7 **Corrow** Ag & B
247 K4 **Corry** Highld
109 L7 **Cors-y-Gedol** Gwynd
12 E3 **Corscombe** Devon
15 L2 **Corscombe** Dorset
64 A2 **Corse** Gloucs
64 B1 **Corse Lawn** Gloucs
46 C5 **Corsham** Wilts
244 F2 **Corsindae** Abers
32 D2 **Corsley** Wilts
32 D2 **Corsley Heath** Wilts
185 J7 **Corsock** D & G
45 K6 **Corston** BaNES
46 D2 **Corston** Wilts
211 G4 **Corstorphine** C Edin
234 B3 **Cortachy** Angus
107 L4 **Corton** Suffk
32 F3 **Corton** Wilts
31 K6 **Corton Denham** Somset
229 H2 **Coruanan Lodge** Highld
111 L3 **Corwen** Denbgs
16 B5 **Coryates** Dorset
12 B6 **Coryton** Devon
52 F2 **Coryton** Thurr

100 C4 **Cosby** Leics
97 L4 **Coseley** Dudley
97 H2 **Cosford** Shrops
84 F6 **Cosgrove** Nhants
19 L3 **Cosham** C Port
55 G6 **Cosheston** Pembks
231 L5 **Coshieville** P & K
116 E3 **Cossall** Notts
116 E3 **Cossall Marsh** Notts
100 D1 **Cossington** Leics
30 E3 **Cossington** Somset
106 D1 **Costessey** Norfk
116 F6 **Costock** Notts
117 M7 **Coston** Leics
106 B2 **Coston** Norfk
65 M6 **Cote** Oxon
30 E2 **Cote** Somset
130 B6 **Cotebrook** Ches
166 B1 **Cotehill** Cumb
157 G5 **Cotes** Cumb
116 F7 **Cotes** Leics
114 C4 **Cotes** Staffs
114 C4 **Cotes Heath** Staffs
100 C7 **Cotesbach** Leics
117 H4 **Cotgrave** Notts
256 F8 **Cothal** Abers
117 L2 **Cotham** Notts
30 B4 **Cothelstone** Somset
168 C6 **Cotherstone** Dur
66 C7 **Cothill** Oxon
14 E2 **Cotleigh** Devon
116 D3 **Cotmanhay** Derbys
87 H3 **Coton** Cambs
84 D1 **Coton** Nhants
113 J4 **Coton** Shrops
114 C7 **Coton** Staffs
114 F5 **Coton** Staffs
98 F2 **Coton** Staffs
114 D7 **Coton Clanford** Staffs
114 F5 **Coton Hayes** Staffs
96 B1 **Coton Hill** Shrops
115 K5 **Coton in the Clay** Staffs
115 L8 **Coton in the Elms** Derbys
115 M7 **Coton Park** Derbys
8 B3 **Cott** Devon
34 E2 **Cottage End** Hants
152 F3 **Cottam** E R Yk
139 G1 **Cottam** Lancs
135 G4 **Cottam** Notts
87 J2 **Cottenham** Cambs
158 E4 **Cotterdale** N York
69 J1 **Cottered** Herts
98 D7 **Cotteridge** Birm
102 A5 **Cotterstock** Nhants
100 F8 **Cottesbrooke** Nhants
101 K1 **Cottesmore** Rutlnd
144 D1 **Cottingham** E R Yk
101 J5 **Cottingham** Nhants
149 K8 **Cottingley** Brad
66 E1 **Cottisford** Oxon
90 C2 **Cotton** Suffk
86 B6 **Cotton End** Beds
148 F7 **Cotton Tree** Lancs
255 K6 **Cottown** Abers
256 D8 **Cottown** Abers
256 E4 **Cottown of Gight** Abers
43 G6 **Cottrell** V Glam
6 E2 **Cotts** Devon
113 K8 **Cotwall** Wrekin
114 E4 **Cotwalton** Staffs
5 K3 **Couch's Mill** Cnwll
63 H3 **Coughton** Herefs
82 C3 **Coughton** Warwks
206 A6 **Coulaghailtro** Ag & B
248 F3 **Coulags** Highld
155 H1 **Coulderton** Cumb
244 B3 **Coull** Abers
207 L2 **Coulport** Ag & B
51 J7 **Coulsdon** Gt Lon
46 D8 **Coulston** Wilts
199 H6 **Coulter** S Lans
21 G3 **Coultershaw Bridge** W Susx
30 C3 **Coultings** Somset
161 K7 **Coulton** N York
222 F3 **Coultra** Fife
96 D2 **Cound** Shrops
96 D2 **Coundlane** Shrops
169 G5 **Coundon** Dur
169 G5 **Coundon Grange** Dur
159 G5 **Countersett** N York
33 K2 **Countess** Wilts
72 C1 **Countess Cross** Essex
13 M4 **Countess Wear** Devon
100 D4 **Countesthorpe** Leics
28 C1 **Countisbury** Devon

139 H2 **Coup Green** Lancs
233 K7 **Coupar Angus** P & K
167 G7 **Coupland** Cumb
202 E7 **Coupland** Nthumb
194 C2 **Cour** Ag & B
187 G8 **Courance** D & G
59 G4 **Court Henry** Carmth
40 E8 **Court-at-Street** Kent
237 K1 **Courteachan** Highld
84 E4 **Courteenhall** Nhants
72 F8 **Courtsend** Essex
30 B4 **Courtway** Somset
211 L5 **Cousland** Mdloth
39 G6 **Cousley Wood** E Susx
207 L3 **Cove** Ag & B
213 G4 **Cove** Border
29 G7 **Cove** Devon
49 L7 **Cove** Hants
260 C2 **Cove** Highld
245 L3 **Cove Bay** C Aber
107 K7 **Cove Bottom** Suffk
107 L7 **Covehithe** Suffk
97 K2 **Coven** Staffs
97 K2 **Coven Lawn** Staffs
103 K7 **Coveney** Cambs
136 F1 **Covenham St Bartholomew** Lincs
136 F1 **Covenham St Mary** Lincs
99 J7 **Coventry** Covtry
3 K7 **Coverack** Cnwll
3 H5 **Coverack Bridges** Cnwll
159 K5 **Coverham** N York
85 L1 **Covington** Cambs
199 G5 **Covington** S Lans
90 C2 **Cow Green** Suffk
82 D6 **Cow Honeybourne** Worcs
157 K7 **Cowan Bridge** Lancs
23 K4 **Cowbeech** E Susx
119 H7 **Cowbit** Lincs
42 F6 **Cowbridge** V Glam
132 B5 **Cowdale** Derbys
38 C5 **Cowden** Kent
38 C5 **Cowden Pound** Kent
38 D5 **Cowden Station** Kent
211 G1 **Cowdenbeath** Fife
116 A2 **Cowers Lane** Derbys
19 H4 **Cowes** IOW
161 G5 **Cowesby** N York
37 K6 **Cowfield Green** Wilts
37 K6 **Cowfold** W Susx
158 C5 **Cowgill** Cumb
45 J1 **Cowhill** S Glos
209 M1 **Cowie** Stirlg
152 E3 **Cowlam** E R Yk
133 G4 **Cowley** Derbys
13 L3 **Cowley** Devon
64 D4 **Cowley** Gloucs
50 D3 **Cowley** Gt Lon
66 D6 **Cowley** Oxon
67 G2 **Cowley** Oxon
139 J4 **Cowling** Lancs
149 H7 **Cowling** N York
160 C5 **Cowling** N York
88 E4 **Cowlinge** Suffk
141 J4 **Cowmes** Kirk
140 C4 **Cowpe** Lancs
181 H3 **Cowpen** Nthumb
170 B5 **Cowpen Bewley** S on T
19 M2 **Cowplain** Hants
167 K3 **Cowshill** Dur
44 F6 **Cowslip Green** N Som
150 F5 **Cowthorpe** N York
107 H7 **Cox Common** Suffk
95 J8 **Coxall** Shrops
113 L3 **Coxbank** Ches
116 C3 **Coxbench** Derbys
31 J3 **Coxbridge** Somset
11 H3 **Coxford** Cnwll
121 J5 **Coxford** Norfk
97 H6 **Coxgreen** Staffs
39 J3 **Coxheath** Kent
169 J3 **Coxhoe** Dur
31 H2 **Coxley** Somset
141 L4 **Coxley** Wakefd
31 H2 **Coxley Wick** Somset
12 A8 **Coxpark** Cnwll
70 E7 **Coxtie Green** Essex
161 H7 **Coxwold** N York
42 E6 **Coychurch** Brdgnd
196 E7 **Coylton** S Ayrs
242 B1 **Coylumbridge** Highld
42 D4 **Coytrahen** Brdgnd
17 L1 **Crab Orchard** Dorset
82 B2 **Crabbs Cross** Worcs
37 K6 **Crabtree** W Susx

112 E3 **Crabtree Green** Wrexhm
166 F6 **Crackenthorpe** Cumb
11 G3 **Crackington Haven** Cnwll
114 C2 **Crackley** Staffs
99 J8 **Crackley** Warwks
97 G1 **Crackleybank** Shrops
159 H3 **Crackpot** N York
149 H4 **Cracoe** N York
29 K8 **Craddock** Devon
70 C3 **Cradle End** Herts
97 L6 **Cradley** Dudley
81 G6 **Cradley** Herefs
97 L6 **Cradley Heath** Sandw
60 F1 **Cradoc** Powys
6 D4 **Crafthole** Cnwll
67 L3 **Crafton** Bucks
157 G7 **Crag Foot** Lancs
150 B8 **Cragg Hill** Leeds
140 F3 **Cragg Vale** Calder
253 K6 **Craggan** Highld
180 F8 **Craghead** Dur
60 D2 **Crai** Powys
267 K4 **Craibstone** Moray
234 D6 **Craichie** Angus
235 H4 **Craig** Angus
249 H2 **Craig** Highld
57 K4 **Craig Llangiwg** Neath
42 E6 **Craig Penllyn** V Glam
88 E7 **Craig's End** Essex
57 K4 **Craig-y-Duke** Neath
60 C4 **Craig-y-nos** Powys
197 H8 **Craigbank** E Ayrs
200 B2 **Craigburn** Border
57 J4 **Craigcefnparc** Swans
177 K2 **Craigcleuch** D & G
256 F5 **Craigdam** Abers
216 C6 **Craigdhu** Ag & B
245 G1 **Craigearn** Abers
254 F3 **Craigellachie** Moray
221 K3 **Craigend** P & K
208 D5 **Craigend** Rens
208 A3 **Craigendoran** Ag & B
173 K1 **Craighlaw** D & G
205 H3 **Craighouse** Ag & B
233 H6 **Craigie** P & K
196 E4 **Craigie** S Ayrs
269 G3 **Craigiefold** Abers
175 J3 **Craigley** D & G
211 H5 **Craiglockhart** C Edin
267 G5 **Craiglug** Moray
211 J4 **Craigmillar** C Edin
112 C4 **Craignant** Shrops
185 J5 **Craigneston** D & G
209 K6 **Craigneuk** N Lans
209 K7 **Craigneuk** N Lans
227 L5 **Craignure** Ag & B
235 H3 **Craigo** Angus
222 F5 **Craigrothie** Fife
219 H3 **Craigruie** Stirlg
234 D7 **Craigton** Angus
245 J3 **Craigton** C Aber
208 E8 **Craigton** E Rens
233 M5 **Craigton of Airlie** Angus
223 L5 **Crail** Fife
189 J1 **Crailing** Border
143 J8 **Craiselound** N Linc
160 C5 **Crakehall** N York
160 F7 **Crakehill** N York
115 H4 **Crakemarsh** Staffs
151 M3 **Crambe** N York
181 G3 **Cramlington** Nthumb
211 G4 **Cramond** C Edin
211 G4 **Cramond Bridge** C Edin
34 E6 **Crampmoor** Hants
130 E6 **Cranage** Ches
114 C4 **Cranberry** Staffs
33 H8 **Cranborne** Dorset
39 J6 **Cranbrook** Kent
39 K5 **Cranbrook Common** Kent
141 M7 **Crane Moor** Barns
105 J1 **Crane's Corner** Norfk
85 J6 **Cranfield** Beds
26 F6 **Cranford** Devon
50 E4 **Cranford** Gt Lon
101 K7 **Cranford St Andrew** Nhants
101 K8 **Cranford St John** Nhants
64 C4 **Cranham** Gloucs
52 C2 **Cranham** Gt Lon
82 D4 **Cranhill** Warwks
139 G7 **Crank** St Hel
37 G3 **Cranleigh** Surrey
89 L1 **Cranmer Green** Suffk
18 F5 **Cranmore** IOW
31 L2 **Cranmore** Somset
101 G4 **Cranoe** Leics

91 H2 **Cransford** Suffk	116 B1 **Crich** Derbys	139 H6 **Crooke** Wigan	156 E5 **Crosslands** Cumb
212 F6 **Cranshaws** Border	116 B1 **Crich Carr** Derbys	63 J3 **Crooked End** Gloucs	112 E7 **Crosslanes** Shrops
154 f2 **Cranstal** IOM	116 B1 **Crich Common** Derbys	178 C6 **Crooked Holme** Cumb	208 C6 **Crosslee** Rens
152 F5 **Cranswick** E R Yk	211 L6 **Crichton** Mdloth	47 L4 **Crooked Soley** Wilts	141 K3 **Crossley** Kirk
4 C3 **Crantock** Cnwll	44 F1 **Crick** Mons	196 E3 **Crookedholm** E Ayrs	175 J2 **Crossmichael** D & G
118 D2 **Cranwell** Lincs	84 B1 **Crick** Nhants	132 F2 **Crookes** Sheff	37 L6 **Crosspost** W Susx
104 F4 **Cranwich** Norfk	78 F6 **Crickadarn** Powys	180 D8 **Crookhall** Dur	244 D2 **Crossroads** Abers
105 K3 **Cranworth** Norfk	15 J1 **Cricket St Thomas** Somset	202 E5 **Crookham** Nthumb	245 G5 **Crossroads** Abers
216 B5 **Craobh Haven** Ag & B	112 D7 **Crickheath** Shrops	48 D6 **Crookham** W Berk	234 E4 **Crosston** Angus
6 F1 **Crapstone** Devon	61 K3 **Crickhowell** Powys	49 J8 **Crookham Village** Hants	62 F3 **Crossway** Mons
216 F7 **Crarae** Ag & B	65 G8 **Cricklade** Wilts	157 H6 **Crooklands** Cumb	75 K4 **Crossway** Pembks
272 D3 **Crask Inn** Highld	51 G2 **Cricklewood** Gt Lon	115 L4 **Cropper** Derbys	78 E4 **Crossway** Powys
250 E3 **Crask of Aigas** Highld	142 E3 **Cridling Stubbs** N York	83 L6 **Cropredy** Oxon	63 G8 **Crossway Green** Mons
191 K2 **Craster** Nthumb	220 F3 **Crieff** P & K	100 C1 **Cropston** Leics	81 J2 **Crossway Green** Worcs
79 K8 **Craswall** Herefs	5 G3 **Criggan** Cnwll	82 B6 **Cropthorne** Worcs	16 E5 **Crossways** Dorset
97 K2 **Crateford** Staffs	112 D8 **Criggion** Powys	162 D5 **Cropton** N York	75 J5 **Crosswell** Pembks
107 G8 **Cratfield** Suffk	141 M4 **Crigglestone** Wakefd	117 H4 **Cropwell Bishop** Notts	156 F4 **Crosthwaite** Cumb
245 G4 **Crathes** Abers	140 C5 **Crimble** Rochdl	117 J4 **Cropwell Butler** Notts	138 F4 **Croston** Lancs
243 J4 **Crathie** Abers	269 K5 **Crimond** Abers	282 h1 **Cros** W Isls	122 E8 **Crostwick** Norfk
241 G5 **Crathie** Highld	104 C3 **Crimplesham** Norfk	195 K1 **Crosbie** N Ayrs	123 G5 **Crostwight** Norfk
161 G1 **Crathorne** N York	82 F5 **Crimscote** Warwks	282 g4 **Crosbost** W Isls	40 D4 **Crouch** Kent
95 K6 **Craven Arms** Shrops	250 D4 **Crinaglack** Highld	164 E3 **Crosby** Cumb	38 F2 **Crouch** Kent
180 D6 **Crawcrook** Gatesd	216 B8 **Crinan** Ag & B	154 d6 **Crosby** IOM	51 J1 **Crouch End** Gt Lon
139 G7 **Crawford** Lancs	209 L7 **Crindledyke** N Lans	143 M5 **Crosby** N Linc	32 B8 **Crouch Hill** Dorset
186 E2 **Crawford** S Lans	106 D2 **Cringleford** Norfk	138 C8 **Crosby** Sefton	33 J6 **Croucheston** Wilts
186 C2 **Crawfordjohn** S Lans	149 J6 **Cringles** Brad	158 C1 **Crosby Garret** Cumb	38 C4 **Crough House Green** Kent
185 K1 **Crawick** D & G	55 K4 **Crinow** Pembks	166 E7 **Crosby Ravensworth** Cumb	84 A8 **Croughton** Nhants
34 F4 **Crawley** Hants	24 D3 **Cripp's Corner** E Susx	164 E3 **Crosby Villa** Cumb	268 E3 **Crovie** Abers
65 M4 **Crawley** Oxon	2 D4 **Cripplesease** Cnwll	31 K2 **Croscombe** Somset	18 B3 **Crow** Hants
37 L4 **Crawley** W Susx	33 J8 **Cripplestyle** Dorset	113 G5 **Crosemere** Shrops	141 J6 **Crow Edge** Barns
38 A6 **Crawley Down** W Susx	62 F1 **Crizeley** Herefs	141 H5 **Crosland Edge** Kirk	87 G4 **Crow End** Cambs
168 C3 **Crawleyside** Dur	251 H6 **Croachy** Highld	141 H5 **Crosland Hill** Kirk	70 E7 **Crow Green** Essex
140 B3 **Crawshawbooth** Lancs	10 E8 **Croanford** Cnwll	44 E8 **Cross** Somset	63 J2 **Crow Hill** Herefs
245 J7 **Crawton** Abers	176 A3 **Crochmore House** D & G	62 E3 **Cross Ash** Mons	71 G2 **Crow's Green** Essex
72 D3 **Craxe's Green** Essex	30 D8 **Crock Street** Somset	85 L4 **Cross Coombe** Cnwll	6 B1 **Crow's Nest** Cnwll
159 G6 **Cray** N York	52 B5 **Crockenhill** Kent	89 G8 **Cross End** Beds	3 G4 **Crowan** Cnwll
48 F3 **Cray's Pond** Oxon	49 H2 **Crocker End** Oxon	89 G8 **Cross End** Essex	38 D7 **Crowborough** E Susx
52 B4 **Crayford** Gt Lon	63 G4 **Crocker's Ash** Herefs	149 K7 **Cross Flatts** Brad	38 D7 **Crowborough Town** E Susx
151 J2 **Crayke** N York	20 F5 **Crockerhill** W Susx	142 B1 **Cross Gates** Leeds	29 L3 **Crowcombe** Somset
122 B5 **Craymere Beck** Norfk	13 H4 **Crockernwell** Devon	11 M5 **Cross Green** Devon	132 B6 **Crowdecote** Derbys
71 H8 **Crays Hill** Essex	32 E2 **Crockerton** Wilts	141 M2 **Cross Green** Leeds	141 G7 **Crowden** Derbys
115 L6 **Craythorne** Staffs	185 K8 **Crocketford** D & G	97 K2 **Cross Green** Staffs	12 C3 **Crowden** Devon
29 H8 **Craze Lowman** Devon	151 K6 **Crockey Hill** York	89 G4 **Cross Green** Suffk	35 G6 **Crowdhill** Hants
49 J3 **Crazies Hill** Wokham	38 C3 **Crockham Hill** Kent	89 H4 **Cross Green** Suffk	52 C7 **Crowdleham** Kent
28 E7 **Creacombe** Devon	39 G4 **Crockhurst Street** Kent	89 K4 **Cross Green** Suffk	67 H7 **Crowell** Oxon
283 c9 **Creag Ghoraidh** W Isls	72 F2 **Crockleford Heath** Essex	59 G6 **Cross Hands** Carmth	84 B7 **Crowfield** Nhants
228 F6 **Creagan Inn** Ag & B	74 D6 **Croes-goch** Pembks	55 H4 **Cross Hands** Pembks	90 D4 **Crowfield** Suffk
283 c9 **Creagorry** W Isls	76 C6 **Croes-lan** Cerdgn	116 C2 **Cross Hill** Derbys	90 D4 **Crowfield Green** Suffk
230 B2 **Creaguaineach Lodge** Highld	62 C8 **Croes-y-mwyalch** Torfn	149 H6 **Cross Hills** N York	123 G7 **Crowgate Street** Norfk
113 H5 **Creamore Bank** Shrops	62 C6 **Croes-y-pant** Mons	96 C5 **Cross Houses** Shrops	213 G4 **Crowhill** E Loth
84 D1 **Creaton** Nhants	42 C3 **Croeserw** Neath	96 F5 **Cross Houses** Shrops	133 G4 **Crowhole** Derbys
177 H5 **Creca** D & G	110 B3 **Croesor** Gwynd	23 J3 **Cross in Hand** E Susx	24 D5 **Crowhurst** E Susx
80 B6 **Credenhill** Herefs	58 D5 **Croesyceiliog** Carmth	76 D4 **Cross Inn** Cerdgn	38 B4 **Crowhurst** Surrey
13 J3 **Crediton** Devon	62 C7 **Croesyceiliog** Torfn	77 G2 **Cross Inn** Cerdgn	38 B4 **Crowhurst Lane End** Surrey
183 J7 **Creebank** D & G	12 C3 **Croford** Devon	55 J5 **Cross Inn** Pembks	102 E2 **Crowland** Lincs
173 K2 **Creebridge** D & G	100 B4 **Croft** Leics	43 G5 **Cross Inn** Rhondd	89 K1 **Crowland** Suffk
30 D5 **Creech Heathfield** Somset	137 J7 **Croft** Lincs	208 B2 **Cross Keys** Ag & B	2 E4 **Crowlas** Cnwll
30 C6 **Creech St Michael** Somset	130 C1 **Croft** Warrtn	46 C5 **Cross Keys** Wilts	143 K5 **Crowle** N Linc
4 F5 **Creed** Cnwll	3 H4 **Croft Michael** Cnwll	19 H5 **Cross Lane** IOW	81 L4 **Crowle** Worcs
13 J2 **Creedy Park** Devon	160 D1 **Croft-on-Tees** N York	97 G4 **Cross Lane Head** Shrops	81 L4 **Crowle Green** Worcs
51 M3 **Creekmouth** Gt Lon	208 E2 **Croftamie** Stirlg	3 H6 **Cross Lanes** Cnwll	48 F1 **Crowmarsh Gifford** Oxon
90 C4 **Creeting St Mary** Suffk	165 J1 **Crofton** Cumb	4 C6 **Cross Lanes** Cnwll	90 F1 **Crown Corner** Suffk
118 D7 **Creeton** Lincs	142 B4 **Crofton** Wakefd	151 H3 **Cross Lanes** N York	6 F3 **Crownhill** C Plym
174 D3 **Creetown** D & G	47 K6 **Crofton** Wilts	112 E2 **Cross Lanes** Wrexhm	36 E2 **Crownpits** Surrey
154 b8 **Cregneash** IOM	175 J2 **Crofts** D & G	115 M2 **Cross o' th' hands** Derbys	106 B3 **Crownthorpe** Norfk
154 e5 **Cregny Baa** IOM	266 F6 **Crofts** Moray	61 H2 **Cross Oak** Powys	3 G5 **Crowntown** Cnwll
79 G5 **Cregrina** Powys	139 M8 **Crofts Bank** Traffd	256 D5 **Cross of Jackston** Abers	2 B5 **Crows-an-Wra** Cnwll
222 E3 **Creich** Fife	267 G4 **Crofts of Dipple** Moray	78 D4 **Cross Roads** Powys	105 J2 **Crowshill** Norfk
43 G5 **Creigiau** Cardif	269 J4 **Crofts of Savoch** Abers	106 D8 **Cross Street** Suffk	95 J3 **Crowsnest** Shrops
3 H4 **Crelly** Cnwll	56 F6 **Crofty** Swans	130 E4 **Cross Town** Ches	49 K6 **Crowthorne** Wokham
6 E4 **Cremyll** Cnwll	111 K4 **Crogen** Gwynd	39 K4 **Cross-at-Hand** Kent	130 B5 **Crowton** Ches
96 D3 **Cressage** Shrops	227 K7 **Croggan** Ag & B	194 C1 **Crossaig** Ag & B	99 G1 **Croxall** Staffs
132 C5 **Cressbrook** Derbys	166 D1 **Croglin** Cumb	224 C6 **Crossapoll** Ag & B	144 F8 **Croxby** NE Lin
55 H5 **Cresselly** Pembks	262 D2 **Croik** Highld	21 H5 **Crossbush** W Susx	169 H3 **Croxdale** Dur
67 K8 **Cressex** Bucks	264 B6 **Cromarty** Highld	164 E3 **Crosscanonby** Cumb	115 H4 **Croxden** Staffs
71 J3 **Cressing** Essex	210 E2 **Crombie** Fife	122 E4 **Crossdale Street** Norfk	68 D7 **Croxley Green** Herts
191 K7 **Cresswell** Nthumb	253 L6 **Cromdale** Highld	138 D4 **Crossens** Sefton	86 E3 **Croxton** Cambs
55 H5 **Cresswell** Pembks	69 J2 **Cromer** Herts	210 E2 **Crossford** Fife	144 E5 **Croxton** N Linc
114 F4 **Cresswell** Staffs	122 E3 **Cromer** Norfk	198 D4 **Crossford** S Lans	121 L5 **Croxton** Norfk
133 K5 **Creswell** Derbys	132 F8 **Cromford** Derbys	11 L5 **Crossgate** Cnwll	105 H6 **Croxton** Norfk
98 D1 **Creswell Green** Staffs	45 K1 **Cromhall** S Glos	119 H6 **Crossgate** Lincs	114 B5 **Croxton** Staffs
90 F3 **Cretingham** Suffk	45 K1 **Cromhall Common** S Glos	114 E4 **Crossgate** Staffs	113 J1 **Croxton Green** Ches
206 A5 **Cretshengan** Ag & B	282 g4 **Cromor** W Isls	211 L5 **Crossgatehall** E Loth	117 L5 **Croxton Kerrial** Leics
112 D8 **Crew Green** Powys	140 E6 **Crompton Fold** Oldham	196 D2 **Crossgates** E Ayrs	114 B5 **Croxtonbank** Staffs
112 F1 **Crewe** Ches	134 F7 **Cromwell** Notts	210 F1 **Crossgates** Fife	252 E2 **Croy** Highld
130 D8 **Crewe** Ches	197 H6 **Cronberry** E Ayrs	163 J6 **Crossgates** N York	209 J4 **Croy** N Lans
130 E8 **Crewe Green** Ches	36 B1 **Crondall** Hants	78 F2 **Crossgates** Powys	27 H3 **Croyde** Devon
15 K1 **Crewkerne** Somset	154 d5 **Cronk-y-Voddy** IOM	147 L3 **Crossgill** Lancs	27 G3 **Croyde Bay** Devon
63 K3 **Crews Hill** Herefs	154 e6 **Cronkbourne** IOM	55 L2 **Crosshands** Carmth	87 G5 **Croydon** Cambs
69 J7 **Crews Hill Station** Herts	129 L2 **Cronton** Knows	196 F5 **Crosshands** E Ayrs	51 J6 **Croydon** Gt Lon
116 C5 **Crewton** C Derb	157 G4 **Crook** Cumb	222 B7 **Crosshill** Fife	241 J5 **Crubenmore** Highld
218 F2 **Crianlarich** Stirlg	168 F4 **Crook** Dur	183 J2 **Crosshill** S Ayrs	95 K2 **Cruckmeole** Shrops
45 H3 **Cribbs Causeway** S Glos	199 J7 **Crook Inn** Border	196 D3 **Crosshouse** E Ayrs	95 K1 **Cruckton** Shrops
76 F5 **Cribyn** Cerdgn	221 J7 **Crook of Devon** P & K	43 K3 **Crosskeys** Caerph	257 K4 **Cruden Bay** Abers
109 J4 **Criccieth** Gwynd	165 G2 **Crookdake** Cumb	279 H2 **Crosskirk** Highld	113 K7 **Crudgington** Wrekin

64 D8 **Crudwell** Wilts
79 H1 **Crug** Powys
94 E7 **Crug-y-byddar** Powys
10 C7 **Crugmeer** Cnwll
77 J7 **Crugybar** Carmth
43 K2 **Crumlin** Caerph
5 L4 **Crumplehorn** Cnwll
140 C7 **Crumpsall** Manch
40 E5 **Crundale** Kent
54 F3 **Crundale** Pembks
55 L5 **Crunwear** Pembks
28 F8 **Cruwys Morchard** Devon
48 B7 **Crux Easton** Hants
16 B3 **Cruxton** Dorset
58 E6 **Crwbin** Carmth
67 L7 **Cryers Hill** Bucks
75 L5 **Crymmych** Pembks
60 B6 **Crynant** Neath
51 J5 **Crystal Palace** Gt Lon
260 A8 **Cuaig** Highld
215 L2 **Cuan Ferry Village** Ag & B
83 H2 **Cubbington** Warwks
4 C3 **Cubert** Cnwll
141 K7 **Cubley** Barns
67 K3 **Cublington** Bucks
79 M7 **Cublington** Herefs
22 D2 **Cuckfield** W Susx
32 C5 **Cucklington** Somset
133 L5 **Cuckney** Notts
53 H4 **Cuckold's Green** Medway
119 G7 **Cuckoo Bridge** Lincs
35 M3 **Cuckoo's Corner** Hants
129 J7 **Cuckoo's Nest** Ches
66 F6 **Cuddesdon** Oxon
67 H5 **Cuddington** Bucks
130 B5 **Cuddington** Ches
113 G2 **Cuddington Heath** Ches
147 J8 **Cuddy Hill** Lancs
51 L7 **Cudham** Gt Lon
12 C6 **Cudliptown** Devon
17 L3 **Cudnell** Bmouth
142 B6 **Cudworth** Barns
30 F8 **Cudworth** Somset
142 B6 **Cudworth Common** Barns
139 H3 **Cuerden Green** Lancs
130 A2 **Cuerdley Cross** Warrtn
49 G7 **Cufaude** Hants
69 J6 **Cuffley** Herts
228 F4 **Cuil** Highld
263 G7 **Culbokie** Highld
28 E1 **Culbone** Somset
250 E3 **Culburnie** Highld
251 J3 **Culcabock** Highld
253 G2 **Culcharry** Highld
130 C1 **Culcheth** Warrtn
255 K5 **Culdrain** Abers
248 A4 **Culduie** Highld
89 G1 **Culford** Suffk
166 E5 **Culgaith** Cumb
66 D8 **Culham** Oxon
270 D2 **Culkein** Highld
270 F1 **Culkein Drumbeg** Highld
64 D7 **Culkerton** Gloucs
267 K3 **Cullen** Moray
181 J4 **Cullercoats** N Tyne
245 G3 **Cullerlie** Abers
263 H7 **Cullicudden** Highld
149 J8 **Cullingworth** Brad
215 L2 **Cullipool House** Ag & B
281 e2 **Cullivoe** Shet
252 D3 **Culloden** Highld
14 B1 **Cullompton** Devon
29 L7 **Culm Davy** Devon
96 B7 **Culmington** Shrops
29 K8 **Culmstock** Devon
270 E7 **Culnacraig** Highld
175 J5 **Culnaightrie** D & G
259 J4 **Culnaknock** Highld
90 F5 **Culpho** Suffk
263 G1 **Culrain** Highld
210 C2 **Culross** Fife
196 C8 **Culroy** S Ayrs
256 B5 **Culsalmond** Abers
174 D5 **Culscadden** D & G
173 H4 **Culshabbin** D & G
281 c6 **Culswick** Shet
257 G7 **Cultercullen** Abers
245 K3 **Cults** C Aber
52 D6 **Culverstone Green** Kent
118 D3 **Culverthorpe** Lincs
84 A6 **Culworth** Nhants
209 K4 **Cumbernauld** N Lans
209 K4 **Cumbernauld Village** N Lans
137 J5 **Cumberworth** Lincs
165 K1 **Cumdivock** Cumb

268 E6 **Cuminestown** Abers
202 B2 **Cumledge** Border
177 L8 **Cummersdale** Cumb
176 F5 **Cummertrees** D & G
266 C2 **Cummingston** Moray
197 H7 **Cumnock** E Ayrs
66 C6 **Cumnor** Oxon
178 D8 **Cumrew** Cumb
176 E2 **Cumrue** D & G
178 B8 **Cumwhinton** Cumb
178 C8 **Cumwhitton** Cumb
150 F1 **Cundall** N York
196 D3 **Cunninghamhead** N Ayrs
222 F4 **Cupar** Fife
222 F4 **Cupar Muir** Fife
132 E5 **Curbar** Derbys
19 J1 **Curbridge** Hants
65 M5 **Curbridge** Oxon
35 H8 **Curdridge** Hants
98 F5 **Curdworth** Warwks
30 C7 **Curland** Somset
48 C4 **Curridge** W Berk
211 G5 **Currie** C Edin
30 E6 **Curry Mallet** Somset
30 F6 **Curry Rivel** Somset
39 L5 **Curteis Corner** Kent
39 J5 **Curtisden Green** Kent
7 L4 **Curtisknowle** Devon
3 H6 **Cury** Cnwll
244 C1 **Cushnie** Abers
30 B5 **Cushuish** Somset
79 J7 **Cusop** Herefs
174 C7 **Cutcloy** D & G
29 G3 **Cutcombe** Somset
140 C5 **Cutgate** Rochdl
110 B8 **Cutiau** Gwynd
70 E1 **Cutler's Green** Essex
5 J2 **Cutmadoc** Cnwll
6 C3 **Cutmere** Cnwll
81 K2 **Cutnall Green** Worcs
65 G1 **Cutsdean** Gloucs
142 C3 **Cutsyke** Wakefd
133 G5 **Cutthorpe** Derbys
6 D2 **Cuttivett** Cnwll
67 G8 **Cuxham** Oxon
52 F5 **Cuxton** Medway
144 F7 **Cuxwold** Lincs
61 J6 **Cwm** Blae G
128 C4 **Cwm** Denbgs
56 E4 **Cwm Capel** Carmth
61 J3 **Cwm Crawnon** Powys
57 H4 **Cwm Dulais** Swans
78 A5 **Cwm Irfon** Powys
93 J2 **Cwm Llinau** Powys
58 B2 **Cwm Morgan** Carmth
110 E2 **Cwm Penmachno** Conwy
56 E4 **Cwm-bach** Carmth
61 K5 **Cwm-celyn** Blae G
93 J1 **Cwm-Cewydd** Gwynd
76 B6 **Cwm-cou** Cerdgn
59 J4 **Cwm-Ifor** Carmth
59 G6 **Cwm-y-glo** Carmth
125 K7 **Cwm-y-glo** Gwynd
57 L6 **Cwmafan** Neath
60 F7 **Cwmaman** Rhondd
77 G6 **Cwmann** Carmth
62 B6 **Cwmavon** Torfn
75 M7 **Cwmbach** Carmth
79 G7 **Cwmbach** Powys
60 F6 **Cwmbach** Rhondd
78 E4 **Cwmbach Llechrhyd** Powys
93 K7 **Cwmbelan** Powys
62 C8 **Cwmbran** Torfn
92 F7 **Cwmbrwyno** Cerdgn
43 K3 **Cwmcarn** Caerph
62 F5 **Cwmcarvan** Mons
60 F6 **Cwmdare** Rhondd
59 H3 **Cwmdu** Carmth
61 J2 **Cwmdu** Powys
57 H6 **Cwmdu** Swans
58 C3 **Cwmduad** Carmth
59 K2 **Cwmdwr** Carmth
42 C4 **Cwmfelin** Brdgnd
61 H6 **Cwmfelin** Myr Td
55 L3 **Cwmfelin Boeth** Carmth
75 L7 **Cwmfelin Mynach** Carmth
43 J3 **Cwmfelinfach** Caerph
58 D5 **Cwmffrwd** Carmth
59 L6 **Cwmgiedd** Powys
57 K3 **Cwmgors** Carmth
57 G3 **Cwmgwili** Carmth
60 C6 **Cwmgwrach** Neath
76 C7 **Cwmhiraeth** Carmth
58 F5 **Cwmisfael** Carmth

59 K6 **Cwmllynfell** Neath
58 F6 **Cwmmawr** Carmth
42 E3 **Cwmparc** Rhondd
58 C2 **Cwmpengraig** Carmth
61 G7 **Cwmpennar** Rhondd
61 J2 **Cwmrhos** Powys
57 J5 **Cwmrhydyceirw** Swans
76 E6 **Cwmsychbant** Cerdgn
61 K6 **Cwmtillery** Blae G
62 C3 **Cwmyoy** Mons
93 G8 **Cwmystwyth** Cerdgn
92 E3 **Cwrt** Gwynd
76 E5 **Cwrt-newydd** Cerdgn
61 K4 **Cwrt-y-gollen** Powys
94 E2 **Cyfronydd** Powys
42 C3 **Cymer** Neath
42 F3 **Cymmer** Rhondd
77 M7 **Cynghordy** Carmth
56 E3 **Cynheidre** Carmth
42 C3 **Cynonville** Neath
111 K3 **Cynwyd** Denbgs
58 C3 **Cynwyl Elfed** Carmth

D

8 D1 **Daccombe** Devon
166 B5 **Dacre** Cumb
150 B4 **Dacre** N York
150 B3 **Dacre Banks** N York
167 K3 **Daddry Shield** Dur
84 C7 **Dadford** Bucks
99 L4 **Dadlington** Leics
56 F4 **Dafen** Carmth
105 J2 **Daffy Green** Norfk
52 B2 **Dagenham** Gt Lon
64 E6 **Daglingworth** Gloucs
68 C4 **Dagnall** Bucks
89 L3 **Dagworth** Suffk
183 H3 **Dailly** S Ayrs
8 C2 **Dainton** Devon
223 G4 **Dairsie** Fife
139 K6 **Daisy Hill** Bolton
141 L2 **Daisy Hill** Leeds
283 b11 **Dalabrog** W Isls
216 F5 **Dalavich** Ag & B
175 L3 **Dalbeattie** D & G
115 M5 **Dalbury** Derbys
154 b6 **Dalby** IOM
137 H5 **Dalby** Lincs
151 K2 **Dalby** N York
232 E4 **Dalcapon** P & K
274 B6 **Dalchalm** Highld
240 A1 **Dalchreichart** Highld
220 C4 **Dalchruin** P & K
221 J2 **Dalcrue** P & K
136 E6 **Dalderby** Lincs
14 B6 **Dalditch** Devon
166 D2 **Dale** Cumb
116 D4 **Dale** Derbys
54 C5 **Dale** Pembks
165 J6 **Dale Bottom** Cumb
132 D7 **Dale End** Derbys
149 G6 **Dale End** N York
39 H7 **Dale Hill** E Susx
171 H7 **Dalehouse** N York
196 B2 **Dalgarven** N Ayrs
211 G2 **Dalgety Bay** Fife
197 G8 **Dalgig** E Ayrs
220 D3 **Dalginross** P & K
232 E6 **Dalguise** P & K
278 F5 **Dalhalvaig** Highld
88 E3 **Dalham** Suffk
283 b11 **Daliburgh** W Isls
211 K5 **Dalkeith** Mdloth
266 C5 **Dallas** Moray
91 G4 **Dallinghoo** Suffk
24 B3 **Dallington** E Susx
84 E3 **Dallington** Nhants
150 B2 **Dallow** N York
217 K2 **Dalmally** Ag & B
219 H8 **Dalmary** Stirlg
184 D2 **Dalmellington** E Ayrs
210 F3 **Dalmeny** C Edin
252 D7 **Dalmigavie** Highld
252 E7 **Dalmigavie Lodge** Highld
263 H6 **Dalmore** Highld
208 E5 **Dalmuir** W Duns
237 K6 **Dalnabreck** Highld
231 K1 **Dalnacardoch** P & K
252 F7 **Dalnahaitnach** Highld
231 J1 **Dalnaspidal** P & K
279 H8 **Dalnawillan Lodge** Highld
231 L4 **Daloist** P & K
221 K6 **Dalqueich** P & K

183 J4 **Dalquhairn** S Ayrs
273 H6 **Dalreavoch Lodge** Highld
196 B1 **Dalry** N Ayrs
196 B8 **Dalrymple** E Ayrs
198 C3 **Dalserf** S Lans
192 D5 **Dalsmeran** Ag & B
165 L1 **Dalston** Cumb
51 J2 **Dalston** Gt Lon
176 B2 **Dalswinton** D & G
157 H7 **Dalton** Cumb
176 F4 **Dalton** D & G
139 G6 **Dalton** Lancs
159 K1 **Dalton** N York
160 F7 **Dalton** N York
180 D4 **Dalton** Nthumb
133 J1 **Dalton** Rothm
133 J1 **Dalton Magna** Rothm
133 J1 **Dalton Parva** Rothm
170 B4 **Dalton Piercy** Hartpl
156 B7 **Dalton-in-Furness** Cumb
169 L1 **Dalton-le-Dale** Dur
160 D1 **Dalton-on-Tees** N York
186 C5 **Dalveen** D & G
219 K2 **Dalveich** Stirlg
241 H6 **Dalwhinnie** Highld
14 F2 **Dalwood** Devon
105 L6 **Dam Green** Norfk
69 H1 **Damask Green** Herts
33 J7 **Damerham** Hants
107 H2 **Damgate** Norfk
53 J6 **Danaway** Kent
71 J6 **Danbury** Essex
162 C1 **Danby** N York
162 B2 **Danby Bottom** N York
160 E3 **Danby Wiske** N York
254 F3 **Dandaleith** Moray
211 J5 **Danderhall** Mdloth
69 J3 **Dane End** Herts
100 C3 **Dane Hills** C Leic
40 D5 **Dane Street** Kent
131 J6 **Danebridge** Ches
38 E6 **Danegate** E Susx
22 F2 **Danehill** E Susx
105 L2 **Danemoor Green** Norfk
97 G5 **Danesford** Shrops
133 H7 **Danesmoor** Derbys
40 C7 **Daniel's Water** Kent
268 C5 **Danshillock** Abers
212 C5 **Danskine** E Loth
145 H1 **Danthorpe** E R Yk
82 D2 **Danzey Green** Warwks
115 G6 **Dapple Heath** Staffs
49 K7 **Darby Green** Hants
139 L6 **Darcy Lever** Bolton
61 K3 **Dardy** Powys
61 K4 **Daren-felen** Mons
52 C5 **Darenth** Kent
130 B3 **Daresbury** Halton
142 C6 **Darfield** Barns
133 L4 **Darfoulds** Notts
40 E3 **Dargate** Kent
6 B1 **Darite** Cnwll
53 G6 **Darland** Medway
129 J8 **Darland** Wrexhm
114 D4 **Darlaston** Staffs
98 B4 **Darlaston** Wsall
98 B4 **Darlaston Green** Wsall
150 B4 **Darley** N York
116 B4 **Darley Abbey** C Derb
132 E7 **Darley Bridge** Derbys
132 E7 **Darley Dale** Derbys
98 F8 **Darley Green** Solhll
150 B4 **Darley Head** N York
68 F3 **Darleyhall** Herts
82 F6 **Darlingscott** Warwks
169 H7 **Darlington** Darltn
113 J5 **Darliston** Shrops
134 F5 **Darlton** Notts
98 E2 **Darnford** Staffs
201 H6 **Darnick** Border
93 H3 **Darowen** Powys
268 D6 **Darra** Abers
26 D8 **Darracott** Cnwll
26 D7 **Darracott** Devon
27 H3 **Darracott** Devon
180 E5 **Darras Hall** Nthumb
142 D4 **Darrington** Wakefd
91 K1 **Darsham** Suffk
31 K2 **Darshill** Somset
52 B4 **Dartford** Kent
8 B2 **Dartington** Devon
12 F7 **Dartmeet** Devon
8 C4 **Dartmouth** Devon
141 M5 **Darton** Barns
197 H3 **Darvel** E Ayrs

24 C3 **Darwell Hole** E Susx
139 K3 **Darwen** Bl w D
50 C3 **Datchet** W & M
69 H3 **Datchworth** Herts
69 H3 **Datchworth Green** Herts
139 L6 **Daubhill** Bolton
46 E3 **Dauntsey** Wilts
253 J4 **Dava** Highld
130 C5 **Davenham** Ches
131 H2 **Davenport** Stockp
131 G4 **Davenport Green** Ches
130 F2 **Davenport Green** Traffd
84 B3 **Daventry** Nhants
52 E6 **David Street** Kent
211 H4 **Davidson's Mains** C Edin
11 G5 **Davidstow** Cnwll
187 K5 **Davington** D & G
40 D3 **Davington Hill** Kent
256 D6 **Daviot** Abers
252 D4 **Daviot** Highld
252 D4 **Daviot House** Highld
23 J4 **Davis's Town** E Susx
267 K6 **Davoch of Grange** Moray
139 M8 **Davyhulme** Traffd
98 C3 **Daw End** Wsall
11 K6 **Daw's House** Cnwll
37 K2 **Dawesgreen** Surrey
96 F2 **Dawley** Wrekin
13 M7 **Dawlish** Devon
14 A6 **Dawlish Warren** Devon
127 G5 **Dawn** Conwy
30 B6 **Daws Green** Somset
53 H1 **Daws Heath** Essex
120 A5 **Dawsmere** Lincs
130 F8 **Day Green** Ches
116 F3 **Daybrook** Notts
114 F5 **Dayhills** Staffs
98 B7 **Dayhouse Bank** Worcs
65 K2 **Daylesford** Gloucs
128 D5 **Ddol** Flints
111 K8 **Ddol-Cownwy** Powys
41 L5 **Deal** Kent
164 E5 **Dean** Cumb
27 L2 **Dean** Devon
28 C1 **Dean** Devon
7 L2 **Dean** Devon
33 G7 **Dean** Dorset
34 F4 **Dean** Hants
35 H7 **Dean** Hants
140 C3 **Dean** Lancs
65 M3 **Dean** Oxon
31 L2 **Dean** Somset
52 C5 **Dean Bottom** Kent
66 C6 **Dean Court** Oxon
33 G7 **Dean End** Dorset
141 L7 **Dean Head** Barns
7 L2 **Dean Prior** Devon
131 G3 **Dean Row** Ches
39 J3 **Dean Street** Kent
188 C4 **Deanburnhaugh** Border
7 L2 **Deancombe** Devon
139 K6 **Deane** Bolton
35 H1 **Deane** Hants
141 G4 **Deanhead** Kirk
33 G7 **Deanland** Dorset
20 B4 **Deanlane End** W Susx
179 J6 **Deanraw** Nthumb
210 D5 **Deans** W Loth
164 E5 **Deanscales** Cumb
84 E7 **Deanshanger** Nhants
267 G6 **Deanshaugh** Moray
220 C6 **Deanston** Stirlg
164 E3 **Dearham** Cumb
140 D4 **Dearnley** Rochdl
90 F4 **Debach** Suffk
87 L8 **Debden** Essex
70 C7 **Debden** Essex
70 E1 **Debden Green** Essex
90 E3 **Debenham** Suffk
81 J5 **Deblin's Green** Worcs
210 D5 **Dechmont** W Loth
210 D5 **Dechmont Road** W Loth
66 C1 **Deddington** Oxon
90 C8 **Dedham** Essex
72 F1 **Dedham Heath** Essex
50 B4 **Dedworth** W & M
101 L5 **Deene** Nhants
101 L5 **Deenethorpe** Nhants
141 L8 **Deepcar** Sheff
49 L7 **Deepcut** Surrey
158 C5 **Deepdale** Cumb
158 F6 **Deepdale** N York
102 C2 **Deeping Gate** C Pete
102 D2 **Deeping St James** Lincs
119 H8 **Deeping St Nicholas** Lincs

64 C1 **Deerhurst** Gloucs
64 C2 **Deerhurst Walton** Gloucs
40 C3 **Deerton Street** Kent
81 L6 **Defford** Worcs
60 D2 **Defynnog** Powys
126 F4 **Deganwy** Conwy
216 B5 **Degnish** Ag & B
160 E2 **Deighton** N York
151 K7 **Deighton** York
125 K7 **Deiniolen** Gwynd
10 F5 **Delabole** Cnwll
130 A6 **Delamere** Ches
257 H7 **Delfrigs** Abers
20 D6 **Dell Quay** W Susx
27 K6 **Delley** Devon
253 L5 **Delliefure** Highld
65 M4 **Delly End** Oxon
39 J7 **Delmonden Green** Kent
254 D4 **Delnashaugh Inn** Moray
263 K5 **Delny** Highld
140 E6 **Delph** Oldham
168 E1 **Delves** Dur
233 H7 **Delvine** P & K
118 D4 **Dembleby** Lincs
5 G2 **Demelza** Cnwll
222 D4 **Den of Lindores** Fife
142 D7 **Denaby** Donc
142 D7 **Denaby Main** Donc
37 H1 **Denbies** Surrey
128 C6 **Denbigh** Denbgs
222 F3 **Denbrae** Fife
8 B1 **Denbury** Devon
116 C2 **Denby** Derbys
116 C2 **Denby Bottles** Derbys
141 K6 **Denby Dale** Kirk
48 A1 **Denchworth** Oxon
146 E2 **Dendron** Cumb
85 K8 **Denel End** Beds
221 G4 **Denfield** P & K
101 L8 **Denford** Nhants
72 E6 **Dengie** Essex
50 D2 **Denham** Bucks
88 E3 **Denham** Suffk
106 D8 **Denham** Suffk
88 F3 **Denham End** Suffk
50 D1 **Denham Green** Bucks
106 D8 **Denham Green** Suffk
269 J5 **Denhead** Abers
223 H4 **Denhead** Fife
222 F1 **Denhead of Gray** C Dund
189 G3 **Denholm** Border
141 G1 **Denholme** Brad
141 G1 **Denholme Clough** Brad
108 F4 **Denio** Gwynd
19 L1 **Denmead** Hants
245 L1 **Denmore** C Aber
37 J5 **Denne Park** W Susx
91 G2 **Dennington** Suffk
209 L3 **Denny** Falk
209 L3 **Dennyloanhead** Falk
140 E5 **Denshaw** Oldham
245 H4 **Denside** Abers
41 G7 **Densole** Kent
88 F5 **Denston** Suffk
115 H3 **Denstone** Staffs
40 E3 **Denstroude** Kent
158 B5 **Dent** Cumb
102 C6 **Denton** Cambs
169 G7 **Denton** Darltn
23 G6 **Denton** E Susx
52 E4 **Denton** Kent
41 G6 **Denton** Kent
117 M5 **Denton** Lincs
149 L6 **Denton** N York
85 G4 **Denton** Nhants
106 F5 **Denton** Norfk
66 E6 **Denton** Oxon
131 H1 **Denton** Tamesd
104 C3 **Denver** Norfk
191 J3 **Denwick** Nthumb
105 L3 **Deopham** Norfk
105 L4 **Deopham Green** Norfk
88 F4 **Depden** Suffk
88 F4 **Depden Green** Suffk
51 K3 **Deptford** Gt Lon
33 H3 **Deptford** Wilts
116 B4 **Derby** C Derb
27 K4 **Derby** Devon
154 C8 **Derbyhaven** IOM
232 C5 **Derculich** P & K
105 K1 **Dereham** Norfk
61 H6 **Deri** Caerph
11 K2 **Derril** Devon
41 G5 **Derringstone** Kent
114 D7 **Derrington** Staffs

11 L2 **Derriton** Devon
46 D5 **Derry Hill** Wilts
143 L6 **Derrythorpe** N Linc
120 F5 **Dersingham** Norfk
226 E2 **Dervaig** Ag & B
111 L2 **Derwen** Denbgs
59 G4 **Derwen Fawr** Carmth
92 F4 **Derwenlas** Powys
59 H5 **Derwydd** Carmth
101 H6 **Desborough** Nhants
100 B3 **Desford** Leics
267 K4 **Deskford** Moray
203 H6 **Detchant** Nthumb
53 G7 **Detling** Kent
96 F6 **Deuxhill** Shrops
62 F7 **Devauden** Mons
92 F8 **Devil's Bridge** Cerdgn
6 C4 **Deviock** Cnwll
99 H5 **Devitts Green** Warwks
46 E6 **Devizes** Wilts
6 E4 **Devonport** C Plym
221 G7 **Devonside** Clacks
3 K3 **Devoran** Cnwll
211 L6 **Dewarton** Mdloth
16 E3 **Dewlish** Dorset
141 K3 **Dewsbury** Kirk
141 K3 **Dewsbury Moor** Kirk
112 C8 **Deytheur** Powys
45 G5 **Dial** N Som
36 D5 **Dial Green** W Susx
139 M2 **Dial Hall** Lancs
21 K3 **Dial Post** W Susx
15 K2 **Dibberford** Dorset
18 F2 **Dibden** Hants
18 F2 **Dibden Purlieu** Hants
98 E8 **Dickens Heath** Solhll
106 D7 **Dickleburgh** Norfk
64 F1 **Didbrook** Gloucs
48 D1 **Didcot** Oxon
86 D2 **Diddington** Cambs
96 C6 **Diddlebury** Shrops
62 F1 **Didley** Herefs
20 D3 **Didling** W Susx
46 B2 **Didmarton** Gloucs
131 G1 **Didsbury** Manch
7 K2 **Didworthy** Devon
135 M8 **Digby** Lincs
259 H3 **Digg** Highld
140 F6 **Diggle** Oldham
139 G6 **Digmoor** Lancs
69 H4 **Digswell** Herts
69 H4 **Digswell Water** Herts
76 E4 **Dihewyd** Cerdgn
123 G6 **Dilham** Norfk
114 F3 **Dilhorne** Staffs
86 C2 **Dillington** Cambs
180 A6 **Dilston** Nthumb
32 E1 **Dilton** Wilts
32 D1 **Dilton Marsh** Wilts
80 A4 **Dilwyn** Herefs
139 L4 **Dimple** Bolton
132 F7 **Dimple** Derbys
58 A3 **Dinas** Carmth
10 C7 **Dinas** Cnwll
108 D4 **Dinas** Gwynd
75 G4 **Dinas** Pembks
42 F3 **Dinas** Rhondd
125 H8 **Dinas Dinlle** Gwynd
43 J7 **Dinas Powys** V Glam
111 G8 **Dinas-Mawddwy** Gwynd
31 J2 **Dinder** Somset
80 C7 **Dinedor** Herefs
62 F5 **Dingestow** Mons
129 J2 **Dingle** Lpool
39 K7 **Dingleden** Kent
101 G6 **Dingley** Nhants
262 F8 **Dingwall** Highld
62 F8 **Dinham** Mons
111 J3 **Dinmael** Conwy
244 A4 **Dinnet** Abers
180 F4 **Dinnington** N u Ty
133 K3 **Dinnington** Rothm
30 F8 **Dinnington** Somset
125 L7 **Dinorwic** Gwynd
67 J5 **Dinton** Bucks
33 H4 **Dinton** Wilts
187 H8 **Dinwoodie** D & G
26 E7 **Dinworthy** Devon
30 B6 **Dipford** Somset
49 H7 **Dipley** Hants
194 B3 **Dippen** Ag & B
195 G6 **Dippen** N Ayrs
36 B2 **Dippenhall** Surrey
12 B1 **Dippermill** Devon
12 B5 **Dippertown** Devon

267 G4 **Dipple** Moray
182 F2 **Dipple** S Ayrs
7 L3 **Diptford** Devon
180 E8 **Dipton** Dur
179 L6 **Diptonmill** Nthumb
212 B2 **Dirleton** E Loth
167 K2 **Dirt Pot** Nthumb
79 K2 **Discoed** Powys
116 D6 **Diseworth** Leics
160 E8 **Dishforth** N York
131 J3 **Disley** Ches
106 C7 **Diss** Norfk
78 E4 **Disserth** Powys
164 D6 **Distington** Cumb
33 J4 **Ditchampton** Wilts
191 G2 **Ditchburn** Nthumb
31 K4 **Ditcheat** Somset
107 G5 **Ditchingham** Norfk
66 A3 **Ditchley** Oxon
22 E4 **Ditchling** E Susx
113 H8 **Ditherington** Shrops
46 B5 **Ditteridge** Wilts
8 C4 **Dittisham** Devon
129 L2 **Ditton** Halton
52 F7 **Ditton** Kent
88 D4 **Ditton Green** Cambs
96 E5 **Ditton Priors** Shrops
64 E1 **Dixton** Gloucs
63 G4 **Dixton** Mons
11 H3 **Dizzard** Cnwll
140 F6 **Dobcross** Oldham
140 D3 **Dobroyd Castle** Calder
5 L2 **Dobwalls** Cnwll
13 H5 **Doccombe** Devon
251 H3 **Dochgarroch** Highld
36 B3 **Dockenfield** Surrey
157 J7 **Docker** Lancs
121 G4 **Docking** Norfk
80 D4 **Docklow** Herefs
165 J1 **Dockray** Cumb
165 L6 **Dockray** Cumb
115 G4 **Dod's Leigh** Staffs
7 L6 **Dodbrooke** Devon
113 K3 **Dodd's Green** Ches
70 E7 **Doddinghurst** Essex
103 H5 **Doddington** Cambs
40 B4 **Doddington** Kent
135 H5 **Doddington** Lincs
202 F6 **Doddington** Nthumb
96 E8 **Doddington** Shrops
13 K5 **Doddiscombsleigh** Devon
120 F5 **Doddshill** Norfk
6 C2 **Doddy Cross** Cnwll
84 B3 **Dodford** Nhants
97 L8 **Dodford** Worcs
45 L3 **Dodington** S Glos
30 A3 **Dodington** Somset
129 J7 **Dodleston** Ches
27 K7 **Dodscott** Devon
208 E8 **Dodside** E Rens
141 M6 **Dodworth** Barns
141 M7 **Dodworth Bottom** Barns
141 M6 **Dodworth Green** Barns
98 E4 **Doe Bank** Birm
133 J6 **Doe Lea** Derbys
14 A3 **Dog Village** Devon
136 D8 **Dogdyke** Lincs
141 J5 **Dogley Lane** Kirk
49 J8 **Dogmersfield** Hants
47 G2 **Dogridge** Wilts
102 D3 **Dogsthorpe** C Pete
93 H2 **Dol-for** Powys
58 D2 **Dol-gran** Carmth
94 C1 **Dolanog** Powys
79 G2 **Dolau** Powys
77 J7 **Dolaucothi** Carmth
109 J3 **Dolbenmaen** Gwynd
114 A5 **Doley** Shrops
93 K3 **Dolfach** Powys
94 D6 **Dolfor** Powys
126 F6 **Dolgarrog** Conwy
110 D7 **Dolgellau** Gwynd
92 E3 **Dolgoch** Gwynd
273 L7 **Doll** Highld
221 G7 **Dollar** Clacks
221 G7 **Dollarfield** Clacks
79 K2 **Dolley Green** Powys
92 E7 **Dollwen** Cerdgn
128 E5 **Dolphin** Flints
147 K5 **Dolphinholme** Lancs
199 J4 **Dolphinton** S Lans
27 K8 **Dolton** Devon
127 H5 **Dolwen** Conwy
110 D1 **Dolwyddelan** Conwy
92 D5 **Dolybont** Cerdgn

79 J4	**Dolyhir** Powys
112 D7	**Domgay** Powys
202 D5	**Donaldson's Lodge** Nthumb
142 F7	**Doncaster** Donc
142 F7	**Doncaster Carr** Donc
32 F6	**Donhead St Andrew** Wilts
32 F6	**Donhead St Mary** Wilts
211 G1	**Donibristle** Fife
29 K2	**Doniford** Somset
119 H4	**Donington** Lincs
136 D3	**Donington on Bain** Lincs
119 G5	**Donington Southing** Lincs
99 J1	**Donisthorpe** Leics
25 L1	**Donkey Street** Kent
50 B6	**Donkey Town** Surrey
65 J2	**Donnington** Gloucs
81 G8	**Donnington** Herefs
96 D2	**Donnington** Shrops
48 C5	**Donnington** W Berk
20 D6	**Donnington** W Susx
113 M8	**Donnington** Wrekin
97 G1	**Donnington Wood** Wrekin
30 E8	**Donyatt** Somset
37 J5	**Doomsday Green** W Susx
196 C7	**Doonfoot** S Ayrs
196 C7	**Doonholm** S Ayrs
253 L8	**Dorback Lodge** Highld
16 D4	**Dorchester** Dorset
66 E8	**Dorchester** Oxon
99 H3	**Dordon** Warwks
132 F3	**Dore** Sheff
251 G5	**Dores** Highld
37 J1	**Dorking** Surrey
89 J7	**Dorking Tye** Suffk
38 B5	**Dormans Land** Surrey
38 B5	**Dormans Park** Surrey
80 D7	**Dormington** Herefs
82 A4	**Dormston** Worcs
82 F8	**Dorn** Gloucs
50 B3	**Dorney** Bucks
248 D6	**Dornie** Highld
264 B2	**Dornoch** Highld
177 H5	**Dornock** D & G
279 J5	**Dorrery** Highld
98 F8	**Dorridge** Solhll
118 E1	**Dorrington** Lincs
96 B3	**Dorrington** Shrops
114 A3	**Dorrington** Shrops
82 D5	**Dorsington** Warwks
79 K7	**Dorstone** Herefs
67 G4	**Dorton** Bucks
99 G3	**Dosthill** Staffs
15 K3	**Dottery** Dorset
5 L2	**Doublebois** Cnwll
46 C1	**Doughton** Gloucs
154 e6	**Douglas** IOM
198 D7	**Douglas** S Lans
234 C8	**Douglas and Angus** C Dund
198 D6	**Douglas Castle** S Lans
217 K7	**Douglas Pier** Ag & B
198 E6	**Douglas Water** S Lans
198 D6	**Douglas West** S Lans
234 B6	**Douglastown** Angus
31 L2	**Doulting** Somset
275 b4	**Dounby** Ork
272 B7	**Doune** Highld
220 C6	**Doune** Stirlg
182 F3	**Dounepark** S Ayrs
263 G2	**Dounie** Highld
7 G1	**Dousland** Devon
112 E7	**Dovaston** Shrops
116 D1	**Dove Green** Notts
131 L4	**Dove Holes** Derbys
164 E4	**Dovenby** Cumb
41 K7	**Dover** Kent
139 J7	**Dover** Wigan
73 K1	**Dovercourt** Essex
81 K2	**Doverdale** Worcs
115 J5	**Doveridge** Derbys
37 L1	**Doversgreen** Surrey
232 F5	**Dowally** P & K
138 E2	**Dowbridge** Lancs
64 E3	**Dowdeswell** Gloucs
61 G5	**Dowlais** Myr Td
12 D1	**Dowland** Devon
30 E8	**Dowlish Ford** Somset
30 E8	**Dowlish Wake** Somset
65 G7	**Down Ampney** Gloucs
64 C3	**Down Hatherley** Gloucs
13 H2	**Down St Mary** Devon
6 F5	**Down Thomas** Devon
11 M4	**Downacarey** Devon
6 C4	**Downderry** Cnwll
51 L6	**Downe** Gt Lon
64 B7	**Downend** Gloucs
19 J6	**Downend** IOW
45 K3	**Downend** S Glos
48 C4	**Downend** W Berk
223 G1	**Downfield** C Dund
11 K8	**Downgate** Cnwll
11 L7	**Downgate** Cnwll
71 H7	**Downham** Essex
51 K4	**Downham** Gt Lon
148 D7	**Downham** Lancs
202 D6	**Downham** Nthumb
104 C3	**Downham Market** Norfk
31 J6	**Downhead** Somset
32 A2	**Downhead** Somset
4 D1	**Downhill** Cnwll
221 K1	**Downhill** P & K
138 D6	**Downholland Cross** Lancs
159 K3	**Downholme** N York
245 K4	**Downies** Abers
128 D4	**Downing** Flints
67 K8	**Downley** Bucks
31 K2	**Downside** Somset
31 L1	**Downside** Somset
50 E7	**Downside** Surrey
18 D5	**Downton** Hants
33 L6	**Downton** Wilts
95 K8	**Downton on the Rock** Herefs
118 F5	**Dowsby** Lincs
102 F2	**Dowsdale** Lincs
72 C2	**Dowsland Green** Essex
114 D6	**Doxey** Staffs
191 H2	**Doxford** Nthumb
45 L4	**Doynton** S Glos
43 K4	**Draethen** Caerph
198 C4	**Draffan** S Lans
143 M5	**Dragonby** N Linc
37 H6	**Dragons Green** W Susx
134 E2	**Drakeholes** Notts
97 J7	**Drakelow** Worcs
196 B3	**Drakemyre** N Ayrs
81 L5	**Drakes Broughton** Worcs
12 B8	**Drakewalls** Cnwll
149 J5	**Draughton** N York
101 G8	**Draughton** Nhants
143 H3	**Drax** N York
143 H3	**Drax Hales** N York
47 J3	**Draycot Foliat** Swindn
83 K1	**Draycote** Warwks
116 D5	**Draycott** Derbys
82 E8	**Draycott** Gloucs
97 H5	**Draycott** Shrops
31 G1	**Draycott** Somset
31 J6	**Draycott** Somset
81 K5	**Draycott** Worcs
115 J6	**Draycott in the Clay** Staffs
114 F3	**Draycott in the Moors** Staffs
28 D8	**Drayford** Devon
5 L1	**Draynes** Cnwll
19 L3	**Drayton** C Port
101 H5	**Drayton** Leics
119 H4	**Drayton** Lincs
106 D1	**Drayton** Norfk
83 K7	**Drayton** Oxon
66 C8	**Drayton** Oxon
30 F6	**Drayton** Somset
97 K8	**Drayton** Worcs
99 G3	**Drayton Bassett** Staffs
67 L5	**Drayton Beauchamp** Bucks
67 K2	**Drayton Parslow** Bucks
66 E7	**Drayton St Leonard** Oxon
149 J4	**Drebley** N York
154 g4	**Dreemskerry** IOM
54 F4	**Dreen Hill** Pembks
76 C7	**Drefach** Carmth
58 F6	**Drefach** Carmth
76 F6	**Drefach** Cerdgn
76 C7	**Drefelin** Carmth
196 C3	**Dreghorn** N Ayrs
41 H7	**Drellingore** Kent
212 B3	**Drem** E Loth
114 E3	**Dresden** C Stke
13 H4	**Drewsteignton** Devon
137 G5	**Driby** Lincs
152 F4	**Driffield** E R Yk
65 G7	**Driffield** Gloucs
64 F7	**Driffield Cross Roads** Gloucs
2 C5	**Drift** Cnwll
155 K3	**Drigg** Cumb
141 K2	**Drighlington** Leeds
227 G2	**Drimnin** Highld
15 K2	**Drimpton** Dorset
238 F7	**Drimsallie** Highld
153 J5	**Dringhoe** E R Yk
151 J6	**Dringhouses** N York
89 H3	**Drinkstone** Suffk
89 J3	**Drinkstone Green** Suffk
135 H5	**Drinsey Nook** Notts
16 B1	**Drive End** Dorset
69 G3	**Driver's End** Herts
115 G6	**Drointon** Staffs
81 K3	**Droitwich** Worcs
221 L4	**Dron** P & K
133 G4	**Dronfield** Derbys
133 G4	**Dronfield Woodhouse** Derbys
196 E7	**Drongan** E Ayrs
234 A8	**Dronley** Angus
16 E1	**Droop** Dorset
35 J7	**Droxford** Hants
140 D8	**Droylsden** Tamesd
111 K3	**Druid** Denbgs
54 E3	**Druidston** Pembks
229 J6	**Druimachoish** Highld
229 H1	**Druimarbin** Highld
206 A5	**Druimdrishaig** Ag & B
237 K4	**Druimindarroch** Highld
206 E4	**Drum** Ag & B
221 J7	**Drum** P & K
198 F5	**Drumalbin** S Lans
270 F2	**Drumbeg** Highld
255 M4	**Drumblade** Abers
172 D6	**Drumbreddon** D & G
248 B5	**Drumbuie** Highld
177 J7	**Drumburgh** Cumb
175 L4	**Drumburn** D & G
208 E5	**Drumchapel** C Glas
231 J4	**Drumchastle** P & K
197 J3	**Drumclog** S Lans
223 G6	**Drumeldrie** Fife
199 K6	**Drumelzier** Border
247 L5	**Drumfearn** Highld
244 F4	**Drumfrennie** Abers
241 L3	**Drumguish** Highld
244 D5	**Drumhead** Abers
254 D5	**Drumin** Moray
184 E3	**Drumjohn** D & G
183 H7	**Drumlamford** S Ayrs
244 E2	**Drumlasie** Abers
177 J8	**Drumleaning** Cumb
192 D4	**Drumlemble** Ag & B
245 H7	**Drumlithie** Abers
173 K6	**Drummoddie** D & G
172 E7	**Drummore** D & G
255 H3	**Drummuir** Moray
250 E5	**Drumnadrochit** Highld
267 L5	**Drumnagorrach** Moray
185 L7	**Drumpark** D & G
271 G7	**Drumrunie Lodge** Highld
195 L8	**Drumshang** S Ayrs
259 G7	**Drumuie** Highld
253 H7	**Drumuillie** Highld
220 B6	**Drumvaich** Stirlg
221 L5	**Drunzie** P & K
191 K7	**Druridge** Nthumb
129 G6	**Drury** Flints
117 M2	**Dry Doddington** Lincs
87 H3	**Dry Drayton** Cambs
66 C7	**Dry Sandford** Oxon
52 E2	**Dry Street** Essex
166 F7	**Drybeck** Cumb
267 J4	**Drybridge** Moray
196 D4	**Drybridge** N Ayrs
63 J4	**Drybrook** Gloucs
201 J6	**Dryburgh** Border
3 G4	**Drym** Cnwll
208 E1	**Drymen** Stirlg
257 G3	**Drymuir** Abers
246 F2	**Drynoch** Highld
59 G5	**Dryslwyn** Carmth
96 D2	**Dryton** Shrops
268 E3	**Dubford** Abers
90 E1	**Dublin** Suffk
271 L4	**Duchally** Highld
85 L6	**Duck End** Beds
86 E2	**Duck End** Cambs
71 G2	**Duck End** Essex
88 D8	**Duck End** Essex
86 C4	**Duck's Cross** Beds
71 H3	**Duckend Green** Essex
113 H1	**Duckington** Ches
65 M5	**Ducklington** Oxon
87 J7	**Duddenhoe End** Essex
211 J4	**Duddingston** C Edin
101 L3	**Duddington** Nhants
30 C6	**Duddlestone** Somset
38 C7	**Duddleswell** E Susx
96 F6	**Duddlewick** Shrops
202 E4	**Duddo** Nthumb
129 L6	**Duddon** Ches
156 B5	**Duddon Bridge** Cumb
112 E4	**Dudleston** Shrops
112 E4	**Dudleston Heath** Shrops
97 L5	**Dudley** Dudley
181 G4	**Dudley** N Tyne
141 J2	**Dudley Hill** Brad
98 B5	**Dudley Port** Sandw
96 E8	**Dudnill** Shrops
17 L3	**Dudsbury** Dorset
68 B5	**Dudswell** Herts
116 B3	**Duffield** Derbys
42 C3	**Duffryn** Neath
255 G4	**Dufftown** Moray
266 D3	**Duffus** Moray
166 F5	**Dufton** Cumb
152 D2	**Duggleby** N York
248 C5	**Duirinish** Highld
247 L6	**Duisdalemore** Highld
239 G8	**Duisky** Highld
90 C6	**Duke Street** Suffk
61 J5	**Dukestown** Blae G
140 E8	**Dukinfield** Tamesd
125 H2	**Dulas** IOA
31 J2	**Dulcote** Somset
14 C1	**Dulford** Devon
232 B5	**Dull** P & K
209 K4	**Dullatur** N Lans
88 C4	**Dullingham** Cambs
88 C4	**Dullingham Ley** Cambs
253 J6	**Dulnain Bridge** Highld
86 D3	**Duloe** Beds
5 M3	**Duloe** Cnwll
29 G5	**Dulverton** Somset
51 J4	**Dulwich** Gt Lon
208 C4	**Dumbarton** W Duns
82 B8	**Dumbleton** Gloucs
176 C4	**Dumfries** D & G
208 E2	**Dumgoyne** Stirlg
35 J2	**Dummer** Hants
41 L2	**Dumpton** Kent
235 G3	**Dun** Angus
231 K4	**Dunalastair** P & K
207 J5	**Dunan** Ag & B
247 J3	**Dunan** Highld
230 E4	**Dunan** P & K
192 E6	**Dunaverty** Ag & B
30 D3	**Dunball** Somset
212 E3	**Dunbar** E Loth
275 G2	**Dunbeath** Highld
228 D8	**Dunbeg** Ag & B
220 D7	**Dunblane** Stirlg
222 D4	**Dunbog** Fife
34 D5	**Dunbridge** Hants
263 G8	**Duncanston** Highld
255 M6	**Duncanstone** Abers
13 K5	**Dunchideock** Devon
83 L1	**Dunchurch** Warwks
84 C5	**Duncote** Nhants
176 C2	**Duncow** D & G
221 L5	**Duncrievie** P & K
20 F3	**Duncton** W Susx
223 G1	**Dundee** C Dund
31 G4	**Dundon** Somset
196 D4	**Dundonald** S Ayrs
261 J2	**Dundonnell** Highld
165 H1	**Dundraw** Cumb
240 B1	**Dundreggan** Highld
175 J5	**Dundrennan** D & G
45 H5	**Dundry** N Som
245 G2	**Dunecht** Abers
210 E2	**Dunfermline** Fife
65 H7	**Dunfield** Gloucs
141 J7	**Dunford Bridge** Barns
40 B3	**Dungate** Kent
197 J3	**Dungavel** S Lans
46 C8	**Dunge** Wilts
132 E2	**Dungworth** Sheff
135 G5	**Dunham** Notts
130 E2	**Dunham Town** Traffd
130 E2	**Dunham Woodhouses** Traffd
129 L5	**Dunham-on-the-Hill** Ches
81 L3	**Dunhampstead** Worcs
81 J2	**Dunhampton** Worcs
135 L4	**Dunholme** Lincs
223 J5	**Dunino** Fife
209 L2	**Dunipace** Falk
38 F3	**Dunk's Green** Kent
232 F6	**Dunkeld** P & K
45 L7	**Dunkerton** BaNES
14 D1	**Dunkeswell** Devon
150 D6	**Dunkeswick** N York
129 J5	**Dunkirk** Ches
40 E3	**Dunkirk** Kent
46 A2	**Dunkirk** S Glos
114 C1	**Dunkirk** Staffs
46 E6	**Dunkirk** Wilts
234 F2	**Dunlappie** Angus

48 C8 **Dunley** Hants
81 H2 **Dunley** Worcs
196 E1 **Dunlop** E Ayrs
251 G7 **Dunmaglass** Highld
5 H1 **Dunmere** Cnwll
210 A1 **Dunmore** Falk
53 G6 **Dunn Street** Kent
280 B2 **Dunnet** Highld
234 D5 **Dunnichen** Angus
221 J4 **Dunning** P & K
153 J5 **Dunnington** E R Yk
82 C4 **Dunnington** Warwks
151 L5 **Dunnington** York
140 B2 **Dunnockshaw** Lancs
207 K4 **Dunoon** Ag & B
253 J2 **Dunphail** Moray
172 E3 **Dunragit** D & G
202 B2 **Duns** Border
66 C2 **Duns Tew** Oxon
132 E5 **Dunsa** Derbys
118 E6 **Dunsby** Lincs
139 L5 **Dunscar** Bolton
185 L6 **Dunscore** D & G
143 G6 **Dunscroft** Donc
170 E6 **Dunsdale** R & Cl
49 H3 **Dunsden Green** Oxon
11 K1 **Dunsdon** Devon
36 F4 **Dunsfold** Surrey
13 J4 **Dunsford** Devon
222 D5 **Dunshalt** Fife
269 H6 **Dunshillock** Abers
133 J7 **Dunsill** Notts
171 K8 **Dunsley** N York
97 J6 **Dunsley** Staffs
67 L6 **Dunsmore** Bucks
148 B6 **Dunsop Bridge** Lancs
68 C3 **Dunstable** Beds
115 K7 **Dunstall** Staffs
81 K6 **Dunstall Common** Worcs
88 E3 **Dunstall Green** Suffk
191 K2 **Dunstan** Nthumb
191 J2 **Dunstan Steads** Nthumb
29 H2 **Dunster** Somset
180 F6 **Dunston** Gatesd
135 L7 **Dunston** Lincs
106 E3 **Dunston** Norfk
114 E8 **Dunston** Staffs
114 E8 **Dunston Heath** Staffs
7 H4 **Dunstone** Devon
13 G7 **Dunstone** Devon
143 G6 **Dunsville** Donc
144 D1 **Dunswell** E R Yk
199 J3 **Dunsyre** S Lans
11 M6 **Dunterton** Devon
65 M2 **Dunthrop** Oxon
64 E5 **Duntisbourne Abbots** Gloucs
64 E6 **Duntisbourne Rouse** Gloucs
16 D1 **Duntish** Dorset
208 E4 **Duntocher** W Duns
86 E6 **Dunton** Beds
67 K2 **Dunton** Bucks
121 J5 **Dunton** Norfk
100 C5 **Dunton Bassett** Leics
38 D2 **Dunton Green** Kent
52 E1 **Dunton Wayletts** Essex
259 G2 **Duntulm** Highld
195 L7 **Dunure** S Ayrs
57 G6 **Dunvant** Swans
258 C7 **Dunvegan** Highld
91 L1 **Dunwich** Suffk
131 J8 **Dunwood** Staffs
177 L8 **Durdar** Cumb
3 K5 **Durgan** Cnwll
169 H2 **Durham** Dur
186 C5 **Durisdeer** D & G
186 C5 **Durisdeermill** D & G
141 M4 **Durkar** Wakefd
30 C4 **Durleigh** Somset
35 G7 **Durley** Hants
47 K6 **Durley** Wilts
35 H7 **Durley Street** Hants
41 J4 **Durlock** Kent
41 J2 **Durlock** Kent
80 E7 **Durlow Common** Gloucs
234 C5 **Durmgley** Angus
140 E4 **Durn** Rochdl
276 F3 **Durness** Highld
228 F4 **Duror** Highld
216 F5 **Durran** Ag & B
21 J6 **Durrington** W Susx
33 K2 **Durrington** Wilts
245 G4 **Durris** Abers
63 M7 **Dursley** Gloucs
63 K3 **Dursley Cross** Gloucs
30 D5 **Durston** Somset

17 G1 **Durweston** Dorset
84 D3 **Duston** Nhants
253 H6 **Duthil** Highld
94 F7 **Dutlas** Powys
70 F2 **Duton Hill** Essex
11 L5 **Dutson** Cnwll
130 B4 **Dutton** Ches
87 K6 **Duxford** Cambs
66 A7 **Duxford** Oxon
126 E4 **Dwygyfylchi** Conwy
125 H6 **Dwyran** IOA
245 K1 **Dyce** C Aber
88 E7 **Dyer's End** Essex
56 E5 **Dyfatty** Carmth
110 D8 **Dyffrydan** Gwynd
42 C3 **Dyffryn** Brdgnd
61 G6 **Dyffryn** Myr Td
43 H7 **Dyffryn** V Glam
109 K7 **Dyffryn Ardudwy** Gwynd
93 G7 **Dyffryn Castell** Cerdgn
60 C5 **Dyffryn Cellwen** Neath
118 E7 **Dyke** Lincs
264 F8 **Dyke** Moray
233 K4 **Dykehead** Angus
234 B3 **Dykehead** Angus
210 A7 **Dykehead** N Lans
219 K7 **Dykehead** Stirlg
235 H2 **Dykelands** Abers
233 K4 **Dykends** Angus
256 C3 **Dykeside** Abers
93 J4 **Dylife** Powys
25 L1 **Dymchurch** Kent
63 K1 **Dymock** Gloucs
45 L4 **Dyrham** S Glos
222 E8 **Dysart** Fife
128 C4 **Dyserth** Denbgs

E

98 C8 **Eachway** Worcs
180 D4 **Eachwick** Nthumb
147 H6 **Eagland Hill** Lancs
135 H6 **Eagle** Lincs
135 H6 **Eagle Barnsdale** Lincs
135 H6 **Eagle Moor** Lincs
169 L7 **Eaglescliffe** S on T
164 E5 **Eaglesfield** Cumb
177 H4 **Eaglesfield** D & G
208 F8 **Eaglesham** E Rens
139 L5 **Eagley** Bolton
154 d6 **Eairy** IOM
84 F5 **Eakley Lanes** M Keyn
134 D7 **Eakring** Notts
143 K5 **Ealand** N Linc
50 F3 **Ealing** Gt Lon
178 F7 **Eals** Nthumb
166 C5 **Eamont Bridge** Cumb
148 F6 **Earby** Lancs
139 K3 **Earcroft** Bl w D
97 G5 **Eardington** Shrops
80 A4 **Eardisland** Herefs
79 K5 **Eardisley** Herefs
112 E6 **Eardiston** Shrops
80 F2 **Eardiston** Worcs
103 H8 **Earith** Cambs
100 A4 **Earl Shilton** Leics
90 F3 **Earl Soham** Suffk
132 B6 **Earl Sterndale** Derbys
90 D3 **Earl Stonham** Suffk
81 K6 **Earl's Croome** Worcs
23 L3 **Earl's Down** E Susx
90 B2 **Earl's Green** Suffk
202 F7 **Earle** Nthumb
130 B1 **Earlestown** St Hel
49 H4 **Earley** Wokham
106 D2 **Earlham** Norfk
258 F4 **Earlish** Highld
85 G3 **Earls Barton** Nhants
71 L1 **Earls Colne** Essex
81 M3 **Earls Common** Worcs
96 E8 **Earlsditton** Shrops
99 J7 **Earlsdon** Covtry
223 H7 **Earlsferry** Fife
51 H4 **Earlsfield** Gt Lon
256 E5 **Earlsford** Abers
141 L3 **Earlsheaton** Kirk
201 J5 **Earlston** Border
196 E4 **Earlston** E Ayrs
37 L1 **Earlswood** Surrey
98 E8 **Earlswood** Warwks
62 F8 **Earlswood Common** Mons
20 D7 **Earnley** W Susx
139 G3 **Earnshaw Bridge** Lancs
181 H4 **Earsdon** N Tyne

191 J7 **Earsdon** Nthumb
107 G5 **Earsham** Norfk
151 K4 **Earswick** York
20 F5 **Eartham** W Susx
45 K2 **Earthcott** S Glos
161 J1 **Easby** N York
215 L1 **Easdale** Ag & B
36 D6 **Easebourne** W Susx
100 A7 **Easenhall** Warwks
36 E2 **Eashing** Surrey
67 G5 **Easington** Bucks
169 L2 **Easington** Dur
145 K4 **Easington** E R Yk
203 J6 **Easington** Nthumb
67 G7 **Easington** Oxon
171 H7 **Easington** R & Cl
169 L2 **Easington Colliery** Dur
169 K2 **Easington Lane** Sundld
151 H2 **Easingwold** N York
41 H5 **Easole Street** Kent
233 M6 **Eassie and Nevay** Angus
42 F8 **East Aberthaw** V Glam
7 M5 **East Allington** Devon
28 F5 **East Anstey** Devon
34 E1 **East Anton** Hants
160 C3 **East Appleton** N York
19 K6 **East Ashey** IOW
20 D5 **East Ashling** W Susx
34 F2 **East Aston** Hants
163 H5 **East Ayton** N York
11 K3 **East Balsdon** Cnwll
61 K6 **East Bank** Blae G
136 C3 **East Barkwith** Lincs
39 H3 **East Barming** Kent
171 J8 **East Barnby** N York
69 H8 **East Barnet** Gt Lon
212 F4 **East Barns** E Loth
121 K5 **East Barsham** Norfk
122 D4 **East Beckham** Norfk
50 D4 **East Bedfont** Gt Lon
90 C8 **East Bergholt** Suffk
141 J2 **East Bierley** Kirk
121 L7 **East Bilney** Norfk
23 H7 **East Blatchington** E Susx
17 H4 **East Bloxworth** Dorset
181 J6 **East Boldon** S Tyne
18 F4 **East Boldre** Hants
191 G3 **East Bolton** Nthumb
30 D3 **East Bower** Somset
105 J2 **East Bradenham** Norfk
44 D8 **East Brent** Somset
117 J3 **East Bridgford** Notts
168 B6 **East Briscoe** Dur
28 B4 **East Buckland** Devon
14 C5 **East Budleigh** Devon
50 B2 **East Burnham** Bucks
16 F5 **East Burton** Dorset
168 E2 **East Butsfield** Dur
143 L6 **East Butterwick** N Linc
210 E5 **East Calder** W Loth
106 D3 **East Carleton** Norfk
150 B7 **East Carlton** Leeds
101 H5 **East Carlton** Nhants
16 F6 **East Chaldon (Chaldon Herring)** Dorset
48 A1 **East Challow** Oxon
7 L6 **East Charleton** Devon
16 A2 **East Chelborough** Dorset
191 K6 **East Chevington** Nthumb
22 F4 **East Chiltington** E Susx
31 H8 **East Chinnock** Somset
47 H8 **East Chisenbury** Wilts
34 C2 **East Cholderton** Hants
50 D8 **East Clandon** Surrey
67 H2 **East Claydon** Bucks
44 E5 **East Clevedon** N Som
31 J8 **East Coker** Somset
29 L4 **East Combe** Somset
31 K3 **East Compton** Somset
8 C4 **East Cornworthy** Devon
176 F7 **East Cote** Cumb
151 L7 **East Cottingwith** E R Yk
19 H4 **East Cowes** IOW
143 G4 **East Cowick** E R Yk
160 D2 **East Cowton** N York
181 G4 **East Cramlington** Nthumb
31 L2 **East Cranmore** Somset
17 H6 **East Creech** Dorset
165 K1 **East Curthwaite** Cumb
23 J7 **East Dean** E Susx
63 K3 **East Dean** Gloucs
34 C5 **East Dean** Hants
20 E4 **East Dean** W Susx
27 L3 **East Down** Devon
134 F4 **East Drayton** Notts

51 J4 **East Dulwich** Gt Lon
45 H5 **East Dundry** N Som
144 D2 **East Ella** C KuH
85 J6 **East End** Beds
86 C4 **East End** Beds
145 G2 **East End** E R Yk
145 H2 **East End** E R Yk
70 B5 **East End** Essex
48 B6 **East End** Hants
18 E4 **East End** Hants
70 C2 **East End** Herts
39 L6 **East End** Kent
53 L4 **East End** Kent
85 J6 **East End** M Keyn
44 F5 **East End** N Som
66 B4 **East End** Oxon
31 L2 **East End** Somset
90 C8 **East End** Suffk
47 J8 **East Everleigh** Wilts
39 J3 **East Farleigh** Kent
100 F6 **East Farndon** Nhants
143 K7 **East Ferry** Lincs
135 K3 **East Firsby** Lincs
212 C3 **East Fortune** E Loth
142 C1 **East Garforth** Leeds
47 M4 **East Garston** W Berk
48 C2 **East Ginge** Oxon
100 E1 **East Goscote** Leics
47 K6 **East Grafton** Wilts
91 J2 **East Green** Suffk
34 B5 **East Grimstead** Wilts
38 B5 **East Grinstead** W Susx
25 H3 **East Guldeford** E Susx
84 C2 **East Haddon** Nhants
48 D1 **East Hagbourne** Oxon
144 E4 **East Halton** N Linc
51 L2 **East Ham** Gt Lon
66 B8 **East Hanney** Oxon
71 J6 **East Hanningfield** Essex
142 D4 **East Hardwick** Wakefd
105 K6 **East Harling** Norfk
160 F3 **East Harlsey** N York
33 K5 **East Harnham** Wilts
45 H7 **East Harptree** BaNES
169 L7 **East Hartburn** S on T
181 G3 **East Hartford** Nthumb
20 C3 **East Harting** W Susx
32 F5 **East Hatch** Wilts
86 F5 **East Hatley** Cambs
159 L4 **East Hauxwell** N York
234 F8 **East Haven** Angus
119 G3 **East Heckington** Lincs
168 F3 **East Hedleyhope** Dur
274 D5 **East Helmsdale** Highld
48 C1 **East Hendred** Oxon
163 G7 **East Heslerton** N York
44 E6 **East Hewish** N Som
23 H4 **East Hoathly** E Susx
17 H5 **East Holme** Dorset
31 J2 **East Horrington** Somset
50 E8 **East Horsley** Surrey
203 G7 **East Horton** Nthumb
17 L3 **East Howe** Bmouth
151 K5 **East Huntington** York
30 E2 **East Huntspill** Somset
68 E4 **East Hyde** Beds
28 C2 **East Ilkerton** Devon
48 C3 **East Ilsley** W Berk
137 G7 **East Keal** Lincs
47 G5 **East Kennett** Wilts
150 E7 **East Keswick** Leeds
209 H8 **East Kilbride** S Lans
12 C3 **East Kimber** Devon
136 F7 **East Kirkby** Lincs
16 F5 **East Knighton** Dorset
28 E6 **East Knowstone** Devon
32 E5 **East Knoyle** Wilts
203 G5 **East Kyloe** Nthumb
31 G7 **East Lambrook** Somset
41 K6 **East Langdon** Kent
100 F5 **East Langton** Leics
229 H4 **East Laroch** Highld
20 D5 **East Lavant** W Susx
20 F4 **East Lavington** W Susx
159 L1 **East Layton** N York
116 F6 **East Leake** Notts
202 D5 **East Learmouth** Nthumb
13 G2 **East Leigh** Devon
7 K4 **East Leigh** Devon
7 L3 **East Leigh** Devon
121 J8 **East Lexham** Norfk
212 D3 **East Linton** E Loth
36 A5 **East Liss** Hants
48 B2 **East Lockinge** Oxon
143 K7 **East Lound** N Linc

17 G6	**East Lulworth** Dorset
152 E2	**East Lutton** N York
30 B5	**East Lydeard** Somset
31 J4	**East Lydford** Somset
39 H2	**East Malling** Kent
39 H2	**East Malling Heath** Kent
20 C4	**East Marden** W Susx
134 E5	**East Markham** Notts
33 J7	**East Martin** Hants
148 F5	**East Marton** N York
35 L6	**East Meon** Hants
29 H7	**East Mere** Devon
72 F4	**East Mersea** Essex
50 F5	**East Molesey** Surrey
17 H3	**East Morden** Dorset
149 K7	**East Morton** Brad
186 C6	**East Morton** D & G
162 B7	**East Ness** N York
153 L8	**East Newton** E R Yk
101 G3	**East Norton** Leics
8 C1	**East Ogwell** Devon
32 D7	**East Orchard** Dorset
202 F3	**East Ord** Nthumb
11 L4	**East Panson** Devon
17 M3	**East Parley** Dorset
39 G4	**East Peckham** Kent
54 F6	**East Pennar** Pembks
31 K3	**East Pennard** Somset
86 C2	**East Perry** Cambs
7 L7	**East Portlemouth** Devon
8 A7	**East Prawle** Devon
21 J6	**East Preston** W Susx
16 D1	**East Pulham** Dorset
26 F7	**East Putford** Devon
29 L2	**East Quantoxhead** Somset
53 H5	**East Rainham** Medway
169 J1	**East Rainton** Sundld
145 G7	**East Ravendale** NE Lin
121 J6	**East Raynham** Norfk
150 E7	**East Rigton** Leeds
44 E6	**East Rolstone** N Som
160 F2	**East Rounton** N York
121 H6	**East Rudham** Norfk
122 D3	**East Runton** Norfk
123 G6	**East Ruston** Norfk
212 B5	**East Saltoun** E Loth
159 K5	**East Scrafton** N York
51 G4	**East Sheen** Gt Lon
48 A4	**East Shefford** W Berk
181 G2	**East Sleekburn** Nthumb
123 K7	**East Somerton** Norfk
134 F1	**East Stockwith** Lincs
17 G5	**East Stoke** Dorset
117 K2	**East Stoke** Notts
32 D6	**East Stour** Dorset
41 H3	**East Stourmouth** Kent
27 L5	**East Stowford** Devon
35 H3	**East Stratton** Hants
41 J5	**East Studdal** Kent
39 L3	**East Sutton** Kent
5 L2	**East Taphouse** Cnwll
191 J6	**East Thirston** Nthumb
52 E3	**East Tilbury** Thurr
35 L4	**East Tisted** Hants
136 B3	**East Torrington** Lincs
106 B1	**East Tuddenham** Norfk
34 C5	**East Tytherley** Hants
46 D4	**East Tytherton** Wilts
13 K2	**East Village** Devon
96 C4	**East Wall** Shrops
121 G8	**East Walton** Norfk
31 J1	**East Water** Somset
12 F4	**East Week** Devon
34 C6	**East Wellow** Hants
222 F7	**East Wemyss** Fife
210 C6	**East Whitburn** W Loth
51 M3	**East Wickham** Gt Lon
55 J6	**East Williamston** Pembks
120 F8	**East Winch** Norfk
34 B4	**East Winterslow** Wilts
20 C7	**East Wittering** W Susx
159 L5	**East Witton** N York
179 L2	**East Woodburn** Nthumb
48 B6	**East Woodhay** Hants
32 C2	**East Woodlands** Somset
35 M3	**East Worldham** Hants
105 J5	**East Wretham** Norfk
26 D7	**East Youlstone** Devon
27 H5	**East-the-Water** Devon
169 J7	**Eastbourne** Darltn
23 K7	**Eastbourne** E Susx
91 K2	**Eastbridge** Suffk
43 J7	**Eastbrook** V Glam
149 J7	**Eastburn** Brad
68 E8	**Eastbury** Herts
47 M3	**Eastbury** W Berk
149 J5	**Eastby** N York
53 L5	**Eastchurch** Kent
64 C6	**Eastcombe** Gloucs
50 E1	**Eastcote** Gt Lon
84 D4	**Eastcote** Nhants
99 G7	**Eastcote** Solhll
26 D7	**Eastcott** Cnwll
46 F7	**Eastcott** Wilts
64 E8	**Eastcourt** Wilts
47 K6	**Eastcourt** Wilts
8 B5	**Eastdown** Devon
72 D8	**Eastend** Essex
198 F5	**Eastend** S Lans
243 J5	**Easter Balmoral** Abers
45 H2	**Easter Compton** S Glos
252 E2	**Easter Dalziel** Highld
211 H6	**Easter Howgate** Mdloth
263 G8	**Easter Kinkell** Highld
250 F3	**Easter Moniack** Highld
245 J3	**Easter Ord** Abers
223 K6	**Easter Pitkierie** Fife
281 d6	**Easter Skeld** Shet
202 B6	**Easter Softlaw** Border
251 H1	**Easter Suddie** Highld
20 F6	**Eastergate** W Susx
209 J6	**Easterhouse** C Glas
99 H7	**Eastern Green** Covtry
46 F8	**Easterton** Wilts
44 D8	**Eastertown** Somset
210 A6	**Eastfield** N Lans
163 J6	**Eastfield** N York
168 B3	**Eastgate** Dur
118 F7	**Eastgate** Lincs
122 C7	**Eastgate** Norfk
129 H4	**Eastham** Wirral
129 J3	**Eastham Ferry** Wirral
49 L5	**Easthampstead** Br For
80 A3	**Easthampton** Herefs
49 J5	**Eastheath** Wokham
96 D4	**Easthope** Shrops
72 C3	**Easthorpe** Essex
117 J1	**Easthorpe** Notts
13 H1	**Eastington** Devon
65 H4	**Eastington** Gloucs
63 M6	**Eastington** Gloucs
185 K8	**Eastlands** D & G
65 J6	**Eastleach Martin** Gloucs
65 J6	**Eastleach Turville** Gloucs
27 J5	**Eastleigh** Devon
34 F7	**Eastleigh** Hants
40 C4	**Eastling** Kent
104 E3	**Eastmoor** Norfk
19 L4	**Eastney** C Port
81 G7	**Eastnor** Herefs
143 K4	**Eastoft** N Linc
86 C1	**Easton** Cambs
177 J7	**Easton** Cumb
13 G5	**Easton** Devon
16 D8	**Easton** Dorset
35 G4	**Easton** Hants
118 B6	**Easton** Lincs
106 C1	**Easton** Norfk
31 H2	**Easton** Somset
91 G3	**Easton** Suffk
48 B4	**Easton** W Berk
46 C5	**Easton** Wilts
46 C2	**Easton Grey** Wilts
85 H3	**Easton Maudit** Nhants
101 M3	**Easton on the Hill** Nhants
47 J7	**Easton Royal** Wilts
45 G4	**Easton-in-Gordano** N Som
11 L4	**Eastpeek** Devon
102 F4	**Eastrea** Cambs
177 H5	**Eastriggs** D & G
143 K2	**Eastrington** E R Yk
65 J8	**Eastrop** Swindn
41 J4	**Eastry** Kent
36 C6	**Eastshaw** W Susx
45 J4	**Eastville** Bristl
137 H8	**Eastville** Lincs
117 K6	**Eastwell** Leics
70 B5	**Eastwick** Herts
140 E3	**Eastwood** Calder
116 D2	**Eastwood** Notts
53 H1	**Eastwood** Sthend
103 J5	**Eastwood End** Cambs
83 J2	**Eathorpe** Warwks
130 B7	**Eaton** Ches
131 G6	**Eaton** Ches
117 L5	**Eaton** Leics
106 D2	**Eaton** Norfk
134 E4	**Eaton** Notts
66 C6	**Eaton** Oxon
95 J5	**Eaton** Shrops
96 B5	**Eaton** Shrops
80 B7	**Eaton Bishop** Herefs
68 B3	**Eaton Bray** Beds
96 D2	**Eaton Constantine** Shrops
86 D3	**Eaton Ford** Beds
68 B3	**Eaton Green** Beds
65 K7	**Eaton Hastings** Oxon
96 C2	**Eaton Mascott** Shrops
86 D3	**Eaton Socon** Cambs
113 L7	**Eaton upon Tern** Shrops
130 C1	**Eaves Brow** Warrtn
99 H6	**Eaves Green** Solhll
162 F6	**Ebberston** N York
33 G6	**Ebbesborne Wake** Wilts
61 J5	**Ebbw Vale** Blae G
180 D7	**Ebchester** Dur
44 D6	**Ebdon** N Som
14 A5	**Ebford** Devon
64 B6	**Ebley** Gloucs
113 H2	**Ebnal** Ches
80 B3	**Ebnall** Herefs
82 E7	**Ebrington** Gloucs
12 C4	**Ebsworthy Town** Devon
48 D7	**Ecchinswell** Hants
213 G5	**Ecclaw** Border
177 G4	**Ecclefechan** D & G
202 B5	**Eccles** Border
52 F6	**Eccles** Kent
140 A8	**Eccles** Salfd
79 L5	**Eccles Green** Herefs
123 H5	**Eccles on Sea** Norfk
105 L5	**Eccles Road** Norfk
132 F3	**Ecclesall** Sheff
133 G1	**Ecclesfield** Sheff
114 C5	**Eccleshall** Staffs
149 M8	**Eccleshill** Brad
210 E4	**Ecclesmachan** W Loth
129 J7	**Eccleston** Ches
139 G4	**Eccleston** Lancs
138 F8	**Eccleston** St Hel
139 G4	**Eccleston Green** Lancs
245 G2	**Echt** Abers
201 L7	**Eckford** Border
133 H4	**Eckington** Derbys
81 L7	**Eckington** Worcs
84 F3	**Ecton** Nhants
132 B8	**Ecton** Staffs
132 B3	**Edale** Derbys
22 C5	**Edburton** W Susx
164 E2	**Edderside** Cumb
263 J3	**Edderton** Highld
41 G2	**Eddington** Kent
200 B4	**Eddleston** Border
209 J8	**Eddlewood** S Lans
156 F7	**Eden Mount** Cumb
51 K5	**Eden Park** Gt Lon
38 C4	**Edenbridge** Kent
140 B4	**Edenfield** Lancs
166 D4	**Edenhall** Cumb
118 E7	**Edenham** Lincs
132 E5	**Edensor** Derbys
218 D8	**Edentaggart** Ag & B
143 G6	**Edenthorpe** Donc
108 E4	**Edern** Gwynd
31 H3	**Edgarley** Somset
98 D6	**Edgbaston** Birm
3 J4	**Edgcombe** Cnwll
67 G3	**Edgcott** Bucks
28 E3	**Edgcott** Somset
64 B5	**Edge** Gloucs
95 K2	**Edge** Shrops
63 H4	**Edge End** Gloucs
113 H1	**Edge Green** Ches
113 J7	**Edgebolton** Shrops
122 B5	**Edgefield** Norfk
122 B4	**Edgefield Green** Norfk
139 L6	**Edgefold** Bolton
83 J5	**Edgehill** Warwks
112 E7	**Edgerley** Shrops
141 H4	**Edgerton** Kirk
140 C3	**Edgeside** Lancs
64 D6	**Edgeworth** Gloucs
28 E8	**Edgeworthy** Devon
8 C2	**Edginswell** Torbay
82 B3	**Edgiock** Worcs
114 A7	**Edgmond** Wrekin
114 A7	**Edgmond Marsh** Wrekin
95 J6	**Edgton** Shrops
51 G1	**Edgware** Gt Lon
139 L4	**Edgworth** Bl w D
258 E6	**Edinbane** Highld
211 J4	**Edinburgh** C Edin
99 G1	**Edingale** Staffs
175 L2	**Edingham** D & G
134 D8	**Edingley** Notts
123 G5	**Edingthorpe** Norfk
122 F5	**Edingthorpe Green** Norfk
202 D2	**Edington** Border
180 E2	**Edington** Nthumb
30 F3	**Edington** Somset
46 D8	**Edington** Wilts
30 F2	**Edington Burtle** Somset
44 D8	**Edingworth** Somset
101 K2	**Edith Weston** Rutlnd
30 E1	**Edithmead** Somset
68 B3	**Edlesborough** Bucks
191 G4	**Edlingham** Nthumb
136 D5	**Edlington** Lincs
178 C7	**Edmond Castle** Cumb
33 J8	**Edmondsham** Dorset
169 G1	**Edmondsley** Dur
117 M8	**Edmondthorpe** Leics
10 D7	**Edmonton** Cnwll
69 J8	**Edmonton** Gt Lon
168 C1	**Edmundbyers** Dur
202 A5	**Ednam** Border
115 L3	**Ednaston** Derbys
232 C5	**Edradynate** P & K
202 C2	**Edrom** Border
113 H5	**Edstaston** Shrops
82 E3	**Edstone** Warwks
80 F3	**Edvin Loach** Herefs
117 G4	**Edwalton** Notts
89 J6	**Edwardstone** Suffk
43 G2	**Edwardsville** Myr Td
59 H2	**Edwinsford** Carmth
134 C6	**Edwinstowe** Notts
86 E7	**Edworth** Beds
80 F4	**Edwyn Ralph** Herefs
234 F2	**Edzell** Angus
234 F2	**Edzell Woods** Angus
43 H5	**Efail Isaf** Rhondd
57 L6	**Efail-fach** Neath
112 A6	**Efail-Rhyd** Powys
108 F4	**Efailnewydd** Gwynd
75 K7	**Efailwen** Carmth
128 D8	**Efenechtyd** Denbgs
187 L7	**Effgill** D & G
50 E8	**Effingham** Surrey
115 K8	**Efflinch** Staffs
13 K2	**Efford** Devon
48 B8	**Egbury** Hants
21 G3	**Egdean** W Susx
139 L5	**Egerton** Bolton
40 B6	**Egerton** Kent
6 F3	**Eggbuckland** C Plym
28 B8	**Eggesford** Devon
68 B2	**Egginton** Beds
115 M6	**Egginton** Derbys
169 L7	**Egglescliffe** S on T
168 C6	**Eggleston** Dur
50 C5	**Egham** Surrey
50 B5	**Egham Wick** Surrey
101 J2	**Egleton** Rutlnd
191 G2	**Eglingham** Nthumb
10 D8	**Egloshayle** Cnwll
11 K5	**Egloskerry** Cnwll
113 G3	**Eglwys Cross** Wrexhm
92 F4	**Eglwys Fach** Cerdgn
42 F7	**Eglwys-Brewis** V Glam
126 F5	**Eglwysbach** Conwy
75 K4	**Eglwyswrw** Pembks
134 E6	**Egmanton** Notts
164 D8	**Egremont** Cumb
129 H1	**Egremont** Wirral
162 E2	**Egton** N York
162 D2	**Egton Bridge** N York
143 L2	**Eight and Forty** E R Yk
72 D2	**Eight Ash Green** Essex
248 C8	**Eilanreach** Highld
93 H6	**Eisteddfa Gurig** Cerdgn
78 C2	**Elan Village** Powys
45 J1	**Elberton** S Glos
20 F6	**Elbridge** W Susx
7 G4	**Elburton** C Plym
47 H3	**Elcombe** Swindn
48 B5	**Elcot** W Berk
88 B8	**Elder Street** Essex
103 G4	**Eldernell** Cambs
64 A1	**Eldersfield** Worcs
208 D6	**Elderslie** Rens
160 F7	**Eldmire** N York
169 G5	**Eldon** Dur
149 L7	**Eldwick** Brad
245 H6	**Elfhill** Abers
203 K7	**Elford** Nthumb
98 F1	**Elford** Staffs
266 E4	**Elgin** Moray

247 H6 **Elgol** Highld
41 G6 **Elham** Kent
223 J7 **Elie** Fife
190 D4 **Elilaw** Nthumb
124 F3 **Elim** IOA
18 F1 **Eling** Hants
134 D4 **Elkesley** Notts
64 D4 **Elkstone** Gloucs
268 B4 **Ella** Abers
8 D2 **Ellacombe** Torbay
141 H4 **Elland** Calder
141 H3 **Elland Lower Edge** Calder
206 A4 **Ellary** Ag & B
115 J3 **Ellastone** Staffs
147 J4 **Ellel** Lancs
212 F7 **Ellemford** Border
37 G4 **Ellen's Green** Surrey
164 D3 **Ellenborough** Cumb
139 L7 **Ellenbrook** Salfd
114 C6 **Ellenhall** Staffs
160 F3 **Ellerbeck** N York
171 J7 **Ellerby** N York
113 K7 **Ellerdine Heath** Wrekin
14 A2 **Ellerhayes** Devon
229 G5 **Elleric** Ag & B
144 A2 **Ellerker** E R Yk
149 H7 **Ellers** N York
151 L7 **Ellerton** E R Yk
160 C3 **Ellerton** N York
113 M6 **Ellerton** Shrops
67 K6 **Ellesborough** Bucks
112 F4 **Ellesmere** Shrops
129 J4 **Ellesmere Port** Ches
29 H2 **Ellicombe** Somset
18 A2 **Ellingham** Hants
107 G5 **Ellingham** Norfk
203 K8 **Ellingham** Nthumb
159 M6 **Ellingstring** N York
86 D1 **Ellington** Cambs
191 K7 **Ellington** Nthumb
86 D1 **Ellington Thorpe** Cambs
32 D2 **Elliots Green** Somset
35 K2 **Ellisfield** Hants
259 H3 **Ellishader** Highld
99 L1 **Ellistown** Leics
257 H5 **Ellon** Abers
166 A4 **Ellonby** Cumb
107 J6 **Ellough** Suffk
144 B2 **Elloughton** E R Yk
63 H5 **Ellwood** Gloucs
103 K2 **Elm** Cambs
71 J6 **Elm Green** Essex
107 K3 **Elm Grove** Norfk
52 B2 **Elm Park** Gt Lon
81 K2 **Elmbridge** Worcs
87 J7 **Elmdon** Essex
98 F6 **Elmdon** Solhll
98 F7 **Elmdon Heath** Solhll
21 G6 **Elmer** W Susx
139 G6 **Elmer's Green** Lancs
51 K5 **Elmers End** Gt Lon
100 A4 **Elmesthorpe** Leics
98 E1 **Elmhurst** Staffs
82 A7 **Elmley Castle** Worcs
81 K1 **Elmley Lovett** Worcs
64 A4 **Elmore** Gloucs
63 M4 **Elmore Back** Gloucs
81 G2 **Elms Green** Worcs
26 D6 **Elmscott** Devon
90 C6 **Elmsett** Suffk
72 F3 **Elmstead Heath** Essex
72 F2 **Elmstead Market** Essex
72 F3 **Elmstead Row** Essex
40 F6 **Elmsted Court** Kent
41 H3 **Elmstone** Kent
64 D2 **Elmstone Hardwicke** Gloucs
152 F4 **Elmswell** E R Yk
89 K2 **Elmswell** Suffk
133 K5 **Elmton** Derbys
271 H6 **Elphin** Highld
211 L5 **Elphinstone** E Loth
245 H2 **Elrick** Abers
173 J6 **Elrig** D & G
179 K6 **Elrington** Nthumb
190 C7 **Elsdon** Nthumb
142 B7 **Elsecar** Barns
70 D2 **Elsenham** Essex
66 D5 **Elsfield** Oxon
144 C5 **Elsham** N Linc
245 K4 **Elsick House** Abers
122 B8 **Elsing** Norfk
149 G6 **Elslack** N York
19 K3 **Elson** Hants

112 F4 **Elson** Shrops
199 J4 **Elsrickle** S Lans
36 D2 **Elstead** Surrey
20 D3 **Elsted** W Susx
118 E6 **Elsthorpe** Lincs
169 J6 **Elstob** Dur
139 J1 **Elston** Lancs
117 K2 **Elston** Notts
33 J2 **Elston** Wilts
28 B7 **Elstone** Devon
85 L6 **Elstow** Beds
68 F8 **Elstree** Herts
145 G1 **Elstronwick** E R Yk
147 H8 **Elswick** Lancs
180 F6 **Elswick** N u Ty
87 G3 **Elsworth** Cambs
156 D2 **Elterwater** Cumb
51 L4 **Eltham** Gt Lon
86 F3 **Eltisley** Cambs
140 B5 **Elton** Bury
102 B4 **Elton** Cambs
129 K4 **Elton** Ches
132 D7 **Elton** Derbys
63 K4 **Elton** Gloucs
80 B1 **Elton** Herefs
117 K4 **Elton** Notts
169 L7 **Elton** S on T
129 K5 **Elton Green** Ches
180 C6 **Eltringham** Nthumb
186 E3 **Elvanfoot** S Lans
116 C5 **Elvaston** Derbys
105 G7 **Elveden** Suffk
49 J7 **Elvetham Heath** Hants
212 A4 **Elvingston** E Loth
41 J5 **Elvington** Kent
151 L6 **Elvington** York
28 B4 **Elwell** Devon
170 B4 **Elwick** Hartpl
203 J5 **Elwick** Nthumb
130 E7 **Elworth** Ches
29 K4 **Elworthy** Somset
103 L7 **Ely** Cambs
43 J6 **Ely** Cardif
85 H5 **Emberton** M Keyn
165 G5 **Embleton** Cumb
169 L5 **Embleton** Dur
191 J2 **Embleton** Nthumb
264 C1 **Embo** Highld
264 C2 **Embo Street** Highld
31 K1 **Emborough** Somset
149 H5 **Embsay** N York
18 D2 **Emery Down** Hants
141 K5 **Emley** Kirk
141 K5 **Emley Moor** Kirk
49 J5 **Emmbrook** Wokham
49 H4 **Emmer Green** Readg
133 J4 **Emmett Carr** Derbys
67 H6 **Emmington** Oxon
103 K2 **Emneth** Cambs
103 K2 **Emneth Hungate** Norfk
101 L2 **Empingham** Rutlnd
35 M4 **Empshott** Hants
35 M5 **Empshott Green** Hants
20 B5 **Emsworth** Hants
48 B6 **Enborne** W Berk
48 C6 **Enborne Row** W Berk
96 B4 **Enchmarsh** Shrops
100 C3 **Enderby** Leics
157 H5 **Endmoor** Cumb
114 E1 **Endon** Staffs
114 E1 **Endon Bank** Staffs
69 K7 **Enfield** Gt Lon
69 K7 **Enfield Lock** Gt Lon
69 K7 **Enfield Wash** Gt Lon
47 H8 **Enford** Wilts
45 K2 **Engine Common** S Glos
80 D5 **England's Gate** Herefs
48 F4 **Englefield** W Berk
50 C4 **Englefield Green** Surrey
114 B1 **Engleseabrook** Ches
63 H4 **English Bicknor** Gloucs
113 G5 **English Frankton** Shrops
45 L6 **Englishcombe** BaNES
4 E1 **Engollan** Cnwll
34 E1 **Enham-Alamein** Hants
30 C4 **Enmore** Somset
32 E6 **Enmore Green** Dorset
164 E7 **Ennerdale Bridge** Cumb
4 F3 **Enniscaven** Cnwll
233 G3 **Enochdhu** P & K
226 D3 **Ensay** Ag & B
17 L3 **Ensbury** Bmouth
112 F8 **Ensdon** Shrops
27 K5 **Ensis** Devon
114 E6 **Enson** Staffs

66 A2 **Enstone** Oxon
186 C5 **Enterkinfoot** D & G
161 G2 **Enterpen** N York
97 J6 **Enville** Staffs
3 K4 **Enys** Cnwll
283 b12 **Eolaigearraidh** W Isls
63 M5 **Epney** Gloucs
117 H2 **Epperstone** Notts
70 C6 **Epping** Essex
70 B6 **Epping Green** Essex
69 J5 **Epping Green** Herts
70 C6 **Epping Upland** Essex
168 F8 **Eppleby** N York
144 C2 **Eppleworth** E R Yk
51 G6 **Epsom** Surrey
83 H7 **Epwell** Oxon
143 K7 **Epworth** N Linc
143 J7 **Epworth Turbary** N Linc
112 E3 **Erbistock** Wrexhm
98 E5 **Erdington** Birm
38 E6 **Eridge Green** E Susx
38 E6 **Eridge Station** E Susx
206 D4 **Erines** Ag & B
3 H7 **Erisey** Cnwll
228 D6 **Eriska** Ag & B
104 E7 **Eriswell** Suffk
52 B3 **Erith** Gt Lon
46 D8 **Erlestoke** Wilts
7 J4 **Ermington** Devon
122 D5 **Erpingham** Norfk
40 B3 **Erriottwood** Kent
250 F7 **Errogie** Highld
222 D3 **Errol** P & K
208 D5 **Erskine** Rens
172 B1 **Ervie** D & G
90 F8 **Erwarton** Suffk
78 F6 **Erwood** Powys
160 D1 **Eryholme** N York
128 E8 **Eryrys** Denbgs
2 B5 **Escalls** Cnwll
168 F4 **Escomb** Dur
29 K3 **Escott** Somset
151 K7 **Escrick** York
58 C3 **Esgair** Carmth
77 G2 **Esgair** Cerdgn
93 G2 **Esgairgeiliog** Powys
77 H7 **Esgyryn** Carmth
126 F4 **Esgyryn** Conwy
169 G2 **Esh** Dur
169 G2 **Esh Winning** Dur
50 F6 **Esher** Surrey
150 A7 **Esholt** Brad
191 J6 **Eshott** Nthumb
149 G4 **Eshton** N York
250 D4 **Eskadale** Highld
211 K5 **Eskbank** Mdloth
155 L3 **Eskdale Green** Cumb
187 K6 **Eskdalemuir** D & G
164 E7 **Eskett** Cumb
145 K8 **Eskham** Lincs
143 G4 **Eskholme** Donc
168 E6 **Esperley Lane Ends** Dur
147 H8 **Esprick** Lancs
102 A1 **Essendine** Rutlnd
69 H5 **Essendon** Herts
251 H4 **Essich** Highld
98 B3 **Essington** Staffs
257 G6 **Esslemont** Abers
170 D7 **Eston** R & Cl
202 E5 **Etal** Nthumb
46 F7 **Etchilhampton** Wilts
24 C2 **Etchingham** E Susx
41 G7 **Etchinghill** Kent
115 G7 **Etchinghill** Staffs
23 H3 **Etchingwood** E Susx
153 L8 **Etherdwick** E R Yk
105 K1 **Etling Green** Norfk
63 K6 **Etloe** Gloucs
50 B3 **Eton** W & M
50 B3 **Eton Wick** W & M
114 D2 **Etruria** C Stke
241 J5 **Etteridge** Highld
167 K5 **Ettersgill** Dur
130 E7 **Ettiley Heath** Ches
97 L4 **Ettingshall** Wolves
83 G5 **Ettington** Warwks
102 C2 **Etton** C Pete
152 F7 **Etton** E R Yk
187 L3 **Ettrick** Border
188 C1 **Ettrickbridge** Border
187 L3 **Ettrickhill** Border
115 M5 **Etwall** Derbys
96 F5 **Eudon George** Shrops
105 H7 **Euston** Suffk
103 K4 **Euximoor Drove** Cambs

139 H4 **Euxton** Lancs
79 J3 **Evancoyd** Powys
263 G6 **Evanton** Highld
118 E2 **Evedon** Lincs
97 G2 **Evelith** Shrops
263 L2 **Evelix** Highld
79 J3 **Evenjobb** Powys
84 B8 **Evenley** Oxon
65 J1 **Evenlode** Gloucs
168 F5 **Evenwood** Dur
168 F6 **Evenwood Gate** Dur
31 L3 **Evercreech** Somset
152 B7 **Everingham** E R Yk
47 J8 **Everleigh** Wilts
163 H5 **Everley** N York
12 B4 **Eversfield** Devon
85 K8 **Eversholt** Beds
16 A2 **Evershot** Dorset
49 J6 **Eversley** Hants
49 J6 **Eversley Cross** Hants
144 A2 **Everthorpe** E R Yk
86 D5 **Everton** Beds
18 D5 **Everton** Hants
129 H1 **Everton** Lpool
134 D2 **Everton** Notts
177 K4 **Evertown** D & G
80 F5 **Evesbatch** Herefs
82 B6 **Evesham** Worcs
100 D3 **Evington** C Leic
141 L8 **Ewden Village** Sheff
97 G4 **Ewdness** Shrops
51 G6 **Ewell** Surrey
41 H6 **Ewell Minnis** Kent
48 F1 **Ewelme** Oxon
64 E7 **Ewen** Gloucs
42 D6 **Ewenny** V Glam
118 F2 **Ewerby** Lincs
118 F2 **Ewerby Thorpe** Lincs
190 F7 **Ewesley** Nthumb
37 G3 **Ewhurst** Surrey
24 E2 **Ewhurst Green** E Susx
37 G3 **Ewhurst Green** Surrey
129 G6 **Ewloe** Flints
129 G6 **Ewloe Green** Flints
139 K3 **Ewood** Bl w D
140 B4 **Ewood Bridge** Lancs
12 B3 **Eworthy** Devon
36 B1 **Ewshot** Hants
62 D2 **Ewyas Harold** Herefs
12 E2 **Exbourne** Devon
19 G4 **Exbury** Hants
23 H7 **Exceat** E Susx
29 G6 **Exebridge** Somset
160 D5 **Exelby** N York
13 L4 **Exeter** Devon
28 E3 **Exford** Somset
95 L2 **Exfordsgreen** Shrops
82 D4 **Exhall** Warwks
99 J6 **Exhall** Warwks
49 G3 **Exlade Street** Oxon
149 J7 **Exley Head** Brad
13 M5 **Exminster** Devon
14 A6 **Exmouth** Devon
88 C2 **Exning** Suffk
41 G6 **Exted** Kent
14 A5 **Exton** Devon
35 J6 **Exton** Hants
101 K1 **Exton** Rutlnd
29 G4 **Exton** Somset
13 L4 **Exwick** Devon
132 D4 **Eyam** Derbys
83 M5 **Eydon** Nhants
102 E3 **Eye** C Pete
80 C2 **Eye** Herefs
106 C8 **Eye** Suffk
102 E3 **Eye Green** C Pete
117 K8 **Eye Kettleby** Leics
213 L6 **Eyemouth** Border
86 E6 **Eyeworth** Beds
39 L2 **Eyhorne Street** Kent
91 H5 **Eyke** Suffk
86 D3 **Eynesbury** Cambs
52 C6 **Eynsford** Kent
66 B5 **Eynsham** Oxon
15 K4 **Eype** Dorset
259 G6 **Eyre** Highld
41 J5 **Eythorne** Kent
80 B3 **Eyton** Herefs
112 F8 **Eyton** Shrops
113 G7 **Eyton** Shrops
95 J6 **Eyton** Shrops
112 E3 **Eyton** Wrexhm
96 D2 **Eyton on Severn** Shrops
113 L8 **Eyton upon the Weald Moors** Wrekin

F

48 A7 **Faccombe** Hants
161 H2 **Faceby** N York
111 K8 **Fachwen** Powys
140 D4 **Facit** Lancs
133 J7 **Fackley** Notts
113 K1 **Faddiley** Ches
161 L5 **Fadmoor** N York
57 J4 **Faerdre** Swans
57 J4 **Fagwyr** Swans
208 E4 **Faifley** W Duns
45 G4 **Failand** N Som
196 F5 **Failford** S Ayrs
140 D7 **Failsworth** Oldham
35 G7 **Fair Oak** Hants
49 G6 **Fair Oak Green** Hants
92 D1 **Fairbourne** Gwynd
142 D2 **Fairburn** N York
131 L5 **Fairfield** Derbys
25 H2 **Fairfield** Kent
97 L8 **Fairfield** Worcs
65 H6 **Fairford** Gloucs
65 H6 **Fairford Park** Gloucs
175 L3 **Fairgirth** D & G
138 C2 **Fairhaven** Lancs
207 L8 **Fairlie** N Ayrs
24 F5 **Fairlight** E Susx
14 C3 **Fairmile** Devon
50 E6 **Fairmile** Surrey
200 F6 **Fairnilee** Border
114 B5 **Fairoak** Staffs
52 D6 **Fairseat** Kent
71 J4 **Fairstead** Essex
122 F6 **Fairstead** Norfk
23 G2 **Fairwarp** E Susx
43 J6 **Fairwater** Cardif
27 G6 **Fairy Cross** Devon
121 K5 **Fakenham** Norfk
105 H8 **Fakenham Magna** Suffk
211 M6 **Fala** Mdloth
211 M6 **Fala Dam** Mdloth
211 L7 **Falahill** Border
77 G5 **Falcondale** Cerdgn
84 B6 **Falcut** Nhants
135 L3 **Faldingworth** Lincs
9 f2 **Faldouet** Jersey
63 K8 **Falfield** S Glos
91 G7 **Falkenham** Suffk
210 A3 **Falkirk** Falk
222 D5 **Falkland** Fife
133 G7 **Fallgate** Derbys
209 L1 **Fallin** Stirlg
191 H2 **Falloden** Nthumb
131 G1 **Fallowfield** Manch
179 L5 **Fallowfield** Nthumb
216 F4 **Falls of Blarghour** Ag & B
22 E5 **Falmer** E Susx
3 K4 **Falmouth** Cnwll
188 C5 **Falnash** Border
163 J5 **Falsgrave** N York
179 G2 **Falstone** Nthumb
276 B6 **Fanagmore** Highld
68 C2 **Fancott** Beds
250 E3 **Fanellan** Highld
161 J4 **Fangdale Beck** N York
152 A5 **Fangfoss** E R Yk
226 E3 **Fanmore** Ag & B
261 L6 **Fannich Lodge** Highld
201 J5 **Fans** Border
85 G8 **Far Bletchley** M Keyn
84 E3 **Far Cotton** Nhants
156 D3 **Far End** Cumb
97 G8 **Far Forest** Worcs
63 M7 **Far Green** Gloucs
139 G7 **Far Moor** Wigan
64 D6 **Far Oakridge** Gloucs
156 E4 **Far Sawrey** Cumb
136 E5 **Far Thorpe** Lincs
102 D4 **Farcet** Cambs
96 D8 **Farden** Shrops
19 K2 **Fareham** Hants
98 D1 **Farewell** Staffs
136 F4 **Farforth** Lincs
65 L8 **Faringdon** Oxon
139 G3 **Farington** Lancs
232 F8 **Farkhill** P & K
178 D7 **Farlam** Cumb
7 L4 **Farleigh** Devon
45 G5 **Farleigh** N Som
51 K7 **Farleigh** Surrey
46 A7 **Farleigh Hungerford** Somset
35 J2 **Farleigh Wallop** Hants
137 J5 **Farlesthorpe** Lincs

157 H6 **Farleton** Cumb
147 L2 **Farleton** Lancs
132 F7 **Farley** Derbys
115 H3 **Farley** Staffs
34 B5 **Farley** Wilts
88 E4 **Farley Green** Suffk
37 G2 **Farley Green** Surrey
49 H6 **Farley Hill** Wokham
63 M4 **Farleys End** Gloucs
19 M3 **Farlington** C Port
151 K2 **Farlington** N York
96 E7 **Farlow** Shrops
116 C8 **Farm Town** Leics
45 K7 **Farmborough** BaNES
70 F5 **Farmbridge End** Essex
64 F1 **Farmcote** Gloucs
97 H5 **Farmcote** Shrops
77 J6 **Farmers** Carmth
65 H4 **Farmington** Gloucs
66 C5 **Farmoor** Oxon
3 H4 **Farms Common** Cnwll
267 K6 **Farmtown** Moray
267 J4 **Farnachty** Moray
116 B2 **Farnah Green** Derbys
51 L6 **Farnborough** Gt Lon
49 L8 **Farnborough** Hants
48 B3 **Farnborough** W Berk
83 K5 **Farnborough** Warwks
49 L7 **Farnborough Park** Hants
49 L7 **Farnborough Street** Hants
36 E2 **Farncombe** Surrey
85 H3 **Farndish** Beds
112 F1 **Farndon** Ches
117 K1 **Farndon** Notts
235 G4 **Farnell** Angus
33 G7 **Farnham** Dorset
70 C2 **Farnham** Essex
150 E4 **Farnham** N York
91 H3 **Farnham** Suffk
36 C2 **Farnham** Surrey
50 B2 **Farnham Common** Bucks
70 C2 **Farnham Green** Essex
50 B2 **Farnham Royal** Bucks
52 C5 **Farningham** Kent
150 B6 **Farnley** Leeds
141 L1 **Farnley** Leeds
141 J5 **Farnley Tyas** Kirk
134 C8 **Farnsfield** Notts
139 L6 **Farnworth** Bolton
129 L2 **Farnworth** Halton
278 B4 **Farr** Highld
251 J5 **Farr** Highld
241 L3 **Farr** Highld
251 G7 **Farraline** Highld
14 B4 **Farringdon** Devon
45 J7 **Farrington Gurney** BaNES
141 K1 **Farsley** Leeds
71 K6 **Farther Howegreen** Essex
39 K4 **Farthing Green** Kent
51 L6 **Farthing Street** Gt Lon
83 M7 **Farthinghoe** Nhants
41 J7 **Farthingloe** Kent
84 B4 **Farthingstone** Nhants
141 J4 **Fartown** Kirk
141 K1 **Fartown** Leeds
14 E3 **Farway Street** Devon
229 G6 **Fasnacloich** Ag & B
250 B6 **Fasnakyle** Highld
239 G7 **Fassfern** Highld
181 H8 **Fatfield** Sundld
178 C7 **Faugh** Cumb
115 K6 **Fauld** Staffs
210 B6 **Fauldhouse** W Loth
71 J4 **Faulkbourne** Essex
45 L8 **Faulkland** Somset
113 K5 **Fauls** Shrops
40 D3 **Faversham** Kent
150 F1 **Fawdington** N York
180 F5 **Fawdon** N u Ty
190 E3 **Fawdon** Nthumb
131 L7 **Fawfieldhead** Staffs
52 C6 **Fawkham Green** Kent
66 A4 **Fawler** Oxon
49 J2 **Fawley** Bucks
19 G3 **Fawley** Hants
48 B3 **Fawley** W Berk
63 H1 **Fawley Chapel** Herefs
128 F6 **Fawnog** Flints
84 A4 **Fawsley** Nhants
143 L3 **Faxfleet** E R Yk
37 G3 **Faygate** W Susx
138 D8 **Fazakerley** Lpool
99 G3 **Fazeley** Staffs
160 B6 **Fearby** N York
264 C4 **Fearn** Highld

231 K6 **Fearnan** P & K
260 B7 **Fearnbeg** Highld
130 C2 **Fearnhead** Warrtn
260 A7 **Fearnmore** Highld
206 E3 **Fearnoch** Ag & B
97 L2 **Featherstone** Staffs
142 C3 **Featherstone** Wakefd
82 B3 **Feckenham** Worcs
72 C3 **Feering** Essex
159 H3 **Feetham** N York
148 D2 **Feizor** N York
38 B5 **Felbridge** Surrey
122 E4 **Felbrigg** Norfk
38 B5 **Felcourt** Surrey
37 H2 **Felday** Surrey
68 D6 **Felden** Herts
76 F4 **Felin Fach** Cerdgn
58 F4 **Felin gwm Isaf** Carmth
58 F4 **Felin gwm Uchaf** Carmth
78 F8 **Felin-newydd** Powys
59 G4 **Felindre** Carmth
59 K3 **Felindre** Carmth
76 C7 **Felindre** Carmth
77 G4 **Felindre** Cerdgn
94 E7 **Felindre** Powys
61 J2 **Felindre** Powys
57 H4 **Felindre** Swans
75 J4 **Felindre Farchog** Pembks
78 F8 **Felinfach** Powys
56 F4 **Felinfoel** Carmth
161 G5 **Felixkirk** N York
91 G8 **Felixstowe** Suffk
91 H7 **Felixstowe Ferry** Suffk
202 E4 **Felkington** Nthumb
142 B5 **Felkirk** Wakefd
156 D2 **Fell Foot** Cumb
149 J7 **Fell Lane** Brad
165 J3 **Fell Side** Cumb
181 G6 **Felling** Gatesd
85 K4 **Felmersham** Beds
122 E5 **Felmingham** Norfk
20 F7 **Felpham** W Susx
89 J4 **Felsham** Suffk
71 G3 **Felsted** Essex
50 E4 **Feltham** Gt Lon
50 E5 **Felthamhill** Gt Lon
122 D7 **Felthorpe** Norfk
80 D5 **Felton** Herefs
45 G6 **Felton** N Som
191 H6 **Felton** Nthumb
112 F8 **Felton Butler** Shrops
104 E5 **Feltwell** Norfk
87 K3 **Fen Ditton** Cambs
87 G2 **Fen Drayton** Cambs
119 H7 **Fen End** Lincs
99 G8 **Fen End** Solhll
105 K4 **Fen Street** Norfk
90 E3 **Fen Street** Suffk
141 J4 **Fenay Bridge** Kirk
148 E8 **Fence** Lancs
133 J3 **Fence** Rothm
169 J1 **Fence Houses** Sundld
160 D4 **Fencote** N York
66 E4 **Fencott** Oxon
137 H7 **Fendike Corner** Lincs
203 H5 **Fenham** Nthumb
139 K2 **Feniscliffe** Bl w D
139 K3 **Feniscowles** Bl w D
14 D3 **Feniton** Devon
97 H6 **Fenn Green** Shrops
53 G4 **Fenn Street** Medway
115 K2 **Fenny Bentley** Derbys
14 D3 **Fenny Bridges** Devon
83 K5 **Fenny Compton** Warwks
99 K4 **Fenny Drayton** Leics
85 G8 **Fenny Stratford** M Keyn
191 H7 **Fenrother** Nthumb
87 G2 **Fenstanton** Cambs
88 F5 **Fenstead End** Suffk
114 D3 **Fenton** C Stke
103 G7 **Fenton** Cambs
178 C7 **Fenton** Cumb
135 G4 **Fenton** Lincs
118 A1 **Fenton** Lincs
134 F3 **Fenton** Notts
202 F6 **Fenton** Nthumb
212 B3 **Fenton Barns** E Loth
142 F4 **Fenwick** Donc
196 F2 **Fenwick** E Ayrs
203 H5 **Fenwick** Nthumb
180 C4 **Fenwick** Nthumb
3 L3 **Feock** Cnwll
205 G3 **Feolin Ferry** Ag & B
196 C2 **Fergushill** N Ayrs
258 B6 **Feriniquarrie** Highld

9 k3 **Fermain Bay** Guern
234 D3 **Fern** Angus
42 F2 **Ferndale** Rhondd
17 L2 **Ferndown** Dorset
253 J3 **Ferness** Moray
65 L8 **Fernham** Oxon
81 K3 **Fernhill Heath** Worcs
36 D5 **Fernhurst** W Susx
222 E4 **Fernie** Fife
209 K8 **Ferniegair** S Lans
246 E2 **Fernilea** Highld
131 K4 **Fernilee** Derbys
79 L5 **Ferny Common** Herefs
150 E4 **Ferrensby** N York
144 B4 **Ferriby Sluice** N Linc
247 L7 **Ferrindonald** Highld
21 J6 **Ferring** W Susx
263 K3 **Ferry Point** Highld
142 D3 **Ferrybridge** Wakefd
235 H4 **Ferryden** Angus
169 H4 **Ferryhill** Dur
56 C3 **Ferryside** Carmth
263 K2 **Ferrytown** Highld
106 B6 **Fersfield** Norfk
240 B7 **Fersit** Highld
241 M3 **Feshiebridge** Highld
50 F7 **Fetcham** Surrey
269 H6 **Fetterangus** Abers
235 G1 **Fettercairn** Abers
66 D2 **Fewcott** Oxon
150 B5 **Fewston** N York
77 K2 **Ffair Rhos** Cerdgn
59 H4 **Ffairfach** Carmth
77 H6 **Ffald-y-Brenin** Carmth
61 K3 **Ffawyddog** Powys
110 D3 **Ffestiniog** Gwynd
128 D6 **Ffordd-las** Denbgs
57 G4 **Fforest** Carmth
62 B3 **Fforest** Mons
57 H5 **Fforest Fach** Swans
57 K4 **Fforest Goch** Neath
76 C5 **Ffostrasol** Cerdgn
129 G8 **Ffrith** Flints
76 F4 **Ffynnon-Oer** Cerdgn
76 C4 **Ffynnonddewi** Cerdgn
128 D3 **Ffynnongroyw** Flints
272 C2 **Fiag Lodge** Highld
51 K6 **Fickleshole** Surrey
64 D1 **Fiddington** Gloucs
30 B3 **Fiddington** Somset
32 D8 **Fiddleford** Dorset
4 D4 **Fiddlers Green** Cnwll
70 C6 **Fiddlers Hamlet** Essex
115 G5 **Field** Staffs
156 E6 **Field Broughton** Cumb
121 M4 **Field Dalling** Norfk
100 B2 **Field Head** Leics
166 B3 **Fieldhead** Cumb
267 H6 **Fife Keith** Moray
32 C6 **Fifehead Magdalen** Dorset
32 C8 **Fifehead Neville** Dorset
16 E1 **Fifehead St Quintin** Dorset
65 K3 **Fifield** Oxon
49 L4 **Fifield** W & M
33 K1 **Fifield** Wilts
33 K1 **Figheldean** Wilts
46 D1 **Filands** Wilts
107 K1 **Filby** Norfk
163 L6 **Filey** N York
85 G5 **Filgrave** M Keyn
65 K6 **Filkins** Oxon
28 B5 **Filleigh** Devon
28 C8 **Filleigh** Devon
135 J3 **Fillingham** Lincs
99 H6 **Fillongley** Warwks
35 K5 **Filmore Hill** Hants
45 J3 **Filton** S Glos
152 D4 **Fimber** E R Yk
234 D4 **Finavon** Angus
104 D2 **Fincham** Norfk
49 J6 **Finchampstead** Wokham
216 D6 **Fincharn** Ag & B
20 B4 **Finchdean** Hants
88 D8 **Finchingfield** Essex
51 H1 **Finchley** Gt Lon
116 A5 **Findern** Derbys
265 G7 **Findhorn** Moray
252 E6 **Findhorn Bridge** Highld
221 H3 **Findo Gask** P & K
267 J3 **Findochty** Moray
245 L4 **Findon** Abers
21 J5 **Findon** W Susx
263 G7 **Findon Mains** Highld
244 D3 **Findrack House** Abers
85 H1 **Finedon** Nhants

101 L4 **Fineshade** Nhants
90 F1 **Fingal Street** Suffk
222 B3 **Fingask** P & K
49 J1 **Fingest** Bucks
160 B5 **Finghall** N York
177 H7 **Fingland** Cumb
197 L7 **Fingland** D & G
41 K4 **Finglesham** Kent
72 F3 **Fingringhoe** Essex
88 D7 **Finkle Green** Essex
141 M7 **Finkle Street** Barns
231 G8 **Finlarig** Stirlg
84 C8 **Finmere** Oxon
230 F4 **Finnart** P & K
90 C2 **Finningham** Suffk
143 H7 **Finningley** Donc
282 e6 **Finsbay** W Isls
82 A1 **Finstall** Worcs
156 E5 **Finsthwaite** Cumb
66 A4 **Finstock** Oxon
275 c4 **Finstown** Ork
268 D5 **Fintry** Abers
209 G2 **Fintry** Stirlg
244 D5 **Finzean** Abers
226 B7 **Fionnphort** Ag & B
282 e6 **Fionnsbhagh** W Isls
168 F4 **Fir Tree** Dur
157 K4 **Firbank** Cumb
133 L2 **Firbeck** Rothm
160 C5 **Firby** N York
152 A3 **Firby** N York
140 D5 **Firgrove** Rochdl
137 H7 **Firsby** Lincs
34 B4 **Firsdown** Dorset
19 J5 **Fishbourne** IOW
20 D6 **Fishbourne** W Susx
169 K4 **Fishburn** Dur
220 F8 **Fishcross** Clacks
20 E6 **Fisher** W Susx
35 G6 **Fisher's Pond** Hants
147 H6 **Fisher's Row** Lancs
256 B4 **Fisherford** Abers
211 K4 **Fisherrow** E Loth
36 E4 **Fisherstreet** W Susx
252 D2 **Fisherton** Highld
196 B7 **Fisherton** S Ayrs
33 G3 **Fisherton de la Mere** Wilts
98 F2 **Fisherwick** Staffs
49 L3 **Fishery Estate** W & M
74 F5 **Fishguard** Pembks
143 G5 **Fishlake** Donc
12 D2 **Fishleigh** Devon
119 J4 **Fishmere End** Lincs
227 J4 **Fishnish Pier** Ag & B
15 J3 **Fishpond Bottom** Dorset
45 J4 **Fishponds** Bristl
140 B6 **Fishpool** Bury
119 K3 **Fishtoft** Lincs
119 K2 **Fishtoft Drove** Lincs
139 H2 **Fishwick** Lancs
246 D2 **Fiskavaig** Highld
135 L5 **Fiskerton** Lincs
117 K1 **Fiskerton** Notts
145 H1 **Fitling** E R Yk
33 K1 **Fittleton** Wilts
21 G3 **Fittleworth** W Susx
103 J1 **Fitton End** Cambs
113 G7 **Fitz** Shrops
29 L5 **Fitzhead** Somset
30 B5 **Fitzroy** Somset
142 C5 **Fitzwilliam** Wakefd
23 H3 **Five Ash Down** E Susx
23 J2 **Five Ashes** E Susx
29 K2 **Five Bells** Somset
80 F6 **Five Bridges** Herefs
44 F1 **Five Lanes** Mons
39 G4 **Five Oak Green** Kent
9 e3 **Five Oaks** Jersey
37 G5 **Five Oaks** W Susx
56 E4 **Five Roads** Carmth
39 K3 **Five Wents** Kent
129 M4 **Fivecrosses** Ches
30 E6 **Fivehead** Somset
11 J6 **Fivelanes** Cnwll
71 J4 **Flack's Green** Essex
49 L1 **Flackwell Heath** Bucks
82 A6 **Fladbury** Worcs
281 e7 **Fladdabister** Shet
132 C6 **Flagg** Derbys
153 K2 **Flamborough** E R Yk
68 D4 **Flamstead** Herts
20 F6 **Flansham** W Susx
141 M4 **Flanshaw** Wakefd
149 J8 **Flappit Spring** Brad
149 G4 **Flasby** N York

131 K6 **Flash** Staffs
258 E6 **Flashader** Highld
68 C7 **Flaunden** Herts
117 K3 **Flawborough** Notts
151 G3 **Flawith** N York
45 G5 **Flax Bourton** N Som
150 E4 **Flaxby** N York
63 K4 **Flaxley** Gloucs
130 A5 **Flaxmere** Ches
29 L4 **Flaxpool** Somset
151 L3 **Flaxton** N York
100 E5 **Fleckney** Leics
83 M3 **Flecknoe** Warwks
134 F5 **Fledborough** Notts
16 C6 **Fleet** Dorset
20 B6 **Fleet** Hants
49 K8 **Fleet** Hants
119 L6 **Fleet** Lincs
119 L6 **Fleet Hargate** Lincs
19 H3 **Fleetend** Hants
146 F6 **Fleetwood** Lancs
42 F7 **Flemingston** V Glam
209 H7 **Flemington** S Lans
89 G1 **Flempton** Suffk
38 E3 **Fletcher Green** Kent
5 J2 **Fletchersbridge** Cnwll
165 G2 **Fletchertown** Cumb
23 G3 **Fletching** E Susx
43 J3 **Fleur-de-lis** Caerph
11 J1 **Flexbury** Cnwll
36 D1 **Flexford** Surrey
164 D4 **Flimby** Cumb
39 H7 **Flimwell** E Susx
128 F5 **Flint** Flints
128 F5 **Flint Mountain** Flints
99 H7 **Flint's Green** Solhll
117 K2 **Flintham** Notts
153 K8 **Flinton** E R Yk
39 J6 **Flishinghurst** Kent
120 F6 **Flitcham** Norfk
85 L8 **Flitton** Beds
85 K8 **Flitwick** Beds
143 L5 **Flixborough** N Linc
143 L5 **Flixborough Stather** N Linc
163 J6 **Flixton** N York
107 G6 **Flixton** Suffk
130 E1 **Flixton** Traffd
141 K5 **Flockton** Kirk
141 L5 **Flockton Green** Kirk
202 E6 **Flodden** Nthumb
259 H2 **Flodigarry** Highld
156 E7 **Flookburgh** Cumb
106 D4 **Flordon** Norfk
84 C3 **Flore** Nhants
190 E5 **Flotterton** Nthumb
23 L5 **Flowers Green** E Susx
90 C6 **Flowton** Suffk
141 L3 **Flushdyke** Wakefd
3 K4 **Flushing** Cnwll
14 C4 **Fluxton** Devon
82 A4 **Flyford Flavell** Worcs
52 F2 **Fobbing** Thurr
267 G4 **Fochabers** Moray
61 H6 **Fochriw** Caerph
143 L4 **Fockerby** N Linc
31 J5 **Foddington** Somset
94 B1 **Foel** Powys
42 C3 **Foel y Dyffryn** Brdgnd
59 G6 **Foelgastell** Carmth
152 A8 **Foggathorpe** E R Yk
202 B3 **Fogo** Border
266 E5 **Fogwatt** Moray
276 B6 **Foindle** Highld
233 J3 **Folda** Angus
115 G4 **Fole** Staffs
99 K7 **Foleshill** Covtry
49 L4 **Foliejon Park** Br For
31 L8 **Folke** Dorset
41 H8 **Folkestone** Kent
118 E5 **Folkingham** Lincs
23 J6 **Folkington** E Susx
102 C5 **Folksworth** Cambs
163 J6 **Folkton** N York
256 C5 **Folla Rule** Abers
150 D5 **Follifoot** N York
12 D3 **Folly Gate** Devon
36 B1 **Folly Hill** Surrey
43 G8 **Fonmon** V Glam
43 G8 **Font-y-gary** V Glam
32 F4 **Fonthill Bishop** Wilts
32 F4 **Fonthill Gifford** Wilts
32 E7 **Fontmell Magna** Dorset
32 D7 **Fontmell Parva** Dorset
20 F5 **Fontwell** W Susx
132 D4 **Foolow** Derbys

52 A5 **Foots Cray** Gt Lon
243 L1 **Forbestown** Abers
168 F8 **Forcett** N York
216 D6 **Ford** Ag & B
67 J5 **Ford** Bucks
133 H4 **Ford** Derbys
27 G6 **Ford** Devon
7 J5 **Ford** Devon
8 B6 **Ford** Devon
65 G1 **Ford** Gloucs
202 E5 **Ford** Nthumb
95 K1 **Ford** Shrops
29 K5 **Ford** Somset
45 H8 **Ford** Somset
115 H1 **Ford** Staffs
21 G6 **Ford** W Susx
46 B4 **Ford** Wilts
33 L4 **Ford** Wilts
71 G4 **Ford End** Essex
147 J6 **Ford Green** Lancs
95 K1 **Ford Heath** Shrops
29 L7 **Ford Street** Somset
90 C2 **Ford's Green** Suffk
12 D4 **Forda** Devon
38 E5 **Fordcombe** Kent
211 G1 **Fordell** Fife
94 F3 **Forden** Powys
12 F4 **Forder Green** Devon
8 B2 **Forder Green** Devon
88 C1 **Fordham** Cambs
72 D2 **Fordham** Essex
104 C3 **Fordham** Norfk
72 D2 **Fordham Heath** Essex
33 K8 **Fordingbridge** Hants
163 J7 **Fordon** E R Yk
245 G8 **Fordoun** Abers
72 D2 **Fordstreet** Essex
13 J3 **Fordton** Devon
65 L4 **Fordwells** Oxon
41 G3 **Fordwich** Kent
267 L3 **Fordyce** Abers
114 E7 **Forebridge** Staffs
116 B6 **Foremark** Derbys
9 J4 **Forest** Guern
160 C3 **Forest** N York
148 D5 **Forest Becks** Lancs
131 J5 **Forest Chapel** Ches
51 L2 **Forest Gate** Gt Lon
37 H3 **Forest Green** Surrey
157 J2 **Forest Hall** Cumb
181 G5 **Forest Hall** N Tyne
178 D7 **Forest Head** Cumb
51 K4 **Forest Hill** Gt Lon
66 E5 **Forest Hill** Oxon
150 D4 **Forest Lane Head** N York
229 M7 **Forest Lodge** Ag & B
221 G8 **Forest Mill** Clacks
38 C6 **Forest Row** E Susx
19 H5 **Forest Side** IOW
133 L7 **Forest Town** Notts
167 K4 **Forest-in-Teesdale** Dur
190 F7 **Forestburn Gate** Nthumb
20 C4 **Forestside** W Susx
234 C5 **Forfar** Angus
221 K3 **Forgandenny** P & K
93 J2 **Forge** Powys
62 B7 **Forge Hammer** Torfn
61 L5 **Forge Side** Torfn
267 H5 **Forgie** Moray
267 H5 **Forgieside** Moray
256 A3 **Forgue** Abers
98 D8 **Forhill** Worcs
138 C6 **Formby** Sefton
106 C4 **Forncett End** Norfk
106 D4 **Forncett St Mary** Norfk
106 D5 **Forncett St Peter** Norfk
89 G2 **Fornham All Saints** Suffk
89 G2 **Fornham St Martin** Suffk
253 H2 **Fornighty** Highld
165 K6 **Fornside** Cumb
265 G8 **Forres** Moray
114 F3 **Forsbrook** Staffs
275 H1 **Forse** Highld
275 H1 **Forse House** Highld
98 E8 **Forshaw Heath** Warwks
278 F7 **Forsinard** Highld
16 C3 **Forston** Dorset
240 C2 **Fort Augustus** Highld
9 i2 **Fort Hommet** Guern
9 k1 **Fort le Marchant** Guern
239 J8 **Fort William** Highld
221 J4 **Forteviot** P & K
198 F2 **Forth** S Lans
64 B1 **Forthampton** Gloucs
231 K6 **Fortingall** P & K

34 F2 **Forton** Hants
147 J5 **Forton** Lancs
113 G8 **Forton** Shrops
15 H1 **Forton** Somset
114 B7 **Forton** Staffs
256 B3 **Fortrie** Abers
263 K8 **Fortrose** Highld
16 D7 **Fortuneswell** Dorset
50 A1 **Forty Green** Bucks
69 J7 **Forty Hill** Gt Lon
90 C3 **Forward Green** Suffk
47 L7 **Fosbury** Wilts
65 K3 **Foscot** Oxon
84 C6 **Foscote** Nhants
119 K5 **Fosdyke** Lincs
119 K5 **Fosdyke Bridge** Lincs
231 L4 **Foss** P & K
76 E3 **Foss-y-ffin** Cerdgn
65 G5 **Fossebridge** Gloucs
70 C5 **Foster Street** Essex
143 G5 **Fosterhouses** Donc
115 K5 **Foston** Derbys
100 D4 **Foston** Leics
117 M3 **Foston** Lincs
151 L3 **Foston** N York
153 H4 **Foston on the Wolds** E R Yk
136 F2 **Fotherby** Lincs
164 D4 **Fothergill** Cumb
102 B5 **Fotheringhay** Nhants
99 H4 **Foul End** Warwks
23 K4 **Foul Mile** E Susx
165 M1 **Foulbridge** Cumb
142 B4 **Foulby** Wakefd
202 E2 **Foulden** Border
104 F4 **Foulden** Norfk
148 F7 **Foulridge** Lancs
122 A6 **Foulsham** Norfk
200 F3 **Fountainhall** Border
98 F8 **Four Ashes** Solhll
97 L2 **Four Ashes** Staffs
97 H6 **Four Ashes** Staffs
89 K1 **Four Ashes** Suffk
9 j3 **Four Cabots** Guern
112 C7 **Four Crosses** Powys
98 B2 **Four Crosses** Staffs
38 C4 **Four Elms** Kent
31 J4 **Four Foot** Somset
30 C3 **Four Forks** Somset
139 J6 **Four Gates** Bolton
120 A8 **Four Gotes** Cambs
141 L7 **Four Lane End** Barns
130 A7 **Four Lane Ends** Ches
3 H3 **Four Lanes** Cnwll
35 K4 **Four Marks** Hants
124 E4 **Four Mile Bridge** IOA
98 E4 **Four Oaks** Birm
24 F2 **Four Oaks** E Susx
63 K2 **Four Oaks** Gloucs
99 H7 **Four Oaks** Solhll
48 E3 **Four Points** W Berk
56 E3 **Four Roads** Carmth
65 K1 **Four Shire Stone** Warwks
39 J7 **Four Throws** Kent
38 F3 **Four Wents** Kent
130 F7 **Fourlanes End** Ches
264 C1 **Fourpenny** Highld
179 K5 **Fourstones** Nthumb
33 H5 **Fovant** Wilts
257 H7 **Foveran** Abers
5 K4 **Fowey** Cnwll
139 K8 **Fowley Common** Warrtn
39 H4 **Fowlhall** Kent
233 M8 **Fowlis** Angus
221 G2 **Fowlis Wester** P & K
87 J6 **Fowlmere** Cambs
80 D8 **Fownhope** Herefs
50 B7 **Fox Corner** Surrey
70 E7 **Fox Hatch** Essex
72 F2 **Fox Street** Essex
208 D6 **Foxbar** Rens
12 C5 **Foxcombe** Devon
64 E3 **Foxcote** Gloucs
45 L7 **Foxcote** Somset
154 c6 **Foxdale** IOM
89 G6 **Foxearth** Essex
52 E5 **Foxendown** Kent
156 B5 **Foxfield** Cumb
46 E3 **Foxham** Wilts
18 E1 **Foxhills** Hants
4 F4 **Foxhole** Cnwll
57 J6 **Foxhole** Swans
163 H8 **Foxholes** N York
23 J4 **Foxhunt Green** E Susx
84 C5 **Foxley** Nhants
122 A7 **Foxley** Norfk

314 Foxley - Garway Common

46 C2 Foxley Wilts
46 C2 Foxley Green Wilts
82 B2 Foxlydiate Worcs
115 G2 Foxt Staffs
87 H5 Foxton Cambs
169 K5 Foxton Dur
100 F5 Foxton Leics
160 F3 Foxton N York
158 F7 Foxup N York
130 C6 Foxwist Green Ches
96 E8 Foxwood Shrops
63 H2 Foy Herefs
250 E7 Foyers Highld
253 G1 Foynesfield Highld
2 F4 Fraddam Cnwll
4 E3 Fraddon Cnwll
98 F1 Fradley Staffs
114 F5 Fradswell Staffs
153 J3 Fraisthorpe E R Yk
23 H3 Framfield E Susx
106 F3 Framingham Earl Norfk
106 F3 Framingham Pigot Norfk
91 G3 Framlingham Suffk
16 B3 Frampton Dorset
119 K4 Frampton Lincs
45 K3 Frampton Cotterell S Glos
64 D6 Frampton Mansell Gloucs
63 L5 Frampton on Severn Gloucs
119 J3 Frampton West End Lincs
90 E3 Framsden Suffk
169 H2 Framwellgate Moor Dur
148 A8 Frances Green Lancs
97 J7 Franche Worcs
130 C4 Frandley Ches
11 M4 Frankaborough Devon
128 F2 Frankby Wirral
122 F6 Frankfort Norfk
80 C6 Franklands Gate Herefs
98 C7 Frankley Worcs
78 F4 Franksbridge Powys
83 K1 Frankton Warwks
38 F6 Frant E Susx
269 J3 Fraserburgh Abers
73 G3 Frating Essex
73 G2 Frating Green Essex
19 L4 Fratton C Port
6 D4 Freathy Cnwll
88 D1 Freckenham Suffk
138 E2 Freckleton Lancs
132 F5 Freebirch Derbys
117 L7 Freeby Leics
35 G1 Freefolk Hants
115 G3 Freehay Staffs
66 B4 Freeland Oxon
107 H2 Freethorpe Norfk
107 H2 Freethorpe Common Norfk
119 L3 Freiston Lincs
27 J4 Fremington Devon
159 J3 Fremington N York
51 M8 French Street Kent
45 J3 Frenchay S Glos
12 F5 Frenchbeer Devon
232 B4 Frenich P & K
36 C3 Frensham Surrey
138 C6 Freshfield Sefton
46 A7 Freshford Wilts
18 E6 Freshwater IoW
18 E6 Freshwater Bay IoW
55 G7 Freshwater East Pembks
106 F7 Fressingfield Suffk
90 E7 Freston Suffk
280 E3 Freswick Highld
63 L5 Fretherne Gloucs
122 E8 Frettenham Norfk
222 E6 Freuchie Fife
54 F4 Freystrop Pembks
98 C4 Friar Park W Mids
16 C5 Friar Waddon Dorset
38 D6 Friar's Gate E Susx
162 C5 Friars' Hill N York
103 K2 Friday Bridge Cambs
23 K6 Friday Street E Susx
90 F3 Friday Street Suffk
91 H5 Friday Street Suffk
91 J3 Friday Street Suffk
37 H2 Friday Street Surrey
152 D4 Fridaythorpe E R Yk
132 C7 Friden Derbys
141 G3 Friendly Calder
69 H8 Friern Barnet Gt Lon
225 G4 Friesland Bay Ag & B
135 M3 Friesthorpe Lincs
118 B2 Frieston Lincs
49 J1 Frieth Bucks
116 D2 Friezeland Notts
66 B7 Frilford Oxon
48 E4 Frilsham W Berk
49 L7 Frimley Surrey
49 L7 Frimley Green Surrey
52 F5 Frindsbury Medway
121 G4 Fring Norfk
66 F1 Fringford Oxon
40 A4 Frinsted Kent
73 K3 Frinton-on-Sea Essex
234 F5 Friockheim Angus
92 D1 Friog Gwynd
117 J8 Frisby on the Wreake Leics
137 J8 Friskney Lincs
137 J8 Friskney Eaudike Lincs
23 J7 Friston E Susx
91 J3 Friston Suffk
116 B1 Fritchley Derbys
119 K2 Frith Bank Lincs
80 F1 Frith Common Worcs
34 B8 Fritham Hants
27 H7 Frithelstock Devon
27 H7 Frithelstock Stone Devon
36 B3 Frithend Hants
68 C5 Frithsden Herts
119 K2 Frithville Lincs
39 K5 Frittenden Kent
8 B6 Frittiscombe Devon
107 K3 Fritton Norfk
106 E5 Fritton Norfk
66 D1 Fritwell Oxon
149 L8 Frizinghall Brad
164 D7 Frizington Cumb
63 M6 Frocester Gloucs
96 C3 Frodesley Shrops
129 M4 Frodsham Ches
87 H6 Frog End Cambs
87 L3 Frog End Cambs
81 J2 Frog Pool Worcs
202 B7 Frogden Border
132 E4 Froggatt Derbys
115 G2 Froghall Staffs
33 L8 Frogham Hants
41 H5 Frogham Kent
7 M6 Frogmore Devon
102 D2 Frognall Lincs
3 J3 Frogpool Cnwll
6 C1 Frogwell Cnwll
100 B5 Frolesworth Leics
32 C1 Frome Somset
16 B2 Frome St Quintin Dorset
16 D4 Frome Whitfield Dorset
80 F6 Fromes Hill Herefs
128 C6 Fron Denbgs
108 F4 Fron Gwynd
109 J1 Fron Gwynd
94 F3 Fron Powys
94 E4 Fron Powys
112 C3 Fron Isaf Wrexhm
111 H4 Fron-goch Gwynd
112 C3 Froncysyllte Denbgs
107 K7 Frostenden Suffk
168 C3 Frosterley Dur
85 J8 Froxfield Beds
47 L5 Froxfield Wilts
35 L5 Froxfield Green Hants
34 F6 Fryern Hill Hants
70 F7 Fryerning Essex
162 B7 Fryton N York
227 J3 Fuinary Highld
118 B2 Fulbeck Lincs
87 L4 Fulbourn Cambs
65 K4 Fulbrook Oxon
35 G5 Fulflood Hants
30 B5 Fulford Somset
114 F4 Fulford Staffs
151 K6 Fulford York
51 H4 Fulham Gt Lon
22 C5 Fulking W Susx
152 A5 Full Sutton E R Yk
28 B3 Fullaford Devon
196 C3 Fullarton N Ayrs
71 H4 Fuller Street Essex
38 E2 Fuller Street Kent
70 D2 Fuller's End Essex
113 H1 Fuller's Moor Ches
34 E3 Fullerton Hants
136 E5 Fulletby Lincs
83 G6 Fullready Warwks
196 E1 Fullwood E Ayrs
50 C2 Fulmer Bucks
121 M5 Fulmodeston Norfk
136 B4 Fulnetby Lincs
119 J6 Fulney Lincs
141 J6 Fulstone Kirk
145 J8 Fulstow Lincs
66 A3 Fulwell Oxon
181 J7 Fulwell Sundld
139 H2 Fulwood Lancs
133 J8 Fulwood Notts
132 F3 Fulwood Sheff
30 B6 Fulwood Somset
106 C4 Fundenhall Norfk
20 C5 Funtington W Susx
19 J2 Funtley Hants
220 C2 Funtullich P & K
15 G2 Furley Devon
217 G7 Furnace Ag & B
56 F4 Furnace Carmth
92 E4 Furnace Cerdgn
99 H5 Furnace End Warwks
22 F2 Furner's Green E Susx
131 K3 Furness Vale Derbys
70 B2 Furneux Pelham Herts
39 M5 Further Quarter Kent
84 E6 Furtho Nhants
49 L3 Furze Platt W & M
28 C2 Furzehill Devon
17 K2 Furzehill Dorset
136 E5 Furzehills Lincs
19 L2 Furzeley Corner Hants
34 C7 Furzley Hants
30 C7 Fyfett Somset
70 E5 Fyfield Essex
34 C2 Fyfield Hants
66 B7 Fyfield Oxon
47 H5 Fyfield Wilts
47 H6 Fyfield Wilts
33 H6 Fyfield Bavant Wilts
66 B7 Fyfield Wick Oxon
163 G2 Fylingthorpe N York
36 B6 Fyning W Susx
256 D4 Fyvie Abers

G

196 E1 Gabroc Hill E Ayrs
100 F1 Gaddesby Leics
68 D4 Gaddesden Row Herts
125 H2 Gadfa IoA
196 E6 Gadgirth S Ayrs
112 E4 Gadlas Shrops
61 J3 Gaer Powys
62 F7 Gaer-llwyd Mons
125 H5 Gaerwen IoA
66 B2 Gagingwell Oxon
196 C4 Gailes N Ayrs
97 K1 Gailey Staffs
168 F7 Gainford Dur
135 G2 Gainsborough Lincs
88 E8 Gainsford End Essex
260 C4 Gairloch Highld
239 K6 Gairlochy Highld
221 L7 Gairneybridge P & K
149 L8 Gaisby Brad
157 K2 Gaisgill Cumb
165 L1 Gaitsgill Cumb
201 G6 Galashiels Border
147 J5 Galgate Lancs
31 K5 Galhampton Somset
216 C2 Gallanach Ag & B
113 H1 Gallantry Bank Ches
222 E8 Gallatown Fife
99 J5 Galley Common Warwks
71 H6 Galleywood Essex
240 F5 Gallovie Highld
234 C7 Gallowfauld Angus
233 J8 Gallowhill P & K
72 D2 Gallows Green Essex
81 L3 Gallows Green Worcs
49 G3 Gallowstree Common Oxon
125 K7 Gallt-y-foel Gwynd
248 C7 Galltair Highld
49 K8 Gally Hill Hants
38 D6 Gallypot Street E Susx
7 K6 Galmpton Devon
8 D4 Galmpton Torbay
150 C1 Galphay N York
196 F4 Galston E Ayrs
16 E5 Galton Dorset
131 L6 Gamballs Green Staffs
71 J4 Gambles Green Essex
166 E3 Gamblesby Cumb
177 H8 Gamelsby Cumb
131 K1 Gamesley Derbys
86 E5 Gamlingay Cambs
86 E4 Gamlingay Cinques Cambs
86 E5 Gamlingay Great Heath Beds
159 J6 Gammersgill N York
268 E4 Gamrie Abers
134 E4 Gamston Notts
117 G4 Gamston Notts
63 G4 Ganarew Herefs
216 D1 Ganavan Bay Ag & B
6 C1 Gang Cnwll
110 D6 Ganllwyd Gwynd
234 F1 Gannachy Angus
144 F1 Ganstead E R Yk
151 L2 Ganthorpe N York
163 H7 Ganton N York
69 H7 Ganwick Corner Herts
13 K7 Gappah Devon
266 F5 Garbity Moray
105 K7 Garboldisham Norfk
243 J2 Garchory Abers
129 H6 Garden City Flints
141 L8 Garden Village Sheff
49 K5 Gardeners Green Wokham
268 E3 Gardenstown Abers
281 d6 Garderhouse Shet
152 E7 Gardham E R Yk
32 C3 Gare Hill Somset
207 L1 Garelochhead Ag & B
66 B7 Garford Oxon
142 B1 Garforth Leeds
142 B1 Garforth Bridge Leeds
149 G5 Gargrave N York
220 B8 Gargunnock Stirlg
126 D4 Garizim Conwy
106 E6 Garlic Street Norfk
174 D5 Garlieston D & G
41 K2 Garlinge Kent
40 F5 Garlinge Green Kent
245 H2 Garlogie Abers
268 E5 Garmond Abers
169 J4 Garmondsway Dur
267 G3 Garmouth Moray
96 E2 Garmston Shrops
108 E5 Garn Gwynd
109 J3 Garn-Dolbenmaen Gwynd
59 J6 Garnant Carmth
157 H3 Garnett Bridge Cumb
209 H5 Garnkirk N Lans
57 H3 Garnswllt Swans
282 h3 Garrabost W Isls
197 G7 Garrallan E Ayrs
3 H6 Garras Cnwll
109 L3 Garreg Gwynd
167 H2 Garrigill Cumb
159 L4 Garriston N York
184 F6 Garroch D & G
172 D7 Garrochtrie D & G
207 H8 Garrochty Ag & B
259 H4 Garros Highld
152 B4 Garrowby Hall E R Yk
158 C5 Garsdale Cumb
158 D4 Garsdale Head Cumb
46 D2 Garsdon Wilts
114 F5 Garshall Green Staffs
66 E6 Garsington Oxon
147 J6 Garstang Lancs
68 E7 Garston Herts
129 J3 Garston Lpool
204 E4 Gartachossan Ag & B
209 J5 Gartcosh N Lans
42 C4 Garth Brdgnd
112 C3 Garth Denbgs
62 D8 Garth Mons
78 C5 Garth Powys
79 K1 Garth Powys
92 E6 Garth Penrhyncoch Cerdgn
157 H3 Garth Row Cumb
209 H5 Garthamlock C Glas
78 E8 Garthbrengy Powys
77 G4 Gartheli Cerdgn
94 F3 Garthmyl Powys
117 L7 Garthorpe Leics
143 L4 Garthorpe N Linc
157 H5 Garths Cumb
255 K5 Gartly Abers
219 H7 Gartmore Stirlg
209 K6 Gartness N Lans
208 E2 Gartness Stirlg
208 D2 Gartocharn W Duns
145 H1 Garton E R Yk
152 F4 Garton-on-the-Wolds E R Yk
274 D5 Gartymore Highld
212 D5 Garvald E Loth
238 F8 Garvan Highld
214 D6 Garvard Ag & B
262 C7 Garve Highld
105 L2 Garvestone Norfk
207 L5 Garvock Inver
62 F3 Garway Herefs
62 F3 Garway Common Herefs

62 F2	**Garway Hill**	Herefs
282 g4	**Garyvard**	W Isls
32 C4	**Gasper**	Wilts
46 C5	**Gastard**	Wilts
105 K7	**Gasthorpe**	Norfk
70 D4	**Gaston Green**	Essex
19 H6	**Gatcombe**	IOW
135 G3	**Gate Burton**	Lincs
151 L5	**Gate Helmsley**	N York
157 J5	**Gatebeck**	Cumb
134 B3	**Gateford**	Notts
142 E2	**Gateforth**	N York
196 D4	**Gatehead**	E Ayrs
179 H1	**Gatehouse**	Nthumb
174 F4	**Gatehouse of Fleet**	D & G
121 L6	**Gateley**	Norfk
160 D5	**Gatenby**	N York
129 L7	**Gates Heath**	Ches
165 G7	**Gatesgarth**	Cumb
189 L2	**Gateshaw**	Border
181 G6	**Gateshead**	Gatesd
234 C6	**Gateside**	Angus
208 E7	**Gateside**	E Rens
222 B5	**Gateside**	Fife
208 B8	**Gateside**	N Ayrs
186 C5	**Gateslack**	D & G
139 G6	**Gathurst**	Wigan
131 G2	**Gatley**	Stockp
51 H8	**Gatton**	Surrey
201 H6	**Gattonside**	Border
78 D2	**Gaufron**	Powys
100 F3	**Gaulby**	Leics
222 F2	**Gauldry**	Fife
233 K5	**Gauldswell**	P & K
139 M3	**Gaulkthorn**	Lancs
103 K2	**Gaultree**	Norfk
17 K2	**Gaunt's Common**	Dorset
70 E2	**Gaunt's End**	Essex
113 J2	**Gaunton's Bank**	Ches
136 C5	**Gautby**	Lincs
202 B3	**Gavinton**	Border
141 M6	**Gawber**	Barns
67 G1	**Gawcott**	Bucks
131 H5	**Gawsworth**	Ches
141 L3	**Gawthorpe**	Wakefd
158 B5	**Gawthrop**	Cumb
156 C5	**Gawthwaite**	Cumb
71 J6	**Gay Bowers**	Essex
21 J3	**Gay Street**	W Susx
83 J4	**Gaydon**	Warwks
85 G6	**Gayhurst**	M Keyn
158 F5	**Gayle**	N York
159 L1	**Gayles**	N York
84 D4	**Gayton**	Nhants
120 F7	**Gayton**	Norfk
114 F6	**Gayton**	Staffs
129 G4	**Gayton**	Wirral
137 H3	**Gayton le Marsh**	Lincs
121 G7	**Gayton Thorpe**	Norfk
120 E7	**Gaywood**	Norfk
88 E2	**Gazeley**	Suffk
3 J6	**Gear**	Cnwll
282 g4	**Gearraidh Bhaird**	W Isls
258 D4	**Geary**	Highld
89 J4	**Gedding**	Suffk
41 H6	**Geddinge**	Kent
101 K6	**Geddington**	Nhants
117 G3	**Gedling**	Notts
119 L6	**Gedney**	Lincs
119 L7	**Gedney Broadgate**	Lincs
120 A5	**Gedney Drove End**	Lincs
119 L6	**Gedney Dyke**	Lincs
103 G1	**Gedney Hill**	Lincs
131 J1	**Gee Cross**	Tamesd
101 L3	**Geeston**	Rutlnd
107 H5	**Geldeston**	Norfk
42 E3	**Gelli**	Rhondd
62 B8	**Gelli**	Torfn
128 D7	**Gellifor**	Denbgs
43 H2	**Gelligaer**	Caerph
43 J3	**Gelligroes**	Caerph
57 K4	**Gelligron**	Neath
110 C4	**Gellilydan**	Gwynd
57 K4	**Gellinudd**	Neath
55 J3	**Gelly**	Carmth
233 G7	**Gellyburn**	P & K
58 A4	**Gellywen**	Carmth
175 J3	**Gelston**	D & G
118 B3	**Gelston**	Lincs
153 H4	**Gembling**	E R Yk
98 D1	**Gentleshaw**	Staffs
50 C3	**George Green**	Bucks
28 B6	**George Nympton**	Devon
187 L7	**Georgefield**	D & G
27 H3	**Georgeham**	Devon

61 J5	**Georgetown**	Blae G
2 D4	**Georgia**	Cnwll
275 c3	**Georth**	Ork
126 C6	**Gerlan**	Gwynd
12 B4	**Germansweek**	Devon
2 F5	**Germoe**	Cnwll
3 M4	**Gerrans**	Cnwll
50 C1	**Gerrards Cross**	Bucks
171 G8	**Gerrick**	R & Cl
89 G7	**Gestingthorpe**	Essex
112 B8	**Geuffordd**	Powys
130 C4	**Gib Hill**	Ches
137 K7	**Gibraltar**	Lincs
117 J2	**Gibsmere**	Notts
46 B4	**Giddeahall**	Wilts
16 F5	**Giddy Green**	Dorset
52 B1	**Gidea Park**	Gt Lon
12 F5	**Gidleigh**	Devon
208 F7	**Giffnock**	E Rens
212 C5	**Gifford**	E Loth
222 E5	**Giffordtown**	Fife
148 D3	**Giggleswick**	N York
143 L2	**Gilberdyke**	E R Yk
35 K4	**Gilbert Street**	Hants
97 J6	**Gilbert's Cross**	Staffs
81 J6	**Gilbert's End**	Worcs
212 B6	**Gilchriston**	E Loth
164 F3	**Gilcrux**	Cumb
141 K2	**Gildersome**	Leeds
133 L3	**Gildingwells**	Rothm
169 J2	**Gilesgate Moor**	Dur
42 F8	**Gileston**	V Glam
43 J2	**Gilfach**	Caerph
42 E4	**Gilfach Goch**	Brdgnd
76 D3	**Gilfachrheda**	Cerdgn
164 D6	**Gilgarran**	Cumb
166 B5	**Gill**	Cumb
39 J7	**Gill's Green**	Kent
162 B4	**Gillamoor**	N York
3 K6	**Gillan**	Cnwll
258 D5	**Gillen**	Highld
187 J7	**Gillesbie**	D & G
161 K7	**Gilling East**	N York
160 B2	**Gilling West**	N York
32 D5	**Gillingham**	Dorset
53 G5	**Gillingham**	Medway
107 H5	**Gillingham**	Norfk
280 B4	**Gillock**	Highld
131 H7	**Gillow Heath**	Staffs
280 D2	**Gills**	Highld
188 B2	**Gilmanscleuch**	Border
211 J5	**Gilmerton**	C Edin
220 F2	**Gilmerton**	P & K
168 C8	**Gilmonby**	Dur
100 C6	**Gilmorton**	Leics
178 E5	**Gilsland**	Nthumb
99 G5	**Gilson**	Warwks
149 L7	**Gilstead**	Brad
70 C4	**Gilston**	Herts
200 F2	**Gilston**	Mdloth
70 B4	**Gilston Park**	Herts
116 E2	**Giltbrook**	Notts
61 L4	**Gilwern**	Mons
122 F4	**Gimingham**	Norfk
131 J4	**Ginclough**	Ches
23 K5	**Gingers Green**	E Susx
90 C3	**Gipping**	Suffk
119 J2	**Gipsey Bridge**	Lincs
196 C3	**Girdle Toll**	N Ayrs
141 H1	**Girlington**	Brad
281 e6	**Girlsta**	Shet
160 E1	**Girsby**	N York
86 D5	**Girtford**	Beds
174 F4	**Girthon**	D & G
87 J3	**Girton**	Cambs
135 G6	**Girton**	Notts
182 F3	**Girvan**	S Ayrs
148 E6	**Gisburn**	Lancs
107 K5	**Gisleham**	Suffk
90 C1	**Gislingham**	Suffk
106 C6	**Gissing**	Norfk
14 D3	**Gittisham**	Devon
79 J4	**Gladestry**	Powys
212 A4	**Gladsmuir**	E Loth
57 K5	**Glais**	Swans
162 D2	**Glaisdale**	N York
234 B6	**Glamis**	Angus
76 F6	**Glan-Duar**	Carmth
109 J3	**Glan-Dwyfach**	Gwynd
57 L3	**Glan-rhyd**	Powys
128 E4	**Glan-y-don**	Flints
43 H5	**Glan-y-llyn**	Rhondd
93 K6	**Glan-y-nant**	Powys
111 H3	**Glan-yr-afon**	Gwynd
111 K3	**Glan-yr-afon**	Gwynd

126 B4	**Glan-yr-afon**	IOA
57 H4	**Glan-yr-afon**	Swans
110 B1	**Glanaber**	Gwynd
54 F3	**Glanafon**	Pembks
59 J6	**Glanaman**	Carmth
122 A3	**Glandford**	Norfk
75 L6	**Glandwr**	Pembks
92 F4	**Glandyfi**	Cerdgn
61 K4	**Glangrwyney**	Powys
42 C3	**Glanllynfi**	Brdgnd
94 E5	**Glanmule**	Powys
75 K4	**Glanrhyd**	Pembks
190 F3	**Glanton**	Nthumb
190 F3	**Glanton Pike**	Nthumb
16 C1	**Glanvilles Wootton**	Dorset
101 M5	**Glapthorn**	Nhants
133 J6	**Glapwell**	Derbys
79 H7	**Glasbury**	Powys
127 K5	**Glascoed**	Denbgs
62 C6	**Glascoed**	Mons
99 G3	**Glascote**	Staffs
79 G5	**Glascwm**	Powys
111 H2	**Glasfryn**	Conwy
209 G6	**Glasgow**	C Glas
125 K6	**Glasinfryn**	Gwynd
237 K2	**Glasnacardoch Bay**	Highld
247 H6	**Glasnakille**	Highld
92 F4	**Glaspwll**	Powys
142 C3	**Glass Houghton**	Wakefd
39 J6	**Glassenbury**	Kent
174 C7	**Glasserton**	D & G
197 L2	**Glassford**	S Lans
63 L3	**Glasshouse**	Gloucs
63 L3	**Glasshouse Hill**	Gloucs
149 L3	**Glasshouses**	N York
177 H6	**Glasson**	Cumb
147 J4	**Glasson**	Lancs
166 D3	**Glassonby**	Cumb
234 F5	**Glasterlaw**	Angus
101 K3	**Glaston**	Rutlnd
31 H3	**Glastonbury**	Somset
102 C6	**Glatton**	Cambs
130 D1	**Glazebrook**	Warrtn
139 K8	**Glazebury**	Warrtn
96 F5	**Glazeley**	Shrops
133 G3	**Gleadless**	Sheff
130 F6	**Gleadsmoss**	Ches
146 E2	**Gleaston**	Cumb
250 F8	**Glebe**	Highld
150 D8	**Gledhow**	Leeds
175 G5	**Gledpark**	D & G
112 D4	**Gledrid**	Shrops
89 G5	**Glemsford**	Suffk
154 f4	**Glen Auldyn**	IOM
242 F7	**Glen Clunie Lodge**	Abers
154 b6	**Glen Maye**	IOM
154 f4	**Glen Mona**	IOM
229 J1	**Glen Nevis House**	Highld
100 C4	**Glen Parva**	Leics
183 K7	**Glen Trool Lodge**	D & G
154 d6	**Glen Vine**	IOM
254 E3	**Glenallachie**	Highld
237 K2	**Glenancross**	Highld
227 G4	**Glenaros House**	Ag & B
192 D1	**Glenbarr**	Ag & B
267 L5	**Glenbarry**	Abers
237 H8	**Glenbeg**	Highld
253 J6	**Glenbeg**	Highld
245 G7	**Glenbervie**	Abers
209 J5	**Glenboig**	N Lans
237 H8	**Glenborrodale**	Highld
217 J7	**Glenbranter**	Ag & B
187 G2	**Glenbreck**	Border
246 F4	**Glenbrittle House**	Highld
198 B7	**Glenbuck**	E Ayrs
234 A3	**Glencally**	Angus
176 C5	**Glencaple**	D & G
249 H2	**Glencarron Lodge**	Highld
222 C3	**Glencarse**	P & K
229 J5	**Glenceitlein**	Highld
229 H4	**Glencoe**	Highld
199 J7	**Glencothe**	Border
222 B8	**Glencraig**	Fife
185 J5	**Glencrosh**	D & G
206 F2	**Glendaruel**	Ag & B
221 H6	**Glendevon**	P & K
240 C2	**Glendoe Lodge**	Highld
222 C3	**Glendoick**	P & K
222 D3	**Glenduckie**	Fife
221 G5	**Gleneagles**	P & K
221 G5	**Gleneagles Hotel**	P & K
204 E6	**Glenegedale**	Ag & B
248 C7	**Glenelg**	Highld
253 K2	**Glenerney**	Moray

221 L5	**Glenfarg**	P & K
241 M5	**Glenfeshie Lodge**	Highld
100 C2	**Glenfield**	Leics
238 E7	**Glenfinnan**	Highld
239 L6	**Glenfintaig Lodge**	Highld
222 B4	**Glenfoot**	P & K
218 B4	**Glenfyne Lodge**	Ag & B
208 B8	**Glengarnock**	N Ayrs
279 K3	**Glengolly**	Highld
226 E1	**Glengorm Castle**	Ag & B
259 G7	**Glengrasco**	Highld
199 J6	**Glenholm**	Border
184 F5	**Glenhoul**	D & G
233 K3	**Glenisla**	Angus
207 J3	**Glenkin**	Ag & B
243 M1	**Glenkindie**	Abers
254 D6	**Glenlivet**	Moray
175 J2	**Glenlochar**	D & G
222 B6	**Glenlomond**	P & K
172 F3	**Glenluce**	D & G
207 H2	**Glenmassen**	Ag & B
209 K5	**Glenmavis**	N Lans
259 G8	**Glenmore**	Highld
242 C2	**Glenmore Lodge**	Highld
234 C3	**Glenquiech**	Angus
206 D5	**Glenralloch**	Ag & B
165 L7	**Glenridding**	Cumb
222 D7	**Glenrothes**	Fife
232 E8	**Glenshee**	P & K
240 F5	**Glenshera Lodge**	Highld
207 H3	**Glenstriven**	Ag & B
135 K2	**Glentham**	Lincs
241 L4	**Glentromie Lodge**	Highld
183 J7	**Glentrool Village**	D & G
241 J4	**Glentruim House**	Highld
135 J2	**Glentworth**	Lincs
237 K5	**Glenuig**	Highld
229 G5	**Glenure**	Ag & B
259 H8	**Glenvarragill**	Highld
182 F8	**Glenwhilly**	D & G
198 D7	**Glespin**	S Lans
63 H3	**Glewstone**	Herefs
102 C2	**Glinton**	C Pete
101 G4	**Glooston**	Leics
203 K6	**Glororum**	Nthumb
131 L1	**Glossop**	Derbys
191 K5	**Gloster Hill**	Nthumb
64 B3	**Gloucester**	Gloucs
149 H6	**Glusburn**	N York
274 D1	**Glutt Lodge**	Highld
4 F2	**Gluvian**	Cnwll
66 B3	**Glympton**	Oxon
112 B4	**Glyn Ceiriog**	Wrexhm
60 D5	**Glyn-Neath**	Neath
76 B5	**Glynarthen**	Cerdgn
60 C7	**Glyncorrwg**	Neath
23 G5	**Glynde**	E Susx
23 G5	**Glyndebourne**	E Susx
112 A3	**Glyndyfrdwy**	Denbgs
43 H4	**Glyntaff**	Rhondd
60 C4	**Glyntawe**	Powys
76 C7	**Glynteg**	Carmth
114 C7	**Gnosall**	Staffs
114 C7	**Gnosall Heath**	Staffs
101 G4	**Goadby**	Leics
117 K6	**Goadby Marwood**	Leics
40 D6	**Goat Lees**	Kent
46 F4	**Goatacre**	Wilts
217 G7	**Goatfield**	Ag & B
24 E3	**Goatham Green**	E Susx
31 L7	**Goathill**	Dorset
162 E2	**Goathland**	N York
30 C4	**Goathurst**	Somset
38 D3	**Goathurst Common**	Kent
112 D5	**Gobowen**	Shrops
36 E2	**Godalming**	Surrey
91 G2	**Goddard's Corner**	Suffk
39 K6	**Goddard's Green**	Kent
14 D2	**Godford Cross**	Devon
66 F2	**Godington**	Bucks
140 E8	**Godley**	Tamesd
86 E1	**Godmanchester**	Cambs
16 C3	**Godmanstone**	Dorset
40 D5	**Godmersham**	Kent
31 H2	**Godney**	Somset
2 F5	**Godolphin Cross**	Cnwll
57 L3	**Godre'r-graig**	Neath
33 L7	**Godshill**	Hants
19 J7	**Godshill**	IOW
115 G5	**Godstone**	Staffs
51 K8	**Godstone**	Surrey
12 C7	**Godsworthy**	Devon
18 B4	**Godwinscroft**	Hants
62 C6	**Goetre**	Mons
69 J6	**Goff's Oak**	Herts

61 L4 **Gofilon** Mons
211 G4 **Gogar** C Edin
92 E7 **Goginan** Cerdgn
109 J3 **Golan** Gwynd
5 K4 **Golant** Cnwll
11 L8 **Golberdon** Cnwll
139 J8 **Golborne** Wigan
141 H4 **Golcar** Kirk
103 L5 **Gold Hill** Cambs
32 D8 **Gold Hill** Dorset
44 D2 **Goldcliff** Newpt
23 J5 **Golden Cross** E Susx
39 G4 **Golden Green** Kent
59 G5 **Golden Grove** Carmth
55 G6 **Golden Hill** Pembks
35 L2 **Golden Pot** Hants
116 C1 **Golden Valley** Derbys
114 D1 **Goldenhill** C Stke
51 H2 **Golders Green** Gt Lon
48 D6 **Goldfinch Bottom** W Berk
72 C5 **Goldhanger** Essex
96 C3 **Golding** Shrops
86 B5 **Goldington** Beds
98 C5 **Golds Green** Sandw
171 J7 **Goldsborough** N York
150 E4 **Goldsborough** N York
2 E5 **Goldsithney** Cnwll
41 J3 **Goldstone** Kent
113 M6 **Goldstone** Shrops
50 C7 **Goldsworth Park** Surrey
142 C7 **Goldthorpe** Barns
27 G6 **Goldworthy** Devon
39 K6 **Golford** Kent
39 K6 **Golford Green** Kent
252 F1 **Gollanfield** Highld
159 L6 **Gollinglith Foot** N York
129 H7 **Golly** Wrexhm
29 J3 **Golsoncott** Somset
273 K8 **Golspie** Highld
33 L4 **Gomeldon** Wilts
141 K3 **Gomersal** Kirk
37 G1 **Gomshall** Surrey
117 H2 **Gonalston** Notts
118 B4 **Gonerby Hill Foot** Lincs
281 d5 **Gonfirth** Shet
70 F5 **Good Easter** Essex
7 G2 **Goodameavy** Devon
104 F3 **Gooderstone** Norfk
27 L4 **Goodleigh** Devon
152 D7 **Goodmanham** E R Yk
51 M2 **Goodmayes** Gt Lon
40 D3 **Goodnestone** Kent
41 H4 **Goodnestone** Kent
63 H3 **Goodrich** Herefs
8 D3 **Goodrington** Torbay
140 B3 **Goodshaw** Lancs
140 B2 **Goodshaw Fold** Lancs
13 H8 **Goodstone** Devon
74 F4 **Goodwick** Pembks
34 D2 **Goodworth Clatford** Hants
99 J6 **Goodyers End** Warwks
143 J3 **Goole** E R Yk
143 J4 **Goole Fields** E R Yk
82 B4 **Goom's Hill** Worcs
4 B5 **Goonbell** Cnwll
4 C4 **Goonhavern** Cnwll
4 B5 **Goonvrea** Cnwll
73 H2 **Goose Green** Essex
73 H2 **Goose Green** Essex
39 G3 **Goose Green** Kent
39 L6 **Goose Green** Kent
45 K4 **Goose Green** S Glos
21 J3 **Goose Green** W Susx
139 H7 **Goose Green** Wigan
80 B7 **Goose Pool** Herefs
245 G7 **Goosecruives** Abers
12 F4 **Gooseford** Devon
26 D7 **Gooseham** Cnwll
81 L3 **Goosehill Green** Worcs
29 G4 **Goosemoor** Somset
47 M1 **Goosey** Oxon
147 L8 **Goosnargh** Lancs
130 F5 **Goostrey** Ches
126 D5 **Gorddinog** Conwy
201 K4 **Gordon** Border
200 C8 **Gordon Arms Hotel** Border
267 L5 **Gordonstown** Abers
256 C4 **Gordonstown** Abers
79 J3 **Gore** Powys
72 C3 **Gore Pit** Essex
41 J2 **Gore Street** Kent
211 K6 **Gorebridge** Mdloth
103 J1 **Gorefield** Cambs
47 G7 **Gores** Wilts
9 f3 **Gorey** Jersey

48 F3 **Goring** Oxon
49 G3 **Goring Heath** Oxon
21 J6 **Goring-by-Sea** W Susx
107 L3 **Gorleston on Sea** Norfk
268 D4 **Gorrachie** Abers
5 G6 **Gorran** Cnwll
5 G6 **Gorran Haven** Cnwll
5 G6 **Gorran High Lanes** Cnwll
76 D6 **Gorrig** Cerdgn
92 D7 **Gors** Cerdgn
47 H2 **Gorse Hill** Swindn
128 E4 **Gorsedd** Flints
57 G5 **Gorseinon** Swans
115 M1 **Gorseybank** Derbys
76 E5 **Gorsgoch** Cerdgn
59 G6 **Gorslas** Carmth
63 K2 **Gorsley** Gloucs
63 K2 **Gorsley Common** Herefs
97 G8 **Gorst Hill** Worcs
130 B5 **Gorstage** Ches
262 C7 **Gorstan** Highld
129 H7 **Gorstello** Ches
115 H6 **Gorsty Hill** Staffs
227 L6 **Gorten** Ag & B
250 F7 **Gorthleck** Highld
140 C8 **Gorton** Manch
90 D4 **Gosbeck** Suffk
119 H5 **Gosberton** Lincs
119 G5 **Gosberton Clough** Lincs
71 J1 **Gosfield** Essex
14 C3 **Gosford** Devon
155 J2 **Gosforth** Cumb
180 F5 **Gosforth** N u Ty
130 B8 **Gosland Green** Ches
31 J4 **Gosling Street** Somset
68 F2 **Gosmore** Herts
97 K4 **Gospel End** Staffs
36 D4 **Gospel Green** W Susx
19 K4 **Gosport** Hants
85 J6 **Gossard's Green** Beds
63 L6 **Gossington** Gloucs
203 G4 **Goswick** Nthumb
116 F5 **Gotham** Notts
64 D1 **Gotherington** Gloucs
30 C5 **Gotton** Somset
39 H6 **Goudhurst** Kent
136 E4 **Goulceby** Lincs
256 D3 **Gourdas** Abers
222 F1 **Gourdie** Angus
235 K1 **Gourdon** Abers
207 L3 **Gourock** Inver
208 F6 **Govan** C Glas
7 L5 **Goveton** Devon
143 G3 **Gowdall** E R Yk
262 E8 **Gower** Highld
57 G5 **Gowerton** Swans
210 E1 **Gowkhall** Fife
152 A5 **Gowthorpe** E R Yk
153 K6 **Goxhill** E R Yk
144 E3 **Goxhill** N Linc
282 g4 **Grabhair** W Isls
118 E5 **Graby** Lincs
3 H8 **Grade** Cnwll
113 K1 **Gradeley Green** Ches
20 F3 **Graffham** W Susx
86 D2 **Grafham** Cambs
36 F3 **Grafham** Surrey
80 C7 **Grafton** Herefs
150 F3 **Grafton** N York
65 K7 **Grafton** Oxon
113 G7 **Grafton** Shrops
80 D3 **Grafton** Worcs
82 A7 **Grafton** Worcs
81 M4 **Grafton Flyford** Worcs
84 E6 **Grafton Regis** Nhants
101 K7 **Grafton Underwood** Nhants
39 L4 **Grafty Green** Kent
128 F8 **Graianrhyd** Denbgs
126 F5 **Graig** Conwy
128 C5 **Graig** Denbgs
112 A1 **Graig-fechan** Denbgs
53 J4 **Grain** Medway
140 E6 **Grains Bar** Oldham
145 H7 **Grainsby** Lincs
145 K8 **Grainthorpe** Lincs
4 F5 **Grampound** Cnwll
4 E5 **Grampound Road** Cnwll
283 C9 **Gramsdal** W Isls
283 C9 **Gramsdale** W Isls
67 J2 **Granborough** Bucks
117 K4 **Granby** Notts
9 e3 **Grand Chemins** Jersey
83 L2 **Grandborough** Warwks
9 j2 **Grandes Rocques** Guern
232 D5 **Grandtully** P & K

165 H7 **Grange** Cumb
53 G5 **Grange** Medway
222 D2 **Grange** P & K
128 F2 **Grange** Wirral
267 K5 **Grange Crossroads** Moray
17 H6 **Grange Gate** Dorset
265 H7 **Grange Hall** Moray
70 C8 **Grange Hill** Gt Lon
141 K4 **Grange Moor** Kirk
222 D4 **Grange of Lindores** Fife
180 F8 **Grange Villa** Dur
156 F7 **Grange-over-Sands** Cumb
199 G4 **Grangehall** S Lans
132 E8 **Grangemill** Derbys
210 B3 **Grangemouth** Falk
210 D3 **Grangepans** Falk
170 D6 **Grangetown** R & Cl
181 K8 **Grangetown** Sundld
153 H4 **Gransmoor** E R Yk
71 G3 **Gransmore Green** Essex
74 E5 **Granston** Pembks
87 J4 **Grantchester** Cambs
118 B4 **Grantham** Lincs
211 H4 **Granton** C Edin
253 K6 **Grantown-on-Spey** Highld
80 C3 **Grantsfield** Herefs
213 H6 **Grantshouse** Border
130 C2 **Grappenhall** Warrtn
144 D6 **Grasby** Lincs
156 D1 **Grasmere** Cumb
88 E7 **Grass Green** Essex
140 E6 **Grasscroft** Oldham
129 J3 **Grassendale** Lpool
165 K2 **Grassgarth** Cumb
149 H3 **Grassington** N York
133 H6 **Grassmoor** Derbys
134 F6 **Grassthorpe** Notts
34 C3 **Grateley** Hants
115 G5 **Gratwich** Staffs
86 E3 **Graveley** Cambs
69 G2 **Graveley** Herts
98 E5 **Gravelly Hill** Birm
95 H3 **Gravelsbank** Shrops
40 D3 **Graveney** Kent
52 E4 **Gravesend** Kent
282 g4 **Gravir** W Isls
144 A8 **Grayingham** Lincs
157 J3 **Grayrigg** Cumb
52 D3 **Grays** Thurr
36 C4 **Grayshott** Hants
164 C5 **Grayson Green** Cumb
36 D4 **Grayswood** Surrey
170 C5 **Graythorpe** Hartpl
49 G5 **Grazeley** Wokham
142 C8 **Greasbrough** Rothm
128 F2 **Greasby** Wirral
116 E2 **Greasley** Notts
87 L5 **Great Abington** Cambs
101 L8 **Great Addington** Nhants
82 D3 **Great Alne** Warwks
138 C6 **Great Altcar** Lancs
69 K4 **Great Amwell** Herts
166 F8 **Great Asby** Cumb
89 K2 **Great Ashfield** Suffk
170 D8 **Great Ayton** N York
71 H6 **Great Baddow** Essex
46 A2 **Great Badminton** S Glos
71 G1 **Great Bardfield** Essex
86 C5 **Great Barford** Beds
98 D4 **Great Barr** Sandw
65 J4 **Great Barrington** Gloucs
129 L6 **Great Barrow** Ches
89 H2 **Great Barton** Suffk
162 C6 **Great Barugh** N York
180 B3 **Great Bavington** Nthumb
90 F5 **Great Bealings** Suffk
47 K6 **Great Bedwyn** Wilts
73 G3 **Great Bentley** Essex
84 F3 **Great Billing** Nhants
121 G5 **Great Bircham** Norfk
90 D5 **Great Blakenham** Suffk
166 B4 **Great Blencow** Cumb
113 L7 **Great Bolas** Wrekin
50 E8 **Great Bookham** Surrey
2 C4 **Great Bosullow** Cnwll
83 K6 **Great Bourton** Oxon
101 G5 **Great Bowden** Leics
88 D4 **Great Bradley** Suffk
72 B4 **Great Braxted** Essex
90 B5 **Great Bricett** Suffk
67 L1 **Great Brickhill** Bucks
114 D6 **Great Bridgeford** Staffs
84 C2 **Great Brington** Nhants
73 G2 **Great Bromley** Essex
164 E4 **Great Broughton** Cumb

161 J2 **Great Broughton** N York
130 C4 **Great Budworth** Ches
169 J7 **Great Burdon** Darltn
71 G8 **Great Burstead** Essex
161 H2 **Great Busby** N York
70 E3 **Great Canfield** Essex
137 H3 **Great Carlton** Lincs
101 M2 **Great Casterton** Rutlnd
46 B6 **Great Chalfield** Wilts
40 C7 **Great Chart** Kent
114 B8 **Great Chatwell** Staffs
114 D1 **Great Chell** C Stke
87 K6 **Great Chesterford** Essex
46 E8 **Great Cheverell** Wilts
87 J7 **Great Chishill** Cambs
73 J4 **Great Clacton** Essex
141 M4 **Great Cliffe** Wakefd
164 D5 **Great Clifton** Cumb
145 G6 **Great Coates** NE Lin
81 L6 **Great Comberton** Worcs
39 G2 **Great Comp** Kent
178 B7 **Great Corby** Cumb
89 H7 **Great Cornard** Suffk
153 L7 **Great Cowden** E R Yk
65 K8 **Great Coxwell** Oxon
101 H8 **Great Cransley** Nhants
105 G3 **Great Cressingham** Norfk
165 J6 **Great Crosthwaite** Cumb
115 K4 **Great Cubley** Derbys
117 K8 **Great Dalby** Leics
85 H2 **Great Doddington** Nhants
63 G4 **Great Doward** Herefs
121 J8 **Great Dunham** Norfk
70 F3 **Great Dunmow** Essex
33 K3 **Great Durnford** Wilts
70 F2 **Great Easton** Essex
101 J5 **Great Easton** Leics
147 H7 **Great Eccleston** Lancs
162 C6 **Great Edstone** N York
105 L4 **Great Ellingham** Norfk
32 C1 **Great Elm** Somset
8 A3 **Great Englebourne** Devon
84 B4 **Great Everdon** Nhants
87 H4 **Great Eversden** Cambs
89 K4 **Great Finborough** Suffk
105 H1 **Great Fransham** Norfk
68 C5 **Great Gaddesden** Herts
102 C6 **Great Gidding** Cambs
152 B5 **Great Givendale** E R Yk
91 H3 **Great Glemham** Suffk
100 E4 **Great Glen** Leics
118 B4 **Great Gonerby** Lincs
86 F4 **Great Gransden** Cambs
86 F6 **Great Green** Cambs
106 F5 **Great Green** Norfk
89 J4 **Great Green** Suffk
89 J2 **Great Green** Suffk
162 D7 **Great Habton** N York
118 F3 **Great Hale** Lincs
70 D3 **Great Hallingbury** Essex
67 K6 **Great Hampden** Bucks
85 G1 **Great Harrowden** Nhants
139 L1 **Great Harwood** Lancs
66 F6 **Great Haseley** Oxon
153 K7 **Great Hatfield** E R Yk
114 F7 **Great Haywood** Staffs
142 F3 **Great Heck** N York
89 H7 **Great Henny** Essex
46 C7 **Great Hinton** Wilts
105 J5 **Great Hockham** Norfk
73 J3 **Great Holland** Essex
72 E1 **Great Horkesley** Essex
69 L1 **Great Hormead** Herts
141 J2 **Great Horton** Brad
67 J1 **Great Horwood** Bucks
142 C6 **Great Houghton** Barns
84 F3 **Great Houghton** Nhants
132 D4 **Great Hucklow** Derbys
153 H4 **Great Kelk** E R Yk
67 K6 **Great Kimble** Bucks
67 L7 **Great Kingshill** Bucks
156 D2 **Great Langdale** Cumb
160 D3 **Great Langton** N York
71 H4 **Great Leighs** Essex
144 E6 **Great Limber** Lincs
85 G6 **Great Linford** M Keyn
89 H1 **Great Livermere** Suffk
132 D5 **Great Longstone** Derbys
169 H1 **Great Lumley** Dur
95 L2 **Great Lyth** Shrops
81 H6 **Great Malvern** Worcs
89 G8 **Great Maplestead** Essex
138 C1 **Great Marton** Bpool
121 H7 **Great Massingham** Norfk
106 C2 **Great Melton** Norfk

128 F2 **Great Meols** Wirral
66 F6 **Great Milton** Oxon
67 L6 **Great Missenden** Bucks
148 C8 **Great Mitton** Lancs
41 K5 **Great Mongeham** Kent
106 D5 **Great Moulton** Norfk
69 K2 **Great Munden** Herts
167 H7 **Great Musgrave** Cumb
112 F7 **Great Ness** Shrops
71 H3 **Great Notley** Essex
62 D5 **Great Oak** Mons
73 J2 **Great Oakley** Essex
101 J6 **Great Oakley** Nhants
68 F2 **Great Offley** Herts
167 G7 **Great Ormside** Cumb
177 K7 **Great Orton** Cumb
150 F3 **Great Ouseburn** N York
100 F6 **Great Oxendon** Nhants
71 G6 **Great Oxney Green** Essex
39 J4 **Great Pattenden** Kent
86 E2 **Great Paxton** Cambs
138 D1 **Great Plumpton** Lancs
106 F2 **Great Plumstead** Norfk
118 B5 **Great Ponton** Lincs
27 J7 **Great Potheridge** Devon
142 B2 **Great Preston** Leeds
83 M7 **Great Purston** Nhants
102 E7 **Great Raveley** Cambs
65 J4 **Great Rissington** Gloucs
65 L1 **Great Rollright** Oxon
54 F3 **Great Rudbaxton** Pembks
121 L6 **Great Ryburgh** Norfk
190 E4 **Great Ryle** Nthumb
96 B3 **Great Ryton** Shrops
71 G2 **Great Saling** Essex
166 D3 **Great Salkeld** Cumb
88 C8 **Great Sampford** Essex
130 B2 **Great Sankey** Warrtn
98 B2 **Great Saredon** Staffs
129 H5 **Great Saughall** Ches
88 F3 **Great Saxham** Suffk
48 A4 **Great Shefford** W Berk
87 J5 **Great Shelford** Cambs
160 E2 **Great Smeaton** N York
121 L4 **Great Snoring** Norfk
46 D2 **Great Somerford** Wilts
114 A5 **Great Soudley** Shrops
169 J6 **Great Stainton** Darltn
53 J1 **Great Stambridge** Essex
86 C2 **Great Staughton** Cambs
137 H6 **Great Steeping** Lincs
45 J3 **Great Stoke** S Glos
41 K3 **Great Stonar** Kent
166 D6 **Great Strickland** Cumb
102 E8 **Great Stukeley** Cambs
136 D4 **Great Sturton** Lincs
129 J4 **Great Sutton** Ches
96 C6 **Great Sutton** Shrops
179 L4 **Great Swinburne** Nthumb
66 B1 **Great Tew** Oxon
72 C2 **Great Tey** Essex
27 J7 **Great Torrington** Devon
190 E6 **Great Tosson** Nthumb
72 B5 **Great Totham** Essex
72 C4 **Great Totham** Essex
136 D2 **Great Tows** Lincs
156 C7 **Great Urswick** Cumb
53 K2 **Great Wakering** Essex
89 J6 **Great Waldingfield** Suffk
121 L4 **Great Walsingham** Norfk
71 G4 **Great Waltham** Essex
130 F4 **Great Warford** Ches
52 C1 **Great Warley** Essex
82 A8 **Great Washbourne** Gloucs
13 G5 **Great Weeke** Devon
101 K5 **Great Weldon** Nhants
89 H3 **Great Welnetham** Suffk
90 C7 **Great Wenham** Suffk
180 B5 **Great Whittington** Nthumb
72 D4 **Great Wigborough** Essex
87 L4 **Great Wilbraham** Cambs
33 J4 **Great Wishford** Wilts
122 C7 **Great Witchingham** Norfk
64 D4 **Great Witcombe** Gloucs
81 H2 **Great Witley** Worcs
82 F8 **Great Wolford** Warwks
88 D5 **Great Wratting** Essex
69 G2 **Great Wymondley** Herts
98 C2 **Great Wyrley** Staffs
113 J7 **Great Wytheford** Shrops
107 L2 **Great Yarmouth** Norfk
88 F7 **Great Yeldham** Essex
47 G2 **Greatfield** Wilts
102 B1 **Greatford** Lincs
115 G3 **Greatgate** Staffs

36 A5 **Greatham** Hants
170 C5 **Greatham** Hartpl
21 H4 **Greatham** W Susx
25 K3 **Greatstone-on-Sea** Kent
84 A6 **Greatworth** Nhants
137 H6 **Grebby** Lincs
154 d6 **Greeba** IOM
128 C6 **Green** Denbgs
156 E6 **Green Bank** Cumb
36 C3 **Green Cross** Surrey
45 H8 **Green Down** Somset
85 K5 **Green End** Beds
86 B2 **Green End** Beds
86 B3 **Green End** Beds
86 C5 **Green End** Beds
102 E8 **Green End** Cambs
87 H4 **Green End** Cambs
87 K2 **Green End** Cambs
87 K3 **Green End** Cambs
102 D6 **Green End** Cambs
69 H1 **Green End** Herts
69 J3 **Green End** Herts
87 G8 **Green End** Herts
99 H6 **Green End** Warwks
151 G4 **Green Hammerton** N York
165 L1 **Green Head** Cumb
98 C1 **Green Heath** Staffs
46 F2 **Green Hill** Wilts
13 H7 **Green Lane** Devon
82 C2 **Green Lane** Warwks
141 L7 **Green Moor** Barns
143 K2 **Green Oak** E R Yk
31 J1 **Green Ore** Somset
157 G2 **Green Quarter** Cumb
24 D5 **Green Street** E Susx
64 C4 **Green Street** Gloucs
70 C3 **Green Street** Herts
69 G7 **Green Street** Herts
81 K5 **Green Street** Worcs
51 M6 **Green Street Green** Gt Lon
52 C5 **Green Street Green** Kent
70 C3 **Green Tye** Herts
210 B7 **Greenburn** W Loth
168 F1 **Greencroft Hall** Dur
65 L3 **Greenend** Oxon
207 L1 **Greenfield** Ag & B
85 L8 **Greenfield** Beds
128 E4 **Greenfield** Flints
239 L3 **Greenfield** Highld
140 F7 **Greenfield** Oldham
49 H1 **Greenfield** Oxon
50 F3 **Greenford** Gt Lon
209 L5 **Greengairs** N Lans
150 B8 **Greengates** Brad
164 F3 **Greengill** Cumb
147 H8 **Greenhalgh** Lancs
29 K6 **Greenham** Somset
48 C6 **Greenham** W Berk
179 J2 **Greenhaugh** Nthumb
178 F6 **Greenhead** Nthumb
139 L7 **Greenheys** Salfd
176 F3 **Greenhill** D & G
209 L3 **Greenhill** Falk
81 G5 **Greenhill** Herefs
40 F2 **Greenhill** Kent
198 F6 **Greenhill** S Lans
116 C2 **Greenhillocks** Derbys
52 C4 **Greenhithe** Kent
197 G3 **Greenholm** E Ayrs
157 J2 **Greenholme** Cumb
188 F2 **Greenhouse** Border
149 K3 **Greenhow Hill** N York
280 B3 **Greenland** Highld
133 H2 **Greenland** Sheff
49 J2 **Greenlands** Bucks
201 L4 **Greenlaw** Border
176 D4 **Greenlea** D & G
220 E5 **Greenloaning** P & K
49 G3 **Greenmoor Hill** Oxon
140 A5 **Greenmount** Bury
207 M4 **Greenock** Inver
156 D6 **Greenodd** Cumb
84 C5 **Greens Norton** Nhants
122 B8 **Greensgate** Norfk
199 H4 **Greenshields** S Lans
180 E6 **Greenside** Gatesd
141 J4 **Greenside** Kirk
72 E2 **Greenstead** Essex
71 K2 **Greenstead Green** Essex
70 D6 **Greensted** Essex
90 B5 **Greenstreet Green** Suffk
81 G8 **Greenway** Gloucs
30 D6 **Greenway** Somset
43 G7 **Greenway** V Glam
81 G1 **Greenway** Worcs

51 K3 **Greenwich** Gt Lon
64 F1 **Greet** Gloucs
80 D1 **Greete** Shrops
136 F5 **Greetham** Lincs
118 B8 **Greetham** Rutlnd
141 G3 **Greetland** Calder
139 J2 **Gregson Lane** Lancs
30 F4 **Greinton** Somset
154 c7 **Grenaby** IOM
85 G3 **Grendon** Nhants
99 H3 **Grendon** Warwks
80 E4 **Grendon Green** Herefs
67 G3 **Grendon Underwood** Bucks
12 C8 **Grenofen** Devon
133 G1 **Grenoside** Sheff
282 e6 **Greosabhagh** W Isls
112 E1 **Gresford** Wrexhm
122 D4 **Gresham** Norfk
258 E6 **Greshornish House Hotel** Highld
121 L8 **Gressenhall** Norfk
121 L8 **Gressenhall Green** Norfk
147 L2 **Gressingham** Lancs
113 M1 **Gresty Green** Ches
168 D8 **Greta Bridge** Dur
177 K5 **Gretna** D & G
177 K5 **Gretna Green** D & G
64 E1 **Gretton** Gloucs
101 K4 **Gretton** Nhants
96 C4 **Gretton** Shrops
160 C7 **Grewelthorpe** N York
91 L1 **Grey Friars** Suffk
143 K6 **Grey Green** N Linc
150 A1 **Greygarth** N York
30 F4 **Greylake** Somset
176 E1 **Greyrigg** D & G
49 H2 **Greys Green** Oxon
164 E5 **Greysouthen** Cumb
166 B4 **Greystoke** Cumb
234 E6 **Greystone** Angus
35 L1 **Greywell** Hants
15 J2 **Gribb** Dorset
143 J1 **Gribthorpe** E R Yk
99 K5 **Griff** Warwks
62 C7 **Griffithstown** Torfn
116 C7 **Griffydam** Leics
36 B4 **Griggs Green** Hants
139 J5 **Grimeford Village** Lancs
133 G2 **Grimesthorpe** Sheff
142 C6 **Grimethorpe** Barns
81 J3 **Grimley** Worcs
183 J1 **Grimmet** S Ayrs
137 G2 **Grimoldby** Lincs
112 E6 **Grimpo** Shrops
139 H1 **Grimsargh** Lancs
145 H5 **Grimsby** NE Lin
84 C4 **Grimscote** Nhants
11 J1 **Grimscott** Cnwll
282 g4 **Grimshader** W Isls
139 L3 **Grimshaw** Bl w D
139 G5 **Grimshaw Green** Lancs
118 D7 **Grimsthorpe** Lincs
145 H1 **Grimston** E R Yk
117 J7 **Grimston** Leics
120 F7 **Grimston** Norfk
134 D6 **Grimston Hill** Notts
16 C4 **Grimstone** Dorset
89 J2 **Grimstone End** Suffk
12 A4 **Grinacombe Moor** Devon
153 J2 **Grindale** E R Yk
97 G3 **Grindle** Shrops
132 E4 **Grindleford** Derbys
148 D6 **Grindleton** Lancs
113 H3 **Grindley Brook** Shrops
132 D4 **Grindlow** Derbys
202 E4 **Grindon** Nthumb
169 K5 **Grindon** S on T
115 H1 **Grindon** Staffs
181 J7 **Grindon** Sundld
179 J5 **Grindon Hill** Nthumb
202 E4 **Grindonrigg** Nthumb
134 E2 **Gringley on the Hill** Notts
177 L7 **Grinsdale** Cumb
113 H6 **Grinshill** Shrops
159 J3 **Grinton** N York
282 g4 **Griomaisiader** W Isls
283 c9 **Griomsaigh** W Isls
224 F3 **Grishipoll** Ag & B
23 G3 **Grisling Common** E Susx
163 K6 **Gristhorpe** N York
105 J4 **Griston** Norfk
275 d5 **Gritley** Ork
46 F2 **Grittenham** Wilts
46 B3 **Grittleton** Wilts
156 C5 **Grizebeck** Cumb

156 D4 **Grizedale** Cumb
100 B2 **Groby** Leics
127 K6 **Groes** Conwy
43 G5 **Groes-faen** Rhondd
43 H4 **Groes-Wen** Caerph
108 D4 **Groesffordd** Powys
127 K5 **Groesffordd Marli** Denbgs
94 F1 **Groeslwyd** Powys
125 H8 **Groeslon** Gwynd
125 J7 **Groeslon** Gwynd
283 c10 **Grogarry** W Isls
194 C2 **Grogport** Ag & B
283 c10 **Groigearraidh** W Isls
91 J3 **Gromford** Suffk
128 C3 **Gronant** Flints
38 E6 **Groombridge** E Susx
282 e6 **Grosebay** W Isls
62 E2 **Grosmont** Mons
162 E2 **Grosmont** N York
89 J7 **Groton** Suffk
140 E6 **Grotton** Oldham
9 e3 **Grouville** Jersey
67 M3 **Grove** Bucks
16 D7 **Grove** Dorset
41 H3 **Grove** Kent
134 E4 **Grove** Notts
48 B1 **Grove** Oxon
55 G6 **Grove** Pembks
39 K2 **Grove Green** Kent
51 L4 **Grove Park** Gt Lon
39 H5 **Grovenhurst** Kent
45 K1 **Grovesend** S Glos
57 G5 **Grovesend** Swans
52 C5 **Grubb Street** Kent
260 F2 **Gruinard** Highld
204 D3 **Gruinart** Ag & B
246 E3 **Grula** Highld
227 G4 **Gruline** Ag & B
2 C5 **Grumbla** Cnwll
90 F5 **Grundisburgh** Suffk
281 c6 **Gruting** Shet
229 J6 **Gualachulain** Highld
103 H2 **Guanockgate** Lincs
223 H3 **Guardbridge** Fife
81 J6 **Guarlford** Worcs
232 F5 **Guay** P & K
24 F4 **Guestling Green** E Susx
24 F4 **Guestling Thorn** E Susx
122 B6 **Guestwick** Norfk
139 L3 **Guide** Bl w D
140 D8 **Guide Bridge** Tamesd
181 G2 **Guide Post** Nthumb
95 H6 **Guilden Down** Shrops
86 F6 **Guilden Morden** Cambs
129 K6 **Guilden Sutton** Ches
36 F1 **Guildford** Surrey
53 H6 **Guildstead** Kent
221 L1 **Guildtown** P & K
84 D1 **Guilsborough** Nhants
94 F1 **Guilsfield** Powys
41 J4 **Guilton** Kent
183 J1 **Guiltreehill** S Ayrs
27 K3 **Guineaford** Devon
170 E7 **Guisborough** R & Cl
150 B7 **Guiseley** Leeds
121 M6 **Guist** Norfk
65 G2 **Guiting Power** Gloucs
212 B2 **Gullane** E Loth
89 G4 **Gulling Green** Suffk
2 D5 **Gulval** Cnwll
12 B8 **Gulworthy** Devon
55 J6 **Gumfreston** Pembks
100 F5 **Gumley** Leics
4 E3 **Gummow's Shop** Cnwll
39 J7 **Gun Green** Kent
23 J4 **Gun Hill** E Susx
99 H5 **Gun Hill** Warwks
143 H1 **Gunby** E R Yk
118 B7 **Gunby** Lincs
137 J6 **Gunby** Lincs
35 J4 **Gundleton** Hants
27 L4 **Gunn** Devon
159 G3 **Gunnerside** N York
179 L4 **Gunnerton** Nthumb
143 L5 **Gunness** N Linc
12 B8 **Gunnislake** Cnwll
281 e6 **Gunnista** Shet
102 D3 **Gunthorpe** C Pete
143 K8 **Gunthorpe** N Linc
121 M4 **Gunthorpe** Norfk
117 H3 **Gunthorpe** Notts
107 L4 **Gunton** Suffk
3 G6 **Gunwalloe** Cnwll
29 H4 **Gupworthy** Somset
19 H4 **Gurnard** IOW

131 H5 **Gurnett** Ches
31 K1 **Gurney Slade** Somset
57 L3 **Gurnos** Powys
40 D4 **Gushmere** Kent
33 G8 **Gussage All Saints** Dorset
33 G8 **Gussage St Andrew** Dorset
33 G8 **Gussage St Michael** Dorset
41 K6 **Guston** Kent
281 f2 **Gutcher** Shet
234 E5 **Guthrie** Angus
32 D6 **Guy's Marsh** Dorset
103 H3 **Guyhirn** Cambs
103 H3 **Guyhirn Gull** Cambs
191 J5 **Guyzance** Nthumb
128 C3 **Gwaenysgor** Flints
125 G4 **Gwalchmai** IOA
126 C8 **Gwastadnant** Gwynd
59 J6 **Gwaun-Cae-Gurwen** Carmth
75 K2 **Gwbert on Sea** Cerdgn
2 F3 **Gwealavellan** Cnwll
3 H6 **Gwealeath** Cnwll
3 H5 **Gweek** Cnwll
62 D6 **Gwehelog** Mons
78 E6 **Gwenddwr** Powys
3 J7 **Gwendreath** Cnwll
3 J3 **Gwennap** Cnwll
3 J7 **Gwenter** Cnwll
128 F6 **Gwernaffield** Flints
62 E6 **Gwernesney** Mons
58 F2 **Gwernogle** Carmth
128 F7 **Gwernymynydd** Flints
112 D1 **Gwersyllt** Wrexhm
128 D3 **Gwespyr** Flints
4 F4 **Gwindra** Cnwll
2 F4 **Gwinear** Cnwll
2 F3 **Gwithian** Cnwll
125 G3 **Gwredog** IOA
61 J7 **Gwrhay** Caerph
111 L2 **Gwyddelwern** Denbgs
58 E2 **Gwyddgrug** Carmth
112 C1 **Gwynfryn** Wrexhm
78 E2 **Gwystre** Powys
127 H7 **Gwytherin** Conwy
112 E3 **Gyfelia** Wrexhm
109 G2 **Gyrn-goch** Gwynd

H

95 K3 **Habberley** Shrops
97 H7 **Habberley** Worcs
140 B1 **Habergham** Lancs
137 J6 **Habertoft** Lincs
36 B6 **Habin** W Susx
144 F5 **Habrough** NE Lin
118 E6 **Hacconby** Lincs
118 D4 **Haceby** Lincs
91 G3 **Hacheston** Suffk
113 L2 **Hack Green** Ches
51 H5 **Hackbridge** Gt Lon
133 H3 **Hackenthorpe** Sheff
106 B3 **Hackford** Norfk
160 C4 **Hackforth** N York
275 c4 **Hackland** Ork
84 F4 **Hackleton** Nhants
41 K4 **Hacklinge** Kent
97 K7 **Hackman's Gate** Worcs
163 H4 **Hackness** N York
30 E2 **Hackness** Somset
51 K2 **Hackney** Gt Lon
135 K3 **Hackthorn** Lincs
166 D6 **Hackthorpe** Cumb
52 C2 **Hacton** Gt Lon
202 B6 **Hadden** Border
67 H5 **Haddenham** Bucks
103 J8 **Haddenham** Cambs
212 B4 **Haddington** E Loth
135 H7 **Haddington** Lincs
107 J4 **Haddiscoe** Norfk
256 E4 **Haddo** Abers
102 C5 **Haddon** Cambs
141 J6 **Hade Edge** Kirk
140 F8 **Hadfield** Derbys
70 B3 **Hadham Cross** Herts
70 B3 **Hadham Ford** Herts
53 H2 **Hadleigh** Essex
89 L6 **Hadleigh** Suffk
89 K7 **Hadleigh Heath** Suffk
81 K2 **Hadley** Worcs
96 F1 **Hadley** Wrekin
115 J7 **Hadley End** Staffs
69 H7 **Hadley Wood** Gt Lon
39 G3 **Hadlow** Kent
23 J2 **Hadlow Down** E Susx
113 H7 **Hadnall** Shrops

88 B6 **Hadstock** Essex
81 L3 **Hadzor** Worcs
39 M5 **Haffenden Quarter** Kent
112 D2 **Hafod-y-bwch** Wrexhm
61 K7 **Hafod-y-coed** Blae G
127 H6 **Hafodunos** Conwy
61 K7 **Hafodyrynys** Caerph
140 C1 **Haggate** Lancs
178 B4 **Haggbeck** Cumb
203 G4 **Haggerston** Nthumb
27 K2 **Haggington Hill** Devon
209 L3 **Haggs** Falk
80 D7 **Hagley** Herefs
97 K7 **Hagley** Worcs
89 J7 **Hagmore Green** Suffk
136 F7 **Hagnaby** Lincs
137 J4 **Hagnaby** Lincs
136 F6 **Hagworthingham** Lincs
139 J6 **Haigh** Wigan
139 H1 **Haighton Green** Lancs
86 D3 **Hail Weston** Cambs
155 J1 **Haile** Cumb
64 F1 **Hailes** Gloucs
69 K5 **Hailey** Herts
48 F2 **Hailey** Oxon
65 M4 **Hailey** Oxon
23 K5 **Hailsham** E Susx
70 C8 **Hainault** Gt Lon
41 K2 **Haine** Kent
122 E7 **Hainford** Norfk
136 C3 **Hainton** Lincs
149 J8 **Hainworth** Brad
153 H3 **Haisthorpe** E R Yk
54 E5 **Hakin** Pembks
117 F1 **Halam** Notts
210 F1 **Halbeath** Fife
29 H8 **Halberton** Devon
280 B4 **Halcro** Highld
157 H7 **Hale** Cumb
129 L3 **Hale** Halton
33 L7 **Hale** Hants
32 C5 **Hale** Somset
36 C1 **Hale** Surrey
130 F2 **Hale** Traffd
129 L3 **Hale Bank** Halton
23 J4 **Hale Green** E Susx
147 G7 **Hale Nook** Lancs
39 G3 **Hale Street** Kent
130 F3 **Halebarns** Traffd
107 H4 **Hales** Norfk
113 M5 **Hales** Staffs
115 K3 **Hales Green** Derbys
40 F3 **Hales Place** Kent
119 K6 **Halesgate** Lincs
98 B6 **Halesowen** Dudley
72 C8 **Halesville** Essex
107 H7 **Halesworth** Suffk
129 K3 **Halewood** Knows
13 J7 **Halford** Devon
95 K6 **Halford** Shrops
83 G6 **Halford** Warwks
157 H5 **Halfpenny** Cumb
97 J5 **Halfpenny Green** Staffs
160 B5 **Halfpenny Houses** N York
59 J3 **Halfway** Carmth
59 M2 **Halfway** Carmth
133 J3 **Halfway** Sheff
48 B5 **Halfway** W Berk
36 D6 **Halfway Bridge** W Susx
95 H1 **Halfway House** Shrops
53 K4 **Halfway Houses** Kent
141 H3 **Halifax** Calder
279 K4 **Halkirk** Highld
128 F5 **Halkyn** Flints
208 C8 **Hall** E Rens
141 L4 **Hall Cliffe** Wakefd
138 E2 **Hall Cross** Lancs
156 B3 **Hall Dunnerdale** Cumb
85 K6 **Hall End** Beds
86 B7 **Hall End** Beds
210 A3 **Hall Glen** Falk
98 E7 **Hall Green** Birm
69 L5 **Hall's Green** Essex
69 H2 **Hall's Green** Herts
116 D4 **Hallam Fields** Derbys
23 H4 **Halland** E Susx
101 H4 **Hallaton** Leics
45 J7 **Hallatrow** BaNES
178 D7 **Hallbankgate** Cumb
157 K5 **Hallbeck** Cumb
45 H3 **Hallen** S Glos
133 H8 **Hallfield Gate** Derbys
169 J2 **Hallgarth** Dur
258 C5 **Hallin** Highld
52 F6 **Halling** Medway

136 F3 **Hallington** Lincs
180 B4 **Hallington** Nthumb
139 L5 **Halliwell** Bolton
117 J1 **Halloughton** Notts
81 J3 **Hallow** Worcs
81 J3 **Hallow Heath** Worcs
8 B7 **Hallsands** Devon
156 A5 **Hallthwaites** Cumb
119 L3 **Halltoft End** Lincs
11 H5 **Hallworthy** Cnwll
199 L5 **Hallyne** Border
114 B2 **Halmer End** Staffs
80 F5 **Halmond's Frome** Herefs
63 K6 **Halmore** Gloucs
20 E5 **Halnaker** W Susx
138 D5 **Halsall** Lancs
84 A7 **Halse** Nhants
29 L5 **Halse** Somset
2 D3 **Halsetown** Cnwll
145 H2 **Halsham** E R Yk
27 J3 **Halsinger** Devon
71 K1 **Halstead** Essex
52 A6 **Halstead** Kent
101 G2 **Halstead** Leics
15 M1 **Halstock** Dorset
29 L3 **Halsway** Somset
165 L3 **Haltcliff Bridge** Cumb
136 D7 **Haltham** Lincs
67 L5 **Halton** Bucks
129 M3 **Halton** Halton
147 K3 **Halton** Lancs
142 A1 **Halton** Leeds
180 B5 **Halton** Nthumb
112 D3 **Halton** Wrexhm
149 J5 **Halton East** N York
137 H7 **Halton Fenside** Lincs
158 F7 **Halton Gill** N York
147 K3 **Halton Green** Lancs
137 H6 **Halton Holegate** Lincs
178 F7 **Halton Lea Gate** Nthumb
6 E2 **Halton Quay** Cnwll
180 B5 **Halton Shields** Nthumb
148 E5 **Halton West** N York
179 G6 **Haltwhistle** Nthumb
107 J2 **Halvergate** Norfk
8 A4 **Halwell** Devon
12 B3 **Halwill** Devon
12 B3 **Halwill Junction** Devon
14 F2 **Ham** Devon
64 E3 **Ham** Gloucs
63 K7 **Ham** Gloucs
50 F4 **Ham** Gt Lon
41 K4 **Ham** Kent
30 D6 **Ham** Somset
31 L1 **Ham** Somset
47 L6 **Ham** Wilts
32 D5 **Ham Common** Dorset
81 H6 **Ham Green** Herefs
53 H5 **Ham Green** Kent
25 G2 **Ham Green** Kent
45 G4 **Ham Green** N Som
82 B3 **Ham Green** Worcs
52 F6 **Ham Hill** Kent
31 J4 **Ham Street** Somset
19 H2 **Hamble-le-Rice** Hants
49 J2 **Hambleden** Bucks
35 K7 **Hambledon** Hants
36 E3 **Hambledon** Surrey
147 G7 **Hambleton** Lancs
142 E2 **Hambleton** N York
147 G7 **Hambleton Moss Side** Lancs
30 F6 **Hambridge** Somset
31 K3 **Hambrook** S Glos
20 C5 **Hambrook** W Susx
136 F6 **Hameringham** Lincs
102 C7 **Hamerton** Cambs
209 J7 **Hamilton** S Lans
16 B1 **Hamlet** Dorset
23 K5 **Hamlins** E Susx
21 H5 **Hammerpot** W Susx
51 G3 **Hammersmith** Gt Lon
98 D2 **Hammerwich** Staffs
38 C5 **Hammerwood** E Susx
69 J6 **Hammond Street** Herts
32 D7 **Hammoon** Dorset
281 d7 **Hamnavoe** Shet
281 e4 **Hamnavoe** Shet
23 K6 **Hampden Park** E Susx
70 E1 **Hamperden End** Essex
65 G4 **Hampnett** Gloucs
142 D5 **Hampole** Donc
17 L3 **Hampreston** Dorset
156 F6 **Hampsfield** Cumb
147 J5 **Hampson Green** Lancs

51 H2 **Hampstead** Gt Lon
48 D4 **Hampstead Norrey's** W Berk
150 C4 **Hampsthwaite** N York
11 M7 **Hampt** Cnwll
102 D4 **Hampton** Cambs
15 G3 **Hampton** Devon
50 F5 **Hampton** Gt Lon
40 F2 **Hampton** Kent
97 G6 **Hampton** Shrops
65 J8 **Hampton** Swindn
82 B6 **Hampton** Worcs
80 D7 **Hampton Bishop** Herefs
64 C7 **Hampton Fields** Gloucs
113 H2 **Hampton Green** Ches
113 H2 **Hampton Heath** Ches
99 G7 **Hampton in Arden** Solhll
97 G6 **Hampton Loade** Shrops
81 K2 **Hampton Lovett** Worcs
82 F4 **Hampton Lucy** Warwks
83 G2 **Hampton Magna** Warwks
82 F2 **Hampton on the Hill** Warwks
66 D4 **Hampton Poyle** Oxon
50 F5 **Hampton Wick** Gt Lon
34 B7 **Hamptworth** Wilts
121 K6 **Hamrow** Norfk
22 F5 **Hamsey** E Susx
51 K7 **Hamsey Green** Gt Lon
115 H7 **Hamstall Ridware** Staffs
98 D5 **Hamstead** Birm
18 F5 **Hamstead** IOW
48 B6 **Hamstead Marshall** W Berk
180 D7 **Hamsterley** Dur
168 E4 **Hamsterley** Dur
40 C8 **Hamstreet** Kent
44 D7 **Hamwood** N Som
17 K4 **Hamworthy** Poole
115 K6 **Hanbury** Staffs
81 M2 **Hanbury** Worcs
118 D5 **Hanby** Lincs
88 C6 **Hanchet End** Suffk
114 C3 **Hanchurch** Staffs
14 B3 **Hand and Pen** Devon
130 A7 **Hand Green** Ches
171 K7 **Handale** R & Cl
129 J6 **Handbridge** Ches
37 L5 **Handcross** W Susx
131 G3 **Handforth** Ches
129 L8 **Handley** Ches
133 G7 **Handley** Derbys
71 G6 **Handley Green** Essex
115 H8 **Handsacre** Staffs
98 D5 **Handsworth** Birm
133 H2 **Handsworth** Sheff
49 K1 **Handy Cross** Bucks
114 D3 **Hanford** C Stke
32 D8 **Hanford** Dorset
101 G8 **Hanging Houghton** Nhants
33 H3 **Hanging Langford** Wilts
22 D6 **Hangleton** Br & H
21 J6 **Hangleton** W Susx
45 J4 **Hanham** S Glos
113 L2 **Hankelow** Ches
46 E1 **Hankerton** Wilts
23 K6 **Hankham** E Susx
114 D2 **Hanley** C Stke
81 J6 **Hanley Castle** Worcs
80 F2 **Hanley Child** Worcs
81 J6 **Hanley Swan** Worcs
80 F2 **Hanley William** Worcs
148 F3 **Hanlith** N York
113 G3 **Hanmer** Wrexhm
27 L5 **Hannaford** Devon
137 J4 **Hannah** Lincs
48 D7 **Hannington** Hants
84 F1 **Hannington** Nhants
65 H8 **Hannington** Swindn
65 H8 **Hannington Wick** Swindn
86 C8 **Hanscombe End** Beds
84 F6 **Hanslope** M Keyn
118 E6 **Hanthorpe** Lincs
50 F3 **Hanwell** Gt Lon
83 K6 **Hanwell** Oxon
95 K2 **Hanwood** Shrops
50 E5 **Hanworth** Gt Lon
122 D4 **Hanworth** Norfk
198 E6 **Happendon** S Lans
123 H5 **Happisburgh** Norfk
123 H5 **Happisburgh Common** Norfk
129 L5 **Hapsford** Ches
140 B2 **Hapton** Lancs
106 D4 **Hapton** Norfk
8 A3 **Harberton** Devon
8 A4 **Harbertonford** Devon
40 F4 **Harbledown** Kent
98 C6 **Harborne** Birm

100 B7 **Harborough Magna** Warwks
190 C5 **Harbottle** Nthumb
7 K2 **Harbourneford** Devon
81 M2 **Harbours Hill** Worcs
18 A2 **Harbridge** Hants
33 K8 **Harbridge Green** Hants
83 J3 **Harbury** Warwks
117 K5 **Harby** Leics
135 H5 **Harby** Notts
13 K6 **Harcombe** Devon
14 D4 **Harcombe** Devon
15 H3 **Harcombe Bottom** Devon
149 K8 **Harden** Brad
98 C3 **Harden** Wsall
46 C4 **Hardenhuish** Wilts
245 H3 **Hardgate** Abers
175 K2 **Hardgate** D & G
150 C3 **Hardgate** N York
208 E4 **Hardgate** W Duns
21 H3 **Hardham** W Susx
147 G8 **Hardhorn** Lancs
105 L3 **Hardingham** Norfk
84 E4 **Hardingstone** Nhants
45 L8 **Hardington** Somset
31 H8 **Hardington Mandeville** Somset
15 L1 **Hardington Marsh** Somset
31 H8 **Hardington Moor** Somset
26 D6 **Hardisworthy** Devon
19 G3 **Hardley** Hants
107 H3 **Hardley Street** Norfk
85 J5 **Hardmead** M Keyn
158 F4 **Hardraw** N York
140 B4 **Hardsough** Lancs
133 J7 **Hardstoft** Derbys
19 K3 **Hardway** Hants
32 B4 **Hardway** Somset
67 K3 **Hardwick** Bucks
87 H3 **Hardwick** Cambs
135 H4 **Hardwick** Lincs
85 G1 **Hardwick** Nhants
106 E5 **Hardwick** Norfk
66 A6 **Hardwick** Oxon
66 E1 **Hardwick** Oxon
133 K3 **Hardwick** Rothm
98 D4 **Hardwick** Wsall
81 J8 **Hardwick Green** Worcs
64 A4 **Hardwicke** Gloucs
64 C2 **Hardwicke** Gloucs
72 D3 **Hardy's Green** Essex
149 K8 **Hare Croft** Brad
73 G2 **Hare Green** Essex
49 J3 **Hare Hatch** Wokham
70 B5 **Hare Street** Essex
70 D7 **Hare Street** Essex
69 K1 **Hare Street** Herts
23 K5 **Harebeating** E Susx
136 F6 **Hareby** Lincs
50 D1 **Harefield** Gt Lon
115 K4 **Harehill** Derbys
141 M1 **Harehills** Leeds
191 G2 **Harehope** Nthumb
188 F2 **Harelaw** Border
178 B3 **Harelaw** D & G
180 E8 **Harelaw** Dur
39 L5 **Hareplain** Kent
166 E2 **Haresceugh** Cumb
64 B5 **Harescombe** Gloucs
64 A5 **Haresfield** Gloucs
34 F4 **Harestock** Hants
150 D6 **Harewood** Leeds
63 G2 **Harewood End** Herefs
7 J3 **Harford** Devon
106 C5 **Hargate** Norfk
132 B4 **Hargatewall** Derbys
129 L7 **Hargrave** Ches
85 K1 **Hargrave** Nhants
88 F3 **Hargrave** Suffk
88 F3 **Hargrave Green** Suffk
177 L6 **Harker** Cumb
90 E8 **Harkstead** Suffk
99 G1 **Harlaston** Staffs
118 A5 **Harlaxton** Lincs
140 C1 **Harle Syke** Lancs
109 K5 **Harlech** Gwynd
113 H8 **Harlescott** Shrops
51 G2 **Harlesden** Gt Lon
133 K4 **Harlesthorpe** Derbys
8 B6 **Harleston** Devon
106 E6 **Harleston** Norfk
89 L3 **Harleston** Suffk
84 D2 **Harlestone** Nhants
142 B8 **Harley** Rothm
96 D3 **Harley** Shrops
68 D1 **Harlington** Beds

142 D7 **Harlington** Donc
50 E3 **Harlington** Gt Lon
258 D8 **Harlosh** Highld
70 C5 **Harlow** Essex
180 C5 **Harlow Hill** Nthumb
152 A8 **Harlthorpe** E R Yk
87 H5 **Harlton** Cambs
10 B7 **Harlyn** Cnwll
17 J6 **Harman's Cross** Dorset
159 L5 **Harmby** N York
69 H4 **Harmer Green** Herts
113 H7 **Harmer Hill** Shrops
50 D3 **Harmondsworth** Gt Lon
135 K7 **Harmston** Lincs
96 D3 **Harnage** Shrops
180 C3 **Harnham** Nthumb
64 F7 **Harnhill** Gloucs
70 D8 **Harold Hill** Gt Lon
52 C1 **Harold Wood** Gt Lon
54 D4 **Haroldston West** Pembks
281 f1 **Haroldswick** Shet
161 L6 **Harome** N York
68 E4 **Harpenden** Herts
14 C4 **Harpford** Devon
153 H3 **Harpham** E R Yk
121 H6 **Harpley** Norfk
80 F3 **Harpley** Worcs
84 D3 **Harpole** Nhants
279 K5 **Harpsdale** Highld
49 J3 **Harpsden** Oxon
135 J2 **Harpswell** Lincs
131 L5 **Harpur Hill** Derbys
140 C7 **Harpurhey** Manch
177 M7 **Harraby** Cumb
27 K5 **Harracott** Devon
247 K4 **Harrapool** Highld
221 H1 **Harrietfield** P & K
39 L3 **Harrietsham** Kent
51 J1 **Harringay** Gt Lon
164 C5 **Harrington** Cumb
137 G5 **Harrington** Lincs
101 G7 **Harrington** Nhants
101 K4 **Harringworth** Nhants
131 G8 **Harriseahead** Staffs
165 G2 **Harriston** Cumb
150 D5 **Harrogate** N York
85 J4 **Harrold** Beds
140 F6 **Harrop Dale** Oldham
50 F1 **Harrow** Gt Lon
89 H4 **Harrow Green** Suffk
50 F2 **Harrow on the Hill** Gt Lon
50 F1 **Harrow Weald** Gt Lon
6 D1 **Harrowbarrow** Cnwll
85 L6 **Harrowden** Beds
169 H7 **Harrowgate Village** Darltn
87 J5 **Harston** Cambs
117 L5 **Harston** Leics
152 C7 **Harswell** E R Yk
170 B4 **Hart** Hartpl
170 B3 **Hart Station** Hartpl
180 D2 **Hartburn** Nthumb
89 G5 **Hartest** Suffk
38 D6 **Hartfield** E Susx
86 E1 **Hartford** Cambs
130 C5 **Hartford** Ches
29 G5 **Hartford** Somset
71 G3 **Hartford End** Essex
49 J7 **Hartfordbridge** Hants
159 L2 **Hartforth** N York
32 D7 **Hartgrove** Dorset
129 L8 **Harthill** Ches
210 B6 **Harthill** N Lans
133 K3 **Harthill** Rothm
132 C7 **Hartington** Derbys
180 B1 **Hartington** Nthumb
26 D6 **Hartland** Devon
26 C6 **Hartland Quay** Devon
81 J1 **Hartlebury** Worcs
170 C4 **Hartlepool** Hartpl
158 D1 **Hartley** Cumb
52 D5 **Hartley** Kent
39 J6 **Hartley** Kent
181 H4 **Hartley** Nthumb
52 D5 **Hartley Green** Kent
114 F5 **Hartley Green** Staffs
49 G7 **Hartley Wespall** Hants
49 J7 **Hartley Wintney** Hants
53 H6 **Hartlip** Kent
53 H6 **Hartlip Hill** Kent
162 C4 **Hartoft End** N York
151 L3 **Harton** N York
181 J6 **Harton** S Tyne
96 B5 **Harton** Shrops
64 A2 **Hartpury** Gloucs
141 J3 **Hartshead** Kirk

114 D2 **Hartshill** C Stke
99 J4 **Hartshill** Warwks
116 B7 **Hartshorne** Derbys
190 D3 **Hartside** Nthumb
165 L8 **Hartsop** Cumb
29 K5 **Hartswell** Somset
84 F5 **Hartwell** Nhants
150 B3 **Hartwith** N York
209 M7 **Hartwood** N Lans
188 D1 **Hartwoodmyres** Border
52 E6 **Harvel** Kent
97 K8 **Harvington** Worcs
82 C5 **Harvington** Worcs
134 D2 **Harwell** Notts
48 C1 **Harwell** Oxon
73 K1 **Harwich** Essex
139 L5 **Harwood** Bolton
167 J4 **Harwood** Dur
190 E8 **Harwood** Nthumb
163 H3 **Harwood Dale** N York
139 L5 **Harwood Lee** Bolton
134 C2 **Harworth** Notts
98 B6 **Hasbury** Dudley
36 F3 **Hascombe** Surrey
100 F7 **Haselbech** Nhants
31 G8 **Haselbury Plucknett** Somset
82 F2 **Haseley** Warwks
82 F1 **Haseley Green** Warwks
82 F1 **Haseley Knob** Warwks
82 D4 **Haselor** Warwks
64 B2 **Hasfield** Gloucs
54 D5 **Hasguard** Pembks
138 D6 **Haskayne** Lancs
90 F5 **Hasketon** Suffk
133 H5 **Hasland** Derbys
133 H6 **Hasland Green** Derbys
36 D4 **Haslemere** Surrey
140 B3 **Haslingden** Lancs
139 M3 **Haslingden Grane** Lancs
87 H5 **Haslingfield** Cambs
130 E8 **Haslington** Ches
130 E8 **Hassall** Ches
130 F7 **Hassall Green** Ches
40 E6 **Hassell Street** Kent
107 H2 **Hassingham** Norfk
165 G7 **Hassness** Cumb
22 D4 **Hassocks** W Susx
132 D5 **Hassop** Derbys
36 D4 **Haste Hill** Surrey
280 D6 **Haster** Highld
137 J5 **Hasthorpe** Lincs
40 E6 **Hastingleigh** Kent
24 E5 **Hastings** E Susx
30 D7 **Hastings** Somset
70 C5 **Hastingwood** Essex
68 A5 **Hastoe** Herts
169 K2 **Haswell** Dur
169 K2 **Haswell Plough** Dur
86 D5 **Hatch** Beds
30 D6 **Hatch Beauchamp** Somset
86 B3 **Hatch End** Beds
50 E1 **Hatch End** Gt Lon
18 F3 **Hatchet Gate** Hants
68 E4 **Hatching Green** Herts
130 A5 **Hatchmere** Ches
145 G7 **Hatcliffe** NE Lin
143 G6 **Hatfield** Donc
80 E3 **Hatfield** Herefs
69 G5 **Hatfield** Herts
81 K5 **Hatfield** Worcs
70 E4 **Hatfield Broad Oak** Essex
70 D4 **Hatfield Heath** Essex
71 J5 **Hatfield Peverel** Essex
143 H6 **Hatfield Woodhouse** Donc
65 M8 **Hatford** Oxon
34 D1 **Hatherden** Hants
12 D2 **Hatherleigh** Devon
116 E7 **Hathern** Leics
65 H6 **Hatherop** Gloucs
132 E3 **Hathersage** Derbys
132 E3 **Hathersage Booths** Derbys
113 L2 **Hatherton** Ches
98 B1 **Hatherton** Staffs
86 F5 **Hatley St George** Cambs
6 D2 **Hatt** Cnwll
131 K1 **Hattersley** Tamesd
35 K3 **Hattingley** Hants
257 K4 **Hatton** Abers
234 C6 **Hatton** Angus
115 L5 **Hatton** Derbys
50 E4 **Hatton** Gt Lon
136 C4 **Hatton** Lincs
95 L5 **Hatton** Shrops
130 B3 **Hatton** Warrtn
82 F2 **Hatton** Warwks

129 K7 **Hatton Heath** Ches
256 F8 **Hatton of Fintray** Abers
196 F6 **Haugh** E Ayrs
137 H4 **Haugh** Lincs
140 D5 **Haugh** Rochdl
202 F7 **Haugh Head** Nthumb
255 H4 **Haugh of Glass** Moray
175 K2 **Haugh of Urr** D & G
136 F3 **Haugham** Lincs
209 J3 **Haughhead** E Duns
89 L3 **Haughley** Suffk
89 L2 **Haughley Green** Suffk
134 D5 **Haughton** Notts
112 D7 **Haughton** Powys
112 F6 **Haughton** Shrops
113 J8 **Haughton** Shrops
97 G2 **Haughton** Shrops
96 F4 **Haughton** Shrops
114 D7 **Haughton** Staffs
131 J1 **Haughton Green** Tamesd
169 J7 **Haughton le Skerne** Darltn
130 B8 **Haughton Moss** Ches
69 J3 **Haultwick** Herts
99 G1 **Haunton** Staffs
9 d1 **Hautes Croix** Jersey
191 K5 **Hauxley** Nthumb
87 J5 **Hauxton** Cambs
131 G6 **Havannah** Ches
20 B5 **Havant** Hants
79 M4 **Haven** Herefs
119 H1 **Haven Bank** Lincs
144 F2 **Haven Side** E R Yk
19 J5 **Havenstreet** IOW
142 B5 **Havercroft** Wakefd
54 F4 **Haverfordwest** Pembks
88 D6 **Haverhill** Suffk
155 L7 **Haverigg** Cumb
70 D8 **Havering-atte-Bower** Essex
84 F6 **Haversham** M Keyn
156 E6 **Haverthwaite** Cumb
170 C6 **Haverton Hill** S on T
44 F6 **Havyat** N Som
31 H3 **Havyatt** Somset
129 H6 **Hawarden** Flints
81 L5 **Hawbridge** Worcs
71 J3 **Hawbush Green** Essex
146 D2 **Hawcoat** Cumb
106 E4 **Hawe's Green** Norfk
76 C6 **Hawen** Cerdgn
158 F5 **Hawes** N York
81 J3 **Hawford** Worcs
188 E3 **Hawick** Border
131 J2 **Hawk Green** Stockp
15 H2 **Hawkchurch** Devon
88 F4 **Hawkedon** Suffk
39 K4 **Hawkenbury** Kent
46 B8 **Hawkeridge** Wilts
14 C5 **Hawkerland** Devon
99 J6 **Hawkes End** Covtry
45 M2 **Hawkesbury** S Glos
99 K6 **Hawkesbury** Warwks
45 M2 **Hawkesbury Upton** S Glos
191 J4 **Hawkhill** Nthumb
39 J7 **Hawkhurst** Kent
23 J4 **Hawkhurst Common** E Susx
41 H7 **Hawkinge** Kent
35 M5 **Hawkley** Hants
28 F5 **Hawkridge** Somset
165 L1 **Hawksdale** Cumb
139 M5 **Hawkshaw** Bury
156 E3 **Hawkshead** Cumb
156 D3 **Hawkshead Hill** Cumb
198 D5 **Hawksland** S Lans
71 G1 **Hawkspur Green** Essex
113 J5 **Hawkstone** Shrops
149 G2 **Hawkswick** N York
149 L7 **Hawksworth** Leeds
117 K3 **Hawksworth** Notts
53 J1 **Hawkwell** Essex
180 C4 **Hawkwell** Nthumb
49 L7 **Hawley** Hants
52 C4 **Hawley** Kent
64 F3 **Hawling** Gloucs
161 J5 **Hawnby** N York
149 J8 **Haworth** Brad
68 B6 **Hawridge** Bucks
89 G3 **Hawstead** Suffk
89 H3 **Hawstead Green** Suffk
169 L2 **Hawthorn** Dur
35 K4 **Hawthorn** Hants
43 H4 **Hawthorn** Rhondd
49 L4 **Hawthorn Hill** Br For
136 D8 **Hawthorn Hill** Lincs
118 D6 **Hawthorpe** Lincs
117 L1 **Hawton** Notts

151 K4 **Haxby** York
151 K4 **Haxby Gates** York
143 J7 **Haxey** N Linc
143 J7 **Haxey Turbary** N Linc
38 C4 **Haxted** Surrey
33 K1 **Haxton** Wilts
4 E4 **Hay** Cnwll
4 F6 **Hay** Cnwll
4 F4 **Hay** Cnwll
10 D8 **Hay** Cnwll
120 C7 **Hay Green** Norfk
69 K2 **Hay Street** Herts
79 J6 **Hay-on-Wye** Powys
139 H8 **Haydock** St Hel
45 K8 **Haydon** BaNES
31 L7 **Haydon** Dorset
30 C6 **Haydon** Somset
179 J6 **Haydon Bridge** Nthumb
47 H2 **Haydon Wick** Swindn
6 C1 **Haye** Cnwll
50 E3 **Hayes** Gt Lon
51 L5 **Hayes** Gt Lon
50 D3 **Hayes End** Gt Lon
217 H2 **Hayfield** Ag & B
131 L2 **Hayfield** Derbys
96 E1 **Haygate** Wrekin
234 E7 **Hayhillock** Angus
2 F4 **Hayle** Cnwll
98 B6 **Hayley Green** Dudley
113 L2 **Haymoor Green** Ches
29 G7 **Hayne** Devon
13 H5 **Hayne** Devon
86 B7 **Haynes (Church End)** Beds
86 B6 **Haynes (Northwood End)** Beds
86 B6 **Haynes (Silver End)** Beds
85 L7 **Haynes (West End)** Beds
74 E7 **Hayscastle** Pembks
74 E7 **Hayscastle Cross** Pembks
38 F4 **Haysden** Kent
164 F2 **Hayton** Cumb
178 C7 **Hayton** Cumb
152 C6 **Hayton** E R Yk
134 E3 **Hayton** Notts
96 C7 **Hayton's Bent** Shrops
13 H7 **Haytor Vale** Devon
26 F7 **Haytown** Devon
22 E2 **Haywards Heath** W Susx
142 F5 **Haywood** Donc
80 B8 **Haywood** Herefs
134 C8 **Haywood Oaks** Notts
24 C5 **Hazards Green** E Susx
131 H2 **Hazel Grove** Stockp
39 H5 **Hazel Street** Kent
88 D6 **Hazel Stub** Suffk
198 D4 **Hazelbank** S Lans
16 E1 **Hazelbury Bryan** Dorset
71 K6 **Hazeleigh** Essex
49 H7 **Hazeley** Hants
117 J2 **Hazelford** Notts
140 E7 **Hazelhurst** Tamesd
98 C1 **Hazelslade** Staffs
222 E3 **Hazelton Walls** Fife
116 B2 **Hazelwood** Derbys
67 L8 **Hazlemere** Bucks
180 F4 **Hazlerigg** N u Ty
114 F2 **Hazles** Staffs
65 G3 **Hazleton** Gloucs
120 E4 **Heacham** Norfk
35 G4 **Headbourne Worthy** Hants
79 K4 **Headbrook** Herefs
39 L4 **Headcorn** Kent
150 C8 **Headingley** Leeds
66 D5 **Headington** Oxon
168 F7 **Headlam** Dur
82 B2 **Headless Cross** Worcs
210 B7 **Headlesscross** N Lans
48 D6 **Headley** Hants
36 B4 **Headley** Hants
51 G8 **Headley** Surrey
36 B4 **Headley Down** Hants
98 D8 **Headley Heath** Worcs
134 E4 **Headon** Notts
197 L2 **Heads** S Lans
178 C7 **Heads Nook** Cumb
116 B2 **Heage** Derbys
159 H3 **Healaugh** N York
151 G6 **Healaugh** N York
131 G3 **Heald Green** Stockp
28 A2 **Heale** Devon
30 C6 **Heale** Somset
30 F5 **Heale** Somset
160 B6 **Healey** N York
180 B7 **Healey** Nthumb
140 C4 **Healey** Rochdl

141 L4 **Healey** Wakefd
168 D1 **Healeyfield** Dur
145 G5 **Healing** NE Lin
2 D5 **Heamoor** Cnwll
116 D2 **Heanor** Derbys
27 J4 **Heanton Punchardon** Devon
139 J4 **Heapey** Lancs
135 H2 **Heapham** Lincs
36 B3 **Hearn** Hants
53 J6 **Hearts Delight** Kent
28 C4 **Heasley Mill** Devon
247 K5 **Heast** Highld
133 J6 **Heath** Derbys
142 A4 **Heath** Wakefd
68 A2 **Heath and Reach** Beds
21 J4 **Heath Common** W Susx
67 L7 **Heath End** Bucks
48 B6 **Heath End** Hants
116 B7 **Heath End** Leics
36 C1 **Heath End** Surrey
82 F3 **Heath End** Warwks
82 C1 **Heath Green** Worcs
176 C3 **Heath Hall** D & G
98 C2 **Heath Hayes & Wimblebury** Staffs
97 H1 **Heath Hill** Shrops
30 F2 **Heath House** Somset
97 L3 **Heath Town** Wolves
113 K6 **Heathbrook** Shrops
132 C7 **Heathcote** Derbys
113 L6 **Heathcote** Shrops
84 D5 **Heathencote** Nhants
99 K1 **Heather** Leics
13 J7 **Heathfield** Devon
23 K3 **Heathfield** E Susx
149 L2 **Heathfield** N York
29 L5 **Heathfield** Somset
66 D4 **Heathfield Village** Oxon
14 F2 **Heathstock** Devon
97 H5 **Heathton** Shrops
115 H6 **Heatley** Staffs
130 D2 **Heatley** Warrtn
139 L6 **Heaton** Bolton
149 L8 **Heaton** Brad
147 J4 **Heaton** Lancs
181 G5 **Heaton** N u Ty
131 J7 **Heaton** Staffs
131 H1 **Heaton Chapel** Stockp
131 G2 **Heaton Mersey** Stockp
131 H2 **Heaton Norris** Stockp
138 E5 **Heaton's Bridge** Lancs
52 C7 **Heaverham** Kent
131 H2 **Heaviley** Stockp
13 L4 **Heavitree** Devon
181 H6 **Hebburn** S Tyne
149 J3 **Hebden** N York
140 F2 **Hebden Bridge** Calder
130 C6 **Hebden Green** Ches
69 J3 **Hebing End** Herts
75 L6 **Hebron** Carmth
125 H3 **Hebron** IOA
191 J8 **Hebron** Nthumb
49 H6 **Heckfield** Hants
106 D8 **Heckfield Green** Suffk
72 D3 **Heckfordbridge** Essex
118 F3 **Heckington** Lincs
141 K3 **Heckmondwike** Kirk
46 E5 **Heddington** Wilts
180 D5 **Heddon-on-the-Wall** Nthumb
107 G5 **Hedenham** Norfk
19 H1 **Hedge End** Hants
50 B2 **Hedgerley** Bucks
50 B2 **Hedgerley Green** Bucks
30 D5 **Hedging** Somset
180 C7 **Hedley on the Hill** Nthumb
98 C1 **Hednesford** Staffs
145 G2 **Hedon** E R Yk
49 L2 **Hedsor** Bucks
80 D4 **Hegdon Hill** Herefs
281 d6 **Heglibister** Shet
169 H6 **Heighington** Darltn
135 L6 **Heighington** Lincs
81 H1 **Heightington** Worcs
201 L7 **Heiton** Border
11 J3 **Hele** Cnwll
27 J2 **Hele** Devon
14 A2 **Hele** Devon
7 L1 **Hele** Devon
30 B6 **Hele** Somset
28 D8 **Hele Lane** Devon
11 J2 **Helebridge** Cnwll
208 A3 **Helensburgh** Ag & B
196 D5 **Helenton** S Ayrs
3 J6 **Helford** Cnwll
3 J5 **Helford Passage** Cnwll

121 J6 **Helhoughton** Norfk
88 C7 **Helions Bumpstead** Essex
48 A6 **Hell Corner** W Berk
133 K1 **Hellaby** Rothm
10 F8 **Helland** Cnwll
10 F8 **Hellandbridge** Cnwll
11 K5 **Hellescott** Cnwll
106 D1 **Hellesdon** Norfk
2 D3 **Hellesveor** Cnwll
83 M4 **Hellidon** Nhants
148 E4 **Hellifield** N York
23 K5 **Hellingly** E Susx
107 G3 **Hellington** Norfk
191 H7 **Helm** Nthumb
84 B6 **Helmdon** Nhants
141 H5 **Helme** Kirk
90 E4 **Helmingham** Suffk
168 F4 **Helmington Row** Dur
274 D5 **Helmsdale** Highld
140 B3 **Helmshore** Lancs
161 K6 **Helmsley** N York
150 F2 **Helperby** N York
152 E2 **Helperthorpe** N York
118 F3 **Helpringham** Lincs
102 C2 **Helpston** C Pete
129 L4 **Helsby** Ches
137 K5 **Helsey** Lincs
3 G5 **Helston** Cnwll
10 F6 **Helstone** Cnwll
166 C6 **Helton** Cumb
159 K2 **Helwith** N York
148 D2 **Helwith Bridge** N York
107 G1 **Hemblington** Norfk
68 D5 **Hemel Hempstead** Herts
7 H3 **Hemerdon** Devon
143 H2 **Hemingbrough** N York
136 D5 **Hemingby** Lincs
142 B7 **Hemingfield** Barns
86 F1 **Hemingford Abbots** Cambs
86 F1 **Hemingford Grey** Cambs
90 D4 **Hemingstone** Suffk
116 D6 **Hemington** Leics
102 B6 **Hemington** Nhants
45 L8 **Hemington** Somset
91 G6 **Hemley** Suffk
170 C7 **Hemlington** Middsb
153 H5 **Hempholme** E R Yk
106 E4 **Hempnall** Norfk
106 E5 **Hempnall Green** Norfk
266 B3 **Hempriggs** Moray
88 C7 **Hempstead** Essex
53 G6 **Hempstead** Medway
122 C4 **Hempstead** Norfk
123 H6 **Hempstead** Norfk
64 B4 **Hempsted** Gloucs
121 K5 **Hempton** Norfk
66 C1 **Hempton** Oxon
123 K8 **Hemsby** Norfk
135 J2 **Hemswell** Lincs
135 J2 **Hemswell Cliff** Lincs
142 C5 **Hemsworth** Wakefd
29 L8 **Hemyock** Devon
45 H3 **Henbury** Bristl
131 H5 **Henbury** Ches
202 A6 **Hendersyde Park** Border
7 L5 **Hendham** Devon
94 F4 **Hendomen** Powys
51 G1 **Hendon** Gt Lon
181 K7 **Hendon** Sundld
3 J4 **Hendra** Cnwll
10 E7 **Hendra** Cnwll
42 E5 **Hendre** Brdgnd
128 E6 **Hendre** Flints
62 F4 **Hendre** Mons
57 G4 **Hendy** Carmth
125 G4 **Heneglwys** IOA
22 C4 **Henfield** W Susx
11 M4 **Henford** Devon
40 B8 **Henghurst** Kent
43 J3 **Hengoed** Caerph
79 J4 **Hengoed** Powys
112 D5 **Hengoed** Shrops
89 G2 **Hengrave** Suffk
70 E2 **Henham** Essex
94 D2 **Heniarth** Powys
30 C6 **Henlade** Somset
16 D2 **Henley** Dorset
64 C4 **Henley** Gloucs
95 L5 **Henley** Shrops
96 C8 **Henley** Shrops
30 F4 **Henley** Somset
90 E5 **Henley** Suffk
36 D5 **Henley** W Susx
99 K7 **Henley Green** Covtry
50 B8 **Henley Park** Surrey

52 E5 **Henley Street** Kent
24 D5 **Henley's Down** E Susx
82 E2 **Henley-in-Arden** Warwks
49 J2 **Henley-on-Thames** Oxon
76 C7 **Henllan** Cerdgn
127 L6 **Henllan** Denbgs
55 L3 **Henllan Amgoed** Carmth
44 B1 **Henllys** Torfn
86 D7 **Henlow** Beds
13 J6 **Hennock** Devon
89 H7 **Henny Street** Essex
75 H6 **Henry's Moat (Castell Hendre)** Pembks
126 F5 **Henryd** Conwy
142 F3 **Hensall** N York
179 H6 **Henshaw** Nthumb
164 C7 **Hensingham** Cumb
107 K6 **Henstead** Suffk
35 G6 **Hensting** Hants
32 B7 **Henstridge** Somset
32 B6 **Henstridge Ash** Somset
32 B6 **Henstridge Marsh** Somset
67 J6 **Henton** Oxon
31 H2 **Henton** Somset
81 J4 **Henwick** Worcs
11 K7 **Henwood** Cnwll
66 C6 **Henwood** Oxon
60 D2 **Heol Senni** Powys
57 J5 **Heol-las** Swans
42 E5 **Heol-y-Cyw** Brdgnd
190 F1 **Hepburn** Nthumb
190 E6 **Hepple** Nthumb
180 F2 **Hepscott** Nthumb
140 E2 **Heptonstall** Calder
141 J6 **Hepworth** Kirk
105 M8 **Hepworth** Suffk
54 E5 **Herbrandston** Pembks
80 C7 **Hereford** Herefs
41 L2 **Hereson** Kent
258 F3 **Heribusta** Highld
200 E2 **Heriot** Border
211 G5 **Hermiston** C Edin
141 M7 **Hermit Hill** Barns
188 E7 **Hermitage** Border
16 C1 **Hermitage** Dorset
20 C5 **Hermitage** Hants
48 D4 **Hermitage** W Berk
125 G6 **Hermon** IOA
75 L6 **Hermon** Pembks
41 G2 **Herne** Kent
41 G2 **Herne Bay** Kent
41 G2 **Herne Common** Kent
51 J4 **Herne Hill** Gt Lon
39 G2 **Herne Pound** Kent
27 K5 **Herner** Devon
40 E3 **Hernhill** Kent
5 L3 **Herodsfoot** Cnwll
41 J4 **Heronden** Kent
52 D1 **Herongate** Essex
182 E6 **Heronsford** S Ayrs
68 C8 **Heronsgate** Herts
35 K2 **Herriard** Hants
86 B6 **Herring's Green** Beds
107 K4 **Herringfleet** Suffk
88 E1 **Herringswell** Suffk
133 J1 **Herringthorpe** Rothm
181 J8 **Herrington** Sundld
41 G3 **Hersden** Kent
11 J1 **Hersham** Cnwll
50 E6 **Hersham** Surrey
23 L5 **Herstmonceux** E Susx
17 K6 **Herston** Dorset
275 c6 **Herston** Ork
69 J4 **Hertford** Herts
69 K5 **Hertford Heath** Herts
69 J5 **Hertingfordbury** Herts
165 K3 **Hesket Newmarket** Cumb
138 F3 **Hesketh Bank** Lancs
147 M7 **Hesketh Lane** Lancs
139 G4 **Heskin Green** Lancs
170 B3 **Hesleden** Dur
158 F7 **Hesleden** N York
134 C1 **Hesley** Donc
179 J2 **Hesleyside** Nthumb
151 K5 **Heslington** York
151 H5 **Hessay** York
6 C3 **Hessenford** Cnwll
89 J3 **Hessett** Suffk
144 C3 **Hessle** E R Yk
142 C4 **Hessle** Wakefd
147 J3 **Hest Bank** Lancs
90 D2 **Hestley Green** Suffk
50 E3 **Heston** Gt Lon
275 b4 **Hestwall** Ork
129 G3 **Heswall** Wirral

66 E1 **Hethe** Oxon
106 C2 **Hethersett** Norfk
178 B5 **Hethersgill** Cumb
178 B5 **Hetherside** Cumb
113 H2 **Hetherson Green** Ches
202 D7 **Hethpool** Nthumb
169 H3 **Hett** Dur
149 G4 **Hetton** N York
203 G6 **Hetton Steads** Nthumb
169 K1 **Hetton-le-Hole** Sundld
180 D4 **Heugh** Nthumb
213 J6 **Heugh Head** Border
243 L1 **Heughhead** Abers
91 H1 **Heveningham** Suffk
38 D4 **Hever** Kent
157 H6 **Heversham** Cumb
122 D7 **Hevingham** Norfk
4 F5 **Hewas Water** Cnwll
63 H6 **Hewelsfield** Gloucs
149 K8 **Hewenden** Brad
44 E6 **Hewish** N Som
15 K1 **Hewish** Somset
15 H2 **Hewood** Dorset
179 L6 **Hexham** Nthumb
52 B5 **Hextable** Kent
142 F7 **Hexthorpe** Donc
68 E1 **Hexton** Herts
11 L6 **Hexworthy** Cnwll
12 F8 **Hexworthy** Devon
148 F7 **Hey** Lancs
138 D2 **Hey Houses** Lancs
71 L5 **Heybridge** Essex
70 F7 **Heybridge** Essex
72 C5 **Heybridge Basin** Essex
6 F5 **Heybrook Bay** Devon
87 J7 **Heydon** Cambs
122 C6 **Heydon** Norfk
118 D4 **Heydour** Lincs
131 G3 **Heyhead** Manch
224 B6 **Heylipoll** Ag & B
281 d4 **Heylor** Shet
140 E7 **Heyrod** Tamesd
147 H4 **Heysham** Lancs
149 L3 **Heyshaw** N York
20 E3 **Heyshott** W Susx
140 D6 **Heyside** Oldham
32 F2 **Heytesbury** Wilts
65 M2 **Heythrop** Oxon
140 C5 **Heywood** Rochdl
46 C8 **Heywood** Wilts
144 B7 **Hibaldstow** N Linc
142 D6 **Hickleton** Donc
123 J6 **Hickling** Norfk
117 J6 **Hickling** Notts
123 H6 **Hickling Green** Norfk
123 H7 **Hickling Heath** Norfk
40 E4 **Hickmans Green** Kent
41 G3 **Hicks Forstal** Kent
22 D3 **Hickstead** W Susx
82 E6 **Hidcote Bartrim** Gloucs
82 E6 **Hidcote Boyce** Gloucs
142 C4 **High Ackworth** Wakefd
180 D2 **High Angerton** Nthumb
172 D5 **High Ardwell** D & G
176 B1 **High Auldgirth** D & G
166 D2 **High Bankhill** Cumb
69 L7 **High Beach** Essex
148 B2 **High Bentham** N York
165 H4 **High Bewaldeth** Cumb
27 L6 **High Bickington** Devon
158 D7 **High Bickwith** N York
157 K7 **High Biggins** Cumb
209 H7 **High Blantyre** S Lans
209 L3 **High Bonnybridge** Falk
156 F3 **High Borrans** Cumb
149 H6 **High Bradley** N York
28 B4 **High Bray** Devon
38 F5 **High Brooms** Kent
27 J6 **High Bullen** Devon
191 J4 **High Buston** Nthumb
180 E5 **High Callerton** Nthumb
157 K7 **High Casterton** Cumb
151 M5 **High Catton** E R Yk
168 F7 **High Close** N York
66 A5 **High Cogges** Oxon
105 K2 **High Common** Norfk
169 G7 **High Coniscliffe** Darltn
178 B6 **High Crosby** Cumb
3 J5 **High Cross** Cnwll
196 D2 **High Cross** E Ayrs
35 L5 **High Cross** Hants
69 K3 **High Cross** Herts
22 C4 **High Cross** W Susx
82 E2 **High Cross** Warwks
115 M8 **High Cross Bank** Derbys

172 E7 **High Drummore** D & G
169 J1 **High Dubmire** Sundld
70 F4 **High Easter** Essex
142 F3 **High Eggborough** N York
160 B6 **High Ellington** N York
113 K8 **High Ercall** Wrekin
168 F5 **High Etherley** Dur
119 K2 **High Ferry** Lincs
141 K6 **High Flats** Kirk
71 J2 **High Garrett** Essex
168 F4 **High Grange** Dur
150 B2 **High Grantley** N York
156 F2 **High Green** Cumb
141 K5 **High Green** Kirk
106 C2 **High Green** Norfk
106 D5 **High Green** Norfk
106 F4 **High Green** Norfk
142 A8 **High Green** Sheff
96 F6 **High Green** Shrops
89 G3 **High Green** Suffk
81 K6 **High Green** Worcs
40 A7 **High Halden** Kent
53 G4 **High Halstow** Medway
30 F4 **High Ham** Somset
164 D5 **High Harrington** Cumb
150 D5 **High Harrogate** N York
169 K2 **High Haswell** Dur
113 K6 **High Hatton** Shrops
163 G1 **High Hawsker** N York
166 B2 **High Hesket** Cumb
141 L5 **High Hoyland** Barns
144 B1 **High Hunsley** E R Yk
23 H2 **High Hurstwood** E Susx
152 A2 **High Hutton** N York
165 H3 **High Ireby** Cumb
122 C3 **High Kelling** Norfk
161 H6 **High Kilburn** N York
163 J6 **High Killerby** N York
166 C6 **High Knipe** Cumb
168 E5 **High Lands** Dur
131 J3 **High Lane** Stockp
2 F4 **High Lanes** Cnwll
70 D5 **High Laver** Essex
130 D3 **High Legh** Ches
170 B8 **High Leven** S on T
45 J7 **High Littleton** BaNES
165 G5 **High Lorton** Cumb
134 F5 **High Marnham** Notts
142 D7 **High Melton** Donc
180 C6 **High Mickley** Nthumb
169 J2 **High Moorsley** Sundld
181 J8 **High Newport** Sundld
156 F6 **High Newton** Cumb
156 D5 **High Nibthwaite** Cumb
114 B6 **High Offley** Staffs
70 E6 **High Ongar** Essex
114 C8 **High Onn** Staffs
72 F3 **High Park Corner** Essex
184 D2 **High Pennyvenie** E Ayrs
33 K4 **High Post** Wilts
70 F4 **High Roding** Essex
165 K3 **High Row** Cumb
165 L6 **High Row** Cumb
147 M3 **High Salter** Lancs
21 K5 **High Salvington** W Susx
165 G2 **High Scales** Cumb
164 D4 **High Seaton** Cumb
158 F4 **High Shaw** N York
165 H4 **High Side** Cumb
180 E7 **High Spen** Gatesd
168 E3 **High Stoop** Dur
5 G4 **High Street** Cnwll
39 J7 **High Street** Kent
91 J1 **High Street** Suffk
91 K4 **High Street** Suffk
170 C4 **High Throston** Hartpl
98 C1 **High Town** Staffs
136 E5 **High Toynton** Lincs
190 E5 **High Trewhitt** Nthumb
181 G8 **High Urpeth** Dur
210 D2 **High Valleyfield** Fife
179 L5 **High Warden** Nthumb
180 D7 **High Westwood** Dur
63 H7 **High Woolaston** Gloucs
160 F1 **High Worsall** N York
156 E3 **High Wray** Cumb
70 C4 **High Wych** Herts
67 L8 **High Wycombe** Bucks
141 M6 **Higham** Barns
133 H7 **Higham** Derbys
38 F4 **Higham** Kent
52 F5 **Higham** Kent
148 E8 **Higham** Lancs
88 E2 **Higham** Suffk
89 L8 **Higham** Suffk

180 D4 **Higham Dykes** Nthumb
85 J2 **Higham Ferrers** Nhants
86 C8 **Higham Gobion** Beds
51 K1 **Higham Hill** Gt Lon
99 K4 **Higham on the Hill** Leics
12 C2 **Highampton** Devon
69 K8 **Highams Park** Gt Lon
34 F6 **Highbridge** Hants
30 D2 **Highbridge** Somset
38 A7 **Highbrook** W Susx
141 J5 **Highburton** Kirk
51 J2 **Highbury** Gt Lon
31 M1 **Highbury** Somset
48 B7 **Highclere** Hants
18 C5 **Highcliffe** Dorset
147 G8 **Highcross** Lancs
31 L3 **Higher Alham** Somset
16 E2 **Higher Ansty** Dorset
138 D2 **Higher Ballam** Lancs
139 G1 **Higher Bartle** Lancs
85 J8 **Higher Berry End** Beds
16 D4 **Higher Bockhampton** Dorset
8 D4 **Higher Brixham** Torbay
14 B3 **Higher Burrowton** Devon
129 M8 **Higher Burwardsley** Ches
15 J1 **Higher Chillington** Somset
26 E6 **Higher Clovelly** Devon
28 F5 **Higher Combe** Somset
15 M4 **Higher Coombe** Dorset
131 J3 **Higher Disley** Ches
139 K7 **Higher Folds** Wigan
8 D1 **Higher Gabwell** Devon
15 L1 **Higher Halstock Leigh** Dorset
148 E8 **Higher Harpers** Lancs
147 H4 **Higher Heysham** Lancs
131 J5 **Higher Hurdsfield** Ches
130 E1 **Higher Irlam** Salfd
15 M3 **Higher Kingcombe** Dorset
129 H7 **Higher Kinnerton** Flints
16 E2 **Higher Melcombe** Dorset
27 K3 **Higher Muddiford** Devon
32 B6 **Higher Nyland** Dorset
140 E5 **Higher Ogden** Rochdl
3 G6 **Higher Pentire** Cnwll
139 G2 **Higher Penwortham** Lancs
148 E2 **Higher Studfold** N York
4 C6 **Higher Town** Cnwll
5 G3 **Higher Town** Cnwll
10 c2 **Higher Town** IOS
6 D4 **Higher Tregantle** Cnwll
139 H2 **Higher Walton** Lancs
130 B3 **Higher Walton** Warrtn
15 G1 **Higher Wambrook** Somset
16 D3 **Higher Waterston** Dorset
17 G2 **Higher Whatcombe** Dorset
139 J3 **Higher Wheelton** Lancs
11 J4 **Higher Whiteleigh** Cnwll
130 B4 **Higher Whitley** Ches
16 A2 **Higher Wraxhall** Dorset
113 H3 **Higher Wych** Ches
148 F7 **Higherford** Lancs
13 G3 **Highfield** Devon
151 M8 **Highfield** E R Yk
180 E7 **Highfield** Gatesd
196 C1 **Highfield** N Ayrs
142 E6 **Highfields** Donc
38 C6 **Highgate** E Susx
51 H2 **Highgate** Gt Lon
131 L2 **Highgate Head** Derbys
189 L7 **Highgreen Manor** Nthumb
131 H6 **Highlane** Ches
133 H3 **Highlane** Derbys
164 F1 **Highlaws** Cumb
63 M2 **Highleadon** Gloucs
20 D7 **Highleigh** W Susx
97 G6 **Highley** Shrops
165 J1 **Highmoor** Cumb
49 H2 **Highmoor** Oxon
49 H2 **Highmoor Cross** Oxon
44 F1 **Highmoor Hill** Mons
64 A3 **Highnam** Gloucs
64 A3 **Highnam Green** Gloucs
45 H5 **Highridge** N Som
41 G2 **Highstead** Kent
40 B3 **Highsted** Kent
40 E3 **Highstreet** Kent
88 F8 **Highstreet Green** Essex
36 E4 **Highstreet Green** Surrey
176 E3 **Hightae** D & G
98 E7 **Highter's Heath** Birm
131 G7 **Hightown** Ches
18 B3 **Hightown** Hants
138 C7 **Hightown** Sefton
89 K4 **Hightown Green** Suffk
80 B5 **Highway** Herefs

46 F4 **Highway** Wilts
13 K8 **Highweek** Devon
115 H5 **Highwood** Staffs
69 G8 **Highwood Hill** Gt Lon
65 J8 **Highworth** Swindn
10 _8 **Hilborough** Norfk
133 J8 **Hilcote** Derbys
38 F4 **Hilden Park** Kent
38 E4 **Hildenborough** Kent
87 L5 **Hildersham** Cambs
114 E4 **Hilderstone** Staffs
153 J3 **Hilderthorpe** E R Yk
16 C2 **Hilfield** Dorset
104 C4 **Hilgay** Norfk
63 J8 **Hill** S Glos
83 K2 **Hill** Warwks
36 B5 **Hill Brow** Hants
114 B4 **Hill Chorlton** Staffs
123 H7 **Hill Common** Norfk
29 L5 **Hill Common** Somset
32 E3 **Hill Deverill** Wilts
119 K2 **Hill Dyke** Lincs
168 C3 **Hill End** Dur
221 J8 **Hill End** Fife
81 K7 **Hill End** Gloucs
53 H6 **Hill Green** Kent
19 J3 **Hill Head** Hants
210 F1 **Hill of Beath** Fife
264 C4 **Hill of Fearn** Highld
115 H8 **Hill Ridware** Staffs
141 J4 **Hill Side** Kirk
81 H3 **Hill Side** Worcs
168 C6 **Hill Top** Dur
18 F3 **Hill Top** Hants
141 G5 **Hill Top** Kirk
133 H1 **Hill Top** Rothm
98 C5 **Hill Top** Sandw
142 A4 **Hill Top** Wakefd
142 D2 **Hillam** N York
167 H7 **Hillbeck** Dur
41 G2 **Hillborough** Kent
17 K2 **Hillbutts** Dorset
115 M2 **Hillclifflane** Derbys
47 G7 **Hillcott** Wilts
210 F2 **Hillend** Fife
211 H5 **Hillend** Mdloth
209 L5 **Hillend** N Lans
56 D6 **Hillend** Swans
63 H4 **Hillersland** Gloucs
13 G3 **Hillerton** Devon
67 G1 **Hillesden** Bucks
45 M1 **Hillesley** Gloucs
29 L6 **Hillfarrance** Somset
36 D5 **Hillgrove** W Susx
80 D6 **Hillhampton** Herefs
8 D4 **Hillhead** Devon
199 G5 **Hillhead** S Lans
257 K3 **Hillhead of Cocklaw** Abers
256 C6 **Hillhead of Durno** Abers
98 F1 **Hilliard's Cross** Staffs
279 L3 **Hilliclay** Highld
50 D2 **Hillingdon** Gt Lon
208 E6 **Hillington** C Glas
120 F6 **Hillington** Norfk
19 H5 **Hillis Corner** IOW
100 C8 **Hillmorton** Warwks
140 A2 **Hillock Vale** Lancs
175 J2 **Hillowton** D & G
97 K8 **Hillpool** Worcs
35 J7 **Hillpound** Hants
133 J5 **Hills Town** Derbys
245 K4 **Hillside** Abers
235 H3 **Hillside** Angus
7 K3 **Hillside** Devon
34 D7 **Hillstreet** Hants
281 c4 **Hillswick** Shet
12 D6 **Hilltown** Devon
211 K5 **Hilltown** E Loth
281 d8 **Hillwell** Shet
46 E4 **Hilmarton** Wilts
46 C7 **Hilperton** Wilts
46 C7 **Hilperton Marsh** Wilts
19 L3 **Hilsea** C Port
145 H1 **Hilston** E R Yk
62 F3 **Hilston Park** Mons
34 F6 **Hiltingbury** Hants
202 D3 **Hilton** Border
86 F2 **Hilton** Cambs
167 G6 **Hilton** Cumb
115 L5 **Hilton** Derbys
16 E2 **Hilton** Dorset
168 F6 **Hilton** Dur
264 D4 **Hilton** Highld
170 B8 **Hilton** S on T
97 H4 **Hilton** Shrops

81 L3 **Himbleton** Worcs
97 K5 **Himley** Staffs
157 H5 **Hincaster** Cumb
50 F6 **Hinchley Wood** Surrey
99 L4 **Hinckley** Leics
105 L8 **Hinderclay** Suffk
171 J7 **Hinderwell** N York
112 E5 **Hindford** Shrops
36 C4 **Hindhead** Surrey
139 L1 **Hindle Fold** Lancs
180 C7 **Hindley** Nthumb
139 J6 **Hindley** Wigan
139 J7 **Hindley Green** Wigan
81 K3 **Hindlip** Worcs
122 A5 **Hindolveston** Norfk
32 F4 **Hindon** Wilts
121 L4 **Hindringham** Norfk
105 L3 **Hingham** Norfk
97 J5 **Hinksford** Staffs
97 G3 **Hinnington** Shrops
113 M6 **Hinstock** Shrops
90 C6 **Hintlesham** Suffk
63 K6 **Hinton** Gloucs
18 C4 **Hinton** Hants
79 L7 **Hinton** Herefs
45 L4 **Hinton** S Glos
95 K2 **Hinton** Shrops
96 E7 **Hinton** Shrops
18 C4 **Hinton Admiral** Hants
35 J5 **Hinton Ampner** Hants
45 H7 **Hinton Blewett** BaNES
45 M7 **Hinton Charterhouse** BaNES
82 B7 **Hinton Green** Worcs
35 J5 **Hinton Marsh** Hants
17 K1 **Hinton Martell** Dorset
82 B7 **Hinton on the Green** Worcs
47 K2 **Hinton Parva** Swindn
30 F8 **Hinton St George** Somset
32 C7 **Hinton St Mary** Dorset
66 A7 **Hinton Waldrist** Oxon
84 A7 **Hinton-in-the-Hedges** Nhants
96 E8 **Hints** Shrops
98 F3 **Hints** Staffs
85 J3 **Hinwick** Beds
40 D6 **Hinxhill** Kent
87 K6 **Hinxton** Cambs
86 E7 **Hinxworth** Herts
141 H3 **Hipperholme** Calder
191 J4 **Hipsburn** Nthumb
160 B3 **Hipswell** N York
245 G3 **Hirn** Abers
111 K7 **Hirnant** Powys
181 G2 **Hirst** Nthumb
142 F3 **Hirst Courtney** N York
128 D7 **Hirwaen** Denbgs
60 E6 **Hirwaun** Rhondd
27 K5 **Hiscott** Devon
87 J3 **Histon** Cambs
89 K5 **Hitcham** Suffk
89 K5 **Hitcham Causeway** Suffk
89 K5 **Hitcham Street** Suffk
68 F1 **Hitchin** Herts
51 K4 **Hither Green** Gt Lon
13 G3 **Hittisleigh** Devon
13 G3 **Hittisleigh Cross** Devon
143 K2 **Hive** E R Yk
114 F6 **Hixon** Staffs
41 J3 **Hoaden** Kent
115 J7 **Hoar Cross** Staffs
63 G1 **Hoarwithy** Herefs
41 G2 **Hoath** Kent
39 G6 **Hoathly** Kent
95 H7 **Hobarris** Shrops
88 D4 **Hobbles Green** Suffk
70 C7 **Hobbs Cross** Essex
70 D5 **Hobbs Cross** Essex
189 G4 **Hobkirk** Border
107 K3 **Hobland Hall** Norfk
116 D2 **Hobsick** Notts
180 E7 **Hobson** Dur
117 H8 **Hoby** Leics
29 K5 **Hoccombe** Somset
106 B1 **Hockering** Norfk
134 E8 **Hockerton** Notts
131 J3 **Hockley** Ches
99 H7 **Hockley** Covtry
71 K8 **Hockley** Essex
99 G3 **Hockley** Staffs
82 E1 **Hockley Heath** Solhll
68 B2 **Hockliffe** Beds
104 E6 **Hockwold cum Wilton** Norfk
29 J7 **Hockworthy** Devon
69 K5 **Hoddesdon** Herts
139 L3 **Hoddlesden** Bl w D
177 G4 **Hoddom Cross** D & G

177 G4 **Hoddom Mains** D & G
131 G5 **Hodgehill** Ches
55 H7 **Hodgeston** Pembks
113 K6 **Hodnet** Shrops
52 D6 **Hodsall Street** Kent
134 C3 **Hodsock** Notts
47 H3 **Hodson** Swindn
133 L4 **Hodthorpe** Derbys
35 H7 **Hoe** Hants
121 M8 **Hoe** Norfk
35 K8 **Hoe Gate** Hants
166 F7 **Hoff** Cumb
25 G4 **Hog Hill** E Susx
40 D4 **Hogben's Hill** Kent
89 H4 **Hoggards Green** Suffk
67 K2 **Hoggeston** Bucks
99 G5 **Hoggrill's End** Warwks
139 J2 **Hoghton** Lancs
139 J2 **Hoghton Bottoms** Lancs
115 L2 **Hognaston** Derbys
137 K5 **Hogsthorpe** Lincs
119 K6 **Holbeach** Lincs
119 K6 **Holbeach Bank** Lincs
119 K6 **Holbeach Clough** Lincs
103 G1 **Holbeach Drove** Lincs
119 L6 **Holbeach Hurn** Lincs
119 K7 **Holbeach St Johns** Lincs
119 L5 **Holbeach St Mark's** Lincs
119 L5 **Holbeach St Matthew** Lincs
133 L5 **Holbeck** Notts
133 L5 **Holbeck Woodhouse** Notts
82 B3 **Holberrow Green** Worcs
7 J5 **Holbeton** Devon
51 J3 **Holborn** Gt Lon
52 F6 **Holborough** Kent
116 B3 **Holbrook** Derbys
133 J3 **Holbrook** Sheff
90 E7 **Holbrook** Suffk
116 B3 **Holbrook Moor** Derbys
203 G6 **Holburn** Nthumb
19 G3 **Holbury** Hants
140 A4 **Holcombe** Bury
13 M7 **Holcombe** Devon
31 L1 **Holcombe** Somset
140 A5 **Holcombe Brook** Bury
29 J7 **Holcombe Rogus** Devon
84 F1 **Holcot** Nhants
148 D6 **Holden** Lancs
140 D3 **Holden Gate** Calder
84 D2 **Holdenby** Nhants
70 F1 **Holder's Green** Essex
96 D5 **Holdgate** Shrops
118 E2 **Holdingham** Lincs
15 H2 **Holditch** Dorset
141 G2 **Holdsworth** Calder
12 A1 **Hole** Devon
39 L6 **Hole Park** Kent
21 K4 **Hole Street** W Susx
63 J2 **Hole-in-the-Wall** Herefs
131 K1 **Holehouse** Derbys
12 A2 **Holemoor** Devon
29 L3 **Holford** Somset
151 J5 **Holgate** York
156 E7 **Holker** Cumb
121 K3 **Holkham** Norfk
11 M2 **Hollacombe** Devon
119 H2 **Holland Fen** Lincs
139 G6 **Holland Lees** Lancs
73 J4 **Holland-on-Sea** Essex
275 f1 **Hollandstoun** Ork
177 J5 **Hollee** D & G
91 H6 **Hollesley** Suffk
8 D2 **Hollicombe** Torbay
97 L7 **Hollies Hill** Worcs
113 K1 **Hollin Green** Ches
39 L2 **Hollingbourne** Kent
22 D5 **Hollingbury** Br & H
67 L2 **Hollingdon** Bucks
142 B2 **Hollingthorpe** Leeds
115 L4 **Hollington** Derbys
115 G4 **Hollington** Staffs
140 F8 **Hollingworth** Tamesd
131 G3 **Hollinlane** Ches
140 B6 **Hollins** Bury
132 F5 **Hollins** Derbys
114 F2 **Hollins** Staffs
133 H3 **Hollins End** Sheff
130 D2 **Hollins Green** Warrtn
147 K5 **Hollins Lane** Lancs
131 L6 **Hollinsclough** Staffs
96 F2 **Hollinswood** Wrekin
113 H4 **Hollinwood** Shrops
24 C3 **Hollingrove** E Susx
27 L8 **Hollocombe** Devon
132 F8 **Holloway** Derbys

51 J2 **Holloway** Gt Lon
32 E5 **Holloway** Wilts
84 D1 **Hollowell** Nhants
129 L6 **Hollowmoor Heath** Ches
177 L3 **Hollows** D & G
103 K2 **Holly End** Norfk
81 K7 **Holly Green** Worcs
61 J6 **Hollybush** Caerph
196 D7 **Hollybush** E Ayrs
81 H7 **Hollybush** Herefs
113 J3 **Hollyhurst** Ches
98 D7 **Hollywood** Worcs
141 H6 **Holmbridge** Kirk
37 H2 **Holmbury St Mary** Surrey
5 H4 **Holmbush** Cnwll
114 E6 **Holmcroft** Staffs
102 D6 **Holme** Cambs
157 H7 **Holme** Cumb
141 H6 **Holme** Kirk
144 A6 **Holme** N Linc
160 E6 **Holme** N York
134 F7 **Holme** Notts
140 C2 **Holme Chapel** Lancs
151 J7 **Holme Green** N York
105 H2 **Holme Hale** Norfk
80 D8 **Holme Lacy** Herefs
79 L4 **Holme Marsh** Herefs
120 F3 **Holme next the Sea** Norfk
152 E6 **Holme on the Wolds** E R Yk
117 G4 **Holme Pierrepont** Notts
164 F1 **Holme St Cuthbert** Cumb
152 B8 **Holme upon Spalding Moor** E R Yk
80 C6 **Holmer** Herefs
67 L7 **Holmer Green** Bucks
130 E6 **Holmes Chapel** Ches
23 J4 **Holmes Hill** E Susx
132 F4 **Holmesfield** Derbys
138 E4 **Holmeswood** Lancs
51 H8 **Holmethorpe** Surrey
133 H6 **Holmewood** Derbys
141 G2 **Holmfield** Calder
141 H6 **Holmfirth** Kirk
133 G7 **Holmgate** Derbys
197 H7 **Holmhead** E Ayrs
145 K3 **Holmpton** E R Yk
155 K3 **Holmrook** Cumb
104 D7 **Holmsey Green** Suffk
23 L2 **Holmshurst** E Susx
169 G1 **Holmside** Dur
166 C1 **Holmwrangle** Cumb
7 K1 **Holne** Devon
16 C1 **Holnest** Dorset
29 G2 **Holnicote** Somset
11 L2 **Holsworthy** Devon
11 L1 **Holsworthy Beacon** Devon
17 K2 **Holt** Dorset
122 B4 **Holt** Norfk
46 B6 **Holt** Wilts
81 J3 **Holt** Worcs
112 F1 **Holt** Wrexhm
82 C1 **Holt End** Worcs
81 J3 **Holt Fleet** Worcs
138 E6 **Holt Green** Lancs
17 L2 **Holt Heath** Dorset
81 J3 **Holt Heath** Worcs
41 H5 **Holt Street** Kent
151 L5 **Holtby** York
66 F5 **Holton** Oxon
31 L5 **Holton** Somset
107 H7 **Holton** Suffk
136 B3 **Holton cum Beckering** Lincs
17 J4 **Holton Heath** Dorset
24 B2 **Holton Hill** E Susx
145 H7 **Holton le Clay** Lincs
144 D8 **Holton le Moor** Lincs
90 C7 **Holton St Mary** Suffk
38 C5 **Holtye** E Susx
128 E4 **Holway** Flints
32 B8 **Holwell** Dorset
86 D8 **Holwell** Herts
117 J6 **Holwell** Leics
65 K5 **Holwell** Oxon
167 L5 **Holwick** Dur
16 E6 **Holworth** Dorset
97 L7 **Holy Cross** Worcs
203 J5 **Holy Island** Nthumb
35 M3 **Holybourne** Hants
69 K6 **Holyfield** Essex
124 D3 **Holyhead** IOA
133 G6 **Holymoorside** Derbys
49 L3 **Holyport** W & M
190 D5 **Holystone** Nthumb
209 K6 **Holytown** N Lans

87 G1 **Holywell** Cambs
4 C3 **Holywell** Cnwll
16 B2 **Holywell** Dorset
128 E4 **Holywell** Flints
181 H4 **Holywell** Nthumb
82 E2 **Holywell** Warwks
141 G4 **Holywell Green** Calder
29 K6 **Holywell Lake** Somset
104 E7 **Holywell Row** Suffk
176 B3 **Holywood** D & G
176 B3 **Holywood Village** D & G
63 H3 **Hom Green** Herefs
96 E3 **Homer** Shrops
138 D7 **Homer Green** Sefton
106 F6 **Homersfield** Suffk
157 J5 **Homescales** Cumb
33 K5 **Homington** Wilts
40 F3 **Honey Hill** Kent
89 J8 **Honey Tye** Suffk
54 F5 **Honeyborough** Pembks
82 D6 **Honeybourne** Worcs
12 E2 **Honeychurch** Devon
47 G6 **Honeystreet** Wilts
82 F1 **Honiley** Warwks
123 G6 **Honing** Norfk
106 C1 **Honingham** Norfk
118 B3 **Honington** Lincs
105 H8 **Honington** Suffk
83 G6 **Honington** Warwks
14 E2 **Honiton** Devon
141 H5 **Honley** Kirk
114 A8 **Honnington** Wrekin
41 J2 **Hoo** Kent
68 F3 **Hoo End** Herts
130 D3 **Hoo Green** Ches
7 G2 **Hoo Meavy** Devon
53 G4 **Hoo St Werburgh** Medway
97 J8 **Hoobrook** Worcs
141 M7 **Hood Green** Barns
142 B8 **Hood Hill** Rothm
6 F4 **Hooe** C Plym
24 C5 **Hooe** E Susx
146 F8 **Hoohill** Bpool
103 J5 **Hook** Cambs
15 G2 **Hook** Devon
143 J3 **Hook** E R Yk
19 H3 **Hook** Hants
49 H8 **Hook** Hants
55 G4 **Hook** Pembks
50 F6 **Hook** Surrey
47 G2 **Hook** Wilts
81 J7 **Hook Bank** Worcs
70 E7 **Hook End** Essex
52 D5 **Hook Green** Kent
39 G6 **Hook Green** Kent
83 H8 **Hook Norton** Oxon
63 K7 **Hook Street** Gloucs
47 G2 **Hook Street** Wilts
95 L2 **Hookagate** Shrops
15 M3 **Hooke** Dorset
114 A4 **Hookgate** Staffs
13 K3 **Hookway** Devon
37 L2 **Hookwood** Surrey
51 H7 **Hooley** Surrey
140 C5 **Hooley Bridge** Rochdl
129 J3 **Hooton** Ches
133 K2 **Hooton Levitt** Rothm
142 D6 **Hooton Pagnell** Donc
142 D8 **Hooton Roberts** Rothm
102 D1 **Hop Pole** Lincs
66 C2 **Hopcrofts Holt** Oxon
132 C3 **Hope** Derbys
7 K6 **Hope** Devon
129 G7 **Hope** Flints
95 G2 **Hope** Powys
95 H3 **Hope** Shrops
96 D8 **Hope** Shrops
132 B8 **Hope** Staffs
95 L5 **Hope Bowdler** Shrops
70 E3 **Hope End Green** Essex
63 J3 **Hope Mansell** Herefs
80 C5 **Hope under Dinmore** Herefs
187 L3 **Hopehouse** Border
266 C2 **Hopeman** Moray
95 J6 **Hopesay** Shrops
142 B3 **Hopetown** Wakefd
151 K5 **Hopgrove** York
150 F4 **Hopperton** N York
99 L6 **Hopsford** Warwks
97 H4 **Hopstone** Shrops
115 L1 **Hopton** Derbys
112 F7 **Hopton** Shrops
114 E6 **Hopton** Staffs
105 K7 **Hopton** Suffk
96 C7 **Hopton Cangeford** Shrops

95 J7 **Hopton Castle** Shrops
107 L3 **Hopton on Sea** Norfk
96 E8 **Hopton Wafers** Shrops
95 J7 **Hoptonheath** Shrops
98 F3 **Hopwas** Staffs
140 C6 **Hopwood** Rochdl
98 C8 **Hopwood** Worcs
23 K4 **Horam** E Susx
118 F4 **Horbling** Lincs
141 L4 **Horbury** Wakefd
65 H7 **Horcott** Gloucs
170 B3 **Horden** Dur
95 K6 **Horderley** Shrops
18 D4 **Hordle** Hants
112 F5 **Hordley** Shrops
56 F4 **Horeb** Carmth
76 D6 **Horeb** Cerdgn
45 H4 **Horfield** Bristl
90 F1 **Horham** Suffk
72 E1 **Horkesley Green** Essex
72 E1 **Horkesley Heath** Essex
144 C4 **Horkstow** N Linc
83 K6 **Horley** Oxon
37 L2 **Horley** Surrey
68 C8 **Horn Hill** Bucks
41 G8 **Horn Street** Kent
31 K4 **Hornblotton Green** Somset
147 L2 **Hornby** Lancs
160 E2 **Hornby** N York
160 B4 **Hornby** N York
136 E6 **Horncastle** Lincs
52 B2 **Hornchurch** Gt Lon
202 E3 **Horncliffe** Nthumb
202 D3 **Horndean** Border
35 L8 **Horndean** Hants
12 C6 **Horndon** Devon
52 E2 **Horndon on the Hill** Thurr
38 A4 **Horne** Surrey
71 J6 **Horne Row** Essex
28 F2 **Horner** Somset
89 K7 **Horners Green** Suffk
23 G2 **Horney Common** E Susx
123 G8 **Horning** Norfk
101 H4 **Horninghold** Leics
115 L6 **Horninglow** Staffs
87 K3 **Horningsea** Cambs
32 D3 **Horningsham** Wilts
121 K6 **Horningtoft** Norfk
6 B3 **Horningtops** Cnwll
27 G6 **Horns Cross** Devon
24 E3 **Horns Cross** E Susx
30 E8 **Hornsbury** Somset
166 C1 **Hornsby** Cumb
166 C1 **Hornsbygate** Cumb
153 K6 **Hornsea** E R Yk
51 J1 **Hornsey** Gt Lon
83 J6 **Hornton** Oxon
47 J2 **Horpit** Swindn
281 e3 **Horra** Shet
7 G1 **Horrabridge** Devon
13 H7 **Horridge** Devon
89 G3 **Horringer** Suffk
19 J6 **Horringford** IOW
139 L5 **Horrocks Fold** Bolton
148 C7 **Horrocksford** Lancs
27 J4 **Horsacott** Devon
12 A7 **Horsebridge** Devon
23 K5 **Horsebridge** E Susx
34 D5 **Horsebridge** Hants
95 J2 **Horsebridge** Shrops
114 F1 **Horsebridge** Staffs
97 K1 **Horsebrook** Staffs
44 E5 **Horsecastle** N Som
3 G4 **Horsedown** Cnwll
102 C2 **Horsegate** Lincs
96 F2 **Horsehay** Wrekin
88 C5 **Horseheath** Cambs
159 J6 **Horsehouse** N York
50 C7 **Horsell** Surrey
113 G3 **Horseman's Green** Wrexhm
67 J6 **Horsenden** Bucks
123 J7 **Horsey** Norfk
30 D3 **Horsey** Somset
123 J6 **Horsey Corner** Norfk
122 D8 **Horsford** Norfk
150 B8 **Horsforth** Leeds
37 J5 **Horsham** W Susx
81 G4 **Horsham** Worcs
122 E8 **Horsham St Faith** Norfk
136 C6 **Horsington** Lincs
32 B6 **Horsington** Somset
116 C3 **Horsley** Derbys
64 B7 **Horsley** Gloucs
190 B6 **Horsley** Nthumb
180 D5 **Horsley** Nthumb

73 H2 **Horsley Cross** Essex
116 C3 **Horsley Woodhouse** Derbys
67 J8 **Horsley's Green** Bucks
132 F4 **Horsley-Gate** Derbys
73 G1 **Horsleycross Street** Essex
188 F2 **Horsleyhill** Border
39 H5 **Horsmonden** Kent
66 E6 **Horspath** Oxon
122 F7 **Horstead** Norfk
22 F2 **Horsted Keynes** W Susx
68 A3 **Horton** Bucks
17 K1 **Horton** Dorset
148 E6 **Horton** Lancs
84 F4 **Horton** Nhants
45 M2 **Horton** S Glos
113 H5 **Horton** Shrops
30 D7 **Horton** Somset
131 J8 **Horton** Staffs
51 G6 **Horton** Surrey
56 E7 **Horton** Swans
50 C4 **Horton** W & M
46 F6 **Horton** Wilts
113 L8 **Horton** Wrekin
30 E7 **Horton Cross** Somset
113 G2 **Horton Green** Ches
35 G7 **Horton Heath** Hants
148 D2 **Horton in Ribblesdale** N York
52 C5 **Horton Kirby** Kent
66 F4 **Horton-cum-Studley** Oxon
139 J5 **Horwich** Bolton
131 K3 **Horwich End** Derbys
27 J5 **Horwood** Devon
138 F5 **Hoscar** Lancs
188 C4 **Hoscote** Border
117 J5 **Hose** Leics
51 M8 **Hosey Hill** Kent
220 E3 **Hosh** P & K
281 e8 **Hoswick** Shet
143 M1 **Hotham** E R Yk
40 C6 **Hothfield** Kent
116 F7 **Hoton** Leics
179 H2 **Hott** Nthumb
113 M1 **Hough** Ches
131 G4 **Hough** Ches
141 K1 **Hough End** Leeds
129 L2 **Hough Green** Halton
118 B2 **Hough-on-the-Hill** Lincs
118 A3 **Hougham** Lincs
86 F1 **Houghton** Cambs
177 L7 **Houghton** Cumb
34 D4 **Houghton** Hants
180 D5 **Houghton** Nthumb
55 G5 **Houghton** Pembks
21 H4 **Houghton** W Susx
85 L7 **Houghton Conquest** Beds
181 H8 **Houghton Gate** Dur
25 G3 **Houghton Green** E Susx
130 C1 **Houghton Green** Warrtn
169 G6 **Houghton le Side** Darltn
169 J1 **Houghton le Spring** Sundld
100 E3 **Houghton on the Hill** Leics
68 C2 **Houghton Regis** Beds
121 K4 **Houghton St Giles** Norfk
49 H7 **Hound Green** Hants
201 K4 **Houndslow** Border
29 L5 **Houndsmoor** Somset
213 J6 **Houndwood** Border
50 F4 **Hounslow** Gt Lon
71 G3 **Hounslow Green** Essex
253 G1 **Househill** Highld
141 K4 **Houses Hill** Kirk
257 G6 **Housieside** Abers
208 C5 **Houston** Rens
275 G1 **Houstry** Highld
275 b5 **Houton** Ork
22 D6 **Hove** Br & H
141 H3 **Hove Edge** Calder
117 J2 **Hoveringham** Notts
122 F7 **Hoveton** Norfk
161 L7 **Hovingham** N York
63 J1 **How Caple** Herefs
85 K7 **How End** Beds
178 C7 **How Mill** Cumb
141 M8 **Howbrook** Barns
143 J2 **Howden** E R Yk
168 F4 **Howden-le-Wear** Dur
280 D4 **Howe** Highld
154 b8 **Howe** IOM
160 E6 **Howe** N York
106 F3 **Howe** Norfk
139 K7 **Howe Bridge** Wigan
71 H6 **Howe Green** Essex
268 E6 **Howe of Teuchar** Abers
71 G4 **Howe Street** Essex
88 D8 **Howe Street** Essex

71 K6 **Howegreen** Essex
118 F2 **Howell** Lincs
177 G5 **Howes** D & G
78 E3 **Howey** Powys
211 H7 **Howgate** Mdloth
148 E6 **Howgill** N York
191 K3 **Howick** Nthumb
168 E5 **Howle** Dur
113 M6 **Howle** Wrekin
63 J3 **Howle Hill** Herefs
88 B8 **Howlett End** Essex
15 G1 **Howley** Somset
283 b10 **Howmore** W Isls
189 L2 **Hownam** Border
165 K1 **Howrigg** Cumb
144 D6 **Howsham** N Linc
151 M3 **Howsham** N York
53 J6 **Howt Green** Kent
202 D6 **Howtel** Nthumb
13 H5 **Howton** Devon
62 E1 **Howton** Herefs
166 B6 **Howwood** Cumb
208 C7 **Howwood** Rens
106 D7 **Hoxne** Suffk
128 F2 **Hoylake** Wirral
142 B7 **Hoyland Common** Barns
142 B7 **Hoyland Nether** Barns
141 L6 **Hoyland Swaine** Barns
20 E3 **Hoyle** W Susx
142 A6 **Hoyle Mill** Barns
159 G7 **Hubberholme** N York
54 E5 **Hubberston** Pembks
119 J3 **Hubbert's Bridge** Lincs
150 C6 **Huby** N York
151 J3 **Huby** N York
12 F7 **Huccaby** Devon
64 C4 **Hucclecote** Gloucs
53 H7 **Hucking** Kent
116 F2 **Hucknall** Notts
141 H4 **Huddersfield** Kirk
81 L4 **Huddington** Worcs
159 L3 **Hudswell** N York
152 D5 **Huggate** E R Yk
99 L1 **Hugglescote** Leics
10 c3 **Hugh Town** IOS
67 L7 **Hughenden Valley** Bucks
96 D4 **Hughley** Shrops
27 J8 **Huish** Devon
47 H6 **Huish** Wilts
29 J5 **Huish Champflower** Somset
31 G5 **Huish Episcopi** Somset
52 B6 **Hulberry** Kent
85 J7 **Hulcote** Beds
67 K4 **Hulcott** Bucks
14 B6 **Hulham** Devon
115 L2 **Hulland** Derbys
115 L2 **Hulland Ward** Derbys
46 C3 **Hullavington** Wilts
71 K8 **Hullbridge** Essex
140 C8 **Hulme** Manch
114 E2 **Hulme** Staffs
130 B2 **Hulme** Warrtn
132 B7 **Hulme End** Staffs
131 G6 **Hulme Walfield** Ches
130 E3 **Hulse Heath** Ches
139 K6 **Hulton Lane Ends** Bolton
105 J1 **Hulver Street** Norfk
107 K6 **Hulver Street** Suffk
18 F6 **Hulverstone** IOW
13 L7 **Humber** Devon
80 C4 **Humber** Herefs
145 J6 **Humberston** NE Lin
100 E2 **Humberstone** C Leic
150 F2 **Humberton** N York
212 A6 **Humbie** E Loth
145 G1 **Humbleton** E R Yk
202 F7 **Humbleton** Nthumb
118 D5 **Humby** Lincs
201 L5 **Hume** Border
179 L4 **Humshaugh** Nthumb
280 E2 **Huna** Highld
140 A2 **Huncoat** Lancs
100 B4 **Huncote** Leics
189 H3 **Hundalee** Border
133 H4 **Hundall** Derbys
168 C6 **Hunderthwaite** Dur
119 H1 **Hundle Houses** Lincs
137 G6 **Hundleby** Lincs
54 F6 **Hundleton** Pembks
88 E5 **Hundon** Suffk
19 K1 **Hundred Acres** Hants
138 E3 **Hundred End** Lancs
78 F4 **Hundred House** Powys
100 F2 **Hungarton** Leics
84 F6 **Hungate End** M Keyn

139 K6 **Hunger Hill** Bolton
139 G5 **Hunger Hill** Lancs
33 L8 **Hungerford** Hants
29 J3 **Hungerford** Somset
47 M5 **Hungerford** W Berk
47 M4 **Hungerford Newtown**
    W Berk
80 B8 **Hungerstone** Herefs
118 A5 **Hungerton** Lincs
113 L6 **Hungryhatton** Shrops
163 K7 **Hunmanby** N York
83 J2 **Hunningham** Warwks
98 B7 **Hunnington** Worcs
84 E4 **Hunsbury Hill** Nhants
69 L4 **Hunsdon** Herts
150 F5 **Hunsingore** N York
141 M2 **Hunslet** Leeds
166 D4 **Hunsonby** Cumb
120 E3 **Hunstanton** Norfk
168 B1 **Hunstanworth** Dur
113 M2 **Hunsterson** Ches
89 K2 **Hunston** Suffk
20 D6 **Hunston** W Susx
89 K2 **Hunston Green** Suffk
45 J6 **Hunstrete** BaNES
141 J2 **Hunsworth** Kirk
82 B2 **Hunt End** Worcs
105 L5 **Hunt's Corner** Norfk
129 K3 **Hunt's Cross** Lpool
28 B1 **Hunter's Inn** Devon
207 K3 **Hunter's Quay** Ag & B
30 E5 **Huntham** Somset
234 D1 **Hunthill Lodge** Angus
86 E1 **Huntingdon** Cambs
107 G8 **Huntingfield** Suffk
32 D5 **Huntingford** Dorset
129 K6 **Huntington** Ches
212 B4 **Huntington** E Loth
79 J4 **Huntington** Herefs
80 B6 **Huntington** Herefs
98 B1 **Huntington** Staffs
151 K4 **Huntington** York
63 L3 **Huntley** Gloucs
255 L4 **Huntly** Abers
35 G3 **Hunton** Hants
39 H3 **Hunton** Kent
160 B4 **Hunton** N York
68 D7 **Hunton Bridge** Herts
67 L6 **Hunts Green** Bucks
98 F4 **Hunts Green** Warwks
29 G2 **Huntscott** Somset
29 H6 **Huntsham** Devon
27 J6 **Huntshaw** Devon
27 J6 **Huntshaw Cross** Devon
30 D2 **Huntspill** Somset
30 C4 **Huntstile** Somset
30 D4 **Huntworth** Somset
168 F4 **Hunwick** Dur
122 B4 **Hunworth** Norfk
30 F7 **Hurcott** Somset
33 L4 **Hurdcott** Wilts
131 H5 **Hurdsfield** Ches
49 K2 **Hurley** W & M
99 H4 **Hurley** Warwks
49 K2 **Hurley Bottom** W & M
99 H4 **Hurley Common** Warwks
196 E4 **Hurlford** E Ayrs
138 E5 **Hurlston Green** Lancs
18 A4 **Hurn** Dorset
119 M2 **Hurn's End** Lincs
34 F6 **Hursley** Hants
16 F4 **Hurst** Dorset
159 J2 **Hurst** N York
31 G7 **Hurst** Somset
49 J4 **Hurst** Wokham
24 D2 **Hurst Green** E Susx
73 G4 **Hurst Green** Essex
148 B8 **Hurst Green** Lancs
51 K8 **Hurst Green** Surrey
97 L4 **Hurst Hill** Dudley
22 D4 **Hurst Wickham** W Susx
34 F2 **Hurstbourne Priors** Hants
48 A8 **Hurstbourne Tarrant** Hants
79 L5 **Hurstley** Herefs
22 D4 **Hurstpierpoint** W Susx
79 K5 **Hurstway Common** Herefs
140 C2 **Hurstwood** Lancs
275 d5 **Hurtiso** Ork
36 E2 **Hurtmore** Surrey
169 L4 **Hurworth Burn** Dur
160 D1 **Hurworth Place** Darltn
169 J8 **Hurworth-on-Tees** Darltn
168 B6 **Hury** Dur
100 E6 **Husbands Bosworth** Leics
85 J8 **Husborne Crawley** Beds

161 H7 **Husthwaite** N York
142 F3 **Hut Green** N York
8 A5 **Hutcherleigh** Devon
161 G2 **Huthwaite** N York
133 J7 **Huthwaite** Notts
137 K4 **Huttoft** Lincs
202 E2 **Hutton** Border
166 B5 **Hutton** Cumb
152 F5 **Hutton** E R Yk
70 F8 **Hutton** Essex
139 G2 **Hutton** Lancs
44 D7 **Hutton** N Som
160 E3 **Hutton Bonville** N York
163 H6 **Hutton Buscel** N York
160 D7 **Hutton Conyers** N York
153 G5 **Hutton Cranswick** E R Yk
166 B3 **Hutton End** Cumb
170 E7 **Hutton Hall** R & Cl
159 L5 **Hutton Hang** N York
169 L3 **Hutton Henry** Dur
170 E7 **Hutton Lowcross** R & Cl
168 E8 **Hutton Magna** Dur
162 E1 **Hutton Mulgrave** N York
165 L4 **Hutton Roof** Cumb
157 J7 **Hutton Roof** Cumb
161 G2 **Hutton Rudby** N York
161 G7 **Hutton Sessay** N York
151 H5 **Hutton Wandesley** N York
162 B4 **Hutton-le-Hole** N York
13 M3 **Huxham** Devon
31 K4 **Huxham Green** Somset
129 L7 **Huxley** Ches
129 K2 **Huyton** Knows
155 K5 **Hycemoor** Cumb
64 C6 **Hyde** Gloucs
33 L8 **Hyde** Hants
131 J1 **Hyde** Tamesd
49 H5 **Hyde End** Wokham
68 B7 **Hyde Heath** Bucks
114 E7 **Hyde Lea** Staffs
30 D4 **Hyde Park Corner** Somset
36 E3 **Hydestile** Surrey
135 J6 **Hykeham Moor** Lincs
198 F5 **Hyndford Bridge** S Lans
224 C7 **Hynish** Ag & B
95 H4 **Hyssington** Powys
63 K7 **Hystfield** Gloucs
19 G2 **Hythe** Hants
41 G8 **Hythe** Kent
44 F8 **Hythe** Somset
50 C4 **Hythe End** W & M
155 K5 **Hyton** Cumb

I

16 F1 **Ibberton** Dorset
132 E8 **Ible** Derbys
18 A2 **Ibsley** Hants
99 L2 **Ibstock** Leics
67 J8 **Ibstone** Bucks
48 A8 **Ibthorpe** Hants
162 F1 **Iburndale** N York
48 E7 **Ibworth** Hants
44 D6 **Icelton** N Som
105 G4 **Ickburgh** Norfk
50 D2 **Ickenham** Gt Lon
66 F5 **Ickford** Bucks
41 H4 **Ickham** Kent
68 F1 **Ickleford** Herts
24 F4 **Icklesham** E Susx
87 K6 **Ickleton** Cambs
88 F1 **Icklingham** Suffk
149 G7 **Ickornshaw** N York
86 C6 **Ickwell Green** Beds
65 J3 **Icomb** Gloucs
65 K3 **Idbury** Oxon
12 D1 **Iddesleigh** Devon
13 L4 **Ide** Devon
38 D3 **Ide Hill** Kent
13 K7 **Ideford** Devon
25 G3 **Iden** E Susx
39 J6 **Iden Green** Kent
39 K7 **Iden Green** Kent
149 M8 **Idle** Brad
4 D5 **Idless** Cnwll
83 G6 **Idlicote** Warwks
33 L3 **Idmiston** Wilts
115 M2 **Idridgehay** Derbys
258 F4 **Idrigill** Highld
47 K2 **Idstone** Oxon
66 D6 **Iffley** Oxon
37 K3 **Ifield** W Susx
36 F4 **Ifold** W Susx
18 A5 **Iford** Bmouth

22 F5 **Iford** E Susx
44 F1 **Ifton** Mons
112 E4 **Ifton Heath** Shrops
113 K4 **Ightfield** Shrops
38 F2 **Ightham** Kent
91 J4 **Iken** Suffk
115 J2 **Ilam** Staffs
31 H6 **Ilchester** Somset
190 E2 **Ilderton** Nthumb
51 L2 **Ilford** Gt Lon
30 E7 **Ilford** Somset
27 J2 **Ilfracombe** Devon
116 D3 **Ilkeston** Derbys
107 H6 **Ilketshall St Andrew** Suffk
107 G6 **Ilketshall St Margaret** Suffk
149 K6 **Ilkley** Brad
11 K6 **Illand** Cnwll
98 B7 **Illey** Dudley
130 F7 **Illidge Green** Ches
141 G2 **Illingworth** Calder
3 H2 **Illogan** Cnwll
100 F3 **Illston on the Hill** Leics
67 J6 **Ilmer** Bucks
82 F6 **Ilmington** Warwks
30 E7 **Ilminster** Somset
13 H7 **Ilsington** Devon
16 E4 **Ilsington** Dorset
57 G6 **Ilston** Swans
160 B7 **Ilton** N York
30 E7 **Ilton** Somset
194 D3 **Imachar** N Ayrs
144 F5 **Immingham** NE Lin
145 G4 **Immingham Dock** NE Lin
87 J3 **Impington** Cambs
129 K4 **Ince** Ches
138 C7 **Ince Blundell** Sefton
139 J6 **Ince-in-Makerfield** Wigan
262 C6 **Inchbae Lodge Hotel** Highld
234 F2 **Inchbare** Angus
266 F5 **Inchberry** Moray
261 G7 **Incheril** Highld
208 E5 **Inchinnan** Rens
239 K3 **Inchlaggan** Highld
222 D2 **Inchmichael** P & K
240 C2 **Inchnacardoch Hotel** Highld
271 H4 **Inchnadamph** Highld
222 D2 **Inchture** P & K
249 L4 **Inchvuilt** Highld
222 C3 **Inchyra** P & K
4 E3 **Indian Queens** Cnwll
107 J5 **Ingate Place** Suffk
70 F7 **Ingatestone** Essex
141 K6 **Ingbirchworth** Barns
150 C3 **Ingerthorpe** N York
114 F6 **Ingestre** Staffs
135 J3 **Ingham** Lincs
123 H6 **Ingham** Norfk
89 G1 **Ingham** Suffk
123 H6 **Ingham Corner** Norfk
120 B8 **Ingleborough** Norfk
116 B6 **Ingleby** Derbys
161 G3 **Ingleby Arncliffe** N York
170 B7 **Ingleby Barwick** S on T
161 G3 **Ingleby Cross** N York
161 J2 **Ingleby Greenhow** N York
12 E1 **Ingleigh Green** Devon
45 L6 **Inglesbatch** BaNES
65 J7 **Inglesham** Swindn
176 C6 **Ingleston** D & G
168 F6 **Ingleton** Dur
158 B8 **Ingleton** N York
147 L7 **Inglewhite** Lancs
157 K4 **Ingmire Hall** Cumb
180 C4 **Ingoe** Nthumb
139 G1 **Ingol** Lancs
120 F5 **Ingoldisthorpe** Norfk
137 K6 **Ingoldmells** Lincs
118 D5 **Ingoldsby** Lincs
190 E3 **Ingram** Nthumb
52 D1 **Ingrave** Essex
149 J7 **Ingrow** Brad
157 G3 **Ings** Cumb
45 H2 **Ingst** S Glos
101 M2 **Ingthorpe** Rutlnd
122 D5 **Ingworth** Norfk
82 B4 **Inkberrow** Worcs
168 E3 **Inkerman** Dur
257 G4 **Inkhorn** Abers
48 A6 **Inkpen** W Berk
280 C2 **Inkstack** Highld
46 D6 **Inmarsh** Wilts
207 J5 **Innellan** Ag & B
200 D6 **Innerleithen** Border
222 F7 **Innerleven** Fife
172 D2 **Innermessan** D & G

212 F4 **Innerwick** E Loth
266 F3 **Innesmill** Moray
256 A6 **Insch** Abers
241 L3 **Insh** Highld
147 J8 **Inskip** Lancs
147 J8 **Inskip Moss Side** Lancs
27 H5 **Instow** Devon
6 E4 **Insworke** Cnwll
133 H3 **Intake** Sheff
243 H5 **Inver** Abers
264 D3 **Inver** Highld
232 F7 **Inver** P & K
268 B3 **Inver-boyndie** Abers
238 B7 **Inverailort** Highld
260 D8 **Inveralligin** Highld
269 J3 **Inverallochy** Abers
272 E8 **Inveran** Highld
217 H5 **Inveraray** Ag & B
247 H2 **Inverarish** Highld
234 C6 **Inverarity** Angus
218 D3 **Inverarnan** Stirlg
260 C3 **Inverasdale** Highld
210 C3 **Inveravon** Falk
217 G1 **Inverawe** Ag & B
218 E7 **Inverbeg** Ag & B
235 K1 **Inverbervie** Abers
261 K3 **Inverbroom** Highld
229 G6 **Invercreran House Hotel** Ag & B
242 B1 **Inverdruie** Highld
211 K5 **Inveresk** E Loth
228 F8 **Inveresragan** Ag & B
242 E5 **Inverey** Abers
250 F7 **Inverfarigaig** Highld
228 E6 **Inverfolla** Ag & B
240 A3 **Invergarry** Highld
220 C2 **Invergeldie** P & K
239 L6 **Invergloy** Highld
263 J6 **Invergordon** Highld
222 F1 **Invergowrie** P & K
238 B2 **Inverguseran** Highld
231 J4 **Inverhadden** P & K
218 E2 **Inverherive Hotel** Stirlg
238 B3 **Inverie** Highld
216 F4 **Inverinan** Ag & B
248 E7 **Inverinate** Highld
235 G5 **Inverkeilor** Angus
210 F2 **Inverkeithing** Fife
268 A6 **Inverkeithny** Abers
207 K4 **Inverkip** Inver
270 E4 **Inverkirkaig** Highld
261 K3 **Inverlael** Highld
240 B7 **Inverlair** Highld
216 D6 **Inverliever Lodge** Ag & B
217 K2 **Inverlochy** Ag & B
244 A7 **Invermark** Angus
255 J4 **Invermarkie** Abers
250 D8 **Invermoriston** Highld
251 H3 **Inverness** Highld
217 J7 **Invernoaden** Ag & B
229 M7 **Inveroran Hotel** Ag & B
234 B4 **Inverquharity** Angus
257 J2 **Inverquhomery** Abers
239 M7 **Inverroy** Highld
228 E3 **Inversanda** Highld
248 F7 **Invershiel** Highld
272 E8 **Invershin** Highld
275 H1 **Invershore** Highld
218 E5 **Inversnaid Hotel** Stirlg
269 L6 **Inverugie** Abers
218 D5 **Inveruglas** Ag & B
241 L3 **Inveruglass** Highld
256 D7 **Inverurie** Abers
12 D3 **Inwardleigh** Devon
72 C3 **Inworth** Essex
283 b9 **Iochdar** W Isls
36 C6 **Iping** W Susx
8 B2 **Ipplepen** Devon
48 F2 **Ipsden** Oxon
115 G2 **Ipstones** Staffs
90 E6 **Ipswich** Suffk
128 F3 **Irby** Wirral
137 J7 **Irby in the Marsh** Lincs
145 G6 **Irby upon Humber** NE Lin
85 H2 **Irchester** Nhants
165 H3 **Ireby** Cumb
157 L7 **Ireby** Lancs
86 C7 **Ireland** Beds
156 B7 **Ireleth** Cumb
167 K3 **Ireshopeburn** Dur
115 M2 **Ireton Wood** Derbys
130 E1 **Irlam** Salfd
118 D6 **Irnham** Lincs
45 K2 **Iron Acton** S Glos
103 K4 **Iron Bridge** Cambs

82 C5 **Iron Cross** Warwks
96 F3 **Ironbridge** Wrekin
185 G7 **Ironmacannie** D & G
37 K2 **Irons Bottom** Surrey
116 D1 **Ironville** Derbys
123 H7 **Irstead** Norfk
178 C6 **Irthington** Cumb
85 J1 **Irthlingborough** Nhants
163 H6 **Irton** N York
196 C3 **Irvine** N Ayrs
279 G3 **Isauld** Highld
281 d3 **Isbister** Shet
23 G4 **Isfield** E Susx
101 J8 **Isham** Nhants
36 B2 **Isington** Hants
97 K7 **Islandpool** Worcs
30 E6 **Isle Abbotts** Somset
30 E6 **Isle Brewers** Somset
51 K3 **Isle of Dogs** Gt Lon
174 D7 **Isle of Whithorn** D & G
104 C8 **Isleham** Cambs
247 L6 **Isleornsay** Highld
176 C4 **Islesteps** D & G
9 k2 **Islet Village** Guern
50 F4 **Isleworth** Gt Lon
116 C6 **Isley Walton** Leics
282 d3 **Islibhig** W Isls
51 J2 **Islington** Gt Lon
101 L7 **Islip** Nhants
66 D4 **Islip** Oxon
282 d3 **Islivig** W Isls
96 E1 **Isombridge** Wrekin
52 D5 **Istead Rise** Kent
35 H4 **Itchen Abbas** Hants
35 H4 **Itchen Stoke** Hants
37 H5 **Itchingfield** W Susx
45 K2 **Itchington** S Glos
122 C5 **Itteringham** Norfk
12 F3 **Itton** Devon
62 F8 **Itton** Mons
165 M2 **Ivegill** Cumb
159 G3 **Ivelet** N York
50 D3 **Iver** Bucks
50 C2 **Iver Heath** Bucks
168 E1 **Iveston** Dur
68 B4 **Ivinghoe** Bucks
68 B3 **Ivinghoe Aston** Bucks
80 B4 **Ivington** Herefs
80 B4 **Ivington Green** Herefs
32 E6 **Ivy Cross** Dorset
38 F3 **Ivy Hatch** Kent
105 H2 **Ivy Todd** Norfk
7 J4 **Ivybridge** Devon
25 J2 **Ivychurch** Kent
40 A2 **Iwade** Kent
32 E8 **Iwerne Courtney or Shroton** Dorset
32 E8 **Iwerne Minster** Dorset
89 J1 **Ixworth** Suffk
89 J1 **Ixworth Thorpe** Suffk

J

139 J3 **Jack Green** Lancs
150 B5 **Jack Hill** N York
34 C3 **Jack's Bush** Hants
14 B3 **Jack-in-the-Green** Devon
116 D1 **Jacksdale** N York
141 J6 **Jackson Bridge** Kirk
209 G8 **Jackton** S Lans
50 C8 **Jacobs Well** Surrey
11 H3 **Jacobstow** Cnwll
12 E2 **Jacobstowe** Devon
55 H7 **Jameston** Pembks
262 E8 **Jamestown** Highld
208 C3 **Jamestown** W Duns
280 D6 **Janets-town** Highld
275 G2 **Janetstown** Highld
176 E1 **Jardine Hall** D & G
181 H6 **Jarrow** S Tyne
38 E7 **Jarvis Brook** E Susx
71 H2 **Jasper's Green** Essex
209 M4 **Jawcraig** Falk
73 H4 **Jaywick** Essex
49 L4 **Jealott's Hill** Br For
160 F4 **Jeater Houses** N York
189 H2 **Jedburgh** Border
55 J5 **Jeffreyston** Pembks
263 K7 **Jemimaville** Highld
9 k4 **Jerbourg** Guern
135 J5 **Jerusalem** Lincs
181 G5 **Jesmond** N u Ty
23 J7 **Jevington** E Susx
62 F5 **Jingle Street** Mons

68 D4 **Jockey End** Herts
130 F5 **Jodrell Bank** Ches
280 E2 **John o'Groats** Highld
24 D3 **John's Cross** E Susx
166 B4 **Johnby** Cumb
235 K2 **Johnshaven** Abers
123 H8 **Johnson's Street** Norfk
54 F5 **Johnston** Pembks
187 K6 **Johnstone** D & G
208 D6 **Johnstone** Rens
187 G7 **Johnstonebridge** D & G
58 D5 **Johnstown** Carmth
112 D2 **Johnstown** Wrexhm
211 K4 **Joppa** C Edin
77 G2 **Joppa** Cerdgn
196 E7 **Joppa** S Ayrs
50 B1 **Jordans** Bucks
74 F5 **Jordanston** Pembks
133 G3 **Jordanthorpe** Sheff
52 B4 **Joyden's Wood** Kent
39 L4 **Jubilee Corner** Kent
142 B7 **Jump** Barns
38 C6 **Jumper's Town** E Susx
179 L7 **Juniper** Nthumb
211 G5 **Juniper Green** C Edin
154 e3 **Jurby** IOM
13 G5 **Jurston** Devon

K

167 J8 **Kaber** Cumb
199 G4 **Kaimend** S Lans
206 F5 **Kames** Ag & B
197 K5 **Kames** E Ayrs
4 C6 **Kea** Cnwll
143 L5 **Keadby** N Linc
137 G7 **Keal Cotes** Lincs
150 E6 **Kearby Town End** N York
139 M6 **Kearsley** Bolton
180 B4 **Kearsley** Nthumb
41 J6 **Kearsney** Kent
157 K6 **Kearstwick** Cumb
159 H3 **Kearton** N York
148 C3 **Keasden** N York
6 C1 **Keason** Cnwll
7 J4 **Keaton** Devon
130 B3 **Keckwick** Halton
136 F2 **Keddington** Lincs
137 G2 **Keddington Corner** Lincs
88 E6 **Kedington** Suffk
116 A3 **Kedleston** Derbys
144 F5 **Keelby** Lincs
114 C3 **Keele** Staffs
114 C3 **Keele University** Staffs
85 K6 **Keeley Green** Beds
141 G1 **Keelham** Brad
54 E3 **Keeston** Pembks
46 D7 **Keevil** Wilts
116 E6 **Kegworth** Leics
3 G3 **Kehelland** Cnwll
256 A7 **Keig** Abers
149 J7 **Keighley** Brad
220 F8 **Keilarsbrae** Clacks
221 H2 **Keillour** P & K
243 G5 **Keiloch** Abers
205 H3 **Keils** Ag & B
31 J5 **Keinton Mandeville** Somset
186 C7 **Keir Mill** D & G
179 H8 **Keirsleywell Row** Nthumb
118 D6 **Keisby** Lincs
167 G6 **Keisley** Cumb
280 D4 **Keiss** Highld
267 J6 **Keith** Moray
233 J7 **Keithick** P & K
234 F3 **Keithock** Angus
262 F8 **Keithtown** Highld
148 F7 **Kelbrook** Lancs
207 L7 **Kelburn** N Ayrs
118 D3 **Kelby** Lincs
166 D7 **Keld** Cumb
158 F3 **Keld** N York
162 D5 **Keld Head** N York
162 C5 **Keldholme** N York
143 L7 **Kelfield** N Linc
151 J8 **Kelfield** N York
134 F8 **Kelham** Notts
176 F5 **Kelhead** D & G
12 A5 **Kellacott** Devon
138 E2 **Kellamergh** Lancs
234 C8 **Kellas** Angus
266 D5 **Kellas** Moray
8 B7 **Kellaton** Devon
157 L2 **Kelleth** Cumb
122 B3 **Kelling** Norfk

142 E3 **Kellington** N York
169 K3 **Kelloe** Dur
185 J1 **Kelloholm** D & G
164 C7 **Kells** Cumb
11 M6 **Kelly** Devon
11 L8 **Kelly Bray** Cnwll
101 G7 **Kelmarsh** Nhants
65 K7 **Kelmscot** Oxon
91 J2 **Kelsale** Suffk
129 M6 **Kelsall** Ches
87 G7 **Kelshall** Herts
165 G1 **Kelsick** Cumb
201 M6 **Kelso** Border
133 G7 **Kelstedge** Derbys
136 D2 **Kelstern** Lincs
129 G5 **Kelsterton** Flints
45 K5 **Kelston** BaNES
231 L5 **Keltneyburn** P & K
176 C5 **Kelton** D & G
221 L8 **Kelty** Fife
72 C3 **Kelvedon** Essex
70 E7 **Kelvedon Hatch** Essex
2 B5 **Kelynack** Cnwll
28 B2 **Kemacott** Devon
223 G4 **Kemback** Fife
97 G3 **Kemberton** Shrops
64 E7 **Kemble** Gloucs
64 E7 **Kemble Wick** Gloucs
81 L7 **Kemerton** Worcs
62 D6 **Kemeys Commander** Mons
256 D8 **Kemnay** Abers
22 E6 **Kemp Town** Br & H
40 D6 **Kempe's Corner** Kent
63 K1 **Kempley** Gloucs
63 K1 **Kempley Green** Gloucs
82 D1 **Kemps Green** Warwks
81 J5 **Kempsey** Worcs
65 H7 **Kempsford** Gloucs
35 J1 **Kempshott** Hants
85 K5 **Kempston** Beds
85 K6 **Kempston Hardwick** Beds
95 J6 **Kempton** Shrops
52 C7 **Kemsing** Kent
40 B2 **Kemsley** Kent
53 H6 **Kemsley Street** Kent
25 H1 **Kenardington** Kent
80 B6 **Kenchester** Herefs
65 K6 **Kencot** Oxon
157 H4 **Kendal** Cumb
62 E2 **Kenderchurch** Herefs
45 K3 **Kendleshire** S Glos
42 B5 **Kenfig** Brdgnd
42 C5 **Kenfig Hill** Brdgnd
2 B4 **Kenidjack** Cnwll
83 G1 **Kenilworth** Warwks
51 J7 **Kenley** Gt Lon
96 D3 **Kenley** Shrops
260 B8 **Kenmore** Highld
231 L6 **Kenmore** P & K
13 L5 **Kenn** Devon
44 E5 **Kenn** N Som
206 C6 **Kennacraig** Ag & B
11 K6 **Kennards House** Cnwll
2 F5 **Kenneggy** Cnwll
13 J1 **Kennerleigh** Devon
138 D7 **Kennessee Green** Sefton
210 B1 **Kennet** Clacks
255 L6 **Kennethmont** Abers
88 D2 **Kennett** Cambs
13 L5 **Kennford** Devon
105 L6 **Kenninghall** Norfk
40 D6 **Kennington** Kent
66 D6 **Kennington** Oxon
222 F6 **Kennoway** Fife
30 D7 **Kenny** Somset
104 D7 **Kennyhill** Suffk
152 B3 **Kennythorpe** N York
224 C6 **Kenovay** Ag & B
259 G6 **Kensaleyre** Highld
39 K7 **Kensham Green** Kent
51 H3 **Kensington** Gt Lon
68 C3 **Kensworth** Beds
68 C3 **Kensworth Common** Beds
64 F8 **Kent End** Wilts
131 G8 **Kent Green** Ches
24 E4 **Kent Street** E Susx
39 G2 **Kent Street** Kent
63 L2 **Kent's Green** Gloucs
34 D6 **Kent's Oak** Hants
228 F4 **Kentallen** Highld
62 E2 **Kentchurch** Herefs
88 E2 **Kentford** Suffk
14 C1 **Kentisbeare** Devon
27 L2 **Kentisbury** Devon
27 L2 **Kentisbury Ford** Devon

51 H2 **Kentish Town** Gt Lon
157 G2 **Kentmere** Cumb
13 M6 **Kenton** Devon
50 F1 **Kenton** Gt Lon
180 F5 **Kenton** N u Ty
90 E2 **Kenton** Suffk
180 F5 **Kenton Bankfoot** N u Ty
237 J6 **Kentra** Highld
156 F7 **Kents Bank** Cumb
112 F5 **Kenwick** Shrops
4 D5 **Kenwyn** Cnwll
139 J8 **Kenyon** Ches
276 F3 **Keoldale** Highld
248 E6 **Keppoch** Highld
161 G4 **Kepwick** N York
99 J7 **Keresley** Covtry
99 J6 **Keresley Green** Covtry
3 K4 **Kergilliack** Cnwll
8 B6 **Kernborough** Devon
63 H3 **Kerne Bridge** Herefs
131 J4 **Kerridge** Ches
131 J4 **Kerridge-end** Ches
2 C5 **Kerris** Cnwll
94 E5 **Kerry** Powys
207 J6 **Kerrycroy** Ag & B
134 E7 **Kersall** Notts
14 C6 **Kersbrook** Devon
27 L5 **Kerscott** Devon
89 K6 **Kersey** Suffk
89 K6 **Kersey Tye** Suffk
89 K6 **Kersey Upland** Suffk
282 f4 **Kershader** W Isls
178 B2 **Kershopefoot** Cumb
82 A7 **Kersoe** Worcs
14 C1 **Kerswell** Devon
81 K6 **Kerswell Green** Worcs
2 F4 **Kerthen Wood** Cnwll
90 F6 **Kesgrave** Suffk
107 L6 **Kessingland** Suffk
107 L6 **Kessingland Beach** Suffk
5 G5 **Kestle** Cnwll
4 D3 **Kestle Mill** Cnwll
51 L6 **Keston** Gt Lon
165 J6 **Keswick** Cumb
106 E2 **Keswick** Norfk
137 G4 **Ketsby** Lincs
101 J7 **Kettering** Nhants
106 D3 **Ketteringham** Norfk
233 K7 **Kettins** Angus
69 L3 **Kettle Green** Herts
89 K5 **Kettlebaston** Suffk
222 E5 **Kettlebridge** Fife
99 G3 **Kettlebrook** Staffs
91 G3 **Kettleburgh** Suffk
176 F3 **Kettleholm** D & G
171 J7 **Kettleness** N York
131 K4 **Kettleshulme** Ches
150 B4 **Kettlesing** N York
150 B4 **Kettlesing Bottom** N York
121 L5 **Kettlestone** Norfk
135 G4 **Kettlethorpe** Lincs
275 e2 **Kettletoft** Ork
149 H2 **Kettlewell** N York
101 L3 **Ketton** Rutlnd
50 F4 **Kew** Gt Lon
44 C6 **Kewstoke** N Som
141 M6 **Kexbrough** Barns
135 H3 **Kexby** Lincs
151 L5 **Kexby** York
131 H7 **Key Green** Ches
162 D2 **Key Green** N York
53 J6 **Key Street** Kent
137 J8 **Key's Toft** Lincs
100 E2 **Keyham** Leics
18 D5 **Keyhaven** Hants
145 H3 **Keyingham** E R Yk
22 D4 **Keymer** W Susx
45 K5 **Keynsham** BaNES
86 B3 **Keysoe** Beds
86 B3 **Keysoe Row** Beds
102 A8 **Keyston** Cambs
117 G5 **Keyworth** Notts
30 B6 **Kibbear** Somset
181 G7 **Kibblesworth** Gatesd
100 F4 **Kibworth Beauchamp** Leics
100 F4 **Kibworth Harcourt** Leics
51 L4 **Kidbrooke** Gt Lon
164 E6 **Kidburngill** Cumb
106 C3 **Kidd's Moor** Norfk
97 J2 **Kiddemore Green** Staffs
97 J8 **Kidderminster** Worcs
66 B3 **Kiddington** Oxon
66 D4 **Kidlington** Oxon
49 G3 **Kidmore End** Oxon
174 C7 **Kidsdale** D & G

131 G8 **Kidsgrove** Staffs
159 G6 **Kidstones** N York
56 D3 **Kidwelly** Carmth
228 D7 **Kiel Crofts** Ag & B
189 H7 **Kielder** Nthumb
204 F3 **Kiells** Ag & B
208 C6 **Kilbarchan** Rens
247 K7 **Kilbeg** Highld
206 A6 **Kilberry** Ag & B
208 A8 **Kilbirnie** N Ayrs
216 C2 **Kilbride** Ag & B
215 L8 **Kilbride** Ag & B
207 G5 **Kilbride** Ag & B
266 B4 **Kilbuiack** Moray
116 C2 **Kilburn** Derbys
51 H2 **Kilburn** Gt Lon
161 H6 **Kilburn** N York
100 D4 **Kilby** Leics
206 C6 **Kilchamaig** Ag & B
214 D5 **Kilchattan** Ag & B
207 H8 **Kilchattan** Ag & B
228 C7 **Kilcheran** Ag & B
236 F7 **Kilchoan** Highld
204 B4 **Kilchoman** Ag & B
217 G3 **Kilchrenan** Ag & B
223 H6 **Kilconquhar** Fife
63 K2 **Kilcot** Gloucs
251 G2 **Kilcoy** Highld
207 L3 **Kilcreggan** Ag & B
161 K1 **Kildale** N York
192 F4 **Kildalloig** Ag & B
263 K5 **Kildary** Highld
206 F6 **Kildavaig** Ag & B
207 G5 **Kildavanan** Ag & B
274 B4 **Kildonan** Highld
195 G6 **Kildonan** N Ayrs
274 B4 **Kildonan Lodge** Highld
236 F3 **Kildonnan** Highld
172 D4 **Kildrochet House** D & G
255 J8 **Kildrummy** Abers
149 H6 **Kildwick** N York
206 E3 **Kilfinan** Ag & B
239 M4 **Kilfinnan** Highld
128 C6 **Kilford** Denbgs
55 K5 **Kilgetty** Pembks
183 G3 **Kilgrammie** S Ayrs
62 F7 **Kilgwrrwg Common** Mons
153 G3 **Kilham** E R Yk
202 D6 **Kilham** Nthumb
224 B6 **Kilkenneth** Ag & B
192 D3 **Kilkenzie** Ag & B
192 E4 **Kilkerran** Ag & B
26 D8 **Kilkhampton** Cnwll
133 J3 **Killamarsh** Derbys
57 H6 **Killay** Swans
208 E2 **Killearn** Stirlg
263 J8 **Killen** Highld
169 G6 **Killerby** Darltn
14 A3 **Killerton** Devon
231 G4 **Killichonan** P & K
227 G4 **Killiechronan** Ag & B
232 D3 **Killiecrankie** P & K
248 F5 **Killilan** Highld
231 G8 **Killin** Stirlg
150 C4 **Killinghall** N York
157 K5 **Killington** Cumb
28 B2 **Killington** Devon
181 G5 **Killingworth** N Tyne
4 C6 **Killiow** Cnwll
4 C5 **Killivose** Cnwll
200 F4 **Killochyett** Border
208 B5 **Kilmacolm** Inver
219 K5 **Kilmahog** Stirlg
216 B8 **Kilmahumaig** Ag & B
259 G2 **Kilmaluag** Highld
222 F3 **Kilmany** Fife
196 E3 **Kilmarnock** E Ayrs
216 C7 **Kilmartin** Ag & B
196 E3 **Kilmaurs** E Ayrs
216 C4 **Kilmelford** Ag & B
45 K8 **Kilmersdon** Somset
35 J5 **Kilmeston** Hants
192 E4 **Kilmichael** Ag & B
216 D8 **Kilmichael Glassary** Ag & B
206 B2 **Kilmichael of Inverlussa** Ag & B
15 G3 **Kilmington** Devon
32 C3 **Kilmington** Wilts
32 C4 **Kilmington Common** Wilts
32 C4 **Kilmington Street** Wilts
250 E3 **Kilmorack** Highld
216 D2 **Kilmore** Ag & B
247 K7 **Kilmore** Highld
205 M2 **Kilmory** Ag & B
237 G6 **Kilmory** Highld

193 K4 **Kilmory** N Ayrs
258 D7 **Kilmuir** Highld
258 F3 **Kilmuir** Highld
251 J2 **Kilmuir** Highld
263 K5 **Kilmuir** Highld
207 K3 **Kilmun** Ag & B
49 K3 **Kiln Green** Wokham
180 C7 **Kiln Pit Hill** Nthumb
204 D2 **Kilnave** Ag & B
198 E3 **Kilncadzow** S Lans
39 H6 **Kilndown** Kent
165 H4 **Kilnhill** Cumb
130 C6 **Kilnhouses** Ches
142 C8 **Kilnhurst** Rothm
216 C3 **Kilninver** Ag & B
145 L4 **Kilnsea** E R Yk
149 H2 **Kilnsey** N York
152 F6 **Kilnwick** E R Yk
152 C6 **Kilnwick Percy** E R Yk
214 D5 **Kiloran** Ag & B
194 D5 **Kilpatrick** N Ayrs
62 F1 **Kilpeck** Herefs
143 K2 **Kilpin** E R Yk
143 J2 **Kilpin Pike** E R Yk
223 K6 **Kilrenny** Fife
84 A1 **Kilsby** Nhants
222 C2 **Kilspindie** P & K
172 E7 **Kilstay** D & G
209 J3 **Kilsyth** N Lans
250 E3 **Kiltarlity** Highld
171 G7 **Kilton** R & Cl
171 G7 **Kilton Thorpe** R & Cl
258 F3 **Kilvaxter** Highld
29 L2 **Kilve** Somset
117 L3 **Kilvington** Notts
196 B2 **Kilwinning** N Ayrs
106 B3 **Kimberley** Norfk
116 E3 **Kimberley** Notts
133 H1 **Kimberworth** Rothm
67 J5 **Kimble Wick** Bucks
169 H1 **Kimblesworth** Dur
86 B2 **Kimbolton** Cambs
80 C3 **Kimbolton** Herefs
100 D6 **Kimcote** Leics
17 H6 **Kimmeridge** Dorset
202 E6 **Kimmerston** Nthumb
34 C2 **Kimpton** Hants
68 F3 **Kimpton** Herts
26 E8 **Kimworthy** Devon
273 L2 **Kinbrace** Highld
220 D6 **Kinbuck** Stirlg
223 H3 **Kincaple** Fife
210 B2 **Kincardine** Fife
263 G2 **Kincardine** Highld
244 D4 **Kincardine O'Neil** Abers
233 H7 **Kinclaven** P & K
245 L3 **Kincorth** C Aber
265 G7 **Kincorth House** Moray
241 M2 **Kincraig** Highld
232 E5 **Kincraigie** P & K
232 E5 **Kindallachan** P & K
205 L5 **Kinerarach** Ag & B
65 G2 **Kineton** Gloucs
83 H5 **Kineton** Warwks
222 B3 **Kinfauns** P & K
196 D4 **Kinfold** S Ayrs
132 B5 **King Sterndale** Derbys
80 B7 **King's Acre** Herefs
115 J8 **King's Bromley** Staffs
101 M4 **King's Cliffe** Nhants
82 C3 **King's Coughton** Warwks
98 D7 **King's Heath** Birm
99 J8 **King's Hill** Warwks
98 C4 **King's Hill** Wsall
120 D7 **King's Lynn** Norfk
9 i3 **King's Mills** Guern
139 G7 **King's Moss** Lancs
116 C6 **King's Newton** Derbys
98 D7 **King's Norton** Birm
100 F3 **King's Norton** Leics
28 B7 **King's Nympton** Devon
80 B5 **King's Pyon** Herefs
34 D4 **King's Somborne** Hants
32 B8 **King's Stag** Dorset
64 A6 **King's Stanley** Gloucs
83 L8 **King's Sutton** Oxon
68 F2 **King's Walden** Herts
207 H7 **Kingarth** Ag & B
245 J3 **Kingcausie** Abers
62 E6 **Kingcoed** Mons
135 L1 **Kingerby** Lincs
11 K1 **Kingford** Devon
65 K2 **Kingham** Oxon
176 C4 **Kingholm Quay** D & G
211 J2 **Kinghorn** Fife

222 C7 **Kinglassie** Fife
233 M4 **Kingoldrum** Angus
222 F1 **Kingoodie** P & K
57 G5 **Kings Bridge** Swans
63 H2 **Kings Caple** Herefs
81 H8 **Kings Green** Gloucs
39 H2 **Kings Hill** Kent
229 L4 **Kings House Hotel** Highld
68 D6 **Kings Langley** Herts
166 E6 **Kings Meaburn** Cumb
200 B5 **Kings Muir** Border
99 M7 **Kings Newnham** Warwks
102 F8 **Kings Ripton** Cambs
45 G3 **Kings Weston** Bristl
35 G4 **Kings Worthy** Hants
6 E5 **Kingsand** Cnwll
67 L6 **Kingsash** Bucks
223 K5 **Kingsbarns** Fife
7 L6 **Kingsbridge** Devon
29 H3 **Kingsbridge** Somset
258 F5 **Kingsburgh** Highld
51 G1 **Kingsbury** Gt Lon
99 G4 **Kingsbury** Warwks
31 G6 **Kingsbury Episcopi** Somset
48 D7 **Kingsclere** Hants
64 B7 **Kingscote** Gloucs
27 K7 **Kingscott** Devon
195 G5 **Kingscross** N Ayrs
31 H5 **Kingsdon** Somset
41 L5 **Kingsdown** Kent
47 H1 **Kingsdown** Swindn
46 A5 **Kingsdown** Wilts
210 F1 **Kingseat** Fife
67 H6 **Kingsey** Bucks
37 J4 **Kingsfold** W Susx
245 J2 **Kingsford** C Aber
196 E2 **Kingsford** E Ayrs
97 J7 **Kingsford** Worcs
41 L1 **Kingsgate** Kent
89 J3 **Kingshall Street** Suffk
27 K3 **Kingsheanton** Devon
219 J3 **Kingshouse Hotel** Stirlg
98 F5 **Kingshurst** Solhll
177 G8 **Kingside Hill** Cumb
8 C1 **Kingskerswell** Devon
222 E5 **Kingskettle** Fife
15 K3 **Kingsland** Dorset
80 B3 **Kingsland** Herefs
124 D3 **Kingsland** IOA
130 A5 **Kingsley** Ches
36 B3 **Kingsley** Hants
115 G2 **Kingsley** Staffs
36 D5 **Kingsley Green** W Susx
84 E3 **Kingsley Park** Nhants
97 H4 **Kingslow** Shrops
35 J8 **Kingsmead** Hants
234 D5 **Kingsmuir** Angus
223 J5 **Kingsmuir** Fife
40 C7 **Kingsnorth** Kent
98 D4 **Kingstanding** Birm
13 K7 **Kingsteignton** Devon
63 G1 **Kingsthorne** Herefs
84 E3 **Kingsthorpe** Nhants
87 G4 **Kingston** Cambs
11 L7 **Kingston** Cnwll
7 J5 **Kingston** Devon
14 C5 **Kingston** Devon
16 E1 **Kingston** Dorset
17 J6 **Kingston** Dorset
212 C3 **Kingston** E Loth
21 J6 **Kingston** E Susx
18 A3 **Kingston** Hants
19 H7 **Kingston** IOW
41 G5 **Kingston** Kent
66 B7 **Kingston Bagpuize** Oxon
67 H7 **Kingston Blount** Oxon
32 D3 **Kingston Deverill** Wilts
47 L2 **Kingston Lisle** Oxon
22 F5 **Kingston near Lewes** E Susx
116 E6 **Kingston on Soar** Notts
267 G3 **Kingston on Spey** Moray
16 A4 **Kingston Russell** Dorset
44 E5 **Kingston Seymour** N Som
30 B5 **Kingston St Mary** Somset
67 H7 **Kingston Stert** Oxon
144 E2 **Kingston upon Hull** C KuH
50 F5 **Kingston upon Thames** Gt Lon
80 A8 **Kingstone** Herefs
30 E8 **Kingstone** Somset
115 H5 **Kingstone** Staffs
47 K2 **Kingstone Winslow** Oxon
177 L7 **Kingstown** Cumb
8 C4 **Kingswear** Devon
245 J2 **Kingswells** C Aber

97 K5 **Kingswinford** Dudley
67 G3 **Kingswood** Bucks
63 L8 **Kingswood** Gloucs
39 L3 **Kingswood** Kent
94 F3 **Kingswood** Powys
45 J4 **Kingswood** S Glos
29 K3 **Kingswood** Somset
51 H7 **Kingswood** Surrey
82 E1 **Kingswood** Warwks
82 E1 **Kingswood Brook** Warwks
79 K4 **Kingswood Common** Herefs
97 J3 **Kingswood Common** Staffs
136 B4 **Kingthorpe** Lincs
79 K4 **Kington** Herefs
45 J1 **Kington** S Glos
82 A4 **Kington** Worcs
46 D3 **Kington Langley** Wilts
32 C6 **Kington Magna** Dorset
46 C3 **Kington St Michael** Wilts
241 K3 **Kingussie** Highld
31 H5 **Kingweston** Somset
257 G5 **Kinharrachie** Abers
176 B5 **Kinharvie** D & G
221 G4 **Kinkell Bridge** P & K
257 J3 **Kinknockie** Abers
211 G5 **Kinleith** C Edin
97 G7 **Kinlet** Shrops
271 K1 **Kinloch** Highld
277 J5 **Kinloch** Highld
246 E8 **Kinloch** Highld
233 H6 **Kinloch** P & K
233 L6 **Kinloch** P & K
238 F2 **Kinloch Hourn** Highld
231 J4 **Kinloch Rannoch** P & K
219 G6 **Kinlochard** Stirlg
276 C5 **Kinlochbervie** Highld
238 F7 **Kinlocheil** Highld
261 G7 **Kinlochewe** Highld
240 F5 **Kinlochlaggan** Highld
229 K3 **Kinlochleven** Highld
237 K6 **Kinlochmoidart** Highld
237 L4 **Kinlochnanuagh** Highld
265 H7 **Kinloss** Moray
127 K4 **Kinmel Bay** Conwy
256 E7 **Kinmuck** Abers
256 F8 **Kinmundy** Abers
204 D7 **Kinnabus** Ag & B
257 H3 **Kinnadie** Abers
232 E4 **Kinnaird** P & K
235 G4 **Kinnaird Castle** Angus
266 E2 **Kinneddar** Moray
245 J8 **Kinneff** Abers
186 F6 **Kinnelhead** D & G
234 F5 **Kinnell** Angus
112 E7 **Kinnerley** Shrops
79 L5 **Kinnersley** Herefs
81 K6 **Kinnersley** Worcs
79 J3 **Kinnerton** Powys
95 J4 **Kinnerton** Shrops
129 H7 **Kinnerton Green** Flints
222 B6 **Kinnesswood** P & K
168 D6 **Kinninvie** Dur
234 B4 **Kinnordy** Angus
117 H5 **Kinoulton** Notts
221 K6 **Kinross** P & K
222 C1 **Kinrossie** P & K
68 E4 **Kinsbourne Green** Herts
113 L3 **Kinsey Heath** Ches
79 L2 **Kinsham** Herefs
81 L8 **Kinsham** Worcs
142 C5 **Kinsley** Wakefd
17 L3 **Kinson** Bmouth
48 A5 **Kintbury** W Berk
264 F7 **Kintessack** Moray
221 L4 **Kintillo** P & K
95 K8 **Kinton** Herefs
112 E7 **Kinton** Shrops
256 E8 **Kintore** Abers
205 G6 **Kintour** Ag & B
226 C7 **Kintra** Ag & B
216 C6 **Kintraw** Ag & B
253 D7 **Kinveachy** Highld
97 J6 **Kinver** Staffs
160 C3 **Kiplin** N York
142 C2 **Kippax** Leeds
219 L8 **Kippen** Stirlg
175 L4 **Kippford or Scaur** D & G
39 G5 **Kipping's Cross** Kent
275 c5 **Kirbister** Ork
199 K4 **Kirburd** Border
106 F2 **Kirby Bedon** Norfk
117 J7 **Kirby Bellars** Leics
107 H4 **Kirby Cane** Norfk
99 J8 **Kirby Corner** Covtry
73 J3 **Kirby Cross** Essex

100 B3 **Kirby Fields** Leics
152 D2 **Kirby Grindalythe** N York
159 L2 **Kirby Hill** N York
150 E2 **Kirby Hill** N York
161 G5 **Kirby Knowle** N York
73 J3 **Kirby le Soken** Essex
162 D6 **Kirby Misperton** N York
100 B3 **Kirby Muxloe** Leics
107 H5 **Kirby Row** Norfk
160 F4 **Kirby Sigston** N York
152 B4 **Kirby Underdale** E R Yk
160 E5 **Kirby Wiske** N York
36 F5 **Kirdford** W Susx
280 C4 **Kirk** Highld
143 G5 **Kirk Bramwith** Donc
150 F5 **Kirk Deighton** N York
144 C2 **Kirk Ella** E R Yk
116 D3 **Kirk Hallam** Derbys
151 G5 **Kirk Hammerton** N York
115 M2 **Kirk Ireton** Derbys
115 M4 **Kirk Langley** Derbys
169 H4 **Kirk Merrington** Dur
154 d4 **Kirk Michael** IOM
209 M6 **Kirk of Shotts** N Lans
142 F6 **Kirk Sandall** Donc
142 E4 **Kirk Smeaton** N York
202 C7 **Kirk Yetholm** Border
281 e7 **Kirkabister** Shet
174 F5 **Kirkandrews** D & G
177 K7 **Kirkandrews upon Eden** Cumb
177 J7 **Kirkbampton** Cumb
176 C7 **Kirkbean** D & G
177 H7 **Kirkbride** Cumb
160 C4 **Kirkbridge** N York
234 D6 **Kirkbuddo** Angus
200 C5 **Kirkburn** Border
152 F5 **Kirkburn** E R Yk
141 K5 **Kirkburton** Kirk
138 E7 **Kirkby** Knows
135 L1 **Kirkby** Lincs
161 H2 **Kirkby** N York
160 D4 **Kirkby Fleetham** N York
136 A8 **Kirkby Green** Lincs
160 C3 **Kirkby Hall** N York
133 K8 **Kirkby in Ashfield** Notts
118 E2 **Kirkby la Thorpe** Lincs
157 K7 **Kirkby Lonsdale** Cumb
148 F4 **Kirkby Malham** N York
99 M3 **Kirkby Mallory** Leics
160 C7 **Kirkby Malzeard** N York
162 C5 **Kirkby Mills** N York
136 D7 **Kirkby on Bain** Lincs
150 D6 **Kirkby Overblow** N York
158 D1 **Kirkby Stephen** Cumb
166 E5 **Kirkby Thore** Cumb
118 E6 **Kirkby Underwood** Lincs
151 H7 **Kirkby Wharf** N York
116 E1 **Kirkby Woodhouse** Notts
156 B6 **Kirkby-in-Furness** Cumb
162 B5 **Kirkbymoorside** N York
211 J1 **Kirkcaldy** Fife
178 C5 **Kirkcambeck** Cumb
175 G4 **Kirkchrist** D & G
172 C1 **Kirkcolm** D & G
197 L8 **Kirkconnel** D & G
176 C5 **Kirkconnell** D & G
175 G3 **Kirkconnell** D & G
173 J3 **Kirkcowan** D & G
175 H5 **Kirkcudbright** D & G
129 H1 **Kirkdale** Lpool
198 E4 **Kirkfieldbank** S Lans
175 L2 **Kirkgunzeon** D & G
138 E1 **Kirkham** Lancs
151 M3 **Kirkham** N York
141 L3 **Kirkhamgate** Wakefd
180 B2 **Kirkharle** Nthumb
167 G1 **Kirkhaugh** Nthumb
141 J4 **Kirkheaton** Kirk
180 B3 **Kirkheaton** Nthumb
250 F3 **Kirkhill** Highld
186 E5 **Kirkhope** S Lans
178 D7 **Kirkhouse** Cumb
143 G5 **Kirkhouse Green** Donc
247 H5 **Kirkibost** Highld
233 L6 **Kirkinch** P & K
174 C4 **Kirkinner** D & G
209 H4 **Kirkintilloch** E Duns
164 E7 **Kirkland** Cumb
166 F4 **Kirkland** Cumb
197 L8 **Kirkland** D & G
185 K5 **Kirkland** D & G
186 F8 **Kirkland** D & G
165 G3 **Kirkland Guards** Cumb
170 E6 **Kirkleatham** R & Cl

160 F1 **Kirklevington** S on T
107 L5 **Kirkley** Suffk
160 D6 **Kirklington** N York
134 D8 **Kirklington** Notts
178 B5 **Kirklinton** Cumb
210 F4 **Kirkliston** C Edin
174 D4 **Kirkmabreck** D & G
172 E7 **Kirkmaiden** D & G
233 G3 **Kirkmichael** P & K
183 J1 **Kirkmichael** S Ayrs
198 C4 **Kirkmuirhill** S Lans
202 E7 **Kirknewton** Nthumb
210 F5 **Kirknewton** W Loth
255 K5 **Kirkney** Abers
166 D3 **Kirkoswald** Cumb
183 G2 **Kirkoswald** S Ayrs
186 D8 **Kirkpatrick** D & G
175 K1 **Kirkpatrick Durham** D & G
177 J5 **Kirkpatrick-Fleming** D & G
155 L6 **Kirksanton** Cumb
150 C8 **Kirkstall** Leeds
136 C7 **Kirkstead** Lincs
255 L5 **Kirkstile** Abers
188 C8 **Kirkstile** D & G
156 F1 **Kirkstone Pass Inn** Cumb
280 D2 **Kirkstyle** Highld
142 B3 **Kirkthorpe** Wakefd
256 B6 **Kirkton** Abers
256 E3 **Kirkton** Abers
176 C3 **Kirkton** D & G
222 F2 **Kirkton** Fife
248 C6 **Kirkton** Highld
248 E3 **Kirkton** Highld
221 G3 **Kirkton** P & K
200 B5 **Kirkton Manor** Border
233 M5 **Kirkton of Airlie** Angus
234 A7 **Kirkton of Auchterhouse** Angus
252 F2 **Kirkton of Barevan** Highld
222 C1 **Kirkton of Collace** P & K
255 H8 **Kirkton of Glenbuchat** Abers
257 H6 **Kirkton of Logie Buchan** Abers
234 E3 **Kirkton of Menmuir** Angus
234 D7 **Kirkton of Monikie** Angus
256 C5 **Kirkton of Rayne** Abers
245 H2 **Kirkton of Skene** Abers
234 B8 **Kirkton of Strathmartine** Angus
234 B7 **Kirkton of Tealing** Angus
244 D1 **Kirkton of Tough** Abers
269 J3 **Kirktown** Abers
269 K6 **Kirktown** Abers
256 E6 **Kirktown of Bourtie** Abers
245 J6 **Kirktown of Fetteresso** Abers
254 F4 **Kirktown of Mortlach** Moray
257 J6 **Kirktown of Slains** Abers
199 K4 **Kirkurd** Border
275 C4 **Kirkwall** Ork
180 B2 **Kirkwhelpington** Nthumb
130 F6 **Kirmincham** Ches
144 E5 **Kirmington** N Linc
136 C1 **Kirmond le Mire** Lincs
207 K3 **Kirn** Ag & B
234 B4 **Kirriemuir** Angus
106 F4 **Kirstead Green** Norfk
177 H4 **Kirtlebridge** D & G
88 D4 **Kirtling** Cambs
88 D4 **Kirtling Green** Suffk
66 D3 **Kirtlington** Oxon
278 C3 **Kirtomy** Highld
119 J4 **Kirton** Lincs
134 D6 **Kirton** Notts
91 G7 **Kirton** Suffk
119 J3 **Kirton End** Lincs
119 J3 **Kirton Holme** Lincs
144 B8 **Kirton in Lindsey** N Linc
208 C4 **Kirtonhill** W Duns
173 K4 **Kirwaugh** D & G
248 D4 **Kishorn** Highld
84 D3 **Kislingbury** Nhants
82 E2 **Kite Green** Warwks
65 K1 **Kitebrook** Warwks
83 L2 **Kites Hardwick** Warwks
11 J3 **Kitleigh** Cnwll
139 H6 **Kitt Green** Wigan
98 F6 **Kitt's Green** Birm
29 K6 **Kittisford** Somset
57 G7 **Kittle** Swans
245 K2 **Kittybrewster** C Aber
35 K4 **Kitwood** Hants
62 F1 **Kivernoll** Herefs
133 K3 **Kiveton Park** Rothm
135 G3 **Knaith** Lincs

135 G3 **Knaith Park** Lincs
32 D6 **Knap Corner** Dorset
50 B7 **Knaphill** Surrey
28 F4 **Knaplock** Somset
30 D5 **Knapp** Somset
34 E6 **Knapp Hill** Hants
134 E7 **Knapthorpe** Notts
162 F7 **Knapton** N York
122 F5 **Knapton** Norfk
151 J5 **Knapton** York
80 B5 **Knapton Green** Herefs
87 G3 **Knapwell** Cambs
150 E4 **Knaresborough** N York
178 F8 **Knarsdale** Nthumb
257 G3 **Knaven** Abers
160 F5 **Knayton** N York
69 H3 **Knebworth** Herts
143 J2 **Knedlington** E R Yk
134 D6 **Kneesall** Notts
87 G6 **Kneesworth** Cambs
117 J2 **Kneeton** Notts
56 E7 **Knelston** Swans
114 E4 **Knenhall** Staffs
105 K7 **Knettishall** Suffk
28 B3 **Knightacott** Devon
83 J4 **Knightcote** Warwks
114 C6 **Knightley** Staffs
114 C6 **Knightley Dale** Staffs
100 D3 **Knighton** C Leic
7 G5 **Knighton** Devon
31 K8 **Knighton** Dorset
17 L3 **Knighton** Poole
79 K1 **Knighton** Powys
30 B2 **Knighton** Somset
114 A3 **Knighton** Staffs
114 B6 **Knighton** Staffs
47 L4 **Knighton** Wilts
80 E1 **Knighton on Teme** Worcs
64 C2 **Knightsbridge** Gloucs
10 F6 **Knightsmill** Cnwll
81 G4 **Knightwick** Worcs
79 K3 **Knill** Herefs
117 L5 **Knipton** Leics
168 E1 **Knitsley** Dur
115 K2 **Kniveton** Derbys
166 F5 **Knock** Cumb
247 L6 **Knock** Highld
267 L5 **Knock** Moray
282 g3 **Knock** W Isls
207 K6 **Knock Castle** N Ayrs
274 F2 **Knockally** Highld
271 H6 **Knockan** Highld
254 D3 **Knockando** Moray
250 F3 **Knockbain** Highld
263 H8 **Knockbain** Highld
279 L4 **Knockdee** Highld
46 B1 **Knockdown** Wilts
183 H4 **Knockeen** S Ayrs
195 G5 **Knockenkelly** N Ayrs
196 D3 **Knockentiber** E Ayrs
52 C4 **Knockhall** Kent
51 M7 **Knockholt** Kent
52 A7 **Knockholt Pound** Kent
112 E7 **Knockin** Shrops
196 E3 **Knockinlaw** E Ayrs
52 C6 **Knockmill** Kent
172 B2 **Knocknain** D & G
184 F6 **Knocksheen** D & G
175 J1 **Knockvennie Smithy** D & G
91 K3 **Knodishall** Suffk
31 G6 **Knole** Somset
45 H2 **Knole Park** S Glos
130 F4 **Knolls Green** Ches
112 F4 **Knolton** Wrexhm
32 F3 **Knook** Wilts
101 H2 **Knossington** Leics
147 G6 **Knott End-on-Sea** Lancs
85 K3 **Knotting** Beds
85 K3 **Knotting Green** Beds
142 D3 **Knottingley** Wakefd
129 J1 **Knotty Ash** Lpool
68 B8 **Knotty Green** Bucks
96 D8 **Knowbury** Shrops
183 H8 **Knowe** D & G
184 F5 **Knowehead** D & G
195 L8 **Knoweside** S Ayrs
88 F7 **Knowl Green** Essex
49 K3 **Knowl Hill** W & M
45 J5 **Knowle** Bristl
27 J3 **Knowle** Devon
13 H2 **Knowle** Devon
14 B1 **Knowle** Devon
14 B6 **Knowle** Devon
96 D8 **Knowle** Shrops
98 F8 **Knowle** Solhll

29 H2 **Knowle** Somset
14 B3 **Knowle Cross** Devon
148 A8 **Knowle Green** Lancs
50 C5 **Knowle Hill** Surrey
30 E8 **Knowle St Giles** Somset
19 J2 **Knowle Village** Hants
177 L7 **Knowlefield** Cumb
17 K1 **Knowlton** Dorset
41 J4 **Knowlton** Kent
138 E8 **Knowsley** Knows
28 E6 **Knowstone** Devon
150 C4 **Knox** N York
39 K5 **Knox Bridge** Kent
95 G6 **Knucklas** Powys
85 H2 **Knuston** Nhants
130 E4 **Knutsford** Ches
114 C2 **Knutton** Staffs
131 H6 **Knypersley** Staffs
141 G4 **Krumlin** Calder
3 J7 **Kuggar** Cnwll
248 B6 **Kyle of Lochalsh** Highld
248 B6 **Kyleakin** Highld
248 C7 **Kylerhea** Highld
282 f6 **Kyles Scalpay** W Isls
271 H1 **Kylesku** Highld
238 C5 **Kylesmorar** Highld
271 H1 **Kylestrome** Highld
203 G5 **Kyloe** Nthumb
80 E8 **Kynaston** Herefs
112 E7 **Kynaston** Shrops
113 L3 **Kynnersley** Wrekin
80 E3 **Kyre Green** Worcs
80 E3 **Kyre Park** Worcs
80 E2 **Kyrewood** Worcs
29 J6 **Kyrle** Somset

L

9 k1 **L'Ancresse** Guern
9 h3 **L'Eree** Guern
9 a2 **L'Etacq** Jersey
9 j3 **La Bellieuse** Guern
9 k1 **La Fontenelle** Guern
9 j4 **La Fosse** Guern
9 k2 **La Greve** Guern
9 b1 **La Greve de Lecq** Jersey
9 e3 **La Hougue Bie** Jersey
9 h3 **La Houguette** Guern
9 j2 **La Passee** Guern
9 a3 **La Pulente** Jersey
9 f4 **La Rocque** Jersey
9 j2 **La Rousaillerie** Guern
9 j3 **La Villette** Guern
282 g3 **Lacadal** W Isls
282 f4 **Lacasaigh** W Isls
145 G6 **Laceby** NE Lin
67 K7 **Lacey Green** Bucks
130 D5 **Lach Dennis** Ches
170 D6 **Lackenby** R & Cl
88 F1 **Lackford** Suffk
88 F1 **Lackford Green** Suffk
46 C5 **Lacock** Wilts
83 K3 **Ladbroke** Warwks
114 F1 **Ladderedge** Staffs
39 H4 **Laddingford** Kent
119 L1 **Lade Bank** Lincs
4 E5 **Ladock** Cnwll
275 e2 **Lady** Ork
156 B5 **Lady Hall** Cumb
88 E3 **Lady's Green** Suffk
222 E5 **Ladybank** Fife
11 L5 **Ladycross** Cnwll
198 F7 **Ladygill** S Lans
202 D3 **Ladykirk** Border
63 H1 **Ladyridge** Herefs
98 D6 **Ladywood** Birm
81 K3 **Ladywood** Worcs
185 L5 **Lag** D & G
237 J8 **Laga** Highld
204 F7 **Lagavulin** Ag & B
193 K4 **Lagg** N Ayrs
240 A4 **Laggan** Highld
241 G5 **Laggan** Highld
277 G4 **Laid** Highld
260 E2 **Laide** Highld
236 F3 **Laig** Highld
196 F2 **Laigh Clunch** E Ayrs
196 F3 **Laigh Fenwick** E Ayrs
197 J7 **Laigh Glenmuir** E Ayrs
209 J8 **Laighstonehall** S Lans
52 E1 **Laindon** Essex
272 E6 **Lairg** Highld
141 J1 **Laisterdyke** Brad
166 B4 **Laithes** Cumb

27 K4 **Lake** Devon
12 C5 **Lake** Devon
19 K7 **Lake** IOW
17 J4 **Lake** Poole
33 K3 **Lake** Wilts
104 E6 **Lakenheath** Suffk
36 F4 **Laker's Green** Surrey
103 L4 **Lakesend** Norfk
156 E5 **Lakeside** Cumb
50 D5 **Laleham** Surrey
42 C5 **Laleston** Brdgnd
199 L3 **Lamancha** Border
3 J5 **Lamanva** Cnwll
89 H8 **Lamarsh** Essex
122 E7 **Lamas** Norfk
148 C8 **Lamb Roe** Lancs
202 A4 **Lambden** Border
39 H6 **Lamberhurst** Kent
39 G6 **Lamberhurst Down** Kent
213 L7 **Lamberton** Border
51 J3 **Lambeth** Gt Lon
88 E4 **Lambfair Green** Suffk
117 H2 **Lambley** Notts
178 F7 **Lambley** Nthumb
47 L3 **Lambourn** W Berk
70 C8 **Lambourne End** Essex
37 K3 **Lambs Green** W Susx
54 E3 **Lambston** Pembks
6 A2 **Lamellion** Cnwll
12 B7 **Lamerton** Devon
181 G7 **Lamesley** Gatesd
199 G7 **Lamington** S Lans
195 G5 **Lamlash** N Ayrs
165 L3 **Lamonby** Cumb
5 H2 **Lamorick** Cnwll
2 C6 **Lamorna** Cnwll
4 E6 **Lamorran** Cnwll
5 L2 **Lampen** Cnwll
77 G5 **Lampeter** Cerdgn
55 K4 **Lampeter Velfrey** Pembks
55 G6 **Lamphey** Pembks
164 E6 **Lamplugh** Cumb
101 G8 **Lamport** Nhants
31 L4 **Lamyatt** Somset
11 K1 **Lana** Devon
11 L3 **Lana** Devon
198 E4 **Lanark** S Lans
3 K6 **Lanarth** Cnwll
147 J3 **Lancaster** Lancs
63 G7 **Lancaut** Gloucs
168 F1 **Lanchester** Dur
21 L6 **Lancing** W Susx
2 A6 **Land's End** Cnwll
275 G2 **Land-hallow** Highld
87 K2 **Landbeach** Cambs
27 H6 **Landcross** Devon
245 G3 **Landerberry** Abers
34 B7 **Landford** Wilts
56 E6 **Landimore** Swans
27 L4 **Landkey** Devon
27 L4 **Landkey Town** Devon
57 J5 **Landore** Swans
6 D3 **Landrake** Cnwll
7 M2 **Landscove** Devon
55 G4 **Landshipping** Pembks
11 L6 **Landue** Cnwll
6 E3 **Landulph** Cnwll
88 C2 **Landwade** Suffk
98 C2 **Landywood** Staffs
4 D3 **Lane** Cnwll
140 C1 **Lane Bottom** Lancs
49 K1 **Lane End** Bucks
5 H1 **Lane End** Cnwll
35 H5 **Lane End** Hants
52 C4 **Lane End** Kent
148 F6 **Lane End** Lancs
130 D2 **Lane End** Warrtn
32 D2 **Lane End** Wilts
155 K4 **Lane End Waberthwaite** Cumb
115 L4 **Lane Ends** Derbys
168 F4 **Lane Ends** Dur
140 B2 **Lane Ends** Lancs
149 H7 **Lane Ends** N York
97 K3 **Lane Green** Staffs
168 E8 **Lane Head** Dur
139 J8 **Lane Head** Wigan
98 B3 **Lane Head** Wsall
147 H7 **Lane Heads** Lancs
140 B3 **Lane Side** Lancs
11 J5 **Laneast** Cnwll
134 F4 **Laneham** Notts
167 J2 **Lanehead** Dur
179 H2 **Lanehead** Nthumb
149 G7 **Laneshaw Bridge** Lancs

328 Langaford - Lenton

12 A3 **Langaford** Devon
30 C5 **Langaller** Somset
117 J4 **Langar** Notts
208 C4 **Langbank** Rens
149 K5 **Langbar** N York
170 D8 **Langbaurgh** N York
148 E3 **Langcliffe** N York
163 G4 **Langdale End** N York
11 K4 **Langdon** Cnwll
167 K4 **Langdon Beck** Dur
19 G2 **Langdown** Hants
222 E6 **Langdyke** Fife
72 E3 **Langenhoe** Essex
86 D7 **Langford** Beds
14 B2 **Langford** Devon
71 K5 **Langford** Essex
44 F6 **Langford** N Som
135 G7 **Langford** Notts
65 K6 **Langford** Oxon
29 K6 **Langford Budville** Somset
32 C5 **Langham** Dorset
89 L8 **Langham** Essex
121 M3 **Langham** Norfk
101 J1 **Langham** Rutlnd
89 K1 **Langham** Suffk
72 E1 **Langham Moor** Essex
72 F1 **Langham Wick** Essex
139 L1 **Langho** Lancs
177 L2 **Langholm** D & G
57 H7 **Langland** Swans
201 G6 **Langlee** Border
131 J5 **Langley** Ches
116 D2 **Langley** Derbys
64 E2 **Langley** Gloucs
19 G3 **Langley** Hants
69 G3 **Langley** Herts
39 K3 **Langley** Kent
179 J6 **Langley** Nthumb
65 L4 **Langley** Oxon
140 C6 **Langley** Rochdl
50 C3 **Langley** Slough
29 K5 **Langley** Somset
36 B5 **Langley** W Susx
82 E3 **Langley** Warwks
46 D4 **Langley Burrell** Wilts
179 J6 **Langley Castle** Nthumb
115 M4 **Langley Common** Derbys
115 M4 **Langley Green** Derbys
72 C3 **Langley Green** Essex
82 E3 **Langley Green** Warwks
87 J8 **Langley Lower Green** Essex
29 K5 **Langley Marsh** Somset
116 D2 **Langley Mill** Derbys
169 H3 **Langley Moor** Dur
169 G2 **Langley Park** Dur
107 H3 **Langley Street** Norfk
87 J8 **Langley Upper Green** Essex
68 D7 **Langleybury** Herts
23 L6 **Langney** E Susx
134 B2 **Langold** Notts
11 K5 **Langore** Cnwll
30 F5 **Langport** Somset
119 J2 **Langrick** Lincs
45 L5 **Langridge** BaNES
27 K6 **Langridge Ford** Devon
165 G2 **Langrigg** Cumb
35 L6 **Langrish** Hants
141 K7 **Langsett** Barns
220 D4 **Langside** P & K
20 B6 **Langstone** Hants
44 D1 **Langstone** Newpt
160 C4 **Langthorne** N York
150 E2 **Langthorpe** N York
159 H2 **Langthwaite** N York
152 F3 **Langtoft** E R Yk
102 C1 **Langtoft** Lincs
168 F6 **Langton** Dur
136 D6 **Langton** Lincs
137 G5 **Langton** Lincs
152 B2 **Langton** N York
136 C4 **Langton by Wragby** Lincs
38 E5 **Langton Green** Kent
106 C8 **Langton Green** Suffk
16 B6 **Langton Herring** Dorset
17 K6 **Langton Matravers** Dorset
27 H7 **Langtree** Devon
27 H7 **Langtree Week** Devon
166 D4 **Langwathby** Cumb
274 F3 **Langwell House** Highld
135 L4 **Langworth** Lincs
12 C4 **Langworthy** Devon
5 H2 **Lanivet** Cnwll
5 G4 **Lanjeth** Cnwll
10 F7 **Lank** Cnwll
5 J3 **Lanlivery** Cnwll
3 J3 **Lanner** Cnwll
11 K7 **Lanoy** Cnwll
5 L3 **Lanreath** Cnwll
5 K4 **Lansallos** Cnwll
10 F6 **Lanteglos** Cnwll
5 K4 **Lanteglos Highway** Cnwll
189 G2 **Lanton** Border
202 E6 **Lanton** Nthumb
13 G1 **Lapford** Devon
204 F7 **Laphroaig** Ag & B
97 K1 **Lapley** Staffs
82 E1 **Lapworth** Warwks
227 K3 **Larachbeg** Highld
209 M3 **Larbert** Falk
147 H7 **Larbreck** Lancs
256 A5 **Largie** Abers
206 E2 **Largiemore** Ag & B
223 H5 **Largoward** Fife
207 K7 **Largs** N Ayrs
195 G6 **Largybeg** N Ayrs
195 G6 **Largymore** N Ayrs
14 C3 **Larkbeare** Devon
207 L4 **Larkfield** Inver
52 F7 **Larkfield** Kent
198 C3 **Larkhall** S Lans
33 K2 **Larkhill** Wilts
105 K5 **Larling** Norfk
168 C7 **Lartington** Dur
64 B8 **Lasborough** Gloucs
35 K2 **Lasham** Hants
12 B2 **Lashbrook** Devon
39 L5 **Lashenden** Kent
131 H8 **Lask Edge** Staffs
221 K8 **Lassodie** Fife
211 J6 **Lasswade** Mdloth
162 C4 **Lastingham** N York
31 G2 **Latcham** Somset
69 K3 **Latchford** Herts
67 G6 **Latchford** Oxon
72 C7 **Latchingdon** Essex
12 A7 **Latchley** Cnwll
139 K8 **Lately Common** Warrtn
85 G6 **Lathbury** M Keyn
275 G2 **Latheron** Highld
275 G2 **Latheronwheel** Highld
223 H5 **Lathones** Fife
68 C7 **Latimer** Bucks
45 K2 **Latteridge** S Glos
32 B5 **Lattiford** Somset
65 G7 **Latton** Wilts
201 H4 **Lauder** Border
56 B3 **Laugharne** Carmth
135 G4 **Laughterton** Lincs
23 H4 **Laughton** E Susx
100 E5 **Laughton** Leics
143 L8 **Laughton** Lincs
118 E5 **Laughton** Lincs
133 K2 **Laughton-en-le-Morthen** Rothm
11 J2 **Launcells** Cnwll
11 K2 **Launcells Cross** Cnwll
11 L5 **Launceston** Cnwll
66 F3 **Launton** Oxon
235 H1 **Laurencekirk** Abers
175 H2 **Laurieston** D & G
210 B3 **Laurieston** Falk
85 H4 **Lavendon** M Keyn
89 J5 **Lavenham** Suffk
43 J8 **Lavernock** V Glam
178 B6 **Laversdale** Cumb
33 L5 **Laverstock** Wilts
35 G1 **Laverstoke** Hants
82 C8 **Laverton** Gloucs
160 B7 **Laverton** N York
45 M8 **Laverton** Somset
129 J8 **Lavister** Wrexhm
209 L8 **Law** S Lans
209 L8 **Law Hill** S Lans
231 J7 **Lawers** P & K
73 G1 **Lawford** Essex
29 L4 **Lawford** Somset
221 K2 **Lawgrove** P & K
11 L6 **Lawhitton** Cnwll
148 D3 **Lawkland** N York
148 D3 **Lawkland Green** N York
96 F2 **Lawley** Wrekin
114 C6 **Lawnhead** Staffs
68 F3 **Lawrence End** Herts
55 G5 **Lawrenny** Pembks
89 H4 **Lawshall** Suffk
89 H4 **Lawshall Green** Suffk
80 B3 **Lawton** Herefs
282 f4 **Laxay** W Isls
282 g3 **Laxdale** W Isls
154 f5 **Laxey** IOM
91 G1 **Laxfield** Suffk
276 C7 **Laxford Bridge** Highld
281 e5 **Laxo** Shet
143 K3 **Laxton** E R Yk
101 L4 **Laxton** Nhants
134 E6 **Laxton** Notts
149 J7 **Laycock** Brad
72 D3 **Layer Breton** Essex
72 D4 **Layer Marney** Essex
72 D3 **Layer-de-la-Haye** Essex
89 L7 **Layham** Suffk
48 A5 **Layland's Green** W Berk
15 J2 **Laymore** Dorset
50 C1 **Layter's Green** Bucks
152 A7 **Laytham** E R Yk
177 H7 **Laythes** Cumb
170 D6 **Lazenby** R & Cl
166 D3 **Lazonby** Cumb
9 i4 **Le Bigard** Guern
9 j4 **Le Bourg** Guern
9 f4 **Le Bourg** Jersey
9 i3 **Le Gron** Guern
9 e4 **Le Haguais** Jersey
9 e4 **Le Hocq** Jersey
9 j2 **Le Villocq** Guern
132 F8 **Lea** Derbys
63 K3 **Lea** Herefs
135 G2 **Lea** Lincs
95 K2 **Lea** Shrops
95 J5 **Lea** Shrops
46 D2 **Lea** Wilts
132 F8 **Lea Bridge** Derbys
115 G6 **Lea Heath** Staffs
99 G5 **Lea Marston** Warwks
138 F2 **Lea Town** Lancs
158 D5 **Lea Yeat** Cumb
251 H3 **Leachkin** Highld
200 B2 **Leadburn** Mdloth
70 E4 **Leaden Roding** Essex
118 B1 **Leadenham** Lincs
180 D8 **Leadgate** Dur
180 D7 **Leadgate** Gatesd
186 C3 **Leadhills** S Lans
39 M3 **Leadingcross Green** Kent
132 E3 **Leadmill** Derbys
65 L4 **Leafield** Oxon
68 D2 **Leagrave** Luton
130 D6 **Leahead** Ches
160 F4 **Leake** N York
119 L1 **Leake Common Side** Lincs
162 D1 **Lealholm** N York
162 D1 **Lealholm Side** N York
259 H4 **Lealt** Highld
132 E4 **Leam** Derbys
83 K2 **Leamington Hastings** Warwks
83 H2 **Leamington Spa** Warwks
169 J1 **Leamside** Dur
23 K5 **Leap Cross** E Susx
157 H6 **Leasgill** Cumb
118 E2 **Leasingham** Lincs
169 H4 **Leasingthorne** Dur
50 F7 **Leatherhead** Surrey
150 B6 **Leathley** N York
113 G7 **Leaton** Shrops
96 E1 **Leaton** Wrekin
40 C4 **Leaveland** Kent
89 J7 **Leavenheath** Suffk
152 B3 **Leavening** N York
51 L6 **Leaves Green** Gt Lon
163 K6 **Lebberston** N York
65 J7 **Lechlade on Thames** Gloucs
204 D3 **Lecht Gruinart** Ag & B
157 K7 **Leck** Lancs
231 K7 **Leckbuie** P & K
34 E3 **Leckford** Hants
84 D7 **Leckhampstead** Bucks
48 B4 **Leckhampstead** W Berk
48 B4 **Leckhampstead Thicket** W Berk
64 D3 **Leckhampton** Gloucs
261 K2 **Leckmelm** Highld
43 J6 **Leckwith** V Glam
152 F7 **Leconfield** E R Yk
228 E7 **Ledaig** Ag & B
67 L3 **Ledburn** Bucks
81 G7 **Ledbury** Herefs
80 F8 **Leddington** Gloucs
80 A5 **Ledgemoor** Herefs
80 A3 **Ledicot** Herefs
271 H5 **Ledmore Junction** Highld
129 H5 **Ledsham** Ches
142 C2 **Ledsham** Leeds
142 C2 **Ledston** Leeds
142 C2 **Ledston Luck** Leeds
7 L5 **Ledstone** Devon
66 B2 **Ledwell** Oxon
27 H2 **Lee** Devon
51 K4 **Lee** Gt Lon
34 D7 **Lee** Hants
112 F5 **Lee** Shrops
113 J6 **Lee Brockhurst** Shrops
52 E2 **Lee Chapel** Essex
67 M6 **Lee Clump** Bucks
67 M6 **Lee Common** Bucks
130 C7 **Lee Green** Ches
7 H4 **Lee Mill** Devon
7 H3 **Lee Moor** Devon
37 L2 **Lee Street** Surrey
19 J3 **Lee-on-the-Solent** Hants
96 B4 **Leebotwood** Shrops
146 E2 **Leece** Cumb
68 B2 **Leedon** Beds
39 K3 **Leeds** Kent
141 L1 **Leeds** Leeds
2 F4 **Leedstown** Cnwll
131 K8 **Leek** Staffs
83 G2 **Leek Wootton** Warwks
141 G1 **Leeming** Brad
160 D5 **Leeming** N York
160 D4 **Leeming Bar** N York
149 J8 **Lees** Brad
115 L4 **Lees** Derbys
140 E6 **Lees** Oldham
115 L4 **Lees Green** Derbys
178 D5 **Lees Hill** Cumb
101 H1 **Leesthorpe** Leics
129 G7 **Leeswood** Flints
222 C3 **Leetown** P & K
130 C5 **Leftwich** Ches
61 K4 **Legar** Powys
137 G3 **Legbourne** Lincs
165 K6 **Legburthwaite** Cumb
201 J4 **Legerwood** Border
136 B3 **Legsby** Lincs
100 D3 **Leicester** C Leic
100 B3 **Leicester Forest East** Leics
28 C8 **Leigh** Devon
16 B1 **Leigh** Dorset
64 C2 **Leigh** Gloucs
38 E4 **Leigh** Kent
95 H3 **Leigh** Shrops
37 K2 **Leigh** Surrey
139 K7 **Leigh** Wigan
64 F8 **Leigh** Wilts
81 H4 **Leigh** Worcs
53 H2 **Leigh Beck** Essex
46 C3 **Leigh Delamere** Wilts
40 A8 **Leigh Green** Kent
197 J1 **Leigh Knoweglass** S Lans
17 K3 **Leigh Park** Dorset
81 H5 **Leigh Sinton** Worcs
31 M2 **Leigh upon Mendip** Somset
45 H4 **Leigh Woods** N Som
53 H2 **Leigh-on-Sea** Sthend
29 J4 **Leighland Chapel** Somset
98 D3 **Leighswood** W Mids
46 B1 **Leighterton** Gloucs
159 L6 **Leighton** N York
94 F2 **Leighton** Powys
96 E2 **Leighton** Shrops
32 B2 **Leighton** Somset
102 C8 **Leighton Bromswold** Cambs
68 A2 **Leighton Buzzard** Beds
80 B2 **Leinthall Earls** Herefs
80 A1 **Leinthall Starkes** Herefs
95 K8 **Leintwardine** Herefs
100 B5 **Leire** Leics
91 K3 **Leiston** Suffk
233 L6 **Leitfie** P & K
211 J4 **Leith** C Edin
202 B4 **Leitholm** Border
2 E4 **Lelant** Cnwll
145 G1 **Lelley** E R Yk
97 G8 **Lem Hill** Worcs
191 G4 **Lemmington Hall** Nthumb
202 B6 **Lempitlaw** Border
282 g5 **Lemreway** W Isls
69 G4 **Lemsford** Herts
82 B6 **Lenchwick** Worcs
182 E5 **Lendalfoot** S Ayrs
219 J6 **Lendrick** Stirlg
257 L3 **Lendrum Terrace** Abers
40 A5 **Lenham** Kent
40 B5 **Lenham Heath** Kent
250 F6 **Lenie** Highld
202 C5 **Lennel** Border
174 F4 **Lennox Plunton** D & G
209 G3 **Lennoxtown** E Duns
50 A3 **Lent** Bucks
116 F4 **Lenton** C Nott

118 D5 **Lenton** Lincs
122 B7 **Lenwade** Norfk
209 H4 **Lenzie** E Duns
244 C2 **Leochel-Cushnie** Abers
98 E2 **Leomansley** Staffs
80 C3 **Leominster** Herefs
64 A6 **Leonard Stanley** Gloucs
9 b2 **Leoville** Jersey
19 G4 **Lepe** Hants
258 B6 **Lephin** Highld
152 A4 **Leppington** N York
141 K5 **Lepton** Kirk
5 K3 **Lerryn** Cnwll
281 e6 **Lerwick** Shet
9 h3 **Les Arquets** Guern
9 k3 **Les Hubits** Guern
9 I3 **Les Lohiers** Guern
9 i4 **Les Murchez** Guern
9 j4 **Les Nicolles** Guern
9 J2 **Les Quartiers** Guern
9 b3 **Les Quennevais** Jersey
9 I3 **Les Sages** Guern
9 i4 **Les Villets** Guern
191 J4 **Lesbury** Nthumb
255 M6 **Leslie** Abers
222 D6 **Leslie** Fife
198 D5 **Lesmahagow** S Lans
11 G4 **Lesnewth** Cnwll
123 H6 **Lessingham** Norfk
165 H1 **Lessonhall** Cumb
3 K6 **Lestowder** Cnwll
172 C2 **Leswalt** D & G
68 F7 **Letchmore Heath** Herts
86 E8 **Letchworth Garden City** Herts
48 A2 **Letcombe Bassett** Oxon
48 A2 **Letcombe Regis** Oxon
234 E5 **Letham** Angus
189 J4 **Letham** Border
210 B2 **Letham** Falk
222 E4 **Letham** Fife
235 G6 **Letham Grange** Angus
233 H7 **Lethenty** P & K
255 M7 **Lethenty** Abers
256 E4 **Lethenty** Abers
91 G4 **Letheringham** Suffk
122 B4 **Letheringsett** Norfk
51 M7 **Lett's Green** Kent
13 G5 **Lettaford** Devon
260 F5 **Letterewe** Highld
248 D7 **Letterfearn** Highld
239 L5 **Letterfinlay Lodge Hotel** Highld
237 L3 **Lettermorar** Highld
261 K2 **Letters** Highld
186 D2 **Lettershaw** S Lans
74 F6 **Letterston** Pembks
253 K7 **Lettoch** Highld
254 B5 **Lettoch** Highld
79 L6 **Letton** Herefs
79 L1 **Letton** Herefs
69 H5 **Letty Green** Herts
133 L2 **Letwell** Rothm
223 H3 **Leuchars** Fife
282 g5 **Leumrabhagh** W Isls
282 g4 **Leurbost** W Isls
5 G5 **Levalsa Meor** Cnwll
114 D8 **Levedale** Staffs
70 C2 **Level's Green** Essex
153 H6 **Leven** E R Yk
222 F7 **Leven** Fife
157 G5 **Levens** Cumb
69 K3 **Levens Green** Herts
131 G1 **Levenshulme** Manch
281 d8 **Levenwick** Shet
282 d6 **Leverburgh** W Isls
103 J1 **Leverington** Cambs
68 D5 **Leverstock Green** Herts
119 L2 **Leverton** Lincs
90 F7 **Levington** Suffk
162 E4 **Levisham** N York
65 L6 **Lew** Oxon
11 K6 **Lewannick** Cnwll
12 B5 **Lewdown** Devon
22 F5 **Lewes** E Susx
31 K8 **Leweston** Dorset
54 F2 **Leweston** Pembks
79 L4 **Lewis Wych** Herefs
51 K4 **Lewisham** Gt Lon
250 F6 **Lewiston** Highld
67 H7 **Lewknor** Oxon
11 L2 **Leworthy** Devon
28 B3 **Leworthy** Devon
40 C3 **Lewson Street** Kent
147 J8 **Lewth** Lancs

12 B5 **Lewtrenchard** Devon
72 D2 **Lexden** Essex
30 C4 **Lexworthy** Somset
5 K2 **Ley** Cnwll
68 C6 **Ley Hill** Bucks
52 E7 **Leybourne** Kent
159 K4 **Leyburn** N York
114 B2 **Leycett** Staffs
68 F2 **Leygreen** Herts
139 H3 **Leyland** Lancs
139 H7 **Leyland Green** St Hel
245 G1 **Leylodge** Abers
269 J5 **Leys** Abers
233 K7 **Leys** Angus
234 B5 **Leys of Cossans** Angus
53 M5 **Leysdown-on-Sea** Kent
234 F6 **Leysmill** Angus
80 D2 **Leysters** Herefs
51 K2 **Leyton** Gt Lon
51 K2 **Leytonstone** Gt Lon
11 L6 **Lezant** Cnwll
154 f3 **Lezayre** IOM
3 H4 **Lezerea** Cnwll
266 F4 **Lhanbryde** Moray
60 F2 **Libanus** Powys
199 G4 **Libberton** S Lans
211 J5 **Liberton** C Edin
98 E2 **Lichfield** Staffs
98 C8 **Lickey** Worcs
81 M1 **Lickey End** Worcs
98 B8 **Lickey Rock** Worcs
36 D5 **Lickfold** W Susx
12 B6 **Liddaton Green** Devon
228 B3 **Liddesdale** Highld
47 J3 **Liddington** Swindn
132 F4 **Lidgate** Derbys
88 E4 **Lidgate** Suffk
143 G7 **Lidget** Donc
134 C6 **Lidgett** Notts
24 F4 **Lidham Hill** E Susx
85 K7 **Lidlington** Beds
53 G6 **Lidsing** Kent
222 E1 **Liff** Angus
98 D7 **Lifford** Birm
11 M5 **Lifton** Devon
11 M5 **Liftondown** Devon
140 F4 **Lighthazles** Calder
83 H4 **Lighthorne** Warwks
83 H4 **Lighthorne Heath** Warwks
50 B6 **Lightwater** Surrey
114 E3 **Lightwood** C Stke
113 L3 **Lightwood Green** Ches
112 F3 **Lightwood Green** Wrexhm
100 C8 **Lilbourne** Nhants
190 E1 **Lilburn Tower** Nthumb
114 A8 **Lilleshall** Wrekin
68 E2 **Lilley** Herts
48 C3 **Lilley** W Berk
201 H8 **Lilliesleaf** Border
84 D7 **Lillingstone Dayrell** Bucks
84 D7 **Lillingstone Lovell** Bucks
31 K8 **Lillington** Dorset
17 K4 **Lilliput** Poole
29 L2 **Lilstock** Somset
97 G1 **Lilyhurst** Shrops
139 J4 **Limbrick** Lancs
68 D2 **Limbury** Luton
64 A1 **Lime Street** Worcs
79 L2 **Limebrook** Herefs
140 B5 **Limefield** Bury
197 K1 **Limekilnburn** S Lans
210 E2 **Limekilns** Fife
209 M5 **Limerigg** Falk
19 G7 **Limerstone** IOW
167 J1 **Limestone Brae** Nthumb
31 J6 **Limington** Somset
197 J5 **Limmerhaugh** E Ayrs
107 H3 **Limpenhoe** Norfk
45 M6 **Limpley Stoke** Wilts
51 L8 **Limpsfield** Surrey
51 L8 **Limpsfield Chart** Surrey
116 F1 **Linby** Notts
36 C5 **Linchmere** W Susx
176 C3 **Lincluden** D & G
135 K5 **Lincoln** Lincs
81 J2 **Lincomb** Worcs
7 L6 **Lincombe** Devon
156 C7 **Lindal in Furness** Cumb
156 F6 **Lindale** Cumb
22 E2 **Lindfield** W Susx
36 B4 **Lindford** Hants
141 H4 **Lindley** Kirk
150 B6 **Lindley Green** N York
130 F4 **Lindow End** Ches
80 F2 **Lindridge** Worcs

70 F2 **Lindsell** Essex
89 K6 **Lindsey** Suffk
89 K6 **Lindsey Tye** Suffk
30 E4 **Liney** Somset
18 B2 **Linford** Hants
52 E3 **Linford** Thurr
149 K8 **Lingbob** Brad
170 F7 **Lingdale** R & Cl
79 L2 **Lingen** Herefs
38 B4 **Lingfield** Surrey
130 A2 **Lingley Green** Warrtn
107 G2 **Lingwood** Norfk
258 D2 **Linicro** Highld
64 B1 **Linkend** Worcs
48 A7 **Linkenholt** Hants
24 E2 **Linkhill** Kent
11 L7 **Linkinhorne** Cnwll
211 J1 **Linktown** Fife
266 E4 **Linkwood** Moray
95 J5 **Linley** Shrops
80 F4 **Linley Green** Herefs
96 F4 **Linleygreen** Shrops
210 C4 **Linlithgow** W Loth
190 C5 **Linshiels** Nthumb
272 D8 **Linsidemore** Highld
67 M2 **Linslade** Beds
107 G7 **Linstead Parva** Suffk
178 A7 **Linstock** Cumb
82 B1 **Linthurst** Worcs
141 H5 **Linthwaite** Kirk
213 H7 **Lintlaw** Border
267 K3 **Lintmill** Moray
202 B7 **Linton** Border
88 B6 **Linton** Cambs
115 M8 **Linton** Derbys
63 K2 **Linton** Herefs
39 J3 **Linton** Kent
150 E6 **Linton** Leeds
149 H3 **Linton** N York
191 K7 **Linton** Nthumb
115 M8 **Linton Heath** Derbys
63 K2 **Linton Hill** Gloucs
151 G4 **Linton-on-Ouse** N York
18 B2 **Linwood** Hants
136 B2 **Linwood** Lincs
208 D6 **Linwood** Rens
283 c9 **Lionacleit** W Isls
282 h1 **Lional** W Isls
23 J4 **Lions Green** E Susx
36 C4 **Liphook** Hants
114 A5 **Lipley** Shrops
129 G1 **Liscard** Wirral
28 F4 **Liscombe** Somset
6 B2 **Liskeard** Cnwll
36 A5 **Liss** Hants
36 A5 **Liss Forest** Hants
153 J4 **Lissett** E R Yk
136 B3 **Lissington** Lincs
89 G6 **Liston** Essex
43 J5 **Lisvane** Cardif
44 D2 **Liswerry** Newpt
121 J8 **Litcham** Norfk
42 D5 **Litchard** Brdgnd
84 C4 **Litchborough** Nhants
48 C8 **Litchfield** Hants
138 D8 **Litherland** Sefton
87 G6 **Litlington** Cambs
23 J7 **Litlington** E Susx
87 L5 **Little Abington** Cambs
101 L8 **Little Addington** Nhants
173 K5 **Little Airies** D & G
69 G2 **Little Almshoe** Herts
82 D3 **Little Alne** Warwks
138 C6 **Little Altcar** Sefton
69 K5 **Little Amwell** Herts
158 B1 **Little Asby** Cumb
98 E3 **Little Aston** Staffs
19 G7 **Little Atherfield** IOW
170 D8 **Little Ayton** N York
71 J5 **Little Baddow** Essex
46 A2 **Little Badminton** S Glos
177 J7 **Little Bampton** Cumb
71 G1 **Little Bardfield** Essex
86 D4 **Little Barford** Beds
122 C5 **Little Barningham** Norfk
65 J4 **Little Barrington** Gloucs
129 L5 **Little Barrow** Ches
162 D6 **Little Barugh** N York
180 B3 **Little Bavington** Nthumb
99 K6 **Little Bayton** Warwks
90 F5 **Little Bealings** Suffk
47 L5 **Little Bedwyn** Wilts
73 G2 **Little Bentley** Essex
69 H5 **Little Berkhamsted** Herts
84 F3 **Little Billing** Nhants

68 B3 **Little Billington** Beds
63 G1 **Little Birch** Herefs
146 F7 **Little Bispham** Bpool
90 C5 **Little Blakenham** Suffk
166 B4 **Little Blencow** Cumb
98 C3 **Little Bloxwich** Wsall
21 G3 **Little Bognor** W Susx
116 A1 **Little Bolehill** Derbys
130 E2 **Little Bollington** Ches
50 E8 **Little Bookham** Surrey
83 K6 **Little Bourton** Oxon
101 G6 **Little Bowden** Leics
88 D5 **Little Bradley** Suffk
79 K3 **Little Brampton** Herefs
95 J7 **Little Brampton** Shrops
71 K4 **Little Braxted** Essex
234 F3 **Little Brechin** Angus
85 H8 **Little Brickhill** M Keyn
114 D6 **Little Bridgeford** Staffs
84 C3 **Little Brington** Nhants
73 G2 **Little Bromley** Essex
164 E4 **Little Broughton** Cumb
130 B6 **Little Budworth** Ches
71 G8 **Little Burstead** Essex
118 D7 **Little Bytham** Lincs
70 E3 **Little Canfield** Essex
137 G3 **Little Carlton** Lincs
134 F8 **Little Carlton** Notts
101 M2 **Little Casterton** Rutlnd
153 H6 **Little Catwick** E R Yk
86 B1 **Little Catworth** Cambs
137 G3 **Little Cawthorpe** Lincs
46 B6 **Little Chalfield** Wilts
68 C7 **Little Chalfont** Bucks
30 C3 **Little Charlinch** Somset
40 B6 **Little Chart** Kent
87 L7 **Little Chesterford** Essex
39 H4 **Little Cheveney** Kent
46 E8 **Little Cheverell** Wilts
87 J7 **Little Chishill** Cambs
73 H3 **Little Clacton** Essex
65 K6 **Little Clanfield** Oxon
164 E5 **Little Clifton** Cumb
145 H6 **Little Coates** NE Lin
81 M6 **Little Comberton** Worcs
24 C5 **Little Common** E Susx
39 G2 **Little Comp** Kent
65 K1 **Little Compton** Warwks
178 B7 **Little Corby** Cumb
89 H7 **Little Cornard** Suffk
80 E5 **Little Cowarne** Herefs
65 L8 **Little Coxwell** Oxon
160 C4 **Little Crakehall** N York
101 H8 **Little Cransley** Nhants
105 H3 **Little Cressingham** Norfk
138 C7 **Little Crosby** Sefton
165 H5 **Little Crosthwaite** Cumb
115 J4 **Little Cubley** Derbys
117 K8 **Little Dalby** Leics
257 K3 **Little Dens** Abers
63 G1 **Little Dewchurch** Herefs
88 D3 **Little Ditton** Cambs
63 G4 **Little Doward** Herefs
103 L6 **Little Downham** Cambs
152 F4 **Little Driffield** E R Yk
105 H1 **Little Dunham** Norfk
232 F7 **Little Dunkeld** P & K
71 G3 **Little Dunmow** Essex
33 K4 **Little Durnford** Wilts
70 F2 **Little Easton** Essex
116 B3 **Little Eaton** Derbys
105 K3 **Little Ellingham** Norfk
32 B2 **Little Elm** Somset
84 B4 **Little Everdon** Nhants
87 H4 **Little Eversden** Cambs
65 J6 **Little Faringdon** Oxon
160 D4 **Little Fencote** N York
142 E1 **Little Fenton** N York
105 H1 **Little Fransham** Norfk
68 C4 **Little Gaddesden** Herts
62 F2 **Little Garway** Herefs
102 C7 **Little Gidding** Cambs
91 H4 **Little Glemham** Suffk
63 K2 **Little Gorsley** Herefs
86 F4 **Little Gransden** Cambs
117 J3 **Little Green** Notts
32 B1 **Little Green** Somset
136 F2 **Little Grimsby** Lincs
134 E3 **Little Gringley** Notts
162 C7 **Little Habton** N York
70 B3 **Little Hadham** Herts
118 F3 **Little Hale** Lincs
116 D3 **Little Hallam** Derbys
70 D4 **Little Hallingbury** Essex
67 L6 **Little Hampden** Bucks

32 D8 **Little Hanford** Dorset
85 G1 **Little Harrowden** Nhants
66 F7 **Little Haseley** Oxon
153 J7 **Little Hatfield** E R Yk
122 E7 **Little Hautbois** Norfk
54 D4 **Little Haven** Pembks
98 E3 **Little Hay** Staffs
131 K2 **Little Hayfield** Derbys
115 G7 **Little Haywood** Staffs
99 K7 **Little Heath** Covtry
114 D8 **Little Heath** Staffs
49 G4 **Little Heath** W Berk
80 D2 **Little Hereford** Herefs
52 F5 **Little Hermitage** Kent
72 D1 **Little Horkesley** Essex
69 L1 **Little Hormead** Herts
23 H4 **Little Horsted** E Susx
141 J2 **Little Horton** Brad
46 F6 **Little Horton** Wilts
67 J1 **Little Horwood** Bucks
142 C6 **Little Houghton** Barns
84 F3 **Little Houghton** Nhants
132 C4 **Little Hucklow** Derbys
139 L7 **Little Hulton** Salfd
48 D4 **Little Hungerford** W Berk
161 G7 **Little Hutton** N York
114 F6 **Little Ingestre** Staffs
85 H2 **Little Irchester** Nhants
153 H4 **Little Kelk** E R Yk
32 C2 **Little Keyford** Somset
67 K5 **Little Kimble** Bucks
83 H5 **Little Kineton** Warwks
67 L7 **Little Kingshill** Bucks
175 K3 **Little Knox** D & G
156 D2 **Little Langdale** Cumb
33 H4 **Little Langford** Wilts
12 A1 **Little Lashbrook** Devon
70 E5 **Little Laver** Essex
130 B4 **Little Leigh** Ches
71 H4 **Little Leighs** Essex
139 M6 **Little Lever** Bolton
85 G6 **Little Linford** M Keyn
87 L5 **Little Linton** Cambs
31 G6 **Little Load** Somset
150 B7 **Little London** Brad
66 F4 **Little London** Bucks
103 J4 **Little London** Cambs
23 J3 **Little London** E Susx
70 C1 **Little London** Essex
88 D8 **Little London** Essex
63 L3 **Little London** Gloucs
34 E1 **Little London** Hants
48 F7 **Little London** Hants
119 H7 **Little London** Lincs
136 F5 **Little London** Lincs
119 M6 **Little London** Lincs
120 C7 **Little London** Norfk
94 C5 **Little London** Powys
132 D5 **Little Longstone** Derbys
114 B3 **Little Madeley** Staffs
81 H7 **Little Malvern** Worcs
129 H6 **Little Mancot** Flints
89 G8 **Little Maplestead** Essex
80 F7 **Little Marcle** Herefs
27 J8 **Little Marland** Devon
49 L2 **Little Marlow** Bucks
121 H6 **Little Massingham** Norfk
106 D2 **Little Melton** Norfk
62 C6 **Little Mill** Mons
66 F7 **Little Milton** Oxon
68 A7 **Little Missenden** Bucks
41 K5 **Little Mongeham** Kent
30 D4 **Little Moor** Somset
167 H8 **Little Musgrave** Cumb
112 F7 **Little Ness** Shrops
129 G4 **Little Neston** Ches
75 G6 **Little Newcastle** Pembks
168 E7 **Little Newsham** Dur
31 G7 **Little Norton** Somset
73 J1 **Little Oakley** Essex
101 K6 **Little Oakley** Nhants
85 J4 **Little Odell** Beds
68 E2 **Little Offley** Herts
114 C8 **Little Onn** Staffs
167 G7 **Little Ormside** Cumb
177 K7 **Little Orton** Cumb
104 C5 **Little Ouse** Cambs
150 F4 **Little Ouseburn** N York
100 F6 **Little Oxendon** Nhants
99 G6 **Little Packington** Warwks
39 J4 **Little Pattenden** Kent
86 D3 **Little Paxton** Cambs
10 C8 **Little Petherick** Cnwll
138 D1 **Little Plumpton** Lancs
107 G1 **Little Plumstead** Norfk

118 B5 **Little Ponton** Lincs
19 J3 **Little Posbrook** Hants
27 J8 **Little Potheridge** Devon
142 B2 **Little Preston** Leeds
84 B4 **Little Preston** Nhants
102 E7 **Little Raveley** Cambs
143 K3 **Little Reedness** E R Yk
150 E5 **Little Ribston** N York
65 J3 **Little Rissington** Gloucs
65 L1 **Little Rollright** Oxon
132 E6 **Little Rowsley** Derbys
121 L6 **Little Ryburgh** Norfk
190 E4 **Little Ryle** Nthumb
96 B3 **Little Ryton** Shrops
166 D3 **Little Salkeld** Cumb
88 C8 **Little Sampford** Essex
49 K6 **Little Sandhurst** Br For
97 L2 **Little Saredon** Staffs
129 J6 **Little Saughall** Ches
88 F3 **Little Saxham** Suffk
262 C8 **Little Scatwell** Highld
161 G7 **Little Sessay** N York
87 J5 **Little Shelford** Cambs
13 K2 **Little Silver** Devon
13 L1 **Little Silver** Devon
147 G7 **Little Singleton** Lancs
151 K8 **Little Skipwith** N York
142 E4 **Little Smeaton** N York
121 L5 **Little Snoring** Norfk
45 M2 **Little Sodbury** S Glos
45 L2 **Little Sodbury End** S Glos
34 E4 **Little Somborne** Hants
46 D2 **Little Somerford** Wilts
114 A6 **Little Soudley** Shrops
148 E2 **Little Stainforth** N York
169 K6 **Little Stainton** Darltn
129 J5 **Little Stanney** Ches
86 B3 **Little Staughton** Beds
137 H7 **Little Steeping** Lincs
90 D3 **Little Stonham** Suffk
100 E3 **Little Stretton** Leics
95 K5 **Little Stretton** Shrops
166 D6 **Little Strickland** Cumb
102 E8 **Little Stukeley** Cambs
114 C5 **Little Sugnall** Staffs
129 J4 **Little Sutton** Ches
96 C6 **Little Sutton** Shrops
179 M3 **Little Swinburne** Nthumb
175 H4 **Little Sypland** D & G
66 A2 **Little Tew** Oxon
72 C2 **Little Tey** Essex
103 L8 **Little Thetford** Cambs
161 G7 **Little Thirkleby** N York
122 B4 **Little Thornage** Norfk
147 G7 **Little Thornton** Lancs
169 L2 **Little Thorpe** Dur
88 D5 **Little Thurlow** Suffk
88 D5 **Little Thurlow Green** Suffk
52 D3 **Little Thurrock** Thurr
27 J7 **Little Torrington** Devon
72 C5 **Little Totham** Essex
165 H6 **Little Town** Cumb
148 B8 **Little Town** Lancs
130 C1 **Little Town** Warrtn
99 J2 **Little Twycross** Leics
156 C7 **Little Urswick** Cumb
53 K1 **Little Wakering** Essex
87 L7 **Little Walden** Essex
89 J6 **Little Waldingfield** Suffk
121 K4 **Little Walsingham** Norfk
71 H4 **Little Waltham** Essex
52 D1 **Little Warley** Essex
82 A8 **Little Washbourne** Gloucs
144 B1 **Little Weighton** E R Yk
101 K5 **Little Weldon** Nhants
89 H3 **Little Welnetham** Suffk
136 F2 **Little Welton** Lincs
90 C7 **Little Wenham** Suffk
96 E2 **Little Wenlock** Wrekin
31 K5 **Little Weston** Somset
19 K5 **Little Whitefield** IOW
180 B5 **Little Whittington** Nthumb
87 L3 **Little Wilbraham** Cambs
64 C4 **Little Witcombe** Gloucs
81 H3 **Little Witley** Worcs
66 E8 **Little Wittenham** Oxon
83 G8 **Little Wolford** Warwks
51 H6 **Little Woodcote** Surrey
88 D6 **Little Wratting** Suffk
85 J2 **Little Wymington** Beds
69 G2 **Little Wymondley** Herts
98 C2 **Little Wyrley** Staffs
113 J7 **Little Wytheford** Shrops
88 F7 **Little Yeldham** Essex
162 F2 **Littlebeck** N York

28 E8 **Littleborough** Devon
135 G3 **Littleborough** Notts
140 E4 **Littleborough** Rochdl
41 G4 **Littlebourne** Kent
16 B5 **Littlebredy** Dorset
251 H1 **Littleburn** Highld
87 L7 **Littlebury** Essex
87 K7 **Littlebury Green** Essex
47 H8 **Littlecott** Wilts
63 K4 **Littledean** Gloucs
47 M7 **Littledown** Hants
27 H6 **Littleham** Devon
14 B6 **Littleham** Devon
21 H6 **Littlehampton** W Susx
180 B2 **Littleharle Tower** Nthumb
37 J4 **Littlehaven** W Susx
8 B2 **Littlehempston** Devon
191 J3 **Littlehoughton** Nthumb
243 K4 **Littlemill** Abers
253 H2 **Littlemill** Highld
133 G7 **Littlemoor** Derbys
66 D6 **Littlemore** Oxon
116 B5 **Littleover** C Derb
104 B6 **Littleport** Cambs
104 B6 **Littleport Bridge** Cambs
130 C6 **Littler** Ches
25 K2 **Littlestone-on-Sea** Kent
100 C4 **Littlethorpe** Leics
150 D2 **Littlethorpe** N York
233 M5 **Littleton** Angus
45 H6 **Littleton** BaNES
129 K6 **Littleton** Ches
175 G4 **Littleton** D & G
17 H2 **Littleton** Dorset
34 F4 **Littleton** Hants
31 H5 **Littleton** Somset
36 E2 **Littleton** Surrey
50 D5 **Littleton** Surrey
46 B3 **Littleton Drew** Wilts
46 E8 **Littleton Pannell** Wilts
45 H1 **Littleton-on-Severn** S Glos
169 J2 **Littletown** Dur
19 J5 **Littletown** IOW
49 K3 **Littlewick Green** W & M
15 K2 **Littlewindsor** Dorset
98 C2 **Littlewood** Staffs
67 L3 **Littleworth** Bucks
65 L7 **Littleworth** Oxon
114 E7 **Littleworth** Staffs
98 C1 **Littleworth** Staffs
21 L3 **Littleworth** W Susx
81 K5 **Littleworth** Worcs
82 B3 **Littleworth** Worcs
50 B2 **Littleworth Common** Bucks
86 E2 **Littleworth End** Cambs
71 G4 **Littley Green** Essex
45 H8 **Litton** BaNES
132 C4 **Litton** Derbys
158 F7 **Litton** N York
16 A4 **Litton Cheney** Dorset
282 g4 **Liurbost** W Isls
129 H2 **Liverpool** Lpool
141 J3 **Liversedge** Kirk
13 J7 **Liverton** Devon
171 G7 **Liverton** R & Cl
171 G7 **Liverton Mines** R & Cl
39 L3 **Liverton Street** Kent
210 E5 **Livingston** W Loth
210 D5 **Livingston Village** W Loth
7 K5 **Lixton** Devon
128 E5 **Lixwm** Flints
3 H8 **Lizard** Cnwll
124 D3 **Llaingoch** IOA
94 C7 **Llaithddu** Powys
93 J3 **Llan** Powys
112 F1 **Llan-y-pwll** Wrexhm
109 L7 **Llanaber** Gwynd
109 G3 **Llanaelhaearn** Gwynd
77 J1 **Llanafan** Cerdgn
78 D5 **Llanafan-fechan** Powys
125 J3 **Llanallgo** IOA
109 G4 **Llanarmon** Gwynd
112 A5 **Llanarmon Dyffryn Ceiriog** Wrexhm
128 E8 **Llanarmon-yn-Ial** Denbgs
76 D4 **Llanarth** Cerdgn
62 D5 **Llanarth** Mons
58 F5 **Llanarthne** Carmth
128 D3 **Llanasa** Flints
124 F2 **Llanbabo** IOA
92 D7 **Llanbadarn Fawr** Cerdgn
94 D7 **Llanbadarn Fynydd** Powys
78 F5 **Llanbadarn-y-garreg** Powys
62 D7 **Llanbadoc** Mons
124 F1 **Llanbadrig** IOA

44 D1 **Llanbeder** Newpt
109 K6 **Llanbedr** Gwynd
79 G6 **Llanbedr** Powys
61 K3 **Llanbedr** Powys
128 D7 **Llanbedr-Dyffryn-Clwyd** Denbgs
126 E6 **Llanbedr-y-Cennin** Conwy
125 J4 **Llanbedrgoch** IOA
108 F5 **Llanbedrog** Gwynd
125 K7 **Llanberis** Gwynd
43 G7 **Llanbethery** V Glam
94 D8 **Llanbister** Powys
42 F7 **Llanblethian** V Glam
55 L2 **Llanboidy** Carmth
43 J4 **Llanbradach** Caerph
93 K3 **Llanbrynmair** Powys
42 F8 **Llancadle** V Glam
43 G7 **Llancarfan** V Glam
62 D6 **Llancayo** Mons
62 D2 **Llancillo** Herefs
63 G3 **Llancloudy** Herefs
92 E5 **Llancynfelyn** Cerdgn
43 J6 **Llandaff** Cardif
109 K6 **Llandanwg** Gwynd
58 A6 **Llandawke** Carmth
125 J3 **Llanddanielfab** IOA
58 F5 **Llanddarog** Carmth
77 G1 **Llanddeiniol** Cerdgn
125 K6 **Llanddeiniolen** Gwynd
111 J4 **Llandderfel** Gwynd
59 L4 **Llanddeusant** Carmth
124 F3 **Llanddeusant** IOA
61 G1 **Llanddew** Powys
56 E7 **Llanddewi** Swans
77 J4 **Llanddewi Brefi** Cerdgn
62 D4 **Llanddewi Rhydderch** Mons
55 K4 **Llanddewi Velfrey** Pembks
78 F2 **Llanddewi Ystradenni** Powys
78 E5 **Llanddewi'r Cwm** Powys
126 F7 **Llanddoget** Conwy
125 K4 **Llanddona** IOA
55 M4 **Llanddowror** Carmth
127 H4 **Llanddulas** Conwy
109 K7 **Llanddwywe** Gwynd
125 J4 **Llanddyfnan** IOA
110 B4 **Llandecwyn** Gwynd
60 F1 **Llandefaelog** Powys
61 H1 **Llandefaelog-Trer-Graig** Powys
78 F8 **Llandefalle** Powys
125 K5 **Llandegfan** IOA
112 B1 **Llandegla** Denbgs
79 G3 **Llandegley** Powys
62 C8 **Llandegveth** Mons
108 D5 **Llandegwning** Gwynd
59 H4 **Llandeilo** Carmth
78 F6 **Llandeilo Graban** Powys
78 B8 **Llandeilo'r Fan** Powys
74 D6 **Llandeloy** Pembks
62 E6 **Llandenny** Mons
44 E1 **Llandevaud** Newpt
44 E2 **Llandevenny** Mons
63 G2 **Llandinabo** Herefs
94 B5 **Llandinam** Powys
55 J3 **Llandissilio** Pembks
63 G6 **Llandogo** Mons
42 F7 **Llandough** V Glam
43 J7 **Llandough** V Glam
59 L2 **Llandovery** Carmth
42 E7 **Llandow** V Glam
77 J6 **Llandre** Carmth
92 D6 **Llandre** Cerdgn
75 K6 **Llandre Isaf** Pembks
111 K4 **Llandrillo** Denbgs
127 G4 **Llandrillo-yn-Rhos** Conwy
78 E3 **Llandrindod Wells** Powys
112 D8 **Llandrinio** Powys
126 F3 **Llandudno** Conwy
126 F4 **Llandudno Junction** Conwy
108 D4 **Llandudwen** Gwynd
78 B7 **Llandulas** Powys
125 H8 **Llandwrog** Gwynd
59 H6 **Llandybie** Carmth
58 D6 **Llandyfaelog** Carmth
59 H5 **Llandyfan** Carmth
76 B7 **Llandyfriog** Cerdgn
125 H3 **Llandyfrydog** IOA
126 B5 **Llandygai** Gwynd
75 M3 **Llandygwydd** Cerdgn
112 B3 **Llandynan** Denbgs
128 D6 **Llandyrnog** Denbgs
94 F4 **Llandyssil** Powys
76 D7 **Llandysul** Cerdgn
43 K5 **Llanedeyrn** Cardif
57 G3 **Llanedi** Carmth

78 E7 **Llaneglwys** Powys
92 D2 **Llanegryn** Gwynd
58 F4 **Llanegwad** Carmth
125 H1 **Llaneilian** IOA
127 G4 **Llaneilian-yn-Rhos** Conwy
111 L2 **Llanelidan** Denbgs
79 H8 **Llanelieu** Powys
62 C5 **Llanellen** Mons
56 F5 **Llanelli** Carmth
110 D7 **Llanelltyd** Gwynd
61 K4 **Llanelly** Mons
78 E5 **Llanelwedd** Powys
109 L6 **Llanenddwyn** Gwynd
108 E6 **Llanengan** Gwynd
111 G8 **Llanerch** Gwynd
95 H4 **Llanerch** Powys
125 G3 **Llanerchymedd** IOA
94 B2 **Llanerfyl** Powys
124 E3 **Llanfachraeth** IOA
110 E7 **Llanfachreth** Gwynd
124 F5 **Llanfaelog** IOA
108 C6 **Llanfaelrhys** Gwynd
62 E4 **Llanfaenor** Mons
126 B4 **Llanfaes** IOA
61 G2 **Llanfaes** Powys
124 E2 **Llanfaethlu** IOA
109 K5 **Llanfair** Gwynd
94 D2 **Llanfair Caereinion** Powys
77 H5 **Llanfair Clydogau** Cerdgn
128 D8 **Llanfair Dyffryn Clwyd** Denbgs
62 D5 **Llanfair Kilgeddin** Mons
125 J5 **Llanfair P G** IOA
127 J5 **Llanfair Talhaiarn** Conwy
94 F8 **Llanfair Waterdine** Shrops
125 J6 **Llanfair-is-gaer** Gwynd
75 K5 **Llanfair-Nant-Gwyn** Pembks
125 H6 **Llanfair-yn-Cwmwd** IOA
124 E4 **Llanfair-yn-Neubwll** IOA
126 D5 **Llanfairfechan** Conwy
124 E2 **Llanfairynghornwy** IOA
55 K3 **Llanfallteg** Carmth
55 K3 **Llanfallteg West** Carmth
92 D7 **Llanfarian** Cerdgn
112 B7 **Llanfechain** Powys
124 F2 **Llanfechell** IOA
128 E7 **Llanferres** Denbgs
124 F2 **Llanfflewyn** IOA
124 F3 **Llanfigael** IOA
111 J2 **Llanfihangel Glyn Myfyr** Conwy
78 C8 **Llanfihangel Nant Bran** Powys
79 G2 **Llanfihangel Rhydithon** Powys
44 F2 **Llanfihangel Rogiet** Mons
61 H2 **Llanfihangel Tal-y-llyn** Powys
124 E4 **Llanfihangel yn Nhowyn** IOA
76 E7 **Llanfihangel-ar-Arth** Carmth
79 H4 **Llanfihangel-nant-Melan** Powys
58 E4 **Llanfihangel-uwch-Gwili** Carmth
92 E8 **Llanfihangel-y-Creuddyn** Cerdgn
109 J3 **Llanfihangel-y-pennant** Gwynd
92 E2 **Llanfihangel-y-pennant** Gwynd
109 L4 **Llanfihangel-y-traethau** Gwynd
111 L8 **Llanfihangel-yng-Ngwynfa** Powys
78 F8 **Llanfilo** Powys
62 B4 **Llanfoist** Mons
111 H4 **Llanfor** Gwynd
62 C8 **Llanfrechfa** Torfn
110 B3 **Llanfrothen** Gwynd
61 G2 **Llanfrynach** Powys
128 D8 **Llanfwrog** Denbgs
124 E3 **Llanfwrog** IOA
112 A7 **Llanfyllin** Powys
59 G3 **Llanfynydd** Carmth
129 G8 **Llanfynydd** Flints
75 L6 **Llanfyrnach** Pembks
94 B1 **Llangadfan** Powys
56 D3 **Llangadog** Carmth
59 K3 **Llangadog** Carmth
125 G6 **Llangadwaladr** IOA
112 B5 **Llangadwaladr** Powys
125 H6 **Llangaffo** IOA
58 C6 **Llangain** Carmth
78 C6 **Llangammarch Wells** Powys
42 E6 **Llangan** V Glam
63 G3 **Llangarron** Herefs

61 H2 **Llangasty-Talyllyn** Powys
59 G4 **Llangathen** Carmth
61 K3 **Llangattock** Powys
62 D3 **Llangattock Lingoed** Mons
62 F4 **Llangattock-Vibon-Avel** Mons
112 B6 **Llangedwyn** Powys
125 H4 **Llangefni** IOA
42 D4 **Llangeinor** Brdgnd
125 H6 **Llangeinwen** IOA
77 H3 **Llangeitho** Cerdgn
76 C7 **Llangeler** Carmth
92 C2 **Llangelynin** Gwynd
58 E6 **Llangendeirne** Carmth
57 G4 **Llangennech** Carmth
56 D6 **Llangennith** Swans
61 K3 **Llangenny** Powys
127 H6 **Llangernyw** Conwy
108 E5 **Llangian** Gwynd
57 K4 **Llangiwg** Neath
74 E5 **Llangloffan** Pembks
75 L6 **Llanglydwen** Carmth
126 C4 **Llangoed** IOA
75 L3 **Llangoedmor** Cerdgn
112 B3 **Llangollen** Denbgs
75 J6 **Llangolman** Pembks
61 H2 **Llangors** Powys
62 F6 **Llangovan** Mons
111 G5 **Llangower** Gwynd
76 B4 **Llangranog** Cerdgn
125 H5 **Llangristiolus** IOA
63 G3 **Llangrove** Herefs
62 E2 **Llangua** Mons
79 H1 **Llangunllo** Powys
58 D5 **Llangunnor** Carmth
93 K7 **Llangurig** Powys
111 J3 **Llangwm** Conwy
62 E7 **Llangwm** Mons
55 G5 **Llangwm** Pembks
62 E7 **Llangwm-isaf** Mons
108 C5 **Llangwnnadl** Gwynd
128 D6 **Llangwyfan** Denbgs
125 H4 **Llangwyllog** IOA
77 H1 **Llangwyryfon** Cerdgn
77 H4 **Llangybi** Cerdgn
109 G3 **Llangybi** Gwynd
62 D7 **Llangybi** Mons
57 H5 **Llangyfelach** Swans
128 D7 **Llangynhafal** Denbgs
61 J3 **Llangynidr** Powys
55 M3 **Llangynin** Carmth
76 C6 **Llangynllo** Cerdgn
58 C6 **Llangynog** Carmth
111 K6 **Llangynog** Powys
78 E6 **Llangynog** Powys
42 C4 **Llangynwyd** Brdgnd
61 H2 **Llanhamlach** Powys
42 F5 **Llanharan** Rhondd
42 F5 **Llanharry** Rhondd
62 D8 **Llanhennock** Mons
61 K7 **Llanhilleth** Blae G
125 J6 **Llanidan** IOA
93 L6 **Llanidloes** Powys
108 D5 **Llaniestyn** Gwynd
79 H7 **Llanigon** Powys
92 D8 **Llanilar** Cerdgn
42 E5 **Llanilid** Rhondd
76 D3 **Llanina** Cerdgn
77 H4 **Llanio** Cerdgn
43 J5 **Llanishen** Cardif
62 F6 **Llanishen** Mons
126 C6 **Llanllechid** Gwynd
78 C5 **Llanlleonfel** Powys
62 D7 **Llanllowell** Mons
94 C3 **Llanllugan** Powys
58 C5 **Llanllwch** Carmth
94 D5 **Llanllwchaiarn** Powys
76 E7 **Llanllwni** Carmth
109 H1 **Llanllyfni** Gwynd
56 D6 **Llanmadoc** Swans
42 E7 **Llanmaes** V Glam
44 E1 **Llanmartin** Newpt
94 E5 **Llanmerewig** Powys
42 E7 **Llanmihangel** V Glam
55 M5 **Llanmiloe** Carmth
56 F6 **Llanmorlais** Swans
127 K5 **Llannefydd** Conwy
56 F3 **Llannon** Carmth
108 F4 **Llannor** Gwynd
76 F2 **Llanon** Cerdgn
62 C5 **Llanover** Mons
58 D3 **Llanpumsaint** Carmth
111 M6 **Llanrhaeadr-ym-Mochnant** Powys
74 D6 **Llanrhian** Pembks
56 F6 **Llanrhidian** Swans

126 F4 **Llanrhos** Conwy
126 F7 **Llanrhychwyn** Conwy
124 F2 **Llanrhyddlad** IOA
76 F1 **Llanrhystud** Cerdgn
62 F3 **Llanrothal** Herefs
125 J7 **Llanrug** Gwynd
43 K5 **Llanrumney** Cardif
126 F7 **Llanrwst** Conwy
56 A3 **Llansadurnen** Carmth
59 J3 **Llansadwrn** Carmth
125 K4 **Llansadwrn** IOA
56 C3 **Llansaint** Carmth
57 J5 **Llansamlet** Swans
126 F4 **Llansanffraid Glan Conwy** Conwy
127 J6 **Llansannan** Conwy
42 F6 **Llansannor** V Glam
61 H2 **Llansantffraed** Powys
78 D2 **Llansantffraed-Cwmdeuddwr** Powys
78 F4 **Llansantffraed-in-Elvel** Powys
76 F2 **Llansantffraid** Cerdgn
112 C7 **Llansantffraid-ym-Mechain** Powys
59 H2 **Llansawel** Carmth
112 B6 **Llansilin** Powys
62 E6 **Llansoy** Mons
60 F2 **Llanspyddid** Powys
54 F6 **Llanstadwell** Pembks
56 C3 **Llansteffan** Carmth
78 F6 **Llanstephan** Powys
62 C8 **Llantarnam** Torfn
55 L5 **Llanteg** Pembks
62 D4 **Llanthewy Skirrid** Mons
62 B2 **Llanthony** Mons
62 C4 **Llantilio Pertholey** Mons
62 E4 **Llantilio-Crossenny** Mons
124 F3 **Llantrisant** IOA
62 D7 **Llantrisant** Mons
43 G5 **Llantrisant** Rhondd
43 G7 **Llantrithyd** V Glam
43 G4 **Llantwit Fardre** Rhondd
42 E7 **Llantwit Major** V Glam
112 B3 **Llantysilio** Denbgs
111 G5 **Llanuwchllyn** Gwynd
44 E1 **Llanvaches** Newpt
62 F8 **Llanvair Discoed** Mons
62 D4 **Llanvapley** Mons
62 D4 **Llanvetherine** Mons
62 C1 **Llanveynoe** Herefs
62 C3 **Llanvihangel Crucorney** Mons
62 D5 **Llanvihangel Gobion** Mons
62 E4 **Llanvihangel-Ystern-Llewern** Mons
63 G2 **Llanwarne** Herefs
111 K1 **Llanwddyn** Powys
62 B4 **Llanwenarth** Mons
76 F6 **Llanwenog** Cerdgn
44 D2 **Llanwern** Newpt
58 A4 **Llanwinio** Carmth
125 H8 **Llanwnda** Gwynd
74 F4 **Llanwnda** Pembks
76 F6 **Llanwnnen** Cerdgn
94 B4 **Llanwnog** Powys
42 F3 **Llanwonno** Rhondd
59 K3 **Llanwrda** Carmth
93 G3 **Llanwrin** Powys
78 D3 **Llanwrthwl** Powys
78 B5 **Llanwrtyd** Powys
78 B6 **Llanwrtyd Wells** Powys
94 C3 **Llanwyddelan** Powys
112 C7 **Llanyblodwel** Shrops
58 B6 **Llanybri** Carmth
76 F6 **Llanybydder** Carmth
55 J2 **Llanycefn** Pembks
75 G5 **Llanychaer Bridge** Pembks
77 H6 **Llanycrwys** Carmth
111 G7 **Llanymawddwy** Gwynd
112 C7 **Llanymynech** Powys
124 E3 **Llanynghenedl** IOA
128 C7 **Llanynys** Denbgs
78 E3 **Llanyre** Powys
109 H4 **Llanystumdwy** Gwynd
61 H2 **Llanywern** Powys
55 H3 **Llawhaden** Pembks
112 C5 **Llawnt** Shrops
93 K5 **Llawryglyn** Powys
129 H8 **Llay** Wrexhm
125 G3 **Llechcynfarwy** IOA
61 G2 **Llechfaen** Powys
61 H5 **Llechrhyd** Caerph
75 L3 **Llechryd** Cerdgn
124 F4 **Llechylched** IOA

77 H1 **Lledrod** Cerdgn
111 G4 **Llidiardau** Gwynd
111 M3 **Llidiart-y-parc** Denbgs
77 G7 **Llidiartnenog** Carmth
108 F3 **Lithfaen** Gwynd
128 D4 **Lloc** Flints
129 G7 **Llong** Flints
79 H7 **Llowes** Powys
60 F6 **Llwydcoed** Rhondd
111 K8 **Llwydiarth** Powys
128 C6 **Llwyn** Denbgs
58 A2 **Llwyn-drain** Pembks
62 C4 **Llwyn-du** Mons
60 F5 **Llwyn-on** Myr Td
55 L4 **Llwyn-y-brain** Carmth
77 G4 **Llwyn-y-groes** Cerdgn
76 E3 **Llwyncelyn** Cerdgn
76 C4 **Llwyndafydd** Cerdgn
94 F3 **Llwynderw** Powys
108 F3 **Llwyndyrys** Gwynd
92 D2 **Llwyngwril** Gwynd
56 F5 **Llwynhendy** Carmth
112 C4 **Llwynmawr** Wrexhm
42 F3 **Llwynypia** Rhondd
128 E6 **Llyn-y-pandy** Flints
112 D6 **Llynclys** Shrops
125 G4 **Llynfaes** IOA
55 H2 **Llys-y-fran** Pembks
127 H4 **Llysfaen** Conwy
76 E3 **Llyswen** Cerdgn
79 G7 **Llyswen** Powys
42 E6 **Llysworney** V Glam
60 C1 **Llywel** Powys
132 E2 **Load Brook** Sheff
210 C4 **Loan** Falk
202 E3 **Loanend** Nthumb
211 J6 **Loanhead** Mdloth
176 C7 **Loaningfoot** D & G
196 C4 **Loans** S Ayrs
27 H3 **Lobb** Devon
12 B5 **Lobhillcross** Devon
283 c11 **Loch Baghasdail** W Isls
283 c8 **Loch Euphoirt** W Isls
219 H5 **Loch Katrine Pier** Stirlg
260 E6 **Loch Maree Hotel** Highld
283 d8 **Loch nam Madadh** W Isls
238 B7 **Lochailort** Highld
227 K3 **Lochaline** Highld
172 D3 **Lochans** D & G
176 C3 **Locharbriggs** D & G
216 E4 **Lochavich** Ag & B
217 J2 **Lochawe** Ag & B
283 c11 **Lochboisdale** W Isls
227 H7 **Lochbuie** Ag & B
248 E4 **Lochcarron** Highld
227 L6 **Lochdon** Ag & B
227 L5 **Lochdonhead** Ag & B
206 B3 **Lochead** Ag & B
219 K2 **Lochearnhead** Stirlg
222 F1 **Lochee** C Dund
239 G7 **Locheilside Station** Highld
251 G4 **Lochend** Highld
283 c8 **Locheport** W Isls
176 B4 **Lochfoot** D & G
206 E1 **Lochgair** Ag & B
222 C8 **Lochgelly** Fife
206 D2 **Lochgilphead** Ag & B
217 K7 **Lochgoilhead** Ag & B
222 D4 **Lochieheads** Fife
266 F3 **Lochill** Moray
253 J4 **Lochindorb Lodge** Highld
270 E4 **Lochinver** Highld
262 B7 **Lochluichart** Highld
176 E2 **Lochmaben** D & G
283 d8 **Lochmaddy** W Isls
222 B7 **Lochore** Fife
194 E1 **Lochranza** N Ayrs
235 J3 **Lochside** Abers
176 C3 **Lochside** D & G
252 F1 **Lochside** Highld
183 G7 **Lochton** S Ayrs
234 E3 **Lochty** Angus
223 J5 **Lochty** Fife
228 B4 **Lochuisge** Highld
208 B7 **Lochwinnoch** Rens
187 G6 **Lochwood** D & G
5 H3 **Lockengate** Cnwll
176 F3 **Lockerbie** D & G
47 H5 **Lockeridge** Wilts
34 C5 **Lockerley** Hants
44 D7 **Locking** N Som
130 C1 **Locking Stumps** Warrtn
152 F6 **Lockington** E R Yk
116 D6 **Lockington** Leics
113 M6 **Lockleywood** Shrops

19 H2 **Locks Heath** Hants
51 L6 **Locksbottom** Gt Lon
19 G5 **Locksgreen** IOW
162 E5 **Lockton** N York
101 H3 **Loddington** Leics
101 H7 **Loddington** Nhants
7 L5 **Loddiswell** Devon
107 G4 **Loddon** Norfk
87 L3 **Lode** Cambs
98 F7 **Lode Heath** Solhll
15 L4 **Loders** Dorset
99 H6 **Lodge Green** Solhll
36 D6 **Lodsworth** W Susx
142 A3 **Lofthouse** Leeds
159 K8 **Lofthouse** N York
142 A3 **Lofthouse Gate** Wakefd
171 G7 **Loftus** R & Cl
197 H6 **Logan** E Ayrs
156 A4 **Loganbeck** Cumb
210 C6 **Loganlea** W Loth
114 A4 **Loggerheads** Staffs
235 H3 **Logie** Angus
223 G3 **Logie** Fife
253 K2 **Logie** Moray
243 M3 **Logie Coldstone** Abers
235 G3 **Logie Pert** Angus
232 E5 **Logierait** P & K
257 G6 **Logierieve** Abers
55 K2 **Login** Carmth
87 H2 **Lolworth** Cambs
57 K5 **Lon-las** Swans
259 M6 **Lonbain** Highld
152 C6 **Londesborough** E R Yk
51 H3 **London** Gt Lon
5 G5 **London Apprentice** Cnwll
39 M6 **London Beach** Kent
68 F6 **London Colney** Herts
85 H2 **London End** Nhants
160 D5 **Londonderry** N York
118 C4 **Londonthorpe** Lincs
260 D4 **Londubh** Highld
260 C4 **Lonemore** Highld
45 H5 **Long Ashton** N Som
97 H8 **Long Bank** Worcs
117 L3 **Long Bennington** Lincs
16 A4 **Long Bredy** Dorset
84 C2 **Long Buckby** Nhants
8 B3 **Long Cause** Devon
117 J6 **Long Clawson** Leics
35 G7 **Long Common** Hants
114 D7 **Long Compton** Staffs
83 G8 **Long Compton** Warwks
67 G5 **Long Crendon** Bucks
17 J1 **Long Crichel** Dorset
50 F5 **Long Ditton** Surrey
143 H2 **Long Drax** N York
133 J5 **Long Duckmanton** Derbys
116 E5 **Long Eaton** Derbys
129 L5 **Long Green** Ches
81 J8 **Long Green** Worcs
66 B4 **Long Hanborough** Oxon
119 K2 **Long Hedges** Lincs
83 K2 **Long Itchington** Warwks
113 K8 **Long Lane** Wrekin
100 A8 **Long Lawford** Warwks
31 G6 **Long Load** Somset
67 L4 **Long Marston** Herts
151 H5 **Long Marston** N York
82 E5 **Long Marston** Warwks
166 F5 **Long Marton** Cumb
95 K7 **Long Meadow End** Shrops
89 H6 **Long Melford** Suffk
64 C8 **Long Newnton** Gloucs
212 B6 **Long Newton** E Loth
148 E4 **Long Preston** N York
153 H7 **Long Riston** E R Yk
140 D6 **Long Sight** Oldham
106 D5 **Long Stratton** Norfk
84 F5 **Long Street** M Keyn
35 M2 **Long Sutton** Hants
119 M7 **Long Sutton** Lincs
31 G6 **Long Sutton** Somset
89 K2 **Long Thurlow** Suffk
113 K8 **Long Waste** Wrekin
116 D6 **Long Whatton** Leics
66 E8 **Long Wittenham** Oxon
181 G5 **Longbenton** N Tyne
65 J1 **Longborough** Gloucs
98 C7 **Longbridge** Birm
83 G3 **Longbridge** Warwks
32 E3 **Longbridge Deverill** Wilts
177 J7 **Longburgh** Cumb
31 L8 **Longburton** Dorset
132 D8 **Longcliffe** Derbys
8 C3 **Longcombe** Devon

47 K1 **Longcot** Oxon
177 H7 **Longcroft** Cumb
50 C6 **Longcross** Surrey
95 K2 **Longden** Shrops
95 K2 **Longden Common** Shrops
115 H8 **Longdon** Staffs
81 J7 **Longdon** Worcs
98 D1 **Longdon Green** Staffs
81 J7 **Longdon Heath** Worcs
113 K8 **Longdon upon Tern** Wrekin
13 K4 **Longdown** Devon
3 J4 **Longdowns** Cnwll
52 D5 **Longfield** Kent
99 K6 **Longford** Covtry
115 L4 **Longford** Derbys
64 B3 **Longford** Gloucs
50 D4 **Longford** Gt Lon
38 D2 **Longford** Kent
113 L5 **Longford** Shrops
114 A7 **Longford** Wrekin
222 E1 **Longforgan** P & K
212 F7 **Longformacus** Border
191 G6 **Longframlington** Nthumb
17 L3 **Longham** Dorset
121 L8 **Longham** Norfk
257 L4 **Longhaven** Abers
191 J8 **Longhirst** Nthumb
63 K3 **Longhope** Gloucs
275 b6 **Longhope** Ork
191 H7 **Longhorsley** Nthumb
191 J3 **Longhoughton** Nthumb
165 J3 **Longlands** Cumb
115 L4 **Longlane** Derbys
64 B3 **Longlevens** Gloucs
141 G3 **Longley** Calder
141 J6 **Longley** Kirk
81 G5 **Longley Green** Worcs
233 L6 **Longleys** P & K
268 D4 **Longmanhill** Abers
36 B4 **Longmoor Camp** Hants
266 E4 **Longmorn** Moray
131 H5 **Longmoss** Ches
201 J7 **Longnewton** Border
169 K7 **Longnewton** S on T
63 M4 **Longney** Gloucs
212 A4 **Longniddry** E Loth
96 B3 **Longnor** Shrops
132 B6 **Longnor** Staffs
34 F2 **Longparish** Hants
178 A6 **Longpark** Cumb
147 M8 **Longridge** Lancs
114 E8 **Longridge** Staffs
210 C6 **Longridge** W Loth
209 L5 **Longriggend** N Lans
2 D5 **Longrock** Cnwll
114 F1 **Longsdon** Staffs
139 G7 **Longshaw** Wigan
269 J6 **Longside** Abers
113 L4 **Longslow** Shrops
87 H2 **Longstanton** Cambs
34 D3 **Longstock** Hants
55 K5 **Longstone** Pembks
86 F4 **Longstowe** Cambs
47 H8 **Longstreet** Wilts
102 D4 **Longthorpe** C Pete
166 B6 **Longthwaite** Cumb
114 E3 **Longton** C Stke
138 F3 **Longton** Lancs
177 L5 **Longtown** Cumb
62 C1 **Longtown** Herefs
9 e3 **Longueville** Jersey
96 C4 **Longville in the Dale** Shrops
67 J6 **Longwick** Bucks
180 C1 **Longwitton** Nthumb
175 J5 **Longwood** D & G
96 D2 **Longwood** Shrops
35 H6 **Longwood House** Hants
66 A7 **Longworth** Oxon
212 C6 **Longyester** E Loth
269 J4 **Lonmay** Abers
258 D7 **Lonmore** Highld
6 B4 **Looe** Cnwll
39 J3 **Loose** Kent
13 G2 **Loosebeare** Devon
119 K6 **Loosegate** Lincs
67 K7 **Loosley Row** Bucks
268 A5 **Lootcherbrae** Abers
34 B4 **Lopcombe Corner** Wilts
30 F8 **Lopen** Somset
113 G5 **Loppington** Shrops
190 E5 **Lorbottle** Nthumb
20 C5 **Lordington** W Susx
53 G6 **Lords Wood** Medway
104 B1 **Lordsbridge** Norfk
233 J6 **Lornty** P & K

116 C2 **Loscoe** Derbys
15 L3 **Loscombe** Dorset
266 E2 **Lossiemouth** Moray
113 K5 **Lostford** Shrops
130 D5 **Lostock Gralam** Ches
130 D5 **Lostock Green** Ches
139 H3 **Lostock Hall** Lancs
139 K6 **Lostock Hall Fold** Bolton
139 K6 **Lostock Junction** Bolton
5 J3 **Lostwithiel** Cnwll
274 C6 **Lothbeg** Highld
149 G6 **Lothersdale** N York
274 C6 **Lothmore** Highld
49 L1 **Loudwater** Bucks
116 F7 **Loughborough** Leics
57 G5 **Loughor** Swans
70 B7 **Loughton** Essex
85 G7 **Loughton** M Keyn
96 E6 **Loughton** Shrops
118 E7 **Lound** Lincs
134 D2 **Lound** Notts
107 K4 **Lound** Suffk
13 J7 **Lounston** Devon
116 C7 **Lount** Leics
136 F2 **Louth** Lincs
140 B2 **Love Clough** Lancs
19 M1 **Lovedean** Hants
34 B6 **Lover** Wilts
142 F8 **Loversall** Donc
70 F6 **Loves Green** Essex
160 E3 **Lovesome Hill** N York
55 J5 **Loveston** Pembks
31 K5 **Lovington** Somset
142 C4 **Low Ackworth** Wakefd
180 D2 **Low Angerton** Nthumb
172 C2 **Low Barbeth** D & G
136 A5 **Low Barlings** Lincs
162 C3 **Low Bell End** N York
148 A2 **Low Bentham** N York
157 K7 **Low Biggins** Cumb
157 K2 **Low Borrowbridge** Cumb
132 E2 **Low Bradfield** Sheff
149 H6 **Low Bradley** N York
166 A2 **Low Braithwaite** Cumb
143 K7 **Low Burnham** N Linc
191 J5 **Low Buston** Nthumb
151 L5 **Low Catton** E R Yk
169 H7 **Low Coniscliffe** Darltn
178 B7 **Low Crosby** Cumb
169 K8 **Low Dinsdale** Darltn
142 E3 **Low Eggborough** N York
160 B6 **Low Ellington** N York
181 G7 **Low Fell** Gatesd
208 D2 **Low Gartachorrans** Stirlg
179 L6 **Low Gate** Nthumb
178 C7 **Low Gettbridge** Cumb
150 B2 **Low Grantley** N York
150 B4 **Low Green** N York
97 H7 **Low Habberley** Worcs
30 F5 **Low Ham** Somset
150 C5 **Low Harrogate** N York
163 G1 **Low Hawsker** N York
166 B2 **Low Hesket** Cumb
97 J8 **Low Hill** Worcs
152 A2 **Low Hutton** N York
166 C6 **Low Knipe** Cumb
150 B3 **Low Laithe** N York
136 C4 **Low Langton** Lincs
131 K3 **Low Leighton** Derbys
164 F5 **Low Lorton** Cumb
134 F6 **Low Marnham** Notts
203 H6 **Low Middleton** Nthumb
161 L4 **Low Mill** N York
141 J2 **Low Moor** Brad
148 C7 **Low Moor** Lancs
169 J2 **Low Moorsley** Sundld
152 D2 **Low Mowthorpe** N York
156 F6 **Low Newton** Cumb
164 F5 **Low Rogerscales** Cumb
165 G2 **Low Row** Cumb
165 K3 **Low Row** Cumb
178 D6 **Low Row** Cumb
159 H3 **Low Row** N York
172 C2 **Low Salchrie** D & G
144 B5 **Low Santon** N Linc
123 G6 **Low Street** Norfk
52 E3 **Low Street** Thurr
106 D4 **Low Tharston** Norfk
210 D2 **Low Torry** Fife
136 E5 **Low Toynton** Lincs
142 B7 **Low Valley** Barns
169 G7 **Low Walworth** Darltn
156 E6 **Low Wood** Cumb
160 F1 **Low Worsall** N York
156 E2 **Low Wray** Cumb

63 M1 **Lowbands** Gloucs
164 C6 **Lowca** Cumb
117 H2 **Lowdham** Notts
113 H5 **Lowe** Shrops
131 K8 **Lowe Hill** Staffs
30 B4 **Lower Aisholt** Somset
16 E2 **Lower Ansty** Dorset
64 B2 **Lower Apperley** Gloucs
66 F3 **Lower Arncott** Oxon
13 K5 **Lower Ashton** Devon
49 H2 **Lower Assendon** Oxon
138 D2 **Lower Ballam** Lancs
79 M4 **Lower Barewood** Herefs
139 G1 **Lower Bartle** Lancs
48 F3 **Lower Basildon** W Berk
37 K5 **Lower Beeding** W Susx
101 L5 **Lower Benefield** Nhants
82 A2 **Lower Bentley** Worcs
97 H5 **Lower Beobridge** Shrops
116 D1 **Lower Birchwood** Derbys
83 L5 **Lower Boddington** Nhants
2 B4 **Lower Boscaswell** Cnwll
36 C2 **Lower Bourne** Surrey
83 H7 **Lower Brailes** Warwks
247 L4 **Lower Breakish** Highld
131 H2 **Lower Bredbury** Stockp
81 J4 **Lower Broadheath** Worcs
80 E8 **Lower Buckenhill** Herefs
80 C7 **Lower Bullingham** Herefs
33 K7 **Lower Burgate** Hants
14 B3 **Lower Burrowton** Devon
80 A4 **Lower Burton** Herefs
86 D6 **Lower Caldecote** Beds
63 L7 **Lower Cam** Gloucs
44 D7 **Lower Canada** N Som
83 M3 **Lower Catesby** Nhants
78 E8 **Lower Chapel** Powys
33 G5 **Lower Chicksgrove** Wilts
47 L8 **Lower Chute** Wilts
51 K2 **Lower Clapton** Gt Lon
97 L7 **Lower Clent** Worcs
82 E6 **Lower Clopton** Warwks
13 K2 **Lower Creedy** Devon
131 L4 **Lower Crossings** Derbys
141 K6 **Lower Cumberworth** Kirk
57 L3 **Lower Cwmtwrch** Powys
139 K3 **Lower Darwen** Bl w D
85 L2 **Lower Dean** Beds
141 K6 **Lower Denby** Kirk
260 C7 **Lower Diabaig** Highld
23 J5 **Lower Dicker** E Susx
95 L6 **Lower Dinchope** Shrops
95 H6 **Lower Down** Shrops
150 F3 **Lower Dunsforth** N York
80 E6 **Lower Egleton** Herefs
131 L8 **Lower Elkstone** Staffs
115 J3 **Lower Ellastone** Staffs
67 G5 **Lower End** Bucks
85 H7 **Lower End** M Keyn
85 H3 **Lower End** Nhants
47 J8 **Lower Everleigh** Wilts
19 G4 **Lower Exbury** Hants
41 J5 **Lower Eythorne** Kent
45 G4 **Lower Failand** N Som
35 L4 **Lower Farringdon** Hants
50 E4 **Lower Feltham** Gt Lon
21 G3 **Lower Fittleworth** W Susx
154 c6 **Lower Foxdale** IOM
112 E5 **Lower Frankton** Shrops
54 F4 **Lower Freystrop** Pembks
36 A2 **Lower Froyle** Hants
8 D1 **Lower Gabwell** Devon
263 G2 **Lower Gledfield** Highld
31 G2 **Lower Godney** Somset
97 L5 **Lower Gornal** Dudley
86 C8 **Lower Gravenhurst** Beds
86 D8 **Lower Green** Herts
87 J8 **Lower Green** Herts
38 E5 **Lower Green** Kent
39 G5 **Lower Green** Kent
84 F3 **Lower Green** Nhants
121 L4 **Lower Green** Norfk
97 K2 **Lower Green** Staffs
88 E2 **Lower Green** Suffk
139 L7 **Lower Green** Wigan
91 H4 **Lower Hacheston** Suffk
50 E5 **Lower Halliford** Surrey
15 M1 **Lower Halstock Leigh** Dorset
53 J5 **Lower Halstow** Kent
17 K4 **Lower Hamworthy** Poole
40 F5 **Lower Hardres** Kent
79 K3 **Lower Harpton** Herefs
85 H6 **Lower Hartlip** Kent
116 C1 **Lower Hartshay** Derbys
67 J4 **Lower Hartwell** Bucks

Lower Hatton - Maesmynis 333

114 C4 **Lower Hatton** Staffs
156 B5 **Lower Hawthwaite** Cumb
79 K4 **Lower Hergest** Herefs
66 C2 **Lower Heyford** Oxon
147 H4 **Lower Heysham** Lancs
52 F4 **Lower Higham** Kent
90 E8 **Lower Holbrook** Suffk
112 F5 **Lower Hordley** Shrops
21 G3 **Lower Horncroft** W Susx
141 J5 **Lower Houses** Kirk
81 H5 **Lower Howsell** Worcs
130 D1 **Lower Irlam** Salfd
116 C3 **Lower Kilburn** Derbys
46 A1 **Lower Kilcott** Gloucs
204 D7 **Lower Killeyan** Ag & B
16 A3 **Lower Kingcombe** Dorset
51 H8 **Lower Kingswood** Surrey
129 H7 **Lower Kinnerton** Ches
44 F6 **Lower Langford** N Som
223 G6 **Lower Largo** Fife
115 G4 **Lower Leigh** Staffs
82 F8 **Lower Lemington** Gloucs
78 C2 **Lower Llanfadog** Powys
27 J5 **Lower Lovacott** Devon
27 L3 **Lower Loxhore** Devon
63 H4 **Lower Lydbrook** Gloucs
79 M2 **Lower Lye** Herefs
43 K4 **Lower Machen** Newpt
62 D1 **Lower Maes-coed** Herefs
17 L2 **Lower Mannington** Dorset
32 C2 **Lower Marston** Somset
63 H6 **Lower Meend** Gloucs
30 B4 **Lower Merridge** Somset
83 L7 **Lower Middleton Cheney** Nhants
31 J2 **Lower Milton** Somset
82 A6 **Lower Moor** Worcs
63 J8 **Lower Morton** S Glos
69 K6 **Lower Nazeing** Essex
82 F3 **Lower Norton** Warwks
32 C6 **Lower Nyland** Dorset
43 J7 **Lower Penarth** V Glam
97 K4 **Lower Penn** Staffs
18 E5 **Lower Pennington** Hants
139 G2 **Lower Penwortham** Lancs
130 E5 **Lower Peover** Ches
140 D5 **Lower Place** Rochdl
67 H4 **Lower Pollicott** Bucks
82 E6 **Lower Quinton** Warwks
53 H5 **Lower Rainham** Medway
90 B7 **Lower Raydon** Suffk
29 J3 **Lower Roadwater** Somset
147 M3 **Lower Salter** Lancs
46 D3 **Lower Seagry** Wilts
70 C4 **Lower Sheering** Essex
85 K6 **Lower Shelton** Beds
49 J3 **Lower Shiplake** Oxon
83 L3 **Lower Shuckburgh** Warwks
65 H3 **Lower Slaughter** Gloucs
141 L3 **Lower Soothill** Kirk
63 K5 **Lower Soudley** Gloucs
41 H7 **Lower Standen** Kent
46 D3 **Lower Stanton St Quintin** Wilts
53 H4 **Lower Stoke** Medway
63 K8 **Lower Stone** Gloucs
98 D3 **Lower Stonnall** Staffs
105 K4 **Lower Stow Bedon** Norfk
17 G3 **Lower Street** Dorset
24 C5 **Lower Street** E Susx
122 F4 **Lower Street** Norfk
88 F5 **Lower Street** Suffk
90 D5 **Lower Street** Suffk
130 C3 **Lower Stretton** Warrtn
15 K3 **Lower Stroud** Dorset
68 D2 **Lower Sundon** Beds
19 H2 **Lower Swanwick** Hants
65 H2 **Lower Swell** Gloucs
83 J7 **Lower Tadmarton** Oxon
14 C2 **Lower Tale** Devon
115 G4 **Lower Tean** Staffs
107 J3 **Lower Thurlton** Norfk
3 G5 **Lower Town** Cnwll
13 G7 **Lower Town** Devon
80 E6 **Lower Town** Herefs
74 F5 **Lower Town** Pembks
11 L7 **Lower Trebullett** Cnwll
6 D4 **Lower Tregantle** Cnwll
3 K4 **Lower Treluswell** Cnwll
83 H6 **Lower Tysoe** Warwks
91 G5 **Lower Ufford** Suffk
13 K6 **Lower Upcott** Devon
35 H7 **Lower Upham** Hants
53 G5 **Lower Upnor** Medway
29 L4 **Lower Vexford** Somset
130 B3 **Lower Walton** Warrtn
16 E3 **Lower Waterston** Dorset
44 E8 **Lower Weare** Somset
84 C3 **Lower Weedon** Nhants
79 K5 **Lower Welson** Herefs
81 L7 **Lower Westmancote** Worcs
17 G2 **Lower Whatcombe** Dorset
32 B2 **Lower Whatley** Somset
130 B4 **Lower Whitley** Ches
63 L7 **Lower Wick** Gloucs
81 J5 **Lower Wick** Worcs
35 K3 **Lower Wield** Hants
23 K6 **Lower Willingdon** E Susx
130 F5 **Lower Withington** Ches
49 K2 **Lower Woodend** Bucks
33 K4 **Lower Woodford** Wilts
16 A2 **Lower Wraxhall** Dorset
81 H6 **Lower Wyche** Worcs
141 J3 **Lower Wyke** Brad
140 B1 **Lowerhouse** Lancs
100 F2 **Lowesby** Leics
107 L5 **Lowestoft** Suffk
164 F6 **Loweswater** Cumb
37 L3 **Lowfield Heath** W Susx
157 K3 **Lowgill** Cumb
148 A3 **Lowgill** Lancs
156 D5 **Lowick** Cumb
101 L7 **Lowick** Nhants
203 G5 **Lowick** Nthumb
156 D5 **Lowick Bridge** Cumb
156 D5 **Lowick Green** Cumb
168 E5 **Lowlands** Dur
62 C7 **Lowlands** Torfn
82 E2 **Lowsonford** Warwks
166 D6 **Lowther** Cumb
166 C6 **Lowther Castle** Cumb
153 H4 **Lowthorpe** E R Yk
12 F2 **Lowton** Devon
30 B7 **Lowton** Somset
139 J8 **Lowton** Wigan
139 J8 **Lowton Common** Wigan
139 J8 **Lowton St Mary's** Wigan
29 G7 **Loxbeare** Devon
36 F3 **Loxhill** Surrey
27 L3 **Loxhore** Devon
27 L3 **Loxhore Cott** Devon
83 G4 **Loxley** Warwks
115 H5 **Loxley Green** Staffs
81 G7 **Loxter** Herefs
44 D7 **Loxton** N Som
36 F4 **Loxwood** W Susx
277 L7 **Loyal Lodge** Highld
100 F6 **Lubenham** Leics
50 B7 **Lucas Green** Surrey
119 M2 **Lucasgate** Lincs
29 G2 **Luccombe** Somset
19 K7 **Luccombe Village** IOW
203 J7 **Lucker** Nthumb
11 M7 **Luckett** Cnwll
89 G8 **Lucking Street** Essex
46 B2 **Luckington** Wilts
46 B4 **Lucknam** Wilts
28 F3 **Luckwell Bridge** Somset
80 B2 **Lucton** Herefs
169 G8 **Lucy Cross** N York
283 c12 **Ludag** W Isls
145 H8 **Ludborough** Lincs
7 J4 **Ludbrook** Devon
55 K4 **Ludchurch** Pembks
141 G3 **Luddenden** Calder
140 F3 **Luddenden Foot** Calder
40 C3 **Luddenham Court** Kent
52 E5 **Luddesdown** Kent
143 L4 **Luddington** N Linc
82 E5 **Luddington** Warwks
102 C6 **Luddington in the Brook** Nhants
136 D2 **Ludford** Lincs
96 C8 **Ludford** Shrops
67 G4 **Ludgershall** Bucks
34 B1 **Ludgershall** Wilts
2 D4 **Ludgvan** Cnwll
123 H7 **Ludham** Norfk
96 C8 **Ludlow** Shrops
30 F8 **Ludney** Somset
32 F6 **Ludwell** Wilts
169 K2 **Ludworth** Dur
69 J1 **Luffenhall** Herts
11 L4 **Luffincott** Devon
212 B3 **Luffness** E Loth
197 H6 **Lugar** E Ayrs
80 B3 **Lugg Green** Herefs
212 D4 **Luggate Burn** E Loth
209 K4 **Luggiebank** N Lans
129 M3 **Lugsdale** Halton
208 C8 **Lugton** E Ayrs
80 D7 **Lugwardine** Herefs
247 J3 **Luib** Highld
80 A7 **Lulham** Herefs
99 H1 **Lullington** Derbys
23 J6 **Lullington** E Susx
45 M8 **Lullington** Somset
45 G6 **Lulsgate Bottom** N Som
81 G4 **Lulsley** Worcs
16 F6 **Lulworth Camp** Dorset
140 F3 **Lumb** Calder
140 C3 **Lumb** Lancs
140 E3 **Lumbutts** Calder
142 D2 **Lumby** N York
209 H5 **Lumloch** E Duns
244 D3 **Lumphanan** Abers
222 B8 **Lumphinnans** Fife
255 K7 **Lumsden** Abers
235 H5 **Lunan** Angus
234 D5 **Lunanhead** Angus
221 K1 **Luncarty** P & K
152 E6 **Lund** E R Yk
143 G1 **Lund** N York
233 L8 **Lundie** Angus
220 C6 **Lundie** Stirlg
223 G6 **Lundin Links** Fife
223 G6 **Lundin Mill** Fife
106 E5 **Lundy Green** Norfk
281 e4 **Lunna** Shet
52 F7 **Lunsford** Kent
24 C5 **Lunsford's Cross** E Susx
138 D7 **Lunt** Sefton
79 M4 **Luntley** Herefs
14 E1 **Luppitt** Devon
7 L4 **Lupridge** Devon
141 M4 **Lupset** Wakefd
157 J6 **Lupton** Cumb
36 D5 **Lurgashall** W Susx
29 G7 **Lurley** Devon
136 F6 **Lusby** Lincs
8 B3 **Luscombe** Devon
7 H5 **Luson** Devon
218 E8 **Luss** Ag & B
258 D5 **Lusta** Highld
13 H6 **Lustleigh** Devon
80 B3 **Luston** Herefs
235 G2 **Luthermuir** Abers
222 E3 **Luthrie** Fife
97 L6 **Lutley** Dudley
14 C2 **Luton** Devon
13 L7 **Luton** Devon
68 E3 **Luton** Luton
53 G5 **Luton** Medway
100 C6 **Lutterworth** Leics
7 H3 **Lutton** Devon
7 K3 **Lutton** Devon
119 M6 **Lutton** Lincs
102 C6 **Lutton** Nhants
29 H3 **Luxborough** Somset
5 H3 **Luxulyan** Cnwll
140 E7 **Luzley** Tamesd
275 H1 **Lybster** Highld
95 J6 **Lydbury North** Shrops
28 B4 **Lydcott** Devon
25 K3 **Lydd** Kent
41 H6 **Lydden** Kent
41 K2 **Lydden** Kent
101 J4 **Lyddington** Rutlnd
49 H7 **Lyde Green** Hants
29 L4 **Lydeard St Lawrence** Somset
46 F7 **Lydeway** Wilts
12 C5 **Lydford** Devon
31 J5 **Lydford on Fosse** Somset
140 D3 **Lydgate** Calder
140 E4 **Lydgate** Rochdl
95 H5 **Lydham** Shrops
47 G2 **Lydiard Green** Wilts
47 G2 **Lydiard Millicent** Wilts
47 G2 **Lydiard Tregoze** Swindn
138 D7 **Lydiate** Sefton
98 B8 **Lydiate Ash** Worcs
32 B8 **Lydlinch** Dorset
63 J6 **Lydney** Gloucs
55 J7 **Lydstep** Pembks
97 L6 **Lye** Dudley
44 F6 **Lye Cross** N Som
68 B6 **Lye Green** Bucks
38 D6 **Lye Green** E Susx
82 E2 **Lye Green** Warwks
97 G8 **Lye Head** Worcs
32 D2 **Lye's Green** Wilts
66 B8 **Lyford** Oxon
40 F6 **Lymbridge Green** Kent
15 H4 **Lyme Regis** Dorset
40 F7 **Lyminge** Kent
18 E4 **Lymington** Hants
21 H6 **Lyminster** W Susx
130 D2 **Lymm** Warrtn
40 F8 **Lympne** Kent
44 C8 **Lympsham** Somset
14 A5 **Lympstone** Devon
28 C1 **Lynbridge** Devon
28 F2 **Lynch** Somset
106 C2 **Lynch Green** Norfk
241 L3 **Lynchat** Highld
18 D2 **Lyndhurst** Hants
101 K3 **Lyndon** Rutlnd
98 F6 **Lyndon Green** Birm
199 L5 **Lyne** Border
50 C5 **Lyne** Surrey
63 J1 **Lyne Down** Herefs
245 G2 **Lyne of Skene** Abers
113 G5 **Lyneal** Shrops
13 K6 **Lyneham** Devon
65 K3 **Lyneham** Oxon
46 F3 **Lyneham** Wilts
178 C4 **Lyneholmford** Cumb
191 K7 **Lynemouth** Nthumb
275 b6 **Lyness** Ork
122 B7 **Lyng** Norfk
30 E5 **Lyng** Somset
79 K4 **Lynhales** Herefs
28 C1 **Lynmouth** Devon
98 D3 **Lynn** Staffs
114 B8 **Lynn** Wrekin
254 E6 **Lynn of Shenval** Moray
40 B3 **Lynsted** Kent
11 H2 **Lynstone** Cnwll
28 C1 **Lynton** Devon
16 C2 **Lyon's Gate** Dorset
79 L4 **Lyonshall** Herefs
17 J3 **Lytchett Matravers** Dorset
17 J4 **Lytchett Minster** Dorset
280 C4 **Lyth** Highld
138 D2 **Lytham** Lancs
138 D2 **Lytham St Anne's** Lancs
95 L2 **Lythbank** Shrops
171 K8 **Lythe** N York
279 J3 **Lythmore** Highld

M

3 J4 **Mabe Burnthouse** Cnwll
176 C5 **Mabie** D & G
137 J3 **Mablethorpe** Lincs
131 H5 **Macclesfield** Ches
268 C3 **Macduff** Abers
192 E6 **Macharioch** Ag & B
43 K4 **Machen** Caerph
194 D4 **Machrie** N Ayrs
192 D4 **Machrihanish** Ag & B
214 D5 **Machrins** Ag & B
93 G3 **Machynlleth** Powys
56 F5 **Machynys** Carmth
116 A4 **Mackworth** Derbys
211 M4 **Macmerry** E Loth
12 D4 **Maddaford** Devon
221 G3 **Madderty** P & K
33 J2 **Maddington** Wilts
210 B4 **Maddiston** Falk
21 G5 **Madehurst** W Susx
114 B3 **Madeley** Staffs
96 F3 **Madeley** Wrekin
114 B2 **Madeley Heath** Staffs
29 L8 **Madford** Devon
87 H3 **Madingley** Cambs
80 A7 **Madley** Herefs
81 J5 **Madresfield** Worcs
2 C5 **Madron** Cnwll
76 C3 **Maen-y-groes** Cerdgn
125 H3 **Maenaddwyn** IOA
126 F6 **Maenan** Conwy
75 J6 **Maenclochog** Pembks
42 F6 **Maendy** V Glam
3 K5 **Maenporth** Cnwll
110 C3 **Maentwrog** Gwynd
11 H1 **Maer** Cnwll
114 B4 **Maer** Staffs
59 J3 **Maerdy** Carmth
42 E2 **Maerdy** Rhondd
44 C2 **Maes-glas** Newpt
112 D7 **Maesbrook** Shrops
112 D6 **Maesbury** Shrops
112 D6 **Maesbury Marsh** Shrops
55 L2 **Maesgwynne** Carmth
128 E7 **Maeshafn** Denbgs
76 C6 **Maesllyn** Cerdgn
78 D6 **Maesmynis** Powys
78 E5 **Maesmynis** Powys

42 C3 **Maesteg** Brdgnd
59 G5 **Maesybont** Carmth
43 J3 **Maesycwmmer** Caerph
70 D5 **Magdalen Laver** Essex
254 F3 **Maggieknockater** Moray
70 C2 **Maggots End** Essex
23 K5 **Magham Down** E Susx
138 D7 **Maghull** Sefton
44 E2 **Magor** Mons
32 D3 **Maiden Bradley** Wilts
45 H5 **Maiden Head** N Som
168 F1 **Maiden Law** Dur
16 B3 **Maiden Newton** Dorset
55 G7 **Maiden Wells** Pembks
37 L4 **Maidenbower** W Susx
8 D1 **Maidencombe** Torbay
15 G3 **Maidenhayne** Devon
49 L3 **Maidenhead** W & M
182 F1 **Maidens** S Ayrs
49 L4 **Maidens Green** Br For
136 F4 **Maidenwell** Lincs
84 B5 **Maidford** Nhants
84 D8 **Maids Moreton** Bucks
39 J2 **Maidstone** Kent
101 G8 **Maidwell** Nhants
44 C1 **Maindee** Newpt
234 D3 **Mains of Balhall** Angus
244 E8 **Mains of Balnakettle** Abers
254 B5 **Mains of Dalvey** Highld
235 H1 **Mains of Haulkerton** Abers
169 J4 **Mainsforth** Dur
176 B7 **Mainsriddle** D & G
95 G6 **Mainstone** Shrops
64 A3 **Maisemore** Gloucs
98 E7 **Major's Green** Worcs
116 B3 **Makeney** Derbys
7 K7 **Malborough** Devon
131 L3 **Malcoff** Derbys
51 G5 **Malden** Surrey
50 F6 **Malden Rushett** Gt Lon
71 K5 **Maldon** Essex
148 F3 **Malham** N York
237 K1 **Mallaig** Highld
237 K1 **Mallaigvaig** Highld
211 G6 **Malleny Mills** C Edin
70 C2 **Mallows Green** Essex
125 G6 **Malltraeth** IOA
93 J1 **Mallwyd** Gwynd
46 D2 **Malmesbury** Wilts
28 D1 **Malmsmead** Somset
113 H2 **Malpas** Ches
4 D6 **Malpas** Cnwll
44 C1 **Malpas** Newpt
63 L2 **Malswick** Gloucs
136 F3 **Maltby** Lincs
133 K1 **Maltby** Rothm
170 B8 **Maltby** S on T
137 J3 **Maltby le Marsh** Lincs
72 E3 **Malting Green** Essex
40 B6 **Maltman's Hill** Kent
152 B2 **Malton** N York
81 H5 **Malvern Link** Worcs
81 H6 **Malvern Wells** Worcs
173 K4 **Malzie** D & G
80 F1 **Mamble** Worcs
62 C6 **Mamhilad** Mons
3 J6 **Manaccan** Cnwll
94 D3 **Manafon** Powys
282 e6 **Manais** W Isls
13 H6 **Manaton** Devon
137 G2 **Manby** Lincs
99 J4 **Mancetter** Warwks
140 C8 **Manchester** Manch
129 H6 **Mancot** Flints
240 A3 **Mandally** Highld
103 K5 **Manea** Cambs
98 E4 **Maney** Birm
169 G8 **Manfield** N York
15 L3 **Mangerton** Dorset
45 K4 **Mangotsfield** S Glos
68 E2 **Mangrove Green** Herts
3 H5 **Manhay** Cnwll
282 e6 **Manish** W Isls
140 E3 **Mankinholes** Calder
129 L5 **Manley** Ches
61 J6 **Manmoel** Caerph
224 C7 **Mannel** Ag & B
37 K5 **Manning's Heath** W Susx
47 H7 **Manningford Bohune** Wilts
47 H7 **Manningford Bruce** Wilts
141 J1 **Manningham** Brad
17 L2 **Mannington** Dorset
73 G1 **Manningtree** Essex
245 K3 **Mannofield** C Aber
51 L2 **Manor Park** Gt Lon

55 H7 **Manorbier** Pembks
55 H6 **Manorbier Newton** Pembks
59 J4 **Manordeilo** Carmth
201 K6 **Manorhill** Border
74 F5 **Manorowen** Pembks
79 M6 **Mansell Gamage** Herefs
80 A6 **Mansell Lacy** Herefs
157 K6 **Mansergh** Cumb
197 J8 **Mansfield** E Ayrs
133 K7 **Mansfield** Notts
133 L7 **Mansfield Woodhouse** Notts
156 D6 **Mansriggs** Cumb
32 D7 **Manston** Dorset
41 K2 **Manston** Kent
142 B1 **Manston** Leeds
17 J1 **Manswood** Dorset
118 B4 **Manthorpe** Lincs
118 E8 **Manthorpe** Lincs
144 A7 **Manton** N Linc
134 C4 **Manton** Notts
101 J3 **Manton** Rutlnd
47 H5 **Manton** Wilts
70 C2 **Manuden** Essex
70 E4 **Manwood Green** Essex
31 L5 **Maperton** Somset
68 C8 **Maple Cross** Herts
134 E7 **Maplebeck** Notts
49 G4 **Mapledurham** Oxon
49 G8 **Mapledurwell** Hants
37 J6 **Maplehurst** W Susx
52 C6 **Maplescombe** Kent
115 K2 **Mapleton** Derbys
38 C3 **Mapleton** Kent
116 D3 **Mapperley** Derbys
117 G3 **Mapperley Park** C Nott
15 L3 **Mapperton** Dorset
82 C2 **Mappleborough Green** Warwks
153 K7 **Mappleton** E R Yk
141 M5 **Mapplewell** Barns
16 E1 **Mappowder** Dorset
4 C5 **Marazanvose** Cnwll
2 E5 **Marazion** Cnwll
113 J2 **Marbury** Ches
103 J4 **March** Cambs
186 E3 **March** S Lans
66 C7 **Marcham** Oxon
113 K5 **Marchamley** Shrops
113 K5 **Marchamley Wood** Shrops
115 J5 **Marchington** Staffs
115 J6 **Marchington Woodlands** Staffs
108 E6 **Marchros** Gwynd
112 E2 **Marchwiel** Wrexhm
18 F2 **Marchwood** Hants
42 D7 **Marcross** V Glam
80 C6 **Marden** Herefs
39 J4 **Marden** Kent
47 G7 **Marden** Wilts
70 E6 **Marden Ash** Essex
39 J5 **Marden Beech** Kent
39 J5 **Marden Thorn** Kent
38 D7 **Mardens Hill** E Susx
69 H3 **Mardlebury** Herts
62 C4 **Mardy** Mons
101 G2 **Marefield** Leics
136 E7 **Mareham le Fen** Lincs
136 E6 **Mareham on the Hill** Lincs
116 C2 **Marehay** Derbys
21 H3 **Marehill** W Susx
23 G2 **Maresfield** E Susx
144 F2 **Marfleet** C KuH
129 H8 **Marford** Wrexhm
57 L7 **Margam** Neath
32 D7 **Margaret Marsh** Dorset
70 F5 **Margaret Roding** Essex
71 G6 **Margaretting** Essex
71 G7 **Margaretting Tye** Essex
41 K1 **Margate** Kent
195 G4 **Margnaheglish** N Ayrs
174 F5 **Margrie** D & G
170 F7 **Margrove Park** R & Cl
104 E2 **Marham** Norfk
11 J2 **Marhamchurch** Cnwll
102 C3 **Marholm** C Pete
125 J3 **Marian-glas** IOA
28 C6 **Mariansleigh** Devon
53 K4 **Marine Town** Kent
244 F2 **Marionburgh** Abers
259 H4 **Marishader** Highld
6 F2 **Maristow** Devon
176 E2 **Marjoriebanks** D & G
30 E1 **Mark** Somset
30 E2 **Mark Causeway** Somset
38 F7 **Mark Cross** E Susx

19 H5 **Mark's Corner** IOW
38 D5 **Markbeech** Kent
137 J4 **Markby** Lincs
116 B4 **Markeaton** C Derb
99 L3 **Market Bosworth** Leics
102 C2 **Market Deeping** Lincs
113 L5 **Market Drayton** Shrops
100 F6 **Market Harborough** Leics
46 E8 **Market Lavington** Wilts
118 A8 **Market Overton** Rutlnd
136 B2 **Market Rasen** Lincs
136 D4 **Market Stainton** Lincs
152 D7 **Market Weighton** E R Yk
105 K7 **Market Weston** Suffk
100 B2 **Markfield** Leics
61 J6 **Markham** Caerph
134 E5 **Markham Moor** Notts
222 E6 **Markinch** Fife
150 C3 **Markington** N York
212 C3 **Markle** E Loth
72 C2 **Marks Tey** Essex
45 K6 **Marksbury** BaNES
6 D3 **Markwell** Cnwll
68 D4 **Markyate** Herts
81 H7 **Marl Bank** Worcs
47 J5 **Marlborough** Wilts
80 C4 **Marlbrook** Herefs
98 B8 **Marlbrook** Worcs
82 C5 **Marlcliff** Warwks
8 C2 **Marldon** Devon
23 K4 **Marle Green** E Susx
91 H3 **Marlesford** Suffk
41 G5 **Marley** Kent
41 K4 **Marley** Kent
113 J2 **Marley Green** Ches
180 F7 **Marley Hill** Gatesd
106 C2 **Marlingford** Norfk
54 C5 **Marloes** Pembks
49 K2 **Marlow** Bucks
95 K8 **Marlow** Herefs
49 K1 **Marlow Bottom** Bucks
38 C4 **Marlpit Hill** Kent
38 C7 **Marlpits** E Susx
24 C4 **Marlpits** E Susx
116 D3 **Marlpool** Derbys
32 C7 **Marnhull** Dorset
131 J2 **Marple** Stockp
131 J2 **Marple Bridge** Stockp
142 E6 **Marr** Donc
159 K3 **Marrick** N York
55 L5 **Marros** Carmth
141 G5 **Marsden** Kirk
181 K6 **Marsden** S Tyne
148 F8 **Marsden Height** Lancs
158 F5 **Marsett** N York
149 J8 **Marsh** Brad
67 K5 **Marsh** Bucks
30 C8 **Marsh** Devon
66 E7 **Marsh Baldon** Oxon
48 B5 **Marsh Benham** W Berk
145 K7 **Marsh Chapel** Lincs
66 F3 **Marsh Gibbon** Bucks
14 B4 **Marsh Green** Devon
38 C4 **Marsh Green** Kent
131 H7 **Marsh Green** Staffs
113 K8 **Marsh Green** Wrekin
133 H4 **Marsh Lane** Derbys
63 H5 **Marsh Lane** Gloucs
29 H2 **Marsh Street** Somset
68 F4 **Marshall's Heath** Herts
68 F5 **Marshalswick** Herts
122 D6 **Marsham** Norfk
41 J4 **Marshborough** Kent
95 K5 **Marshbrook** Shrops
43 L5 **Marshfield** Newpt
45 M4 **Marshfield** S Glos
11 G4 **Marshgate** Cnwll
103 L2 **Marshland St James** Norfk
138 D4 **Marshside** Sefton
15 J3 **Marshwood** Dorset
159 K3 **Marske** N York
170 E6 **Marske-by-the-Sea** R & Cl
139 K7 **Marsland Green** Wigan
130 D5 **Marston** Ches
79 L4 **Marston** Herefs
118 A3 **Marston** Lincs
66 D5 **Marston** Oxon
97 J1 **Marston** Staffs
114 E6 **Marston** Staffs
99 G4 **Marston** Warwks
46 D7 **Marston** Wilts
98 F6 **Marston Green** Solhll
99 K5 **Marston Jabbet** Warwks
31 K6 **Marston Magna** Somset
65 H7 **Marston Meysey** Wilts

115 J4 **Marston Montgomery** Derbys
85 K7 **Marston Moretaine** Beds
115 L5 **Marston on Dove** Derbys
83 M6 **Marston St Lawrence** Nhants
80 D4 **Marston Stannett** Herefs
100 F6 **Marston Trussell** Nhants
63 H3 **Marstow** Herefs
68 A4 **Marsworth** Bucks
47 L7 **Marten** Wilts
130 F4 **Marthall** Ches
123 J7 **Martham** Norfk
33 J7 **Martin** Hants
41 K6 **Martin** Kent
136 B7 **Martin** Lincs
136 D6 **Martin** Lincs
136 C7 **Martin Dales** Lincs
33 H6 **Martin Drove End** Hants
81 K3 **Martin Hussingtree** Worcs
166 B6 **Martindale** Cumb
28 B1 **Martinhoe** Devon
130 C2 **Martinscroft** Warrtn
16 C5 **Martinstown** Dorset
90 F6 **Martlesham** Suffk
90 F6 **Martlesham Heath** Suffk
55 H5 **Martletwy** Pembks
81 H3 **Martley** Worcs
31 G7 **Martock** Somset
130 C6 **Marton** Ches
131 G6 **Marton** Ches
156 C7 **Marton** Cumb
153 J7 **Marton** E R Yk
153 K2 **Marton** E R Yk
135 G3 **Marton** Lincs
170 C7 **Marton** Middsb
150 F3 **Marton** N York
162 C6 **Marton** N York
95 G3 **Marton** Shrops
83 J2 **Marton** Warwks
150 E2 **Marton-le-Moor** N York
35 G4 **Martyr Worthy** Hants
50 E7 **Martyr's Green** Surrey
275 b3 **Marwick** Ork
27 K3 **Marwood** Devon
12 C6 **Mary Tavy** Devon
250 E1 **Marybank** Highld
262 F8 **Maryburgh** Highld
245 J4 **Maryculter** Abers
213 H7 **Marygold** Border
256 E3 **Maryhill** Abers
208 F5 **Maryhill** C Glas
235 H2 **Marykirk** Abers
63 G6 **Maryland** Mons
51 H3 **Marylebone** Gt Lon
139 H6 **Marylebone** Wigan
254 D4 **Marypark** Moray
164 D3 **Maryport** Cumb
172 E7 **Maryport** D & G
12 B6 **Marystow** Devon
235 H4 **Maryton** Angus
244 D4 **Marywell** Abers
245 L4 **Marywell** Abers
235 G6 **Marywell** Angus
160 B6 **Masham** N York
71 G5 **Mashbury** Essex
180 F4 **Mason** N u Ty
157 L7 **Masongill** N York
133 J4 **Mastin Moor** Derbys
70 D5 **Matching** Essex
70 D5 **Matching Green** Essex
70 D5 **Matching Tye** Essex
180 C4 **Matfen** Nthumb
39 G5 **Matfield** Kent
45 G1 **Mathern** Mons
81 G6 **Mathon** Herefs
74 E6 **Mathry** Pembks
122 C4 **Matlask** Norfk
132 F7 **Matlock** Derbys
132 F7 **Matlock Bank** Derbys
132 F8 **Matlock Bath** Derbys
132 F7 **Matlock Dale** Derbys
64 B4 **Matson** Gloucs
165 L6 **Matterdale End** Cumb
134 D2 **Mattersey** Notts
134 D2 **Mattersey Thorpe** Notts
49 H7 **Mattingley** Hants
105 L1 **Mattishall** Norfk
105 L1 **Mattishall Burgh** Norfk
196 F5 **Mauchline** E Ayrs
269 G6 **Maud** Abers
9 e2 **Maufant** Jersey
65 J2 **Maugersbury** Gloucs
154 g4 **Maughold** IOM
250 C4 **Mauld** Highld
85 L7 **Maulden** Beds
166 E7 **Maulds Meaburn** Cumb

160 E5 **Maunby** N York
80 D5 **Maund Bryan** Herefs
29 J5 **Maundown** Somset
107 K1 **Mautby** Norfk
115 H8 **Mavesyn Ridware** Staffs
137 G6 **Mavis Enderby** Lincs
130 D8 **Maw Green** Ches
164 E1 **Mawbray** Cumb
139 G5 **Mawdesley** Lancs
42 B5 **Mawdlam** Brdgnd
3 H6 **Mawgan** Cnwll
3 H6 **Mawgan Cross** Cnwll
4 D2 **Mawgan Porth** Cnwll
4 A5 **Mawla** Cnwll
3 K5 **Mawnan** Cnwll
3 K5 **Mawnan Smith** Cnwll
137 J5 **Mawthorpe** Lincs
102 C2 **Maxey** C Pete
99 G6 **Maxstoke** Warwks
40 F6 **Maxted Street** Kent
201 J7 **Maxton** Border
41 J7 **Maxton** Kent
176 C4 **Maxwell Town** D & G
11 J4 **Maxworthy** Cnwll
114 D2 **May Bank** Staffs
49 H3 **May's Green** Oxon
50 E7 **May's Green** Surrey
57 H6 **Mayals** Swans
183 H1 **Maybole** S Ayrs
50 C7 **Maybury** Surrey
37 H3 **Mayes Green** Surrey
23 K2 **Mayfield** E Susx
211 K6 **Mayfield** Mdloth
115 J2 **Mayfield** Staffs
50 C7 **Mayford** Surrey
72 D6 **Mayland** Essex
72 C6 **Maylandsea** Essex
23 K3 **Maynard's Green** E Susx
98 D7 **Maypole** Birm
41 G2 **Maypole** Kent
62 F4 **Maypole** Mons
107 J4 **Maypole Green** Norfk
89 J3 **Maypole Green** Suffk
91 G2 **Maypole Green** Suffk
26 C7 **Mead** Devon
45 K7 **Meadgate** BaNES
67 K6 **Meadle** Bucks
169 H3 **Meadowfield** Dur
95 H3 **Meadowtown** Shrops
12 A6 **Meadwell** Devon
157 H4 **Meal Bank** Cumb
164 F2 **Mealrigg** Cumb
165 H2 **Mealsgate** Cumb
150 C8 **Meanwood** Leeds
148 E4 **Mearbeck** N York
31 G3 **Meare** Somset
30 E5 **Meare Green** Somset
30 D6 **Meare Green** Somset
208 F7 **Mearns** E Rens
85 G2 **Mears Ashby** Nhants
99 J1 **Measham** Leics
156 F6 **Meathop** Cumb
153 H7 **Meaux** E R Yk
7 G2 **Meavy** Devon
101 H5 **Medbourne** Leics
26 D7 **Meddon** Devon
134 B5 **Meden Vale** Notts
136 F8 **Medlam** Lincs
147 H8 **Medlar** Lancs
49 K2 **Medmenham** Bucks
180 D7 **Medomsley** Dur
35 K3 **Medstead** Hants
79 L5 **Meer Common** Herefs
131 K7 **Meerbrook** Staffs
70 B1 **Meesden** Herts
113 L7 **Meeson** Wrekin
12 D1 **Meeth** Devon
88 E4 **Meeting Green** Suffk
122 F6 **Meeting House Hill** Norfk
58 B5 **Meidrim** Carmth
94 E1 **Meifod** Powys
233 L6 **Meigle** P & K
186 A3 **Meikle Carco** D & G
209 J8 **Meikle Earnock** S Lans
207 G6 **Meikle Kilmory** Ag & B
232 F7 **Meikle Obney** P & K
256 C5 **Meikle Wartle** Abers
233 J7 **Meikleour** P & K
56 E3 **Meinciau** Carmth
114 E3 **Meir** C Stke
114 E3 **Meir Heath** Staffs
87 H6 **Melbourn** Cambs
116 C6 **Melbourne** Derbys
152 A7 **Melbourne** E R Yk
26 F7 **Melbury** Devon

32 E6 **Melbury Abbas** Dorset
16 B1 **Melbury Bubb** Dorset
16 A1 **Melbury Osmond** Dorset
16 A2 **Melbury Sampford** Dorset
85 K2 **Melchbourne** Beds
16 E2 **Melcombe Bingham** Dorset
12 D4 **Meldon** Devon
180 D2 **Meldon** Nthumb
180 D2 **Meldon Park** Nthumb
87 H6 **Meldreth** Cambs
220 C7 **Meldrum** Stirlg
4 F4 **Meledor** Cnwll
216 C4 **Melfort** Ag & B
234 E4 **Melgund Castle** Angus
128 C3 **Meliden** Denbgs
60 B6 **Melin Court** Neath
93 H4 **Melin-byrhedyn** Powys
127 G7 **Melin-y-coed** Conwy
94 D2 **Melin-y-ddol** Powys
111 K2 **Melin-y-wig** Denbgs
55 K4 **Melinau** Pembks
166 D5 **Melkinthorpe** Cumb
179 G6 **Melkridge** Nthumb
46 C6 **Melksham** Wilts
48 C3 **Mell Green** W Berk
3 H5 **Mellangoose** Cnwll
166 B2 **Mellguards** Cumb
147 M2 **Melling** Lancs
138 E7 **Melling** Sefton
138 E7 **Melling Mount** Sefton
95 G5 **Mellington** Powys
106 B8 **Mellis** Suffk
260 D2 **Mellon Charles** Highld
260 E1 **Mellon Udrigle** Highld
139 K2 **Mellor** Lancs
131 K2 **Mellor** Stockp
139 J2 **Mellor Brook** Lancs
32 B1 **Mells** Somset
107 H8 **Mells** Suffk
166 E3 **Melmerby** Cumb
159 K5 **Melmerby** N York
160 E7 **Melmerby** N York
277 K4 **Melness** Highld
89 G4 **Melon Green** Suffk
15 L3 **Melplash** Dorset
201 H6 **Melrose** Border
275 b6 **Melsetter** Ork
160 B1 **Melsonby** N York
141 H5 **Meltham** Kirk
141 H5 **Meltham Mills** Kirk
144 B3 **Melton** E R Yk
91 G5 **Melton** Suffk
122 A5 **Melton Constable** Norfk
117 K7 **Melton Mowbray** Leics
144 D5 **Melton Ross** N Linc
152 B5 **Meltonby** E R Yk
260 B3 **Melvaig** Highld
112 E8 **Melverley** Shrops
112 E7 **Melverley Green** Shrops
278 E3 **Melvich** Highld
15 G2 **Membury** Devon
269 H4 **Memsie** Abers
234 C4 **Memus** Angus
5 J4 **Menabilly** Cnwll
4 B5 **Menagissey** Cnwll
125 K5 **Menai Bridge** IOA
106 F6 **Mendham** Suffk
90 D2 **Mendlesham** Suffk
90 C3 **Mendlesham Green** Suffk
6 B2 **Menheniot** Cnwll
81 G2 **Menithwood** Worcs
185 K2 **Mennock** D & G
149 L7 **Menston** Brad
220 E7 **Menstrie** Clacks
143 H1 **Menthorpe** N York
67 M3 **Mentmore** Bucks
238 C6 **Meoble** Highld
96 B1 **Meole Brace** Shrops
35 J7 **Meonstoke** Hants
52 D5 **Meopham** Kent
52 D6 **Meopham Green** Kent
52 D5 **Meopham Station** Kent
103 J7 **Mepal** Cambs
86 C8 **Meppershall** Beds
130 E3 **Mere** Ches
32 D4 **Mere** Wilts
138 E4 **Mere Brow** Lancs
98 E4 **Mere Green** Birm
81 L3 **Mere Green** Worcs
130 C5 **Mere Heath** Ches
140 C2 **Mereclough** Lancs
53 H6 **Meresborough** Medway
39 G3 **Mereworth** Kent
99 G7 **Meriden** Solhll
246 E2 **Merkadale** Highld

17 K3 **Merley** Poole
54 F4 **Merlin's Bridge** Pembks
8 B5 **Merrifield** Devon
113 G7 **Merrington** Shrops
54 F7 **Merrion** Pembks
31 G8 **Merriott** Somset
12 D7 **Merrivale** Devon
36 F1 **Merrow** Surrey
17 K2 **Merry Field Hill** Dorset
68 E8 **Merry Hill** Herts
100 A2 **Merry Lees** Leics
97 K4 **Merryhill** Wolves
6 B2 **Merrymeet** Cnwll
40 D7 **Mersham** Kent
51 H8 **Merstham** Surrey
20 E6 **Merston** W Susx
19 J6 **Merstone** IOW
4 D6 **Merther** Cnwll
58 C5 **Merthyr** Carmth
78 D7 **Merthyr Cynog** Powys
43 H7 **Merthyr Dyfan** V Glam
42 D6 **Merthyr Mawr** Brdgnd
61 G6 **Merthyr Tydfil** Myr Td
61 G7 **Merthyr Vale** Myr Td
27 J8 **Merton** Devon
51 H5 **Merton** Gt Lon
105 H4 **Merton** Norfk
66 E3 **Merton** Oxon
28 D7 **Meshaw** Devon
72 C3 **Messing** Essex
143 M6 **Messingham** N Linc
106 F7 **Metfield** Suffk
6 E1 **Metherell** Cnwll
11 G7 **Metherin** Cnwll
135 L7 **Metheringham** Lincs
222 F7 **Methil** Fife
222 F7 **Methilhill** Fife
3 G5 **Methleigh** Cnwll
142 B2 **Methley** Leeds
142 B3 **Methley Junction** Leeds
256 F4 **Methlick** Abers
221 J2 **Methven** P & K
104 E4 **Methwold** Norfk
104 E4 **Methwold Hythe** Norfk
107 H5 **Mettingham** Suffk
122 D4 **Metton** Norfk
5 G6 **Mevagissey** Cnwll
142 D7 **Mexborough** Donc
280 C2 **Mey** Highld
108 D5 **Meyllteyrn** Gwynd
65 G7 **Meysey Hampton** Gloucs
282 e3 **Miabhig** W Isls
282 e3 **Miavaig** W Isls
63 G2 **Michaelchurch** Herefs
79 K8 **Michaelchurch Escley** Herefs
79 J5 **Michaelchurch-on-Arrow** Powys
43 J7 **Michaelston-le-Pit** V Glam
43 K5 **Michaelstone-y-Fedw** Newpt
10 F6 **Michaelstow** Cnwll
7 K1 **Michelcombe** Devon
35 G3 **Micheldever** Hants
35 G2 **Micheldever Station** Hants
34 D5 **Michelmersh** Hants
90 D3 **Mickfield** Suffk
129 K5 **Mickle Trafford** Ches
133 K1 **Micklebring** Donc
171 J8 **Mickleby** N York
142 C1 **Micklefield** Leeds
68 D7 **Micklefield Green** Herts
50 F8 **Mickleham** Surrey
116 A5 **Mickleover** C Derb
149 K7 **Micklethwaite** Brad
165 J1 **Micklethwaite** Cumb
168 B6 **Mickleton** Dur
82 E6 **Mickleton** Gloucs
142 B2 **Mickletown** Leeds
132 F4 **Mickley** Derbys
160 C7 **Mickley** N York
89 G4 **Mickley Green** Suffk
180 C6 **Mickley Square** Nthumb
269 H3 **Mid Ardlaw** Abers
244 E3 **Mid Beltie** Abers
18 B4 **Mid Bockhampton** Hants
210 E5 **Mid Calder** W Loth
280 C8 **Mid Clyth** Highld
37 J2 **Mid Holmwood** Surrey
20 D5 **Mid Lavant** W Susx
250 D4 **Mid Mains** Highld
136 E5 **Mid Thorpe** Lincs
281 e3 **Mid Yell** Shet
275 c2 **Midbea** Ork
49 H2 **Middle Assendon** Oxon
66 C2 **Middle Aston** Oxon
66 B2 **Middle Barton** Oxon

31 G8 **Middle Chinnock** Somset
67 H2 **Middle Claydon** Bucks
64 E6 **Middle Duntisbourne** Gloucs
133 H4 **Middle Handley** Derbys
105 K6 **Middle Harling** Norfk
206 E1 **Middle Kames** Ag & B
82 C6 **Middle Littleton** Worcs
114 B3 **Middle Madeley** Staffs
79 L8 **Middle Maes-coed** Herefs
115 J3 **Middle Mayfield** Staffs
74 C7 **Middle Mill** Pembks
40 A7 **Middle Quarter** Kent
136 A2 **Middle Rasen** Lincs
8 D1 **Middle Rocombe** Devon
147 M3 **Middle Salter** Lancs
30 B6 **Middle Stoford** Somset
53 H4 **Middle Stoke** Medway
30 F1 **Middle Stoughton** Somset
63 M6 **Middle Street** Gloucs
5 K2 **Middle Taphouse** Cnwll
10 b3 **Middle Town** IOS
83 H6 **Middle Tysoe** Warwks
34 C3 **Middle Wallop** Hants
34 B4 **Middle Winterslow** Wilts
33 K4 **Middle Woodford** Wilts
64 B6 **Middle Yard** Gloucs
177 H4 **Middlebie** D & G
232 C2 **Middlebridge** P & K
142 C6 **Middlecliffe** Barns
13 G5 **Middlecott** Devon
159 L5 **Middleham** N York
6 B1 **Middlehill** Cnwll
46 B5 **Middlehill** Wilts
96 B5 **Middlehope** Shrops
16 C1 **Middlemarsh** Dorset
12 C7 **Middlemore** Devon
170 C6 **Middlesbrough** Middsb
165 L2 **Middlesceugh** Cumb
157 J5 **Middleshaw** Cumb
159 K7 **Middlesmoor** N York
169 H4 **Middlestone** Dur
169 H4 **Middlestone Moor** Dur
141 L4 **Middlestown** Wakefd
201 L4 **Middlethird** Border
224 B6 **Middleton** Ag & B
157 K5 **Middleton** Cumb
132 D7 **Middleton** Derbys
132 E8 **Middleton** Derbys
89 H7 **Middleton** Essex
34 F2 **Middleton** Hants
80 D1 **Middleton** Herefs
147 H4 **Middleton** Lancs
141 M2 **Middleton** Leeds
208 C8 **Middleton** N Ayrs
149 L6 **Middleton** N York
162 D5 **Middleton** N York
101 J5 **Middleton** Nhants
120 E8 **Middleton** Norfk
203 H6 **Middleton** Nthumb
180 C2 **Middleton** Nthumb
221 L6 **Middleton** P & K
104 C6 **Middleton** Rochdl
112 D5 **Middleton** Shrops
96 C7 **Middleton** Shrops
91 K2 **Middleton** Suffk
56 D7 **Middleton** Swans
98 F4 **Middleton** Warwks
83 L7 **Middleton Cheney** Nhants
114 F4 **Middleton Green** Staffs
202 F8 **Middleton Hall** Nthumb
91 J2 **Middleton Moor** Suffk
80 C2 **Middleton on the Hill** Herefs
152 E6 **Middleton on the Wolds** E R Yk
169 K8 **Middleton One Row** Darltn
96 E5 **Middleton Priors** Shrops
160 E7 **Middleton Quernhow** N York
96 F6 **Middleton Scriven** Shrops
169 K8 **Middleton St George** Darltn
66 D2 **Middleton Stoney** Oxon
160 B2 **Middleton Tyas** N York
168 B5 **Middleton-in-Teesdale** Dur
161 G1 **Middleton-on-Leven** N York
20 F6 **Middleton-on-Sea** W Susx
155 H1 **Middletown** Cumb
44 F4 **Middletown** N Som
95 H1 **Middletown** Powys
130 D6 **Middlewich** Ches
11 K7 **Middlewood** Cnwll
79 K6 **Middlewood** Herefs
90 C3 **Middlewood Green** Suffk
197 G4 **Middleyard** E Ayrs
30 E4 **Middlezoy** Somset
169 H5 **Middridge** Dur
45 M6 **Midford** BaNES

139 G3 **Midge Hall** Lancs	24 E3 **Millcorner** E Susx	244 C3 **Milton of Auchinhove** Abers	71 H3 **Molehill Green** Essex
178 E7 **Midgeholme** Cumb	263 H5 **Millcraig** Highld	222 E7 **Milton of Balgonie** Fife	152 F7 **Molescroft** E R Yk
48 E5 **Midgham** W Berk	115 J1 **Milldale** Staffs	208 D1 **Milton of Buchanan** Stirlg	180 E2 **Molesden** Nthumb
140 F3 **Midgley** Calder	63 H5 **Millend** Gloucs	209 H4 **Milton of Campsie** E Duns	102 B8 **Molesworth** Cambs
141 L5 **Midgley** Wakefd	63 L7 **Millend** Gloucs	251 J3 **Milton of Leys** Highld	28 E5 **Molland** Devon
141 K7 **Midhopestones** Sheff	132 C5 **Miller's Dale** Derbys	243 L4 **Milton of Tullich** Abers	129 J5 **Mollington** Ches
36 C6 **Midhurst** W Susx	70 E5 **Miller's Green** Essex	32 D5 **Milton on Stour** Dorset	83 K5 **Mollington** Oxon
201 H7 **Midlem** Border	211 K5 **Millerhill** Mdloth	40 A2 **Milton Regis** Kent	209 J4 **Mollinsburn** N Lans
31 H5 **Midney** Somset	115 M1 **Millers Green** Derbys	23 J6 **Milton Street** E Susx	76 F3 **Monachty** Cerdgn
207 G7 **Midpark** Ag & B	209 H5 **Millerston** N Lans	65 K3 **Milton-under-Wychwood** Oxon	245 G7 **Mondynes** Abers
45 K8 **Midsomer Norton** BaNES	140 D4 **Millgate** Lancs	29 L5 **Milverton** Somset	90 F3 **Monewden** Suffk
277 K4 **Midtown** Highld	113 L6 **Millgreen** Shrops	83 H2 **Milverton** Warwks	221 J1 **Moneydie** P & K
137 G8 **Midville** Lincs	79 K5 **Millhalf** Herefs	114 F5 **Milwich** Staffs	49 L3 **Moneyrow Green** W & M
131 H3 **Midway** Ches	14 F2 **Millhayes** Devon	128 E5 **Milwr** Flints	185 J5 **Moniaive** D & G
244 A2 **Migvie** Abers	147 K2 **Millhead** Lancs	216 F7 **Minard** Ag & B	223 J1 **Monifieth** Angus
31 L7 **Milborne Port** Somset	198 B3 **Millheugh** S Lans	33 G7 **Minchington** Dorset	234 D7 **Monikie** Angus
16 F3 **Milborne St Andrew** Dorset	206 F5 **Millhouse** Ag & B	64 C7 **Minchinhampton** Gloucs	222 E4 **Monimail** Fife
31 L6 **Milborne Wick** Somset	165 K3 **Millhouse** Cumb	202 C6 **Mindrum** Nthumb	75 K3 **Monington** Pembks
180 D4 **Milbourne** Nthumb	141 K7 **Millhouse Green** Barns	202 C6 **Mindrum Mill** Nthumb	142 B6 **Monk Bretton** Barns
46 D2 **Milbourne** Wilts	176 F2 **Millhousebridge** D & G	29 H2 **Minehead** Somset	142 D2 **Monk Fryston** N York
166 F5 **Milburn** Cumb	142 C6 **Millhouses** Barns	112 C1 **Minera** Wrexhm	48 F7 **Monk Sherborne** Hants
45 K1 **Milbury Heath** S Glos	133 G3 **Millhouses** Sheff	46 F1 **Minety** Wilts	90 F2 **Monk Soham** Suffk
150 F2 **Milby** N York	208 C6 **Milliken Park** Rens	109 L4 **Minffordd** Gwynd	90 E2 **Monk Soham Green** Suffk
83 K8 **Milcombe** Oxon	55 G4 **Millin Cross** Pembks	237 K6 **Mingarrypark** Highld	70 F1 **Monk Street** Essex
89 J6 **Milden** Suffk	152 C5 **Millington** E R Yk	136 F6 **Miningsby** Lincs	37 K5 **Monk's Gate** W Susx
104 E8 **Mildenhall** Suffk	157 H6 **Millness** Cumb	11 J8 **Minions** Cnwll	69 H7 **Monken Hadley** Gt Lon
47 J5 **Mildenhall** Wilts	155 M6 **Millom** Cumb	196 C8 **Minishant** S Ayrs	80 E6 **Monkhide** Herefs
46 E5 **Mile Elm** Wilts	11 H3 **Millook** Cnwll	111 G8 **Minllyn** Gwynd	177 K7 **Monkhill** Cumb
72 E2 **Mile End** Essex	2 F5 **Millpool** Cnwll	173 K2 **Minnigaff** D & G	96 E5 **Monkhopton** Shrops
63 H5 **Mile End** Gloucs	11 G8 **Millpool** Cnwll	41 J2 **Minnis Bay** Kent	80 B4 **Monkland** Herefs
107 G5 **Mile End** Suffk	207 K8 **Millport** N Ayrs	268 D4 **Minnonie** Abers	27 H6 **Monkleigh** Devon
22 C5 **Mile Oak** Br & H	132 F4 **Millthorpe** Derbys	130 D7 **Minshull Vernon** Ches	42 D7 **Monknash** V Glam
39 H4 **Mile Oak** Kent	157 L4 **Millthrop** Cumb	150 E3 **Minskip** N York	12 E2 **Monkokehampton** Devon
98 F3 **Mile Oak** Staffs	245 J3 **Milltimber** C Aber	18 D2 **Minstead** Hants	151 K5 **Monks Cross** N York
53 K4 **Mile Town** Kent	243 J2 **Milltown** Abers	20 D3 **Minsted** W Susx	89 K5 **Monks Eleigh** Suffk
79 K1 **Milebrook** Powys	255 J8 **Milltown** Abers	53 L4 **Minster** Kent	131 G5 **Monks Heath** Ches
39 J4 **Milebush** Kent	5 J3 **Milltown** Cnwll	41 J2 **Minster** Kent	40 F7 **Monks Horton** Kent
121 K7 **Mileham** Norfk	177 K4 **Milltown** D & G	65 L5 **Minster Lovell** Oxon	100 A6 **Monks Kirby** Warwks
80 D2 **Miles Hope** Herefs	133 G7 **Milltown** Derbys	180 B7 **Minsteracres** Nthumb	67 K6 **Monks Risborough** Bucks
140 C7 **Miles Platting** Manch	27 K3 **Milltown** Devon	95 J2 **Minsterley** Shrops	181 J4 **Monkseaton** N Tyne
210 E1 **Milesmark** Fife	244 E3 **Milltown of Campfield** Abers	63 M4 **Minsterworth** Gloucs	29 K3 **Monksilver** Somset
202 E6 **Milfield** Nthumb	254 F4 **Milltown of Edinville** Moray	16 C2 **Minterne Magna** Dorset	98 E8 **Monkspath** Solhll
116 B3 **Milford** Derbys	244 E3 **Milltown of Learney** Abers	16 C2 **Minterne Parva** Dorset	45 M6 **Monkton Combe** BaNES
26 D6 **Milford** Devon	221 L6 **Milnathort** P & K	136 C5 **Minting** Lincs	32 E3 **Monkton Deverill** Wilts
94 D5 **Milford** Powys	208 F4 **Milngavie** W Duns	269 J6 **Mintlaw** Abers	46 A6 **Monkton Farleigh** Wilts
114 F7 **Milford** Staffs	140 D5 **Milnrow** Rochdl	188 F2 **Minto** Border	30 C5 **Monkton Heathfield** Somset
36 E2 **Milford** Surrey	157 H6 **Milnthorpe** Cumb	95 K5 **Minton** Shrops	33 H8 **Monkton Up Wimborne** Dorset
54 E5 **Milford Haven** Pembks	142 A4 **Milnthorpe** Wakefd	55 H4 **Minwear** Pembks	15 H3 **Monkton Wyld** Dorset
18 D5 **Milford on Sea** Hants	258 B6 **Milovaig** Highld	98 F5 **Minworth** Birm	181 K7 **Monkwearmouth** Sundld
63 H5 **Milkwall** Gloucs	80 E1 **Milson** Shrops	164 C7 **Mirehouse** Cumb	35 K5 **Monkwood** Hants
140 F3 **Mill Bank** Calder	40 A3 **Milstead** Kent	141 K4 **Mirfield** Kirk	97 L4 **Monmore Green** Wolves
131 J2 **Mill Brow** Stockp	33 L2 **Milston** Wilts	64 D5 **Miserden** Gloucs	63 G4 **Monmouth** Mons
107 G3 **Mill Common** Norfk	118 F5 **Milthorpe** Lincs	43 G5 **Miskin** Rhondd	79 L6 **Monnington on Wye** Herefs
107 H7 **Mill Common** Suffk	84 B6 **Milthorpe** Nhants	43 G2 **Miskin** Rhondd	173 J6 **Monreith** D & G
7 L3 **Mill Cross** Devon	114 E2 **Milton** C Stke	134 D1 **Misson** Notts	9 i3 **Mont Saint** Guern
49 J2 **Mill End** Bucks	87 K3 **Milton** Cambs	100 C6 **Misterton** Leics	31 H7 **Montacute** Somset
103 G7 **Mill End** Cambs	178 D6 **Milton** Cumb	134 F1 **Misterton** Notts	139 K5 **Montcliffe** Bolton
87 G8 **Mill End** Herts	172 F4 **Milton** D & G	15 K1 **Misterton** Somset	112 F8 **Montford** Shrops
88 C6 **Mill Green** Cambs	175 L1 **Milton** D & G	73 G1 **Mistley** Essex	113 G8 **Montford Bridge** Shrops
70 F6 **Mill Green** Essex	116 A6 **Milton** Derbys	73 H1 **Mistley Heath** Essex	255 L8 **Montgarrie** Abers
69 G5 **Mill Green** Herts	280 D6 **Milton** Highld	51 H5 **Mitcham** Gt Lon	197 G5 **Montgarswood** E Ayrs
119 H6 **Mill Green** Lincs	248 A3 **Milton** Highld	62 F5 **Mitchel Troy** Mons	94 F4 **Montgomery** Powys
106 C6 **Mill Green** Norfk	250 E5 **Milton** Highld	63 K3 **Mitcheldean** Gloucs	196 C2 **Montgreenan** N Ayrs
98 D3 **Mill Green** Staffs	251 G2 **Milton** Highld	4 D4 **Mitchell** Cnwll	140 A7 **Monton** Salfd
115 H7 **Mill Green** Staffs	263 K5 **Milton** Highld	186 E7 **Mitchellslacks** D & G	235 H4 **Montrose** Angus
89 J6 **Mill Green** Suffk	208 B5 **Milton** Inver	180 E2 **Mitford** Nthumb	34 C2 **Monxton** Hants
89 K4 **Mill Green** Suffk	52 E4 **Milton** Kent	4 B5 **Mithian** Cnwll	132 C6 **Monyash** Derbys
90 D3 **Mill Green** Suffk	267 K3 **Milton** Moray	114 D8 **Mitton** Staffs	256 C8 **Monymusk** Abers
91 H3 **Mill Green** Suffk	44 D6 **Milton** N Som	84 B8 **Mixbury** Oxon	220 F2 **Monzie** P & K
23 L6 **Mill Hill** E Susx	44 D1 **Milton** Newpt	141 G2 **Mixenden** Calder	209 J5 **Moodiesburn** N Lans
69 G8 **Mill Hill** Gt Lon	134 E5 **Milton** Notts	131 L8 **Mixon** Staffs	222 F4 **Moonzie** Fife
114 C5 **Mill Meece** Staffs	83 K8 **Milton** Oxon	90 B4 **Moats Tye** Suffk	150 D8 **Moor Allerton** Leeds
220 E4 **Mill of Drummond** P & K	66 C8 **Milton** Oxon	130 F4 **Mobberley** Ches	17 K1 **Moor Crichel** Dorset
208 C3 **Mill of Haldane** W Duns	233 H4 **Milton** P & K	115 G3 **Mobberley** Staffs	68 B3 **Moor End** Beds
157 G6 **Mill Side** Cumb	55 H6 **Milton** Pembks	79 L6 **Moccas** Herefs	141 G2 **Moor End** Calder
39 H2 **Mill Street** Kent	31 G6 **Milton** Somset	127 G4 **Mochdre** Conwy	12 F1 **Moor End** Devon
121 M7 **Mill Street** Norfk	219 H7 **Milton** Stirlg	94 C5 **Mochdre** Powys	152 B8 **Moor End** E R Yk
122 B7 **Mill Street** Norfk	208 D4 **Milton** W Duns	173 J5 **Mochrum** D & G	147 G6 **Moor End** Lancs
90 C1 **Mill Street** Suffk	16 F2 **Milton Abbas** Dorset	18 B2 **Mockbeggar** Hants	151 J8 **Moor End** N York
9 a1 **Millais** Jersey	12 A6 **Milton Abbot** Devon	39 H4 **Mockbeggar** Kent	69 J2 **Moor End** Herts
36 B5 **Milland** W Susx	211 H6 **Milton Bridge** Mdloth	164 E6 **Mockerkin** Cumb	141 K2 **Moor Head** Leeds
36 C5 **Milland Marsh** W Susx	68 B1 **Milton Bryan** Beds	7 J4 **Modbury** Devon	151 H4 **Moor Monkton** N York
165 H5 **Millbeck** Cumb	31 L3 **Milton Clevedon** Somset	114 E4 **Moddershall** Staffs	164 D7 **Moor Row** Cumb
257 J3 **Millbreck** Abers	6 F2 **Milton Combe** Devon	125 J8 **Moel Tryfan** Gwynd	165 H1 **Moor Row** Cumb
256 E3 **Millbrex** Abers	67 G6 **Milton Common** Oxon	125 J2 **Moelfre** IOA	168 F7 **Moor Row** Dur
36 C2 **Millbridge** Surrey	27 G8 **Milton Damerel** Devon	112 B6 **Moelfre** Powys	147 K8 **Moor Side** Lancs
85 K7 **Millbrook** Beds	63 L5 **Milton End** Gloucs	187 G5 **Moffat** D & G	138 E1 **Moor Side** Lancs
34 E8 **Millbrook** C Sotn	65 H7 **Milton End** Gloucs	86 C5 **Mogerhanger** Beds	
6 E4 **Millbrook** Cnwll	85 K4 **Milton Ernest** Beds	116 A8 **Moira** Leics	
9 c3 **Millbrook** Jersey	129 K7 **Milton Green** Ches	246 F6 **Mol-chlach** Highld	
140 E7 **Millbrook** Tamesd	48 C1 **Milton Hill** Oxon	40 D5 **Molash** Kent	
245 H2 **Millbuie** Abers	85 G7 **Milton Keynes** M Keyn	128 F7 **Mold** Flints	
250 F1 **Millbuie** Highld	47 J7 **Milton Lilbourne** Wilts	141 J4 **Moldgreen** Kirk	
196 E5 **Millburn** S Ayrs	84 E4 **Milton Malsor** Nhants	70 E2 **Molehill Green** Essex	
8 B5 **Millcombe** Devon	231 H8 **Milton Morenish** P & K		

136 E8 **Moor Side** Lincs
98 C6 **Moor Street** Birm
53 H6 **Moor Street** Medway
15 K3 **Moorbath** Dorset
136 E6 **Moorby** Lincs
79 L4 **Moorcot** Herefs
17 L4 **Moordown** Bmouth
130 B3 **Moore** Halton
63 L6 **Moorend** Gloucs
143 H4 **Moorends** Donc
35 G7 **Moorgreen** Hants
116 E2 **Moorgreen** Notts
132 F5 **Moorhall** Derbys
79 M6 **Moorhampton** Herefs
149 L8 **Moorhead** Brad
177 H8 **Moorhouse** Cumb
177 K7 **Moorhouse** Cumb
142 D5 **Moorhouse** Donc
134 E6 **Moorhouse** Notts
51 L8 **Moorhouse Bank** Surrey
30 E4 **Moorland** Somset
30 F3 **Moorlinch** Somset
170 F7 **Moorsholm** R & Cl
155 K2 **Moorside** Cumb
32 D7 **Moorside** Dorset
150 C8 **Moorside** Leeds
140 E6 **Moorside** Oldham
40 E7 **Moorstock** Kent
5 M2 **Moorswater** Cnwll
142 C5 **Moorthorpe** Wakefd
12 C7 **Moortown** Devon
18 A3 **Moortown** Hants
19 G7 **Moortown** IOW
150 D7 **Moortown** Leeds
144 D7 **Moortown** Lincs
113 K7 **Moortown** Wrekin
263 K3 **Morangie** Highld
237 H2 **Morar** Highld
102 C5 **Morborne** Cambs
13 H1 **Morchard Bishop** Devon
15 J4 **Morcombelake** Dorset
101 K3 **Morcott** Rutlnd
112 D6 **Morda** Shrops
17 H3 **Morden** Dorset
51 H5 **Morden** Gt Lon
80 D7 **Mordiford** Herefs
169 J5 **Mordon** Dur
95 H5 **More** Shrops
29 G6 **Morebath** Devon
189 K1 **Morebattle** Border
147 H3 **Morecambe** Lancs
47 H2 **Moredon** Swindn
261 J1 **Morefield** Highld
41 G7 **Morehall** Kent
7 L4 **Moreleigh** Devon
231 H8 **Morenish** P & K
164 C6 **Moresby** Cumb
164 C6 **Moresby Parks** Cumb
35 G6 **Morestead** Hants
16 F4 **Moreton** Dorset
70 D5 **Moreton** Essex
80 C2 **Moreton** Herefs
67 G6 **Moreton** Oxon
114 B8 **Moreton** Staffs
115 J5 **Moreton** Staffs
129 G2 **Moreton** Wirral
113 J6 **Moreton Corbet** Shrops
80 E5 **Moreton Jeffries** Herefs
83 H4 **Moreton Morrell** Warwks
80 C6 **Moreton on Lugg** Herefs
83 H4 **Moreton Paddox** Warwks
84 B5 **Moreton Pinkney** Nhants
113 K4 **Moreton Say** Shrops
63 M5 **Moreton Valence** Gloucs
65 J1 **Moreton-in-Marsh** Gloucs
13 H5 **Moretonhampstead** Devon
113 J7 **Moretonmill** Shrops
76 B4 **Morfa** Cerdgn
109 K4 **Morfa Bychan** Gwynd
125 H8 **Morfa Dinlle** Gwynd
60 C6 **Morfa Glas** Neath
108 E3 **Morfa Nefyn** Gwynd
33 L6 **Morgan's Vale** Wilts
43 H5 **Morganstown** Cardif
212 C5 **Morham** E Loth
92 D7 **Moriah** Cerdgn
166 E6 **Morland** Cumb
130 F3 **Morley** Ches
116 C3 **Morley** Derbys
168 E5 **Morley** Dur
141 L2 **Morley** Leeds
130 F3 **Morley Green** Ches
106 B3 **Morley St Botolph** Norfk
11 L8 **Mornick** Cnwll
211 H5 **Morningside** C Edin

209 L7 **Morningside** N Lans
106 E5 **Morningthorpe** Norfk
180 F2 **Morpeth** Nthumb
235 H3 **Morphie** Abers
115 J7 **Morrey** Staffs
115 G1 **Morridge Side** Staffs
131 K6 **Morridge Top** Staffs
57 J5 **Morriston** Swans
121 M3 **Morston** Norfk
27 H2 **Mortehoe** Devon
133 J2 **Morthen** Rothm
49 G6 **Mortimer** W Berk
49 G6 **Mortimer Common** W Berk
48 F6 **Mortimer West End** Hants
80 A3 **Mortimer's Cross** Herefs
51 G4 **Mortlake** Gt Lon
177 L7 **Morton** Cumb
166 B3 **Morton** Cumb
133 H7 **Morton** Derbys
19 K6 **Morton** IOW
134 F1 **Morton** Lincs
118 E6 **Morton** Lincs
117 J1 **Morton** Notts
112 D6 **Morton** Shrops
135 H7 **Morton Hall** Lincs
122 C8 **Morton on the Hill** Norfk
168 F6 **Morton Tinmouth** Dur
160 D4 **Morton-on-Swale** N York
2 B4 **Morvah** Cnwll
6 B3 **Morval** Cnwll
248 F7 **Morvich** Highld
96 F4 **Morville** Shrops
96 F4 **Morville Heath** Shrops
26 C7 **Morwenstow** Cnwll
133 H3 **Mosborough** Sheff
196 F3 **Moscow** E Ayrs
97 G5 **Mose** Shrops
165 K4 **Mosedale** Cumb
98 D6 **Moseley** Birm
97 L4 **Moseley** Wolves
81 J3 **Moseley** Worcs
139 L6 **Moses Gate** Bolton
224 B6 **Moss** Ag & B
142 F5 **Moss** Donc
112 D1 **Moss** Wrexhm
139 G8 **Moss Bank** St Hel
147 H7 **Moss Edge** Lancs
130 D4 **Moss End** Ches
177 G8 **Moss Side** Cumb
138 D2 **Moss Side** Lancs
138 D7 **Moss Side** Sefton
253 G1 **Moss-side** Highld
255 K7 **Mossat** Abers
281 e4 **Mossbank** Shet
164 C5 **Mossbay** Cumb
196 D6 **Mossblown** S Ayrs
130 D2 **Mossbrow** Traffd
189 H3 **Mossburnford** Border
175 G1 **Mossdale** D & G
184 D2 **Mossdale** E Ayrs
209 K7 **Mossend** N Lans
164 F5 **Mosser Mains** Cumb
131 H7 **Mossley** Ches
140 E7 **Mossley** Tamesd
188 C6 **Mosspaul Hotel** Border
267 G4 **Mosstodloch** Moray
139 G5 **Mossy Lea** Lancs
174 E4 **Mossyard** D & G
15 K2 **Mosterton** Dorset
140 C7 **Moston** Manch
113 J6 **Moston** Shrops
130 E7 **Moston Green** Ches
128 E4 **Mostyn** Flints
32 E6 **Motcombe** Dorset
7 H5 **Mothecombe** Devon
166 A5 **Motherby** Cumb
209 K7 **Motherwell** N Lans
51 G5 **Motspur Park** Gt Lon
51 L4 **Mottingham** Gt Lon
34 D5 **Mottisfont** Hants
18 F7 **Mottistone** IOW
140 F8 **Mottram in Longdendale** Tamesd
131 G4 **Mottram St Andrew** Ches
9 j3 **Mouilpied** Guern
129 L5 **Mouldsworth** Ches
232 D3 **Moulin** P & K
22 E6 **Moulsecoomb** Br & H
48 E2 **Moulsford** Oxon
85 H7 **Moulsoe** M Keyn
263 H5 **Moultavie** Highld
130 C5 **Moulton** Ches
119 J6 **Moulton** Lincs
160 C2 **Moulton** N York
84 F2 **Moulton** Nhants

88 D2 **Moulton** Suffk
43 G7 **Moulton** V Glam
119 J7 **Moulton Chapel** Lincs
119 K6 **Moulton Seas End** Lincs
107 H2 **Moulton St Mary** Norfk
4 C4 **Mount** Cnwll
5 K1 **Mount** Cnwll
141 H4 **Mount** Kirk
4 B6 **Mount Ambrose** Cnwll
89 H8 **Mount Bures** Essex
4 B5 **Mount Hawke** Cnwll
3 H7 **Mount Hermon** Cnwll
200 C2 **Mount Lothian** Mdloth
131 G8 **Mount Pleasant** Ches
116 B2 **Mount Pleasant** Derbys
169 H4 **Mount Pleasant** Dur
23 G4 **Mount Pleasant** E Susx
105 K4 **Mount Pleasant** Norfk
88 E5 **Mount Pleasant** Suffk
82 B2 **Mount Pleasant** Worcs
33 H6 **Mount Sorrel** Wilts
141 G2 **Mount Tabor** Calder
141 G2 **Mountain** Brad
61 G7 **Mountain Ash** Rhondd
199 K4 **Mountain Cross** Border
40 E5 **Mountain Street** Kent
24 D3 **Mountfield** E Susx
263 G7 **Mountgerald House** Highld
4 E3 **Mountjoy** Cnwll
70 F7 **Mountnessing** Essex
63 G8 **Mounton** Mons
116 F8 **Mountsorrel** Leics
36 E3 **Mousehill** Surrey
2 D5 **Mousehole** Cnwll
176 E4 **Mouswald** D & G
131 G8 **Mow Cop** Ches
189 L2 **Mowhaugh** Border
100 D2 **Mowmacre Hill** C Leic
100 E5 **Mowsley** Leics
245 J6 **Mowtie** Abers
252 E5 **Moy** Highld
240 D7 **Moy** Highld
248 D7 **Moy** Highld
18 B2 **Moyles Court** Hants
75 J3 **Moylgrove** Pembks
205 L8 **Muasdale** Ag & B
63 G1 **Much Birch** Herefs
80 E6 **Much Cowarne** Herefs
62 F1 **Much Dewchurch** Herefs
70 B3 **Much Hadham** Herts
138 F3 **Much Hoole** Lancs
138 F3 **Much Hoole Town** Lancs
80 F8 **Much Marcle** Herefs
96 E3 **Much Wenlock** Shrops
245 K5 **Muchalls** Abers
30 F6 **Muchelney** Somset
31 G6 **Muchelney Ham** Somset
5 L3 **Muchlarnick** Cnwll
52 E3 **Mucking** Thurr
52 E3 **Muckingford** Thurr
16 C4 **Muckleford** Dorset
114 A4 **Mucklestone** Staffs
96 E4 **Muckley** Shrops
137 G3 **Muckton** Lincs
53 M4 **Mud Row** Kent
27 K3 **Muddiford** Devon
23 J4 **Muddles Green** E Susx
18 B5 **Mudeford** Dorset
31 J7 **Mudford** Somset
31 J7 **Mudford Sock** Somset
31 G2 **Mudgley** Somset
208 F4 **Mugdock** Stirlg
246 F1 **Mugeary** Highld
115 M3 **Mugginton** Derbys
115 M3 **Muggintonlane End** Derbys
168 D1 **Muggleswick** Dur
244 C1 **Muir of Fowlis** Abers
266 D4 **Muir of Miltonduff** Moray
250 F2 **Muir of Ord** Highld
233 G7 **Muir of Thorn** P & K
268 C5 **Muirden** Abers
234 E7 **Muirdrum** Angus
268 C6 **Muiresk** Abers
233 M8 **Muirhead** Angus
222 D6 **Muirhead** Fife
209 J5 **Muirhead** N Lans
197 K5 **Muirkirk** E Ayrs
209 J2 **Muirmill** Stirlg
239 J7 **Muirshearlich** Highld
257 J4 **Muirtack** Abers
221 G5 **Muirton** P & K
250 E1 **Muirton Mains** Highld
233 J6 **Muirton of Ardblair** P & K
158 F3 **Muker** N York
106 D3 **Mulbarton** Norfk

267 G6 **Mulben** Moray
2 C4 **Mulfra** Cnwll
27 J2 **Mullacott Cross** Devon
3 H7 **Mullion** Cnwll
3 H7 **Mullion Cove** Cnwll
137 K5 **Mumby** Lincs
80 F5 **Munderfield Row** Herefs
80 F5 **Munderfield Stocks** Herefs
123 G4 **Mundesley** Norfk
104 F4 **Mundford** Norfk
107 G4 **Mundham** Norfk
72 C6 **Mundon Hill** Essex
40 B6 **Mundy Bois** Kent
165 L4 **Mungrisdale** Cumb
251 H1 **Munlochy** Highld
195 L1 **Munnoch** N Ayrs
80 F7 **Munsley** Herefs
96 C6 **Munslow** Shrops
13 G5 **Murchington** Devon
82 C7 **Murcot** Worcs
66 E4 **Murcott** Oxon
46 D1 **Murcott** Wilts
279 L3 **Murkle** Highld
239 G5 **Murlaggan** Highld
49 H7 **Murrell Green** Hants
234 C8 **Murroes** Angus
103 H2 **Murrow** Cambs
67 K2 **Mursley** Bucks
40 B2 **Murston** Kent
234 C4 **Murthill** Angus
233 G7 **Murthly** P & K
167 G6 **Murton** Cumb
169 K1 **Murton** Dur
181 H5 **Murton** N Tyne
202 F3 **Murton** Nthumb
151 K5 **Murton** York
15 G4 **Musbury** Devon
162 B6 **Muscoates** N York
211 K4 **Musselburgh** E Loth
117 L4 **Muston** Leics
163 K6 **Muston** N York
97 K8 **Mustow Green** Worcs
51 H1 **Muswell Hill** Gt Lon
175 H5 **Mutehill** D & G
107 K5 **Mutford** Suffk
220 F4 **Muthill** P & K
14 B2 **Mutterton** Devon
114 A8 **Muxton** Wrekin
279 L5 **Mybster** Highld
59 L3 **Myddfai** Carmth
113 G6 **Myddle** Shrops
76 E4 **Mydroilyn** Cerdgn
147 K7 **Myerscough** Lancs
3 L4 **Mylor** Cnwll
3 K4 **Mylor Bridge** Cnwll
75 K6 **Mynachlog ddu** Pembks
128 D5 **Myndd-llan** Flints
95 J5 **Myndtown** Shrops
92 F8 **Mynydd Buch** Cerdgn
128 F7 **Mynydd Isa** Flints
126 B6 **Mynydd Llandygai** Gwynd
62 F8 **Mynydd-bach** Mons
57 J5 **Mynydd-Bach** Swans
56 D3 **Mynyddgarreg** Carmth
108 E5 **Mynytho** Gwynd
245 G4 **Myrebird** Abers
189 G6 **Myredykes** Border
49 L7 **Mytchett** Surrey
140 E2 **Mytholm** Calder
140 F3 **Mytholmroyd** Calder
138 D1 **Mythop** Lancs
150 F3 **Myton-on-Swale** N York

N

282 d6 **Na Buirgh** W Isls
260 C3 **Naast** Highld
139 J2 **Nab's Head** Lancs
151 J6 **Naburn** York
40 D6 **Naccolt** Kent
40 F4 **Nackington** Kent
90 F7 **Nacton** Suffk
153 G4 **Nafferton** E R Yk
64 C7 **Nag's Head** Gloucs
63 J4 **Nailbridge** Gloucs
30 B5 **Nailsbourne** Somset
44 F5 **Nailsea** N Som
99 L2 **Nailstone** Leics
64 B7 **Nailsworth** Gloucs
264 D8 **Nairn** Highld
37 K2 **Nalderswood** Surrey
3 G4 **Nancegollan** Cnwll
2 D4 **Nancledra** Cnwll
108 E5 **Nanhoron** Gwynd

128 E5 **Nannerch** Flints
116 E8 **Nanpantan** Leics
4 F4 **Nanpean** Cnwll
2 B5 **Nanquidno** Cnwll
5 H2 **Nanstallon** Cnwll
110 B2 **Nant Gwynant** Gwynd
126 B7 **Nant Peris** Gwynd
60 F4 **Nant-ddu** Powys
78 D2 **Nant-glas** Powys
61 H5 **Nant-y-Bwch** Blae G
58 E5 **Nant-y-caws** Carmth
62 C6 **Nant-y-derry** Mons
112 C5 **Nant-y-gollen** Shrops
42 D3 **Nant-y-moel** Brdgnd
126 D5 **Nant-y-pandy** Conwy
76 C4 **Nanternis** Cerdgn
58 F4 **Nantgaredig** Carmth
43 H4 **Nantgarw** Rhondd
127 K7 **Nantglyn** Denbgs
93 L8 **Nantgwyn** Powys
109 J1 **Nantlle** Gwynd
112 C6 **Nantmawr** Shrops
78 E2 **Nantmel** Powys
109 L2 **Nantmor** Gwynd
113 L1 **Nantwich** Ches
42 C3 **Nantyffyllon** Brdgnd
61 K5 **Nantyglo** Blae G
67 K7 **Naphill** Bucks
81 K5 **Napleton** Worcs
148 E5 **Nappa** N York
83 L3 **Napton on the Hill** Warwks
55 J4 **Narberth** Pembks
100 C4 **Narborough** Leics
104 E1 **Narborough** Norfk
6 C4 **Narkurs** Cnwll
109 H2 **Nasareth** Gwynd
100 F7 **Naseby** Nhants
84 F8 **Nash** Bucks
51 L6 **Nash** Gt Lon
79 K3 **Nash** Herefs
44 D2 **Nash** Newpt
80 E1 **Nash** Shrops
97 H7 **Nash End** Worcs
67 K5 **Nash Lee** Bucks
52 D5 **Nash Street** Kent
35 K2 **Nash's Green** Hants
102 B4 **Nassington** Nhants
64 A6 **Nastend** Gloucs
69 K2 **Nasty** Herts
158 D1 **Nateby** Cumb
147 J7 **Nateby** Lancs
157 H5 **Natland** Cumb
89 L5 **Naughton** Suffk
65 G2 **Naunton** Gloucs
81 K7 **Naunton** Worcs
81 M5 **Naunton Beauchamp** Worcs
135 K8 **Navenby** Lincs
70 D7 **Navestock** Essex
70 E7 **Navestock Side** Essex
274 D5 **Navidale House Hotel** Highld
264 B7 **Navity** Highld
161 L5 **Nawton** N York
89 K8 **Nayland** Suffk
69 L6 **Nazeing** Essex
69 L6 **Nazeing Gate** Essex
18 B4 **Neacroft** Hants
99 J6 **Neal's Green** Warwks
281 e5 **Neap** Shet
115 H2 **Near Cotton** Staffs
156 E3 **Near Sawrey** Cumb
51 G2 **Neasden** Gt Lon
169 J8 **Neasham** Darltn
57 L5 **Neath** Neath
35 M3 **Neatham** Hants
123 G7 **Neatishead** Norfk
77 G2 **Nebo** Cerdgn
127 G8 **Nebo** Conwy
109 H2 **Nebo** Gwynd
125 H2 **Nebo** IOA
105 H2 **Necton** Norfk
270 F2 **Nedd** Highld
180 F2 **Nedderton** Nthumb
89 K5 **Nedging** Suffk
89 L5 **Nedging Tye** Suffk
106 E7 **Needham** Norfk
90 C4 **Needham Market** Suffk
88 E2 **Needham Street** Suffk
87 G1 **Needingworth** Cambs
96 F7 **Neen Savage** Shrops
80 F1 **Neen Sollars** Shrops
96 E6 **Neenton** Shrops
108 E3 **Nefyn** Gwynd
208 E7 **Neilston** E Rens
43 H3 **Nelson** Caerph
148 F8 **Nelson** Lancs

198 E4 **Nemphlar** S Lans
45 G7 **Nempnett Thrubwell** BaNES
167 H2 **Nenthall** Cumb
167 H2 **Nenthead** Cumb
201 L5 **Nenthorn** Border
13 J3 **Neopardy** Devon
22 B4 **Nep Town** W Susx
128 F7 **Nercwys** Flints
204 C5 **Nereabolls** Ag & B
209 H7 **Nerston** S Lans
202 F6 **Nesbit** Nthumb
149 K6 **Nesfield** N York
129 G4 **Ness** Ches
112 F7 **Nesscliffe** Shrops
129 G4 **Neston** Ches
46 B5 **Neston** Wilts
96 E5 **Netchwood** Shrops
131 G4 **Nether Alderley** Ches
201 H4 **Nether Blainslie** Border
117 J6 **Nether Broughton** Notts
16 C3 **Nether Cerne** Dorset
31 K7 **Nether Compton** Dorset
256 E7 **Nether Crimond** Abers
267 G3 **Nether Dallachy** Moray
13 L3 **Nether Exe** Devon
186 D4 **Nether Fingland** S Lans
133 H4 **Nether Handley** Derbys
234 B7 **Nether Handwick** Angus
142 C8 **Nether Haugh** Rothm
134 E4 **Nether Headon** Notts
116 B2 **Nether Heage** Derbys
84 C3 **Nether Heyford** Nhants
186 F4 **Nether Howcleugh** S Lans
147 K2 **Nether Kellet** Lancs
257 K3 **Nether Kinmundy** Abers
133 K5 **Nether Langwith** Notts
133 G6 **Nether Moor** Derbys
132 E4 **Nether Padley** Derbys
151 J5 **Nether Poppleton** York
165 K3 **Nether Row** Cumb
161 G4 **Nether Silton** N York
95 G8 **Nether Skyborry** Shrops
30 B3 **Nether Stowey** Somset
70 E5 **Nether Street** Essex
34 C4 **Nether Wallop** Hants
155 L2 **Nether Wasdale** Cumb
165 K2 **Nether Welton** Cumb
65 J3 **Nether Westcote** Gloucs
99 G5 **Nether Whitacre** Warwks
186 B2 **Nether Whitecleuch** S Lans
67 H4 **Nether Winchendon** Bucks
33 K1 **Netheravon** Wilts
268 E4 **Netherbrae** Abers
198 C4 **Netherburn** S Lans
15 L3 **Netherbury** Dorset
177 L4 **Netherby** Cumb
150 D6 **Netherby** N York
176 F2 **Nethercleuch** D & G
83 M2 **Nethercote** Warwks
27 H3 **Nethercott** Devon
11 L3 **Nethercott** Devon
63 H7 **Netherend** Gloucs
24 C3 **Netherfield** E Susx
117 G8 **Netherfield** Leics
117 G3 **Netherfield** Notts
24 D4 **Netherfield Road** E Susx
143 J7 **Nethergate** N Linc
122 B5 **Nethergate** Norfk
33 K5 **Netherhampton** Wilts
15 J2 **Netherhay** Dorset
115 H5 **Netherland Green** Staffs
175 J6 **Netherlaw** D & G
245 J5 **Netherley** Abers
176 D1 **Nethermill** D & G
257 G3 **Nethermuir** Abers
141 H4 **Netheroyd Hill** Kirk
208 E7 **Netherplace** E Rens
99 H1 **Netherseal** Derbys
46 E6 **Netherstreet** Wilts
141 H6 **Netherthong** Kirk
133 J5 **Netherthorpe** Derbys
234 E4 **Netherton** Angus
13 L8 **Netherton** Devon
97 L5 **Netherton** Dudley
48 A7 **Netherton** Hants
63 G2 **Netherton** Herefs
141 H5 **Netherton** Kirk
209 K8 **Netherton** N Lans
190 E4 **Netherton** Nthumb
66 B7 **Netherton** Oxon
233 H5 **Netherton** P & K
97 G6 **Netherton** Shrops
208 F3 **Netherton** Stirlg
141 L4 **Netherton** Wakefd
82 A7 **Netherton** Worcs

155 H1 **Nethertown** Cumb
280 E1 **Nethertown** Highld
148 C8 **Nethertown** Lancs
115 J8 **Nethertown** Staffs
199 K4 **Netherurd** Border
191 G8 **Netherwitton** Nthumb
253 J7 **Nethy Bridge** Highld
19 G2 **Netley** Hants
34 D8 **Netley Marsh** Hants
13 L3 **Nettacott** Devon
49 G2 **Nettlebed** Oxon
31 L1 **Nettlebridge** Somset
15 L3 **Nettlecombe** Dorset
19 J7 **Nettlecombe** IOW
68 C5 **Nettleden** Herts
135 K4 **Nettleham** Lincs
39 H3 **Nettlestead** Kent
39 H3 **Nettlestead Green** Kent
19 L5 **Nettlestone** IOW
169 H1 **Nettlesworth** Dur
144 E7 **Nettleton** Lincs
46 B3 **Nettleton** Wilts
46 B3 **Nettleton Shrub** Wilts
7 G5 **Netton** Devon
33 K3 **Netton** Wilts
59 K4 **Neuadd** Carmth
77 K7 **Neuadd Fawr** Carmth
93 K8 **Neuadd-ddu** Powys
53 G1 **Nevendon** Essex
75 J4 **Nevern** Pembks
101 H4 **Nevill Holt** Leics
176 C5 **New Abbey** D & G
268 F3 **New Aberdour** Abers
51 K6 **New Addington** Gt Lon
35 J4 **New Alresford** Hants
233 K6 **New Alyth** P & K
153 G7 **New Arram** E R Yk
52 D6 **New Ash Green** Kent
117 L1 **New Balderton** Notts
52 D5 **New Barn** Kent
69 H7 **New Barnet** Gt Lon
85 G2 **New Barton** Nhants
190 F2 **New Bewick** Nthumb
100 B8 **New Bilton** Warwks
136 F8 **New Bolingbroke** Lincs
135 K5 **New Boultham** Lincs
84 F7 **New Bradwell** M Keyn
133 G5 **New Brampton** Derbys
169 G2 **New Brancepeth** Dur
162 D5 **New Bridge** N York
128 F6 **New Brighton** Flints
129 G1 **New Brighton** Wirral
116 D2 **New Brinsley** Notts
171 G6 **New Brotton** R & Cl
112 D1 **New Broughton** Wrexhm
106 B5 **New Buckenham** Norfk
139 L6 **New Bury** Bolton
268 E5 **New Byth** Abers
106 D2 **New Costessey** Norfk
164 F2 **New Cowper** Cumb
142 B4 **New Crofton** Wakefd
92 D8 **New Cross** Cerdgn
51 K4 **New Cross** Gt Lon
30 F7 **New Cross** Somset
197 J8 **New Cumnock** E Ayrs
24 E4 **New Cut** E Susx
268 F6 **New Deer** Abers
181 H3 **New Delaval** Nthumb
140 F6 **New Delph** Oldham
50 D2 **New Denham** Bucks
84 D3 **New Duston** Nhants
151 K5 **New Earswick** York
116 D2 **New Eastwood** Notts
142 E7 **New Edlington** Donc
266 E4 **New Elgin** Moray
153 J7 **New Ellerby** E R Yk
51 L4 **New Eltham** Gt Lon
82 C3 **New End** Worcs
102 D3 **New England** C Pete
88 E6 **New England** Essex
141 L2 **New Farnley** Leeds
129 H3 **New Ferry** Wirral
102 D4 **New Fletton** C Pete
142 C2 **New Fryston** Wakefd
185 G7 **New Galloway** D & G
223 G5 **New Gilston** Fife
10 b2 **New Grimsby** IOS
181 H3 **New Hartley** Nthumb
50 D6 **New Haw** Surrey
55 K6 **New Hedges** Pembks
181 H8 **New Herrington** Sundld
121 J4 **New Holkham** Norfk
144 D3 **New Holland** N Linc
133 K6 **New Houghton** Derbys
121 H6 **New Houghton** Norfk

158 D7 **New Houses** N York
139 H7 **New Houses** Wigan
157 J4 **New Hutton** Cumb
52 F7 **New Hythe** Kent
58 E2 **New Inn** Carmth
62 C7 **New Inn** Torfn
95 H8 **New Invention** Shrops
106 E2 **New Lakenham** Norfk
198 E4 **New Lanark** S Lans
138 E5 **New Lane** Lancs
130 C1 **New Lane End** Warrtn
177 K2 **New Langholm** D & G
137 G8 **New Leake** Lincs
269 H5 **New Leeds** Abers
142 A6 **New Lodge** Barns
139 G3 **New Longton** Lancs
172 F2 **New Luce** D & G
51 G5 **New Malden** Gt Lon
170 E6 **New Marske** R & Cl
66 D5 **New Marston** Oxon
112 E4 **New Marton** Shrops
245 H7 **New Mill** Abers
2 D4 **New Mill** Cnwll
68 A4 **New Mill** Herts
141 J6 **New Mill** Kirk
4 E4 **New Mills** Cnwll
131 K3 **New Mills** Derbys
94 D3 **New Mills** Powys
18 C4 **New Milton** Hants
73 H1 **New Mistley** Essex
75 H7 **New Moat** Pembks
134 D6 **New Ollerton** Notts
98 E4 **New Oscott** Birm
268 F5 **New Pitsligo** Abers
10 C6 **New Polzeath** Cnwll
196 C6 **New Prestwick** S Ayrs
76 D3 **New Quay** Cerdgn
72 F2 **New Quay** Essex
106 F1 **New Rackheath** Norfk
79 H3 **New Radnor** Powys
166 B3 **New Rent** Cumb
180 C7 **New Ridley** Nthumb
149 H7 **New Road Side** N York
25 K2 **New Romney** Kent
143 G8 **New Rossington** Donc
92 F8 **New Row** Cerdgn
148 A8 **New Row** Lancs
220 F8 **New Sauchie** Clacks
142 B4 **New Sharlston** Wakefd
203 K6 **New Shoreston** Nthumb
181 J8 **New Silksworth** Sundld
170 F7 **New Skelton** R & Cl
118 B4 **New Somerby** Lincs
137 H6 **New Spilsby** Lincs
139 J6 **New Springs** Wigan
209 K7 **New Stevenston** N Lans
79 L4 **New Street** Herefs
116 D8 **New Swannington** Leics
53 G1 **New Thundersley** Essex
86 D6 **New Town** Beds
32 F7 **New Town** Dorset
17 K1 **New Town** Dorset
33 G7 **New Town** Dorset
23 H3 **New Town** E Susx
101 L7 **New Town** Nhants
47 L4 **New Town** Wilts
61 J6 **New Tredegar** Caerph
198 D5 **New Trows** S Lans
133 H6 **New Tupton** Derbys
143 L2 **New Village** E R Yk
103 K2 **New Walsoken** Cambs
145 H6 **New Waltham** NE Lin
133 H4 **New Whittington** Derbys
211 M5 **New Winton** E Loth
66 A4 **New Yatt** Oxon
136 D8 **New York** Lincs
181 H5 **New York** N Tyne
150 B3 **New York** N York
150 B6 **Newall** Leeds
102 E3 **Newark** C Pete
275 f2 **Newark** Ork
117 L1 **Newark-on-Trent** Notts
209 L7 **Newarthill** N Lans
40 F7 **Newbarn** Kent
211 K6 **Newbattle** Mdloth
177 G6 **Newbie** D & G
166 B5 **Newbiggin** Cumb
166 D1 **Newbiggin** Cumb
166 E5 **Newbiggin** Cumb
155 K4 **Newbiggin** Cumb
146 E2 **Newbiggin** Cumb
167 L5 **Newbiggin** Dur
168 F1 **Newbiggin** Dur
159 G4 **Newbiggin** N York
159 H5 **Newbiggin** N York

181 H1 **Newbiggin-by-the-Sea** Nthumb
158 C2 **Newbiggin-on-Lune** Cumb
233 L7 **Newbigging** Angus
234 C7 **Newbigging** Angus
234 D8 **Newbigging** Angus
199 H4 **Newbigging** S Lans
133 G5 **Newbold** Derbys
116 C7 **Newbold** Leics
100 B7 **Newbold on Avon** Warwks
82 F6 **Newbold on Stour** Warwks
83 G4 **Newbold Pacey** Warwks
99 M7 **Newbold Revel** Warwks
99 L3 **Newbold Verdon** Leics
102 D2 **Newborough** C Pete
125 G6 **Newborough** IOA
115 J6 **Newborough** Staffs
83 M7 **Newbottle** Nhants
181 H8 **Newbottle** Sundld
91 G6 **Newbourne** Suffk
210 F4 **Newbridge** C Edin
43 K2 **Newbridge** Caerph
76 F3 **Newbridge** Cerdgn
2 C5 **Newbridge** Cnwll
4 C6 **Newbridge** Cnwll
176 C3 **Newbridge** D & G
34 C7 **Newbridge** Hants
18 F6 **Newbridge** IOW
66 B6 **Newbridge** Oxon
74 F6 **Newbridge** Pembks
112 D3 **Newbridge** Wrexhm
81 J7 **Newbridge Green** Worcs
78 E4 **Newbridge on Wye** Powys
62 D8 **Newbridge-on-Usk** Mons
179 K5 **Newbrough** Nthumb
13 J2 **Newbuildings** Devon
269 H4 **Newburgh** Abers
257 J6 **Newburgh** Abers
222 C3 **Newburgh** Fife
138 F5 **Newburgh** Lancs
161 J7 **Newburgh Priory** N York
180 E6 **Newburn** N u Ty
32 B1 **Newbury** Somset
48 C5 **Newbury** W Berk
32 D3 **Newbury** Wilts
51 L1 **Newbury Park** Gt Lon
166 E6 **Newby** Cumb
148 E6 **Newby** Lancs
170 C8 **Newby** N York
148 C2 **Newby** N York
163 J4 **Newby** N York
156 E5 **Newby Bridge** Cumb
177 L8 **Newby Cross** Cumb
178 B7 **Newby East** Cumb
166 E6 **Newby Head** Cumb
177 L8 **Newby West** Cumb
160 E5 **Newby Wiske** N York
62 F4 **Newcastle** Mons
95 G7 **Newcastle** Shrops
76 B7 **Newcastle Emlyn** Carmth
181 G6 **Newcastle upon Tyne** N u Ty
114 D2 **Newcastle-under-Lyme** Staffs
178 C2 **Newcastleton** Border
75 L4 **Newchapel** Pembks
131 G8 **Newchapel** Staffs
38 A5 **Newchapel** Surrey
61 J5 **Newchurch** Blae G
79 L5 **Newchurch** Herefs
19 J6 **Newchurch** IOW
25 K1 **Newchurch** Kent
62 F7 **Newchurch** Mons
79 H5 **Newchurch** Powys
115 J7 **Newchurch** Staffs
148 E7 **Newchurch in Pendle** Lancs
211 K4 **Newcraighall** C Edin
37 J3 **Newdigate** Surrey
49 L5 **Newell Green** Br For
24 F2 **Newenden** Kent
63 L2 **Newent** Gloucs
169 G4 **Newfield** Dur
181 G8 **Newfield** Dur
264 B4 **Newfield** Highld
48 E8 **Newfound** Hants
54 D2 **Newgale** Pembks
122 A3 **Newgate** Norfk
69 J6 **Newgate Street** Herts
113 K2 **Newhall** Ches
115 M7 **Newhall** Derbys
203 K7 **Newham** Nthumb
211 H4 **Newhaven** C Edin
132 C7 **Newhaven** Derbys
23 G7 **Newhaven** E Susx
140 E5 **Newhey** Rochdl
171 K8 **Newholm** N York
209 L6 **Newhouse** N Lans

22 F3 **Newick** E Susx
40 F8 **Newingreen** Kent
53 J6 **Newington** Kent
41 G7 **Newington** Kent
66 F7 **Newington** Oxon
95 K6 **Newington** Shrops
64 B8 **Newington Bagpath** Gloucs
144 D2 **Newland** C KuH
156 D6 **Newland** Cumb
143 K2 **Newland** E R Yk
63 H5 **Newland** Gloucs
143 H3 **Newland** N York
66 A5 **Newland** Oxon
28 E3 **Newland** Somset
81 H5 **Newland** Worcs
211 L6 **Newlandrig** Mdloth
188 E7 **Newlands** Border
165 K3 **Newlands** Cumb
180 D7 **Newlands** Nthumb
266 F6 **Newlands of Dundurcas** Moray
2 D5 **Newlyn** Cnwll
4 D3 **Newlyn East** Cnwll
256 F7 **Newmachar** Abers
209 L7 **Newmains** N Lans
70 D4 **Newman's End** Essex
89 H6 **Newman's Green** Suffk
88 C3 **Newmarket** Suffk
282 g3 **Newmarket** W Isls
188 D4 **Newmill** Border
267 J5 **Newmill** Moray
234 C3 **Newmill of Inshewan** Angus
141 M4 **Newmillerdam** Wakefd
211 G5 **Newmills** C Edin
210 D2 **Newmills** Fife
63 G5 **Newmills** Mons
221 L1 **Newmiln** P & K
197 G3 **Newmilns** E Ayrs
112 F5 **Newnes** Shrops
71 G5 **Newney Green** Essex
63 K5 **Newnham** Gloucs
49 H8 **Newnham** Hants
86 E7 **Newnham** Herts
40 B4 **Newnham** Kent
84 B3 **Newnham** Nhants
80 E2 **Newnham** Worcs
100 B6 **Newnham Paddox** Warwks
11 L5 **Newport** Cnwll
27 K4 **Newport** Devon
17 G3 **Newport** Dorset
143 L2 **Newport** E R Yk
87 L8 **Newport** Essex
63 K7 **Newport** Gloucs
274 F3 **Newport** Highld
19 H6 **Newport** IOW
44 C1 **Newport** Newpt
123 K8 **Newport** Norfk
75 H4 **Newport** Pembks
114 A7 **Newport** Wrekin
85 G6 **Newport Pagnell** M Keyn
223 G2 **Newport-on-Tay** Fife
37 G5 **Newpound Common** W Susx
4 D3 **Newquay** Cnwll
142 B2 **Newsam Green** Leeds
131 G6 **Newsbank** Ches
256 C5 **Newseat** Abers
147 K8 **Newsham** Lancs
168 E8 **Newsham** N York
160 E5 **Newsham** N York
181 H3 **Newsham** Nthumb
143 H2 **Newsholme** E R Yk
148 E5 **Newsholme** Lancs
141 J5 **Newsome** Kirk
201 H6 **Newstead** Border
116 E1 **Newstead** Notts
203 J7 **Newstead** Nthumb
267 J7 **Newtack** Moray
142 D1 **Newthorpe** N York
116 E2 **Newthorpe** Notts
22 D4 **Newtimber** W Susx
135 L2 **Newtoft** Lincs
217 G7 **Newton** Ag & B
86 E6 **Newton** Beds
189 G2 **Newton** Border
42 C6 **Newton** Brdgnd
119 M8 **Newton** Cambs
87 J5 **Newton** Cambs
43 K6 **Newton** Cardif
129 J6 **Newton** Ches
129 L7 **Newton** Ches
129 M4 **Newton** Ches
146 D2 **Newton** Cumb
133 J7 **Newton** Derbys
79 L8 **Newton** Herefs
79 L1 **Newton** Herefs

80 C4 **Newton** Herefs
251 G2 **Newton** Highld
252 D2 **Newton** Highld
263 L6 **Newton** Highld
147 G8 **Newton** Lancs
157 J7 **Newton** Lancs
148 B5 **Newton** Lancs
142 C2 **Newton** Leeds
118 D4 **Newton** Lincs
211 K5 **Newton** Mdloth
266 C3 **Newton** Moray
267 G4 **Newton** Moray
152 D1 **Newton** N York
101 J6 **Newton** Nhants
121 H8 **Newton** Norfk
117 J3 **Newton** Notts
190 D5 **Newton** Nthumb
180 C6 **Newton** Nthumb
209 H6 **Newton** S Lans
198 F6 **Newton** S Lans
98 C4 **Newton** Sandw
112 F4 **Newton** Shrops
29 K3 **Newton** Somset
115 G6 **Newton** Staffs
89 J7 **Newton** Suffk
210 E3 **Newton** W Loth
100 C7 **Newton** Warwks
34 B6 **Newton** Wilts
13 K8 **Newton Abbot** Devon
177 G7 **Newton Arlosh** Cumb
169 H5 **Newton Aycliffe** Dur
170 B5 **Newton Bewley** Hartpl
85 H5 **Newton Blossomville** M Keyn
85 K2 **Newton Bromswold** Beds
99 K2 **Newton Burgoland** Leics
135 L2 **Newton by Toft** Lincs
6 C2 **Newton Ferrers** Cnwll
7 G5 **Newton Ferrers** Devon
282 c7 **Newton Ferry** W Isls
106 E4 **Newton Flotman** Norfk
45 G1 **Newton Green** Mons
100 E4 **Newton Harcourt** Leics
140 C7 **Newton Heath** Manch
141 M3 **Newton Hill** Wakefd
151 G6 **Newton Kyme** N York
67 K1 **Newton Longville** Bucks
208 F7 **Newton Mearns** E Rens
160 C1 **Newton Morrell** N York
55 G5 **Newton Mountain** Pembks
171 H7 **Newton Mulgrave** N York
222 B5 **Newton of Balcanquhal** P & K
223 J6 **Newton of Balcormo** Fife
151 H4 **Newton on Ouse** N York
113 H7 **Newton on the Hill** Shrops
135 G5 **Newton on Trent** Lincs
14 C4 **Newton Poppleford** Devon
66 F1 **Newton Purcell** Oxon
99 H2 **Newton Regis** Warwks
166 B4 **Newton Reigny** Cumb
280 D6 **Newton Row** Highld
115 M6 **Newton Solney** Derbys
13 K3 **Newton St Cyres** Devon
122 E8 **Newton St Faith** Norfk
45 L6 **Newton St Loe** BaNES
27 G8 **Newton St Petrock** Devon
34 E3 **Newton Stacey** Hants
173 K2 **Newton Stewart** D & G
34 B3 **Newton Tony** Wilts
27 J5 **Newton Tracey** Devon
170 D8 **Newton under Roseberry** R & Cl
180 C2 **Newton Underwood** Nthumb
151 M6 **Newton upon Derwent** E R Yk
35 L4 **Newton Valence** Hants
187 H4 **Newton Wamphray** D & G
138 F2 **Newton with Scales** Lancs
203 L8 **Newton-by-the-Sea** Nthumb
160 B5 **Newton-le-Willows** N York
139 H8 **Newton-le-Willows** St Hel
162 K4 **Newton-on-Rawcliffe** N York
191 H5 **Newton-on-the-Moor** Nthumb
255 M4 **Newtongarry Croft** Abers
211 K6 **Newtongrange** Mdloth
245 K5 **Newtonhill** Abers
211 K6 **Newtonloan** Mdloth
234 F3 **Newtonmill** Angus
241 J4 **Newtonmore** Highld
61 J5 **Newtown** Blae G
113 K2 **Newtown** Ches
131 H7 **Newtown** Ches
129 M4 **Newtown** Ches
2 F5 **Newtown** Cnwll
3 J6 **Newtown** Cnwll

5 J4 **Newtown** Cnwll
11 K6 **Newtown** Cnwll
164 E1 **Newtown** Cumb
178 C6 **Newtown** Cumb
166 C6 **Newtown** Cumb
177 L6 **Newtown** Cumb
185 J1 **Newtown** D & G
131 K3 **Newtown** Derbys
14 C3 **Newtown** Devon
28 D6 **Newtown** Devon
15 L2 **Newtown** Dorset
63 K6 **Newtown** Gloucs
18 D2 **Newtown** Hants
48 C6 **Newtown** Hants
35 J8 **Newtown** Hants
80 B4 **Newtown** Herefs
80 C8 **Newtown** Herefs
80 E6 **Newtown** Herefs
81 G7 **Newtown** Herefs
240 B3 **Newtown** Highld
19 G5 **Newtown** IOW
139 G4 **Newtown** Lancs
202 F6 **Newtown** Nthumb
190 E6 **Newtown** Nthumb
203 G8 **Newtown** Nthumb
17 K4 **Newtown** Poole
94 D5 **Newtown** Powys
61 G7 **Newtown** Rhondd
112 F7 **Newtown** Shrops
113 H5 **Newtown** Shrops
30 C8 **Newtown** Somset
98 C3 **Newtown** Staffs
139 H6 **Newtown** Wigan
32 F5 **Newtown** Wilts
47 L6 **Newtown** Wilts
81 K4 **Newtown** Worcs
98 B7 **Newtown** Worcs
100 B2 **Newtown Linford** Leics
208 C7 **Newtown of Beltrees** Rens
201 J6 **Newtown St Boswells** Border
100 B3 **Newtown Unthank** Leics
233 L7 **Newtyle** Angus
50 D1 **Newyears Green** Gt Lon
216 F5 **Newyork** Ag & B
79 L4 **Nextend** Herefs
54 F6 **Neyland** Pembks
154 D6 **Niarbyl** IOM
63 K5 **Nibley** Gloucs
45 K3 **Nibley** S Glos
63 L7 **Nibley Green** Gloucs
29 K7 **Nicholashayne** Devon
56 F7 **Nicholaston** Swans
178 D5 **Nickies Hill** Cumb
150 D4 **Nidd** N York
245 L3 **Nigg** C Aber
264 C5 **Nigg** Highld
28 F5 **Nightcott** Somset
45 L5 **Nimlet** BaNES
47 G2 **Nine Elms** Swindn
74 C7 **Nine Wells** Pembks
179 H8 **Ninebanks** Nthumb
80 E2 **Nineveh** Worcs
24 C5 **Ninfield** E Susx
18 F6 **Ningwood** IOW
201 L8 **Nisbet** Border
202 B3 **Nisbet Hill** Border
19 H8 **Niton** IOW
208 L7 **Nitshill** C Glas
113 H2 **No Man's Heath** Ches
99 H2 **No Man's Heath** Warwks
4 F1 **No Man's Land** Cnwll
6 B3 **No Man's Land** Cnwll
52 C7 **Noah's Ark** Kent
52 E1 **Noak Bridge** Essex
70 D8 **Noak Hill** Essex
141 L6 **Noblethorpe** Barns
95 L2 **Nobold** Shrops
84 C3 **Nobottle** Nhants
135 L6 **Nocton** Lincs
107 H3 **Nogdam End** Norfk
66 E4 **Noke** Oxon
54 E3 **Nolton** Pembks
54 D3 **Nolton Haven** Pembks
28 E8 **Nomansland** Devon
34 B7 **Nomansland** Wilts
113 H6 **Noneley** Shrops
41 H5 **Nonington** Kent
178 B3 **Nook** Cumb
157 H6 **Nook** Cumb
51 G5 **Norbiton** Gt Lon
146 F7 **Norbreck** Bpool
81 G6 **Norbridge** Herefs
113 J2 **Norbury** Ches
115 J3 **Norbury** Derbys
51 J5 **Norbury** Gt Lon

95 J5 **Norbury** Shrops
114 B6 **Norbury** Staffs
113 J2 **Norbury Common** Ches
114 B7 **Norbury Junction** Staffs
81 J2 **Norchard** Worcs
130 B4 **Norcott Brook** Ches
146 F7 **Norcross** Lancs
103 L3 **Nordelph** Norfk
140 C5 **Norden** Rochdl
96 F4 **Nordley** Shrops
202 D4 **Norham** Nthumb
141 G3 **Norland Town** Calder
130 B5 **Norley** Ches
18 E4 **Norleywood** Hants
23 G4 **Norlington** E Susx
102 D5 **Norman Cross** Cambs
24 C6 **Norman's Bay** E Susx
14 C2 **Norman's Green** Devon
135 K2 **Normanby** Lincs
143 M4 **Normanby** N Linc
162 C6 **Normanby** N York
170 D7 **Normanby** R & Cl
136 B1 **Normanby le Wold** Lincs
50 B8 **Normandy** Surrey
116 B5 **Normanton** C Derb
117 L3 **Normanton** Leics
118 B2 **Normanton** Lincs
134 E8 **Normanton** Notts
101 K2 **Normanton** Rutlnd
142 B3 **Normanton** Wakefd
33 K3 **Normanton** Wilts
99 K1 **Normanton le Heath** Leics
116 E7 **Normanton on Soar** Notts
117 G5 **Normanton on the Wolds** Notts
134 F6 **Normanton on Trent** Notts
147 G8 **Normoss** Lancs
36 E2 **Norney** Surrey
46 C6 **Norrington Common** Wilts
6 E1 **Norris Green** Cnwll
141 K3 **Norristhorpe** Kirk
133 K3 **North Anston** Rothm
49 M5 **North Ascot** Br For
66 C1 **North Aston** Oxon
34 E6 **North Baddesley** Hants
229 G3 **North Ballachulish** Highld
31 K5 **North Barrow** Somset
121 K4 **North Barsham** Norfk
53 G1 **North Benfleet** Essex
20 F6 **North Bersted** W Susx
212 C2 **North Berwick** E Loth
168 F4 **North Bitchburn** Dur
181 H2 **North Blyth** Nthumb
19 K2 **North Boarhunt** Hants
18 B4 **North Bockhampton** Hants
13 H5 **North Bovey** Devon
46 B7 **North Bradley** Wilts
12 C6 **North Brentor** Devon
32 B3 **North Brewham** Somset
36 E3 **North Bridge** Surrey
86 F6 **North Brook End** Cambs
27 H3 **North Buckland** Devon
107 H2 **North Burlingham** Norfk
31 K5 **North Cadbury** Somset
135 J4 **North Carlton** Lincs
134 B3 **North Carlton** Notts
143 M1 **North Cave** E R Yk
64 E5 **North Cerney** Gloucs
22 F3 **North Chailey** E Susx
33 L7 **North Charford** Hants
191 H2 **North Charlton** Nthumb
51 G6 **North Cheam** Gt Lon
31 M5 **North Cheriton** Somset
15 K4 **North Chideock** Dorset
152 D8 **North Cliffe** E R Yk
135 G5 **North Clifton** Notts
169 H4 **North Close** Dur
137 G2 **North Cockerington** Lincs
228 E8 **North Connel** Ag & B
42 B5 **North Cornelly** Brdgnd
3 K7 **North Corner** Cnwll
228 C5 **North Corry** Highld
145 K7 **North Cotes** Lincs
4 A6 **North Country** Cnwll
107 K5 **North Cove** Suffk
160 D2 **North Cowton** N York
85 H6 **North Crawley** M Keyn
52 A4 **North Cray** Gt Lon
121 J4 **North Creake** Norfk
30 D6 **North Curry** Somset
152 E5 **North Dalton** E R Yk
150 E5 **North Deighton** N York
151 L8 **North Duffield** N York
259 G2 **North Duntulm** Highld
41 G6 **North Elham** Kent

136 E2 **North Elkington** Lincs
121 L7 **North Elmham** Norfk
142 D5 **North Elmsall** Wakefd
19 L3 **North End** C Port
177 K7 **North End** Cumb
32 D5 **North End** Dorset
153 K7 **North End** E R Yk
145 H2 **North End** E R Yk
71 G3 **North End** Essex
33 J7 **North End** Hants
35 J5 **North End** Hants
116 F8 **North End** Leics
145 J7 **North End** Lincs
144 D7 **North End** Lincs
119 H3 **North End** Lincs
137 H2 **North End** Lincs
144 E3 **North End** N Linc
44 E5 **North End** N Som
85 J2 **North End** Nhants
105 K5 **North End** Norfk
191 G6 **North End** Nthumb
138 C6 **North End** Sefton
21 G6 **North End** W Susx
21 J5 **North End** W Susx
260 B4 **North Erradale** Highld
100 D3 **North Evington** C Leic
71 K7 **North Fambridge** Essex
144 C3 **North Ferriby** E R Yk
153 H5 **North Frodingham** E R Yk
33 L8 **North Gorley** Hants
106 E5 **North Green** Suffk
91 G3 **North Green** Suffk
91 J2 **North Green** Suffk
152 C2 **North Grimston** N York
52 F6 **North Halling** Medway
20 B6 **North Hayling** Hants
203 G6 **North Hazelrigg** Nthumb
28 C4 **North Heasley** Devon
37 G6 **North Heath** W Susx
29 J6 **North Hele** Somset
11 K7 **North Hill** Cnwll
50 D2 **North Hillingdon** Gt Lon
66 C6 **North Hinksey** Oxon
37 J2 **North Holmwood** Surrey
7 K3 **North Huish** Devon
135 J6 **North Hykeham** Lincs
144 D7 **North Kelsey** Lincs
251 H2 **North Kessock** Highld
144 F4 **North Killingholme** N Linc
160 F5 **North Kilvington** N York
100 D6 **North Kilworth** Leics
18 B3 **North Kingston** Hants
118 F1 **North Kyme** Lincs
153 L2 **North Landing** E R Yk
67 K5 **North Lee** Bucks
160 D7 **North Lees** N York
40 F6 **North Leigh** Kent
66 A4 **North Leigh** Oxon
134 F3 **North Leverton with Habblesthorpe** Notts
82 C5 **North Littleton** Worcs
105 L6 **North Lopham** Norfk
101 K3 **North Luffenham** Rutlnd
20 C4 **North Marden** W Susx
67 J3 **North Marston** Bucks
211 K7 **North Middleton** Mdloth
190 E1 **North Middleton** Nthumb
172 D4 **North Milmain** D & G
28 C5 **North Molton** Devon
48 E1 **North Moreton** Oxon
20 E6 **North Mundham** W Susx
134 F7 **North Muskham** Notts
152 D8 **North Newbald** E R Yk
83 K7 **North Newington** Oxon
47 H7 **North Newnton** Wilts
30 D4 **North Newton** Somset
63 L7 **North Nibley** Gloucs
48 D8 **North Oakley** Hants
52 C2 **North Ockendon** Gt Lon
170 C6 **North Ormesby** Middsb
136 E1 **North Ormsby** Lincs
160 E5 **North Otterington** N York
135 L1 **North Owersby** Lincs
15 L1 **North Perrott** Somset
30 D4 **North Petherton** Somset
11 K4 **North Petherwin** Cnwll
105 H2 **North Pickenham** Norfk
81 M4 **North Piddle** Worcs
7 M6 **North Pool** Devon
15 M3 **North Poorton** Dorset
18 B2 **North Poulner** Hants
29 G3 **North Quarme** Somset
210 F3 **North Queensferry** C Edin
28 C4 **North Radworthy** Devon
118 D2 **North Rauceby** Lincs

137 G3 **North Reston** Lincs
150 C6 **North Rigton** N York
18 B4 **North Ripley** Hants
131 H6 **North Rode** Ches
165 H4 **North Row** Cumb
120 E8 **North Runcton** Norfk
146 C2 **North Scale** Cumb
135 G6 **North Scarle** Lincs
181 H2 **North Seaton** Nthumb
181 H2 **North Seaton Colliery** Nthumb
228 E6 **North Shian** Ag & B
181 J5 **North Shields** N Tyne
53 K2 **North Shoebury** Sthend
146 F8 **North Shore** Bpool
102 F3 **North Side** C Pete
164 C5 **North Side** Cumb
170 F7 **North Skelton** R & Cl
145 L8 **North Somercotes** Lincs
160 D7 **North Stainley** N York
167 J7 **North Stainmore** Cumb
52 D3 **North Stifford** Thurr
45 L5 **North Stoke** BaNES
48 F2 **North Stoke** Oxon
21 H5 **North Stoke** W Susx
88 B2 **North Street** Cambs
33 K7 **North Street** Hants
35 K4 **North Street** Hants
40 D4 **North Street** Kent
53 H4 **North Street** Medway
48 F4 **North Street** W Berk
203 K6 **North Sunderland** Nthumb
11 K3 **North Tamerton** Cnwll
12 F2 **North Tawton** Devon
209 K1 **North Third** Stirlg
145 H8 **North Thoresby** Lincs
34 B1 **North Tidworth** Wilts
12 C1 **North Town** Devon
31 J2 **North Town** Somset
49 L3 **North Town** W & M
122 A8 **North Tuddenham** Norfk
180 E5 **North Walbottle** N u Ty
122 F5 **North Walsham** Norfk
35 H2 **North Waltham** Hants
49 H8 **North Warnborough** Hants
70 D6 **North Weald Bassett** Essex
134 F3 **North Wheatley** Notts
8 C2 **North Whilborough** Devon
45 H6 **North Wick** BaNES
45 H7 **North Widcombe** BaNES
136 C2 **North Willingham** Lincs
133 H6 **North Wingfield** Derbys
118 B7 **North Witham** Lincs
31 L7 **North Wootton** Dorset
120 E6 **North Wootton** Norfk
31 J3 **North Wootton** Somset
46 B4 **North Wraxall** Wilts
47 H3 **North Wroughton** Swindn
105 J4 **Northacre** Norfk
68 B3 **Northall** Bucks
121 M8 **Northall Green** Norfk
160 E4 **Northallerton** N York
19 G1 **Northam** C Sotn
27 H5 **Northam** Devon
84 E3 **Northampton** Nhants
81 J2 **Northampton** Worcs
69 H6 **Northaw** Herts
30 D8 **Northay** Somset
102 C2 **Northborough** C Pete
41 K5 **Northbourne** Kent
24 D2 **Northbridge Street** E Susx
35 G3 **Northbrook** Hants
66 D3 **Northbrook** Oxon
36 E5 **Northchapel** W Susx
68 B5 **Northchurch** Herts
29 K8 **Northcott** Devon
14 D1 **Northcott** Devon
11 L4 **Northcott** Devon
66 D7 **Northcourt** Oxon
41 L1 **Northdown** Kent
133 G6 **Northedge** Derbys
67 H8 **Northend** Bucks
83 J5 **Northend** Warwks
49 L1 **Northend Woods** Bucks
131 G2 **Northenden** Manch
98 C7 **Northfield** Birm
245 K2 **Northfield** C Aber
144 C2 **Northfield** E R Yk
102 A2 **Northfields** Lincs
52 D4 **Northfleet** Kent
24 E2 **Northiam** E Susx
86 C6 **Northill** Beds
63 L5 **Northington** Gloucs
35 H3 **Northington** Hants
119 K1 **Northlands** Lincs

65 G4 **Northleach** Gloucs
27 L4 **Northleigh** Devon
14 E3 **Northleigh** Devon
12 C3 **Northlew** Devon
31 H3 **Northload Bridge** Somset
66 B6 **Northmoor** Oxon
28 F5 **Northmoor** Somset
234 B4 **Northmuir** Angus
20 B6 **Northney** Hants
50 E2 **Northolt** Gt Lon
128 F6 **Northop** Flints
129 G6 **Northop Hall** Flints
141 K3 **Northorpe** Kirk
143 M8 **Northorpe** Lincs
118 E8 **Northorpe** Lincs
119 G4 **Northorpe** Lincs
31 H3 **Northover** Somset
31 H6 **Northover** Somset
141 H2 **Northowram** Calder
17 H5 **Northport** Dorset
122 E4 **Northrepps** Norfk
282 d6 **Northton** W Isls
29 L5 **Northway** Somset
57 G7 **Northway** Swans
130 C5 **Northwich** Ches
45 H2 **Northwick** S Glos
30 E1 **Northwick** Somset
81 J4 **Northwick** Worcs
104 E4 **Northwold** Norfk
114 D2 **Northwood** C Stke
132 E6 **Northwood** Derbys
50 E1 **Northwood** Gt Lon
19 H5 **Northwood** IOW
113 G5 **Northwood** Shrops
63 L4 **Northwood Green** Gloucs
5 J1 **Norton** Cnwll
142 E5 **Norton** Donc
23 G7 **Norton** E Susx
64 B2 **Norton** Gloucs
130 A3 **Norton** Halton
86 E8 **Norton** Herts
18 E6 **Norton** IOW
62 F3 **Norton** Mons
44 D6 **Norton** N Som
152 B2 **Norton** N York
84 B3 **Norton** Nhants
133 L5 **Norton** Notts
79 K2 **Norton** Powys
170 B6 **Norton** S on T
133 G3 **Norton** Sheff
96 D2 **Norton** Shrops
97 G3 **Norton** Shrops
95 L7 **Norton** Shrops
96 E6 **Norton** Shrops
89 J2 **Norton** Suffk
57 H7 **Norton** Swans
20 F5 **Norton** W Susx
46 C2 **Norton** Wilts
81 K5 **Norton** Worcs
82 B5 **Norton** Worcs
32 F2 **Norton Bavant** Wilts
114 D5 **Norton Bridge** Staffs
98 C2 **Norton Canes** Staffs
79 M6 **Norton Canon** Herefs
122 B6 **Norton Corner** Norfk
135 H7 **Norton Disney** Lincs
32 C4 **Norton Ferris** Wilts
30 B5 **Norton Fitzwarren** Somset
18 E6 **Norton Green** IOW
45 H6 **Norton Hawkfield** BaNES
70 F6 **Norton Heath** Essex
113 M4 **Norton in Hales** Shrops
114 D1 **Norton in the Moors** C Stke
82 F3 **Norton Lindsey** Warwks
89 K2 **Norton Little Green** Suffk
45 J6 **Norton Malreward** BaNES
70 E6 **Norton Mandeville** Essex
45 M7 **Norton St Philip** Somset
31 G7 **Norton sub Hamdon** Somset
107 H4 **Norton Subcourse** Norfk
79 L5 **Norton Wood** Herefs
99 J2 **Norton-Juxta-Twycross** Leics
150 F2 **Norton-le-Clay** N York
134 F7 **Norwell** Notts
134 E7 **Norwell Woodhouse** Notts
106 E2 **Norwich** Norfk
281 f1 **Norwick** Shet
220 F8 **Norwood** Clacks
133 J3 **Norwood** Derbys
25 K1 **Norwood** Kent
70 E5 **Norwood End** Essex
141 H2 **Norwood Green** Calder
50 E3 **Norwood Green** Gt Lon
37 K2 **Norwood Hill** Surrey
103 H4 **Norwoodside** Cambs

101 G4	**Noseley** Leics	
7 G5	**Noss Mayo** Devon	
160 C6	**Nosterfield** N York	
88 C6	**Nosterfield End** Cambs	
248 D6	**Nostie** Highld	
65 G3	**Notgrove** Gloucs	
42 B6	**Nottage** Brdgnd	
6 D3	**Notter** Cnwll	
116 F4	**Nottingham** C Nott	
16 C6	**Nottington** Dorset	
142 A5	**Notton** Wakefd	
46 C5	**Notton** Wilts	
63 L3	**Nottswood Hill** Gloucs	
71 J5	**Nounsley** Essex	
81 J2	**Noutard's Green** Worcs	
89 H3	**Nowton** Suffk	
95 K1	**Nox** Shrops	
49 G2	**Nuffield** Oxon	
151 H4	**Nun Monkton** N York	
152 C6	**Nunburnholme** E R Yk	
116 E1	**Nuncargate** Notts	
166 C2	**Nunclose** Cumb	
99 K5	**Nuneaton** Warwks	
66 E7	**Nuneham Courtenay** Oxon	
51 K4	**Nunhead** Gt Lon	
153 J6	**Nunkeeling** E R Yk	
32 B2	**Nunney** Somset	
32 B2	**Nunney Catch** Somset	
80 D6	**Nunnington** Herefs	
161 L6	**Nunnington** N York	
190 F7	**Nunnykirk** Nthumb	
145 H6	**Nunsthorpe** NE Lin	
170 C7	**Nunthorpe** Middsb	
151 J6	**Nunthorpe** York	
170 D8	**Nunthorpe Village** Middsb	
33 K5	**Nunton** Wilts	
160 D7	**Nunwick** N York	
179 K4	**Nunwick** Nthumb	
67 L3	**Nup End** Bucks	
63 J7	**Nupdown** S Glos	
64 A5	**Nupend** Gloucs	
49 L4	**Nuptow** Br For	
34 E7	**Nursling** Hants	
36 A6	**Nursted** Hants	
46 F6	**Nursteed** Wilts	
97 J3	**Nurton** Staffs	
20 C6	**Nutbourne** W Susx	
21 J3	**Nutbourne** W Susx	
37 M1	**Nutfield** Surrey	
116 E3	**Nuthall** Notts	
87 H8	**Nuthampstead** Herts	
37 J5	**Nuthurst** W Susx	
23 G2	**Nutley** E Susx	
35 J2	**Nutley** Hants	
140 B4	**Nuttal Lane** Bury	
143 G7	**Nutwell** Donc	
280 E3	**Nybster** Highld	
20 E7	**Nyetimber** W Susx	
36 B6	**Nyewood** W Susx	
13 G1	**Nymet Rowland** Devon	
13 G2	**Nymet Tracey** Devon	
64 A7	**Nympsfield** Gloucs	
29 L6	**Nynehead** Somset	
30 F4	**Nythe** Somset	
20 F5	**Nyton** W Susx	

53 J6	**Oad Street** Kent	
100 D3	**Oadby** Leics	
12 D3	**Oak Cross** Devon	
169 K8	**Oak Tree** Darltn	
81 J3	**Oakall Green** Worcs	
115 G3	**Oakamoor** Staffs	
210 E5	**Oakbank** W Loth	
43 J2	**Oakdale** Caerph	
29 L6	**Oake** Somset	
97 J3	**Oaken** Staffs	
147 K6	**Oakenclough** Lancs	
96 F1	**Oakengates** Wrekin	
129 G5	**Oakenholt** Flints	
169 G3	**Oakenshaw** Dur	
141 J2	**Oakenshaw** Kirk	
132 E7	**Oaker Side** Derbys	
133 H8	**Oakerthorpe** Derbys	
76 E4	**Oakford** Cerdgn	
29 G6	**Oakford** Devon	
29 G6	**Oakfordbridge** Devon	
131 H6	**Oakgrove** Ches	
101 J2	**Oakham** Rutlnd	
114 B1	**Oakhanger** Ches	
36 A4	**Oakhanger** Hants	
31 K2	**Oakhill** Somset	
38 E3	**Oakhurst** Kent	

87 H2	**Oakington** Cambs	
78 E5	**Oaklands** Powys	
63 M4	**Oakle Street** Gloucs	
85 K4	**Oakley** Beds	
66 F4	**Oakley** Bucks	
210 D1	**Oakley** Fife	
35 H1	**Oakley** Hants	
67 H7	**Oakley** Oxon	
17 K3	**Oakley** Poole	
106 D7	**Oakley** Suffk	
50 A4	**Oakley Green** W & M	
93 L6	**Oakley Park** Powys	
64 C6	**Oakridge** Gloucs	
168 F5	**Oaks** Dur	
139 K1	**Oaks** Lancs	
95 K2	**Oaks** Shrops	
115 J5	**Oaks Green** Derbys	
64 E8	**Oaksey** Wilts	
178 C4	**Oakshaw** Cumb	
35 M5	**Oakshott** Hants	
99 J1	**Oakthorpe** Leics	
116 C4	**Oakwood** C Derb	
179 L5	**Oakwood** Nthumb	
37 H3	**Oakwoodhill** Surrey	
149 J8	**Oakworth** Brad	
40 C3	**Oare** Kent	
28 D2	**Oare** Somset	
47 H6	**Oare** Wilts	
118 D4	**Oasby** Lincs	
30 F5	**Oath** Somset	
234 D4	**Oathlaw** Angus	
50 E6	**Oatlands Park** Surrey	
216 D1	**Oban** Ag & B	
95 H7	**Obley** Shrops	
232 F7	**Obney** P & K	
31 L7	**Oborne** Dorset	
118 E8	**Obthorpe** Lincs	
90 D1	**Occold** Suffk	
275 J1	**Occumster** Highld	
196 F6	**Ochiltree** E Ayrs	
116 C4	**Ockbrook** Derbys	
98 B4	**Ocker Hill** Sandw	
81 H3	**Ockeridge** Worcs	
50 D7	**Ockham** Surrey	
237 G6	**Ockle** Highld	
37 H3	**Ockley** Surrey	
80 E6	**Ocle Pychard** Herefs	
153 G2	**Octon** E R Yk	
31 H7	**Odcombe** Somset	
45 L6	**Odd Down** BaNES	
81 L3	**Oddingley** Worcs	
65 J2	**Oddington** Gloucs	
66 E4	**Oddington** Oxon	
85 J4	**Odell** Beds	
12 C2	**Odham** Devon	
35 M1	**Odiham** Hants	
141 J2	**Odsal** Brad	
86 F7	**Odsey** Herts	
33 K5	**Odstock** Wilts	
99 K2	**Odstone** Leics	
83 J2	**Offchurch** Warwks	
82 C6	**Offenham** Worcs	
131 H2	**Offerton** Gt Man	
181 J7	**Offerton** Sundld	
22 F5	**Offham** E Susx	
39 G2	**Offham** Kent	
21 H5	**Offham** W Susx	
114 B5	**Offleymarsh** Shrops	
86 E2	**Offord Cluny** Cambs	
86 E2	**Offord Darcy** Cambs	
90 C5	**Offton** Suffk	
14 E3	**Offwell** Devon	
47 J4	**Ogbourne Maizey** Wilts	
47 J4	**Ogbourne St Andrew** Wilts	
47 J4	**Ogbourne St George** Wilts	
141 G2	**Ogden** Calder	
180 E3	**Ogle** Nthumb	
129 K3	**Oglet** Lpool	
42 D6	**Ogmore** V Glam	
42 E4	**Ogmore Vale** Brdgnd	
42 C6	**Ogmore-by-Sea** V Glam	
126 D6	**Ogwen Bank** Gwynd	
32 D8	**Okeford Fitzpaine** Dorset	
12 E3	**Okehampton** Devon	
13 K7	**Olchard** Devon	
84 F1	**Old** Nhants	
245 L2	**Old Aberdeen** C Aber	
35 J4	**Old Alresford** Hants	
185 J3	**Old Auchenbrack** D & G	
116 F3	**Old Basford** C Nott	
49 G8	**Old Basing** Hants	
190 F2	**Old Bewick** Nthumb	
136 F6	**Old Bolingbroke** Lincs	
49 L5	**Old Bracknell** Br For	
150 B7	**Old Bramhope** Leeds	

133 G5	**Old Brampton** Derbys	
175 J1	**Old Bridge of Urr** D & G	
106 B5	**Old Buckenham** Norfk	
48 C7	**Old Burghclere** Hants	
161 J5	**Old Byland** N York	
143 G7	**Old Cantley** Donc	
169 J3	**Old Cassop** Dur	
42 D6	**Old Castle** Brdgnd	
95 G4	**Old Churchstoke** Powys	
145 H6	**Old Clee** NE Lin	
29 J3	**Old Cleeve** Somset	
134 C6	**Old Clipstone** Notts	
127 G4	**Old Colwyn** Conwy	
183 G3	**Old Dailly** S Ayrs	
117 H6	**Old Dalby** Leics	
132 B4	**Old Dam** Derbys	
269 H6	**Old Deer** Abers	
31 H1	**Old Ditch** Somset	
142 E8	**Old Edlington** Donc	
169 H5	**Old Eldon** Dur	
153 J8	**Old Ellerby** E R Yk	
91 H8	**Old Felixstowe** Suffk	
102 D4	**Old Fletton** C Pete	
63 H3	**Old Forge** Herefs	
62 F2	**Old Furnace** Herefs	
131 L1	**Old Glossop** Derbys	
143 J3	**Old Goole** E R Yk	
10 b2	**Old Grimsby** IOS	
69 K3	**Old Hall Green** Herts	
122 F5	**Old Hall Street** Norfk	
70 C5	**Old Harlow** Essex	
72 E3	**Old Heath** Essex	
120 F3	**Old Hunstanton** Norfk	
102 F7	**Old Hurst** Cambs	
157 J5	**Old Hutton** Cumb	
4 D6	**Old Kea** Cnwll	
208 D4	**Old Kilpatrick** W Duns	
69 G3	**Old Knebworth** Herts	
106 E2	**Old Lakenham** Norfk	
148 B8	**Old Langho** Lancs	
154 f5	**Old Laxey** IOM	
119 L2	**Old Leake** Lincs	
152 B1	**Old Malton** N York	
142 C1	**Old Micklefield** Leeds	
83 G2	**Old Milverton** Warwks	
90 B3	**Old Newton** Suffk	
169 J3	**Old Quarrington** Dur	
116 F3	**Old Radford** C Nott	
79 J3	**Old Radnor** Powys	
256 B6	**Old Rayne** Abers	
25 J2	**Old Romney** Kent	
22 B6	**Old Shoreham** W Susx	
38 F3	**Old Soar** Kent	
45 L3	**Old Sodbury** S Glos	
118 C5	**Old Somerby** Lincs	
84 E7	**Old Stratford** Nhants	
97 K6	**Old Swinford** Dudley	
157 K2	**Old Tebay** Cumb	
160 F6	**Old Thirsk** N York	
140 F2	**Old Town** Calder	
166 B2	**Old Town** Cumb	
157 J6	**Old Town** Cumb	
23 K7	**Old Town** E Susx	
10 c3	**Old Town** IOS	
190 B7	**Old Town** Nthumb	
140 B8	**Old Trafford** Traffd	
133 H6	**Old Tupton** Derbys	
86 C6	**Old Warden** Beds	
102 B7	**Old Weston** Cambs	
280 E6	**Old Wick** Highld	
50 C4	**Old Windsor** W & M	
40 E4	**Old Wives Lees** Kent	
50 C7	**Old Woking** Surrey	
84 F7	**Old Wolverton** M Keyn	
113 G7	**Old Woods** Shrops	
270 E2	**Oldany** Highld	
82 D2	**Oldberrow** Warwks	
38 F2	**Oldbury** Kent	
98 C5	**Oldbury** Sandw	
97 G5	**Oldbury** Shrops	
99 J4	**Oldbury** Warwks	
63 J8	**Oldbury Naite** S Glos	
46 B1	**Oldbury on the Hill** Gloucs	
63 J8	**Oldbury-on-Severn** S Glos	
62 C2	**Oldcastle** Mons	
113 G2	**Oldcastle Heath** Ches	
134 B2	**Oldcotes** Notts	
149 H8	**Oldfield** Brad	
81 J2	**Oldfield** Worcs	
32 C1	**Oldford** Somset	
89 H4	**Oldhall Green** Suffk	
140 D6	**Oldham** Oldham	
213 G6	**Oldhamstocks** E Loth	
45 K4	**Oldland** S Glos	
256 E6	**Oldmeldrum** Abers	

11 M7	**Oldmill** Cnwll	
44 C7	**Oldmixon** N Som	
13 J3	**Oldridge** Devon	
276 C4	**Oldshoremore** Highld	
161 H6	**Oldstead** N York	
178 B6	**Oldwall** Cumb	
56 E6	**Oldwalls** Swans	
28 F6	**Oldways End** Somset	
115 J7	**Olive Green** Staffs	
187 G1	**Oliver** Border	
34 F5	**Oliver's Battery** Hants	
281 d4	**Ollaberry** Shet	
247 H1	**Ollach** Highld	
130 F4	**Ollerton** Ches	
134 D6	**Ollerton** Notts	
113 L6	**Ollerton** Shrops	
77 H4	**Olmarch** Cerdgn	
88 C7	**Olmstead Green** Cambs	
85 H5	**Olney** M Keyn	
279 L3	**Olrig House** Highld	
98 E7	**Olton** Solhll	
45 J2	**Olveston** S Glos	
81 J3	**Ombersley** Worcs	
134 D6	**Ompton** Notts	
179 H5	**Once Brewed** Nthumb	
154 e6	**Onchan** IOM	
131 L8	**Onecote** Staffs	
89 K3	**Onehouse** Suffk	
62 E4	**Onen** Mons	
79 M2	**Ongar Street** Herefs	
95 L7	**Onibury** Shrops	
229 G3	**Onich** Highld	
60 C5	**Onllwyn** Neath	
114 B3	**Onneley** Staffs	
36 E1	**Onslow Village** Surrey	
130 B5	**Onston** Ches	
116 B2	**Openwoodgate** Derbys	
260 B5	**Opinan** Highld	
266 F5	**Orbliston** Moray	
258 D7	**Orbost** Highld	
137 J6	**Orby** Lincs	
30 C6	**Orchard Portman** Somset	
33 J2	**Orcheston** Wilts	
62 F2	**Orcop** Herefs	
62 F2	**Orcop Hill** Herefs	
268 A4	**Ord** Abers	
244 E2	**Ordhead** Abers	
244 A3	**Ordie** Abers	
267 G5	**Ordiequish** Moray	
179 L7	**Ordley** Nthumb	
134 D4	**Ordsall** Notts	
24 F5	**Ore** E Susx	
80 B2	**Oreleton Common** Herefs	
96 E7	**Oreton** Shrops	
91 K5	**Orford** Suffk	
130 B2	**Orford** Warrtn	
17 H4	**Organford** Dorset	
115 J8	**Orgreave** Staffs	
40 C8	**Orlestone** Kent	
80 C2	**Orleton** Herefs	
81 G2	**Orleton** Worcs	
85 G1	**Orlingbury** Nhants	
165 J5	**Ormathwaite** Cumb	
170 C7	**Ormesby** R & Cl	
123 K8	**Ormesby St Margaret** Norfk	
123 K8	**Ormesby St Michael** Norfk	
260 D2	**Ormiscaig** Highld	
211 M5	**Ormiston** E Loth	
236 F7	**Ormsaigmore** Highld	
206 A4	**Ormsary** Ag & B	
138 E6	**Ormskirk** Lancs	
168 F1	**Ornsby Hill** Dur	
214 C6	**Oronsay** Ag & B	
275 D2	**Orphir** Ork	
51 M5	**Orpington** Gt Lon	
138 D8	**Orrell** Sefton	
139 G7	**Orrell** Wigan	
139 G7	**Orrell Post** Wigan	
154 d4	**Orrisdale** IOM	
175 J5	**Orroland** D & G	
52 D3	**Orsett** Thurr	
114 C8	**Orslow** Staffs	
117 K3	**Orston** Notts	
165 H4	**Orthwaite** Cumb	
147 K5	**Orton** Cumb	
157 K1	**Orton** Cumb	
101 H7	**Orton** Nhants	
97 K4	**Orton** Staffs	
102 D4	**Orton Longueville** C Pete	
177 K8	**Orton Rigg** Cumb	
102 C4	**Orton Waterville** C Pete	
99 J3	**Orton-on-the-Hill** Leics	
87 H5	**Orwell** Cambs	
139 K2	**Osbaldeston** Lancs	
139 K1	**Osbaldeston Green** Lancs	

151 K5 **Osbaldwick** York
99 L3 **Osbaston** Leics
112 D7 **Osbaston** Shrops
19 H5 **Osborne** IOW
118 E4 **Osbournby** Lincs
129 L6 **Oscroft** Ches
258 E8 **Ose** Highld
116 D7 **Osgathorpe** Leics
135 M1 **Osgodby** Lincs
143 G1 **Osgodby** N York
163 J5 **Osgodby** N York
247 H1 **Oskaig** Highld
226 E4 **Oskamull** Ag & B
115 K3 **Osmaston** Derbys
16 D6 **Osmington** Dorset
16 D6 **Osmington Mills** Dorset
142 A1 **Osmondthorpe** Leeds
161 G3 **Osmotherley** N York
66 D6 **Osney** Oxon
40 C3 **Ospringe** Kent
141 L4 **Ossett** Wakefd
134 E6 **Ossington** Notts
72 D7 **Ostend** Essex
50 F3 **Osterley** Gt Lon
161 K6 **Oswaldkirk** N York
139 L2 **Oswaldtwistle** Lancs
112 D5 **Oswestry** Shrops
52 B7 **Otford** Kent
39 K3 **Otham** Kent
39 K3 **Otham Hole** Kent
30 F4 **Othery** Somset
150 B6 **Otley** Leeds
90 E4 **Otley** Suffk
90 F4 **Otley Green** Suffk
206 E2 **Otter Ferry** Ag & B
34 F6 **Otterbourne** Hants
148 F4 **Otterburn** N York
190 C7 **Otterburn** Nthumb
11 H4 **Otterham** Cnwll
53 H5 **Otterham Quay** Kent
30 C2 **Otterhampton** Somset
282 c7 **Otternish** W Isls
50 C6 **Ottershaw** Surrey
281 e3 **Otterswick** Shet
14 C5 **Otterton** Devon
18 F3 **Otterwood** Hants
12 B7 **Ottery** Devon
14 C3 **Ottery St Mary** Devon
41 G6 **Ottinge** Kent
145 H3 **Ottringham** E R Yk
177 J7 **Oughterby** Cumb
158 F6 **Oughtershaw** N York
164 F3 **Oughterside** Cumb
132 F1 **Oughtibridge** Sheff
130 D2 **Oughtrington** Warrtn
161 J7 **Oulston** N York
177 H8 **Oulton** Cumb
142 B2 **Oulton** Leeds
122 C6 **Oulton** Norfk
114 B7 **Oulton** Staffs
114 E4 **Oulton** Staffs
107 L4 **Oulton** Suffk
107 L5 **Oulton Broad** Suffk
122 C6 **Oulton Street** Norfk
102 A5 **Oundle** Nhants
97 K5 **Ounsdale** Staffs
166 E4 **Ousby** Cumb
88 E3 **Ousden** Suffk
143 L3 **Ousefleet** E R Yk
181 G8 **Ouston** Dur
41 G5 **Out Elmstead** Kent
145 K3 **Out Newton** E R Yk
147 H7 **Out Rawcliffe** Lancs
203 J6 **Outchester** Nthumb
156 E3 **Outgate** Cumb
158 D2 **Outhgill** Cumb
82 D2 **Outhill** Warwks
114 B5 **Outlands** Staffs
141 G4 **Outlane** Kirk
103 K3 **Outwell** Norfk
33 K7 **Outwick** Hants
37 M2 **Outwood** Surrey
142 A3 **Outwood** Wakefd
140 B6 **Outwood Gate** Bury
116 C7 **Outwoods** Leics
114 B7 **Outwoods** Staffs
99 H6 **Outwoods** Warwks
142 A3 **Ouzlewell Green** Leeds
141 G2 **Ovenden** Calder
87 H1 **Over** Cambs
130 C6 **Over** Ches
64 A3 **Over** Gloucs
45 H2 **Over** S Glos
115 L4 **Over Burrows** Derbys
31 K7 **Over Compton** Dorset

102 B5 **Over End** Cambs
98 F4 **Over Green** Warwks
132 D6 **Over Haddon** Derbys
147 K2 **Over Kellet** Lancs
66 B3 **Over Kiddington** Oxon
63 G4 **Over Monnow** Mons
65 L2 **Over Norton** Oxon
130 F5 **Over Peover** Ches
161 G4 **Over Silton** N York
30 B3 **Over Stowey** Somset
31 G7 **Over Stratton** Somset
130 E4 **Over Tabley** Ches
34 C3 **Over Wallop** Hants
99 H5 **Over Whitacre** Warwks
133 J5 **Over Woodhouse** Derbys
66 B1 **Over Worton** Oxon
81 M7 **Overbury** Worcs
16 D6 **Overcombe** Dorset
132 F5 **Overgreen** Derbys
31 G4 **Overleigh** Somset
115 J8 **Overley** Staffs
129 J4 **Overpool** Ches
272 B3 **Overscaig Hotel** Highld
116 A8 **Overseal** Derbys
40 D4 **Oversland** Kent
82 C4 **Oversley Green** Warwks
84 F2 **Overstone** Nhants
122 E3 **Overstrand** Norfk
33 J3 **Overstreet** Wilts
83 L7 **Overthorpe** Nhants
245 J1 **Overton** C Aber
129 M4 **Overton** Ches
35 G1 **Overton** Hants
147 H4 **Overton** Lancs
151 J5 **Overton** N York
80 C1 **Overton** Shrops
56 E7 **Overton** Swans
141 L4 **Overton** Wakefd
112 E3 **Overton** Wrexhm
112 E3 **Overton Bridge** Wrexhm
130 F7 **Overton Green** Ches
157 K7 **Overtown** Lancs
209 L8 **Overtown** N Lans
47 H3 **Overtown** Swindn
142 A4 **Overtown** Wakefd
66 E8 **Overy** Oxon
67 J3 **Oving** Bucks
20 E6 **Oving** W Susx
22 E6 **Ovingdean** Br & H
180 D6 **Ovingham** Nthumb
168 E7 **Ovington** Dur
88 F6 **Ovington** Essex
35 H4 **Ovington** Hants
105 J3 **Ovington** Norfk
180 C6 **Ovington** Nthumb
34 D7 **Ower** Hants
19 H3 **Ower** Hants
16 E5 **Owermoigne** Dorset
91 G1 **Owl's Green** Suffk
95 H5 **Owlbury** Shrops
133 G2 **Owlerton** Sheff
64 A7 **Owlpen** Gloucs
49 K6 **Owlsmoor** Br For
67 J6 **Owlswick** Bucks
144 D6 **Owmby** Lincs
135 K2 **Owmby** Lincs
35 G6 **Owslebury** Hants
142 E5 **Owston** Donc
101 G2 **Owston** Leics
143 K7 **Owston Ferry** N Linc
145 H1 **Owstwick** E R Yk
145 J2 **Owthorne** E R Yk
117 H5 **Owthorpe** Notts
104 E3 **Oxborough** Norfk
15 L3 **Oxbridge** Dorset
136 F4 **Oxcombe** Lincs
133 J5 **Oxcroft** Derbys
71 G1 **Oxen End** Essex
156 D5 **Oxen Park** Cumb
157 H5 **Oxenholme** Cumb
140 F1 **Oxenhope** Brad
31 G3 **Oxenpill** Somset
64 D1 **Oxenton** Gloucs
47 L7 **Oxenwood** Wilts
66 D6 **Oxford** Oxon
68 E8 **Oxhey** Herts
180 F8 **Oxhill** Dur
83 H6 **Oxhill** Warwks
97 K3 **Oxley** Wolves
72 C4 **Oxley Green** Essex
24 C3 **Oxley's Green** E Susx
103 K6 **Oxlode** Cambs
189 J3 **Oxnam** Border
122 E6 **Oxnead** Norfk
50 F6 **Oxshott** Surrey

50 E6 **Oxshott Heath** Surrey
141 L7 **Oxspring** Barns
51 K8 **Oxted** Surrey
201 G2 **Oxton** Border
151 H7 **Oxton** N York
117 G1 **Oxton** Notts
56 F7 **Oxwich** Swans
56 F7 **Oxwich Green** Swans
121 K6 **Oxwick** Norfk
271 L7 **Oykel Bridge Hotel** Highld
256 B6 **Oyne** Abers
57 H7 **Oystermouth** Swans
64 A8 **Ozleworth** Gloucs

P

282 h3 **Pabail** W Isls
16 D1 **Packers Hill** Dorset
116 B8 **Packington** Leics
114 D1 **Packmoor** C Stke
83 G2 **Packmores** Warwks
234 C5 **Padanaram** Angus
67 H1 **Padbury** Bucks
51 H3 **Paddington** Gt Lon
130 C2 **Paddington** Warrtn
52 E6 **Paddlesworth** Kent
41 G7 **Paddlesworth** Kent
39 G4 **Paddock Wood** Kent
113 H5 **Paddolgreen** Shrops
129 G2 **Padeswood** Flints
140 F8 **Padfield** Derbys
130 C2 **Padgate** Warrtn
70 F7 **Padhams Green** Essex
140 B1 **Padiham** Lancs
149 L4 **Padside** N York
10 C7 **Padstow** Cnwll
48 F5 **Padworth** W Berk
169 G4 **Page Bank** Dur
20 E7 **Pagham** W Susx
72 D8 **Paglesham** Essex
8 C3 **Paignton** Torbay
100 A7 **Pailton** Warwks
23 K3 **Paine's Cross** E Susx
115 G5 **Painleyhill** Staffs
79 G6 **Painscastle** Powys
180 C6 **Painshawfield** Nthumb
152 B4 **Painsthorpe** E R Yk
64 C5 **Painswick** Gloucs
40 C3 **Painter's Forstal** Kent
208 E6 **Paisley** Rens
107 L5 **Pakefield** Suffk
89 J2 **Pakenham** Suffk
111 J4 **Pale** Gwynd
88 D6 **Pale Green** Essex
34 B3 **Palestine** Hants
49 L4 **Paley Street** W & M
98 C4 **Palfrey** Wsall
106 C7 **Palgrave** Suffk
16 F4 **Pallington** Dorset
69 J8 **Palmers Green** Gt Lon
11 H7 **Palmersbridge** Cnwll
196 F7 **Palmerston** E Ayrs
43 H7 **Palmerstown** V Glam
175 K3 **Palnackie** D & G
174 C2 **Palnure** D & G
133 J6 **Palterton** Derbys
48 F7 **Pamber End** Hants
48 F7 **Pamber Green** Hants
48 F6 **Pamber Heath** Hants
81 L8 **Pamington** Gloucs
17 K3 **Pamphill** Dorset
87 K5 **Pampisford** Cambs
31 G2 **Panborough** Somset
234 E8 **Panbride** Angus
11 K2 **Pancrasweek** Devon
43 G7 **Pancross** V Glam
43 J4 **Pandy** Caerph
92 D3 **Pandy** Gwynd
111 G5 **Pandy** Gwynd
62 C3 **Pandy** Mons
93 K3 **Pandy** Powys
112 B4 **Pandy** Wrexhm
127 G6 **Pandy Tudur** Conwy
111 L2 **Pandy'r Capel** Denbgs
71 H2 **Panfield** Essex
48 F4 **Pangbourne** W Berk
22 D5 **Pangdean** W Susx
80 E5 **Panks Bridge** Herefs
150 D5 **Pannal** N York
150 C5 **Pannal Ash** N York
243 L4 **Pannanich Wells Hotel** Abers
112 D7 **Pant** Shrops
109 H2 **Pant Glas** Gwynd
93 J7 **Pant Mawr** Powys

42 E5 **Pant-ffrwyth** Brdgnd
59 G4 **Pant-Gwyn** Carmth
57 J5 **Pant-lasau** Swans
128 B7 **Pant-pastynog** Denbgs
93 L8 **Pant-y-dwr** Powys
94 E3 **Pant-y-ffridd** Powys
42 D3 **Pant-y-gog** Brdgnd
128 E6 **Pant-y-mwyn** Flints
128 E4 **Pantasaph** Flints
74 F5 **Panteg** Pembks
5 K1 **Pantersbridge** Cnwll
93 G4 **Pantglas** Powys
136 C4 **Panton** Lincs
93 G3 **Pantperthog** Gwynd
57 H3 **Pantyffynnon** Carmth
61 L7 **Pantygaseg** Torfn
75 K7 **Pantymenyn** Carmth
107 G1 **Panxworth** Norfk
164 F4 **Papcastle** Cumb
280 E6 **Papigoe** Highld
212 D4 **Papple** E Loth
116 F1 **Papplewick** Notts
86 F3 **Papworth Everard** Cambs
86 F2 **Papworth St Agnes** Cambs
5 H4 **Par** Cnwll
41 J3 **Paramour Street** Kent
139 G5 **Parbold** Lancs
31 J4 **Parbrook** Somset
37 G6 **Parbrook** W Susx
111 G5 **Parc** Gwynd
44 E1 **Parc Seymour** Newpt
75 M2 **Parcllyn** Cerdgn
164 E5 **Pardshaw** Cumb
91 G3 **Parham** Suffk
245 H4 **Park** Abers
186 D7 **Park** D & G
178 F6 **Park** Nthumb
3 H3 **Park Bottom** Cnwll
140 F7 **Park Bridge** Tamesd
38 E6 **Park Corner** E Susx
49 G1 **Park Corner** Oxon
49 K2 **Park Corner** W & M
85 K4 **Park End** Beds
179 K4 **Park End** Nthumb
114 B1 **Park End** Staffs
40 D7 **Park Farm** Kent
19 J2 **Park Gate** Hants
150 A7 **Park Gate** Leeds
81 L1 **Park Gate** Worcs
70 C2 **Park Green** Essex
90 D2 **Park Green** Suffk
166 D2 **Park Head** Cumb
116 B1 **Park Head** Derbys
63 H7 **Park Hill** Gloucs
51 G3 **Park Royal** Gt Lon
68 F6 **Park Street** Herts
37 H4 **Park Street** W Susx
63 J5 **Parkend** Gloucs
38 F4 **Parkers Green** Kent
73 K1 **Parkeston** Essex
90 F8 **Parkeston Quay** Essex
6 C2 **Parkfield** Cnwll
129 G4 **Parkgate** Ches
165 H1 **Parkgate** Cumb
176 D7 **Parkgate** D & G
24 C4 **Parkgate** E Susx
71 G1 **Parkgate** Essex
52 B6 **Parkgate** Kent
39 L6 **Parkgate** Kent
37 K2 **Parkgate** Surrey
208 E4 **Parkhall** W Duns
27 G6 **Parkham** Devon
26 F6 **Parkham Ash** Devon
117 J1 **Parkhill** Notts
245 K1 **Parkhill House** Abers
63 G6 **Parkhouse** Mons
57 G7 **Parkmill** Swans
169 L1 **Parkside** Dur
209 L7 **Parkside** N Lans
129 J8 **Parkside** Wrexhm
17 K4 **Parkstone** Poole
17 M3 **Parley Green** Dorset
150 F8 **Parlington** Leeds
49 J1 **Parmoor** Bucks
70 B5 **Parndon** Essex
28 B2 **Parracombe** Devon
75 H4 **Parrog** Pembks
103 H2 **Parson Drove** Cambs
133 G1 **Parson's Cross** Sheff
72 F2 **Parson's Heath** Essex
116 A6 **Parson's Hill** Derbys
164 F3 **Parsonby** Cumb
208 F5 **Partick** C Glas
130 D2 **Partington** Traffd
137 H6 **Partney** Lincs

164 C6 **Parton** Cumb
22 B3 **Partridge Green** W Susx
62 B3 **Partrishow** Powys
115 K1 **Parwich** Derbys
70 E6 **Paslow Wood Common** Essex
84 F7 **Passenham** Nhants
36 B4 **Passfield** Hants
70 D7 **Passingford Bridge** Essex
102 D3 **Paston** C Pete
123 G4 **Paston** Norfk
114 F6 **Pasturefields** Staffs
12 B3 **Patchacott** Devon
22 D5 **Patcham** Br & H
68 F7 **Patchetts Green** Herts
21 J5 **Patching** W Susx
27 L2 **Patchole** Devon
45 J3 **Patchway** S Glos
149 L3 **Pateley Bridge** N York
72 D4 **Paternoster Heath** Essex
80 C3 **Pateshall** Herefs
221 K5 **Path of Condie** P & K
30 F5 **Pathe** Somset
222 E8 **Pathhead** Fife
211 L6 **Pathhead** Mdloth
82 E3 **Pathlow** Warwks
70 B2 **Patmore Heath** Herts
183 K1 **Patna** E Ayrs
47 G7 **Patney** Wilts
154 c5 **Patrick** IOM
160 B4 **Patrick Brompton** N York
139 M8 **Patricroft** Salfd
145 J3 **Patrington** E R Yk
145 J3 **Patrington Haven** E R Yk
41 G4 **Patrixbourne** Kent
165 L7 **Patterdale** Cumb
97 J4 **Pattingham** Staffs
84 C4 **Pattishall** Nhants
71 K2 **Pattiswick Green** Essex
96 D4 **Patton** Shrops
2 D5 **Paul** Cnwll
33 K4 **Paul's Dene** Wilts
84 D6 **Paulerspury** Bucks
144 F3 **Paull** E R Yk
45 K7 **Paulton** BaNES
80 F5 **Paunton** Herefs
191 G6 **Pauperhaugh** Nthumb
114 B8 **Pave Lane** Wrekin
85 K4 **Pavenham** Beds
30 D2 **Pawlett** Somset
202 C6 **Pawston** Nthumb
82 E7 **Paxford** Gloucs
202 E3 **Paxton** Border
40 B4 **Payden Street** Kent
14 C2 **Payhembury** Devon
148 E5 **Paythorne** Lancs
80 A1 **Paytoe** Herefs
22 F7 **Peacehaven** E Susx
132 B4 **Peak Dale** Derbys
132 B4 **Peak Forest** Derbys
119 J8 **Peak Hill** Lincs
102 D2 **Peakirk** C Pete
237 K4 **Peanmeanach** Highld
39 H4 **Pearson's Green** Kent
80 E8 **Peartree Green** Herefs
37 L4 **Pease Pottage** W Susx
45 K7 **Peasedown St John** BaNES
116 C2 **Peasehill** Derbys
122 B8 **Peaseland Green** Norfk
48 C3 **Peasemore** W Berk
91 H2 **Peasenhall** Suffk
37 G2 **Peaslake** Surrey
129 M1 **Peasley Cross** St Hel
25 G3 **Peasmarsh** E Susx
30 E8 **Peasmarsh** Somset
36 E2 **Peasmarsh** Surrey
223 H5 **Peat Inn** Fife
269 G3 **Peathill** Abers
100 D5 **Peatling Magna** Leics
100 D5 **Peatling Parva** Leics
96 C6 **Peaton** Shrops
89 G6 **Pebmarsh** Essex
82 D6 **Pebworth** Worcs
140 F2 **Pecket Well** Calder
129 M8 **Peckforton** Ches
51 J4 **Peckham** Gt Lon
100 A3 **Peckleton** Leics
111 M6 **Pedairffordd** Powys
40 F8 **Pedlinge** Kent
97 K7 **Pedmore** Dudley
30 F4 **Pedwell** Somset
200 B5 **Peebles** Border
154 c5 **Peel** IOM
138 D2 **Peel** Lancs
19 K3 **Peel Common** Hants
41 G7 **Peene** Kent

39 M7 **Peening Quarter** Kent
116 C7 **Peggs Green** Leics
68 E1 **Pegsdon** Beds
180 F2 **Pegswood** Nthumb
41 K3 **Pegwell** Kent
247 H2 **Peinchorran** Highld
259 G5 **Peinlich** Highld
54 F3 **Pelcomb** Pembks
54 F3 **Pelcomb Bridge** Pembks
54 F3 **Pelcomb Cross** Pembks
72 E4 **Peldon** Essex
39 G6 **Pell Green** E Susx
98 C3 **Pelsall** Wsall
98 C3 **Pelsall Wood** Wsall
181 G8 **Pelton** Dur
181 G8 **Pelton Fell** Dur
164 F1 **Pelutho** Cumb
5 L4 **Pelynt** Cnwll
56 F5 **Pemberton** Carmth
139 H7 **Pemberton** Wigan
39 M4 **Pembles Cross** Kent
56 D4 **Pembrey** Carmth
79 M4 **Pembridge** Herefs
55 G6 **Pembroke** Pembks
54 F6 **Pembroke Dock** Pembks
39 G5 **Pembury** Kent
57 K3 **Pen Rhiwfawr** Neath
92 E6 **Pen-bont Rhydybeddau** Cerdgn
55 J2 **Pen-ffordd** Pembks
62 C5 **Pen-groes-oped** Mons
124 F3 **Pen-llyn** IOA
125 G6 **Pen-lôn** IOA
75 M4 **Pen-rhiw** Pembks
61 K7 **Pen-twyn** Caerph
63 G5 **Pen-twyn** Mons
61 L6 **Pen-twyn** Torfn
112 B6 **Pen-y-bont** Powys
111 L6 **Pen-y-bont-fawr** Powys
42 C5 **Pen-y-bryn** Neath
75 L4 **Pen-y-bryn** Pembks
60 C4 **Pen-y-cae** Powys
62 E8 **Pen-y-cae-mawr** Mons
128 D4 **Pen-y-cefn** Flints
62 F5 **Pen-y-clawdd** Mons
43 G4 **Pen-y-coedcae** Rhondd
54 D2 **Pen-y-cwn** Pembks
61 G5 **Pen-y-darren** Myr Td
42 D5 **Pen-y-fai** Brdgnd
128 D5 **Pen-y-felin** Flints
92 D6 **Pen-y-garn** Cerdgn
111 L6 **Pen-y-Garnedd** Powys
61 J1 **Pen-y-genffordd** Powys
108 C5 **Pen-y-graig** Gwynd
126 D8 **Pen-y-Gwryd** Gwynd
42 F6 **Pen-y-lan** V Glam
126 C8 **Pen-y-pass** Gwynd
112 B1 **Pen-y-stryt** Denbgs
62 E5 **Pen-yr-Heol** Mons
60 F6 **Pen-yr-Heolgerrig** Myr Td
4 D5 **Penair** Cnwll
63 G5 **Penallt** Mons
55 J7 **Penally** Pembks
63 H1 **Penalt** Herefs
5 G6 **Penare** Cnwll
43 J7 **Penarth** V Glam
55 J4 **Penblewin** Pembks
76 B5 **Penbryn** Cerdgn
58 E2 **Pencader** Carmth
109 G3 **Pencaenewydd** Gwynd
212 A5 **Pencaitland** E Loth
4 D6 **Pencalenick** Cnwll
124 F5 **Pencarnisiog** IOA
76 F6 **Pencarreg** Carmth
10 F6 **Pencarrow** Cnwll
61 H2 **Pencelli** Powys
57 G5 **Penclawdd** Swans
42 E5 **Pencoed** Brdgnd
80 E5 **Pencombe** Herefs
63 G2 **Pencoyd** Herefs
63 H3 **Pencraig** Herefs
111 K6 **Pencraig** Powys
2 B4 **Pendeen** Cnwll
60 E5 **Penderyn** Rhondd
55 L5 **Pendine** Carmth
140 B7 **Pendlebury** Salfd
148 D7 **Pendleton** Lancs
81 H8 **Pendock** Worcs
10 E6 **Pendoggett** Cnwll
31 H8 **Pendomer** Somset
43 G6 **Pendoylan** V Glam
42 D5 **Pendre** Brdgnd
93 G3 **Penegoes** Powys
3 K3 **Penelewey** Cnwll
43 J2 **Pengam** Caerph

43 K6 **Pengam** Cardif
51 K5 **Penge** Gt Lon
4 D4 **Pengelly** Cnwll
10 F6 **Pengelly** Cnwll
125 H1 **Pengorffwysfa** IOA
6 B2 **Pengover Green** Cnwll
5 G5 **Pengrugla** Cnwll
127 K4 **Pengwern** Denbgs
3 H7 **Penhale** Cnwll
4 E3 **Penhale** Cnwll
5 J3 **Penhale** Cnwll
6 E4 **Penhale** Cnwll
4 C4 **Penhallow** Cnwll
3 H3 **Penhalurick** Cnwll
3 H3 **Penhalvean** Cnwll
47 H1 **Penhill** Swindn
44 E1 **Penhow** Newpt
24 C4 **Penhurst** E Susx
92 D2 **Peniarth** Gwynd
58 D4 **Peniel** Carmth
127 L7 **Peniel** Denbgs
259 H8 **Penifiler** Highld
192 F3 **Peninver** Ag & B
125 K7 **Penisar Waun** Gwynd
141 K7 **Penistone** Barns
3 K5 **Penjerrick** Cnwll
5 L4 **Penkelly** Cnwll
130 A2 **Penketh** Warrtn
183 G3 **Penkill** S Ayrs
97 L1 **Penkridge** Staffs
11 H3 **Penlean** Cnwll
112 F3 **Penley** Wrexhm
57 H5 **Penllergaer** Swans
42 E6 **Penllyn** V Glam
110 E2 **Penmachno** Conwy
43 J2 **Penmaen** Caerph
56 F7 **Penmaen** Swans
126 E4 **Penmaenan** Conwy
126 E4 **Penmaenmawr** Conwy
110 C7 **Penmaenpool** Gwynd
43 G7 **Penmark** V Glam
126 C3 **Penmon** IOA
109 K3 **Penmorfa** Gwynd
125 J5 **Penmynydd** IOA
67 M8 **Penn** Bucks
97 K4 **Penn** Wolves
68 A7 **Penn Street** Bucks
92 F3 **Pennal** Gwynd
268 F3 **Pennan** Abers
76 F3 **Pennant** Cerdgn
111 K5 **Pennant** Denbgs
93 J4 **Pennant** Powys
111 K6 **Pennant-Melangell** Powys
57 G7 **Pennard** Swans
95 J3 **Pennerley** Shrops
13 K2 **Pennicott** Devon
156 C7 **Pennington** Cumb
18 D4 **Pennington** Hants
139 J6 **Pennington Green** Wigan
61 H2 **Pennorth** Powys
45 L4 **Pennsylvania** S Glos
156 D6 **Penny Bridge** Cumb
55 G6 **Penny Bridge** Pembks
133 L4 **Penny Green** Notts
119 K6 **Penny Hill** Lincs
226 F7 **Pennycross** Ag & B
123 G7 **Pennygate** Norfk
227 G7 **Pennyghael** Ag & B
183 H1 **Pennyglen** S Ayrs
28 F8 **Pennymoor** Devon
75 L3 **Penparc** Cerdgn
92 D7 **Penparcau** Cerdgn
43 J2 **Penpedairheol** Caerph
62 C6 **Penpedairheol** Mons
62 C6 **Penperlleni** Mons
10 F5 **Penpethy** Cnwll
5 J4 **Penpillick** Cnwll
3 K3 **Penpol** Cnwll
5 K4 **Penpoll** Cnwll
3 G3 **Penponds** Cnwll
10 F7 **Penpont** Cnwll
186 C7 **Penpont** D & G
60 E2 **Penpont** Powys
7 J4 **Penquit** Devon
11 L7 **Penrest** Cnwll
76 B7 **Penrherber** Carmth
76 C6 **Penrhiw-pal** Cerdgn
43 G2 **Penrhiwceiber** Rhondd
76 C6 **Penrhiwllan** Cerdgn
108 F5 **Penrhos** Gwynd
124 D3 **Penrhos** IOA
62 E5 **Penrhos** Mons
59 L6 **Penrhos** Powys
125 K5 **Penrhos garnedd** Gwynd

127 G3 **Penrhyn Bay** Conwy
126 F3 **Penrhyn-side** Conwy
92 D6 **Penrhyncoch** Cerdgn
109 L4 **Penrhyndeudraeth** Gwynd
56 F7 **Penrice** Swans
194 D2 **Penrioch** N Ayrs
166 C4 **Penrith** Cumb
10 B8 **Penrose** Cnwll
11 J5 **Penrose** Cnwll
166 A5 **Penruddock** Cumb
3 K4 **Penryn** Cnwll
58 D5 **Pensarn** Carmth
127 J4 **Pensarn** Conwy
81 G2 **Pensax** Worcs
129 G3 **Pensby** Wirral
32 C4 **Penselwood** Somset
45 J6 **Pensford** BaNES
81 L6 **Pensham** Worcs
181 H8 **Penshaw** Sundld
38 E4 **Penshurst** Kent
38 E4 **Penshurst Station** Kent
6 B1 **Pensilva** Cnwll
97 K5 **Pensnett** Dudley
13 H3 **Penstone** Devon
94 C5 **Penstrowed** Powys
5 G5 **Pentewan** Cnwll
125 K6 **Pentir** Gwynd
4 C3 **Pentire** Cnwll
55 J5 **Pentlepoir** Pembks
89 G6 **Pentlow** Essex
89 G6 **Pentlow Street** Essex
120 F8 **Pentney** Norfk
34 D2 **Penton Grafton** Hants
34 D2 **Penton Mewsey** Hants
178 B3 **Pentonbridge** Cumb
125 J4 **Pentraeth** IOA
128 C7 **Pentre** Denbgs
129 H6 **Pentre** Flints
62 C6 **Pentre** Mons
94 C6 **Pentre** Powys
94 E5 **Pentre** Powys
95 G5 **Pentre** Powys
42 E2 **Pentre** Rhondd
112 E7 **Pentre** Shrops
112 D3 **Pentre** Wrexhm
77 G6 **Pentre Bach** Cerdgn
128 F4 **Pentre Bach** Flints
125 H5 **Pentre Berw** IOA
128 F5 **Pentre Ffwrndan** Flints
109 L6 **Pentre Gwynfryn** Gwynd
128 E5 **Pentre Halkyn** Flints
95 H7 **Pentre Hodrey** Shrops
127 K5 **Pentre Isaf** Conwy
128 C7 **Pentre Llanrhaeadr** Denbgs
94 E4 **Pentre Llifior** Powys
42 E6 **Pentre Meyrick** V Glam
127 L7 **Pentre Saron** Denbgs
59 M2 **Pentre ty gwyn** Carmth
126 F6 **Pentre'r Felin** Conwy
77 H5 **Pentre'r-felin** Cerdgn
60 D1 **Pentre'r-felin** Powys
76 D4 **Pentre'rbryn** Cerdgn
78 B8 **Pentre-bach** Powys
110 D1 **Pentre-bont** Conwy
76 C7 **Pentre-cagel** Cerdgn
112 A1 **Pentre-celyn** Denbgs
93 J2 **Pentre-celyn** Powys
57 J6 **Pentre-chwyth** Swans
112 D5 **Pentre-clawdd** Shrops
76 D7 **Pentre-cwrt** Carmth
57 J5 **Pentre-dwr** Swans
59 H5 **Pentre-Gwenlais** Carmth
78 C4 **Pentre-llwyn-llwyd** Powys
92 D8 **Pentre-llyn** Cerdgn
111 J1 **Pentre-llyn-cymmer** Conwy
93 J3 **Pentre-Maw** Powys
62 B6 **Pentre-piod** Torfn
44 B2 **Pentre-poeth** Newpt
126 F7 **Pentre-tafarn-y-fedw** Conwy
61 G6 **Pentrebach** Myr Td
94 E1 **Pentrebeirdd** Powys
112 B2 **Pentredwr** Denbgs
109 J4 **Pentrefelin** Gwynd
125 H1 **Pentrefelin** IOA
111 G1 **Pentrefoelas** Conwy
75 L6 **Pentregalar** Pembks
76 C5 **Pentregat** Cerdgn
116 C1 **Pentrich** Derbys
33 H7 **Pentridge Hill** Dorset
43 K2 **Pentwynmaur** Caerph
43 H5 **Pentyrch** Cardif
5 H4 **Penwithick** Cnwll
48 C6 **Penwood** Hants
60 C4 **Penwyllt** Powys
59 H4 **Penybanc** Carmth

78 F2	**Penybont** Powys	
112 D3	**Penycae** Wrexhm	
108 C6	**Penycaerau** Gwynd	
129 G7	**Penyffordd** Flints	
42 F3	**Penygraig** Rhondd	
59 G6	**Penygroes** Carmth	
109 H1	**Penygroes** Gwynd	
125 H2	**Penysarn** IOA	
60 E6	**Penywaun** Rhondd	
57 L3	**Penywern** Neath	
2 D5	**Penzance** Cnwll	
81 L5	**Peopleton** Worcs	
130 F5	**Peover Heath** Ches	
36 D2	**Peper Harow** Surrey	
113 K6	**Peplow** Shrops	
70 F5	**Pepper's Green** Essex	
67 G5	**Peppershill** Oxon	
68 D3	**Pepperstock** Beds	
196 C3	**Perceton** N Ayrs	
244 D5	**Percie** Abers	
269 H3	**Percyhorner** Abers	
9 i3	**Perelle** Guern	
29 G2	**Periton** Somset	
50 F2	**Perivale** Gt Lon	
14 B4	**Perkins Village** Devon	
181 G8	**Perkinsville** Dur	
134 C5	**Perlethorpe** Notts	
3 K3	**Perran Wharf** Cnwll	
3 K3	**Perranarworthal** Cnwll	
4 B4	**Perranporth** Cnwll	
2 E5	**Perranuthnoe** Cnwll	
3 K3	**Perranwell** Cnwll	
4 C4	**Perranwell** Cnwll	
4 C4	**Perranzabuloe** Cnwll	
64 E6	**Perrott's Brook** Gloucs	
98 D5	**Perry** Birm	
98 D5	**Perry Barr** Birm	
71 K3	**Perry Green** Essex	
70 B4	**Perry Green** Herts	
46 E1	**Perry Green** Wilts	
15 H2	**Perry Street** Somset	
114 C5	**Pershall** Staffs	
81 L6	**Pershore** Worcs	
86 B2	**Pertenhall** Beds	
221 K3	**Perth** P & K	
112 E5	**Perthy** Shrops	
80 E7	**Perton** Herefs	
97 J3	**Perton** Staffs	
32 E4	**Pertwood** Wilts	
40 E6	**Pet Street** Kent	
12 C7	**Peter Tavy** Devon	
68 F3	**Peter's Green** Herts	
102 D4	**Peterborough** C Pete	
79 L7	**Peterchurch** Herefs	
245 J3	**Peterculter** C Aber	
257 L2	**Peterhead** Abers	
169 L2	**Peterlee** Dur	
27 H8	**Peters Marland** Devon	
35 M6	**Petersfield** Hants	
50 F4	**Petersham** Gt Lon	
43 G6	**Peterston-super-Ely** V Glam	
43 L5	**Peterstone Wentlooge** Newpt	
63 H2	**Peterstow** Herefs	
40 F5	**Petham** Kent	
11 K5	**Petherwin Gate** Cnwll	
12 C1	**Petrockstow** Devon	
85 H5	**Petsoe End** M Keyn	
24 F4	**Pett** E Susx	
40 F5	**Pett Bottom** Kent	
90 E3	**Pettaugh** Suffk	
234 C7	**Petterden** Angus	
198 F4	**Pettinain** S Lans	
91 G4	**Pettistree** Suffk	
29 H6	**Petton** Devon	
113 G6	**Petton** Shrops	
51 M5	**Petts Wood** Gt Lon	
46 A2	**Petty France** S Glos	
211 J2	**Pettycur** Fife	
257 G7	**Pettymuk** Abers	
36 E6	**Petworth** W Susx	
23 L6	**Pevensey** E Susx	
24 B6	**Pevensey Bay** E Susx	
47 H7	**Pewsey** Wilts	
49 J2	**Pheasant's Hill** Bucks	
81 L3	**Phepson** Worcs	
181 H8	**Philadelphia** Sundld	
26 D6	**Philham** Devon	
200 F7	**Philiphaugh** Border	
2 F3	**Phillack** Cnwll	
3 L3	**Philleigh** Cnwll	
70 F3	**Philpot End** Essex	
210 E4	**Philpstoun** W Loth	
63 J2	**Phocle Green** Herefs	
49 J7	**Phoenix Green** Hants	
241 J5	**Phoines** Highld	
31 G5	**Pibsbury** Somset	
164 D6	**Pica** Cumb	
99 G4	**Piccadilly** Warwks	
68 D5	**Piccotts End** Herts	
142 E6	**Pickburn** Donc	
162 D6	**Pickering** N York	
34 E2	**Picket Piece** Hants	
18 B2	**Picket Post** Hants	
99 H7	**Pickford** Covtry	
99 H7	**Pickford Green** Covtry	
160 E6	**Pickhill** N York	
95 K3	**Picklescott** Shrops	
130 D4	**Pickmere** Ches	
30 B5	**Pickney** Somset	
114 A6	**Pickstock** Wrekin	
139 L3	**Pickup Bank** Bl w D	
27 H3	**Pickwell** Devon	
101 G1	**Pickwell** Leics	
46 B5	**Pickwick** Wilts	
101 L1	**Pickworth** Lincs	
118 D5	**Pickworth** Lincs	
63 H2	**Pict's Cross** Herefs	
256 D8	**Pictillum** Abers	
129 K5	**Picton** Ches	
128 D3	**Picton** Flints	
160 F1	**Picton** N York	
58 A5	**Picton Ferry** Carmth	
23 G6	**Piddinghoe** E Susx	
67 K8	**Piddington** Bucks	
84 F4	**Piddington** M Keyn	
66 F4	**Piddington** Oxon	
16 D3	**Piddlehinton** Dorset	
16 D3	**Piddletrenthide** Dorset	
103 G7	**Pidley** Cambs	
80 F3	**Pie Corner** Herefs	
169 G7	**Piercebridge** Darltn	
275 c1	**Pierowall** Ork	
64 C2	**Piff's Elm** Gloucs	
17 K2	**Pig Oak** Dorset	
79 L5	**Pig Street** Herefs	
180 E1	**Pigdon** Nthumb	
82 F3	**Pigeon Green** Warwks	
132 D7	**Pikehall** Derbys	
17 K2	**Pilford** Dorset	
70 E7	**Pilgrims Hatch** Essex	
135 H1	**Pilham** Lincs	
45 G4	**Pill** N Som	
6 D2	**Pillaton** Cnwll	
6 D2	**Pillatonmill** Cnwll	
83 G5	**Pillerton Hersey** Warwks	
83 G5	**Pillerton Priors** Warwks	
79 J2	**Pilleth** Powys	
142 A7	**Pilley** Barns	
18 E4	**Pilley** Hants	
18 E4	**Pilley Bailey** Hants	
44 C2	**Pillgwenlly** Newpt	
27 H5	**Pillhead** Devon	
147 H6	**Pilling** Lancs	
147 G6	**Pilling Lane** Lancs	
45 H2	**Pilning** S Glos	
25 K4	**Pilot Inn** Kent	
132 B7	**Pilsbury** Derbys	
15 J3	**Pilsdon** Dorset	
102 B2	**Pilsgate** C Pete	
132 E5	**Pilsley** Derbys	
133 H7	**Pilsley** Derbys	
107 H1	**Pilson Green** Norfk	
23 G3	**Piltdown** E Susx	
27 K4	**Pilton** Devon	
101 M6	**Pilton** Nhants	
101 K3	**Pilton** Rutlnd	
31 K3	**Pilton** Somset	
56 E7	**Pilton Green** Swans	
148 C7	**Pimlico** Lancs	
84 B7	**Pimlico** Nhants	
17 H1	**Pimperne** Dorset	
69 H2	**Pin Green** Herts	
90 E7	**Pin Mill** Suffk	
119 H6	**Pinchbeck** Lincs	
119 G6	**Pinchbeck Bars** Lincs	
119 G6	**Pinchbeck West** Lincs	
143 G4	**Pincheon Green** Donc	
170 D7	**Pinchinthorpe** R & Cl	
139 H4	**Pincock** Lancs	
84 F5	**Pindon End** M Keyn	
138 E5	**Pinfold** Lancs	
89 G3	**Pinford End** Suffk	
56 D4	**Pinged** Carmth	
49 G5	**Pingewood** W Berk	
13 M4	**Pinhoe** Devon	
99 H7	**Pinkett's Booth** Covtry	
46 B2	**Pinkney** Wilts	
99 K7	**Pinley** Covtry	
82 F2	**Pinley Green** Warwks	
182 F4	**Pinminnoch** S Ayrs	
182 F4	**Pinmore** S Ayrs	
14 C5	**Pinn** Devon	
50 E1	**Pinner** Gt Lon	
50 E1	**Pinner Green** Gt Lon	
113 K2	**Pinsley Green** Ches	
81 M5	**Pinvin** Worcs	
182 F5	**Pinwherry** S Ayrs	
133 J8	**Pinxton** Derbys	
80 C6	**Pipe and Lyde** Herefs	
114 A3	**Pipe Gate** Shrops	
98 E2	**Pipehill** Staffs	
253 G2	**Piperhill** Highld	
11 J5	**Pipers Pool** Cnwll	
101 J6	**Pipewell** Nhants	
27 J3	**Pippacott** Devon	
139 H3	**Pippin Street** Lancs	
79 G7	**Pipton** Powys	
50 B7	**Pirbright** Surrey	
50 B7	**Pirbright Camp** Surrey	
201 K7	**Pirnie** Border	
194 D2	**Pirnmill** N Ayrs	
68 F1	**Pirton** Herts	
81 K5	**Pirton** Worcs	
92 E7	**Pisgah** Cerdgn	
49 H1	**Pishill** Oxon	
108 E3	**Pistyll** Gwynd	
232 B2	**Pitagowan** P & K	
269 H3	**Pitblae** Abers	
221 J2	**Pitcairngreen** P & K	
264 C5	**Pitcalnie** Highld	
256 C6	**Pitcaple** Abers	
233 M2	**Pitcarity** Angus	
67 J6	**Pitch Green** Bucks	
36 C3	**Pitch Place** Surrey	
50 B8	**Pitch Place** Surrey	
64 B5	**Pitchcombe** Gloucs	
67 J3	**Pitchcott** Bucks	
119 J5	**Pitcher Row** Lincs	
96 C3	**Pitchford** Shrops	
254 D4	**Pitchroy** Moray	
31 L4	**Pitcombe** Somset	
42 D6	**Pitcot** V Glam	
212 E4	**Pitcox** E Loth	
256 B8	**Pitfichie** Abers	
256 C3	**Pitglassie** Abers	
264 B2	**Pitgrudy** Highld	
234 E4	**Pitkennedy** Angus	
222 E5	**Pitlessie** Fife	
232 D4	**Pitlochry** P & K	
256 B6	**Pitmachie** Abers	
241 K3	**Pitmain** Highld	
256 F6	**Pitmedden** Abers	
30 B7	**Pitminster** Somset	
234 E5	**Pitmuies** Angus	
256 B8	**Pitmunie** Abers	
31 G5	**Pitney** Somset	
222 C2	**Pitroddie** P & K	
223 G4	**Pitscottie** Fife	
52 F1	**Pitsea** Essex	
140 E7	**Pitses** Oldham	
84 E2	**Pitsford** Nhants	
68 B4	**Pitstone** Bucks	
29 J7	**Pitt** Devon	
34 F5	**Pitt** Hants	
63 L7	**Pitt Court** Gloucs	
38 F3	**Pitt's Wood** Kent	
245 G8	**Pittarrow** Abers	
223 K6	**Pittenweem** Fife	
222 D7	**Pitteuchar** Fife	
169 J2	**Pittington** Dur	
256 C6	**Pittodrie House Hotel** Abers	
34 B4	**Pitton** Wilts	
269 H3	**Pittulie** Abers	
169 H2	**Pity Me** Dur	
10 C7	**Pityme** Cnwll	
40 B6	**Pivington** Kent	
106 E8	**Pixey Green** Suffk	
37 J1	**Pixham** Surrey	
10 D6	**Plain Street** Cnwll	
209 L5	**Plains** N Lans	
96 C4	**Plaish** Shrops	
133 G8	**Plaistow** Derbys	
51 L2	**Plaistow** Gt Lon	
80 F7	**Plaistow** Herefs	
36 F5	**Plaistow** W Susx	
34 C7	**Plaitford** Hants	
139 J7	**Plank Lane** Wigan	
124 E4	**Plas Cymyran** IOA	
48 D6	**Plastow Green** Hants	
39 G2	**Platt** Kent	
139 J7	**Platt Bridge** Wigan	
113 H4	**Platt Lane** Shrops	
39 L3	**Platts Heath** Kent	
169 H1	**Plawsworth** Dur	
38 F3	**Plaxtol** Kent	
49 H4	**Play Hatch** Oxon	
25 G3	**Playden** E Susx	
90 F5	**Playford** Suffk	
4 C6	**Playing Place** Cnwll	
63 M1	**Playley Green** Gloucs	
95 K2	**Plealey** Shrops	
209 M2	**Plean** Stirlg	
222 C4	**Pleasance** Fife	
139 J2	**Pleasington** Bl w D	
133 K6	**Pleasley** Derbys	
133 K6	**Pleasleyhill** Notts	
32 B8	**Pleck** Dorset	
70 E2	**Pledgdon Green** Essex	
142 A4	**Pledwick** Wakefd	
9 j2	**Pleinheaume** Guern	
9 a1	**Plemont** Jersey	
129 K5	**Plemstall** Ches	
179 G6	**Plenmeller** Nthumb	
71 G4	**Pleshey** Essex	
248 C5	**Plockton** Highld	
95 J6	**Plowden** Shrops	
95 J3	**Plox Green** Shrops	
40 B6	**Pluckley** Kent	
40 B6	**Pluckley Station** Kent	
40 B6	**Pluckley Thorne** Kent	
41 J3	**Plucks Gutter** Kent	
164 F3	**Plumbland** Cumb	
157 G4	**Plumgarths** Cumb	
130 E5	**Plumley** Ches	
166 C3	**Plumpton** Cumb	
156 D7	**Plumpton** Cumb	
22 E4	**Plumpton** E Susx	
84 B5	**Plumpton** Nhants	
84 D6	**Plumpton End** Nhants	
22 E4	**Plumpton Green** E Susx	
166 C4	**Plumpton Head** Cumb	
51 L3	**Plumstead** Gt Lon	
122 C4	**Plumstead** Norfk	
122 C4	**Plumstead Green** Norfk	
117 G5	**Plumtree** Notts	
39 K4	**Plumtree Green** Kent	
117 K5	**Plungar** Leics	
40 B7	**Plurenden** Kent	
16 D2	**Plush** Dorset	
11 J6	**Plusha** Cnwll	
11 K8	**Plushabridge** Cnwll	
76 C5	**Plwmp** Cerdgn	
6 F4	**Plymouth** C Plym	
7 G4	**Plympton** C Plym	
7 G4	**Plymstock** C Plym	
14 B2	**Plymtree** Devon	
161 K5	**Pockley** N York	
152 B6	**Pocklington** E R Yk	
119 H7	**Pode Hole** Lincs	
31 J6	**Podimore** Somset	
85 J3	**Podington** Beds	
114 B4	**Podmore** Staffs	
73 G4	**Point Clear** Essex	
118 F5	**Pointon** Lincs	
18 A5	**Pokesdown** Bmouth	
11 L4	**Polapit Tamar** Cnwll	
270 C6	**Polbain** Highld	
6 C3	**Polbathic** Cnwll	
210 D6	**Polbeth** W Loth	
5 G1	**Polbrock** Cnwll	
81 J5	**Pole Elm** Worcs	
141 G4	**Pole Moor** Kirk	
102 B6	**Polebrook** Nhants	
23 K6	**Polegate** E Susx	
130 C4	**Polelane Ends** Ches	
99 H3	**Polesworth** Warwks	
2 B6	**Polgigga** Cnwll	
270 D6	**Polglass** Highld	
5 G5	**Polgooth** Cnwll	
185 H2	**Polgown** D & G	
21 H6	**Poling** W Susx	
21 H5	**Poling Corner** W Susx	
5 J4	**Polkerris** Cnwll	
123 G5	**Pollard Street** Norfk	
142 F4	**Pollington** E R Yk	
228 B2	**Polloch** Highld	
208 F6	**Pollokshaws** C Glas	
208 F6	**Pollokshields** C Glas	
5 G5	**Polmassick** Cnwll	
5 J4	**Polmear** Cnwll	
210 B3	**Polmont** Falk	
237 L4	**Polnish** Highld	
5 L4	**Polperro** Cnwll	
5 K5	**Polruan** Cnwll	
31 H2	**Polsham** Somset	
89 K7	**Polstead** Suffk	
89 K7	**Polstead Heath** Suffk	
216 C7	**Poltalloch** Ag & B	
3 J7	**Poltescoe** Cnwll	

Poltimore - Preston Street 345

13 M3 Poltimore Devon
211 J6 Polton Mdloth
202 A3 Polwarth Border
11 J6 Polyphant Cnwll
10 C6 Polzeath Cnwll
211 H7 Pomathorn Mdloth
132 B6 Pomeroy Derbys
78 F7 Ponde Powys
69 K7 Ponders End Gt Lon
102 F5 Pondersbridge Cambs
3 J3 Ponsanooth Cnwll
155 J2 Ponsonby Cumb
3 J7 Ponsongath Cnwll
13 G7 Ponsworthy Devon
126 E8 Pont Cyfyng Conwy
126 F6 Pont Dolgarrog Conwy
56 F3 Pont Morlais Carmth
126 C7 Pont Pen-y-benglog Gwynd
111 G6 Pont Rhyd-sarn Gwynd
42 C4 Pont Rhyd-y-cyff Brdgnd
94 D1 Pont Robert Powys
60 D6 Pont Walby Neath
58 F4 Pont-ar-gothi Carmth
60 C2 Pont-ar-Hydfer Powys
59 K4 Pont-ar-llechau Carmth
44 C2 Pont-Ebbw Newpt
78 D8 Pont-faen Powys
60 D5 Pont-Nedd-Fechan Neath
42 B3 Pont-rhyd-y-fen Neath
125 J7 Pont-rug Gwynd
112 D4 Pont-y-blew Wrexhm
110 E1 Pont-y-pant Conwy
74 E7 Pont-yr-hafod Pembks
42 D4 Pont-yr-Rhyl Brdgnd
9 e4 Pontac Jersey
59 H6 Pontamman Carmth
58 E6 Pontantwn Carmth
57 K4 Pontardawe Neath
57 G4 Pontarddulais Swans
58 E3 Pontarsais Carmth
129 G7 Pontblyddyn Flints
94 B5 Pontdolgoch Powys
142 C3 Pontefract Wakefd
180 E4 Ponteland Nthumb
93 G7 Ponterwyd Cerdgn
95 K2 Pontesbury Shrops
95 K2 Pontesbury Hill Shrops
95 K2 Pontesford Shrops
112 C4 Pontfadog Wrexhm
75 H5 Pontfaen Pembks
76 B4 Pontgarreg Cerdgn
75 K4 Pontgarreg Pembks
56 E3 Ponthenry Carmth
62 C8 Ponthir Torfn
76 A6 Ponthirwaun Cerdgn
43 J3 Pontllanfraith Caerph
57 H5 Pontlliw Swans
61 H6 Pontlottyn Caerph
109 H1 Pontlyfni Gwynd
62 B7 Pontnewydd Torfn
62 B6 Pontnewynydd Torfn
180 E8 Pontop Dur
77 K2 Pontrhydfendigaid Cerdgn
77 K1 Pontrhydygroes Cerdgn
62 C7 Pontrhydyrun Torfn
62 E2 Pontrilas Herefs
24 B4 Ponts Green E Susx
76 D6 Pontshaen Cerdgn
63 J3 Pontshill Herefs
61 G5 Pontsticill Powys
76 D7 Pontwelly Carmth
56 E3 Pontyates Carmth
58 F6 Pontyberem Carmth
129 G7 Pontybodkin Flints
42 F5 Pontyclun Rhondd
42 D3 Pontycymer Brdgnd
75 K5 Pontyglasier Pembks
42 F3 Pontygwaith Rhondd
75 K5 Pontygynon Pembks
62 C7 Pontymoel Torfn
62 B7 Pontypool Torfn
62 C7 Pontypool Road Torfn
43 G4 Pontypridd Rhondd
43 K3 Pontywaun Caerph
3 H3 Pool Cnwll
10 b2 Pool IOS
150 C6 Pool Leeds
80 D5 Pool Head Herefs
221 H7 Pool of Muckhart Clacks
95 G1 Pool Quay Powys
88 F7 Pool Street Essex
17 K4 Poole Poole
64 E8 Poole Keynes Gloucs
260 D4 Poolewe Highld
166 B6 Pooley Bridge Cumb
105 L7 Pooley Street Norfk
131 H7 Poolfold Staffs
63 L1 Poolhill Gloucs
38 C3 Pooting's Kent
35 H2 Popham Hants
51 K3 Poplar Gt Lon
91 K2 Poplar Street Suffk
81 G1 Porchbrook Worcs
19 G5 Porchfield IOW
106 F3 Poringland Norfk
3 H4 Porkellis Cnwll
28 F2 Porlock Somset
28 F1 Porlock Weir Somset
228 D6 Port Appin Ag & B
205 G3 Port Askaig Ag & B
207 H5 Port Bannatyne Ag & B
177 H6 Port Carlisle Cumb
204 C4 Port Charlotte Ag & B
170 C6 Port Clarence S on T
206 F4 Port Driseach Ag & B
154 g4 Port e Vallen IOM
56 E7 Port Einon Swans
204 E7 Port Ellen Ag & B
256 D7 Port Elphinstone Abers
154 b8 Port Erin IOM
10 D6 Port Gaverne Cnwll
208 B4 Port Glasgow Inver
260 B5 Port Henderson Highld
10 D6 Port Isaac Cnwll
172 D6 Port Logan D & G
236 E4 Port Mor Highld
171 J7 Port Mulgrave N York
282 h3 Port nan Giuran W Isls
282 c7 Port nan Long W Isls
282 h1 Port Nis W Isls
219 J7 Port of Menteith Stirlg
282 h1 Port of Ness W Isls
10 D6 Port Quin Cnwll
228 D6 Port Ramsay Ag & B
154 d7 Port Soderick IOM
19 L3 Port Solent Hants
154 b8 Port St Mary IOM
129 H3 Port Sunlight Wirral
57 L7 Port Talbot Neath
57 J6 Port Tennant Swans
204 B6 Port Wemyss Ag & B
173 J6 Port William D & G
248 B5 Port-an-Eorna Highld
206 B7 Portachoillan Ag & B
206 E5 Portavadie Ag & B
45 G4 Portbury N Som
19 K3 Portchester Hants
10 D6 Porteath Cnwll
182 C8 Portencalzie D & G
195 K1 Portencross N Ayrs
16 B5 Portesham Dorset
267 J3 Portessie Moray
54 F4 Portfield Gate Pembks
12 A5 Portgate Devon
267 H3 Portgordon Moray
274 D5 Portgower Highld
4 D2 Porth Cnwll
42 F3 Porth Rhondd
108 D3 Porth Dinllaen Gwynd
3 J5 Porth Navas Cnwll
112 C6 Porth-y-Waen Shrops
3 K6 Porthallow Cnwll
5 L4 Porthallow Cnwll
42 B6 Porthcawl Brdgnd
10 B8 Porthcothan Cnwll
2 B6 Porthcurno Cnwll
74 D5 Porthgain Pembks
2 B6 Porthgwarra Cnwll
114 D2 Porthill Staffs
4 D6 Porthkea Cnwll
43 G8 Porthkerry V Glam
3 G6 Porthleven Cnwll
109 K4 Porthmadog Gwynd
2 C4 Porthmeor Cnwll
4 F6 Portholland Cnwll
3 K6 Porthoustock Cnwll
5 H5 Porthpean Cnwll
4 A5 Porthtowan Cnwll
112 F2 Porthwgan Wrexhm
58 F5 Porthyrhyd Carmth
218 C8 Portincaple Ag & B
9 a1 Portinfer Jersey
143 K2 Portington E R Yk
216 F5 Portinnisherrich Ag & B
165 H6 Portinscale Cumb
44 F4 Portishead N Som
267 K3 Portknockie Moray
16 D8 Portland Dorset
245 K4 Portlethen Abers
175 L4 Portling D & G
4 F7 Portloe Cnwll
6 A4 Portlooe Cnwll
264 E3 Portmahomack Highld
5 G6 Portmellon Cnwll
18 E4 Portmore Hants
228 E6 Portnacroish Ag & B
282 h3 Portnaguran W Isls
204 B6 Portnahaven Ag & B
246 D2 Portnalong Highld
211 J4 Portobello C Edin
181 G7 Portobello Gatesd
98 B4 Portobello Wolves
33 L4 Porton Wilts
12 A7 Portontown Devon
172 B4 Portpatrick D & G
3 G2 Portreath Cnwll
259 H7 Portree Highld
3 M4 Portscatho Cnwll
19 L4 Portsea C Port
278 E3 Portskerra Highld
45 G1 Portskewett Mons
22 C6 Portslade Br & H
22 C6 Portslade-by-Sea Br & H
172 B3 Portslogan D & G
19 L4 Portsmouth C Port
140 D3 Portsmouth Calder
217 G3 Portsonachan Hotel Ag & B
267 M3 Portsoy Abers
34 F8 Portswood C Sotn
236 E7 Portuairk Highld
80 B6 Portway Herefs
80 C8 Portway Herefs
98 B6 Portway Sandw
82 C1 Portway Worcs
6 D4 Portwrinkle Cnwll
174 D7 Portyerrock D & G
13 J3 Posbury Devon
96 E3 Posenhall Shrops
88 F5 Poslingford Suffk
199 L6 Posso Border
17 J4 Post Green Dorset
12 F6 Postbridge Devon
67 H7 Postcombe Oxon
40 F7 Postling Kent
106 F2 Postwick Norfk
244 D4 Potarch Abers
5 G5 Pothole Cnwll
68 B1 Potsgrove Beds
120 F7 Pott Row Norfk
131 J4 Pott Shrigley Ches
72 C3 Pott's Green Essex
68 C5 Potten End Herts
41 H2 Potten Street Kent
163 H7 Potter Brompton N York
123 J7 Potter Heigham Norfk
67 L6 Potter Row Bucks
115 J4 Potter Somersal Derbys
97 J6 Potter's Cross Staffs
39 M4 Potter's Forstal Kent
23 H3 Potter's Green E Susx
69 K3 Potter's Green Herts
106 D5 Pottergate Street Norfk
135 L6 Potterhanworth Lincs
135 M6 Potterhanworth Booths Lincs
46 E7 Potterne Wilts
46 E7 Potterne Wick Wilts
69 H6 Potters Bar Herts
147 J5 Potters Brook Lancs
68 E6 Potters Crouch Herts
99 K7 Potters Green Covtry
100 B4 Potters Marston Leics
69 G3 Pottersheath Herts
84 E6 Potterspury Nhants
257 H8 Potterton Abers
150 F8 Potterton Leeds
121 L7 Potthorpe Norfk
32 D3 Pottle Street Wilts
161 G2 Potto N York
86 E5 Potton Beds
11 J1 Poughill Cnwll
13 K1 Poughill Devon
18 B2 Poulner Hants
46 E7 Poulshot Wilts
7 M4 Poulston Devon
65 G7 Poulton Gloucs
129 G2 Poulton Wirral
65 G7 Poulton Priory Gloucs
147 G7 Poulton-le-Fylde Lancs
97 G8 Pound Bank Worcs
23 H3 Pound Green E Susx
88 E4 Pound Green Suffk
97 G7 Pound Green Worcs
37 L3 Pound Hill W Susx
48 C6 Pound Street Hants
57 G6 Poundffald Swans
38 D7 Poundgate E Susx
66 F2 Poundon Bucks
38 E5 Poundsbridge Kent
13 G8 Poundsgate Devon
11 H3 Poundstock Cnwll
23 J3 Pounsley E Susx
174 C5 Pouton D & G
91 H1 Pouy Street Suffk
37 L3 Povey Cross Surrey
81 G6 Pow Green Herefs
190 F3 Powburn Nthumb
13 M5 Powderham Devon
15 L3 Powerstock Dorset
176 F5 Powfoot D & G
177 H7 Powhill Cumb
81 J5 Powick Worcs
221 J7 Powmill P & K
16 E5 Poxwell Dorset
50 C4 Poyle Slough
22 C5 Poynings W Susx
3 H2 Poynter's Lane End Cnwll
31 L6 Poyntington Dorset
131 H3 Poynton Ches
113 J8 Poynton Wrekin
113 J7 Poynton Green Wrekin
55 G3 Poyston Cross Pembks
89 K4 Poystreet Green Suffk
2 F5 Praa Sands Cnwll
52 A6 Pratt's Bottom Gt Lon
3 G4 Praze-an-Beeble Cnwll
3 H7 Predannack Wollas Cnwll
113 J5 Prees Shrops
113 J5 Prees Green Shrops
113 J4 Prees Heath Shrops
113 J4 Prees Higher Heath Shrops
113 J5 Prees Lower Heath Shrops
147 G6 Preesall Lancs
112 D4 Preesgweene Shrops
76 D6 Pren-gwyn Cerdgn
190 E4 Prendwick Nthumb
109 K3 Prenteg Gwynd
129 G2 Prenton Wirral
129 L1 Prescot Knows
29 K8 Prescott Devon
112 F7 Prescott Shrops
96 F7 Prescott Shrops
233 J2 Presnerb Angus
202 C6 Pressen Nthumb
128 C3 Prestatyn Denbgs
131 H4 Prestbury Ches
64 E2 Prestbury Gloucs
79 K2 Presteigne Powys
31 K3 Prestleigh Somset
139 M6 Prestolee Bolton
213 H7 Preston Border
22 D6 Preston Br & H
7 L4 Preston Devon
13 K7 Preston Devon
16 D6 Preston Dorset
212 D3 Preston E Loth
144 F2 Preston E R Yk
80 F8 Preston Gloucs
64 F7 Preston Gloucs
68 F2 Preston Herts
40 D3 Preston Kent
41 H3 Preston Kent
139 G2 Preston Lancs
203 K8 Preston Nthumb
101 J3 Preston Rutlnd
96 C1 Preston Shrops
29 K4 Preston Somset
89 J5 Preston Suffk
8 D3 Preston Torbay
46 F3 Preston Wilts
47 K4 Preston Wilts
82 E2 Preston Bagot Warwks
67 G1 Preston Bissett Bucks
29 L5 Preston Bowyer Somset
113 J6 Preston Brockhurst Shrops
130 B4 Preston Brook Halton
35 J3 Preston Candover Hants
84 B4 Preston Capes Nhants
48 F1 Preston Crowmarsh Oxon
84 F4 Preston Deanery Nhants
82 E2 Preston Green Warwks
113 H7 Preston Gubbals Shrops
113 G8 Preston Montford Shrops
82 F5 Preston on Stour Warwks
169 L7 Preston on Tees S on T
130 B3 Preston on the Hill Halton
79 M7 Preston on Wye Herefs
157 H6 Preston Patrick Cumb
31 H7 Preston Plucknett Somset
41 H3 Preston Street Kent

113 L8 **Preston upon the Weald Moors** Wrekin
80 D6 **Preston Wynne** Herefs
159 K4 **Preston-under-Scar** N York
211 L4 **Prestonpans** E Loth
140 B6 **Prestwich** Bury
180 E4 **Prestwick** Nthumb
196 C6 **Prestwick** S Ayrs
67 L7 **Prestwood** Bucks
97 K6 **Prestwood** Staffs
42 E3 **Price Town** Brdgnd
104 B7 **Prickwillow** Cambs
31 H1 **Priddy** Somset
157 H7 **Priest Hutton** Lancs
12 B1 **Priestacott** Devon
132 C5 **Priestcliffe** Derbys
132 C5 **Priestcliffe Ditch** Derbys
67 G6 **Priestend** Bucks
197 H3 **Priestland** E Ayrs
141 H3 **Priestley Green** Calder
95 H4 **Priestweston** Shrops
52 E6 **Priestwood Green** Kent
100 B5 **Primethorpe** Leics
122 B8 **Primrose Green** Norfk
103 H5 **Primrose Hill** Cambs
133 J8 **Primrose Hill** Derbys
97 L6 **Primrose Hill** Dudley
138 E6 **Primrose Hill** Lancs
213 H7 **Primrosehill** Border
202 C7 **Primsidemill** Border
55 K4 **Princes Gate** Pembks
67 K6 **Princes Risborough** Bucks
83 J1 **Princethorpe** Warwks
12 E7 **Princetown** Devon
20 C5 **Prinsted** W Susx
128 C7 **Prion** Denbgs
178 B5 **Prior Rigg** Cumb
96 B8 **Priors Halton** Shrops
83 L4 **Priors Hardwick** Warwks
83 L4 **Priors Marston** Warwks
64 C2 **Priors Norton** Gloucs
47 H1 **Priory Vale** Swindn
79 J6 **Priory Wood** Herefs
42 F6 **Prisk** V Glam
45 K7 **Priston** BaNES
106 C5 **Pristow Green** Norfk
53 J2 **Prittlewell** Sthend
35 L5 **Privett** Hants
27 K3 **Prixford** Devon
4 E5 **Probus** Cnwll
212 B3 **Prora** E Loth
164 F3 **Prospect** Cumb
3 G5 **Prospidnick** Cnwll
268 E3 **Protstonhill** Abers
45 G5 **Providence** N Som
180 D6 **Prudhoe** Nthumb
2 E5 **Prussia Cove** Cnwll
45 J6 **Publow** BaNES
69 K2 **Puckeridge** Herts
30 E7 **Puckington** Somset
45 K4 **Pucklechurch** S Glos
81 K7 **Puckrup** Gloucs
130 E5 **Puddinglake** Ches
129 H5 **Puddington** Ches
28 E8 **Puddington** Devon
105 L5 **Puddledock** Norfk
68 C2 **Puddlehill** Herts
16 E4 **Puddletown** Dorset
80 D3 **Pudleston** Herefs
141 K1 **Pudsey** Leeds
21 H3 **Pulborough** W Susx
114 A7 **Puleston** Wrekin
129 J7 **Pulford** Ches
16 D1 **Pulham** Dorset
106 D6 **Pulham Market** Norfk
106 E6 **Pulham St Mary** Norfk
63 J8 **Pullens Green** S Glos
96 B2 **Pulley** Shrops
85 L8 **Pulloxhill** Beds
210 E5 **Pumpherston** W Loth
77 J7 **Pumsaint** Carmth
75 G6 **Puncheston** Pembks
15 M5 **Puncknowle** Dorset
23 K3 **Punnett's Town** E Susx
19 M2 **Purbrook** Hants
52 C3 **Purfleet** Thurr
30 D3 **Puriton** Somset
71 K6 **Purleigh** Essex
51 J6 **Purley** Gt Lon
49 G4 **Purley** W Berk
95 G7 **Purlogue** Shrops
46 C5 **Purlpit** Wilts
103 K6 **Purls Bridge** Cambs
32 B7 **Purse Caundle** Dorset
81 K1 **Purshull Green** Worcs

95 J7 **Purslow** Shrops
142 C4 **Purston Jaglin** Wakefd
15 J1 **Purtington** Somset
63 K6 **Purton** Gloucs
63 K6 **Purton** Gloucs
47 G2 **Purton** Wilts
47 G1 **Purton Stoke** Wilts
84 D6 **Pury End** Nhants
65 M7 **Pusey** Oxon
80 E7 **Putley** Herefs
80 F7 **Putley Green** Herefs
63 M5 **Putloe** Gloucs
51 G4 **Putney** Gt Lon
9 k3 **Putron Village** Guern
27 H3 **Putsborough** Devon
67 L4 **Puttenham** Herts
36 D2 **Puttenham** Surrey
89 G7 **Puttock End** Essex
70 E3 **Puttock's End** Essex
16 C6 **Putton** Dorset
84 E6 **Puxley** Nhants
44 E6 **Puxton** N Som
56 E4 **Pwll** Carmth
58 A5 **Pwll Trap** Carmth
61 L5 **Pwll-du** Mons
111 M1 **Pwll-glas** Denbgs
42 B3 **Pwll-y-glaw** Neath
54 F6 **Pwllcrochan** Pembks
78 E8 **Pwllgloyw** Powys
108 F4 **Pwllheli** Gwynd
63 G8 **Pwllmeyric** Mons
126 F4 **Pydew** Conwy
116 D1 **Pye Bridge** Derbys
44 D2 **Pye Corner** Newpt
114 F8 **Pye Green** Staffs
22 D4 **Pyecombe** W Susx
42 B5 **Pyle** Brdgnd
29 L5 **Pyleigh** Somset
31 K3 **Pylle** Somset
103 K6 **Pymoor** Cambs
15 L4 **Pymore** Dorset
50 D7 **Pyrford** Surrey
67 G7 **Pyrton** Oxon
101 J8 **Pytchley** Nhants
11 K2 **Pyworthy** Devon

94 F7 **Quabbs** Shrops
119 H5 **Quadring** Lincs
119 H5 **Quadring Eaudike** Lincs
67 H3 **Quainton** Bucks
43 H3 **Quaker's Yard** Myr Td
180 F8 **Quaking Houses** Dur
34 C2 **Quarley** Hants
116 B3 **Quarndon** Derbys
19 K5 **Quarr Hill** IOW
208 B5 **Quarrier's Village** Inver
118 E3 **Quarrington** Lincs
169 J3 **Quarrington Hill** Dur
97 L6 **Quarry Bank** Dudley
130 A6 **Quarrybank** Ches
266 D3 **Quarrywood** Moray
207 K6 **Quarter** N Ayrs
197 L1 **Quarter** S Lans
97 G5 **Quatford** Shrops
97 G5 **Quatt** Shrops
168 F2 **Quebec** Dur
64 A4 **Quedgeley** Gloucs
104 B7 **Queen Adelaide** Cambs
31 K6 **Queen Camel** Somset
45 J5 **Queen Charlton** BaNES
28 E7 **Queen Dart** Devon
32 C4 **Queen Oak** Dorset
39 H4 **Queen Street** Kent
46 F2 **Queen Street** Wilts
19 J6 **Queen's Bower** IOW
112 E6 **Queen's Head** Shrops
85 L5 **Queen's Park** Beds
84 E3 **Queen's Park** Nhants
53 K4 **Queenborough** Kent
81 K7 **Queenhill** Worcs
141 H2 **Queensbury** Brad
129 H6 **Queensferry** Flints
209 H6 **Queenslie** C Glas
209 J3 **Queenzieburn** N Lans
70 D1 **Quendon** Essex
100 E1 **Queniborough** Leics
65 H6 **Quenington** Gloucs
147 K4 **Quernmore** Lancs
147 K3 **Quernmore Park Hall** Lancs
98 D4 **Queslett** Birm
6 C2 **Quethiock** Cnwll
48 E4 **Quick's Green** W Berk

105 L6 **Quidenham** Norfk
35 G1 **Quidhampton** Hants
33 K5 **Quidhampton** Wilts
113 H5 **Quina Brook** Shrops
84 B5 **Quinbury End** Nhants
98 C6 **Quinton** Dudley
84 E4 **Quinton** Nhants
84 F4 **Quinton Green** Nhants
4 D3 **Quintrell Downs** Cnwll
12 B6 **Quither** Devon
115 H3 **Quixhall** Staffs
213 H6 **Quixwood** Border
12 A3 **Quoditch** Devon
116 F8 **Quorn** Leics
199 G5 **Quothquan** S Lans
275 d5 **Quoyburray** Ork
275 b4 **Quoyloo** Ork

R

39 K4 **Rabbit's Cross** Kent
69 G3 **Rableyheath** Herts
177 G8 **Raby** Cumb
129 H4 **Raby** Wirral
199 K6 **Rachan Mill** Border
126 C6 **Rachub** Gwynd
28 E7 **Rackenford** Devon
21 H4 **Rackham** W Susx
122 F8 **Rackheath** Norfk
176 D4 **Racks** D & G
275 a5 **Rackwick** Ork
115 M4 **Radbourne** Derbys
140 B6 **Radcliffe** Bury
191 K5 **Radcliffe** Nthumb
117 H4 **Radcliffe on Trent** Notts
84 D8 **Radclive** Bucks
65 L7 **Radcot** Oxon
263 J7 **Radernie** Fife
29 J5 **Raddington** Somset
223 H5 **Radernie** Fife
83 H2 **Radford Semele** Warwks
30 B3 **Radlet** Somset
68 F7 **Radlett** Herts
28 C6 **Radley** Devon
66 D7 **Radley** Oxon
70 F6 **Radley Green** Essex
130 B8 **Radmore Green** Ches
67 J7 **Radnage** Bucks
45 K8 **Radstock** BaNES
84 B7 **Radstone** Nhants
83 J5 **Radway** Warwks
114 B1 **Radway Green** Ches
85 K4 **Radwell** Beds
86 E8 **Radwell** Herts
88 C7 **Radwinter** Essex
88 C7 **Radwinter End** Essex
43 H5 **Radyr** Cardif
118 D2 **RAF College (Cranwell)** Lincs
265 H8 **Rafford** Moray
117 H7 **Ragdale** Leics
95 L5 **Ragdon** Shrops
2 D6 **Raginnis** Cnwll
62 E5 **Raglan** Mons
134 F5 **Ragnall** Notts
252 F6 **Raigbeg** Highld
81 K4 **Rainbow Hill** Worcs
138 F7 **Rainford** St Hel
52 B3 **Rainham** Gt Lon
53 H6 **Rainham** Medway
129 L2 **Rainhill** St Hel
129 L2 **Rainhill Stoops** St Hel
131 J4 **Rainow** Ches
140 B7 **Rainsough** Bury
160 E7 **Rainton** N York
134 B8 **Rainworth** Notts
157 K1 **Raisbeck** Cumb
167 G2 **Raise** Cumb
152 C3 **Raisthorpe** N York
222 C2 **Rait** P & K
136 F3 **Raithby** Lincs
137 G6 **Raithby** Lincs
171 K8 **Raithwaite** N York
36 B5 **Rake** W Susx
140 E5 **Rakewood** Rochdl
241 J4 **Ralia** Highld
77 G6 **Ram** Carmth
45 K3 **Ram Hill** S Glos
40 C6 **Ram Lane** Kent
258 B7 **Ramasaig** Highld
3 J4 **Rame** Cnwll
6 E5 **Rame** Cnwll
16 A2 **Rampisham** Dorset
146 E3 **Rampside** Cumb
87 J2 **Rampton** Cambs

134 F4 **Rampton** Notts
140 B4 **Ramsbottom** Bury
47 K4 **Ramsbury** Wilts
274 F3 **Ramscraigs** Highld
35 L6 **Ramsdean** Hants
48 E7 **Ramsdell** Hants
65 M4 **Ramsden** Oxon
81 L6 **Ramsden** Worcs
71 H8 **Ramsden Bellhouse** Essex
71 H7 **Ramsden Heath** Essex
102 F6 **Ramsey** Cambs
73 J1 **Ramsey** Essex
154 f3 **Ramsey** IOM
102 F6 **Ramsey Forty Foot** Cambs
102 E6 **Ramsey Heights** Cambs
72 D6 **Ramsey Island** Essex
102 F5 **Ramsey Mereside** Cambs
102 E6 **Ramsey St Mary's** Cambs
41 L2 **Ramsgate** Kent
149 K2 **Ramsgill** N York
168 B1 **Ramshaw** Dur
91 H7 **Ramsholt** Suffk
189 K5 **Ramshope** Nthumb
115 H3 **Ramshorn** Staffs
12 F4 **Ramsley** Devon
36 E4 **Ramsnest Common** Surrey
136 D4 **Ranby** Lincs
134 C3 **Ranby** Notts
136 B4 **Rand** Lincs
64 B5 **Randwick** Gloucs
208 C6 **Ranfurly** Rens
115 K7 **Rangemore** Staffs
45 K2 **Rangeworthy** S Glos
71 H3 **Rank's Green** Essex
196 E8 **Rankinston** E Ayrs
101 H1 **Ranksborough** Rutlnd
139 L3 **Rann** Bl w D
230 D4 **Rannoch Station** P & K
29 G2 **Ranscombe** Somset
134 C2 **Ranskill** Notts
114 D6 **Ranton** Staffs
114 D7 **Ranton Green** Staffs
123 G8 **Ranworth** Norfk
220 D8 **Raploch** Stirlg
275 d2 **Rapness** Ork
30 E7 **Rapps** Somset
175 K5 **Rascarrel** D & G
207 J2 **Rashfield** Ag & B
81 L2 **Rashwood** Worcs
151 G2 **Raskelf** N York
61 J5 **Rassau** Blae G
141 H3 **Rastrick** Calder
248 E7 **Ratagan** Highld
100 B2 **Ratby** Leics
99 J3 **Ratcliffe Culey** Leics
116 E6 **Ratcliffe on Soar** Notts
117 G8 **Ratcliffe on the Wreake** Leics
33 L2 **Ratfyn** Wilts
269 J4 **Rathen** Abers
222 F3 **Rathillet** Fife
148 D4 **Rathmell** N York
210 F5 **Ratho** C Edin
267 J3 **Rathven** Moray
34 E6 **Ratlake** Hants
83 J5 **Ratley** Warwks
41 H4 **Ratling** Kent
95 K4 **Ratlinghope** Shrops
120 B8 **Rattar** Norfk
280 C2 **Rattar** Highld
165 K3 **Ratten Row** Cumb
165 L1 **Ratten Row** Cumb
147 H7 **Ratten Row** Lancs
7 L3 **Rattery** Devon
89 K3 **Rattlesden** Suffk
23 K7 **Ratton Village** E Susx
233 J6 **Rattray** P & K
165 L1 **Raughton** Cumb
165 L2 **Raughton Head** Cumb
85 K1 **Raunds** Nhants
138 C6 **Raven Meols** Sefton
133 J1 **Ravenfield** Rothm
155 K3 **Ravenglass** Cumb
81 G4 **Ravenhills Green** Worcs
107 H4 **Raveningham** Norfk
163 H2 **Ravenscar** N York
114 C1 **Ravenscliffe** C Stke
154 e4 **Ravensdale** IOM
86 B4 **Ravensden** Beds
133 L8 **Ravenshead** Notts
113 K2 **Ravensmoor** Ches
141 K4 **Ravensthorpe** Kirk
84 C1 **Ravensthorpe** Nhants
99 L1 **Ravenstone** Leics
85 G5 **Ravenstone** M Keyn
158 C2 **Ravenstonedale** Cumb

198 F4 **Ravenstruther** S Lans
159 L1 **Ravensworth** N York
163 G2 **Raw** N York
143 H3 **Rawcliffe** E R Yk
151 J5 **Rawcliffe** York
143 H3 **Rawcliffe Bridge** E R Yk
150 B7 **Rawdon** Leeds
40 B3 **Rawling Street** Kent
142 C8 **Rawmarsh** Rothm
98 C1 **Rawnsley** Staffs
71 J8 **Rawreth** Essex
14 E1 **Rawridge** Devon
140 B3 **Rawtenstall** Lancs
90 B7 **Raydon** Suffk
190 C7 **Raylees** Nthumb
53 H1 **Rayleigh** Essex
15 H3 **Raymond's Hill** Devon
71 H3 **Rayne** Essex
51 G5 **Raynes Park** Gt Lon
64 A4 **Rea** Gloucs
88 B2 **Reach** Cambs
140 A1 **Read** Lancs
49 H4 **Reading** Readg
25 G1 **Reading Street** Kent
41 L2 **Reading Street** Kent
166 E7 **Reagill** Cumb
263 K1 **Rearquhar** Highld
117 H8 **Rearsby** Leics
113 L1 **Rease Heath** Shrops
279 G3 **Reay** Highld
41 H2 **Reculver** Kent
29 K7 **Red Ball** Somset
131 G8 **Red Bull** Ches
87 K4 **Red Cross** Cambs
11 K2 **Red Cross** Cnwll
165 H2 **Red Dial** Cumb
17 L3 **Red Hill** Bmouth
82 D4 **Red Hill** Warwks
88 D1 **Red Lodge** Suffk
140 C4 **Red Lumb** Rochdl
139 H6 **Red Rock** Wigan
55 L4 **Red Roses** Carmth
191 K6 **Red Row** Nthumb
114 C1 **Red Street** Staffs
125 J3 **Red Wharf Bay** IOA
55 J6 **Redberth** Pembks
68 E4 **Redbourn** Herts
144 B7 **Redbourne** N Linc
63 G5 **Redbrook** Gloucs
113 H3 **Redbrook** Wrexhm
40 B8 **Redbrook Street** Kent
253 H2 **Redburn** Highld
179 H6 **Redburn** Nthumb
170 E6 **Redcar** R & Cl
175 K2 **Redcastle** D & G
251 G2 **Redcastle** Highld
210 B3 **Redding** Falk
210 B3 **Reddingmuirhead** Falk
131 H1 **Reddish** Stockp
82 B2 **Redditch** Worcs
88 F4 **Rede** Suffk
106 F6 **Redenhall** Norfk
34 C1 **Redenham** Hants
179 K3 **Redesmouth** Nthumb
235 J2 **Redford** Abers
234 E6 **Redford** Angus
36 C5 **Redford** W Susx
188 C3 **Redfordgreen** Border
42 F4 **Redgate** Rhondd
221 K2 **Redgorton** P & K
105 L7 **Redgrave** Suffk
245 H3 **Redhill** Abers
86 F8 **Redhill** Herts
45 G6 **Redhill** N Som
37 L1 **Redhill** Surrey
107 H6 **Redisham** Suffk
45 H4 **Redland** Bristl
275 c3 **Redland** Ork
90 E1 **Redlingfield** Suffk
90 E1 **Redlingfield Green** Suffk
32 B4 **Redlynch** Somset
33 L6 **Redlynch** Wilts
164 F4 **Redmain** Cumb
81 H2 **Redmarley** Worcs
63 L1 **Redmarley D'Abitot** Gloucs
169 K6 **Redmarshall** S on T
117 L4 **Redmile** Leics
159 J4 **Redmire** N York
245 G8 **Redmyre** Abers
98 C8 **Rednal** Birm
112 E6 **Rednal** Shrops
201 J6 **Redpath** Border
260 B6 **Redpoint** Highld
4 A6 **Redruth** Cnwll
46 D6 **Redstocks** Wilts

233 J8 **Redstone** P & K
55 J4 **Redstone Cross** Pembks
140 B6 **Redvales** Bury
44 E2 **Redwick** Newpt
45 H2 **Redwick** S Glos
169 G6 **Redworth** Darltn
87 H8 **Reed** Herts
107 J3 **Reedham** Norfk
143 K3 **Reedness** E R Yk
136 D6 **Reeds Beck** Lincs
140 B3 **Reeds Holme** Lancs
135 L5 **Reepham** Lincs
122 B7 **Reepham** Norfk
159 J3 **Reeth** N York
99 H7 **Reeves Green** Solhll
154 f3 **Regaby** IOM
270 C5 **Reiff** Highld
37 L1 **Reigate** Surrey
163 L7 **Reighton** N York
256 F7 **Reisque** Abers
280 D5 **Reiss** Highld
4 C4 **Rejerrah** Cnwll
3 G4 **Releath** Cnwll
2 F4 **Relubbus** Cnwll
253 J2 **Relugas** Moray
49 J2 **Remenham** Wokham
49 J2 **Remenham Hill** Wokham
116 F6 **Rempstone** Notts
64 E5 **Rendcomb** Gloucs
91 H2 **Rendham** Suffk
91 H4 **Rendlesham** Suffk
208 E5 **Renfrew** Rens
86 B5 **Renhold** Beds
133 J4 **Renishaw** Derbys
191 J3 **Rennington** Nthumb
208 C3 **Renton** W Duns
166 E2 **Renwick** Cumb
123 J8 **Repps** Norfk
116 A6 **Repton** Derbys
251 J3 **Resaurie** Highld
5 G6 **Rescassa** Cnwll
5 G5 **Rescorla** Cnwll
237 L7 **Resipole** Highld
3 G3 **Reskadinnick** Cnwll
263 J6 **Resolis** Highld
60 C6 **Resolven** Neath
218 C5 **Rest and be thankful** Ag & B
213 J6 **Reston** Border
3 K4 **Restronguet** Cnwll
234 D5 **Reswallie** Angus
4 F2 **Reterth** Cnwll
4 F3 **Retew** Cnwll
134 D3 **Retford** Notts
5 G2 **Retire** Cnwll
71 J7 **Rettendon** Essex
4 E3 **Retyn** Cnwll
136 E7 **Revesby** Lincs
13 H8 **Rew** Devon
7 K7 **Rew** Devon
19 H5 **Rew Street** IOW
13 M3 **Rewe** Devon
12 A5 **Rexon** Devon
107 K7 **Reydon** Suffk
105 L2 **Reymerston** Norfk
55 J5 **Reynalton** Pembks
56 E6 **Reynoldston** Swans
11 L7 **Rezare** Cnwll
62 D6 **Rhadyr** Mons
77 L6 **Rhandirmwyn** Carmth
78 D2 **Rhayader** Powys
250 F2 **Rheindown** Highld
128 E5 **Rhes-y-cae** Flints
128 D7 **Rhewl** Denbgs
112 B3 **Rhewl** Denbgs
128 D4 **Rhewl Mostyn** Flints
128 D3 **Rhewl-fawr** Flints
270 E3 **Rhicarn** Highld
276 D5 **Rhiconich** Highld
263 J5 **Rhicullen** Highld
60 D6 **Rhigos** Rhondd
261 G1 **Rhireavach** Highld
273 K7 **Rhives** Highld
43 J5 **Rhiwbina** Cardif
110 D2 **Rhiwbryfdir** Gwynd
43 L4 **Rhiwderyn** Newpt
125 K7 **Rhiwen** Gwynd
42 F4 **Rhiwinder** Rhondd
125 K6 **Rhiwlas** Gwynd
111 H4 **Rhiwlas** Gwynd
112 B5 **Rhiwlas** Powys
43 G5 **Rhiwsaeson** Cardif
30 C4 **Rhode** Somset
39 H4 **Rhoden Green** Kent
140 C6 **Rhodes** Bury
40 F6 **Rhodes Minnis** Kent

133 L4 **Rhodesia** Notts
74 C6 **Rhodiad-y-brenin** Pembks
175 J3 **Rhonehouse** D & G
43 G8 **Rhoose** V Glam
58 C2 **Rhos** Carmth
128 D7 **Rhos** Denbgs
57 K4 **Rhos** Neath
61 J1 **Rhos** Powys
76 F2 **Rhos Haminiog** Cerdgn
125 J2 **Rhos Lligwy** IOA
111 M7 **Rhos y-brithdir** Powys
109 G4 **Rhos-fawr** Gwynd
127 G3 **Rhos-on-Sea** Conwy
77 H1 **Rhos-y-garth** Cerdgn
111 H4 **Rhos-y-gwaliau** Gwynd
108 D4 **Rhos-y-llan** Gwynd
79 K1 **Rhos-y-meirch** Powys
125 G2 **Rhosbeirio** IOA
125 J4 **Rhoscefnhir** IOA
124 D4 **Rhoscolyn** IOA
54 E6 **Rhoscrowther** Pembks
128 F6 **Rhosesmor** Flints
125 J8 **Rhosgadfan** Gwynd
125 G2 **Rhosgoch** IOA
79 H5 **Rhosgoch** Powys
75 L4 **Rhoshill** Pembks
108 C5 **Rhoshirwaun** Gwynd
109 H3 **Rhoslan** Gwynd
92 C2 **Rhoslefain** Gwynd
112 D2 **Rhosllanerchrugog** Wrexhm
59 H4 **Rhosmaen** Carmth
125 H4 **Rhosmeirch** IOA
124 E5 **Rhosneigr** IOA
112 E2 **Rhosnesni** Wrexhm
112 E1 **Rhosrobin** Wrexhm
56 D7 **Rhossili** Swans
125 J8 **Rhostryfan** Gwynd
112 D2 **Rhostyllen** Wrexhm
125 G2 **Rhosybol** IOA
112 D4 **Rhosygadfa** Shrops
112 D3 **Rhosymedre** Wrexhm
207 M2 **Rhu** Ag & B
128 C5 **Rhualit** Denbgs
207 G4 **Rhubodach** Ag & B
130 A7 **Rhuddall Heath** Ches
76 F6 **Rhuddlan** Cerdgn
127 L4 **Rhuddlan** Denbgs
79 G5 **Rhulen** Powys
205 M6 **Rhunahaorine** Ag & B
110 B3 **Rhyd** Gwynd
109 K1 **Rhyd-Ddu** Gwynd
111 G2 **Rhyd-lydan** Conwy
111 G4 **Rhyd-uchaf** Gwynd
92 D6 **Rhyd-y pennau** Cerdgn
108 E4 **Rhyd-y-clafdy** Gwynd
127 H4 **Rhyd-y-foel** Conwy
125 K6 **Rhyd-y-groes** Gwynd
62 C5 **Rhyd-y-meirch** Mons
110 C3 **Rhyd-y-sarn** Gwynd
92 D3 **Rhyd-yr-onnen** Gwynd
58 D4 **Rhydargaeau** Carmth
77 G7 **Rhydcymerau** Carmth
81 J6 **Rhydd** Worcs
57 K5 **Rhydding** Neath
127 K6 **Rhydgaled** Conwy
110 F1 **Rhydlanfair** Conwy
76 C5 **Rhydlewis** Cerdgn
108 C5 **Rhydlios** Gwynd
76 E6 **Rhydowen** Cerdgn
77 G2 **Rhydrosser** Cerdgn
79 J6 **Rhydspence** Herefs
128 F8 **Rhydtalog** Flints
112 C5 **Rhydycroesau** Shrops
92 D7 **Rhydyfelin** Cerdgn
43 H4 **Rhydyfelin** Rhondd
57 K4 **Rhydyfro** Neath
110 F7 **Rhydymain** Gwynd
128 E6 **Rhydymwyn** Flints
127 K3 **Rhyl** Denbgs
61 H5 **Rhymney** Caerph
222 B3 **Rhynd** P & K
255 K6 **Rhynie** Abers
264 C4 **Rhynie** Highld
97 H8 **Ribbesford** Worcs
139 H2 **Ribbleton** Lancs
138 E2 **Ribby** Lancs
139 K1 **Ribchester** Lancs
132 F7 **Riber** Derbys
144 F6 **Riby** Lincs
151 K8 **Riccall** N York
188 F7 **Riccarton** Border
196 E4 **Riccarton** E Ayrs
29 L4 **Rich's Holford** Somset
80 C1 **Richards Castle** Herefs
50 C3 **Richings Park** Bucks

50 F4 **Richmond** Gt Lon
159 M2 **Richmond** N York
133 H3 **Richmond** Sheff
9 i2 **Richmond Fort** Guern
114 E7 **Rickerscote** Staffs
44 F7 **Rickford** N Som
7 L7 **Rickham** Devon
105 L8 **Rickinghall** Suffk
70 D1 **Rickling** Essex
70 D1 **Rickling Green** Essex
68 D8 **Rickmansworth** Herts
188 E1 **Riddell** Border
177 L4 **Riddings** Cumb
116 C1 **Riddings** Derbys
27 L8 **Riddlecombe** Devon
149 K7 **Riddlesden** Brad
45 H7 **Ridge** BaNES
17 H5 **Ridge** Dorset
69 G7 **Ridge** Herts
33 G4 **Ridge** Wilts
37 L1 **Ridge Green** Surrey
99 J4 **Ridge Lane** Warwks
41 G6 **Ridge Row** Kent
78 E3 **Ridgebourne** Powys
45 G6 **Ridgehill** N Som
116 B1 **Ridgeway** Derbys
133 H3 **Ridgeway** Derbys
82 C3 **Ridgeway** Worcs
81 G5 **Ridgeway Cross** Herefs
88 E7 **Ridgewell** Essex
23 H3 **Ridgewood** E Susx
85 J8 **Ridgmont** Beds
180 B6 **Riding Mill** Nthumb
52 D6 **Ridley** Kent
179 H6 **Ridley** Nthumb
113 J1 **Ridley Green** Ches
123 G5 **Ridlington** Norfk
101 J3 **Ridlington** Rutlnd
123 G5 **Ridlington Street** Norfk
179 L2 **Ridsdale** Nthumb
161 J5 **Rievaulx** N York
177 J5 **Rigg** D & G
209 K5 **Riggend** N Lans
253 G2 **Righoul** Highld
157 K5 **Rigmadon Park** Cumb
137 H4 **Rigsby** Lincs
198 E6 **Rigside** S Lans
139 J3 **Riley Green** Lancs
115 J8 **Rileyhill** Staffs
11 K7 **Rilla Mill** Cnwll
11 K7 **Rillaton** Cnwll
162 E7 **Rillington** N York
148 D6 **Rimington** Lancs
31 K6 **Rimpton** Somset
145 J2 **Rimswell** E R Yk
75 G7 **Rinaston** Pembks
97 G4 **Rindleford** Shrops
138 F5 **Ring o'Bells** Lancs
103 H3 **Ring's End** Cambs
175 H3 **Ringford** D & G
132 F3 **Ringinglow** Sheff
106 C1 **Ringland** Norfk
23 H3 **Ringles Cross** E Susx
39 L2 **Ringlestone** Kent
139 M6 **Ringley** Bolton
23 G5 **Ringmer** E Susx
7 J5 **Ringmore** Devon
13 L8 **Ringmore** Devon
254 E3 **Ringorm** Moray
107 H5 **Ringsfield** Suffk
107 H6 **Ringsfield Corner** Suffk
68 C4 **Ringshall** Bucks
90 B4 **Ringshall** Suffk
90 B5 **Ringshall Stocks** Suffk
101 L8 **Ringstead** Nhants
120 F3 **Ringstead** Norfk
18 A3 **Ringwood** Hants
41 K5 **Ringwould** Kent
2 F5 **Rinsey** Cnwll
2 F5 **Rinsey Croft** Cnwll
23 H5 **Ripe** E Susx
116 C2 **Ripley** Derbys
18 B4 **Ripley** Hants
150 C4 **Ripley** N York
50 D7 **Ripley** Surrey
144 B2 **Riplingham** E R Yk
35 K6 **Riplington** Hants
150 D2 **Ripon** N York
118 E6 **Rippingale** Lincs
41 K5 **Ripple** Kent
81 K7 **Ripple** Worcs
140 F4 **Ripponden** Calder
204 D7 **Risabus** Ag & B
80 D4 **Risbury** Herefs
144 A5 **Risby** N Linc

88 F2 **Risby** Suffk
43 K3 **Risca** Caerph
153 J7 **Rise** E R Yk
38 F7 **Riseden** E Susx
39 H6 **Riseden** Kent
119 H5 **Risegate** Lincs
135 K5 **Riseholme** Lincs
164 D4 **Risehow** Cumb
85 L3 **Riseley** Beds
49 H6 **Riseley** Wokham
90 E2 **Rishangles** Suffk
139 L2 **Rishton** Lancs
140 F4 **Rishworth** Calder
140 A3 **Rising Bridge** Lancs
116 D4 **Risley** Derbys
130 C1 **Risley** Warrtn
150 B2 **Risplith** N York
47 L6 **Rivar** Wilts
71 K4 **Rivenhall End** Essex
41 J6 **River** Kent
36 D6 **River** W Susx
87 L2 **River Bank** Cambs
250 F1 **Riverford** Highld
38 D2 **Riverhead** Kent
32 C8 **Rivers Corner** Dorset
139 J5 **Rivington** Lancs
146 D3 **Roa Island** Cumb
28 E6 **Roachill** Devon
46 C7 **Road Ashton** Wilts
106 F4 **Road Green** Norfk
84 E5 **Roade** Nhants
178 C4 **Roadhead** Cumb
198 E3 **Roadmeetings** S Lans
197 H7 **Roadside** E Ayrs
279 L4 **Roadside** Highld
29 J3 **Roadwater** Somset
258 D7 **Roag** Highld
183 H2 **Roan of Craigoch** S Ayrs
87 J8 **Roast Green** Essex
43 K6 **Roath** Cardif
188 D3 **Roberton** Border
198 F7 **Roberton** S Lans
24 D3 **Robertsbridge** E Susx
141 J3 **Roberttown** Kirk
55 J4 **Robeston Wathen** Pembks
177 H4 **Robgill Tower** D & G
131 H8 **Robin Hill** Staffs
139 G5 **Robin Hood** Lancs
141 M2 **Robin Hood** Leeds
163 G2 **Robin Hood's Bay** N York
88 E7 **Robinhood End** Essex
27 K7 **Roborough** Devon
6 F2 **Roborough** Devon
129 K2 **Roby** Knows
139 G6 **Roby Mill** Lancs
115 J4 **Rocester** Staffs
54 E3 **Roch** Pembks
54 E3 **Roch Gate** Pembks
140 D5 **Rochdale** Rochdl
5 G3 **Roche** Cnwll
52 F5 **Rochester** Medway
189 M6 **Rochester** Nthumb
53 J1 **Rochford** Essex
80 E2 **Rochford** Worcs
10 C7 **Rock** Cnwll
57 L6 **Rock** Neath
191 J2 **Rock** Nthumb
21 K4 **Rock** W Susx
81 G1 **Rock** Worcs
129 H2 **Rock Ferry** Wirral
81 L1 **Rock Hill** Worcs
14 B3 **Rockbeare** Devon
33 K7 **Rockbourne** Hants
177 K6 **Rockcliffe** Cumb
175 L4 **Rockcliffe** D & G
177 K6 **Rockcliffe Cross** Cumb
8 D2 **Rockend** Torbay
2 B6 **Rockestal** Cnwll
264 E3 **Rockfield** Highld
62 F4 **Rockfield** Mons
28 D1 **Rockford** Devon
18 B2 **Rockford** Hants
96 C8 **Rockgreen** Shrops
63 K8 **Rockhampton** S Glos
10 F5 **Rockhead** Cnwll
95 G7 **Rockhill** Shrops
101 J5 **Rockingham** Nhants
105 K4 **Rockland All Saints** Norfk
107 G3 **Rockland St Mary** Norfk
105 K4 **Rockland St Peter** Norfk
134 E5 **Rockley** Notts
47 H4 **Rockley** Wilts
140 C3 **Rockliffe** Lancs
207 L1 **Rockville** Ag & B
49 J1 **Rockwell End** Bucks

29 L6 **Rockwell Green** Somset
64 B6 **Rodborough** Gloucs
47 H2 **Rodbourne** Swindn
46 D2 **Rodbourne** Wilts
79 K3 **Rodd** Herefs
190 E2 **Roddam** Nthumb
16 B5 **Rodden** Dorset
168 F3 **Roddymoor** Dur
46 A8 **Rode** Somset
130 F8 **Rode Heath** Ches
131 G6 **Rode Heath** Ches
282 d7 **Rodel** W Isls
113 J8 **Roden** Wrekin
29 J3 **Rodhuish** Somset
113 K8 **Rodington** Wrekin
113 K8 **Rodington Heath** Wrekin
63 L5 **Rodley** Gloucs
150 B8 **Rodley** Leeds
64 D7 **Rodmarton** Gloucs
22 F6 **Rodmell** E Susx
40 B3 **Rodmersham** Kent
40 B3 **Rodmersham Green** Kent
31 H1 **Rodney Stoke** Somset
115 K3 **Rodsley** Derbys
30 C3 **Rodway** Somset
140 E8 **Roe Cross** Tamesd
69 G5 **Roe Green** Herts
87 G8 **Roe Green** Herts
139 M7 **Roe Green** Salfd
150 E3 **Roecliffe** N York
51 G4 **Roehampton** Gt Lon
37 J4 **Roffey** W Susx
273 H7 **Rogart** Highld
36 B6 **Rogate** W Susx
156 E3 **Roger Ground** Cumb
44 B2 **Rogerstone** Newpt
282 d7 **Roghadal** W Isls
44 F2 **Rogiet** Mons
66 F8 **Roke** Oxon
181 K7 **Roker** Sundld
123 J8 **Rollesby** Norfk
100 F3 **Rolleston** Leics
117 K1 **Rolleston** Notts
115 L6 **Rolleston** Staffs
153 K6 **Rolston** E R Yk
44 D6 **Rolstone** N Som
39 L7 **Rolvenden** Kent
39 L7 **Rolvenden Layne** Kent
168 C6 **Romaldkirk** Dur
160 E4 **Romanby** N York
199 K3 **Romanno Bridge** Border
28 C6 **Romansleigh** Devon
40 A7 **Romden Castle** Kent
258 F6 **Romesdal** Highld
17 L1 **Romford** Dorset
52 B1 **Romford** Gt Lon
131 J2 **Romiley** Stockp
52 C6 **Romney Street** Kent
34 D6 **Romsey** Hants
97 H6 **Romsley** Shrops
98 B7 **Romsley** Worcs
206 B8 **Ronachan** Ag & B
167 L2 **Rookhope** Dur
19 H6 **Rookley** IOW
19 H7 **Rookley Green** IOW
44 D8 **Rooks Bridge** Somset
29 K4 **Rooks Nest** Somset
160 B5 **Rookwith** N York
145 H2 **Roos** E R Yk
146 D2 **Roose** Cumb
146 E2 **Roosebeck** Cumb
86 B4 **Roothams Green** Beds
35 K4 **Ropley** Hants
35 K4 **Ropley Dean** Hants
35 K4 **Ropley Soke** Hants
118 C5 **Ropsley** Lincs
269 K6 **Rora** Abers
95 H3 **Rorrington** Shrops
267 H6 **Rosarie** Moray
3 G3 **Roscroggan** Cnwll
4 C4 **Rose** Cnwll
28 D6 **Rose Ash** Devon
72 C2 **Rose Green** Essex
89 J7 **Rose Green** Suffk
89 K6 **Rose Green** Suffk
20 E7 **Rose Green** W Susx
23 G4 **Rose Hill** E Susx
140 B2 **Rose Hill** Lancs
147 H8 **Roseacre** Lancs
198 D3 **Rosebank** S Lans
75 J6 **Rosebush** Pembks
11 H3 **Rosecare** Cnwll
4 D3 **Rosecliston** Cnwll
162 C3 **Rosedale Abbey** N York
272 C7 **Rosehall** Highld

269 G3 **Rosehearty** Abers
113 G8 **Rosehill** Shrops
266 C3 **Roseisle** Moray
23 K7 **Roselands** E Susx
54 F5 **Rosemarket** Pembks
263 K8 **Rosemarkie** Highld
29 L7 **Rosemary Lane** Devon
233 J6 **Rosemount** P & K
4 F2 **Rosenannon** Cnwll
3 K6 **Rosenithon** Cnwll
23 J3 **Roser's Cross** E Susx
5 H3 **Rosevean** Cnwll
3 M4 **Rosevine** Cnwll
2 F4 **Rosewarne** Cnwll
211 J6 **Rosewell** Mdloth
169 L6 **Roseworth** S on T
3 G3 **Roseworthy** Cnwll
166 D7 **Rosgill** Cumb
258 D7 **Roskhill** Highld
3 K6 **Roskorwell** Cnwll
3 J4 **Roskrow** Cnwll
165 K2 **Rosley** Cumb
211 J6 **Roslin** Mdloth
115 L8 **Rosliston** Derbys
207 L2 **Rosneath** Ag & B
175 G6 **Ross** D & G
203 J5 **Ross** Nthumb
63 J2 **Ross-on-Wye** Herefs
129 J8 **Rossett** Wrexhm
150 D5 **Rossett Green** N York
143 G8 **Rossington** Donc
208 D5 **Rossland** Rens
280 C8 **Roster** Highld
130 E3 **Rostherne** Ches
165 H7 **Rosthwaite** Cumb
115 J3 **Roston** Derbys
2 E5 **Rosudgeon** Cnwll
210 F2 **Rosyth** Fife
190 F6 **Rothbury** Nthumb
117 H8 **Rotherby** Leics
38 E7 **Rotherfield** E Susx
49 H3 **Rotherfield Greys** Oxon
49 H3 **Rotherfield Peppard** Oxon
133 H1 **Rotherham** Rothm
84 D4 **Rothersthorpe** Nhants
49 H7 **Rotherwick** Hants
266 F6 **Rothes** Moray
207 H6 **Rothesay** Ag & B
256 D4 **Rothiebrisbane** Abers
267 L6 **Rothiemay** Moray
242 C2 **Rothiemurchus Lodge** Highld
256 C4 **Rothienorman** Abers
100 D1 **Rothley** Leics
180 C1 **Rothley** Nthumb
256 B5 **Rothmaise** Abers
142 A2 **Rothwell** Leeds
144 F7 **Rothwell** Lincs
101 H7 **Rothwell** Nhants
142 A2 **Rothwell Haigh** Leeds
153 G5 **Rotsea** E R Yk
234 B2 **Rottal Lodge** Angus
22 F6 **Rottingdean** Br & H
164 C8 **Rottington** Cumb
176 D3 **Roucan** D & G
19 H7 **Roud** IOW
114 E4 **Rough Close** Staffs
40 F3 **Rough Common** Kent
121 H7 **Rougham** Norfk
89 H3 **Rougham Green** Suffk
148 E7 **Roughlee** Lancs
243 K1 **Roughpark** Abers
136 D6 **Roughton** Lincs
122 E4 **Roughton** Norfk
97 G4 **Roughton** Shrops
38 F3 **Roughway** Kent
68 F7 **Round Bush** Herts
68 E3 **Round Green** Luton
52 E5 **Round Street** Kent
72 B6 **Roundbush** Essex
70 E4 **Roundbush Green** Essex
15 K1 **Roundham** Somset
150 D8 **Roundhay** Leeds
98 C5 **Rounds Green** Sandw
37 G5 **Roundstreet Common** W Susx
46 E6 **Roundway** Wilts
234 B5 **Roundyhill** Angus
82 B4 **Rous Lench** Worcs
15 G4 **Rousdon** Devon
66 C2 **Rousham** Oxon
67 J7 **Rout's Green** Bucks
165 G4 **Routenbeck** Cumb
207 K6 **Routenburn** N Ayrs
153 H7 **Routh** E R Yk
10 F7 **Row** Cnwll

166 E4 **Row** Cumb
157 G5 **Row** Cumb
35 H8 **Row Ash** Hants
71 H3 **Row Green** Essex
50 D6 **Row Town** Surrey
177 L3 **Rowanburn** D & G
218 E7 **Rowardennan Hotel** Stirlg
218 E7 **Rowardennan Lodge** Stirlg
131 K2 **Rowarth** Derbys
44 F7 **Rowberrow** Somset
19 G6 **Rowborough** IOW
46 E6 **Rowde** Wilts
12 F3 **Rowden** Devon
126 E5 **Rowen** Conwy
115 K2 **Rowfield** Derbys
178 F6 **Rowfoot** Nthumb
30 C5 **Rowford** Somset
72 F3 **Rowhedge** Essex
37 H4 **Rowhook** W Susx
82 F2 **Rowington** Warwks
132 D5 **Rowland** Derbys
20 B5 **Rowland's Castle** Hants
180 E7 **Rowland's Gill** Gatesd
36 B2 **Rowledge** Surrey
168 E1 **Rowley** Dur
144 B1 **Rowley** E R Yk
95 H2 **Rowley** Shrops
99 K6 **Rowley Green** Covtry
141 J5 **Rowley Hill** Kirk
98 B6 **Rowley Regis** Sandw
62 D2 **Rowlstone** Herefs
37 G3 **Rowly** Surrey
19 K3 **Rowner** Hants
82 B1 **Rowney Green** Worcs
34 E7 **Rownhams** Hants
164 E7 **Rowrah** Cumb
131 G4 **Rows of Trees** Ches
67 K3 **Rowsham** Bucks
132 E6 **Rowsley** Derbys
48 C1 **Rowstock** Oxon
136 A8 **Rowston** Lincs
133 J6 **Rowthorne** Derbys
129 K6 **Rowton** Ches
95 H1 **Rowton** Shrops
95 K7 **Rowton** Shrops
113 K7 **Rowton** Wrekin
201 L7 **Roxburgh** Border
144 A4 **Roxby** N Linc
171 H7 **Roxby** N York
86 C4 **Roxton** Beds
70 F5 **Roxwell** Essex
239 M7 **Roy Bridge** Highld
169 G6 **Royal Oak** Dur
138 E7 **Royal Oak** Lancs
113 K3 **Royal's Green** Ches
141 K5 **Roydhouse** Kirk
69 L5 **Roydon** Essex
120 F7 **Roydon** Norfk
106 C7 **Roydon** Norfk
69 L5 **Roydon Hamlet** Essex
142 B5 **Royston** Barns
87 G7 **Royston** Herts
140 D6 **Royton** Oldham
9 e2 **Rozel** Jersey
112 D3 **Ruabon** Wrexhm
224 D5 **Ruaig** Ag & B
4 E6 **Ruan High Lanes** Cnwll
4 E6 **Ruan Lanihorne** Cnwll
3 H7 **Ruan Major** Cnwll
3 J8 **Ruan Minor** Cnwll
63 J3 **Ruardean** Gloucs
63 J4 **Ruardean Hill** Gloucs
63 J4 **Ruardean Woodside** Gloucs
98 C7 **Rubery** Birm
283 c12 **Rubha Ban** W Isls
166 C2 **Ruckcroft** Cumb
80 B7 **Ruckhall** Herefs
80 B7 **Ruckhall Common** Herefs
40 D8 **Ruckinge** Kent
136 F4 **Ruckland** Lincs
96 C3 **Ruckley** Shrops
161 G1 **Rudby** N York
180 D5 **Rudchester** Nthumb
116 F5 **Ruddington** Notts
63 K5 **Ruddle** Gloucs
5 G4 **Ruddlemoor** Cnwll
63 M3 **Rudford** Gloucs
46 B8 **Rudge** Somset
45 J2 **Rudgeway** S Glos
37 G4 **Rudgwick** W Susx
63 J2 **Rudhall** Herefs
130 D5 **Rudheath** Ches
71 K6 **Rudley Green** Essex
46 B5 **Rudloe** Wilts
43 K4 **Rudry** Caerph

153 H2 **Rudston** E R Yk
131 J8 **Rudyard** Staffs
189 G2 **Ruecastle** Border
138 F4 **Rufford** Lancs
151 H5 **Rufforth** York
111 K3 **Rug** Denbgs
100 B8 **Rugby** Warwks
115 G7 **Rugeley** Staffs
27 K2 **Ruggaton** Devon
30 C6 **Ruishton** Somset
50 E2 **Ruislip** Gt Lon
267 H5 **Rumbach** Moray
221 J7 **Rumbling Bridge** P & K
107 G7 **Rumburgh** Suffk
168 F4 **Rumby Hill** Dur
4 E1 **Rumford** Cnwll
210 B4 **Rumford** Falk
43 K6 **Rumney** Cardif
30 B6 **Rumwell** Somset
129 L3 **Runcorn** Halton
20 E6 **Runcton** W Susx
104 C2 **Runcton Holme** Norfk
36 C2 **Runfold** Surrey
105 L2 **Runhall** Norfk
107 J1 **Runham** Norfk
107 L2 **Runham** Norfk
29 L6 **Runnington** Somset
71 J6 **Runsell Green** Essex
139 G4 **Runshaw Moor** Lancs
171 J7 **Runswick** N York
233 L2 **Runtaleave** Angus
71 J8 **Runwell** Essex
49 J4 **Ruscombe** Wokham
73 H4 **Rush Green** Essex
52 B2 **Rush Green** Gt Lon
69 G2 **Rush Green** Herts
69 J2 **Rush Green** Herts
130 D2 **Rush Green** Warrtn
80 E8 **Rushall** Herefs
106 D6 **Rushall** Norfk
47 H7 **Rushall** Wilts
98 C3 **Rushall** Wsall
89 H3 **Rushbrooke** Suffk
96 C5 **Rushbury** Shrops
69 J1 **Rushden** Herts
85 J2 **Rushden** Nhants
53 K5 **Rushenden** Kent
38 F7 **Rusher's Cross** E Susx
36 F2 **Rushett Common** Surrey
12 B7 **Rushford** Devon
105 J7 **Rushford** Norfk
23 L3 **Rushlake Green** E Susx
107 K6 **Rushmere** Suffk
90 E6 **Rushmere St Andrew** Suffk
36 C3 **Rushmoor** Surrey
79 K3 **Rushock** Herefs
81 K1 **Rushock** Worcs
131 G1 **Rusholme** Manch
130 B7 **Rushton** Ches
101 J6 **Rushton** Nhants
96 D2 **Rushton** Shrops
131 J7 **Rushton Spencer** Staffs
81 J4 **Rushwick** Worcs
169 H5 **Rushyford** Dur
219 K7 **Ruskie** Stirlg
118 E1 **Ruskington** Lincs
156 E5 **Rusland** Cumb
37 K3 **Rusper** W Susx
63 K5 **Ruspidge** Gloucs
37 K3 **Russ Hill** Surrey
90 F1 **Russel's Green** Suffk
71 H4 **Russell Green** Essex
49 H1 **Russell's Water** Oxon
38 E5 **Rusthall** Kent
21 H6 **Rustington** W Susx
163 G6 **Ruston** N York
153 G3 **Ruston Parva** E R Yk
162 F1 **Ruswarp** N York
96 D5 **Ruthall** Shrops
201 K7 **Rutherford** Border
209 G6 **Rutherglen** S Lans
5 G2 **Ruthernbridge** Cnwll
128 D8 **Ruthin** Denbgs
245 K3 **Ruthrieston** C Aber
267 K6 **Ruthven** Abers
233 L5 **Ruthven** Angus
241 K4 **Ruthven** Highld
233 L6 **Ruthven House** Angus
4 F3 **Ruthvoes** Cnwll
165 H3 **Ruthwaite** Cumb
176 E5 **Ruthwell** D & G
52 A5 **Ruxley Corner** Gt Lon
63 G3 **Ruxton Green** Herefs
112 F7 **Ruyton-XI-Towns** Shrops
180 B4 **Ryal** Nthumb

15 J3 **Ryall** Dorset
81 K7 **Ryall** Worcs
52 E7 **Ryarsh** Kent
67 G6 **Rycote** Oxon
156 E2 **Rydal** Cumb
19 K5 **Ryde** IOW
25 G3 **Rye** E Susx
81 H8 **Rye Cross** Worcs
25 G3 **Rye Foreign** E Susx
25 H3 **Rye Harbour** E Susx
81 H8 **Rye Street** Worcs
113 H5 **Ryebank** Shrops
63 J3 **Ryeford** Herefs
145 G3 **Ryehill** E R Yk
49 H5 **Ryeish Green** Wokham
102 A1 **Ryhall** Rutlnd
142 B5 **Ryhill** Wakefd
181 K8 **Ryhope** Sundld
133 J6 **Rylah** Derbys
135 K4 **Ryland** Lincs
116 F4 **Rylands** Notts
149 H4 **Rylstone** N York
31 J8 **Ryme Intrinseca** Dorset
151 J7 **Ryther** N York
180 E6 **Ryton** Gatesd
162 D7 **Ryton** N York
97 G3 **Ryton** Shrops
99 L6 **Ryton** Warwks
180 E6 **Ryton Woodside** Gatesd
99 K8 **Ryton-on-Dunsmore** Warwks

S

148 D8 **Sabden** Lancs
70 E7 **Sabine's Green** Essex
69 J3 **Sacombe** Herts
69 J3 **Sacombe Green** Herts
169 G1 **Sacriston** Dur
169 J7 **Sadberge** Darltn
194 B4 **Saddell** Ag & B
100 E5 **Saddington** Leics
120 D8 **Saddle Bow** Norfk
22 D5 **Saddlescombe** W Susx
157 G2 **Sadgill** Cumb
87 L7 **Saffron Walden** Essex
55 H6 **Sageston** Pembks
105 H3 **Saham Hills** Norfk
105 H3 **Saham Toney** Norfk
129 K7 **Saighton** Ches
213 K5 **St Abbs** Border
212 F6 **St Agnes** Border
4 B5 **St Agnes** Cnwll
68 F5 **St Albans** Herts
4 D5 **St Allen** Cnwll
9 j3 **St Andrew** Guern
43 H7 **St Andrew's Major** V Glam
223 J4 **St Andrews** Fife
15 L4 **St Andrews Well** Dorset
187 G7 **St Ann's** D & G
12 A8 **St Ann's Chapel** Cnwll
7 J5 **St Ann's Chapel** Devon
138 C2 **St Anne's** Lancs
3 K6 **St Anthony** Cnwll
23 L7 **St Anthony's Hill** E Susx
63 G7 **St Arvans** Mons
128 B5 **St Asaph** Denbgs
42 F8 **St Athan** V Glam
9 c3 **St Aubin** Jersey
5 G4 **St Austell** Cnwll
164 C8 **St Bees** Cumb
5 H4 **St Blazey** Cnwll
5 H4 **St Blazey Gate** Cnwll
201 J7 **St Boswells** Border
9 b3 **St Brelade** Jersey
9 b3 **St Brelade's Bay** Jersey
10 D8 **St Breock** Cnwll
10 F7 **St Breward** Cnwll
63 H6 **St Briavels** Gloucs
42 D6 **St Bride's Major** V Glam
54 C5 **St Brides** Pembks
44 E1 **St Brides Netherwent** Mons
43 H6 **St Brides super-Ely** V Glam
44 C3 **St Brides Wentlooge** Newpt
6 E3 **St Budeaux** C Plym
2 C6 **St Buryan** Cnwll
45 M5 **St Catherine** BaNES
217 J5 **St Catherines** Ag & B
64 B6 **St Chloe** Gloucs
58 A5 **St Clears** Carmth
6 A1 **St Cleer** Cnwll
4 D6 **St Clement** Cnwll
9 e4 **St Clement** Jersey
11 H5 **St Clether** Cnwll
207 G5 **St Colmac** Ag & B

4 E2 **St Columb Major** Cnwll
4 D2 **St Columb Minor** Cnwll
4 E3 **St Columb Road** Cnwll
269 K4 **St Combs** Abers
106 F6 **St Cross South Elmham** Suffk
235 J2 **St Cyrus** Abers
221 G3 **St David's** P & K
74 B7 **St David's** Pembks
4 B6 **St Day** Cnwll
29 K2 **St Decumans** Somset
4 F3 **St Dennis** Cnwll
62 E1 **St Devereux** Herefs
75 K3 **St Dogmaels** Cerdgn
75 G6 **St Dogwells** Pembks
6 D1 **St Dominick** Cnwll
42 E8 **St Donats** V Glam
46 E6 **St Edith's Marsh** Wilts
10 D6 **St Endellion** Cnwll
4 E3 **St Enoder** Cnwll
4 D5 **St Erme** Cnwll
6 D3 **St Erney** Cnwll
2 E4 **St Erth** Cnwll
2 F4 **St Erth Praze** Cnwll
10 B8 **St Ervan** Cnwll
5 G5 **St Ewe** Cnwll
43 H6 **St Fagans** Cardif
269 K6 **St Fergus** Abers
220 B2 **St Fillans** P & K
55 J6 **St Florence** Pembks
11 G3 **St Gennys** Cnwll
127 K4 **St George** Conwy
43 H6 **St George's** V Glam
50 D6 **St George's Hill** Surrey
44 D6 **St Georges** N Som
6 D3 **St Germans** Cnwll
27 J7 **St Giles in the Wood** Devon
11 L4 **St Giles-on-the-Heath** Cnwll
3 K4 **St Gluvia's** Cnwll
78 D1 **St Harmon** Powys
168 F5 **St Helen Auckland** Dur
122 D8 **St Helena** Norfk
164 D4 **St Helens** Cumb
24 E5 **St Helens** E Susx
19 L6 **St Helens** IOW
139 G8 **St Helens** St Hel
51 H5 **St Helier** Gt Lon
9 d3 **St Helier** Jersey
2 E5 **St Hilary** Cnwll
42 F7 **St Hilary** V Glam
14 C1 **St Hill** Devon
38 B6 **St Hill** W Susx
61 K6 **St Illtyd** Blae G
69 G2 **St Ippollitts** Herts
54 D5 **St Ishmael's** Pembks
10 C8 **St Issey** Cnwll
6 C2 **St Ive** Cnwll
87 G1 **St Ives** Cambs
2 E3 **St Ives** Cnwll
17 M2 **St Ives** Dorset
122 F7 **St James** Norfk
107 G7 **St James South Elmham** Suffk
84 E3 **St James's End** Nhants
6 E4 **St John** Cnwll
9 c1 **St John** Jersey
154 c5 **St John's** IOM
27 J5 **St John's Chapel** Devon
167 K3 **St John's Chapel** Dur
103 L1 **St John's Fen End** Norfk
120 C8 **St John's Highway** Norfk
199 G6 **St John's Kirk** S Lans
184 F6 **St John's Town of Dalry** D & G
51 H2 **St John's Wood** Gt Lon
168 D4 **St Johns** Dur
38 E2 **St Johns** Kent
50 C7 **St Johns** Surrey
81 J4 **St Johns** Worcs
154 e3 **St Jude's** IOM
2 B5 **St Just** Cnwll
3 L4 **St Just Lane** Cnwll
3 L4 **St Just-in-Roseland** Cnwll
256 D5 **St Katherines** Abers
3 K6 **St Keverne** Cnwll
10 E7 **St Kew** Cnwll
10 E7 **St Kew Highway** Cnwll
6 A3 **St Keyne** Cnwll
5 H2 **St Lawrence** Cnwll
72 D6 **St Lawrence** Essex
19 J8 **St Lawrence** IOW
9 c2 **St Lawrence** Jersey
41 K2 **St Lawrence** Kent
39 H2 **St Leonard's Street** Kent
67 M5 **St Leonards** Bucks
17 M2 **St Leonards** Dorset
24 E5 **St Leonards** E Susx

2 B6 **St Levan** Cnwll
43 H7 **St Lythans** V Glam
10 E7 **St Mabyn** Cnwll
222 C3 **St Madoes** P & K
107 G6 **St Margaret South Elmham** Suffk
41 K6 **St Margaret's at Cliffe** Kent
275 C6 **St Margaret's Hope** Ork
79 L8 **St Margarets** Herefs
69 K5 **St Margarets** Herts
154 d7 **St Marks** IOM
6 B4 **St Martin** Cnwll
3 J6 **St Martin** Cnwll
9 j3 **St Martin** Guern
9 e2 **St Martin** Jersey
221 L1 **St Martin's** P & K
112 D4 **St Martin's Moor** Shrops
112 D4 **St Martins** Shrops
9 c2 **St Mary** Jersey
34 F1 **St Mary Bourne** Hants
42 F7 **St Mary Church** V Glam
52 A5 **St Mary Cray** Gt Lon
42 E6 **St Mary Hill** V Glam
25 K2 **St Mary in the Marsh** Kent
275 d5 **St Mary's** Ork
25 K2 **St Mary's Bay** Kent
44 F5 **St Mary's Grove** N Som
53 H4 **St Mary's Hoo** Medway
8 D2 **St Marychurch** Torbay
62 F4 **St Maughans** Mons
62 F4 **St Maughans Green** Mons
3 L4 **St Mawes** Cnwll
4 E2 **St Mawgan** Cnwll
6 D2 **St Mellion** Cnwll
43 K5 **St Mellons** Cardif
10 B7 **St Merryn** Cnwll
5 G4 **St Mewan** Cnwll
4 F6 **St Michael Caerhays** Cnwll
30 D5 **St Michael Church** Somset
4 D6 **St Michael Penkevil** Cnwll
107 G6 **St Michael South Elmham** Suffk
147 J7 **St Michael's on Wyre** Lancs
39 M6 **St Michaels** Kent
80 D2 **St Michaels** Worcs
10 D7 **St Minver** Cnwll
223 J6 **St Monans** Fife
5 L1 **St Neot** Cnwll
86 D3 **St Neots** Cambs
74 E5 **St Nicholas** Pembks
43 H6 **St Nicholas** V Glam
41 J2 **St Nicholas at Wade** Kent
209 L1 **St Ninians** Stirlg
107 J3 **St Olaves** Norfk
73 H4 **St Osyth** Essex
9 b2 **St Ouen** Jersey
63 G2 **St Owens Cross** Herefs
69 G3 **St Paul's Walden** Herts
52 A5 **St Pauls Cray** Gt Lon
9 b2 **St Peter** Jersey
9 k3 **St Peter Port** Guern
9 i3 **St Peter's** Guern
41 L2 **St Peter's** Kent
86 E1 **St Peter's Hill** Cambs
55 G7 **St Petrox** Pembks
5 L2 **St Pinnock** Cnwll
196 D6 **St Quivox** S Ayrs
3 J8 **St Ruan** Cnwll
9 k2 **St Sampson** Guern
9 i3 **St Saviour** Guern
9 d3 **St Saviour** Jersey
4 F4 **St Stephen** Cnwll
4 F4 **St Stephen's Coombe** Cnwll
11 L5 **St Stephens** Cnwll
6 E3 **St Stephens** Cnwll
10 F6 **St Teath** Cnwll
10 F7 **St Tudy** Cnwll
54 F7 **St Twynnells** Pembks
5 K4 **St Veep** Cnwll
235 G6 **St Vigeans** Angus
5 G4 **St Wenn** Cnwll
63 G2 **St Weonards** Herefs
43 H6 **St y-Nyll** V Glam
82 D7 **Saintbury** Gloucs
229 G5 **Salachail** Ag & B
7 L7 **Salcombe** Devon
14 D5 **Salcombe Regis** Devon
72 D4 **Salcott** Essex
130 F2 **Sale** Traffd
81 L4 **Sale Green** Worcs
137 J4 **Saleby** Lincs
24 D2 **Salehurst** E Susx
59 H4 **Salem** Carmth
92 E6 **Salem** Cerdgn
125 K8 **Salem** Gwynd

227 H4 **Salen** Ag & B
237 K7 **Salen** Highld
139 K1 **Salesbury** Lancs
85 J7 **Salford** Beds
65 L2 **Salford** Oxon
140 B8 **Salford** Salfd
82 C5 **Salford Priors** Warwks
37 L2 **Salfords** Surrey
123 G8 **Salhouse** Norfk
221 J8 **Saline** Fife
33 K5 **Salisbury** Wilts
166 D3 **Salkeld Dykes** Cumb
122 C6 **Salle** Norfk
136 F5 **Salmonby** Lincs
65 G3 **Salperton** Gloucs
86 B5 **Salph End** Beds
209 L6 **Salsburgh** N Lans
114 F6 **Salt** Staffs
177 G8 **Salt Cotes** Cumb
164 E2 **Salta** Cumb
149 L8 **Saltaire** Brad
6 E3 **Saltash** Cnwll
263 K6 **Saltburn** Highld
170 F6 **Saltburn-by-the-Sea** R & Cl
117 M6 **Saltby** Leics
155 K3 **Saltcoats** Cumb
195 L3 **Saltcoats** N Ayrs
138 D2 **Saltcotes** Lancs
22 F6 **Saltdean** Br & H
164 C5 **Salterbeck** Cumb
148 F6 **Salterforth** Lancs
130 C6 **Salterswall** Ches
33 K4 **Salterton** Wilts
137 H1 **Saltfleet** Lincs
137 H2 **Saltfleetby All Saints** Lincs
137 J1 **Saltfleetby St Clement** Lincs
137 H2 **Saltfleetby St Peter** Lincs
45 K5 **Saltford** BaNES
122 B3 **Salthouse** Norfk
98 E5 **Saltley** Birm
44 D2 **Saltmarsh** Newpt
143 K3 **Saltmarshe** E R Yk
129 J6 **Saltney** Flints
162 C6 **Salton** N York
27 H6 **Saltrens** Devon
180 E3 **Saltwick** Nthumb
40 F8 **Saltwood** Kent
21 K6 **Salvington** W Susx
81 K3 **Salwarpe** Worcs
15 K3 **Salwayash** Dorset
82 C3 **Sambourne** Warwks
113 M6 **Sambrook** Wrekin
139 H2 **Samlesbury** Lancs
139 J2 **Samlesbury Bottoms** Lancs
29 K7 **Sampford Arundel** Somset
29 K3 **Sampford Brett** Somset
12 F2 **Sampford Courtenay** Devon
29 K7 **Sampford Moor** Somset
29 J8 **Sampford Peverell** Devon
12 D8 **Sampford Spiney** Devon
73 G3 **Samson's Corner** Essex
275 e3 **Samsonlane** Ork
212 B5 **Samuelston** E Loth
204 C2 **Sanaigmore** Ag & B
2 C5 **Sancreed** Cnwll
152 D7 **Sancton** E R Yk
31 G2 **Sand** Somset
150 E7 **Sand Hills** Leeds
152 B8 **Sand Hole** E R Yk
151 L4 **Sand Hutton** N York
156 B6 **Sand Side** Cumb
247 M8 **Sandaig** Highld
142 A4 **Sandal Magna** Wakefd
165 H3 **Sandale** Cumb
236 F4 **Sandavore** Highld
130 E7 **Sandbach** Ches
207 K3 **Sandbank** Ag & B
17 K5 **Sandbanks** Poole
267 L3 **Sandend** Abers
51 J6 **Sanderstead** Gt Lon
167 G7 **Sandford** Cumb
13 J2 **Sandford** Devon
17 H5 **Sandford** Dorset
18 B3 **Sandford** Hants
19 J7 **Sandford** IOW
44 E7 **Sandford** N Som
197 L2 **Sandford** S Lans
112 E6 **Sandford** Shrops
113 J5 **Sandford** Shrops
31 K6 **Sandford Orcas** Dorset
66 B2 **Sandford St Martin** Oxon
66 D6 **Sandford-on-Thames** Oxon
41 G8 **Sandgate** Kent
269 H3 **Sandhaven** Abers
172 D5 **Sandhead** D & G

142 C8 **Sandhill** Rothm
16 B3 **Sandhills** Dorset
31 L8 **Sandhills** Dorset
66 E5 **Sandhills** Oxon
36 D3 **Sandhills** Surrey
180 A5 **Sandhoe** Nthumb
216 F7 **Sandhole** Ag & B
143 L2 **Sandholme** E R Yk
119 K4 **Sandholme** Lincs
49 K6 **Sandhurst** Br For
64 B2 **Sandhurst** Gloucs
39 K7 **Sandhurst** Kent
24 E2 **Sandhurst Cross** Kent
160 E6 **Sandhutton** N York
116 E4 **Sandiacre** Derbys
137 K3 **Sandilands** Lincs
130 B5 **Sandiway** Ches
33 K7 **Sandleheath** Hants
66 C6 **Sandleigh** Oxon
32 C6 **Sandley** Dorset
53 G7 **Sandling** Kent
130 F6 **Sandlow Green** Ches
281 c5 **Sandness** Shet
71 H6 **Sandon** Essex
87 G8 **Sandon** Herts
114 E5 **Sandon** Staffs
114 E6 **Sandon Bank** Staffs
19 K6 **Sandown** IOW
6 A3 **Sandplace** Cnwll
68 F5 **Sandridge** Herts
46 D6 **Sandridge** Wilts
120 F5 **Sandringham** Norfk
67 K8 **Sands** Bucks
171 K8 **Sandsend** N York
157 G6 **Sandside** Cumb
143 J6 **Sandtoft** N Linc
39 M3 **Sandway** Kent
41 K4 **Sandwich** Kent
166 A6 **Sandwick** Cumb
281 e8 **Sandwick** Shet
282 g3 **Sandwick** W Isls
164 C7 **Sandwith** Cumb
164 C7 **Sandwith Newtown** Cumb
86 D5 **Sandy** Beds
136 E8 **Sandy Bank** Lincs
23 K3 **Sandy Cross** E Susx
80 F4 **Sandy Cross** Herefs
54 D5 **Sandy Haven** Pembks
149 K8 **Sandy Lane** Brad
46 D5 **Sandy Lane** Wilts
112 F3 **Sandy Lane** Wrexhm
13 G4 **Sandy Park** Devon
129 H6 **Sandycroft** Flints
187 J7 **Sandyford** D & G
13 K7 **Sandygate** Devon
154 e3 **Sandygate** IOM
175 M4 **Sandyhills** D & G
147 H3 **Sandylands** Lancs
113 M4 **Sandylane** Staffs
57 G7 **Sandylane** Swans
177 L5 **Sandysike** Cumb
63 G2 **Sandyway** Herefs
277 G3 **Sangobeg** Highld
276 F3 **Sangomore** Highld
130 B2 **Sankey Bridges** Warrtn
81 H2 **Sankyn's Green** Worcs
236 E6 **Sanna Bay** Highld
282 g3 **Sanndabhaig** W Isls
195 G2 **Sannox** N Ayrs
185 K1 **Sanquhar** D & G
155 K2 **Santon** Cumb
154 d7 **Santon** IOM
155 K2 **Santon Bridge** Cumb
105 G6 **Santon Downham** Suffk
100 B5 **Sapcote** Leics
81 G2 **Sapey Common** Herefs
105 J8 **Sapiston** Suffk
102 E8 **Sapley** Cambs
115 K4 **Sapperton** Derbys
64 D6 **Sapperton** Gloucs
118 D5 **Sapperton** Lincs
119 K6 **Saracen's Head** Lincs
280 D7 **Sarclet** Highld
19 H2 **Sarisbury** Hants
42 D5 **Sarn** Brdgnd
108 D5 **Sarn** Gwynd
93 L4 **Sarn** Powys
94 F5 **Sarn** Powys
108 E6 **Sarn-bach** Gwynd
112 D7 **Sarn-wen** Powys
58 B5 **Sarnau** Carmth
76 B5 **Sarnau** Cerdgn
111 J4 **Sarnau** Gwynd
112 C8 **Sarnau** Powys
78 E8 **Sarnau** Powys

79 L5 **Sarnesfield** Herefs
76 C7 **Saron** Carmth
59 H6 **Saron** Carmth
125 J6 **Saron** Gwynd
125 H7 **Saron** Gwynd
68 D7 **Sarratt** Herts
41 H2 **Sarre** Kent
65 L3 **Sarsden** Oxon
34 C2 **Sarson** Hants
168 E2 **Satley** Dur
41 H7 **Satmar** Kent
159 G3 **Satron** N York
28 B6 **Satterleigh** Devon
156 D4 **Satterthwaite** Cumb
49 H2 **Satwell** Oxon
244 F1 **Sauchen** Abers
233 J8 **Saucher** P & K
235 G2 **Sauchieburn** Abers
63 L5 **Saul** Gloucs
134 F2 **Saundby** Notts
55 K6 **Saundersfoot** Pembks
67 J6 **Saunderton** Bucks
27 H3 **Saunton** Devon
137 G6 **Sausthorpe** Lincs
4 C6 **Saveock Water** Cnwll
114 F4 **Saverley Green** Staffs
141 K4 **Savile Town** Kirk
83 L2 **Sawbridge** Warwks
70 C4 **Sawbridgeworth** Herts
163 G5 **Sawdon** N York
116 D5 **Sawley** Derbys
148 D6 **Sawley** Lancs
150 C2 **Sawley** N York
87 K5 **Sawston** Cambs
102 D6 **Sawtry** Cambs
117 L7 **Saxby** Leics
135 K3 **Saxby** Lincs
144 C4 **Saxby All Saints** N Linc
117 J7 **Saxelbye** Leics
90 C3 **Saxham Street** Suffk
135 H4 **Saxilby** Lincs
122 A4 **Saxlingham** Norfk
106 E4 **Saxlingham Green** Norfk
106 E4 **Saxlingham Nethergate** Norfk
106 E4 **Saxlingham Thorpe** Norfk
91 J3 **Saxmundham** Suffk
88 D3 **Saxon Street** Cambs
117 H3 **Saxondale** Notts
91 G2 **Saxtead** Suffk
90 F2 **Saxtead Green** Suffk
90 F2 **Saxtead Little Green** Suffk
122 C5 **Saxthorpe** Norfk
151 G8 **Saxton** N York
22 D4 **Sayers Common** W Susx
161 L8 **Scackleton** N York
134 D2 **Scaftworth** Notts
152 C1 **Scagglethorpe** N York
214 D5 **Scalasaig** Ag & B
143 L2 **Scalby** E R Yk
163 H4 **Scalby** N York
85 L4 **Scald End** Beds
84 E1 **Scaldwell** Nhants
166 E2 **Scale Houses** Cumb
178 B6 **Scaleby** Cumb
178 B6 **Scalebyhill** Cumb
165 K5 **Scales** Cumb
146 E2 **Scales** Cumb
166 B1 **Scalesceugh** Cumb
117 K6 **Scalford** Leics
171 H7 **Scaling** N York
171 H8 **Scaling Dam** R & Cl
281 d7 **Scalloway** Shet
136 E4 **Scamblesby** Lincs
141 G4 **Scammonden** Kirk
228 C1 **Scamodale** Highld
162 F7 **Scampston** N York
135 J4 **Scampton** Lincs
251 H4 **Scaniport** Highld
141 G4 **Scapegoat Hill** Kirk
163 J5 **Scarborough** N York
4 F4 **Scarcewater** Cnwll
133 K6 **Scarcliffe** Derbys
150 E7 **Scarcroft** Leeds
150 E7 **Scarcroft Hill** Leeds
280 C2 **Scarfskerry** Highld
168 D8 **Scargill** Dur
224 D6 **Scarinish** Ag & B
138 D5 **Scarisbrick** Lancs
165 H4 **Scarness** Cumb
105 J1 **Scarning** Norfk
117 J3 **Scarrington** Notts
138 E6 **Scarth Hill** Lancs
151 G8 **Scarthingwell** N York
145 H6 **Scartho** Lincs

144 B6 **Scawby** N Linc
142 E6 **Scawsby** Donc
142 E6 **Scawthorpe** Donc
161 J6 **Scawton** N York
22 F3 **Scayne's Hill** W Susx
61 H2 **Scethrog** Powys
131 G8 **Scholar Green** Ches
141 J6 **Scholes** Kirk
141 J3 **Scholes** Kirk
150 E8 **Scholes** Leeds
142 B8 **Scholes** Rothm
139 J6 **Scholes** Wigan
142 B3 **Scholey Hill** Leeds
169 H6 **School Aycliffe** Dur
141 H1 **School Green** Brad
130 C6 **School Green** Ches
15 J2 **School House** Dorset
49 H5 **Schoolgreen** Wokham
141 L5 **Scissett** Kirk
74 F5 **Scleddau** Pembks
122 F7 **Sco Ruston** Norfk
134 C4 **Scofton** Notts
106 C7 **Scole** Norfk
221 L2 **Scone** P & K
247 H2 **Sconser** Highld
222 F6 **Scoonie** Fife
135 M8 **Scopwick** Lincs
261 G1 **Scoraig** Highld
152 F6 **Scorborough** E R Yk
4 B6 **Scorrier** Cnwll
7 K1 **Scorriton** Devon
147 K6 **Scorton** Lancs
160 C3 **Scorton** N York
114 C2 **Scot Hay** Staffs
139 J6 **Scot Lane End** Bolton
180 C2 **Scot's Gap** Nthumb
178 B7 **Scotby** Cumb
160 B2 **Scotch Corner** N York
147 J4 **Scotforth** Lancs
135 L4 **Scothern** Lincs
150 B7 **Scotland** Leeds
118 C5 **Scotland** Lincs
181 G2 **Scotland Gate** Nthumb
222 C7 **Scotlandwell** P & K
279 K5 **Scotscalder Station** Highld
177 L4 **Scotsdike** Cumb
255 L7 **Scotsmill** Abers
208 F5 **Scotstoun** C Glas
180 F6 **Scotswood** N u Ty
118 D4 **Scott Willoughby** Lincs
143 M7 **Scotter** Lincs
143 L7 **Scotterthorpe** Lincs
118 D7 **Scottlethorpe** Lincs
143 M7 **Scotton** Lincs
160 B3 **Scotton** N York
150 D4 **Scotton** N York
122 F6 **Scottow** Norfk
105 K3 **Scoulton** Norfk
115 H5 **Scounslow Green** Staffs
276 B7 **Scourie** Highld
276 A7 **Scourie More** Highld
281 d8 **Scousburgh** Shet
140 E6 **Scouthead** Oldham
279 K2 **Scrabster** Highld
189 J3 **Scraesburgh** Border
136 F6 **Scrafield** Lincs
190 D4 **Scrainwood** Nthumb
119 L3 **Scrane End** Lincs
100 E2 **Scraptoft** Leics
123 K8 **Scratby** Norfk
151 M4 **Scrayingham** N York
24 D3 **Scrays** E Susx
118 E3 **Scredington** Lincs
137 H6 **Scremby** Lincs
202 F3 **Scremerston** Nthumb
117 J3 **Screveton** Notts
136 E6 **Scrivelsby** Lincs
150 E4 **Scriven** N York
134 C2 **Scrooby** Notts
115 K5 **Scropton** Derbys
136 D8 **Scrub Hill** Lincs
233 K4 **Scruschloch** Angus
160 D4 **Scruton** N York
178 B4 **Scuggate** Cumb
277 L4 **Scullomie** Highld
121 K5 **Sculthorpe** Norfk
143 M5 **Scunthorpe** N Linc
56 E7 **Scurlage** Swans
30 E8 **Sea** Somset
123 J6 **Sea Palling** Norfk
15 K1 **Seaborough** Dorset
114 C3 **Seabridge** Staffs
41 G8 **Seabrook** Kent
181 K6 **Seaburn** Sundld
129 H2 **Seacombe** Wirral

150 E8 **Seacroft** Leeds
137 L7 **Seacroft** Lincs
119 K4 **Seadyke** Lincs
259 H8 **Seafield** Highld
210 D6 **Seafield** W Loth
23 H7 **Seaford** E Susx
138 C8 **Seaforth** Sefton
117 G8 **Seagrave** Leics
46 D3 **Seagry Heath** Wilts
169 L1 **Seaham** Dur
203 L6 **Seahouses** Nthumb
38 E2 **Seal** Kent
170 D6 **Seal Sands** S on T
36 D1 **Seale** Surrey
170 C8 **Seamer** N York
163 J6 **Seamer** N York
195 K2 **Seamill** N Ayrs
144 D6 **Searby** Lincs
40 E2 **Seasalter** Kent
155 J2 **Seascale** Cumb
165 H8 **Seathwaite** Cumb
156 B3 **Seathwaite** Cumb
156 E6 **Seatle** Cumb
165 H7 **Seatoller** Cumb
6 C4 **Seaton** Cnwll
164 D4 **Seaton** Cumb
14 F4 **Seaton** Devon
169 L1 **Seaton** Dur
153 J6 **Seaton** E R Yk
41 H4 **Seaton** Kent
181 H3 **Seaton** Nthumb
101 K4 **Seaton** Rutlnd
181 G4 **Seaton Burn** N Tyne
170 C5 **Seaton Carew** Hartpl
181 H4 **Seaton Delaval** Nthumb
152 B7 **Seaton Ross** E R Yk
181 H3 **Seaton Sluice** Nthumb
15 K4 **Seatown** Dorset
161 J3 **Seave Green** N York
19 L5 **Seaview** IOW
177 G8 **Seaville** Cumb
30 F7 **Seavington St Mary** Somset
30 F7 **Seavington St Michael** Somset
62 C7 **Sebastopol** Torfn
165 K2 **Sebergham** Cumb
99 H2 **Seckington** Warwks
157 L4 **Sedbergh** Cumb
63 H8 **Sedbury** Gloucs
158 F4 **Sedbusk** N York
104 D6 **Sedge Fen** Suffk
82 B7 **Sedgeberrow** Worcs
117 M4 **Sedgebrook** Lincs
169 K5 **Sedgefield** Dur
120 F4 **Sedgeford** Norfk
32 E5 **Sedgehill** Wilts
97 L4 **Sedgley** Dudley
140 B7 **Sedgley Park** Bury
157 H5 **Sedgwick** Cumb
24 E4 **Sedlescombe** E Susx
67 J5 **Sedrup** Bucks
40 B4 **Seed** Kent
46 D6 **Seend** Wilts
46 D6 **Seend Cleeve** Wilts
68 B8 **Seer Green** Bucks
107 G4 **Seething** Norfk
138 D7 **Sefton** Sefton
138 D7 **Sefton Town** Sefton
181 G4 **Seghill** Nthumb
114 D6 **Seighford** Staffs
125 K6 **Seion** Gwynd
97 J4 **Seisdon** Staffs
112 C5 **Selattyn** Shrops
35 M4 **Selborne** Hants
142 F1 **Selby** N York
20 F3 **Selham** W Susx
51 J5 **Selhurst** Gt Lon
201 G7 **Selkirk** Border
63 H2 **Sellack** Herefs
281 e2 **Sellafirth** Shet
2 C5 **Sellan** Cnwll
30 B7 **Sellick's Green** Somset
40 E7 **Sellindge** Kent
40 D4 **Selling** Kent
46 D6 **Sells Green** Wilts
98 D7 **Selly Oak** Birm
23 H6 **Selmeston** E Susx
51 K6 **Selsdon** Gt Lon
20 D8 **Selsey** W Susx
38 A6 **Selsfield Common** W Susx
157 H3 **Selside** Cumb
158 D7 **Selside** N York
64 B6 **Selsley** Gloucs
41 H6 **Selsted** Kent
116 D1 **Selston** Notts

29 G2 **Selworthy** Somset
89 K6 **Semer** Suffk
46 C6 **Semington** Wilts
32 E5 **Semley** Wilts
118 F5 **Sempringham** Lincs
50 C7 **Send** Surrey
50 D7 **Send Marsh** Surrey
43 H3 **Senghenydd** Caerph
2 B6 **Sennen** Cnwll
2 B6 **Sennen Cove** Cnwll
60 D2 **Sennybridge** Powys
134 C2 **Serlby** Notts
161 G7 **Sessay** N York
104 C1 **Setchey** Norfk
18 D3 **Setley** Hants
211 M4 **Seton Mains** E Loth
148 E3 **Settle** N York
179 K5 **Settlingstones** Nthumb
152 C2 **Settrington** N York
29 L4 **Seven Ash** Somset
51 M2 **Seven Kings** Gt Lon
60 B5 **Seven Sisters** Neath
64 D4 **Seven Springs** Gloucs
72 D2 **Seven Star Green** Essex
82 D8 **Seven Wells** Gloucs
64 F3 **Sevenhampton** Gloucs
47 J1 **Sevenhampton** Swindn
38 E2 **Sevenoaks** Kent
38 E3 **Sevenoaks Weald** Kent
45 G2 **Severn Beach** S Glos
81 K6 **Severn Stoke** Worcs
86 B4 **Sevick End** Beds
40 D7 **Sevington** Kent
88 B7 **Sewards End** Essex
69 K7 **Sewardstonebury** Gt Lon
68 C3 **Sewell** Beds
153 K2 **Sewerby** E R Yk
3 H5 **Seworgan** Cnwll
118 A7 **Sewstern** Leics
161 G2 **Sexhow** N York
65 H1 **Sezincote** Gloucs
282 h1 **Sgiogarstaigh** W Isls
67 G5 **Shabbington** Bucks
99 K2 **Shackerstone** Leics
116 C5 **Shacklecross** Derbys
36 D2 **Shackleford** Surrey
140 D3 **Shade** Calder
282 g1 **Shader** W Isls
169 J3 **Shadforth** Dur
107 J6 **Shadingfield** Suffk
40 C7 **Shadoxhurst** Kent
150 D7 **Shadwell** Leeds
105 J6 **Shadwell** Norfk
87 H7 **Shaftenhoe End** Herts
32 E6 **Shaftesbury** Dorset
142 F6 **Shaftholme** Donc
142 B5 **Shafton** Barns
142 B5 **Shafton Two Gates** Barns
139 K7 **Shakerley** Wigan
47 L6 **Shalbourne** Wilts
18 F6 **Shalcombe** IOW
35 L3 **Shalden** Hants
35 L2 **Shalden Green** Hants
13 L8 **Shaldon** Devon
18 F6 **Shalfleet** IOW
71 H1 **Shalford** Essex
36 F2 **Shalford** Surrey
71 H2 **Shalford Green** Essex
114 D5 **Shallowford** Staffs
40 E4 **Shalmsford Street** Kent
84 C7 **Shalstone** Bucks
36 F2 **Shamley Green** Surrey
234 D3 **Shandford** Angus
207 L2 **Shandon** Ag & B
264 D5 **Shandwick** Highld
100 F4 **Shangton** Leics
181 G3 **Shankhouse** Nthumb
19 K7 **Shanklin** IOW
166 D7 **Shap** Cumb
17 H2 **Shapwick** Dorset
30 F3 **Shapwick** Somset
98 F5 **Shard End** Birm
116 D5 **Shardlow** Derbys
97 L2 **Shareshill** Staffs
142 B4 **Sharlston** Wakefd
142 B4 **Sharlston Common** Wakefd
98 E7 **Sharman's Cross** Solhll
53 G4 **Sharnal Street** Medway
85 K3 **Sharnbrook** Beds
140 C3 **Sharneyford** Lancs
100 B5 **Sharnford** Leics
16 D2 **Sharnhill Green** Dorset
139 G1 **Sharoe Green** Lancs
150 D2 **Sharow** N York
123 H7 **Sharp Green** Norfk

68 D1 **Sharpenhoe** Beds
190 D5 **Sharperton** Nthumb
63 K6 **Sharpness** Gloucs
38 B6 **Sharpthorne** W Susx
11 J7 **Sharptor** Cnwll
81 L2 **Sharpway Gate** Worcs
122 A4 **Sharrington** Norfk
97 H7 **Shatterford** Worcs
41 J4 **Shatterling** Kent
132 D3 **Shatton** Derbys
7 G2 **Shaugh Prior** Devon
15 J3 **Shave Cross** Dorset
113 M1 **Shavington** Ches
140 F1 **Shaw** Brad
140 D6 **Shaw** Oldham
47 G2 **Shaw** Swindn
48 C5 **Shaw** W Berk
46 C6 **Shaw** Wilts
63 K2 **Shaw Common** Gloucs
69 J1 **Shaw Green** Herts
139 G4 **Shaw Green** Lancs
150 C5 **Shaw Green** N York
139 H4 **Shaw Hill** Lancs
150 C3 **Shaw Mills** N York
282 f2 **Shawbost** W Isls
113 J7 **Shawbury** Shrops
140 D5 **Shawclough** Rochdl
190 F3 **Shawdon Hill** Nthumb
100 C7 **Shawell** Leics
34 F6 **Shawford** Hants
140 D4 **Shawforth** Lancs
185 L7 **Shawhead** D & G
198 C3 **Shawsburn** S Lans
32 E3 **Shear Cross** Wilts
176 D5 **Shearington** D & G
100 D5 **Shearsby** Leics
30 D5 **Shearston** Somset
12 B1 **Shebbear** Devon
114 B6 **Shebdon** Staffs
279 H3 **Shebster** Highld
208 F7 **Sheddens** E Rens
35 H8 **Shedfield** Hants
132 B7 **Sheen** Derbys
180 E7 **Sheep Hill** Dur
133 G5 **Sheepbridge** Derbys
141 J4 **Sheepridge** Kirk
141 M1 **Sheepscar** Leeds
64 C5 **Sheepscombe** Gloucs
7 G1 **Sheepstor** Devon
12 C1 **Sheepwash** Devon
181 G2 **Sheepwash** Nthumb
45 G4 **Sheepway** N Som
99 J3 **Sheepy Magna** Leics
99 J3 **Sheepy Parva** Leics
70 D4 **Sheering** Essex
53 K4 **Sheerness** Kent
50 D6 **Sheerwater** Surrey
36 A6 **Sheet** Hants
2 D5 **Sheffield** Cnwll
133 G2 **Sheffield** Sheff
49 G5 **Sheffield Bottom** W Berk
22 F2 **Sheffield Green** E Susx
86 C7 **Shefford** Beds
276 B4 **Sheigra** Highld
96 E3 **Sheinton** Shrops
95 K7 **Shelderton** Shrops
98 F6 **Sheldon** Birm
132 C6 **Sheldon** Derbys
14 D1 **Sheldon** Devon
40 D4 **Sheldwich** Kent
40 D4 **Sheldwich Lees** Kent
141 H2 **Shelf** Calder
106 C6 **Shelfanger** Norfk
82 D3 **Shelfield** Warwks
98 C3 **Shelfield** Wsall
82 D3 **Shelfield Green** Warwks
117 H3 **Shelford** Notts
99 L5 **Shelford** Warwks
202 D4 **Shellacres** Border
70 E6 **Shelley** Essex
141 K5 **Shelley** Kirk
89 L7 **Shelley** Suffk
141 K5 **Shelley Far Bank** Kirk
65 L8 **Shellingford** Oxon
70 F5 **Shellow Bowells** Essex
81 G3 **Shelsley Beauchamp** Worcs
81 G3 **Shelsley Walsh** Worcs
85 K2 **Shelton** Beds
106 E5 **Shelton** Norfk
117 K3 **Shelton** Notts
95 L1 **Shelton** Shrops
106 E5 **Shelton Green** Norfk
116 C5 **Shelton Lock** C Derb
114 C4 **Shelton Under Harley** Staffs
95 H4 **Shelve** Shrops

80 C6 **Shelwick** Herefs
70 F8 **Shenfield** Essex
83 J6 **Shenington** Oxon
68 F7 **Shenley** Herts
85 G8 **Shenley Brook End** M Keyn
85 G7 **Shenley Church End** M Keyn
68 F6 **Shenleybury** Herts
79 M7 **Shenmore** Herefs
173 J2 **Shennanton** D & G
98 E3 **Shenstone** Staffs
97 J8 **Shenstone** Worcs
98 E3 **Shenstone Woodend** Staffs
99 K3 **Shenton** Leics
102 F1 **Shepeau Stow** Lincs
69 H2 **Shephall** Herts
51 G3 **Shepherd's Bush** Gt Lon
49 H2 **Shepherd's Green** Oxon
4 D4 **Shepherds** Cnwll
63 L6 **Shepherds Patch** Gloucs
41 H5 **Shepherdswell** Kent
141 J6 **Shepley** Kirk
63 J8 **Shepperdine** S Glos
50 D5 **Shepperton** Surrey
50 D5 **Shepperton Green** Surrey
87 H5 **Shepreth** Cambs
116 E7 **Shepshed** Leics
30 F7 **Shepton Beauchamp** Somset
31 K2 **Shepton Mallet** Somset
31 L4 **Shepton Montague** Somset
39 J3 **Shepway** Kent
170 B4 **Sheraton** Dur
31 L7 **Sherborne** Dorset
65 H4 **Sherborne** Gloucs
45 H7 **Sherborne** Somset
32 D6 **Sherborne Causeway** Dorset
48 F7 **Sherborne St John** Hants
83 G3 **Sherbourne** Warwks
169 J2 **Sherburn** Dur
163 G7 **Sherburn** N York
169 J2 **Sherburn Hill** Dur
142 D1 **Sherburn in Elmet** N York
37 G1 **Shere** Surrey
121 K5 **Shereford** Norfk
34 C6 **Sherfield English** Hants
49 G7 **Sherfield on Loddon** Hants
140 B3 **Sherfin** Lancs
8 A6 **Sherford** Devon
17 H4 **Sherford** Dorset
151 K3 **Sheriff Hutton** N York
97 G1 **Sheriffhales** Shrops
122 D3 **Sheringham** Norfk
85 H6 **Sherington** M Keyn
22 B3 **Shermanbury** W Susx
120 F5 **Shernborne** Norfk
33 G3 **Sherrington** Wilts
46 B2 **Sherston** Wilts
116 F3 **Sherwood** C Nott
209 H6 **Shettleston** C Glas
139 H6 **Shevington** Wigan
139 H5 **Shevington Moor** Wigan
139 G6 **Shevington Vale** Wigan
6 D4 **Sheviock** Cnwll
141 H2 **Shibden Head** Brad
19 H6 **Shide** IOW
202 C5 **Shidlaw** Nthumb
248 F7 **Shiel Bridge** Highld
248 C1 **Shieldaig** Highld
176 D2 **Shieldhill** D & G
210 B4 **Shieldhill** Falk
199 G5 **Shieldhill House Hotel** S Lans
209 K7 **Shields** N Lans
237 J6 **Shielfoot** Highld
234 C4 **Shielhill** Angus
207 L4 **Shielhill** Inver
66 A6 **Shifford** Oxon
97 G2 **Shifnal** Shrops
191 J4 **Shilbottle** Nthumb
169 G5 **Shildon** Dur
208 D7 **Shillford** E Rens
29 H6 **Shillingford** Devon
66 E8 **Shillingford** Oxon
13 L5 **Shillingford Abbot** Devon
13 L5 **Shillingford St George** Devon
32 D8 **Shillingstone** Dorset
86 C8 **Shillington** Beds
190 B4 **Shillmoor** Nthumb
65 K5 **Shilton** Oxon
99 L6 **Shilton** Warwks
16 B5 **Shilvinghampton** Dorset
106 D6 **Shimpling** Norfk
89 H5 **Shimpling** Suffk
89 H4 **Shimpling Street** Suffk
169 H3 **Shincliffe** Dur
181 H8 **Shiney Row** Sundld
49 H5 **Shinfield** Wokham

86 F6 **Shingay** Cambs
91 J6 **Shingle Street** Suffk
8 B2 **Shinnersbridge** Devon
272 D5 **Shinness** Highld
38 F3 **Shipbourne** Kent
130 D5 **Shipbrookhill** Ches
105 J2 **Shipdham** Norfk
44 E7 **Shipham** Somset
8 D2 **Shiphay** Torbay
49 J3 **Shiplake** Oxon
49 H3 **Shiplake Row** Oxon
44 D7 **Shiplate** N Som
149 L8 **Shipley** Brad
116 D3 **Shipley** Derbys
97 H4 **Shipley** Shrops
37 H6 **Shipley** W Susx
37 M3 **Shipley Bridge** Surrey
40 C7 **Shipley Hatch** Kent
107 H5 **Shipmeadow** Suffk
104 C6 **Shippea Hill Station** Cambs
66 C7 **Shippon** Oxon
83 G7 **Shipston on Stour** Warwks
67 J2 **Shipton** Bucks
64 F3 **Shipton** Gloucs
151 H4 **Shipton** N York
96 D5 **Shipton** Shrops
34 B2 **Shipton Bellinger** Hants
15 L4 **Shipton Gorge** Dorset
20 C7 **Shipton Green** W Susx
46 C1 **Shipton Moyne** Gloucs
66 C4 **Shipton-on-Cherwell** Oxon
65 L3 **Shipton-under-Wychwood** Oxon
152 C7 **Shiptonthorpe** E R Yk
67 G7 **Shirburn** Oxon
138 D5 **Shirdley Hill** Lancs
166 E4 **Shire** Cumb
98 D3 **Shire Oak** Wsall
133 K6 **Shirebrook** Derbys
133 G1 **Shiregreen** Sheff
45 G4 **Shirehampton** Bristl
181 H4 **Shiremoor** N Tyne
62 F8 **Shirenewton** Mons
133 L3 **Shireoaks** Notts
40 B8 **Shirkoak** Kent
80 A3 **Shirl Heath** Herefs
133 H8 **Shirland** Derbys
96 E4 **Shirlett** Shrops
34 E8 **Shirley** C Sotn
115 L3 **Shirley** Derbys
51 K6 **Shirley** Gt Lon
98 E7 **Shirley** Solhll
35 H8 **Shirrell Heath** Hants
206 D2 **Shirvan** Ag & B
27 L3 **Shirwell** Devon
27 L3 **Shirwell Cross** Devon
194 E5 **Shiskine** N Ayrs
168 C3 **Shittlehope** Dur
79 M3 **Shobdon** Herefs
18 B2 **Shobley** Hants
13 K2 **Shobrooke** Devon
117 H7 **Shoby** Leics
113 G2 **Shocklach** Ches
113 G2 **Shocklach Green** Ches
53 K2 **Shoeburyness** Sthend
41 K5 **Sholden** Kent
19 G2 **Sholing** C Sotn
164 D5 **Shoose** Cumb
95 K1 **Shoot Hill** Shrops
26 D7 **Shop** Cnwll
10 B7 **Shop** Cnwll
90 F2 **Shop Street** Suffk
20 E6 **Shopwyke** W Susx
140 D4 **Shore** Rochdl
51 J2 **Shoreditch** Gt Lon
30 C6 **Shoreditch** Somset
52 B6 **Shoreham** Kent
22 C6 **Shoreham-by-Sea** W Susx
202 E4 **Shoreswood** Nthumb
35 J5 **Shorley** Hants
64 F7 **Shorncote** Gloucs
52 E5 **Shorne** Kent
52 E5 **Shorne Ridgeway** Kent
98 E5 **Short Heath** Birm
98 B3 **Short Heath** Wsall
6 B3 **Shorta Cross** Cnwll
23 G3 **Shortbridge** E Susx
36 C2 **Shortfield Common** Surrey
23 H4 **Shortgate** E Susx
36 A4 **Shortheath** Hants
4 C5 **Shortlanesend** Cnwll
86 B6 **Shortstown** Beds
19 G7 **Shorwell** IOW
45 L7 **Shoscombe** BaNES
106 E4 **Shotesham** Norfk

71 J8 **Shotgate** Essex
90 F8 **Shotley** Suffk
180 D8 **Shotley Bridge** Dur
90 F8 **Shotley Gate** Suffk
90 F8 **Shotley Street** Suffk
180 C8 **Shotleyfield** Nthumb
40 D4 **Shottenden** Kent
36 C4 **Shottermill** Surrey
82 E4 **Shottery** Warwks
83 K6 **Shotteswell** Warwks
91 H6 **Shottisham** Suffk
116 A2 **Shottle** Derbys
116 A2 **Shottlegate** Derbys
169 K5 **Shotton** Dur
169 L3 **Shotton** Dur
129 H6 **Shotton** Flints
202 C7 **Shotton** Nthumb
180 F3 **Shotton** Nthumb
169 K3 **Shotton Colliery** Dur
210 A7 **Shotts** N Lans
129 H5 **Shotwick** Ches
266 D5 **Shougle** Moray
104 D2 **Shouldham** Norfk
104 D2 **Shouldham Thorpe** Norfk
81 J3 **Shoulton** Worcs
39 G7 **Shover's Green** E Susx
114 B2 **Shraleybrook** Staffs
112 F8 **Shrawardine** Shrops
81 J2 **Shrawley** Worcs
50 J3 **Shreding Green** Bucks
82 F2 **Shrewley** Warwks
96 B1 **Shrewsbury** Shrops
33 J2 **Shrewton** Wilts
20 F6 **Shripney** W Susx
47 K1 **Shrivenham** Oxon
105 K5 **Shropham** Norfk
72 E2 **Shrub End** Essex
80 D6 **Shucknall** Herefs
88 C6 **Shudy Camps** Cambs
64 D3 **Shurdington** Gloucs
49 K4 **Shurlock Row** W & M
82 B3 **Shurnock** Worcs
279 J4 **Shurrery** Highld
279 J5 **Shurrery Lodge** Highld
30 B2 **Shurton** Somset
99 G5 **Shustoke** Warwks
114 D7 **Shut Heath** Staffs
13 L3 **Shute** Devon
14 F3 **Shute** Devon
83 J7 **Shutford** Oxon
81 K8 **Shuthonger** Gloucs
84 E5 **Shutlanger** Nhants
97 K2 **Shutt Green** Staffs
13 M6 **Shutterton** Devon
99 H2 **Shuttington** Warwks
133 J5 **Shuttlewood** Derbys
133 J5 **Shuttlewood Common** Derbys
140 B4 **Shuttleworth** Bury
282 f2 **Siabost** W Isls
282 g1 **Siadar** W Isls
100 E6 **Sibbertoft** Nhants
95 K6 **Sibdon Carwood** Shrops
83 H7 **Sibford Ferris** Oxon
83 H7 **Sibford Gower** Oxon
88 F8 **Sible Hedingham** Essex
70 F2 **Sibley's Green** Essex
11 J7 **Siblyback** Cnwll
119 K2 **Sibsey** Lincs
119 K1 **Sibsey Fenside** Lincs
102 B4 **Sibson** Cambs
99 K3 **Sibson** Leics
280 D5 **Sibster** Highld
134 E5 **Sibthorpe** Notts
117 K2 **Sibthorpe** Notts
91 J2 **Sibton** Suffk
89 H3 **Sicklesmere** Suffk
150 E6 **Sicklinghall** N York
142 B6 **Sid Cop** Barns
30 C5 **Sidbrook** Somset
14 D4 **Sidbury** Devon
96 F6 **Sidbury** Shrops
44 E7 **Sidcot** N Som
51 M4 **Sidcup** Gt Lon
164 D4 **Siddick** Cumb
131 G5 **Siddington** Ches
64 F7 **Siddington** Gloucs
81 L1 **Sidemoor** Worcs
122 F3 **Sidestrand** Norfk
14 D4 **Sidford** Devon
20 D7 **Sidlesham** W Susx
20 D6 **Sidlesham Common** W Susx
24 D5 **Sidley** E Susx
14 D5 **Sidmouth** Devon
96 B6 **Siefton** Shrops

13 H7 **Sigford** Devon
153 J6 **Sigglesthorne** E R Yk
42 E7 **Sigingstone** V Glam
65 K5 **Signet** Oxon
48 F6 **Silchester** Hants
117 G8 **Sileby** Leics
155 L6 **Silecroft** Cumb
106 C3 **Silfield** Norfk
77 G5 **Silian** Cerdgn
118 E3 **Silk Willoughby** Lincs
34 F6 **Silkstead** Hants
141 L6 **Silkstone** Barns
141 L6 **Silkstone Common** Barns
181 J8 **Silksworth** Sundld
176 F8 **Silloth** Cumb
163 H4 **Silpho** N York
149 J6 **Silsden** Brad
86 B8 **Silsoe** Beds
32 C5 **Silton** Dorset
71 K3 **Silver End** Essex
53 J7 **Silver Street** Kent
31 J4 **Silver Street** Somset
211 G7 **Silverburn** Mdloth
157 G7 **Silverdale** Lancs
114 C2 **Silverdale** Staffs
157 G7 **Silverdale Green** Lancs
268 D3 **Silverford** Abers
122 D6 **Silvergate** Norfk
91 H3 **Silverlace Green** Suffk
106 F8 **Silverley's Green** Suffk
84 C6 **Silverstone** Nhants
13 M2 **Silverton** Devon
4 B5 **Silverwell** Cnwll
96 E7 **Silvington** Shrops
131 K1 **Simmondley** Derbys
179 K4 **Simonburn** Nthumb
29 L7 **Simons Burrow** Devon
28 D3 **Simonsbath** Somset
140 A1 **Simonstone** Lancs
158 F4 **Simonstone** N York
202 C4 **Simprim** Border
85 H8 **Simpson** M Keyn
54 E3 **Simpson Cross** Pembks
202 C3 **Sinclair's Hill** Border
196 F7 **Sinclairston** E Ayrs
160 E6 **Sinderby** N York
179 K8 **Sinderhope** Nthumb
130 E2 **Sinderland Green** Traffd
49 J5 **Sindlesham** Wokham
116 B5 **Sinfin** C Derb
51 L7 **Single Street** Gt Lon
67 J1 **Singleborough** Bucks
147 G8 **Singleton** Lancs
20 E4 **Singleton** W Susx
52 E5 **Singlewell** Kent
39 K5 **Sinkhurst Green** Kent
244 B1 **Sinnarhard** Abers
162 C5 **Sinnington** N York
81 J3 **Sinton** Worcs
81 J3 **Sinton Green** Worcs
50 D3 **Sipson** Gt Lon
61 J5 **Sirhowy** Blae G
39 K6 **Sissinghurst** Kent
45 K4 **Siston** S Glos
11 L4 **Sitcott** Devon
3 G5 **Sithney** Cnwll
3 G5 **Sithney Common** Cnwll
3 G5 **Sithney Green** Cnwll
40 B3 **Sittingbourne** Kent
97 H5 **Six Ashes** Staffs
61 K6 **Six Bells** Blae G
88 B4 **Six Mile Bottom** Cambs
9 c2 **Six Rues** Jersey
136 C2 **Sixhills** Lincs
40 F6 **Sixmile Cottages** Kent
33 G7 **Sixpenny Handley** Dorset
91 J2 **Sizewell** Suffk
275 d5 **Skaill** Ork
197 G7 **Skares** E Ayrs
245 K5 **Skateraw** Abers
213 G4 **Skateraw** E Loth
259 G7 **Skeabost** Highld
160 B2 **Skeeby** N York
101 G3 **Skeffington** Leics
145 K8 **Skeffling** E R Yk
133 K7 **Skegby** Notts
134 F5 **Skegby** Notts
137 L7 **Skegness** Lincs
264 B1 **Skelbo** Highld
264 B1 **Skelbo Street** Highld
142 D5 **Skelbrooke** Donc
119 K4 **Skeldyke** Lincs
135 J5 **Skellingthorpe** Lincs
131 H3 **Skellorm Green** Ches
142 E5 **Skellow** Donc

141 K5 **Skelmanthorpe** Kirk
138 F6 **Skelmersdale** Lancs
207 K5 **Skelmorlie** N Ayrs
278 B5 **Skelpick** Highld
185 K5 **Skelston** D & G
166 B4 **Skelton** Cumb
143 J3 **Skelton** E R Yk
159 K3 **Skelton** N York
150 E2 **Skelton** N York
170 F7 **Skelton** R & Cl
151 J4 **Skelton** York
156 E2 **Skelwith Bridge** Cumb
137 H5 **Skendleby** Lincs
245 G2 **Skene House** Abers
62 F3 **Skenfrith** Mons
153 G5 **Skerne** E R Yk
277 L4 **Skerray** Highld
276 C6 **Skerricha** Highld
147 J3 **Skerton** Lancs
99 L5 **Sketchley** Leics
57 H6 **Sketty** Swans
57 K5 **Skewen** Neath
151 K2 **Skewsby** N York
122 E6 **Skeyton** Norfk
122 E6 **Skeyton Corner** Norfk
279 H3 **Skiall** Highld
137 H1 **Skidbrooke** Lincs
137 H1 **Skidbrooke North End** Lincs
144 C1 **Skidby** E R Yk
282 h1 **Skigersta** W Isls
29 H5 **Skilgate** Somset
118 A6 **Skillington** Lincs
176 F7 **Skinburness** Cumb
210 B2 **Skinflats** Falk
258 C7 **Skinidin** Highld
48 C6 **Skinners Green** W Berk
171 G6 **Skinningrove** R & Cl
206 E7 **Skipness** Ag & B
177 L2 **Skipper's Bridge** Cumb
165 L2 **Skiprigg** Cumb
153 J5 **Skipsea** E R Yk
153 J5 **Skipsea Brough** E R Yk
149 H5 **Skipton** N York
160 E6 **Skipton-on-Swale** N York
151 L8 **Skipwith** N York
153 J7 **Skirlaugh** E R Yk
199 J5 **Skirling** Border
49 J1 **Skirmett** Bucks
152 A4 **Skirpenbeck** E R Yk
166 E4 **Skirwith** Cumb
158 C7 **Skirwith** N York
280 E3 **Skirza** Highld
178 B5 **Skitby** Cumb
67 J6 **Skittle Green** Bucks
247 L4 **Skulamus** Highld
95 G8 **Skyborry Green** Shrops
72 C3 **Skye Green** Essex
253 J6 **Skye of Curr** Highld
149 J4 **Skyreholme** N York
140 E2 **Slack** Calder
133 G7 **Slack** Derbys
157 G6 **Slack Head** Cumb
140 E6 **Slackcote** Oldham
137 K5 **Slackholme End** Lincs
256 F3 **Slacks of Cairnbanno** Abers
64 C5 **Slad** Gloucs
27 J2 **Slade** Devon
14 D1 **Slade** Devon
28 E5 **Slade** Somset
48 E1 **Slade End** Oxon
52 B4 **Slade Green** Kent
97 L2 **Slade Heath** Staffs
133 K2 **Slade Hooton** Rothm
81 J8 **Slades Green** Worcs
10 E8 **Sladesbridge** Cnwll
178 F8 **Slaggyford** Nthumb
150 D7 **Slaid Hill** Leeds
148 C5 **Slaidburn** Lancs
141 G5 **Slaithwaite** Kirk
132 E8 **Slaley** Derbys
180 A7 **Slaley** Nthumb
209 M4 **Slamannan** Falk
68 B3 **Slapton** Bucks
8 B6 **Slapton** Devon
84 C6 **Slapton** Nhants
140 D6 **Slattocks** Rochdl
37 L5 **Slaugham** W Susx
46 B4 **Slaughterford** Wilts
101 G4 **Slawston** Leics
36 B3 **Sleaford** Hants
118 E2 **Sleaford** Lincs
166 E6 **Sleagill** Cumb
113 H6 **Sleap** Shrops
113 L8 **Sleapford** Wrekin
69 G5 **Sleapshyde** Herts

272 F8 **Sleasdairidh** Highld
81 J8 **Sledge Green** Worcs
152 E3 **Sledmere** E R Yk
17 J3 **Sleight** Dorset
168 B8 **Sleightholme** Dur
162 F1 **Sleights** N York
17 H4 **Slepe** Dorset
280 C3 **Slickly** Highld
193 J4 **Sliddery** N Ayrs
247 G3 **Sligachan** Highld
207 K1 **Sligrachan** Ag & B
63 L6 **Slimbridge** Gloucs
114 C5 **Slindon** Staffs
20 F5 **Slindon** W Susx
37 H4 **Slinfold** W Susx
126 B6 **Sling** Gwynd
162 B7 **Slingsby** N York
68 D3 **Slip End** Beds
86 F7 **Slip End** Herts
101 L7 **Slipton** Nhants
115 G8 **Slitting Mill** Staffs
216 C7 **Slockavullin** Ag & B
175 G1 **Slogarie** D & G
122 F6 **Sloley** Norfk
13 H5 **Sloncombe** Devon
137 J5 **Sloothby** Lincs
50 C3 **Slough** Slough
30 C7 **Slough Green** Somset
37 L5 **Slough Green** W Susx
248 E4 **Slumbay** Highld
50 C8 **Slyfield Green** Surrey
147 J3 **Slyne** Lancs
201 K6 **Smailholm** Border
22 C5 **Small Dole** W Susx
98 E6 **Small Heath** Birm
25 G1 **Small Hythe** Kent
147 H6 **Small Wood Hey** Lancs
140 D5 **Smallbridge** Rochdl
13 K3 **Smallbrook** Devon
63 H7 **Smallbrook** Gloucs
123 G6 **Smallburgh** Norfk
132 B4 **Smalldale** Derbys
132 C3 **Smalldale** Derbys
116 C3 **Smalley** Derbys
116 C3 **Smalley Common** Derbys
116 C3 **Smalley Green** Derbys
37 M2 **Smallfield** Surrey
15 G2 **Smallridge** Devon
114 D2 **Smallthorne** C Stke
168 E8 **Smallways** N York
130 F7 **Smallwood** Ches
105 K7 **Smallworth** Norfk
34 E1 **Smannell** Hants
158 C1 **Smardale** Cumb
39 L5 **Smarden** Kent
39 L5 **Smarden Bell** Kent
38 E5 **Smart's Hill** Kent
203 H5 **Smeafield** Nthumb
237 J5 **Smearisary** Highld
30 B8 **Smeatharpe** Devon
40 E7 **Smeeth** Kent
100 E5 **Smeeton Westerby** Leics
150 B3 **Smelthouses** N York
275 G2 **Smerral** Highld
97 J5 **Smestow** Staffs
98 C6 **Smethwick** Sandw
130 F7 **Smethwick Green** Ches
116 B7 **Smisby** Derbys
81 H5 **Smith End Green** Worcs
147 J5 **Smith Green** Lancs
87 H7 **Smith's End** Herts
70 E3 **Smith's Green** Essex
88 D7 **Smith's Green** Essex
19 J5 **Smitheciose** IOW
178 B6 **Smithfield** Cumb
142 A6 **Smithies** Barns
29 J8 **Smithincott** Devon
260 C4 **Smithstown** Highld
252 D3 **Smithton** Highld
140 D5 **Smithy Bridge** Rochdl
130 E5 **Smithy Green** Ches
131 G3 **Smithy Green** Stockp
116 C2 **Smithy Houses** Derbys
99 M5 **Smockington** Leics
277 G3 **Smoo** Highld
72 D3 **Smythe's Green** Essex
185 L5 **Snade** D & G
95 J3 **Snailbeach** Shrops
88 C2 **Snailwell** Cambs
163 G6 **Snainton** N York
143 G3 **Snaith** E R Yk
132 B2 **Snake Pass Inn** Derbys
160 C6 **Snape** N York
91 J3 **Snape** Suffk
138 D5 **Snape Green** Lancs

91 J4 **Snape Street** Suffk
51 L1 **Snaresbrook** Gt Lon
99 K2 **Snarestone** Leics
135 L3 **Snarford** Lincs
25 J2 **Snargate** Kent
25 J1 **Snave** Kent
81 L4 **Sneachill** Worcs
95 H5 **Snead** Powys
106 D5 **Sneath Common** Norfk
162 F1 **Sneaton** N York
162 F2 **Sneatonthorpe** N York
135 M4 **Snelland** Lincs
130 F5 **Snelson** Ches
115 J3 **Snelston** Derbys
105 K5 **Snetterton** Norfk
120 F4 **Snettisham** Norfk
116 C8 **Snibston** Leics
64 A1 **Snig's End** Gloucs
190 E5 **Snitter** Nthumb
135 K1 **Snitterby** Lincs
82 F3 **Snitterfield** Warwks
132 E7 **Snitterton** Derbys
165 H3 **Snittlegarth** Cumb
96 D8 **Snitton** Shrops
40 B6 **Snoadhill** Kent
79 K7 **Snodhill** Herefs
52 F6 **Snodland** Kent
39 G4 **Snoll Hatch** Kent
69 L1 **Snow End** Herts
106 B7 **Snow Street** Norfk
141 L7 **Snowden Hill** Barns
82 C8 **Snowshill** Gloucs
19 L2 **Soake** Hants
43 H5 **Soar** Cardif
7 K7 **Soar** Devon
60 E1 **Soar** Powys
35 J7 **Soberton** Hants
35 J8 **Soberton Heath** Hants
166 C5 **Sockbridge** Cumb
160 E1 **Sockburn** Darltn
128 C5 **Sodom** Denbgs
112 E3 **Sodylt Bank** Shrops
104 B8 **Soham** Cambs
104 B8 **Soham Cotes** Cambs
282 C7 **Solas** W Isls
54 E4 **Solbury** Pembks
26 E8 **Soldon** Devon
11 L1 **Soldon Cross** Devon
35 K4 **Soldridge** Hants
52 E5 **Sole Street** Kent
40 E5 **Sole Street** Kent
98 F7 **Solihull** Solhll
80 A4 **Sollers Dilwyn** Herefs
80 E8 **Sollers Hope** Herefs
138 F4 **Sollom** Lancs
74 C7 **Solva** Pembks
177 J3 **Solwaybank** D & G
101 G1 **Somerby** Leics
144 D6 **Somerby** Lincs
116 C1 **Somercotes** Derbys
18 B5 **Somerford** Dorset
64 E8 **Somerford Keynes** Gloucs
20 D7 **Somerley** W Susx
107 K4 **Somerleyton** Suffk
115 J4 **Somersal Herbert** Derbys
136 F5 **Somersby** Lincs
103 G7 **Somersham** Cambs
90 C5 **Somersham** Suffk
66 D2 **Somerton** Oxon
31 H5 **Somerton** Somset
89 G4 **Somerton** Suffk
113 J8 **Somerwood** Shrops
21 K6 **Sompting** W Susx
49 J4 **Sonning** Wokham
49 H3 **Sonning Common** Oxon
49 H4 **Sonning Eye** Oxon
112 E2 **Sontley** Wrexhm
18 B4 **Sopley** Hants
46 B2 **Sopworth** Wilts
174 C5 **Sorbie** D & G
279 L4 **Sordale** Highld
225 H3 **Sorisdale** Ag & B
197 G5 **Sorn** E Ayrs
280 C4 **Sortat** Highld
164 E6 **Sosgill** Cumb
136 D4 **Sotby** Lincs
136 B6 **Sots Hole** Lincs
107 J6 **Sotterley** Suffk
128 F6 **Soughton** Flints
67 L2 **Soulbury** Bucks
166 B5 **Soulby** Cumb
167 H8 **Soulby** Cumb
66 D1 **Souldern** Oxon
85 J3 **Souldrop** Beds
267 G5 **Sound Muir** Moray

45 J4 **Soundwell** S Glos
12 D4 **Sourton** Devon
156 B6 **Soutergate** Cumb
121 H8 **South Acre** Norfk
41 H7 **South Alkham** Kent
8 B7 **South Allington** Devon
210 A1 **South Alloa** Falk
20 F3 **South Ambersham** W Susx
133 K3 **South Anston** Rothm
50 A5 **South Ascot** W & M
40 C7 **South Ashford** Kent
18 E4 **South Baddesley** Hants
170 C6 **South Bank** R & Cl
151 J5 **South Bank** York
31 K5 **South Barrow** Somset
51 H6 **South Beddington** Gt Lon
11 K4 **South Beer** Cnwll
53 G2 **South Benfleet** Essex
20 F6 **South Bersted** W Susx
18 B4 **South Bockhampton** Dorset
15 K3 **South Bowood** Dorset
143 G5 **South Bramwith** Donc
7 K3 **South Brent** Devon
32 B4 **South Brewham** Somset
191 K6 **South Broomhill** Nthumb
107 H2 **South Burlingham** Norfk
31 K5 **South Cadbury** Somset
135 J4 **South Carlton** Lincs
134 B3 **South Carlton** Notts
144 A2 **South Cave** E R Yk
64 F7 **South Cerney** Gloucs
22 F4 **South Chailey** E Susx
15 H2 **South Chard** Somset
191 H2 **South Charlton** Nthumb
32 B6 **South Cheriton** Somset
169 G5 **South Church** Dur
168 E7 **South Cleatlam** Dur
152 D8 **South Cliffe** E R Yk
135 G5 **South Clifton** Notts
137 G2 **South Cockerington** Lincs
42 B5 **South Cornelly** Brdgnd
107 K7 **South Cove** Suffk
121 J4 **South Creake** Norfk
141 H5 **South Crosland** Kirk
100 F2 **South Croxton** Leics
152 E6 **South Dalton** E R Yk
52 C5 **South Darenth** Kent
143 H1 **South Duffield** N York
136 E2 **South Elkington** Lincs
142 D5 **South Elmsall** Wakefd
145 K4 **South End** E R Yk
33 J7 **South End** Hants
81 G6 **South End** Herefs
144 E4 **South End** N Linc
105 K5 **South End** Norfk
260 B5 **South Erradale** Highld
72 B8 **South Fambridge** Essex
48 A3 **South Fawley** W Berk
144 B4 **South Ferriby** N Linc
144 C3 **South Field** E R Yk
38 A4 **South Godstone** Surrey
18 B2 **South Gorley** Hants
181 G5 **South Gosforth** N u Ty
72 F3 **South Green** Essex
71 G8 **South Green** Essex
53 J7 **South Green** Kent
105 L1 **South Green** Norfk
106 D8 **South Green** Suffk
211 G4 **South Gyle** C Edin
71 H7 **South Hanningfield** Essex
20 C3 **South Harting** W Susx
20 B6 **South Hayling** Hants
203 G6 **South Hazelrigg** Nthumb
67 M6 **South Heath** Bucks
23 G6 **South Heighton** E Susx
169 K2 **South Hetton** Dur
142 B5 **South Hiendley** Wakefd
11 L7 **South Hill** Cnwll
31 G5 **South Hill** Somset
66 D6 **South Hinksey** Oxon
26 C6 **South Hole** Devon
37 J2 **South Holmwood** Surrey
52 B2 **South Hornchurch** Gt Lon
31 J2 **South Horrington** Somset
7 K6 **South Huish** Devon
135 J6 **South Hykeham** Lincs
181 J7 **South Hylton** Sundld
144 D8 **South Kelsey** Lincs
251 H2 **South Kessock** Highld
144 F4 **South Killingholme** N Linc
160 F6 **South Kilvington** N York
100 D7 **South Kilworth** Nhants
142 C5 **South Kirkby** Wakefd
13 J8 **South Knighton** Devon
119 G2 **South Kyme** Lincs

65 L4 **South Lawn** Oxon
66 B5 **South Leigh** Oxon
134 F3 **South Leverton** Notts
82 C6 **South Littleton** Worcs
105 L7 **South Lopham** Norfk
101 K3 **South Luffenham** Rutlnd
23 G5 **South Malling** E Susx
47 J2 **South Marston** Swindn
51 H8 **South Merstham** Surrey
190 E2 **South Middleton** Nthumb
142 D2 **South Milford** N York
7 K6 **South Milton** Devon
69 G6 **South Mimms** Herts
28 C5 **South Molton** Devon
180 F8 **South Moor** Dur
48 E1 **South Moreton** Oxon
20 E6 **South Mundham** W Susx
134 F8 **South Muskham** Notts
152 D8 **South Newbald** E R Yk
83 J8 **South Newington** Oxon
33 J4 **South Newton** Wilts
133 J8 **South Normanton** Derbys
51 J5 **South Norwood** Gt Lon
37 M1 **South Nutfield** Surrey
52 D2 **South Ockendon** Thurr
137 G4 **South Ormsby** Lincs
141 L4 **South Ossett** Wakefd
160 E5 **South Otterington** N York
135 L1 **South Owersby** Lincs
37 K1 **South Park** Surrey
15 L1 **South Perrott** Dorset
31 G7 **South Petherton** Somset
11 K6 **South Petherwin** Cnwll
105 G3 **South Pickenham** Norfk
6 E3 **South Pill** Cnwll
7 M6 **South Pool** Devon
15 M3 **South Poorton** Dorset
210 F3 **South Queensferry** C Edin
28 C4 **South Radworthy** Devon
118 D2 **South Rauceby** Lincs
121 J6 **South Raynham** Norfk
131 H1 **South Reddish** Stockp
137 G3 **South Reston** Lincs
104 C2 **South Runcton** Norfk
135 G7 **South Scarle** Notts
228 E7 **South Shian** Ag & B
181 J5 **South Shields** S Tyne
138 C1 **South Shore** Bpool
137 H1 **South Somercotes** Lincs
150 D3 **South Stainley** N York
52 D3 **South Stifford** Thurr
45 L6 **South Stoke** BaNES
48 F2 **South Stoke** Oxon
21 H5 **South Stoke** W Susx
40 D7 **South Stour** Kent
52 D6 **South Street** Kent
40 D4 **South Street** Kent
40 F2 **South Street** Kent
199 H3 **South Tarbrax** S Lans
12 F4 **South Tawton** Devon
137 G4 **South Thoresby** Lincs
168 E7 **South Thorpe** Dur
35 K4 **South Town** Hants
107 H1 **South Walsham** Norfk
35 L2 **South Warnborough** Hants
70 E8 **South Weald** Essex
67 H7 **South Weston** Oxon
11 J4 **South Wheatley** Cnwll
45 H7 **South Widcombe** BaNES
100 D4 **South Wigston** Leics
40 D7 **South Willesborough** Kent
136 C3 **South Willingham** Lincs
169 L4 **South Wingate** Dur
133 G8 **South Wingfield** Derbys
118 B7 **South Witham** Lincs
34 F4 **South Wonston** Hants
71 K7 **South Woodham Ferrers** Essex
120 E7 **South Wootton** Norfk
46 B6 **South Wraxall** Wilts
12 F4 **South Zeal** Devon
50 E3 **Southall** Gt Lon
64 E2 **Southam** Gloucs
83 K3 **Southam** Warwks
19 G1 **Southampton** C Sotn
51 L5 **Southborough** Gt Lon
38 F5 **Southborough** Kent
18 A5 **Southbourne** Bmouth
20 C5 **Southbourne** W Susx
17 G4 **Southbrook** Dorset
105 K2 **Southburgh** Norfk
152 F5 **Southburn** E R Yk
53 J2 **Southchurch** Sthend
11 H3 **Southcott** Cnwll
27 H7 **Southcott** Devon

12 D3 **Southcott** Devon
13 H6 **Southcott** Devon
47 H7 **Southcott** Wilts
67 K5 **Southcourt** Bucks
23 G6 **Southease** E Susx
192 E6 **Southend** Ag & B
47 J4 **Southend** Wilts
53 J2 **Southend-on-Sea** Sthend
165 L3 **Southernby** Cumb
39 L4 **Southernden** Kent
42 D7 **Southerndown** V Glam
176 C7 **Southerness** D & G
14 C4 **Southerton** Devon
104 C4 **Southery** Norfk
209 M4 **Southfield** Falk
52 D5 **Southfleet** Kent
19 J7 **Southford** IOW
69 J8 **Southgate** Gt Lon
120 E5 **Southgate** Norfk
121 J4 **Southgate** Norfk
122 C6 **Southgate** Norfk
57 G7 **Southgate** Swans
86 C6 **Southill** Beds
35 G1 **Southington** Hants
14 E4 **Southleigh** Devon
72 D7 **Southminster** Essex
66 B7 **Southmoor** Oxon
234 B5 **Southmuir** Angus
86 D2 **Southoe** Cambs
90 E2 **Southolt** Suffk
102 B3 **Southorpe** C Pete
16 B4 **Southover** Dorset
24 B2 **Southover** E Susx
141 H3 **Southowram** Calder
138 D4 **Southport** Sefton
122 E4 **Southrepps** Norfk
136 B6 **Southrey** Lincs
65 J6 **Southrop** Gloucs
35 K2 **Southrope** Hants
19 L4 **Southsea** C Port
112 D1 **Southsea** Wrexhm
168 E5 **Southside** Dur
107 L2 **Southtown** Norfk
30 D7 **Southtown** Somset
166 B2 **Southwaite** Cumb
51 J3 **Southwark** Gt Lon
37 J5 **Southwater** W Susx
37 H5 **Southwater Street** W Susx
31 H2 **Southway** Somset
16 D8 **Southwell** Dorset
117 J1 **Southwell** Notts
19 L2 **Southwick** Hants
101 M5 **Southwick** Nhants
30 E2 **Southwick** Somset
181 J7 **Southwick** Sundld
22 C6 **Southwick** W Susx
46 B7 **Southwick** Wilts
107 K8 **Southwold** Suffk
107 H2 **Southwood** Norfk
31 J4 **Southwood** Somset
99 K6 **Sowe Common** Covtry
147 G7 **Sower Carr** Lancs
141 G3 **Sowerby** Kirk
160 F6 **Sowerby** N York
141 G3 **Sowerby Bridge** Calder
165 L3 **Sowerby Row** Cumb
28 F6 **Sowerhill** Somset
62 B7 **Sowhill** Torfn
88 D5 **Sowley Green** Suffk
141 G4 **Sowood** Calder
6 F2 **Sowton** Devon
14 A4 **Sowton** Devon
140 F4 **Soyland Town** Calder
122 F5 **Spa Common** Norfk
88 D7 **Spain's End** Essex
119 H7 **Spalding** Lincs
143 J1 **Spaldington** E R Yk
86 C1 **Spaldwick** Cambs
135 G6 **Spalford** Notts
118 E4 **Spanby** Lincs
49 G7 **Spanish Green** Hants
122 B7 **Sparham** Norfk
122 B7 **Sparhamill** Norfk
156 D5 **Spark Bridge** Cumb
166 B5 **Sparket** Cumb
31 K5 **Sparkford** Somset
98 E6 **Sparkhill** Birm
7 H3 **Sparkwell** Devon
121 L8 **Sparrow Green** Norfk
132 B4 **Sparrowpit** Derbys
39 G6 **Sparrows Green** E Susx
34 F4 **Sparsholt** Hants
47 M2 **Sparsholt** Oxon
167 K1 **Spartylea** Cumb
115 H4 **Spath** Staffs

162 C5 **Spaunton** N York
30 C3 **Spaxton** Somset
239 L7 **Spean Bridge** Highld
21 K3 **Spear Hill** W Susx
34 D5 **Spearywell** Hants
67 K7 **Speen** Bucks
48 C5 **Speen** W Berk
163 L7 **Speeton** N York
129 K3 **Speke** Lpool
38 E5 **Speldhurst** Kent
70 C4 **Spellbrook** Herts
39 H6 **Spelmonden** Kent
65 M3 **Spelsbury** Oxon
141 K3 **Spen** Kirk
130 F7 **Spen Green** Ches
49 H5 **Spencers Wood** Wokham
159 L5 **Spennithorne** N York
169 H4 **Spennymoor** Dur
82 C3 **Spernall** Warwks
13 G3 **Spestos** Devon
81 K4 **Spetchley** Worcs
17 H2 **Spetisbury** Dorset
107 H7 **Spexhall** Suffk
267 G3 **Spey Bay** Moray
253 K6 **Speybridge** Highld
254 E3 **Speyview** Moray
137 G6 **Spilsby** Lincs
203 J6 **Spindlestone** Nthumb
133 J4 **Spinkhill** Derbys
263 J2 **Spinningdale** Highld
133 L6 **Spion Kop** Notts
46 E4 **Spirthill** Wilts
129 H3 **Spital** Wirral
134 C1 **Spital Hill** Donc
135 K2 **Spital in the Street** Lincs
23 G4 **Spithurst** E Susx
212 A4 **Spittal** E Loth
152 B5 **Spittal** E R Yk
279 L5 **Spittal** Highld
202 F3 **Spittal** Nthumb
55 G2 **Spittal** Pembks
243 K6 **Spittal of Glenmuick** Abers
233 H2 **Spittal of Glenshee** P & K
189 G2 **Spittal-on-Rule** Border
233 H7 **Spittalfield** P & K
122 E8 **Spixworth** Norfk
10 C7 **Splatt** Cnwll
11 J5 **Splatt** Cnwll
12 E2 **Splatt** Devon
23 G2 **Splayne's Green** E Susx
43 K6 **Splottlands** Cardif
130 E5 **Spodegreen** Ches
150 E5 **Spofforth** N York
129 G7 **Spon Green** Flints
116 C4 **Spondon** C Derb
106 B4 **Spooner Row** Norfk
105 G1 **Sporle** Norfk
212 E4 **Spott** E Loth
201 J3 **Spottiswoode** Border
84 D1 **Spratton** Nhants
36 B3 **Spreakley** Surrey
13 G3 **Spreyton** Devon
7 G4 **Spriddlestone** Devon
135 K3 **Spridlington** Lincs
168 F5 **Spring Gardens** Dur
141 L7 **Spring Vale** Barns
209 G5 **Springburn** C Glas
177 K5 **Springfield** D & G
71 H5 **Springfield** Essex
222 F5 **Springfield** Fife
98 D2 **Springhill** Staffs
98 B3 **Springhill** Staffs
175 K1 **Springholm** D & G
196 D3 **Springside** N Ayrs
135 H2 **Springthorpe** Lincs
181 G7 **Springwell** Sundld
145 L7 **Sproatley** E R Yk
130 E6 **Sproston Green** Ches
142 E7 **Sprotbrough** Donc
90 D6 **Sproughton** Suffk
202 B6 **Sprouston** Border
106 E1 **Sprowston** Norfk
117 M6 **Sproxton** Leics
161 K6 **Sproxton** N York
12 A5 **Sprytown** Devon
112 F5 **Spunhill** Shrops
130 A8 **Spurstow** Ches
15 M4 **Spyway** Dorset
74 D6 **Square & Compass** Pembks
97 G4 **Stableford** Shrops
114 C4 **Stableford** Staffs
132 F2 **Stacey Bank** Sheff
148 E3 **Stackhouse** N York
55 G7 **Stackpole** Pembks
105 L5 **Stacksford** Norfk

140 C3 **Stacksteads** Lancs
7 G4 **Staddiscombe** C Plym
143 L2 **Staddlethorpe** E R Yk
131 L5 **Staden** Derbys
66 F7 **Stadhampton** Oxon
283 b10 **Stadhlaigearraidh** W Isls
166 D2 **Staffield** Cumb
259 H3 **Staffin** Highld
114 E7 **Stafford** Staffs
85 J5 **Stagsden** Beds
141 M7 **Stainborough** Barns
164 D5 **Stainburn** Cumb
150 C6 **Stainburn** N York
118 B7 **Stainby** Lincs
141 M5 **Staincross** Barns
168 E6 **Staindrop** Dur
50 D5 **Staines** Surrey
118 E6 **Stainfield** Lincs
136 B5 **Stainfield** Lincs
143 G5 **Stainforth** Donc
148 E2 **Stainforth** N York
147 G8 **Staining** Lancs
141 G4 **Stainland** Calder
163 G1 **Stainsacre** N York
133 J6 **Stainsby** Derbys
177 L7 **Stainton** Cumb
166 C5 **Stainton** Cumb
157 H5 **Stainton** Cumb
133 L1 **Stainton** Donc
168 D7 **Stainton** Dur
170 B7 **Stainton** Middsb
159 K3 **Stainton** N York
135 L4 **Stainton by Langworth** Lincs
136 C1 **Stainton le Vale** Lincs
146 E1 **Stainton with Adgarley** Cumb
163 H3 **Staintondale** N York
165 H6 **Stair** Cumb
196 E6 **Stair** E Ayrs
142 B6 **Stairfoot** Barns
172 F4 **Stairhaven** D & G
171 H7 **Staithes** N York
147 H6 **Stake Pool** Lancs
181 G2 **Stakeford** Nthumb
19 M2 **Stakes** Hants
32 B7 **Stalbridge** Dorset
32 B7 **Stalbridge Weston** Dorset
123 H6 **Stalham** Norfk
123 H6 **Stalham Green** Norfk
40 B5 **Stalisfield Green** Kent
31 K7 **Stallen** Dorset
159 G5 **Stalling Busk** N York
145 J2 **Stallingborough** NE Lin
114 E4 **Stallington** Staffs
147 G6 **Stalmine** Lancs
147 G6 **Stalmine Moss Side** Lancs
140 E8 **Stalybridge** Tamesd
88 E7 **Stambourne** Essex
88 D7 **Stambourne Green** Essex
102 A2 **Stamford** Lincs
191 J2 **Stamford** Nthumb
129 L6 **Stamford Bridge** Ches
151 M5 **Stamford Bridge** E R Yk
51 J2 **Stamford Hill** Gt Lon
180 C4 **Stamfordham** Nthumb
147 G7 **Stanah** Lancs
69 G5 **Stanborough** Herts
68 B2 **Stanbridge** Beds
17 K2 **Stanbridge** Dorset
149 H8 **Stanbury** Brad
140 B6 **Stand** Bury
209 K5 **Stand** N Lans
210 B4 **Standburn** Falk
97 K2 **Standeford** Staffs
39 L5 **Standen** Kent
39 K7 **Standen Street** Kent
32 D1 **Standerwick** Somset
36 B4 **Standford** Hants
164 D4 **Standingstone** Cumb
64 A5 **Standish** Gloucs
139 H5 **Standish** Wigan
139 H6 **Standish Lower Ground** Wigan
66 B6 **Standlake** Oxon
34 F5 **Standon** Hants
69 K3 **Standon** Herts
114 C4 **Standon** Staffs
69 K3 **Standon Green End** Herts
90 D1 **Standwell Green** Suffk
210 A7 **Stane** N Lans
121 K7 **Stanfield** Norfk
86 D7 **Stanford** Beds
40 F7 **Stanford** Kent
95 H1 **Stanford** Shrops
80 F5 **Stanford Bishop** Herefs

81 G2 **Stanford Bridge** Worcs
113 M6 **Stanford Bridge** Wrekin
48 E4 **Stanford Dingley** W Berk
65 M8 **Stanford in the Vale** Oxon
52 E3 **Stanford le Hope** Thurr
100 D7 **Stanford on Avon** Nhants
116 F7 **Stanford on Soar** Notts
81 G2 **Stanford on Teme** Worcs
70 D7 **Stanford Rivers** Essex
133 J5 **Stanfree** Derbys
170 F7 **Stanghow** R & Cl
102 D4 **Stanground** C Pete
139 L2 **Stanhill** Lancs
121 H4 **Stanhoe** Norfk
199 K7 **Stanhope** Border
168 C3 **Stanhope** Dur
115 M7 **Stanhope Bretby** Derbys
101 K6 **Stanion** Nhants
97 J8 **Stanklin** Worcs
116 C3 **Stanley** Derbys
180 F8 **Stanley** Dur
133 J7 **Stanley** Notts
221 K1 **Stanley** P & K
97 G6 **Stanley** Shrops
114 E1 **Stanley** Staffs
142 A3 **Stanley** Wakefd
116 C3 **Stanley Common** Derbys
168 F3 **Stanley Crook** Dur
142 A3 **Stanley Ferry** Wakefd
138 F6 **Stanley Gate** Lancs
114 E1 **Stanley Moor** Staffs
64 E1 **Stanley Pontlarge** Gloucs
22 E5 **Stanmer** Br & H
68 F8 **Stanmore** Gt Lon
34 F5 **Stanmore** Hants
48 C3 **Stanmore** W Berk
179 G2 **Stannersburn** Nthumb
89 H4 **Stanningfield** Suffk
141 K1 **Stanningley** Leeds
180 F3 **Stannington** Nthumb
132 F2 **Stannington** Sheff
180 F3 **Stannington Station** Nthumb
79 L3 **Stansbatch** Herefs
88 F5 **Stansfield** Suffk
115 J1 **Stanshope** Staffs
89 G5 **Stanstead** Suffk
69 K5 **Stanstead Abbotts** Herts
89 G5 **Stanstead Street** Suffk
52 D6 **Stansted** Kent
70 D2 **Stansted Mountfitchet** Essex
115 M7 **Stanton** Derbys
7 K5 **Stanton** Devon
82 C8 **Stanton** Gloucs
62 C3 **Stanton** Mons
191 G8 **Stanton** Nthumb
115 J2 **Stanton** Staffs
105 K8 **Stanton** Suffk
116 B6 **Stanton by Bridge** Derbys
116 D4 **Stanton by Dale** Derbys
45 H6 **Stanton Drew** BaNES
47 J1 **Stanton Fitzwarren** Swindn
66 B6 **Stanton Harcourt** Oxon
133 J7 **Stanton Hill** Notts
132 E6 **Stanton in Peak** Derbys
96 B7 **Stanton Lacy** Shrops
132 E7 **Stanton Lees** Derbys
96 D5 **Stanton Long** Shrops
117 G5 **Stanton on the Wolds** Notts
45 K6 **Stanton Prior** BaNES
47 G6 **Stanton St Bernard** Wilts
66 E5 **Stanton St John** Oxon
46 C3 **Stanton St Quintin** Wilts
89 J2 **Stanton Street** Suffk
100 A1 **Stanton under Bardon** Leics
113 J6 **Stanton upon Hine Heath** Shrops
45 J6 **Stanton Wick** BaNES
63 L4 **Stantway** Gloucs
112 F6 **Stanwardine in the Field** Shrops
113 G6 **Stanwardine in the Wood** Shrops
72 D2 **Stanway** Essex
64 F1 **Stanway** Gloucs
72 D2 **Stanway Green** Essex
90 F1 **Stanway Green** Suffk
50 D4 **Stanwell** Surrey
50 D4 **Stanwell Moor** Surrey
85 J1 **Stanwick** Nhants
177 L7 **Stanwix** Cumb
283 b10 **Staoinebrig** W Isls
162 D4 **Stape** N York
17 L2 **Stapehill** Dorset
113 L2 **Stapeley** Ches
115 L7 **Stapenhill** Staffs

Staple - Stoneywood 355

41 J4 Staple Kent
29 K3 Staple Somset
29 J6 Staple Cross Devon
24 E3 Staple Cross E Susx
30 C7 Staple Fitzpaine Somset
98 B8 Staple Hill Worcs
37 L5 Staplefield W Susx
87 K5 Stapleford Cambs
69 J4 Stapleford Herts
117 L7 Stapleford Leics
135 H8 Stapleford Lincs
116 E4 Stapleford Notts
33 J3 Stapleford Wilts
70 D8 Stapleford Abbotts Essex
70 D7 Stapleford Tawney Essex
30 B5 Staplegrove Somset
30 B6 Staplehay Somset
39 K5 Staplehurst Kent
19 H6 Staplers IOW
40 D3 Staplestreet Kent
178 C4 Staplet Cumb
79 L2 Stapleton Herefs
99 L4 Stapleton Leics
169 H8 Stapleton N York
95 L3 Stapleton Shrops
31 G6 Stapleton Somset
30 B8 Stapley Somset
86 C3 Staploe Beds
80 F7 Staplow Herefs
222 E6 Star Fife
75 M5 Star Pembks
44 E7 Star Somset
150 D4 Starbeck N York
159 G7 Starbotton N York
14 A6 Starcross Devon
83 H1 Stareton Warwks
132 F7 Starkholmes Derbys
140 A5 Starling Bury
70 C1 Starlings Green Essex
24 D4 Starr's Green E Susx
106 E6 Starston Norfk
8 B6 Start Devon
168 D7 Startforth Dur
46 D3 Startley Wilts
41 J4 Statenborough Kent
130 D2 Statham Warrtn
30 E5 Stathe Somset
117 K5 Stathern Leics
169 L3 Station Town Dur
86 C2 Staughton Green Cambs
86 C2 Staughton Highway Cambs
63 H4 Staunton Gloucs
64 A1 Staunton Gloucs
79 L3 Staunton Green Herefs
117 L3 Staunton in the Vale Notts
79 L3 Staunton on Arrow Herefs
79 L6 Staunton on Wye Herefs
156 E5 Staveley Cumb
157 G3 Staveley Cumb
133 H5 Staveley Derbys
150 E3 Staveley N York
8 B2 Staverton Devon
64 C2 Staverton Gloucs
83 M3 Staverton Nhants
46 B6 Staverton Wilts
64 C3 Staverton Bridge Gloucs
30 E3 Stawell Somset
29 J6 Stawley Somset
280 E5 Staxigoe Highld
163 J6 Staxton N York
92 E5 Staylittle Cerdgn
93 J5 Staylittle Powys
147 G7 Staynall Lancs
117 K1 Staythorpe Notts
149 L6 Stead Brad
159 K8 Stean N York
84 A7 Steane Nhants
151 K2 Stearsby N York
30 C2 Steart Somset
71 G2 Stebbing Essex
71 G2 Stebbing Green Essex
71 G2 Stebbing Park Essex
98 E6 Stechford Birm
39 L5 Stede Quarter Kent
36 C6 Stedham W Susx
179 L7 Steel Nthumb
38 E7 Steel Cross E Susx
155 L6 Steel Green Cumb
113 J4 Steel Heath Shrops
188 F7 Steele Road Border
210 D1 Steelend Fife
80 C4 Steen's Bridge Herefs
35 M6 Steep Hants
140 F3 Steep Lane Calder
19 J8 Steephill IOW
17 H6 Steeple Dorset
72 D6 Steeple Essex
46 C7 Steeple Ashton Wilts
66 C2 Steeple Aston Oxon
66 C2 Steeple Barton Oxon
88 D7 Steeple Bumpstead Essex
67 H2 Steeple Claydon Bucks
102 C7 Steeple Gidding Cambs
33 H3 Steeple Langford Wilts
86 F6 Steeple Morden Cambs
149 J7 Steeton Brad
258 D5 Stein Highld
180 E6 Stella Gatesd
40 F6 Stelling Minnis Kent
30 F6 Stembridge Somset
5 G3 Stenalees Cnwll
185 K4 Stenhouse D & G
210 A2 Stenhousemuir Falk
136 D3 Stenigot Lincs
259 H3 Stenscholl Highld
212 D4 Stenton E Loth
282 g3 Steornabhagh W Isls
55 K5 Stepaside Pembks
51 K3 Stepney Gt Lon
131 H2 Stepping Hill Stockp
85 K8 Steppingley Beds
209 H5 Stepps N Lans
91 J3 Sternfield Suffk
27 K2 Sterridge Devon
46 F7 Stert Wilts
88 C3 Stetchworth Cambs
24 C4 Steven's Crouch E Susx
69 G2 Stevenage Herts
196 B3 Stevenston N Ayrs
35 H1 Steventon Hants
48 C1 Steventon Oxon
88 B6 Steventon End Essex
85 K4 Stevington Beds
85 K6 Stewartby Beds
209 G7 Stewartfield S Lans
196 E2 Stewarton E Ayrs
67 K2 Stewkley Bucks
30 D7 Stewley Somset
137 G2 Stewton Lincs
19 L6 Steyne Cross IOW
21 L4 Steyning W Susx
54 E5 Steynton Pembks
26 C8 Stibb Cnwll
27 G7 Stibb Cross Devon
47 J6 Stibb Green Wilts
121 L6 Stibbard Norfk
102 B4 Stibbington Cambs
201 L5 Stichill Border
5 G5 Sticker Cnwll
136 F7 Stickford Lincs
12 F4 Sticklepath Devon
29 J4 Sticklepath Somset
87 K8 Stickling Green Essex
136 F8 Stickney Lincs
53 J6 Stiff Street Kent
121 L3 Stiffkey Norfk
81 G5 Stifford's Bridge Herefs
39 J4 Stile Bridge Kent
31 G3 Stileway Somset
283 b10 Stilligarry W Isls
151 J7 Stillingfleet N York
151 J2 Stillington N York
169 K6 Stillington S on T
102 D5 Stilton Cambs
63 L7 Stinchcombe Gloucs
16 D4 Stinsford Dorset
95 J3 Stiperstones Shrops
98 D7 Stirchley Birm
96 F2 Stirchley Wrekin
257 L3 Stirling Abers
220 D8 Stirling Stirlg
86 D2 Stirtloe Cambs
149 H5 Stirton N York
71 J2 Stisted Essex
47 K5 Stitchcombe Wilts
3 J4 Stithians Cnwll
99 J8 Stivichall Covtry
136 C6 Stixwould Lincs
129 K5 Stoak Ches
199 L5 Stobo Border
17 H5 Stoborough Dorset
17 H5 Stoborough Green Dorset
188 E4 Stobs Castle Border
191 J7 Stobswood Nthumb
71 G7 Stock Essex
44 F6 Stock N Som
82 A3 Stock Green Worcs
82 B3 Stock Wood Worcs
34 D4 Stockbridge Hants
198 C6 Stockbriggs S Lans
53 H6 Stockbury Kent
48 B5 Stockcross W Berk
3 K4 Stockdale Cnwll
165 L2 Stockdalewath Cumb
40 C5 Stocker's Hill Kent
101 H4 Stockerston Leics
63 J1 Stocking Herefs
84 F5 Stocking Green M Keyn
70 C1 Stocking Pelham Herts
99 J5 Stockingford Warwks
14 F2 Stockland Devon
30 C2 Stockland Bristol Somset
38 E5 Stockland Green Kent
13 K1 Stockleigh English Devon
13 K2 Stockleigh Pomeroy Devon
46 E5 Stockley Wilts
79 L7 Stockley Hill Herefs
30 F7 Stocklinch Somset
79 M4 Stockmoor Herefs
131 H2 Stockport Stockp
141 L8 Stocksbridge Sheff
180 C6 Stocksfield Nthumb
71 K3 Stockstreet Essex
80 C3 Stockton Herefs
107 H4 Stockton Norfk
95 G3 Stockton Shrops
97 G3 Stockton Shrops
83 K3 Stockton Warwks
33 G3 Stockton Wilts
114 B8 Stockton Wrekin
114 E1 Stockton Brook Staffs
130 B3 Stockton Heath Warrtn
81 G2 Stockton on Teme Worcs
151 L4 Stockton on the Forest York
170 B6 Stockton-on-Tees S on T
64 D4 Stockwell Gloucs
97 K3 Stockwell End Wolves
115 G7 Stockwell Heath Staffs
45 J5 Stockwood Bristl
16 B1 Stockwood Dorset
147 J4 Stodday Lancs
41 H3 Stodmarsh Kent
122 B4 Stody Norfk
270 D2 Stoer Highld
31 J8 Stoford Somset
33 J4 Stoford Wilts
29 K3 Stogumber Somset
30 B2 Stogursey Somset
99 K7 Stoke Covtry
26 D6 Stoke Devon
48 B8 Stoke Hants
20 B6 Stoke Hants
53 H4 Stoke Medway
15 K2 Stoke Abbott Dorset
101 H5 Stoke Albany Nhants
90 D1 Stoke Ash Suffk
117 H3 Stoke Bardolph Notts
80 F3 Stoke Bliss Worcs
84 E5 Stoke Bruerne Nhants
88 E6 Stoke by Clare Suffk
13 L3 Stoke Canon Devon
35 G3 Stoke Charity Hants
11 L7 Stoke Climsland Cnwll
80 E5 Stoke Cross Herefs
50 E7 Stoke D'Abernon Surrey
102 A6 Stoke Doyle Nhants
101 J4 Stoke Dry Rutlnd
80 E7 Stoke Edith Herefs
98 F4 Stoke End Warwks
33 H5 Stoke Farthing Wilts
104 D3 Stoke Ferry Norfk
8 C5 Stoke Fleming Devon
8 C3 Stoke Gabriel Devon
45 J3 Stoke Gifford S Glos
99 L4 Stoke Golding Leics
85 G5 Stoke Goldington M Keyn
50 B3 Stoke Green Bucks
67 L1 Stoke Hammond Bucks
99 K7 Stoke Heath Covtry
113 L5 Stoke Heath Shrops
81 L2 Stoke Heath Worcs
106 E3 Stoke Holy Cross Norfk
80 E5 Stoke Lacy Herefs
66 E2 Stoke Lyne Oxon
67 K5 Stoke Mandeville Bucks
51 J2 Stoke Newington Gt Lon
64 D2 Stoke Orchard Gloucs
50 B2 Stoke Poges Bucks
81 M2 Stoke Pound Worcs
80 C4 Stoke Prior Herefs
81 L2 Stoke Prior Worcs
27 L4 Stoke Rivers Devon
118 B6 Stoke Rochford Lincs
49 G2 Stoke Row Oxon
30 E5 Stoke St Gregory Somset
30 C6 Stoke St Mary Somset
31 L2 Stoke St Michael Somset
96 D7 Stoke St Milborough Shrops
31 G7 Stoke sub Hamdon Somset
67 G7 Stoke Talmage Oxon
32 B5 Stoke Trister Somset
113 L6 Stoke upon Tern Shrops
16 E1 Stoke Wake Dorset
81 L2 Stoke Wharf Worcs
89 K7 Stoke-by-Nayland Suffk
114 D2 Stoke-on-Trent C Stke
114 D3 Stoke-upon-Trent C Stke
17 G5 Stokeford Dorset
134 F4 Stokeham Notts
13 L8 Stokeinteignhead Devon
67 J7 Stokenchurch Bucks
8 B6 Stokenham Devon
95 K7 Stokesay Shrops
107 J1 Stokesby Norfk
161 H1 Stokesley N York
30 C2 Stolford Somset
45 J8 Ston Easton Somset
70 E7 Stondon Massey Essex
67 J4 Stone Bucks
63 K8 Stone Gloucs
52 C4 Stone Kent
25 H2 Stone Kent
133 L2 Stone Rothm
31 J4 Stone Somset
114 E5 Stone Staffs
97 J8 Stone Worcs
30 F1 Stone Allerton Somset
102 F3 Stone Bridge Corner C Pete
141 H2 Stone Chair Calder
38 D7 Stone Cross E Susx
23 K6 Stone Cross E Susx
39 G7 Stone Cross E Susx
38 E5 Stone Cross Kent
40 D7 Stone Cross Kent
41 K4 Stone Cross Kent
143 H6 Stone Hill Donc
158 D5 Stone House Cumb
38 F2 Stone Street Kent
89 K7 Stone Street Suffk
89 K6 Stone Street Suffk
107 H6 Stone Street Suffk
44 F4 Stone-edge-Batch N Som
103 J5 Stonea Cambs
44 D7 Stonebridge N Som
105 J5 Stonebridge Norfk
99 G6 Stonebridge Solhll
133 H7 Stonebroom Derbys
89 G4 Stonecross Green Suffk
39 H6 Stonecrouch Kent
144 E2 Stoneferry C KuH
206 D5 Stonefield Castle Hotel Ag & B
39 G7 Stonegate E Susx
162 D1 Stonegate N York
161 L7 Stonegrave N York
81 K5 Stonehall Worcs
179 J4 Stonehaugh Nthumb
245 J6 Stonehaven Abers
52 B5 Stonehill Green Gt Lon
6 F4 Stonehouse C Plym
129 L5 Stonehouse Ches
175 K1 Stonehouse D & G
64 A6 Stonehouse Gloucs
179 G7 Stonehouse Nthumb
198 C4 Stonehouse S Lans
83 H1 Stoneleigh Warwks
113 K1 Stoneley Green Ches
86 C2 Stonely Cambs
35 M5 Stoner Hill Hants
73 H2 Stones Green Essex
117 L6 Stonesby Leics
66 B4 Stonesfield Oxon
40 E7 Stonestreet Green Kent
165 J7 Stonethwaite Cumb
266 F3 Stonewells Moray
52 D4 Stonewood Kent
18 D1 Stoney Cross Hants
132 E4 Stoney Middleton Derbys
100 B4 Stoney Stanton Leics
32 B4 Stoney Stoke Somset
31 L3 Stoney Stratton Somset
95 J2 Stoney Stretton Shrops
283 b10 Stoneybridge W Isls
97 L8 Stoneybridge Worcs
210 C6 Stoneyburn W Loth
100 D3 Stoneygate C Leic
72 D7 Stoneyhills Essex
172 D4 Stoneykirk D & G
245 K1 Stoneywood C Aber
209 L2 Stoneywood Falk

90 D3 **Stonham Aspal** Suffk
98 D3 **Stonnall** Staffs
49 H1 **Stonor** Oxon
101 G4 **Stonton Wyville** Leics
80 D2 **Stony Cross** Herefs
81 G5 **Stony Cross** Herefs
133 K6 **Stony Houghton** Derbys
84 F7 **Stony Stratford** M Keyn
34 D7 **Stonyford** Hants
98 D1 **Stonywell** Staffs
28 B4 **Stoodleigh** Devon
29 G7 **Stoodleigh** Devon
21 H3 **Stopham** W Susx
68 E2 **Stopsley** Luton
10 C7 **Stoptide** Cnwll
129 G3 **Storeton** Wirral
81 G6 **Storeyard Green** Herefs
138 F6 **Stormy Corner** Lancs
282 g3 **Stornoway** W Isls
81 H5 **Storridge** Herefs
21 J4 **Storrington** W Susx
157 G6 **Storth** Cumb
151 M7 **Storwood** E R Yk
266 E2 **Stotfield** Moray
86 E7 **Stotfold** Beds
96 F6 **Stottesdon** Shrops
100 E3 **Stoughton** Leics
50 C8 **Stoughton** Surrey
20 C4 **Stoughton** W Susx
238 B5 **Stoul** Highld
81 L5 **Stoulton** Worcs
32 C6 **Stour Provost** Dorset
32 D6 **Stour Row** Dorset
97 K6 **Stourbridge** Dudley
17 G1 **Stourpaine** Dorset
81 J1 **Stourport-on-Severn** Worcs
141 M2 **Stourton** Leeds
97 K6 **Stourton** Staffs
83 G7 **Stourton** Warwks
32 C4 **Stourton** Wilts
32 B7 **Stourton Caundle** Dorset
31 G4 **Stout** Somset
281 e8 **Stove** Shet
107 J7 **Stoven** Suffk
200 F4 **Stow** Border
135 H3 **Stow** Lincs
104 C2 **Stow Bardolph** Norfk
105 J4 **Stow Bedon** Norfk
86 C1 **Stow Longa** Cambs
71 K7 **Stow Maries** Essex
87 L3 **Stow-cum-Quy** Cambs
65 J2 **Stow-on-the-Wold** Gloucs
104 B2 **Stowbridge** Norfk
63 H5 **Stowe** Gloucs
95 H8 **Stowe** Shrops
114 F6 **Stowe by Chartley** Staffs
84 C3 **Stowehill** Nhants
31 L6 **Stowell** Somset
45 H7 **Stowey** BaNES
12 B3 **Stowford** Devon
28 B3 **Stowford** Devon
12 B5 **Stowford** Devon
14 D4 **Stowford** Devon
89 J2 **Stowlangtoft** Suffk
90 B3 **Stowmarket** Suffk
40 F7 **Stowting** Kent
40 F6 **Stowting Common** Kent
90 C3 **Stowupland** Suffk
253 J8 **Straanruie** Moray
244 F5 **Strachan** Abers
217 H6 **Strachur** Ag & B
234 F2 **Stracthro Hospital** Angus
106 E8 **Stradbroke** Suffk
46 D8 **Stradbrook** Wilts
88 E5 **Stradishall** Suffk
104 D2 **Stradsett** Norfk
118 B1 **Stragglethorpe** Lincs
117 H4 **Stragglethorpe** Notts
47 L4 **Straight Soley** Wilts
211 J5 **Straiton** Mdloth
183 K2 **Straiton** S Ayrs
256 F7 **Straloch** Abers
232 F3 **Straloch** P & K
115 H4 **Stramshall** Staffs
154 e6 **Strang** IOM
140 B7 **Strangeways** Salfd
63 H2 **Strangford** Herefs
172 C3 **Stranraer** D & G
77 K2 **Strata Florida** Cerdgn
49 G6 **Stratfield Mortimer** W Berk
49 G6 **Stratfield Saye** Hants
49 G7 **Stratfield Turgis** Hants
86 D5 **Stratford** Beds
51 K2 **Stratford** Gt Lon
91 H3 **Stratford St Andrew** Suffk

90 B8 **Stratford St Mary** Suffk
33 K4 **Stratford sub Castle** Wilts
33 J5 **Stratford Tony** Wilts
82 F4 **Stratford-upon-Avon** Warwks
260 C4 **Strath** Highld
270 E4 **Strathan** Highld
277 K3 **Strathan** Highld
197 K2 **Strathaven** S Lans
208 F3 **Strathblane** Stirlg
270 F7 **Strathcanaird** Highld
248 F3 **Strathcarron** Highld
227 K6 **Strathcoil** Ag & B
243 K1 **Strathdon** Abers
223 H4 **Strathkinness** Fife
210 B4 **Strathloanhead** W Loth
241 G5 **Strathmashie House** Highld
222 C5 **Strathmiglo** Fife
262 E8 **Strathpeffer** Highld
232 D4 **Strathtay** P & K
195 G4 **Strathwhillan** N Ayrs
278 E3 **Strathy** Highld
278 E3 **Strathy Inn** Highld
219 J4 **Strathyre** Stirlg
11 J1 **Stratton** Cnwll
16 C4 **Stratton** Dorset
64 E6 **Stratton** Gloucs
66 F2 **Stratton Audley** Oxon
47 H2 **Stratton St Margaret** Swindn
106 D4 **Stratton St Michael** Norfk
122 E7 **Stratton Strawless** Norfk
31 L1 **Stratton-on-the-Fosse** Somset
223 J4 **Stravithie** Fife
29 K3 **Stream** Somset
22 E4 **Streat** E Susx
51 J4 **Streatham** Gt Lon
68 D2 **Streatley** Beds
48 E3 **Streatley** W Berk
14 E5 **Street** Devon
147 K5 **Street** Lancs
162 C2 **Street** N York
31 H3 **Street** Somset
99 M7 **Street Ashton** Warwks
112 E4 **Street Dinas** Shrops
23 K3 **Street End** E Susx
40 F4 **Street End** Kent
20 D7 **Street End** W Susx
180 F7 **Street Gate** Gatesd
171 G6 **Street Houses** N York
151 H6 **Street Houses** N York
116 C2 **Street Lane** Derbys
31 K3 **Street on the Fosse** Somset
98 F1 **Streethay** Staffs
160 D3 **Streetlam** N York
98 D4 **Streetly** Wsall
88 C5 **Streetly End** Cambs
95 K6 **Strefford** Shrops
233 J8 **Strelitz** P & K
116 E3 **Strelley** Notts
151 K4 **Strensall** York
81 L7 **Strensham** Worcs
30 D2 **Stretcholt** Somset
8 C5 **Strete** Devon
80 B4 **Stretford** Herefs
80 C4 **Stretford** Herefs
130 F1 **Stretford** Traffd
87 K7 **Strethall** Essex
103 K8 **Stretham** Cambs
20 E5 **Strettington** W Susx
113 G1 **Stretton** Ches
133 H7 **Stretton** Derbys
118 B8 **Stretton** Rutlnd
97 K1 **Stretton** Staffs
115 L6 **Stretton** Staffs
130 C3 **Stretton** Warrtn
99 J1 **Stretton en le Field** Leics
80 E6 **Stretton Grandison** Herefs
95 J1 **Stretton Heath** Shrops
82 F7 **Stretton on Fosse** Warwks
80 B6 **Stretton Sugwas** Herefs
99 M7 **Stretton under Fosse** Warwks
96 D4 **Stretton Westwood** Shrops
83 K1 **Stretton-on-Dunsmore** Warwks
269 H5 **Strichen** Abers
131 J3 **Strines** Stockp
30 B2 **Stringston** Somset
85 H3 **Strixton** Nhants
63 H7 **Stroat** Gloucs
248 D5 **Stromeferry** Highld
275 b4 **Stromness** Ork
218 F3 **Stronachlachar** Stirlg
207 G3 **Stronafian** Ag & B
271 H4 **Stronchrubie** Highld
207 K3 **Strone** Ag & B

239 J7 **Strone** Highld
239 L6 **Stronenaba** Highld
217 J2 **Stronmilchan** Ag & B
228 C3 **Strontian** Highld
39 L7 **Strood** Kent
52 F5 **Strood** Medway
37 J1 **Strood Green** Surrey
36 F6 **Strood Green** W Susx
64 B6 **Stroud** Gloucs
35 L6 **Stroud** Hants
53 J1 **Stroud Green** Essex
64 A5 **Stroud Green** Gloucs
50 C5 **Stroude** Surrey
118 B5 **Stroxton** Lincs
246 D1 **Struan** Highld
232 B2 **Struan** P & K
137 H3 **Strubby** Lincs
107 G2 **Strumpshaw** Norfk
198 C3 **Strutherhill** S Lans
222 F5 **Struthers** Fife
250 C4 **Struy** Highld
124 F3 **Stryd-y-Facsen** IOA
112 D2 **Stryt-issa** Wrexhm
257 H3 **Stuartfield** Abers
98 D3 **Stubbers Green** Wsall
19 J3 **Stubbington** Hants
140 B4 **Stubbins** N York
106 E4 **Stubbs Green** Norfk
32 F8 **Stubhampton** Dorset
133 G4 **Stubley** Derbys
139 H7 **Stubshaw Cross** Wigan
118 A2 **Stubton** Lincs
84 A6 **Stuchbury** Nhants
29 G6 **Stuckeridge** Devon
33 L8 **Stuckton** Hants
49 L3 **Stud Green** W & M
148 E2 **Studfold** N York
68 C4 **Studham** Beds
177 H7 **Studholme** Cumb
17 K6 **Studland** Dorset
82 C2 **Studley** Warwks
46 D4 **Studley** Wilts
82 C2 **Studley Common** Warwks
150 C2 **Studley Roger** N York
150 C2 **Studley Royal** N York
87 K6 **Stump Cross** Cambs
103 L7 **Stuntney** Cambs
23 K4 **Stunts Green** E Susx
114 C5 **Sturbridge** Staffs
135 H2 **Sturgate** Lincs
88 D6 **Sturmer** Essex
32 C8 **Sturminster Common** Dorset
17 J3 **Sturminster Marshall** Dorset
32 C8 **Sturminster Newton** Dorset
41 G3 **Sturry** Kent
144 B7 **Sturton** N Linc
135 H4 **Sturton by Stow** Lincs
134 F3 **Sturton le Steeple** Notts
106 C7 **Stuston** Suffk
151 G7 **Stutton** N York
90 D8 **Stutton** Suffk
131 G3 **Styal** Ches
148 A8 **Stydd** Lancs
267 G4 **Stynie** Moray
134 C2 **Styrrup** Notts
218 D6 **Succoth** Ag & B
81 G5 **Suckley** Worcs
81 G4 **Suckley Green** Worcs
101 L7 **Sudborough** Nhants
91 J4 **Sudbourne** Suffk
118 C3 **Sudbrook** Lincs
45 G2 **Sudbrook** Mons
135 L4 **Sudbrooke** Lincs
115 K5 **Sudbury** Derbys
50 F2 **Sudbury** Gt Lon
89 H7 **Sudbury** Suffk
140 C5 **Sudden** Rochdl
81 J3 **Suddington** Worcs
64 D5 **Sudgrove** Gloucs
163 H4 **Suffield** N York
122 E5 **Suffield** Norfk
113 K8 **Sugdon** Wrekin
114 B5 **Sugnall** Staffs
80 B6 **Sugwas Pool** Herefs
247 J5 **Suisnish** Highld
154 e3 **Sulby** IOM
84 A6 **Sulgrave** Nhants
48 F4 **Sulham** W Berk
48 F5 **Sulhamstead** W Berk
48 F5 **Sulhamstead Abbots** W Berk
48 F5 **Sulhamstead Bannister** W Berk
21 J4 **Sullington** W Susx
281 d4 **Sullom** Shet
281 d4 **Sullom Voe** Shet

43 J8 **Sully** V Glam
49 H1 **Summer Heath** Bucks
112 D1 **Summer Hill** Wrexhm
150 B3 **Summerbridge** N York
4 E4 **Summercourt** Cnwll
121 G4 **Summerfield** Norfk
97 J8 **Summerfield** Worcs
98 D2 **Summerhill** Staffs
169 G6 **Summerhouse** Darltn
157 H5 **Summerlands** Cumb
133 G4 **Summerley** Derbys
20 D5 **Summersdale** W Susx
140 B5 **Summerseat** Bury
66 D5 **Summertown** Oxon
140 D6 **Summit** Oldham
140 E4 **Summit** Rochdl
157 L1 **Sunbiggin** N York
50 E5 **Sunbury** Surrey
185 K6 **Sundaywell** D & G
204 C3 **Sunderland** Ag & B
165 G4 **Sunderland** Cumb
147 H4 **Sunderland** Lancs
181 K7 **Sunderland** Sundld
169 H3 **Sunderland Bridge** Dur
200 D8 **Sundhope** Border
68 D2 **Sundon Park** Luton
38 D2 **Sundridge** Kent
145 H4 **Sunk Island** E R Yk
50 B5 **Sunningdale** W & M
50 B5 **Sunninghill** W & M
66 D7 **Sunningwell** Oxon
168 F3 **Sunniside** Dur
180 F7 **Sunniside** Gatesd
140 A4 **Sunny Bank** Lancs
169 G4 **Sunny Brow** Dur
116 B5 **Sunnyhill** C Derb
139 K3 **Sunnyhurst** Bl w D
220 D7 **Sunnylaw** Stirlg
66 D5 **Sunnymead** Oxon
47 K8 **Sunton** Wilts
50 F5 **Surbiton** Gt Lon
119 H6 **Surfleet** Lincs
119 J6 **Surfleet Seas End** Lincs
107 G2 **Surlingham** Norfk
72 C3 **Surrex** Essex
122 D4 **Sustead** Norfk
143 L7 **Susworth** Lincs
26 F8 **Sutcombe** Devon
26 F8 **Sutcombemill** Devon
106 B4 **Suton** Norfk
137 G5 **Sutterby** Lincs
119 J4 **Sutterton** Lincs
86 E5 **Sutton** Beds
102 B4 **Sutton** C Pete
103 J7 **Sutton** Cambs
13 G2 **Sutton** Devon
7 K6 **Sutton** Devon
142 E5 **Sutton** Donc
23 H7 **Sutton** E Susx
51 H6 **Sutton** Gt Lon
41 K5 **Sutton** Kent
142 D3 **Sutton** N York
123 H6 **Sutton** Norfk
117 K4 **Sutton** Notts
66 B6 **Sutton** Oxon
54 E4 **Sutton** Pembks
112 E6 **Sutton** Shrops
96 C1 **Sutton** Shrops
113 L5 **Sutton** Shrops
97 G6 **Sutton** Shrops
129 M1 **Sutton** St Hel
114 B7 **Sutton** Staffs
91 G6 **Sutton** Suffk
21 G4 **Sutton** W Susx
52 C5 **Sutton at Hone** Kent
101 G5 **Sutton Bassett** Nhants
46 D3 **Sutton Benger** Wilts
31 J8 **Sutton Bingham** Somset
116 E6 **Sutton Bonington** Notts
120 B7 **Sutton Bridge** Lincs
99 L3 **Sutton Cheney** Leics
98 E4 **Sutton Coldfield** Birm
66 D8 **Sutton Courtenay** Oxon
119 M7 **Sutton Crosses** Lincs
134 D3 **Sutton cum Lound** Notts
116 E6 **Sutton Fields** Notts
160 D7 **Sutton Grange** N York
66 B5 **Sutton Green** Oxon
50 C8 **Sutton Green** Surrey
112 F2 **Sutton Green** Wrexhm
160 D6 **Sutton Howgrave** N York
133 K7 **Sutton in Ashfield** Notts
100 B4 **Sutton in the Elms** Leics
131 H5 **Sutton Lane Ends** Ches
97 G3 **Sutton Maddock** Shrops

30 E3 **Sutton Mallet** Somset
33 G5 **Sutton Mandeville** Wilts
129 L2 **Sutton Manor** St Hel
80 D6 **Sutton Marsh** Herefs
31 K6 **Sutton Montis** Somset
137 K3 **Sutton on Sea** Lincs
115 L5 **Sutton on the Hill** Derbys
134 F6 **Sutton on Trent** Notts
16 D5 **Sutton Poyntz** Dorset
34 F3 **Sutton Scotney** Hants
103 H1 **Sutton St Edmund** Lincs
119 L7 **Sutton St James** Lincs
80 C6 **Sutton St Nicholas** Herefs
39 K2 **Sutton Street** Kent
151 L6 **Sutton upon Derwent** E R Yk
39 K3 **Sutton Valence** Kent
32 E3 **Sutton Veny** Wilts
32 E7 **Sutton Waldron** Dorset
130 A4 **Sutton Weaver** Ches
45 H7 **Sutton Wick** BaNES
66 C8 **Sutton Wick** Oxon
149 H7 **Sutton-in-Craven** N York
144 E1 **Sutton-on-Hull** C KuH
151 J3 **Sutton-on-the-Forest** N York
83 G7 **Sutton-under-Brailes** Warwks
161 G6 **Sutton-under-Whitestonecliffe** N York
137 G4 **Swaby** Lincs
116 A7 **Swadlincote** Derbys
105 G2 **Swaffham** Norfk
87 L3 **Swaffham Bulbeck** Cambs
88 B2 **Swaffham Prior** Cambs
122 F5 **Swafield** Norfk
161 G2 **Swainby** N York
80 B7 **Swainshill** Herefs
106 E3 **Swainsthorpe** Norfk
45 M5 **Swainswick** BaNES
83 J7 **Swalcliffe** Oxon
40 F2 **Swalecliffe** Kent
144 F7 **Swallow** Lincs
135 J6 **Swallow Beck** Lincs
133 J3 **Swallow Nest** Rothm
33 G5 **Swallowcliffe** Wilts
49 H6 **Swallowfield** Wokham
70 F7 **Swallows Cross** Essex
34 E1 **Swampton** Hants
130 E5 **Swan Green** Ches
72 C2 **Swan Street** Essex
98 C5 **Swan Village** Sandw
17 K6 **Swanage** Dorset
67 K2 **Swanbourne** Bucks
43 J8 **Swanbridge** V Glam
97 G4 **Swancote** Shrops
144 C2 **Swanland** E R Yk
52 B5 **Swanley** Kent
52 B5 **Swanley Village** Kent
35 J7 **Swanmore** Hants
116 C8 **Swannington** Leics
122 C7 **Swannington** Norfk
135 J6 **Swanpool Garden Suburb** Lincs
52 D4 **Swanscombe** Kent
57 J6 **Swansea** Swans
122 F6 **Swanton Abbot** Norfk
121 M8 **Swanton Morley** Norfk
121 M5 **Swanton Novers** Norfk
53 J7 **Swanton Street** Kent
116 C1 **Swanwick** Derbys
19 H2 **Swanwick** Hants
118 D3 **Swarby** Lincs
106 D3 **Swardeston** Norfk
116 B6 **Swarkestone** Derbys
191 H6 **Swarland** Nthumb
191 H5 **Swarland Estate** Nthumb
35 H3 **Swarraton** Hants
149 J6 **Swartha** Brad
156 C7 **Swarthmoor** Cumb
118 F4 **Swaton** Lincs
87 G2 **Swavesey** Cambs
18 D4 **Sway** Hants
118 C7 **Swayfield** Lincs
34 F7 **Swaythling** C Sotn
80 F3 **Sweet Green** Worcs
13 K3 **Sweetham** Devon
38 D7 **Sweethaws** E Susx
39 K4 **Sweetlands Corner** Kent
11 G3 **Sweets** Cnwll
5 J3 **Sweetshouse** Cnwll
91 H3 **Swefling** Suffk
99 K1 **Swepstone** Leics
66 A1 **Swerford** Oxon
130 F6 **Swettenham** Ches
61 K7 **Swffryd** Blae G
39 L4 **Swift's Green** Kent
90 E4 **Swilland** Suffk

138 F1 **Swillbrook** Lancs
142 B2 **Swillington** Leeds
27 L5 **Swimbridge** Devon
27 L5 **Swimbridge Newland** Devon
65 L4 **Swinbrook** Oxon
141 K2 **Swincliffe** Kirk
150 C4 **Swincliffe** N York
28 B3 **Swincombe** Devon
148 E5 **Swinden** N York
135 H7 **Swinderby** Lincs
64 D2 **Swindon** Gloucs
190 D6 **Swindon** Nthumb
97 J5 **Swindon** Staffs
47 H2 **Swindon** Swindn
153 J8 **Swine** E R Yk
143 J3 **Swinefleet** E R Yk
45 K5 **Swineford** S Glos
85 L2 **Swineshead** Beds
119 H3 **Swineshead** Lincs
119 H3 **Swineshead Bridge** Lincs
275 H1 **Swiney** Highld
100 C7 **Swinford** Leics
66 C5 **Swinford** Oxon
41 G6 **Swingfield Minnis** Kent
41 H6 **Swingfield Street** Kent
89 K6 **Swingleton Green** Suffk
203 K7 **Swinhoe** Nthumb
145 G8 **Swinhope** Lincs
159 J5 **Swinithwaite** N York
80 F7 **Swinmore Common** Herefs
115 J2 **Swinscoe** Staffs
165 H6 **Swinside** Cumb
118 D7 **Swinstead** Lincs
135 L4 **Swinthorpe** Lincs
202 C4 **Swinton** Border
160 B6 **Swinton** N York
162 D8 **Swinton** N York
142 C7 **Swinton** Rothm
140 A7 **Swinton** Salfd
100 C1 **Swithland** Leics
263 G6 **Swordale** Highld
238 B5 **Swordland** Highld
278 C4 **Swordly** Highld
130 D3 **Sworton Heath** Ches
77 J2 **Swyddffynnon** Cerdgn
114 D4 **Swynnerton** Staffs
15 M5 **Swyre** Dorset
112 B6 **Sycharth** Powys
93 L7 **Sychnant** Powys
94 B2 **Sychtyn** Powys
129 G8 **Sydallt** Flints
64 D5 **Syde** Gloucs
51 K4 **Sydenham** Gt Lon
67 H6 **Sydenham** Oxon
12 A7 **Sydenham Damerel** Devon
36 E4 **Sydenhurst** Surrey
121 H5 **Syderstone** Norfk
16 C3 **Sydling St Nicholas** Dorset
48 C7 **Sydmonton** Hants
97 H2 **Sydnal Lane** Shrops
117 K2 **Syerston** Notts
140 D4 **Syke** Rochdl
143 G4 **Sykehouse** Donc
106 E7 **Syleham** Suffk
56 F3 **Sylen** Carmth
281 e5 **Symbister** Shet
196 D5 **Symington** S Ayrs
199 G6 **Symington** S Lans
63 H4 **Symonds Yat** Herefs
15 K4 **Symondsbury** Dorset
150 A8 **Sympson Green** Brad
15 J2 **Synderford** Dorset
76 D7 **Synod Inn** Cerdgn
278 B7 **Syre** Highld
64 F3 **Syreford** Gloucs
84 C7 **Syresham** Nhants
100 D1 **Syston** Leics
118 B3 **Syston** Lincs
81 J2 **Sytchampton** Worcs
84 F2 **Sywell** Nhants

T

130 E4 **Tabley Hill** Ches
66 C3 **Tackley** Oxon
106 C4 **Tacolneston** Norfk
151 G7 **Tadcaster** N York
132 C5 **Taddington** Derbys
65 G1 **Taddington** Gloucs
27 H7 **Taddiport** Devon
48 F6 **Tadley** Hants
86 F5 **Tadlow** Cambs
83 J7 **Tadmarton** Oxon
45 L5 **Tadwick** BaNES

51 G7 **Tadworth** Surrey
75 J5 **Tafarn-y-bwlch** Pembks
128 E7 **Tafarn-y-Gelyn** Denbgs
61 H5 **Tafarnaubach** Blae G
43 H5 **Taff's Well** Cardif
93 J3 **Tafolwern** Powys
60 F2 **Tai'r Bull** Powys
57 L7 **Taibach** Neath
280 B3 **Tain** Highld
263 L3 **Tain** Highld
282 e5 **Tairbeart** W Isls
70 E3 **Takeley** Essex
70 E3 **Takeley Street** Essex
92 E5 **Tal-y-bont** Cerdgn
126 F6 **Tal-y-Bont** Conwy
109 L7 **Tal-y-bont** Gwynd
126 C5 **Tal-y-bont** Gwynd
126 F5 **Tal-y-Cafn** Conwy
62 E4 **Tal-y-coed** Mons
42 F5 **Tal-y-garn** Rhondd
92 F2 **Tal-y-llyn** Gwynd
61 L6 **Tal-y-Waun** Torfn
78 F8 **Talachddu** Powys
128 D3 **Talacre** Flints
14 C3 **Talaton** Devon
54 D4 **Talbenny** Pembks
43 G5 **Talbot Green** Rhondd
17 L4 **Talbot Village** Bmouth
14 C3 **Taleford** Devon
93 K3 **Talerddig** Powys
76 D5 **Talgarreg** Cerdgn
79 G8 **Talgarth** Powys
246 D3 **Talisker** Highld
114 C1 **Talke** Staffs
114 C1 **Talke Pits** Staffs
178 D7 **Talkin** Cumb
187 H2 **Talla Linnfoots** Border
260 E6 **Talladale** Highld
183 K3 **Tallaminnock** S Ayrs
113 G3 **Tallarn Green** Wrexhm
164 F4 **Tallentire** Cumb
59 H2 **Talley** Carmth
102 B2 **Tallington** Lincs
112 D2 **Tallwrn** Wrexhm
277 K4 **Talmine** Highld
58 B4 **Talog** Carmth
77 G4 **Talsarn** Cerdgn
109 L4 **Talsarnau** Gwynd
4 E2 **Talskiddy** Cnwll
125 J4 **Talwrn** IOA
112 F2 **Talwrn** Wrexhm
61 H3 **Talybont-on-Usk** Powys
109 J1 **Talysarn** Gwynd
93 H3 **Talywern** Powys
139 J7 **Tamer Lane End** Wigan
6 F3 **Tamerton Foliot** C Plym
99 G3 **Tamworth** Staffs
119 L3 **Tamworth Green** Lincs
158 F1 **Tan Hill** N York
110 C3 **Tan-y-Bwlch** Gwynd
127 J6 **Tan-y-fron** Conwy
112 D1 **Tan-y-fron** Wrexhm
110 C3 **Tan-y-Grisiau** Gwynd
76 B5 **Tan-y-groes** Cerdgn
151 G4 **Tancred** N York
74 E7 **Tancredston** Pembks
38 B3 **Tandridge** Surrey
180 F7 **Tanfield** Dur
180 F8 **Tanfield Lea** Dur
54 F3 **Tangiers** Pembks
47 L8 **Tangley** Hants
20 E5 **Tangmere** W Susx
283 b13 **Tangusdale** W Isls
275 d4 **Tankerness** Ork
142 A7 **Tankersley** Barns
40 F2 **Tankerton** Kent
280 D6 **Tannach** Highld
245 H6 **Tannachie** Abers
234 D4 **Tannadice** Angus
98 D8 **Tanner's Green** Worcs
90 F2 **Tannington** Suffk
209 J6 **Tannochside** N Lans
132 F7 **Tansley** Derbys
102 B5 **Tansor** Nhants
180 E7 **Tantobie** Dur
170 C8 **Tanton** N York
97 K8 **Tanwood** Worcs
82 D1 **Tanworth in Arden** Warwks
282 d6 **Taobh Tuath** W Isls
49 M3 **Taplow** Bucks
205 L6 **Tarbert** Ag & B
206 D5 **Tarbert** Ag & B
282 e5 **Tarbert** W Isls
218 D6 **Tarbet** Ag & B
276 B6 **Tarbet** Highld

238 C5 **Tarbet** Highld
129 K2 **Tarbock Green** Knows
196 E5 **Tarbolton** S Ayrs
199 H2 **Tarbrax** S Lans
82 B2 **Tardebigge** Worcs
244 B7 **Tarfside** Angus
244 B3 **Tarland** Abers
138 F4 **Tarleton** Lancs
138 E5 **Tarlscough** Lancs
64 D7 **Tarlton** Gloucs
44 D8 **Tarnock** Somset
164 F1 **Tarns** Cumb
156 F4 **Tarnside** Cumb
130 A7 **Tarporley** Ches
28 F4 **Tarr** Somset
29 K5 **Tarr** Somset
17 H2 **Tarrant Crawford** Dorset
32 F8 **Tarrant Gunville** Dorset
32 F8 **Tarrant Hinton** Dorset
17 H2 **Tarrant Keyneston** Dorset
17 J1 **Tarrant Launceston** Dorset
17 H1 **Tarrant Monkton** Dorset
17 H1 **Tarrant Rawston** Dorset
17 H2 **Tarrant Rushton** Dorset
23 G6 **Tarring Neville** E Susx
80 E7 **Tarrington** Herefs
247 J6 **Tarskavaig** Highld
256 F5 **Tarves** Abers
232 F3 **Tarvie** P & K
129 L6 **Tarvin** Ches
129 L6 **Tarvin Sands** Ches
106 D4 **Tasburgh** Norfk
96 F4 **Tasley** Shrops
65 M3 **Taston** Oxon
115 K7 **Tatenhill** Staffs
84 F6 **Tathall End** M Keyn
147 M2 **Tatham** Lancs
136 F3 **Tathwell** Lincs
51 L7 **Tatsfield** Surrey
129 L7 **Tattenhall** Ches
121 J6 **Tatterford** Norfk
121 J5 **Tattersett** Norfk
136 D8 **Tattershall** Lincs
136 C8 **Tattershall Bridge** Lincs
136 D7 **Tattershall Thorpe** Lincs
90 D7 **Tattingstone** Suffk
90 D7 **Tattingstone White Horse** Suffk
15 H2 **Tatworth** Somset
267 H6 **Tauchers** Moray
30 C6 **Taunton** Somset
122 D8 **Taverham** Norfk
70 E3 **Taverners Green** Essex
55 L4 **Tavernspite** Pembks
12 C7 **Tavistock** Devon
12 F3 **Taw Green** Devon
27 K5 **Tawstock** Devon
131 K4 **Taxal** Derbys
217 G3 **Taychreggan Hotel** Ag & B
205 M7 **Tayinloan** Ag & B
63 L3 **Taynton** Gloucs
65 K4 **Taynton** Oxon
216 F1 **Taynuilt** Ag & B
223 H2 **Tayport** Fife
215 L7 **Tayvallich** Ag & B
136 C2 **Tealby** Lincs
181 G7 **Team Valley** Gatesd
247 K6 **Teangue** Highld
263 G7 **Teanord** Highld
157 K2 **Tebay** Cumb
68 C2 **Tebworth** Beds
13 J4 **Tedburn St Mary** Devon
81 M8 **Teddington** Gloucs
50 F5 **Teddington** Gt Lon
80 F3 **Tedstone Delamere** Herefs
80 F3 **Tedstone Wafer** Herefs
170 D6 **Teesport** R & Cl
170 B7 **Teesside Park** S on T
84 D1 **Teeton** Nhants
33 G4 **Teffont Evias** Wilts
33 G4 **Teffont Magna** Wilts
75 L5 **Tegryn** Pembks
117 M8 **Teigh** Rutlnd
12 F5 **Teigncombe** Devon
13 K7 **Teigngrace** Devon
13 L7 **Teignmouth** Devon
188 D4 **Teindside** Border
96 F2 **Telford** Wrekin
46 A7 **Tellisford** Somset
22 F6 **Telscombe** E Susx
22 F7 **Telscombe Cliffs** E Susx
231 J4 **Tempar** P & K
176 E2 **Templand** D & G
11 G7 **Temple** Cnwll
211 K7 **Temple** Mdloth

99 G8 **Temple Balsall** Solhll
76 F4 **Temple Bar** Cerdgn
45 J7 **Temple Cloud** BaNES
88 D5 **Temple End** Suffk
41 J6 **Temple Ewell** Kent
82 D4 **Temple Grafton** Warwks
65 G2 **Temple Guiting** Gloucs
142 F3 **Temple Hirst** N York
133 H6 **Temple Normanton** Derbys
245 H7 **Temple of Fiddes** Abers
250 F5 **Temple Pier** Highld
166 E5 **Temple Sowerby** Cumb
32 B6 **Templecombe** Somset
28 F8 **Templeton** Devon
55 J4 **Templeton** Pembks
168 E1 **Templetown** Dur
86 D4 **Tempsford** Beds
104 B4 **Ten Mile Bank** Norfk
80 E2 **Tenbury Wells** Worcs
55 K6 **Tenby** Pembks
73 H2 **Tendring** Essex
73 H2 **Tendring Green** Essex
73 H2 **Tendring Heath** Essex
73 G3 **Tenpenny Heath** Essex
39 M6 **Tenterden** Kent
71 J4 **Terling** Essex
113 K8 **Tern** Wrekin
113 L5 **Ternhill** Shrops
176 B3 **Terregles** D & G
151 L2 **Terrington** N York
120 C7 **Terrington St Clement** Norfk
120 C8 **Terrington St John** Norfk
98 E8 **Terry's Green** Warwks
39 H3 **Teston** Kent
34 D7 **Testwood** Hants
64 C8 **Tetbury** Gloucs
64 C8 **Tetbury Upton** Gloucs
112 F5 **Tetchill** Shrops
11 L3 **Tetcott** Devon
136 F5 **Tetford** Lincs
145 J7 **Tetney** Lincs
145 J7 **Tetney Lock** Lincs
67 G6 **Tetsworth** Oxon
97 K3 **Tettenhall** Wolves
97 K3 **Tettenhall Wood** Wolves
86 E4 **Tetworth** Cambs
133 J7 **Teversal** Notts
87 K3 **Teversham** Cambs
188 C5 **Teviothead** Border
69 H4 **Tewin** Herts
81 K8 **Tewkesbury** Gloucs
40 B3 **Teynham** Kent
149 M8 **Thackley** Brad
164 F6 **Thackthwaite** Cumb
166 A5 **Thackthwaite** Cumb
21 J3 **Thakeham** W Susx
67 H6 **Thame** Oxon
50 F5 **Thames Ditton** Surrey
52 A3 **Thamesmead** Gt Lon
40 F4 **Thanington** Kent
199 G5 **Thankerton** S Lans
106 D4 **Tharston** Norfk
48 D5 **Thatcham** W Berk
129 L1 **Thatto Heath** St Hel
70 F1 **Thaxted** Essex
131 G8 **The Bank** Ches
96 E3 **The Bank** Shrops
64 F6 **The Beeches** Gloucs
115 G6 **The Blythe** Staffs
95 J4 **The Bog** Shrops
82 A4 **The Bourne** Worcs
247 H2 **The Braes** Highld
97 K4 **The Bratch** Staffs
80 C3 **The Broad** Herefs
212 F4 **The Brunt** E Loth
154 e5 **The Bungalow** IOM
64 C4 **The Butts** Gloucs
64 C5 **The Camp** Gloucs
113 H3 **The Chequer** Wrexhm
86 C3 **The City** Beds
67 J7 **The City** Bucks
65 L2 **The Common** Oxon
34 B4 **The Common** Wilts
46 F2 **The Common** Wilts
39 H5 **The Corner** Kent
95 K6 **The Corner** Shrops
154 d3 **The Cronk** IOM
196 C1 **The Den** N Ayrs
178 D3 **The Flatt** Cumb
79 L3 **The Forge** Herefs
38 E6 **The Forstal** E Susx
40 A6 **The Forstal** Kent
40 D7 **The Forstal** Kent
113 L5 **The Fouralls** Shrops
156 A5 **The Green** Cumb

71 J3 **The Green** Essex
162 D2 **The Green** N York
81 K7 **The Grove** Worcs
37 G5 **The Haven** W Susx
64 B2 **The Haw** Gloucs
170 C4 **The Headland** Hartpl
156 A6 **The Hill** Cumb
49 K3 **The Holt** Wokham
80 C2 **The Hundred** Herefs
40 C8 **The Leacon** Kent
67 L6 **The Lee** Bucks
154 e2 **The Lhen** IOM
266 F4 **The Lochs** Moray
95 H4 **The Marsh** Powys
180 F8 **The Middles** Dur
39 J7 **The Moor** Kent
57 H7 **The Mumbles** Swans
209 H8 **The Murray** S Lans
81 K8 **The Mythe** Gloucs
63 G6 **The Narth** Mons
245 G4 **The Neuk** Abers
63 L7 **The Quarry** Gloucs
39 M4 **The Quarter** Kent
64 C3 **The Reddings** Gloucs
131 G8 **The Rookery** Staffs
220 D3 **The Ross** P & K
36 C2 **The Sands** Surrey
46 A4 **The Shoe** Wilts
96 F4 **The Smithies** Shrops
87 K5 **The Spike** Cambs
83 G1 **The Spring** Warwks
62 B7 **The Square** Torfn
38 F4 **The Stair** Kent
25 G2 **The Stocks** Kent
36 A3 **The Straits** Hants
46 D7 **The Strand** Wilts
2 E3 **The Towans** Cnwll
80 C5 **The Vauld** Herefs
97 G2 **The Wyke** Shrops
160 D5 **Theakston** N York
143 M4 **Thealby** N Linc
31 G2 **Theale** Somset
48 F5 **Theale** W Berk
153 G8 **Thearne** E R Yk
91 K2 **Theberton** Suffk
35 L3 **Thedden Grange** Hants
100 E6 **Theddingworth** Leics
137 J2 **Theddlethorpe All Saints** Lincs
137 J2 **Theddlethorpe St Helen** Lincs
28 D8 **Thelbridge Cross** Devon
105 L7 **Thelnetham** Suffk
106 D7 **Thelveton** Norfk
130 C2 **Thelwall** Warrtn
122 B6 **Themelthorpe** Norfk
83 M7 **Thenford** Nhants
46 F5 **Theobald's Green** Wilts
87 G7 **Therfield** Herts
105 H6 **Thetford** Norfk
165 L2 **Thethwaite** Cumb
70 C7 **Theydon Bois** Essex
151 L7 **Thicket Priory** E R Yk
46 B4 **Thickwood** Wilts
136 D5 **Thimbleby** Lincs
161 G3 **Thimbleby** N York
129 G3 **Thingwall** Wirral
161 G6 **Thirkleby** N York
161 G6 **Thirlby** N York
201 H4 **Thirlestane** Border
165 K7 **Thirlspot** Cumb
160 B5 **Thirn** N York
160 F6 **Thirsk** N York
144 F1 **Thirtleby** E R Yk
147 H8 **Thistleton** Lancs
118 B7 **Thistleton** Rutlnd
104 D8 **Thistley Green** Suffk
152 C4 **Thixendale** E R Yk
179 M3 **Thockrington** Nthumb
103 H2 **Tholomas Drove** Cambs
151 G2 **Tholthorpe** N York
55 J5 **Thomas Chapel** Pembks
166 B3 **Thomas Close** Cumb
82 C3 **Thomas Town** Warwks
255 M4 **Thomastown** Abers
105 J4 **Thompson** Norfk
52 E5 **Thong** Kent
159 H5 **Thoralby** N York
134 C5 **Thoresby** Notts
137 J4 **Thoresthorpe** Lincs
144 F8 **Thoresway** Lincs
145 G8 **Thorganby** Lincs
151 L7 **Thorganby** N York
162 C3 **Thorgill** N York
107 J8 **Thorington** Suffk
89 K8 **Thorington Street** Suffk

149 H5 **Thorlby** N York
70 C3 **Thorley** Herts
18 F6 **Thorley** IOW
70 C3 **Thorley Houses** Herts
18 F6 **Thorley Street** IOW
161 H7 **Thormanby** N York
170 B7 **Thornaby-on-Tees** S on T
122 B4 **Thornage** Norfk
84 E8 **Thornborough** Bucks
160 D6 **Thornborough** N York
141 J1 **Thornbury** Brad
12 A1 **Thornbury** Devon
80 E3 **Thornbury** Herefs
45 J1 **Thornbury** S Glos
177 J8 **Thornby** Cumb
100 E8 **Thornby** Nhants
131 K7 **Thorncliff** Staffs
15 J2 **Thorncombe** Dorset
36 F3 **Thorncombe Street** Surrey
86 C5 **Thorncott Green** Beds
19 G7 **Thorncross** IOW
90 D1 **Thorndon** Suffk
12 D4 **Thorndon Cross** Devon
143 H5 **Thorne** Donc
31 H7 **Thorne** Somset
29 K6 **Thorne St Margaret** Somset
7 M2 **Thornecroft** Devon
27 G7 **Thornehillhead** Devon
150 E7 **Thorner** Leeds
98 D3 **Thornes** Staffs
141 M4 **Thornes** Wakefd
50 D3 **Thorney** Bucks
102 F3 **Thorney** C Pete
135 G5 **Thorney** Notts
30 F6 **Thorney** Somset
18 B4 **Thorney Hill** Hants
103 G3 **Thorney Toll** Cambs
30 D6 **Thornfalcon** Somset
31 K8 **Thornford** Dorset
179 H6 **Thorngrafton** Nthumb
30 E4 **Thorngrove** Somset
145 G3 **Thorngumbald** E R Yk
121 G3 **Thornham** Norfk
90 C1 **Thornham Magna** Suffk
90 D1 **Thornham Parva** Suffk
102 B3 **Thornhaugh** C Pete
19 G1 **Thornhill** C Sotn
43 J5 **Thornhill** Caerph
186 C7 **Thornhill** D & G
132 D3 **Thornhill** Derbys
141 L4 **Thornhill** Kirk
219 L7 **Thornhill** Stirlg
141 K4 **Thornhill Lees** Kirk
141 J3 **Thornhills** Calder
153 H3 **Thornholme** E R Yk
17 G2 **Thornicombe** Dorset
202 D6 **Thornington** Nthumb
168 E3 **Thornley** Dur
169 K3 **Thornley** Dur
179 J7 **Thornley Gate** Cumb
208 F7 **Thornliebank** E Rens
88 E4 **Thorns** Suffk
130 F3 **Thorns Green** Ches
131 K2 **Thornsett** Derbys
165 H5 **Thornthwaite** Cumb
149 L4 **Thornthwaite** N York
234 B6 **Thornton** Angus
141 H1 **Thornton** Brad
84 E8 **Thornton** Bucks
152 A6 **Thornton** E R Yk
222 E7 **Thornton** Fife
146 F7 **Thornton** Lancs
100 A2 **Thornton** Leics
136 D6 **Thornton** Lincs
170 B7 **Thornton** Middsb
202 E4 **Thornton** Nthumb
54 E5 **Thornton** Pembks
138 D7 **Thornton** Sefton
144 D4 **Thornton Curtis** N Linc
129 K5 **Thornton Green** Ches
51 J5 **Thornton Heath** Gt Lon
129 G3 **Thornton Hough** Wirral
158 B8 **Thornton in Lonsdale** N York
162 E6 **Thornton le Dale** N York
144 D8 **Thornton le Moor** Lincs
159 G5 **Thornton Rust** N York
160 A5 **Thornton Steward** N York
160 C5 **Thornton Watlass** N York
148 F6 **Thornton-in-Craven** N York
160 F4 **Thornton-le-Beans** N York
151 L3 **Thornton-le-Clay** N York
160 F5 **Thornton-le-Moor** N York
129 K5 **Thornton-le-Moors** Ches
160 F5 **Thornton-le-Street** N York
209 G8 **Thorntonhall** S Lans

213 G4 **Thorntonloch** E Loth
70 C6 **Thornwood Common** Essex
201 J3 **Thornydykes** Border
165 L6 **Thornythwaite** Cumb
117 K3 **Thoroton** Notts
150 F6 **Thorp Arch** Leeds
115 J2 **Thorpe** Derbys
152 F6 **Thorpe** E R Yk
137 J3 **Thorpe** Lincs
149 H3 **Thorpe** N York
107 J4 **Thorpe** Norfk
117 K2 **Thorpe** Notts
50 C5 **Thorpe** Surrey
106 D7 **Thorpe Abbotts** Norfk
116 E7 **Thorpe Acre** Leics
117 K7 **Thorpe Arnold** Leics
142 D4 **Thorpe Audlin** Donc
162 F8 **Thorpe Bassett** N York
53 K2 **Thorpe Bay** Sthend
101 K4 **Thorpe by Water** Rutlnd
133 G1 **Thorpe Common** Rothm
99 H2 **Thorpe Constantine** Staffs
106 F1 **Thorpe End** Norfk
73 H3 **Thorpe Green** Essex
139 H3 **Thorpe Green** Lancs
89 J4 **Thorpe Green** Suffk
142 B8 **Thorpe Hesley** Rothm
142 F5 **Thorpe in Balne** Donc
135 H4 **Thorpe in the Fallows** Lincs
101 G5 **Thorpe Langton** Leics
169 K5 **Thorpe Larches** Dur
152 C7 **Thorpe le Street** E R Yk
50 C5 **Thorpe Lea** Surrey
101 H7 **Thorpe Malsor** Nhants
83 M6 **Thorpe Mandeville** Nhants
122 E4 **Thorpe Market** Norfk
122 D8 **Thorpe Marriot** Norfk
89 J4 **Thorpe Morieux** Suffk
141 M2 **Thorpe on the Hill** Leeds
135 H6 **Thorpe on the Hill** Lincs
133 K3 **Thorpe Salvin** Rothm
100 F1 **Thorpe Satchville** Leics
106 F2 **Thorpe St Andrew** Norfk
137 J7 **Thorpe St Peter** Lincs
169 L6 **Thorpe Thewles** S on T
136 B8 **Thorpe Tilney** Lincs
151 G4 **Thorpe Underwood** N York
101 H7 **Thorpe Underwood** Nhants
102 A7 **Thorpe Waterville** Nhants
142 F2 **Thorpe Willoughby** N York
73 J3 **Thorpe-le-Soken** Essex
91 L3 **Thorpeness** Suffk
104 C2 **Thorpland** Norfk
73 G3 **Thorrington** Essex
13 L2 **Thorverton** Devon
68 E4 **Thrales End** Beds
106 C8 **Thrandeston** Suffk
101 M7 **Thrapston** Nhants
165 G3 **Threapland** Cumb
149 H4 **Threapland** N York
113 G3 **Threapwood** Ches
115 G3 **Threapwood** Staffs
115 G3 **Threapwood Head** Staffs
183 J2 **Threave** S Ayrs
63 G3 **Three Ashes** Herefs
37 L3 **Three Bridges** W Susx
4 B5 **Three Burrows** Cnwll
39 K5 **Three Chimneys** Kent
79 G7 **Three Cocks** Powys
57 G6 **Three Crosses** Swans
23 L3 **Three Cups Corner** E Susx
80 F3 **Three Gates** Worcs
11 J5 **Three Hammers** Cnwll
103 K3 **Three Holes** Norfk
140 C6 **Three Lane Ends** Rochdl
39 H7 **Three Leg Cross** E Susx
17 L2 **Three Legged Cross** Dorset
49 H5 **Three Mile Cross** Wokham
4 C6 **Three Mile Stone** Cnwll
210 E4 **Three Miletown** W Loth
24 F4 **Three Oaks** E Susx
123 G7 **Threehammer Common** Norfk
118 E4 **Threekingham** Lincs
201 G4 **Threepwood** Border
165 K5 **Threlkeld** Cumb
149 H3 **Threshfield** N York
107 J1 **Thrigby** Norfk
167 L6 **Thringarth** Dur
116 D8 **Thringstone** Leics
160 D4 **Thrintoft** N York
87 J6 **Thriplow** Cambs
133 K2 **Throapham** Rothm
103 G2 **Throckenhalt** Lincs
69 J1 **Throcking** Herts

180 E5 **Throckley** N u Ty
82 A5 **Throckmorton** Worcs
17 M3 **Throop** Bmouth
16 F4 **Throop** Dorset
180 D2 **Throphill** Nthumb
190 E5 **Thropton** Nthumb
209 M1 **Throsk** Stirlg
64 D5 **Througham** Gloucs
185 L6 **Throughgate** D & G
12 F4 **Throwleigh** Devon
40 C4 **Throwley** Kent
40 C4 **Throwley Forstal** Kent
116 E5 **Thrumpton** Notts
134 D4 **Thrumpton** Notts
280 D7 **Thrumster** Highld
145 J6 **Thrunscoe** NE Lin
190 F4 **Thrunton** Nthumb
65 L7 **Thrup** Oxon
64 B6 **Thrupp** Gloucs
66 C4 **Thrupp** Oxon
12 B5 **Thrushelton** Devon
70 D5 **Thrushesbush** Essex
117 H8 **Thrussington** Leics
34 C2 **Thruxton** Hants
80 B8 **Thruxton** Herefs
142 D8 **Thrybergh** Rothm
116 C5 **Thulston** Derbys
53 G1 **Thundersley** Essex
100 C1 **Thurcaston** Leics
133 K2 **Thurcroft** Rothm
26 E8 **Thurdon** Cnwll
122 D4 **Thurgarton** Norfk
117 J2 **Thurgarton** Notts
141 L7 **Thurgoland** Barns
100 B4 **Thurlaston** Leics
83 L1 **Thurlaston** Warwks
30 C6 **Thurlbear** Somset
135 H7 **Thurlby** Lincs
118 E8 **Thurlby** Lincs
137 J4 **Thurlby** Lincs
85 L3 **Thurleigh** Beds
7 K6 **Thurlestone** Devon
88 D5 **Thurlow** Suffk
30 C5 **Thurloxton** Somset
141 K7 **Thurlstone** Barns
107 J4 **Thurlton** Norfk
130 F8 **Thurlwood** Ches
100 D2 **Thurmaston** Leics
100 E3 **Thurnby** Leics
123 H8 **Thurne** Norfk
53 H7 **Thurnham** Kent
102 B6 **Thurning** Nhants
122 B5 **Thurning** Norfk
142 C6 **Thurnscoe** Barns
165 K1 **Thursby** Cumb
140 D1 **Thursden** Lancs
121 L5 **Thursford** Norfk
36 D3 **Thursley** Surrey
279 K3 **Thurso** Highld
128 F3 **Thurstaston** Wirral
89 J2 **Thurston** Suffk
140 E6 **Thurston Clough** Oldham
89 J2 **Thurston Planch** Suffk
177 K7 **Thurstonfield** Cumb
141 J3 **Thurstonland** Kirk
107 G3 **Thurton** Norfk
115 L4 **Thurvaston** Derbys
105 L2 **Thuxton** Norfk
158 F3 **Thwaite** N York
90 D2 **Thwaite** Suffk
156 E4 **Thwaite Head** Cumb
107 G4 **Thwaite St Mary** Norfk
149 K7 **Thwaites** Brad
149 K7 **Thwaites Brow** Brad
153 G2 **Thwing** E R Yk
221 J3 **Tibbermore** P & K
186 C6 **Tibbers** D & G
63 M3 **Tibberton** Gloucs
81 L4 **Tibberton** Worcs
113 L7 **Tibberton** Wrekin
187 K2 **Tibbie Shiels Inn** Border
106 C5 **Tibenham** Norfk
133 J7 **Tibshelf** Derbys
152 E5 **Tibthorpe** E R Yk
39 H7 **Ticehurst** E Susx
35 H5 **Tichborne** Hants
101 L2 **Tickencote** Rutlnd
44 F4 **Tickenham** N Som
85 H6 **Tickford End** M Keyn
134 B1 **Tickhill** Donc
96 B5 **Ticklerton** Shrops
116 B6 **Ticknall** Derbys
153 G7 **Tickton** E R Yk
98 E8 **Tidbury Green** Solhll
47 L7 **Tidcombe** Wilts

67 G6 **Tiddington** Oxon
82 F4 **Tiddington** Warwks
46 C4 **Tiddleywink** Wilts
38 F7 **Tidebrook** E Susx
6 C3 **Tideford** Cnwll
6 C3 **Tideford Cross** Cnwll
63 H7 **Tidenham** Gloucs
132 C4 **Tideswell** Derbys
48 F4 **Tidmarsh** W Berk
83 G7 **Tidmington** Warwks
33 J7 **Tidpit** Hants
54 E5 **Tiers Cross** Pembks
84 D5 **Tiffield** Nhants
234 E3 **Tigerton** Angus
282 b7 **Tigh a Ghearraidh** W Isls
282 b7 **Tigharry** W Isls
206 F4 **Tighnabruaich** Ag & B
7 L3 **Tigley** Devon
86 B2 **Tilbrook** Cambs
52 D4 **Tilbury** Thurr
88 E7 **Tilbury Green** Essex
88 F7 **Tilbury Juxta Clare** Essex
98 F6 **Tile Cross** Birm
99 H7 **Tile Hill** Covtry
98 F8 **Tilehouse Green** Solhll
49 G4 **Tilehurst** Readg
36 C2 **Tilford** Surrey
37 L4 **Tilgate** W Susx
37 L4 **Tilgate Forest Row** W Susx
31 J4 **Tilham Street** Somset
80 F8 **Tillers Green** Gloucs
221 G7 **Tillicoultry** Clacks
198 D4 **Tillietudlem** S Lans
72 E6 **Tillingham** Essex
80 B6 **Tillington** Herefs
36 E6 **Tillington** W Susx
80 B6 **Tillington Common** Herefs
244 F2 **Tillybirloch** Abers
244 A4 **Tillycairn** Abers
244 E1 **Tillyfourie** Abers
256 F7 **Tillygreig** Abers
221 K6 **Tillyrie** P & K
41 J5 **Tilmanstone** Kent
134 D3 **Tiln** Notts
120 C7 **Tilney All Saints** Norfk
120 C8 **Tilney High End** Norfk
120 C8 **Tilney St Lawrence** Norfk
33 H1 **Tilshead** Wilts
113 J4 **Tilstock** Shrops
113 G1 **Tilston** Ches
130 A7 **Tilstone Bank** Ches
130 A7 **Tilstone Fearnall** Ches
68 B2 **Tilsworth** Beds
101 G2 **Tilton on the Hill** Leics
64 B7 **Tiltups End** Gloucs
70 E2 **Tilty** Essex
136 B7 **Timberland** Lincs
131 H7 **Timbersbrook** Ches
29 G2 **Timberscombe** Somset
149 M5 **Timble** N York
29 H5 **Timewell** Devon
177 K4 **Timpanheck** D & G
130 F2 **Timperley** Traffd
45 K7 **Timsbury** BaNES
34 D6 **Timsbury** Hants
282 d3 **Timsgarry** W Isls
282 d3 **Timsgearraidh** W Isls
89 H2 **Timworth** Suffk
89 H2 **Timworth Green** Suffk
16 E4 **Tincleton** Dorset
178 E7 **Tindale** Cumb
169 G5 **Tindale Crescent** Dur
84 C8 **Tingewick** Bucks
141 L3 **Tingley** Leeds
68 C1 **Tingrith** Beds
12 A5 **Tinhay** Devon
34 E2 **Tinker's Hill** Hants
132 E6 **Tinkersley** Derbys
133 H2 **Tinsley** Sheff
37 L3 **Tinsley Green** W Susx
10 F5 **Tintagel** Cnwll
63 G7 **Tintern Parva** Mons
31 H7 **Tintinhull** Somset
140 F8 **Tintwistle** Derbys
176 D3 **Tinwald** D & G
101 M2 **Tinwell** Rutlnd
103 K4 **Tipp's End** Norfk
28 D2 **Tippacott** Devon
18 C4 **Tiptoe** Hants
97 L5 **Tipton** Sandw
98 B5 **Tipton Green** Sandw
14 C4 **Tipton St John** Devon
72 C4 **Tiptree** Essex
72 C4 **Tiptree Heath** Essex
129 G7 **Tir-y-fron** Flints

78 B7 **Tirabad** Powys
206 A6 **Tiretigan** Ag & B
64 B2 **Tirley** Gloucs
61 H6 **Tirphil** Caerph
166 C5 **Tirril** Cumb
32 F5 **Tisbury** Wilts
37 G4 **Tisman's Common** W Susx
115 K1 **Tissington** Derbys
26 D5 **Titchberry** Devon
19 J3 **Titchfield** Hants
19 J2 **Titchfield Common** Hants
102 A7 **Titchmarsh** Nhants
121 G3 **Titchwell** Norfk
117 J4 **Tithby** Notts
79 L3 **Titley** Herefs
69 G2 **Titmore Green** Herts
51 L7 **Titsey** Surrey
114 D4 **Tittensor** Staffs
121 K7 **Tittleshall** Norfk
81 J1 **Titton** Worcs
130 A7 **Tiverton** Ches
29 G8 **Tiverton** Devon
106 D6 **Tivetshall St Margaret** Norfk
106 D6 **Tivetshall St Mary** Norfk
29 G2 **Tivington** Somset
141 L6 **Tivy Dale** Barns
114 F7 **Tixall** Staffs
101 L3 **Tixover** Rutlnd
133 H8 **Toadhole** Derbys
116 B1 **Toadmoor** Derbys
226 F1 **Tobermory** Ag & B
215 L3 **Toberonochy** Ag & B
283 b10 **Tobha Mor** W Isls
256 C5 **Tocher** Abers
267 H6 **Tochieneal** Moray
46 F3 **Tockenham** Wilts
46 F3 **Tockenham Wick** Wilts
170 E7 **Tocketts** R & Cl
139 K3 **Tockholes** Bl w D
45 J2 **Tockington** S Glos
151 G5 **Tockwith** N York
32 D7 **Todber** Dorset
191 G2 **Todburn** Nthumb
68 C2 **Toddington** Beds
82 B8 **Toddington** Gloucs
69 G2 **Todds Green** Herts
82 F8 **Todenham** Gloucs
234 C7 **Todhills** Angus
177 L6 **Todhills** Cumb
169 G4 **Todhills** Dur
140 E3 **Todmorden** Calder
133 K3 **Todwick** Rothm
87 G4 **Toft** Cambs
130 E4 **Toft** Ches
118 E8 **Toft** Lincs
281 e4 **Toft** Shet
83 L1 **Toft** Warwks
168 F5 **Toft Hill** Dur
136 D7 **Toft Hill** Lincs
107 J4 **Toft Monks** Norfk
135 L2 **Toft next Newton** Lincs
121 K6 **Toftrees** Norfk
105 K1 **Toftwood** Norfk
191 K5 **Togston** Nthumb
247 J6 **Tokavaig** Highld
49 H3 **Tokers Green** Oxon
282 h2 **Tolastadh** W Isls
4 F3 **Toldish** Cnwll
142 E6 **Toll Bar** Donc
29 K4 **Tolland** Somset
32 F7 **Tollard Farnham** Dorset
32 F7 **Tollard Royal** Wilts
99 K8 **Tollbar End** Covtry
16 B3 **Toller Fratrum** Dorset
16 A3 **Toller Porcorum** Dorset
15 L2 **Toller Whelme** Dorset
151 H3 **Tollerton** N York
117 G4 **Tollerton** Notts
72 D5 **Tollesbury** Essex
72 D5 **Tolleshunt D'Arcy** Essex
72 D4 **Tolleshunt Knights** Essex
72 C5 **Tolleshunt Major** Essex
281 d9 **Tolob** Shet
16 F4 **Tolpuddle** Dorset
282 h2 **Tolsta** W Isls
3 H5 **Tolvan** Cnwll
2 D4 **Tolver** Cnwll
51 G5 **Tolworth** Gt Lon
252 E6 **Tomatin** Highld
239 M1 **Tomchrasky** Highld
239 K3 **Tomdoun** Highld
272 F7 **Tomich** Highld
250 B6 **Tomich** Highld
250 F2 **Tomich** Highld
263 J5 **Tomich** Highld

254 D7 **Tomintoul** Moray
83 K3 **Tomlow** Warwks
250 F3 **Tomnacross** Highld
254 D6 **Tomnavoulin** Moray
114 E1 **Tompkin** Staffs
62 C6 **Ton** Mons
62 D7 **Ton** Mons
43 H4 **Ton-teg** Rhondd
38 F4 **Tonbridge** Kent
42 D5 **Tondu** Brdgnd
29 L6 **Tonedale** Somset
141 K2 **Tong** Brad
40 C4 **Tong** Kent
97 H2 **Tong** Shrops
40 C4 **Tong Green** Kent
97 H2 **Tong Norton** Shrops
141 J2 **Tong Street** Brad
116 C7 **Tonge** Leics
36 C1 **Tongham** Surrey
175 H4 **Tongland** D & G
277 K5 **Tongue** Highld
118 F7 **Tongue End** Lincs
43 H5 **Tongwynlais** Cardif
57 L5 **Tonna** Neath
69 J4 **Tonwell** Herts
42 F3 **Tonypandy** Rhondd
42 F4 **Tonyrefail** Rhondd
66 E7 **Toot Baldon** Oxon
70 D6 **Toot Hill** Essex
34 E7 **Toot Hill** Hants
47 G2 **Toothill** Swindn
51 H5 **Tooting** Gt Lon
51 H4 **Tooting Bec** Gt Lon
85 L3 **Top End** Beds
140 C6 **Top of Hebers** Rochdl
128 F7 **Top-y-rhos** Flints
160 F7 **Topcliffe** N York
106 F5 **Topcroft** Norfk
106 F5 **Topcroft Street** Norfk
143 G4 **Topham** Donc
88 E7 **Toppesfield** Essex
139 L5 **Toppings** Bolton
106 D4 **Toprow** Norfk
13 M5 **Topsham** Devon
194 D5 **Torbeg** N Ayrs
273 H8 **Torboll** Highld
251 H3 **Torbreck** Highld
8 B2 **Torbryan** Devon
239 J7 **Torcastle** Highld
8 B6 **Torcross** Devon
251 G1 **Tore** Highld
5 J4 **Torfrey** Cnwll
206 C6 **Torinturk** Ag & B
135 G4 **Torksey** Lincs
45 M3 **Tormarton** S Glos
194 D4 **Tormore** N Ayrs
252 E2 **Tornagrain** Highld
244 D2 **Tornaveen** Abers
251 G6 **Torness** Highld
8 B1 **Tornewton** Devon
169 G4 **Toronto** Dur
227 L5 **Torosay Castle** Ag & B
165 G3 **Torpenhow** Cumb
210 C4 **Torphichen** W Loth
244 E3 **Torphins** Abers
6 E4 **Torpoint** Cnwll
8 D2 **Torquay** Torbay
200 F3 **Torquhan** Border
7 H4 **Torr** Devon
259 K6 **Torran** Highld
209 G4 **Torrance** E Duns
196 D2 **Torranyard** N Ayrs
29 J3 **Torre** Somset
260 E8 **Torridon** Highld
260 D8 **Torridon House** Highld
247 J4 **Torrin** Highld
194 B4 **Torrisdale** Ag & B
278 B4 **Torrisdale** Highld
274 C4 **Torrish** Highld
147 J3 **Torrisholme** Lancs
272 E7 **Torrobull** Highld
245 L3 **Torry** C Aber
210 D2 **Torryburn** Fife
9 h4 **Torteval** Guern
176 D3 **Torthorwald** D & G
21 G6 **Tortington** W Susx
81 J1 **Torton** Worcs
63 L8 **Tortworth** S Glos
259 H7 **Torvaig** Highld
156 C4 **Torver** Cumb
209 M2 **Torwood** Falk
201 G5 **Torwoodlee** Border
134 D2 **Torworth** Notts
247 L1 **Toscaig** Highld
86 E3 **Toseland** Cambs

360 Tosside - Trewavas

148 D4 Tosside N York
89 J3 Tostock Suffk
258 B6 Totaig Highld
259 G6 Tote Highld
259 J4 Tote Highld
36 C6 Tote Hill W Susx
137 H3 Tothill Lincs
18 E6 Totland IOW
132 F4 Totley Sheff
132 F4 Totley Brook Sheff
8 B3 Totnes Devon
116 E4 Toton Notts
224 F4 Totronald Ag & B
258 F3 Totscore Highld
51 J1 Tottenham Gt Lon
104 C1 Tottenhill Norfk
69 H8 Totteridge Gt Lon
68 C3 Totternhoe Beds
140 A5 Tottington Bury
139 L2 Tottleworth Lancs
34 D8 Totton Hants
49 L4 Touchen End W & M
151 G7 Toulston N York
30 B4 Toulton Somset
264 D4 Toulvaddie Highld
39 J3 Tovil Kent
168 E3 Tow Law Dur
10 B7 Towan Cnwll
5 G5 Towan Cnwll
207 J5 Toward Ag & B
207 J5 Toward Quay Ag & B
84 D5 Towcester Nhants
2 D3 Towednack Cnwll
67 H6 Towersey Oxon
244 A1 Towie Abers
103 J4 Town End Cambs
156 C4 Town End Cumb
156 E1 Town End Cumb
166 E5 Town End Cumb
156 E5 Town End Cumb
156 F6 Town End Cumb
138 E6 Town Green Lancs
107 G1 Town Green Norfk
156 F2 Town Head Cumb
148 E4 Town Head N York
149 L6 Town Head N York
169 K3 Town Kelloe Dur
139 K7 Town Lane Wigan
22 F4 Town Littleworth E Susx
139 J8 Town of Lowton Wigan
38 E7 Town Row E Susx
104 F6 Town Street Suffk
202 C7 Town Yetholm Border
208 C4 Townend W Duns
166 C1 Towngate Cumb
102 C1 Towngate Lincs
141 J7 Townhead Barns
164 E3 Townhead Cumb
166 E4 Townhead Cumb
176 D1 Townhead D & G
175 J2 Townhead of Greenlaw D & G
210 F1 Townhill Fife
12 A7 Townlake Devon
48 E7 Towns End Hants
30 E7 Townsend Somset
2 F4 Townshend Cnwll
45 K1 Townwell S Glos
152 D3 Towthorpe E R Yk
151 K4 Towthorpe York
151 G7 Towton N York
127 K4 Towyn Conwy
129 H2 Toxteth Lpool
38 D3 Toy's Hill Kent
137 G7 Toynton All Saints Lincs
137 G7 Toynton Fen Side Lincs
137 G7 Toynton St Peter Lincs
196 E6 Trabboch E Ayrs
196 F6 Trabbochburn E Ayrs
3 J6 Traboe Cnwll
29 K6 Tracebridge Somset
264 D8 Tradespark Highld
76 A5 Traethsaith Cerdgn
60 E1 Trallong Powys
211 L4 Tranent E Loth
129 H2 Tranmere Wirral
2 F4 Trannack Cnwll
278 F5 Trantelbeg Highld
278 F5 Trantlemore Highld
180 F2 Tranwell Nthumb
82 D1 Trap's Green Warwks
59 J5 Trapp Carmth
212 D4 Traprain E Loth
48 A6 Trapshill W Berk
200 D6 Traquair Border
49 G5 Trash Green W Berk
27 L5 Traveller's Rest Devon
148 F8 Trawden Lancs
77 J1 Trawscoed Cerdgn
110 D4 Trawsfynydd Gwynd
43 G7 Tre Aubrey V Glam
92 E5 Tre Taliesin Cerdgn
92 E5 Tre'r-ddol Cerdgn
63 G5 Tre-gagle Mons
60 F6 Tre-Gibbon Rhondd
76 D6 Tre-groes Cerdgn
128 D4 Tre-Mostyn Flints
58 D4 Tre-Vaughan Carmth
62 C3 Tre-wyn Mons
42 F3 Trealaw Rhondd
138 F1 Treales Lancs
4 C4 Treamble Cnwll
124 D3 Trearddur Bay IOA
258 F6 Treaslane Highld
10 C7 Treator Cnwll
42 F4 Trebanog Rhondd
57 K4 Trebanos Neath
11 K7 Trebartha Cnwll
3 H5 Trebarvah Cnwll
10 E5 Trebarwith Cnwll
11 J5 Trebeath Cnwll
2 B6 Trebehor Cnwll
4 D2 Trebelzue Cnwll
10 C7 Trebetherick Cnwll
29 H4 Treborough Somset
4 E3 Trebudannon Cnwll
11 L6 Trebullett Cnwll
10 E6 Treburgett Cnwll
10 B8 Treburick Cnwll
11 L7 Treburley Cnwll
10 B8 Treburrick Cnwll
5 J2 Trebyan Cnwll
60 C1 Trecastle Powys
11 K6 Trecogo Cnwll
12 F3 Trecott Devon
74 F5 Trecwn Pembks
60 F6 Trecynon Rhondd
11 J6 Tredaule Cnwll
2 C5 Tredavoe Cnwll
61 J5 Tredegar Blae G
10 F8 Tredethy Cnwll
64 C1 Tredington Gloucs
83 G6 Tredington Warwks
4 F1 Tredinnick Cnwll
5 H3 Tredinnick Cnwll
5 K2 Tredinnick Cnwll
5 M3 Tredinnick Cnwll
6 B3 Tredinnick Cnwll
61 H1 Tredomen Powys
75 J4 Tredrissi Pembks
10 D7 Tredrizzick Cnwll
62 D8 Tredunhock Mons
61 H1 Tredustan Powys
2 C3 Treen Cnwll
2 B6 Treen Cnwll
5 J4 Treesmill Cnwll
133 J2 Treeton Rothm
74 E4 Trefasser Pembks
125 G5 Trefdraeth IOA
61 J1 Trefecca Powys
93 L5 Trefeglwys Powys
77 H2 Trefenter Cerdgn
54 F2 Treffgarne Pembks
74 E7 Treffgarne Owen Pembks
43 G4 Trefforest Rhondd
74 D6 Treffynnon Pembks
61 H4 Trefil Blae G
77 G4 Trefilan Cerdgn
74 D5 Trefin Pembks
112 C6 Treflach Wood Shrops
112 C8 Trefnannau Powys
128 C5 Trefnant Denbgs
112 C6 Trefonen Shrops
108 F2 Trefor Gwynd
124 F4 Trefor IOA
10 F5 Treforda Cnwll
10 F5 Trefrew Cnwll
126 F7 Trefriw Conwy
11 K6 Tregadillett Cnwll
125 H4 Tregaian IOA
62 E5 Tregare Mons
3 K6 Tregarne Cnwll
77 J3 Tregaron Cerdgn
126 B6 Tregarth Gwynd
4 E2 Tregaswith Cnwll
10 F5 Tregatta Cnwll
5 G2 Tregawne Cnwll
4 E5 Tregear Cnwll
11 J5 Tregeare Cnwll
112 B5 Tregeiriog Wrexhm
124 F1 Tregele IOA
10 E7 Tregellist Cnwll
4 E6 Tregenna Cnwll
10 F7 Tregenna Cnwll
2 B5 Tregeseal Cnwll
3 K4 Tregew Cnwll
3 J6 Tregidden Cnwll
3 H6 Tregiddle Cnwll
4 F5 Tregidgeo Cnwll
5 G5 Tregiskey Cnwll
74 D6 Treglemais Pembks
11 H3 Tregole Cnwll
3 J4 Tregolls Cnwll
10 C7 Tregonce Cnwll
4 F2 Tregonetha Cnwll
4 F6 Tregony Cnwll
11 G6 Tregoodwell Cnwll
3 H6 Tregoose Cnwll
4 F3 Tregoss Cnwll
3 K6 Tregowris Cnwll
79 H7 Tregoyd Powys
5 H4 Tregrehan Mills Cnwll
5 H2 Tregullon Cnwll
10 D7 Tregunna Cnwll
11 J6 Tregunnon Cnwll
4 D2 Tregurrian Cnwll
5 G2 Tregustick Cnwll
94 D4 Tregynon Powys
43 G3 Trehafod Rhondd
6 D3 Trehan Cnwll
43 H2 Treharris Myr Td
10 E6 Treharrock Cnwll
10 B7 Trehemborne Cnwll
77 G6 Treherbert Carmth
42 E2 Treherbert Rhondd
4 C5 Treheveras Cnwll
6 C2 Trehunist Cnwll
11 L6 Trekelland Cnwll
11 L6 Trekenner Cnwll
10 E5 Treknow Cnwll
3 J7 Trelan Cnwll
11 H4 Trelash Cnwll
4 E4 Trelassick Cnwll
5 L4 Trelawne Cnwll
128 C4 Trelawnyd Flints
3 K6 Treleague Cnwll
3 K7 Treleaver Cnwll
58 A3 Trelech Carmth
58 B3 Trelech a'r Betws Carmth
74 B6 Treleddyd-fawr Pembks
3 K4 Trelew Cnwll
43 H2 Trelewis Myr Td
10 E5 Treligga Cnwll
10 D6 Trelights Cnwll
10 E7 Trelill Cnwll
11 K6 Trelinnoe Cnwll
4 F4 Trelion Cnwll
3 L3 Trelissick Cnwll
63 G6 Trelleck Mons
62 F6 Trelleck Grange Mons
128 D4 Trelogan Flints
4 E6 Trelonk Cnwll
4 F1 Trelow Cnwll
3 J6 Trelowarren Cnwll
6 B3 Trelowia Cnwll
3 M3 Treluggan Cnwll
95 G3 Trelystan Powys
109 K3 Tremadog Gwynd
11 H5 Tremail Cnwll
75 M3 Tremain Cerdgn
11 J5 Tremaine Cnwll
6 B1 Tremar Cnwll
6 D3 Trematon Cnwll
6 B2 Trembraze Cnwll
128 C5 Tremeirchion Denbgs
2 C5 Tremethick Cross Cnwll
11 K7 Tremollett Cnwll
5 G2 Tremore Cnwll
3 K6 Trenance Cnwll
4 D1 Trenance Cnwll
10 C8 Trenance Cnwll
3 H7 Trenance Cnwll
5 H5 Trenarren Cnwll
11 K6 Trenault Cnwll
96 F1 Trench Wrekin
49 G3 Trench Green Oxon
4 D3 Trencreek Cnwll
11 H3 Trencreek Cnwll
4 E4 Trendeal Cnwll
2 D3 Trendrine Cnwll
10 D8 Treneague Cnwll
3 H5 Trenear Cnwll
11 H5 Treneglos Cnwll
2 F4 Trenerth Cnwll
5 K4 Trenewan Cnwll
10 F6 Trenewth Cnwll
11 H4 Trengune Cnwll
4 D3 Treninnick Cnwll
4 C3 Trenowah Cnwll
3 J4 Trenoweth Cnwll
31 K7 Trent Dorset
135 G3 Trent Port Lincs
114 D3 Trent Vale C Stke
114 D3 Trentham C Stke
28 A1 Trentishoe Devon
116 E5 Trentlock Derbys
42 E6 Treoes V Glam
42 E2 Treorchy Rhondd
10 E7 Trequite Cnwll
42 F6 Trerhyngyll V Glam
6 C3 Trerulefoot Cnwll
3 J5 Tresahor Cnwll
4 E5 Tresawle Cnwll
97 J4 Trescott Staffs
2 F5 Trescowe Cnwll
4 C3 Tresean Cnwll
46 A1 Tresham Gloucs
4 E5 Tresillian Cnwll
10 F6 Tresinney Cnwll
11 H3 Treskinnick Cross Cnwll
5 K1 Treslea Cnwll
11 J5 Tresmeer Cnwll
11 G4 Tresparrett Cnwll
232 B3 Tressait P & K
281 d6 Tresta Shet
281 f3 Tresta Shet
134 F4 Treswell Notts
3 G3 Treswithian Cnwll
6 B2 Trethawle Cnwll
10 F5 Trethevey Cnwll
2 B6 Trethewey Cnwll
43 J4 Trethomas Caerph
4 F4 Trethosa Cnwll
5 H4 Trethurgy Cnwll
74 C6 Tretio Pembks
63 G2 Tretire Herefs
61 J3 Tretower Powys
128 F8 Treuddyn Flints
11 K6 Trevadlock Cnwll
11 J6 Trevague Cnwll
10 F4 Trevalga Cnwll
129 J8 Trevalyn Wrexhm
10 D7 Trevanger Cnwll
10 D7 Trevanson Cnwll
2 D5 Trevarrack Cnwll
4 E3 Trevarren Cnwll
4 D2 Trevarrian Cnwll
5 G6 Trevarrick Cnwll
3 J3 Trevarth Cnwll
55 L4 Trevaughan Carmth
2 D3 Treveal Cnwll
4 C3 Treveal Cnwll
4 E4 Treveale Cnwll
10 F6 Treveighan Cnwll
4 B4 Trevellas Downs Cnwll
5 L2 Trevelmond Cnwll
4 D3 Trevemper Cnwll
2 E4 Treveneague Cnwll
5 G6 Treveor Cnwll
4 E5 Treverbyn Cnwll
5 G3 Treverbyn Cnwll
3 J5 Treverva Cnwll
2 B6 Trevescan Cnwll
62 B6 Trevethin Torfn
10 F6 Trevia Cnwll
6 C1 Trevigro Cnwll
3 L3 Trevilla Cnwll
4 E1 Trevilledor Cnwll
4 D4 Trevilson Cnwll
4 F4 Treviscoe Cnwll
4 F6 Treviskey Cnwll
5 H5 Trevissick Cnwll
2 D5 Trevithal Cnwll
4 E2 Trevithick Cnwll
4 F6 Trevithick Cnwll
11 H5 Trevivian Cnwll
4 D3 Trevoll Cnwll
10 B7 Trevone Cnwll
112 C3 Trevor Denbgs
2 B6 Trevorgans Cnwll
10 B8 Trevorrick Cnwll
10 C7 Trevorrick Cnwll
10 B7 Trevose Cnwll
3 G5 Trew Cnwll
10 F6 Trewalder Cnwll
61 J1 Trewalkin Powys
11 L6 Trewarlett Cnwll
10 F5 Trewarmett Cnwll
4 E6 Trewarthenick Cnwll
11 G5 Trewassa Cnwll
2 F5 Trewavas Cnwll

11 J6 **Treween** Cnwll
2 B4 **Trewellard** Cnwll
11 J6 **Trewen** Cnwll
10 E7 **Trewen** Cnwll
3 H5 **Trewennack** Cnwll
55 G7 **Trewent** Pembks
95 G1 **Trewern** Powys
10 E6 **Trewetha** Cnwll
10 E7 **Trewethern** Cnwll
6 B3 **Trewidland** Cnwll
3 K7 **Trewillis** Cnwll
3 L4 **Trewince** Cnwll
11 G8 **Trewint** Cnwll
11 J6 **Trewint** Cnwll
6 B2 **Trewint** Cnwll
4 E6 **Trewirgie** Cnwll
3 M4 **Trewithian** Cnwll
11 L8 **Trewoodloe** Cnwll
2 C6 **Trewoofe** Cnwll
3 H7 **Trewoon** Cnwll
5 G4 **Trewoon** Cnwll
4 D5 **Treworgan** Cnwll
4 E7 **Treworlas** Cnwll
11 G4 **Treworld** Cnwll
3 M3 **Treworthal** Cnwll
10 B7 **Treyarnon** Cnwll
20 D3 **Treyford** W Susx
141 G3 **Triangle** Calder
17 L2 **Trickett's Cross** Dorset
178 E5 **Triermain** Cumb
75 G7 **Triffleton** Pembks
11 K4 **Trillacott** Cnwll
169 K4 **Trimdon** Dur
169 K4 **Trimdon Colliery** Dur
169 K3 **Trimdon Grange** Dur
122 F4 **Trimingham** Norfk
91 G7 **Trimley** Suffk
91 G7 **Trimley Lower Street** Suffk
97 H7 **Trimpley** Worcs
70 C4 **Trims Green** Herts
56 E4 **Trimsaran** Carmth
27 J2 **Trimstone** Devon
231 K3 **Trinafour** P & K
61 K7 **Trinant** Caerph
68 A5 **Tring** Herts
68 A4 **Tring Wharf** Herts
67 M4 **Tringford** Herts
234 F3 **Trinity** Angus
9 d2 **Trinity** Jersey
221 G3 **Trinity Gask** P & K
29 G3 **Triscombe** Somset
29 L4 **Triscombe** Somset
239 H8 **Trislaig** Highld
4 D5 **Trispen** Cnwll
191 J7 **Tritlington** Nthumb
4 E3 **Troan** Cnwll
232 E7 **Trochry** P & K
61 H6 **Troedrhiwfuwch** Caerph
76 B6 **Troedyraur** Cerdgn
61 G6 **Troedyrhiw** Myr Td
127 G5 **Trofarth** Conwy
9 c2 **Trois Bois** Jersey
3 G3 **Troon** Cnwll
196 C5 **Troon** S Ayrs
89 H1 **Troston** Suffk
11 J4 **Troswell** Cnwll
81 K4 **Trotshill** Worcs
52 D7 **Trottiscliffe** Kent
36 B6 **Trotton** W Susx
140 D3 **Trough Gate** Lancs
190 B7 **Troughend** Nthumb
165 L5 **Troutbeck** Cumb
156 F2 **Troutbeck** Cumb
156 F3 **Troutbeck Bridge** Cumb
133 H4 **Troway** Derbys
46 B7 **Trowbridge** Wilts
116 E3 **Trowell** Notts
46 B7 **Trowle Common** Wilts
106 E2 **Trowse Newton** Norfk
150 C8 **Troy** Leeds
32 C2 **Trudoxhill** Somset
30 B6 **Trull** Somset
142 F5 **Trumfleet** Donc
258 C4 **Trumpan** Highld
80 F7 **Trumpet** Herefs
87 J4 **Trumpington** Cambs
50 C5 **Trumpsgreen** Surrey
122 F4 **Trunch** Norfk
147 G7 **Trunnah** Lancs
4 D6 **Truro** Cnwll
11 K5 **Truscott** Cnwll
13 K6 **Trusham** Devon
115 L4 **Trusley** Derbys
137 K3 **Trusthorpe** Lincs
97 J4 **Trysull** Staffs

66 B7 **Tubney** Oxon
8 B4 **Tuckenhay** Devon
97 H5 **Tuckhill** Shrops
3 G3 **Tuckingmill** Cnwll
32 F5 **Tuckingmill** Wilts
18 A5 **Tuckton** Bmouth
4 F5 **Tucoyse** Cnwll
88 E1 **Tuddenham** Suffk
90 E5 **Tuddenham** Suffk
38 F4 **Tudeley** Kent
169 H3 **Tudhoe** Dur
63 H3 **Tudorville** Herefs
108 D4 **Tudweiliog** Gwynd
36 E3 **Tuesley** Surrey
64 B4 **Tuffley** Gloucs
34 F2 **Tufton** Hants
75 H6 **Tufton** Pembks
101 G3 **Tugby** Leics
96 D6 **Tugford** Shrops
203 K7 **Tughall** Nthumb
220 E8 **Tullibody** Clacks
251 H6 **Tullich** Highld
264 D4 **Tullich** Highld
232 F5 **Tulliemet** P & K
256 E5 **Tulloch** Abers
219 H3 **Tulloch** Stirlg
240 B7 **Tulloch Station** Highld
216 F8 **Tullochgorm** Ag & B
232 F8 **Tullybeagles Lodge** P & K
255 L7 **Tullynessle** Abers
51 J4 **Tulse Hill** Gt Lon
58 F6 **Tumble** Carmth
71 K2 **Tumbler's Green** Essex
136 D7 **Tumby** Lincs
136 E8 **Tumby Woodside** Lincs
231 L4 **Tummel Bridge** P & K
38 F5 **Tunbridge Wells** Kent
177 G3 **Tundergarth** D & G
122 F5 **Tungate** Norfk
45 K7 **Tunley** BaNES
114 D1 **Tunstall** C Stke
145 J2 **Tunstall** E R Yk
40 A3 **Tunstall** Kent
157 K8 **Tunstall** Lancs
160 B3 **Tunstall** N York
107 J2 **Tunstall** Norfk
114 B6 **Tunstall** Staffs
91 H4 **Tunstall** Suffk
181 J8 **Tunstall** Sundld
132 B5 **Tunstead** Derbys
122 F7 **Tunstead** Norfk
131 K4 **Tunstead Milton** Derbys
35 K1 **Tunworth** Hants
80 C7 **Tupsley** Herefs
100 F4 **Tur Langton** Leics
49 G7 **Turgis Green** Hants
65 G4 **Turkdean** Gloucs
46 A6 **Turleigh** Wilts
97 H6 **Turleygreen** Shrops
140 B4 **Turn** Lancs
79 L7 **Turnastone** Herefs
182 F2 **Turnberry** S Ayrs
6 F4 **Turnchapel** C Plym
116 A2 **Turnditch** Derbys
139 J2 **Turner Green** Lancs
23 L3 **Turner's Green** E Susx
82 E2 **Turner's Green** Warwks
38 A6 **Turner's Hill** W Susx
16 F4 **Turners Puddle** Dorset
69 K6 **Turnford** Herts
211 G4 **Turnhouse** C Edin
16 F1 **Turnworth** Dorset
268 C6 **Turriff** Abers
139 L4 **Turton Bottoms** Bl w D
103 G4 **Turves** Cambs
85 J5 **Turvey** Beds
49 J1 **Turville** Bucks
49 H1 **Turville Heath** Bucks
84 B7 **Turweston** Bucks
187 L3 **Tushielaw Inn** Border
113 H2 **Tushingham cum Grindley** Ches
115 L6 **Tutbury** Staffs
82 A1 **Tutnall** Worcs
63 G8 **Tutshill** Gloucs
122 E6 **Tuttington** Norfk
11 M7 **Tutwell** Cnwll
134 E5 **Tuxford** Notts
275 b3 **Twatt** Ork
281 d6 **Twatt** Shet
209 J4 **Twechar** E Duns
202 F3 **Tweedmouth** Nthumb
187 G1 **Tweedsmuir** Border
24 C3 **Twelve Oaks** E Susx
4 B6 **Twelveheads** Cnwll

130 F6 **Twemlow Green** Ches
118 F7 **Twenty** Lincs
45 L6 **Twerton** BaNES
50 F4 **Twickenham** Gt Lon
64 B3 **Twigworth** Gloucs
22 C3 **Twineham** W Susx
22 C3 **Twineham Green** W Susx
45 L7 **Twinhoe** BaNES
89 H7 **Twinstead** Essex
28 D5 **Twitchen** Devon
95 J7 **Twitchen** Shrops
41 H4 **Twitham** Kent
12 E7 **Two Bridges** Devon
132 E7 **Two Dales** Derbys
99 G3 **Two Gates** Staffs
8 C1 **Two Mile Oak Cross** Devon
27 J2 **Two Pots** Devon
68 D6 **Two Waters** Herts
99 J2 **Twycross** Leics
67 G2 **Twyford** Bucks
35 G6 **Twyford** Hants
100 F2 **Twyford** Leics
118 B6 **Twyford** Lincs
121 M6 **Twyford** Norfk
49 J4 **Twyford** Wokham
80 C8 **Twyford Common** Herefs
61 H5 **Twyn-carno** Caerph
62 E6 **Twyn-y-Sheriff** Mons
43 H7 **Twyn-yr-Odyn** V Glam
175 G4 **Twynholm** D & G
81 K8 **Twyning** Gloucs
81 L7 **Twyning Green** Gloucs
59 L4 **Twynllanan** Carmth
101 L7 **Twywell** Nhants
112 C3 **Ty'n-dwr** Denbgs
42 F4 **Ty'n-y-bryn** Rhondd
43 K4 **Ty'n-y-coedcae** Caerph
126 F5 **Ty'n-y-Groes** Conwy
111 J3 **Ty-nant** Conwy
111 H6 **Ty-nant** Gwynd
79 M7 **Tyberton** Herefs
98 E5 **Tyburn** Birm
57 H3 **Tycroes** Carmth
111 L7 **Tycrwyn** Powys
120 A7 **Tydd Gote** Lincs
119 M8 **Tydd St Giles** Cambs
119 M7 **Tydd St Mary** Lincs
20 B6 **Tye** Hants
70 D2 **Tye Green** Essex
88 B8 **Tye Green** Essex
71 J3 **Tye Green** Essex
141 J1 **Tyersal** Brad
139 K7 **Tyldesley** Wigan
40 F3 **Tyler Hill** Kent
70 D6 **Tyler's Green** Essex
67 L8 **Tylers Green** Bucks
51 K8 **Tylers Green** Surrey
42 F3 **Tylorstown** Rhondd
93 L7 **Tylwch** Powys
43 G4 **Tyn-y-nant** Rhondd
218 E1 **Tyndrum** Stirlg
181 J5 **Tynemouth** N Tyne
60 E7 **Tynewydd** Rhondd
212 D3 **Tyninghame** E Loth
185 K4 **Tynron** D & G
125 J3 **Tynygongl** IOA
77 J1 **Tynygraig** Cerdgn
85 G6 **Tyringham** M Keyn
98 E6 **Tyseley** Birm
42 C6 **Tythegston** Brdgnd
131 H4 **Tytherington** Ches
45 K1 **Tytherington** S Glos
32 C2 **Tytherington** Somset
32 F3 **Tytherington** Wilts
15 H2 **Tytherleigh** Devon
46 D4 **Tytherton Lucas** Wilts
68 F6 **Tyttenhanger** Herts
5 J4 **Tywardreath** Cnwll
5 J4 **Tywardreath Highway** Cnwll
126 F4 **Tywyn** Conwy
92 C3 **Tywyn** Gwynd

U

91 H1 **Ubbeston Green** Suffk
45 G7 **Ubley** BaNES
160 C2 **Uckerby** N York
23 H3 **Uckfield** E Susx
81 K7 **Uckinghall** Worcs
64 C2 **Uckington** Gloucs
96 D2 **Uckington** Shrops
209 J6 **Uddingston** S Lans
198 E6 **Uddington** S Lans
24 F3 **Udimore** E Susx

256 F6 **Udny Green** Abers
257 G6 **Udny Station** Abers
47 H3 **Uffcott** Wilts
29 K8 **Uffculme** Devon
102 B2 **Uffington** Lincs
47 L1 **Uffington** Oxon
96 C1 **Uffington** Shrops
102 B3 **Ufford** C Pete
91 G5 **Ufford** Suffk
83 J3 **Ufton** Warwks
48 F5 **Ufton Nervet** W Berk
194 B5 **Ugadale** Ag & B
7 K4 **Ugborough** Devon
107 J7 **Uggeshall** Suffk
162 F1 **Ugglebarnby** N York
132 E2 **Ughill** Sheff
70 D2 **Ugley** Essex
70 D2 **Ugley Green** Essex
171 J8 **Ugthorpe** N York
224 F4 **Uig** Ag & B
258 B6 **Uig** Highld
258 F4 **Uig** Highld
282 d3 **Uig** W Isls
259 G7 **Uigshader** Highld
226 D8 **Uisken** Ag & B
280 D7 **Ulbster** Highld
165 L6 **Ulcat Row** Cumb
137 H5 **Ulceby** Lincs
144 E5 **Ulceby** N Linc
137 H5 **Ulceby Cross** Lincs
144 E5 **Ulceby Skitter** N Linc
39 L4 **Ulcombe** Kent
165 H3 **Uldale** Cumb
63 M7 **Uley** Gloucs
191 J7 **Ulgham** Nthumb
261 J1 **Ullapool** Highld
82 D2 **Ullenhall** Warwks
64 D4 **Ullenwood** Gloucs
151 H7 **Ulleskelf** N York
100 B6 **Ullesthorpe** Leics
133 J2 **Ulley** Rothm
80 E5 **Ullingswick** Herefs
246 D1 **Ullinish Lodge Hotel** Highld
164 E6 **Ullock** Cumb
156 B4 **Ulpha** Cumb
157 G6 **Ulpha** Cumb
153 J4 **Ulrome** E R Yk
281 e4 **Ulsta** Shet
71 K5 **Ulting Wick** Essex
98 E7 **Ulverley Green** Solhll
156 C7 **Ulverston** Cumb
17 K6 **Ulwell** Dorset
259 K6 **Umachan** Highld
27 L6 **Umberleigh** Devon
271 H2 **Unapool** Highld
178 B2 **Under Burnmouth** Border
38 E3 **Under River** Kent
157 G4 **Underbarrow** Cumb
141 J1 **Undercliffe** Brad
96 B1 **Underdale** Shrops
157 K6 **Underley Hall** Cumb
39 J4 **Underling Green** Kent
116 D2 **Underwood** Notts
104 D7 **Undley** Suffk
44 E2 **Undy** Mons
154 e6 **Union Mills** IOM
39 H7 **Union Street** E Susx
133 G4 **Unstone** Derbys
133 G4 **Unstone Green** Derbys
140 B6 **Unsworth** Bury
165 L1 **Unthank** Cumb
166 B3 **Unthank** Cumb
166 E3 **Unthank** Cumb
132 F4 **Unthank** Derbys
202 F3 **Unthank** Nthumb
166 B4 **Unthank End** Cumb
16 C2 **Up Cerne** Dorset
13 L2 **Up Exe** Devon
139 G6 **Up Holland** Lancs
20 C4 **Up Marden** W Susx
31 J7 **Up Mudford** Somset
49 G8 **Up Nately** Hants
34 E4 **Up Somborne** Hants
16 B2 **Up Sydling** Dorset
47 H7 **Upavon** Wilts
53 H5 **Upchurch** Kent
27 K3 **Upcott** Devon
28 D5 **Upcott** Devon
79 K5 **Upcott** Herefs
28 F6 **Upcott** Somset
50 B6 **Updown Hill** Surrey
88 D3 **Upend** Cambs
122 C7 **Upgate** Norfk
106 B5 **Upgate Street** Norfk
106 F5 **Upgate Street** Norfk

16 A2 **Uphall** Dorset
210 E4 **Uphall** W Loth
13 K1 **Upham** Devon
35 H6 **Upham** Hants
79 M3 **Uphampton** Herefs
81 J2 **Uphampton** Worcs
44 C7 **Uphill** N Som
208 D8 **Uplawmoor** E Rens
63 L2 **Upleadon** Gloucs
170 E6 **Upleatham** R & Cl
40 C2 **Uplees** Kent
15 L4 **Uploders** Dorset
29 J7 **Uplowman** Devon
15 H4 **Uplyme** Devon
52 C2 **Upminster** Gt Lon
14 E1 **Upottery** Devon
12 B6 **Uppaton** Devon
86 C8 **Upper & Lower Stondon** Beds
95 K6 **Upper Affcot** Shrops
263 G2 **Upper Ardchronie** Highld
97 H7 **Upper Arley** Worcs
66 F4 **Upper Arncott** Oxon
83 L7 **Upper Astrop** Nhants
48 F4 **Upper Basildon** W Berk
141 K3 **Upper Batley** Kirk
22 B5 **Upper Beeding** W Susx
101 L5 **Upper Benefield** Nhants
82 B2 **Upper Bentley** Worcs
278 F5 **Upper Bighouse** Highld
133 J8 **Upper Birchwood** Derbys
43 H4 **Upper Boat** Rhondd
83 L5 **Upper Boddington** Nhants
92 D5 **Upper Borth** Cerdgn
83 G7 **Upper Brailes** Warwks
247 L4 **Upper Breakish** Highld
80 B7 **Upper Breinton** Herefs
81 J4 **Upper Broadheath** Worcs
117 J6 **Upper Broughton** Notts
48 D5 **Upper Bucklebury** W Berk
33 K7 **Upper Burgate** Hants
52 E5 **Upper Bush** Medway
86 D6 **Upper Caldecote** Beds
44 D7 **Upper Canada** N Som
18 D1 **Upper Canterton** Hants
83 M3 **Upper Catesby** Nhants
98 B8 **Upper Catshill** Worcs
78 D7 **Upper Chapel** Powys
30 C5 **Upper Cheddon** Somset
33 G5 **Upper Chicksgrove** Wilts
47 L8 **Upper Chute** Wilts
51 K2 **Upper Clapton** Gt Lon
34 D2 **Upper Clatford** Hants
109 H2 **Upper Clynnog** Gwynd
64 E4 **Upper Coberley** Gloucs
21 K6 **Upper Cokeham** W Susx
115 G2 **Upper Cotton** Staffs
96 C2 **Upper Cound** Shrops
142 B5 **Upper Cudworth** Barns
141 K6 **Upper Cumberworth** Kirk
59 L6 **Upper Cwmtwrch** Powys
267 G4 **Upper Dallachy** Moray
41 K5 **Upper Deal** Kent
85 L2 **Upper Dean** Beds
141 K6 **Upper Denby** Kirk
178 E5 **Upper Denton** Cumb
23 J5 **Upper Dicker** E Susx
95 L6 **Upper Dinchope** Shrops
279 H3 **Upper Dounreay** Highld
73 K1 **Upper Dovercourt** Essex
219 L6 **Upper Drumbane** Stirlg
150 F3 **Upper Dunsforth** N York
36 E2 **Upper Eashing** Surrey
263 K7 **Upper Eathie** Highld
80 E6 **Upper Egleton** Herefs
131 L7 **Upper Elkstone** Staffs
115 J3 **Upper Ellastone** Staffs
132 B4 **Upper End** Derbys
34 E1 **Upper Enham** Hants
97 H5 **Upper Farmcote** Shrops
35 L4 **Upper Farringdon** Hants
63 L5 **Upper Framilode** Gloucs
35 M2 **Upper Froyle** Hants
31 H2 **Upper Godney** Somset
86 C8 **Upper Gravenhurst** Beds
88 B8 **Upper Green** Essex
62 D3 **Upper Green** Mons
88 E2 **Upper Green** Suffk
48 A6 **Upper Green** W Berk
63 H2 **Upper Grove Common** Herefs
132 F7 **Upper Hackney** Derbys
36 B1 **Upper Hale** Surrey
50 E5 **Upper Halliford** Surrey
52 E6 **Upper Halling** Medway
101 K2 **Upper Hambleton** Rutlnd
40 F4 **Upper Harbledown** Kent

40 F5 **Upper Hardres Court** Kent
79 M4 **Upper Hardwick** Herefs
38 C6 **Upper Hartfield** E Susx
116 C2 **Upper Hartshay** Derbys
64 D3 **Upper Hatherley** Gloucs
114 C4 **Upper Hatton** Staffs
142 C8 **Upper Haugh** Rothm
96 C7 **Upper Hayton** Shrops
141 J4 **Upper Heaton** Kirk
151 L4 **Upper Helmsley** N York
79 J4 **Upper Hergest** Herefs
84 C3 **Upper Heyford** Nhants
66 D2 **Upper Heyford** Oxon
80 B4 **Upper Hill** Herefs
52 B5 **Upper Hockenden** Kent
141 K4 **Upper Hopton** Kirk
81 H5 **Upper Howsell** Worcs
131 K7 **Upper Hulme** Staffs
36 F4 **Upper Ifold** Surrey
65 J7 **Upper Inglesham** Swindn
46 A1 **Upper Kilcott** Gloucs
57 G6 **Upper Killay** Swans
217 J2 **Upper Kinchrackine** Ag & B
47 L3 **Upper Lambourn** W Berk
98 C2 **Upper Landywood** Staffs
44 F7 **Upper Langford** N Som
133 K6 **Upper Langwith** Derbys
223 G6 **Upper Largo** Fife
115 G4 **Upper Leigh** Staffs
63 L4 **Upper Ley** Gloucs
45 H6 **Upper Littleton** N Som
115 H8 **Upper Longdon** Staffs
97 H4 **Upper Ludstone** Shrops
275 H1 **Upper Lybster** Highld
63 J4 **Upper Lydbrook** Gloucs
80 C6 **Upper Lyde** Herefs
79 M2 **Upper Lye** Herefs
79 L8 **Upper Maes-coed** Herefs
141 K7 **Upper Midhope** Sheff
81 J1 **Upper Milton** Worcs
46 E1 **Upper Minety** Wilts
82 A5 **Upper Moor** Worcs
141 K2 **Upper Moor Side** Leeds
267 G6 **Upper Mulben** Moray
96 E5 **Upper Netchwood** Shrops
115 G4 **Upper Nobut** Staffs
20 F3 **Upper Norwood** W Susx
132 E4 **Upper Padley** Derbys
18 D4 **Upper Pennington** Hants
67 H4 **Upper Pollicott** Bucks
151 J5 **Upper Poppleton** York
82 E6 **Upper Quinton** Warwks
34 D6 **Upper Ratley** Hants
80 E2 **Upper Rochford** Worcs
174 E3 **Upper Ruscoe** D & G
80 F3 **Upper Sapey** Herefs
46 D3 **Upper Seagry** Wilts
85 K6 **Upper Shelton** Beds
122 C3 **Upper Sheringham** Norfk
83 L3 **Upper Shuckburgh** Warwks
207 K5 **Upper Skelmorlie** N Ayrs
65 H3 **Upper Slaughter** Gloucs
63 K5 **Upper Soudley** Gloucs
79 K4 **Upper Spond** Herefs
41 H7 **Upper Standen** Kent
86 C3 **Upper Staploe** Beds
185 L6 **Upper Stepford** D & G
106 E3 **Upper Stoke** Norfk
84 C4 **Upper Stowe** Nhants
33 K7 **Upper Street** Hants
123 G7 **Upper Street** Norfk
123 G8 **Upper Street** Norfk
106 D7 **Upper Street** Norfk
88 F5 **Upper Street** Suffk
90 C5 **Upper Street** Suffk
90 D8 **Upper Street** Suffk
81 K7 **Upper Strensham** Worcs
68 D2 **Upper Sundon** Beds
65 H2 **Upper Swell** Gloucs
142 A7 **Upper Tankersley** Barns
106 E4 **Upper Tasburgh** Norfk
115 G4 **Upper Tean** Staffs
113 G3 **Upper Threapwood** Ches
115 L1 **Upper Town** Derbys
132 E7 **Upper Town** Derbys
168 D3 **Upper Town** Dur
80 D5 **Upper Town** Herefs
45 G6 **Upper Town** N Som
89 J2 **Upper Town** Suffk
59 G6 **Upper Tumble** Carmth
83 H6 **Upper Tysoe** Warwks
91 G4 **Upper Ufford** Suffk
47 J3 **Upper Upham** Wilts
53 G5 **Upper Upnor** Medway
234 E8 **Upper Victoria** Angus

32 B1 **Upper Vobster** Somset
83 L6 **Upper Wardington** Oxon
84 F7 **Upper Weald** M Keyn
84 B3 **Upper Weedon** Nhants
23 G4 **Upper Wellingham** E Susx
45 L5 **Upper Weston** BaNES
106 E7 **Upper Weybread** Suffk
81 J5 **Upper Wick** Worcs
35 K3 **Upper Wield** Hants
67 H4 **Upper Winchendon** Bucks
33 K3 **Upper Woodford** Wilts
48 E7 **Upper Wootton** Hants
46 A4 **Upper Wraxall** Wilts
81 H6 **Upper Wyche** Worcs
177 L8 **Upperby** Cumb
258 E6 **Upperglen** Highld
140 F6 **Uppermill** Oldham
141 H6 **Upperthong** Kirk
133 J4 **Upperthorpe** Derbys
143 J7 **Upperthorpe** N Linc
36 E6 **Upperton** W Susx
132 F6 **Uppertown** Derbys
280 D1 **Uppertown** Highld
64 F7 **Upperup** Gloucs
132 F8 **Upperwood** Derbys
13 L1 **Uppincott** Devon
101 J3 **Uppingham** Rutlnd
96 D2 **Uppington** Shrops
161 G5 **Upsall** N York
202 D4 **Upsettlington** Border
69 L7 **Upshire** Essex
41 H3 **Upstreet** Kent
89 K1 **Upthorpe** Suffk
67 J5 **Upton** Bucks
102 C3 **Upton** C Pete
102 D7 **Upton** Cambs
129 J6 **Upton** Ches
11 H2 **Upton** Cnwll
11 K8 **Upton** Cnwll
165 K3 **Upton** Cumb
14 C2 **Upton** Devon
7 K6 **Upton** Devon
16 E6 **Upton** Dorset
17 J4 **Upton** Dorset
153 J5 **Upton** E R Yk
129 L2 **Upton** Halton
47 M7 **Upton** Hants
34 E7 **Upton** Hants
99 K3 **Upton** Leics
135 H2 **Upton** Lincs
84 D3 **Upton** Nhants
107 H1 **Upton** Norfk
117 J1 **Upton** Notts
134 E4 **Upton** Notts
65 K4 **Upton** Oxon
48 D2 **Upton** Oxon
55 G6 **Upton** Pembks
50 B3 **Upton** Slough
29 H5 **Upton** Somset
31 G5 **Upton** Somset
142 D5 **Upton** Wakefd
82 D4 **Upton** Warwks
32 E4 **Upton** Wilts
129 G2 **Upton** Wirral
63 K2 **Upton Bishop** Herefs
45 K5 **Upton Cheyney** S Glos
96 E5 **Upton Cressett** Shrops
63 J2 **Upton Crews** Herefs
11 K8 **Upton Cross** Cnwll
86 C8 **Upton End** Beds
35 L1 **Upton Grey** Hants
129 K5 **Upton Heath** Ches
13 K2 **Upton Hellions** Devon
32 F3 **Upton Lovell** Wilts
96 C1 **Upton Magna** Shrops
32 B3 **Upton Noble** Somset
13 L3 **Upton Pyne** Devon
32 E1 **Upton Scudamore** Wilts
81 L4 **Upton Snodsbury** Worcs
64 B4 **Upton St Leonards** Gloucs
2 F3 **Upton Towans** Cnwll
81 K7 **Upton upon Severn** Worcs
81 L2 **Upton Warren** Worcs
20 F4 **Upwaltham** W Susx
87 L1 **Upware** Cambs
103 K3 **Upwell** Norfk
16 C5 **Upwey** Dorset
70 C2 **Upwick Green** Herts
102 E6 **Upwood** Cambs
46 F7 **Urchfont** Wilts
80 C5 **Urdimarsh** Herefs
150 D1 **Ure Bank** N York
169 L7 **Urlay Nook** S on T
130 E1 **Urmston** Traffd

266 F4 **Urquhart** Moray
161 J2 **Urra** N York
250 E1 **Urray** Highld
235 H4 **Usan** Angus
169 G2 **Ushaw Moor** Dur
62 D7 **Usk** Mons
136 A1 **Usselby** Lincs
181 H7 **Usworth** Sundld
130 A6 **Utkinton** Ches
149 J7 **Utley** Brad
13 J3 **Uton** Devon
136 F1 **Utterby** Lincs
115 H5 **Uttoxeter** Staffs
108 B6 **Uwchmynydd** Gwynd
50 D2 **Uxbridge** Gt Lon
281 f2 **Uyeasound** Shet
54 F4 **Uzmaston** Pembks

V

9 k2 **Vale** Guern
124 E4 **Valley** IOA
50 B6 **Valley End** Surrey
10 F6 **Valley Truckle** Cnwll
259 J4 **Valtos** Highld
282 e3 **Valtos** W Isls
43 J4 **Van** Caerph
52 F2 **Vange** Essex
61 L6 **Varteg** Torfn
281 e3 **Vatsetter** Shet
258 D7 **Vatten** Highld
61 G5 **Vaynor** Myr Td
9 i2 **Vazon Bay** Guern
79 H7 **Velindre** Powys
29 K3 **Vellow** Somset
26 E6 **Velly** Devon
11 K1 **Venn** Cnwll
8 C5 **Venn** Devon
14 C4 **Venn Ottery** Devon
26 F8 **Venngreen** Devon
95 H2 **Vennington** Shrops
13 J3 **Venny Tedburn** Devon
11 L7 **Venterdon** Cnwll
19 J8 **Ventnor** IOW
7 H3 **Venton** Devon
47 M7 **Vernham Dean** Hants
47 M7 **Vernham Street** Hants
95 L7 **Vernolds Common** Shrops
17 L1 **Verwood** Dorset
4 E7 **Veryan** Cnwll
4 F6 **Veryan Green** Cnwll
146 C2 **Vickerstown** Cumb
141 J6 **Victoria** Barns
61 J5 **Victoria** Blae G
5 G3 **Victoria** Cnwll
281 e5 **Vidlin** Shet
266 F3 **Viewfield** Moray
209 J6 **Viewpark** N Lans
52 D6 **Vigo** Kent
9 a1 **Ville la Bas** Jersey
9 i3 **Villiaze** Guern
24 D3 **Vinehall Street** E Susx
23 K4 **Vines Cross** E Susx
50 C5 **Virginia Water** Surrey
11 M4 **Virginstow** Devon
72 D4 **Virley** Essex
32 B1 **Vobster** Somset
281 d5 **Voe** Shet
79 L7 **Vowchurch** Herefs
130 B1 **Vulcan Village** St Hel

W

168 F6 **Wackerfield** Dur
106 D5 **Wacton** Norfk
81 K5 **Wadborough** Worcs
67 H4 **Waddesdon** Bucks
8 C3 **Waddeton** Devon
138 E7 **Waddicar** Sefton
144 B8 **Waddingham** Lincs
148 C7 **Waddington** Lancs
135 K6 **Waddington** Lincs
13 K6 **Waddon** Devon
16 B5 **Waddon** Dorset
10 D8 **Wadebridge** Cnwll
30 D8 **Wadeford** Somset
101 M6 **Wadenhoe** Nhants
69 K4 **Wadesmill** Herts
39 G7 **Wadhurst** E Susx
132 F5 **Wadshelf** Derbys
46 B5 **Wadswick** Wilts
142 F8 **Wadworth** Donc
127 K7 **Waen** Denbgs

128 D6 **Waen** Denbgs
112 C7 **Waen** Powys
112 B8 **Waen Fach** Powys
125 K6 **Waen-pentir** Gwynd
125 K6 **Waen-wen** Gwynd
95 J3 **Wagbeach** Shrops
44 E5 **Wain's Hill** N Som
62 B6 **Wainfelin** Torfn
137 J7 **Wainfleet All Saints** Lincs
137 J7 **Wainfleet Bank** Lincs
107 G5 **Wainford** Norfk
11 H3 **Wainhouse Corner** Cnwll
52 F5 **Wainscott** Medway
141 G2 **Wainstalls** Calder
158 C1 **Waitby** Cumb
145 H7 **Waithe** Lincs
98 E6 **Wake Green** Birm
142 A4 **Wakefield** Wakefd
101 L3 **Wakerley** Nhants
72 C2 **Wakes Colne** Essex
128 E4 **Wal-wen** Flints
107 K8 **Walberswick** Suffk
21 G5 **Walberton** W Susx
180 E5 **Walbottle** N u Ty
175 J1 **Walbutt** D & G
178 B6 **Walby** Cumb
31 J2 **Walcombe** Somset
118 E4 **Walcot** Lincs
143 M3 **Walcot** N Linc
96 D1 **Walcot** Shrops
95 J6 **Walcot** Shrops
47 H2 **Walcot** Swindn
82 D4 **Walcot** Warwks
106 C7 **Walcot Green** Norfk
100 C4 **Walcote** Leics
136 B8 **Walcott** Lincs
123 G5 **Walcott** Norfk
159 H6 **Walden** N York
159 H6 **Walden Head** N York
142 E4 **Walden Stubbs** N York
53 G6 **Walderslade** Medway
20 C5 **Walderton** W Susx
15 L4 **Walditch** Dorset
115 J4 **Waldley** Derbys
169 H1 **Waldridge** Dur
91 G6 **Waldringfield** Suffk
23 J3 **Waldron** E Susx
133 J3 **Wales** Rothm
31 K6 **Wales** Somset
136 B1 **Walesby** Lincs
134 D5 **Walesby** Notts
79 M1 **Walford** Herefs
63 H3 **Walford** Herefs
113 G7 **Walford** Shrops
114 C5 **Walford** Staffs
113 G7 **Walford Heath** Shrops
113 M2 **Walgherton** Ches
84 F1 **Walgrave** Nhants
18 E4 **Walhampton** Hants
140 C2 **Walk Mill** Lancs
139 L7 **Walkden** Salfd
181 H6 **Walker** N u Ty
148 B7 **Walker Fold** Lancs
80 C5 **Walker's Green** Herefs
98 D7 **Walker's Heath** Birm
200 D5 **Walkerburn** Border
134 F1 **Walkeringham** Notts
134 F1 **Walkerith** Lincs
69 H2 **Walkern** Herts
222 C7 **Walkerton** Fife
18 C5 **Walkford** Dorset
7 G1 **Walkhampton** Devon
152 F8 **Walkington** E R Yk
133 G2 **Walkley** Sheff
82 B2 **Walkwood** Worcs
2 F4 **Wall** Cnwll
179 L5 **Wall** Nthumb
98 E2 **Wall** Staffs
156 B6 **Wall End** Cumb
80 B4 **Wall End** Herefs
97 K5 **Wall Heath** Dudley
180 C5 **Wall Houses** Nthumb
96 C5 **Wall under Haywood** Shrops
183 H2 **Wallacetown** S Ayrs
196 B6 **Wallacetown** S Ayrs
22 F5 **Wallands Park** E Susx
129 G1 **Wallasey** Wirral
53 J4 **Wallend** Medway
80 F7 **Waller's Green** Herefs
178 B6 **Wallhead** Cumb
48 F1 **Wallingford** Oxon
51 H6 **Wallington** Gt Lon
19 K2 **Wallington** Hants
86 F8 **Wallington** Herts
98 C3 **Wallington Heath** Wsall

75 G7 **Wallis** Pembks
17 L4 **Wallisdown** Poole
37 H3 **Walliswood** W Susx
281 c6 **Walls** Shet
181 H5 **Wallsend** N Tyne
165 K5 **Wallthwaite** Cumb
211 L4 **Wallyford** E Loth
41 L5 **Walmer** Kent
138 F3 **Walmer Bridge** Lancs
140 B5 **Walmersley** Bury
41 H3 **Walmestone** Kent
98 F5 **Walmley** Birm
98 F5 **Walmley Ash** Birm
137 G4 **Walmsgate** Lincs
30 D3 **Walpole** Somset
107 H8 **Walpole** Suffk
120 B7 **Walpole Cross Keys** Norfk
120 B8 **Walpole Highway** Norfk
120 B8 **Walpole St Andrew** Norfk
120 B8 **Walpole St Peter** Norfk
30 E2 **Walrow** Somset
98 C4 **Walsall** Wsall
98 D3 **Walsall Wood** Wsall
140 D3 **Walsden** Calder
99 K7 **Walsgrave on Sowe** Covtry
89 K1 **Walsham le Willows** Suffk
140 A5 **Walshaw** Bury
140 E2 **Walshaw** Calder
150 F5 **Walshford** N York
103 K1 **Walsoken** Norfk
199 H4 **Walston** S Lans
69 G1 **Walsworth** Herts
67 K7 **Walter's Ash** Bucks
38 D5 **Walters Green** Kent
43 G7 **Walterston** V Glam
62 D2 **Walterstone** Herefs
40 E5 **Waltham** Kent
145 H7 **Waltham** NE Lin
69 K7 **Waltham Abbey** Essex
35 H7 **Waltham Chase** Hants
69 K7 **Waltham Cross** Herts
117 L6 **Waltham on the Wolds** Leics
49 K4 **Waltham St Lawrence** W & M
71 G1 **Waltham's Cross** Essex
102 D3 **Walton** C Pete
178 C6 **Walton** Cumb
133 G6 **Walton** Derbys
150 F6 **Walton** Leeds
100 D6 **Walton** Leics
85 H7 **Walton** M Keyn
79 J3 **Walton** Powys
95 L7 **Walton** Shrops
31 G4 **Walton** Somset
114 D6 **Walton** Staffs
114 D5 **Walton** Staffs
91 G8 **Walton** Suffk
20 D6 **Walton** W Susx
142 A4 **Walton** Wakefd
83 G4 **Walton** Warwks
113 K7 **Walton** Wrekin
64 C1 **Walton Cardiff** Gloucs
55 H2 **Walton East** Pembks
32 C7 **Walton Elm** Dorset
83 L8 **Walton Grounds** Nhants
51 G7 **Walton on the Hill** Surrey
73 K3 **Walton on the Naze** Essex
117 G7 **Walton on the Wolds** Leics
44 E4 **Walton Park** N Som
54 D4 **Walton West** Pembks
44 E4 **Walton-in-Gordano** N Som
139 H2 **Walton-le-Dale** Lancs
50 E5 **Walton-on-Thames** Surrey
114 F7 **Walton-on-the-Hill** Staffs
115 L7 **Walton-on-Trent** Derbys
128 D4 **Walwen** Flints
128 E5 **Walwen** Flints
179 L5 **Walwick** Nthumb
169 G7 **Walworth** Darltn
51 J3 **Walworth** Gt Lon
169 G6 **Walworth Gate** Darltn
54 E4 **Walwyn's Castle** Pembks
15 G1 **Wambrook** Somset
177 H7 **Wampool** Cumb
36 D1 **Wanborough** Surrey
47 J2 **Wanborough** Swindn
68 E3 **Wandon End** Herts
51 H4 **Wandsworth** Gt Lon
107 J7 **Wangford** Suffk
100 D1 **Wanlip** Leics
186 C4 **Wanlockhead** D & G
23 K6 **Wannock** E Susx
102 B4 **Wansford** C Pete
153 G2 **Wansford** E R Yk
39 J4 **Wanshurst Green** Kent
51 L1 **Wanstead** Gt Lon

32 B3 **Wanstrow** Somset
63 K6 **Wanswell** Gloucs
48 B1 **Wantage** Oxon
81 H4 **Wants Green** Worcs
45 L3 **Wapley** S Glos
83 J2 **Wappenbury** Warwks
84 C6 **Wappenham** Nhants
23 K4 **Warbleton** E Susx
66 F8 **Warborough** Oxon
102 F7 **Warboys** Cambs
146 F8 **Warbreck** Bpool
11 H4 **Warbstow** Cnwll
130 D2 **Warburton** Traffd
167 H7 **Warcop** Cumb
98 E5 **Ward End** Birm
90 B2 **Ward Green** Suffk
53 M5 **Warden** Kent
179 L5 **Warden** Nthumb
169 K1 **Warden Law** Sundld
86 C6 **Warden Street** Beds
85 L8 **Wardhedges** Beds
83 L6 **Wardington** Oxon
130 B8 **Wardle** Ches
140 D4 **Wardle** Rochdl
181 H6 **Wardley** Gatesd
101 H3 **Wardley** Rutlnd
140 A7 **Wardley** Salfd
132 D5 **Wardlow** Derbys
131 J3 **Wardsend** Ches
103 K7 **Wardy Hill** Cambs
69 K4 **Ware** Herts
39 K2 **Ware Street** Kent
17 H5 **Wareham** Dorset
25 J1 **Warehorne** Kent
203 J6 **Waren Mill** Nthumb
203 J7 **Warenford** Nthumb
203 H7 **Warenton** Nthumb
69 K4 **Wareside** Herts
86 E4 **Waresley** Cambs
81 J1 **Waresley** Worcs
49 L4 **Warfield** Br For
8 C5 **Warfleet** Devon
119 H5 **Wargate** Lincs
49 J3 **Wargrave** Wokham
80 B7 **Warham** Herefs
121 L3 **Warham All Saints** Norfk
121 L3 **Warham St Mary** Norfk
202 C5 **Wark** Nthumb
179 K3 **Wark** Nthumb
27 M6 **Warkleigh** Devon
101 K7 **Warkton** Nhants
83 L7 **Warkworth** Nhants
191 K5 **Warkworth** Nthumb
160 E4 **Warlaby** N York
140 E4 **Warland** Calder
5 K1 **Warleggan** Cnwll
46 A6 **Warleigh** BaNES
141 G3 **Warley Town** Calder
51 K7 **Warlingham** Surrey
177 G5 **Warmanbie** D & G
115 M1 **Warmbrook** Derbys
142 B4 **Warmfield** Wakefd
130 D7 **Warmingham** Ches
102 B5 **Warmington** Nhants
83 K5 **Warmington** Warwks
32 E2 **Warminster** Wilts
45 K4 **Warmley** S Glos
142 E7 **Warmsworth** Donc
16 E5 **Warmwell** Dorset
81 K4 **Warndon** Worcs
35 J6 **Warnford** Hants
37 J4 **Warnham** W Susx
37 J4 **Warnham Court** W Susx
21 H5 **Warningcamp** W Susx
37 K5 **Warninglid** W Susx
131 H5 **Warren** Ches
54 F7 **Warren** Pembks
49 K3 **Warren Row** W & M
40 B5 **Warren Street** Kent
69 H2 **Warren's Green** Herts
170 D5 **Warrenby** R & Cl
198 F5 **Warrenhill** S Lans
85 H4 **Warrington** M Keyn
130 B2 **Warrington** Warrtn
211 H4 **Warriston** C Edin
19 H2 **Warsash** Hants
132 B7 **Warslow** Staffs
133 L6 **Warsop** Notts
133 L6 **Warsop Vale** Notts
152 D5 **Warter** E R Yk
152 C6 **Warter Priory** E R Yk
160 B6 **Warthermaske** N York
151 L5 **Warthill** N York
24 B5 **Wartling** E Susx
117 J7 **Wartnaby** Leics

138 E2 **Warton** Lancs
147 K2 **Warton** Lancs
190 E5 **Warton** Nthumb
99 H3 **Warton** Warwks
178 B7 **Warwick** Cumb
83 G2 **Warwick** Warwks
178 B7 **Warwick Bridge** Cumb
178 B3 **Warwicksland** Cumb
275 c3 **Wasbister** Ork
156 B1 **Wasdale Head** Cumb
131 L3 **Wash** Derbys
7 M2 **Wash** Devon
70 C1 **Washall Green** Herts
5 H1 **Washaway** Cnwll
8 B4 **Washbourne** Devon
30 F1 **Washbrook** Somset
90 D6 **Washbrook** Suffk
29 G7 **Washfield** Devon
159 J2 **Washfold** N York
29 J3 **Washford** Somset
28 E8 **Washford Pyne** Devon
135 L5 **Washingborough** Lincs
181 H7 **Washington** Sundld
21 J4 **Washington** W Susx
98 E5 **Washwood Heath** Birm
48 E6 **Wasing** W Berk
168 D2 **Waskerley** Dur
83 G3 **Wasperton** Warwks
135 M6 **Wasps Nest** Lincs
161 J6 **Wass** N York
29 K2 **Watchet** Somset
47 K1 **Watchfield** Oxon
30 E2 **Watchfield** Somset
157 H3 **Watchgate** Cumb
165 G2 **Watchill** Cumb
8 D2 **Watcombe** Torbay
165 J7 **Watendlath** Cumb
13 H6 **Water** Devon
140 C3 **Water** Lancs
66 D5 **Water Eaton** Oxon
97 K1 **Water Eaton** Staffs
85 L7 **Water End** Beds
86 C7 **Water End** Beds
86 C5 **Water End** Beds
152 B8 **Water End** E R Yk
88 B7 **Water End** Essex
68 D5 **Water End** Herts
69 G6 **Water End** Herts
142 D2 **Water Fryston** Wakefd
102 C4 **Water Newton** Cambs
98 F5 **Water Orton** Warwks
84 C8 **Water Stratford** Bucks
42 B5 **Water Street** Neath
156 D5 **Water Yeat** Cumb
139 K6 **Water's Nook** Bolton
87 K2 **Waterbeach** Cambs
20 E5 **Waterbeach** W Susx
177 H3 **Waterbeck** D & G
16 E5 **Watercombe** Dorset
121 J4 **Waterden** Norfk
164 F6 **Waterend** Cumb
115 H1 **Waterfall** Staffs
140 C3 **Waterfoot** Lancs
208 F7 **Waterfoot** S Lans
69 J4 **Waterford** Herts
11 G6 **Watergate** Cnwll
156 E2 **Waterhead** Cumb
197 G8 **Waterhead** E Ayrs
200 B3 **Waterheads** Border
168 F3 **Waterhouses** Dur
115 H2 **Waterhouses** Staffs
39 H3 **Wateringbury** Kent
64 D6 **Waterlane** Gloucs
10 F7 **Waterloo** Cnwll
133 H7 **Waterloo** Derbys
79 L5 **Waterloo** Herefs
247 K4 **Waterloo** Highld
209 L8 **Waterloo** N Lans
122 E7 **Waterloo** Norfk
233 G7 **Waterloo** P & K
55 G6 **Waterloo** Pembks
17 K4 **Waterloo** Poole
138 C8 **Waterloo** Sefton
29 J8 **Waterloo Cross** Devon
125 J6 **Waterloo Port** Gwynd
19 M2 **Waterlooville** Hants
166 B6 **Watermillock** Cumb
66 F6 **Waterperry** Oxon
29 J6 **Waterrow** Somset
113 K7 **Waters Upton** Wrekin
21 G4 **Watersfield** W Susx
139 L3 **Waterside** Bl w D
68 B7 **Waterside** Bucks
165 H2 **Waterside** Cumb
143 H5 **Waterside** Donc

184 C1 **Waterside** E Ayrs
196 F2 **Waterside** E Ayrs
209 H4 **Waterside** E Duns
258 A7 **Waterstein** Highld
66 F6 **Waterstock** Oxon
54 F5 **Waterston** Pembks
68 E7 **Watford** Herts
84 B2 **Watford** Nhants
149 L2 **Wath** N York
160 D7 **Wath** N York
142 C7 **Wath upon Dearne** Rothm
104 C1 **Watlington** Norfk
67 G8 **Watlington** Oxon
116 E2 **Watnall** Notts
280 B5 **Watten** Highld
105 K8 **Wattisfield** Suffk
89 K5 **Wattisham** Suffk
15 K4 **Watton** Dorset
152 F6 **Watton** E R Yk
105 J3 **Watton** Norfk
105 J3 **Watton Green** Norfk
69 J3 **Watton-at-Stone** Herts
70 D8 **Wattons Green** Essex
209 K5 **Wattston** N Lans
42 F3 **Wattstown** Rhondd
43 K3 **Wattsville** Caerph
144 B2 **Wauldby** E R Yk
244 E5 **Waulkmill** Abers
57 H6 **Waunarlwydd** Swans
92 D7 **Waunfawr** Cerdgn
125 J7 **Waunfawr** Gwynd
57 G4 **Waungron** Swans
61 J5 **Waunlwyd** Blae G
85 H7 **Wavendon** M Keyn
165 H1 **Waverbridge** Cumb
129 K7 **Waverton** Ches
165 H1 **Waverton** Cumb
153 H8 **Wawne** E R Yk
123 J6 **Waxham** Norfk
145 J2 **Waxholme** E R Yk
41 K2 **Way** Kent
13 K1 **Way Village** Devon
44 D6 **Way Wick** N Som
13 H8 **Waye** Devon
15 J1 **Wayford** Somset
15 L3 **Waytown** Dorset
29 K3 **Weacombe** Somset
65 L6 **Weald** Oxon
50 F1 **Wealdstone** Gt Lon
150 D7 **Weardley** Leeds
44 E8 **Weare** Somset
27 H6 **Weare Giffard** Devon
167 K3 **Wearhead** Dur
30 F5 **Wearne** Somset
158 B2 **Weasdale** Cumb
121 J7 **Weasenham All Saints** Norfk
121 J7 **Weasenham St Peter** Norfk
140 B8 **Weaste** Salfd
98 D8 **Weatheroak Hill** Worcs
130 B5 **Weaverham** Ches
115 J7 **Weaverslake** Staffs
152 E2 **Weaverthorpe** N York
45 K4 **Webb's Heath** S Glos
44 D7 **Webbington** Somset
82 B2 **Webheath** Worcs
80 A7 **Webton** Herefs
256 F5 **Wedderlairs** Abers
149 G6 **Wedding Hall Fold** N York
41 J3 **Weddington** Kent
99 K5 **Weddington** Warwks
46 F7 **Wedhampton** Wilts
31 G1 **Wedmore** Somset
98 C4 **Wednesbury** Sandw
97 L3 **Wednesfield** Wolves
135 G6 **Weecar** Notts
67 K3 **Weedon** Bucks
84 C3 **Weedon** Nhants
84 B6 **Weedon Lois** Nhants
98 F3 **Weeford** Staffs
27 K5 **Week** Devon
28 C7 **Week** Devon
8 A2 **Week** Devon
29 G4 **Week** Somset
11 J3 **Week St Mary** Cnwll
13 H1 **Weeke** Devon
34 F5 **Weeke** Hants
101 J7 **Weekley** Nhants
153 G7 **Weel** E R Yk
73 H3 **Weeley** Essex
73 H3 **Weeley Heath** Essex
232 B5 **Weem** P & K
114 E7 **Weeping Cross** Staffs
82 C4 **Weethley** Warwks
104 F5 **Weeting** Norfk
145 K4 **Weeton** E R Yk

138 D1 **Weeton** Lancs
150 C6 **Weeton** N York
150 C8 **Weetwood** Leeds
140 C3 **Weir** Lancs
6 E2 **Weir Quay** Devon
112 E6 **Weirbrook** Shrops
133 L5 **Welbeck Abbey** Notts
106 B2 **Welborne** Norfk
118 C1 **Welbourn** Lincs
151 M2 **Welburn** N York
160 F2 **Welbury** N York
118 C4 **Welby** Lincs
103 K6 **Welches Dam** Cambs
26 D7 **Welcombe** Devon
191 G6 **Weldon Bridge** Nthumb
100 E7 **Welford** Nhants
48 B4 **Welford** W Berk
82 D5 **Welford-on-Avon** Warwks
101 G5 **Welham** Leics
134 E3 **Welham** Notts
69 G6 **Welham Green** Herts
36 A2 **Well** Hants
137 H5 **Well** Lincs
160 C6 **Well** N York
49 L1 **Well End** Bucks
69 G7 **Well End** Herts
68 F2 **Well Head** Herts
52 E6 **Well Hill** Kent
13 L1 **Well Town** Devon
81 H7 **Welland** Worcs
81 J7 **Welland Stone** Worcs
234 D7 **Wellbank** Angus
68 F1 **Wellbury** Herts
83 G4 **Wellesbourne** Warwks
83 G4 **Wellesbourne Mountford** Warwks
48 D4 **Wellhouse** W Berk
51 M4 **Welling** Gt Lon
85 H2 **Wellingborough** Nhants
121 J7 **Wellingham** Norfk
135 K8 **Wellingore** Lincs
155 K2 **Wellington** Cumb
80 C5 **Wellington** Herefs
29 L6 **Wellington** Somset
96 E1 **Wellington** Wrekin
81 G7 **Wellington Heath** Herefs
80 C6 **Wellington Marsh** Herefs
45 L7 **Wellow** BaNES
18 F6 **Wellow** IOW
134 D6 **Wellow** Notts
69 L3 **Wellpond Green** Herts
31 J2 **Wells** Somset
113 M1 **Wells Green** Ches
141 G1 **Wells Head** Brad
121 K3 **Wells-next-the-sea** Norfk
99 K3 **Wellsborough** Leics
70 F3 **Wellstye Green** Essex
221 G3 **Welltree** P & K
210 E1 **Wellwood** Fife
103 L4 **Welney** Norfk
63 H4 **Welsh Bicknor** Herefs
113 H4 **Welsh End** Shrops
112 E5 **Welsh Frankton** Shrops
74 F6 **Welsh Hook** Pembks
63 G3 **Welsh Newton** Herefs
42 F6 **Welsh St Donats** V Glam
113 G4 **Welshampton** Shrops
94 F2 **Welshpool** Powys
165 K2 **Welton** Cumb
144 B2 **Welton** E R Yk
135 K4 **Welton** Lincs
84 B2 **Welton** Nhants
137 J6 **Welton le Marsh** Lincs
136 E2 **Welton le Wold** Lincs
145 J3 **Welwick** E R Yk
69 G4 **Welwyn** Herts
69 G4 **Welwyn Garden City** Herts
113 H5 **Wem** Shrops
30 D3 **Wembdon** Somset
50 F2 **Wembley** Gt Lon
7 G5 **Wembury** Devon
12 F1 **Wembworthy** Devon
207 K5 **Wemyss Bay** Inver
77 J1 **Wenallt** Cerdgn
87 K8 **Wendens Ambo** Essex
66 E3 **Wendlebury** Oxon
105 J1 **Wendling** Norfk
67 L5 **Wendover** Bucks
3 H5 **Wendron** Cnwll
87 G5 **Wendy** Cambs
10 F7 **Wenfordbridge** Cnwll
107 J8 **Wenhaston** Suffk
102 E7 **Wennington** Cambs
52 B3 **Wennington** Gt Lon
147 M2 **Wennington** Lancs

132 E7 **Wensley** Derbys
159 K5 **Wensley** N York
142 D4 **Wentbridge** Wakefd
95 J5 **Wentnor** Shrops
103 K7 **Wentworth** Cambs
142 B8 **Wentworth** Rothm
141 M7 **Wentworth Castle** Barns
43 H7 **Wenvoe** V Glam
79 M5 **Weobley** Herefs
80 A5 **Weobley Marsh** Herefs
21 H5 **Wepham** W Susx
104 D3 **Wereham** Norfk
97 K3 **Wergs** Wolves
109 K4 **Wern** Gwynd
93 L1 **Wern** Powys
95 G1 **Wern** Powys
61 H3 **Wern** Powys
112 D4 **Wern** Shrops
128 F6 **Wern-y-gaer** Flints
131 J1 **Werneth Low** Tamesd
56 F6 **Wernffrwd** Swans
102 D3 **Werrington** C Pete
11 L5 **Werrington** Cnwll
114 E2 **Werrington** Staffs
129 K5 **Wervin** Ches
138 E1 **Wesham** Lancs
133 G8 **Wessington** Derbys
42 F8 **West Aberthaw** V Glam
121 G8 **West Acre** Norfk
202 F4 **West Allerdean** Nthumb
7 L6 **West Alvington** Devon
33 K3 **West Amesbury** Wilts
28 E5 **West Anstey** Devon
160 B4 **West Appleton** N York
136 E5 **West Ashby** Lincs
20 D5 **West Ashling** W Susx
46 C7 **West Ashton** Wilts
168 F5 **West Auckland** Dur
163 H5 **West Ayton** N York
30 A4 **West Bagborough** Somset
11 K3 **West Balsdon** Cnwll
61 K6 **West Bank** Blae G
129 L3 **West Bank** Halton
136 C4 **West Barkwith** Lincs
171 J8 **West Barnby** N York
212 E3 **West Barns** E Loth
121 K5 **West Barsham** Norfk
15 K4 **West Bay** Dorset
122 C4 **West Beckham** Norfk
50 D4 **West Bedfont** Surrey
72 D2 **West Bergholt** Essex
15 M5 **West Bexington** Dorset
120 F8 **West Bilney** Norfk
22 D6 **West Blatchington** Br & H
181 J6 **West Boldon** S Tyne
32 C5 **West Bourton** Dorset
141 J2 **West Bowling** Brad
40 E6 **West Brabourne** Kent
105 J2 **West Bradenham** Norfk
148 C7 **West Bradford** Lancs
31 J3 **West Bradley** Somset
141 L5 **West Bretton** Wakefd
117 G4 **West Bridgford** Notts
168 B6 **West Briscoe** Dur
98 C5 **West Bromwich** Sandw
188 B3 **West Buccleuch Hotel** Border
28 B4 **West Buckland** Devon
30 B6 **West Buckland** Somset
159 H5 **West Burton** N York
21 G4 **West Burton** W Susx
168 E2 **West Butsfield** Dur
143 L6 **West Butterwick** N Linc
50 D6 **West Byfleet** Surrey
172 E8 **West Cairngaan** D & G
107 K1 **West Caister** Norfk
210 D6 **West Calder** W Loth
31 J6 **West Camel** Somset
16 E6 **West Chaldon** Dorset
48 A1 **West Challow** Oxon
7 L6 **West Charleton** Devon
15 M2 **West Chelborough** Dorset
191 J6 **West Chevington** Nthumb
21 J3 **West Chiltington** W Susx
31 G8 **West Chinnock** Somset
47 H8 **West Chisenbury** Wilts
50 D8 **West Clandon** Surrey
16 A4 **West Compton** Dorset
151 L7 **West Cottingwith** N York
143 G3 **West Cowick** E R Yk
57 H7 **West Cross** Swans
11 K4 **West Curry** Cnwll

165 K1 **West Curthwaite** Cumb
20 E4 **West Dean** W Susx
34 B5 **West Dean** Wilts
102 C2 **West Deeping** Lincs
129 J1 **West Derby** Lpool
104 D3 **West Dereham** Norfk
27 J3 **West Down** Devon
50 D3 **West Drayton** Gt Lon
134 D5 **West Drayton** Notts
280 B2 **West Dunnet** Highld
144 C2 **West Ella** E R Yk
85 J4 **West End** Beds
49 L5 **West End** Br For
43 K3 **West End** Caerph
87 G2 **West End** Cambs
177 K7 **West End** Cumb
144 A2 **West End** E R Yk
144 F2 **West End** E R Yk
145 H2 **West End** E R Yk
34 F7 **West End** Hants
35 K4 **West End** Hants
69 H5 **West End** Herts
69 J6 **West End** Herts
139 L2 **West End** Lancs
150 B8 **West End** Leeds
145 K8 **West End** Lincs
44 F5 **West End** N Som
149 L4 **West End** N York
151 H7 **West End** N York
105 H2 **West End** Norfk
107 K1 **West End** Norfk
48 E2 **West End** Oxon
45 L1 **West End** S Glos
31 L4 **West End** Somset
50 B6 **West End** Surrey
50 E6 **West End** Surrey
49 K4 **West End** W & M
22 B4 **West End** W Susx
32 F6 **West End** Wilts
46 E3 **West End** Wilts
33 G6 **West End** Wilts
49 G6 **West End Green** Hants
51 G6 **West Ewell** Surrey
39 H3 **West Farleigh** Kent
83 M5 **West Farndon** Nhants
112 E6 **West Felton** Shrops
23 G6 **West Firle** E Susx
135 K3 **West Firsby** Lincs
163 K6 **West Flotmanby** N York
142 B1 **West Garforth** Leeds
48 C2 **West Ginge** Oxon
47 K7 **West Grafton** Wilts
49 H7 **West Green** Hants
33 L5 **West Grimstead** Wilts
37 J6 **West Grinstead** W Susx
142 E2 **West Haddlesey** N York
84 C1 **West Haddon** Nhants
48 D2 **West Hagbourne** Oxon
97 K7 **West Hagley** Worcs
116 D3 **West Hallam** Derbys
116 C3 **West Hallam Common** Derbys
144 A4 **West Halton** N Linc
51 K2 **West Ham** Gt Lon
133 H4 **West Handley** Derbys
66 B8 **West Hanney** Oxon
71 H7 **West Hanningfield** Essex
33 K5 **West Harnham** Wilts
45 H7 **West Harptree** BaNES
20 C3 **West Harting** W Susx
30 D6 **West Hatch** Somset
32 F5 **West Hatch** Wilts
234 E8 **West Haven** Angus
104 B2 **West Head** Norfk
98 C7 **West Heath** Birm
48 E7 **West Heath** Hants
274 D5 **West Helmsdale** Highld
48 C1 **West Hendred** Oxon
163 G7 **West Heslerton** N York
44 D6 **West Hewish** N Som
14 C4 **West Hill** Devon
38 A6 **West Hoathly** W Susx
17 G5 **West Holme** Dorset
52 D1 **West Horndon** Essex
31 J2 **West Horrington** Somset
50 D8 **West Horsley** Surrey
203 G7 **West Horton** Nthumb
41 H7 **West Hougham** Kent
17 L3 **West Howe** Bmouth
29 G4 **West Howetown** Somset
221 K2 **West Huntingtower** P & K
30 D2 **West Huntspill** Somset
68 E4 **West Hyde** Beds
50 C1 **West Hyde** Herts
40 F8 **West Hythe** Kent
28 C2 **West Ilkerton** Devon

48 C3 **West Ilsley** W Berk
20 C6 **West Itchenor** W Susx
137 G7 **West Keal** Lincs
47 G5 **West Kennett** Wilts
195 K1 **West Kilbride** N Ayrs
52 C6 **West Kingsdown** Kent
46 A3 **West Kington** Wilts
128 F2 **West Kirby** Wirral
162 F7 **West Knapton** N York
16 D5 **West Knighton** Dorset
32 E4 **West Knoyle** Wilts
30 F7 **West Lambrook** Somset
41 K6 **West Langdon** Kent
229 H4 **West Laroch** Highld
20 E3 **West Lavington** W Susx
46 E8 **West Lavington** Wilts
168 F8 **West Layton** N York
116 E6 **West Leake** Notts
202 C5 **West Learmouth** Nthumb
161 G2 **West Lees** N York
13 G2 **West Leigh** Devon
7 L3 **West Leigh** Devon
29 L5 **West Leigh** Somset
121 J8 **West Lexham** Norfk
151 K3 **West Lilling** N York
199 K3 **West Linton** Border
45 M4 **West Littleton** S Glos
48 B2 **West Lockinge** Oxon
16 F6 **West Lulworth** Dorset
152 E2 **West Lutton** N York
31 J4 **West Lydford** Somset
28 C1 **West Lyn** Devon
30 D5 **West Lyng** Somset
120 D7 **West Lynn** Norfk
52 E7 **West Malling** Kent
81 H6 **West Malvern** Worcs
20 C4 **West Marden** W Susx
134 E5 **West Markham** Notts
145 H5 **West Marsh** NE Lin
148 F5 **West Marton** N York
32 E6 **West Melbury** Dorset
142 C7 **West Melton** Rothm
35 K6 **West Meon** Hants
35 K5 **West Meon Hut** Hants
35 K5 **West Meon Woodlands** Hants
72 E4 **West Mersea** Essex
180 C6 **West Mickley** Nthumb
15 L3 **West Milton** Dorset
53 K4 **West Minster** Kent
50 E5 **West Molesey** Surrey
30 C5 **West Monkton** Somset
17 L2 **West Moors** Dorset
17 H3 **West Morden** Dorset
201 J5 **West Morriston** Border
149 K7 **West Morton** Brad
31 J6 **West Mudford** Somset
162 B6 **West Ness** N York
169 K7 **West Newbiggin** Darltn
153 K8 **West Newton** E R Yk
120 F6 **West Newton** Norfk
30 D5 **West Newton** Somset
51 J4 **West Norwood** Gt Lon
8 B1 **West Ogwell** Devon
32 D7 **West Orchard** Dorset
47 H5 **West Overton** Wilts
11 L4 **West Panson** Devon
17 L3 **West Parley** Dorset
39 G3 **West Peckham** Kent
180 F8 **West Pelton** Dur
31 J3 **West Pennard** Somset
4 C3 **West Pentire** Cnwll
86 C2 **West Perry** Cambs
28 F2 **West Porlock** Somset
7 M7 **West Prawle** Devon
16 D1 **West Pulham** Dorset
26 F7 **West Putford** Devon
29 K3 **West Quantoxhead** Somset
13 L2 **West Raddon** Devon
169 J1 **West Rainton** Dur
135 L2 **West Rasen** Lincs
145 G7 **West Ravendale** NE Lin
121 J6 **West Raynham** Norfk
134 D3 **West Retford** Notts
160 F7 **West Rounton** N York
104 D8 **West Row** Suffk
121 H6 **West Rudham** Norfk
122 D3 **West Runton** Norfk
212 A5 **West Saltoun** E Loth
13 J2 **West Sandford** Devon
281 e3 **West Sandwick** Shet
159 K6 **West Scrafton** N York
181 G2 **West Sleekburn** Nthumb
123 K7 **West Somerton** Norfk
16 D4 **West Stafford** Dorset
134 F1 **West Stockwith** Notts

20 D5 **West Stoke** W Susx
158 F2 **West Stonesdale** N York
30 F1 **West Stoughton** Somset
32 C6 **West Stour** Dorset
41 H3 **West Stourmouth** Kent
89 G1 **West Stow** Suffk
47 H6 **West Stowell** Wilts
35 H3 **West Stratton** Hants
40 A4 **West Street** Kent
41 K4 **West Street** Kent
52 F4 **West Street** Medway
89 K1 **West Street** Suffk
160 C7 **West Tanfield** N York
5 K2 **West Taphouse** Cnwll
206 D5 **West Tarbert** Ag & B
21 J6 **West Tarring** W Susx
191 H6 **West Thirston** Nthumb
20 C6 **West Thorney** W Susx
117 G6 **West Thorpe** Notts
52 C3 **West Thurrock** Thurr
52 E3 **West Tilbury** Thurr
35 K5 **West Tisted** Hants
136 B3 **West Torrington** Lincs
45 G6 **West Town** BaNES
20 B7 **West Town** Hants
80 B3 **West Town** Herefs
44 F5 **West Town** N Som
31 J4 **West Town** Somset
32 B3 **West Town** Somset
34 C5 **West Tytherley** Hants
103 K1 **West Walton** Norfk
103 K1 **West Walton Highway** Norfk
34 C7 **West Wellow** Hants
7 G5 **West Wembury** Devon
222 E8 **West Wemyss** Fife
44 D6 **West Wick** N Som
88 C5 **West Wickham** Cambs
51 K5 **West Wickham** Gt Lon
55 H5 **West Williamston** Pembks
120 E8 **West Winch** Norfk
34 B4 **West Winterslow** Wilts
20 C7 **West Wittering** W Susx
159 J5 **West Witton** N York
179 K2 **West Woodburn** Nthumb
48 B6 **West Woodhay** W Berk
32 C2 **West Woodlands** Somset
165 J1 **West Woodside** Cumb
35 M3 **West Worldham** Hants
21 K6 **West Worthing** W Susx
88 C5 **West Wratting** Essex
67 K8 **West Wycombe** Bucks
180 D6 **West Wylam** Nthumb
46 B4 **West Yatton** Wilts
52 D5 **West Yoke** Kent
26 D7 **West Youlstone** Cnwll
41 G3 **Westbere** Kent
117 M3 **Westborough** Lincs
17 L4 **Westbourne** Bmouth
20 B5 **Westbourne** W Susx
41 K1 **Westbrook** Kent
48 B4 **Westbrook** W Berk
46 D5 **Westbrook** Wilts
84 B8 **Westbury** Bucks
95 J2 **Westbury** Shrops
46 C8 **Westbury** Wilts
32 E1 **Westbury Leigh** Wilts
63 L4 **Westbury on Severn** Gloucs
45 K4 **Westbury-on-Trym** Bristl
31 H1 **Westbury-sub-Mendip** Somset
138 D2 **Westby** Lancs
53 J2 **Westcliff-on-Sea** Sthend
31 L3 **Westcombe** Somset
65 J3 **Westcote** Gloucs
66 B2 **Westcote Barton** Oxon
67 H4 **Westcott** Bucks
14 B2 **Westcott** Devon
28 F6 **Westcott** Somset
37 H1 **Westcott** Surrey
47 J6 **Westcourt** Wilts
23 J7 **Westdean** E Susx
33 H2 **Westdown Camp** Wilts
10 F6 **Westdowns** Cnwll
52 B5 **Wested** Kent
64 A5 **Westend** Gloucs
179 H6 **Westend Town** Nthumb
40 F7 **Westenhanger** Kent
251 G5 **Wester Drumashie** Highld
210 D4 **Wester Ochiltree** W Loth
223 K6 **Wester Pitkierie** Fife
279 K6 **Westerdale** Highld
161 L2 **Westerdale** N York
90 E5 **Westerfield** Suffk
20 F6 **Westergate** W Susx
51 L8 **Westerham** Kent

180 F5 **Westerhope** N u Ty
8 C2 **Westerland** Devon
45 K3 **Westerleigh** S Glos
235 G4 **Westerton** Angus
20 E5 **Westerton** W Susx
45 K8 **Westfield** BaNES
164 C5 **Westfield** Cumb
24 E4 **Westfield** E Susx
279 J3 **Westfield** Highld
209 J4 **Westfield** N Lans
105 K2 **Westfield** Norfk
210 B4 **Westfield** W Loth
53 G6 **Westfield Sole** Kent
16 D1 **Westfields** Dorset
80 C7 **Westfields** Herefs
233 J6 **Westfields of Rattray** P & K
29 L6 **Westford** Somset
167 L3 **Westgate** Dur
143 K6 **Westgate** N Linc
121 L3 **Westgate** Norfk
141 K2 **Westgate Hill** Brad
41 K1 **Westgate on Sea** Kent
122 D7 **Westgate Street** Norfk
107 J7 **Westhall** Suffk
16 C6 **Westham** Dorset
23 L6 **Westham** E Susx
30 F2 **Westham** Somset
20 E5 **Westhampnett** W Susx
31 G2 **Westhay** Somset
138 F6 **Westhead** Lancs
80 D6 **Westhide** Herefs
245 J2 **Westhill** Abers
31 J3 **Westholme** Somset
80 B5 **Westhope** Herefs
95 L6 **Westhope** Shrops
83 L5 **Westhorp** Nhants
119 H5 **Westhorpe** Lincs
90 B2 **Westhorpe** Suffk
139 K6 **Westhoughton** Bolton
157 L7 **Westhouse** N York
133 H8 **Westhouses** Derbys
50 F8 **Westhumble** Surrey
7 J4 **Westlake** Devon
70 B3 **Westland Green** Herts
27 H5 **Westleigh** Devon
29 J7 **Westleigh** Devon
91 K2 **Westleton** Suffk
95 J2 **Westley** Shrops
89 G2 **Westley** Suffk
88 C4 **Westley Waterless** Cambs
67 J5 **Westlington** Bucks
177 L6 **Westlinton** Cumb
41 J3 **Westmarsh** Kent
22 E4 **Westmeston** E Susx
69 K2 **Westmill** Herts
69 J4 **Westmill** Herts
51 J3 **Westminster** Gt Lon
234 A5 **Westmuir** Angus
164 F2 **Westnewton** Cumb
181 J5 **Westoe** S Tyne
45 L5 **Weston** BaNES
114 A1 **Weston** Ches
14 D3 **Weston** Devon
14 E5 **Weston** Devon
16 D8 **Weston** Dorset
129 L3 **Weston** Halton
35 M6 **Weston** Hants
79 L4 **Weston** Herefs
69 H1 **Weston** Herts
119 J6 **Weston** Lincs
149 M6 **Weston** N York
84 B6 **Weston** Nhants
134 F6 **Weston** Notts
96 D5 **Weston** Shrops
112 D6 **Weston** Shrops
95 H8 **Weston** Shrops
114 F6 **Weston** Staffs
48 B4 **Weston** W Berk
80 D7 **Weston Beggard** Herefs
101 G5 **Weston by Welland** Nhants
35 G3 **Weston Colley** Hants
88 C4 **Weston Colville** Cambs
35 L2 **Weston Corbett** Hants
114 E3 **Weston Coyney** C Stke
84 F3 **Weston Favell** Nhants
88 C5 **Weston Green** Cambs
97 H1 **Weston Heath** Shrops
119 J7 **Weston Hills** Lincs
99 K6 **Weston in Arden** Warwks
114 B6 **Weston Jones** Staffs
122 C8 **Weston Longville** Norfk
112 F6 **Weston Lullingfields** Shrops
35 L2 **Weston Patrick** Hants
112 D4 **Weston Rhyn** Shrops
82 D7 **Weston Subedge** Gloucs

67 K5 **Weston Turville** Bucks
63 J3 **Weston under Penyard** Herefs
83 J1 **Weston under Wetherley** Warwks
115 M3 **Weston Underwood** Derbys
85 G5 **Weston Underwood** M Keyn
44 F4 **Weston-in-Gordano** N Som
66 D3 **Weston-on-the-Green** Oxon
44 C6 **Weston-Super-Mare** N Som
97 H1 **Weston-under-Lizard** Staffs
113 J5 **Weston-under-Redcastle** Shrops
116 C6 **Weston-upon-Trent** Derbys
46 B1 **Westonbirt** Gloucs
85 K8 **Westoning** Beds
68 C1 **Westoning Woodend** Beds
30 E4 **Westonzoyland** Somset
152 A3 **Westow** N York
11 L4 **Westpeek** Devon
30 F6 **Westport** Somset
210 B3 **Westquarter** Falk
43 J7 **Westra** V Glam
48 E3 **Westridge Green** W Berk
210 B5 **Westrigg** W Loth
65 J8 **Westrop** Swindn
201 K3 **Westruther** Border
103 H4 **Westry** Cambs
133 J4 **Westthorpe** Derbys
165 J2 **Westward** Cumb
27 G5 **Westward Ho!** Devon
40 C6 **Westwell** Kent
65 J5 **Westwell** Oxon
40 C5 **Westwell Leacon** Kent
87 J2 **Westwick** Cambs
168 D7 **Westwick** Dur
122 F6 **Westwick** Norfk
14 B3 **Westwood** Devon
52 D5 **Westwood** Kent
41 K2 **Westwood** Kent
116 D1 **Westwood** Notts
179 H6 **Westwood** Nthumb
46 A7 **Westwood** Wilts
99 H8 **Westwood Heath** Covtry
143 J7 **Westwoodside** N Linc
53 H5 **Wetham Green** Kent
178 B7 **Wetheral** Cumb
150 F6 **Wetherby** Leeds
89 K3 **Wetherden** Suffk
90 D2 **Wetheringsett** Suffk
71 H1 **Wethersfield** Essex
90 D2 **Wetherup Street** Suffk
114 F2 **Wetley Rocks** Staffs
130 C7 **Wettenhall** Ches
132 B8 **Wetton** Staffs
152 E4 **Wetwang** E R Yk
114 B5 **Wetwood** Staffs
47 K7 **Wexcombe** Wilts
50 C3 **Wexham** Slough
50 C2 **Wexham Street** Bucks
122 C3 **Weybourne** Norfk
106 E7 **Weybread** Suffk
106 E7 **Weybread Street** Suffk
50 D6 **Weybridge** Surrey
15 G3 **Weycroft** Devon
279 L3 **Weydale** Highld
34 D2 **Weyhill** Hants
16 C6 **Weymouth** Dorset
84 F8 **Whaddon** Bucks
87 G6 **Whaddon** Cambs
64 B4 **Whaddon** Gloucs
46 C6 **Whaddon** Wilts
33 L5 **Whaddon** Wilts
166 C6 **Whale** Cumb
133 K5 **Whaley** Derbys
131 K3 **Whaley Bridge** Derbys
133 K5 **Whaley Thorns** Derbys
280 D8 **Whaligoe** Highld
148 C8 **Whalley** Lancs
139 L1 **Whalley Banks** Lancs
180 D3 **Whalton** Nthumb
119 K6 **Whaplode** Lincs
103 G1 **Whaplode Drove** Lincs
83 K5 **Wharf** Warwks
148 D2 **Wharfe** N York
147 J8 **Wharles** Lancs
85 J6 **Wharley End** Beds
179 K5 **Wharmley** Nthumb
132 F1 **Wharncliffe Side** Sheff
152 C3 **Wharram-le-Street** N York
130 C6 **Wharton** Ches
80 C4 **Wharton** Herefs
159 L2 **Whashton** N York
159 L2 **Whashton Green** N York
157 H6 **Whasset** Cumb

83 G6 **Whatcote** Warwks
99 G3 **Whateley** Warwks
89 L6 **Whatfield** Suffk
15 H1 **Whatley** Somset
32 B2 **Whatley** Somset
45 K3 **Whatley's End** S Glos
24 D4 **Whatlington** E Susx
40 F6 **Whatsole Street** Kent
116 B1 **Whatstandwell** Derbys
117 K4 **Whatton** Notts
173 K5 **Whauphill** D & G
159 H2 **Whaw** N York
4 B6 **Wheal Rose** Cnwll
107 J4 **Wheatacre** Norfk
67 G7 **Wheatfield** Oxon
68 F4 **Wheathampstead** Herts
96 E7 **Wheathill** Shrops
31 J5 **Wheathill** Somset
141 G3 **Wheatley** Calder
36 A3 **Wheatley** Hants
66 E6 **Wheatley** Oxon
169 K3 **Wheatley Hill** Dur
142 F6 **Wheatley Hills** Donc
148 E8 **Wheatley Lane** Lancs
97 J1 **Wheaton Aston** Staffs
112 D1 **Wheatsheaf** Wrexhm
29 G3 **Wheddon Cross** Somset
3 H6 **Wheel Inn** Cnwll
40 F6 **Wheelbarrow Town** Kent
49 J4 **Wheeler's Green** Oxon
39 L4 **Wheeler's Street** Kent
67 K8 **Wheelerend Common** Bucks
36 E3 **Wheelerstreet** Surrey
130 E7 **Wheelock** Ches
130 E8 **Wheelock Heath** Ches
139 J3 **Wheelton** Lancs
142 C3 **Wheldale** Wakefd
151 L6 **Wheldrake** York
65 H7 **Whelford** Gloucs
68 C6 **Whelpley Hill** Bucks
165 J3 **Whelpo** Cumb
128 F4 **Whelston** Flints
69 J3 **Whempstead** Herts
151 K2 **Whenby** N York
89 G4 **Whepstead** Suffk
90 E7 **Wherstead** Suffk
34 E3 **Wherwell** Hants
132 C4 **Wheston** Derbys
39 G4 **Whetsted** Kent
69 H8 **Whetstone** Gt Lon
100 C4 **Whetstone** Leics
165 G1 **Wheyrigg** Cumb
155 L6 **Whicham** Cumb
83 H8 **Whichford** Warwks
180 F6 **Whickham** Gatesd
12 B3 **Whiddon** Devon
13 G4 **Whiddon Down** Devon
90 D6 **Whight's Corner** Suffk
234 D6 **Whigstreet** Angus
84 C2 **Whilton** Nhants
11 L2 **Whimble** Devon
14 B3 **Whimple** Devon
123 H5 **Whimpwell Green** Norfk
147 H7 **Whin Lane End** Lancs
105 K2 **Whinburgh** Norfk
175 H4 **Whinnie Liggate** D & G
177 J8 **Whinnow** Cumb
169 K6 **Whinny Hill** S on T
257 K5 **Whinnyfold** Abers
19 H5 **Whippingham** IOW
68 C3 **Whipsnade** Beds
13 M4 **Whipton** Devon
132 F3 **Whirlow** Sheff
135 H6 **Whisby** Lincs
117 L8 **Whissendine** Rutlnd
121 K7 **Whissonsett** Norfk
218 C8 **Whistlefield** Ag & B
217 J8 **Whistlefield Inn** Ag & B
49 J4 **Whistley Green** Wokham
129 L2 **Whiston** Knows
85 G3 **Whiston** Nhants
133 J2 **Whiston** Rothm
114 D8 **Whiston** Staffs
115 G2 **Whiston** Staffs
97 H3 **Whiston Cross** Shrops
115 G2 **Whiston Eaves** Staffs
129 L2 **Whiston Lane End** Knows
99 H5 **Whitacre Fields** Warwks
155 K5 **Whitbeck** Cumb
81 G4 **Whitbourne** Herefs
181 K6 **Whitburn** S Tyne
210 C6 **Whitburn** W Loth
129 J4 **Whitby** Ches
171 K8 **Whitby** N York
129 J5 **Whitbyheath** Ches

212 F7 **Whitchester** Border
45 J5 **Whitchurch** BaNES
67 J3 **Whitchurch** Bucks
43 J5 **Whitchurch** Cardif
12 C8 **Whitchurch** Devon
34 F1 **Whitchurch** Hants
63 H4 **Whitchurch** Herefs
48 F3 **Whitchurch** Oxon
74 C7 **Whitchurch** Pembks
113 J3 **Whitchurch** Shrops
15 J3 **Whitchurch Canonicorum** Dorset
48 F3 **Whitchurch Hill** Oxon
16 D5 **Whitcombe** Dorset
95 J5 **Whitcot** Shrops
95 G6 **Whitcott Keysett** Shrops
29 K7 **White Ball** Somset
147 L7 **White Chapel** Lancs
82 C7 **White Chapel** Worcs
72 C1 **White Colne** Essex
139 J4 **White Coppice** Lancs
3 H6 **White Cross** Cnwll
81 H8 **White End** Worcs
168 C3 **White Kirkley** Dur
16 D3 **White Lackington** Dorset
81 L4 **White Ladies Aston** Worcs
58 E4 **White Mill** Carmth
71 J3 **White Notley** Essex
45 L7 **White Ox Mead** BaNES
137 G4 **White Pit** Lincs
70 E4 **White Roding** Essex
139 G3 **White Stake** Lancs
80 D6 **White Stone** Herefs
49 K3 **White Waltham** W & M
180 E7 **White-le-Head** Dur
40 E5 **Whiteacre** Kent
99 G5 **Whiteacre Heath** Warwks
71 J1 **Whiteash Green** Essex
139 L2 **Whitebirk** Bl w D
250 E8 **Whitebridge** Highld
63 G6 **Whitebrook** Mons
257 D8 **Whitecairns** Abers
51 J3 **Whitechapel** Gt Lon
75 K5 **Whitechurch** Pembks
63 H5 **Whitecliffe** Gloucs
211 K5 **Whitecraig** E Loth
63 J6 **Whitecroft** Gloucs
172 F3 **Whitecrook** D & G
2 E4 **Whitecross** Cnwll
10 D8 **Whitecross** Cnwll
210 C4 **Whitecross** Falk
263 J2 **Whiteface** Highld
194 D3 **Whitefarland** N Ayrs
183 H1 **Whitefaulds** S Ayrs
140 B6 **Whitefield** Bury
28 C4 **Whitefield** Devon
29 K5 **Whitefield** Somset
129 K2 **Whitefield Lane End** Knows
256 C6 **Whiteford** Abers
130 C6 **Whitegate** Ches
49 H8 **Whitehall** Hants
275 e3 **Whitehall** Ork
37 H6 **Whitehall** W Susx
164 C7 **Whitehaven** Cumb
36 B4 **Whitehill** Hants
40 C3 **Whitehill** Kent
99 L1 **Whitehill** Leics
268 B3 **Whitehills** Abers
256 A8 **Whitehouse** Abers
206 C6 **Whitehouse** Ag & B
98 E4 **Whitehouse Common** Birm
212 D3 **Whitekirk** E Loth
30 F7 **Whitelackington** Somset
19 J2 **Whiteley** Hants
19 J7 **Whiteley Bank** IOW
131 H4 **Whiteley Green** Ches
50 E6 **Whiteley Village** Surrey
22 D2 **Whitemans Green** W Susx
253 J1 **Whitemire** Moray
116 F3 **Whitemoor** C Nott
5 G3 **Whitemoor** Cnwll
116 B2 **Whitemoor** Derbys
131 H7 **Whitemoor** Staffs
281 d6 **Whiteness** Shet
65 M4 **Whiteoak Green** Oxon
34 B6 **Whiteparish** Wilts
256 F7 **Whiterashes** Abers
280 E6 **Whiterow** Highld
265 G8 **Whiterow** Moray
64 B5 **Whiteshill** Gloucs
23 J4 **Whitesmith** E Susx
30 D8 **Whitestaunton** Somset
13 K4 **Whitestone** Devon
13 L4 **Whitestone Cross** Devon
89 K7 **Whitestreet Green** Suffk

152 B2 **Whitewall Corner** N York
45 L6 **Whiteway** BaNES
64 C5 **Whiteway** Gloucs
148 B6 **Whitewell** Lancs
12 E8 **Whiteworks** Devon
41 J6 **Whitfield** Kent
84 B7 **Whitfield** Nhants
179 H7 **Whitfield** Nthumb
63 K8 **Whitfield** S Glos
179 H7 **Whitfield Hall** Nthumb
14 F3 **Whitford** Devon
128 D4 **Whitford** Flints
143 K3 **Whitgift** E R Yk
114 D6 **Whitgreave** Staffs
174 C6 **Whithorn** D & G
195 G6 **Whiting Bay** N Ayrs
142 B1 **Whitkirk** Leeds
55 L3 **Whitland** Carmth
188 E4 **Whitlaw** Border
196 D6 **Whitletts** S Ayrs
142 E4 **Whitley** N York
49 H5 **Whitley** Readg
133 G1 **Whitley** Sheff
46 C5 **Whitley** Wilts
181 J4 **Whitley Bay** N Tyne
179 L7 **Whitley Chapel** Nthumb
114 C6 **Whitley Heath** Staffs
141 K4 **Whitley Lower** Kirk
38 D3 **Whitley Row** Kent
98 E8 **Whitlock's End** Solhll
63 M5 **Whitminster** Gloucs
17 L1 **Whitmore** Dorset
114 C3 **Whitmore** Staffs
29 J7 **Whitnage** Devon
83 H3 **Whitnash** Warwks
79 J5 **Whitney-on-Wye** Herefs
165 G3 **Whitrigg** Cumb
177 H7 **Whitrigg** Cumb
177 H7 **Whitrigglees** Cumb
33 K7 **Whitsbury** Hants
28 B4 **Whitsford** Devon
202 D3 **Whitsome** Border
44 D2 **Whitson** Newpt
40 E2 **Whitstable** Kent
11 K3 **Whitstone** Cnwll
190 F4 **Whittingham** Nthumb
95 K5 **Whittingslow** Shrops
133 H4 **Whittington** Derbys
64 E3 **Whittington** Gloucs
157 K7 **Whittington** Lancs
104 E3 **Whittington** Norfk
112 E5 **Whittington** Shrops
98 F2 **Whittington** Staffs
97 J6 **Whittington** Staffs
99 J4 **Whittington** Warwks
81 K4 **Whittington** Worcs
133 G5 **Whittington Moor** Derbys
139 H3 **Whittle-le-Woods** Lancs
84 D6 **Whittlebury** Nhants
102 F4 **Whittlesey** Cambs
87 K5 **Whittlesford** Cambs
139 L4 **Whittlestone Head** Bl w D
143 M3 **Whitton** N Linc
190 F6 **Whitton** Nthumb
79 J2 **Whitton** Powys
169 K6 **Whitton** S on T
80 D1 **Whitton** Shrops
90 D5 **Whitton** Suffk
47 L4 **Whittonditch** Wilts
180 C7 **Whittonstall** Nthumb
48 C7 **Whitway** Hants
133 K4 **Whitwell** Derbys
68 F3 **Whitwell** Herts
19 J8 **Whitwell** IOW
160 D3 **Whitwell** N York
101 K2 **Whitwell** Rutlnd
122 B7 **Whitwell Street** Norfk
151 M3 **Whitwell-on-the-Hill** N York
116 D8 **Whitwick** Leics
142 B3 **Whitwood** Wakefd
140 D4 **Whitworth** Lancs
113 H4 **Whixall** Shrops
150 F4 **Whixley** N York
168 E7 **Whorlton** Dur
161 G2 **Whorlton** N York
80 D3 **Whyle** Herefs
51 J7 **Whyteleafe** Surrey
63 H7 **Wibdon** Gloucs
141 J2 **Wibsey** Brad
100 B6 **Wibtoft** Warwks
81 H3 **Wichenford** Worcs
40 B4 **Wichling** Kent
18 B5 **Wick** Bmouth
14 E2 **Wick** Devon
280 E6 **Wick** Highld

45 K4 **Wick** S Glos
30 B2 **Wick** Somset
30 F5 **Wick** Somset
42 D7 **Wick** V Glam
21 H6 **Wick** W Susx
33 L6 **Wick** Wilts
81 M6 **Wick** Worcs
85 K5 **Wick End** Beds
44 D6 **Wick St Lawrence** N Som
88 B1 **Wicken** Cambs
84 E7 **Wicken** Nhants
87 K8 **Wicken Bonhunt** Essex
136 A3 **Wickenby** Lincs
89 K6 **Wicker Street Green** Suffk
133 J2 **Wickersley** Rothm
71 H8 **Wickford** Essex
19 K2 **Wickham** Hants
48 B5 **Wickham** W Berk
71 K5 **Wickham Bishops** Essex
90 C2 **Wickham Green** Suffk
48 B4 **Wickham Green** W Berk
48 B5 **Wickham Heath** W Berk
91 G4 **Wickham Market** Suffk
90 C2 **Wickham Skeith** Suffk
89 G7 **Wickham St Paul** Essex
88 F4 **Wickham Street** Suffk
90 C1 **Wickham Street** Suffk
41 H3 **Wickhambreaux** Kent
88 E4 **Wickhambrook** Suffk
82 C7 **Wickhamford** Worcs
107 J2 **Wickhampton** Norfk
106 B3 **Wicklewood** Norfk
122 D5 **Wickmere** Norfk
23 J5 **Wickstreet** E Susx
45 L1 **Wickwar** S Glos
70 D1 **Widdington** Essex
140 D1 **Widdop** Calder
191 K7 **Widdrington** Nthumb
191 J7 **Widdrington Station** Nthumb
181 G4 **Wide Open** N Tyne
13 G7 **Widecombe in the Moor** Devon
6 B3 **Widegates** Cnwll
11 H2 **Widemouth Bay** Cnwll
71 G6 **Widford** Essex
70 B4 **Widford** Herts
65 K5 **Widford** Oxon
47 G1 **Widham** Wilts
19 M2 **Widley** Hants
67 L7 **Widmer End** Bucks
117 G2 **Widmerpool** Notts
51 L5 **Widmore** Gt Lon
129 L3 **Widnes** Halton
14 F3 **Widworthy** Devon
139 H6 **Wigan** Wigan
31 G7 **Wigborough** Somset
14 C4 **Wiggaton** Devon
120 D8 **Wiggenhall St Germans** Norfk
104 B1 **Wiggenhall St Mary Magdalen** Norfk
104 B1 **Wiggenhall St Mary the Virgin** Norfk
88 D6 **Wiggens Green** Essex
132 B7 **Wiggenstall** Staffs
112 E4 **Wiggington** Shrops
68 B5 **Wigginton** Herts
83 J8 **Wigginton** Oxon
99 G2 **Wigginton** Staffs
151 J4 **Wigginton** York
68 B5 **Wigginton Bottom** Herts
148 E4 **Wigglesworth** N York
64 F6 **Wiggold** Gloucs
177 J8 **Wiggonby** Cumb
21 H3 **Wiggonholt** W Susx
151 G6 **Wighill** N York
121 L3 **Wighton** Norfk
97 K4 **Wightwick** Wolves
132 F5 **Wigley** Derbys
34 D7 **Wigley** Hants
80 A2 **Wigmore** Herefs
53 G6 **Wigmore** Medway
135 G5 **Wigsley** Notts
102 A6 **Wigsthorpe** Nhants
100 D4 **Wigston** Leics
100 D3 **Wigston Fields** Leics
100 A5 **Wigston Parva** Leics
134 B3 **Wigthorpe** Notts
119 J4 **Wigtoft** Lincs
165 H1 **Wigton** Cumb
174 C4 **Wigtown** D & G
141 L8 **Wigtwizzle** Sheff
150 D7 **Wike** Leeds
101 H5 **Wilbarston** Nhants
151 M5 **Wilberfoss** E R Yk
103 K8 **Wilburton** Cambs

85 G2 **Wilby** Nhants
105 L5 **Wilby** Norfk
90 F1 **Wilby** Suffk
47 H6 **Wilcot** Wilts
112 F7 **Wilcott** Shrops
44 E2 **Wilcrick** Newpt
132 F5 **Wilday Green** Derbys
131 K6 **Wildboarclough** Ches
86 B4 **Wilden** Beds
81 J1 **Wilden** Worcs
34 D1 **Wildhern** Hants
69 H5 **Wildhill** Herts
209 L8 **Wildmanbridge** S Lans
98 B8 **Wildmoor** Worcs
143 K8 **Wildsworth** Lincs
116 F4 **Wilford** C Nott
113 K3 **Wilkesley** Ches
264 E3 **Wilkhaven** Highld
210 F5 **Wilkieston** W Loth
69 G5 **Wilkin's Green** Herts
136 E7 **Wilksby** Lincs
29 J8 **Willand** Devon
24 C2 **Willards Hill** E Susx
129 H4 **Willaston** Ches
113 L1 **Willaston** Ches
85 G7 **Willen** M Keyn
99 K8 **Willenhall** Covtry
98 B4 **Willenhall** Wsall
144 C2 **Willerby** E R Yk
163 H6 **Willerby** N York
82 D7 **Willersey** Gloucs
79 K6 **Willersley** Herefs
40 D7 **Willesborough** Kent
40 D7 **Willesborough Lees** Kent
51 G2 **Willesden** Gt Lon
27 L4 **Willesleigh** Devon
46 B1 **Willesley** Wilts
29 K4 **Willett** Somset
96 F3 **Willey** Shrops
100 B6 **Willey** Warwks
50 B8 **Willey Green** Surrey
83 L6 **Williamscot** Oxon
42 F4 **Williamstown** Rhondd
69 G1 **Willian** Herts
82 E5 **Willicote** Warwks
70 E5 **Willingale** Essex
23 K6 **Willingdon** E Susx
87 H1 **Willingham** Cambs
135 H3 **Willingham by Stow** Lincs
88 C4 **Willingham Green** Cambs
86 C5 **Willington** Beds
116 A6 **Willington** Derbys
169 G4 **Willington** Dur
39 K3 **Willington** Kent
83 G7 **Willington** Warwks
129 M6 **Willington Corner** Ches
181 H5 **Willington Quay** N Tyne
143 J1 **Willitoft** E R Yk
29 K3 **Williton** Somset
137 J5 **Willoughby** Lincs
83 M2 **Willoughby** Warwks
119 K2 **Willoughby Hills** Lincs
100 C5 **Willoughby Waterleys** Leics
117 H6 **Willoughby-on-the-Wolds** Notts
135 J1 **Willoughton** Lincs
130 B4 **Willow Green** Ches
71 H3 **Willows Green** Essex
45 K5 **Willsbridge** S Glos
12 D6 **Willsworthy** Devon
30 F6 **Willtown** Somset
82 E4 **Wilmcote** Warwks
45 K6 **Wilmington** BaNES
14 F3 **Wilmington** Devon
23 J6 **Wilmington** E Susx
52 B4 **Wilmington** Kent
131 G3 **Wilmslow** Ches
99 G3 **Wilnecote** Staffs
139 K1 **Wilpshire** Lancs
149 K8 **Wilsden** Brad
118 D3 **Wilsford** Lincs
47 G7 **Wilsford** Wilts
33 K3 **Wilsford** Wilts
28 D1 **Wilsham** Devon
141 H6 **Wilshaw** Kirk
150 A3 **Wilsill** N York
39 K6 **Wilsley Green** Kent
39 K6 **Wilsley Pound** Kent
63 H2 **Wilson** Herefs
116 C6 **Wilson** Leics
198 F2 **Wilsontown** S Lans
85 L6 **Wilstead** Beds
102 B1 **Wilsthorpe** Lincs
67 L4 **Wilstone** Herts
67 M4 **Wilstone Green** Herts

164 D8 **Wilton** Cumb
63 H2 **Wilton** Herefs
162 F6 **Wilton** N York
170 D6 **Wilton** R & Cl
33 J4 **Wilton** Wilts
47 K6 **Wilton** Wilts
188 E3 **Wilton Dean** Border
88 B7 **Wimbish** Essex
88 C8 **Wimbish Green** Essex
51 G5 **Wimbledon** Gt Lon
103 J5 **Wimblington** Cambs
130 D7 **Wimboldsley** Ches
17 K3 **Wimborne Minster** Dorset
33 H8 **Wimborne St Giles** Dorset
104 C2 **Wimbotsham** Norfk
87 G5 **Wimpole** Cambs
82 F5 **Wimpstone** Warwks
32 B5 **Wincanton** Somset
136 F6 **Winceby** Lincs
130 C4 **Wincham** Ches
210 E4 **Winchburgh** W Loth
64 F2 **Winchcombe** Gloucs
25 G4 **Winchelsea** E Susx
25 G4 **Winchelsea Beach** E Susx
35 G5 **Winchester** Hants
39 J5 **Winchet Hill** Kent
49 J8 **Winchfield** Hants
68 B8 **Winchmore Hill** Bucks
69 J8 **Winchmore Hill** Gt Lon
131 J6 **Wincle** Ches
133 G1 **Wincobank** Sheff
164 D7 **Winder** Cumb
156 F3 **Windermere** Cumb
83 H7 **Winderton** Warwks
250 F2 **Windhill** Highld
131 J3 **Windlehurst** Stockp
50 A6 **Windlesham** Surrey
10 B7 **Windmill** Cnwll
132 C4 **Windmill** Derbys
23 L5 **Windmill Hill** E Susx
30 D7 **Windmill Hill** Somset
65 J4 **Windrush** Gloucs
267 L4 **Windsole** Abers
50 B4 **Windsor** W & M
89 H4 **Windsor Green** Suffk
64 B7 **Windsoredge** Gloucs
83 G1 **Windy Arbour** Warwks
129 G8 **Windy Hill** Wrexhm
222 F7 **Windygates** Fife
131 G5 **Windyharbour** Ches
22 C3 **Wineham** W Susx
145 J3 **Winestead** E R Yk
148 F7 **Winewall** Lancs
106 C6 **Winfarthing** Norfk
19 J6 **Winford** IOW
45 G6 **Winford** N Som
79 K6 **Winforton** Herefs
16 F5 **Winfrith Newburgh** Dorset
67 L3 **Wing** Bucks
101 K3 **Wing** Rutlnd
169 L3 **Wingate** Dur
139 K6 **Wingates** Bolton
191 J6 **Wingates** Nthumb
133 G6 **Wingerworth** Derbys
68 C2 **Wingfield** Beds
106 E7 **Wingfield** Suffk
46 B7 **Wingfield** Wilts
106 E7 **Wingfield Green** Suffk
41 H4 **Wingham** Kent
41 G6 **Wingmore** Kent
67 L3 **Wingrave** Bucks
134 E7 **Winkburn** Notts
49 L4 **Winkfield** Br For
49 L5 **Winkfield Row** Br For
49 L4 **Winkfield Street** Br For
115 H1 **Winkhill** Staffs
38 D3 **Winkhurst Green** Kent
12 F1 **Winkleigh** Devon
150 C2 **Winksley** N Yorks
18 B4 **Winkton** Dorset
180 E6 **Winlaton** Gatesd
180 E6 **Winlaton Mill** Gatesd
280 D5 **Winless** Highld
112 C7 **Winllan** Powys
147 J6 **Winmarleigh** Lancs
35 G5 **Winnall** Hants
81 J2 **Winnall** Worcs
49 J5 **Winnersh** Wokham
130 C5 **Winnington** Ches
164 D5 **Winscales** Cumb
44 E7 **Winscombe** N Som
130 C6 **Winsford** Ches
28 F4 **Winsford** Somset
27 J3 **Winsham** Devon
15 J1 **Winsham** Somset

115 M7 **Winshill** Staffs
57 J5 **Winshwen** Swans
166 D4 **Winskill** Cumb
35 K1 **Winslade** Hants
46 A6 **Winsley** Wilts
67 J2 **Winslow** Bucks
65 G5 **Winson** Gloucs
34 D8 **Winsor** Hants
156 F4 **Winster** Cumb
132 E7 **Winster** Derbys
168 F7 **Winston** Dur
90 E3 **Winston** Suffk
90 E3 **Winston Green** Suffk
64 D5 **Winstone** Gloucs
27 J8 **Winswell** Devon
16 D5 **Winterborne Came** Dorset
17 G2 **Winterborne Clenston** Dorset
16 D5 **Winterborne Herringston** Dorset
16 F2 **Winterborne Houghton** Dorset
17 G3 **Winterborne Kingston** Dorset
16 C5 **Winterborne Monkton** Dorset
16 F2 **Winterborne Stickland** Dorset
17 G3 **Winterborne Tomson** Dorset
17 G2 **Winterborne Whitechurch** Dorset
17 H3 **Winterborne Zelston** Dorset
45 J3 **Winterbourne** S Glos
48 C4 **Winterbourne** W Berk
16 B4 **Winterbourne Abbas** Dorset
47 L4 **Winterbourne Bassett** Wilts
33 L4 **Winterbourne Dauntsey** Wilts
33 L4 **Winterbourne Earls** Wilts
33 L4 **Winterbourne Gunner** Wilts
47 L4 **Winterbourne Monkton** Wilts
16 B4 **Winterbourne Steepleton** Dorset
33 J3 **Winterbourne Stoke** Wilts
48 F1 **Winterbrook** Oxon
149 G4 **Winterburn** N York
144 A3 **Winteringham** N Linc
130 E8 **Winterley** Ches
142 B4 **Wintersett** Wakefd
34 B4 **Winterslow** Wilts
144 A4 **Winterton** N Linc
123 K7 **Winterton-on-Sea** Norfk
137 K6 **Winthorpe** Lincs
135 G8 **Winthorpe** Notts
17 L4 **Winton** Bmouth
167 H8 **Winton** Cumb
23 H6 **Winton** E Susx
160 F3 **Winton** N York
162 F8 **Wintringham** N York
102 B7 **Winwick** Cambs
100 D8 **Winwick** Nhants
130 B1 **Winwick** Warrtn
115 M1 **Wirksworth** Derbys
113 J3 **Wirswall** Ches
103 J2 **Wisbech** Cambs
103 J2 **Wisbech St Mary** Cambs
37 G5 **Wisborough Green** W Susx
55 K5 **Wiseman's Bridge** Pembks
134 E2 **Wiseton** Notts
64 D5 **Wishanger** Gloucs
209 L7 **Wishaw** N Lans
98 F4 **Wishaw** Warwks
50 D7 **Wisley** Surrey
136 D5 **Wispington** Lincs
40 B7 **Wissenden** Kent
107 H7 **Wissett** Suffk
104 D4 **Wissington** Norfk
89 J8 **Wissington** Suffk
95 K6 **Wistanstow** Shrops
113 L5 **Wistanswick** Shrops
113 L1 **Wistaston** Ches
130 D8 **Wistaston Green** Ches
131 G5 **Wisterfield** Ches
55 H3 **Wiston** Pembks
198 F6 **Wiston** S Lans
21 K4 **Wiston** W Susx
102 F5 **Wistow** Cambs
100 E4 **Wistow** Leics
142 F1 **Wistow** N York
148 C8 **Wiswell** Lancs
103 J7 **Witcham** Cambs
17 J1 **Witchampton** Dorset
103 K7 **Witchford** Cambs
31 G6 **Witcombe** Somset
71 K4 **Witham** Essex
32 B3 **Witham Friary** Somset
118 D8 **Witham on the Hill** Lincs
135 H7 **Witham St Hughs** Lincs

136 E3 **Withcall** Lincs
22 D5 **Withdean** Br & H
23 L2 **Witherenden Hill** E Susx
28 D8 **Witheridge** Devon
99 J4 **Witherley** Leics
137 H3 **Withern** Lincs
145 J2 **Withernsea** E R Yk
153 K7 **Withernwick** E R Yk
106 F7 **Withersdale Street** Suffk
88 D5 **Withersfield** Essex
156 F5 **Witherslack** Cumb
156 F5 **Witherslack Hall** Cumb
5 G2 **Withiel** Cnwll
29 H4 **Withiel Florey** Somset
5 G2 **Withielgoose** Cnwll
64 F4 **Withington** Gloucs
80 D6 **Withington** Herefs
131 G1 **Withington** Manch
96 D1 **Withington** Shrops
115 G4 **Withington** Staffs
130 F5 **Withington Green** Ches
80 D6 **Withington Marsh** Herefs
28 F8 **Withleigh** Devon
139 J3 **Withnell** Lancs
45 K7 **Withy Mills** BaNES
82 B1 **Withybed Green** Worcs
99 L6 **Withybrook** Warwks
29 J3 **Withycombe** Somset
38 D6 **Withyham** E Susx
28 E4 **Withypool** Somset
45 H5 **Withywood** Bristl
36 E3 **Witley** Surrey
90 E5 **Witnesham** Suffk
65 M5 **Witney** Oxon
102 B3 **Wittering** C Pete
25 G2 **Wittersham** Kent
98 D5 **Witton** Birm
107 G2 **Witton** Norfk
123 G5 **Witton** Norfk
169 G2 **Witton Gilbert** Dur
107 J3 **Witton Green** Norfk
168 F4 **Witton le Wear** Dur
168 F4 **Witton Park** Dur
29 K5 **Wiveliscombe** Somset
35 K3 **Wivelrod** Hants
22 E3 **Wivelsfield** E Susx
22 E3 **Wivelsfield Green** E Susx
22 E3 **Wivelsfield Station** W Susx
72 F3 **Wivenhoe** Essex
72 F2 **Wivenhoe Cross** Essex
122 A3 **Wiveton** Norfk
73 H2 **Wix** Essex
73 H2 **Wix Green** Essex
82 C4 **Wixford** Warwks
113 J6 **Wixhill** Shrops
88 E6 **Wixoe** Essex
85 J8 **Woburn** Beds
85 H8 **Woburn Sands** M Keyn
49 G6 **Wokefield Park** W Berk
50 C7 **Woking** Surrey
49 K5 **Wokingham** Wokham
8 C1 **Wolborough** Devon
163 J8 **Wold Newton** E R Yk
145 G8 **Wold Newton** NE Lin
51 K7 **Woldingham** Surrey
179 G7 **Wolf Hills** Nthumb
74 F6 **Wolf's Castle** Pembks
199 H6 **Wolfclyde** S Lans
80 F3 **Wolferlow** Herefs
120 E6 **Wolferton** Norfk
83 M2 **Wolfhampcote** Warwks
233 H8 **Wolfhill** P & K
54 F3 **Wolfsdale** Pembks
97 K6 **Wollaston** Dudley
85 H3 **Wollaston** Nhants
95 H1 **Wollaston** Shrops
116 E4 **Wollaton** C Nott
13 J6 **Wolleigh** Devon
113 K5 **Wollerton** Shrops
97 L6 **Wollescote** Dudley
115 G7 **Wolseley Bridge** Staffs
168 D3 **Wolsingham** Dur
114 D2 **Wolstanton** Staffs
140 C5 **Wolstenholme** Rochdl
99 L8 **Wolston** Warwks
176 E8 **Wolsty** Cumb
66 D5 **Wolvercote** Oxon
97 K4 **Wolverhampton** Wolves
113 G5 **Wolverley** Shrops
97 J7 **Wolverley** Worcs
48 E7 **Wolverton** Hants
41 H6 **Wolverton** Kent
84 F7 **Wolverton** M Keyn
82 F3 **Wolverton** Warwks
32 C4 **Wolverton** Wilts

48 E7 **Wolverton Common** Hants
62 F7 **Wolvesnewton** Mons
99 L6 **Wolvey** Warwks
99 L5 **Wolvey Heath** Warwks
170 B5 **Wolviston** S on T
161 L6 **Wombleton** N York
97 K5 **Wombourne** Staffs
142 B7 **Wombwell** Barns
41 H5 **Womenswold** Kent
142 E4 **Womersley** N York
62 F5 **Wonastow** Mons
36 F2 **Wonersh** Surrey
13 L4 **Wonford** Devon
12 F4 **Wonson** Devon
35 G3 **Wonston** Hants
49 M2 **Wooburn** Bucks
49 M1 **Wooburn Green** Bucks
49 M1 **Wooburn Moor** Bucks
82 C4 **Wood Bevington** Warwks
84 D6 **Wood Burcot** Nhants
122 B6 **Wood Dalling** Norfk
114 C7 **Wood Eaton** Staffs
85 K6 **Wood End** Beds
86 B2 **Wood End** Beds
103 H8 **Wood End** Cambs
50 E3 **Wood End** Gt Lon
69 J2 **Wood End** Herts
82 D1 **Wood End** Warwks
99 H4 **Wood End** Warwks
99 J6 **Wood End** Warwks
97 L3 **Wood End** Wolves
136 E6 **Wood Enderby** Lincs
51 J1 **Wood Green** Gt Lon
97 L3 **Wood Hayes** Wolves
112 F5 **Wood Lane** Shrops
114 C2 **Wood Lane** Staffs
121 M6 **Wood Norton** Norfk
142 B2 **Wood Row** Leeds
123 H7 **Wood Street** Norfk
36 E1 **Wood Street** Surrey
147 L7 **Wood Top** Lancs
102 E7 **Wood Walton** Cambs
24 B3 **Wood's Corner** E Susx
39 G6 **Wood's Green** E Susx
159 J6 **Woodale** N York
133 J3 **Woodall** Rothm
123 G8 **Woodbastwick** Norfk
134 F4 **Woodbeck** Notts
117 G2 **Woodborough** Notts
47 G7 **Woodborough** Wilts
14 E3 **Woodbridge** Devon
32 E7 **Woodbridge** Dorset
91 G5 **Woodbridge** Suffk
14 B5 **Woodbury** Devon
14 B5 **Woodbury Salterton** Devon
64 B6 **Woodchester** Gloucs
40 B8 **Woodchurch** Kent
129 G2 **Woodchurch** Wirral
29 G2 **Woodcombe** Somset
51 J6 **Woodcote** Gt Lon
48 F3 **Woodcote** Oxon
114 B8 **Woodcote** Wrekin
81 L1 **Woodcote Green** Worcs
48 B7 **Woodcott** Hants
63 G7 **Woodcroft** Gloucs
33 G7 **Woodcutts** Dorset
88 D3 **Woodditton** Cambs
66 D5 **Woodeaton** Oxon
55 J6 **Wooden** Pembks
228 B3 **Woodend** Highld
84 B5 **Woodend** Nhants
115 K6 **Woodend** Staffs
210 B5 **Woodend** W Loth
20 D5 **Woodend** W Susx
70 E2 **Woodend Green** Essex
33 L6 **Woodfalls** Wilts
26 C8 **Woodford** Cnwll
8 B5 **Woodford** Devon
63 K7 **Woodford** Gloucs
69 L8 **Woodford** Gt Lon
101 L8 **Woodford** Nhants
131 H3 **Woodford** Stockp
70 B8 **Woodford Bridge** Gt Lon
84 A5 **Woodford Halse** Nhants
69 L8 **Woodford Wells** Gt Lon
98 C6 **Woodgate** Birm
29 K7 **Woodgate** Devon
121 K8 **Woodgate** Norfk
121 M8 **Woodgate** Norfk
20 F6 **Woodgate** W Susx
81 M2 **Woodgate** Worcs
33 L7 **Woodgreen** Hants
66 A5 **Woodgreen** Oxon
136 D6 **Woodhall** Lincs
159 H4 **Woodhall** N York

141 K1 **Woodhall Hill** Leeds
136 C7 **Woodhall Spa** Lincs
67 H3 **Woodham** Bucks
169 H5 **Woodham** Dur
50 D6 **Woodham** Surrey
71 J7 **Woodham Ferrers** Essex
71 K6 **Woodham Mortimer** Essex
71 K5 **Woodham Walter** Essex
256 E4 **Woodhead** Abers
30 E5 **Woodhill** Somset
181 H1 **Woodhorn** Nthumb
181 H1 **Woodhorn Demesne** Nthumb
141 L1 **Woodhouse** Leeds
116 F8 **Woodhouse** Leics
133 H3 **Woodhouse** Sheff
142 B3 **Woodhouse** Wakefd
116 F8 **Woodhouse Eaves** Leics
131 H7 **Woodhouse Green** Staffs
133 H3 **Woodhouse Mill** Sheff
211 H6 **Woodhouselee** Mdloth
177 L4 **Woodhouselees** D & G
177 K8 **Woodhouses** Cumb
140 D7 **Woodhouses** Oldham
98 D2 **Woodhouses** Staffs
115 J7 **Woodhouses** Staffs
8 D4 **Woodhuish** Devon
103 G8 **Woodhurst** Cambs
22 E6 **Woodingdean** Br & H
141 L3 **Woodkirk** Leeds
256 F7 **Woodland** Abers
8 B1 **Woodland** Devon
7 J4 **Woodland** Devon
168 D5 **Woodland** Dur
40 F7 **Woodland** Kent
182 F4 **Woodland** S Ayrs
13 H3 **Woodland Head** Devon
31 J3 **Woodland Street** Somset
132 F2 **Woodland View** Sheff
245 H4 **Woodlands** Abers
142 E6 **Woodlands** Donc
17 L1 **Woodlands** Dorset
18 E1 **Woodlands** Hants
52 C6 **Woodlands** Kent
150 D5 **Woodlands** N York
29 L3 **Woodlands** Somset
49 L3 **Woodlands Park** W & M
47 M4 **Woodlands St Mary** W Berk
7 L5 **Woodleigh** Devon
142 B2 **Woodlesford** Leeds
131 J1 **Woodley** Stockp
49 J4 **Woodley** Wokham
64 E2 **Woodmancote** Gloucs
64 E5 **Woodmancote** Gloucs
63 M7 **Woodmancote** Gloucs
20 C5 **Woodmancote** W Susx
22 C4 **Woodmancote** W Susx
81 L6 **Woodmancote** Worcs
35 H2 **Woodmancott** Hants
153 G8 **Woodmansey** E R Yk
36 C5 **Woodmansgreen** W Susx
51 H7 **Woodmansterne** Surrey
14 B5 **Woodmanton** Devon
46 B7 **Woodmarsh** Wilts
115 J7 **Woodmill** Staffs
33 H6 **Woodminton** Wilts
41 J4 **Woodnesborough** Kent
102 A4 **Woodnewton** Nhants
116 D1 **Woodnook** Notts
139 G1 **Woodplumpton** Lancs
105 K3 **Woodrising** Norfk
97 K8 **Woodrow** Worcs
113 M5 **Woodseaves** Shrops
114 B6 **Woodseaves** Staffs
47 J4 **Woodsend** Wilts
133 L3 **Woodsetts** Rothm
16 E4 **Woodsford** Dorset
50 B5 **Woodside** Br For
164 D4 **Woodside** Cumb
70 C6 **Woodside** Essex
223 G5 **Woodside** Fife
51 J5 **Woodside** Gt Lon
18 E5 **Woodside** Hants
69 H5 **Woodside** Herts
233 J7 **Woodside** P & K
40 B4 **Woodside Green** Kent
66 C4 **Woodstock** Oxon
75 H7 **Woodstock** Pembks
102 D4 **Woodston** C Pete
133 J5 **Woodthorpe** Derbys
116 F8 **Woodthorpe** Leics
137 H4 **Woodthorpe** Lincs
106 F4 **Woodton** Norfk
27 G6 **Woodtown** Devon
138 C5 **Woodvale** Sefton
116 A7 **Woodville** Derbys

114 B5 **Woodwall Green** Staffs
28 B1 **Woody Bay** Devon
33 H7 **Woodyates** Dorset
80 C2 **Woofferton** Shrops
31 H2 **Wookey** Somset
31 H2 **Wookey Hole** Somset
17 G5 **Wool** Dorset
27 H2 **Woolacombe** Devon
41 H5 **Woolage Green** Kent
41 H5 **Woolage Village** Kent
63 H7 **Woolaston** Gloucs
63 H6 **Woolaston Common** Gloucs
30 E3 **Woolavington** Somset
36 C6 **Woolbeding** W Susx
14 D5 **Woolbrook** Devon
29 H4 **Woolcotts** Somset
141 J6 **Wooldale** Kirk
202 F7 **Wooler** Nthumb
26 F6 **Woolfardisworthy** Devon
13 J1 **Woolfardisworthy** Devon
140 B5 **Woolfold** Bury
199 G2 **Woolfords** S Lans
48 E5 **Woolhampton** W Berk
28 B2 **Woolhanger** Devon
80 E8 **Woolhope** Herefs
16 E1 **Woolland** Dorset
45 J6 **Woollard** BaNES
69 K5 **Woollensbrook** Herts
45 L5 **Woolley** BaNES
102 C8 **Woolley** Cambs
26 D7 **Woolley** Cnwll
133 G7 **Woolley** Derbys
141 M5 **Woolley** Wakefd
131 K1 **Woolley Bridge** Derbys
49 K3 **Woolley Green** W & M
69 H3 **Woolmer Green** Herts
81 M3 **Woolmere Green** Worcs
30 D4 **Woolmerston** Somset
15 J1 **Woolminstone** Somset
39 L6 **Woolpack** Kent
89 K3 **Woolpit** Suffk
89 K3 **Woolpit Green** Suffk
83 L2 **Woolscott** Warwks
13 J2 **Woolsgrove** Devon
180 F5 **Woolsington** N u Ty
95 L4 **Woolstaston** Shrops
117 L5 **Woolsthorpe** Lincs
118 B6 **Woolsthorpe-by-Colsterworth** Lincs
19 G2 **Woolston** C Sotn
7 L6 **Woolston** Devon
7 L5 **Woolston** Devon
112 E6 **Woolston** Shrops
95 K6 **Woolston** Shrops
29 K3 **Woolston** Somset
31 L5 **Woolston** Somset
130 C2 **Woolston** Warrtn
8 A2 **Woolston Green** Devon
64 D1 **Woolstone** Gloucs
85 G7 **Woolstone** M Keyn
47 L2 **Woolstone** Oxon
129 K2 **Woolton** Lpool
48 B6 **Woolton Hill** Hants
90 E7 **Woolverstone** Suffk
46 A8 **Woolverton** Somset
51 L3 **Woolwich** Gt Lon
79 L5 **Woonton** Herefs
80 D3 **Woonton** Herefs
190 F2 **Wooperton** Nthumb
114 A3 **Woore** Shrops
90 F1 **Wootten Green** Suffk
85 K6 **Wootton** Beds
18 C4 **Wootton** Hants
79 L4 **Wootton** Herefs
19 J5 **Wootton** IOW
41 H6 **Wootton** Kent
144 D4 **Wootton** N Linc
84 E4 **Wootton** Nhants
66 B3 **Wootton** Oxon
66 C6 **Wootton** Oxon
112 E6 **Wootton** Shrops
114 C6 **Wootton** Staffs
115 H3 **Wootton** Staffs
46 F3 **Wootton Bassett** Wilts
19 J5 **Wootton Bridge** IOW
85 K6 **Wootton Broadmead** Beds
19 J5 **Wootton Common** IOW
29 G2 **Wootton Courtenay** Somset
15 J3 **Wootton Fitzpaine** Dorset
47 J6 **Wootton Rivers** Wilts
48 E8 **Wootton St Lawrence** Hants
82 E3 **Wootton Wawen** Warwks
81 K4 **Worcester** Worcs
51 G6 **Worcester Park** Gt Lon
97 K6 **Wordsley** Dudley

97 G4 **Worfield** Shrops
17 H5 **Worgret** Dorset
86 B5 **Workhouse End** Beds
164 D5 **Workington** Cumb
134 B4 **Worksop** Notts
136 F4 **Worlaby** Lincs
144 C5 **Worlaby** N Linc
48 C3 **World's End** W Berk
67 L5 **Worlds End** Bucks
19 L1 **Worlds End** Hants
22 E3 **Worlds End** W Susx
44 D6 **Worle** N Som
130 C8 **Worleston** Ches
107 J5 **Worlingham** Suffk
28 D8 **Worlington** Devon
104 D8 **Worlington** Suffk
90 F2 **Worlingworth** Suffk
150 D3 **Wormald Green** N York
62 E1 **Wormbridge** Herefs
104 D1 **Wormegay** Norfk
62 F1 **Wormelow Tump** Herefs
132 C5 **Wormhill** Derbys
80 A7 **Wormhill** Herefs
72 D1 **Wormingford** Essex
66 F5 **Worminghall** Bucks
82 B7 **Wormington** Gloucs
31 J2 **Worminster** Somset
223 G2 **Wormit** Fife
83 K4 **Wormleighton** Warwks
69 K6 **Wormley** Herts
36 E3 **Wormley** Surrey
143 G4 **Wormley Hill** Donc
69 K6 **Wormleybury** Herts
39 M2 **Wormshill** Kent
80 A5 **Wormsley** Herefs
50 B8 **Worplesdon** Surrey
132 F1 **Worrall** Sheff
63 J4 **Worrall Hill** Gloucs
142 A7 **Worsbrough** Barns
142 A7 **Worsbrough Bridge** Barns
142 B7 **Worsbrough Dale** Barns
139 M7 **Worsley** Salfd
139 H7 **Worsley Mesnes** Wigan
122 F6 **Worstead** Norfk
140 C1 **Worsthorne** Lancs
7 H4 **Worston** Devon
148 D7 **Worston** Lancs
41 K4 **Worth** Kent
31 H2 **Worth** Somset
37 L4 **Worth** W Susx
37 M4 **Worth Abbey** Surrey
17 J7 **Worth Matravers** Dorset
106 B7 **Wortham** Suffk
95 H2 **Worthen** Shrops
112 F2 **Worthenbury** Wrexhm
121 M7 **Worthing** Norfk
21 K6 **Worthing** W Susx
116 C7 **Worthington** Leics
62 F5 **Worthybrook** Mons
48 F8 **Worting** Hants
141 M7 **Wortley** Barns
141 L1 **Wortley** Leeds
159 G5 **Worton** N York
46 E7 **Worton** Wilts
106 F6 **Wortwell** Norfk
95 G3 **Wotherton** Shrops
101 M2 **Wothorpe** C Pete
7 H3 **Wotter** Devon
37 H2 **Wotton** Surrey
67 G4 **Wotton Underwood** Bucks
63 M8 **Wotton-under-Edge** Gloucs
85 G7 **Woughton on the Green** M Keyn
52 F6 **Wouldham** Kent
97 H5 **Woundale** Shrops
73 J1 **Wrabness** Essex
27 J4 **Wrafton** Devon
136 B4 **Wragby** Lincs
142 C4 **Wragby** Wakefd
106 C2 **Wramplingham** Norfk
7 K3 **Wrangaton** Devon
142 D5 **Wrangbrook** Wakefd
119 M2 **Wrangle** Lincs
119 M1 **Wrangle Common** Lincs
119 M1 **Wrangle Lowgate** Lincs
29 L7 **Wrangway** Somset
30 D6 **Wrantage** Somset
144 C6 **Wrawby** N Linc
44 F4 **Wraxall** N Som
31 K4 **Wraxall** Somset
147 M2 **Wray** Lancs
156 E3 **Wray Castle** Cumb
50 C4 **Wraysbury** W & M
147 M2 **Wrayton** Lancs
138 E2 **Wrea Green** Lancs

156 B5 **Wreaks End** Cumb
166 B1 **Wreay** Cumb
166 B6 **Wreay** Cumb
36 B2 **Wrecclesham** Surrey
181 G7 **Wrekenton** Gatesd
162 D5 **Wrelton** N York
113 K2 **Wrenbury** Ches
163 H5 **Wrench Green** N York
106 D4 **Wreningham** Norfk
107 K6 **Wrentham** Suffk
141 M3 **Wrenthorpe** Wakefd
95 K3 **Wrentnall** Shrops
143 H2 **Wressle** E R Yk
144 B6 **Wressle** N Linc
86 E5 **Wrestlingworth** Beds
104 D3 **Wretton** Norfk
112 E2 **Wrexham** Wrexhm
97 H8 **Wribbenhall** Worcs
96 E6 **Wrickton** Shrops
70 D4 **Wright's Green** Essex
139 G5 **Wrightington Bar** Lancs
114 B2 **Wrinehill** Staffs
44 F6 **Wrington** N Som
6 B3 **Wringworthy** Cnwll
45 K8 **Writhlington** BaNES
71 G6 **Writtle** Essex
96 E1 **Wrockwardine** Wrekin
143 H7 **Wroot** N Linc
149 L8 **Wrose** Brad
52 D7 **Wrotham** Kent
52 D7 **Wrotham Heath** Kent
97 J3 **Wrottesley** Staffs
47 H3 **Wroughton** Swindn
19 J7 **Wroxall** IOW
82 F1 **Wroxall** Warwks
96 D2 **Wroxeter** Shrops
122 F8 **Wroxham** Norfk
83 K7 **Wroxton** Oxon
115 K3 **Wyaston** Derbys
70 F7 **Wyatt's Green** Essex
119 K3 **Wyberton East** Lincs
119 J3 **Wyberton West** Lincs
86 D4 **Wyboston** Beds
113 M2 **Wybunbury** Ches
15 L4 **Wych** Dorset
38 C7 **Wych Cross** E Susx
81 L2 **Wychbold** Worcs
115 K8 **Wychnor** Staffs
35 M3 **Wyck** Hants
65 J3 **Wyck Rissington** Gloucs
168 E7 **Wycliffe** Dur
149 G8 **Wycoller** Lancs
117 K6 **Wycomb** Leics
67 L8 **Wycombe Marsh** Bucks
69 K1 **Wyddial** Herts
40 D6 **Wye** Kent
63 G5 **Wyesham** Mons
117 L7 **Wyfordby** Leics
141 J2 **Wyke** Brad
13 K3 **Wyke** Devon
15 G3 **Wyke** Devon
32 D5 **Wyke** Dorset
96 E3 **Wyke** Shrops
50 A8 **Wyke** Surrey
31 L4 **Wyke Champflower** Somset
16 C7 **Wyke Regis** Dorset
162 E7 **Wykeham** N York
163 H6 **Wykeham** N York
99 K7 **Wyken** Covtry
97 H4 **Wyken** Shrops
112 F6 **Wykey** Shrops
99 L4 **Wykin** Leics
180 D6 **Wylam** Nthumb
98 E4 **Wylde Green** Birm
33 H3 **Wylye** Wilts
117 G6 **Wymeswold** Leics
85 J2 **Wymington** Beds
117 M7 **Wymondham** Leics
106 C3 **Wymondham** Norfk
42 E3 **Wyndham** Brdgnd
16 B3 **Wynford Eagle** Dorset
169 L5 **Wynyard Park** S on T
169 L5 **Wynyard Village** S on T
81 M5 **Wyre Piddle** Worcs
117 G6 **Wysall** Notts
80 C2 **Wyson** Herefs
98 D8 **Wythall** Worcs
66 C5 **Wytham** Oxon
165 K7 **Wythburn** Cumb
131 G2 **Wythenshawe** Manch
165 G5 **Wythop Mill** Cumb
86 F1 **Wyton** Cambs
144 F1 **Wyton** E R Yk
90 B2 **Wyverstone** Suffk
89 L2 **Wyverstone Street** Suffk

118 A5 **Wyville** Lincs

Y

125 J6 **Y Felinheli** Gwynd
75 L2 **Y Ferwig** Cerdgn
109 G4 **Y Ffor** Gwynd
128 C8 **Y Gyffylliog** Denbgs
111 K3 **Y Maerdy** Conwy
112 D2 **Y Nant** Wrexhm
108 D6 **Y Rhiw** Gwynd
143 M6 **Yaddlethorpe** N Linc
19 G7 **Yafford** IOW
160 E4 **Yafforth** N York
8 C3 **Yalberton** Torbay
39 H3 **Yalding** Kent
166 C5 **Yanwath** Cumb
65 G4 **Yanworth** Gloucs
152 B5 **Yapham** E R Yk
21 G6 **Yapton** W Susx
44 D7 **Yarborough** N Som
19 K6 **Yarbridge** IOW
136 F1 **Yarburgh** Lincs
14 F1 **Yarcombe** Devon
28 D6 **Yard** Devon
98 E6 **Yardley** Birm
84 E6 **Yardley Gobion** Nhants
85 G4 **Yardley Hastings** Nhants
98 E7 **Yardley Wood** Birm
79 J3 **Yardro** Powys
30 B5 **Yarford** Somset
80 E6 **Yarkhill** Herefs
31 H2 **Yarley** Somset
31 L5 **Yarlington** Somset
148 C2 **Yarlsber** N York
169 L8 **Yarm** S on T
18 E5 **Yarmouth** IOW
27 L5 **Yarnacott** Devon
46 C7 **Yarnbrook** Wilts
13 H7 **Yarner** Devon
114 D5 **Yarnfield** Staffs
27 K6 **Yarnscombe** Devon
66 C5 **Yarnton** Oxon
80 B2 **Yarpole** Herefs
200 D7 **Yarrow** Border
30 E2 **Yarrow** Somset
200 D7 **Yarrow Feus** Border
200 E7 **Yarrowford** Border
80 A6 **Yarsop** Herefs
102 B4 **Yarwell** Nhants
45 L3 **Yate** S Glos
49 K6 **Yateley** Hants
46 F4 **Yatesbury** Wilts
48 E4 **Yattendon** W Berk
80 A2 **Yatton** Herefs
63 J1 **Yatton** Herefs
44 E6 **Yatton** N Som
46 C4 **Yatton Keynell** Wilts
19 K6 **Yaverland** IOW
15 H4 **Yawl** Devon
135 H1 **Yawthorpe** Lincs
105 K1 **Yaxham** Norfk
102 D5 **Yaxley** Cambs
106 C8 **Yaxley** Suffk
79 M6 **Yazor** Herefs
50 E3 **Yeading** Gt Lon
150 B7 **Yeadon** Leeds
157 H7 **Yealand Conyers** Lancs
157 H7 **Yealand Redmayne** Lancs
157 H7 **Yealand Storrs** Lancs
7 H4 **Yealmbridge** Devon
7 H4 **Yealmpton** Devon
170 E6 **Yearby** R & Cl
164 F2 **Yearngill** Cumb
161 J7 **Yearsley** N York
113 G7 **Yeaton** Shrops
115 K3 **Yeaveley** Derbys
202 E7 **Yeavering** Nthumb
162 F6 **Yedingham** N York
66 A6 **Yelford** Oxon
27 J4 **Yelland** Devon
86 F3 **Yelling** Cambs
100 D8 **Yelvertoft** Nhants
7 G1 **Yelverton** Devon
106 F3 **Yelverton** Norfk
32 B6 **Yenston** Somset
28 E5 **Yeo Mill** Somset
27 G6 **Yeo Vale** Devon
13 H3 **Yeoford** Devon
11 L5 **Yeolmbridge** Cnwll
31 J7 **Yeovil** Somset
31 J7 **Yeovil Marsh** Somset
31 J6 **Yeovilton** Somset
55 H5 **Yerbeston** Pembks

275 b4 **Yesnaby** Ork
190 E4 **Yetlington** Nthumb
31 K8 **Yetminster** Dorset
8 B4 **Yetson** Devon
14 B5 **Yettington** Devon
221 H6 **Yetts o' Muckhart** Clacks
82 F2 **Yew Green** Warwks
98 C4 **Yew Tree** W Mids
141 H2 **Yews Green** Brad
85 K2 **Yielden** Beds
97 K7 **Yieldingtree** Worcs
198 E3 **Yieldshields** S Lans
50 D3 **Yiewsley** Gt Lon
43 G3 **Ynysboeth** Rhondd
43 J3 **Ynysddu** Caerph
57 J5 **Ynysforgan** Swans
42 F3 **Ynyshir** Rhondd
92 D5 **Ynyslas** Cerdgn
42 F5 **Ynysmaerdy** Rhondd
57 K4 **Ynysmeudwy** Neath
57 J5 **Ynystawe** Swans
60 C4 **Ynyswen** Powys
42 E2 **Ynyswen** Rhondd
43 G3 **Ynysybwl** Rhondd
92 D3 **Ynysymaengwyn** Gwynd
158 F6 **Yockenthwaite** N York
95 K2 **Yockleton** Shrops
143 K3 **Yokefleet** E R Yk
208 E5 **Yoker** C Glas
139 L1 **York** Lancs
151 J5 **York** York
49 L7 **York Town** Surrey
40 E3 **Yorkletts** Kent
63 J5 **Yorkley** Gloucs
113 H7 **Yorton Heath** Shrops
132 D6 **Youlgreave** Derbys
152 B5 **Youlthorpe** E R Yk
151 G3 **Youlton** N York
71 H3 **Young's End** Essex
69 K3 **Youngsbury** Herts
115 J7 **Yoxall** Staffs
91 J2 **Yoxford** Suffk
91 J1 **Yoxford Little Street** Suffk
93 G7 **Ysbyty Cynfyn** Cerdgn
110 F2 **Ysbyty Ifan** Conwy
77 K1 **Ysbyty Ystwyth** Cerdgn
128 D5 **Ysceifiog** Flints
92 D4 **Ysgubor-y-Coed** Cerdgn
57 L3 **Ystalyfera** Powys
42 F3 **Ystrad** Rhondd
76 F4 **Ystrad Aeron** Cerdgn
77 L6 **Ystrad Ffin** Carmth
77 K2 **Ystrad Meurig** Cerdgn
43 J3 **Ystrad Mynach** Caerph
60 D4 **Ystradfellte** Powys
60 B5 **Ystradgynlais** Powys
42 F6 **Ystradowen** V Glam
92 F7 **Ystumtuen** Cerdgn
257 G5 **Ythanbank** Abers
256 B4 **Ythanwells** Abers
256 F5 **Ythsie** Abers

Z

13 G2 **Zeal Monachorum** Devon
32 C4 **Zeals** Wilts
4 C4 **Zelah** Cnwll
2 C3 **Zennor** Cnwll
3 J7 **Zoar** Cnwll
116 E6 **Zouch** Notts